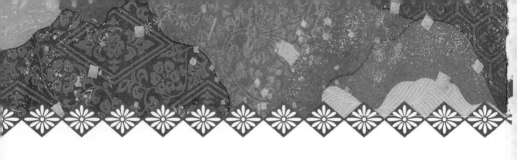

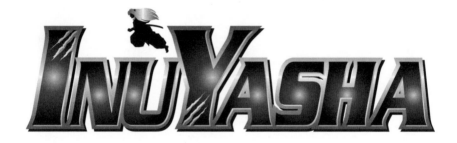

Story & Art by
Rumiko Takahashi

INUYASHA

Volume 15
VIZBIG Edition

Story and Art by RUMIKO TAKAHASHI

INUYASHA Vol. 15
by Rumiko TAKAHASHI

Original Japanese edition published by SHOGAKUKAN.
English translation rights in the United States of America, Canada, the United Kingdom, Ireland, Australia and New Zealand arranged with SHOGAKUKAN.

Translation/Mari Morimoto
Transcription/David Smith
Touch-up Art & Lettering/Bill Schuch, Leonard Clark
VIZ Media Series Design/Yuki Ameda
VIZBIG Edition Design/Sam Elzway
Shonen Sunday Edition Editor/Annette Roman
VIZBIG Edition Editor/Annette Roman

Printed in China

Published by VIZ Media, LLC
P.O. Box 77010
San Francisco, CA 94107

10 9 8 7 6 5 4 3
First printing, May 2013
Third printing, April 2021

大 VIZBIG EDITION

viz media
www.viz.com

SHONEN SUNDAY
WWW.SHONENSUNDAY.COM

RATED T+ FOR OLDER TEEN

PARENTAL ADVISORY
INUYASHA is rated T+ for Older Teen and is recommended for ages 16 and up. This volume contains fantasy violence and partial nudity.
ratings.viz.com

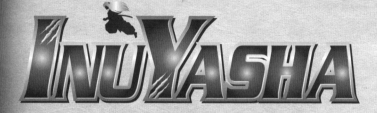

Volume 43
Assimilation

Volume 44
Koga's Decision

Volume 45
Absorption

Story & Art by
Rumiko Takahashi

Shonen Sunday Manga / VIZBIG Edition

CONTENTS

Volume 45: Absorption

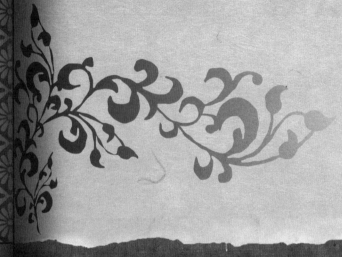

CAST OF CHARACTERS

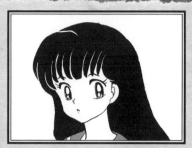

Kagome

A modern-day Japanese schoolgirl who is the reincarnation of Kikyo, the priestess who imprisoned Inuyasha for fifty years with her enchanted arrow. As Kikyo's reincarnation, Kagome has the power to see the Shikon Jewel shards.

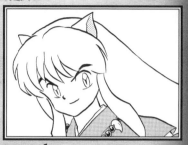

Inuyasha

A half-human, half-demon hybrid, Inuyasha has doglike ears and demonic strength. He assists Kagome in her search for the shards of the Shikon Jewel, mostly because a charmed necklace allows Kagome to restrain him with a single word.

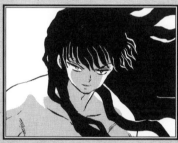

Naraku

This enigmatic demon is responsible for both Miroku's curse and for turning Kikyo and Inuyasha against each other.

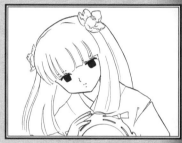

Kanna

Kanna is Naraku's first incarnation and the one he trusts the most. Her demonic mirror steals souls and the powers of those it reflects.

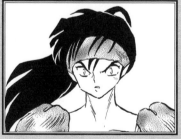

Koga

A wolf demon and leader of the wolf clan. Koga has Shikon shards in his legs, giving him super speed.

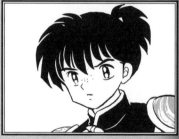

Kohaku

Naraku controlled Kohaku with a Shikon shard, then resurrected him after he was killed and used him as a puppet. Kohaku has regained his memories and is trying to redeem himself.

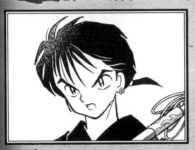

Miroku

An easygoing Buddhist priest of questionable morals. Miroku bears a curse passed down from his grandfather and is searching for the demon Naraku, who first inflicted the curse.

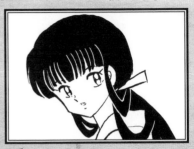

Kikyo

A village priestess who was the original protector of the Shikon Jewel. She died fifty years ago.

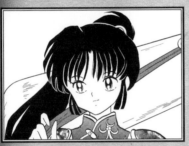

Sango

A proud Demon Slayer from the village where the first Shikon Jewel was born. Her clan and family lost, she fights on against the demonic Naraku along with Inuyasha.

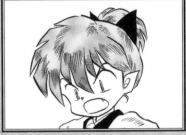

Shippo

A young orphan fox demon. The mischievous Shippo enjoys goading Inuyasha and playing tricks with his shape-shifting abilities.

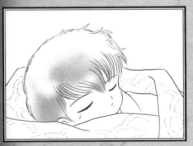

The Infant

Naraku's heart is safely housed inside the body of the Infant that he created. The Infant enables Naraku to avoid being influenced by the heart's feelings and to survive even if his primary body is killed.

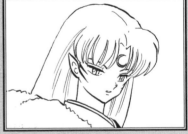

Sesshomaru

Inuyasha's half brother by the same demon father, Sesshomaru is a pureblood demon who covets the sword left to Inuyasha by their father.

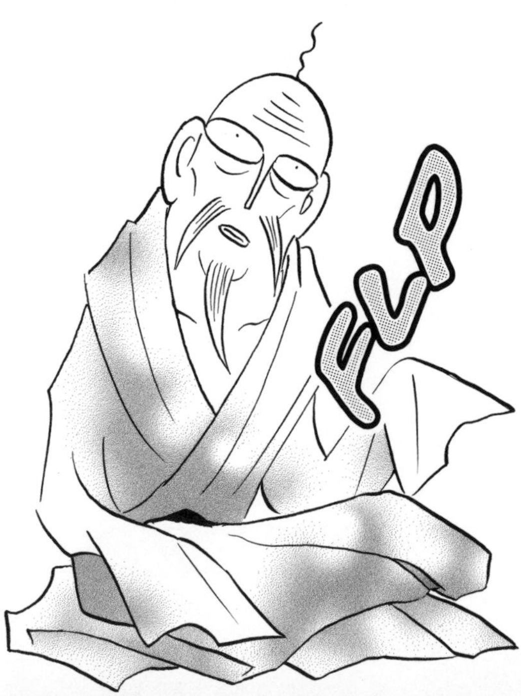
FLIP

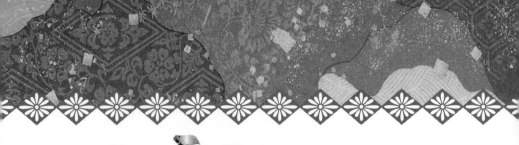

INUYASHA

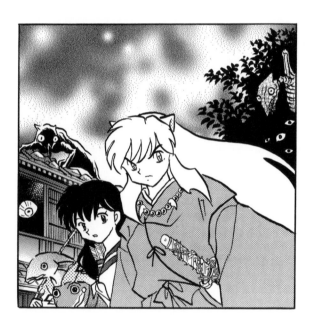

Volume 43
Assimilation

SCROLL ONE
THE ENTRAPPED BROTHERS

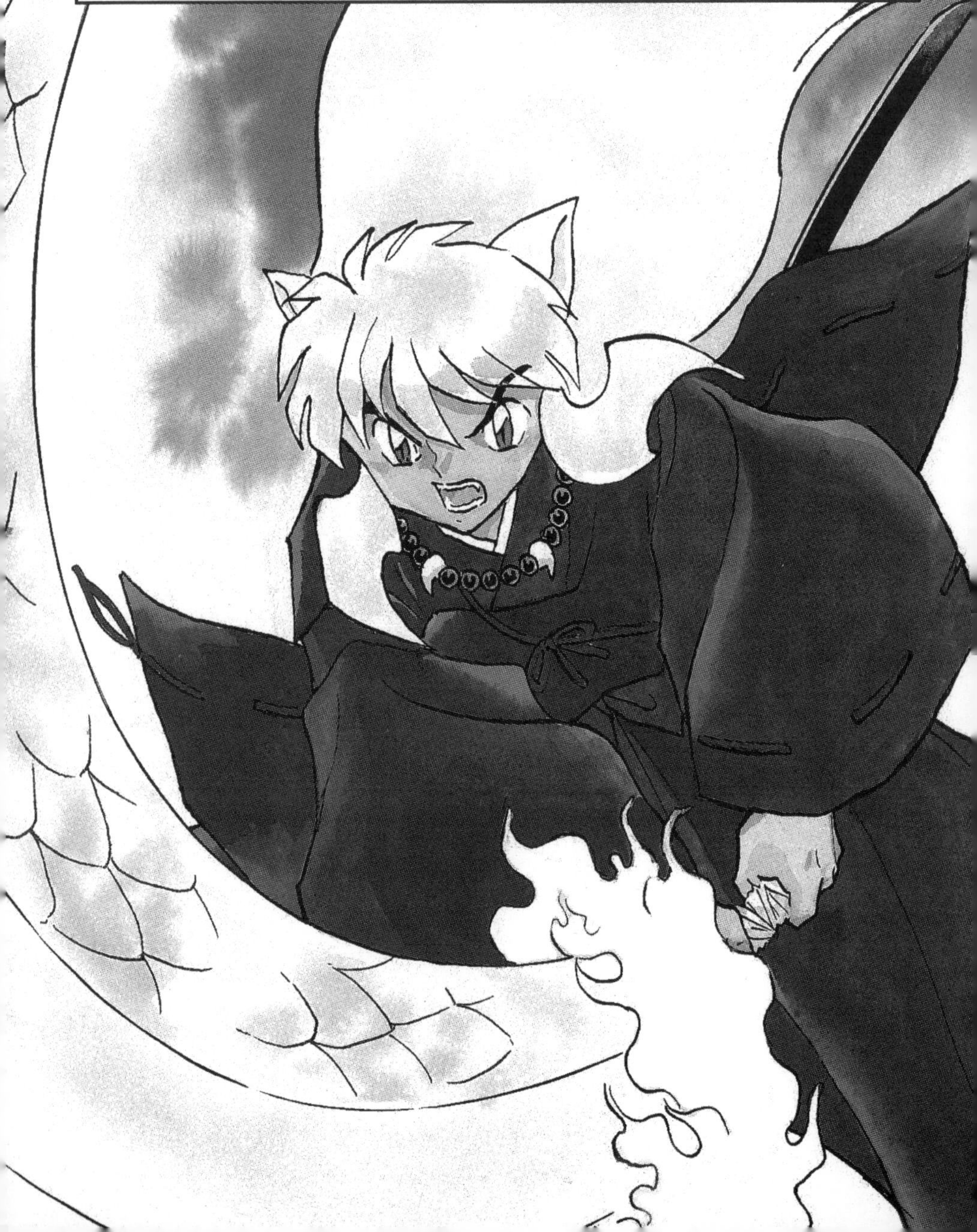

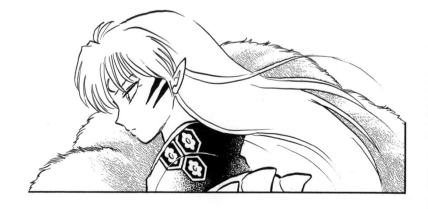

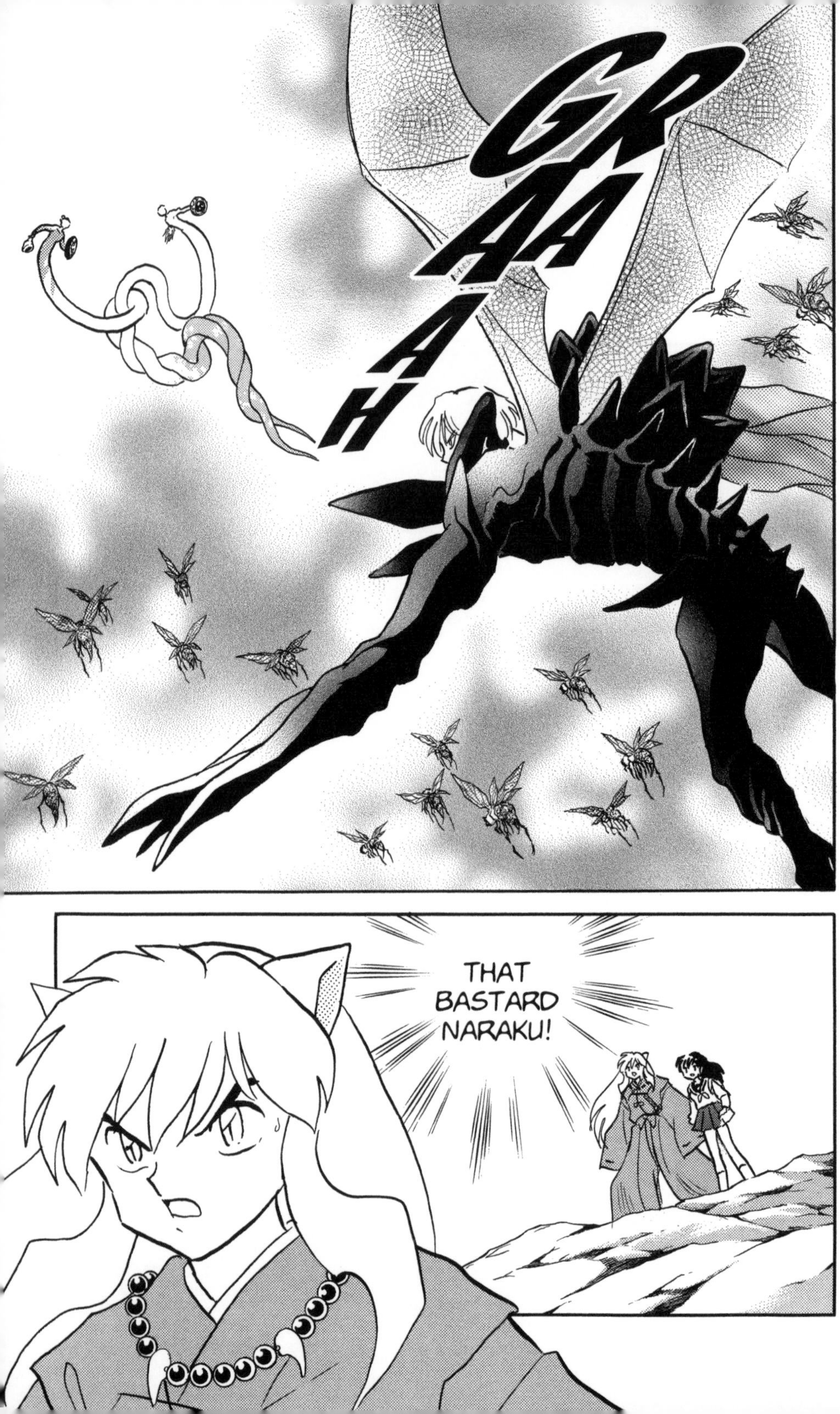
GRAAAH
THAT BASTARD NARAKU!

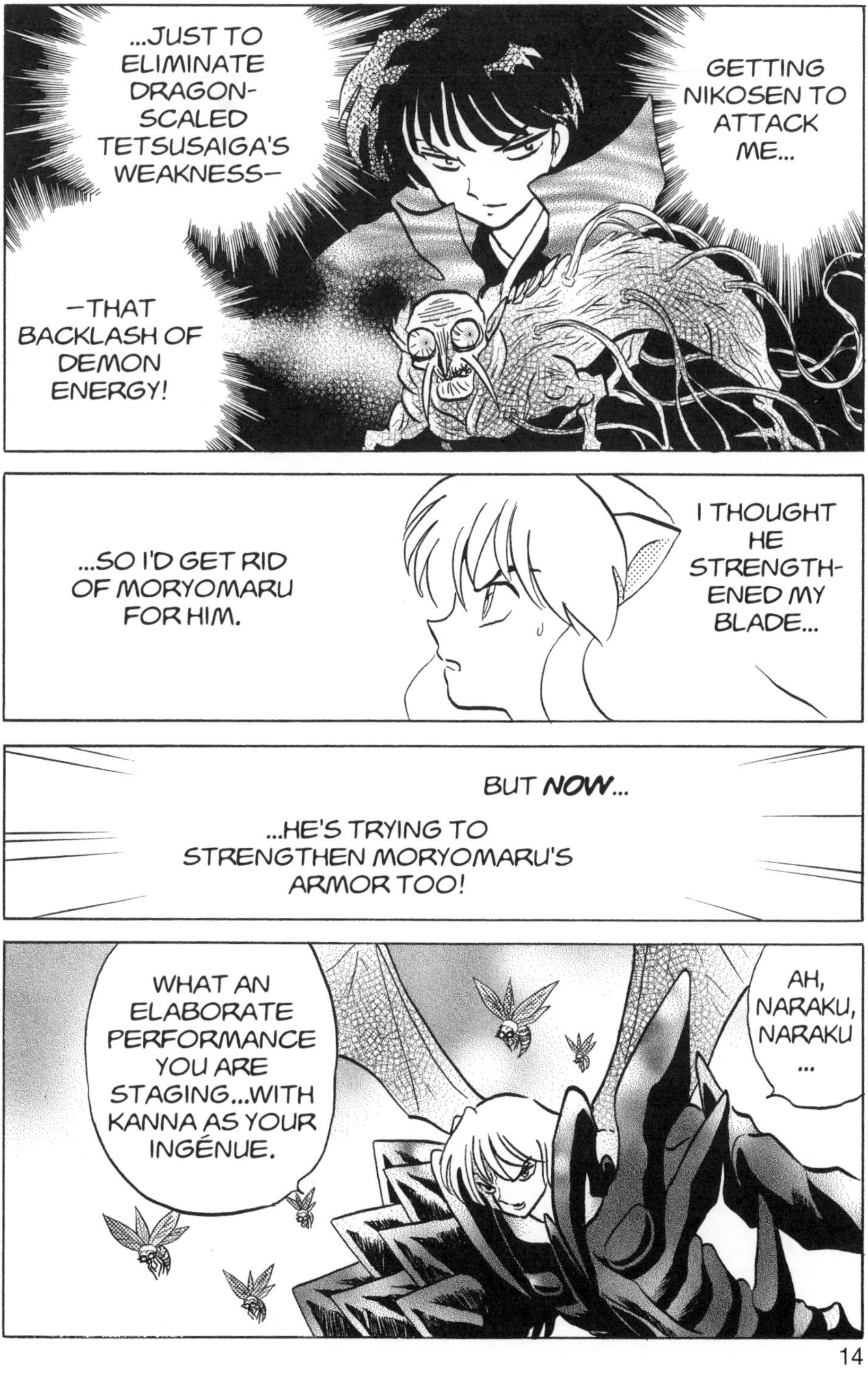
GETTING NIKOSEN TO ATTACK ME...
...JUST TO ELIMINATE DRAGON-SCALED TETSUSAIGA'S WEAKNESS—
—THAT BACKLASH OF DEMON ENERGY!
I THOUGHT HE STRENGTH-ENED MY BLADE...
...SO I'D GET RID OF MORYOMARU FOR HIM.
BUT *NOW*...
...HE'S TRYING TO STRENGTHEN MORYOMARU'S ARMOR TOO!
AH, NARAKU, NARAKU...
WHAT AN ELABORATE PERFORMANCE YOU ARE STAGING...WITH KANNA AS YOUR INGÉNUE.

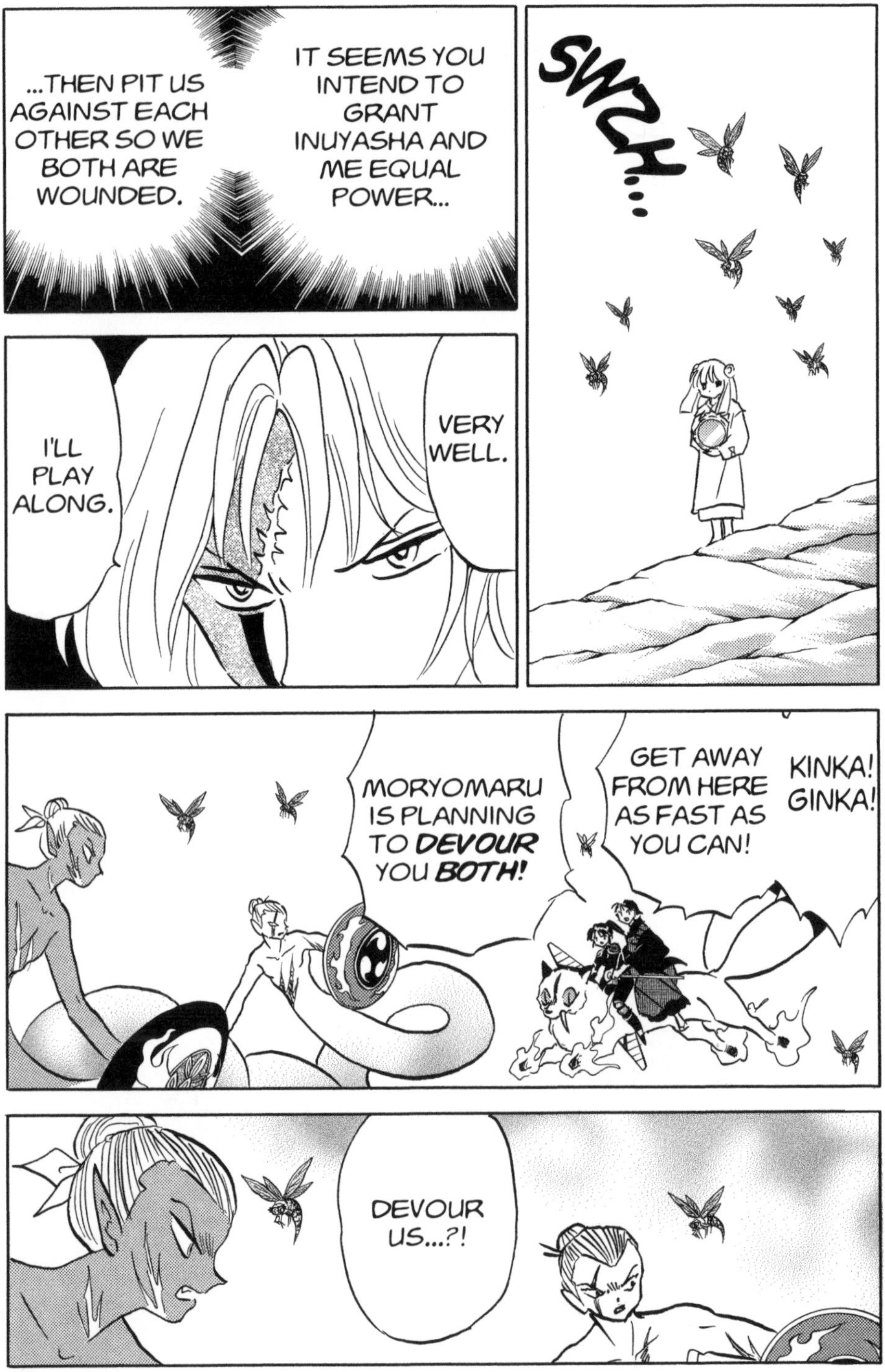
SWZH...
IT SEEMS YOU INTEND TO GRANT INUYASHA AND ME EQUAL POWER...
...THEN PIT US AGAINST EACH OTHER SO WE BOTH ARE WOUNDED.
VERY WELL.
I'LL PLAY ALONG.
KINKA! GINKA!
GET AWAY FROM HERE AS FAST AS YOU CAN!
MORYOMARU IS PLANNING TO **DEVOUR** YOU **BOTH**!
DEVOUR US...?!

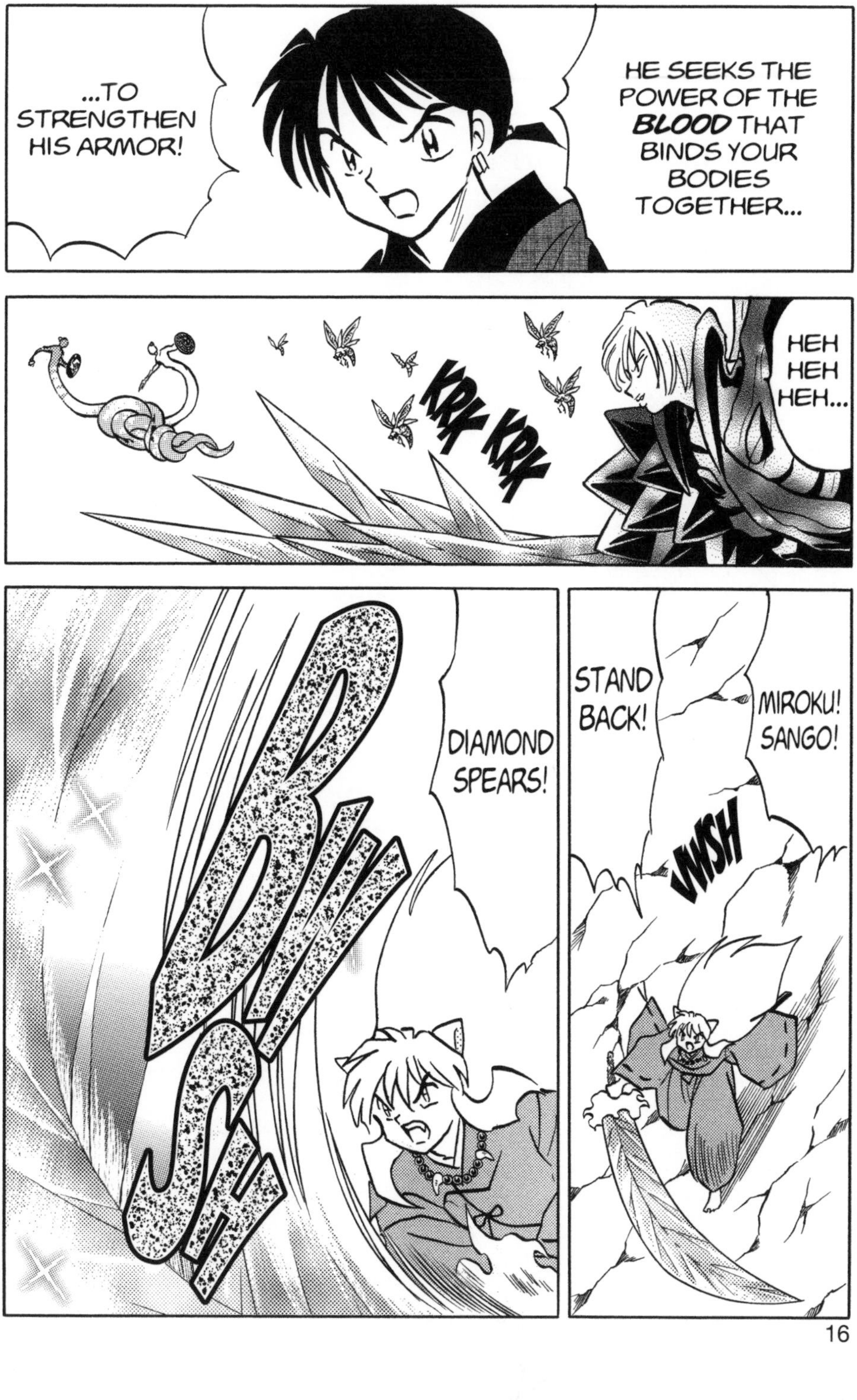
HE SEEKS THE POWER OF THE **BLOOD** THAT BINDS YOUR BODIES TOGETHER...
...TO STRENGTHEN HIS ARMOR!
HEH HEH HEH...
KRK KRK
MIROKU! SANGO!
STAND BACK!
VWSH
DIAMOND SPEARS!

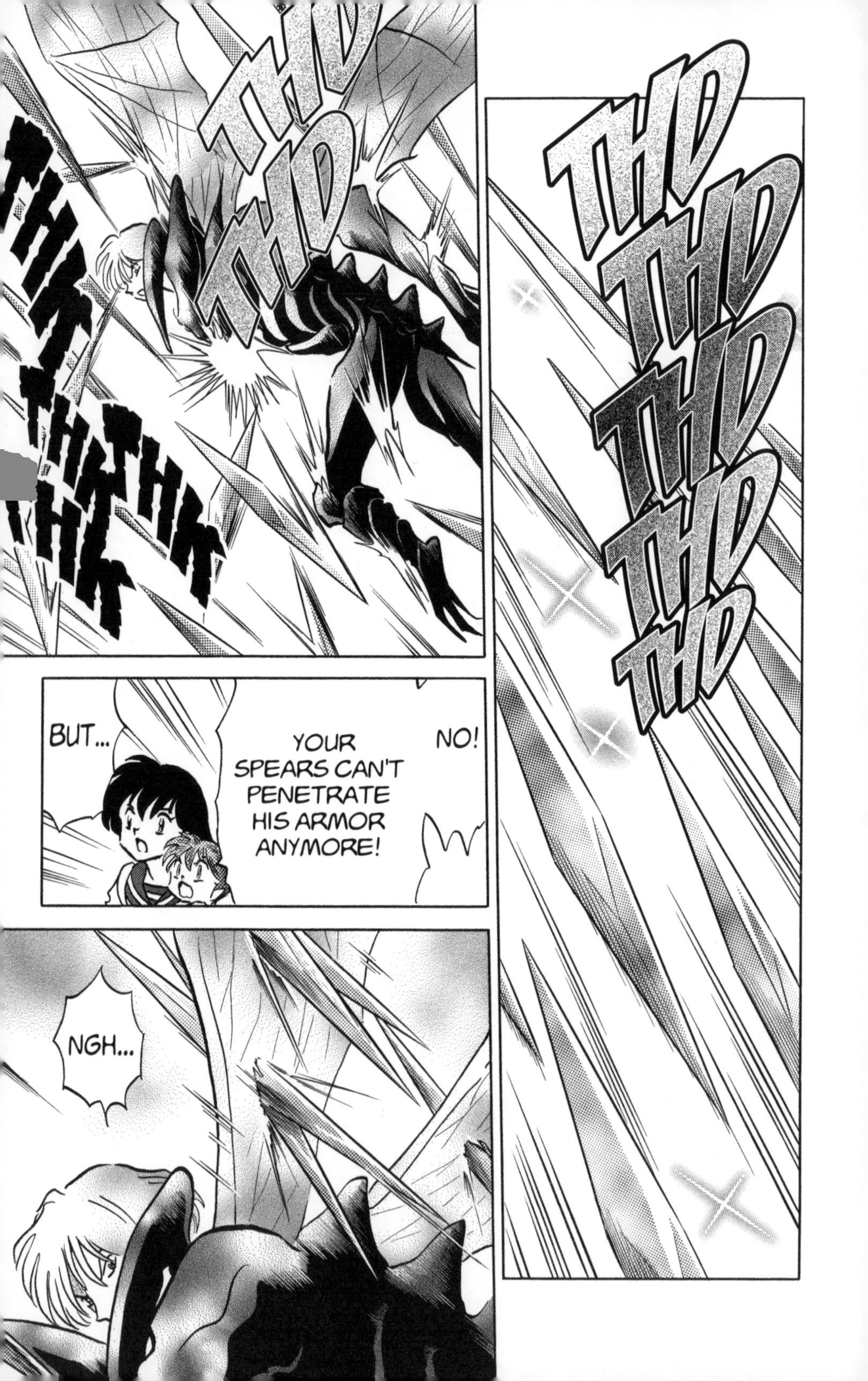
THD THD THD THD THD
THD THD
THK THK THK THK
NO!
YOUR SPEARS CAN'T PENETRATE HIS ARMOR ANYMORE!
BUT...
NGH...

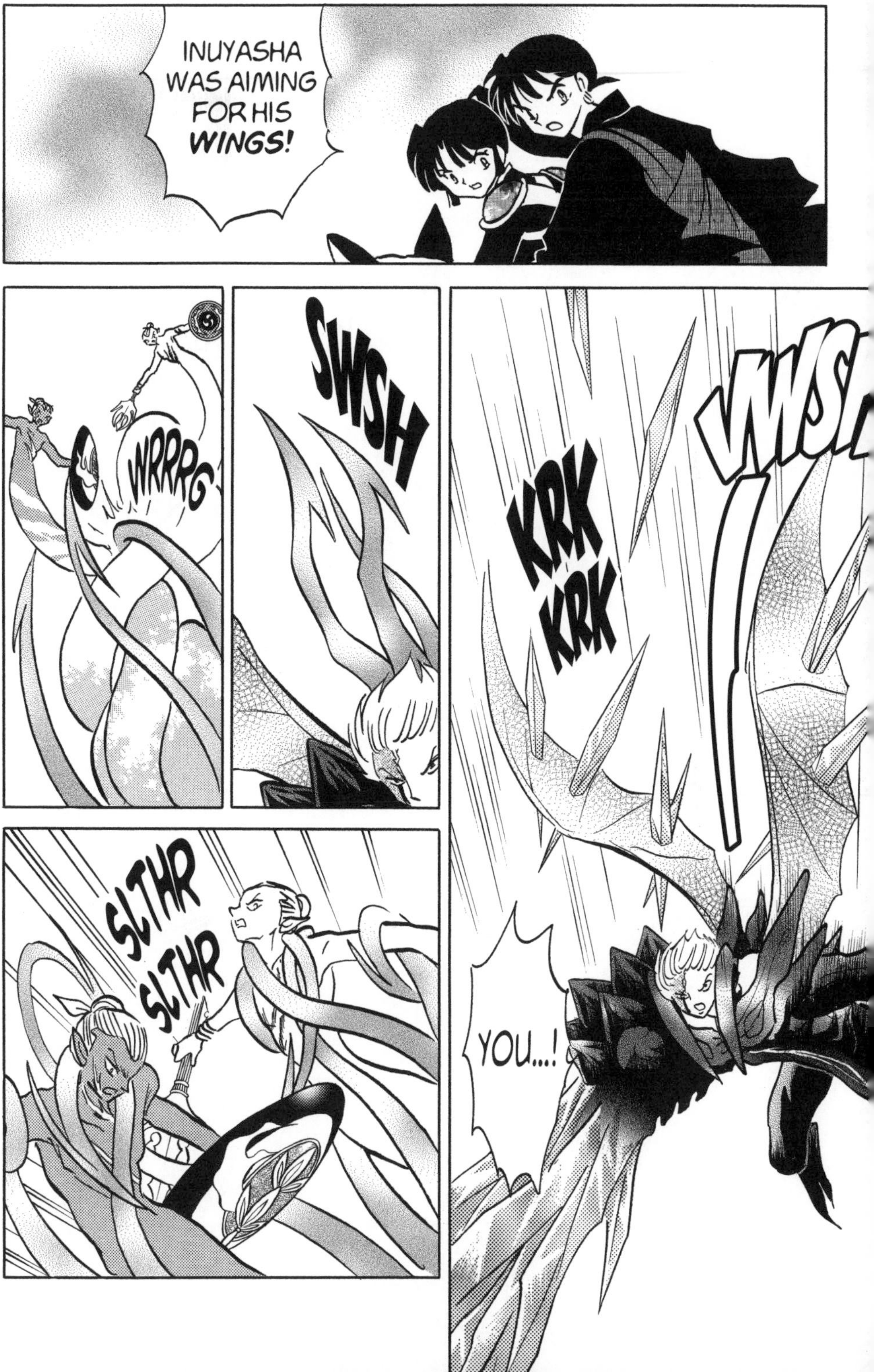

INUYASHA WAS AIMING FOR HIS WINGS!
VWS
KRK KRK
YOU...!
SWSH
WRRRG
SLTHR SLTHR

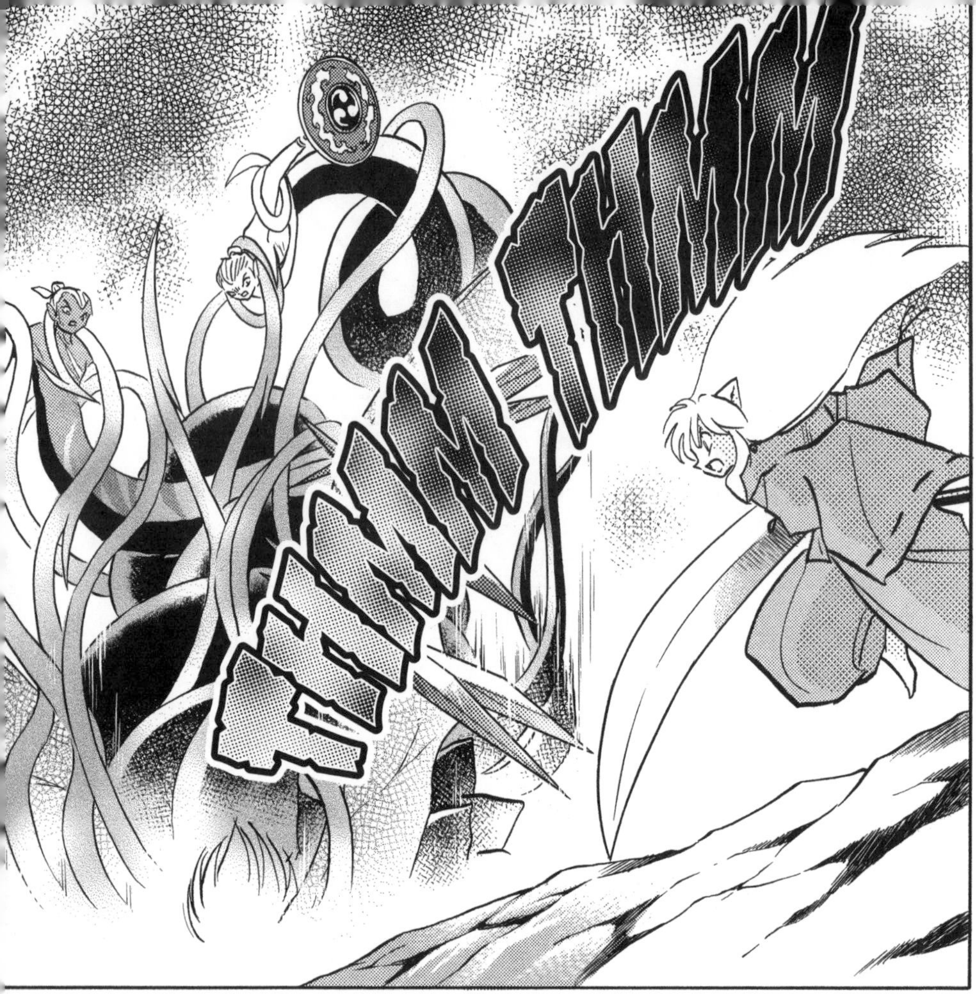
THMM THMM
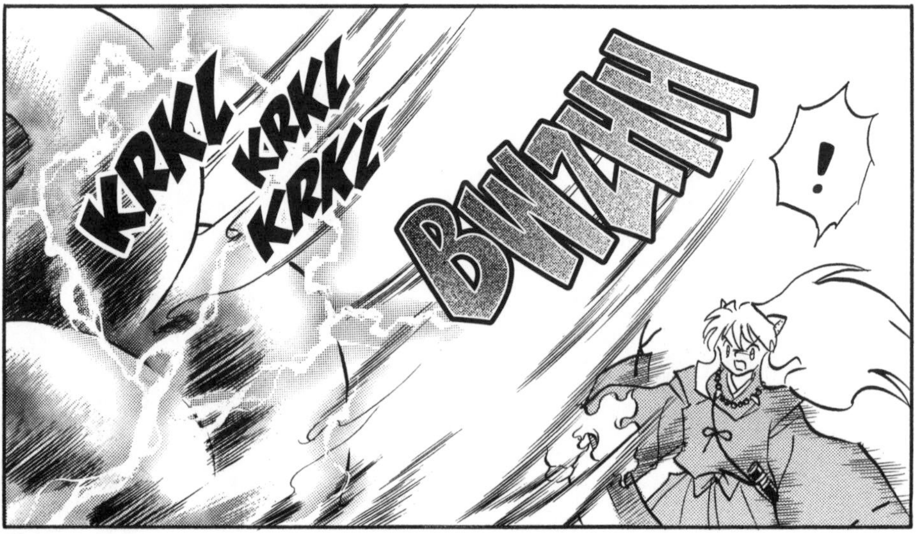
!
BWZHH
KRKL
KRKL
KRKL

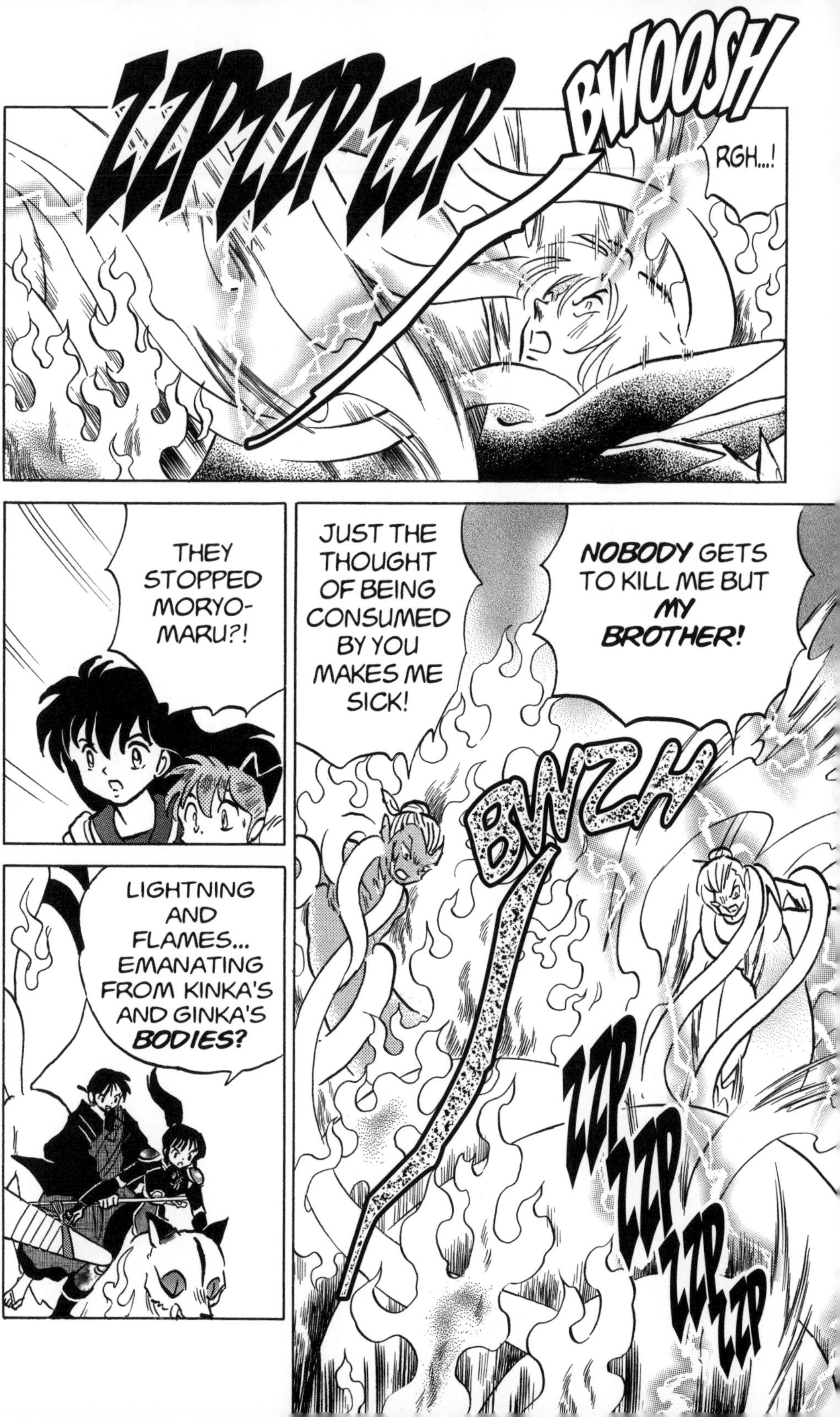
BWOOSH
RGH...!
ZZIP ZZIP ZZIP
NOBODY GETS TO KILL ME BUT MY BROTHER!
JUST THE THOUGHT OF BEING CONSUMED BY YOU MAKES ME SICK!
BWZH
ZZIP ZZIP ZZIP ZZIP
THEY STOPPED MORYO-MARU?!
LIGHTNING AND FLAMES... EMANATING FROM KINKA'S AND GINKA'S BODIES?

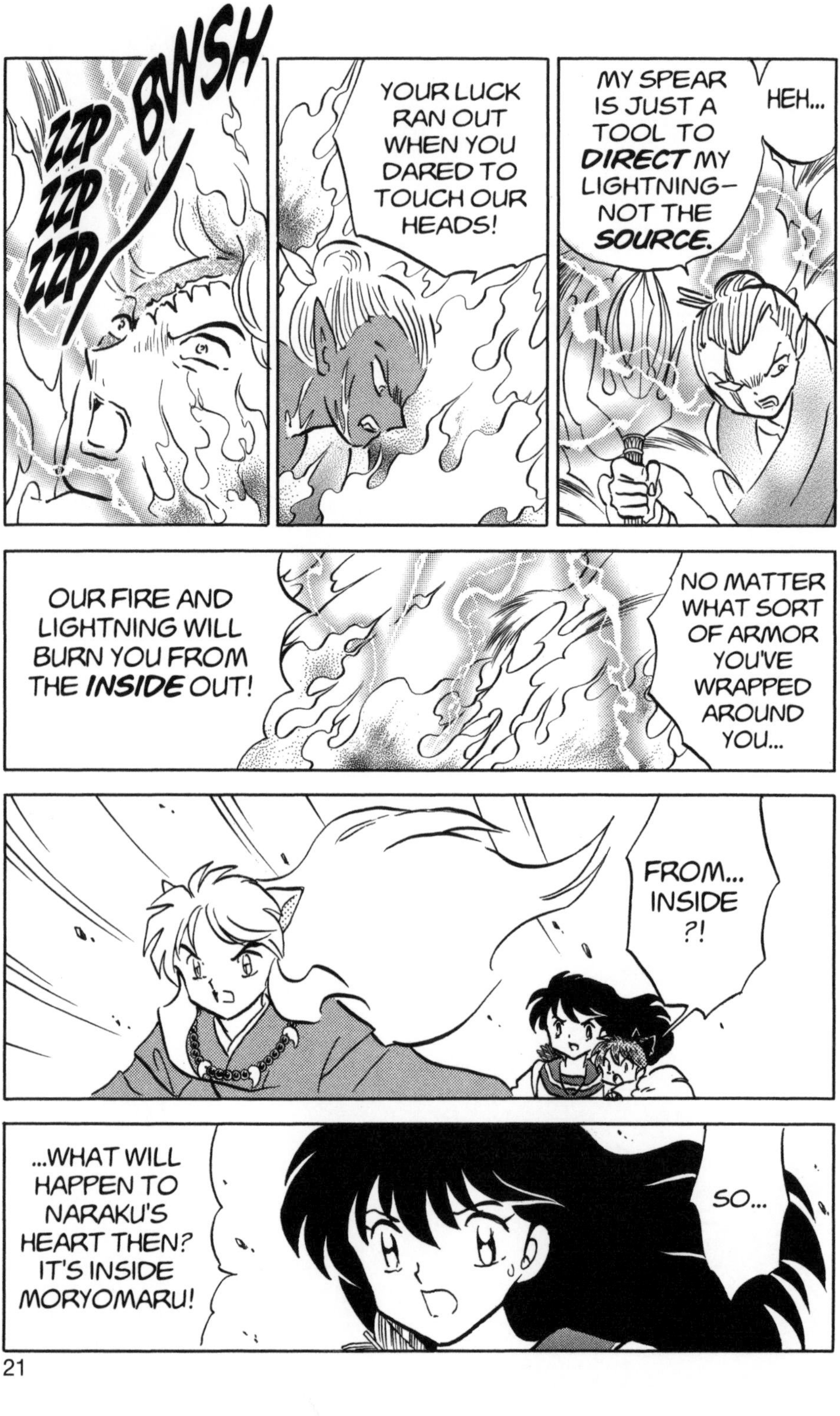
HEH...
MY SPEAR IS JUST A TOOL TO **DIRECT** MY LIGHTNING— NOT THE **SOURCE.**
YOUR LUCK RAN OUT WHEN YOU DARED TO TOUCH OUR HEADS!
BWSH
ZZP ZZP ZZP
NO MATTER WHAT SORT OF ARMOR YOU'VE WRAPPED AROUND YOU...
OUR FIRE AND LIGHTNING WILL BURN YOU FROM THE **INSIDE** OUT!
FROM... INSIDE ?!
SO...
...WHAT WILL HAPPEN TO NARAKU'S HEART THEN? IT'S INSIDE MORYOMARU!

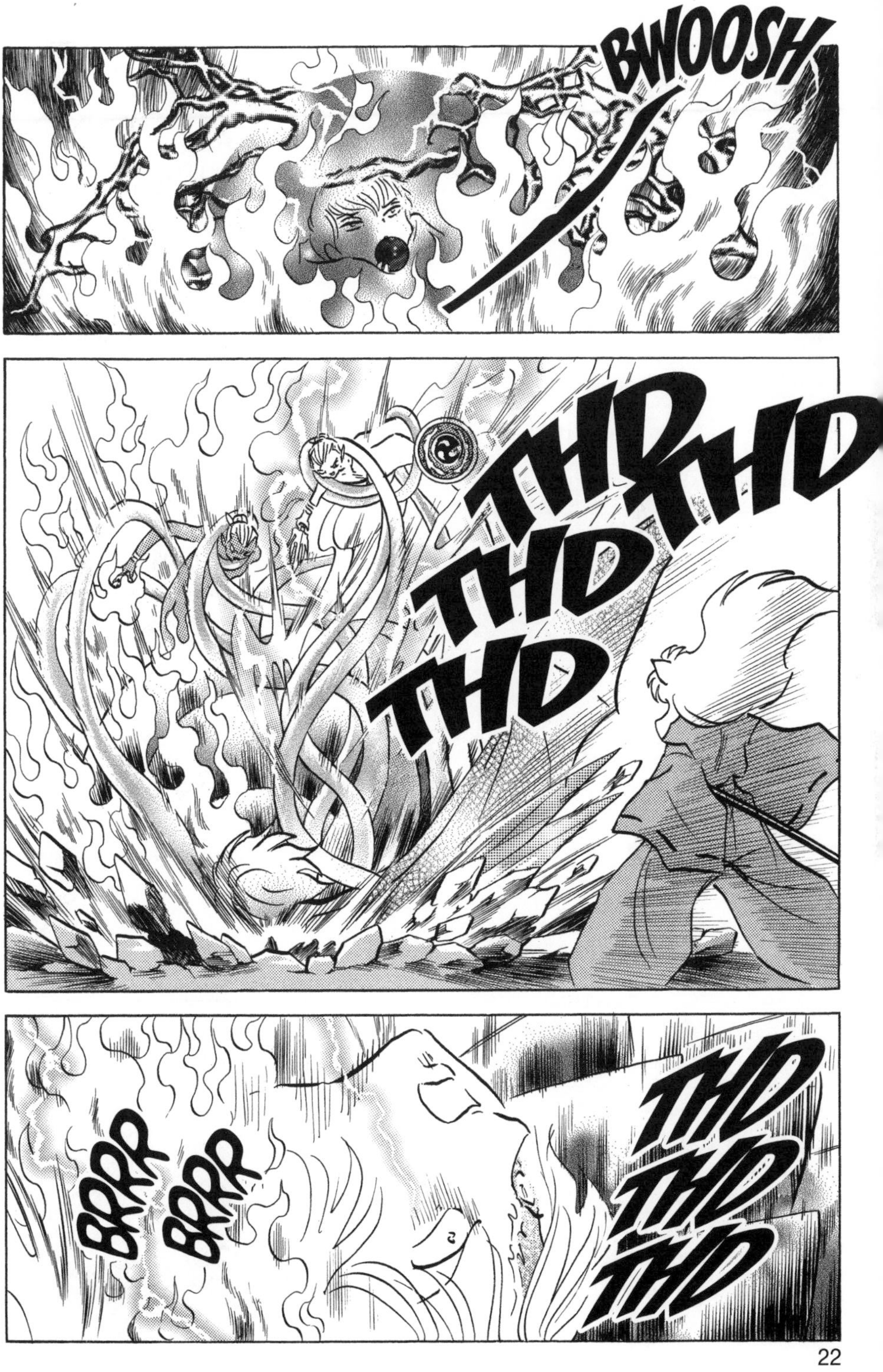
BWOOSH
THD THD
THD
THD
THD
THD
THD
BRRR
BRRR

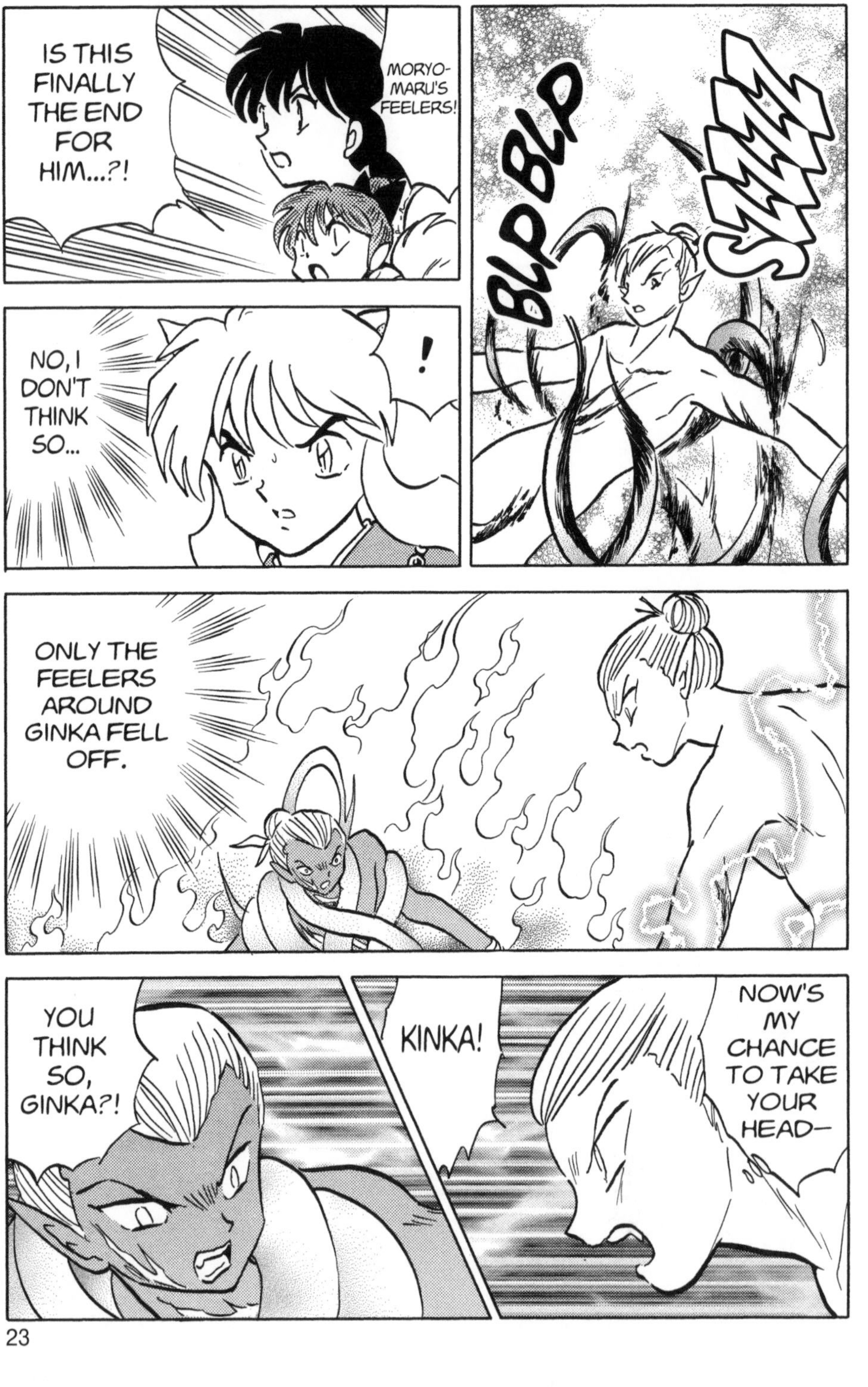
BLP BLP
SZZZZ
MORYO-MARU'S FEELERS!
IS THIS FINALLY THE END FOR HIM...?!
!
NO, I DON'T THINK SO...
ONLY THE FEELERS AROUND GINKA FELL OFF.
NOW'S MY CHANCE TO TAKE YOUR HEAD—
KINKA!
YOU THINK SO, GINKA?!

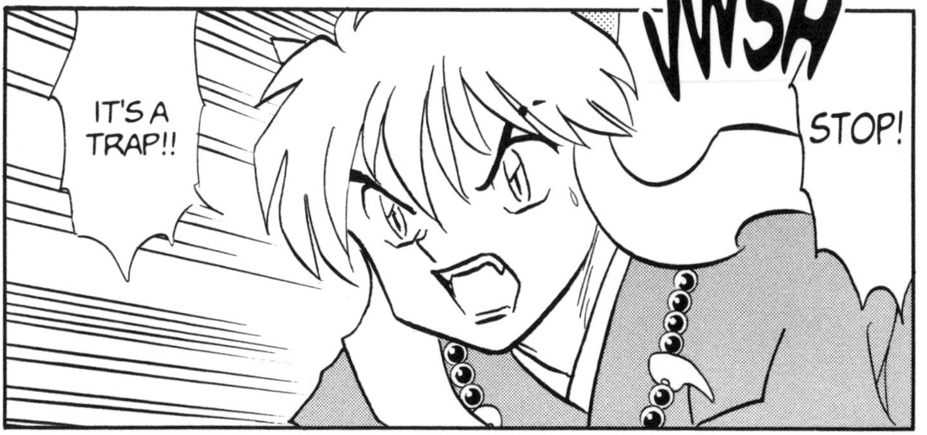
VVNSH
STOP!
IT'S A TRAP!!
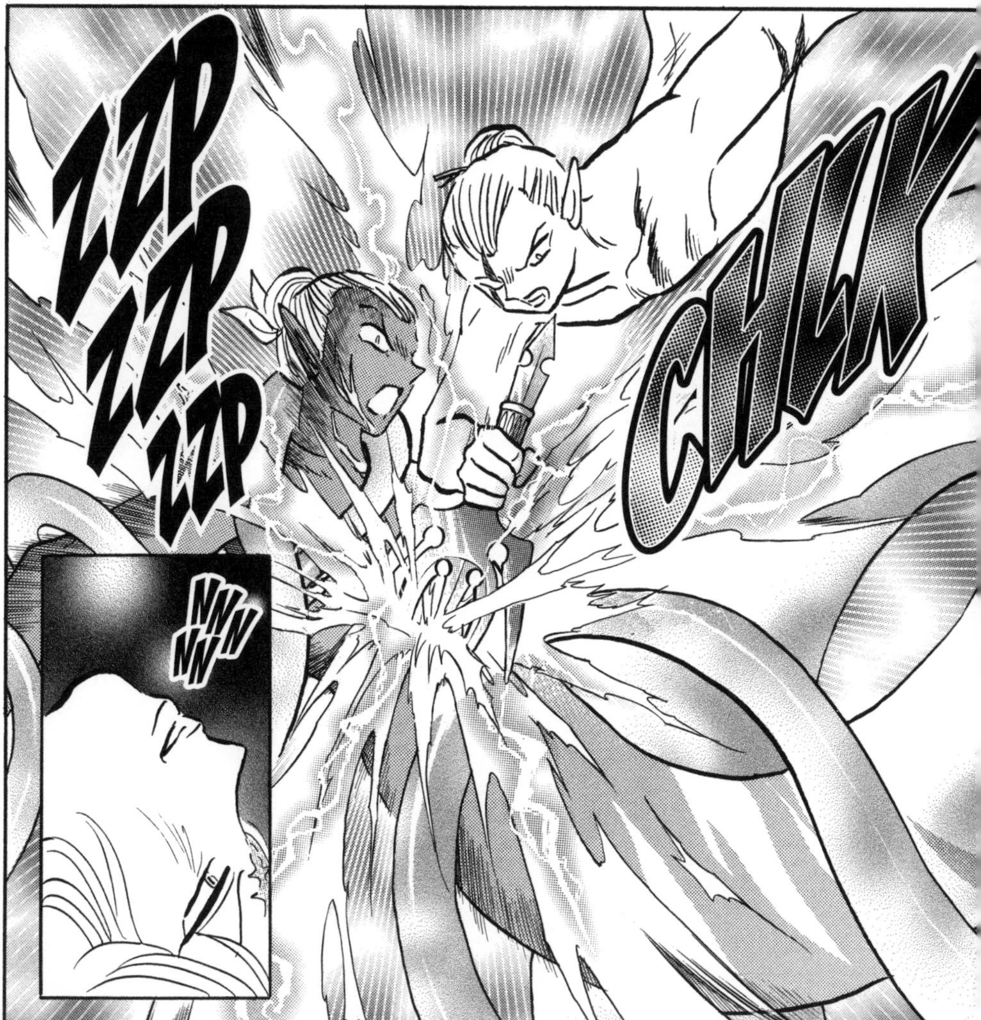
CHINK
ZZP ZZP ZZP
NNNNN

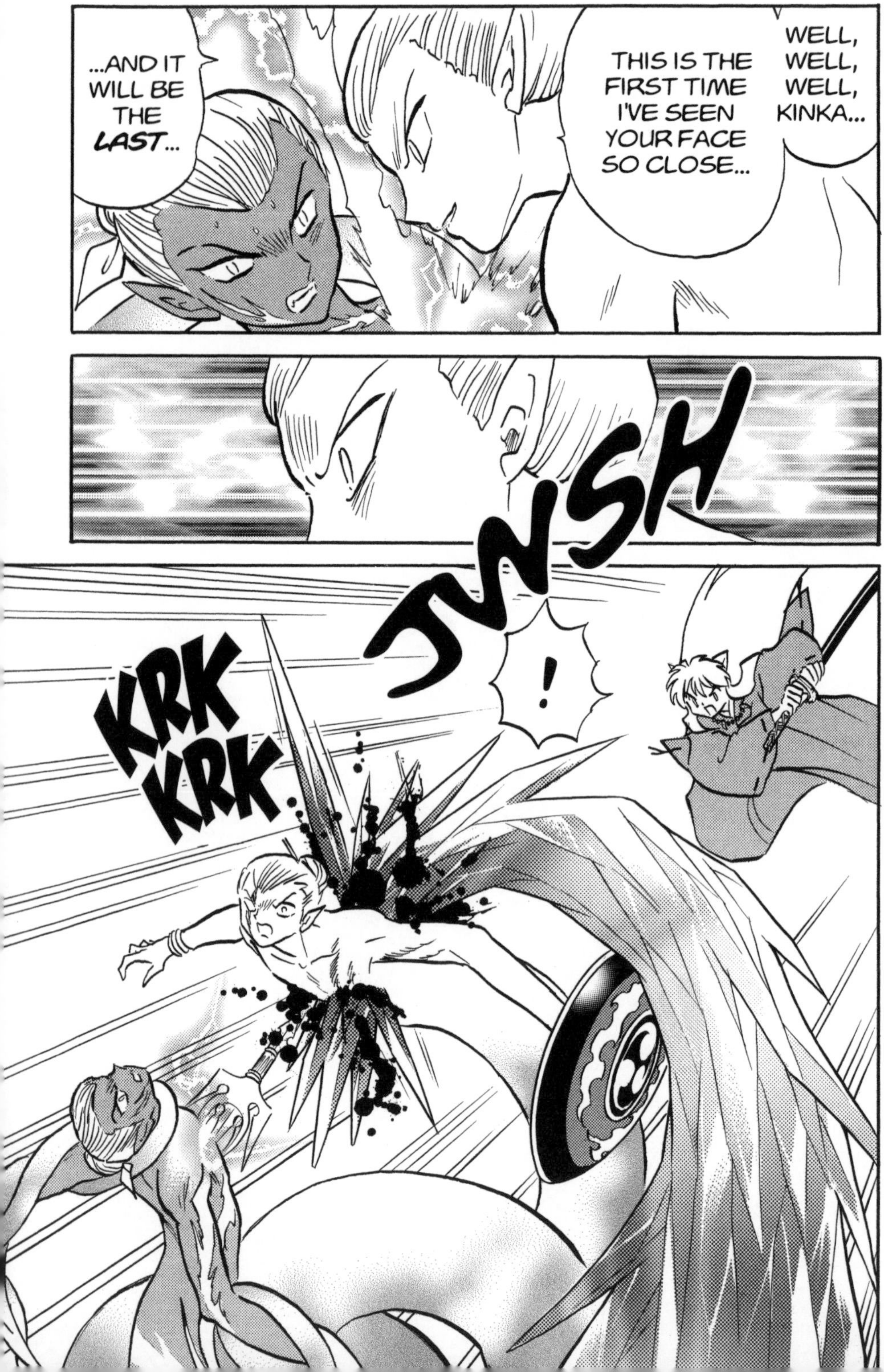
WELL, WELL, WELL, KINKA...
THIS IS THE FIRST TIME I'VE SEEN YOUR FACE SO CLOSE...
...AND IT WILL BE THE *LAST*...
JWSH
!
KRK KRK

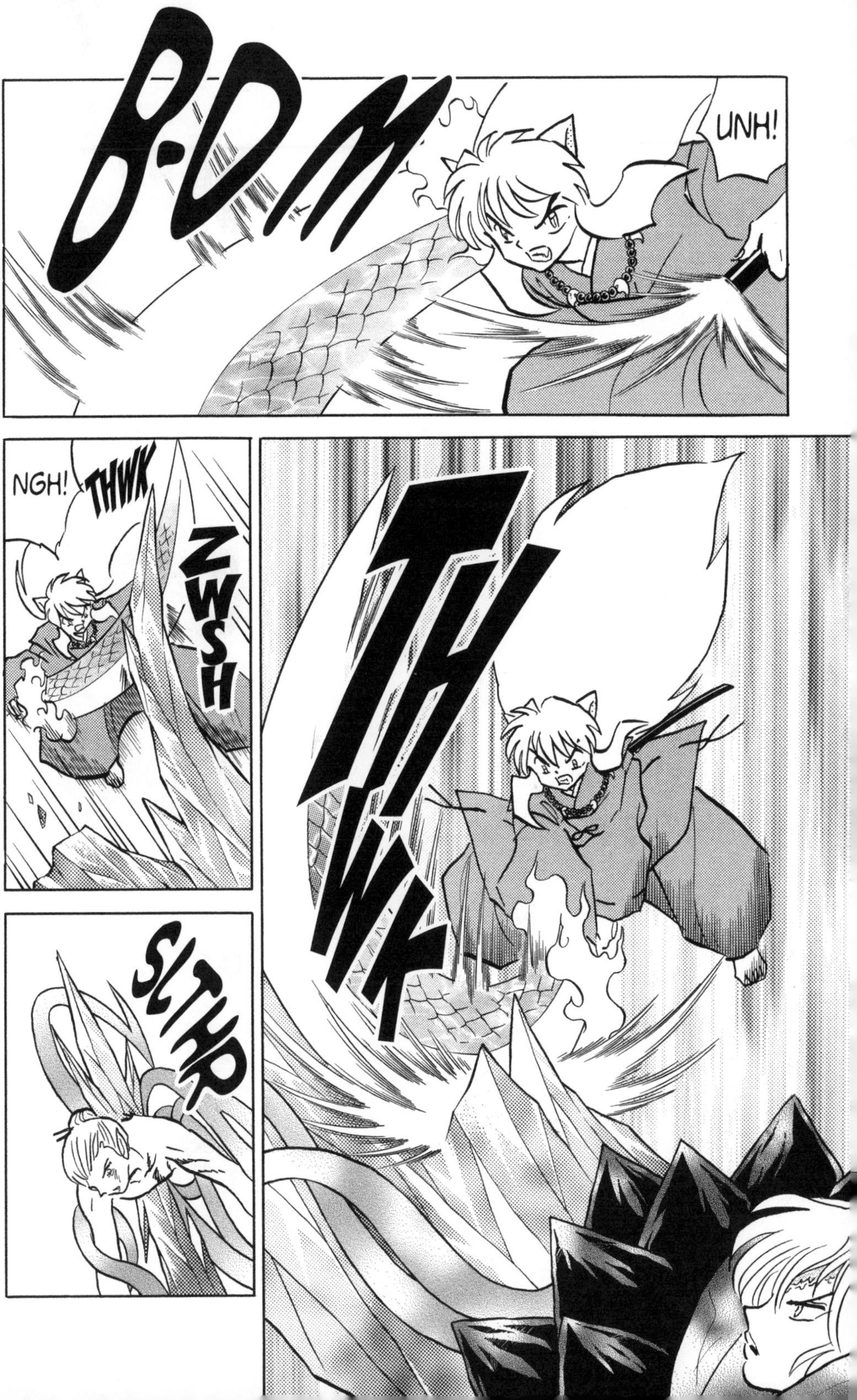
UNH!
B-D-M
THWK
THWK
NGH!
ZWSH
SLTHR

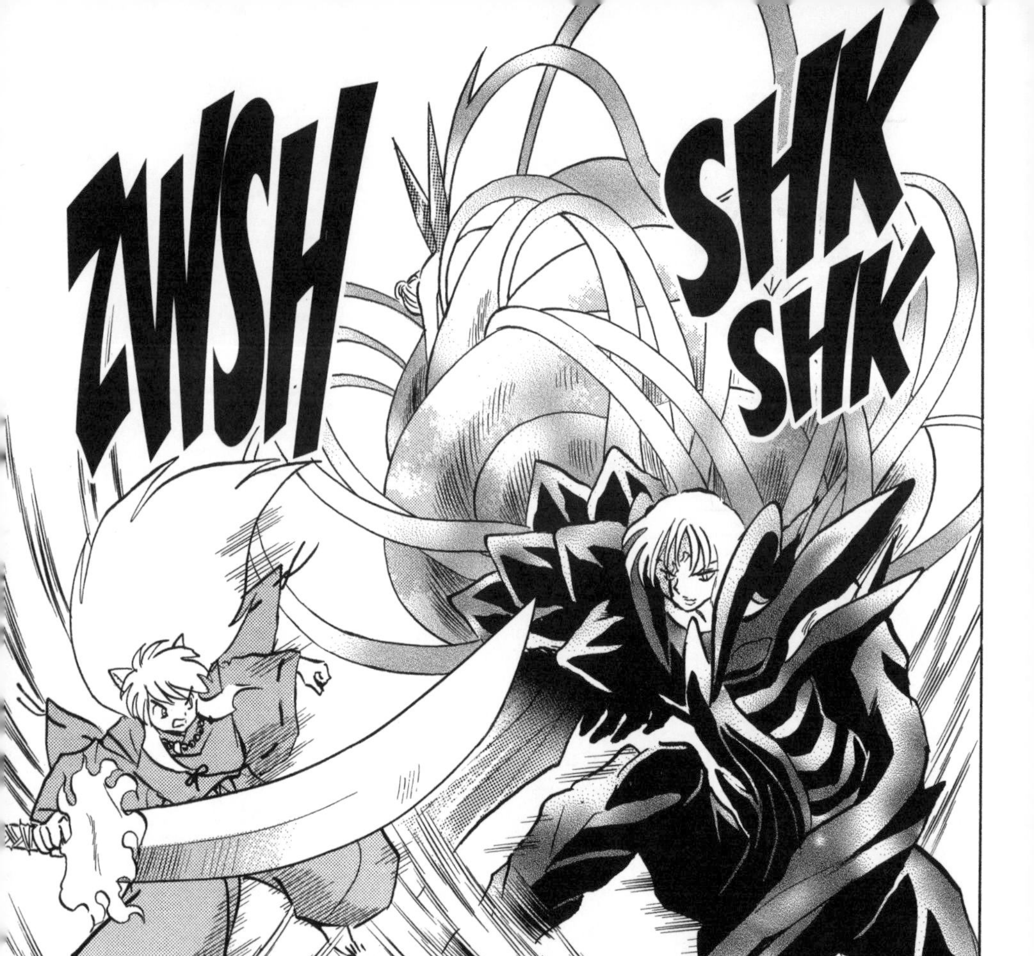
SHK SHK
ZWSH

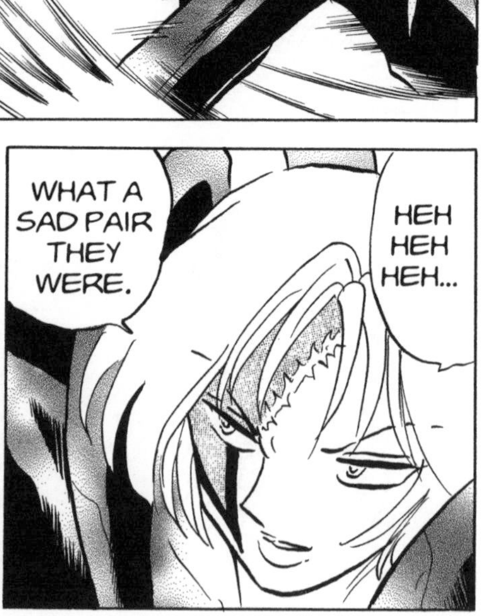
HEH HEH HEH...
WHAT A SAD PAIR THEY WERE.

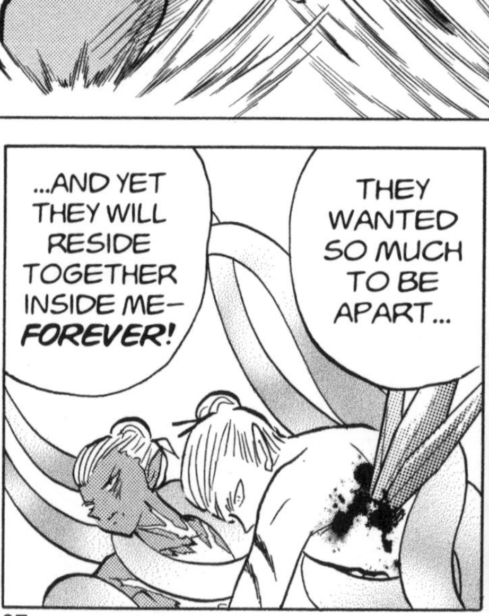
THEY WANTED SO MUCH TO BE APART...
...AND YET THEY WILL RESIDE TOGETHER INSIDE ME—**FOREVER!**

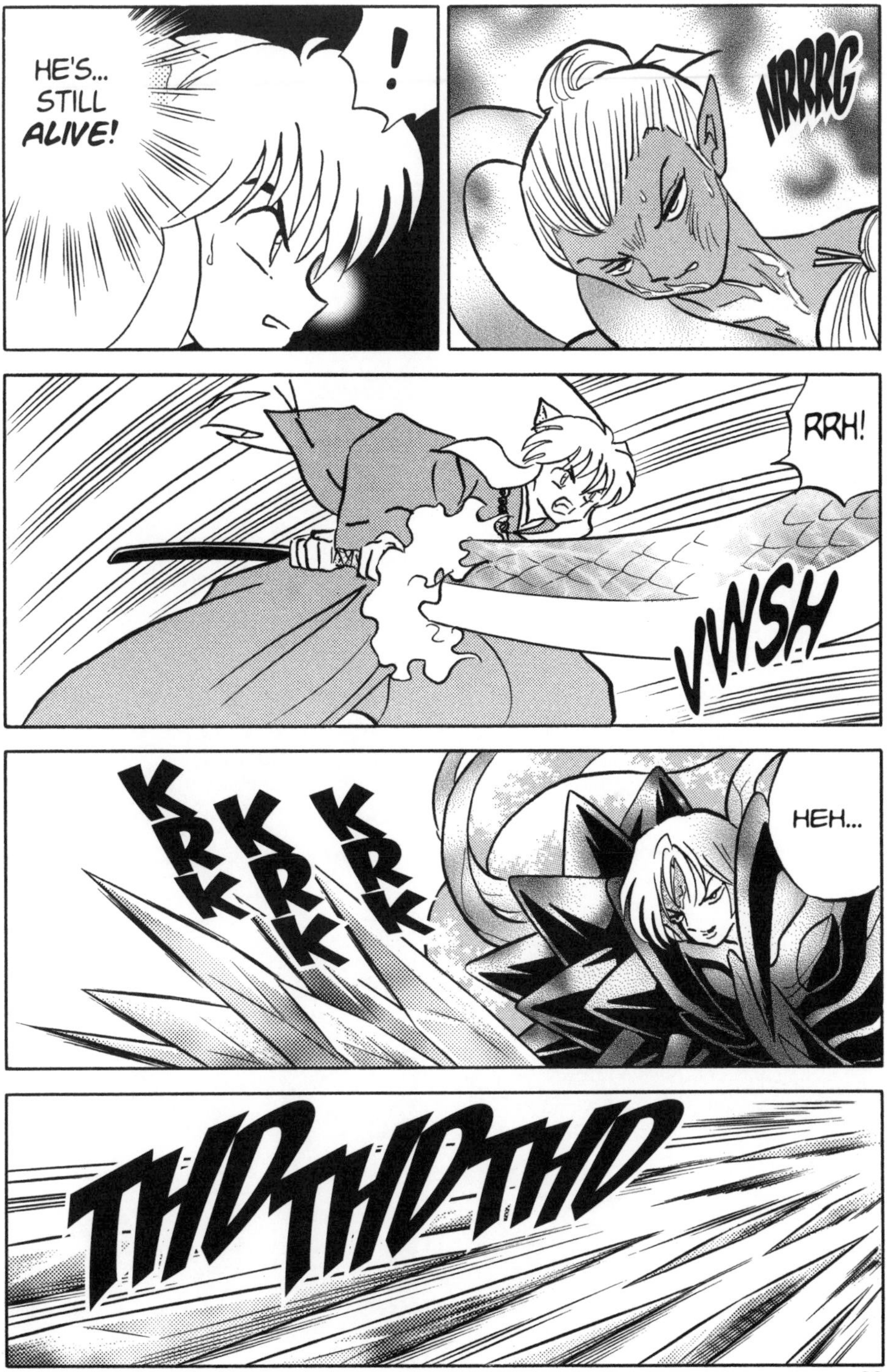
NRRRG
!
HE'S... STILL ALIVE!
RRH!
VWSH
HEH...
KRK
KRK
KRK
THD THD THD

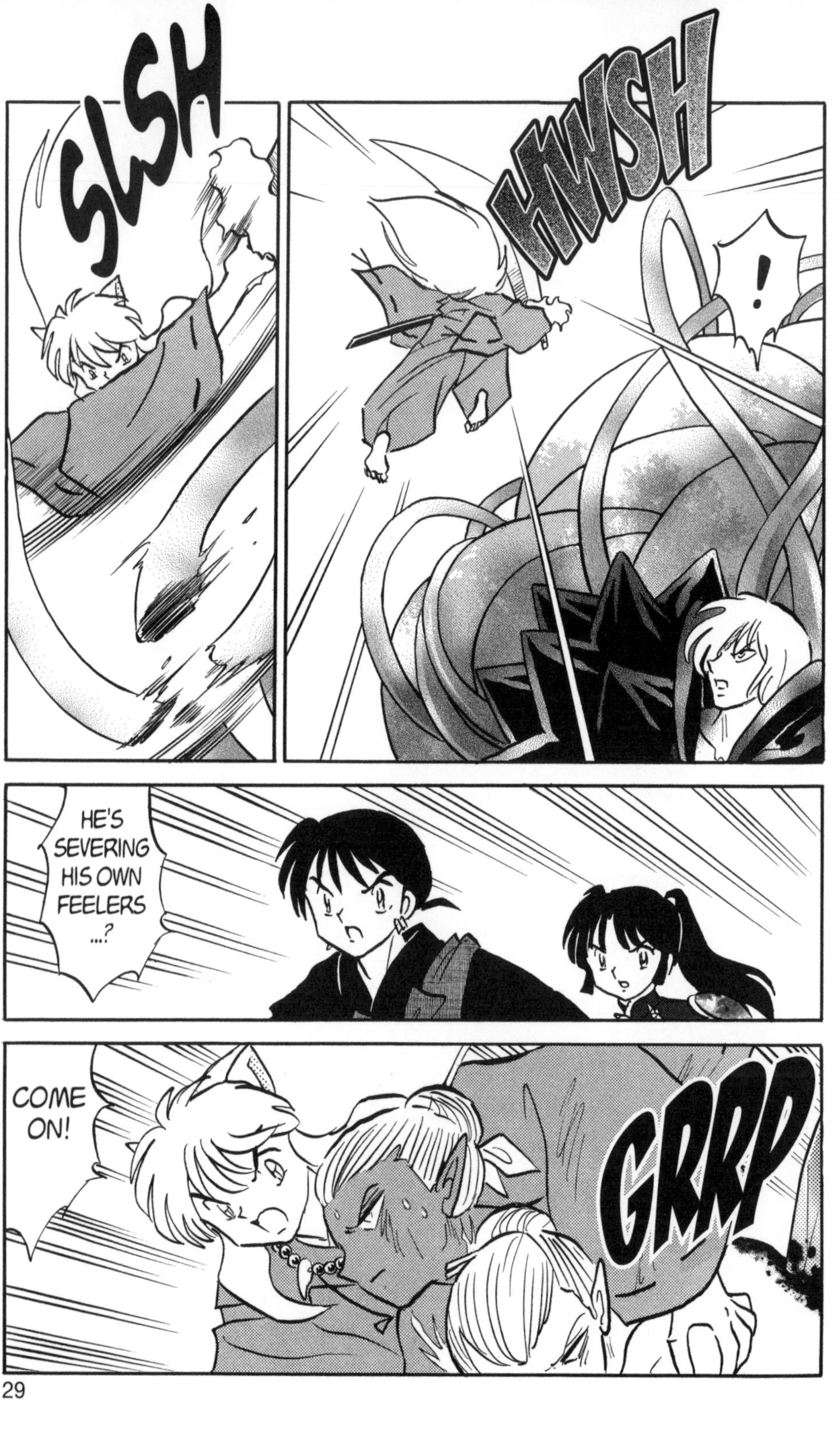
HWSH
!
SLSH
HE'S SEVERING HIS OWN FEELERS ...?
GRRP
COME ON!

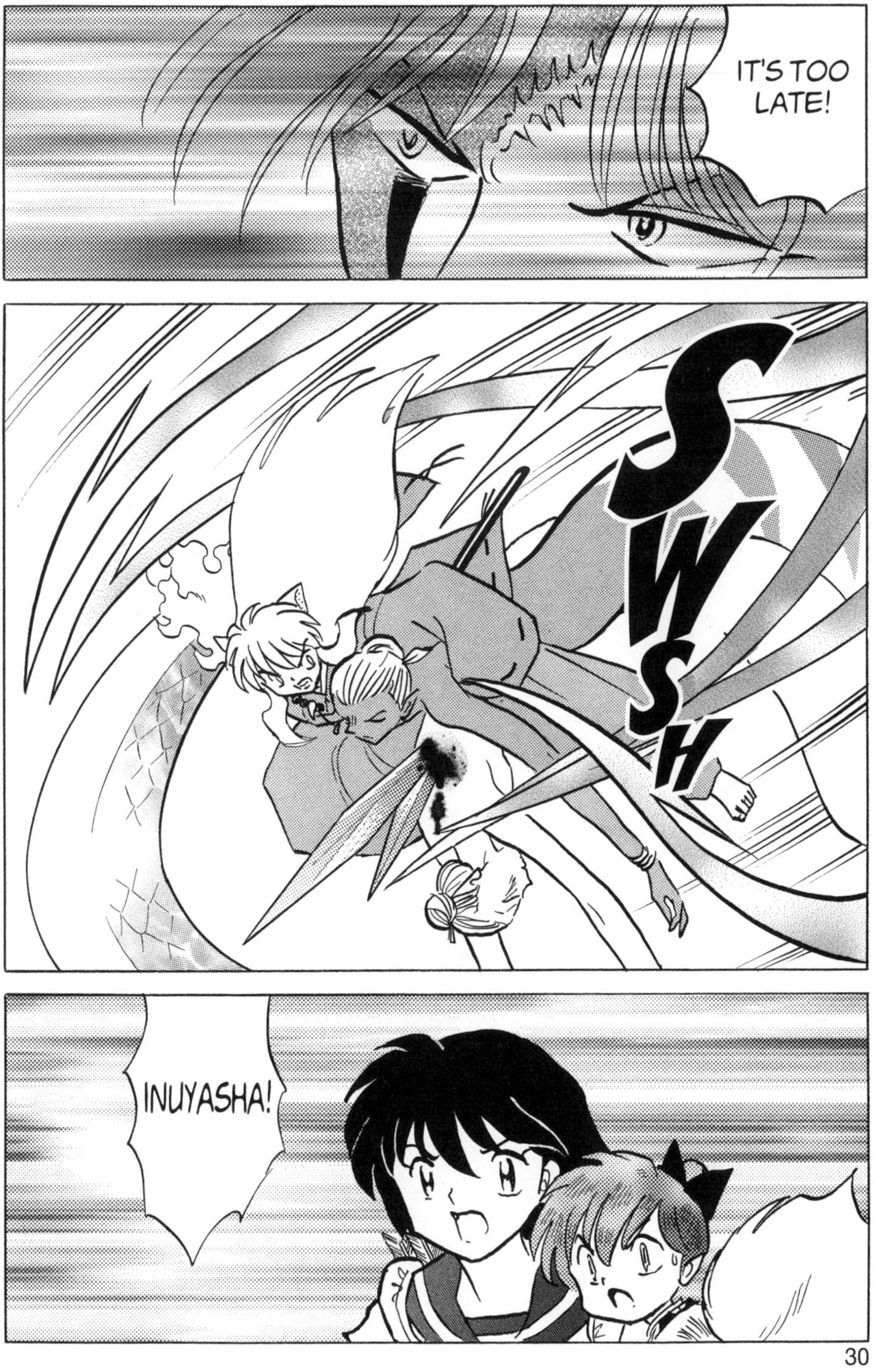
IT'S TOO LATE!
SWSH
INUYASHA!

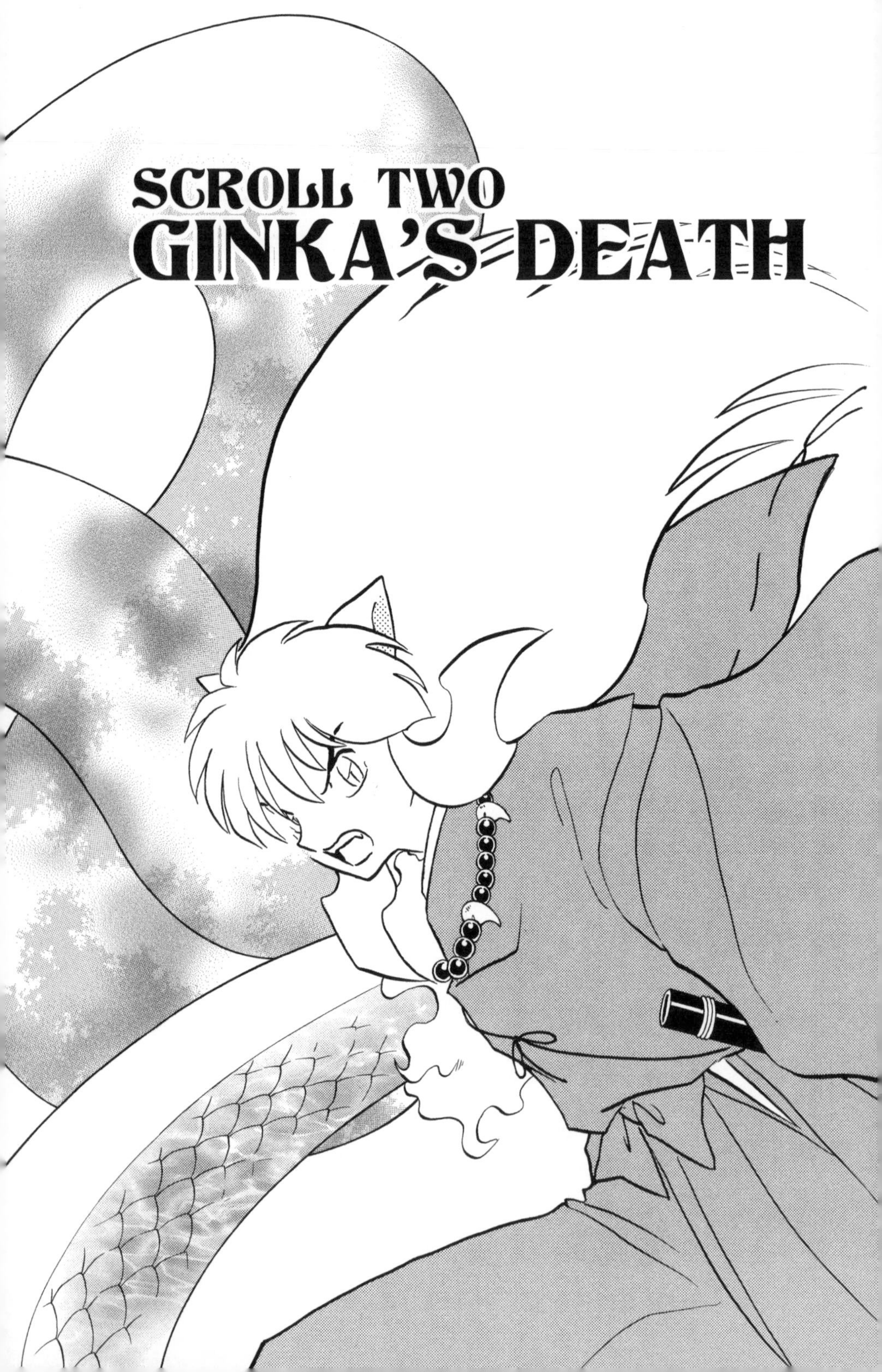
SCROLL TWO
GINKA'S DEATH

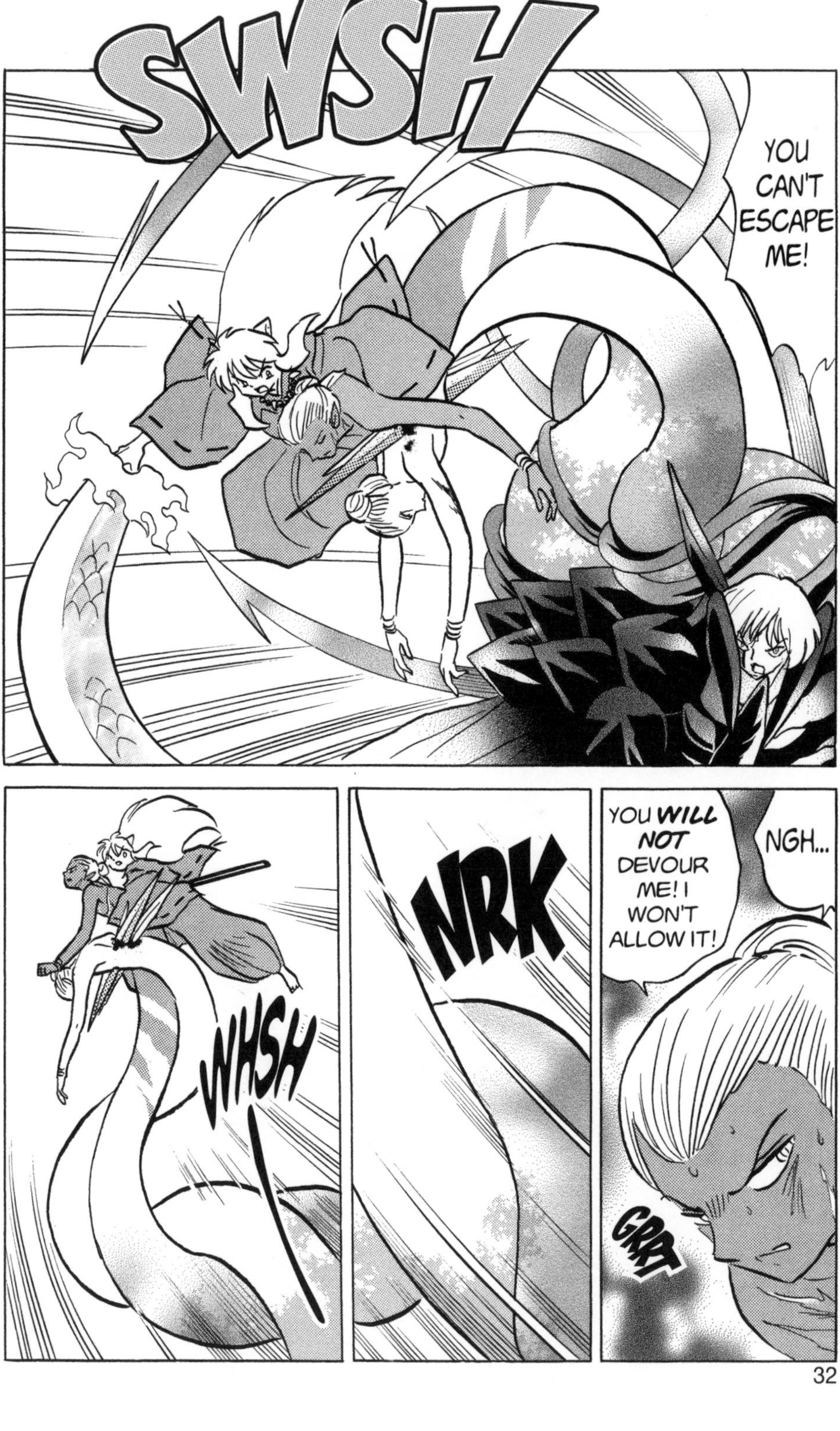
SWSH
YOU CAN'T ESCAPE ME!
NGH...
YOU **WILL NOT** DEVOUR ME! I WON'T ALLOW IT!
GRRT
NRK
WHSH

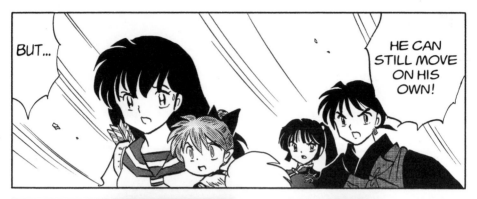

BUT...

HE CAN STILL MOVE ON HIS OWN!

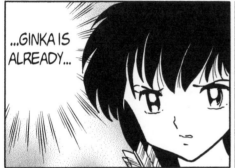

...GINKA IS ALREADY...

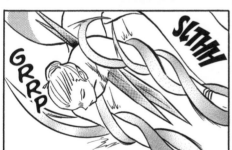

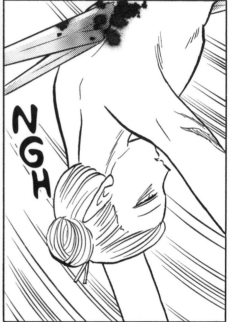

NGH

GRRP

SLTHH

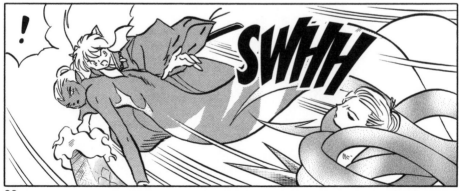

!

SWHH

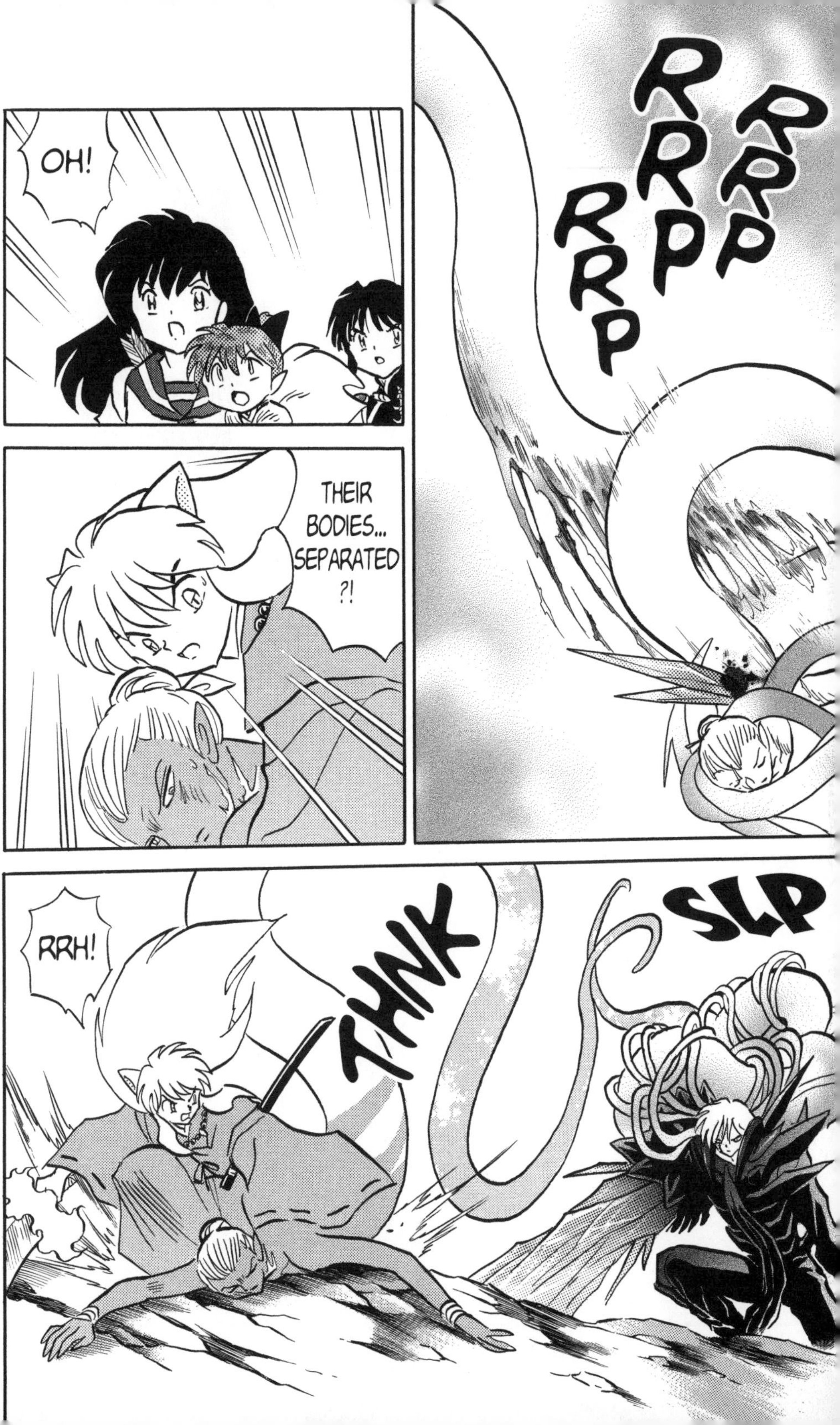
RRP
RRP
RRP
OH!
THEIR BODIES... SEPARATED ?!
SLP
THNK
RRH!

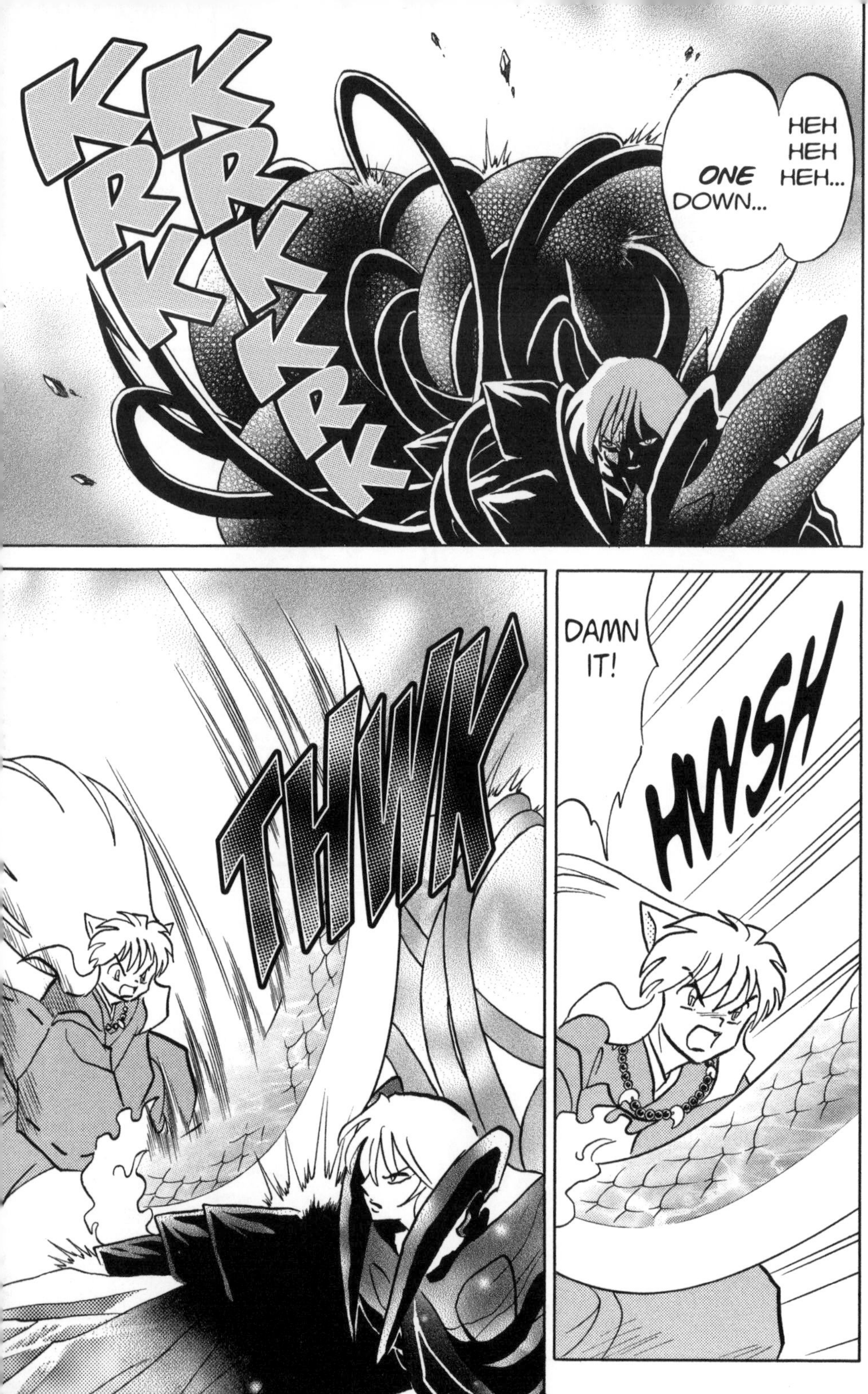
HEH HEH HEH...
ONE DOWN...
DAMN IT!
HWSH
THWK

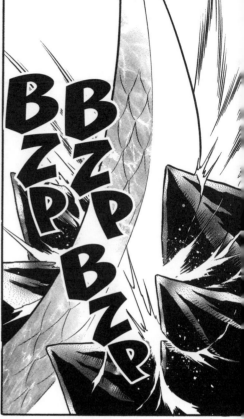

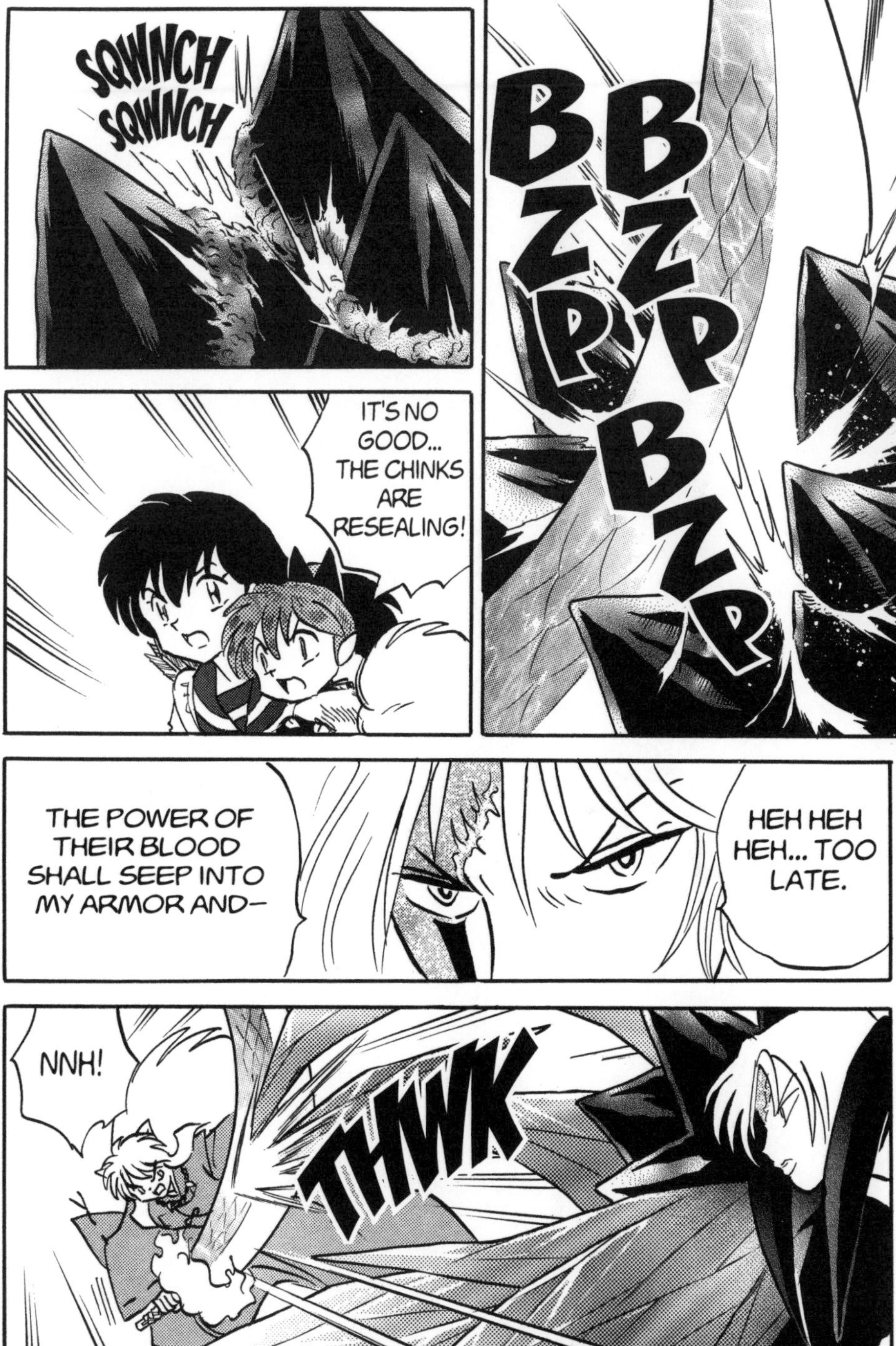
BZP BZP BZP
SQWNCH SQWNCH
IT'S NO GOOD... THE CHINKS ARE RESEALING!
HEH HEH HEH... TOO LATE.
THE POWER OF THEIR BLOOD SHALL SEEP INTO MY ARMOR AND–
THWK
NNH!

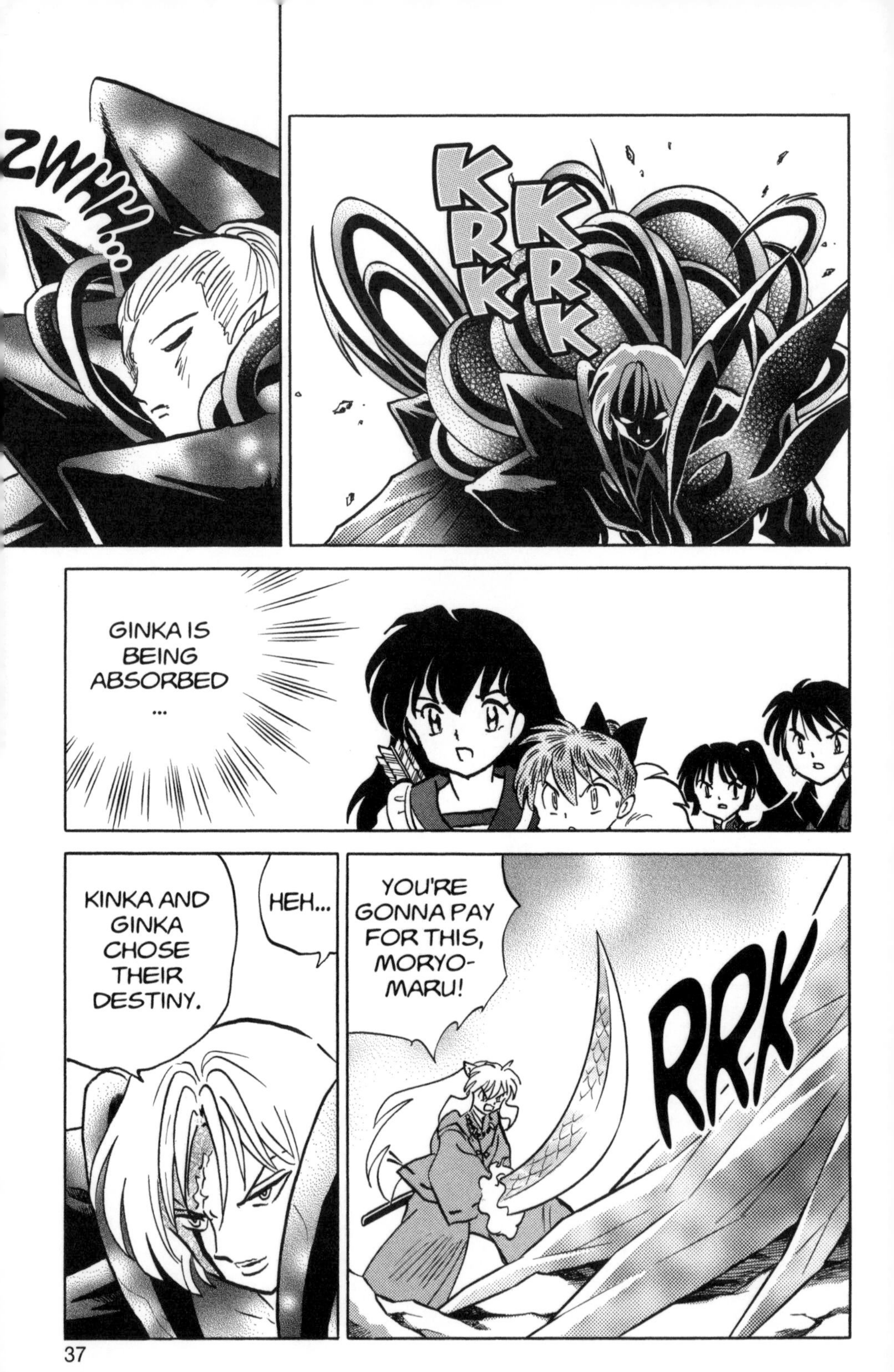
KRKRKK
ZWHHOOO
GINKA IS BEING ABSORBED ...
YOU'RE GONNA PAY FOR THIS, MORYO-MARU!
RRK
HEH...
KINKA AND GINKA CHOSE THEIR DESTINY.

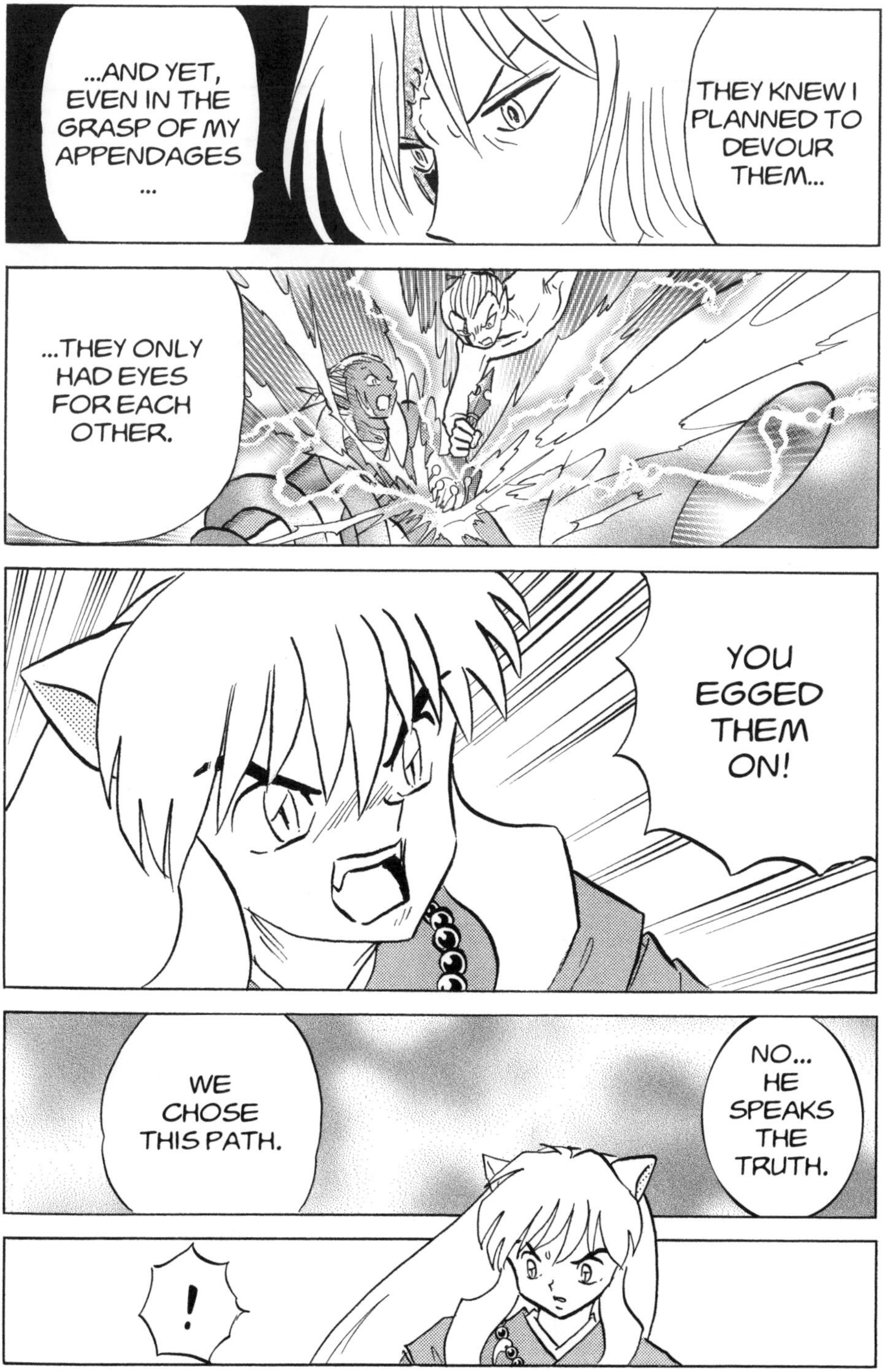
THEY KNEW I PLANNED TO DEVOUR THEM...
...AND YET, EVEN IN THE GRASP OF MY APPENDAGES ...
...THEY ONLY HAD EYES FOR EACH OTHER.
YOU EGGED THEM ON!
NO... HE SPEAKS THE TRUTH.
WE CHOSE THIS PATH.
!

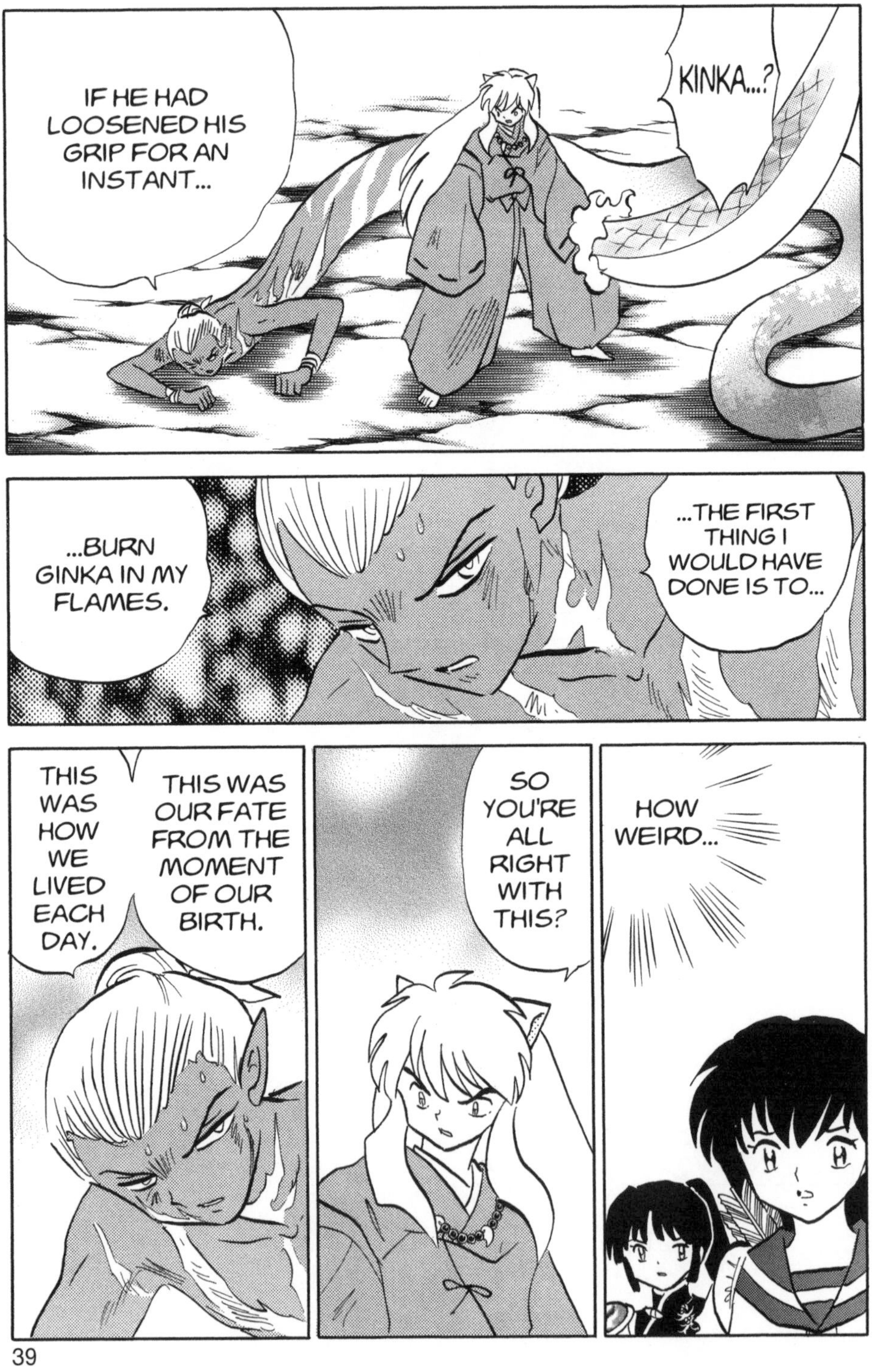
KINKA...?
IF HE HAD LOOSENED HIS GRIP FOR AN INSTANT...
...THE FIRST THING I WOULD HAVE DONE IS TO...
...BURN GINKA IN MY FLAMES.
HOW WEIRD...
SO YOU'RE ALL RIGHT WITH THIS?
THIS WAS OUR FATE FROM THE MOMENT OF OUR BIRTH.
THIS WAS HOW WE LIVED EACH DAY.

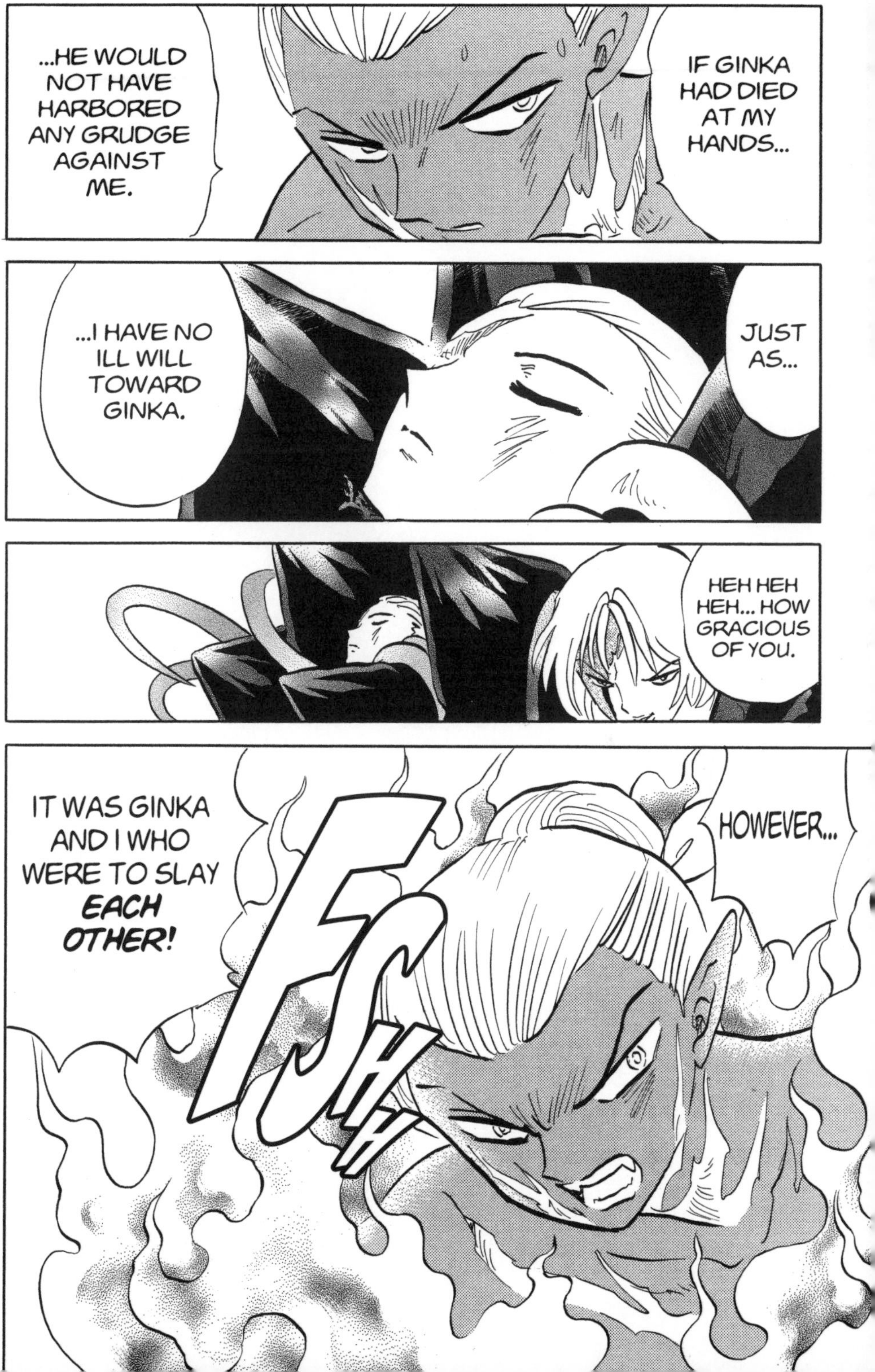
IF GINKA HAD DIED AT MY HANDS...
...HE WOULD NOT HAVE HARBORED ANY GRUDGE AGAINST ME.
JUST AS...
...I HAVE NO ILL WILL TOWARD GINKA.
HEH HEH HEH... HOW GRACIOUS OF YOU.
HOWEVER...
FSHH
IT WAS GINKA AND I WHO WERE TO SLAY EACH OTHER!

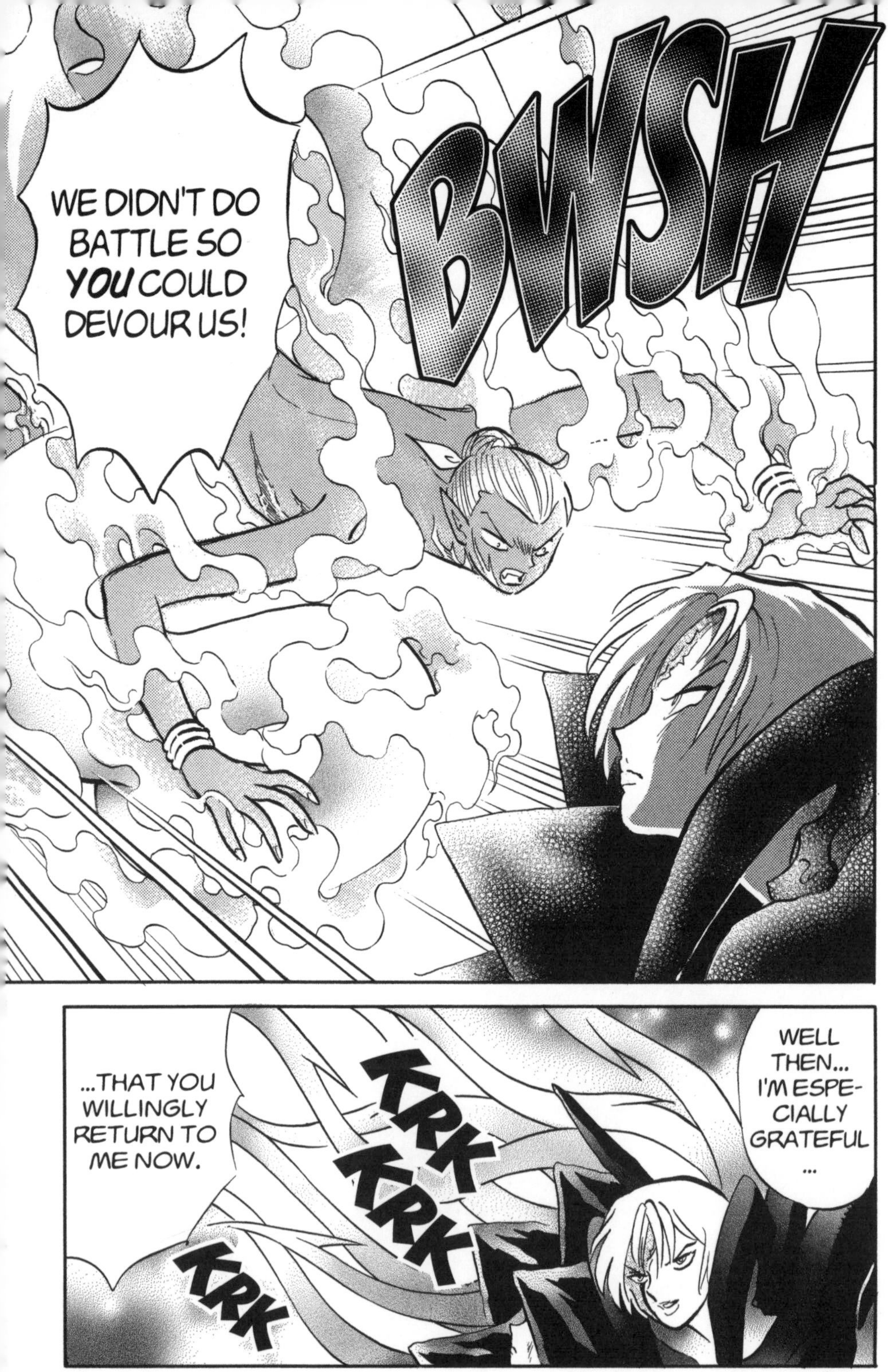
BWSH
WE DIDN'T DO BATTLE SO **YOU** COULD DEVOUR US!
WELL THEN... I'M ESPE-CIALLY GRATEFUL ...
...THAT YOU WILLINGLY RETURN TO ME NOW.
KRK KRK KRK

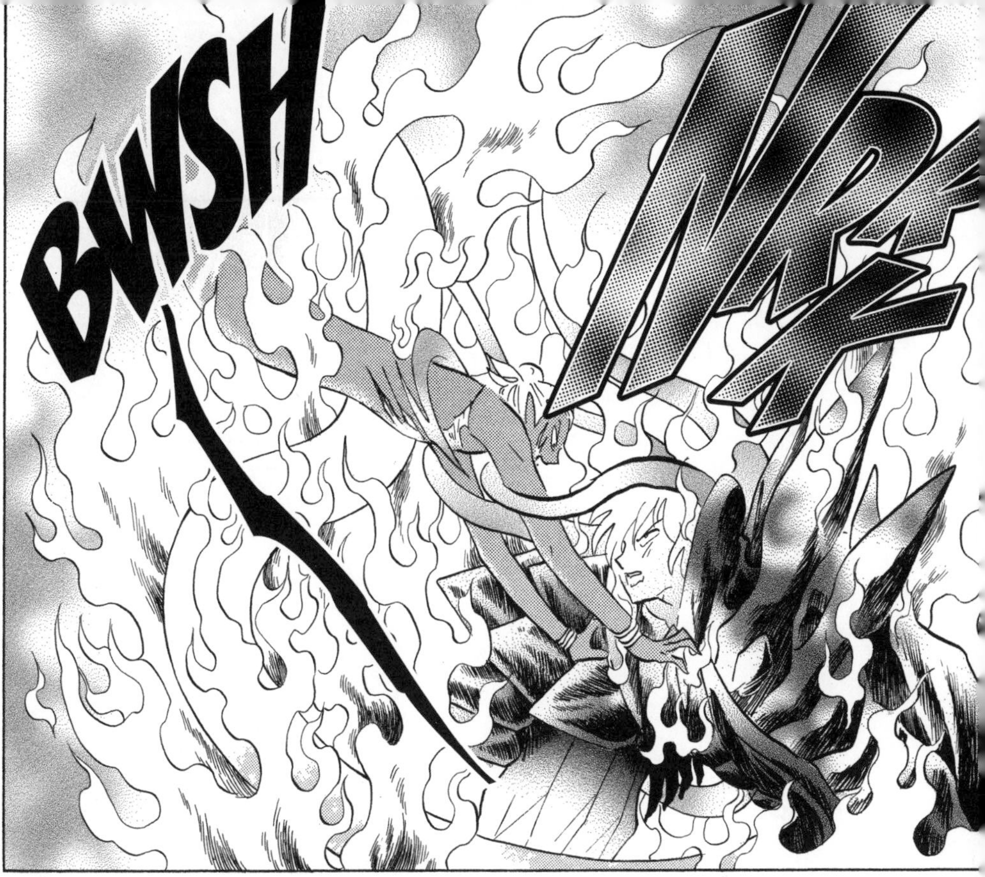
BWSH

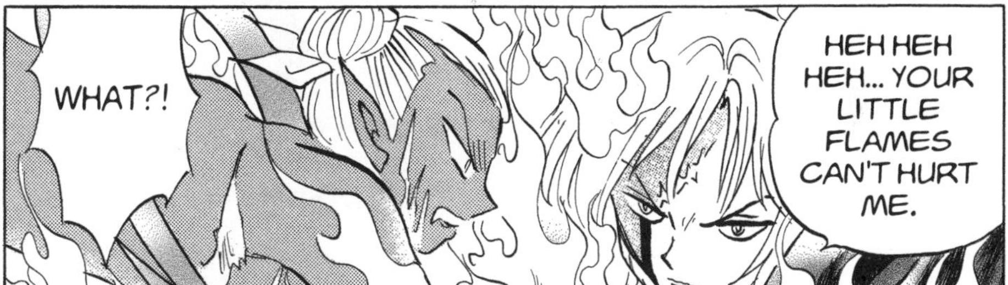
HEH HEH HEH... YOUR LITTLE FLAMES CAN'T HURT ME.
WHAT?!

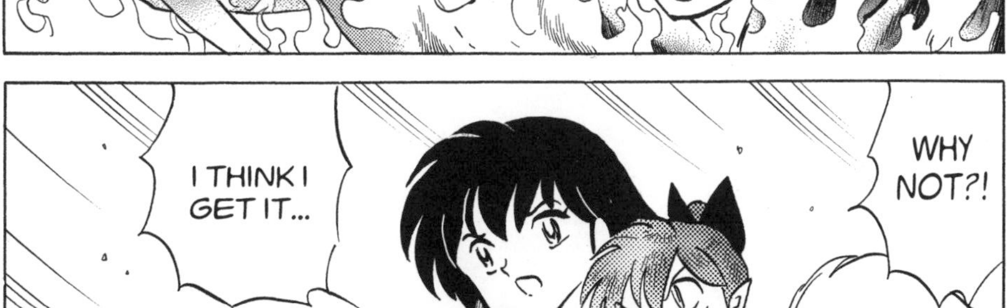
WHY NOT?!
I THINK I GET IT...

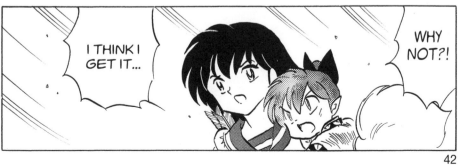

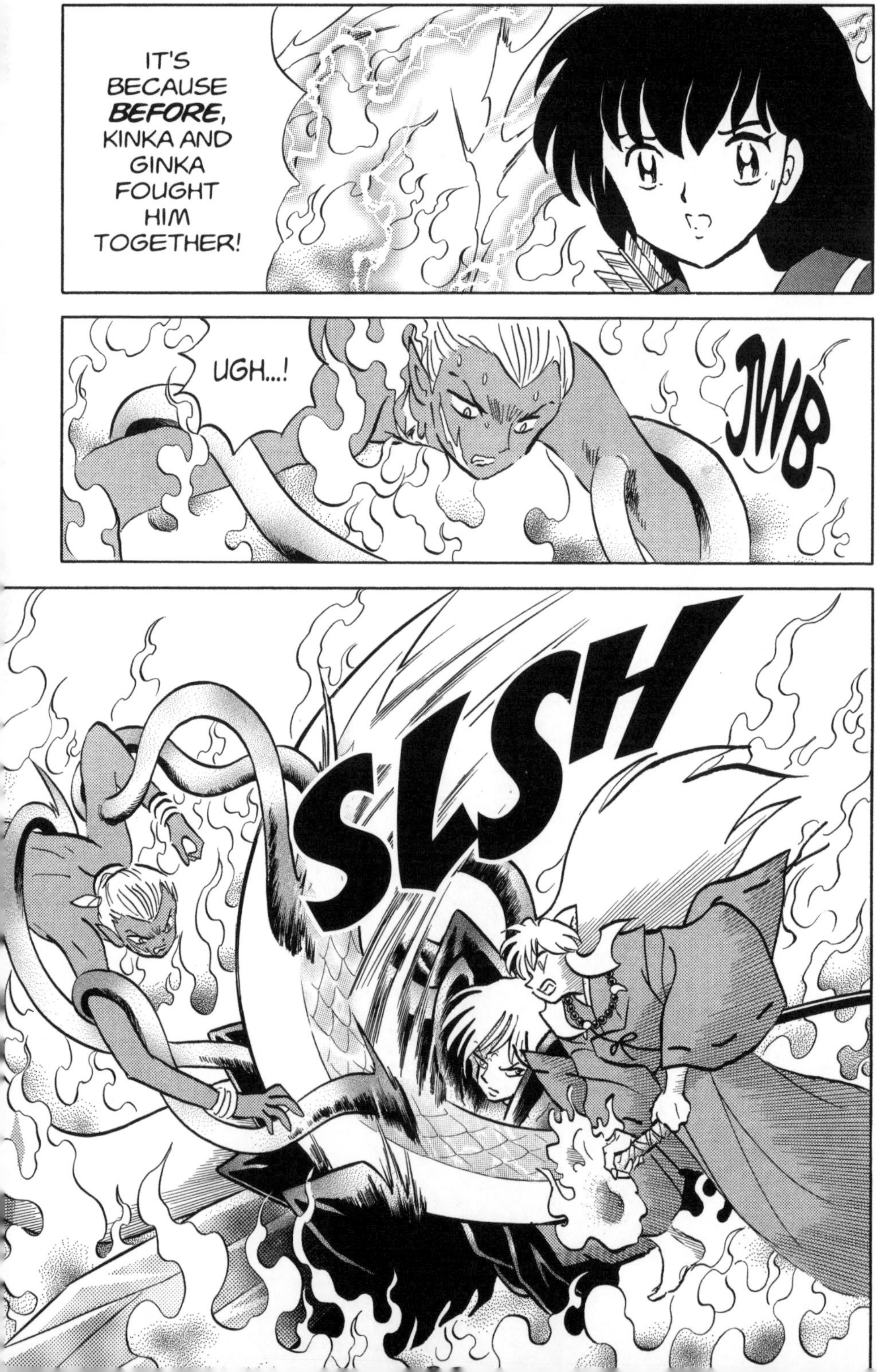
IT'S BECAUSE *BEFORE*, KINKA AND GINKA FOUGHT HIM TOGETHER!
JWB
UGH...!
SLSH

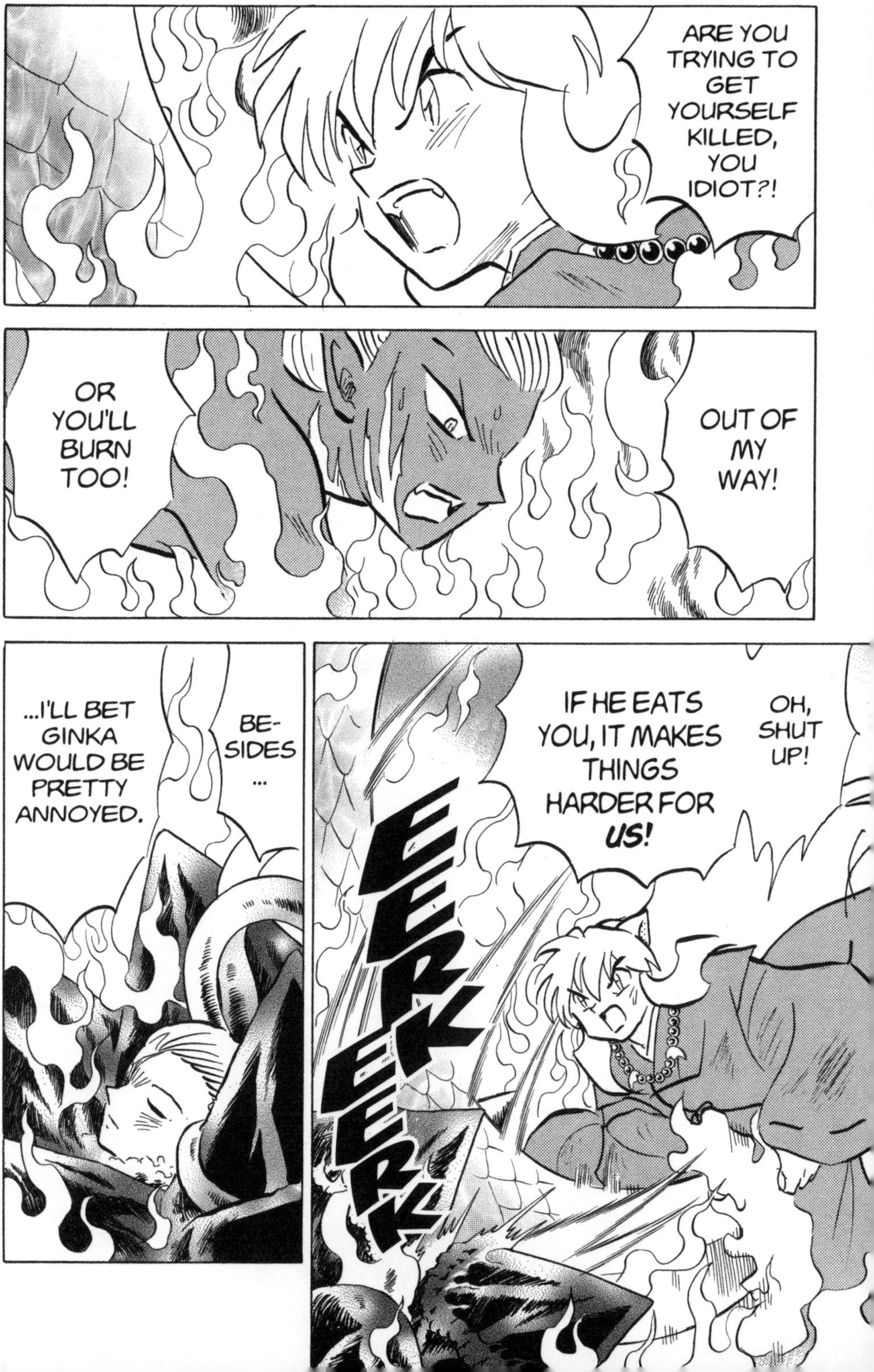
ARE YOU TRYING TO GET YOURSELF KILLED, YOU IDIOT?!
OUT OF MY WAY!
OR YOU'LL BURN TOO!
OH, SHUT UP!
IF HE EATS YOU, IT MAKES THINGS HARDER FOR *US!*
EERK EERK
BE-SIDES...
...I'LL BET GINKA WOULD BE PRETTY ANNOYED.

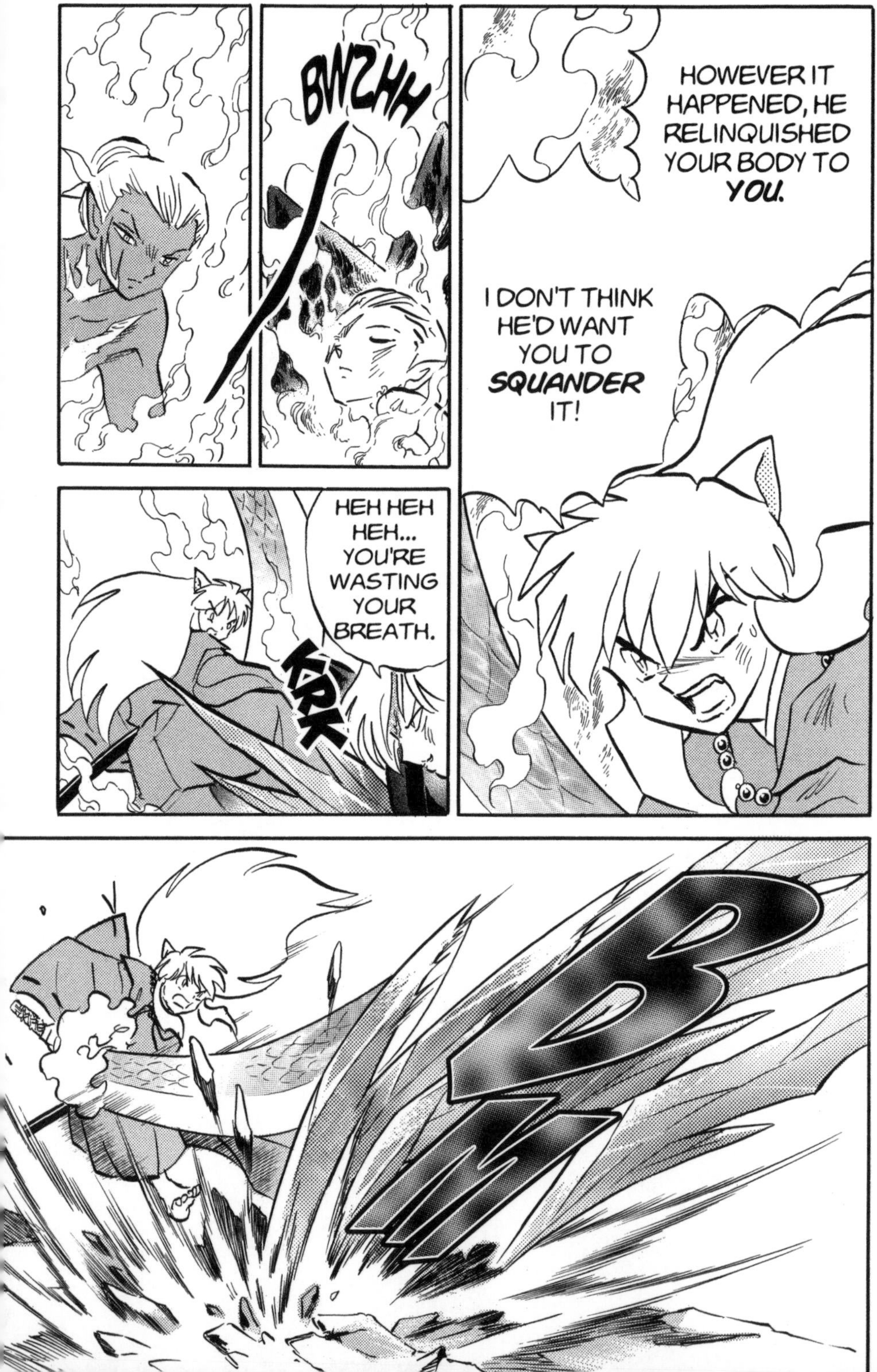
HOWEVER IT HAPPENED, HE RELINQUISHED YOUR BODY TO **YOU.**
I DON'T THINK HE'D WANT YOU TO **SQUANDER** IT!
BWZHH
HEH HEH HEH... YOU'RE WASTING YOUR BREATH.
KRRK

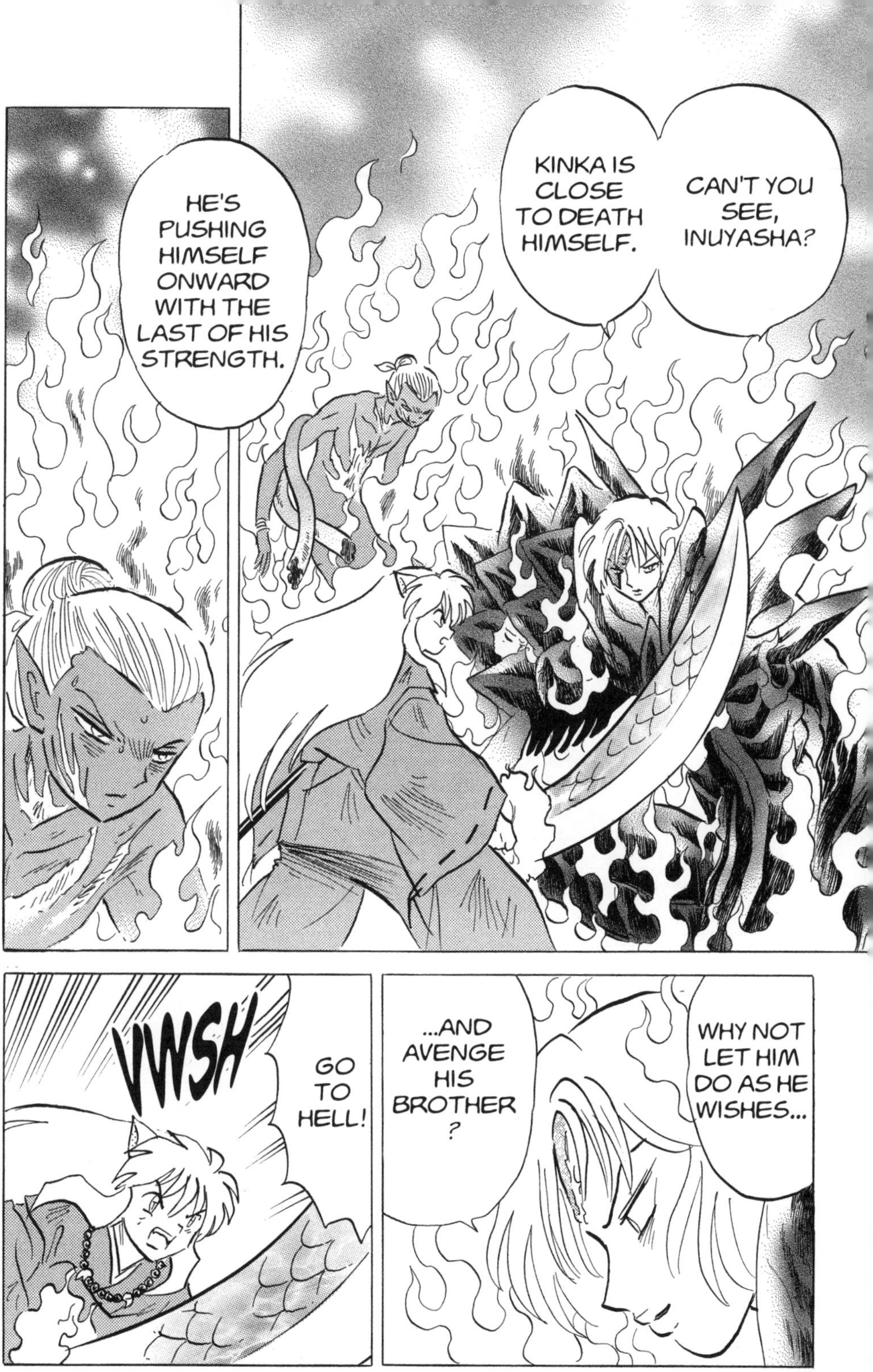
CAN'T YOU SEE, INUYASHA?
KINKA IS CLOSE TO DEATH HIMSELF.
HE'S PUSHING HIMSELF ONWARD WITH THE LAST OF HIS STRENGTH.
WHY NOT LET HIM DO AS HE WISHES...
...AND AVENGE HIS BROTHER?
VWSH
GO TO HELL!

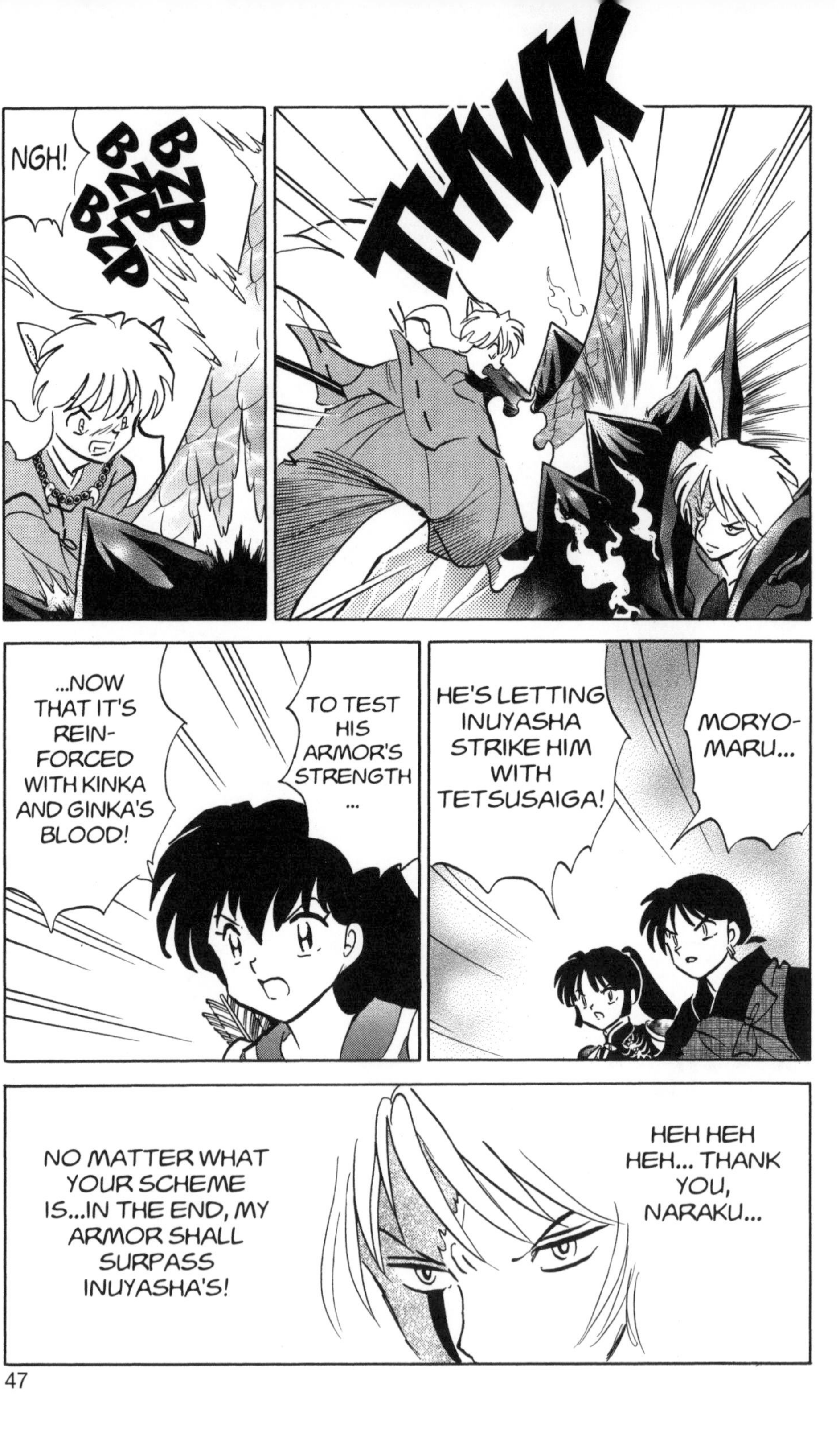
THWK
BZZP BZZP BZZP
NGH!
MORYO-MARU...
HE'S LETTING INUYASHA STRIKE HIM WITH TETSUSAIGA!
TO TEST HIS ARMOR'S STRENGTH...
...NOW THAT IT'S REIN-FORCED WITH KINKA AND GINKA'S BLOOD!
HEH HEH HEH... THANK YOU, NARAKU...
NO MATTER WHAT YOUR SCHEME IS...IN THE END, MY ARMOR SHALL SURPASS INUYASHA'S!

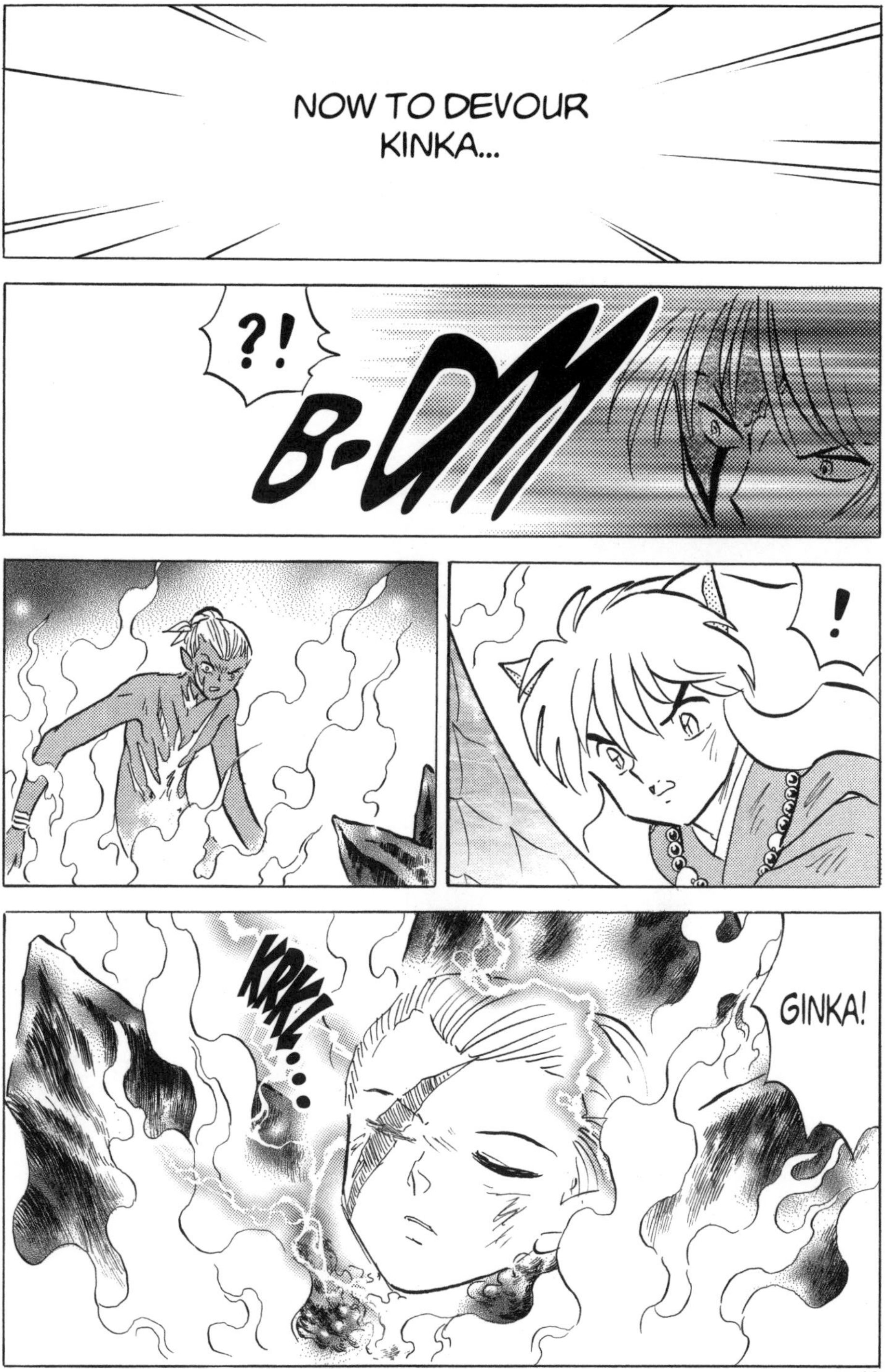
NOW TO DEVOUR KINKA...
?!
B-DM
!
GINKA!
KRKL...

SCROLL THREE
ASSIMILATION

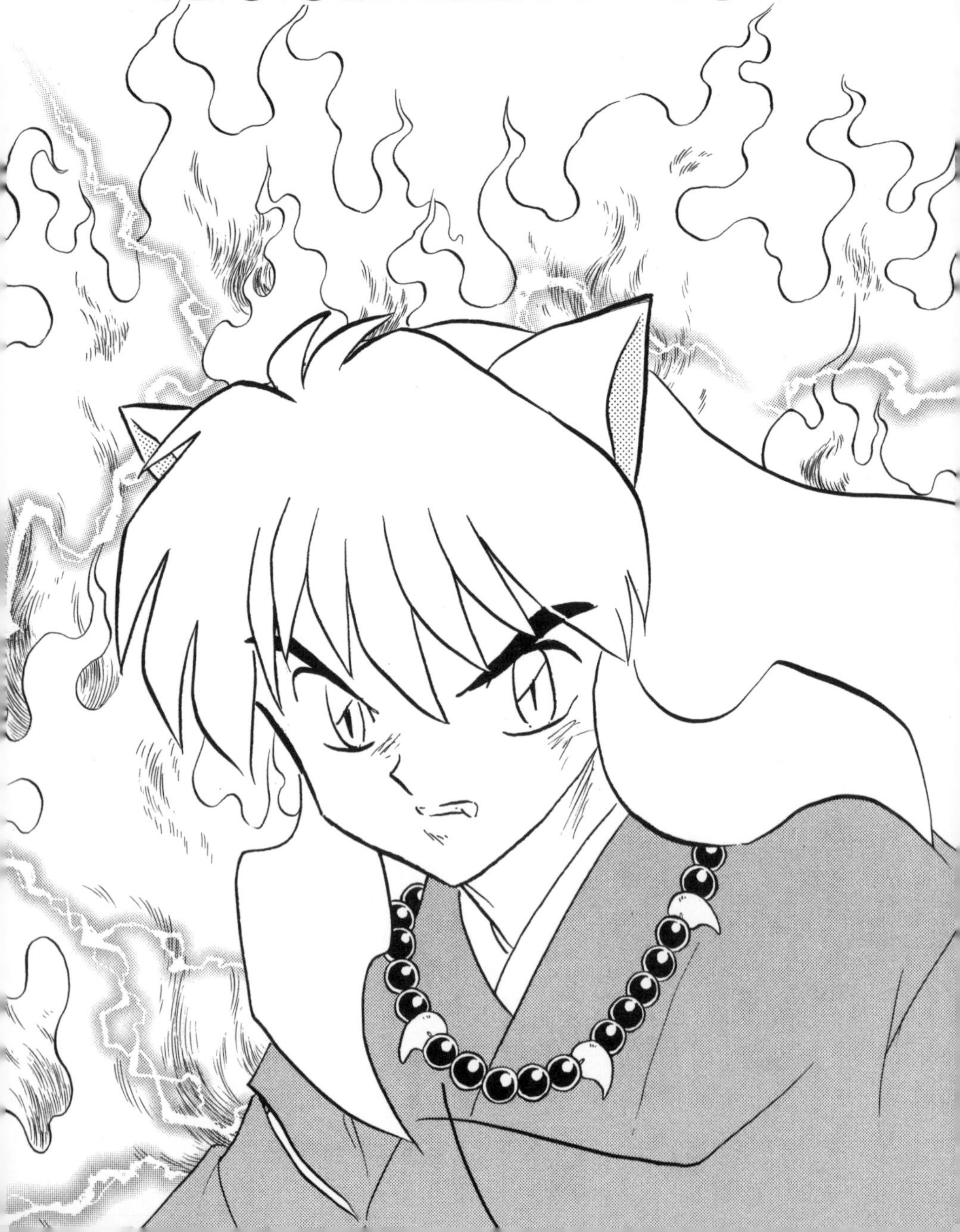

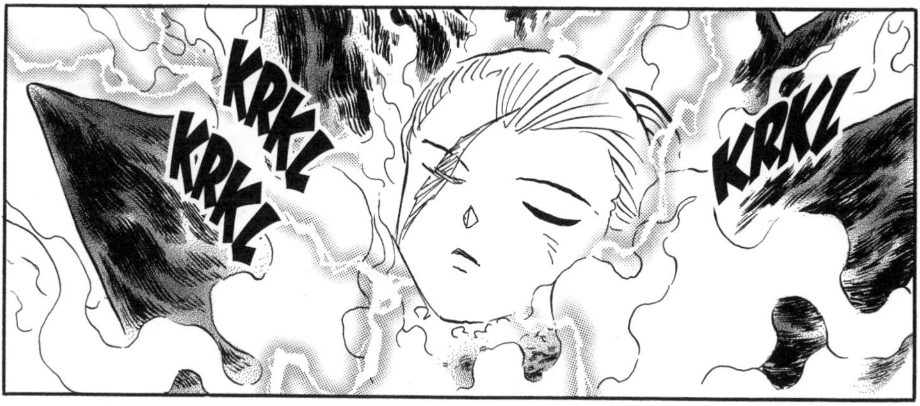
KRKL
KRKL
KRKL
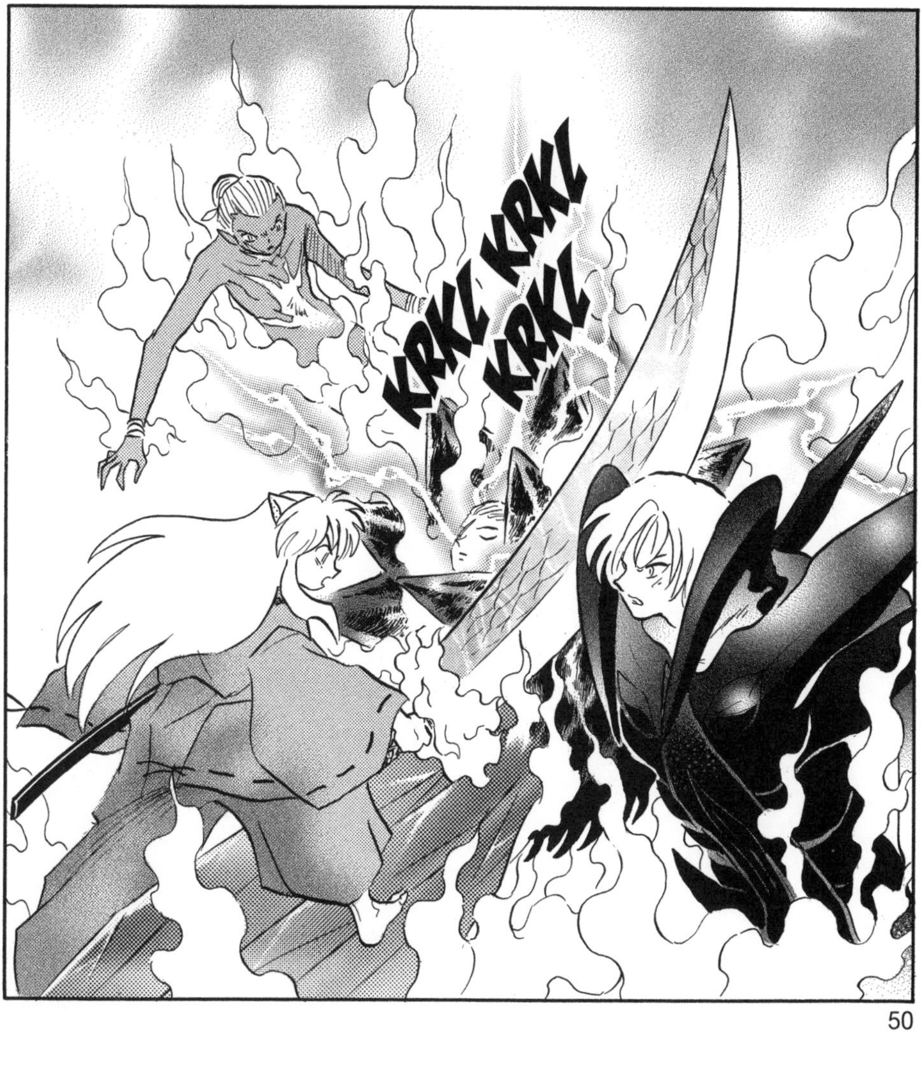
KRKL KRKL
KRKL KRKL

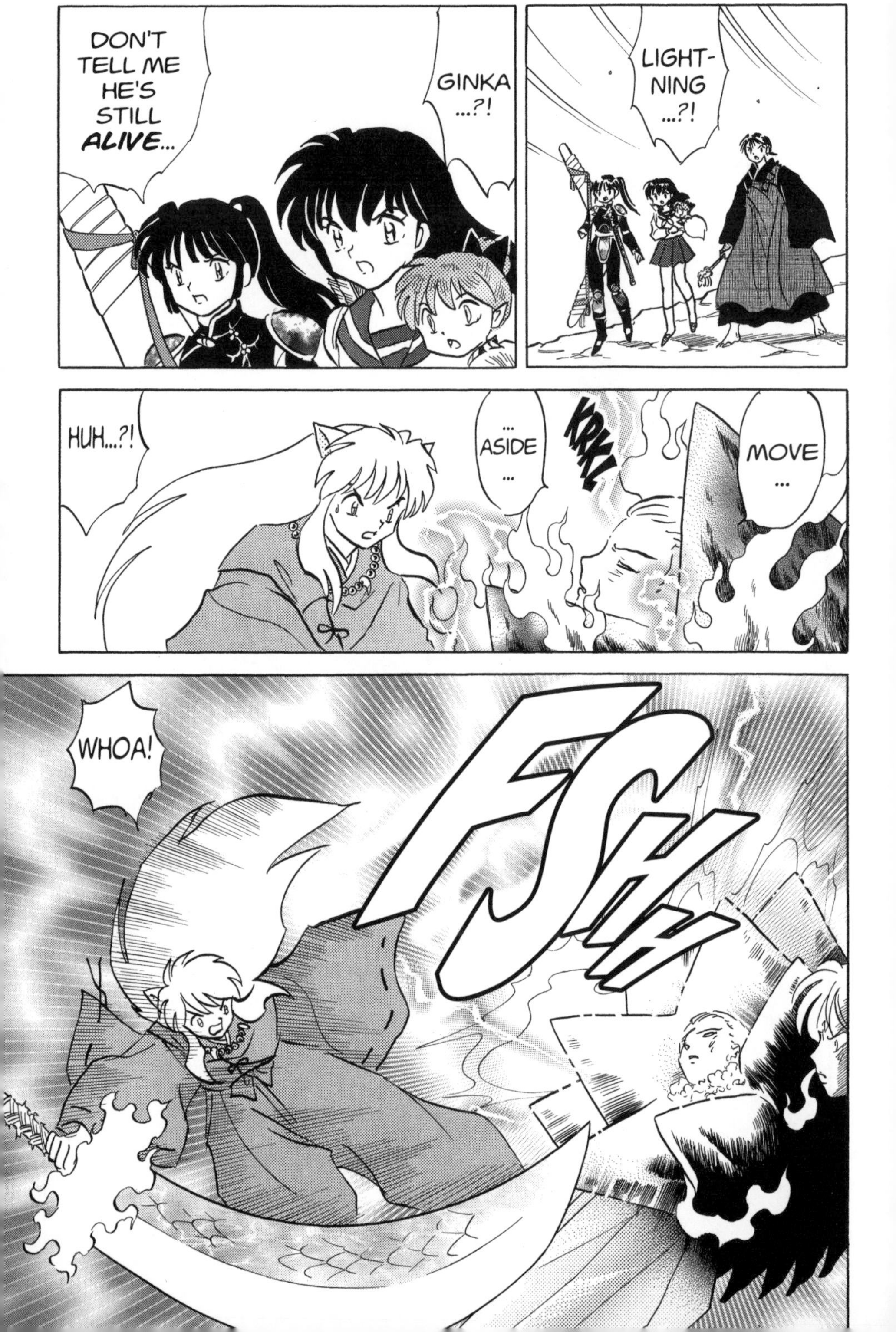
LIGHT-NING ...?!
GINKA ...?!
DON'T TELL ME HE'S STILL **ALIVE**...
MOVE ...
KRK!
... ASIDE ...
HUH...?!
FSHHH
WHOA!

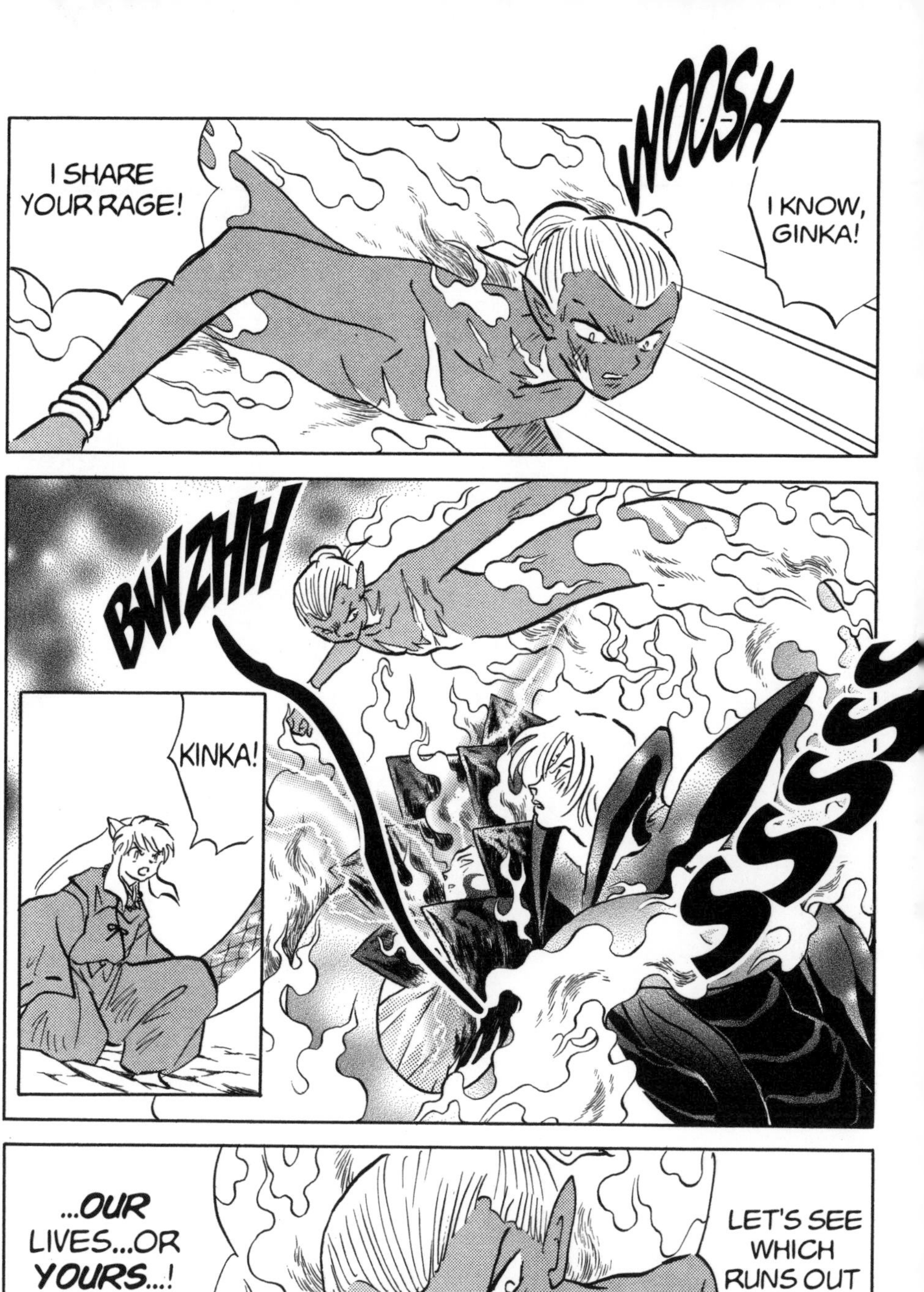
WOOSH
I KNOW, GINKA!
I SHARE YOUR RAGE!
SSSSS
BWZHH
KINKA!
LET'S SEE WHICH RUNS OUT FIRST...
...**OUR** LIVES...OR ***YOURS***...!

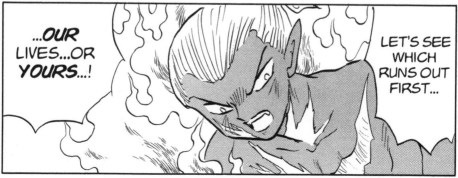

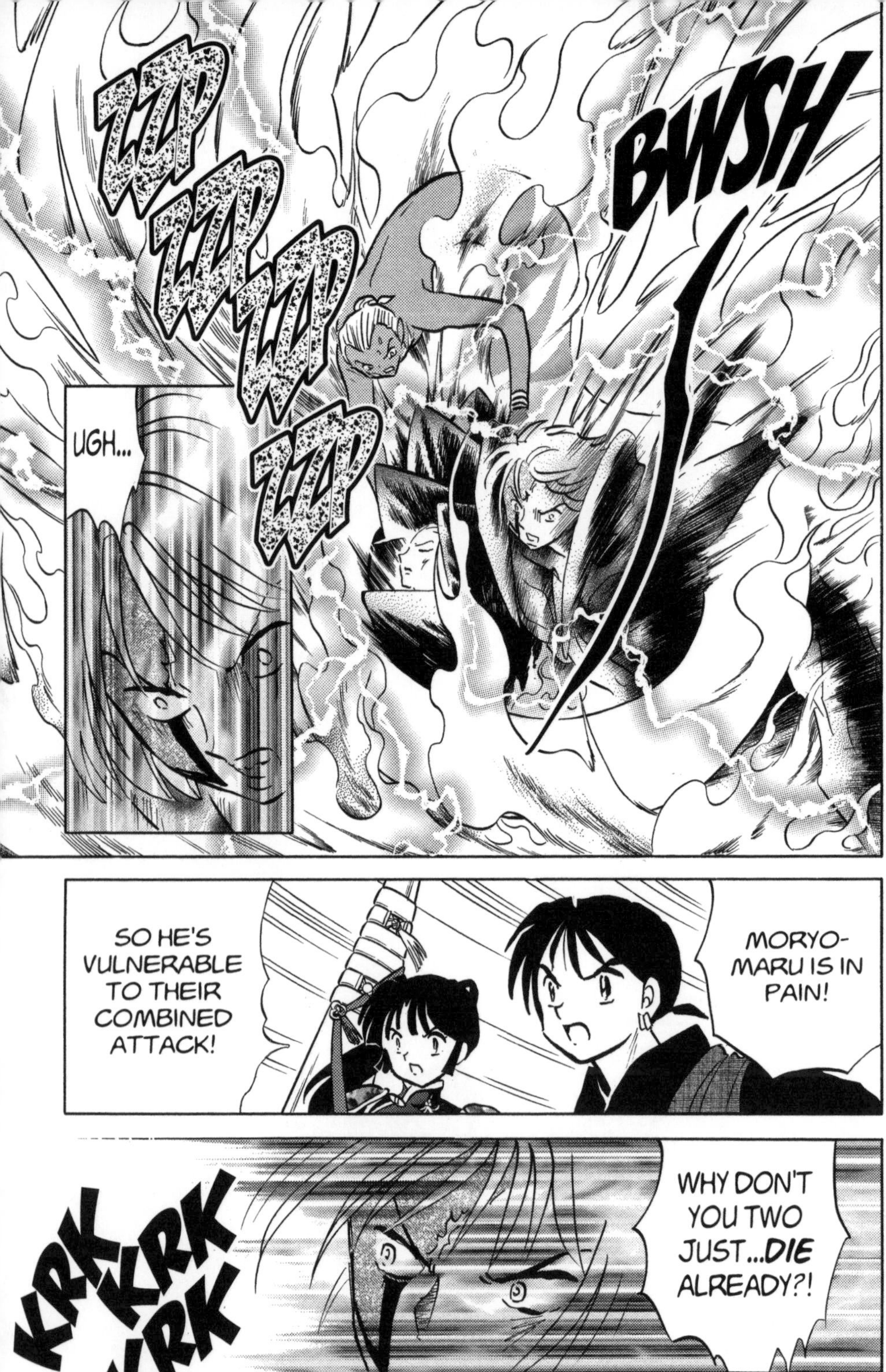
BWSH
ZZAP
ZZAP
ZZAP
ZZAP
UGH...
MORYO-MARU IS IN PAIN!
SO HE'S VULNERABLE TO THEIR COMBINED ATTACK!
WHY DON'T YOU TWO JUST...**DIE** ALREADY?!
KRK KRK KRK

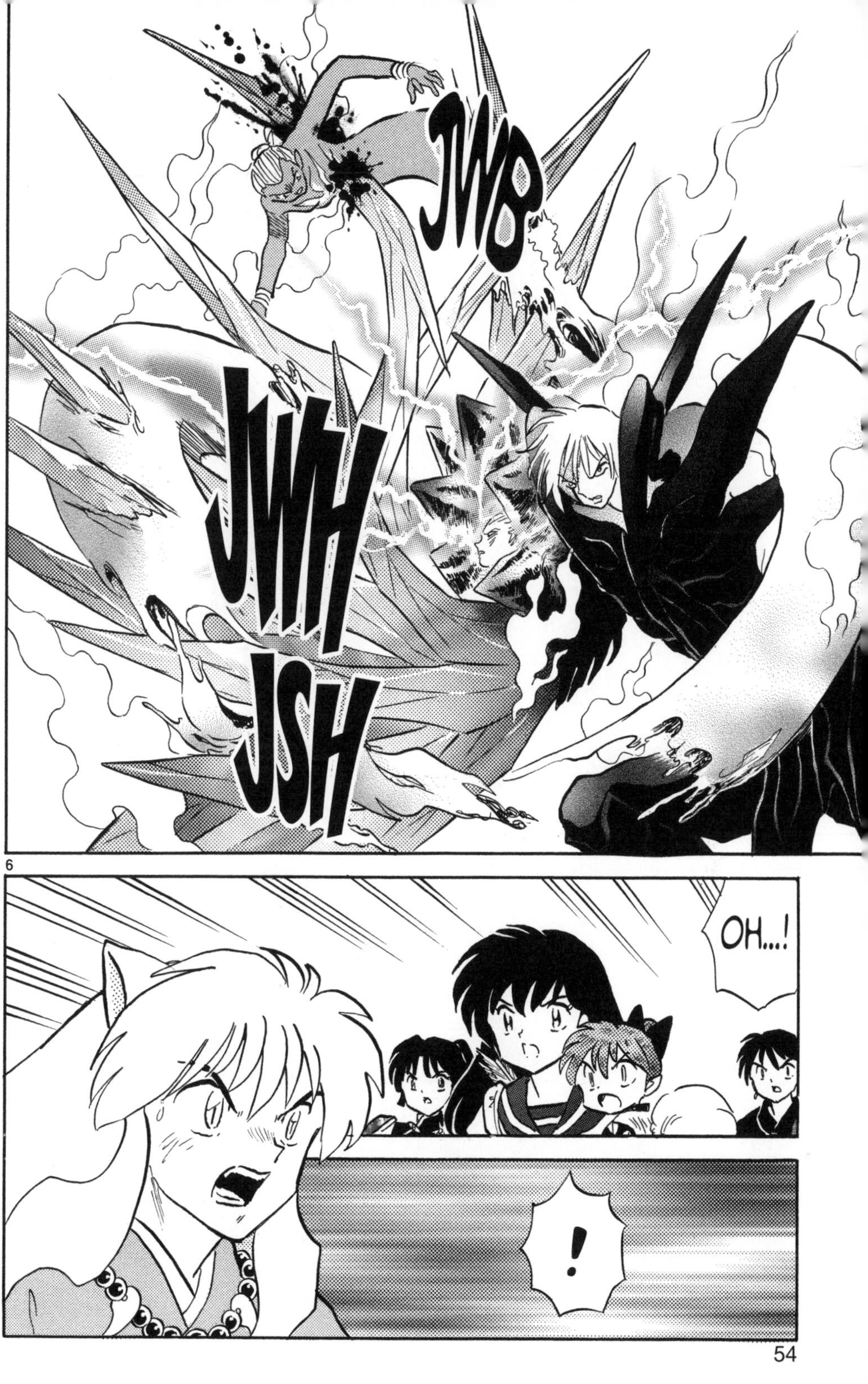
JWB
JWH
JSH
6
OH...!
!

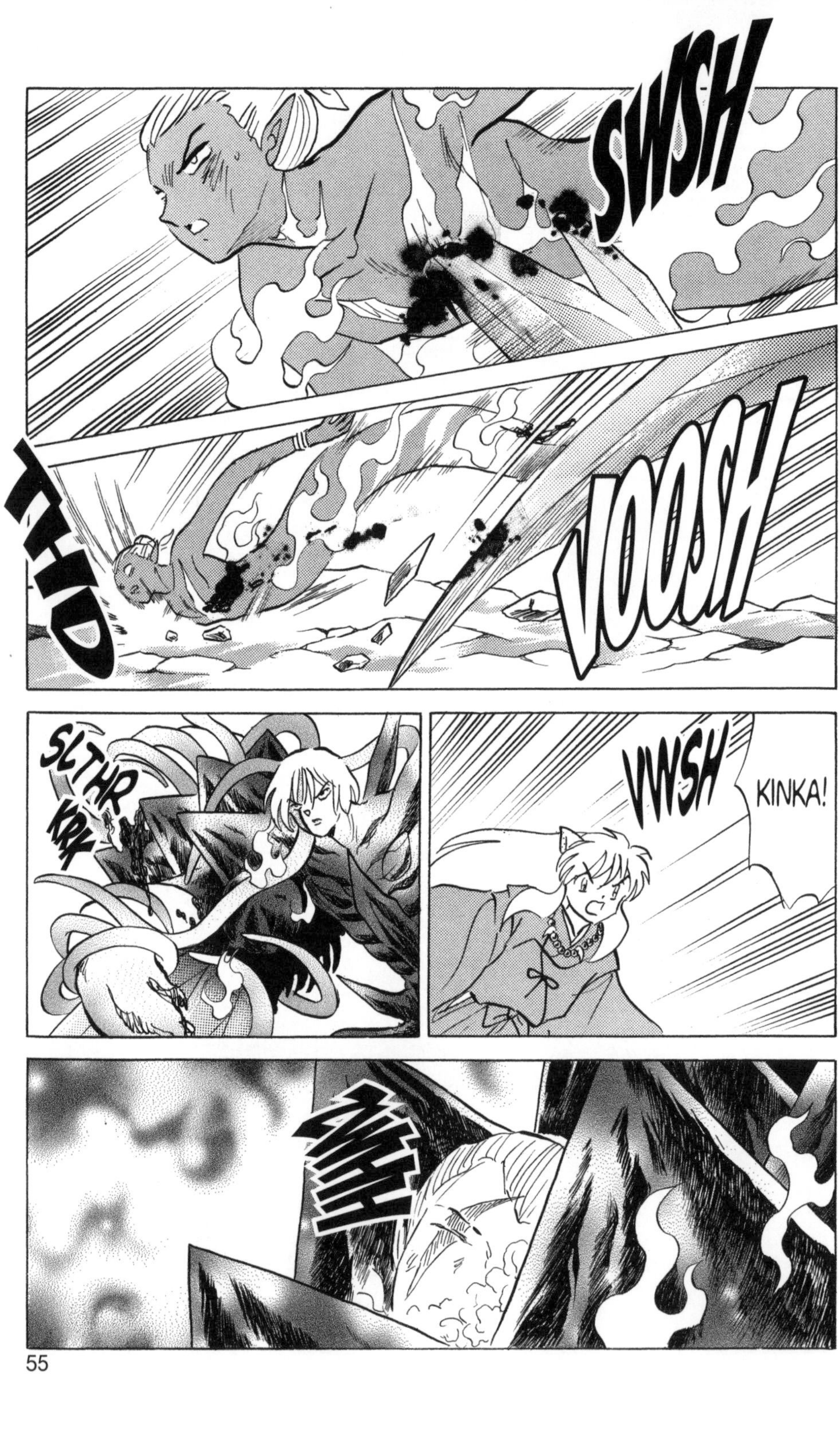
SWISH
VOOSH
THUD
VWSH
KINKA!
SLTHR
KRK
ZWHH!

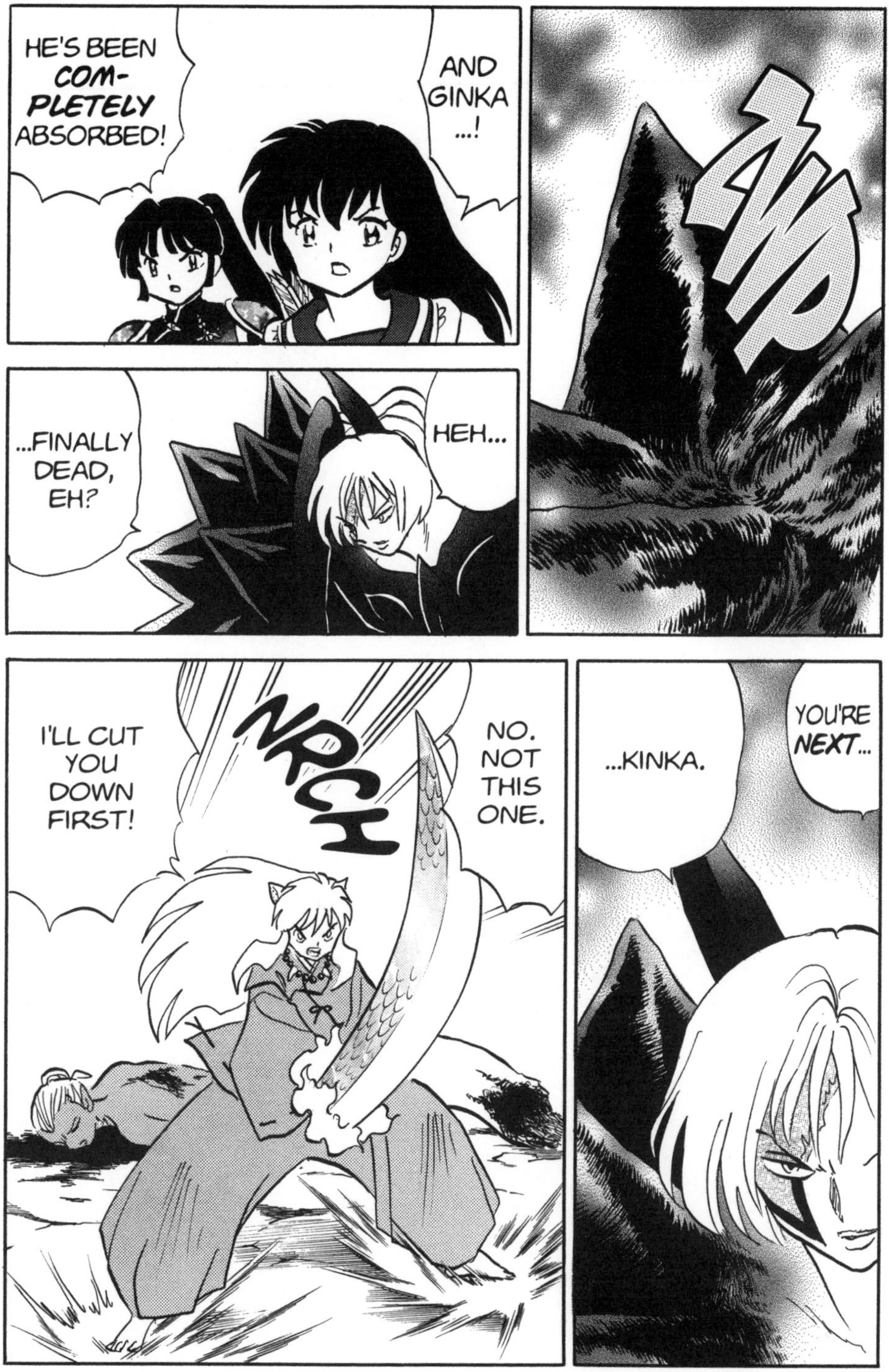
ZWIP
HE'S BEEN COMPLETELY ABSORBED!
AND GINKA ...!
HEH...
...FINALLY DEAD, EH?
YOU'RE NEXT...
...KINKA.
NO. NOT THIS ONE.
NRCH
I'LL CUT YOU DOWN FIRST!

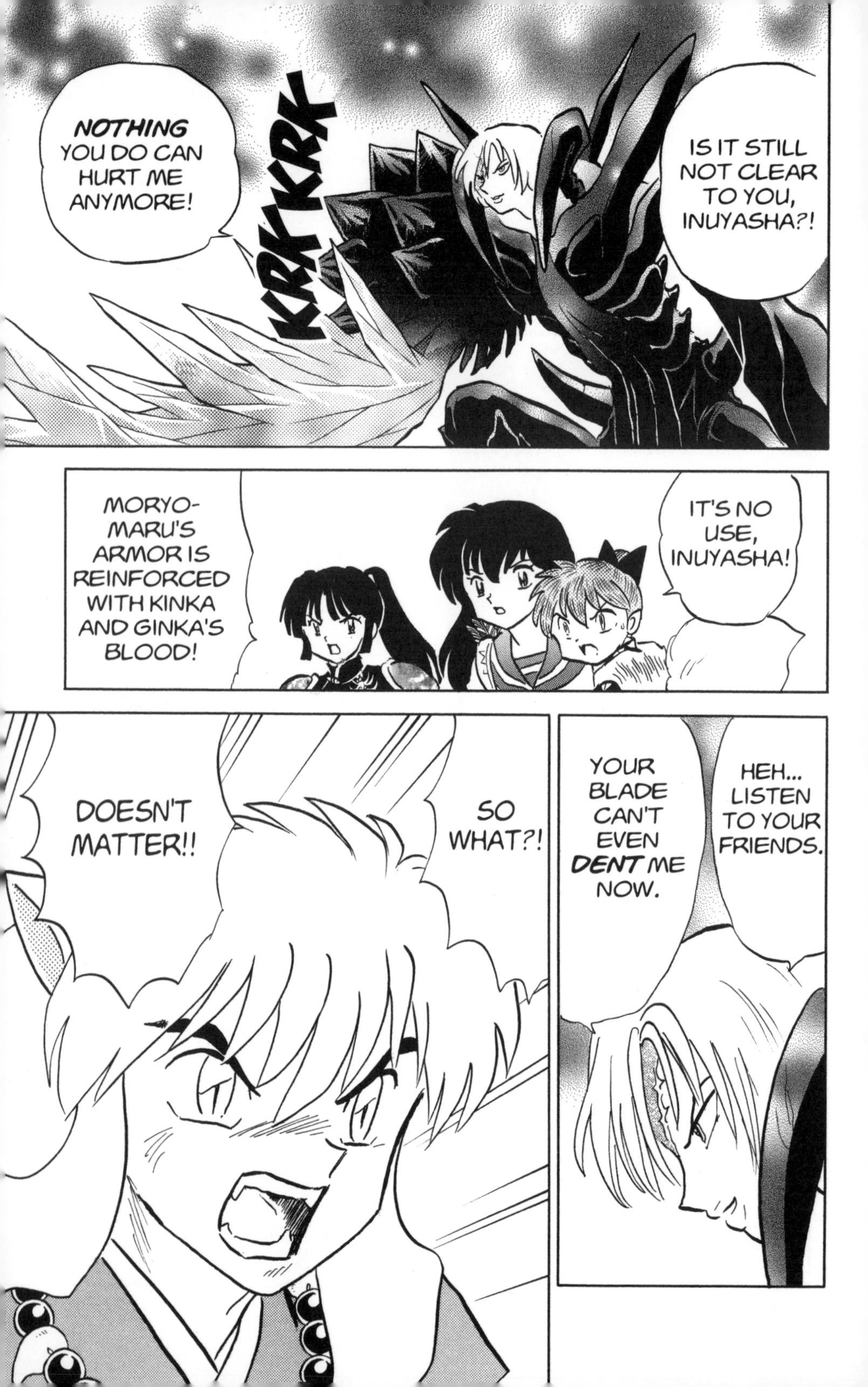
IS IT STILL NOT CLEAR TO YOU, INUYASHA?!
NOTHING YOU DO CAN HURT ME ANYMORE!
KRK KRK
IT'S NO USE, INUYASHA!
MORYO-MARU'S ARMOR IS REINFORCED WITH KINKA AND GINKA'S BLOOD!
HEH... LISTEN TO YOUR FRIENDS.
YOUR BLADE CAN'T EVEN DENT ME NOW.
SO WHAT?!
DOESN'T MATTER!!

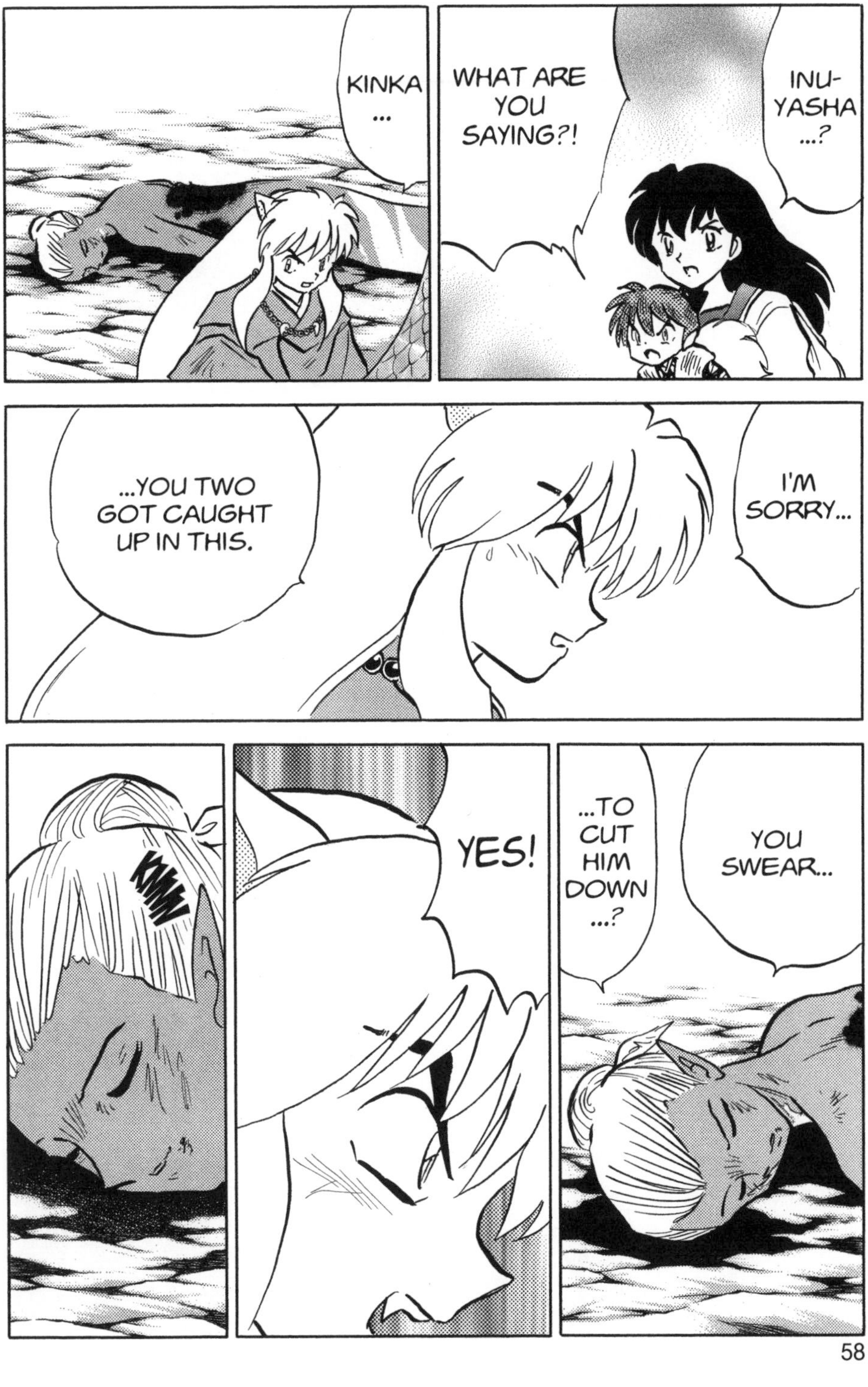
INU-YASHA ...?
WHAT ARE YOU SAYING?!
KINKA ...
I'M SORRY...
...YOU TWO GOT CAUGHT UP IN THIS.
YOU SWEAR...
...TO CUT HIM DOWN ...?
YES!
KMW

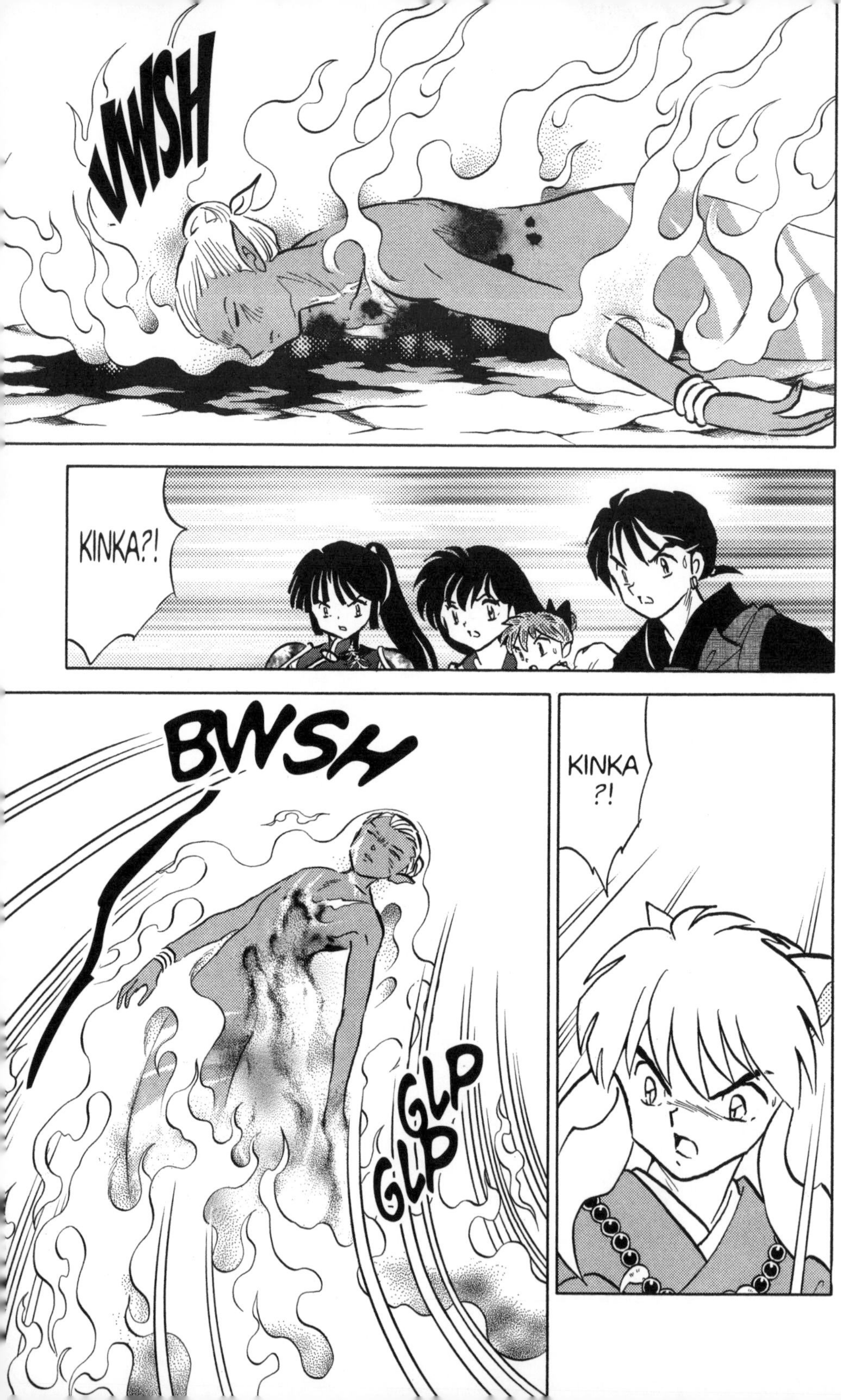
VWSH
KINKA?!
KINKA ?!
BWSH
GLP GLP

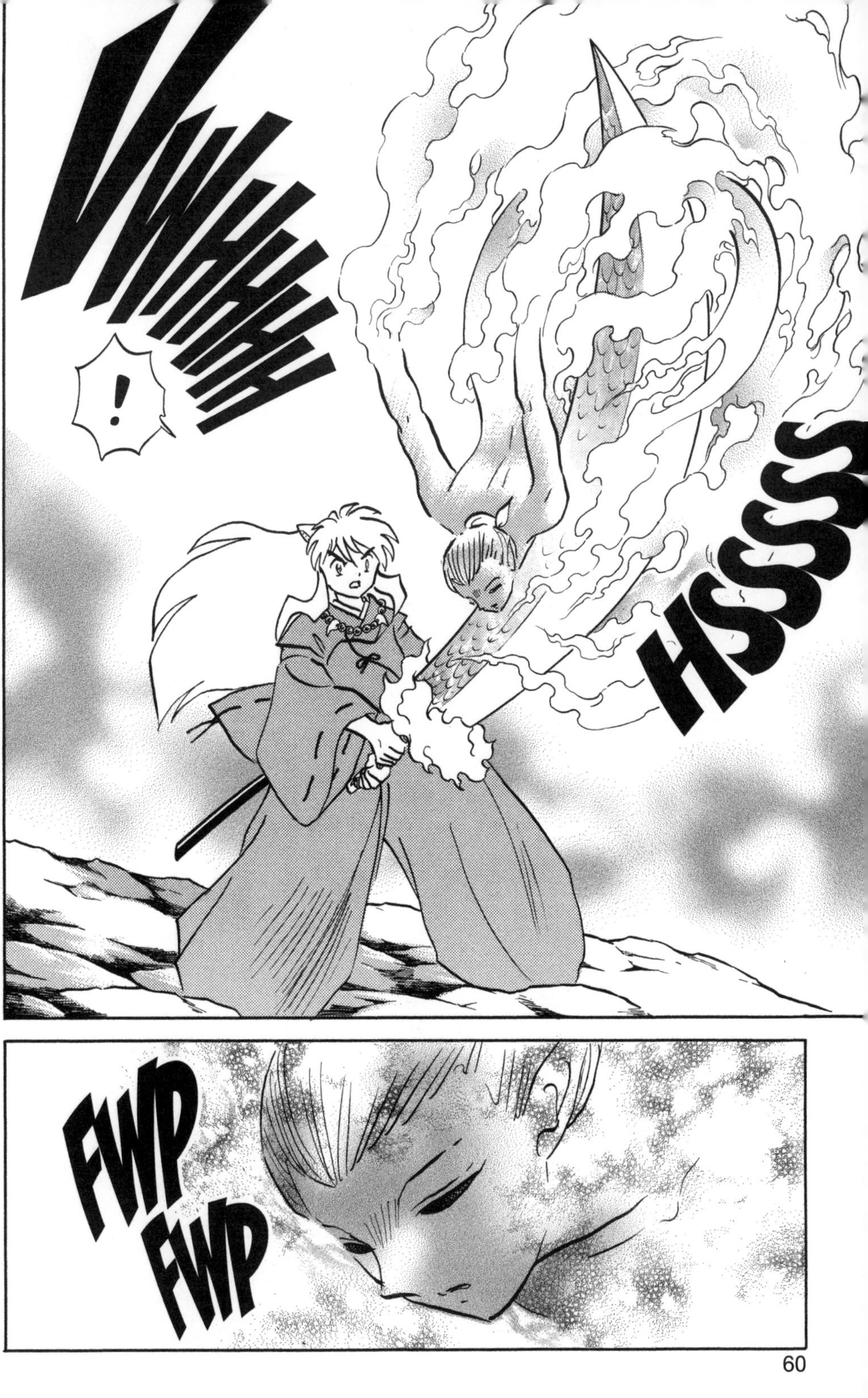
HSSSSS
VWHHH
!
FWP FWP

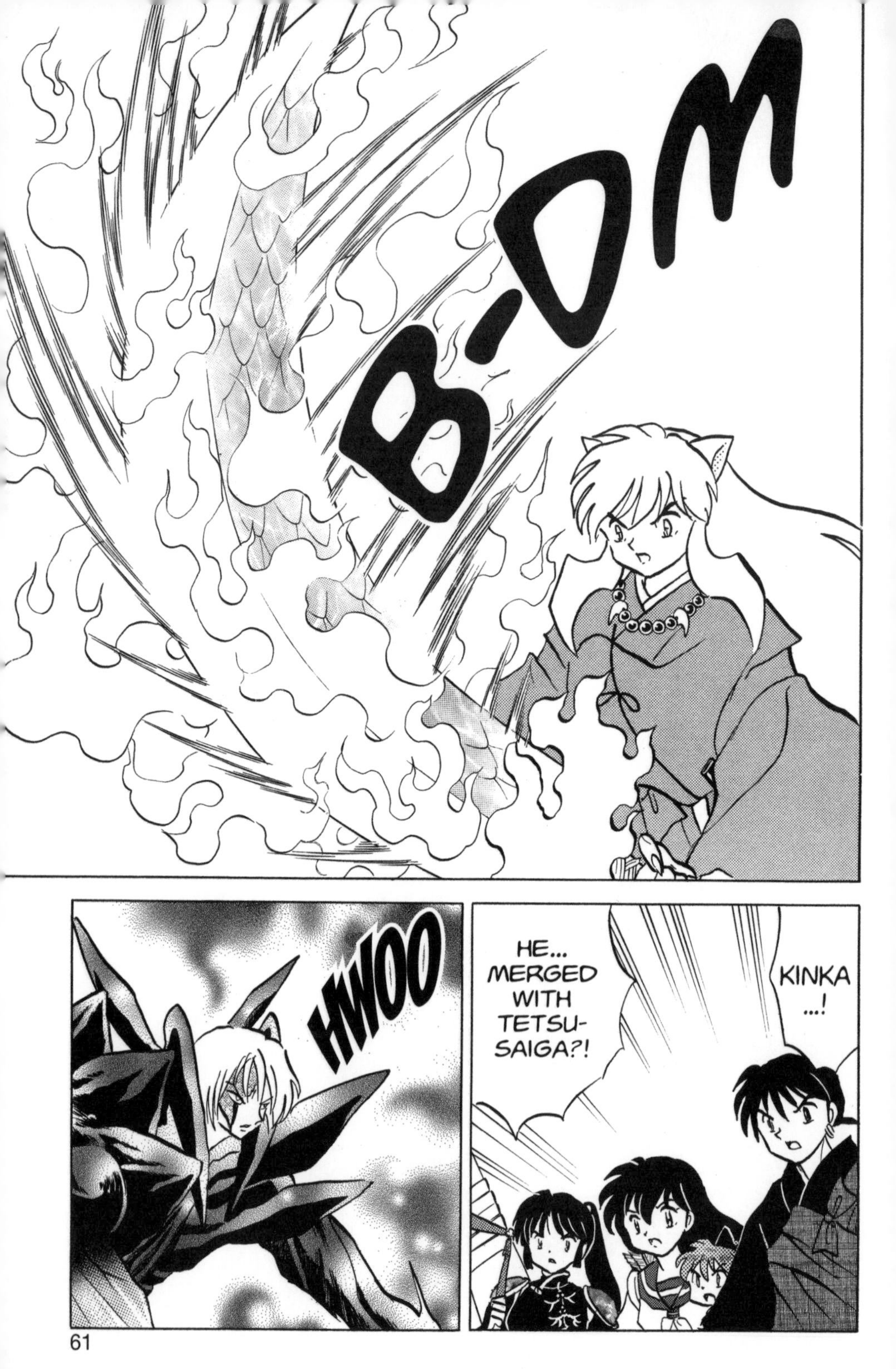
B-DM
HE... MERGED WITH TETSU-SAIGA?!
KINKA ...!
HWOO

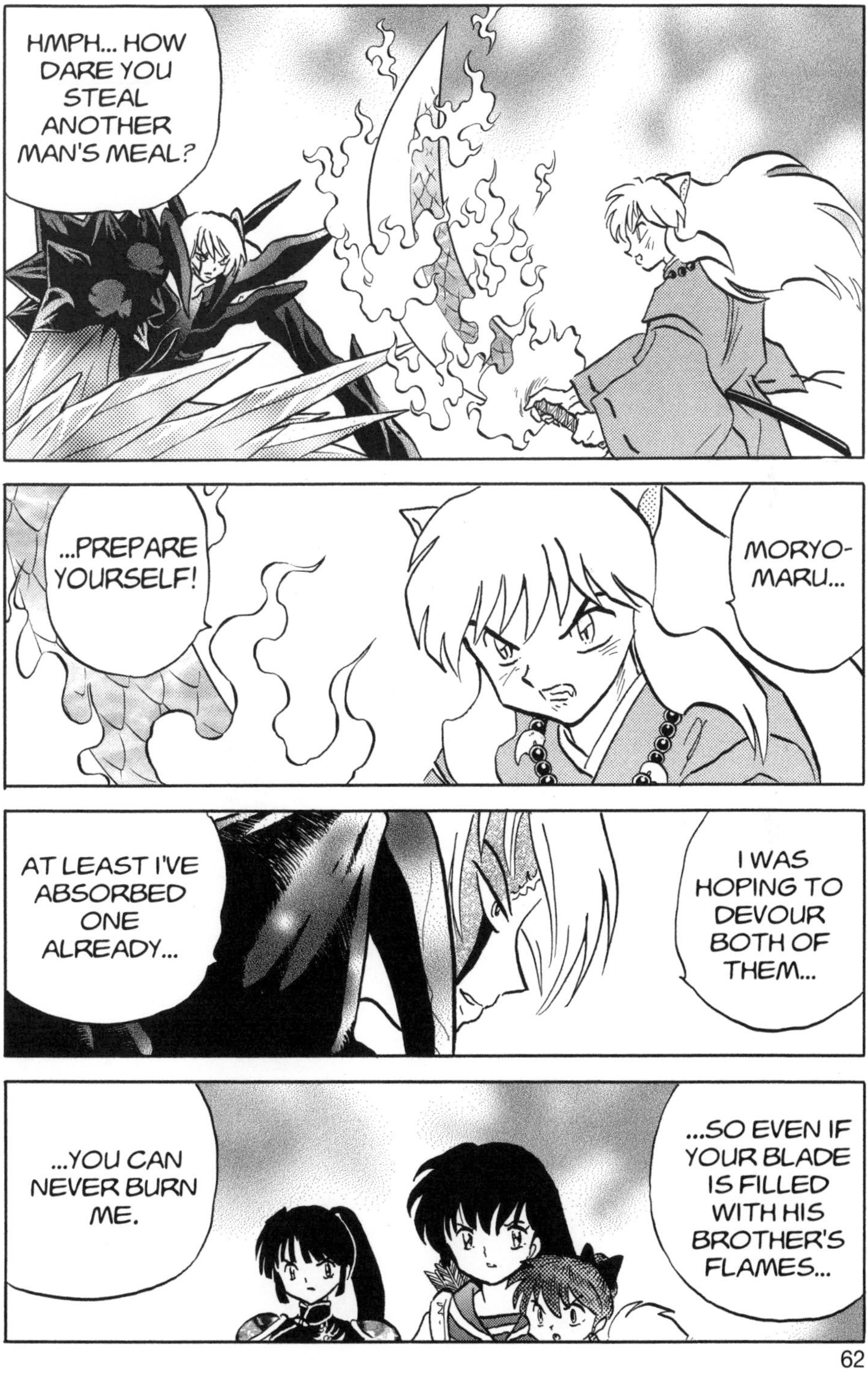
HMPH... HOW DARE YOU STEAL ANOTHER MAN'S MEAL?
MORYO-MARU...
...PREPARE YOURSELF!
I WAS HOPING TO DEVOUR BOTH OF THEM...
AT LEAST I'VE ABSORBED ONE ALREADY...
...SO EVEN IF YOUR BLADE IS FILLED WITH HIS BROTHER'S FLAMES...
...YOU CAN NEVER BURN ME.

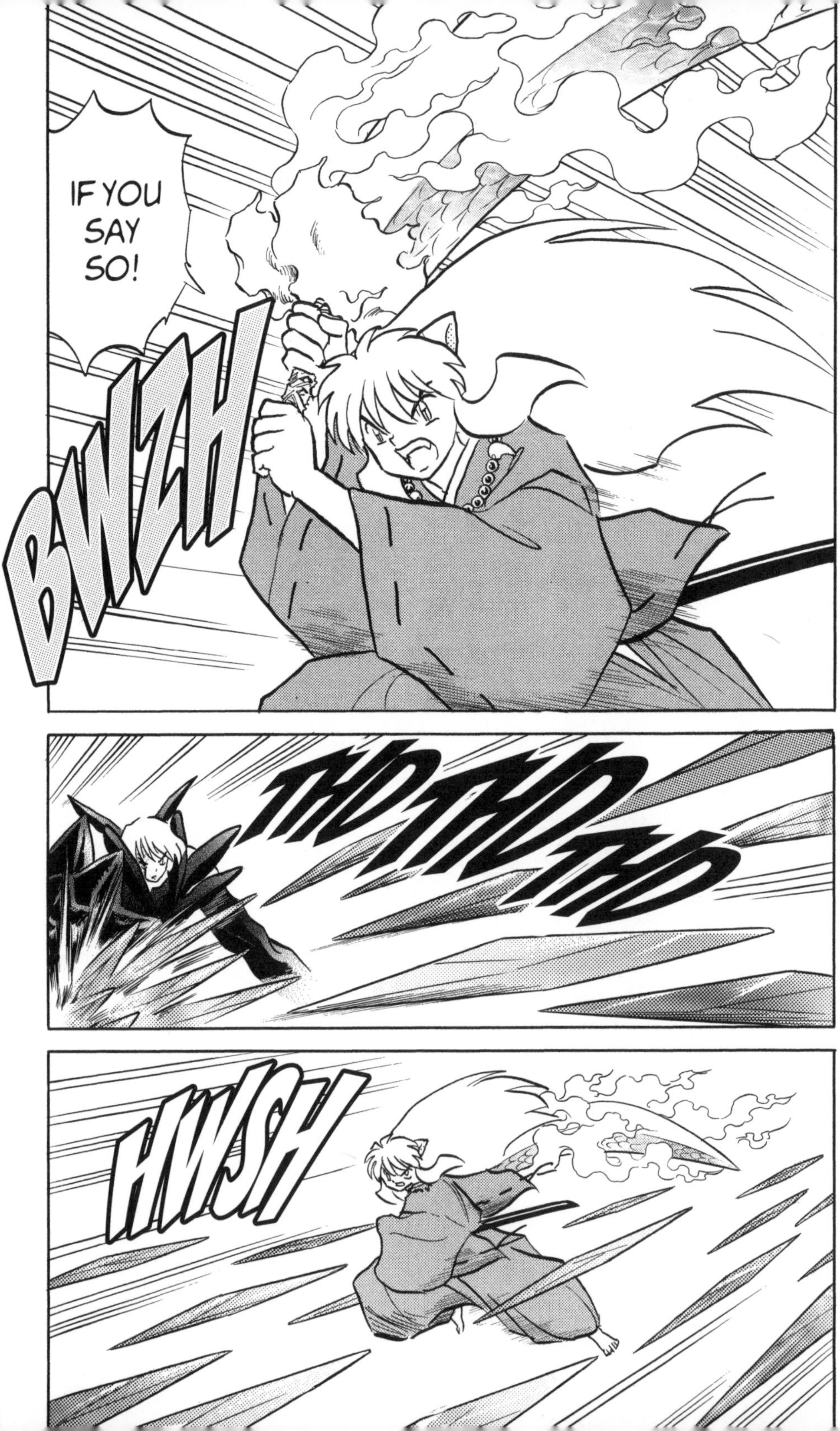
IF YOU SAY SO!
BWZH
THD THD THD
HWSH

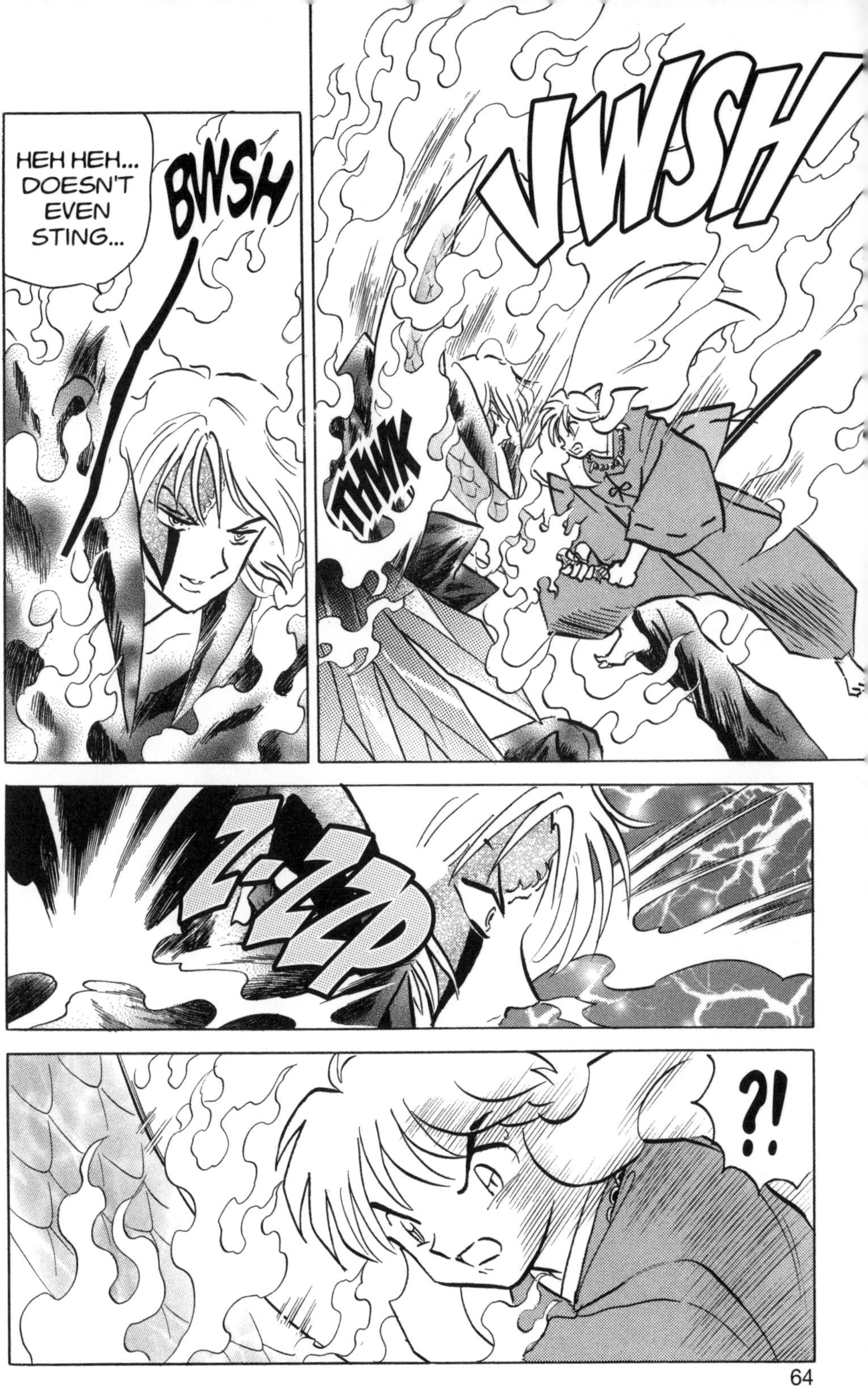
VWSH
THWK
HEH HEH... DOESN'T EVEN STING...
BWSH
Z-ZIP
?!

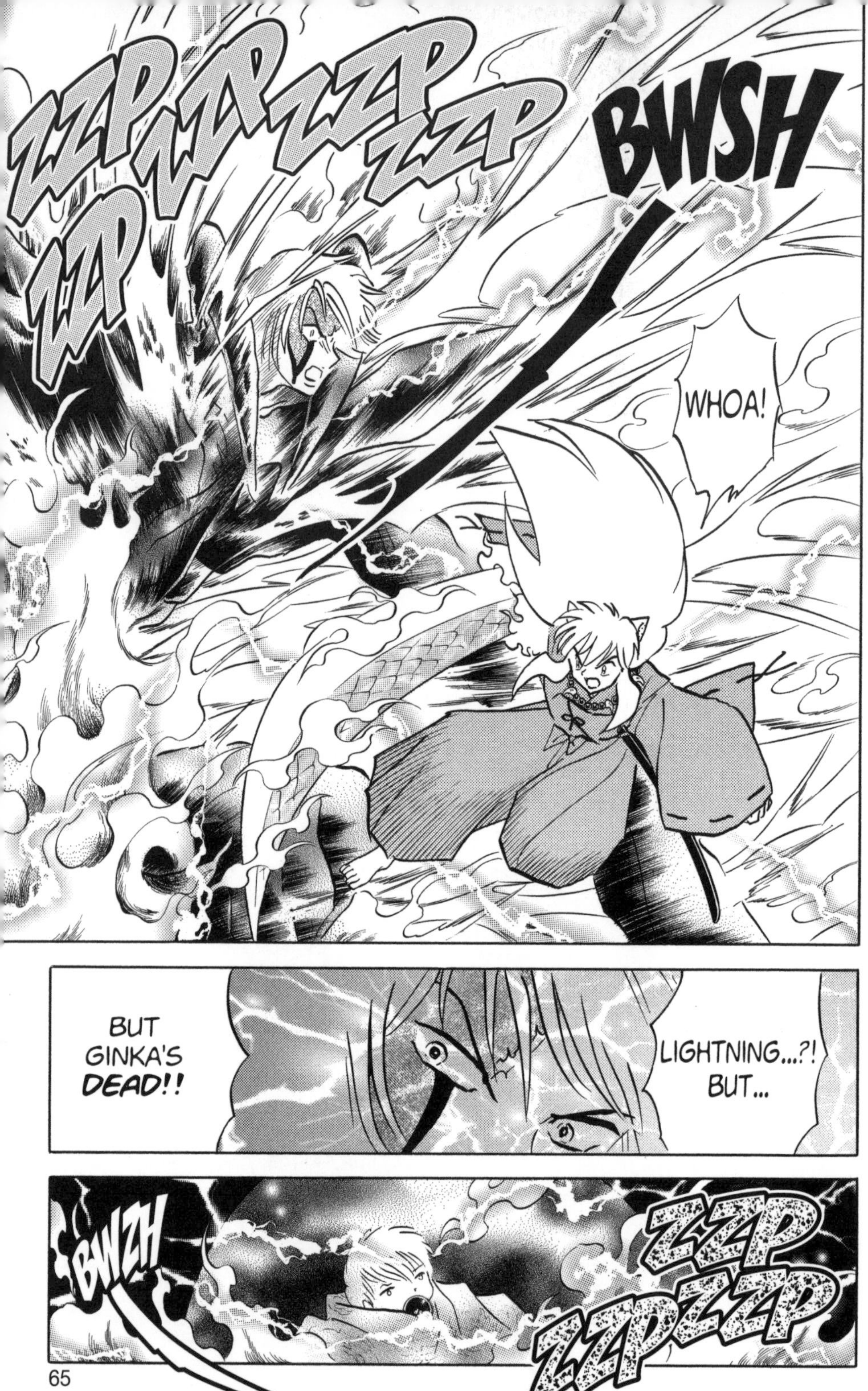
BWSH
WHOA!
ZZZP ZZZP ZZZP ZZZP ZZZP
LIGHTNING...?! BUT...
BUT GINKA'S DEAD!!
ZZZP ZZZPZZZP
BWZH

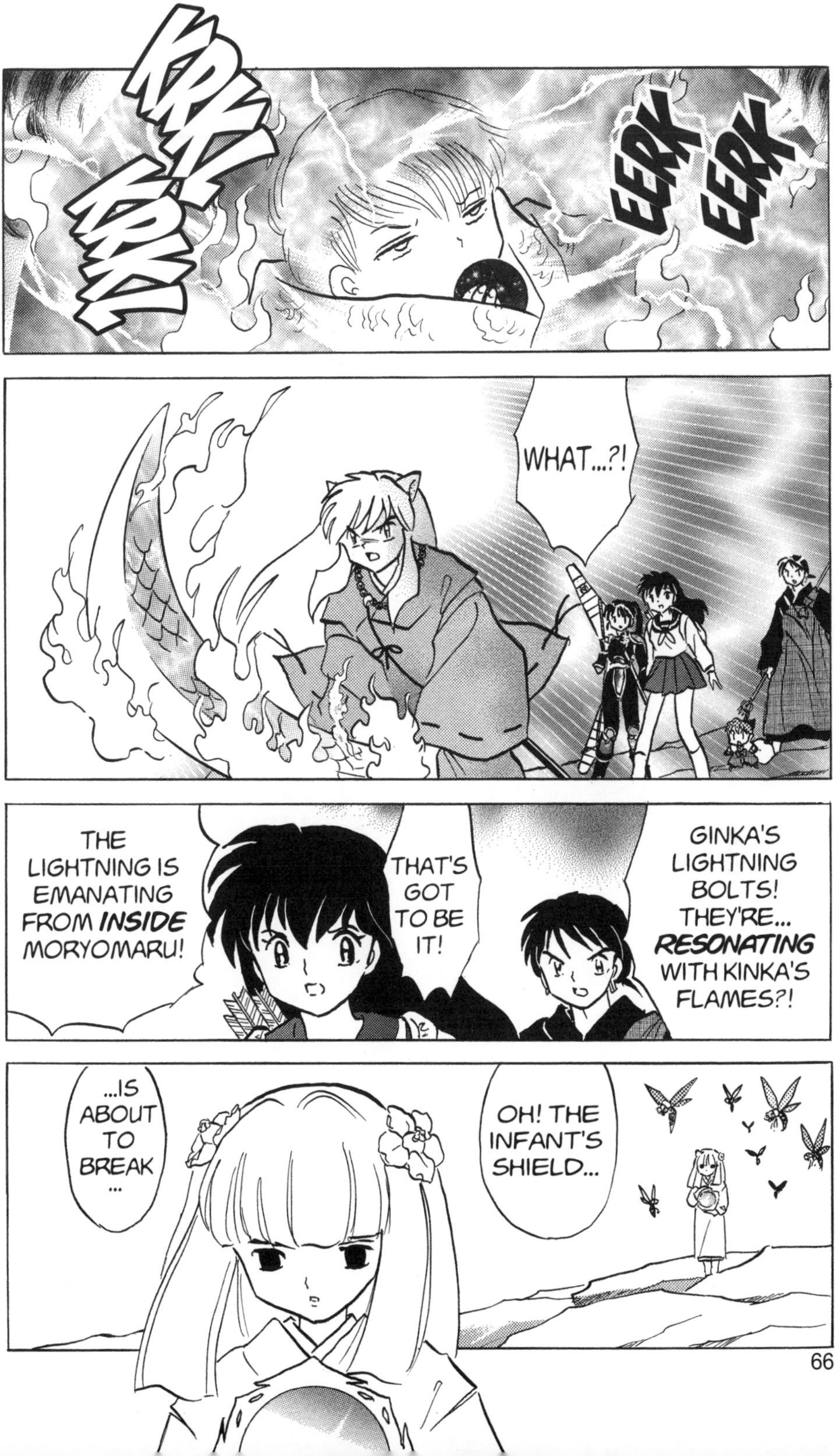
EERK EERK
KRK! KRK!
WHAT...?!
GINKA'S LIGHTNING BOLTS! THEY'RE... **RESONATING** WITH KINKA'S FLAMES?!
THAT'S GOT TO BE IT!
THE LIGHTNING IS EMANATING FROM **INSIDE** MORYOMARU!
OH! THE INFANT'S SHIELD...
...IS ABOUT TO BREAK ...

SCROLL FOUR
TETSUSAIGA'S FLAMES

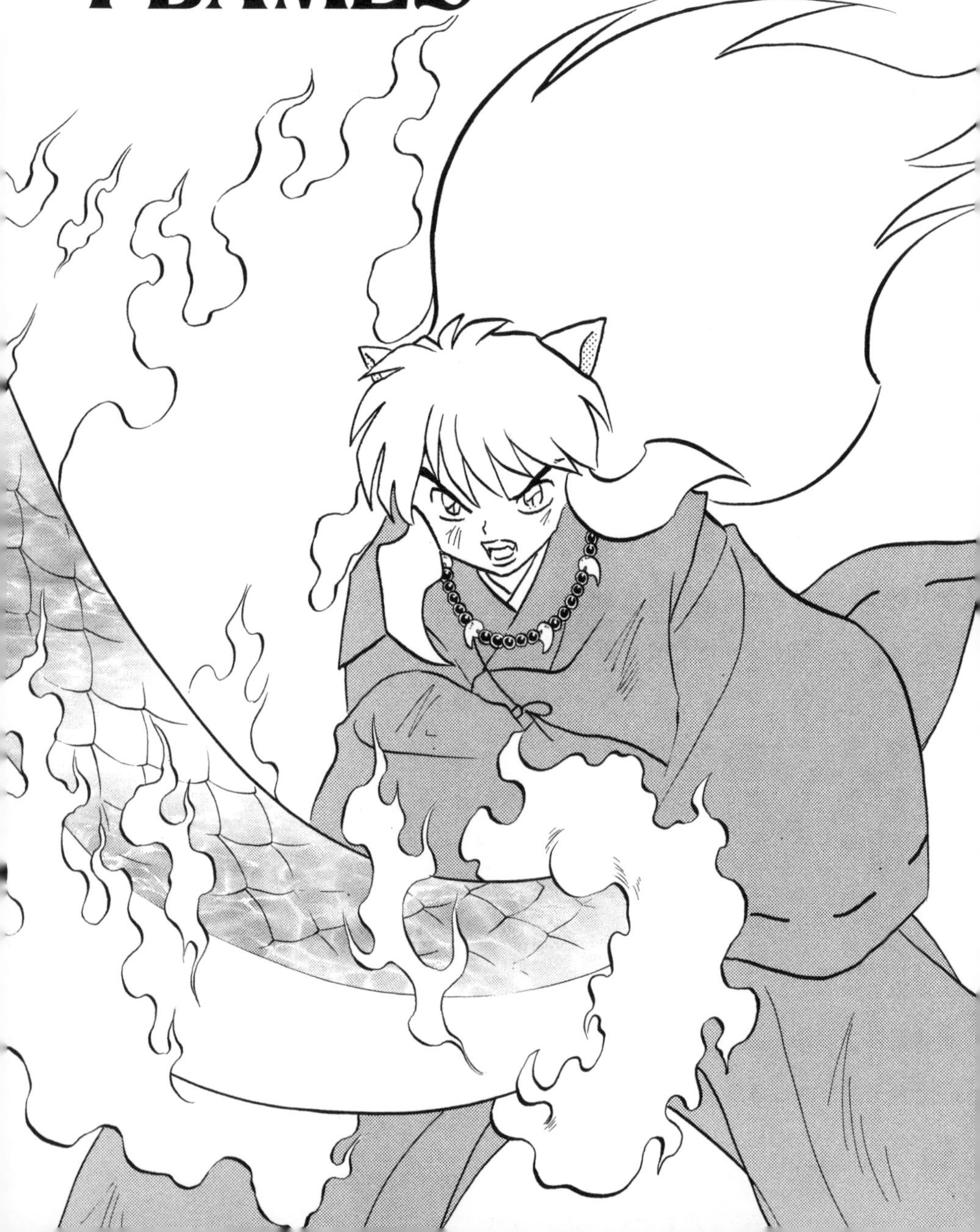

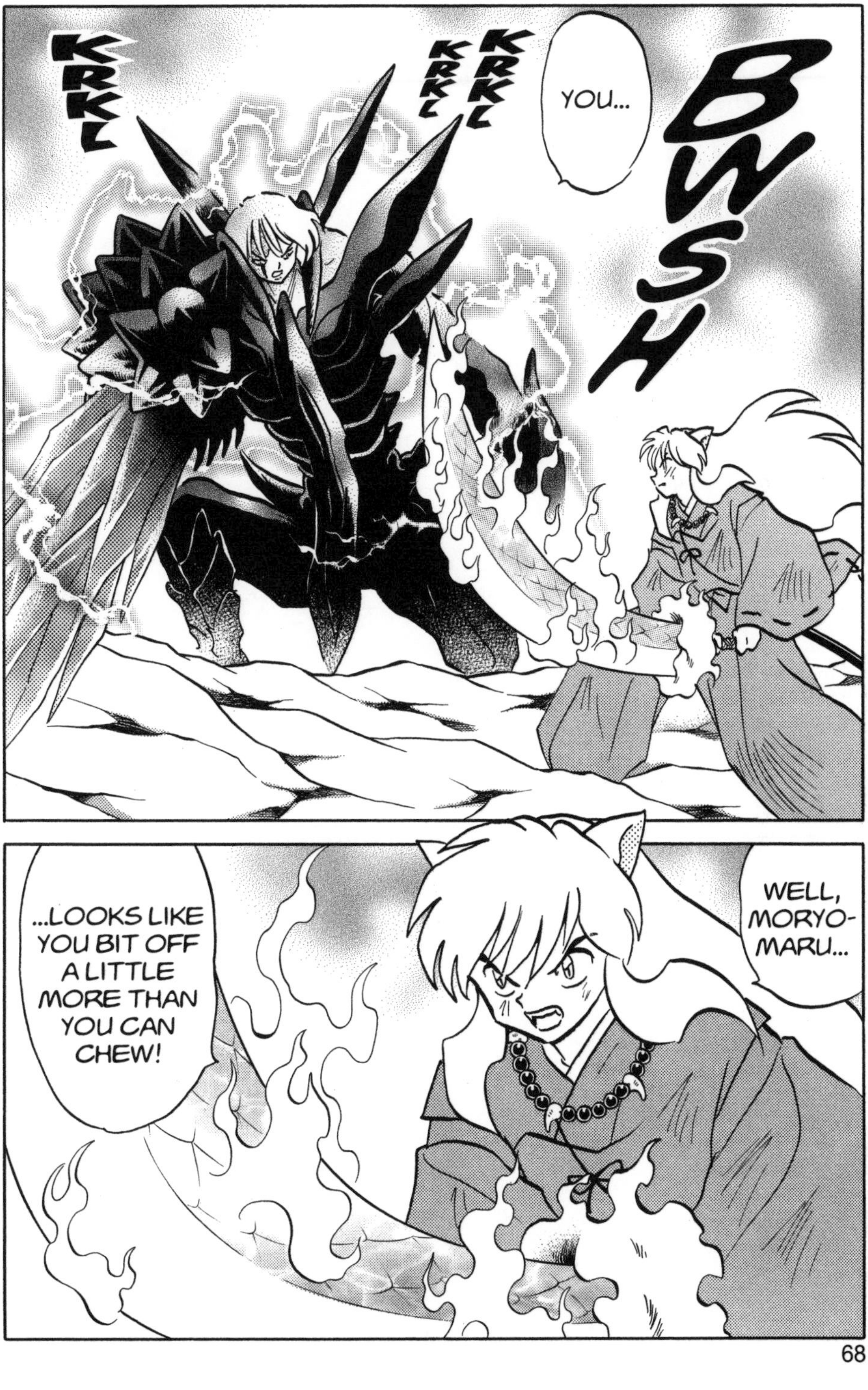
BWSH
YOU...
KRKL KRKL
KRKL
WELL, MORYO-MARU...
...LOOKS LIKE YOU BIT OFF A LITTLE MORE THAN YOU CAN CHEW!

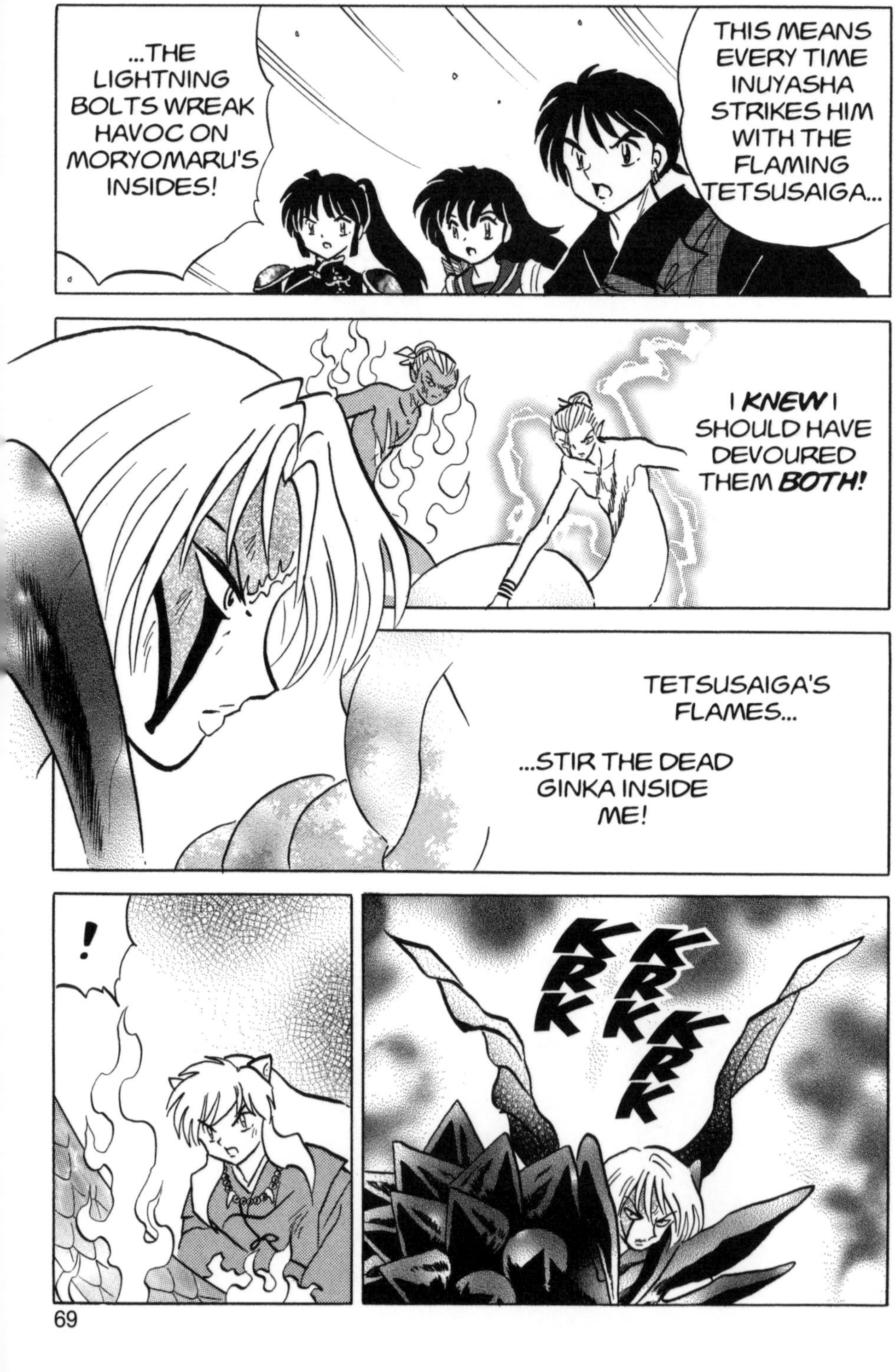
THIS MEANS EVERY TIME INUYASHA STRIKES HIM WITH THE FLAMING TETSUSAIGA...
...THE LIGHTNING BOLTS WREAK HAVOC ON MORYOMARU'S INSIDES!
I **KNEW** I SHOULD HAVE DEVOURED THEM **BOTH!**
TETSUSAIGA'S FLAMES...
...STIR THE DEAD GINKA INSIDE ME!
KRK KRK KRK KRK
!

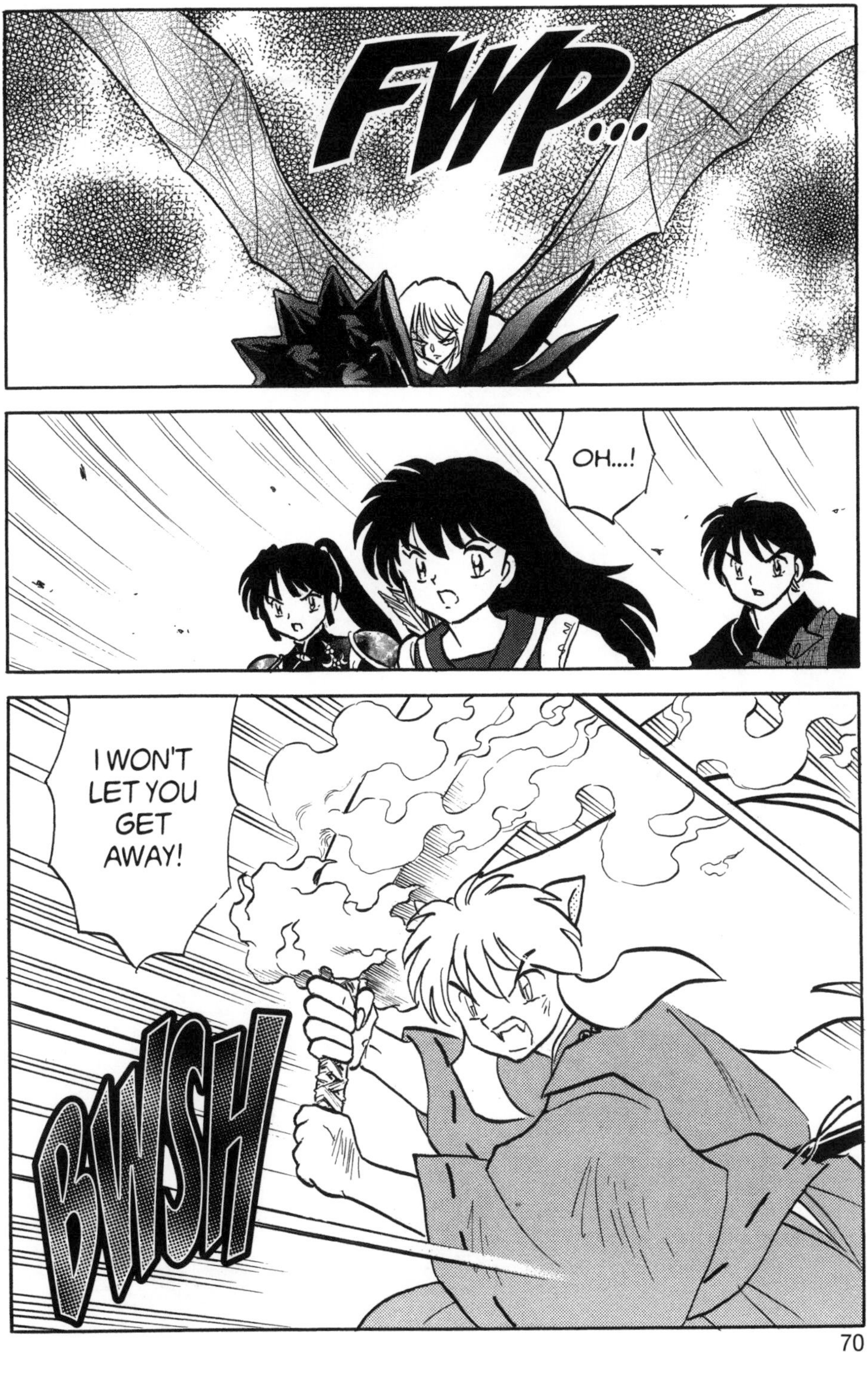
FWP...
OH...!
I WON'T LET YOU GET AWAY!
BWSH

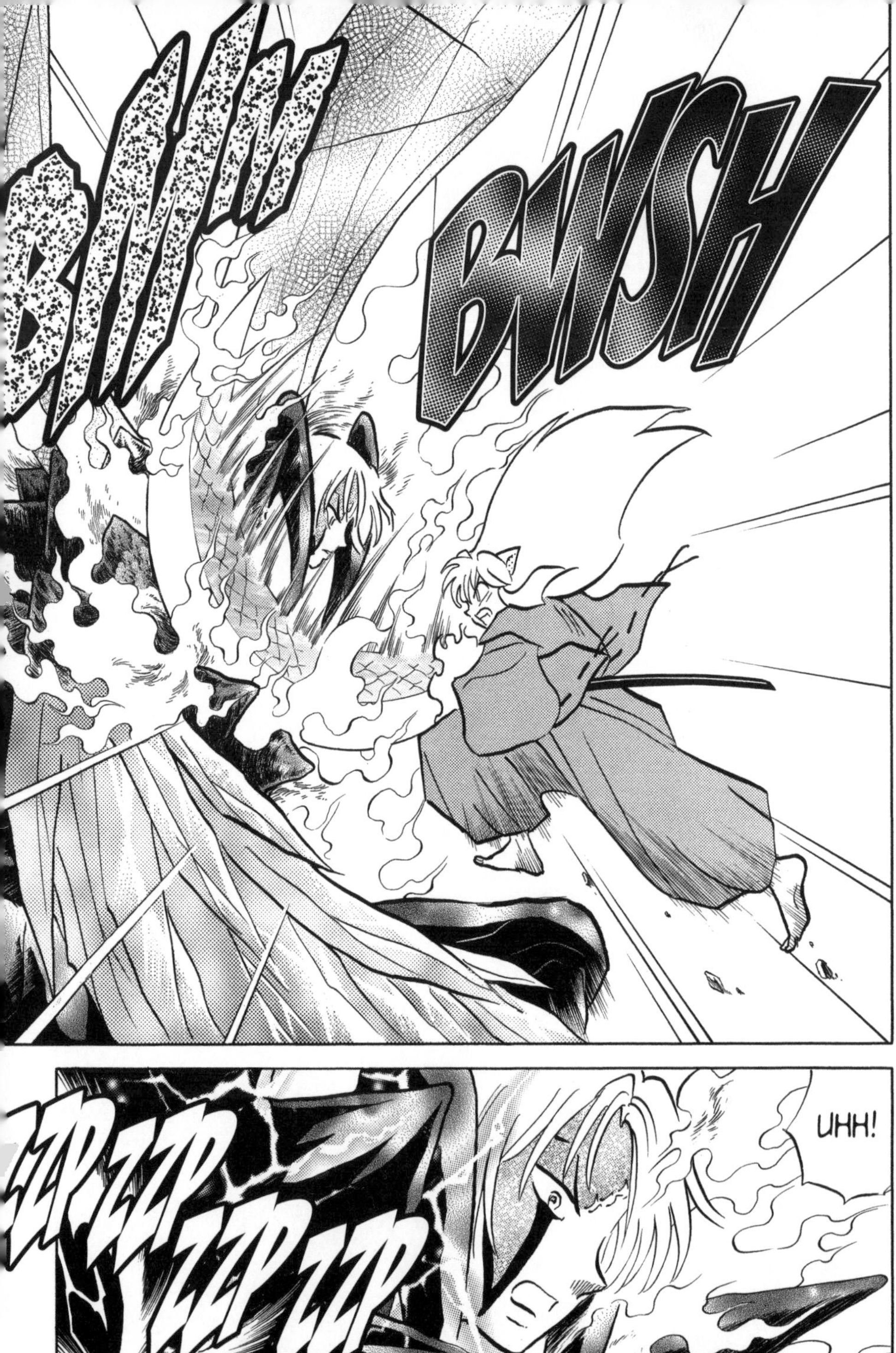
UHH!

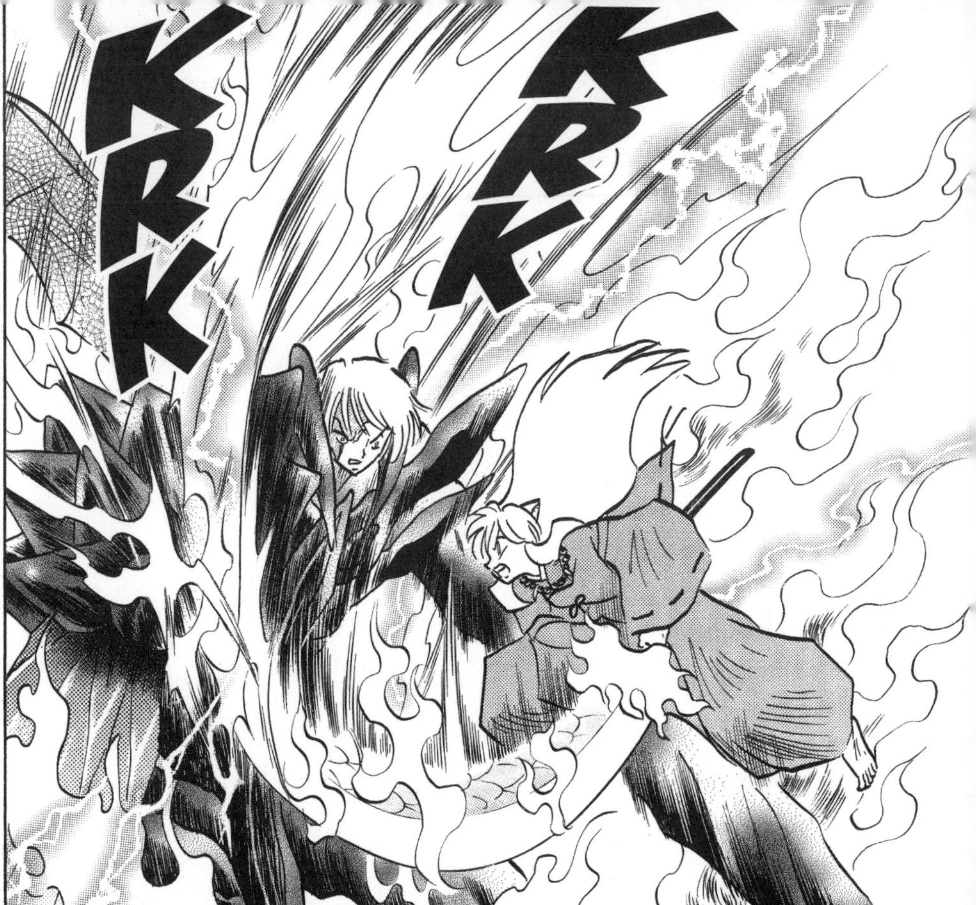
KRK
KRK

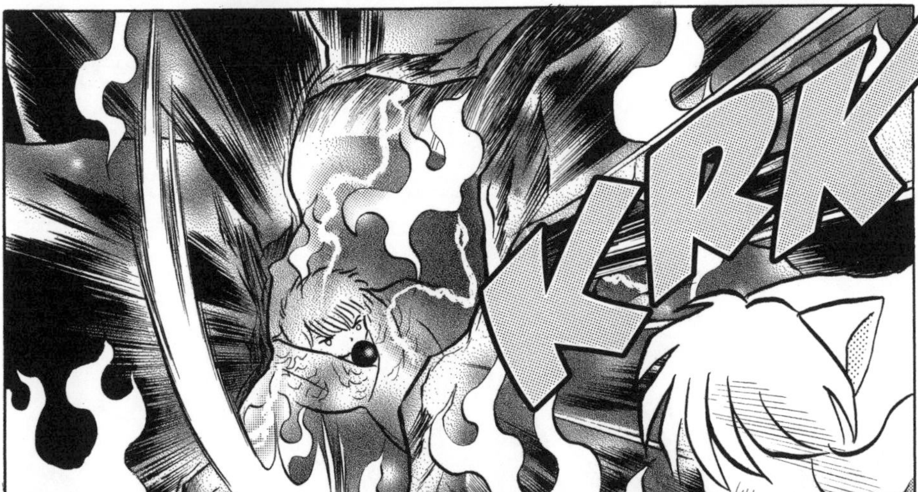
KRK

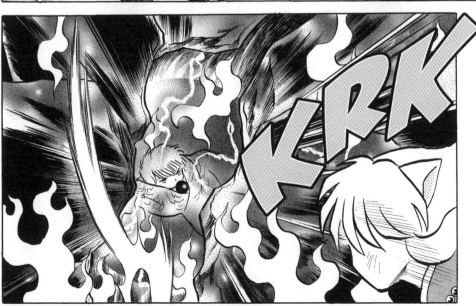

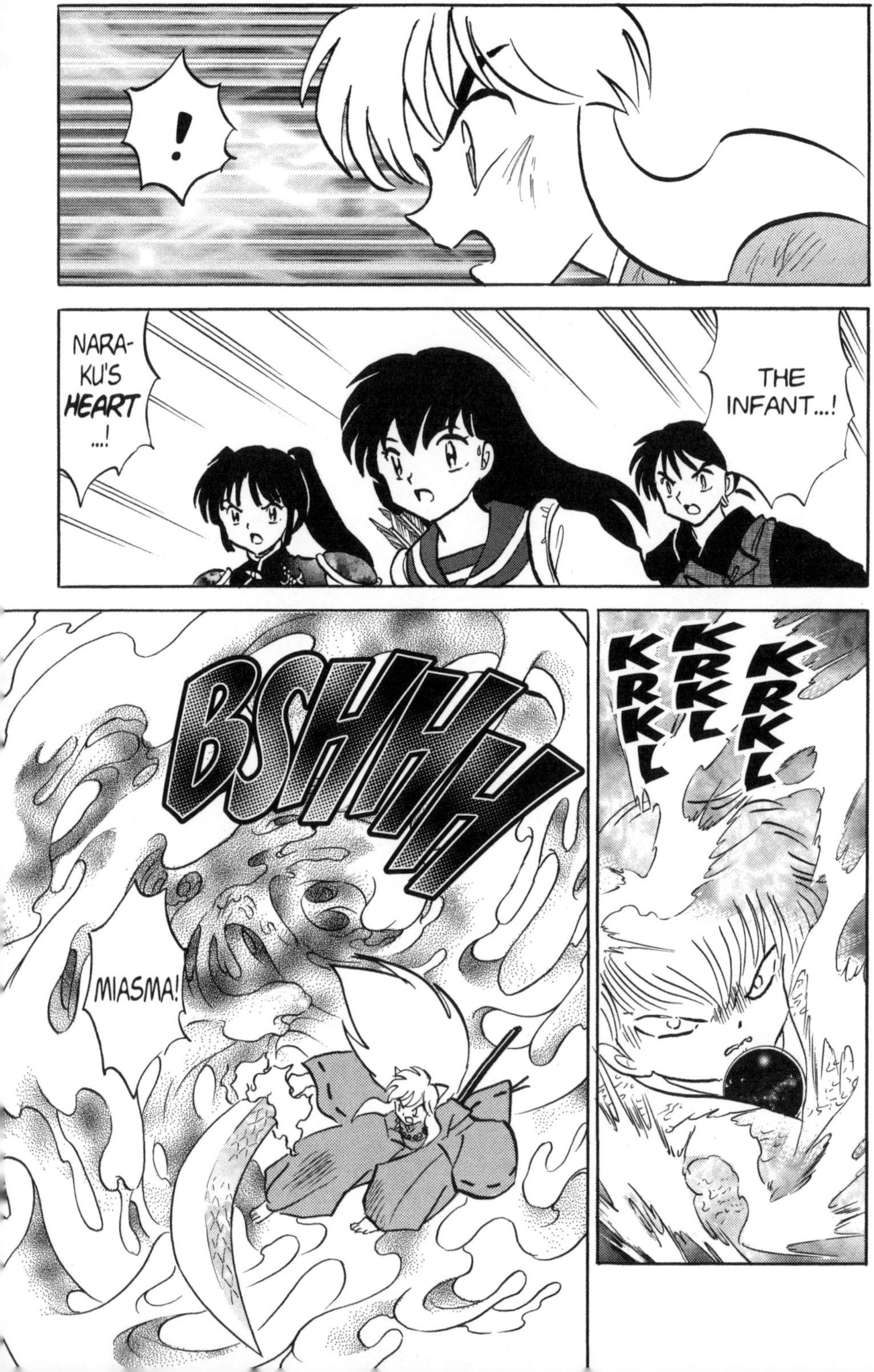
!
THE INFANT...!
NARAKU'S HEART ...!
KRKL KRKL KRKL
BSHHH
MIASMA!

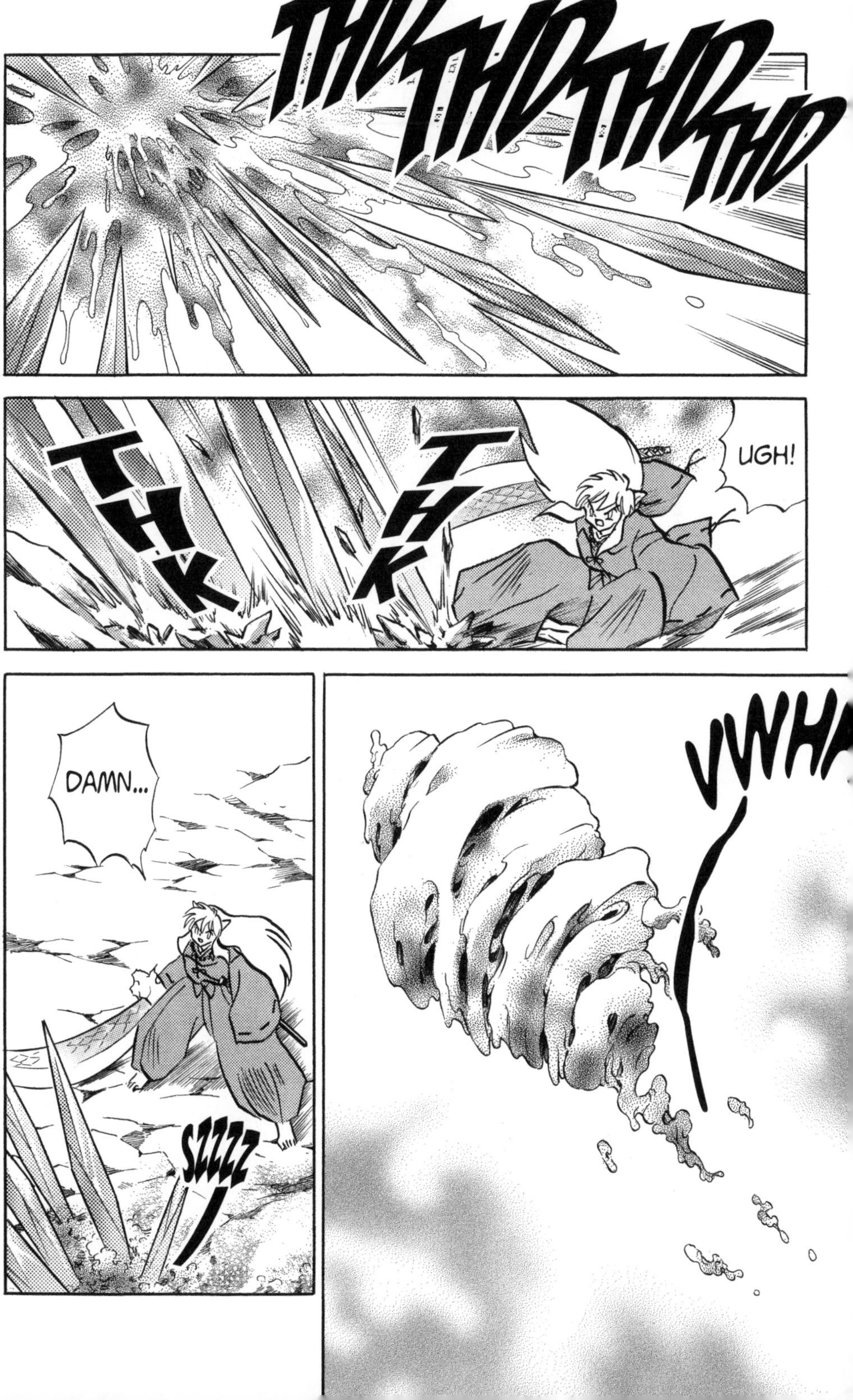
THD THD THD THD
UGH!
THK
THK
VWH
DAMN...
SZZZZ

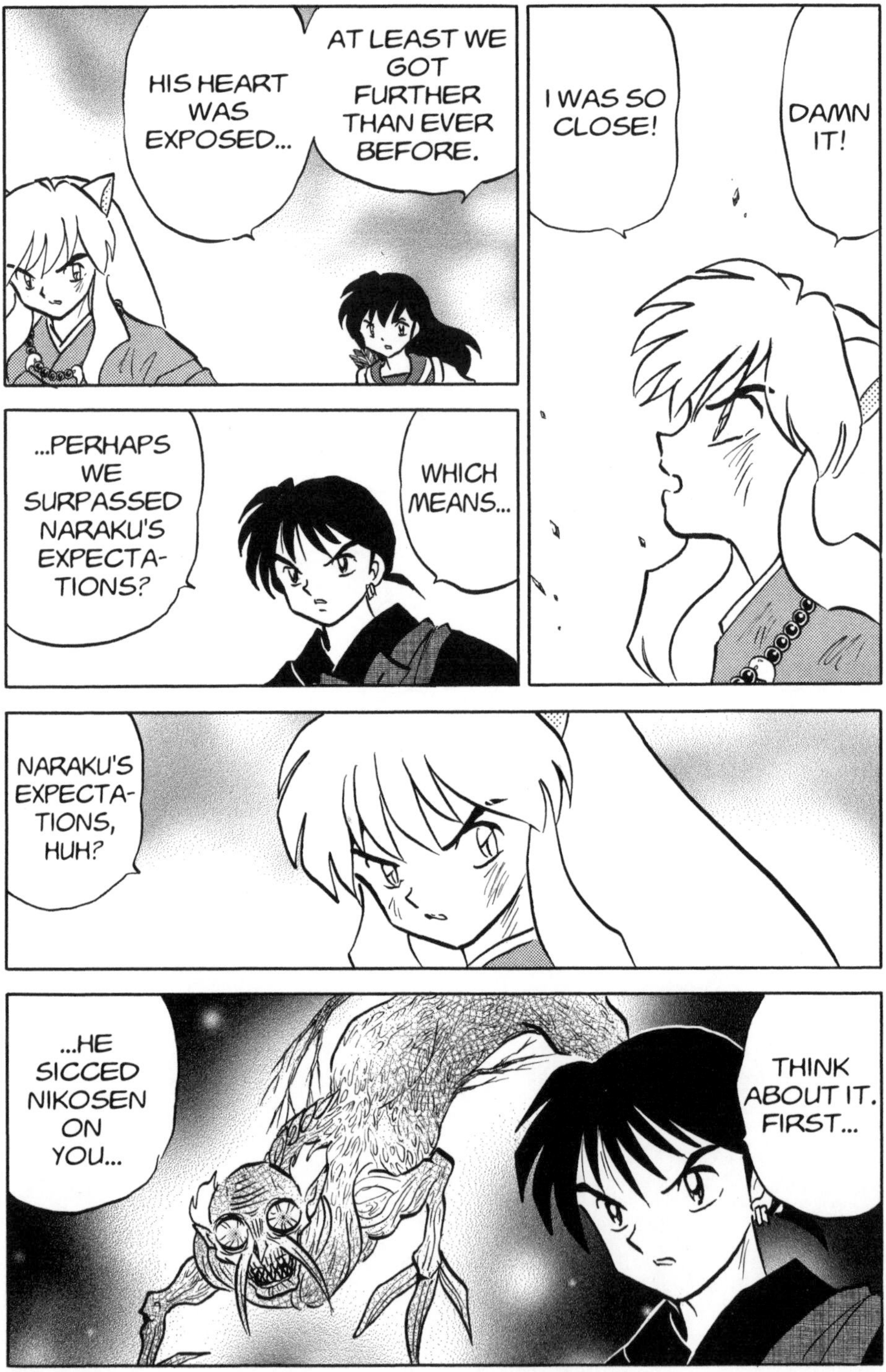
DAMN IT!
I WAS SO CLOSE!
AT LEAST WE GOT FURTHER THAN EVER BEFORE.
HIS HEART WAS EXPOSED...
WHICH MEANS...
...PERHAPS WE SURPASSED NARAKU'S EXPECTA-TIONS?
NARAKU'S EXPECTA-TIONS, HUH?
THINK ABOUT IT. FIRST...
...HE SICCED NIKOSEN ON YOU...

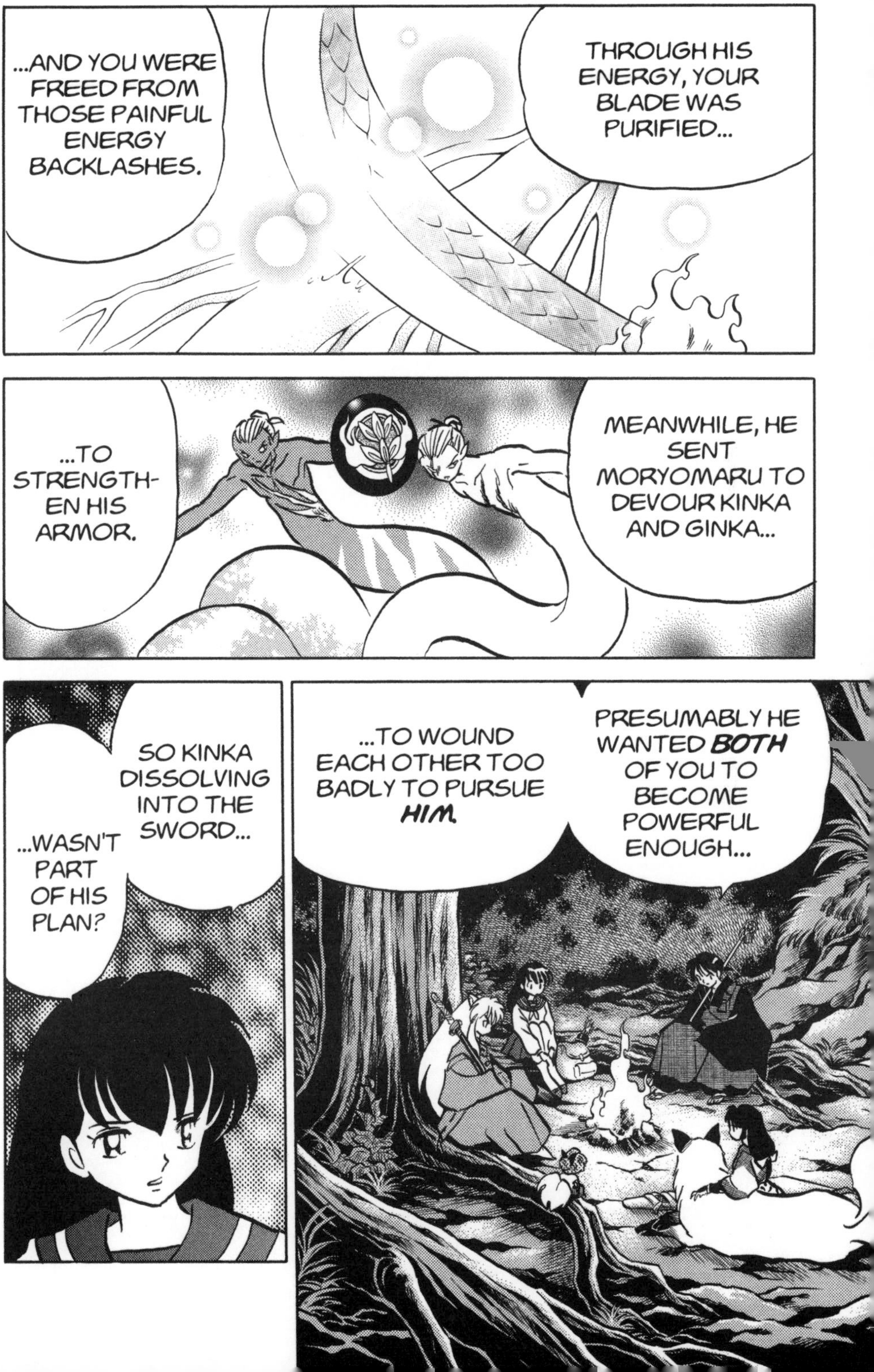
THROUGH HIS ENERGY, YOUR BLADE WAS PURIFIED...
...AND YOU WERE FREED FROM THOSE PAINFUL ENERGY BACKLASHES.
MEANWHILE, HE SENT MORYOMARU TO DEVOUR KINKA AND GINKA...
...TO STRENGTH-EN HIS ARMOR.
PRESUMABLY HE WANTED **BOTH** OF YOU TO BECOME POWERFUL ENOUGH...
...TO WOUND EACH OTHER TOO BADLY TO PURSUE ***HIM.***
SO KINKA DISSOLVING INTO THE SWORD...
...WASN'T PART OF HIS PLAN?

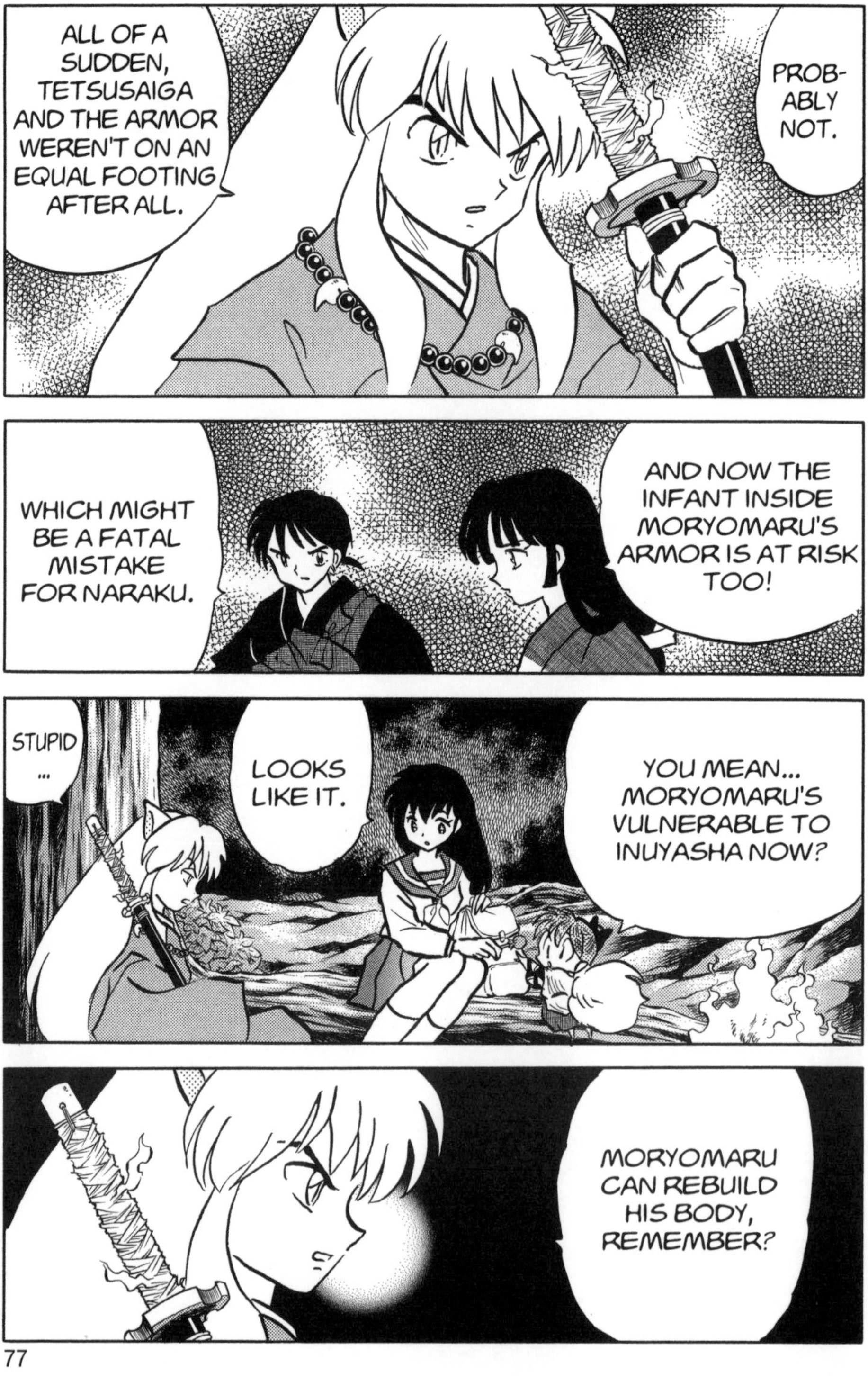
PROB-ABLY NOT.
ALL OF A SUDDEN, TETSUSAIGA AND THE ARMOR WEREN'T ON AN EQUAL FOOTING AFTER ALL.
AND NOW THE INFANT INSIDE MORYOMARU'S ARMOR IS AT RISK TOO!
WHICH MIGHT BE A FATAL MISTAKE FOR NARAKU.
YOU MEAN... MORYOMARU'S VULNERABLE TO INUYASHA NOW?
LOOKS LIKE IT.
STUPID ...
MORYOMARU CAN REBUILD HIS BODY, REMEMBER?

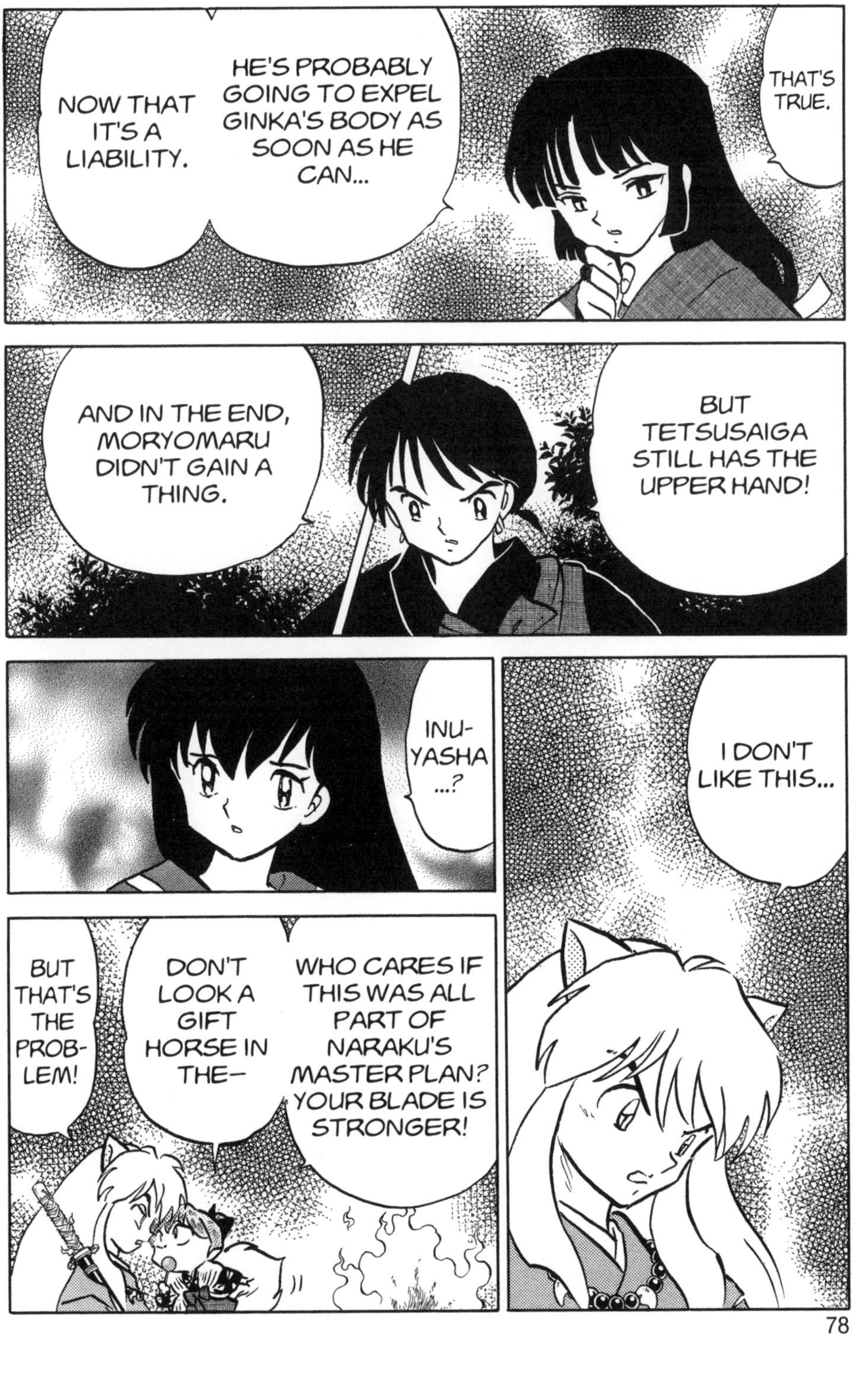
THAT'S TRUE.
HE'S PROBABLY GOING TO EXPEL GINKA'S BODY AS SOON AS HE CAN...
NOW THAT IT'S A LIABILITY.
BUT TETSUSAIGA STILL HAS THE UPPER HAND!
AND IN THE END, MORYOMARU DIDN'T GAIN A THING.
I DON'T LIKE THIS...
INU-YASHA ...?
WHO CARES IF THIS WAS ALL PART OF NARAKU'S MASTER PLAN? YOUR BLADE IS STRONGER!
DON'T LOOK A GIFT HORSE IN THE–
BUT THAT'S THE PROB-LEM!

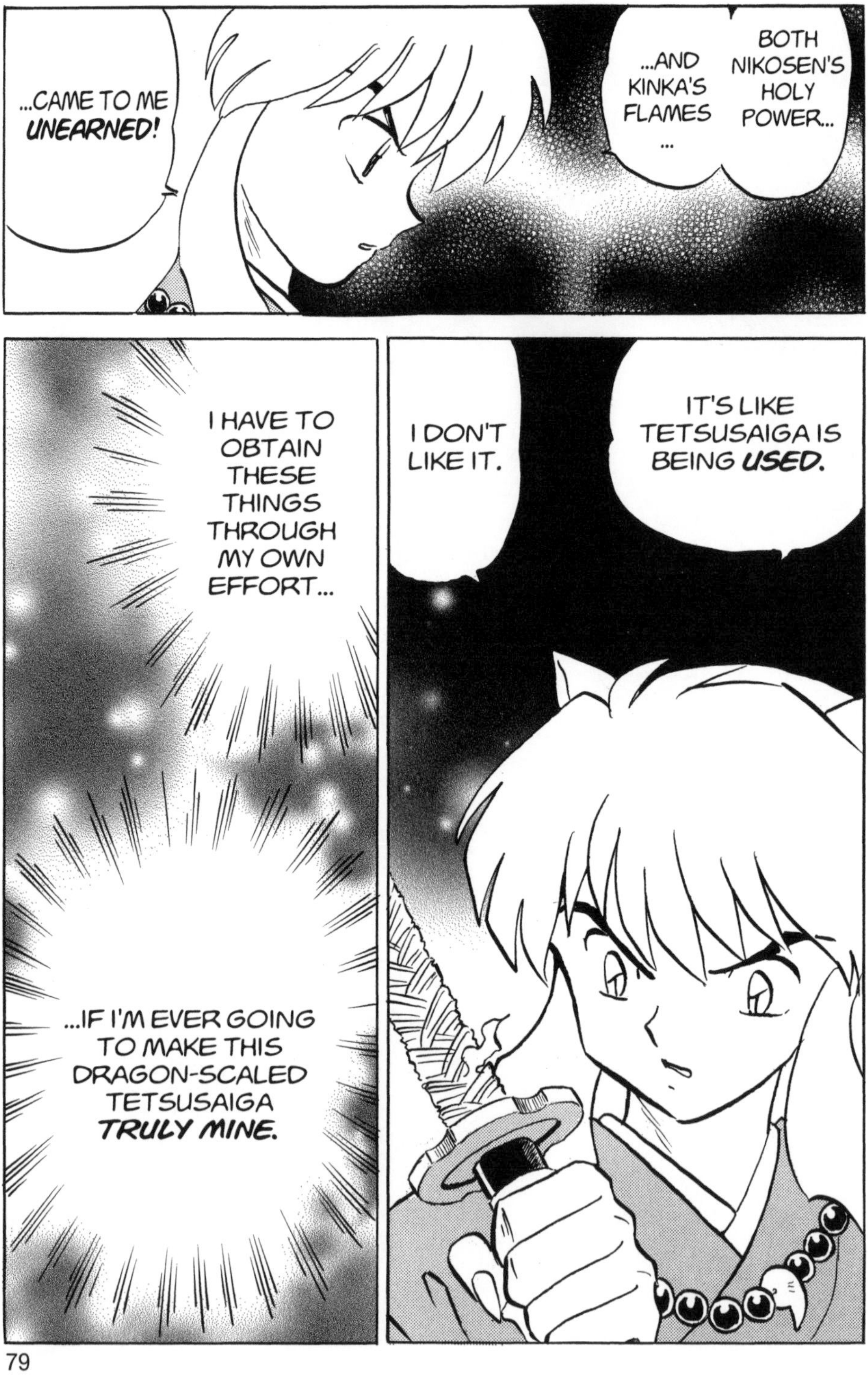
BOTH NIKOSEN'S HOLY POWER...
...AND KINKA'S FLAMES ...
...CAME TO ME **UNEARNED!**
IT'S LIKE TETSUSAIGA IS BEING **USED.**
I DON'T LIKE IT.
I HAVE TO OBTAIN THESE THINGS THROUGH MY OWN EFFORT...
...IF I'M EVER GOING TO MAKE THIS DRAGON-SCALED TETSUSAIGA **TRULY MINE.**

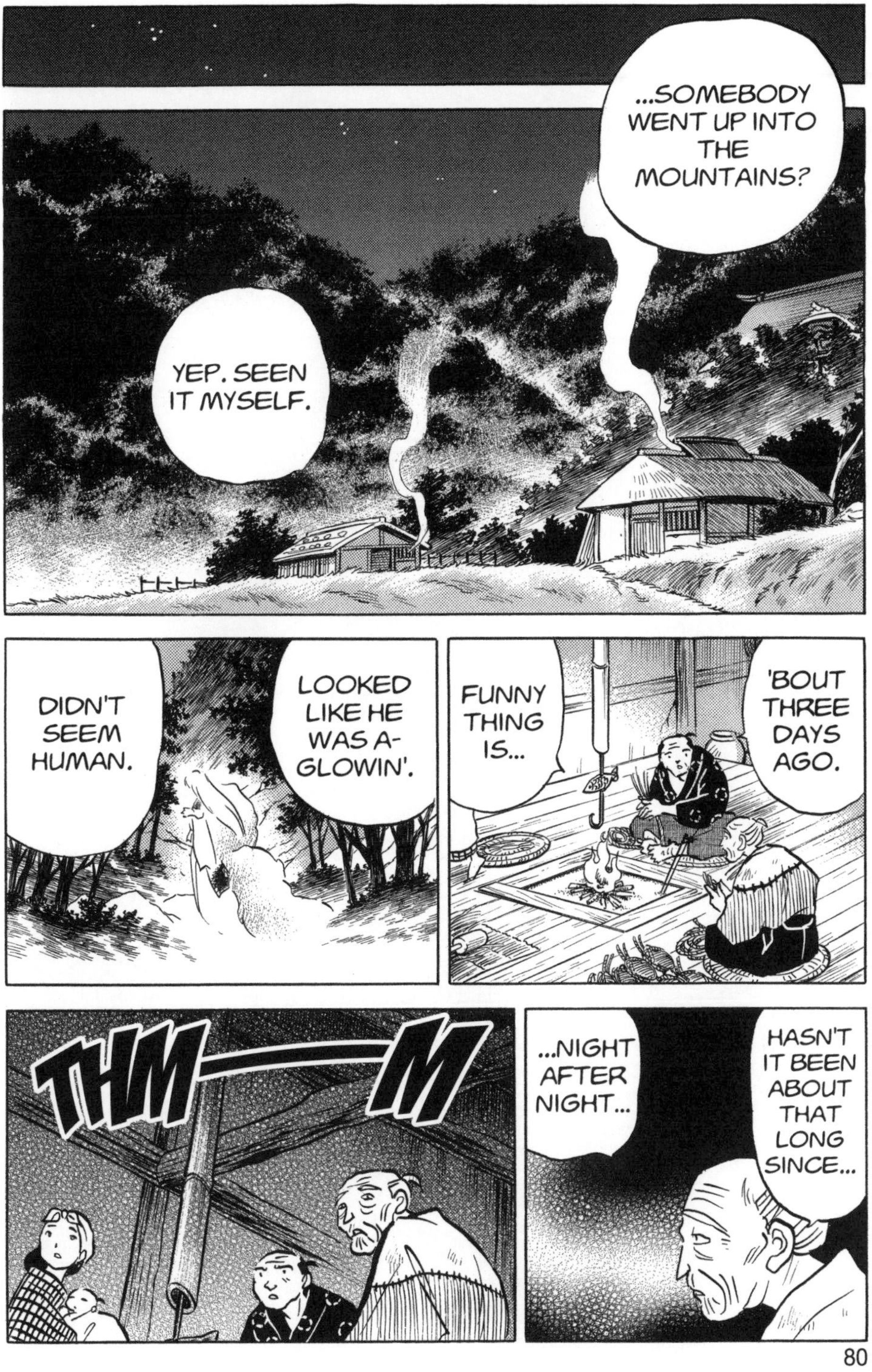
...SOMEBODY WENT UP INTO THE MOUNTAINS?
YEP. SEEN IT MYSELF.
'BOUT THREE DAYS AGO.
FUNNY THING IS...
LOOKED LIKE HE WAS A-GLOWIN'.
DIDN'T SEEM HUMAN.
HASN'T IT BEEN ABOUT THAT LONG SINCE...
...NIGHT AFTER NIGHT...
THM——M

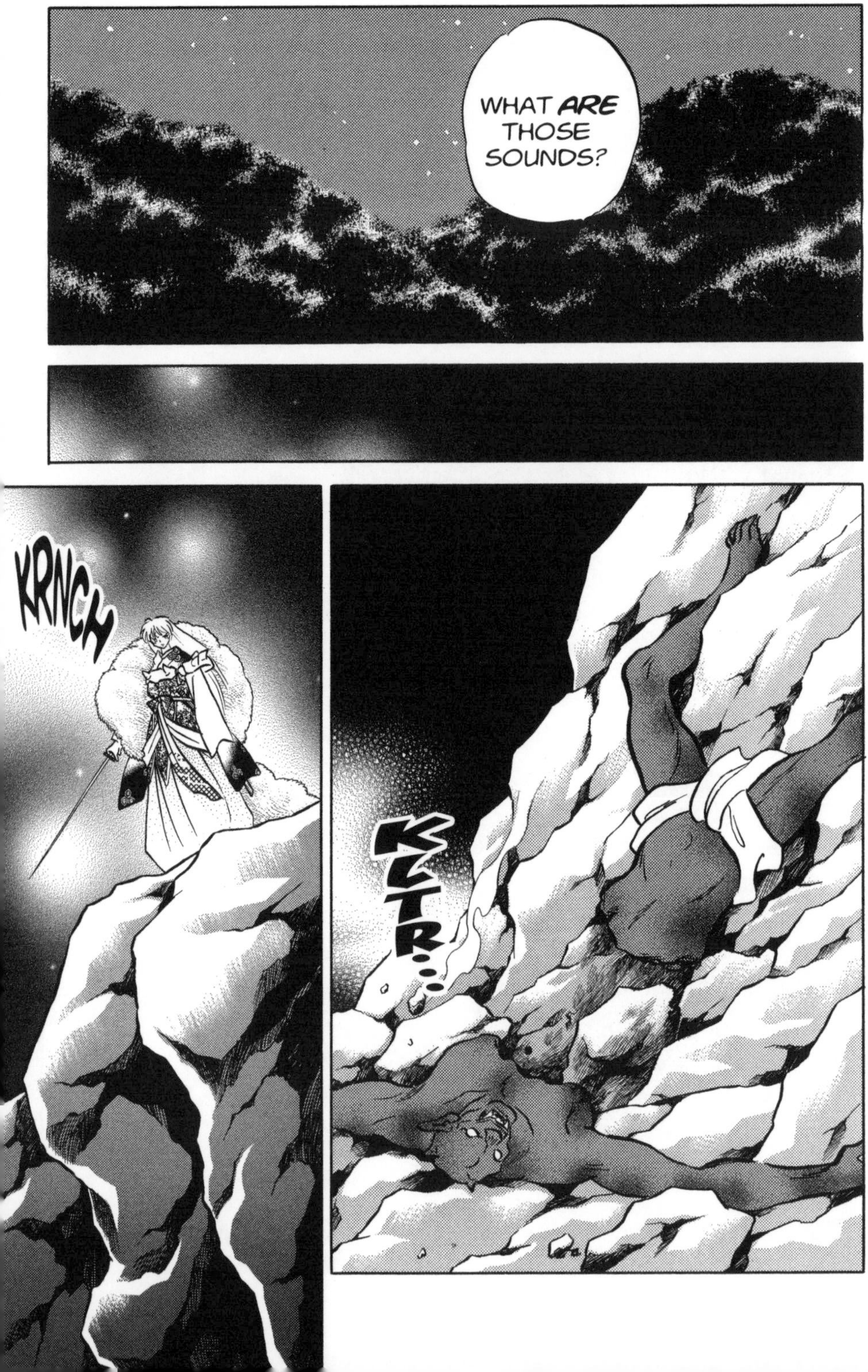
WHAT **ARE** THOSE SOUNDS?
KLTR...
KRNCH

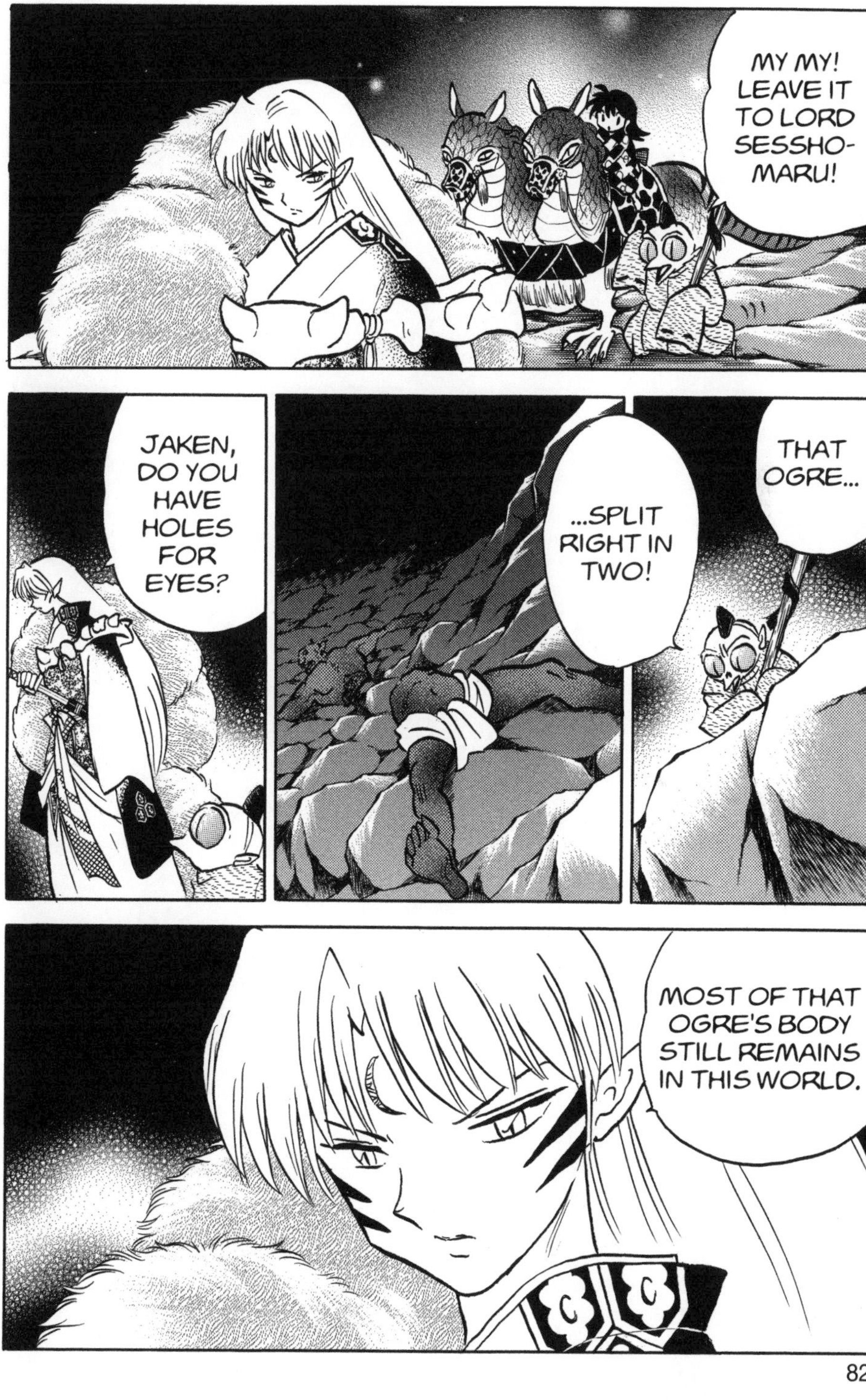
MY MY! LEAVE IT TO LORD SESSHO-MARU!
THAT OGRE...
...SPLIT RIGHT IN TWO!
JAKEN, DO YOU HAVE HOLES FOR EYES?
MOST OF THAT OGRE'S BODY STILL REMAINS IN THIS WORLD.

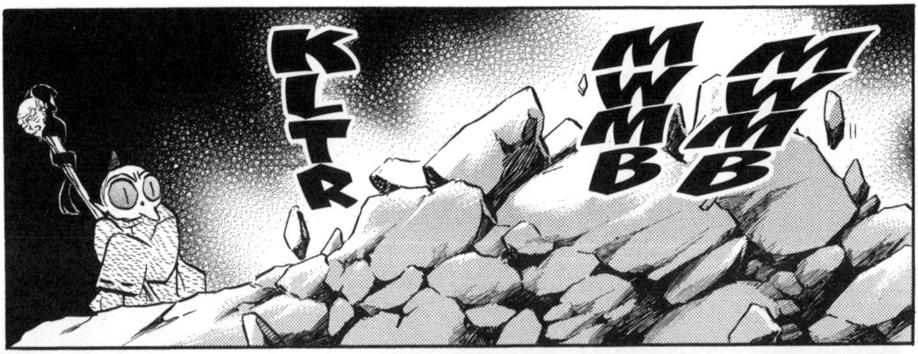
MWMB MWMB
KLTR
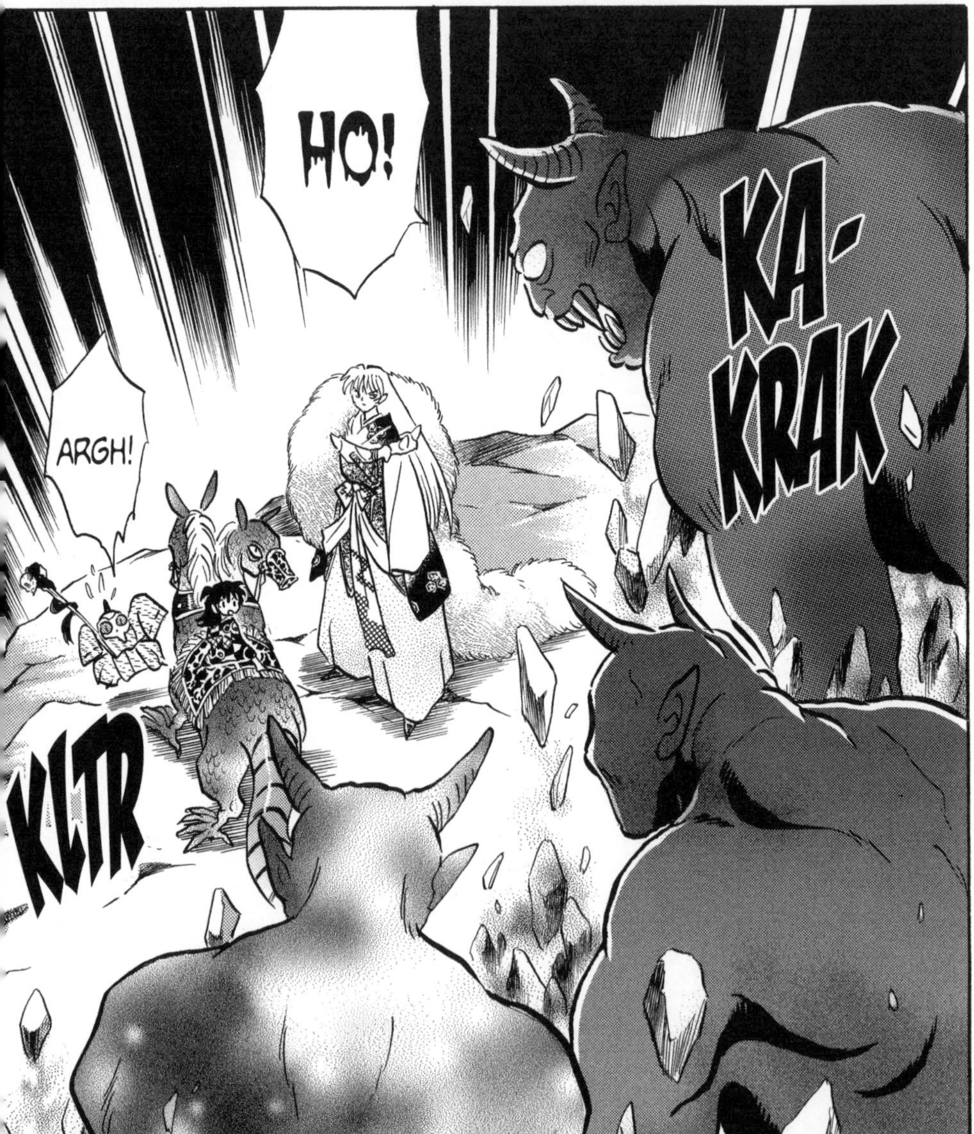
KA-
KRAK
HO!
ARGH!
KLTR

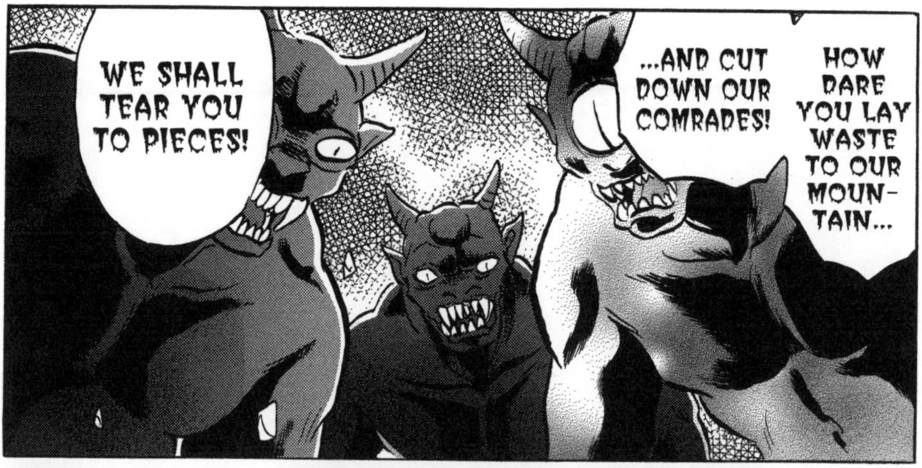
HOW DARE YOU LAY WASTE TO OUR MOUNTAIN...
...AND CUT DOWN OUR COMRADES!
WE SHALL TEAR YOU TO PIECES!

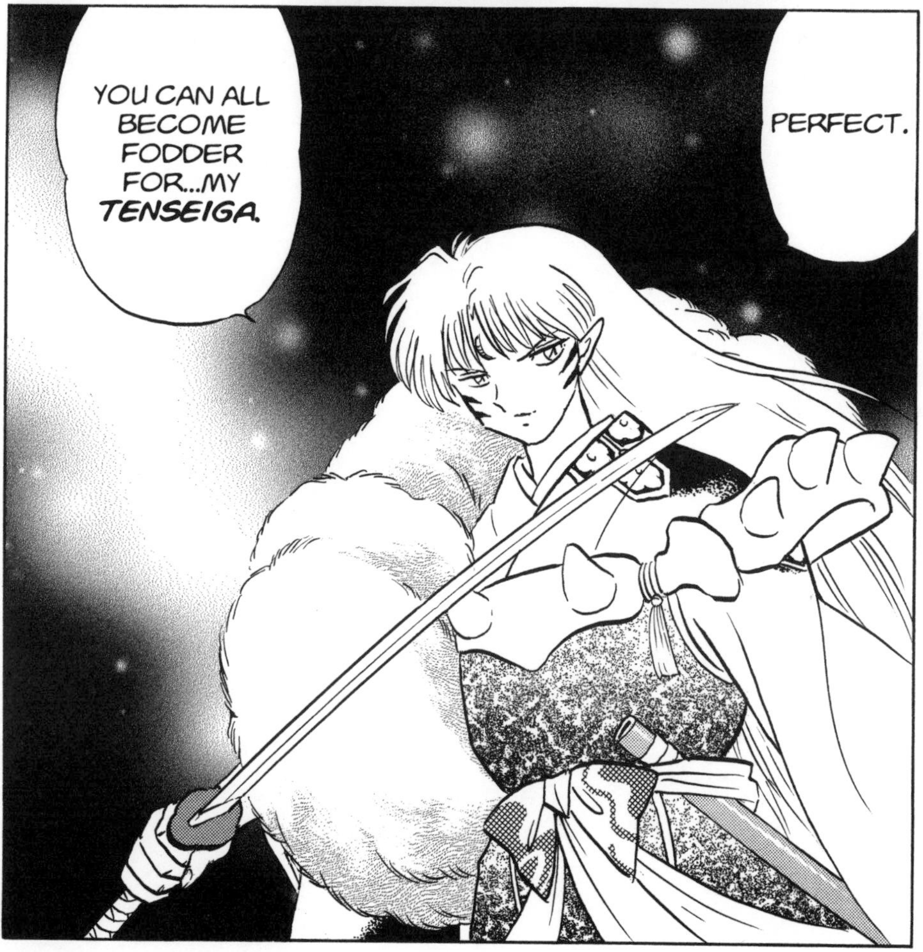
PERFECT.
YOU CAN ALL BECOME FODDER FOR...MY *TENSEIGA*.

SCROLL FIVE
THE NUMAWATARI

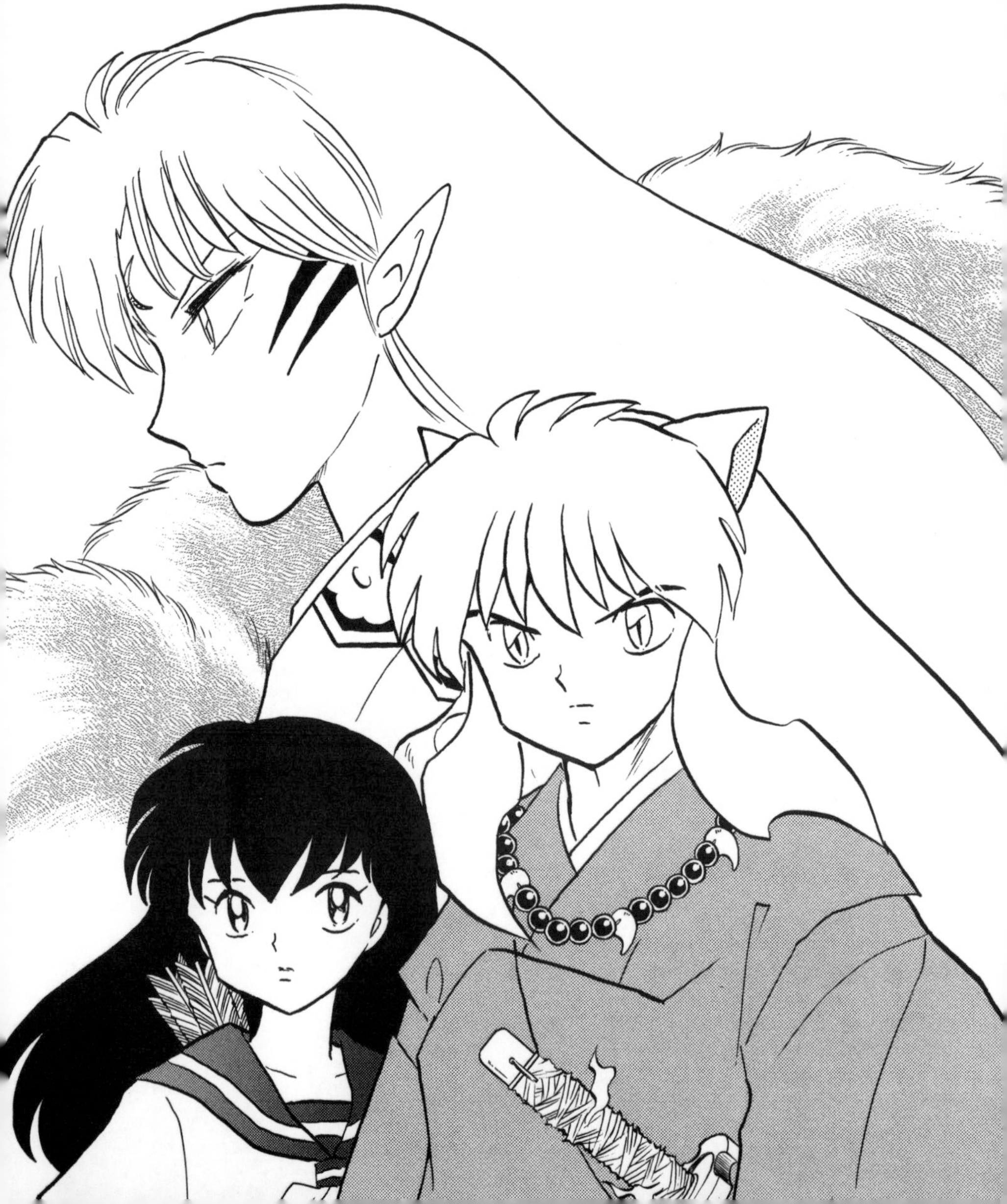

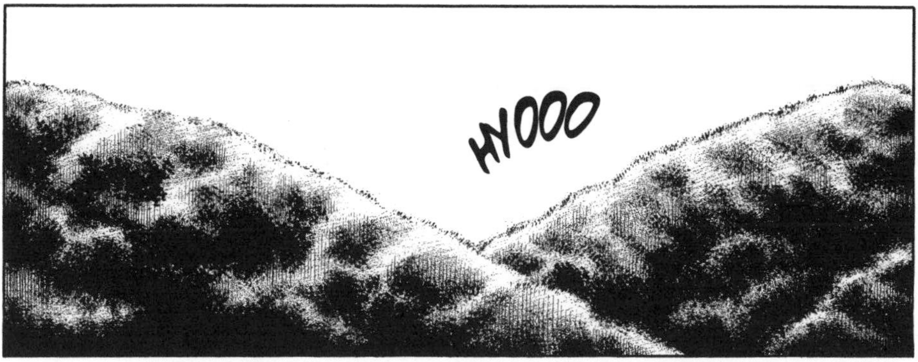
HYOOO
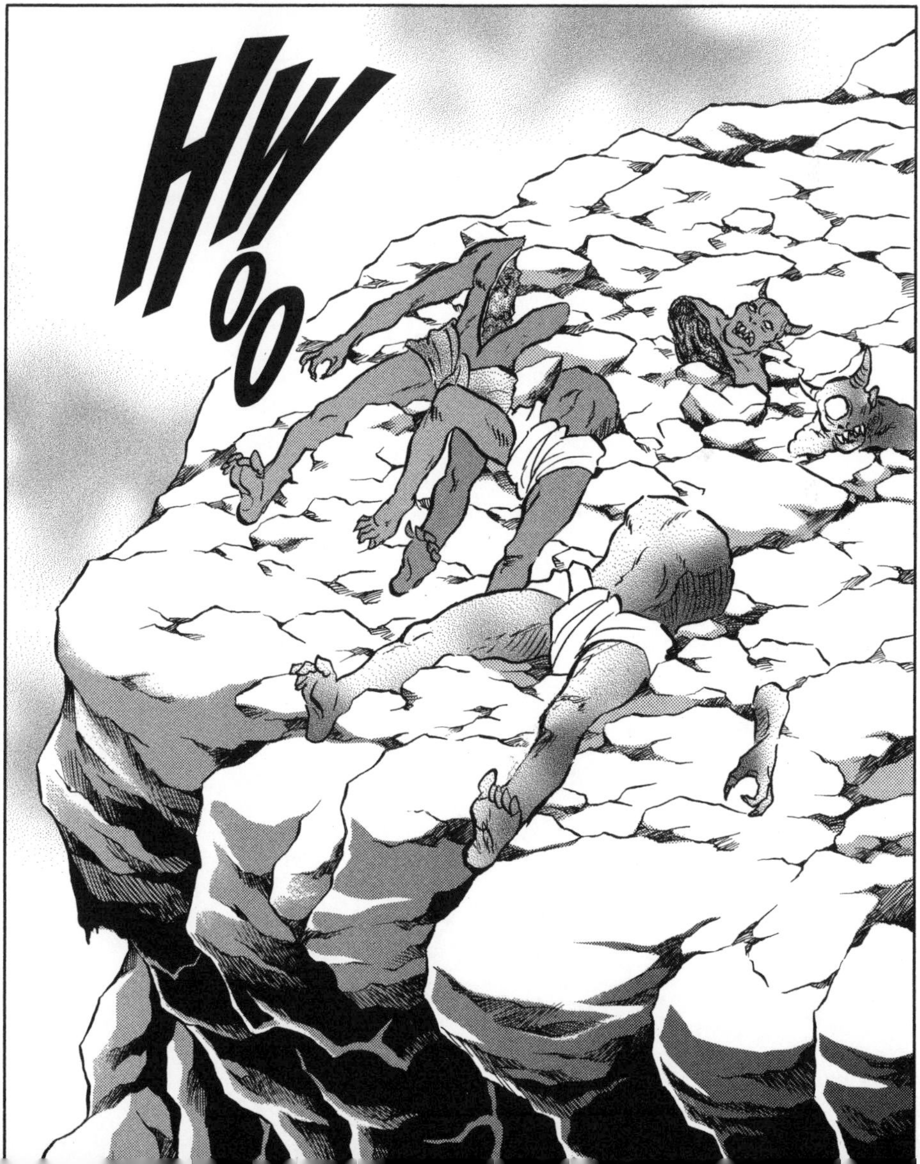
HWOO

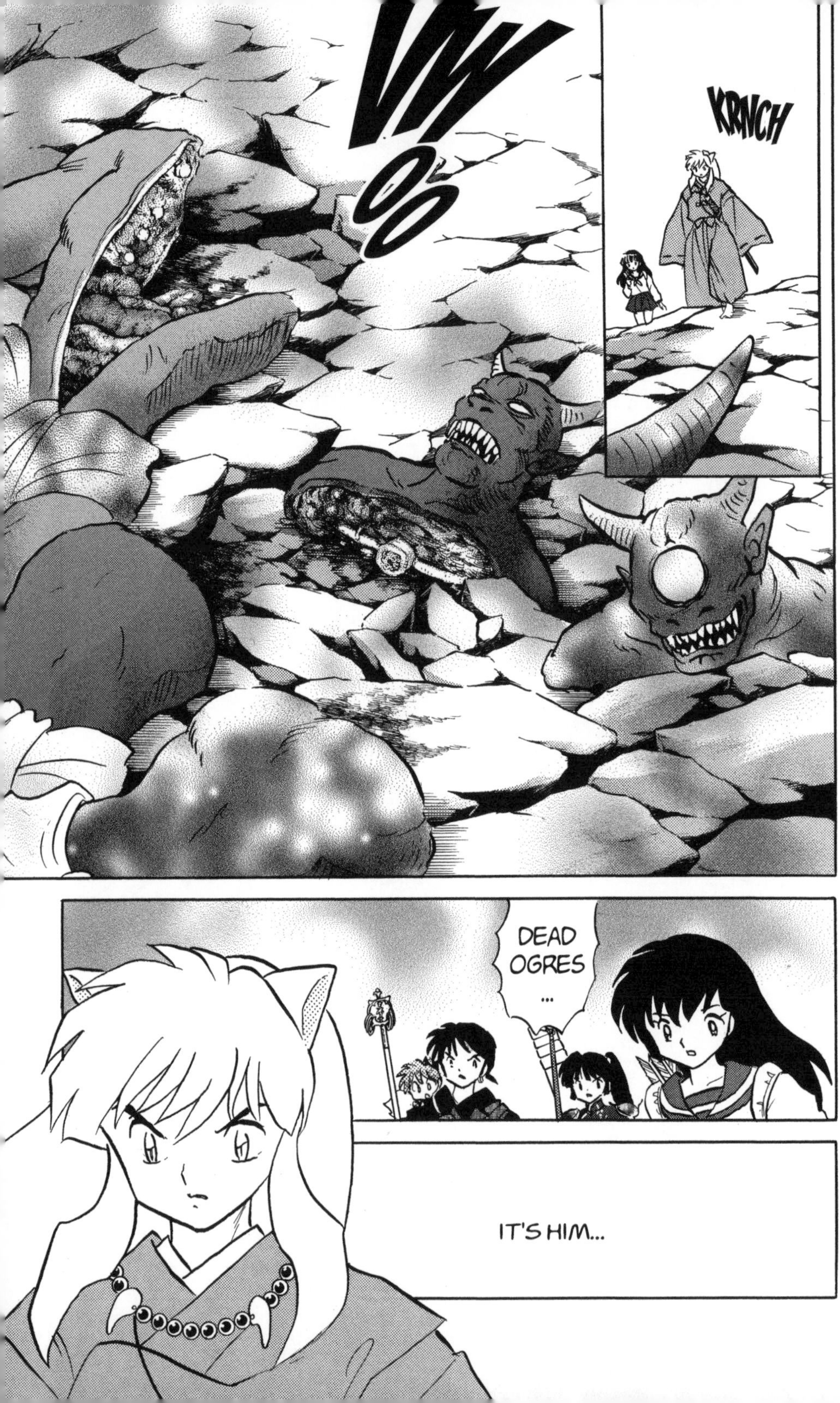
KRNCH
VWOOO
DEAD OGRES ...
IT'S HIM...

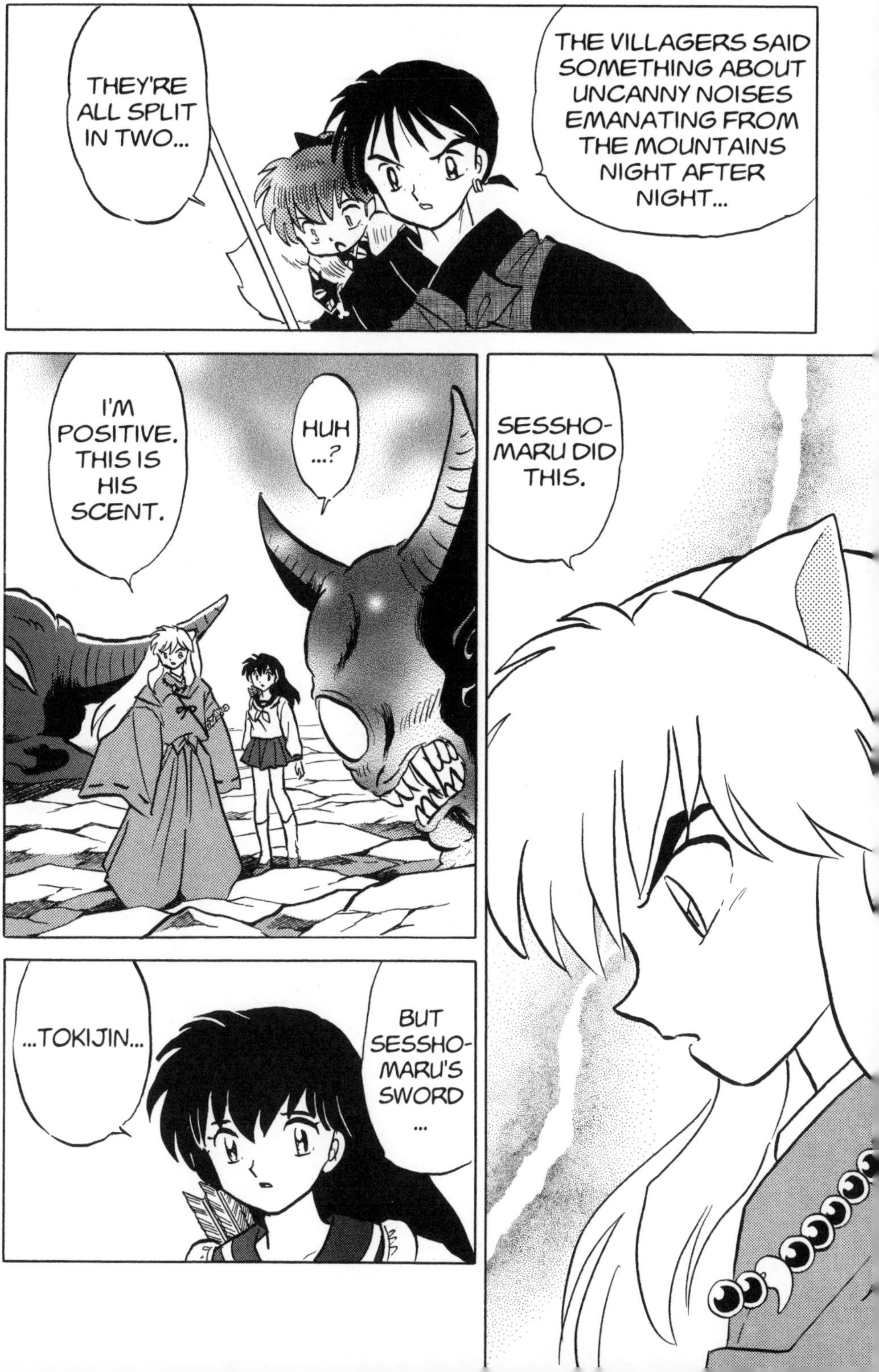
THE VILLAGERS SAID SOMETHING ABOUT UNCANNY NOISES EMANATING FROM THE MOUNTAINS NIGHT AFTER NIGHT...
THEY'RE ALL SPLIT IN TWO...
SESSHO-MARU DID THIS.
HUH ...?
I'M POSITIVE. THIS IS HIS SCENT.
BUT SESSHO-MARU'S SWORD ...
...TOKIJIN...

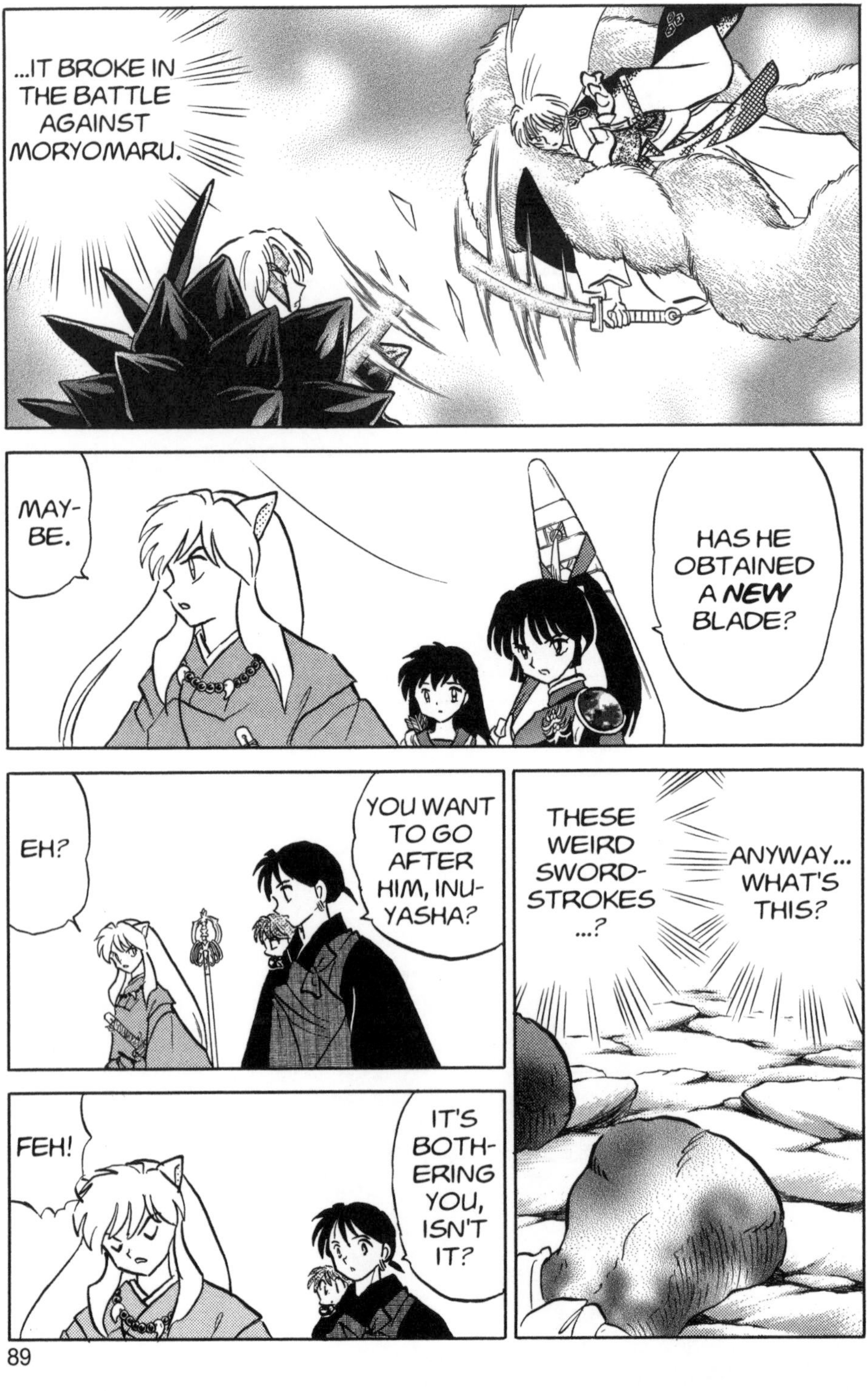
...IT BROKE IN THE BATTLE AGAINST MORYOMARU.
HAS HE OBTAINED A **NEW** BLADE?
MAY-BE.
ANYWAY... WHAT'S THIS?
THESE WEIRD SWORD-STROKES ...?
YOU WANT TO GO AFTER HIM, INU-YASHA?
EH?
IT'S BOTH-ERING YOU, ISN'T IT?
FEH!

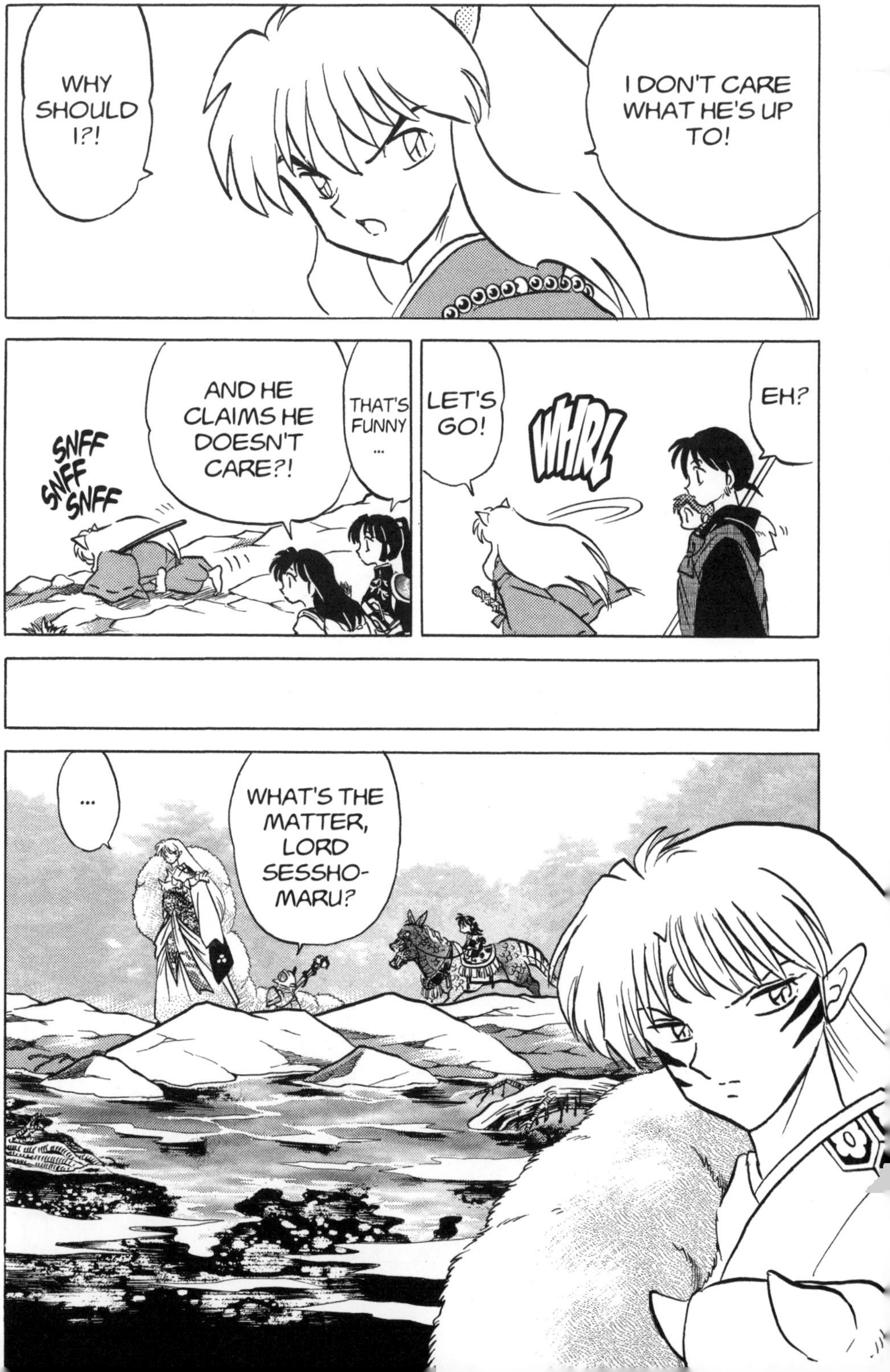
I DON'T CARE WHAT HE'S UP TO!
WHY SHOULD I?!
EH?
WHRL
LET'S GO!
THAT'S FUNNY ...
AND HE CLAIMS HE DOESN'T CARE?!
SNFF SNFF SNFF
WHAT'S THE MATTER, LORD SESSHO-MARU?
...

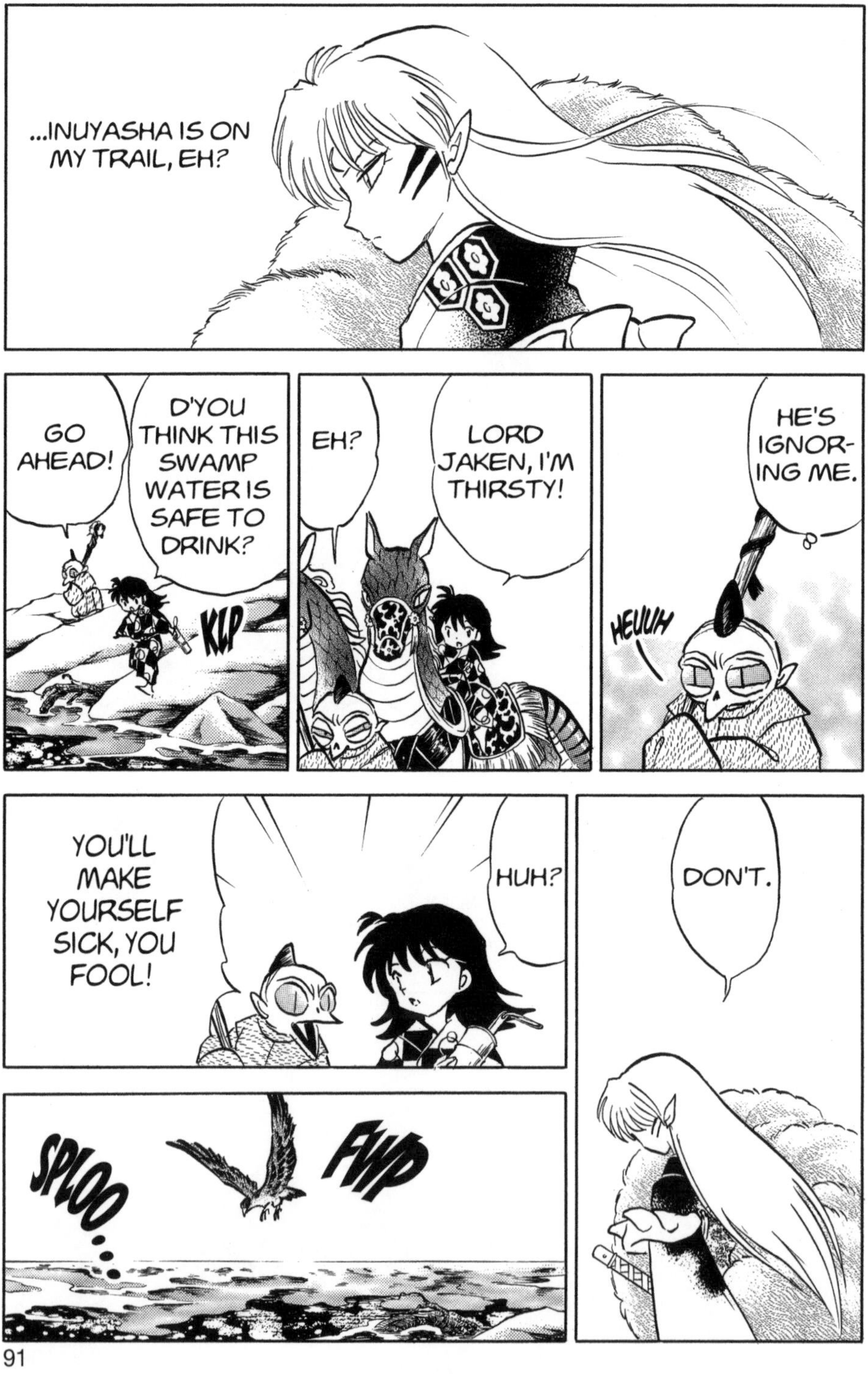
...INUYASHA IS ON MY TRAIL, EH?
HE'S IGNORING ME.
HEUUH
LORD JAKEN, I'M THIRSTY!
EH?
D'YOU THINK THIS SWAMP WATER IS SAFE TO DRINK?
GO AHEAD!
KLP
DON'T.
HUH?
YOU'LL MAKE YOURSELF SICK, YOU FOOL!
FWP
SPLOO...

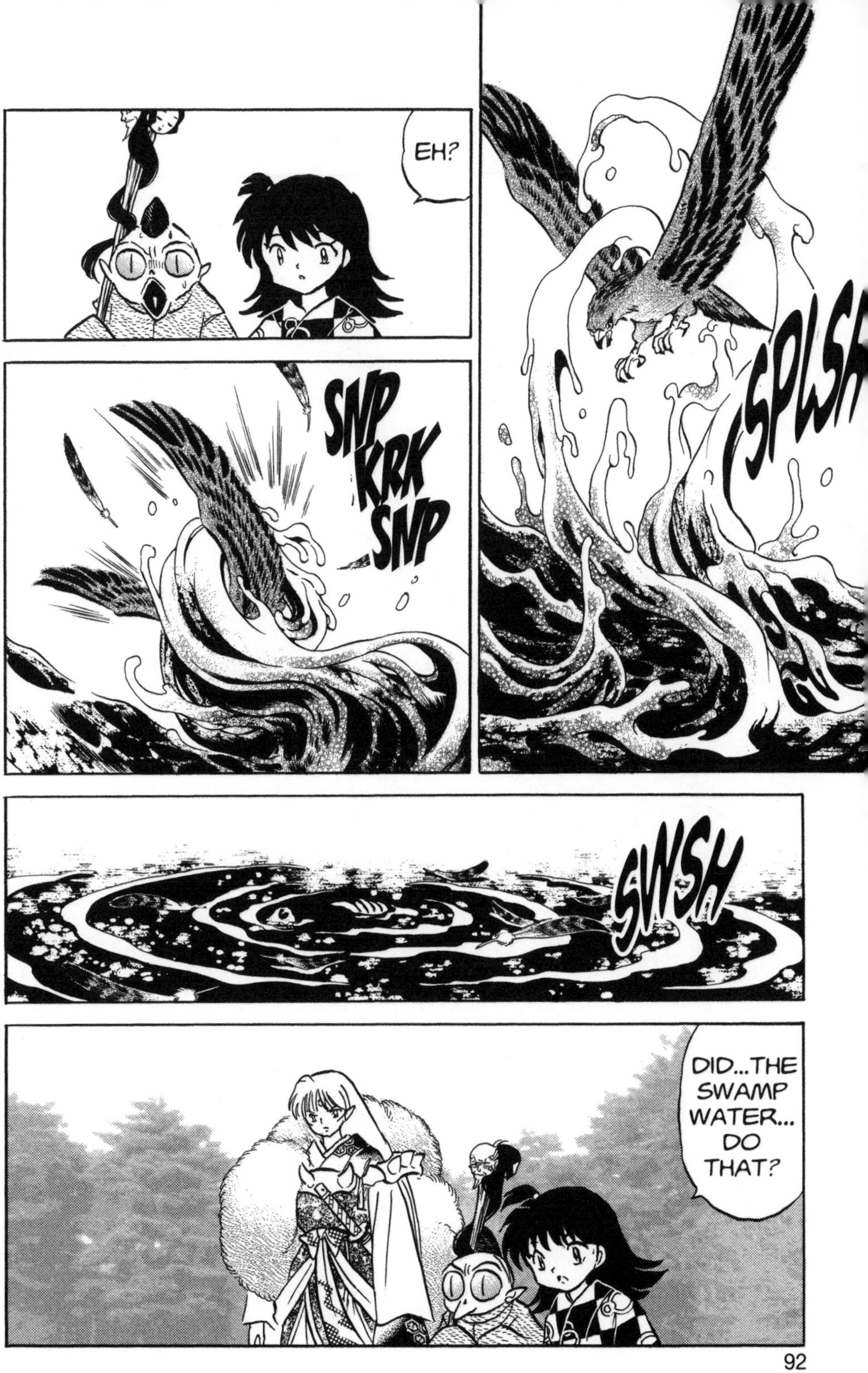
SPLSH
EH?
SNP KRK SNP
SWSH
DID...THE SWAMP WATER... DO THAT?

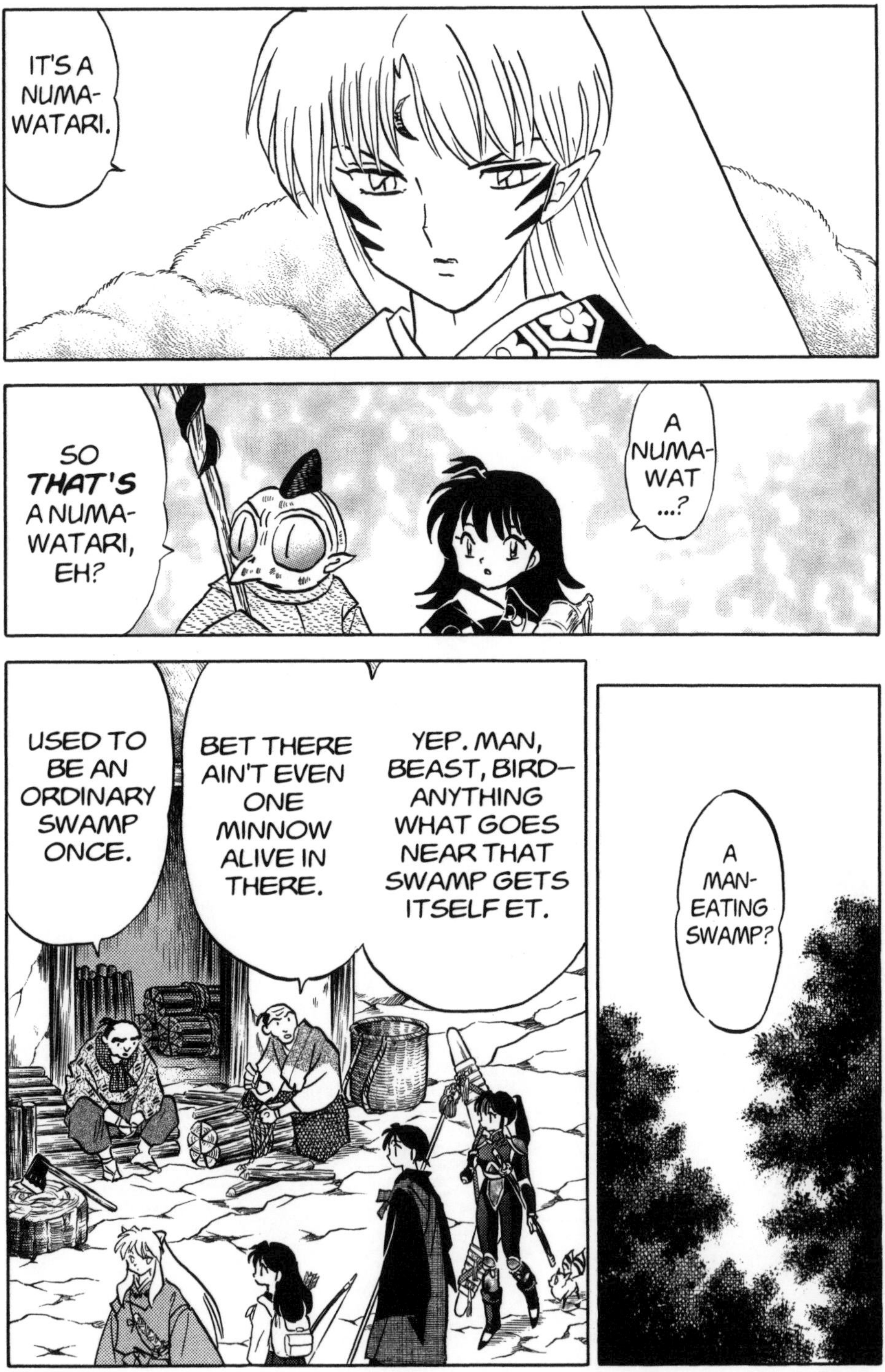
IT'S A NUMA-WATARI.
A NUMA-WAT...?
SO ***THAT'S*** A NUMA-WATARI, EH?
A MAN-EATING SWAMP?
YEP. MAN, BEAST, BIRD—ANYTHING WHAT GOES NEAR THAT SWAMP GETS ITSELF ET.
BET THERE AIN'T EVEN ONE MINNOW ALIVE IN THERE.
USED TO BE AN ORDINARY SWAMP ONCE.

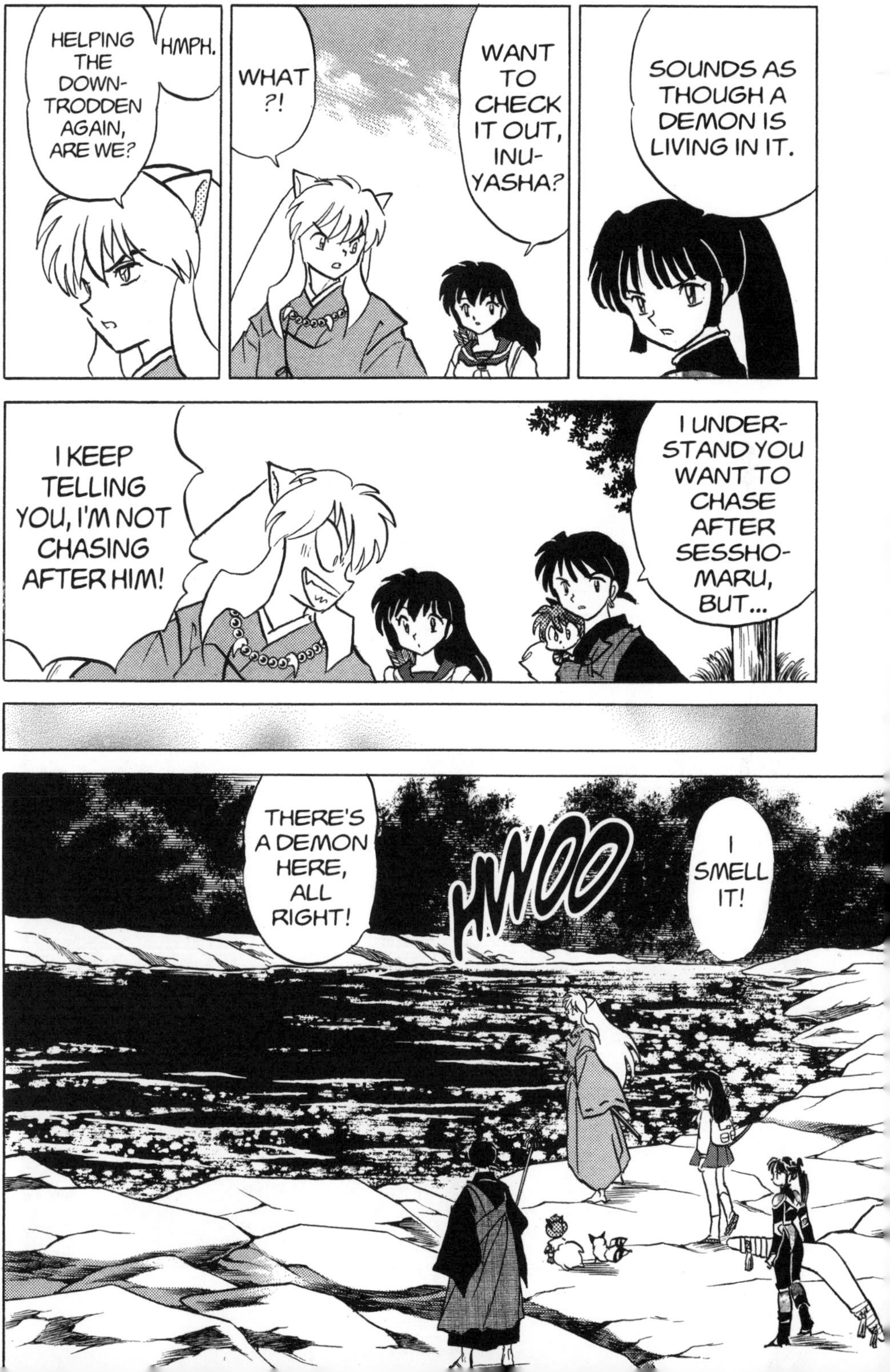
SOUNDS AS THOUGH A DEMON IS LIVING IN IT.
WANT TO CHECK IT OUT, INU-YASHA?
WHAT ?!
HMPH.
HELPING THE DOWN-TRODDEN AGAIN, ARE WE?
I UNDER-STAND YOU WANT TO CHASE AFTER SESSHO-MARU, BUT...
I KEEP TELLING YOU, I'M NOT CHASING AFTER HIM!
I SMELL IT!
HWOO
THERE'S A DEMON HERE, ALL RIGHT!

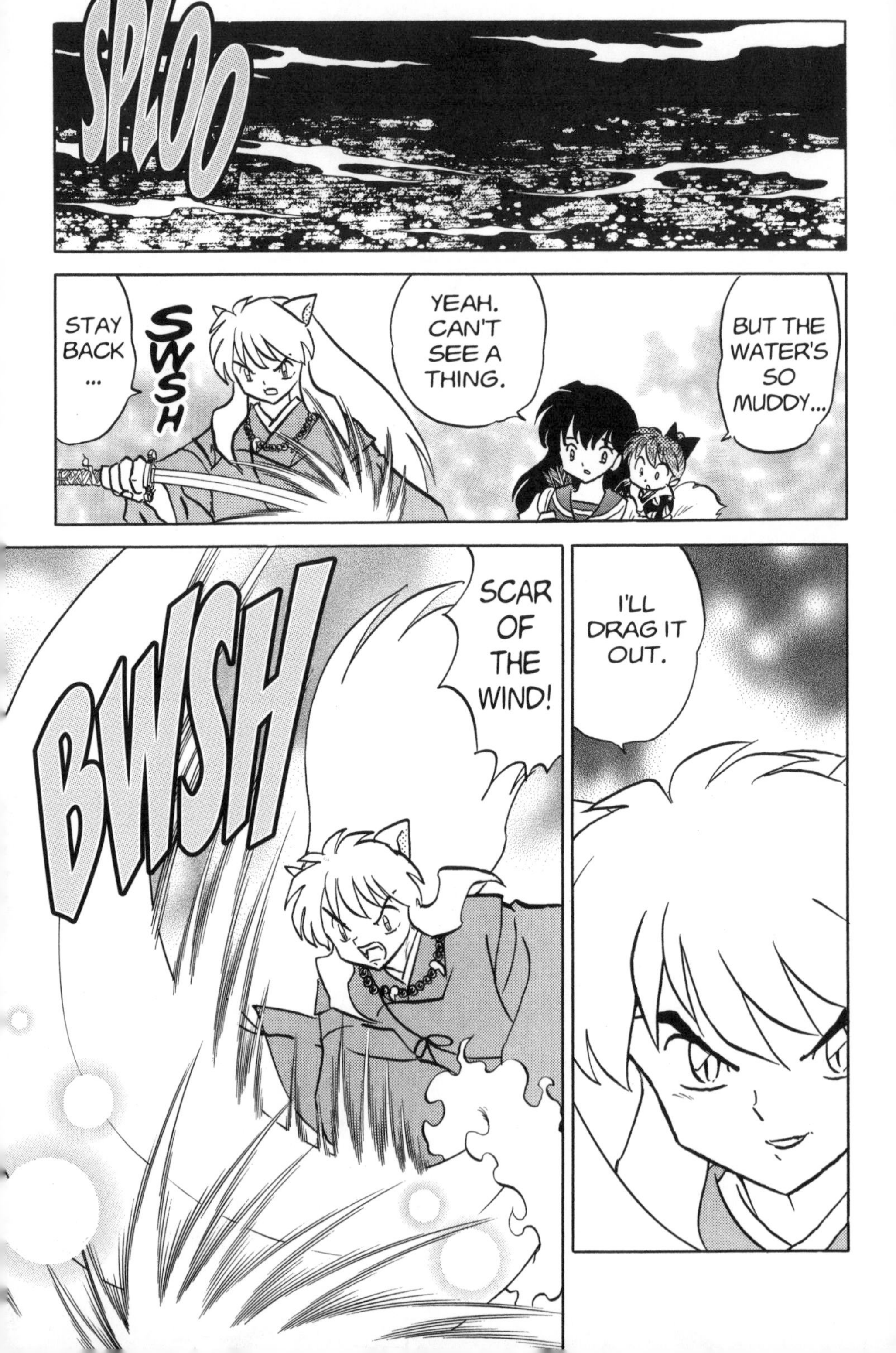
SPLOO
BUT THE WATER'S SO MUDDY...
YEAH. CAN'T SEE A THING.
SWSH
STAY BACK ...
I'LL DRAG IT OUT.
SCAR OF THE WIND!
BWSH

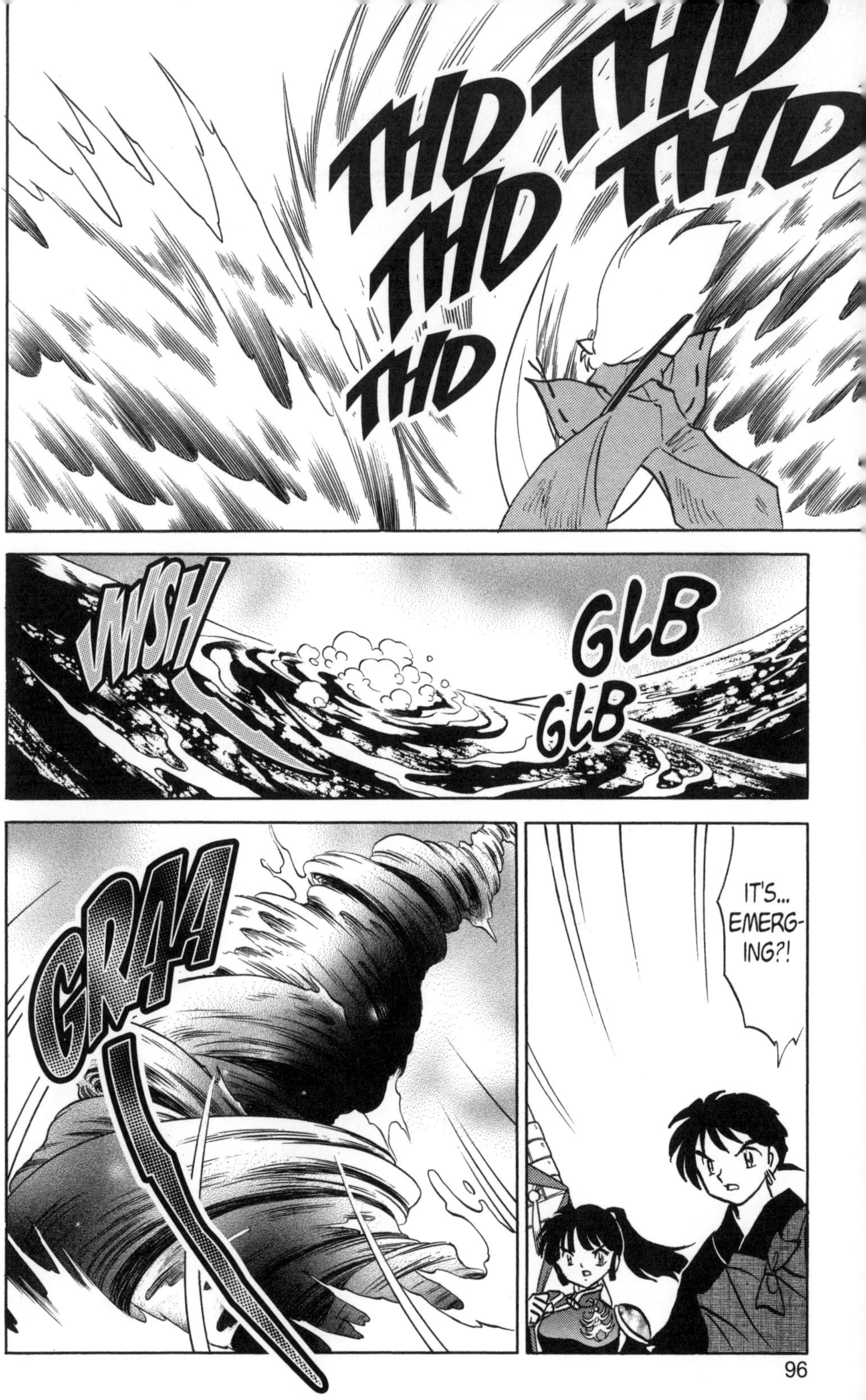
THD THD THD THD THD
JWSH
GLB GLB
IT'S... EMERG-ING?!
GRAA

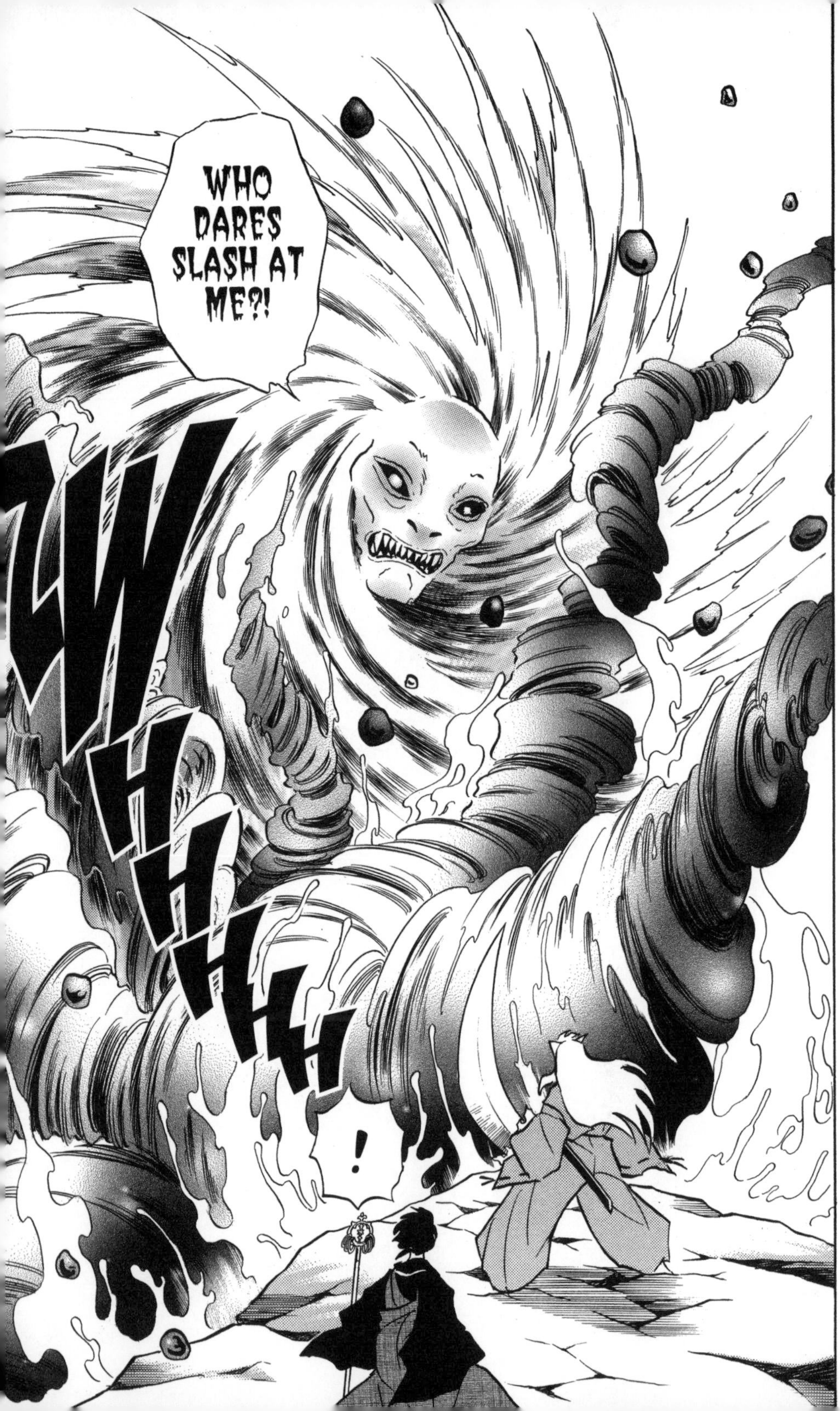
WHO DARES SLASH AT ME?!
!

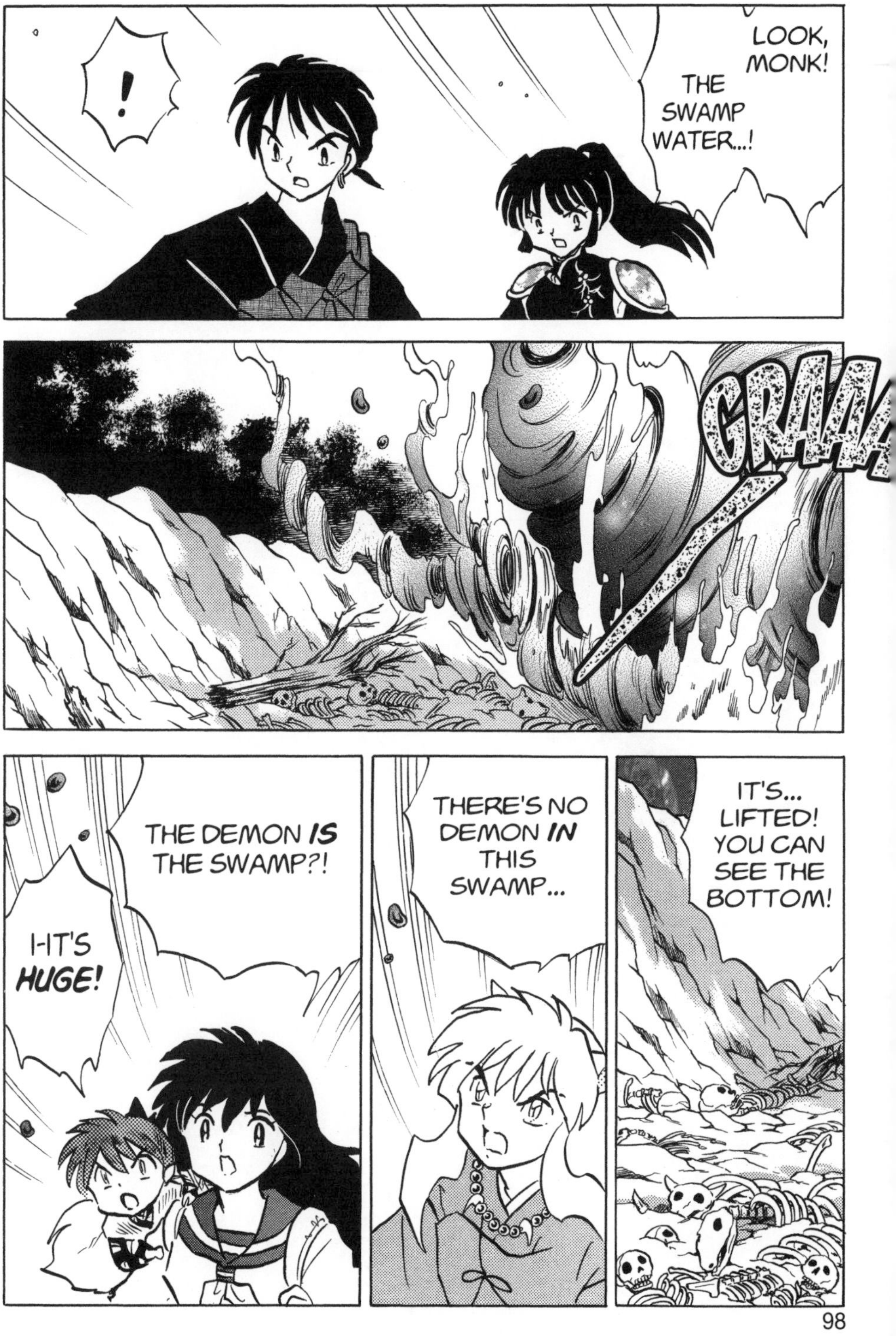
LOOK, MONK! THE SWAMP WATER...!
!
GRAAA
IT'S... LIFTED! YOU CAN SEE THE BOTTOM!
THERE'S NO DEMON IN THIS SWAMP...
THE DEMON IS THE SWAMP?!
I-IT'S HUGE!

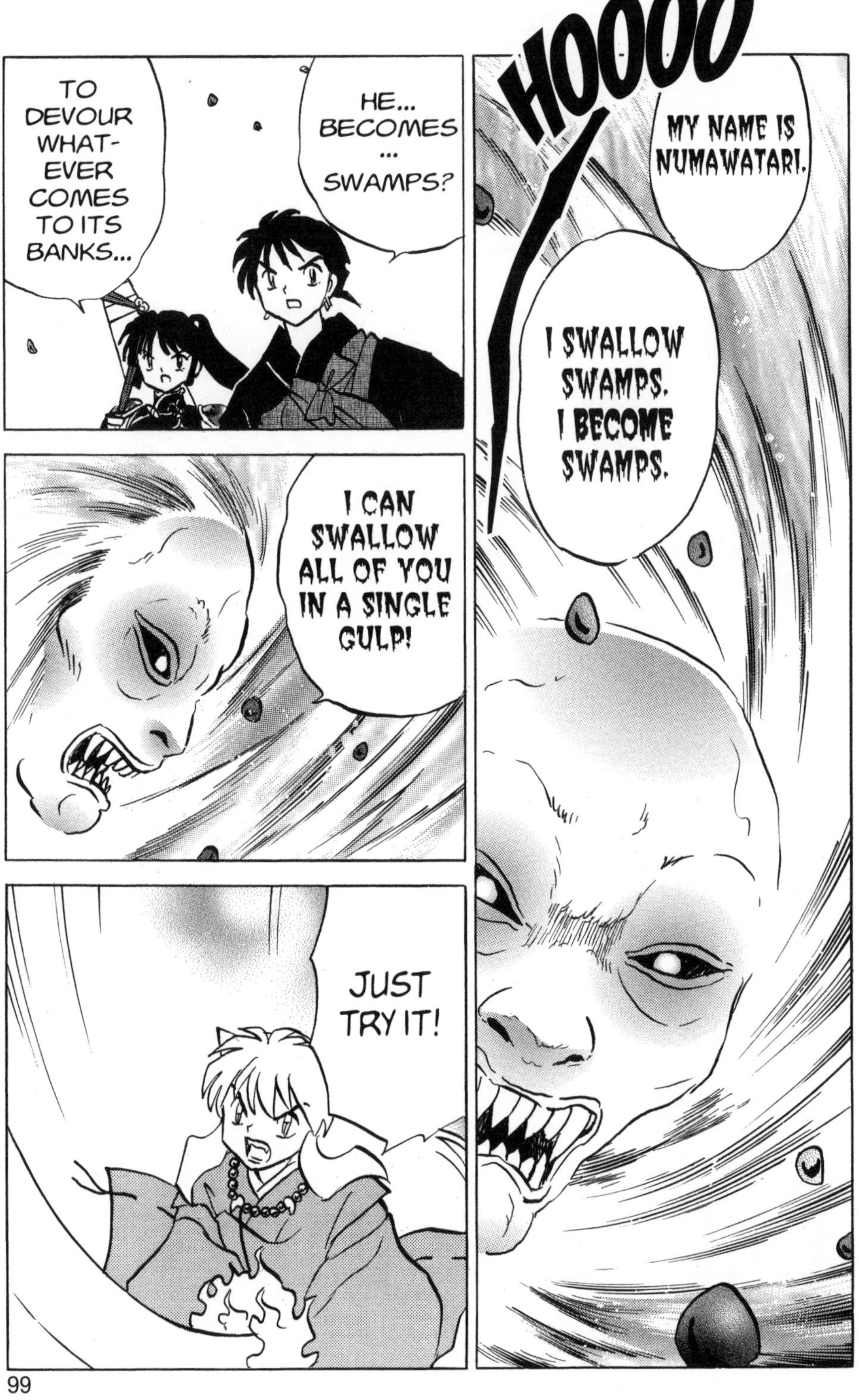
HOOOO
MY NAME IS NUMAWATARI.
I SWALLOW SWAMPS. I BECOME SWAMPS.
HE... BECOMES ... SWAMPS?
TO DEVOUR WHAT-EVER COMES TO ITS BANKS...
I CAN SWALLOW ALL OF YOU IN A SINGLE GULP!
JUST TRY IT!

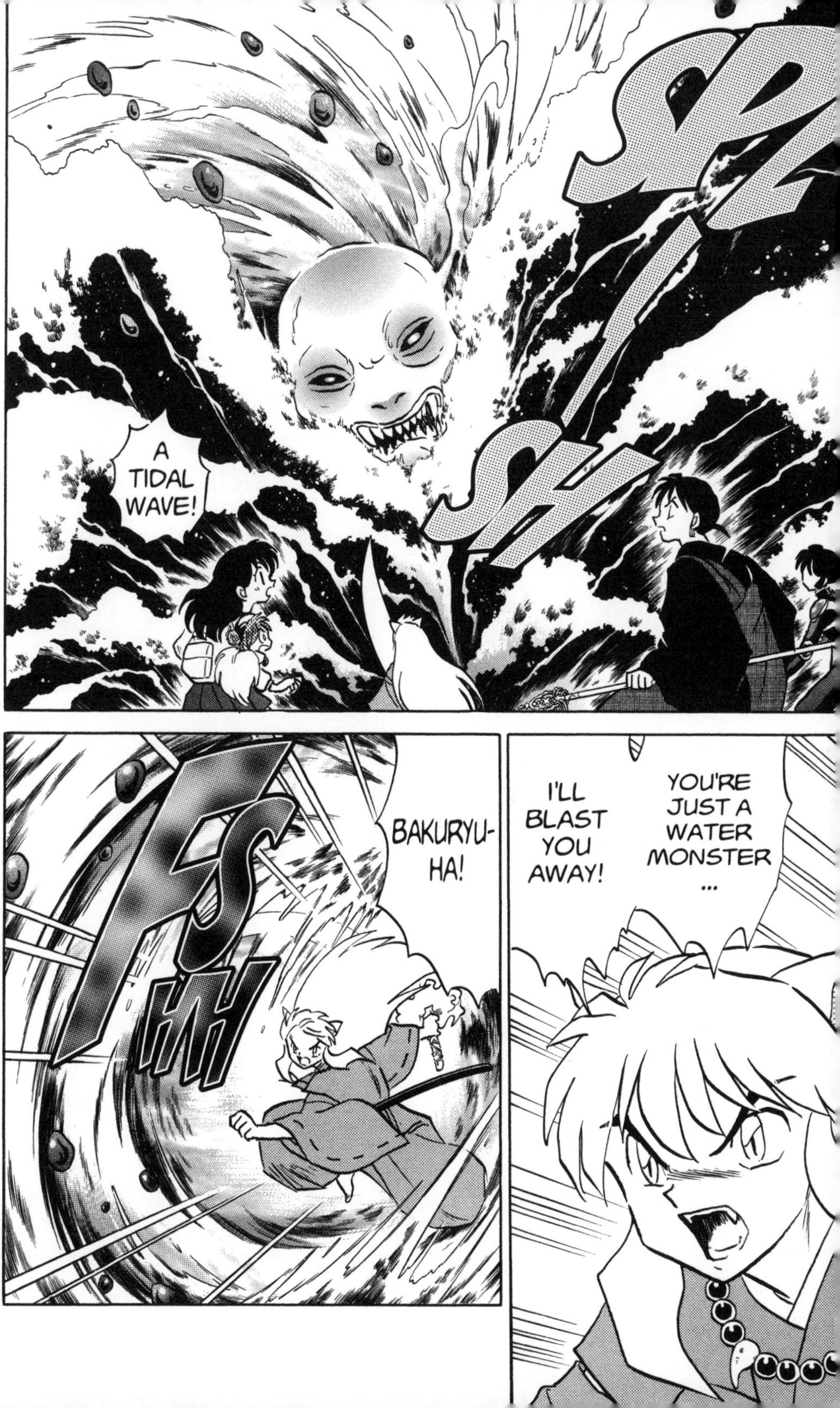
A TIDAL WAVE!
YOU'RE JUST A WATER MONSTER ...
I'LL BLAST YOU AWAY!
BAKURYU-HA!

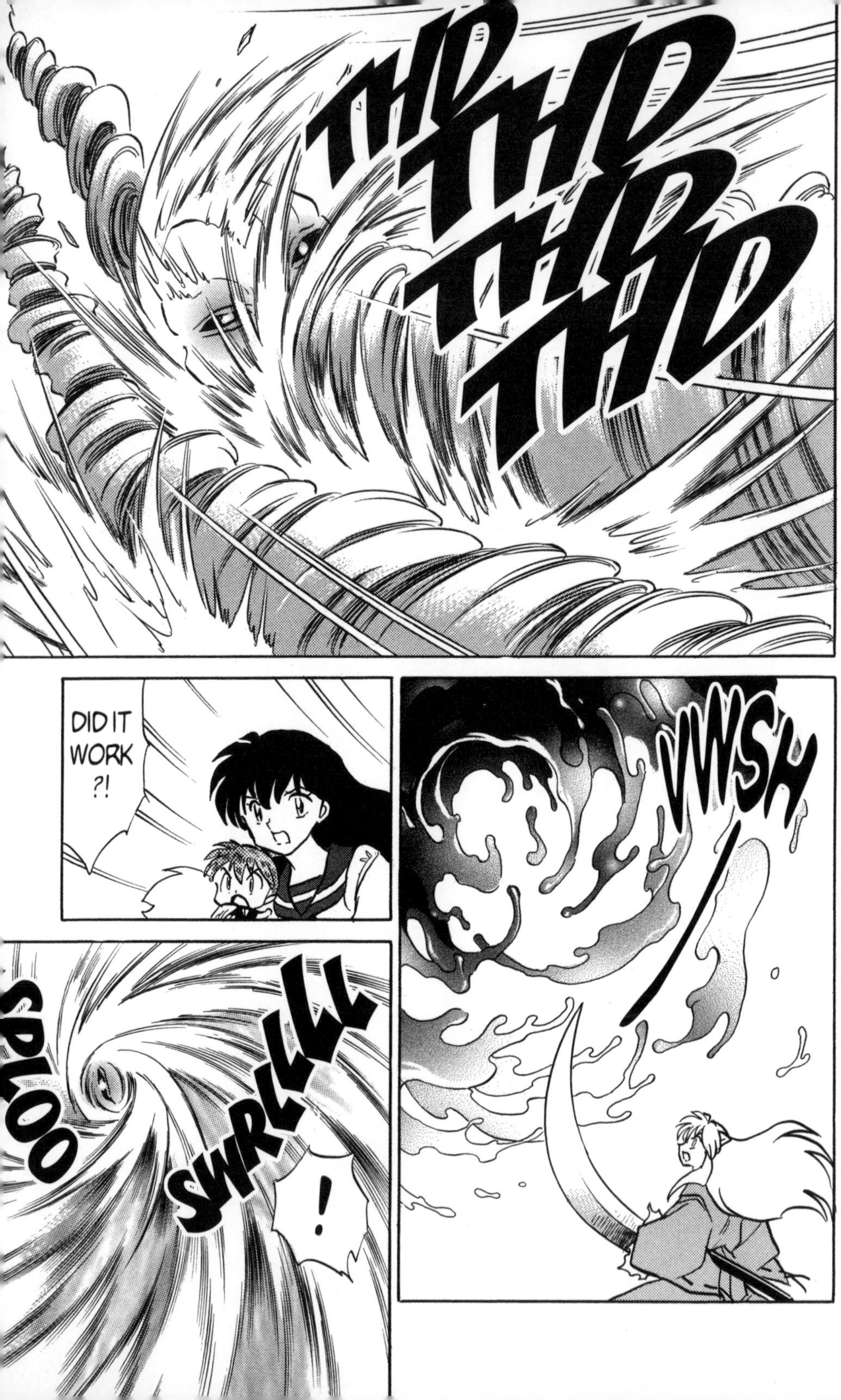
THD
THD
THD
VWSH
DID IT WORK ?!
SPLOO
SWRLLL
!

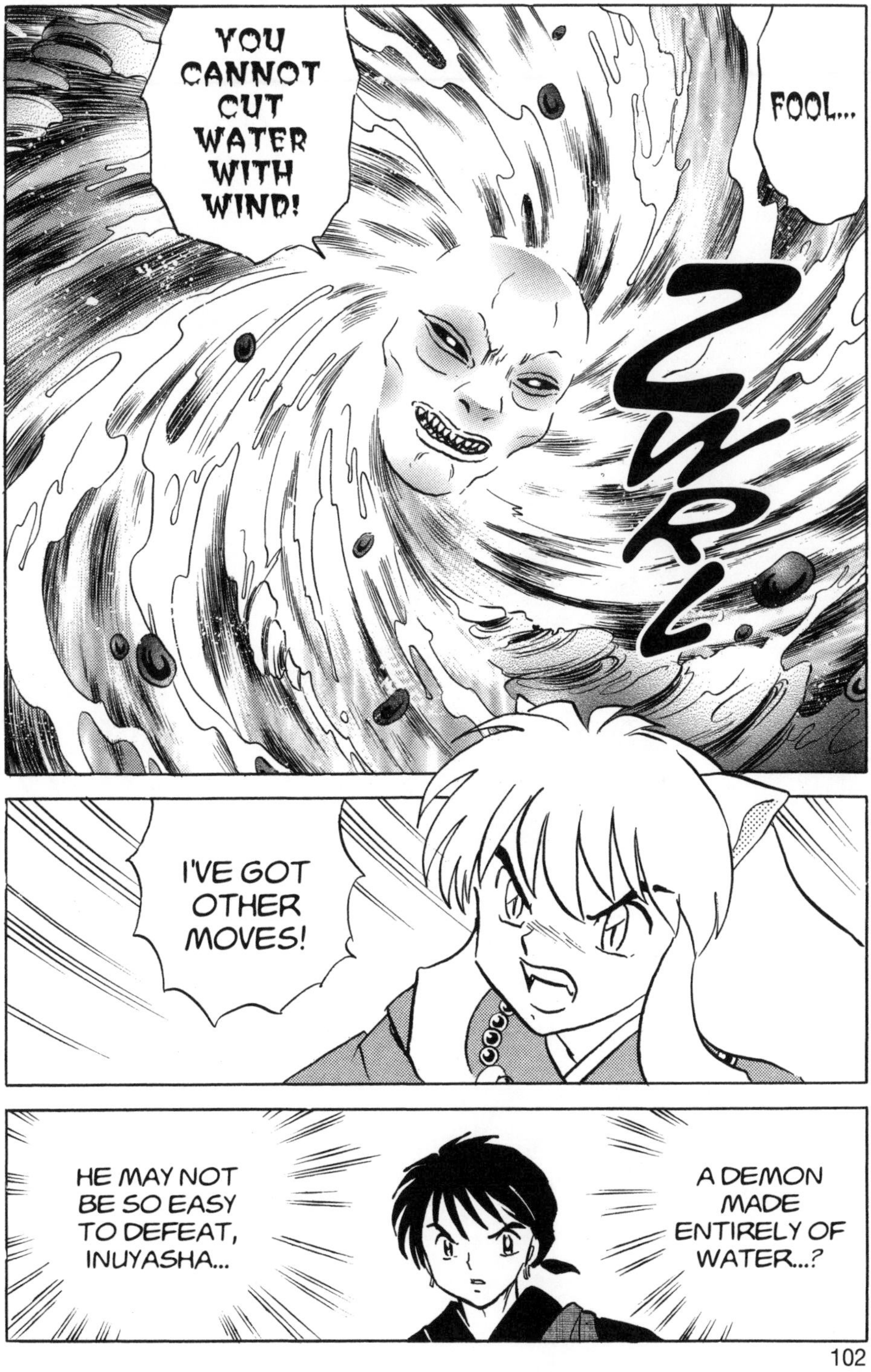
FOOL...
YOU CANNOT CUT WATER WITH WIND!
ZWRL
I'VE GOT OTHER MOVES!
A DEMON MADE ENTIRELY OF WATER...?
HE MAY NOT BE SO EASY TO DEFEAT, INUYASHA...

SCROLL SIX
THE TRANSFORMING WATERS

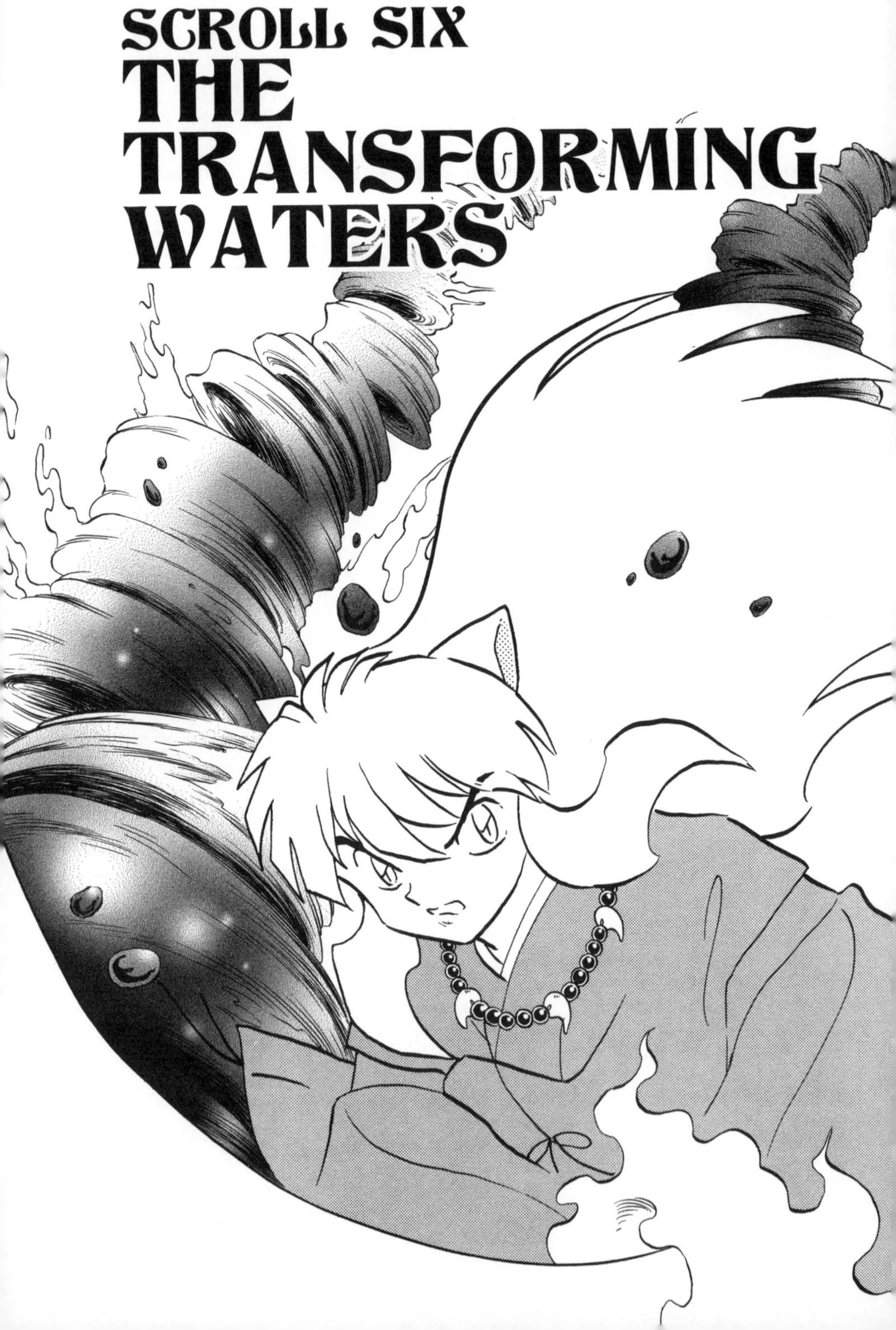

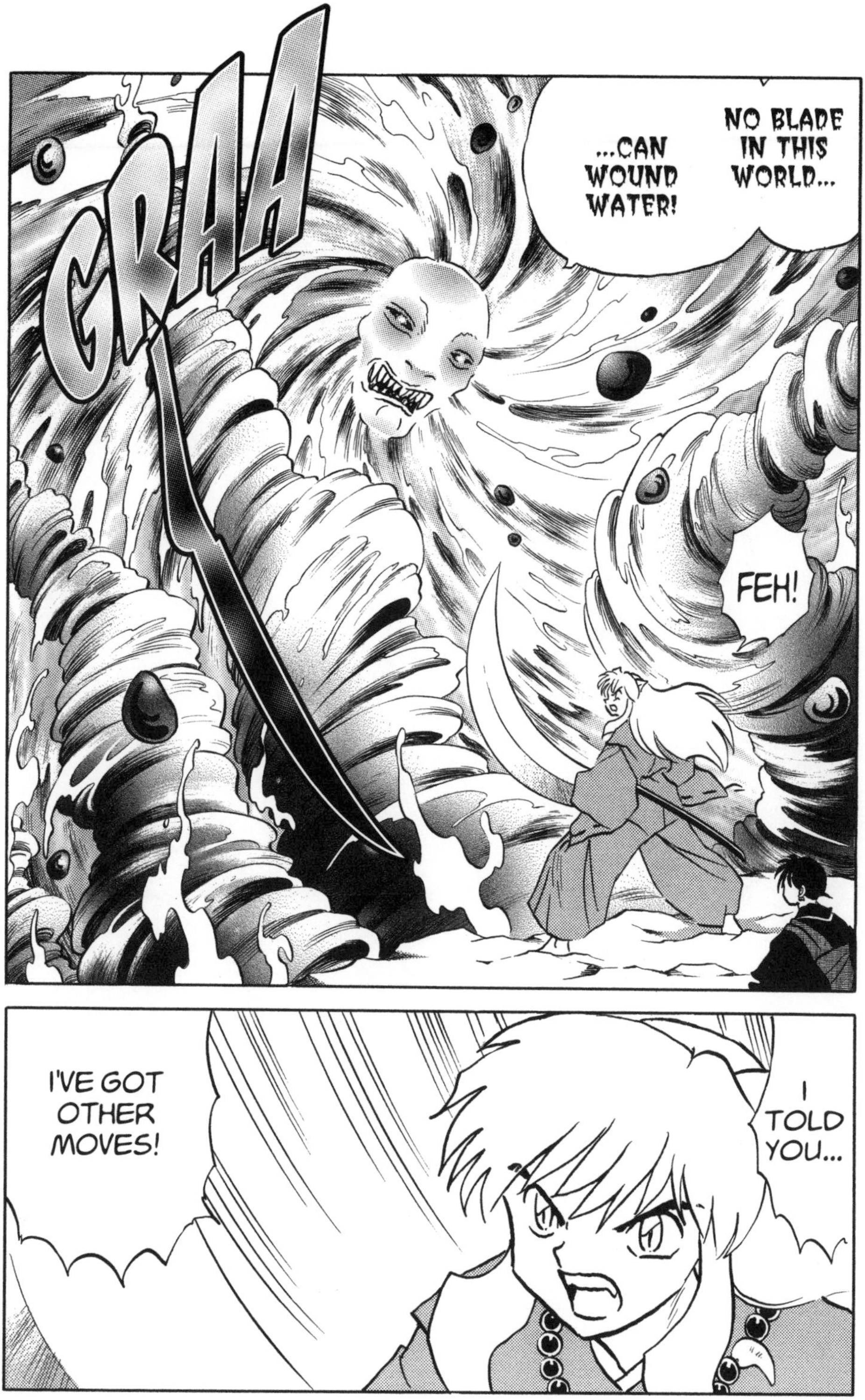
NO BLADE IN THIS WORLD...
...CAN WOUND WATER!
GRAA
FEH!
I TOLD YOU...
I'VE GOT OTHER MOVES!

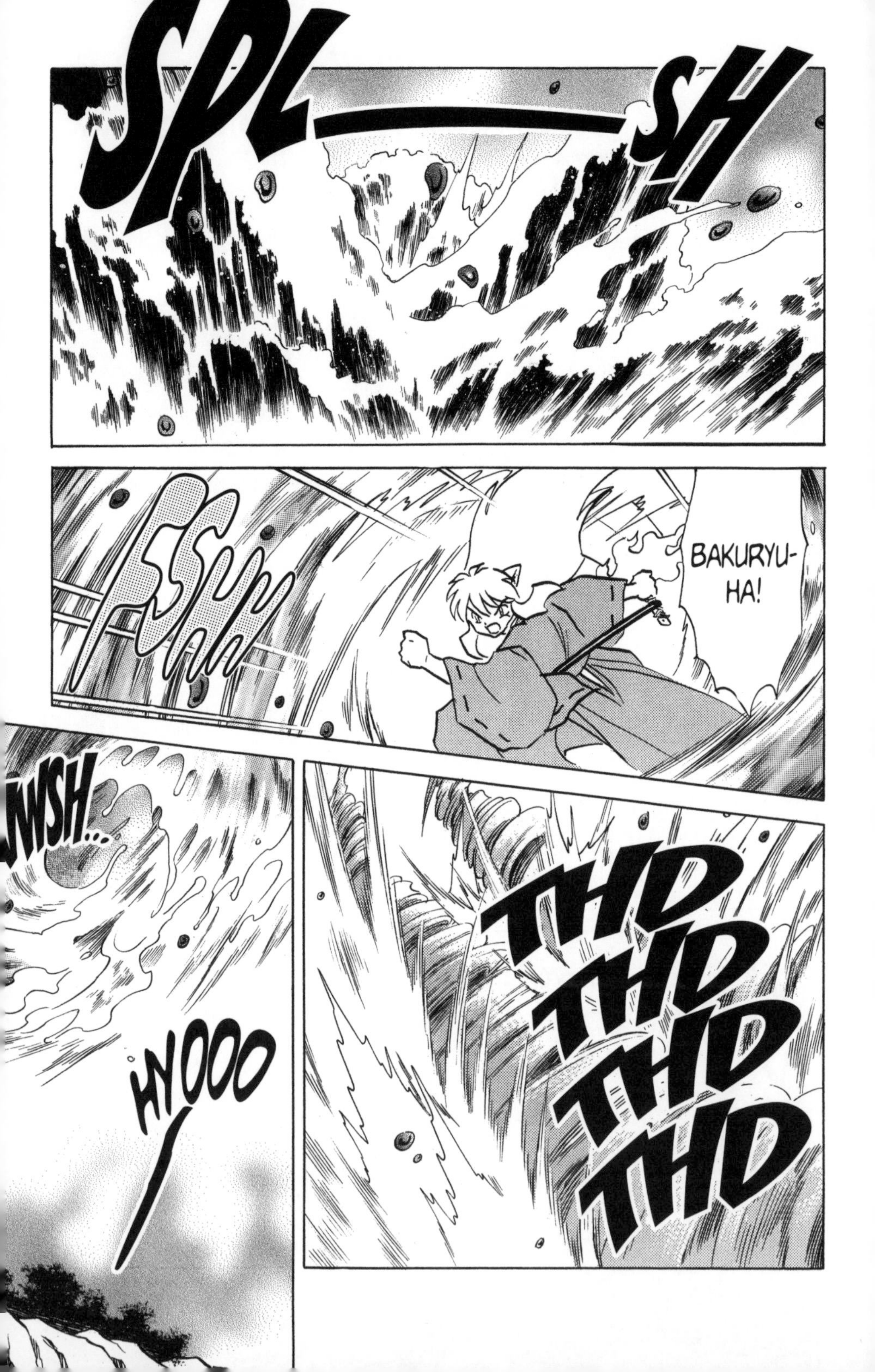
SPL—SH
BAKURYU-HA!
FSSHH
THD THD THD THD
WSH...
HYOOO

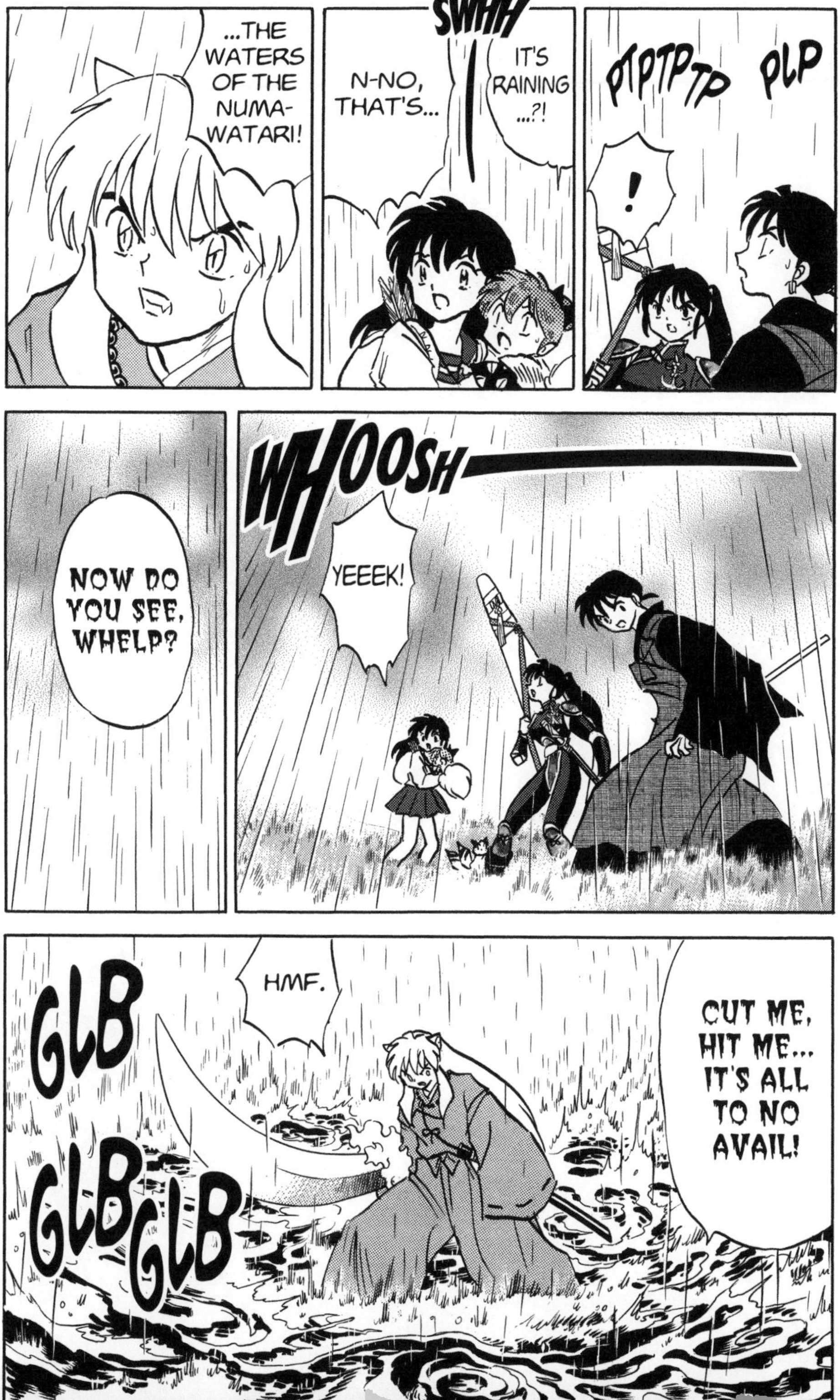
PTPTPTP
PLP
!
SWHH
IT'S RAINING ...?!
N-NO, THAT'S...
...THE WATERS OF THE NUMA-WATARI!
WHOOSH
YEEEK!
NOW DO YOU SEE, WHELP?
CUT ME, HIT ME... IT'S ALL TO NO AVAIL!
HMF.
GLB
GLB GLB

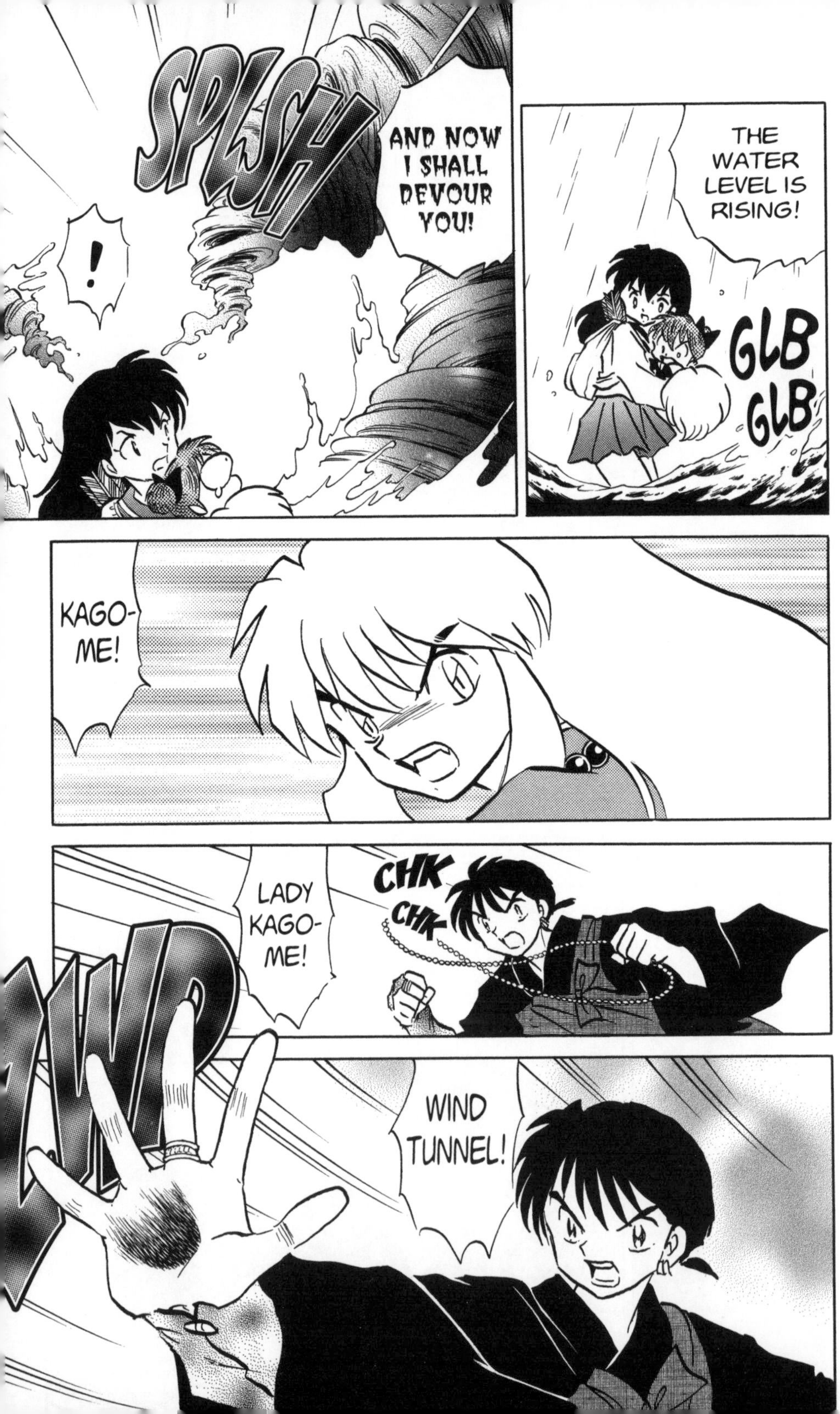
THE WATER LEVEL IS RISING!
GLB GLB
SPLSH
AND NOW I SHALL DEVOUR YOU!
!
KAGO-ME!
CHK CHK
LADY KAGO-ME!
ZWP
WIND TUNNEL!

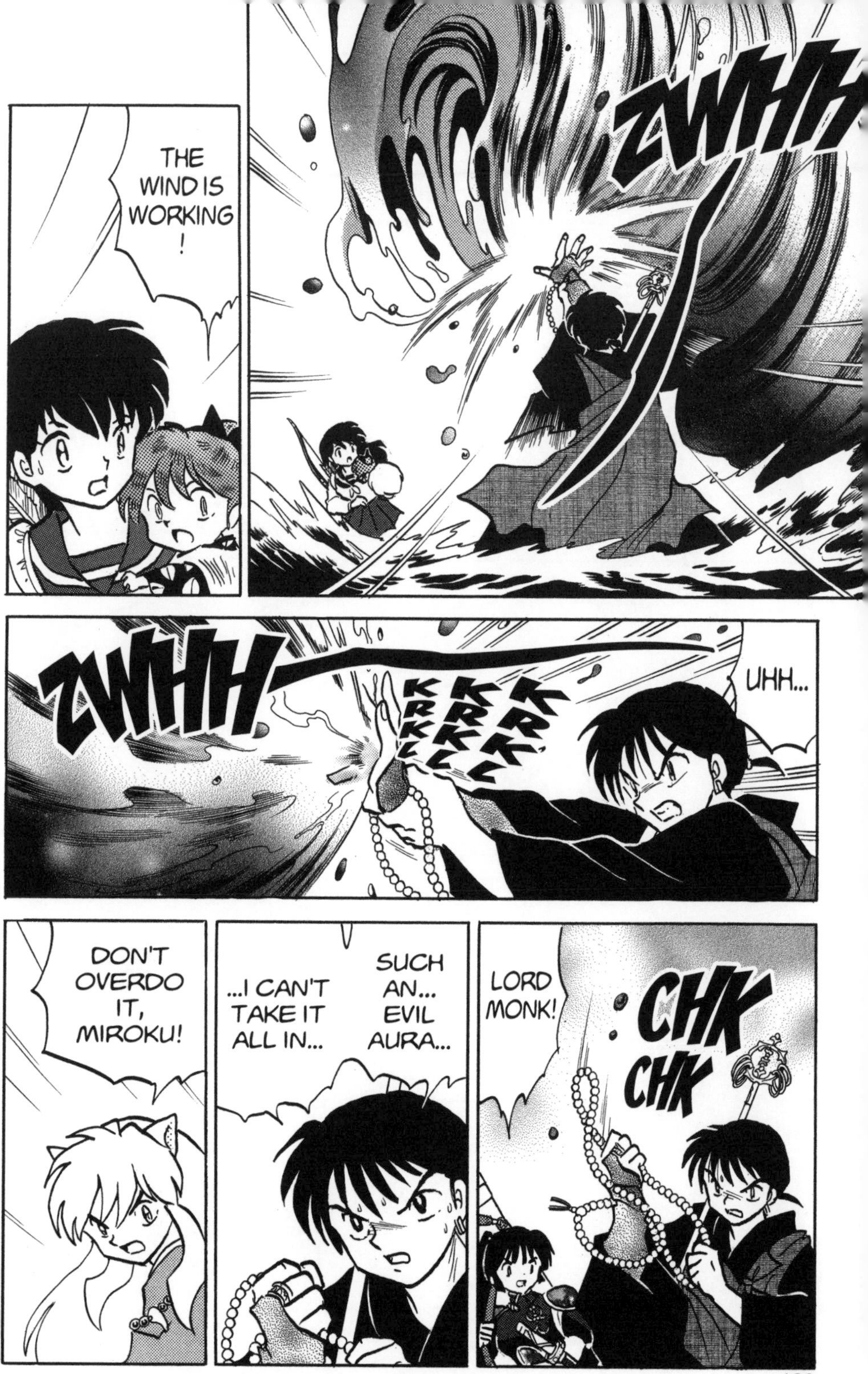
ZWHH
THE WIND IS WORKING!
UHH...
ZWHH
LORD MONK!
CHK CHK
SUCH AN... EVIL AURA...
...I CAN'T TAKE IT ALL IN...
DON'T OVERDO IT, MIROKU!

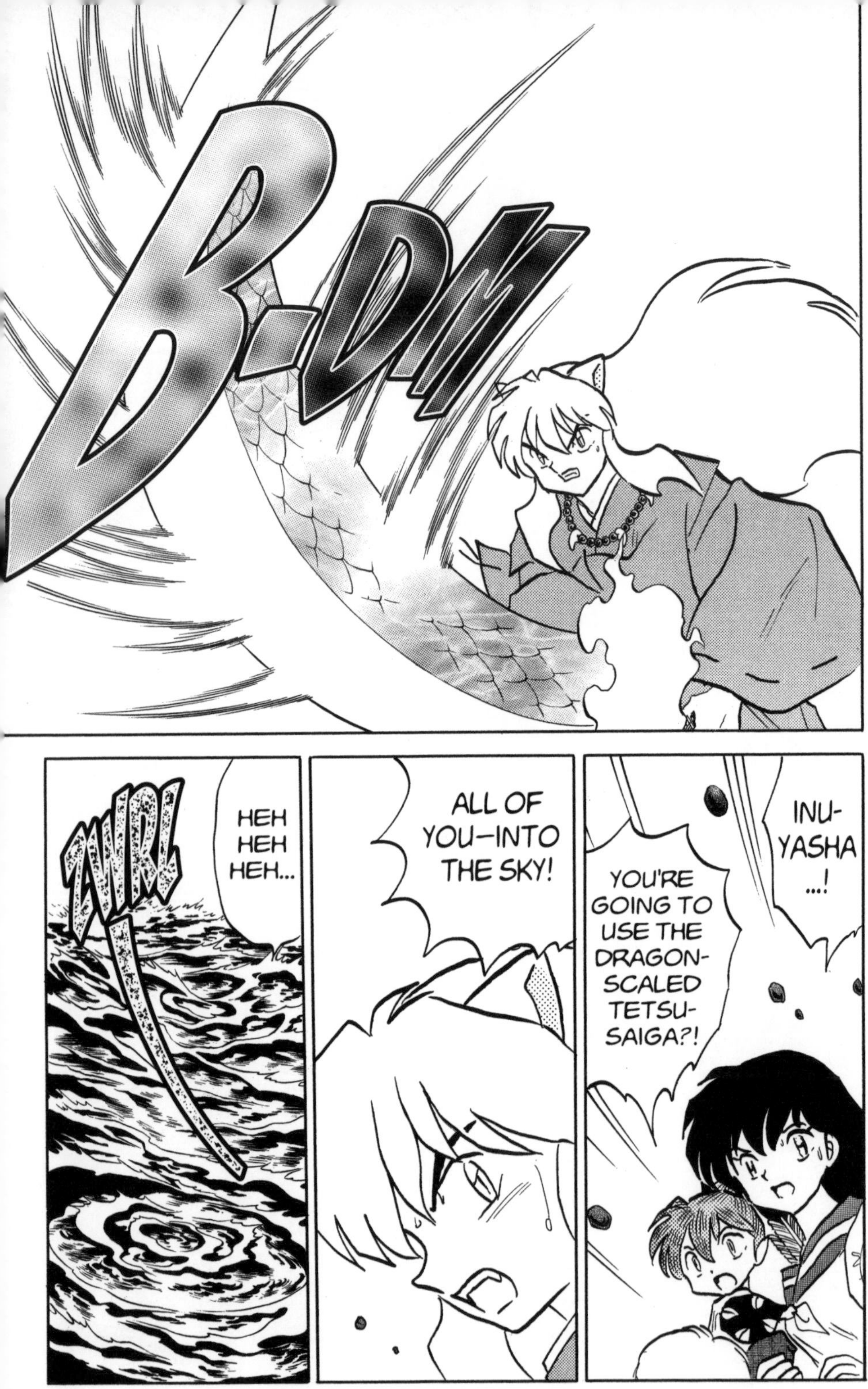
B-DM
INU-YASHA ...!
YOU'RE GOING TO USE THE DRAGON-SCALED TETSU-SAIGA?!
ALL OF YOU—INTO THE SKY!
HEH HEH HEH...
ZWR!

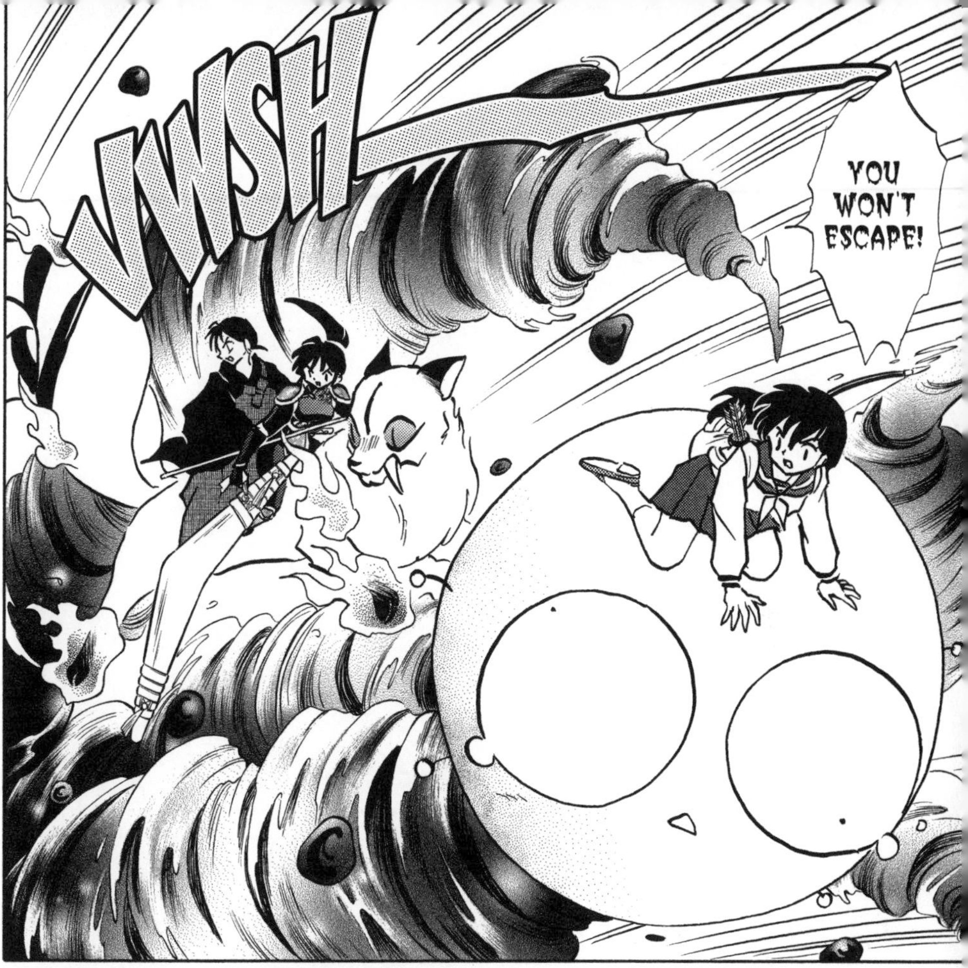
VWSH
YOU WON'T ESCAPE!

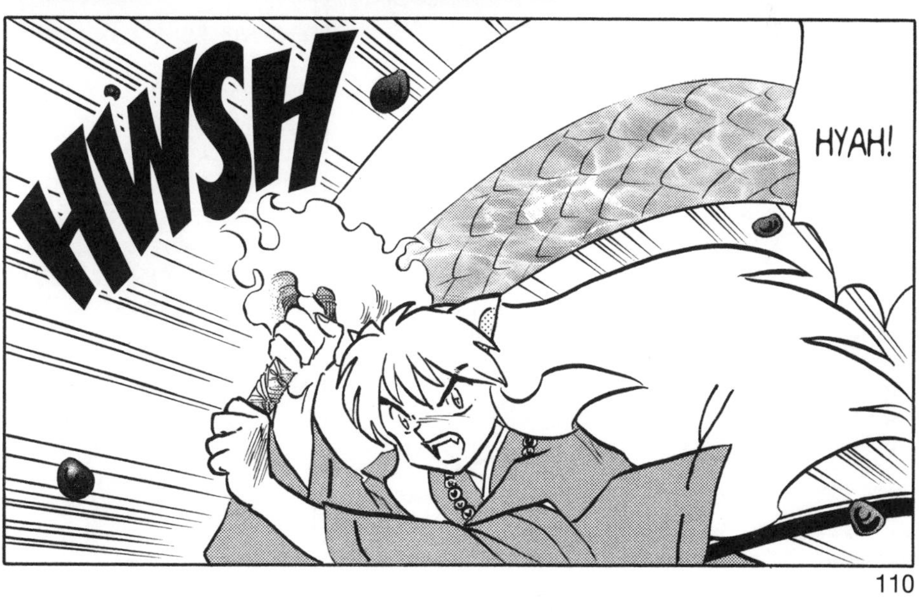
HYAH!
HWSH

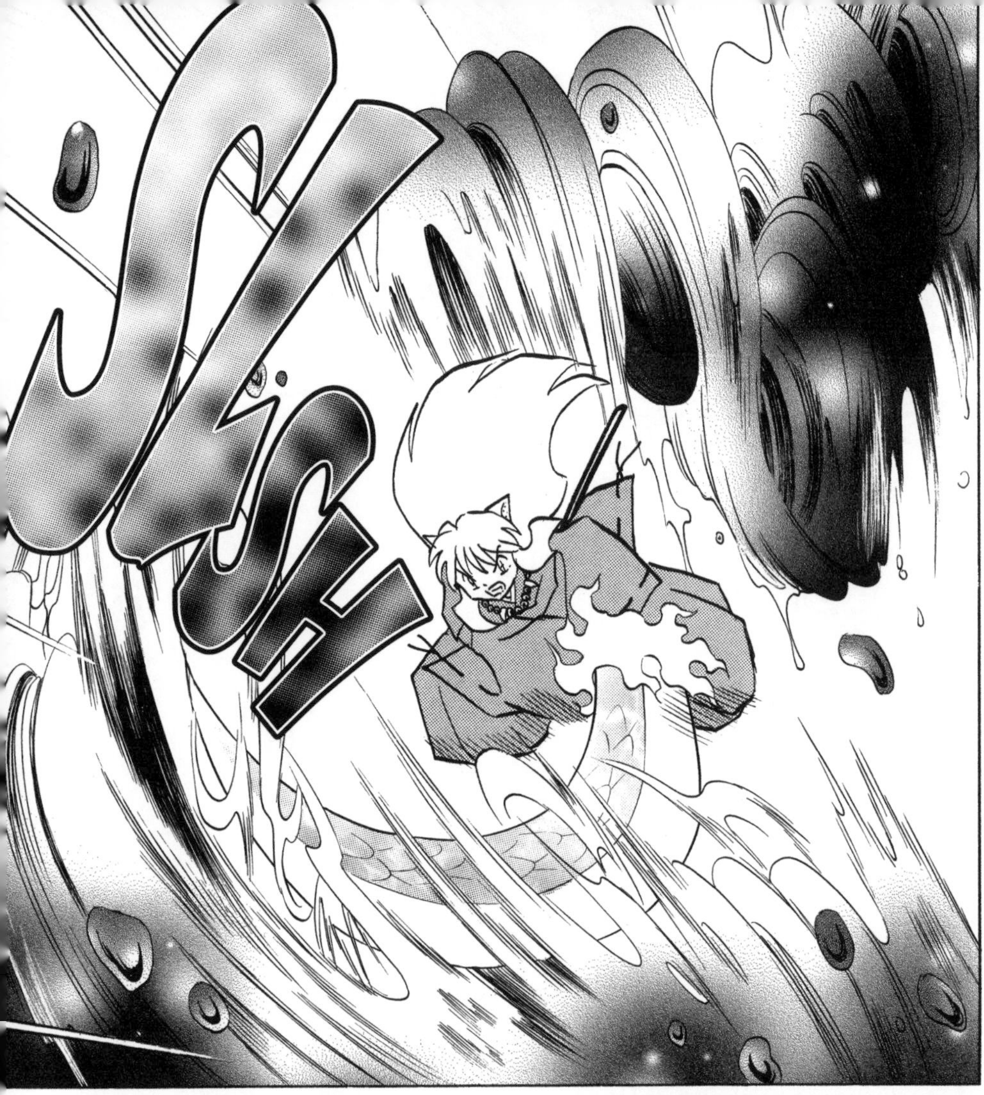
SLISH!
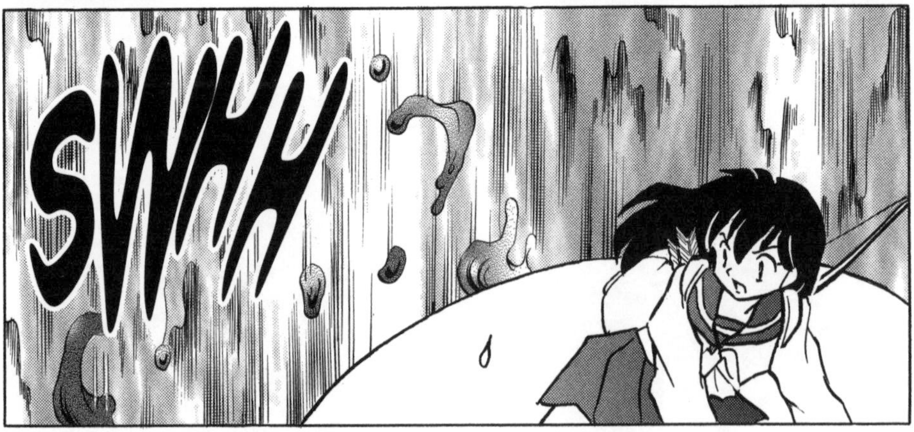
SWHH

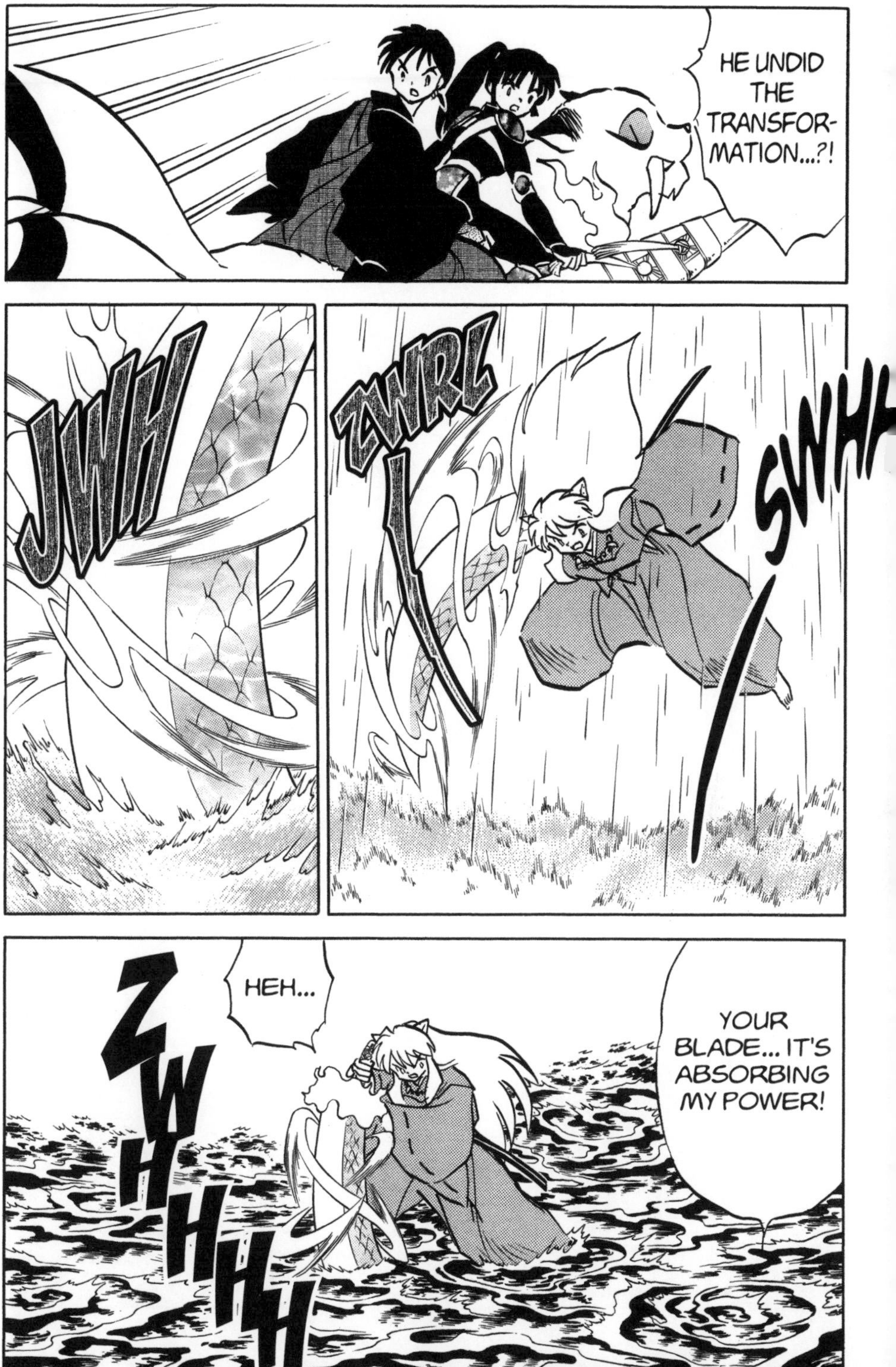
HE UNDID THE TRANSFORMATION...?!
SWH
ZWRL
JWH
YOUR BLADE... IT'S ABSORBING MY POWER!
HEH...
ZWHHHHH

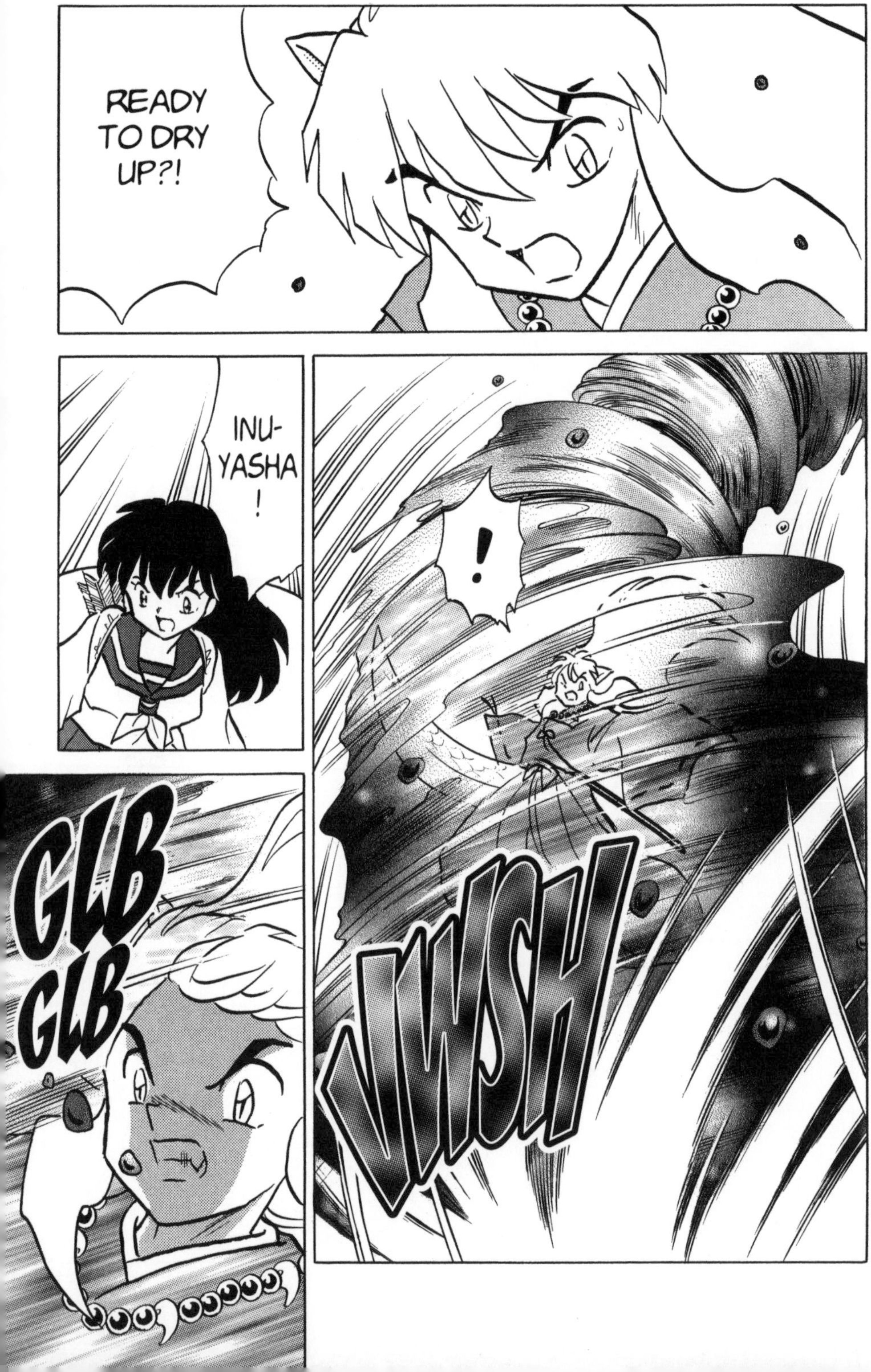
READY TO DRY UP?!
!
VWSH
INU-YASHA!
GLB GLB

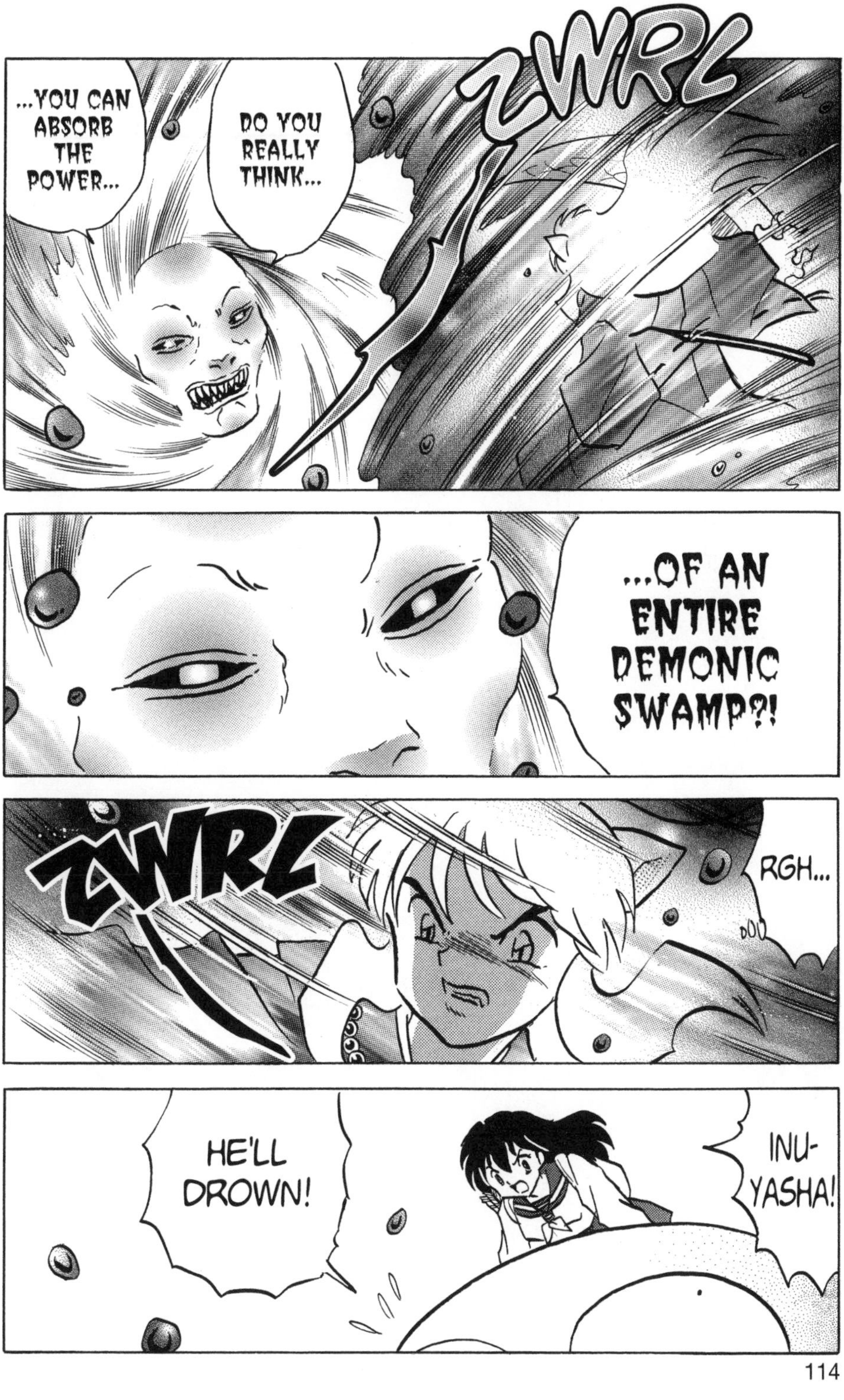
ZWRL
DO YOU REALLY THINK...
...YOU CAN ABSORB THE POWER...
...OF AN ENTIRE DEMONIC SWAMP?!
RGH...
ZWRL
INU-YASHA!
HE'LL DROWN!

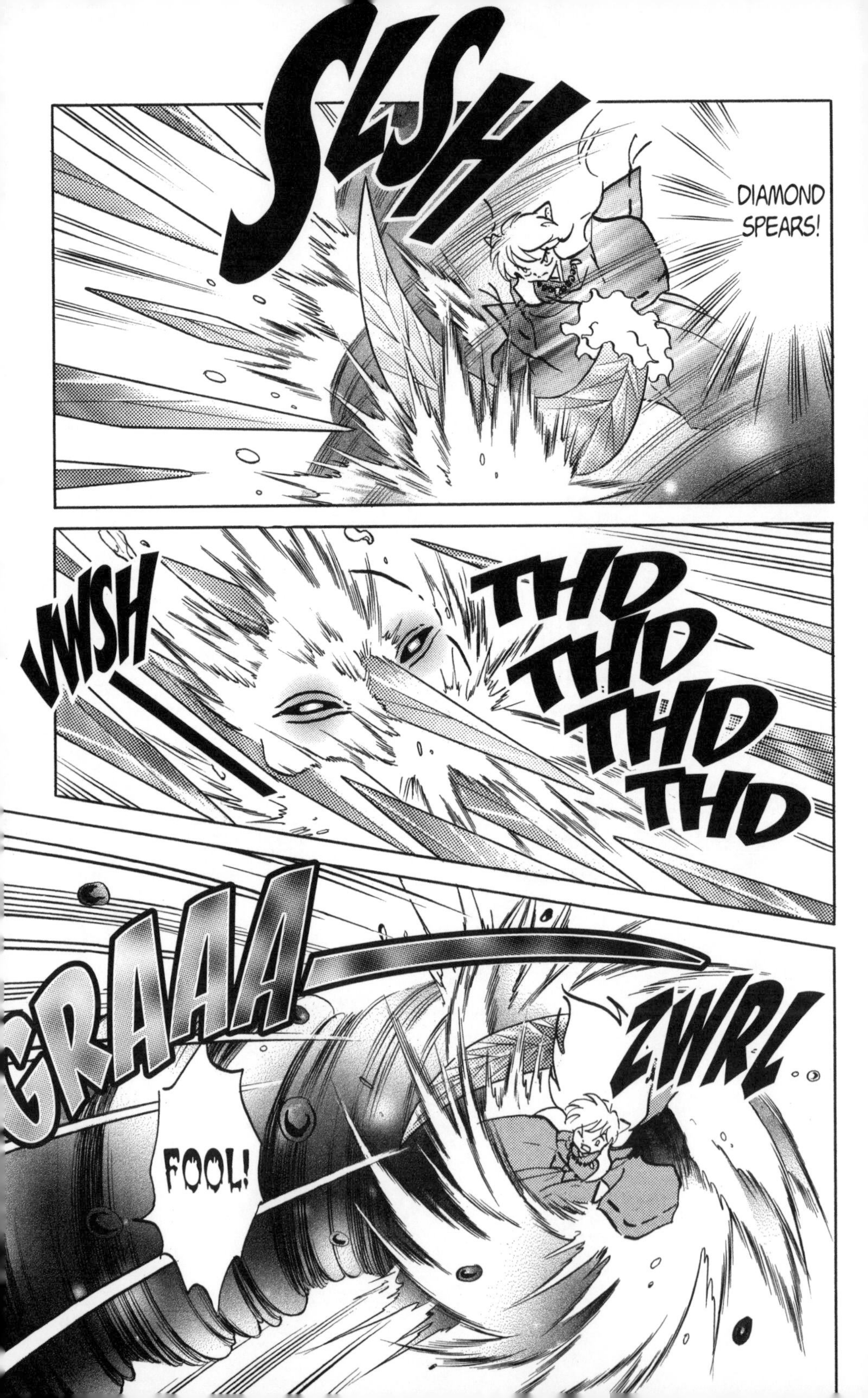
SLSH
DIAMOND SPEARS!
THD THD THD THD
VWSH
ZWRL
GRAAAA
FOOL!

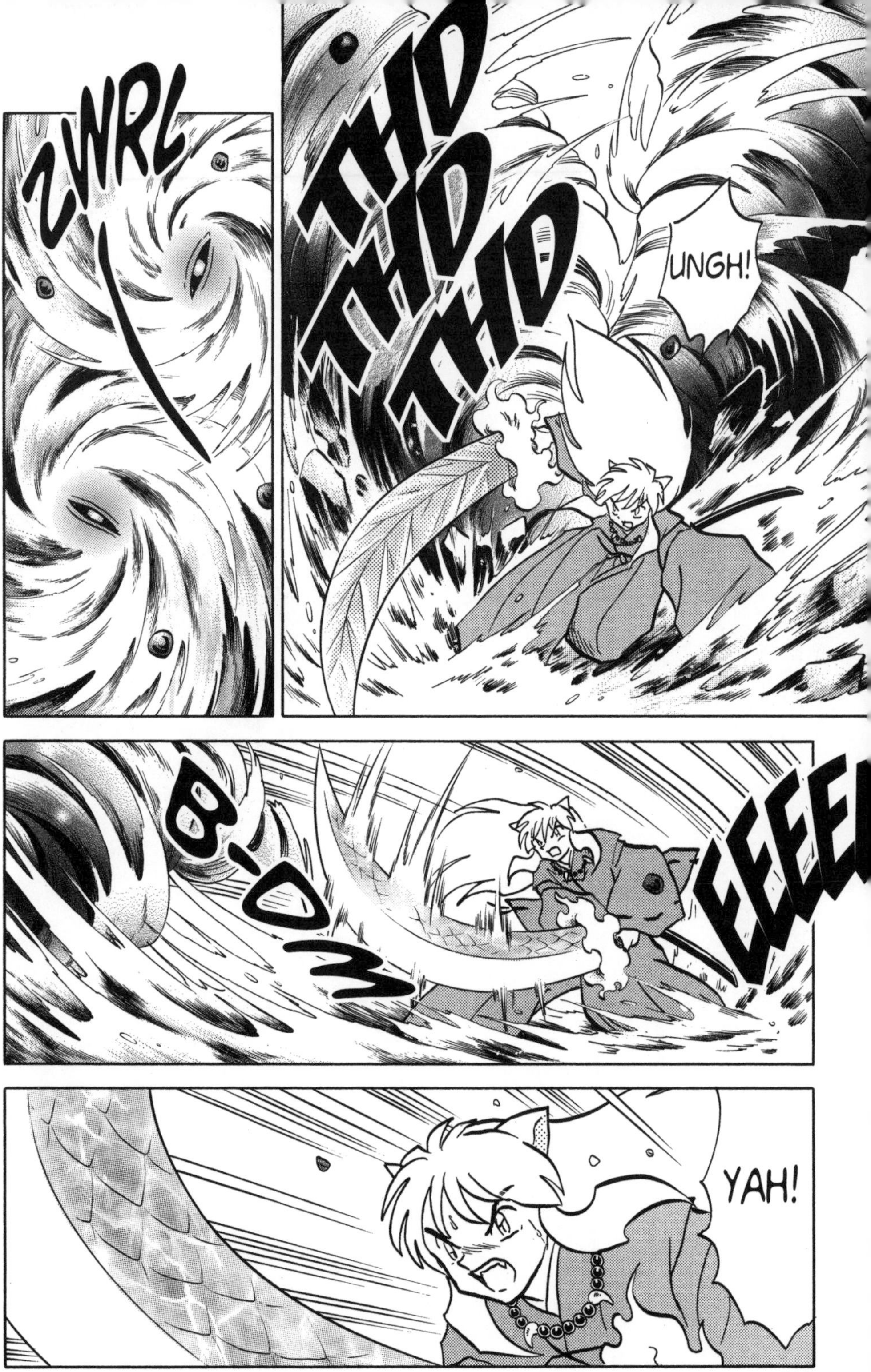
THD THD THD
UNGH!
ZWRL
EEEE
B'DOM
YAH!

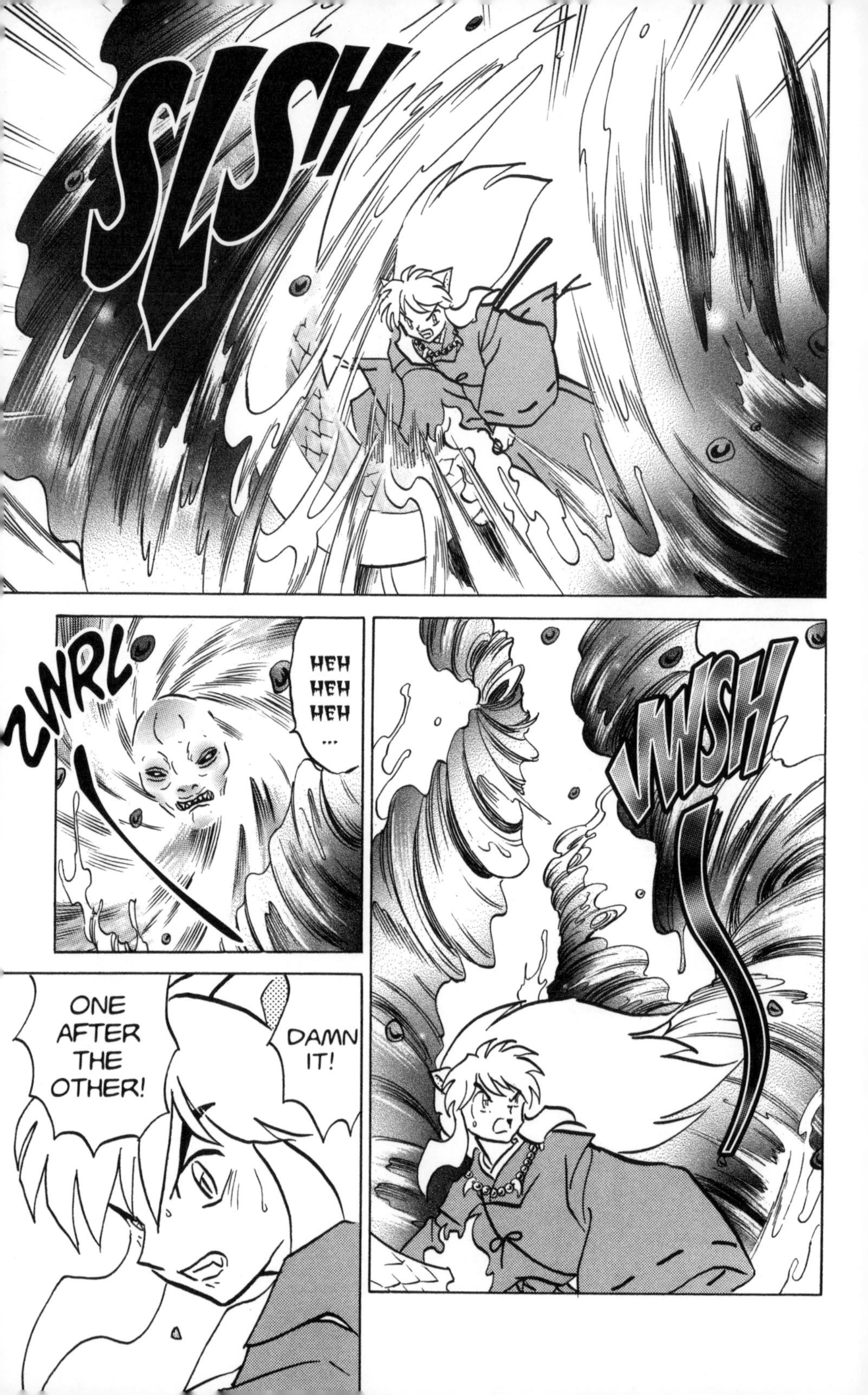
SLISH
HEH HEH HEH...
ZWRL
WHSH
DAMN IT!
ONE AFTER THE OTHER!

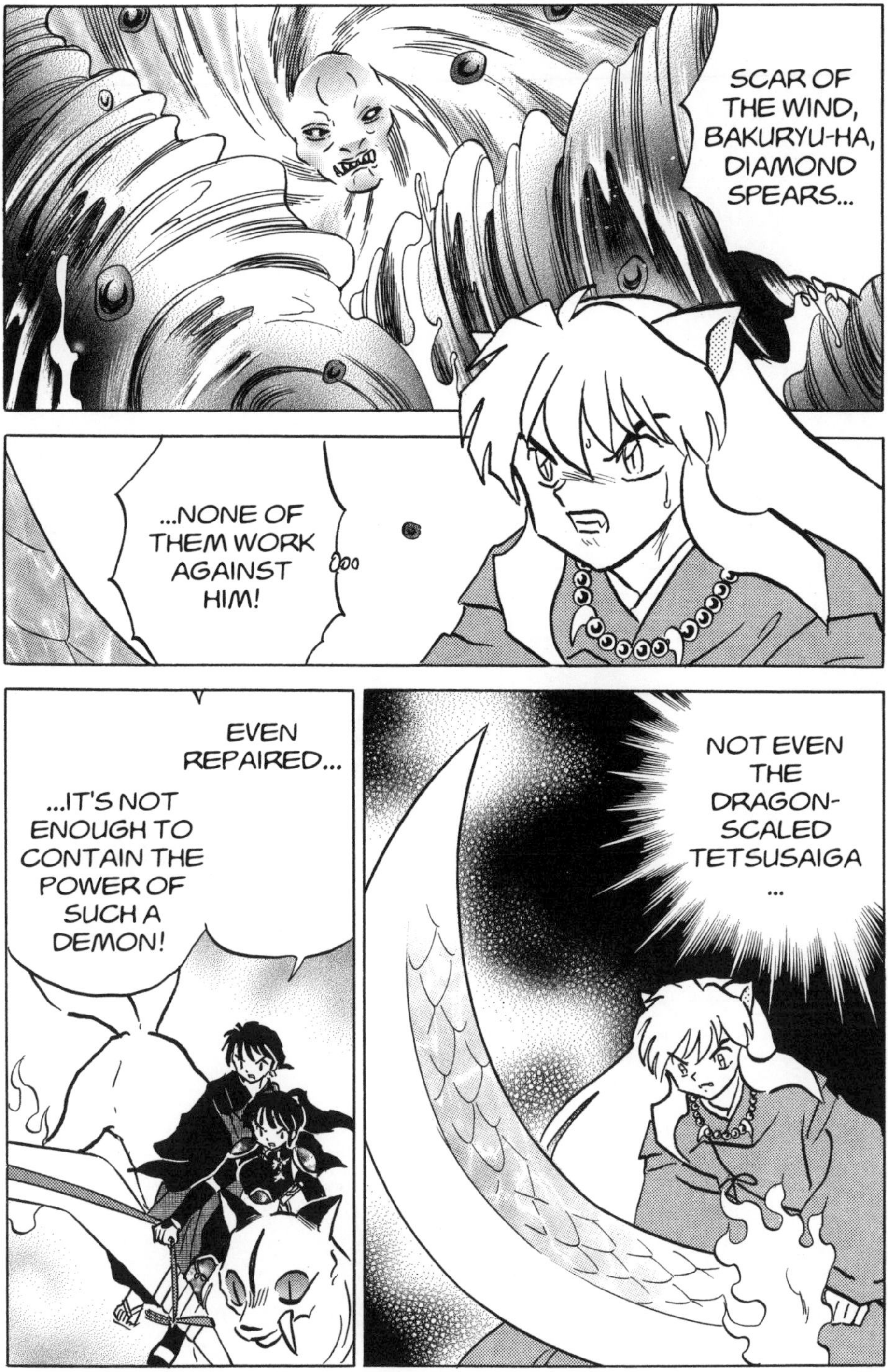
SCAR OF THE WIND, BAKURYU-HA, DIAMOND SPEARS...
...NONE OF THEM WORK AGAINST HIM!
NOT EVEN THE DRAGON-SCALED TETSUSAIGA ...
EVEN REPAIRED...
...IT'S NOT ENOUGH TO CONTAIN THE POWER OF SUCH A DEMON!

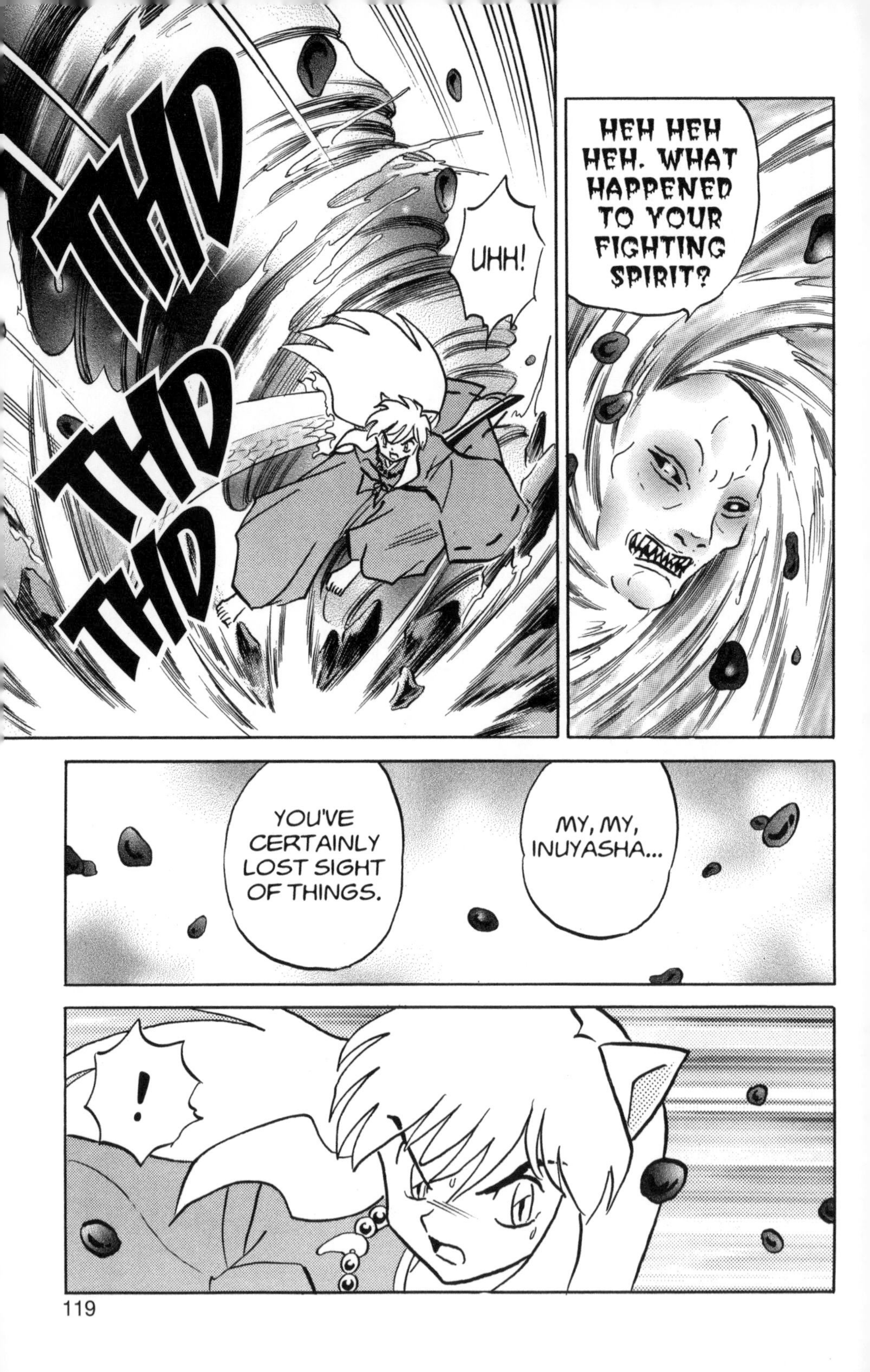
HEH HEH HEH. WHAT HAPPENED TO YOUR FIGHTING SPIRIT?
THD
THD
THD
UHH!
MY, MY, INUYASHA...
YOU'VE CERTAINLY LOST SIGHT OF THINGS.
!

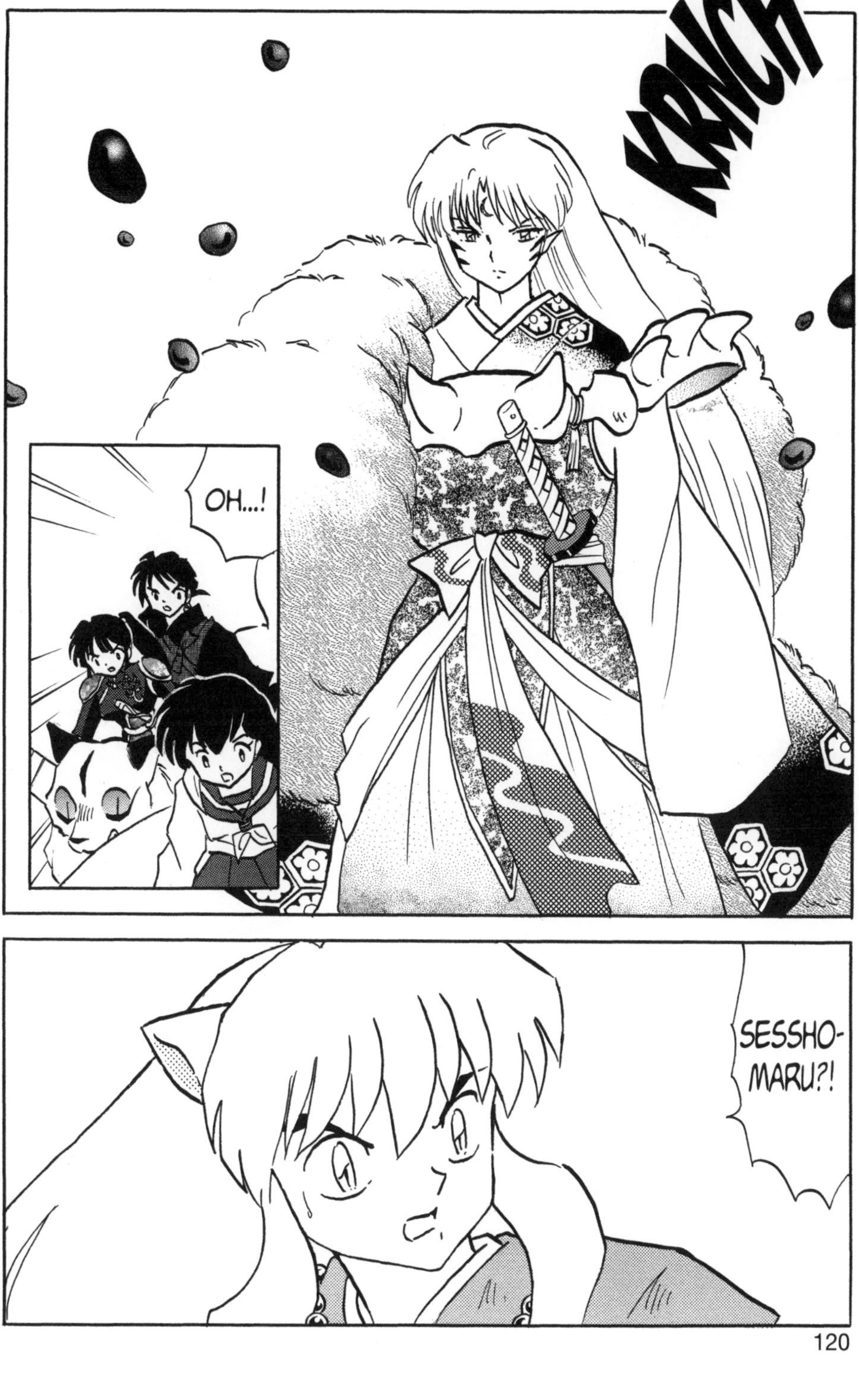
KRNCH
OH...!
SESSHO-
MARU?!

SCROLL SEVEN
THE BLADE'S MATURATION

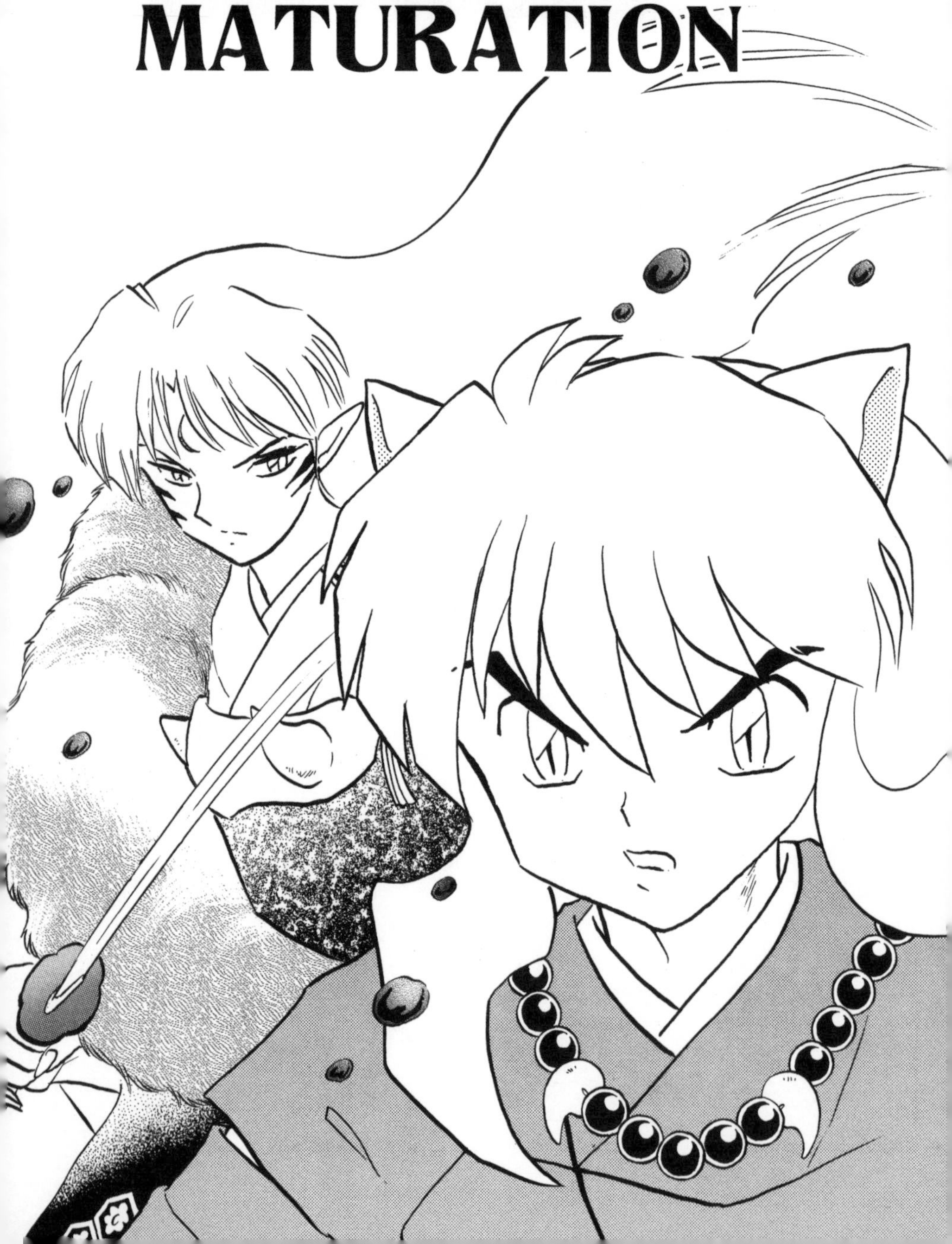

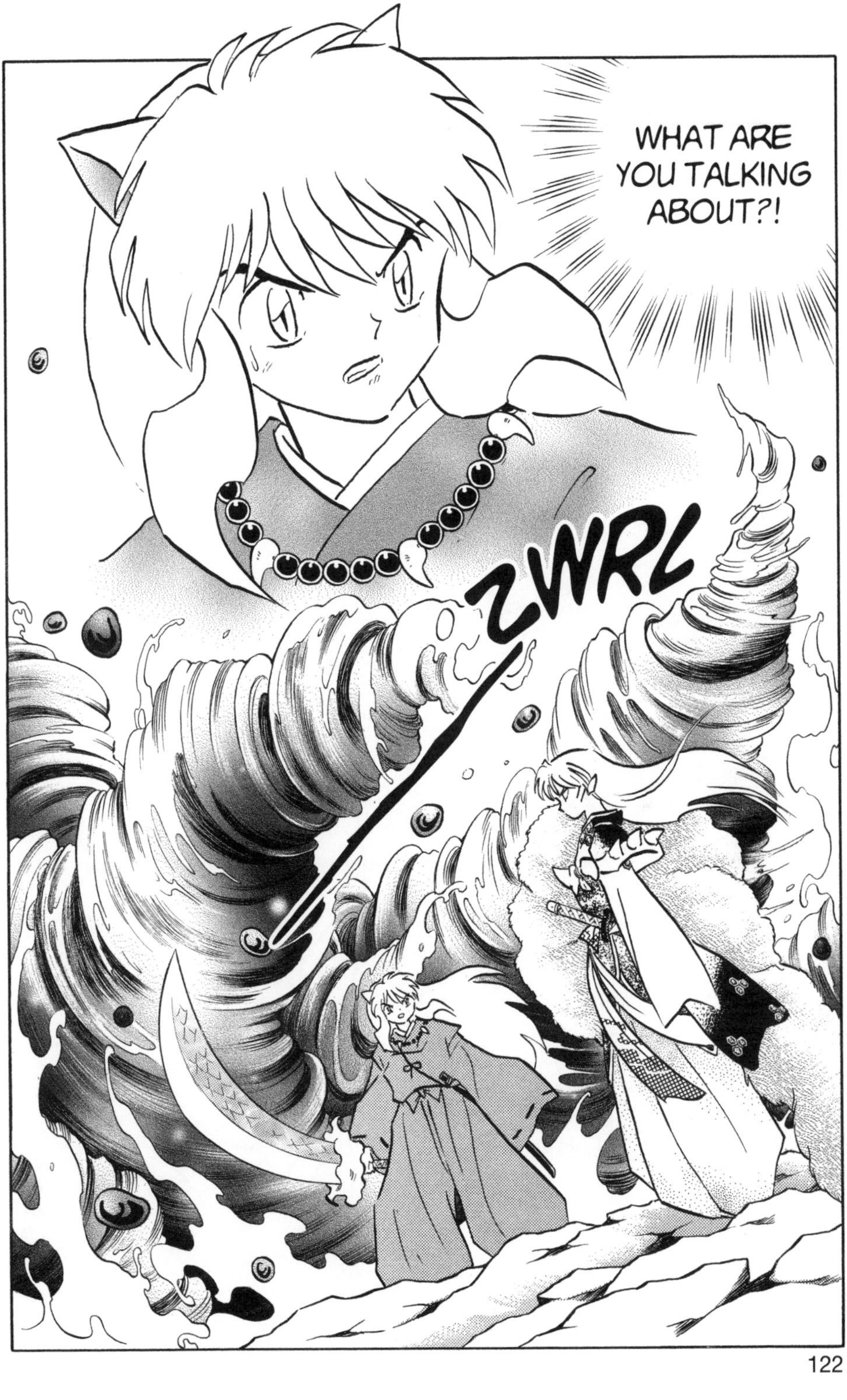
WHAT ARE YOU TALKING ABOUT?!
ZWRL

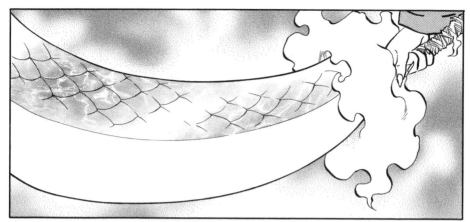

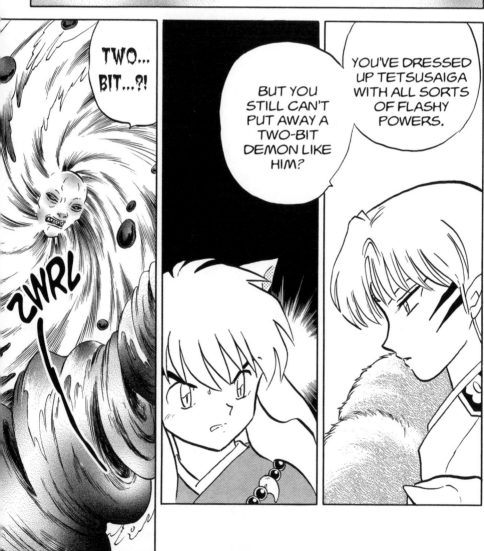

TWO... BIT...?!

ZWRL

YOU'VE DRESSED UP TETSUSAIGA WITH ALL SORTS OF FLASHY POWERS.

BUT YOU STILL CAN'T PUT AWAY A TWO-BIT DEMON LIKE HIM?

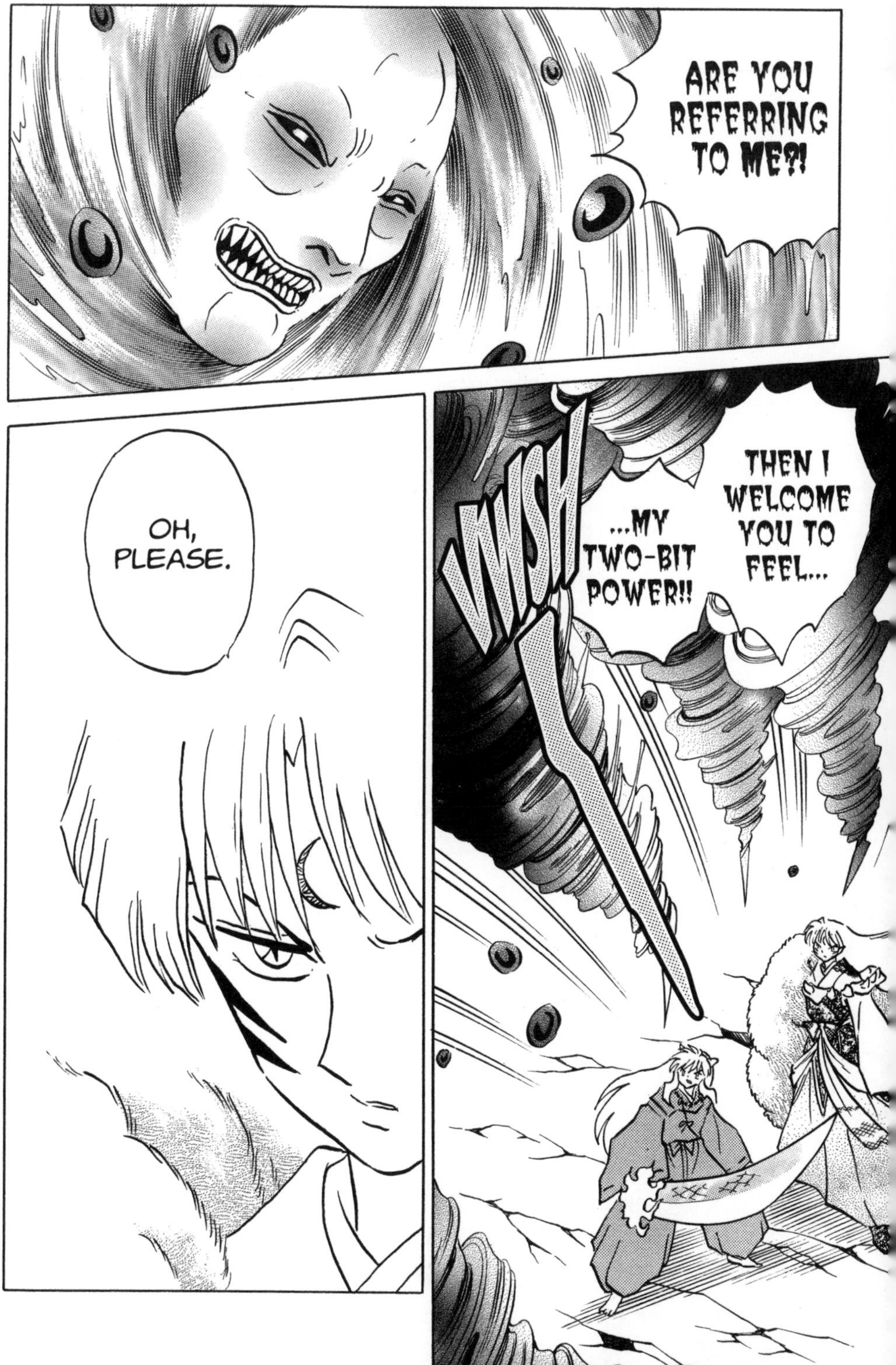
ARE YOU REFERRING TO ME?!
VWSH
THEN I WELCOME YOU TO FEEL...
...MY TWO-BIT POWER!!
OH, PLEASE.

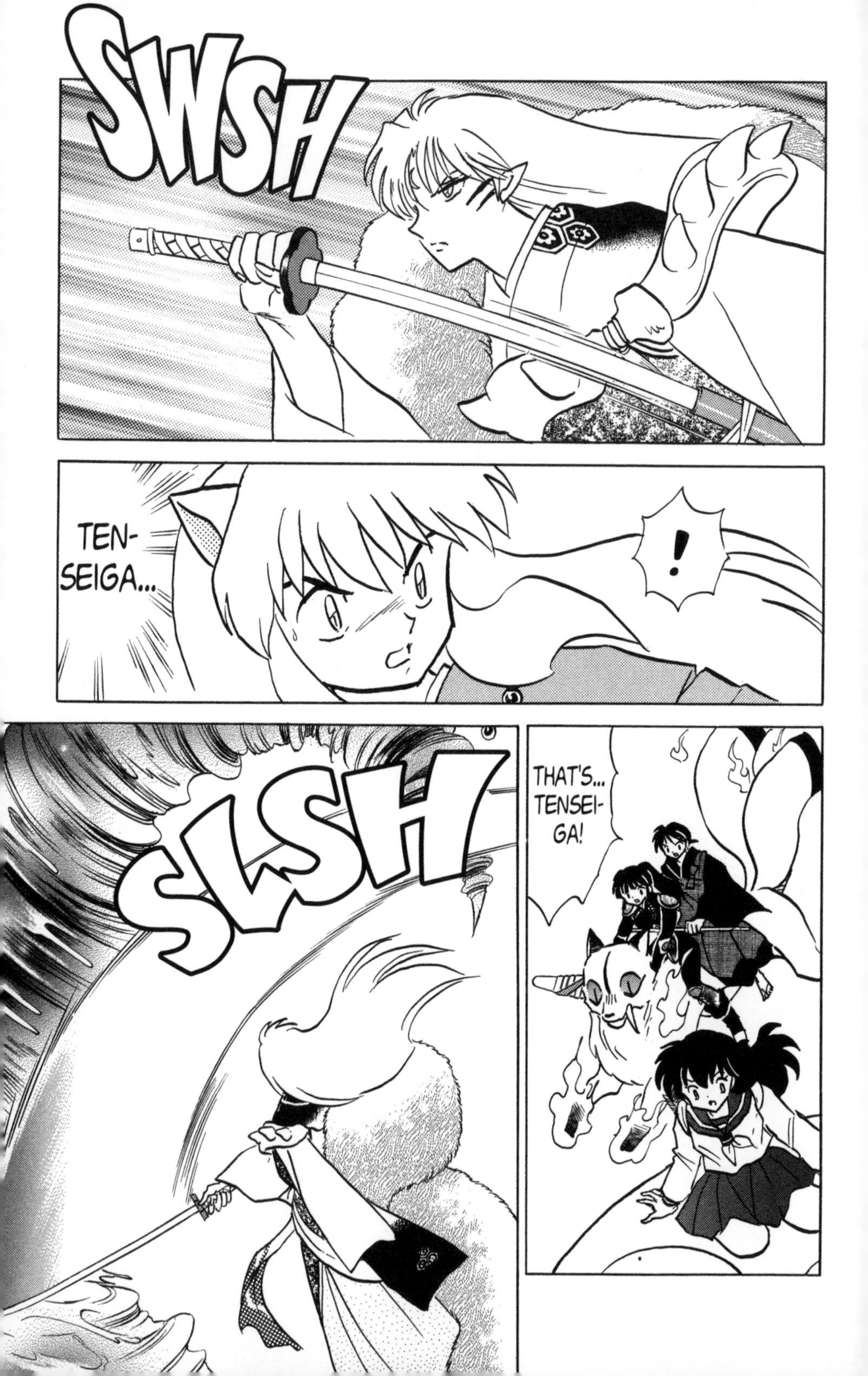
SWSH
!
TEN-SEIGA...
THAT'S... TENSEI-GA!
SLSH

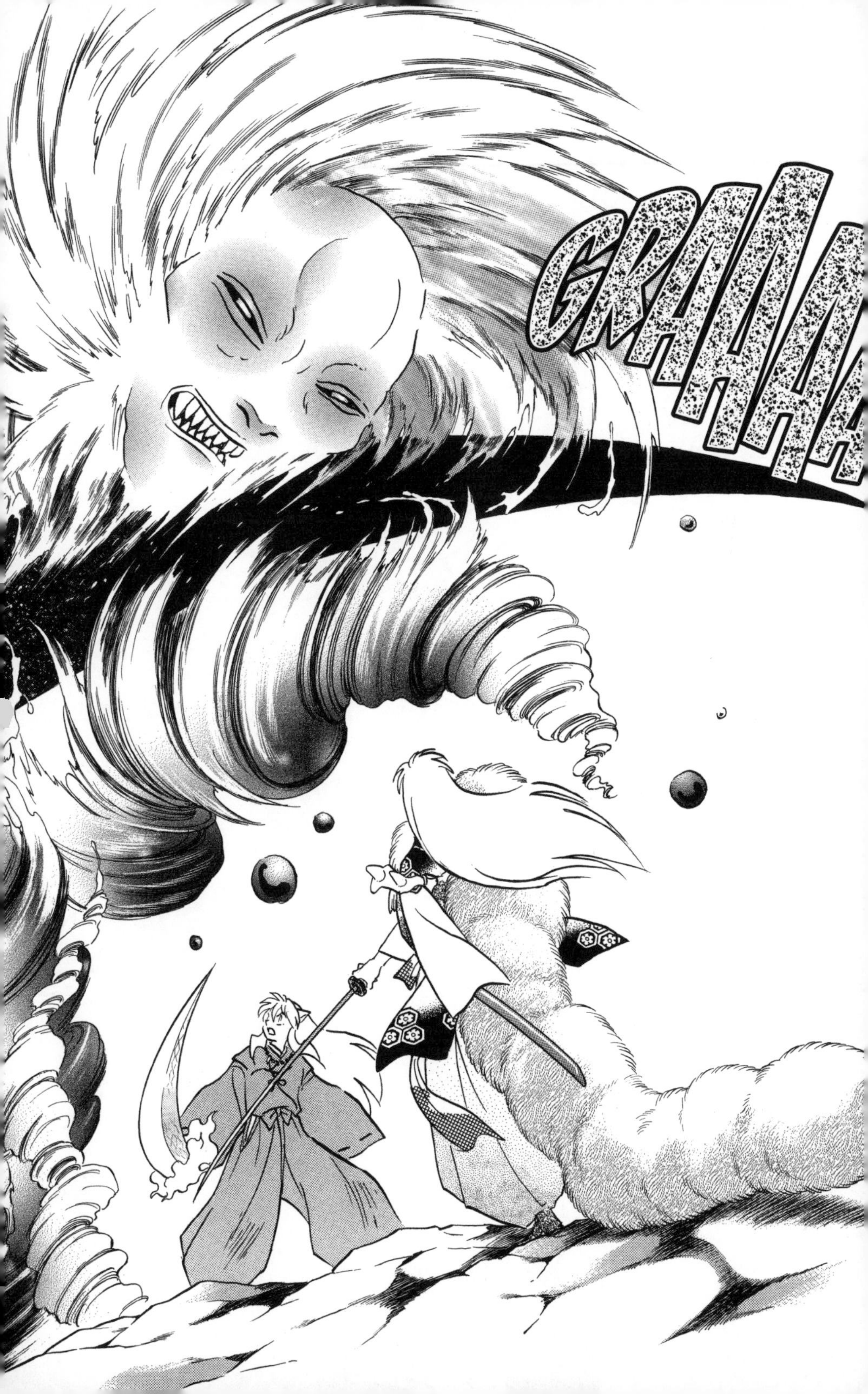
GRAAAA

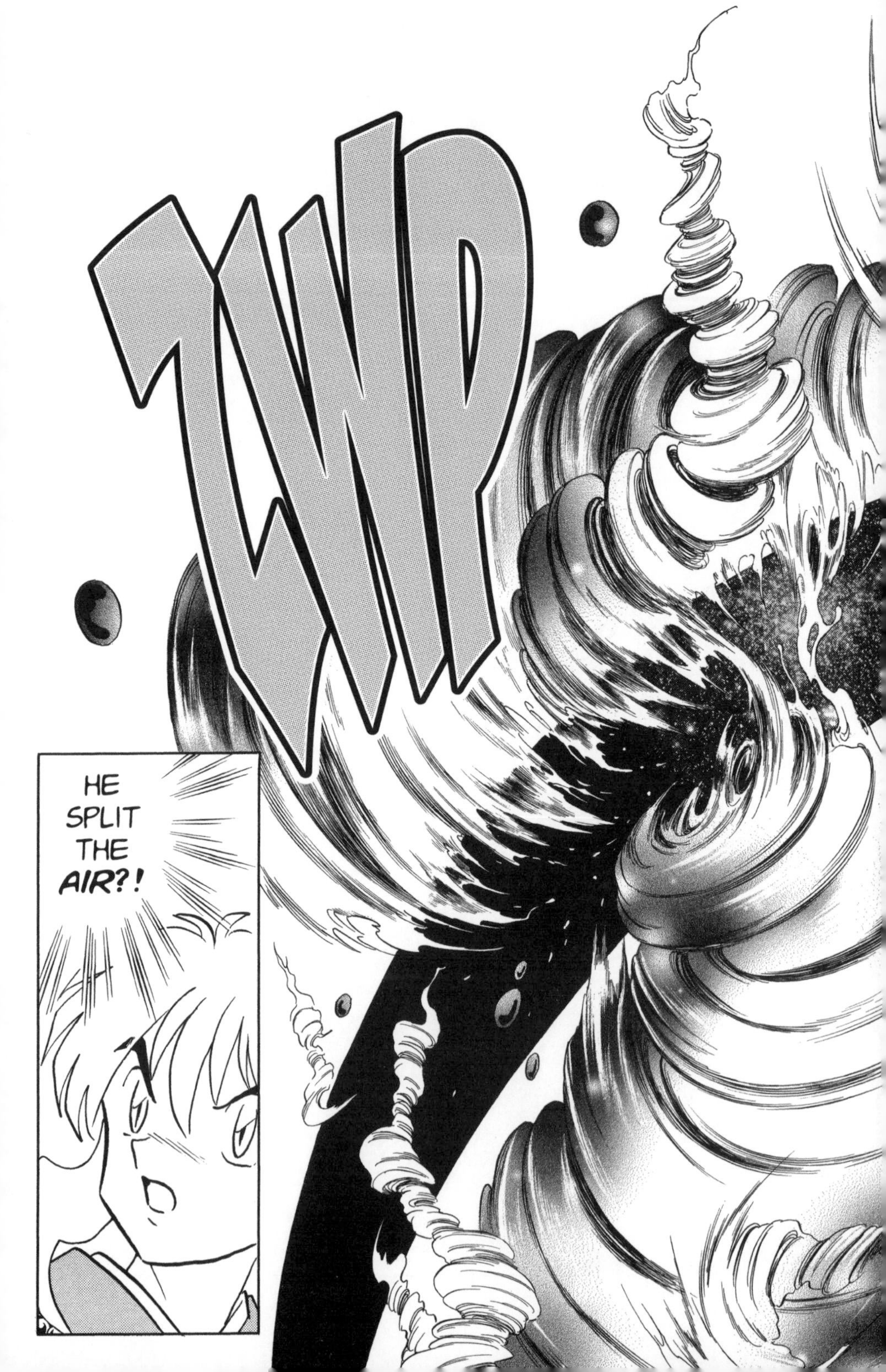
ZWIP
HE SPLIT THE AIR?!

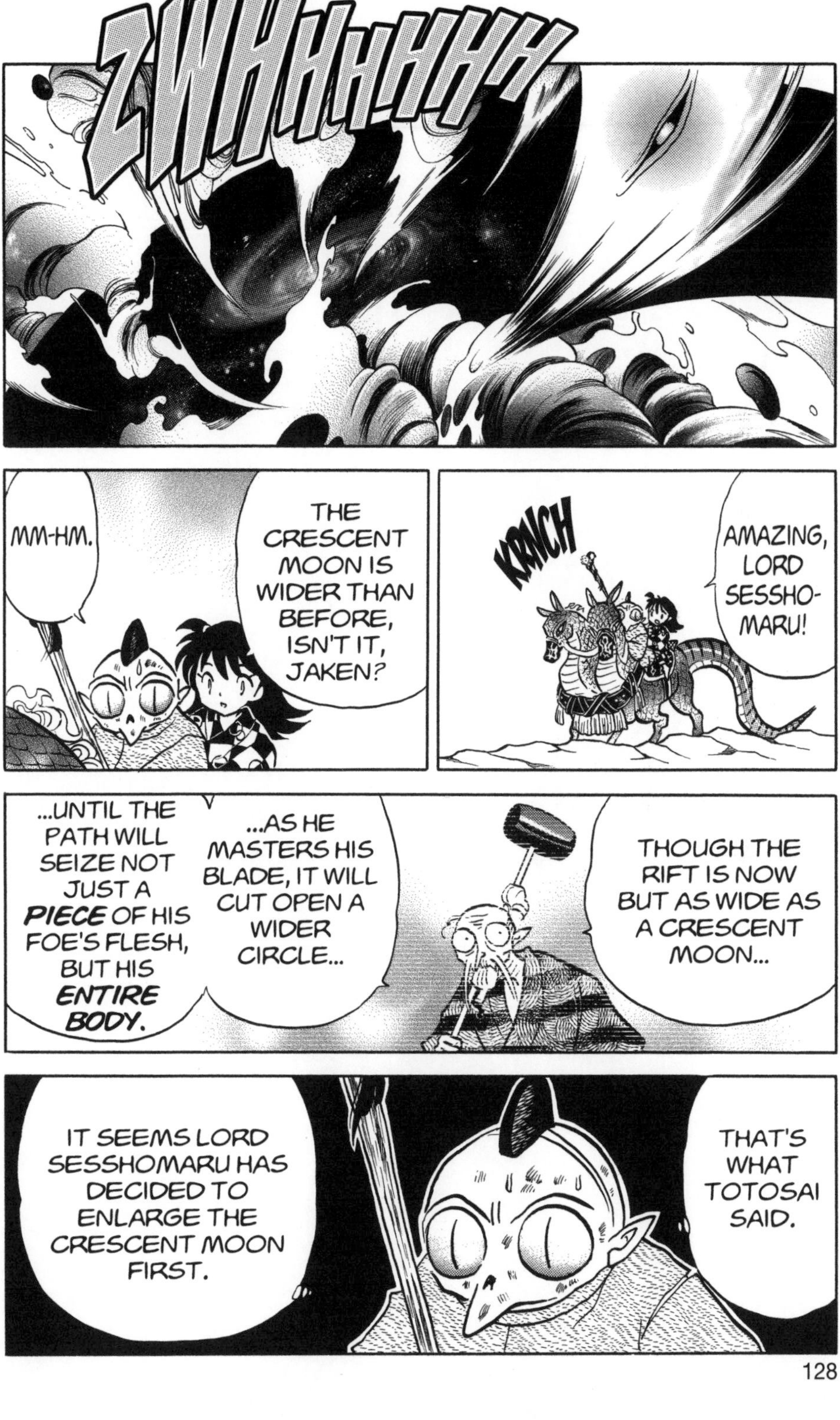
ZWHHHHHHH
AMAZING, LORD SESSHO-MARU!
KRNCH
THE CRESCENT MOON IS WIDER THAN BEFORE, ISN'T IT, JAKEN?
MM-HM.
THOUGH THE RIFT IS NOW BUT AS WIDE AS A CRESCENT MOON...
...AS HE MASTERS HIS BLADE, IT WILL CUT OPEN A WIDER CIRCLE...
...UNTIL THE PATH WILL SEIZE NOT JUST A PIECE OF HIS FOE'S FLESH, BUT HIS ENTIRE BODY.
THAT'S WHAT TOTOSAI SAID.
IT SEEMS LORD SESSHOMARU HAS DECIDED TO ENLARGE THE CRESCENT MOON FIRST.

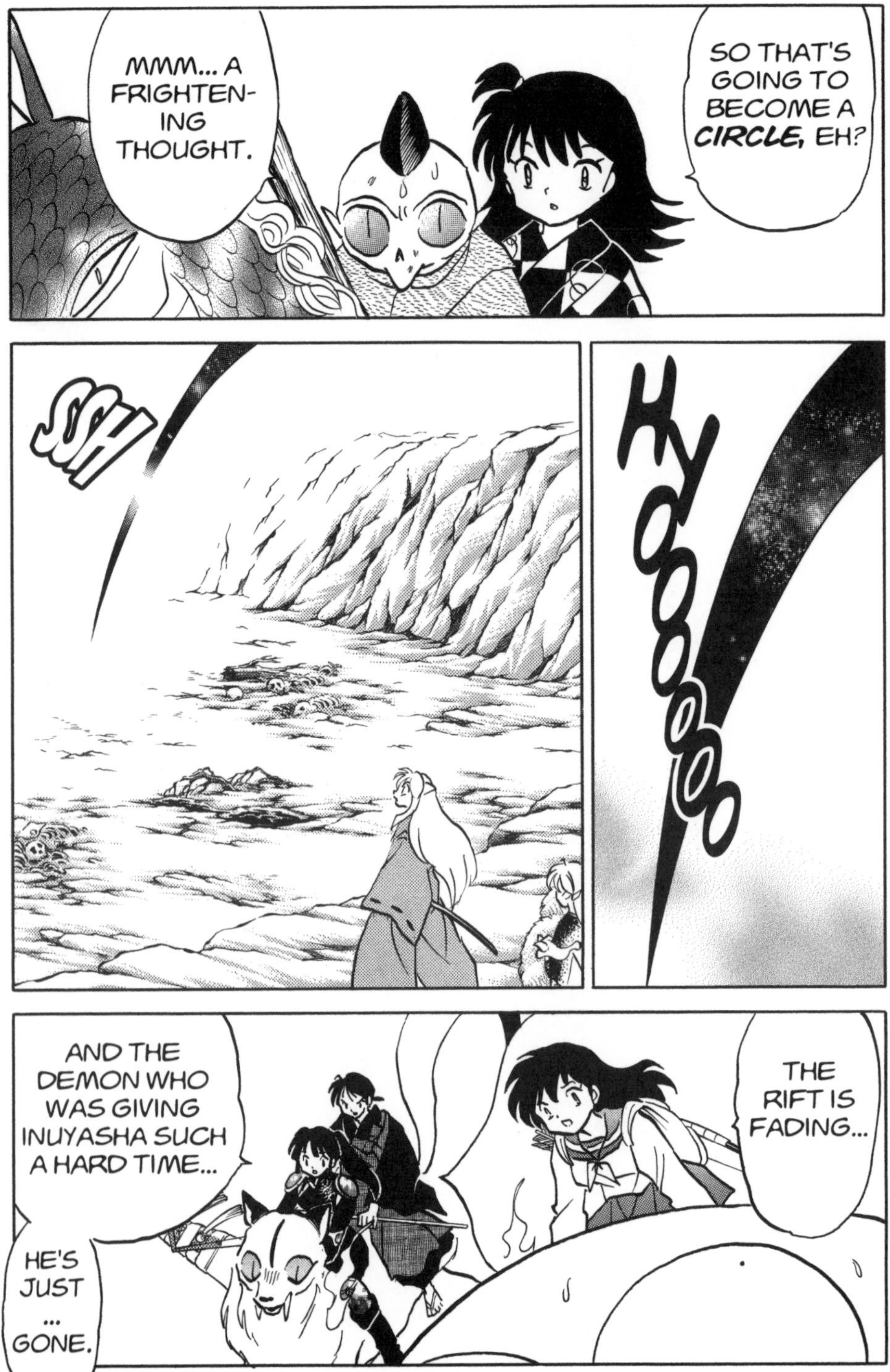
SO THAT'S GOING TO BECOME A CIRCLE, EH?
MMM... A FRIGHTEN-ING THOUGHT.
HYOOOOOOO
SH
THE RIFT IS FADING...
AND THE DEMON WHO WAS GIVING INUYASHA SUCH A HARD TIME...
HE'S JUST ... GONE.

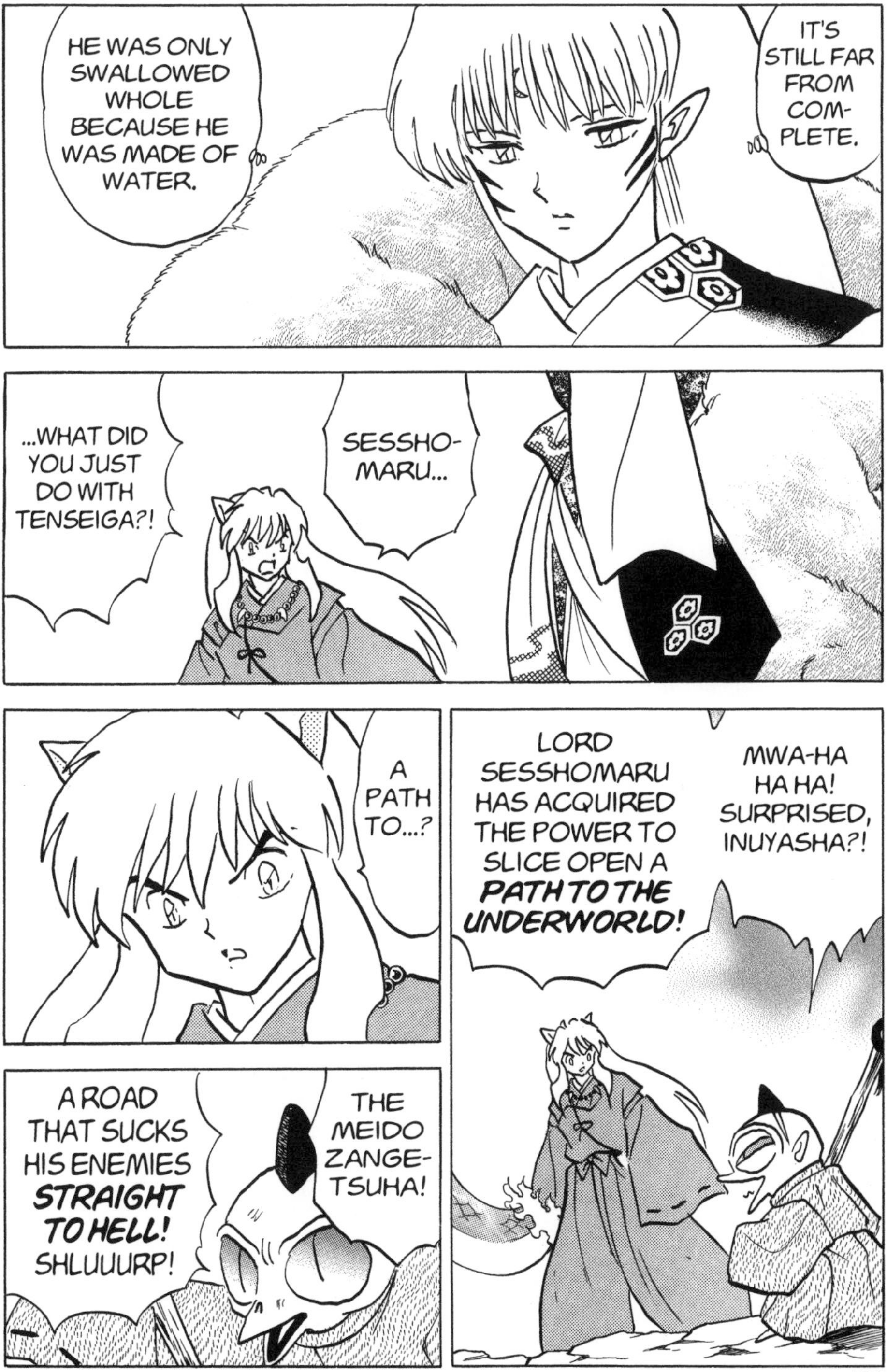
IT'S STILL FAR FROM COM-PLETE.
HE WAS ONLY SWALLOWED WHOLE BECAUSE HE WAS MADE OF WATER.
SESSHO-MARU...
...WHAT DID YOU JUST DO WITH TENSEIGA?!
MWA-HA HA HA! SURPRISED, INUYASHA?!
LORD SESSHOMARU HAS ACQUIRED THE POWER TO SLICE OPEN A ***PATH TO THE UNDERWORLD!***
A PATH TO...?
THE MEIDO ZANGE-TSUHA!
A ROAD THAT SUCKS HIS ENEMIES ***STRAIGHT TO HELL!*** SHLUUURP!

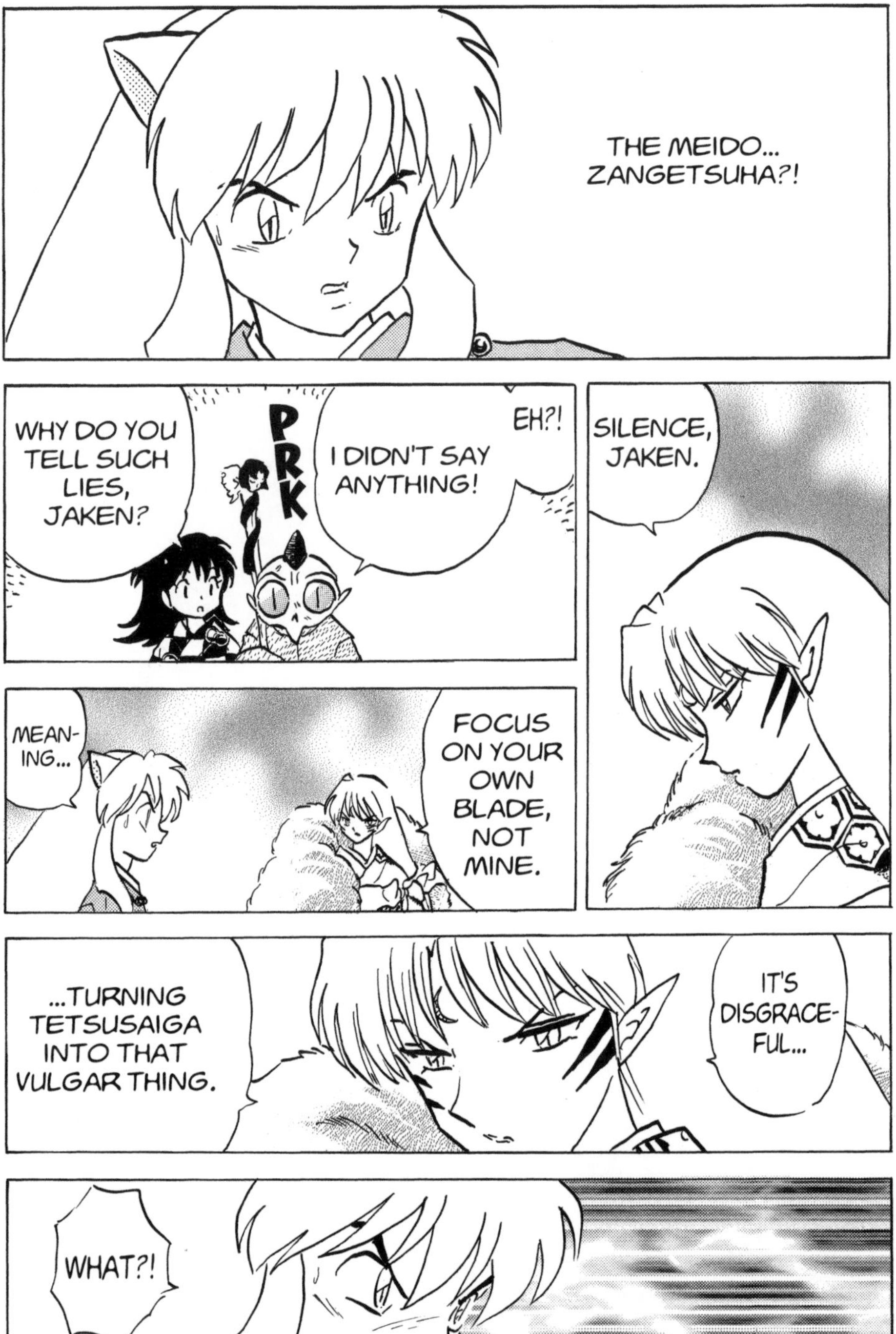
THE MEIDO... ZANGETSUHA?!
SILENCE, JAKEN.
EH?!
I DIDN'T SAY ANYTHING!
PRK
WHY DO YOU TELL SUCH LIES, JAKEN?
FOCUS ON YOUR OWN BLADE, NOT MINE.
MEAN-ING...
IT'S DISGRACE-FUL...
...TURNING TETSUSAIGA INTO THAT VULGAR THING.
WHAT?!

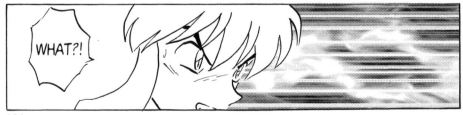

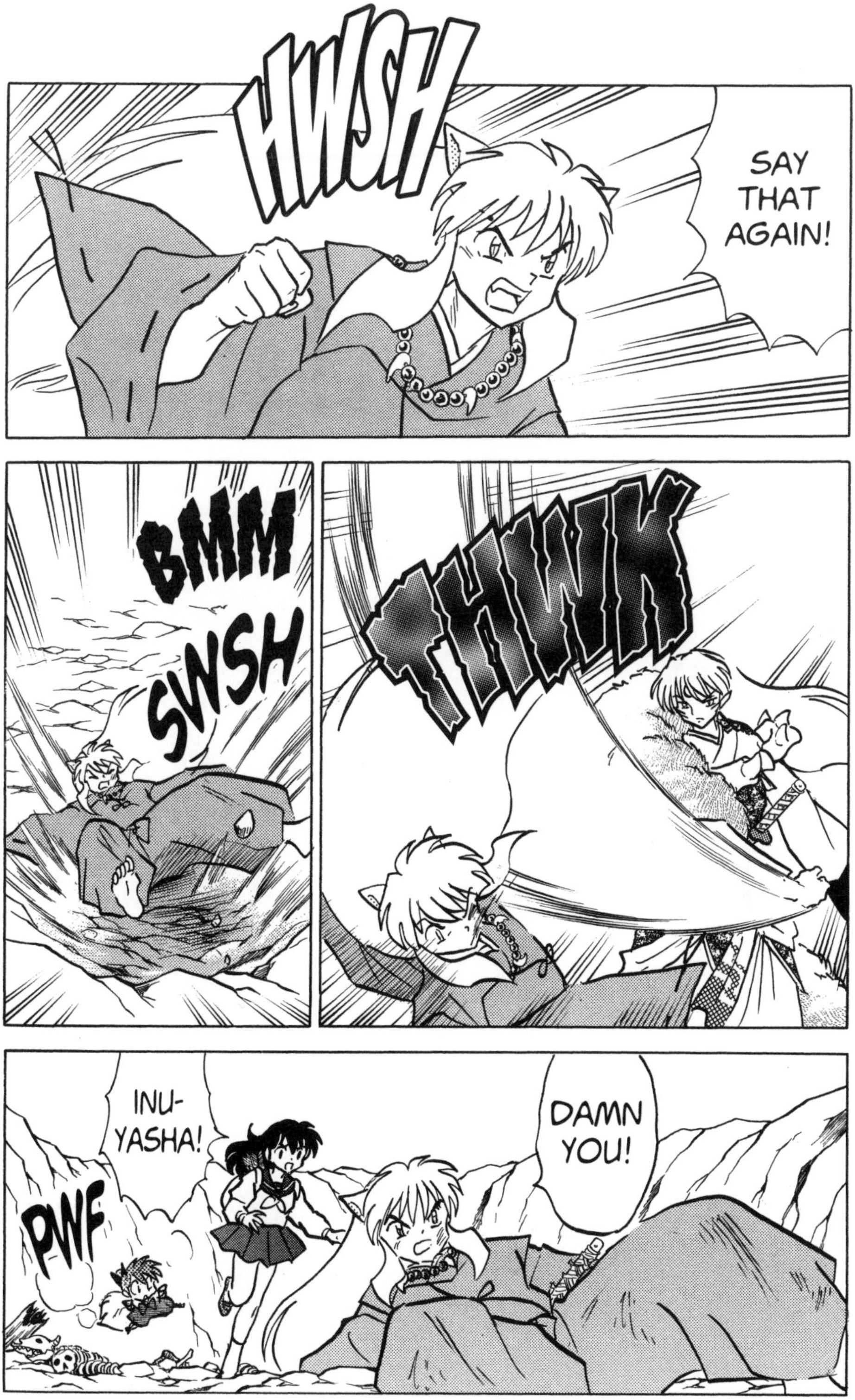
HWSH
SAY THAT AGAIN!
THWK
BMM
SWSH
DAMN YOU!
INU-YASHA!
PWF

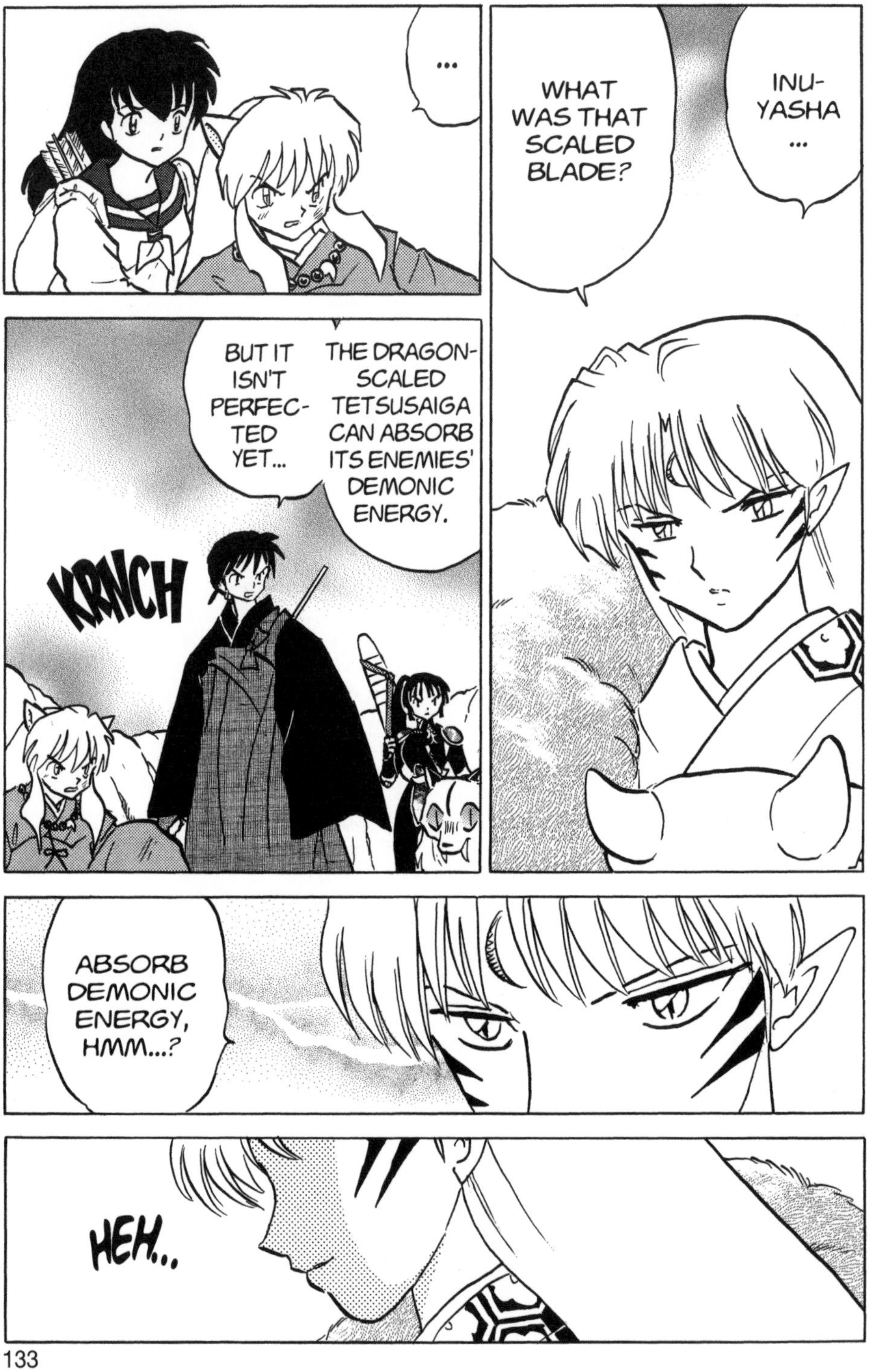
INU-YASHA...
WHAT WAS THAT SCALED BLADE?
...
THE DRAGON-SCALED TETSUSAIGA CAN ABSORB ITS ENEMIES' DEMONIC ENERGY.
BUT IT ISN'T PERFECTED YET...
KRNCH
ABSORB DEMONIC ENERGY, HMM...?
HEH...

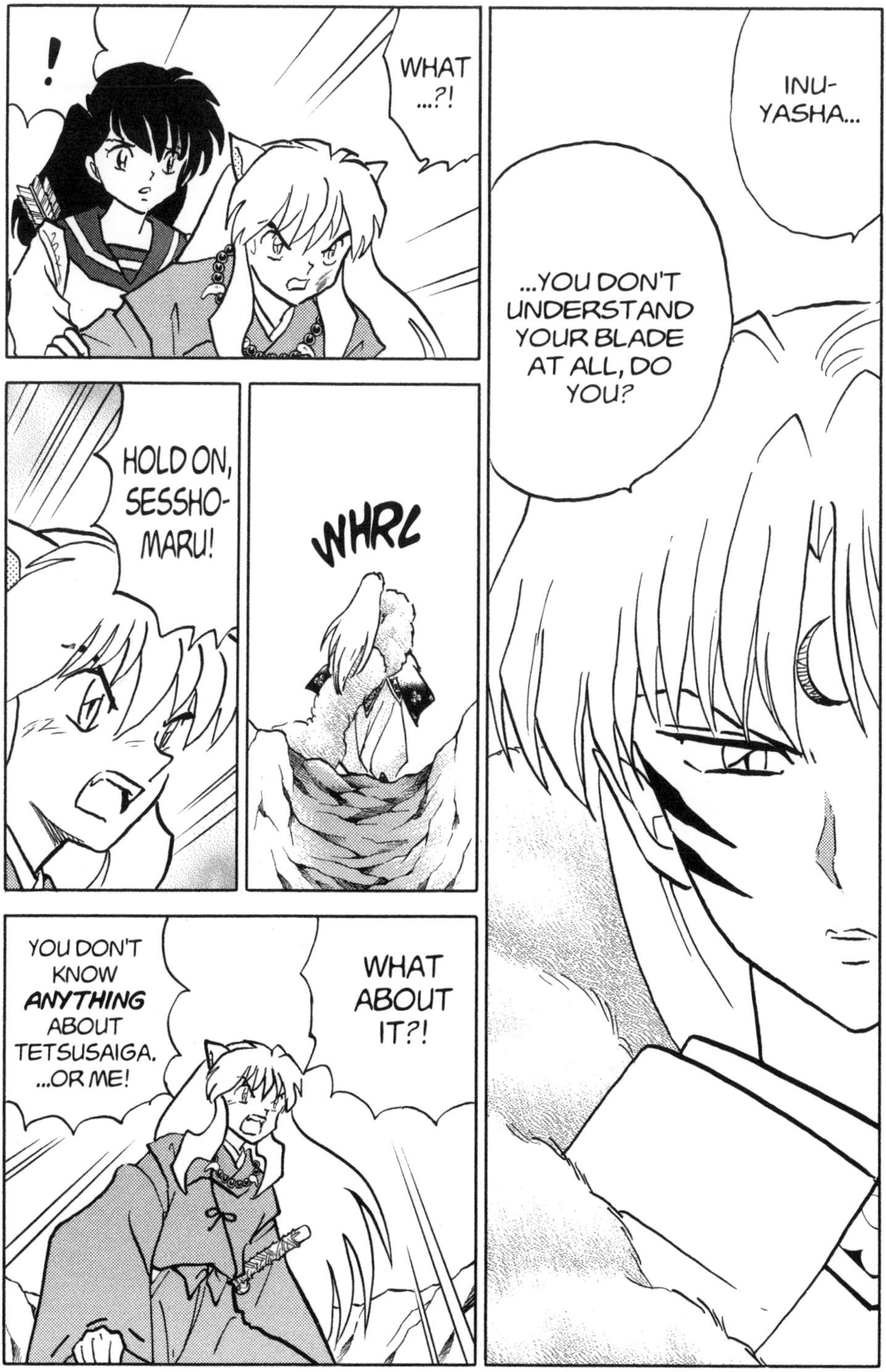
INU-YASHA...
...YOU DON'T UNDERSTAND YOUR BLADE AT ALL, DO YOU?
!
WHAT ...?!
WHRL
HOLD ON, SESSHO-MARU!
WHAT ABOUT IT?!
YOU DON'T KNOW **ANYTHING** ABOUT TETSUSAIGA. ...OR ME!

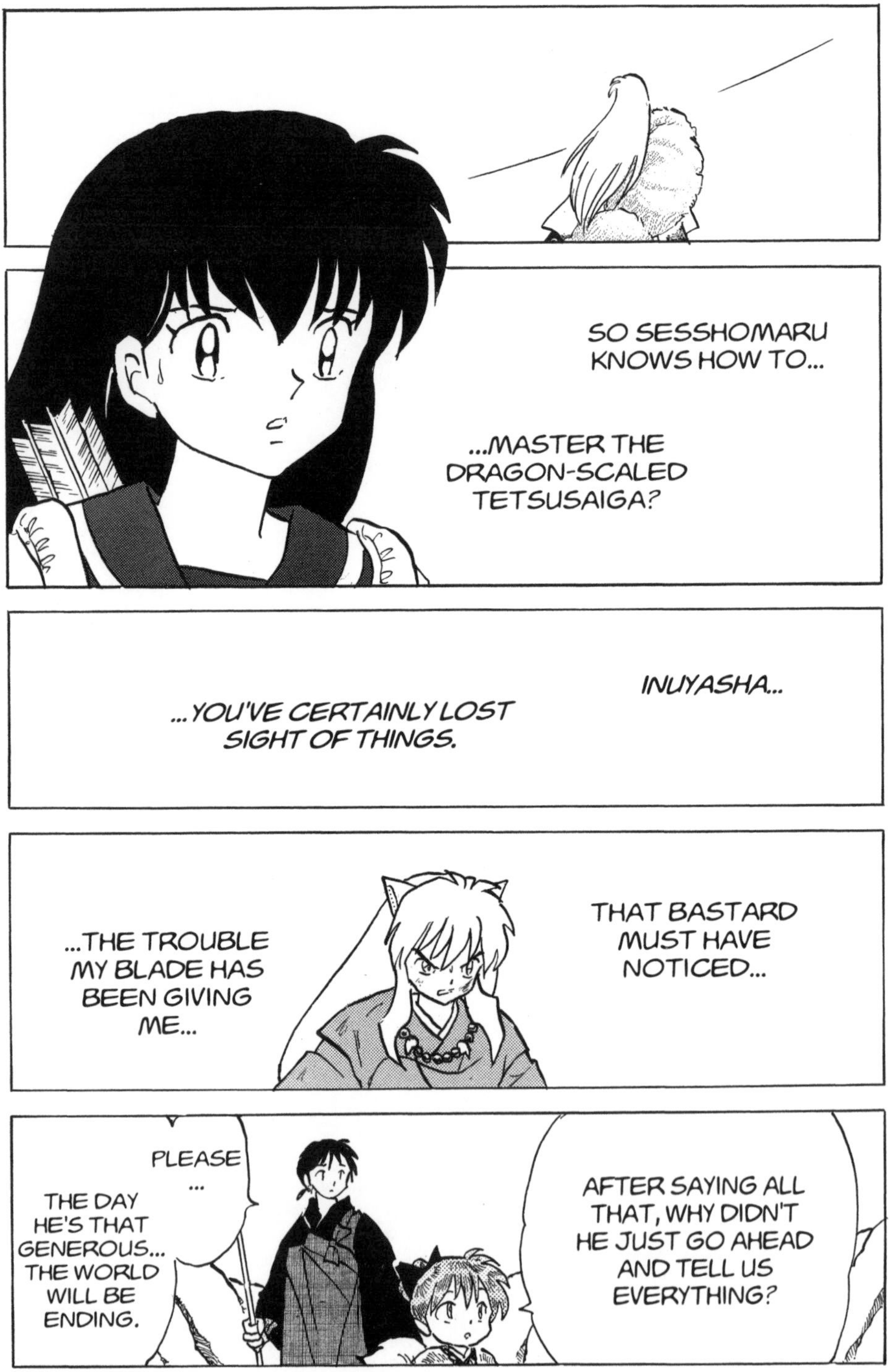
SO SESSHOMARU KNOWS HOW TO...
...MASTER THE DRAGON-SCALED TETSUSAIGA?
INUYASHA...
...YOU'VE CERTAINLY LOST SIGHT OF THINGS.
THAT BASTARD MUST HAVE NOTICED...
...THE TROUBLE MY BLADE HAS BEEN GIVING ME...
AFTER SAYING ALL THAT, WHY DIDN'T HE JUST GO AHEAD AND TELL US EVERYTHING?
PLEASE...
THE DAY HE'S THAT GENEROUS... THE WORLD WILL BE ENDING.

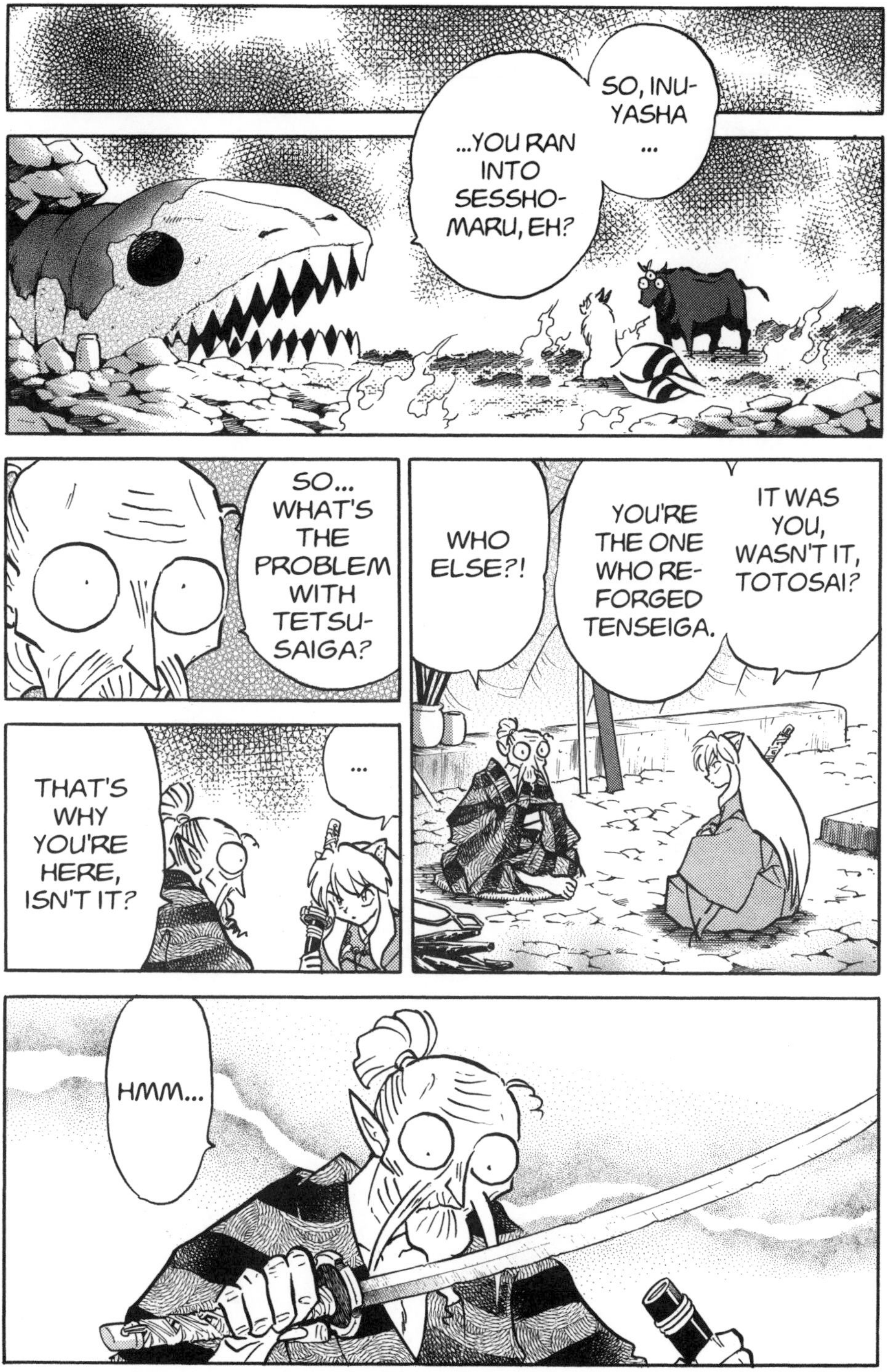
SO, INU-YASHA ...
...YOU RAN INTO SESSHO-MARU, EH?
IT WAS YOU, WASN'T IT, TOTOSAI?
YOU'RE THE ONE WHO RE-FORGED TENSEIGA.
WHO ELSE?!
SO... WHAT'S THE PROBLEM WITH TETSU-SAIGA?
...
THAT'S WHY YOU'RE HERE, ISN'T IT?
HMM...

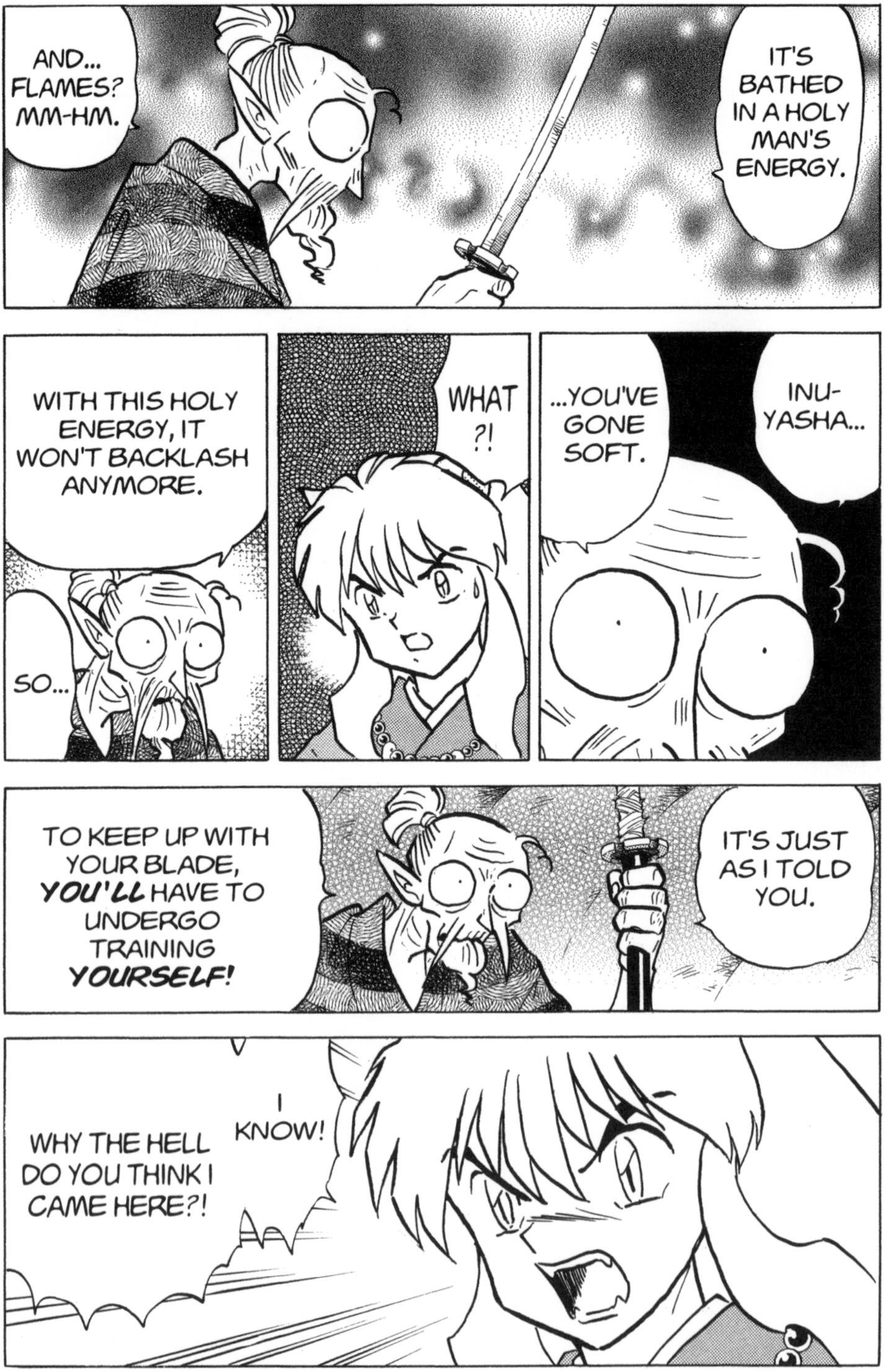
IT'S BATHED IN A HOLY MAN'S ENERGY.
AND... FLAMES? MM-HM.
INU-YASHA...
...YOU'VE GONE SOFT.
WHAT?!
WITH THIS HOLY ENERGY, IT WON'T BACKLASH ANYMORE.
SO...
IT'S JUST AS I TOLD YOU.
TO KEEP UP WITH YOUR BLADE, YOU'LL HAVE TO UNDERGO TRAINING YOURSELF!
I KNOW!
WHY THE HELL DO YOU THINK I CAME HERE?!

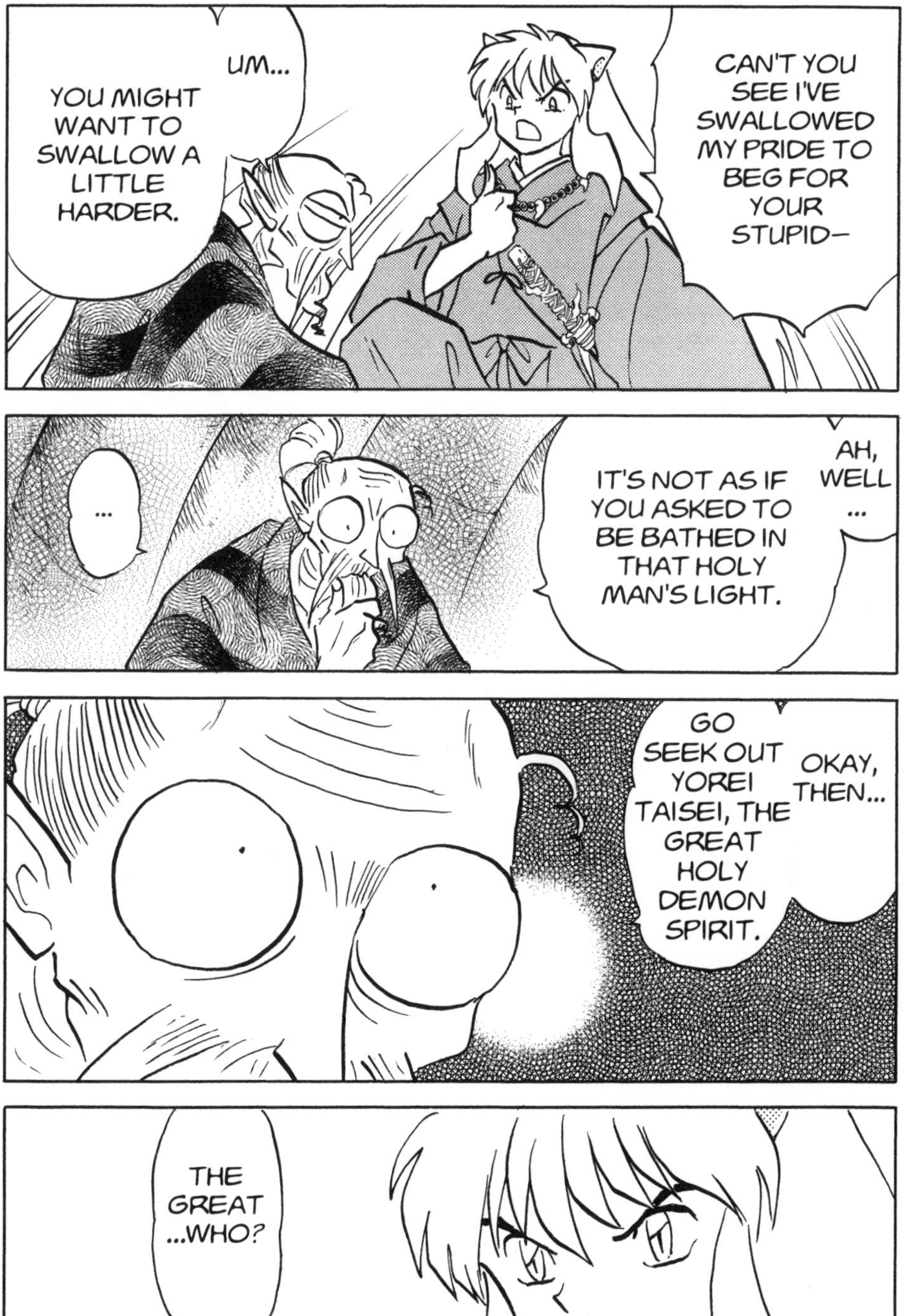
CAN'T YOU SEE I'VE SWALLOWED MY PRIDE TO BEG FOR YOUR STUPID–
UM... YOU MIGHT WANT TO SWALLOW A LITTLE HARDER.
AH, WELL ... IT'S NOT AS IF YOU ASKED TO BE BATHED IN THAT HOLY MAN'S LIGHT.
...
OKAY, THEN... GO SEEK OUT YOREI TAISEI, THE GREAT HOLY DEMON SPIRIT.
THE GREAT ...WHO?

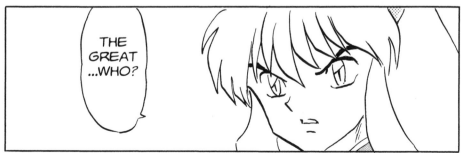

SCROLL EIGHT
YOREI TAISEI

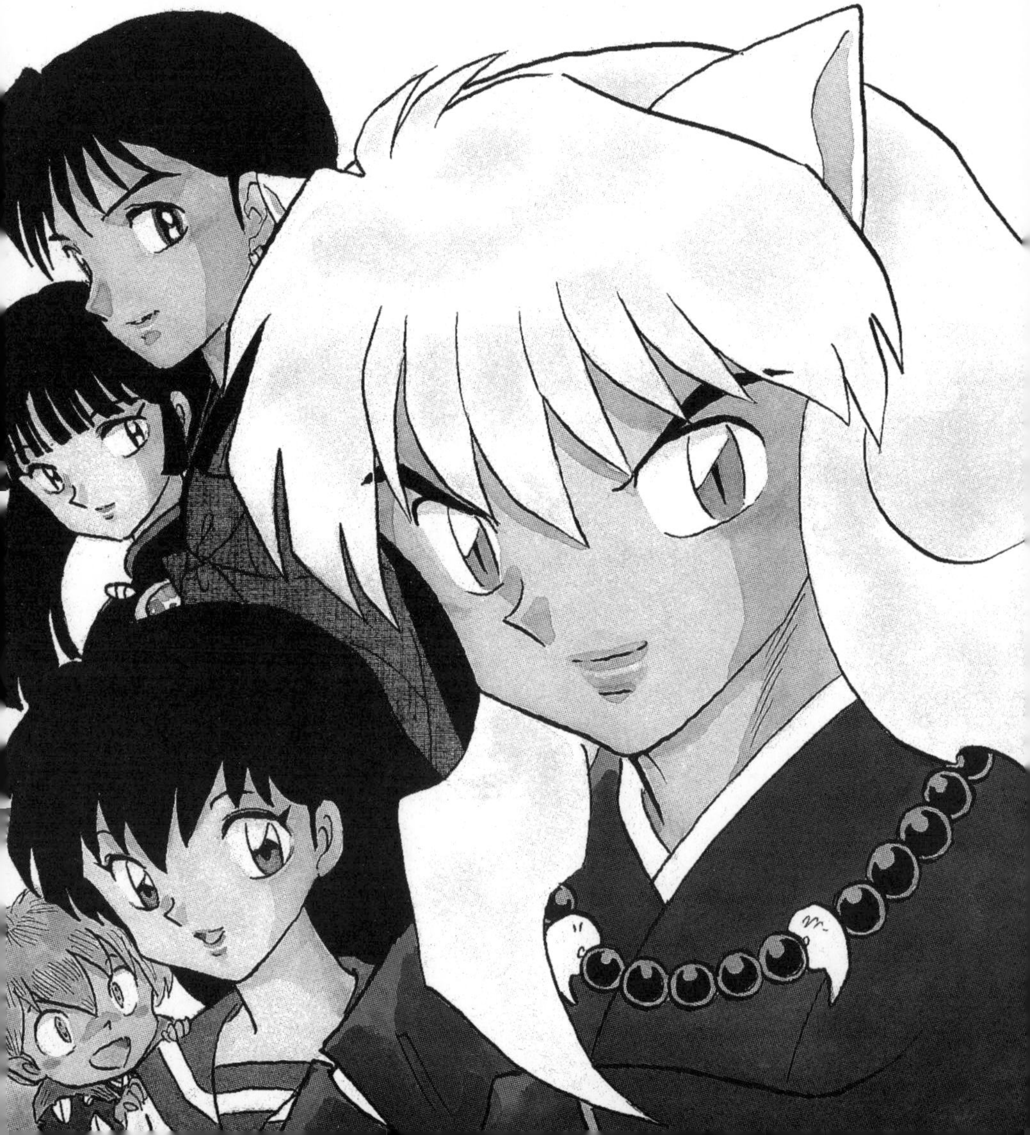

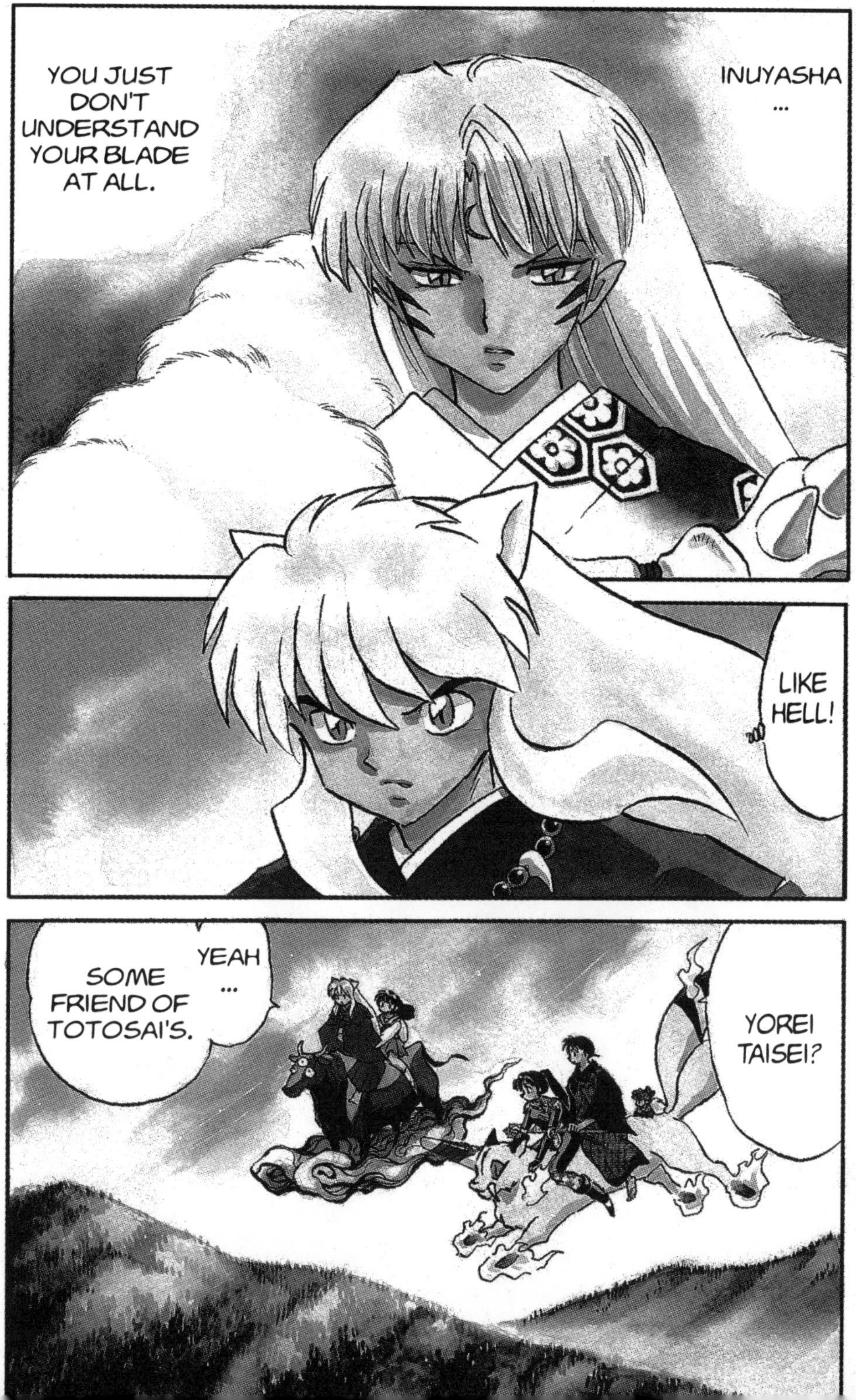
INUYASHA ...
YOU JUST DON'T UNDERSTAND YOUR BLADE AT ALL.
LIKE HELL!
YOREI TAISEI?
YEAH ... SOME FRIEND OF TOTOSAI'S.

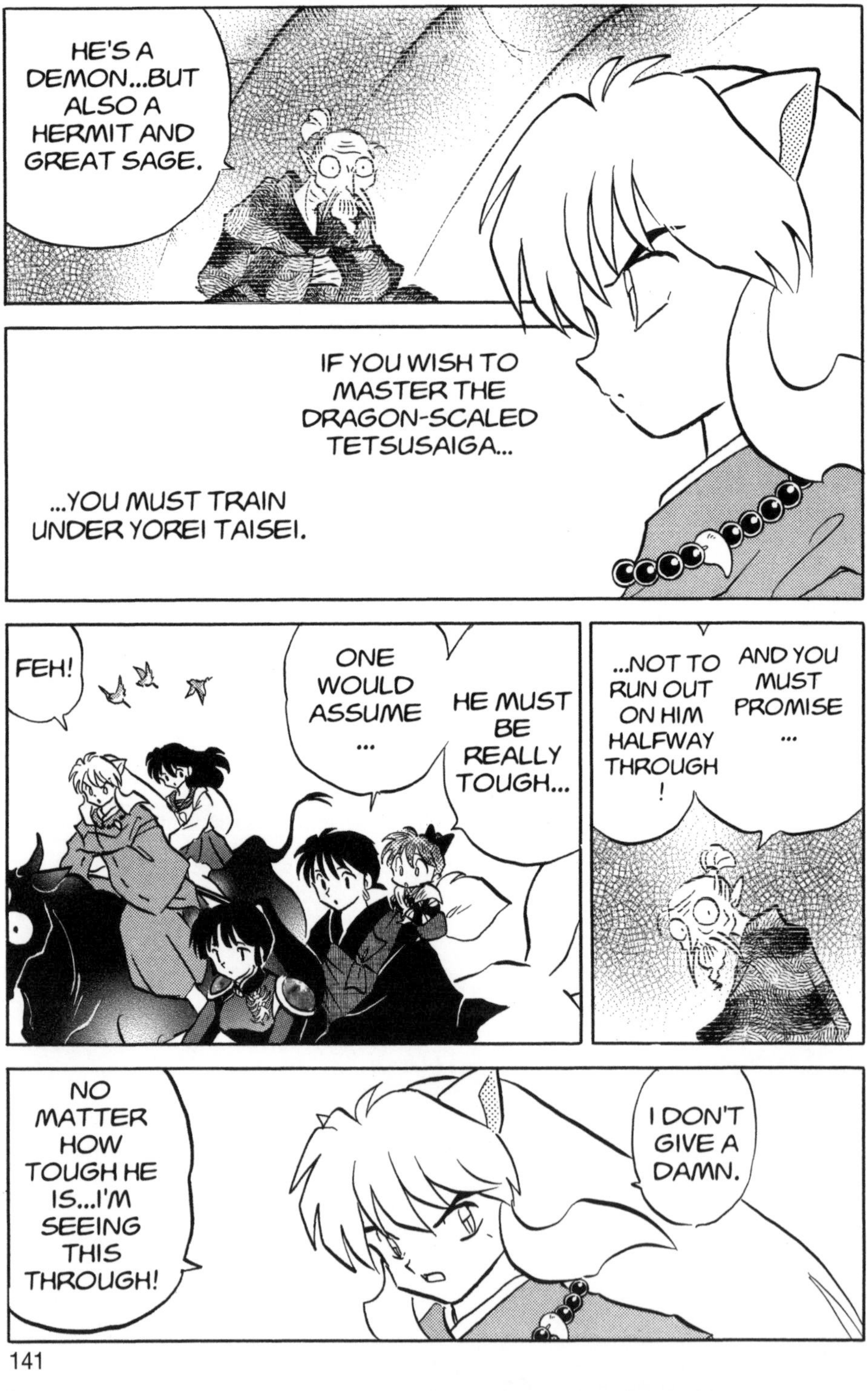
HE'S A DEMON...BUT ALSO A HERMIT AND GREAT SAGE.
IF YOU WISH TO MASTER THE DRAGON-SCALED TETSUSAIGA...
...YOU MUST TRAIN UNDER YOREI TAISEI.
AND YOU MUST PROMISE...
...NOT TO RUN OUT ON HIM HALFWAY THROUGH!
HE MUST BE REALLY TOUGH...
ONE WOULD ASSUME...
FEH!
I DON'T GIVE A DAMN.
NO MATTER HOW TOUGH HE IS...I'M SEEING THIS THROUGH!

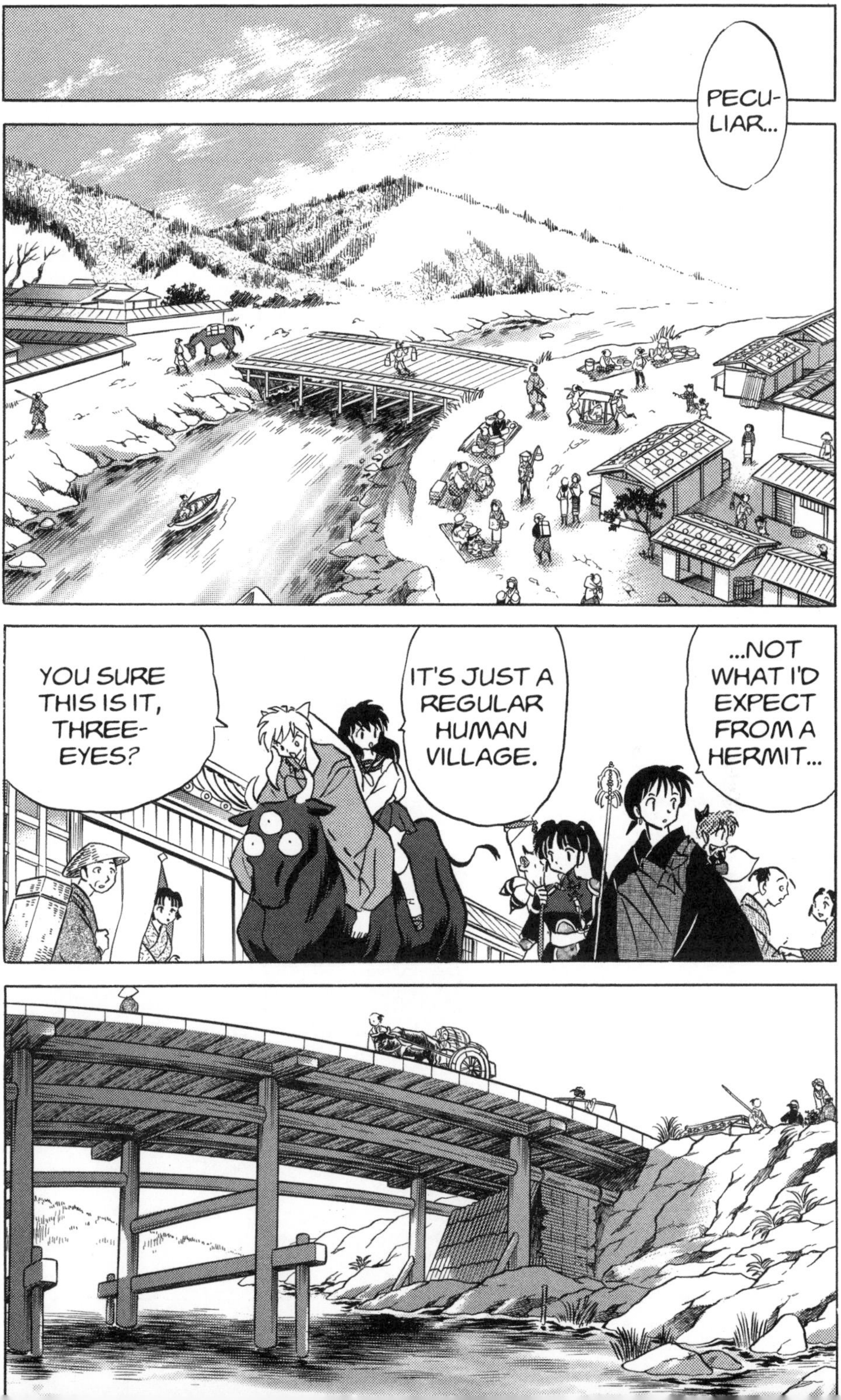
PECULIAR...
...NOT WHAT I'D EXPECT FROM A HERMIT...
IT'S JUST A REGULAR HUMAN VILLAGE.
YOU SURE THIS IS IT, THREE-EYES?

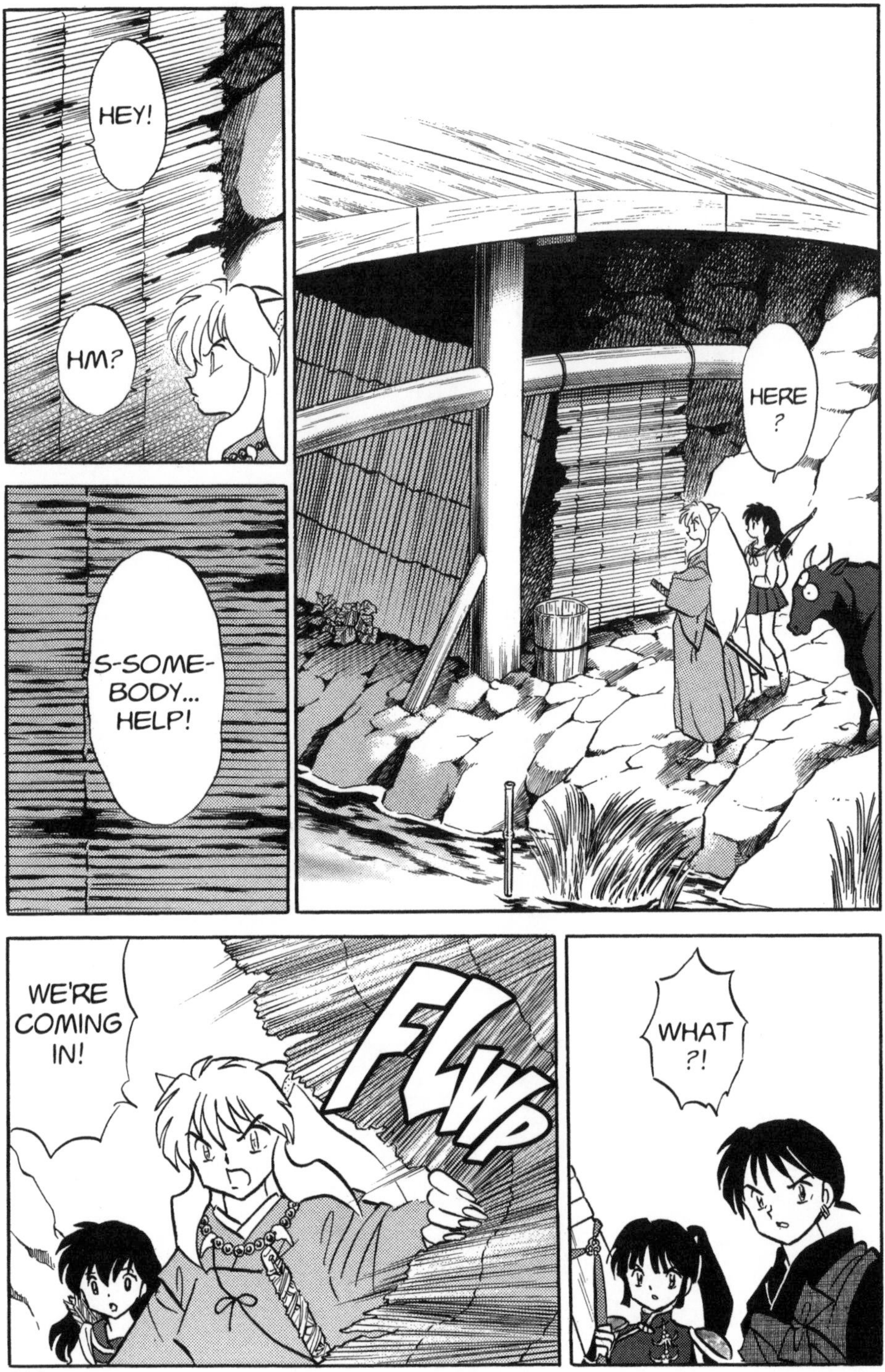
HERE?
HEY!
HM?
S-SOME-BODY... HELP!
WHAT?!
WE'RE COMING IN!
FLWP

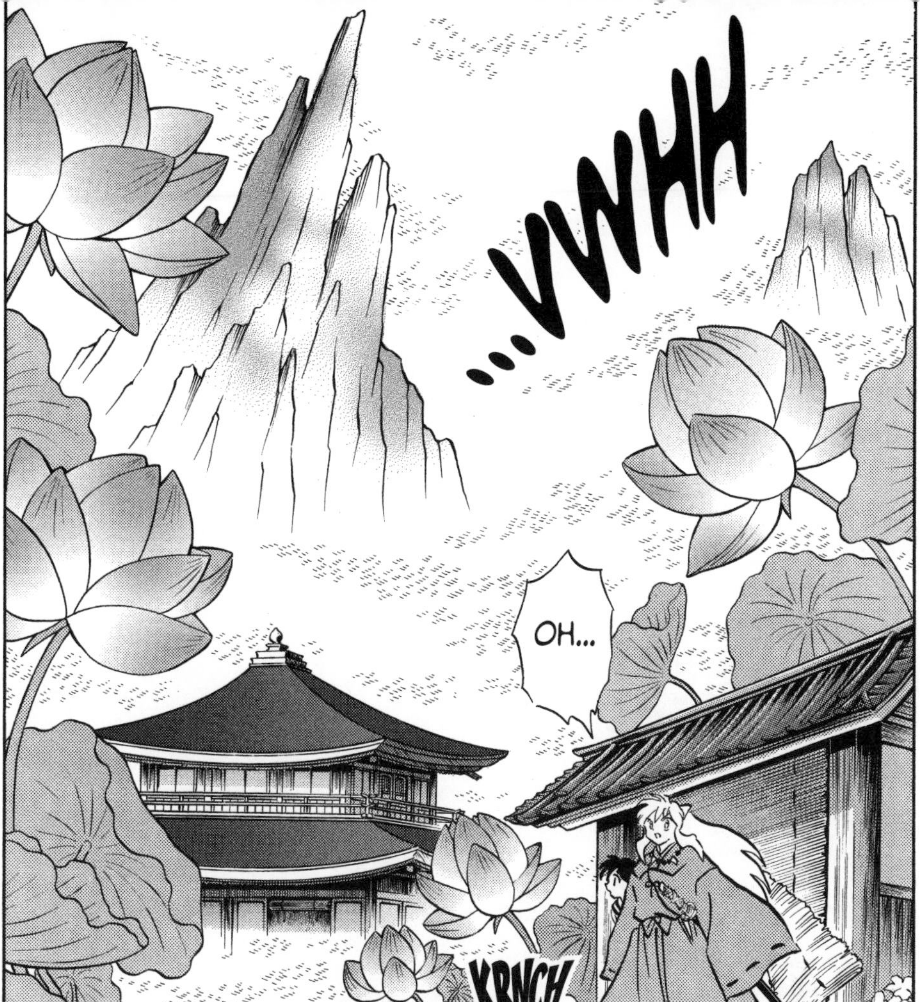
...VWHH
OH...
KRNCH
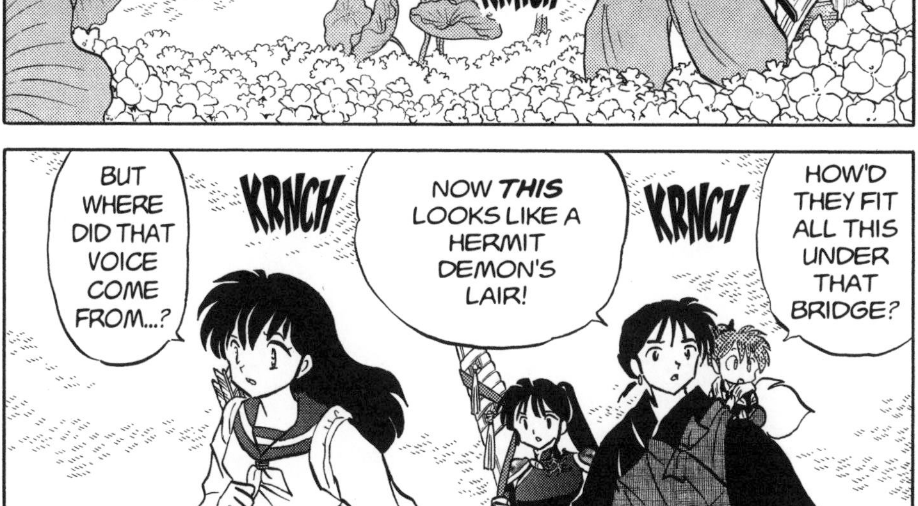
HOW'D THEY FIT ALL THIS UNDER THAT BRIDGE?
KRNCH
NOW *THIS* LOOKS LIKE A HERMIT DEMON'S LAIR!
KRNCH
BUT WHERE DID THAT VOICE COME FROM...?

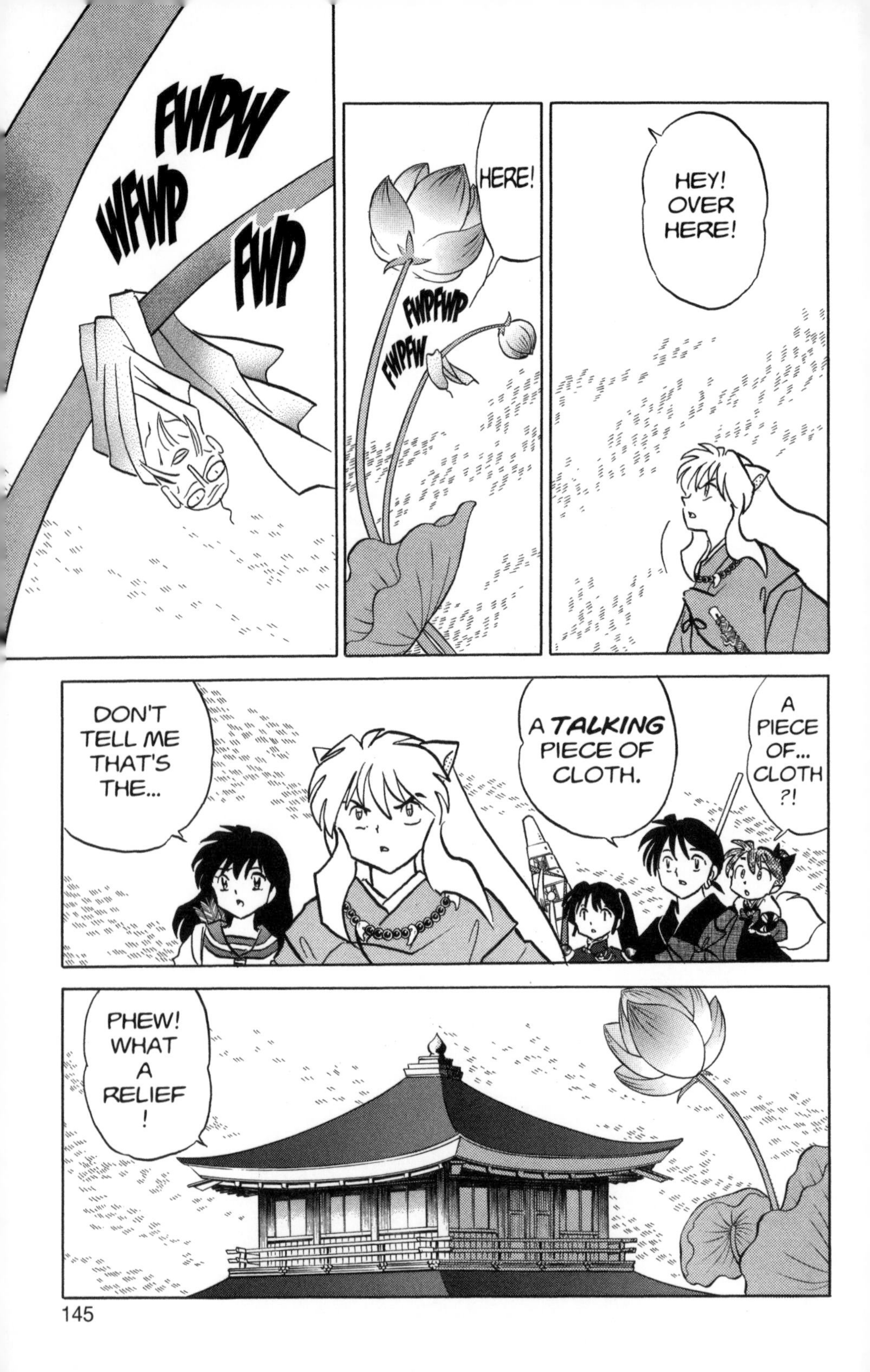
HEY! OVER HERE!
HERE!
FWPFWP
FWPFW
FWPW
WFWP
FWP
A PIECE OF... CLOTH ?!
A *TALKING* PIECE OF CLOTH.
DON'T TELL ME THAT'S THE...
PHEW! WHAT A RELIEF!

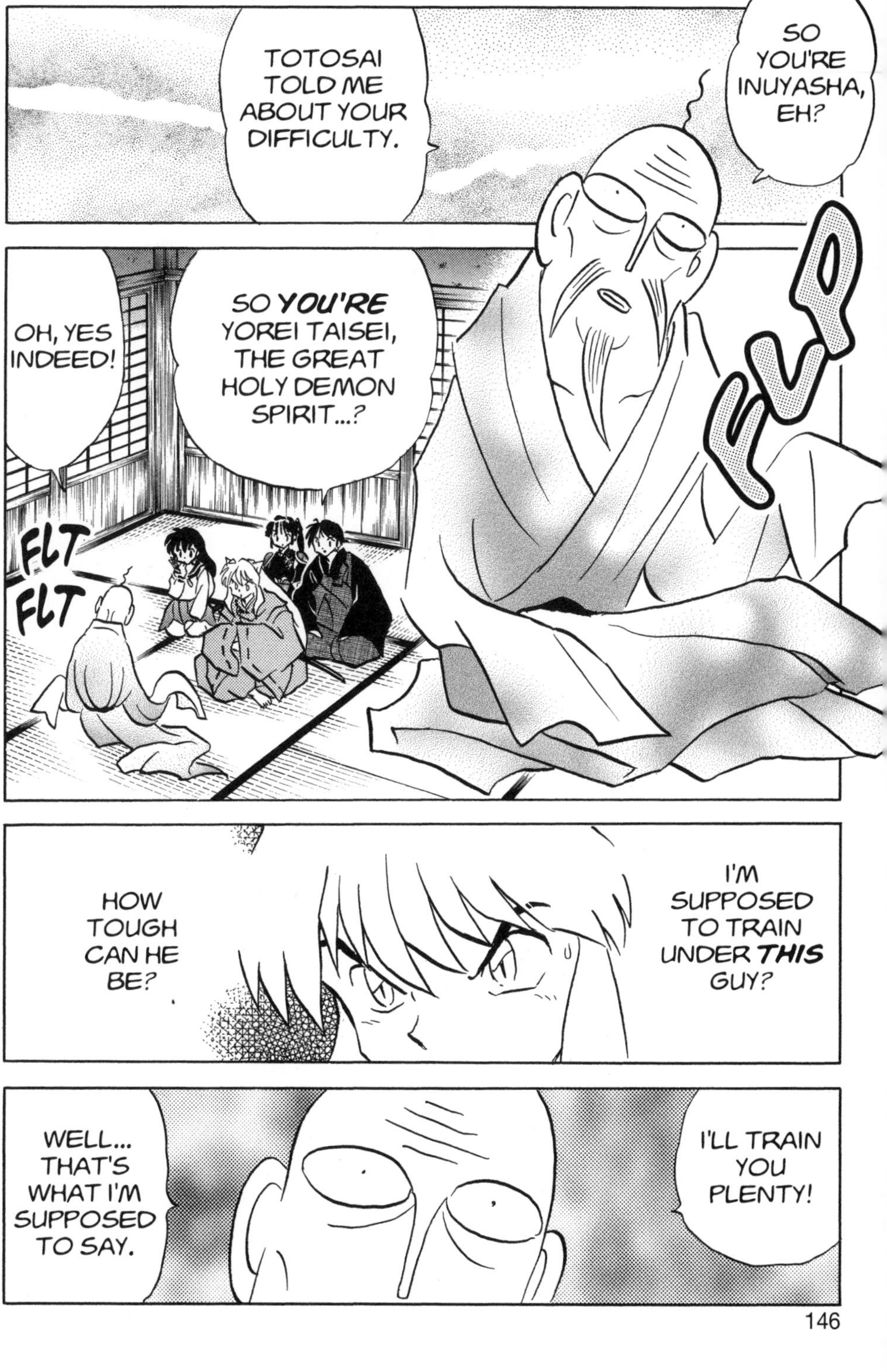
SO YOU'RE INUYASHA, EH?
TOTOSAI TOLD ME ABOUT YOUR DIFFICULTY.
FLOP
SO **YOU'RE** YOREI TAISEI, THE GREAT HOLY DEMON SPIRIT...?
OH, YES INDEED!
FLT FLT
I'M SUPPOSED TO TRAIN UNDER **THIS** GUY?
HOW TOUGH CAN HE BE?
I'LL TRAIN YOU PLENTY!
WELL... THAT'S WHAT I'M SUPPOSED TO SAY.

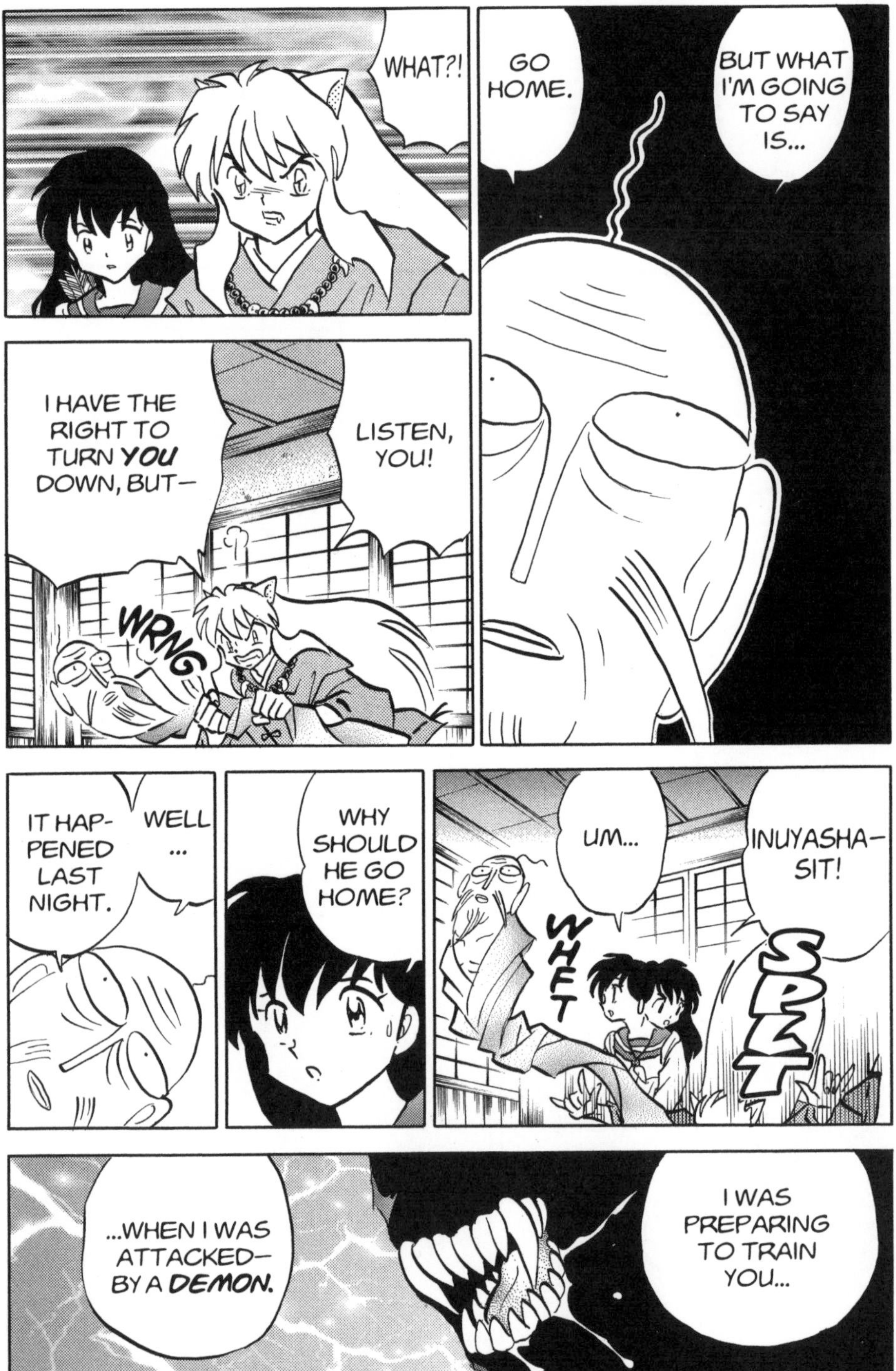
BUT WHAT I'M GOING TO SAY IS...
GO HOME.
WHAT?!
LISTEN, YOU!
I HAVE THE RIGHT TO TURN **YOU** DOWN, BUT—
WRNG
INUYASHA-SIT!
SPLT
UM...
WHFT
WHY SHOULD HE GO HOME?
WELL...
IT HAPPENED LAST NIGHT.
I WAS PREPARING TO TRAIN YOU...
...WHEN I WAS ATTACKED—BY A **DEMON**.

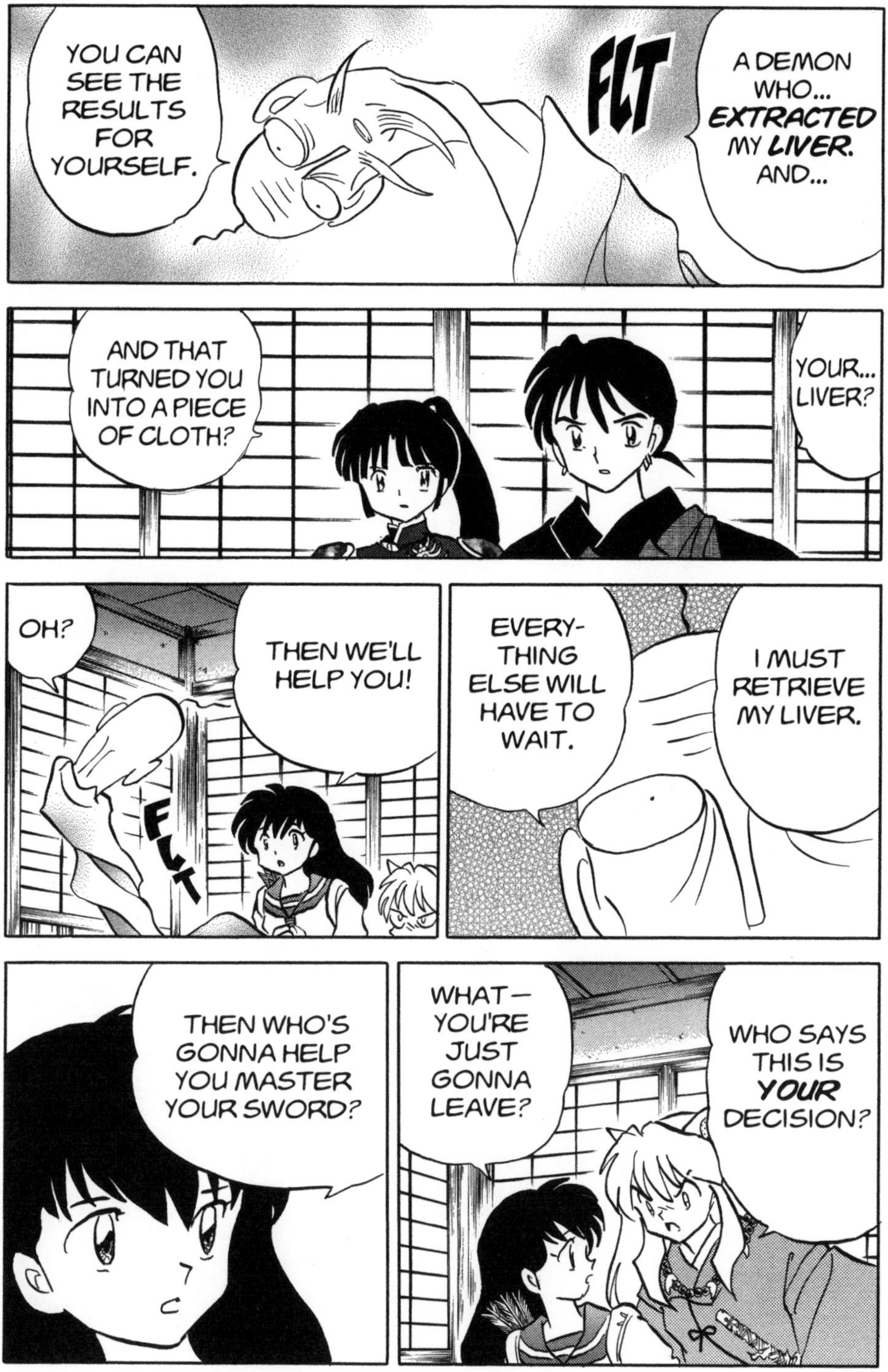
A DEMON WHO... EXTRACTED MY LIVER. AND...
FLT
YOU CAN SEE THE RESULTS FOR YOURSELF.
YOUR... LIVER?
AND THAT TURNED YOU INTO A PIECE OF CLOTH?
I MUST RETRIEVE MY LIVER.
EVERY-THING ELSE WILL HAVE TO WAIT.
THEN WE'LL HELP YOU!
OH?
FLT
WHO SAYS THIS IS YOUR DECISION?
WHAT— YOU'RE JUST GONNA LEAVE?
THEN WHO'S GONNA HELP YOU MASTER YOUR SWORD?

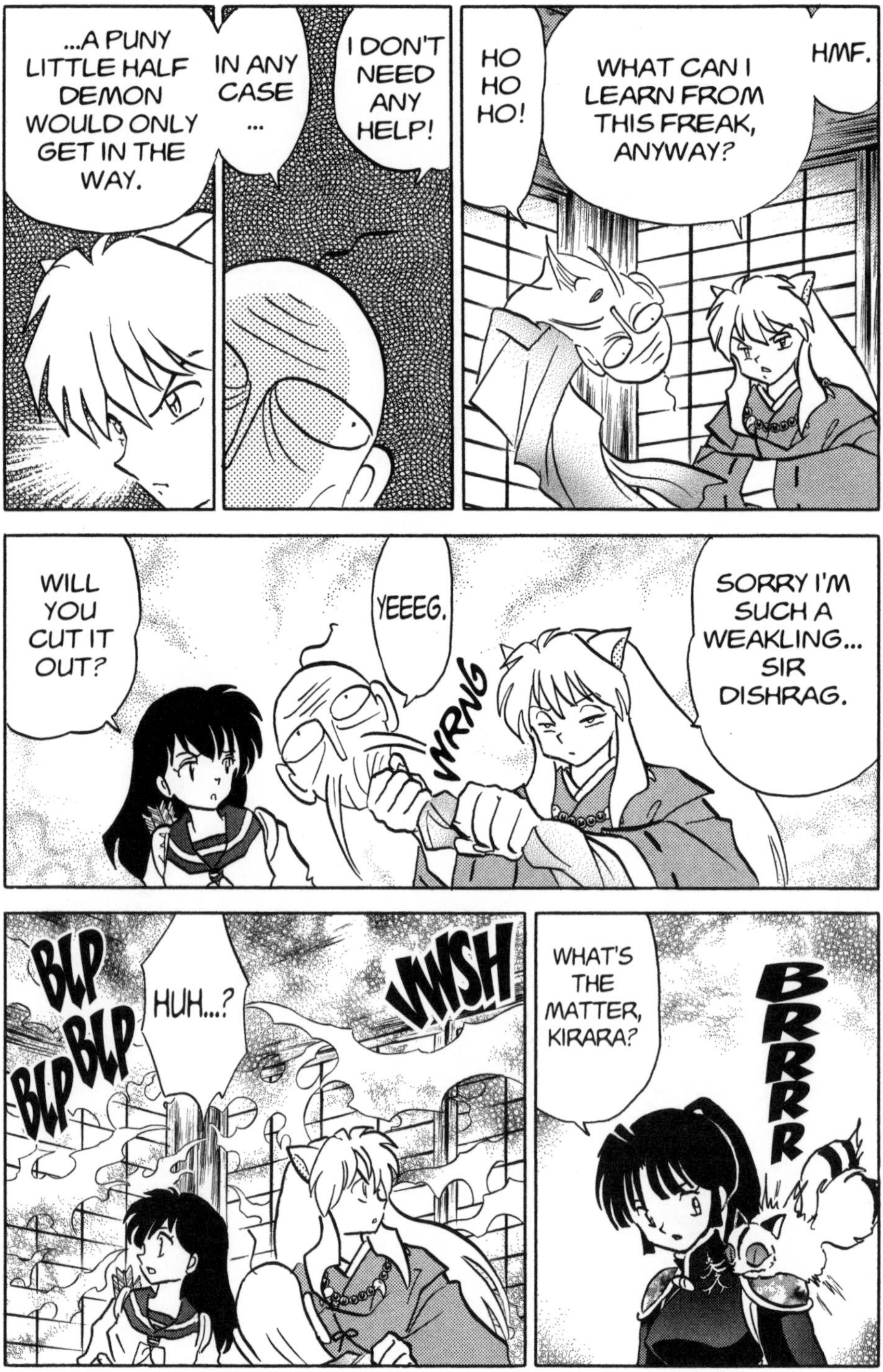
HMF.
WHAT CAN I LEARN FROM THIS FREAK, ANYWAY?
HO HO HO!
I DON'T NEED ANY HELP!
IN ANY CASE ...
...A PUNY LITTLE HALF DEMON WOULD ONLY GET IN THE WAY.
SORRY I'M SUCH A WEAKLING... SIR DISHRAG.
WRNG
YEEEG.
WILL YOU CUT IT OUT?
BRRRR
WHAT'S THE MATTER, KIRARA?
VWSH
HUH...?
BLP BLP
BLP BLP

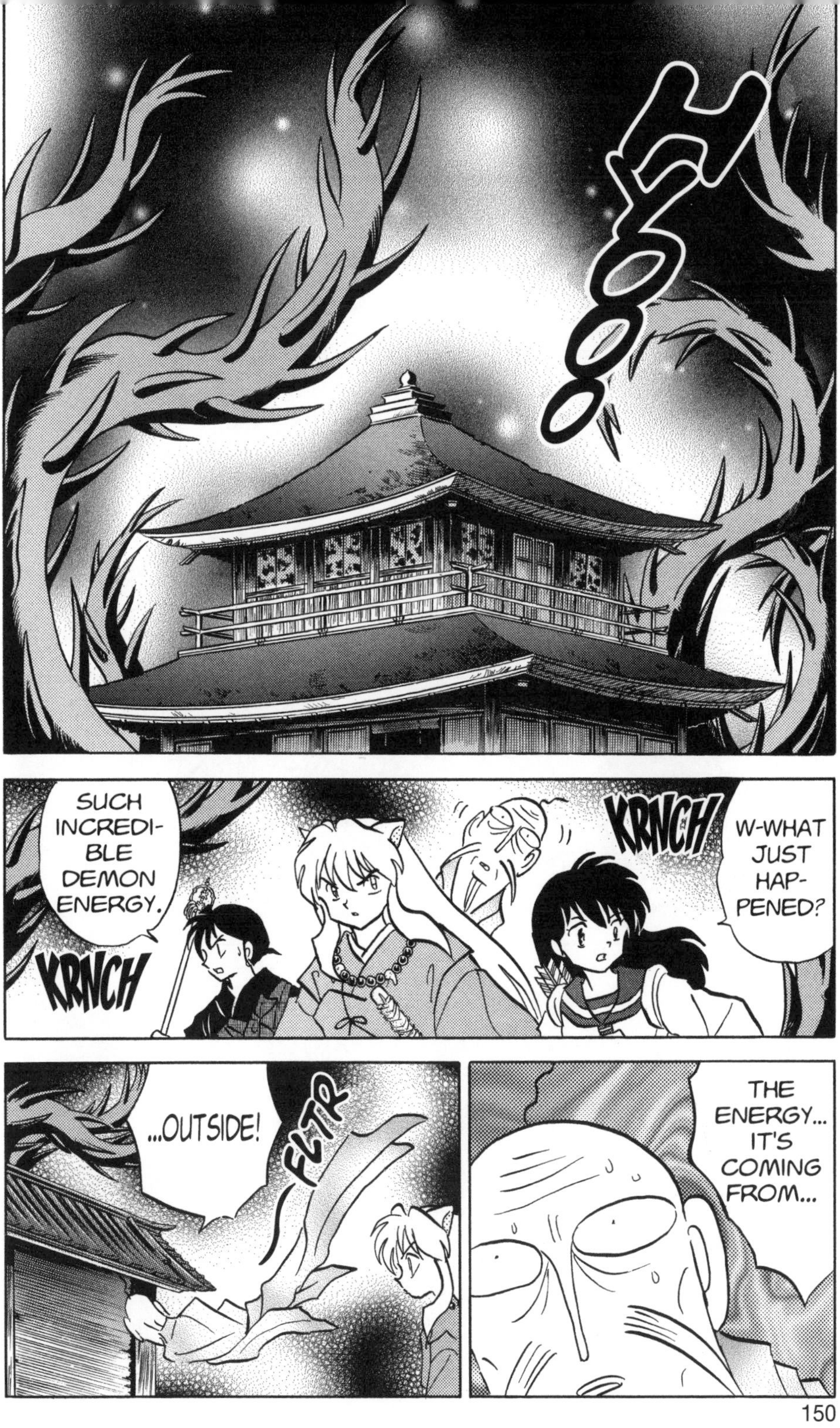
KRNCH
W-WHAT JUST HAP-PENED?
SUCH INCREDI-BLE DEMON ENERGY.
KRNCH
THE ENERGY... IT'S COMING FROM...
...OUTSIDE!
FLTR

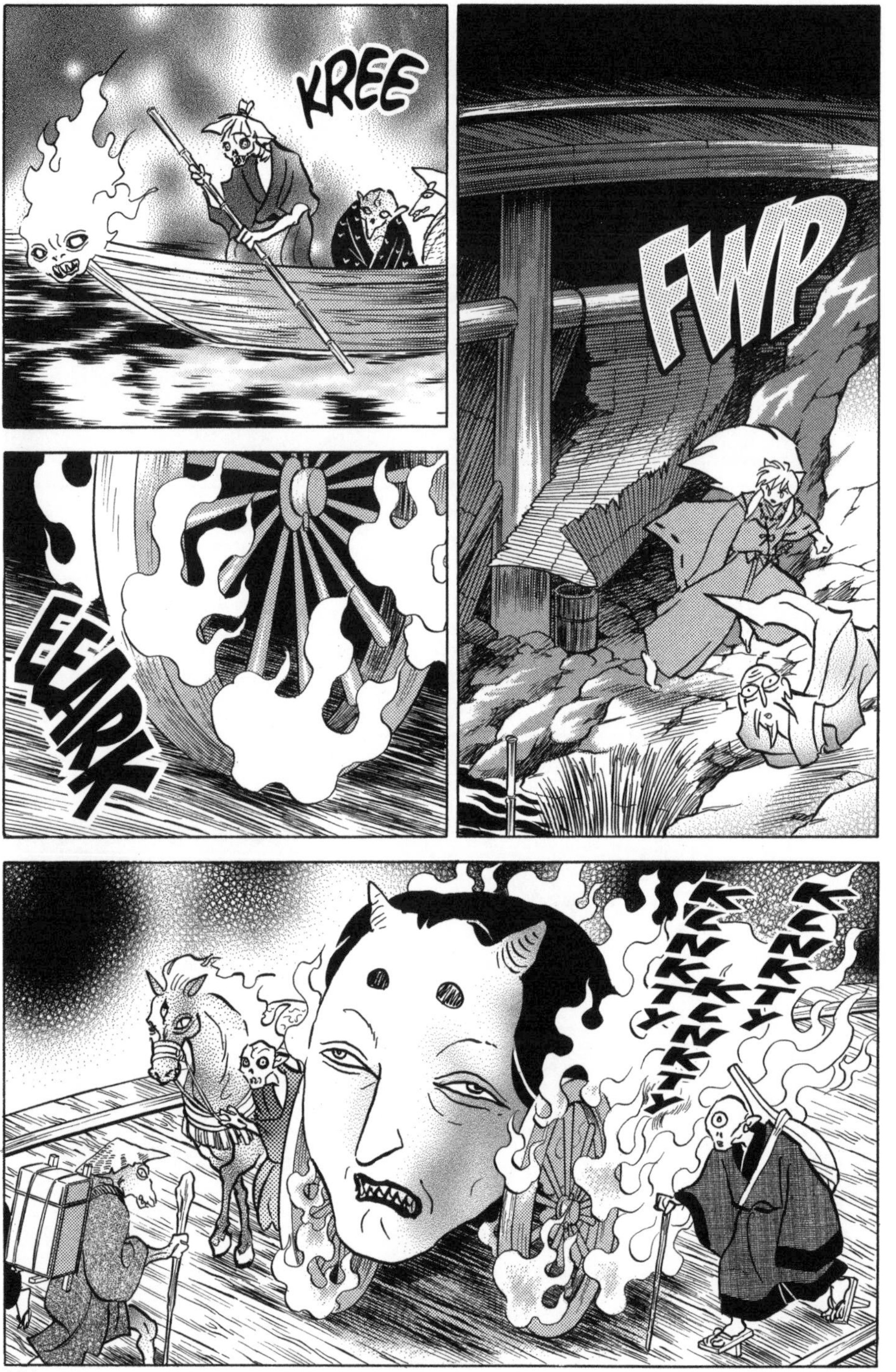
FWP
KREE
EEARK
KENKTY
KENKTY
KENKTY

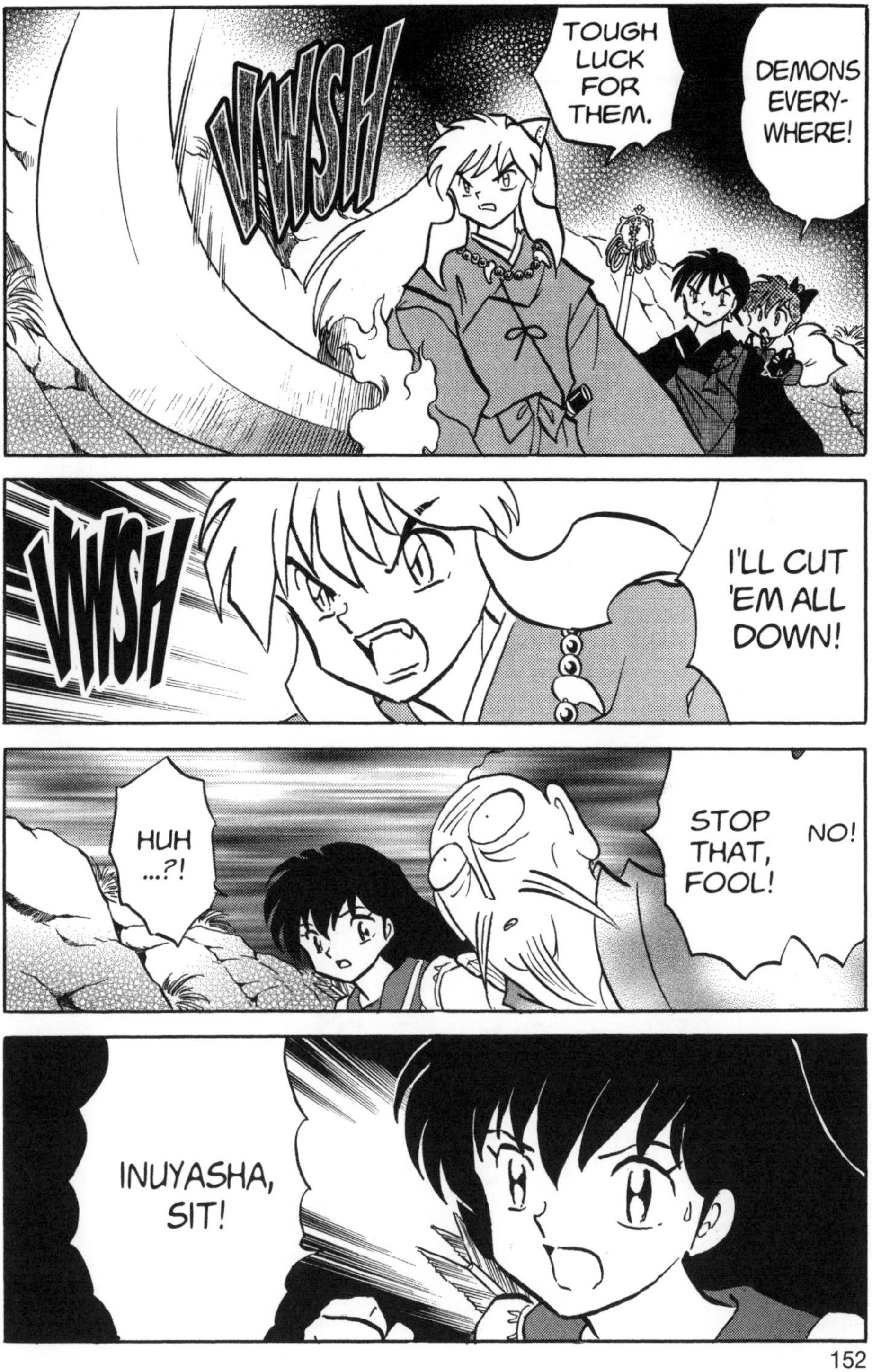
DEMONS EVERY-WHERE!
TOUGH LUCK FOR THEM.
VWSH
I'LL CUT 'EM ALL DOWN!
VWSH
NO!
STOP THAT, FOOL!
HUH ...?!
INUYASHA, SIT!

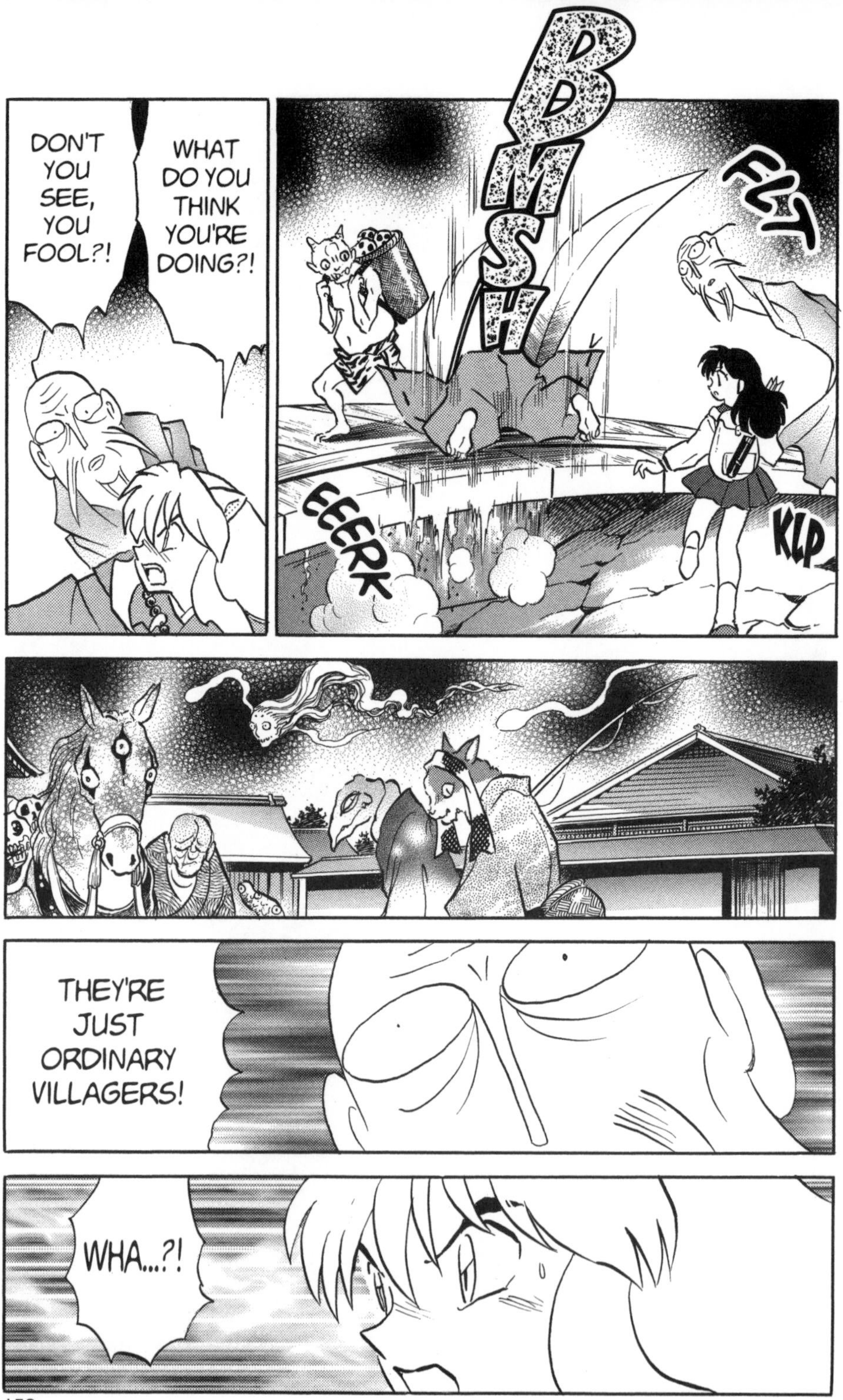
BMSH
FLIT
KLP
EEERK
WHAT DO YOU THINK YOU'RE DOING?!
DON'T YOU SEE, YOU FOOL?!
THEY'RE JUST ORDINARY VILLAGERS!
WHA...?!

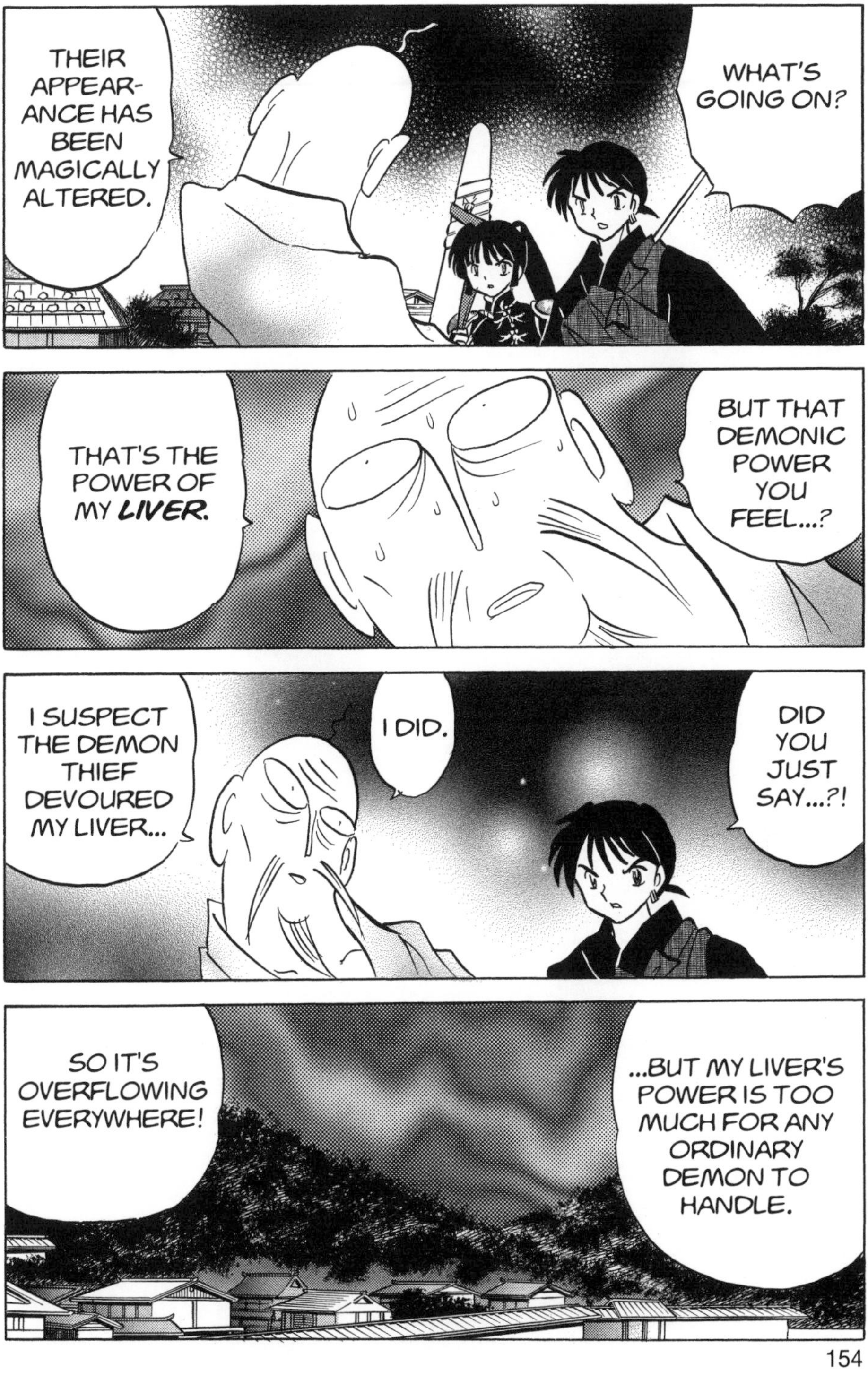
WHAT'S GOING ON?
THEIR APPEARANCE HAS BEEN MAGICALLY ALTERED.
BUT THAT DEMONIC POWER YOU FEEL...?
THAT'S THE POWER OF MY ***LIVER***.
DID YOU JUST SAY...?!
I DID.
I SUSPECT THE DEMON THIEF DEVOURED MY LIVER...
...BUT MY LIVER'S POWER IS TOO MUCH FOR ANY ORDINARY DEMON TO HANDLE.
SO IT'S OVERFLOWING EVERYWHERE!

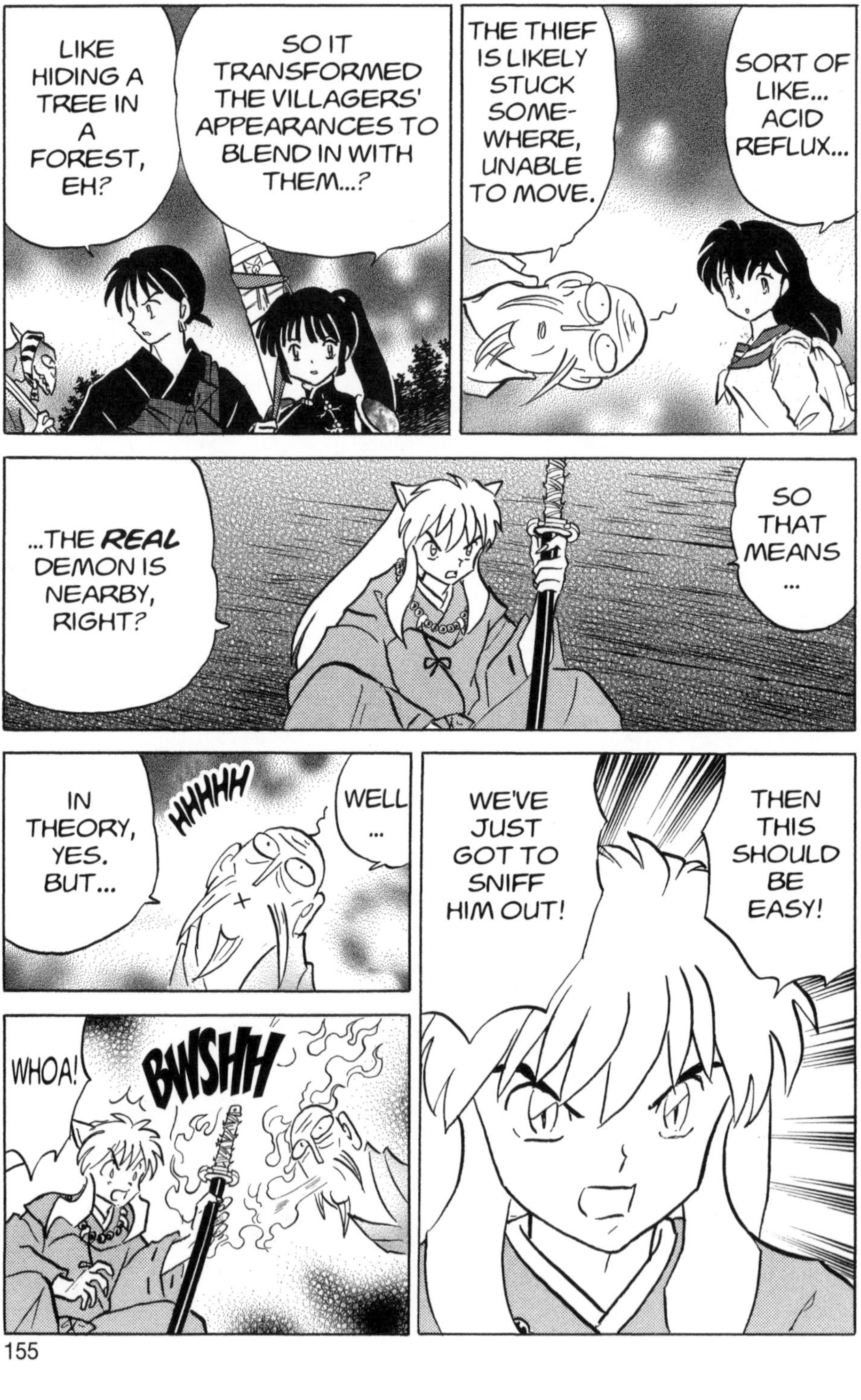
SORT OF LIKE... ACID REFLUX...
THE THIEF IS LIKELY STUCK SOME- WHERE, UNABLE TO MOVE.
SO IT TRANSFORMED THE VILLAGERS' APPEARANCES TO BLEND IN WITH THEM...?
LIKE HIDING A TREE IN A FOREST, EH?
SO THAT MEANS ...
...THE ***REAL*** DEMON IS NEARBY, RIGHT?
THEN THIS SHOULD BE EASY!
WE'VE JUST GOT TO SNIFF HIM OUT!
WELL ...
HHHHH
IN THEORY, YES. BUT...
BWSHH
WHOA!

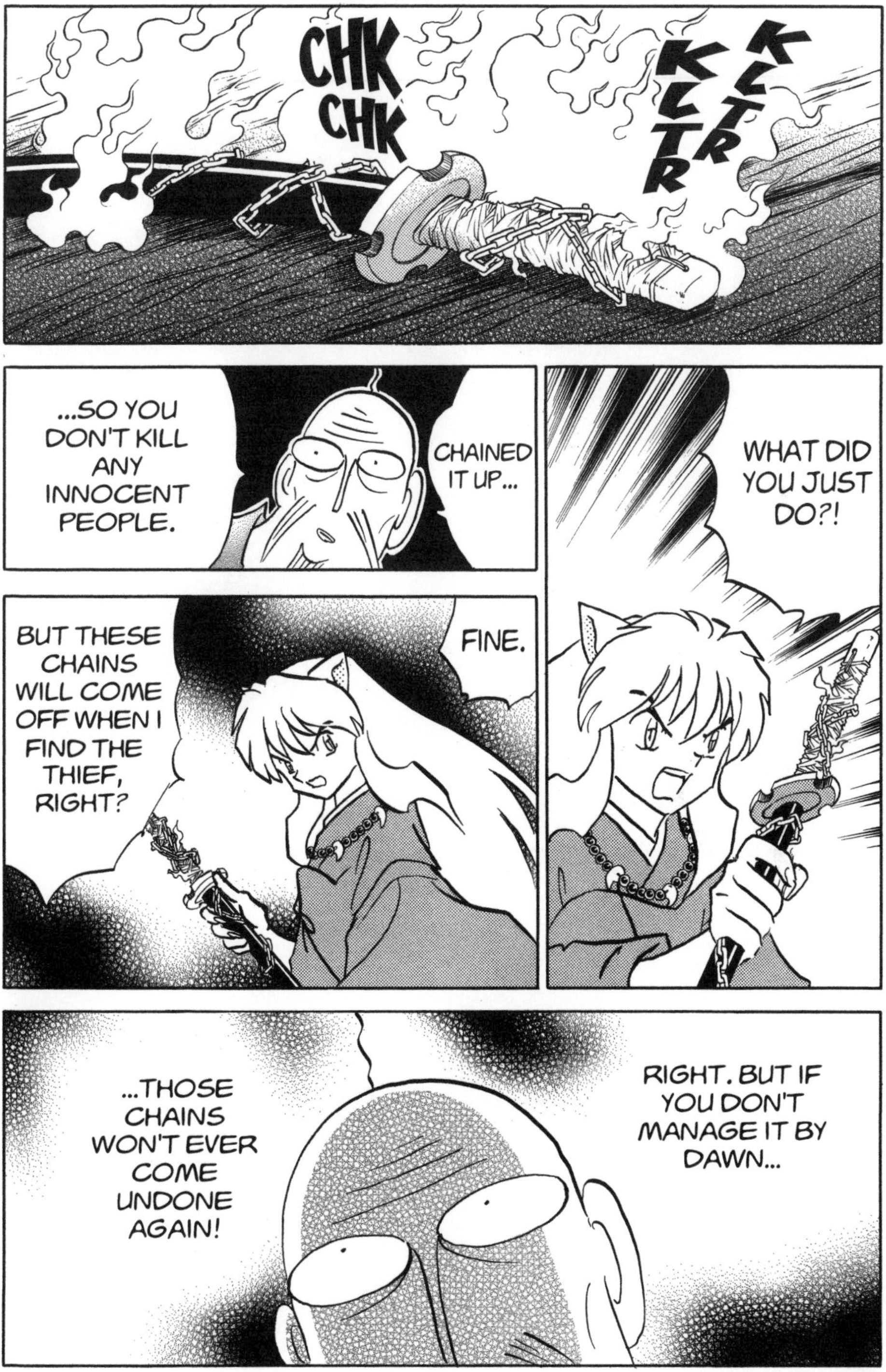
KLTR
KLTR
CHK CHK
WHAT DID YOU JUST DO?!
CHAINED IT UP...
...SO YOU DON'T KILL ANY INNOCENT PEOPLE.
FINE.
BUT THESE CHAINS WILL COME OFF WHEN I FIND THE THIEF, RIGHT?
RIGHT. BUT IF YOU DON'T MANAGE IT BY DAWN...
...THOSE CHAINS WON'T EVER COME UNDONE AGAIN!

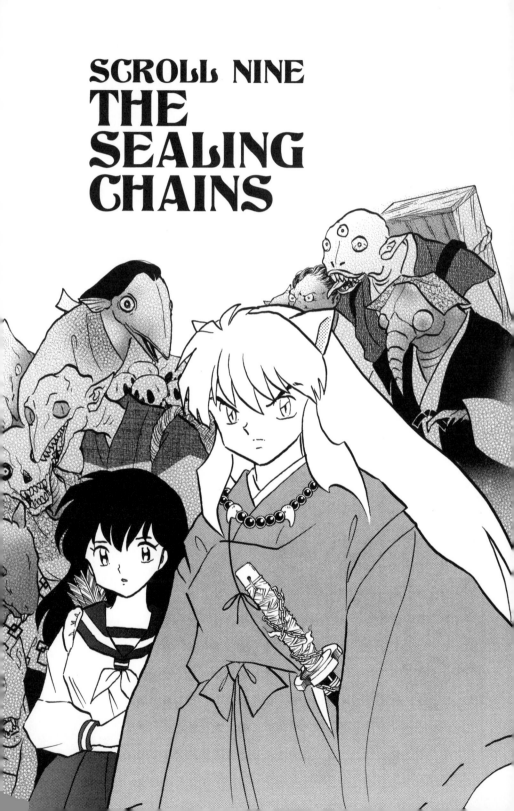

SCROLL NINE
THE SEALING CHAINS

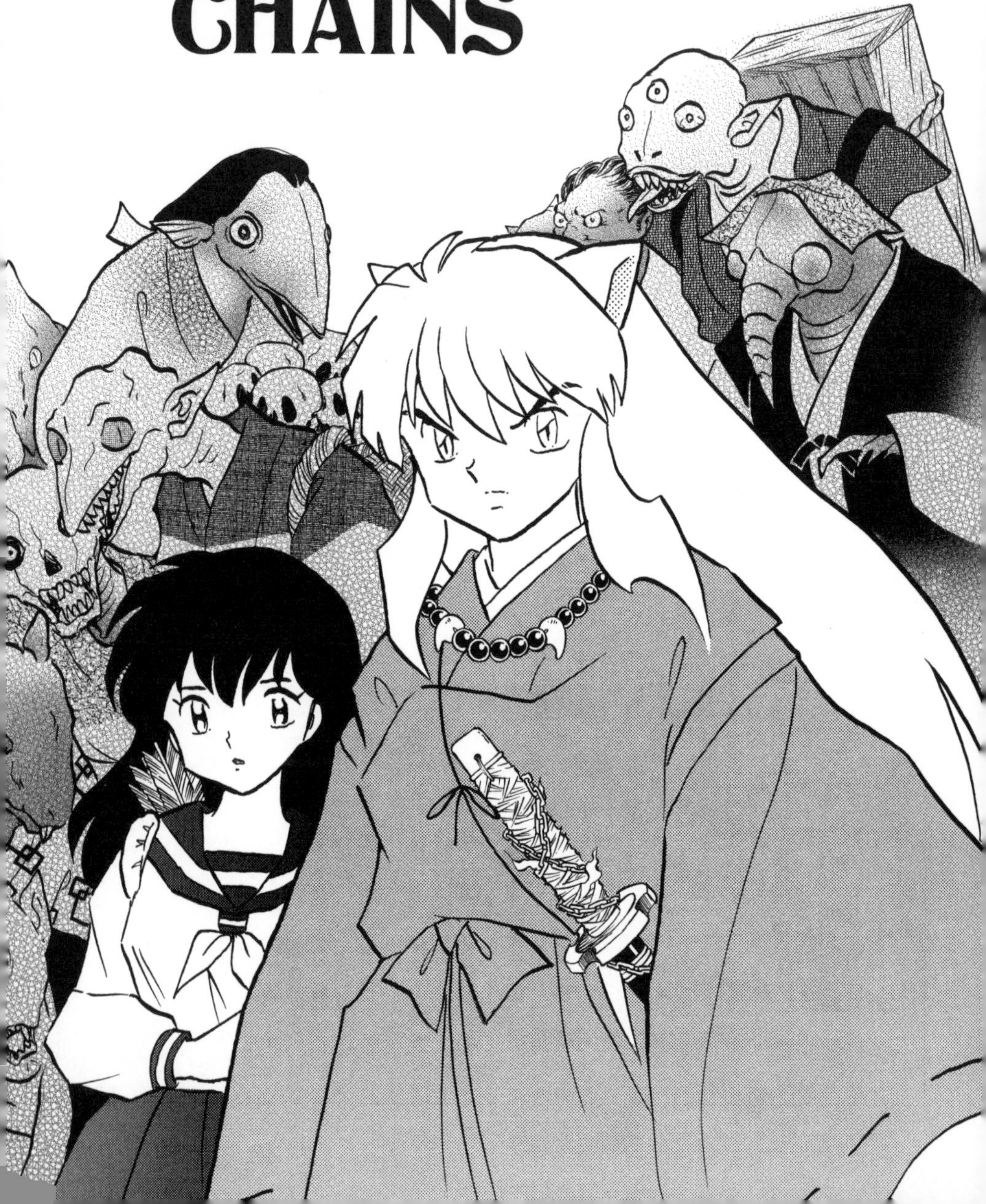

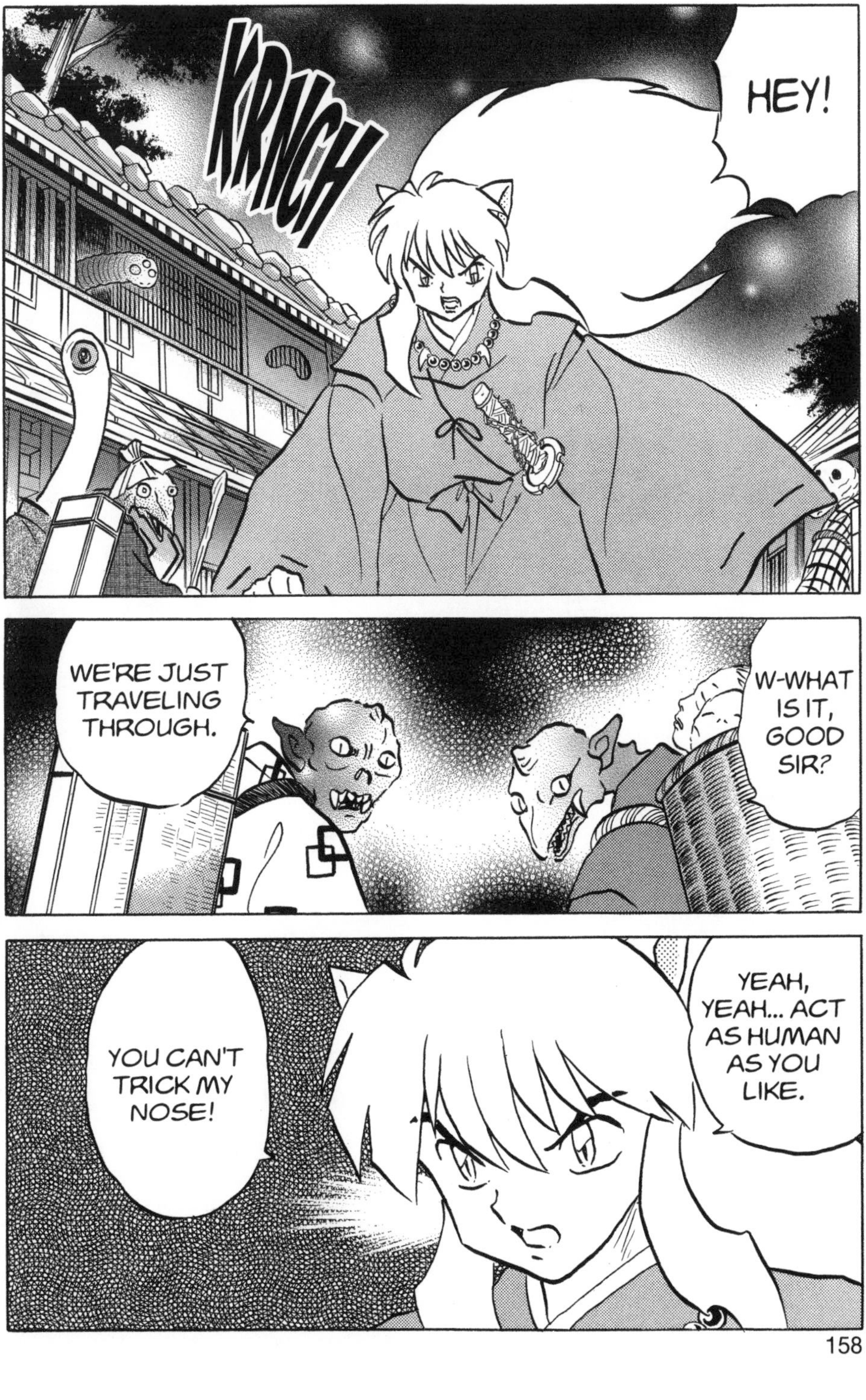
HEY!
KRNCH
W-WHAT IS IT, GOOD SIR?
WE'RE JUST TRAVELING THROUGH.
YEAH, YEAH... ACT AS HUMAN AS YOU LIKE.
YOU CAN'T TRICK MY NOSE!

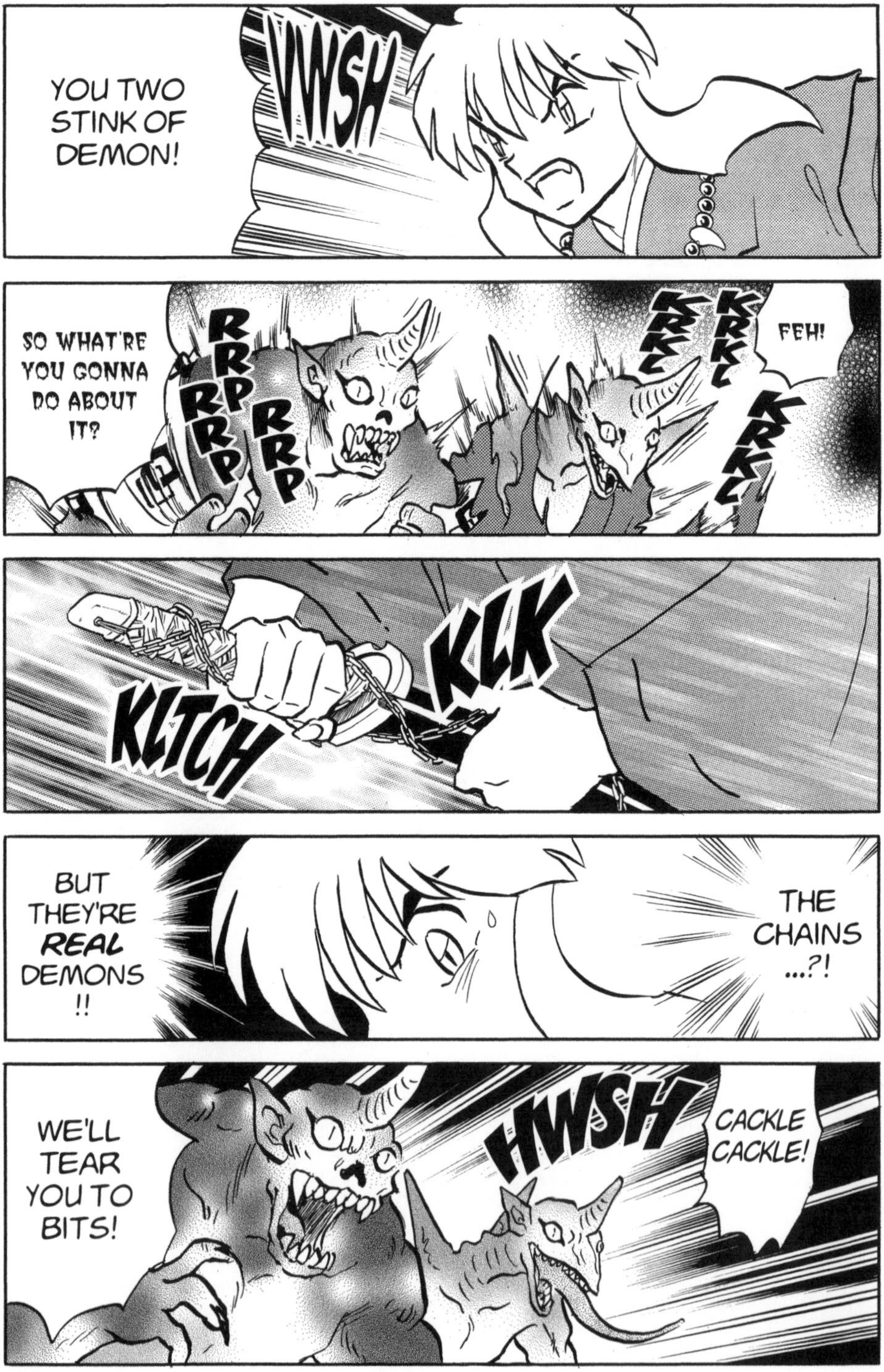
VWSH
YOU TWO STINK OF DEMON!
FEH!
KRKL
KRKL
KRKL
SO WHAT'RE YOU GONNA DO ABOUT IT?
RRP
RRRP
RRP
KLK
KLTCH
THE CHAINS ...?!
BUT THEY'RE ***REAL*** DEMONS !!
CACKLE CACKLE!
HWSH
WE'LL TEAR YOU TO BITS!

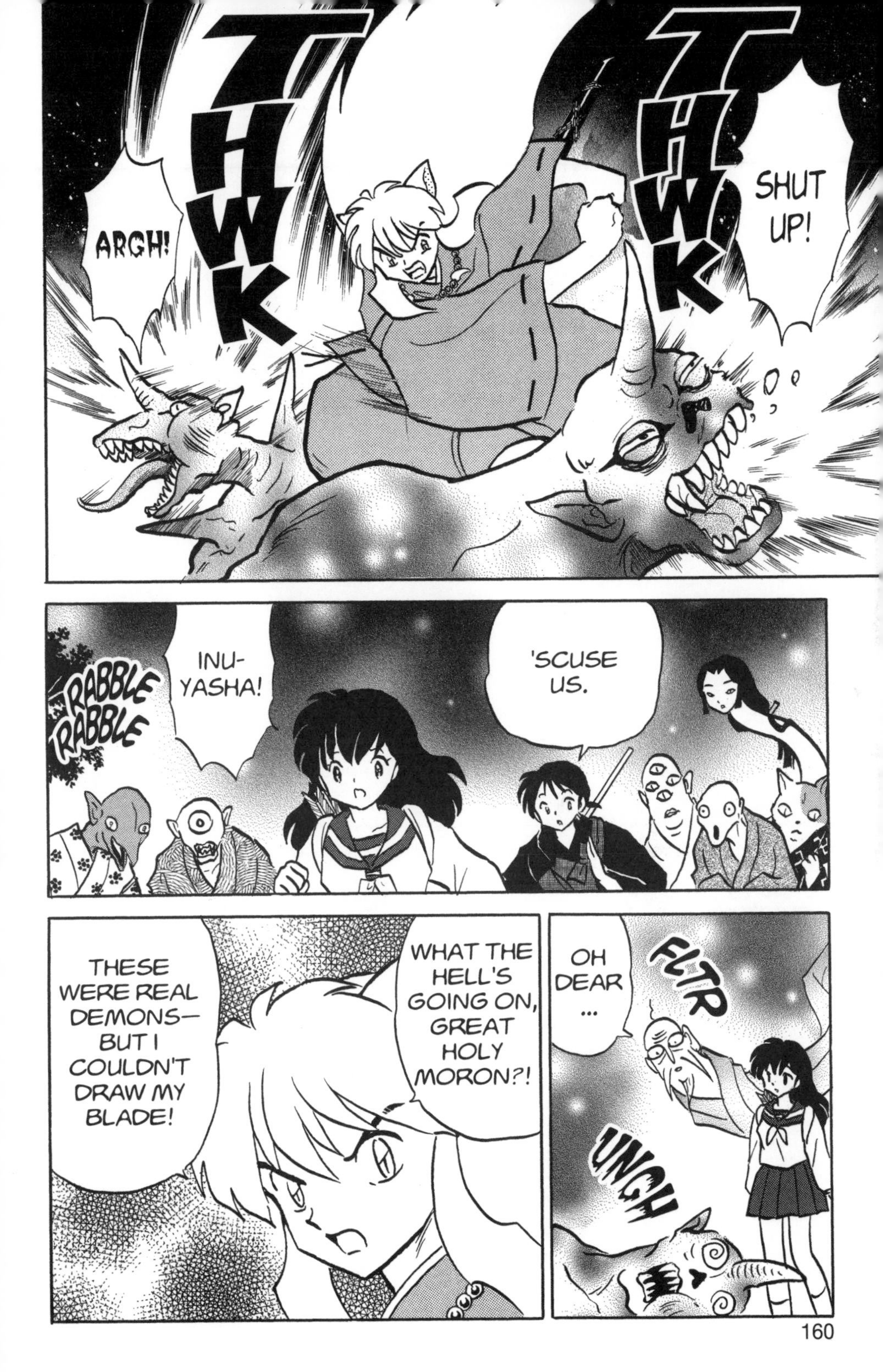
THWK
SHUT UP!
THWK
ARGH!
'SCUSE US.
INU-YASHA!
RABBLE RABBLE
OH DEAR ...
FLTR
UNGH
WHAT THE HELL'S GOING ON, GREAT HOLY MORON?!
THESE WERE REAL DEMONS— BUT I COULDN'T DRAW MY BLADE!

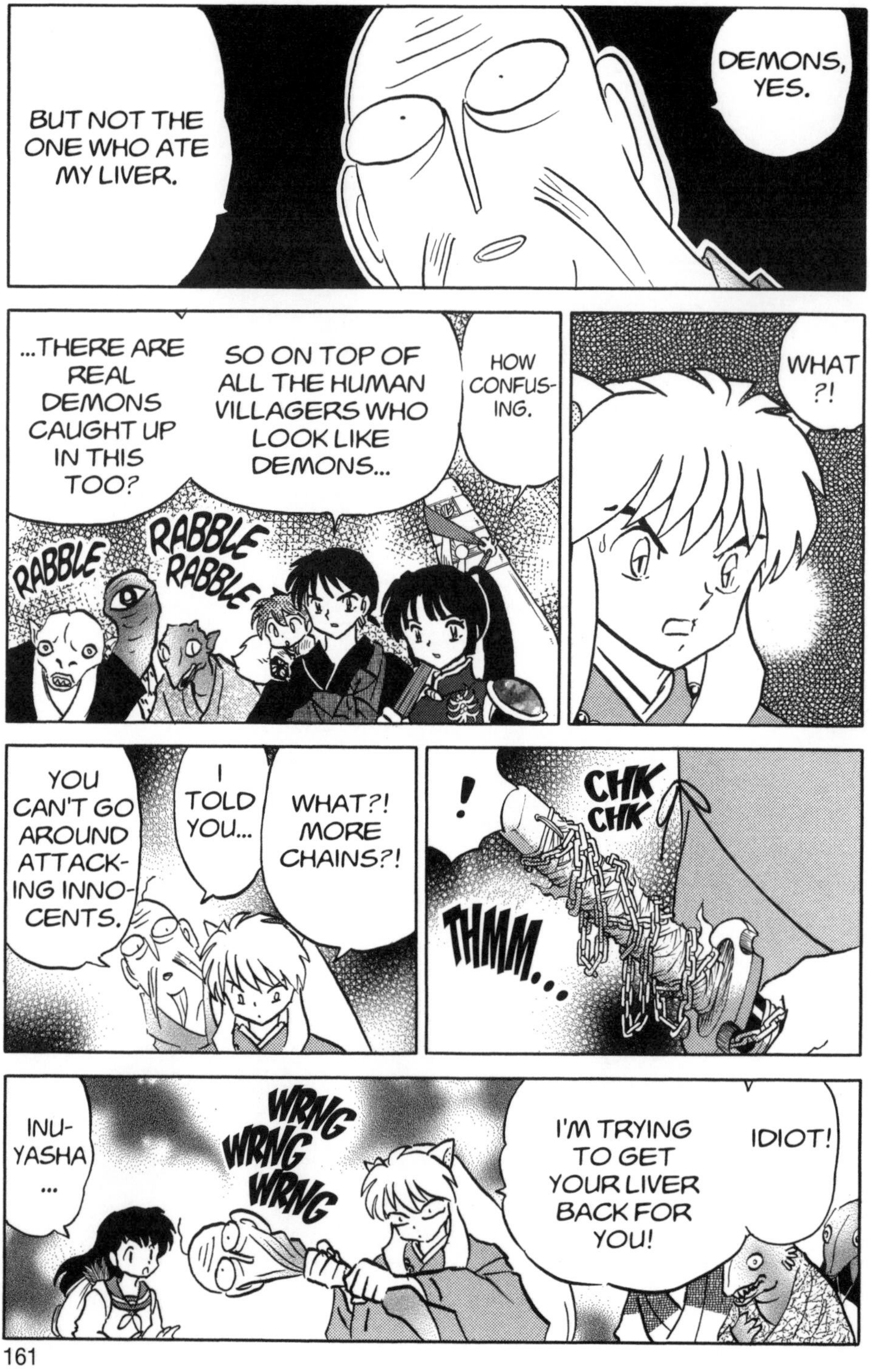
DEMONS, YES.
BUT NOT THE ONE WHO ATE MY LIVER.
WHAT ?!
HOW CONFUSING.
SO ON TOP OF ALL THE HUMAN VILLAGERS WHO LOOK LIKE DEMONS...
...THERE ARE REAL DEMONS CAUGHT UP IN THIS TOO?
RABBLE RABBLE
RABBLE
RABBLE
!
CHK CHK
THMM...
WHAT?! MORE CHAINS?!
I TOLD YOU...
YOU CAN'T GO AROUND ATTACKING INNOCENTS.
IDIOT!
I'M TRYING TO GET YOUR LIVER BACK FOR YOU!
WRNG WRNG WRNG
INU-YASHA...

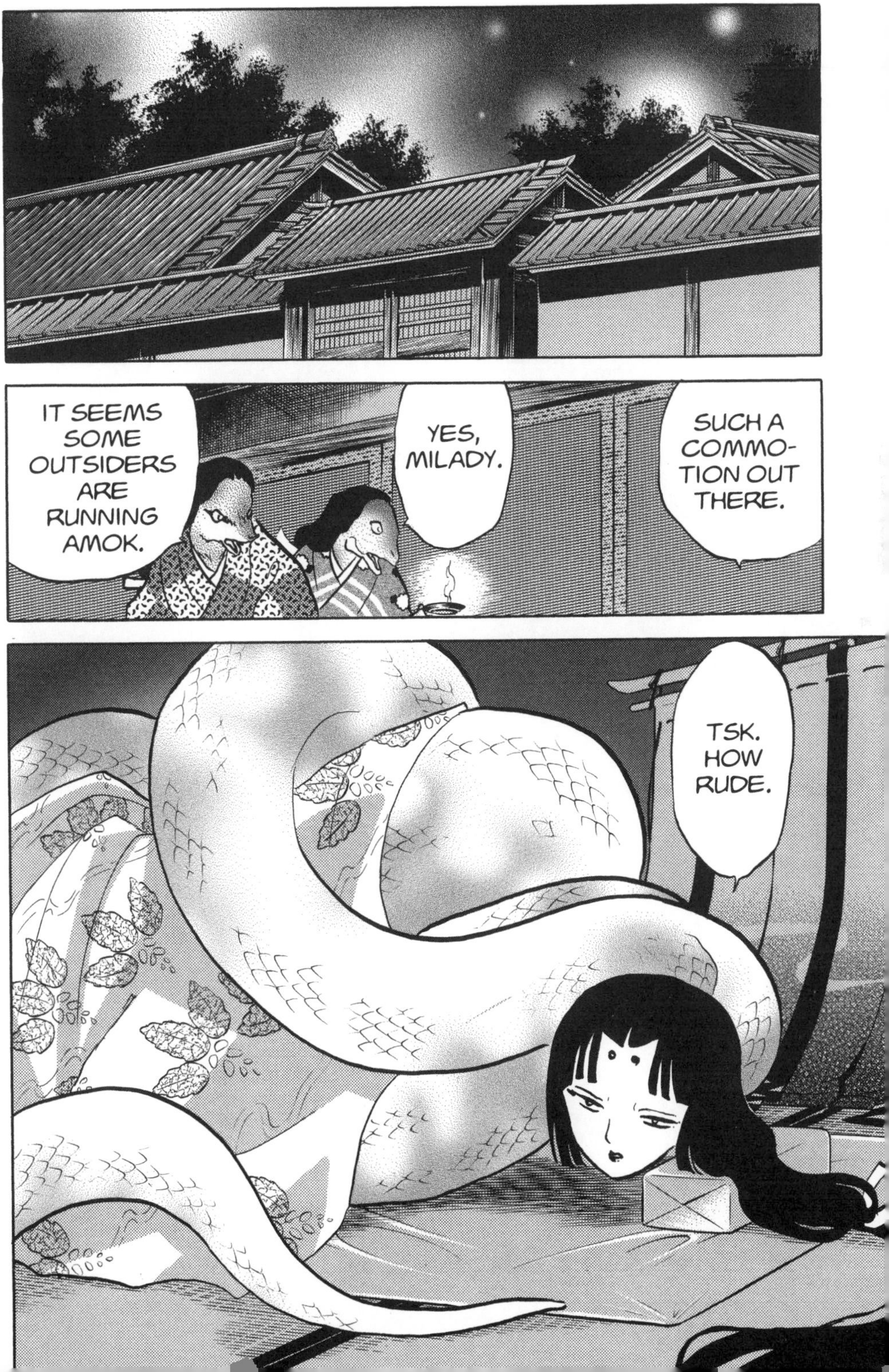
SUCH A COMMO-TION OUT THERE.
YES, MILADY.
IT SEEMS SOME OUTSIDERS ARE RUNNING AMOK.
TSK. HOW RUDE.

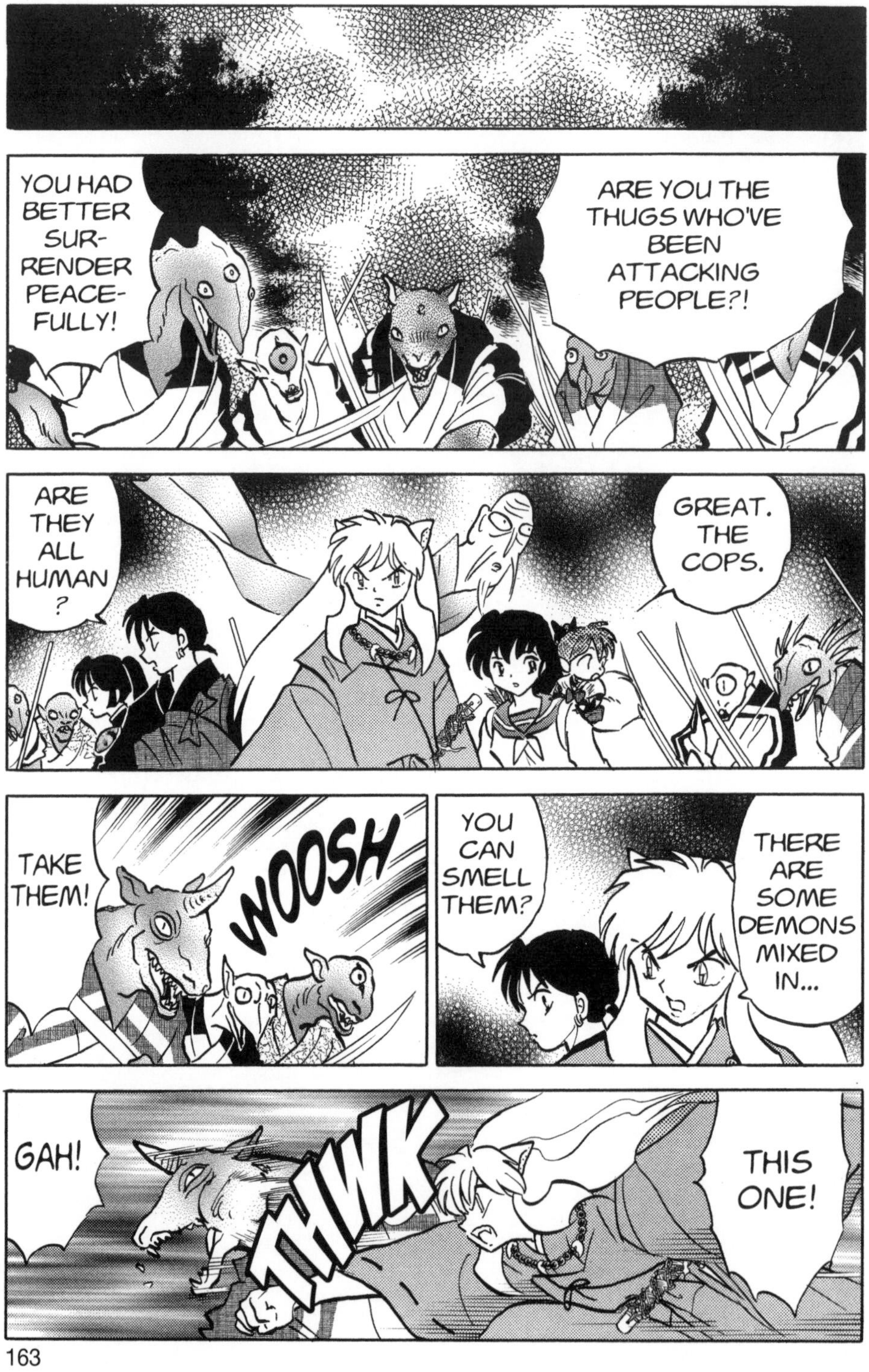
ARE YOU THE THUGS WHO'VE BEEN ATTACKING PEOPLE?!
YOU HAD BETTER SUR-RENDER PEACE-FULLY!
GREAT. THE COPS.
ARE THEY ALL HUMAN?
THERE ARE SOME DEMONS MIXED IN...
YOU CAN SMELL THEM?
TAKE THEM!
WOOSH
THIS ONE!
THWK
GAH!

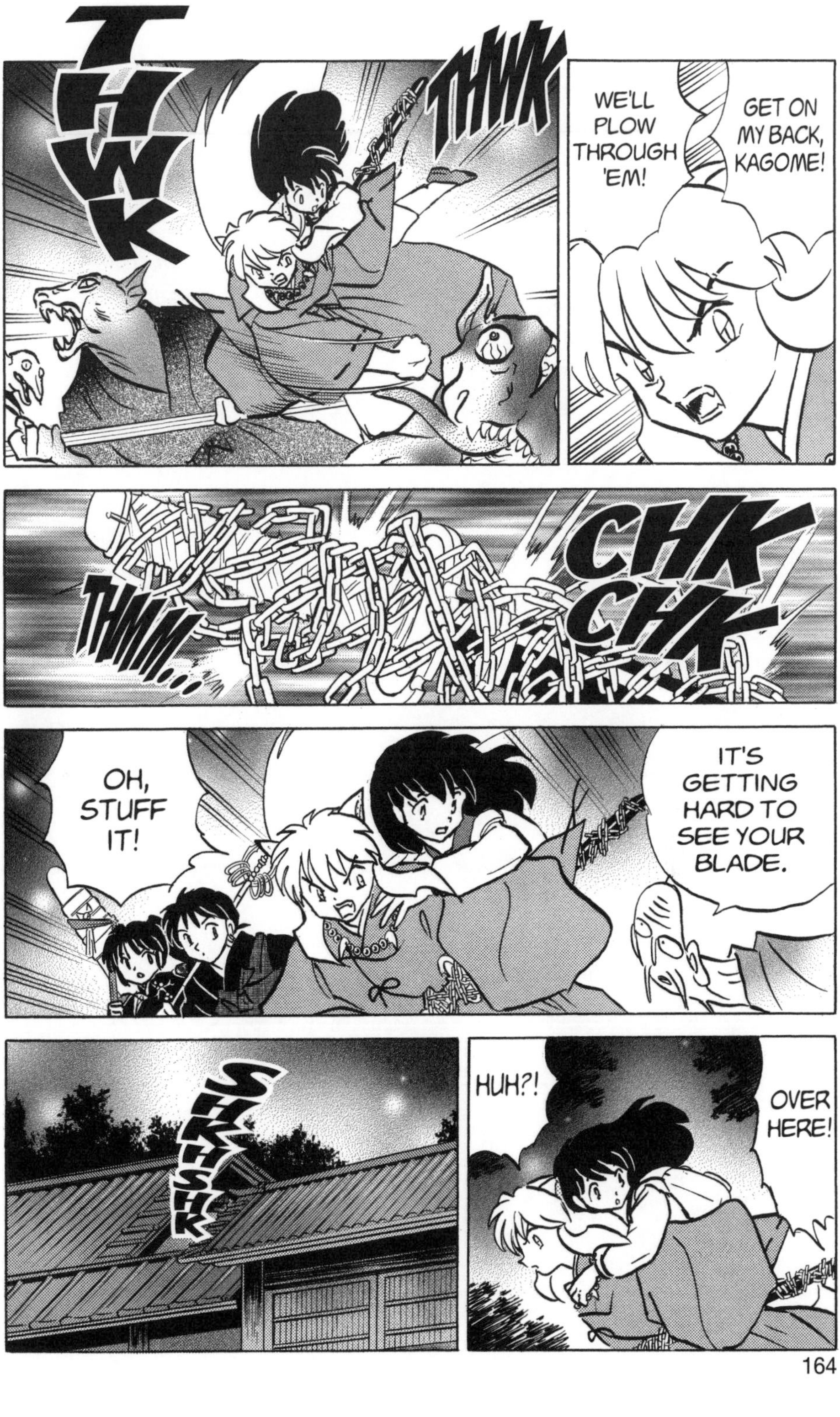

GET ON MY BACK, KAGOME!
WE'LL PLOW THROUGH 'EM!
THWK
THWK
CHK CHK
THMM...
IT'S GETTING HARD TO SEE YOUR BLADE.
OH, STUFF IT!
OVER HERE!
HUH?!
SHKSHK

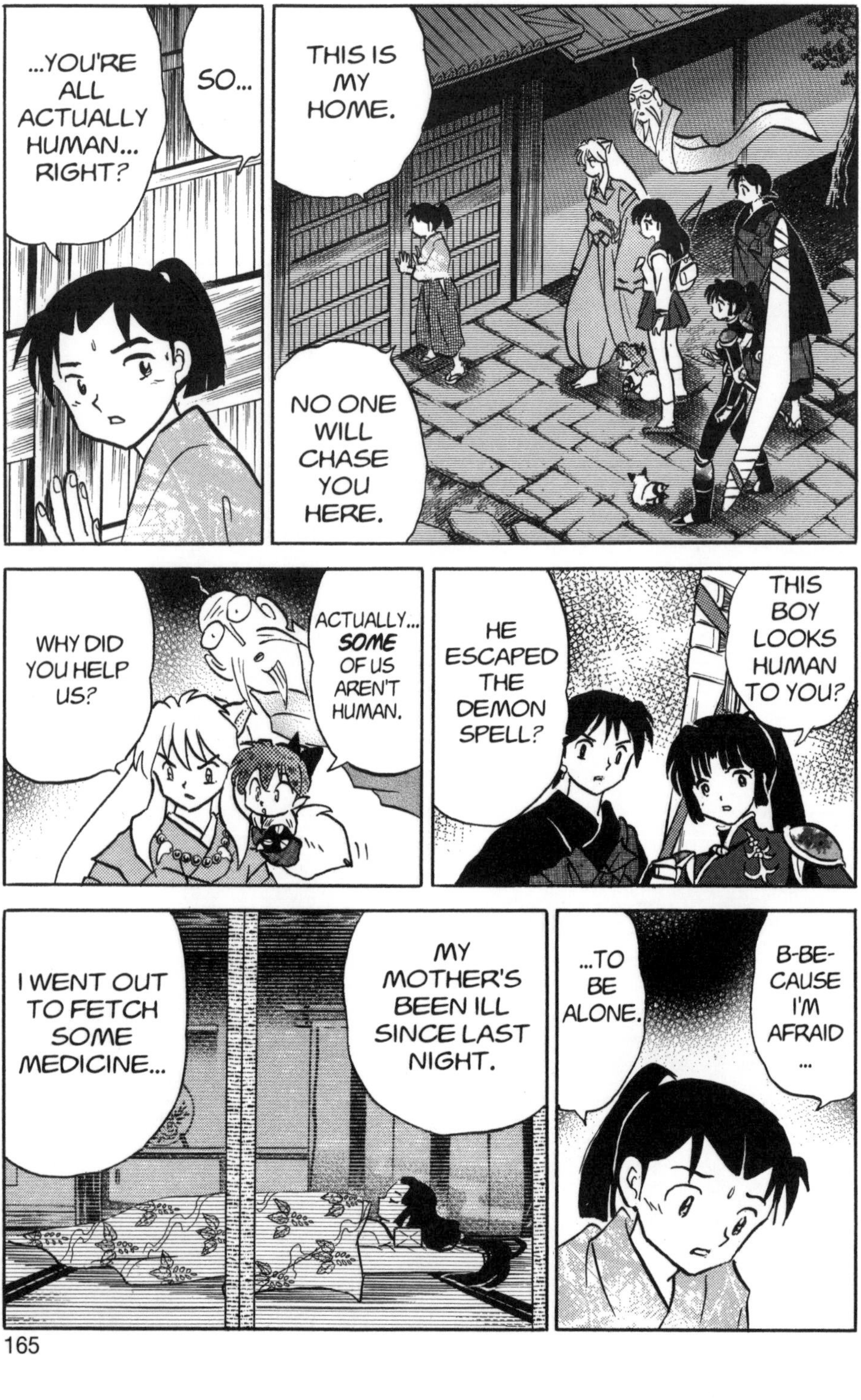
THIS IS MY HOME.
NO ONE WILL CHASE YOU HERE.
SO...
...YOU'RE ALL ACTUALLY HUMAN... RIGHT?
THIS BOY LOOKS HUMAN TO YOU?
HE ESCAPED THE DEMON SPELL?
ACTUALLY... **SOME** OF US AREN'T HUMAN.
WHY DID YOU HELP US?
B-BE-CAUSE I'M AFRAID ...
...TO BE ALONE.
MY MOTHER'S BEEN ILL SINCE LAST NIGHT.
I WENT OUT TO FETCH SOME MEDICINE...

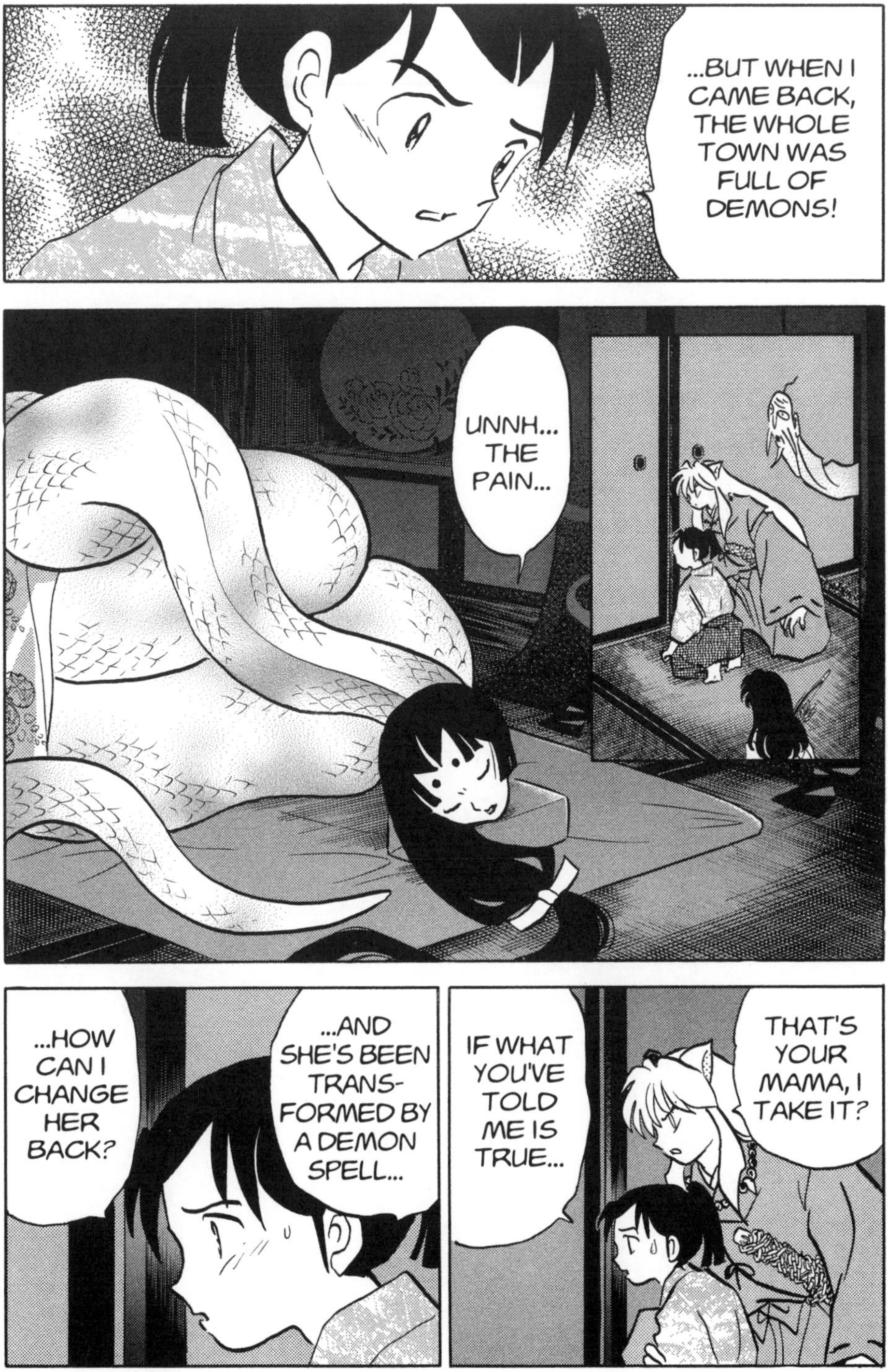
...BUT WHEN I CAME BACK, THE WHOLE TOWN WAS FULL OF DEMONS!
UNNH... THE PAIN...
THAT'S YOUR MAMA, I TAKE IT?
IF WHAT YOU'VE TOLD ME IS TRUE...
...AND SHE'S BEEN TRANS-FORMED BY A DEMON SPELL...
...HOW CAN I CHANGE HER BACK?

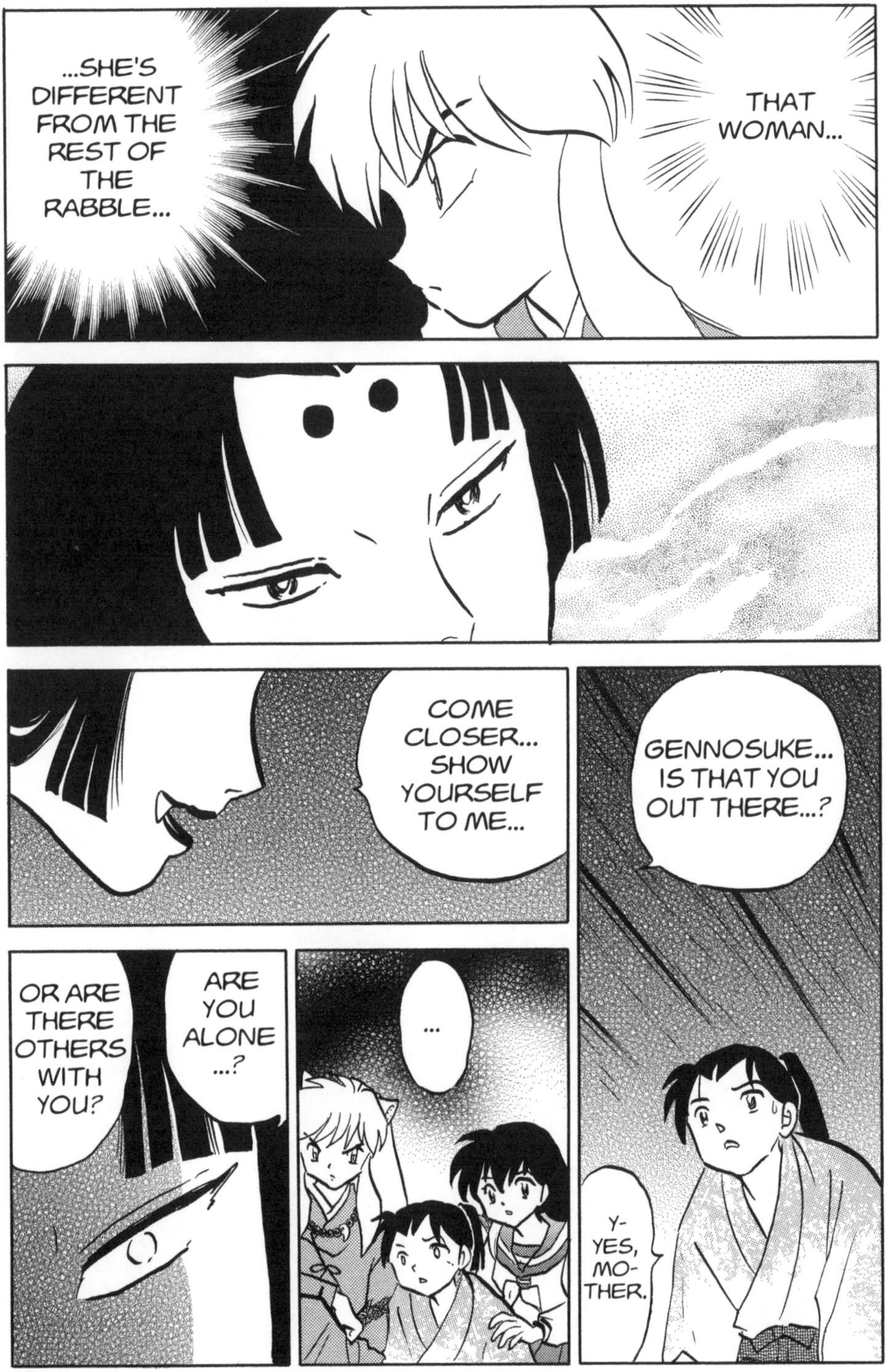
THAT WOMAN...
...SHE'S DIFFERENT FROM THE REST OF THE RABBLE...
GENNOSUKE... IS THAT YOU OUT THERE...?
Y-YES, MO-THER.
COME CLOSER... SHOW YOURSELF TO ME...
...
ARE YOU ALONE ...?
OR ARE THERE OTHERS WITH YOU?

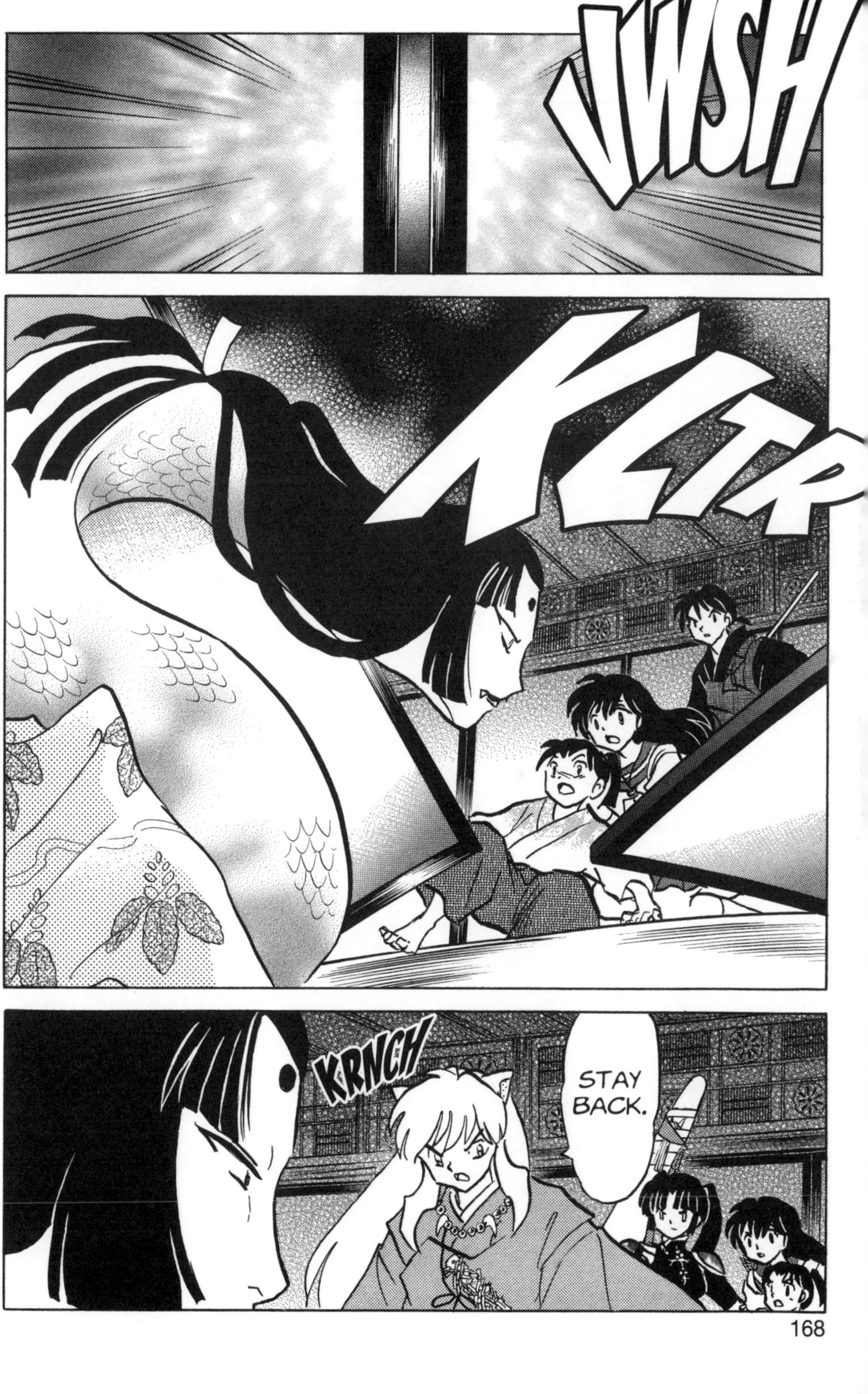
VWSH
KLTR
STAY BACK.
KRNCH

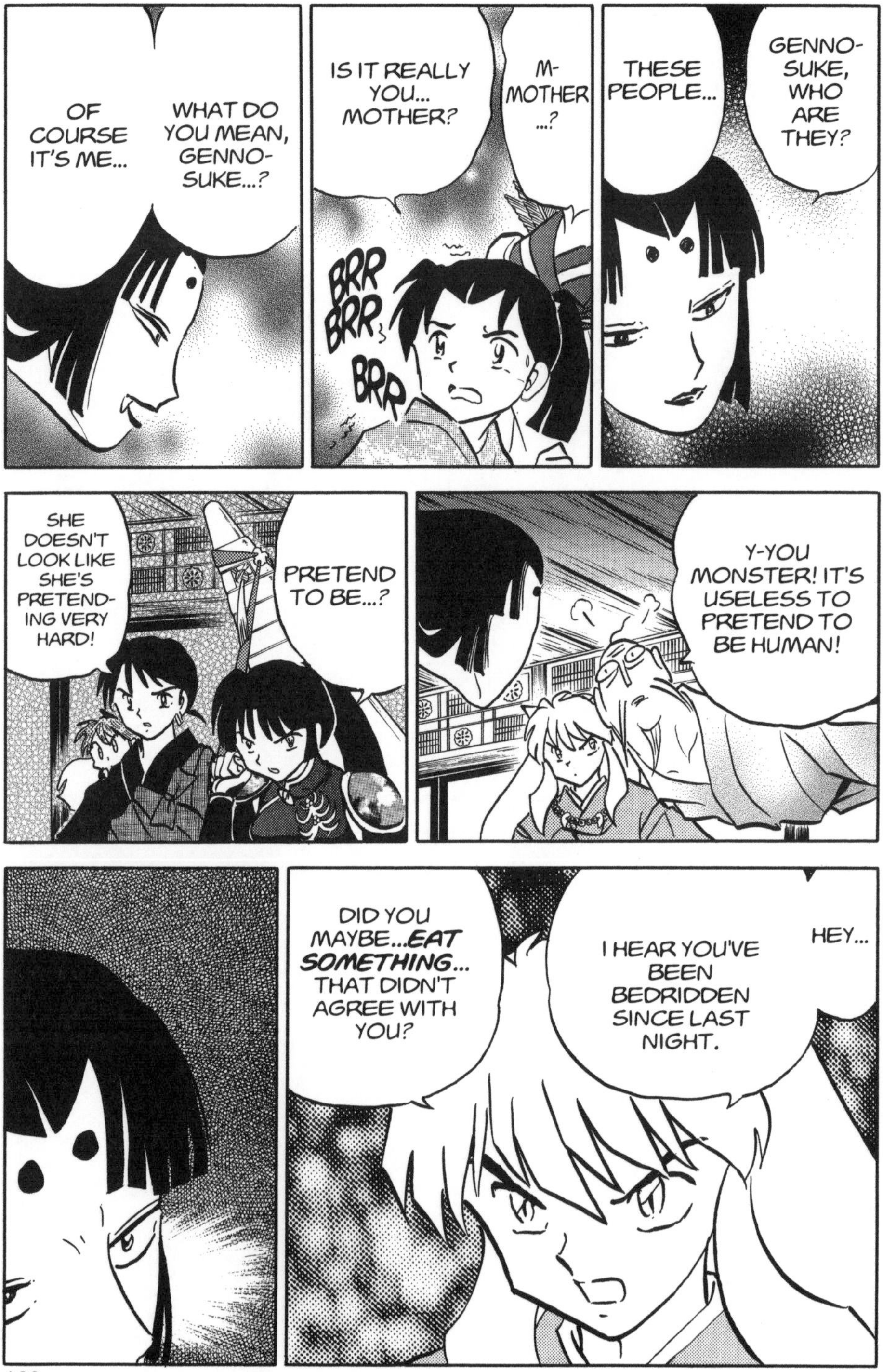
GENNO-SUKE, WHO ARE THEY?
THESE PEOPLE...
M-MOTHER ...?
IS IT REALLY YOU... MOTHER?
BRR BRR BRR
WHAT DO YOU MEAN, GENNO-SUKE...?
OF COURSE IT'S ME...
Y-YOU MONSTER! IT'S USELESS TO PRETEND TO BE HUMAN!
PRETEND TO BE...?
SHE DOESN'T LOOK LIKE SHE'S PRETENDING VERY HARD!
HEY...
I HEAR YOU'VE BEEN BEDRIDDEN SINCE LAST NIGHT.
DID YOU MAYBE...**EAT SOMETHING**... THAT DIDN'T AGREE WITH YOU?

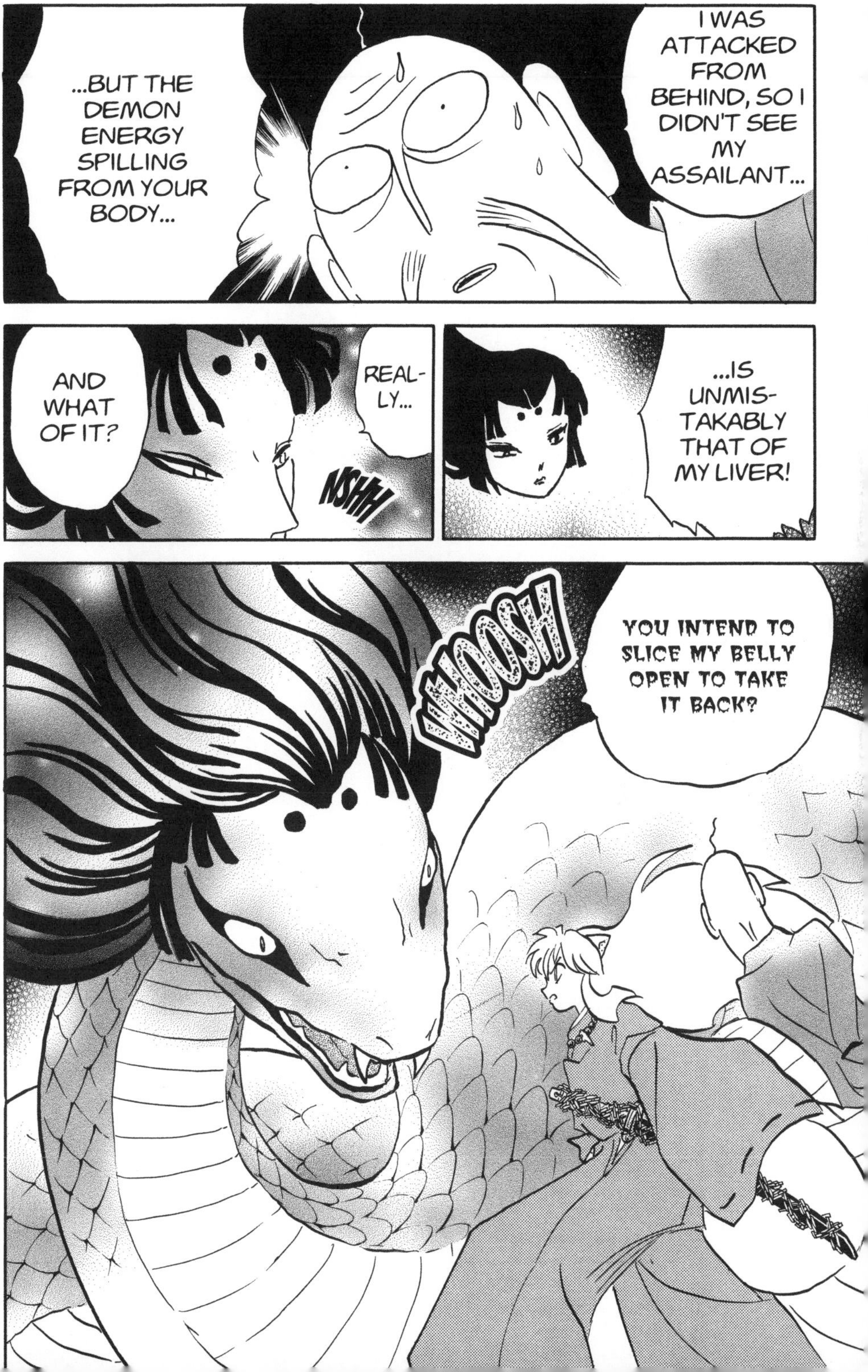
I WAS ATTACKED FROM BEHIND, SO I DIDN'T SEE MY ASSAILANT...
...BUT THE DEMON ENERGY SPILLING FROM YOUR BODY...
...IS UNMISTAKABLY THAT OF MY LIVER!
REALLY...
NSHH
AND WHAT OF IT?
WHOOSH
YOU INTEND TO SLICE MY BELLY OPEN TO TAKE IT BACK?

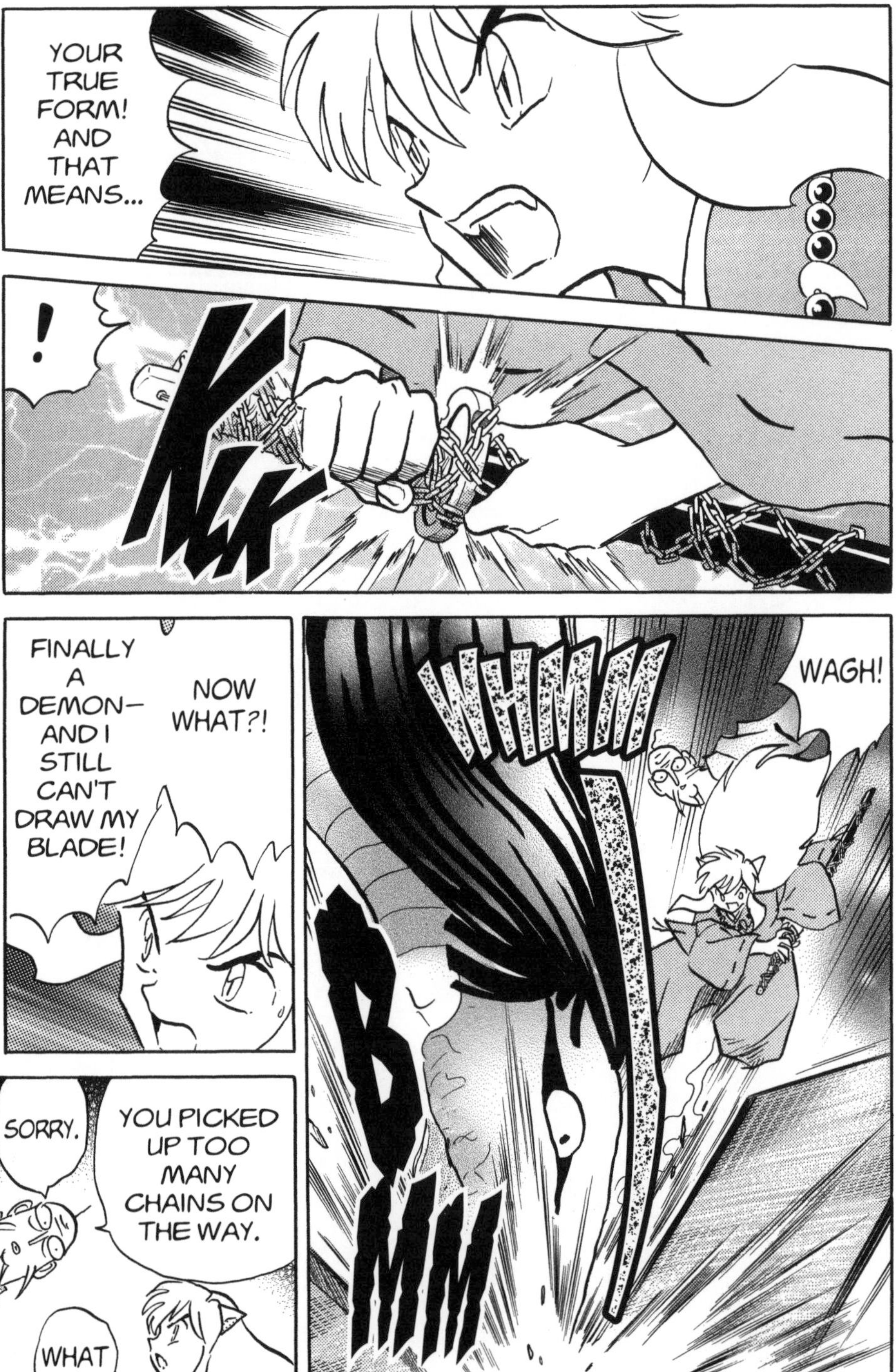
YOUR TRUE FORM! AND THAT MEANS...
!
KNK
WAGH!
WHMMM
BMM
NOW WHAT?!
FINALLY A DEMON— AND I STILL CAN'T DRAW MY BLADE!
YOU PICKED UP TOO MANY CHAINS ON THE WAY.
SORRY.
WHAT ...?!

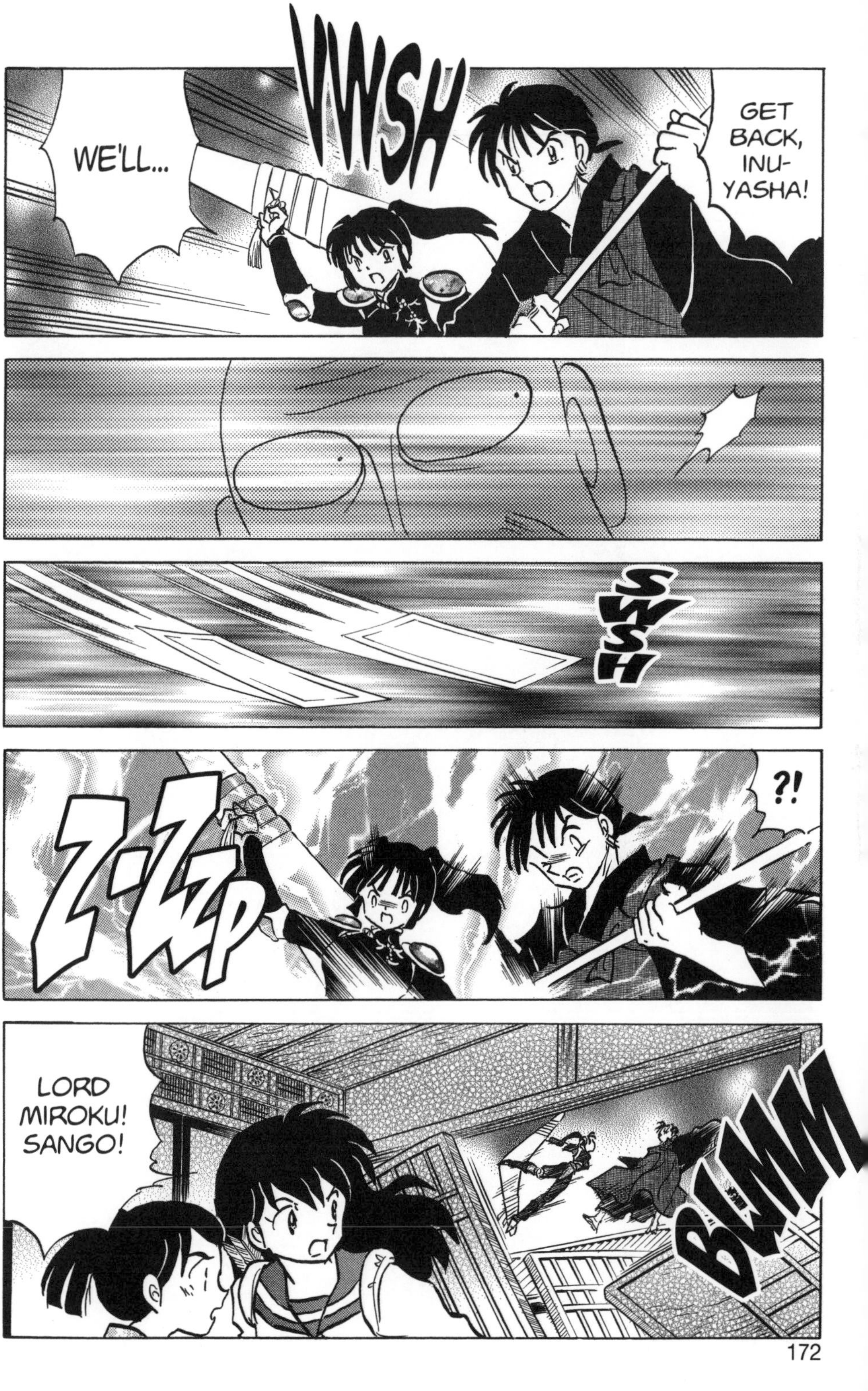
GET BACK, INU-YASHA!
VWSH
WE'LL...
SWSH
?!
Z-ZZP
BMMM
LORD MIROKU! SANGO!

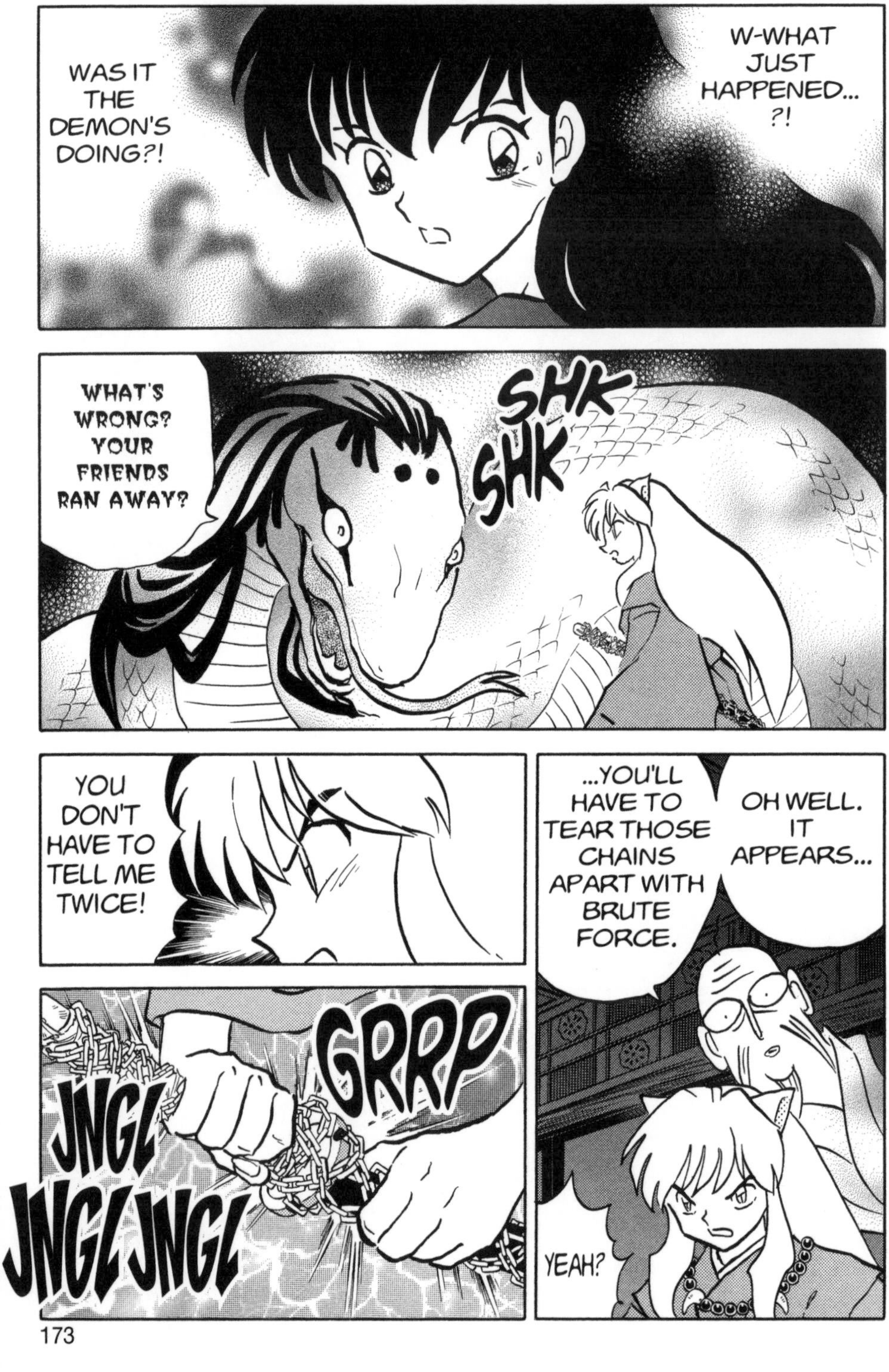
W-WHAT JUST HAPPENED... ?!
WAS IT THE DEMON'S DOING?!
SHK SHK
WHAT'S WRONG? YOUR FRIENDS RAN AWAY?
OH WELL. IT APPEARS...
...YOU'LL HAVE TO TEAR THOSE CHAINS APART WITH BRUTE FORCE.
YEAH?
YOU DON'T HAVE TO TELL ME TWICE!
GRRP
JNGL JNGL JNGL

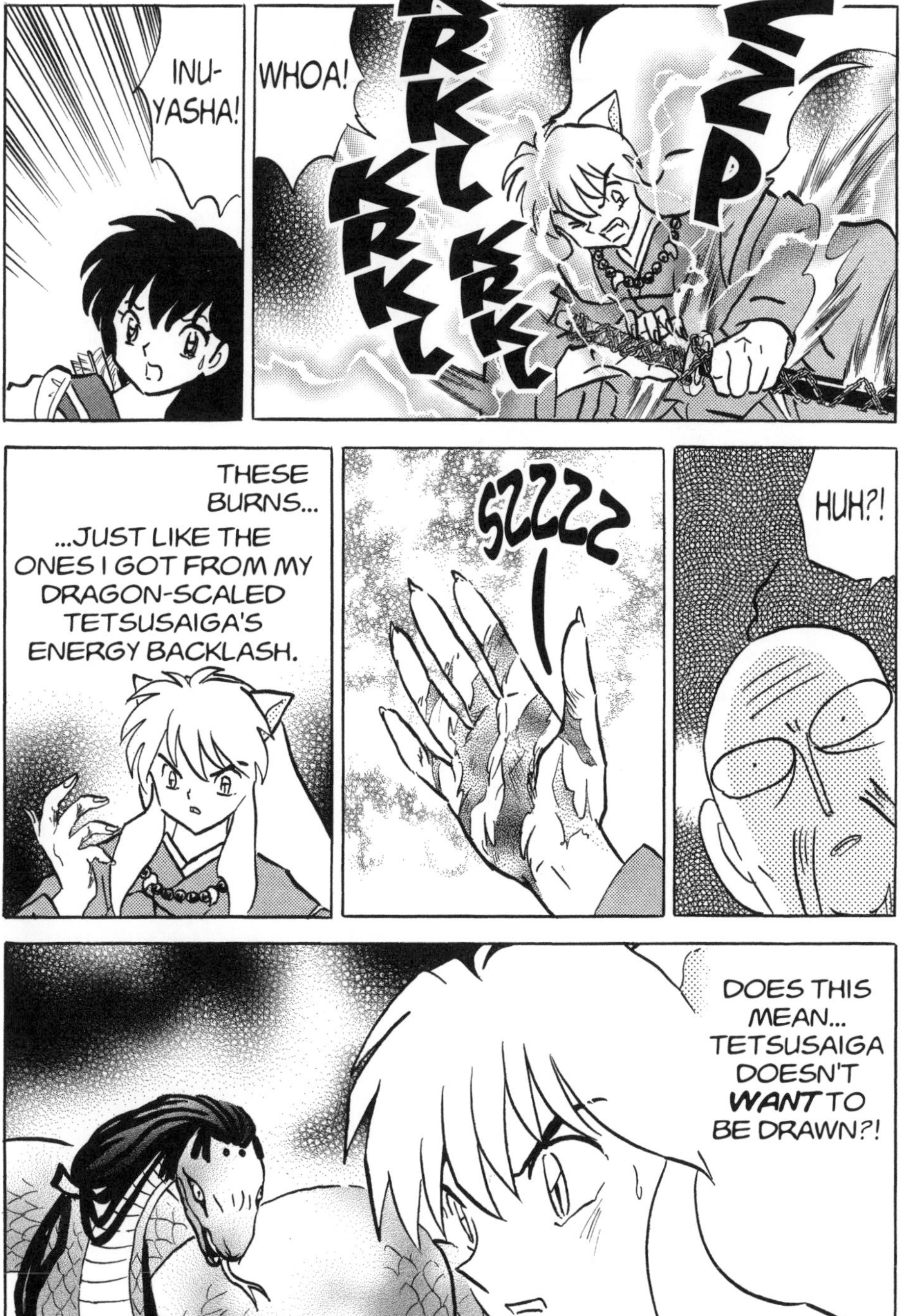
ZZZP
KRKL
KRKL
KRKL
WHOA!
INU-YASHA!
HUH?!
SZZZZ
THESE BURNS...
...JUST LIKE THE ONES I GOT FROM MY DRAGON-SCALED TETSUSAIGA'S ENERGY BACKLASH.
DOES THIS MEAN... TETSUSAIGA DOESN'T *WANT* TO BE DRAWN?!

SCROLL TEN
DEMON VORTEX

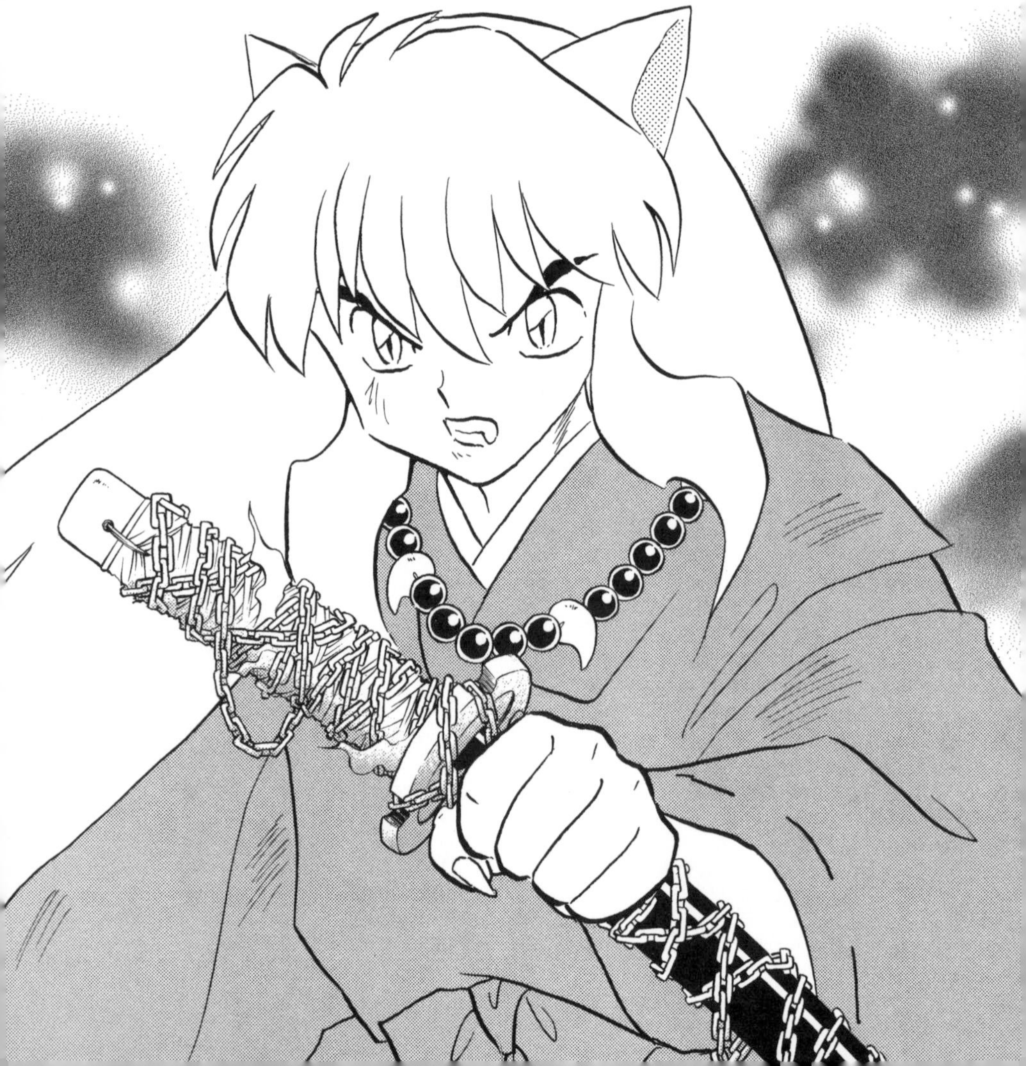

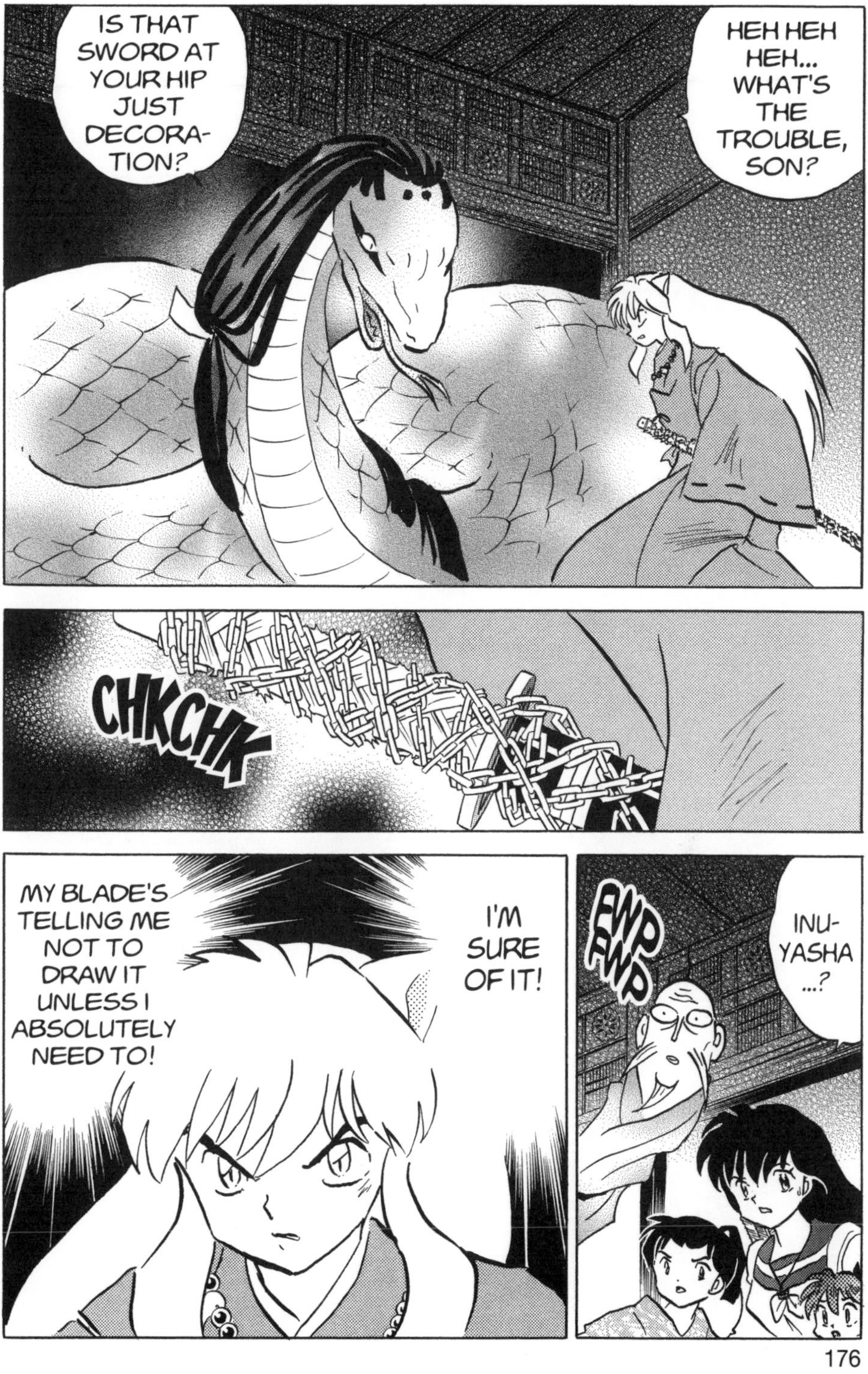
HEH HEH HEH... WHAT'S THE TROUBLE, SON?
IS THAT SWORD AT YOUR HIP JUST DECORA-TION?
CHKCHK
INU-YASHA ...?
FWP FWP
MY BLADE'S TELLING ME NOT TO DRAW IT UNLESS I ABSOLUTELY NEED TO!
I'M SURE OF IT!

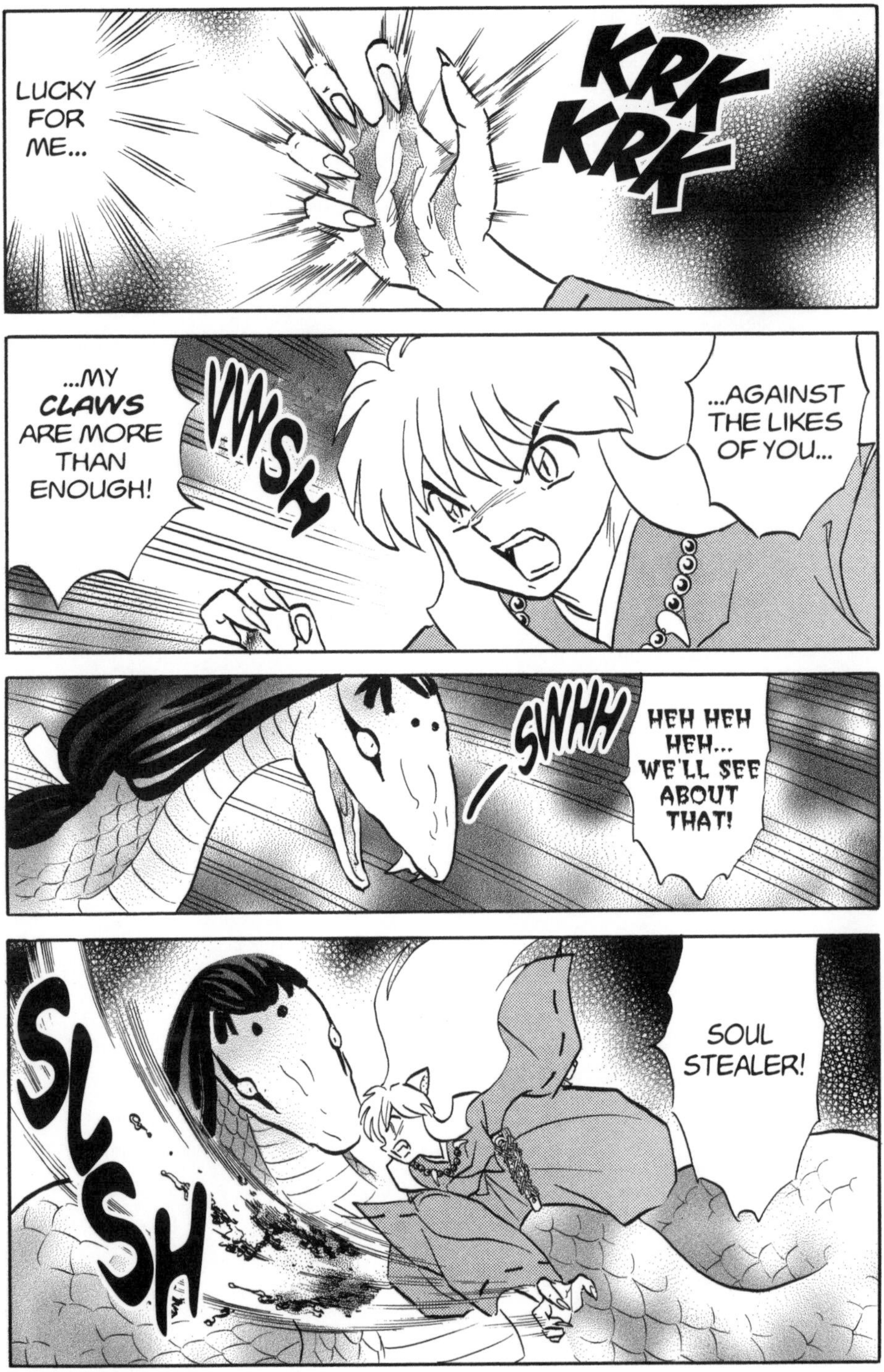
KRK KRK
LUCKY FOR ME...
...AGAINST THE LIKES OF YOU...
VWSH
...MY **CLAWS** ARE MORE THAN ENOUGH!
HEH HEH HEH... WE'LL SEE ABOUT THAT!
SWHH
SOUL STEALER!
SLSH

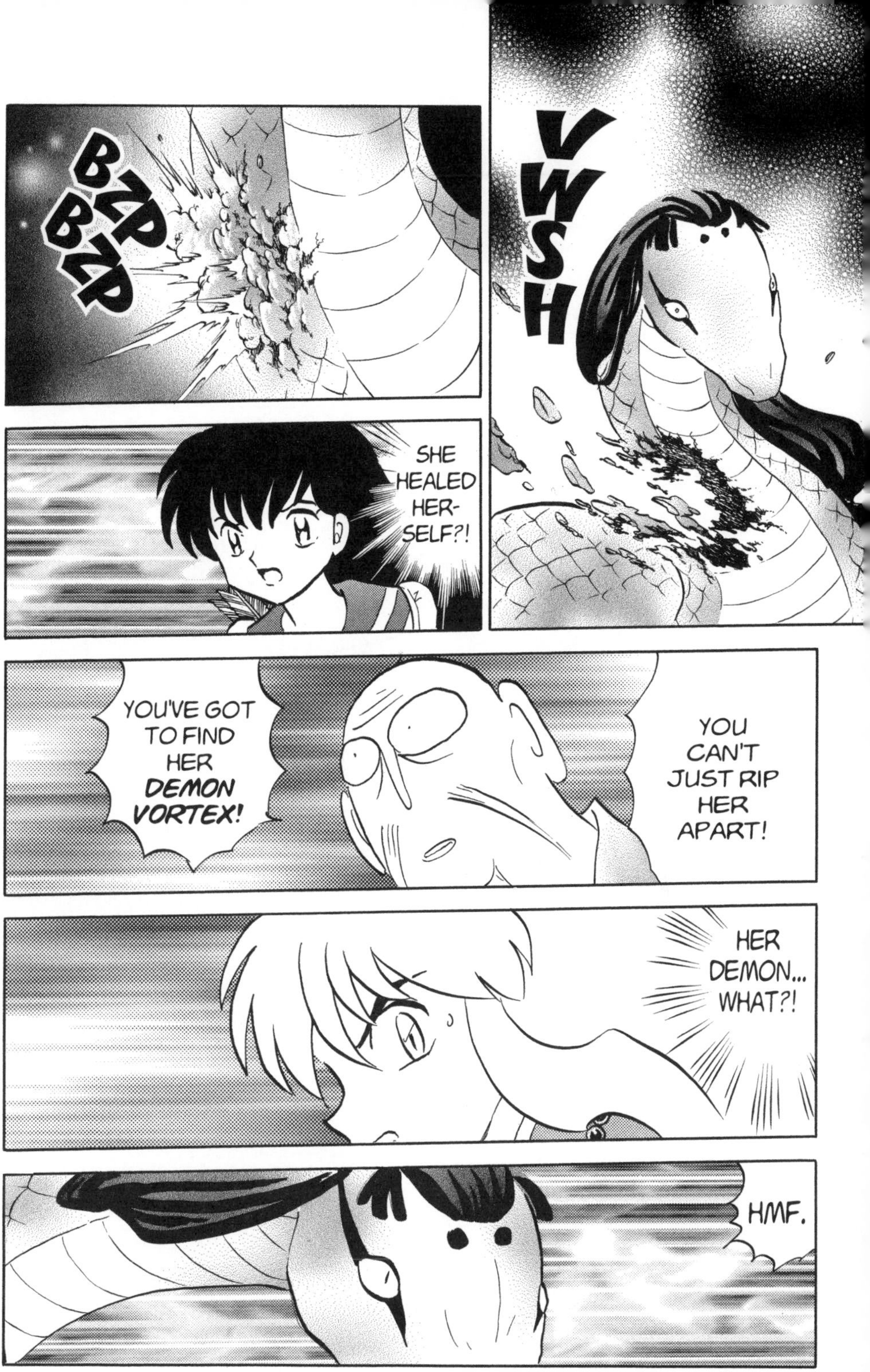
VWSH
BZP BZP
SHE HEALED HER-SELF?!
YOU CAN'T JUST RIP HER APART!
YOU'VE GOT TO FIND HER *DEMON VORTEX!*
HER DEMON... WHAT?!
HMF.

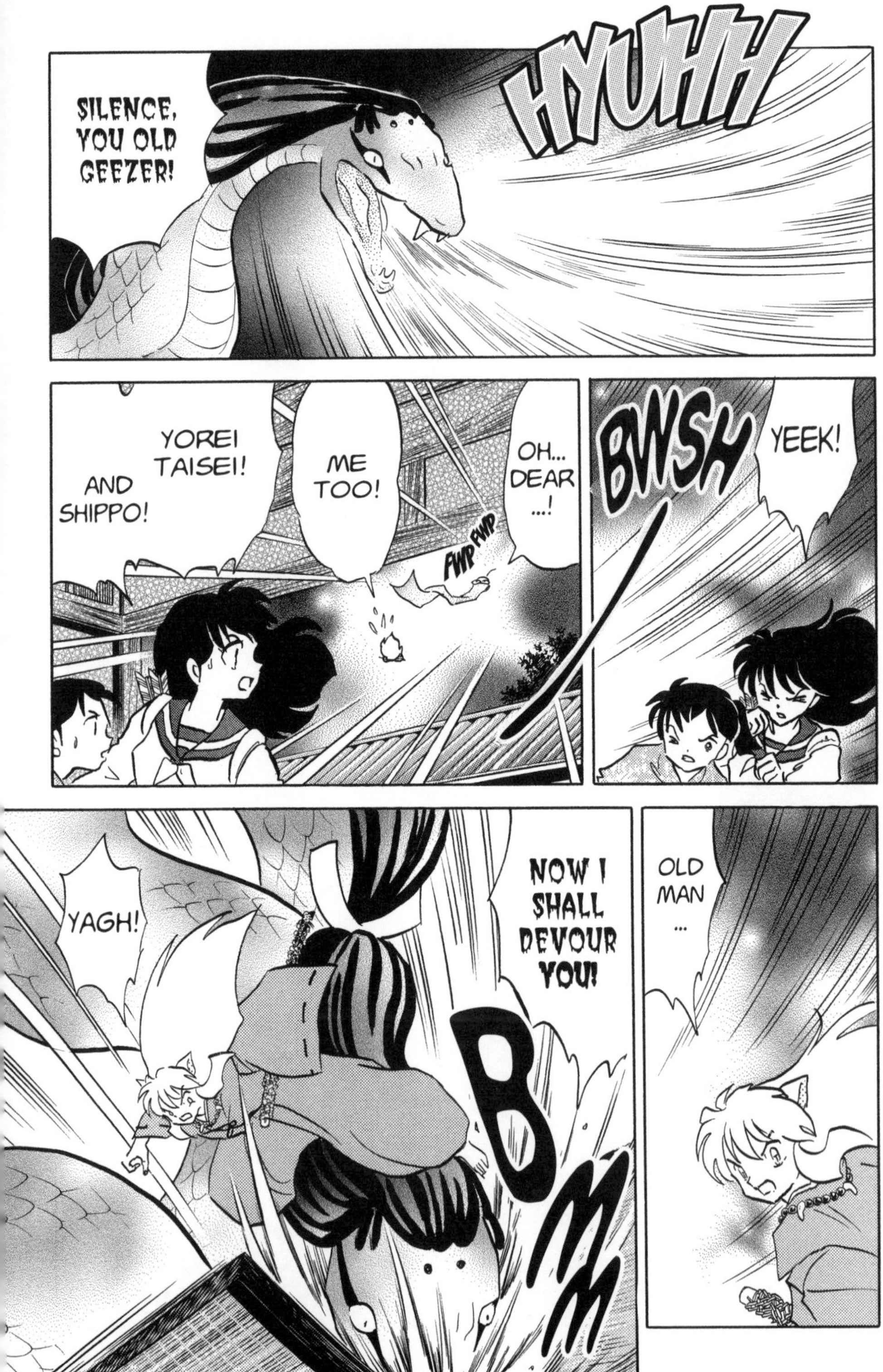
HYUHH
SILENCE, YOU OLD GEEZER!
BWSH
YEEK!
OH... DEAR ...!
ME TOO!
YOREI TAISEI!
AND SHIPPO!
FWP FWP
OLD MAN ...
NOW I SHALL DEVOUR YOU!
YAGH!
BMM

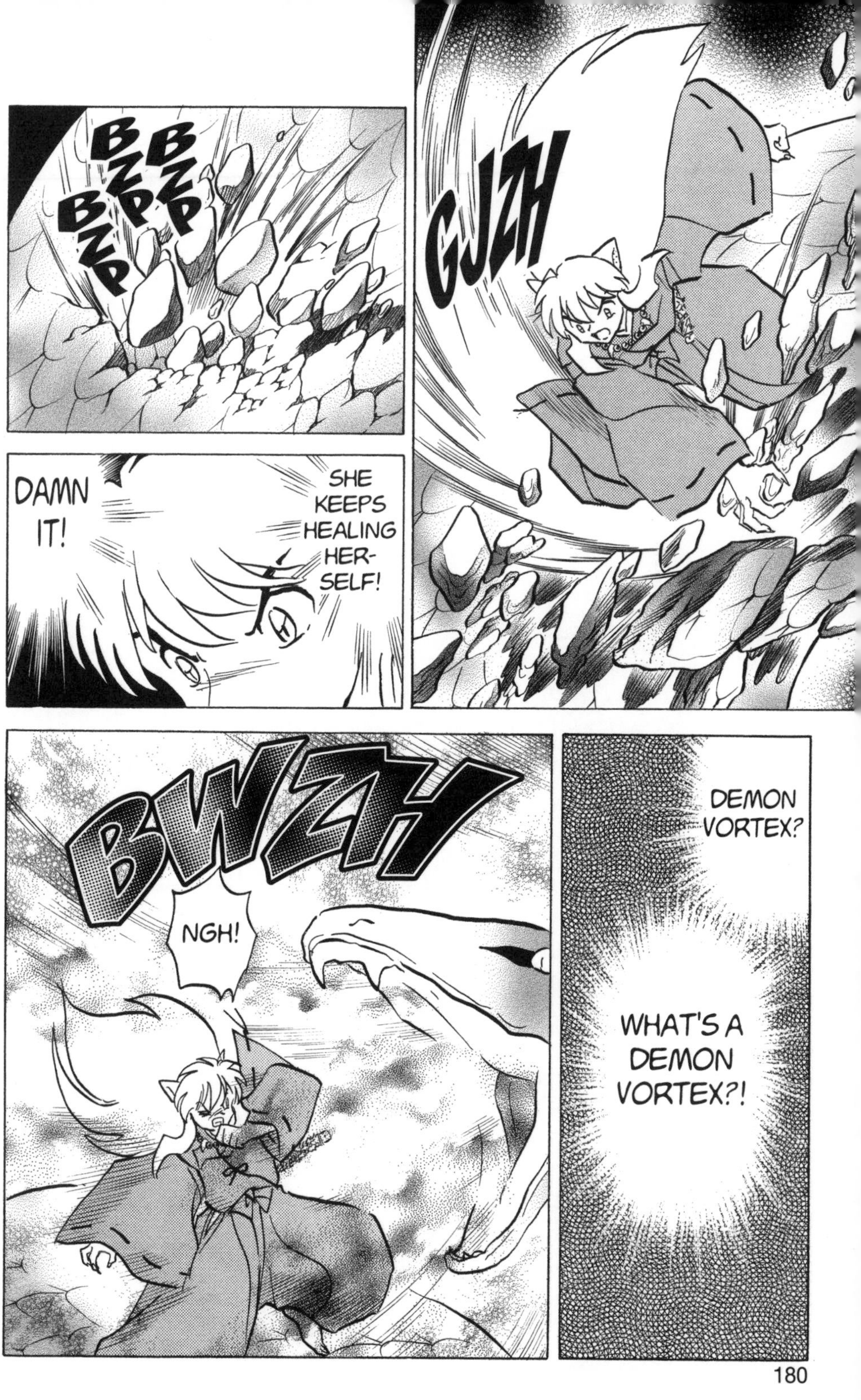
GJZH
BZP BZP BZP
SHE KEEPS HEALING HER-SELF!
DAMN IT!
DEMON VORTEX?
WHAT'S A DEMON VORTEX?!
BWZH
NGH!

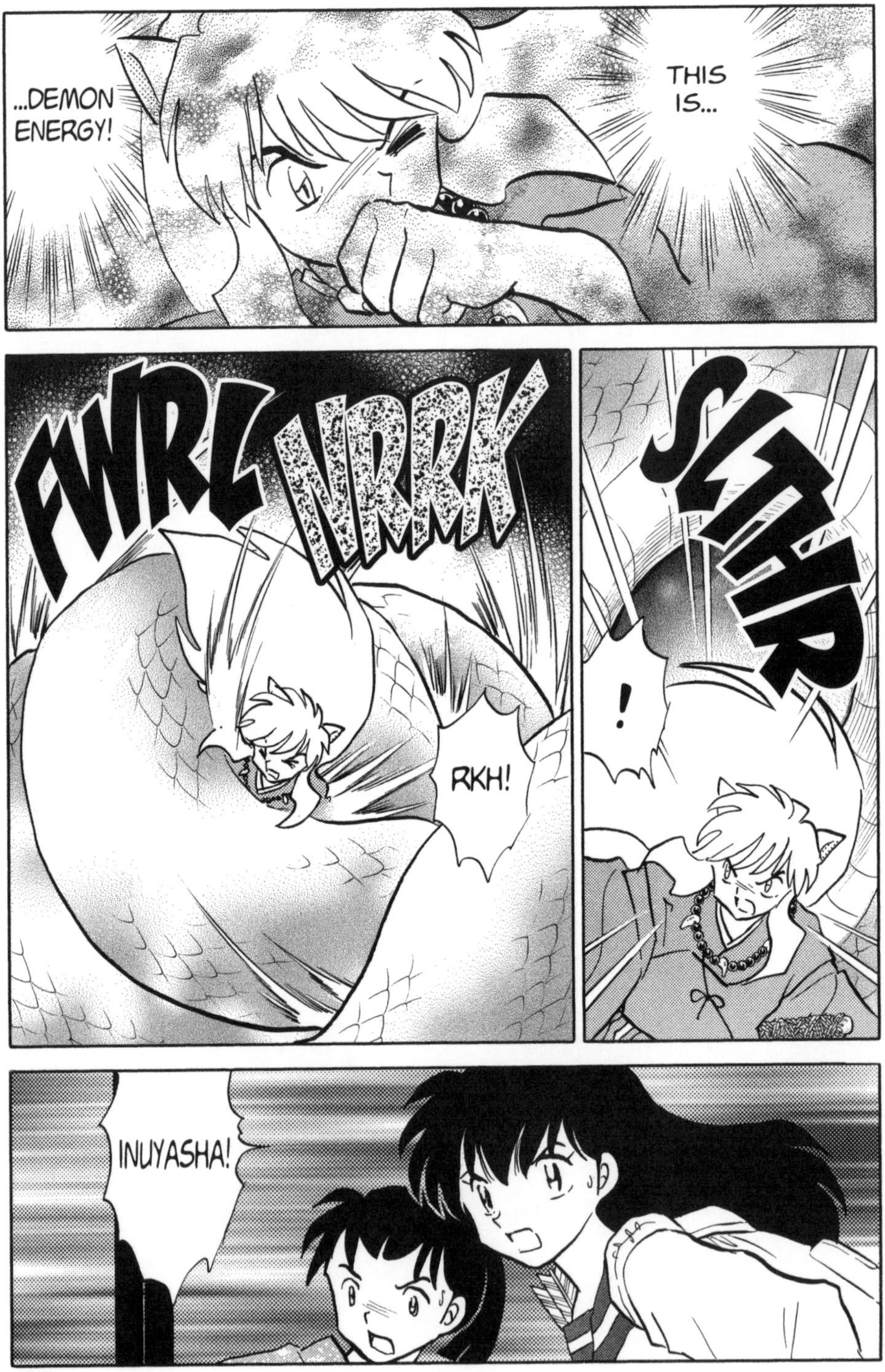
THIS IS...
...DEMON ENERGY!
SHTAR
!
FWRL
NRRK
RKH!
INUYASHA!

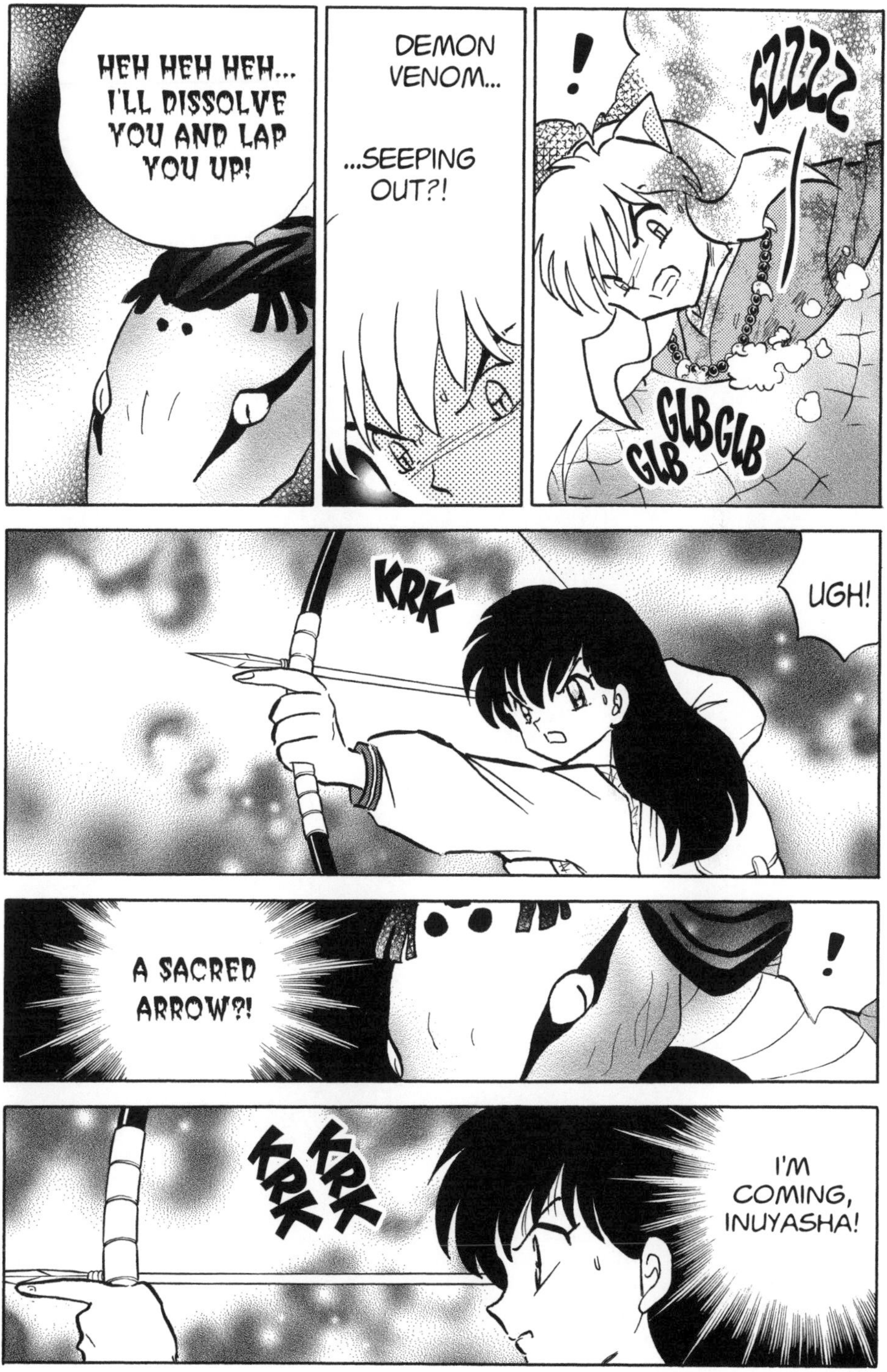
!
SZZZZ
GLB GLBGLB
DEMON VENOM...
...SEEPING OUT?!
HEH HEH HEH... I'LL DISSOLVE YOU AND LAP YOU UP!
UGH!
KRK
!
A SACRED ARROW?!
I'M COMING, INUYASHA!
KRK KRK

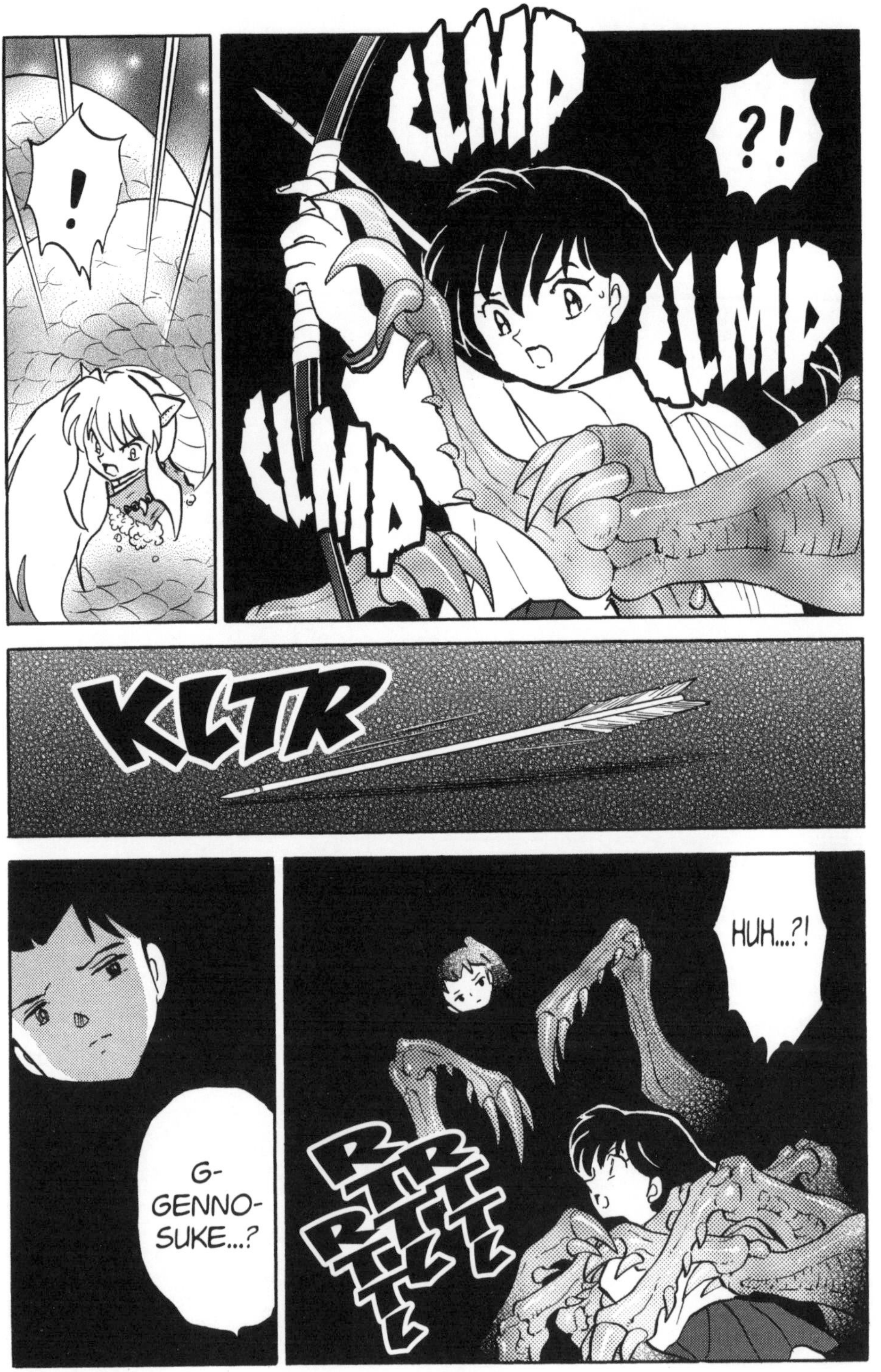
CLMP
?!
CLMP
CLMP
!
KLTR
HUH...?!
G-GENNO-SUKE...?

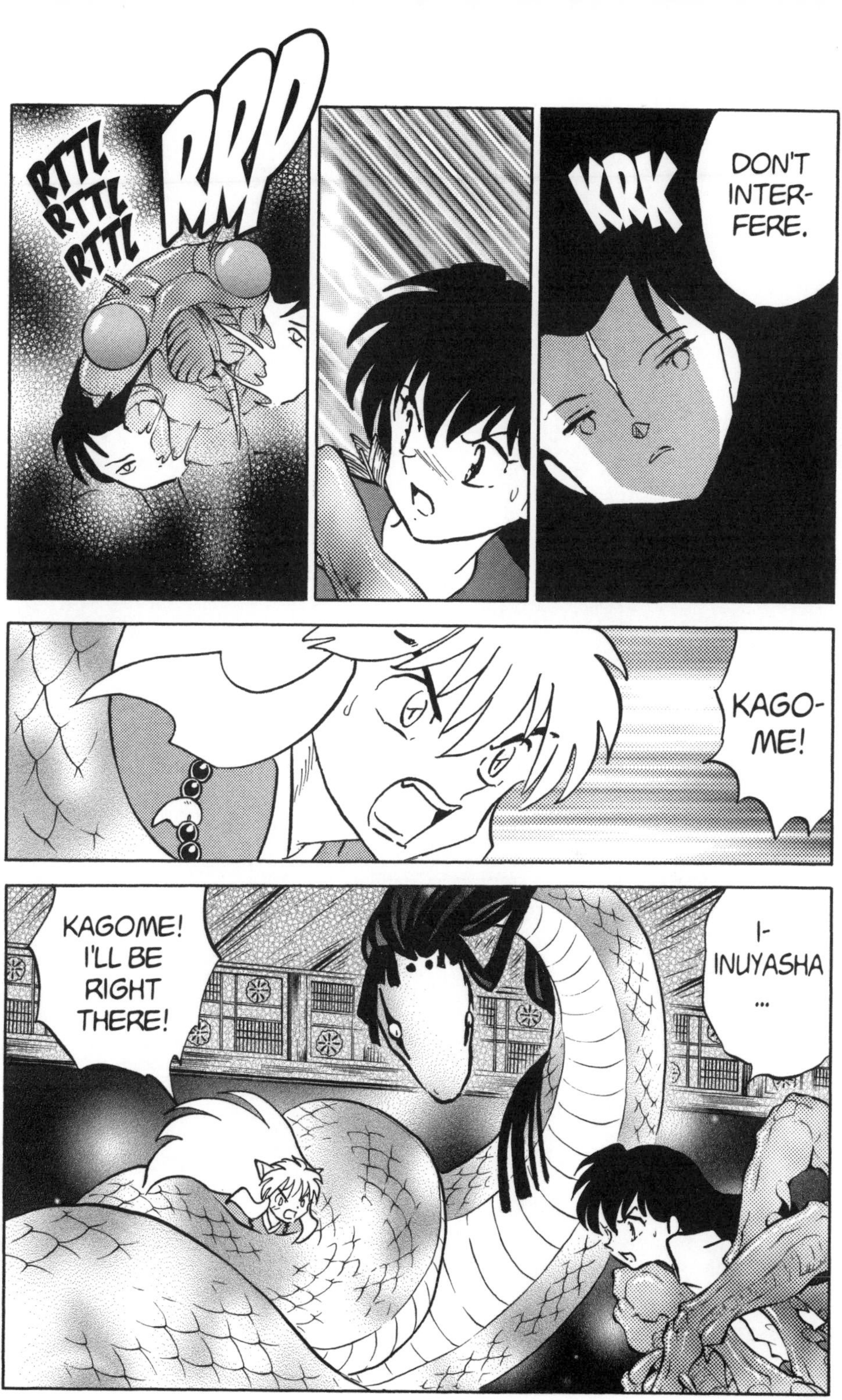
KRK
DON'T INTERFERE.
RRP
RTTL RTTL RTTL
KAGOME!
I- INUYASHA ...
KAGOME! I'LL BE RIGHT THERE!

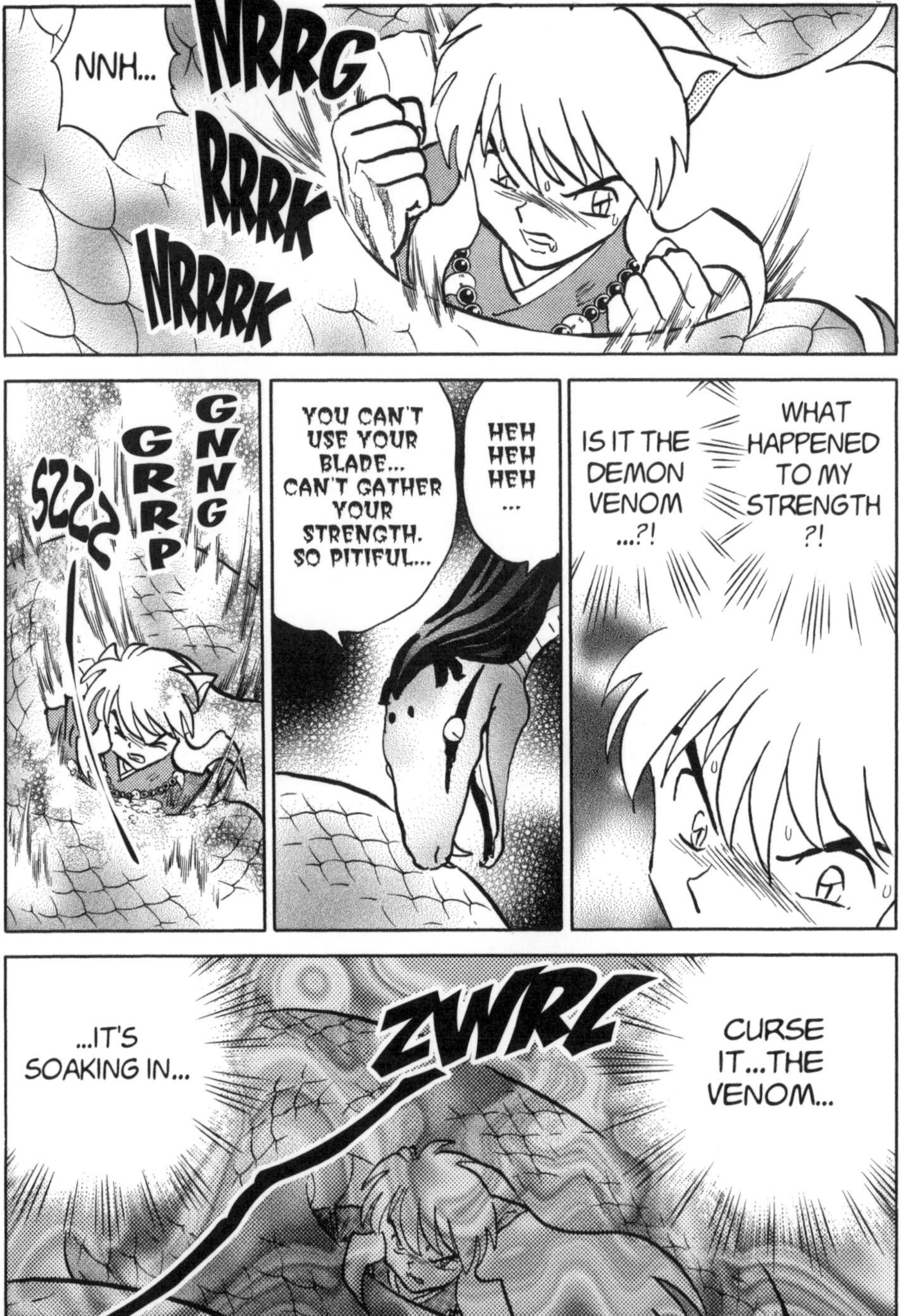
NRRG
RRRK
NRRRRK
NNH...
WHAT HAPPENED TO MY STRENGTH?!
IS IT THE DEMON VENOM...?!
HEH HEH HEH...
YOU CAN'T USE YOUR BLADE... CAN'T GATHER YOUR STRENGTH. SO PITIFUL...
GNNG
GRRP
SZZZ
CURSE IT...THE VENOM...
ZWRL
...IT'S SOAKING IN...

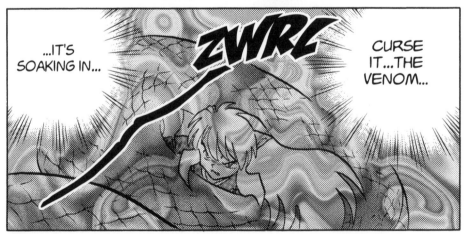

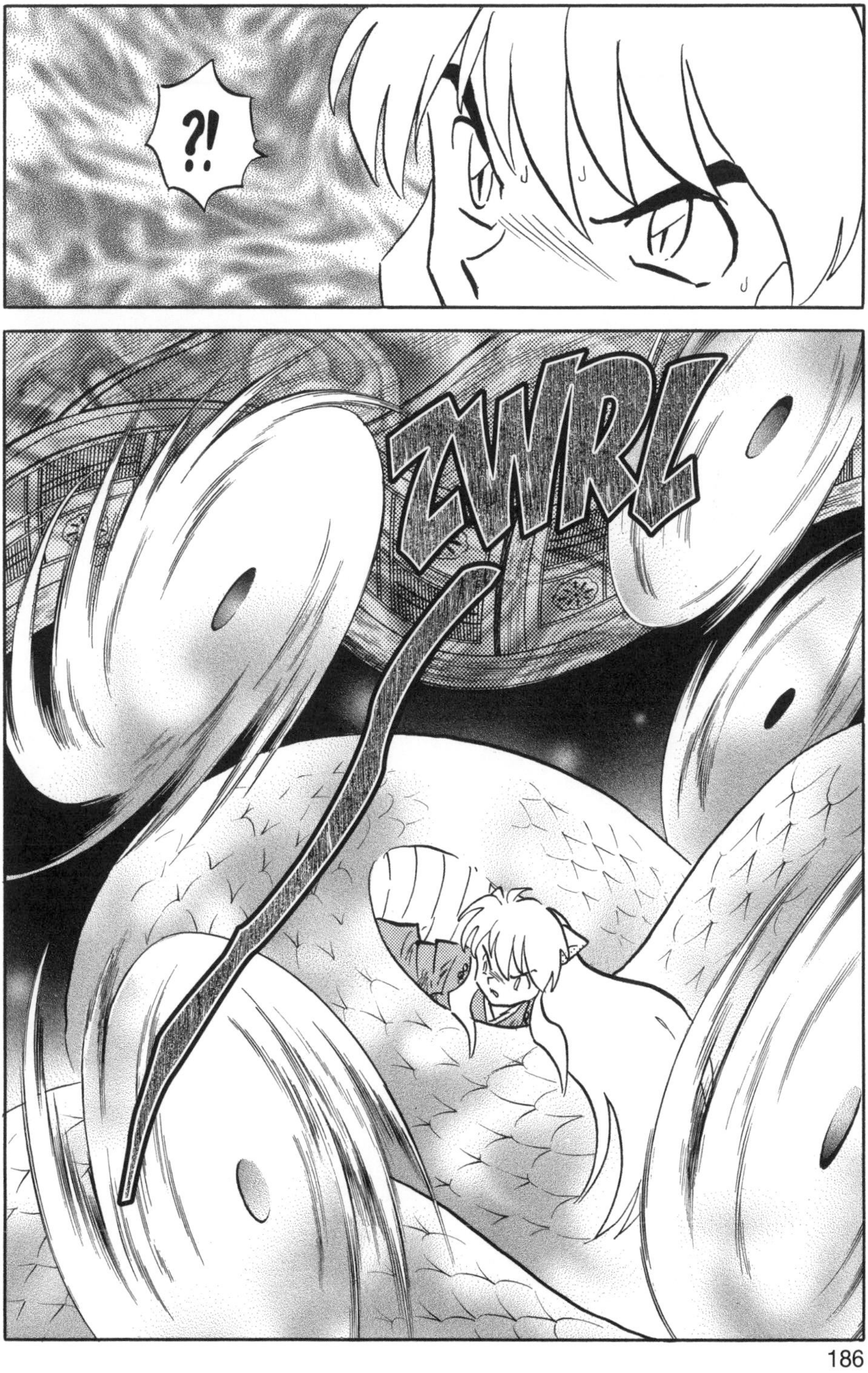
?!
ZWRL

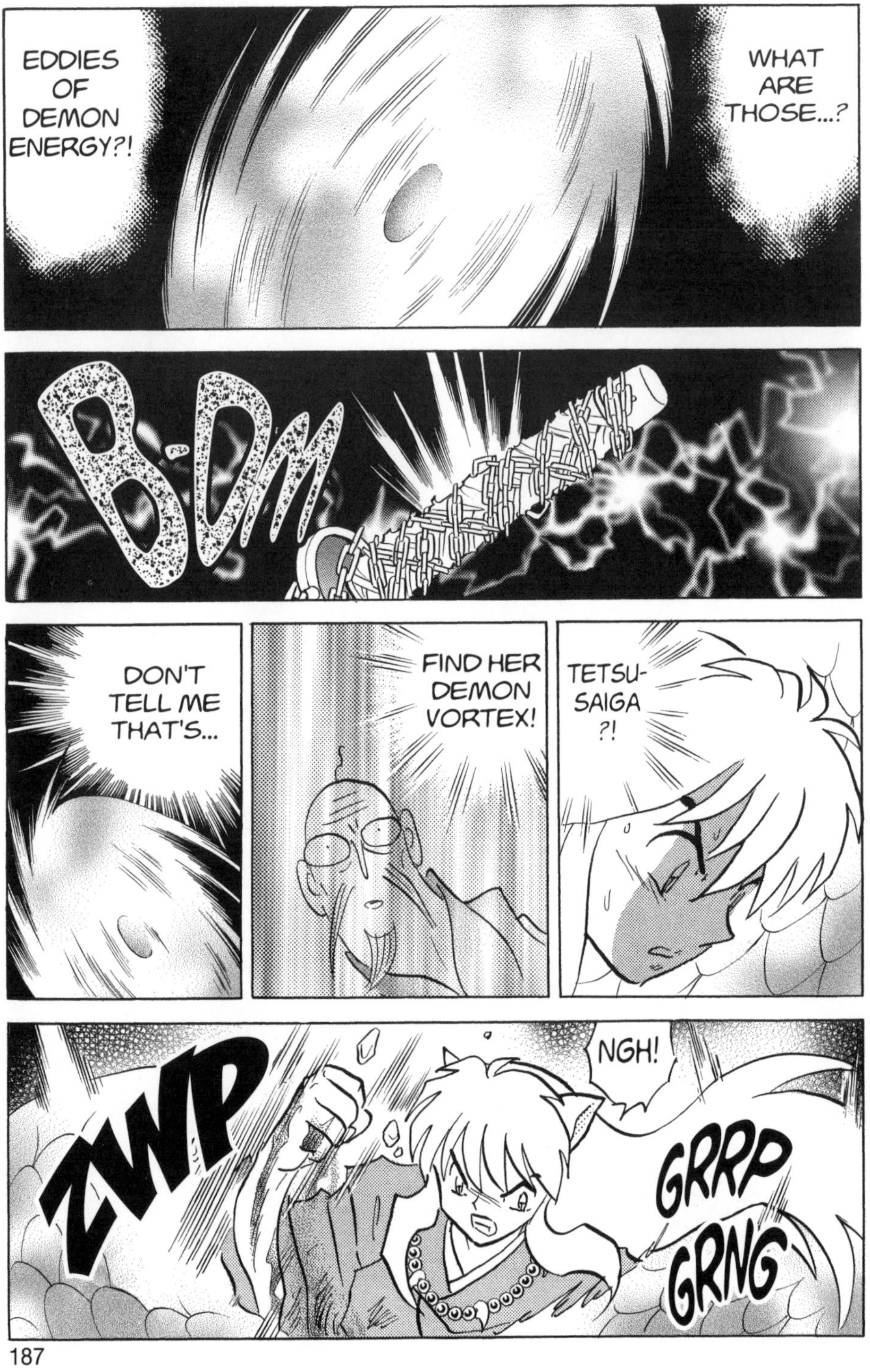
WHAT ARE THOSE...?
EDDIES OF DEMON ENERGY?!
B-DM
TETSU-SAIGA?!
FIND HER DEMON VORTEX!
DON'T TELL ME THAT'S...
NGH!
GRRP GRNG
ZWP

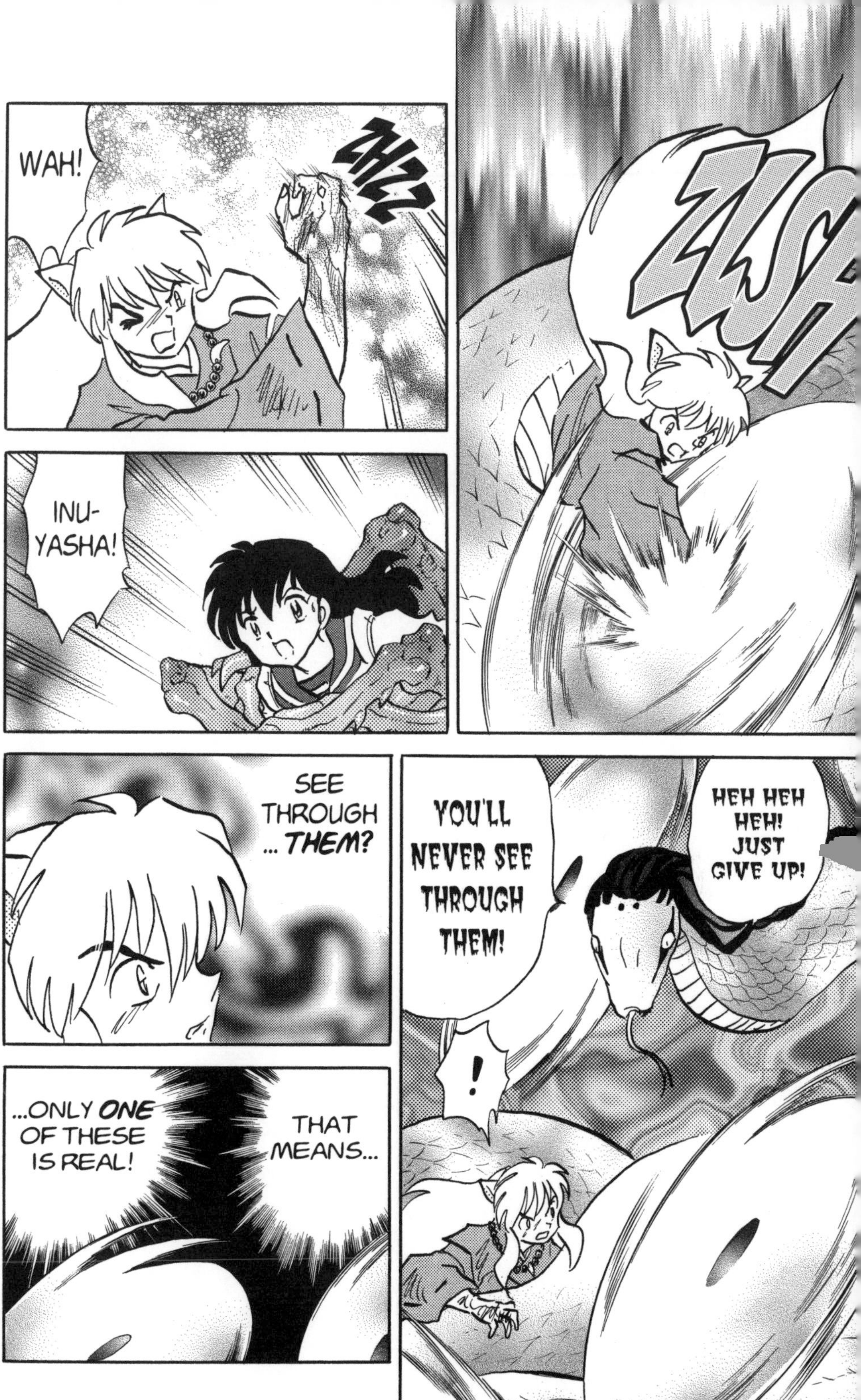

ZUSA
WAH!
INU-YASHA!
HEH HEH HEH! JUST GIVE UP!
YOU'LL NEVER SEE THROUGH THEM!
!
SEE THROUGH ...THEM?
THAT MEANS...
...ONLY ONE OF THESE IS REAL!

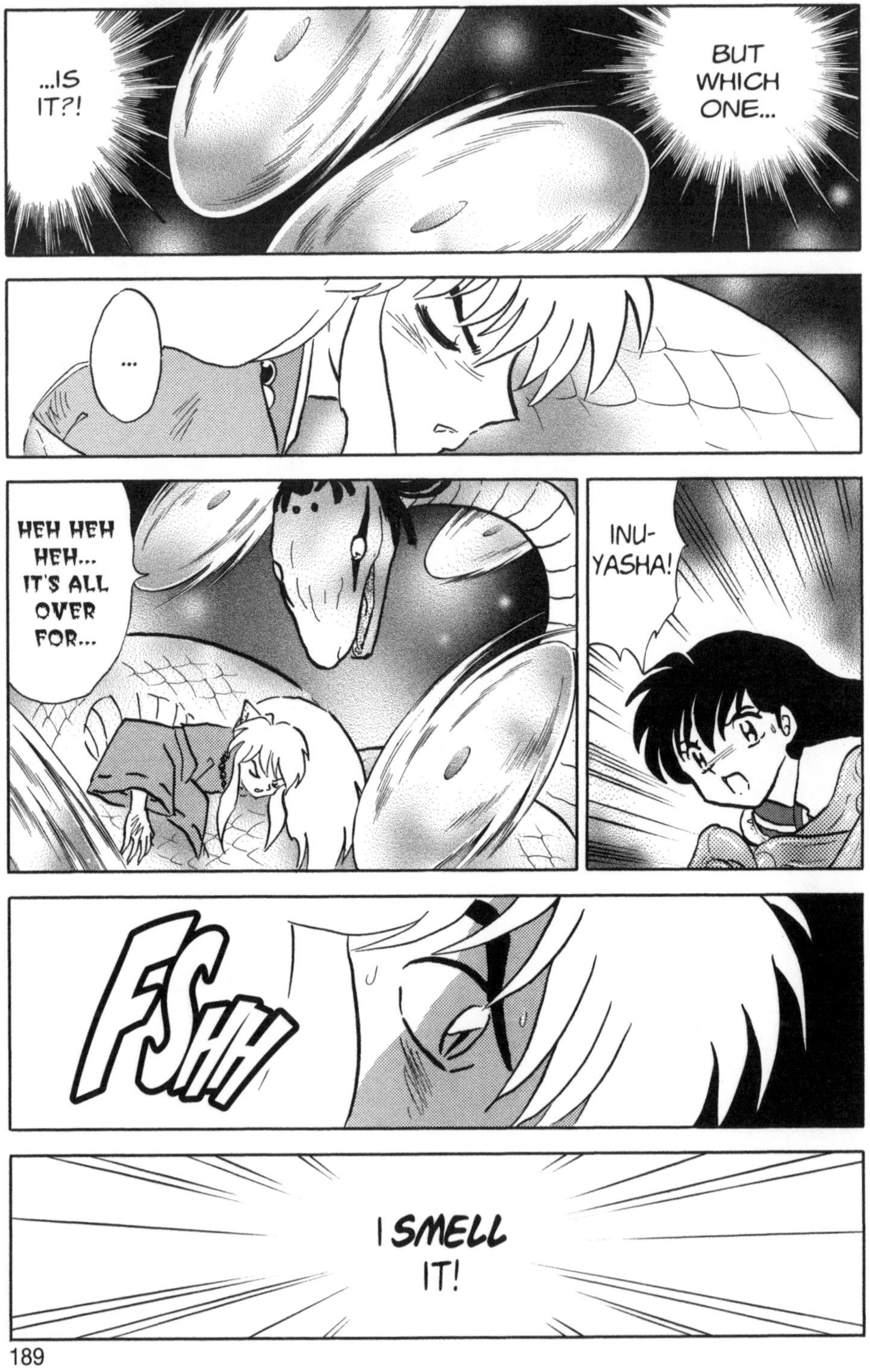
BUT WHICH ONE...
...IS IT?!
...
INU-YASHA!
HEH HEH HEH... IT'S ALL OVER FOR...
FSHH
I SMELL IT!

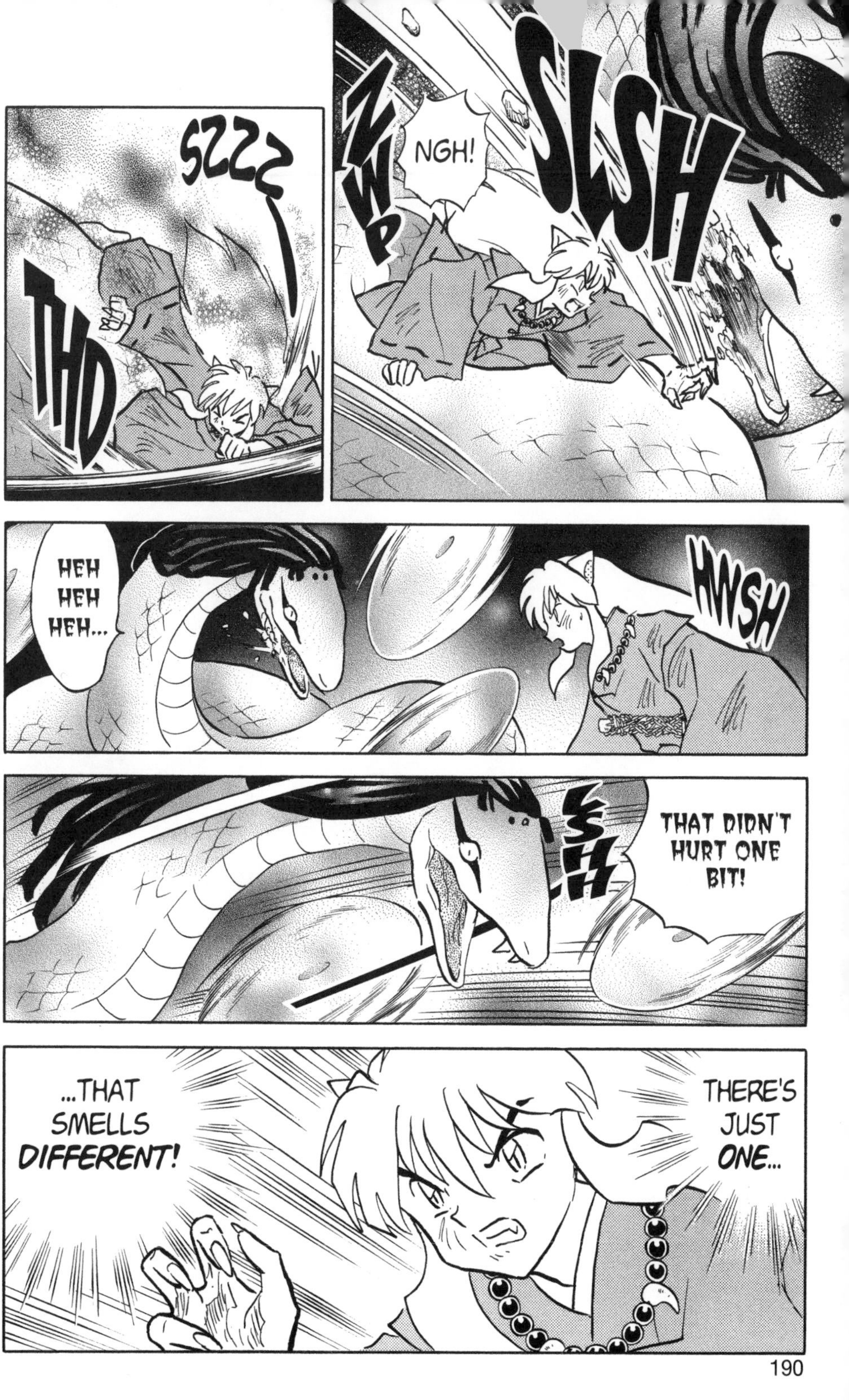
SLSH
NGH!
WMP
SZZZ
THD
HWSH
HEH HEH HEH...
THAT DIDN'T HURT ONE BIT!
SHH
THERE'S JUST **ONE**...
...THAT SMELLS **DIFFERENT!**

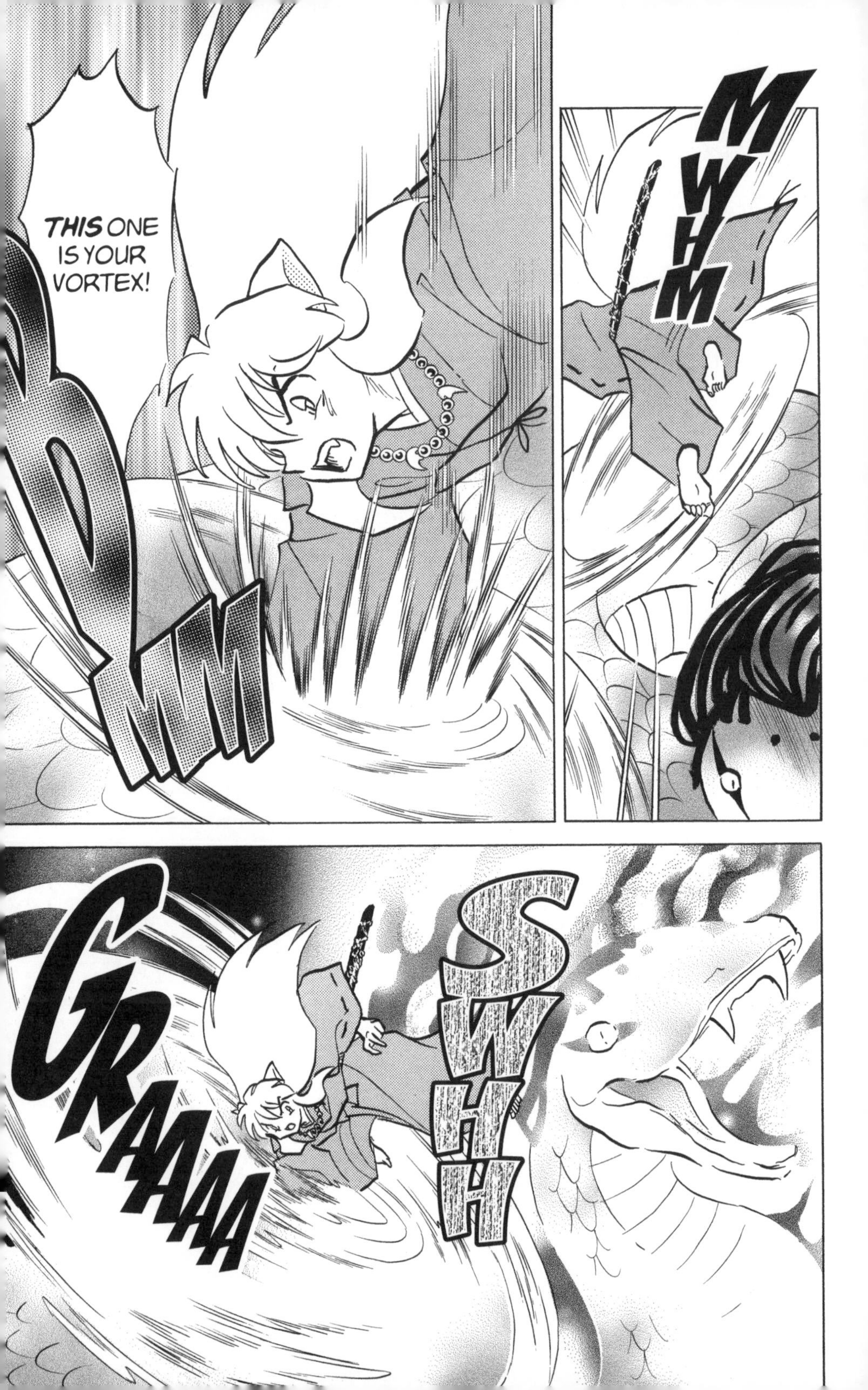
MWHM
THIS ONE IS YOUR VORTEX!
SWHHH
GRAAAAA

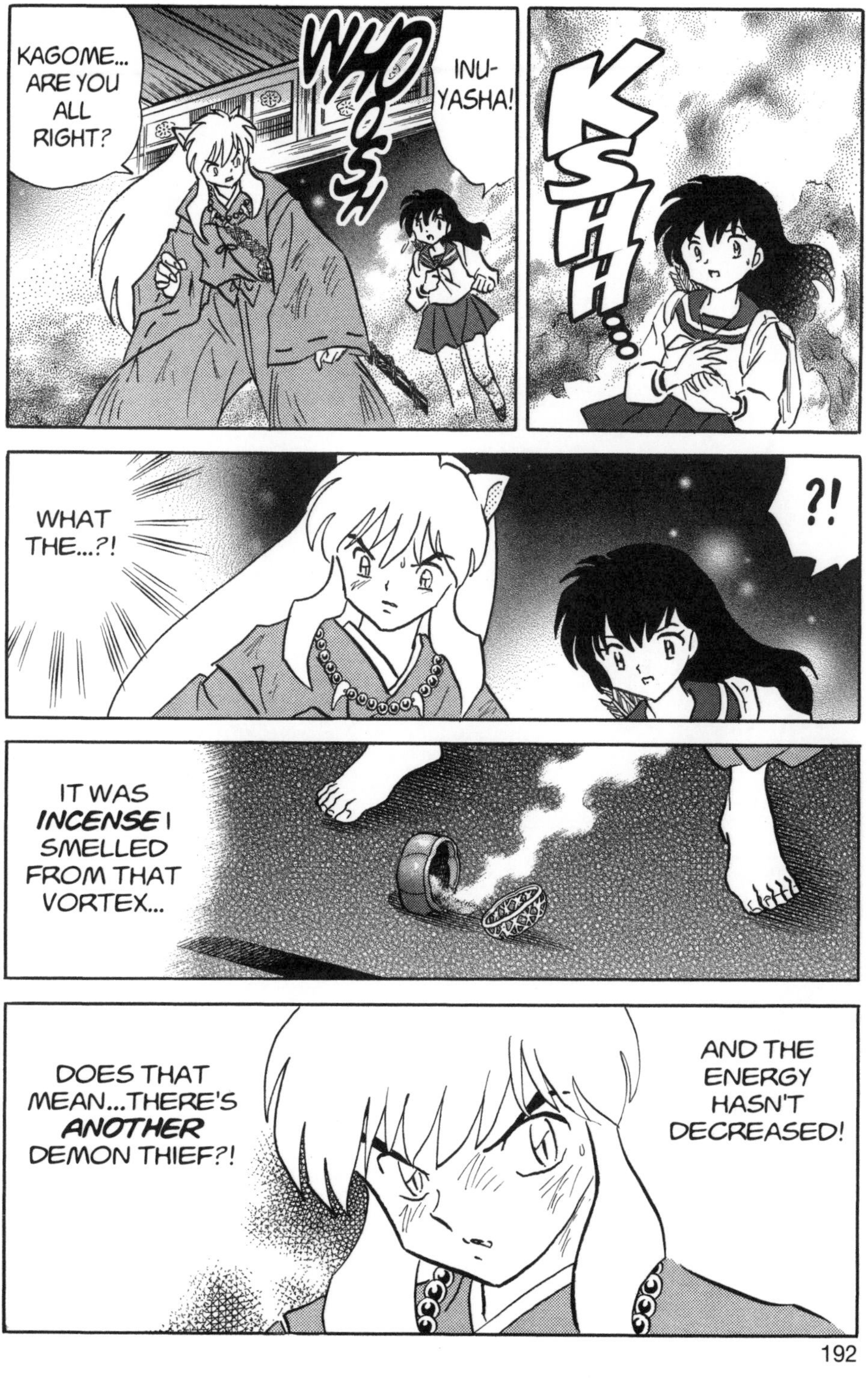
KSHH...
INU-YASHA!
WHOOSH
KAGOME... ARE YOU ALL RIGHT?
?!
WHAT THE...?!
IT WAS *INCENSE* I SMELLED FROM THAT VORTEX...
AND THE ENERGY HASN'T DECREASED!
DOES THAT MEAN...THERE'S *ANOTHER* DEMON THIEF?!

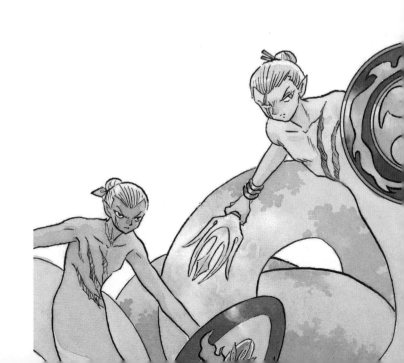

InuYasha

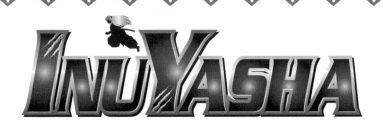

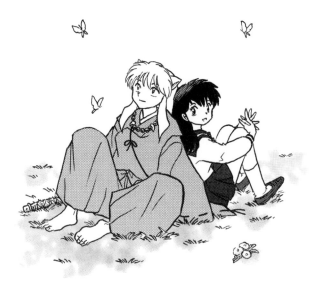

Volume 44

Koga's Decision

SCROLL ONE
THE TRUE FOE

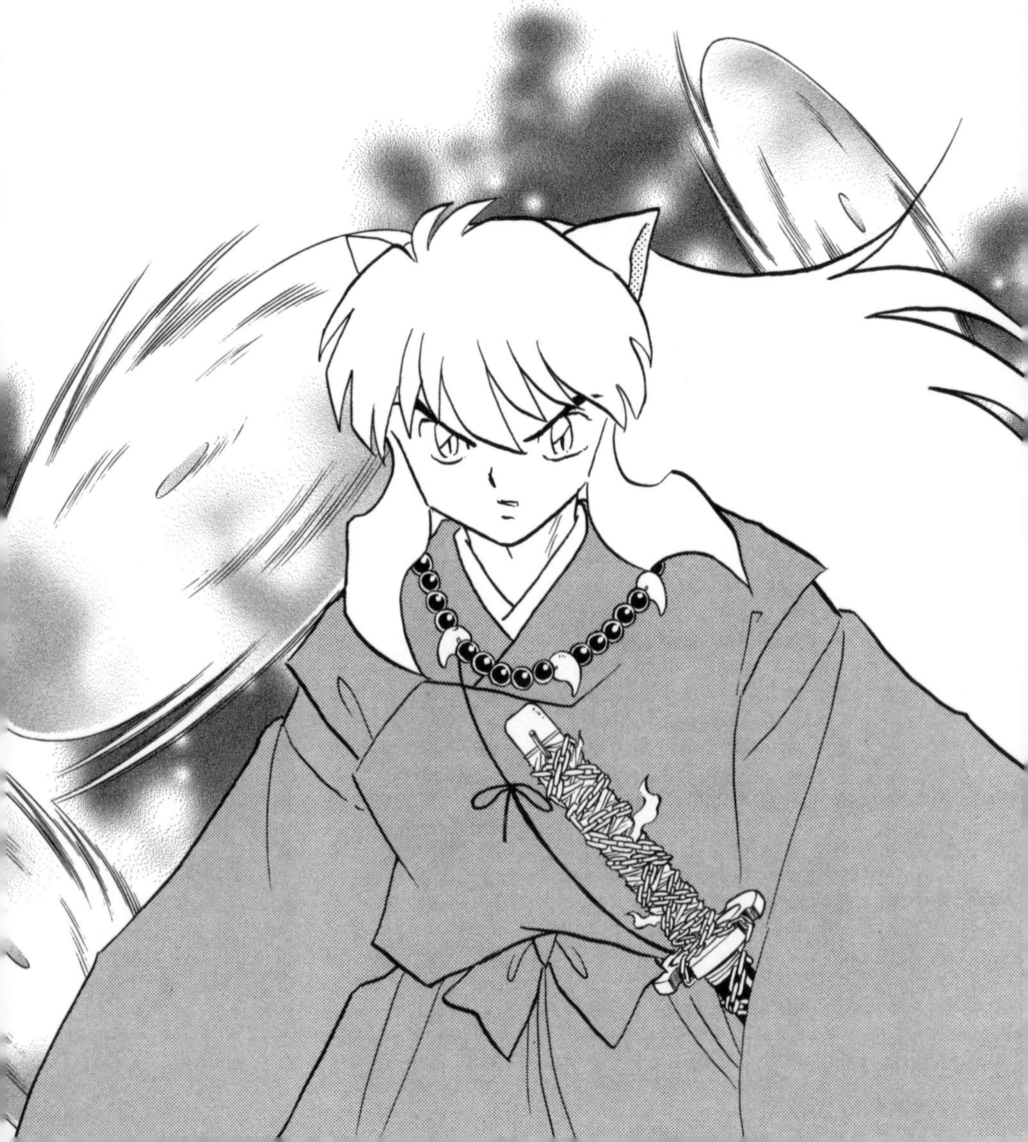

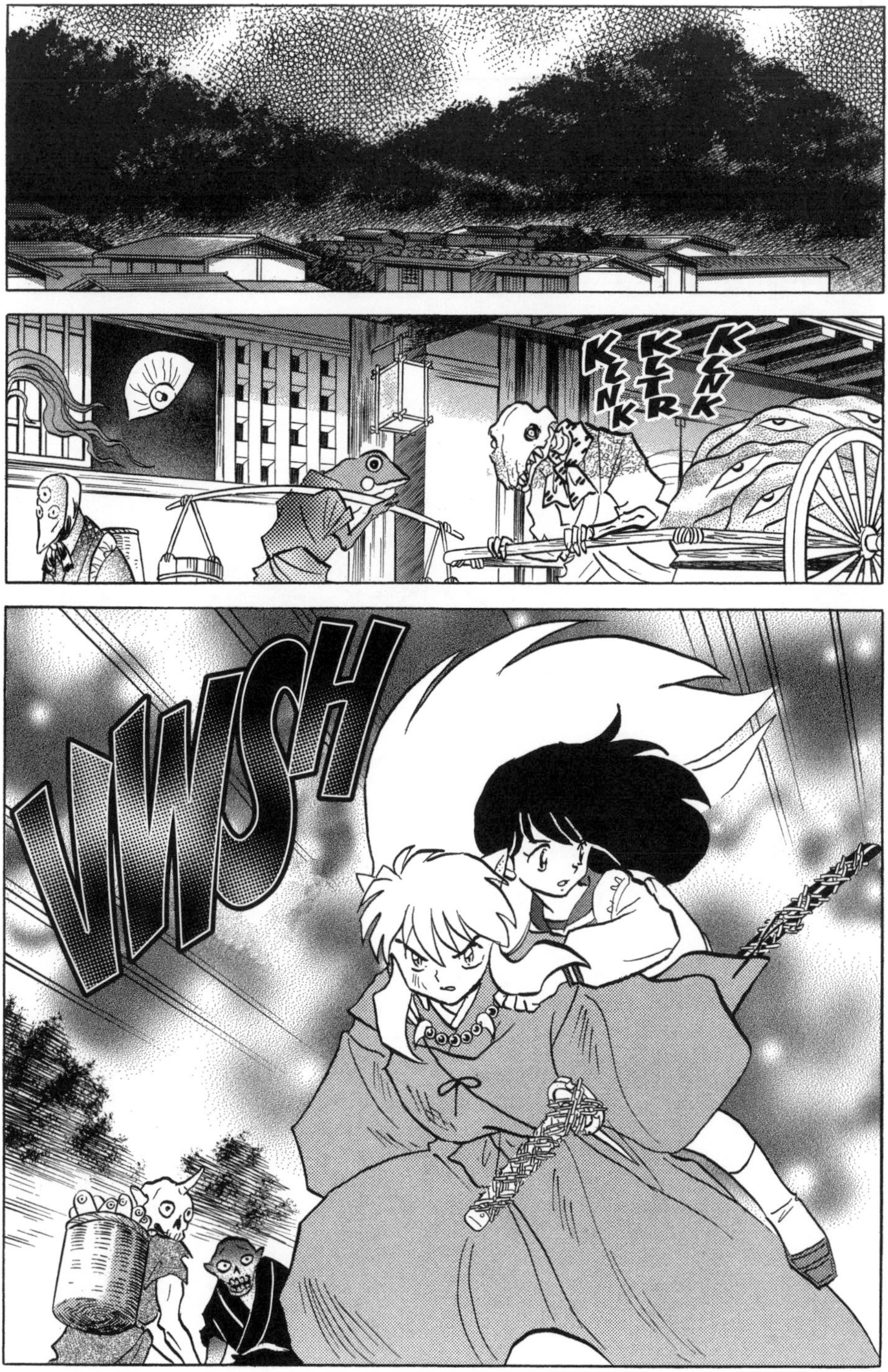
KLNK
KLTR
KLNK
VWSH

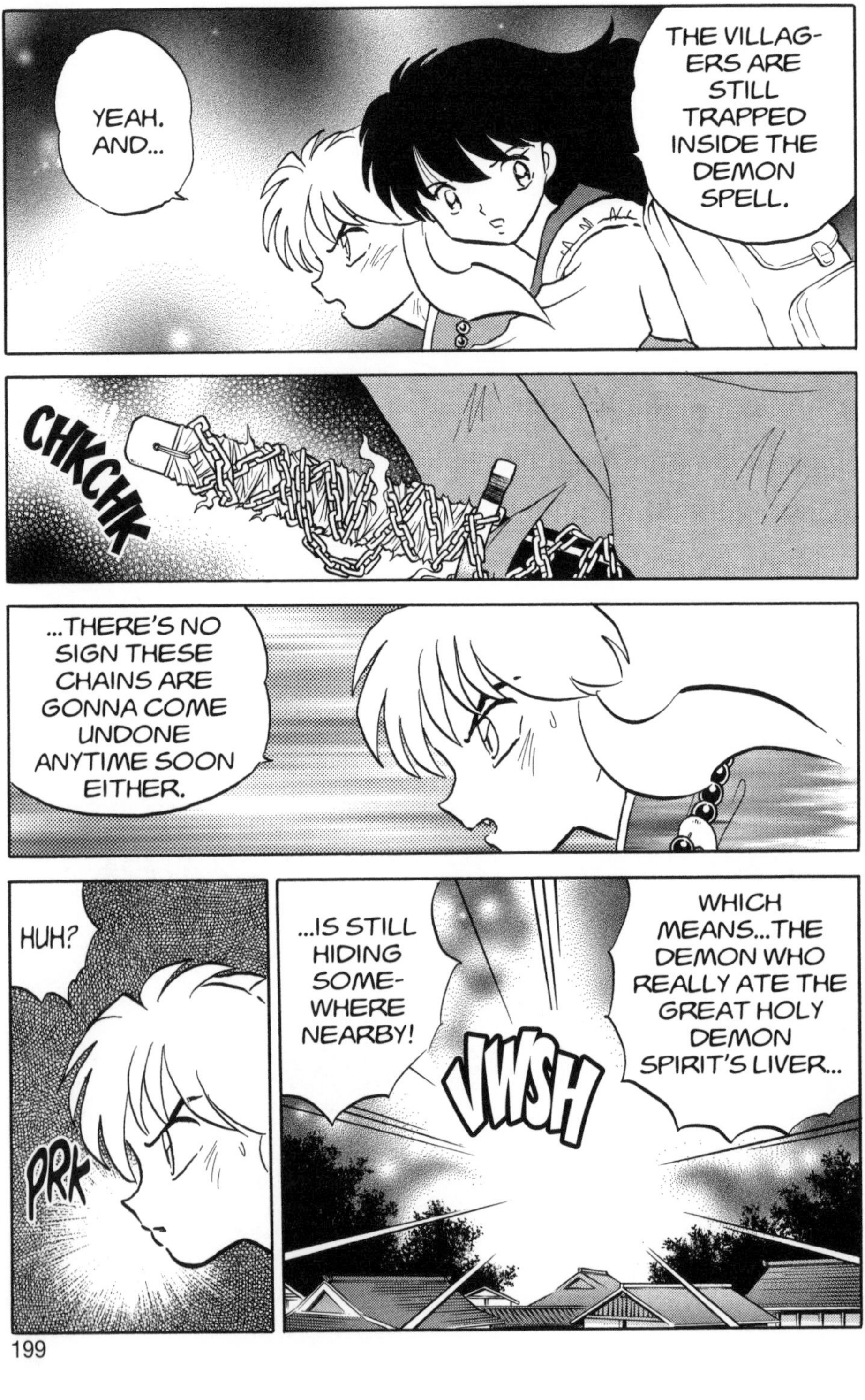
THE VILLAG-ERS ARE STILL TRAPPED INSIDE THE DEMON SPELL.
YEAH. AND...
CHKCHIK
...THERE'S NO SIGN THESE CHAINS ARE GONNA COME UNDONE ANYTIME SOON EITHER.
WHICH MEANS...THE DEMON WHO REALLY ATE THE GREAT HOLY DEMON SPIRIT'S LIVER...
...IS STILL HIDING SOME-WHERE NEARBY!
JWSH
HUH?
PRK

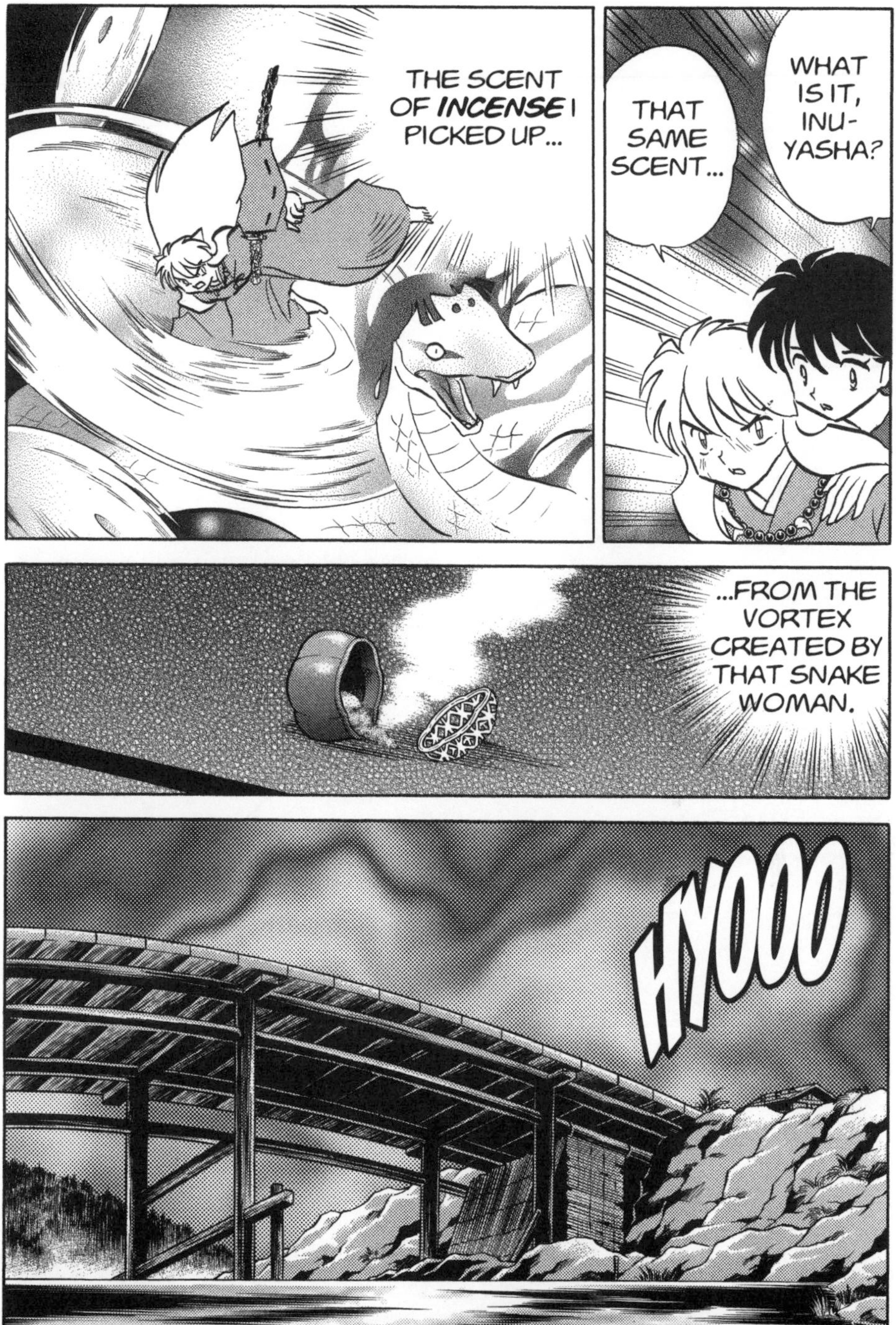
WHAT IS IT, INU-YASHA?
THAT SAME SCENT...
THE SCENT OF **INCENSE** I PICKED UP...
...FROM THE VORTEX CREATED BY THAT SNAKE WOMAN.
HYOOO

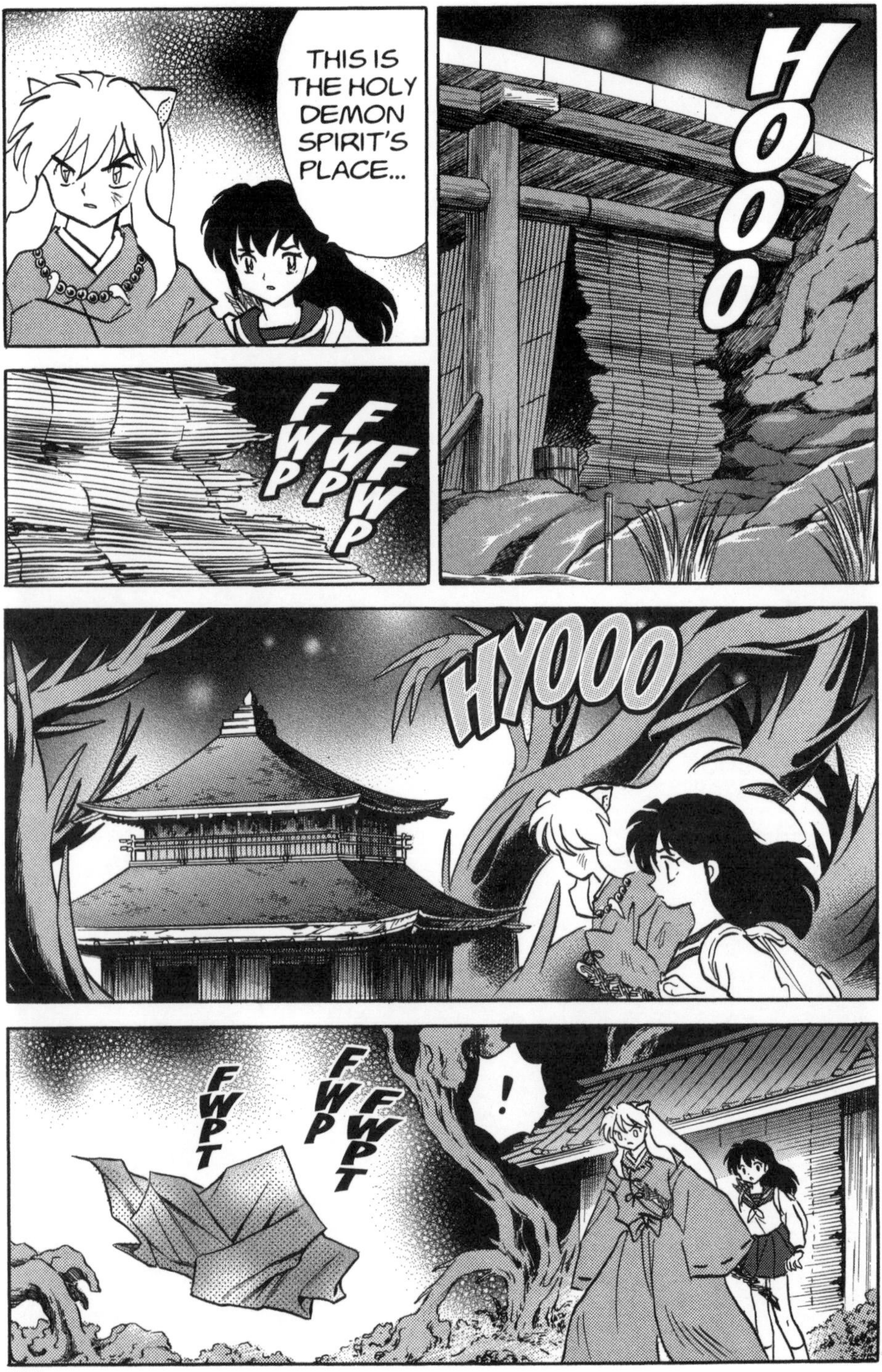
HOOOO
THIS IS THE HOLY DEMON SPIRIT'S PLACE...
FWP
FWP
FWP
HYOOO
!
FWP
FWPT
FWPT

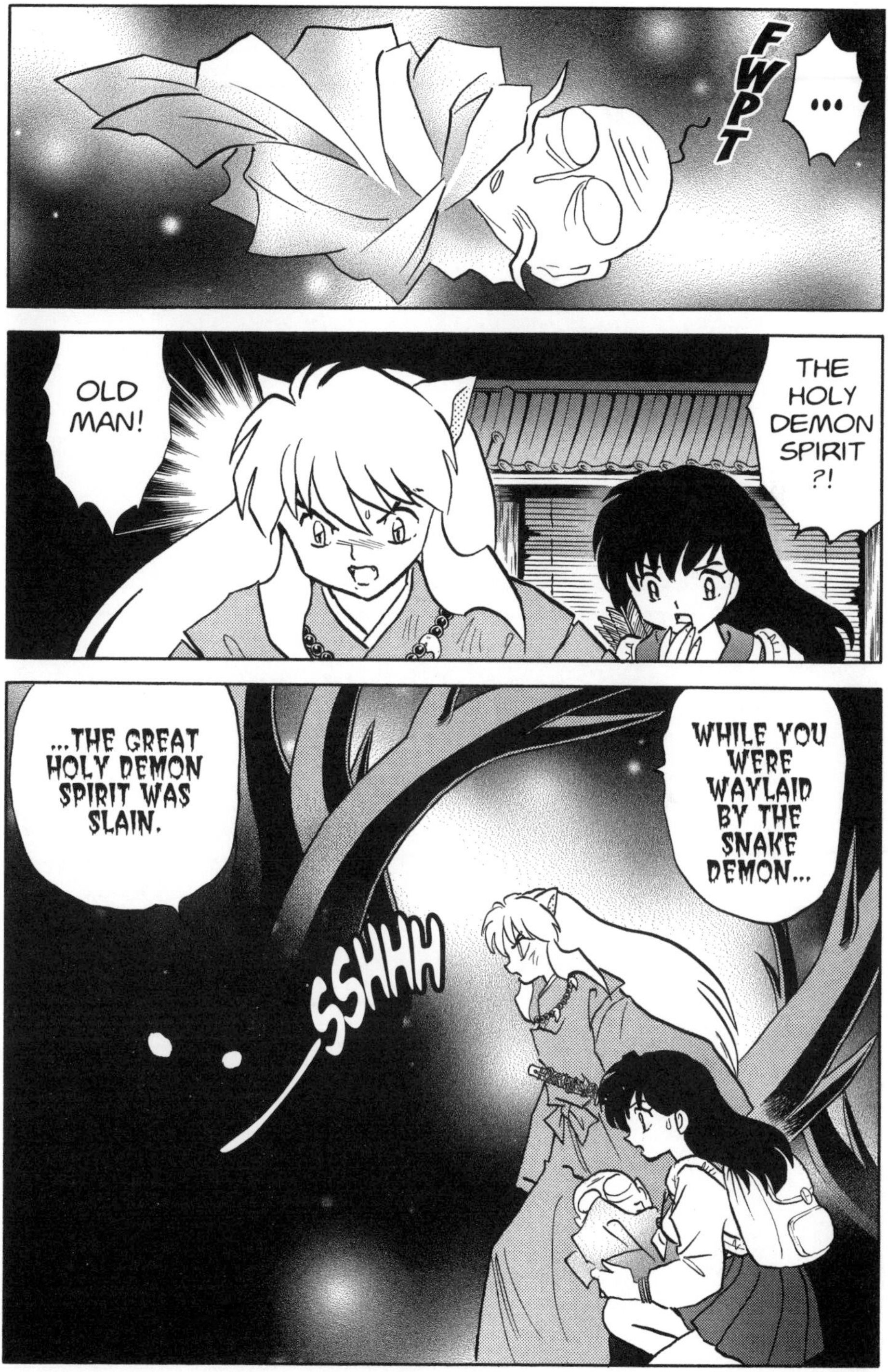
...
FWPT
THE HOLY DEMON SPIRIT?!
OLD MAN!
WHILE YOU WERE WAYLAID BY THE SNAKE DEMON...
...THE GREAT HOLY DEMON SPIRIT WAS SLAIN.
SSHHH

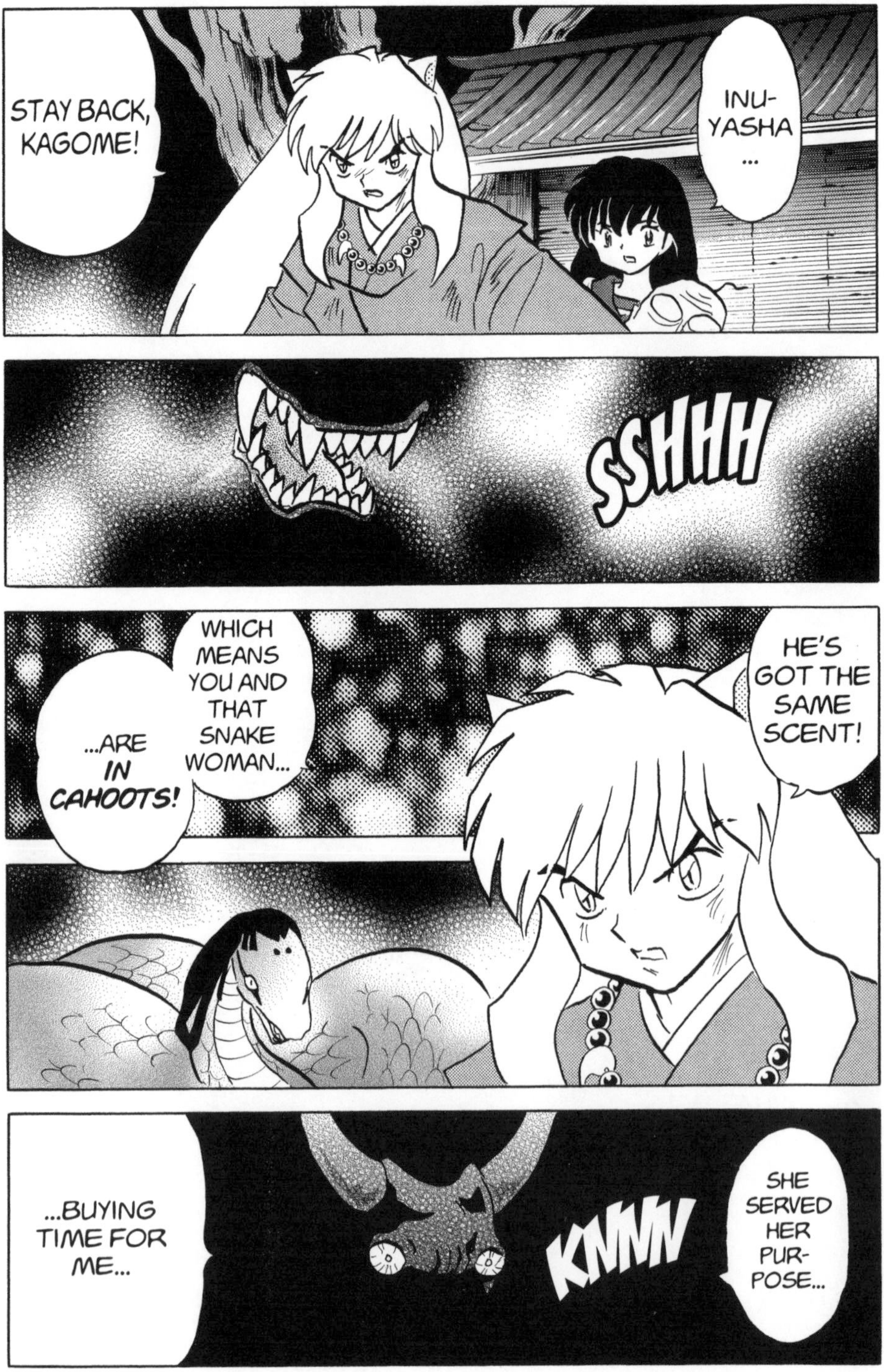
INU-YASHA ...
STAY BACK, KAGOME!
SSHHH
HE'S GOT THE SAME SCENT!
WHICH MEANS YOU AND THAT SNAKE WOMAN...
...ARE **IN CAHOOTS!**
SHE SERVED HER PUR-POSE...
KNNN
...BUYING TIME FOR ME...

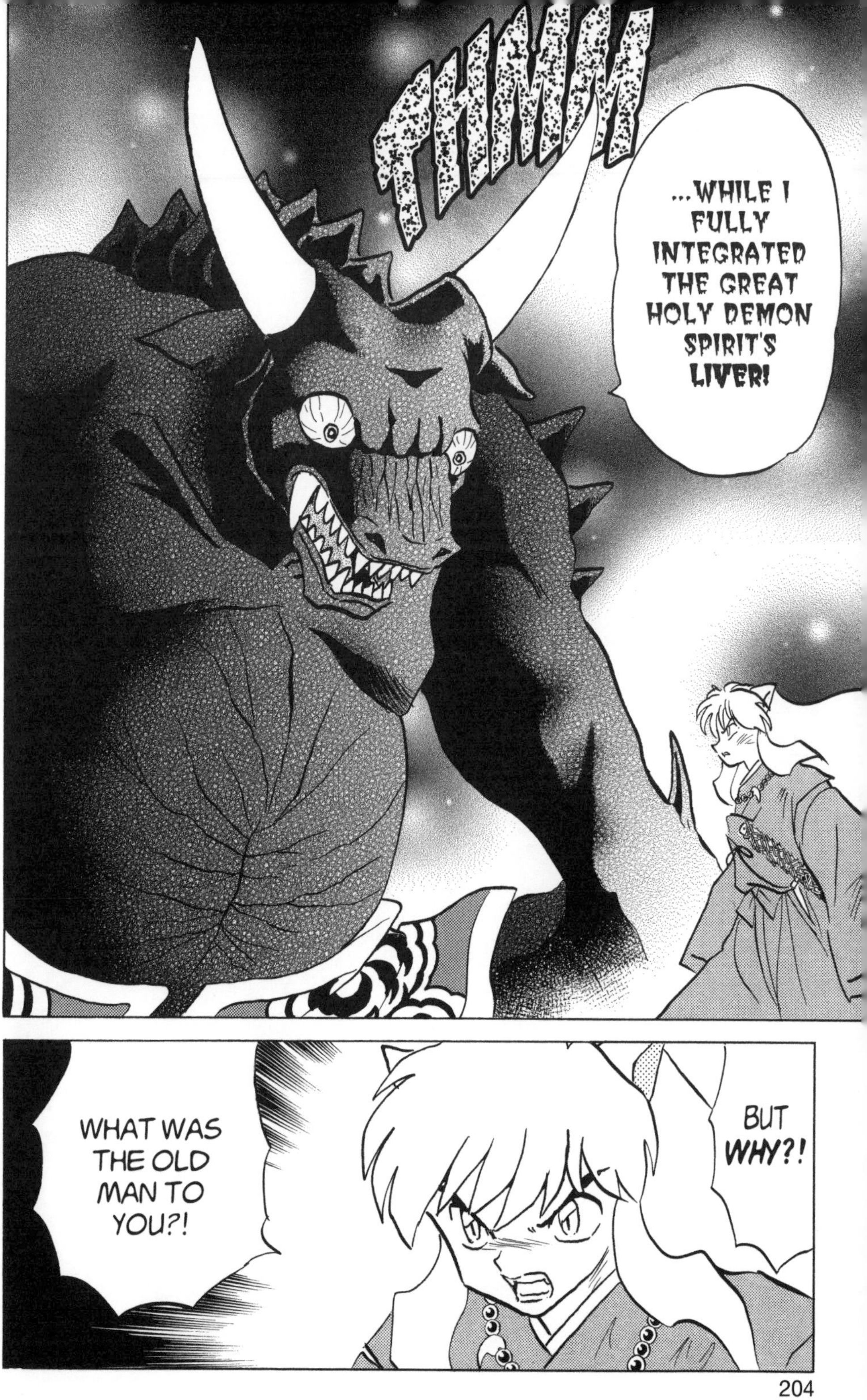
THMM
...WHILE I FULLY INTEGRATED THE GREAT HOLY DEMON SPIRIT'S LIVER!
BUT WHY?!
WHAT WAS THE OLD MAN TO YOU?!

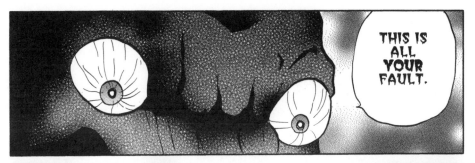

THIS IS ALL YOUR FAULT.
?!
HE'D BE ALIVE YET IF YOU HADN'T COME HERE TO TRAIN WITH HIM.
IT'S THAT BLADE OF YOURS.
!
IT ABSORBS OTHER DEMONS' DEMONIC ENERGY, YES?
CAN'T LEAVE A DANGEROUS BLADE LIKE THAT ON THE LOOSE...
...MUCH LESS LET IT KEEP GROWING STRONGER.

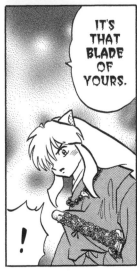

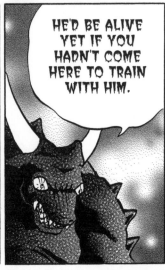

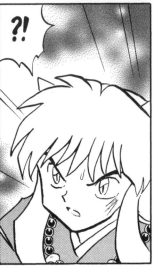

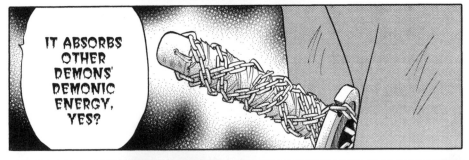

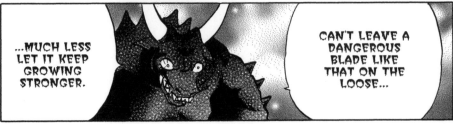

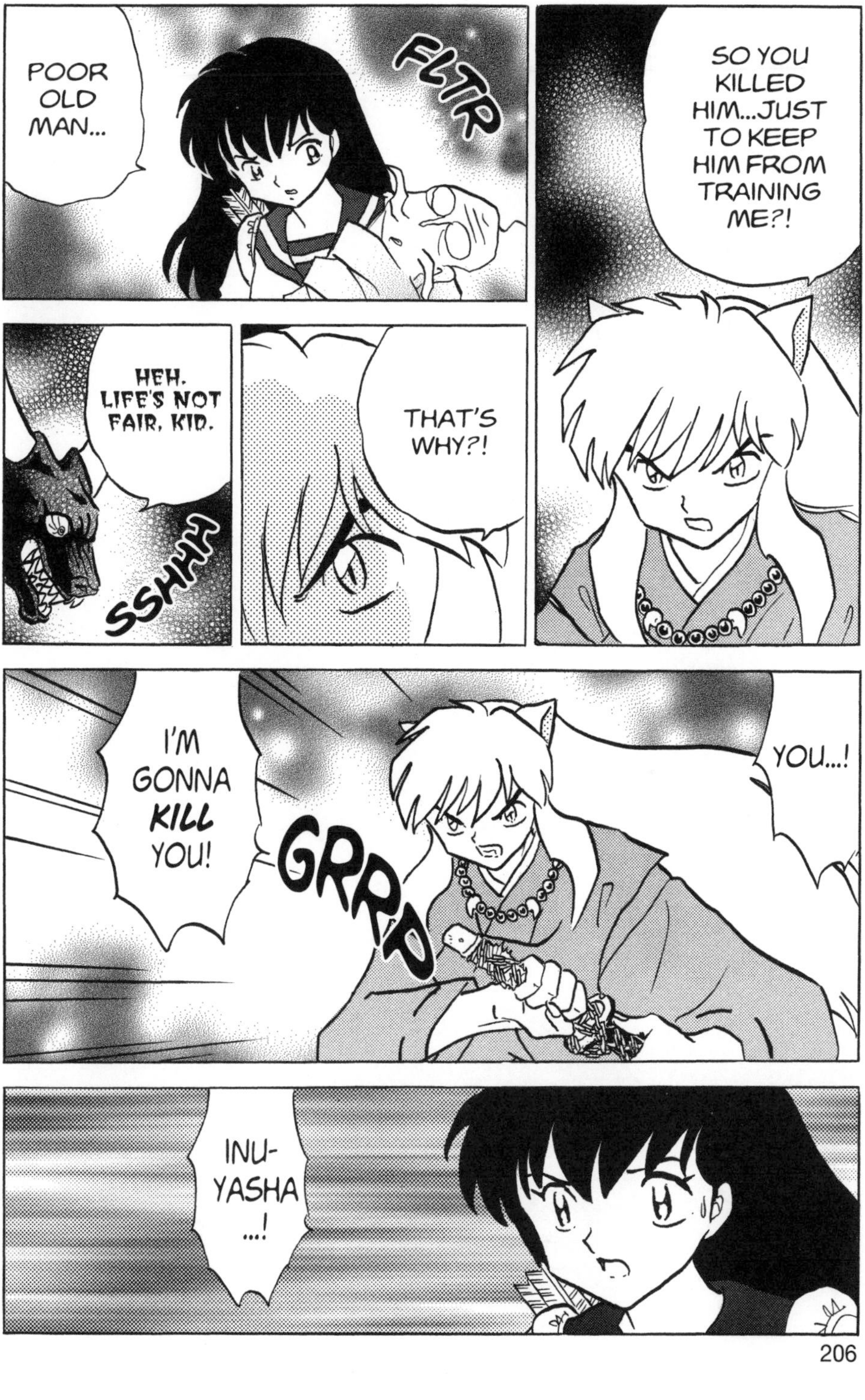
SO YOU KILLED HIM...JUST TO KEEP HIM FROM TRAINING ME?!
FLTR
POOR OLD MAN...
THAT'S WHY?!
HEH. LIFE'S NOT FAIR, KID.
SSHHH
YOU...!
GRRP
I'M GONNA **KILL** YOU!
INU-YASHA ...!

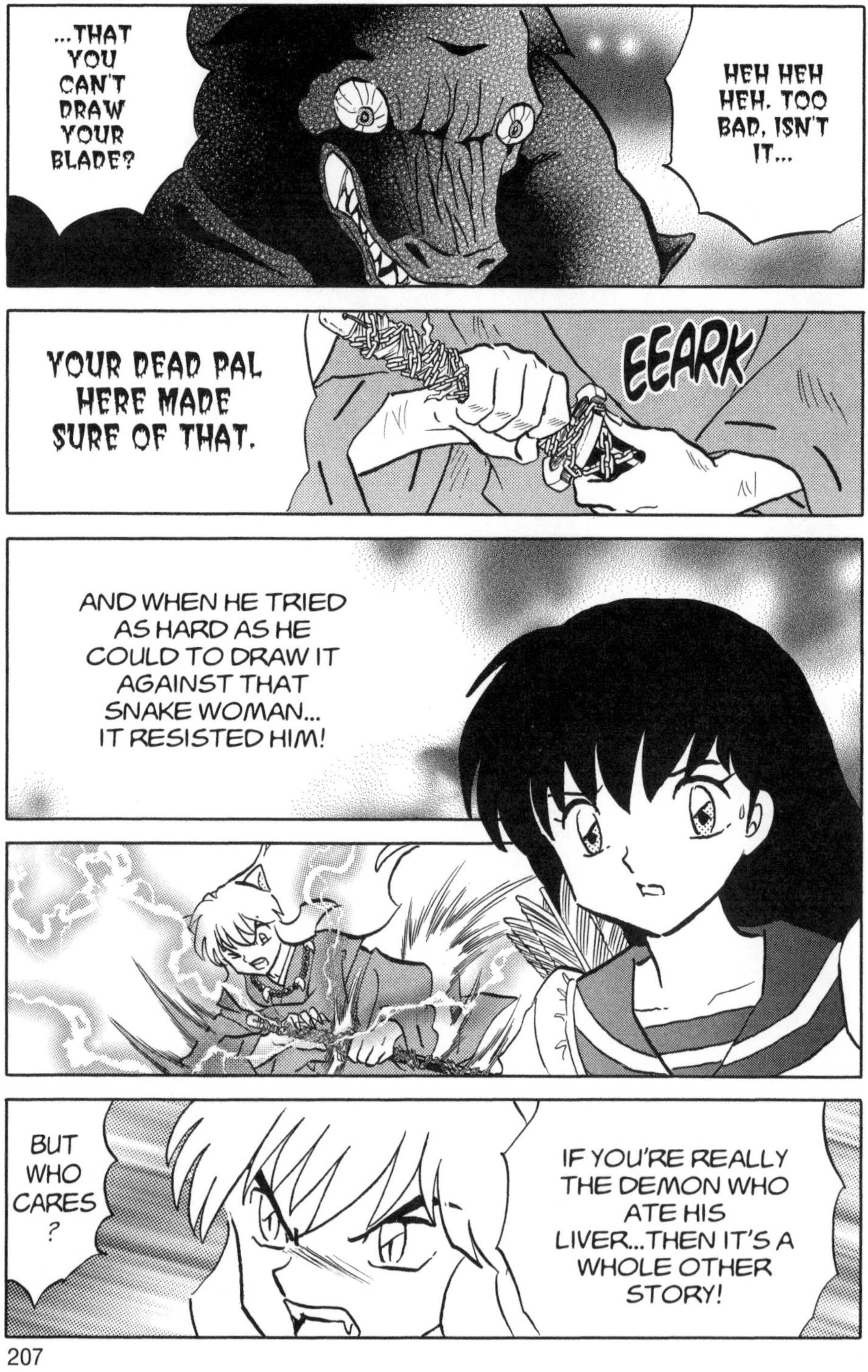
HEH HEH HEH. TOO BAD, ISN'T IT...
...THAT YOU CAN'T DRAW YOUR BLADE?
EEARK
YOUR DEAD PAL HERE MADE SURE OF THAT.
AND WHEN HE TRIED AS HARD AS HE COULD TO DRAW IT AGAINST THAT SNAKE WOMAN... IT RESISTED HIM!
IF YOU'RE REALLY THE DEMON WHO ATE HIS LIVER...THEN IT'S A WHOLE OTHER STORY!
BUT WHO CARES?

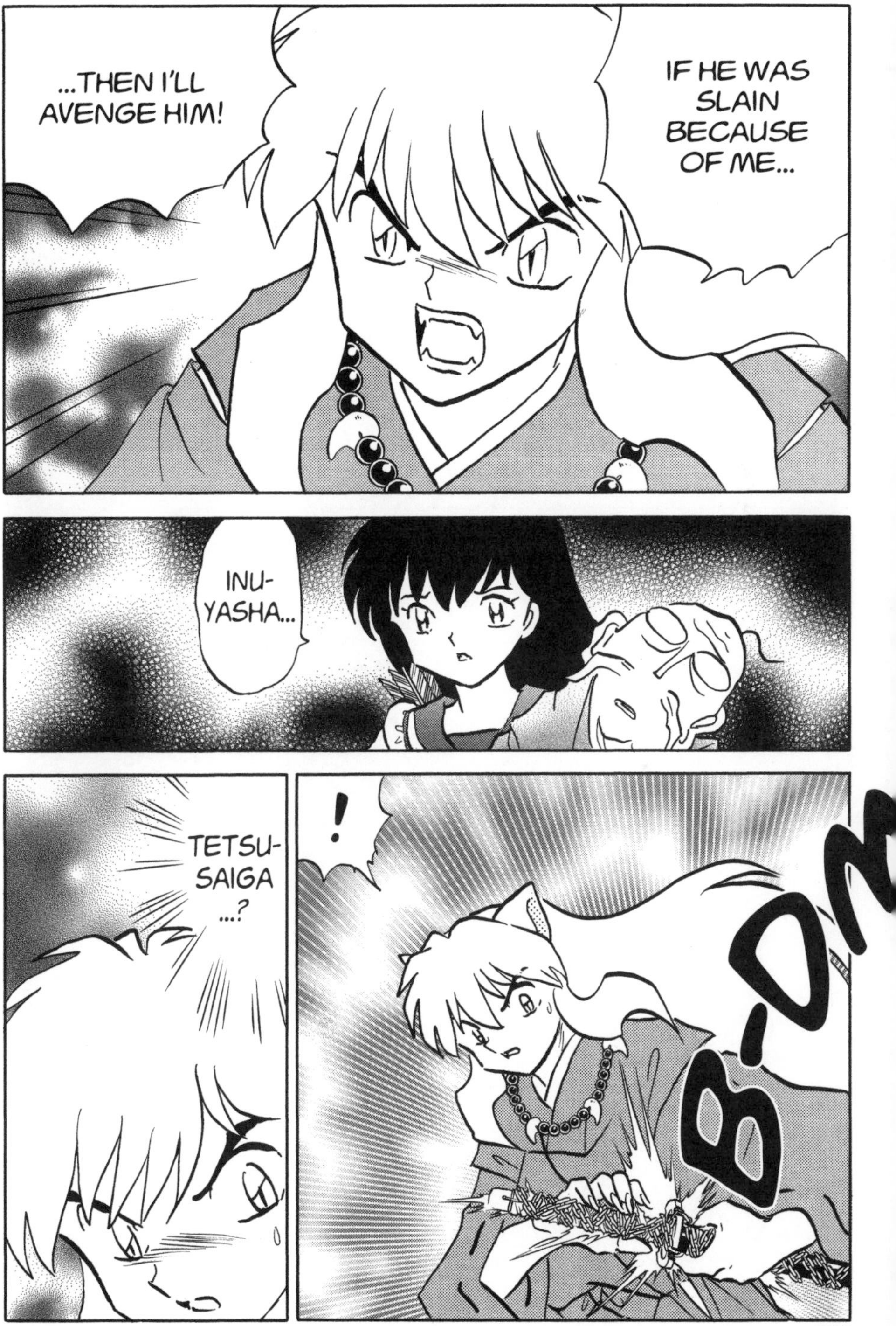
IF HE WAS SLAIN BECAUSE OF ME...
...THEN I'LL AVENGE HIM!
INU-YASHA...
!
B-DM
TETSU-SAIGA ...?

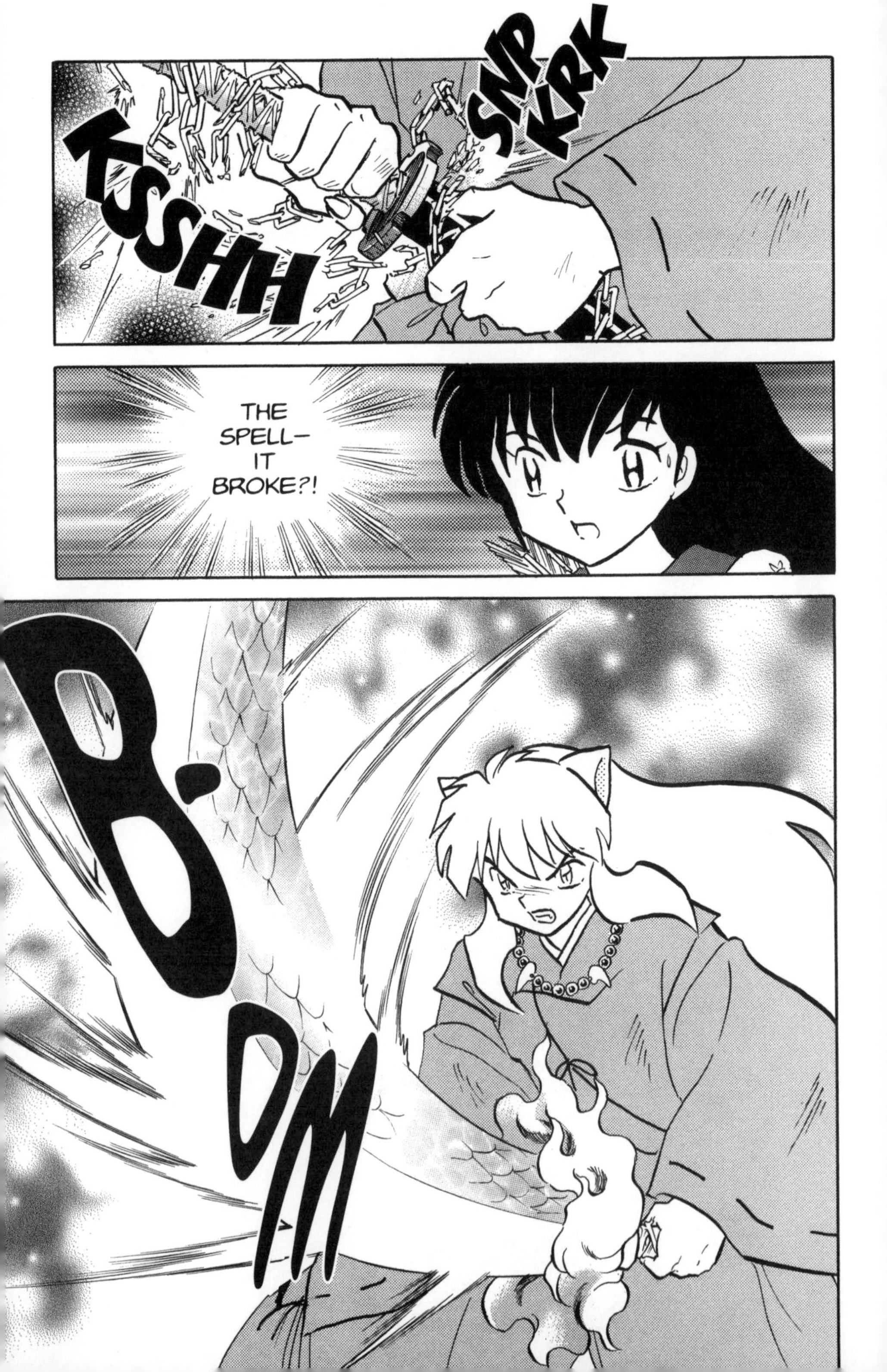
SNIP KRK
KSSHH
THE SPELL—IT BROKE?!
B-DM

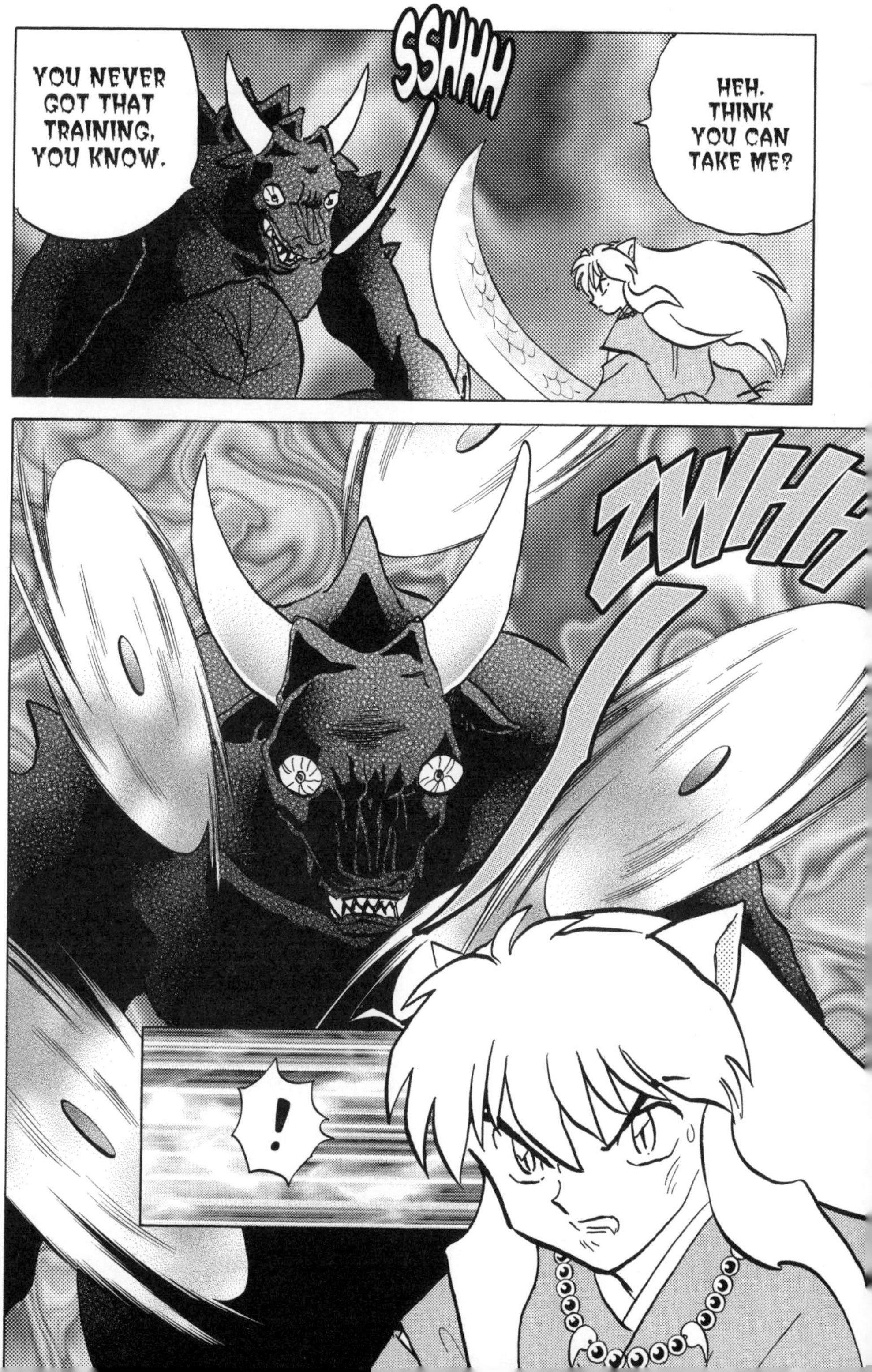
HEH. THINK YOU CAN TAKE ME?
SSHHH
YOU NEVER GOT THAT TRAINING, YOU KNOW.
ZWHH
!

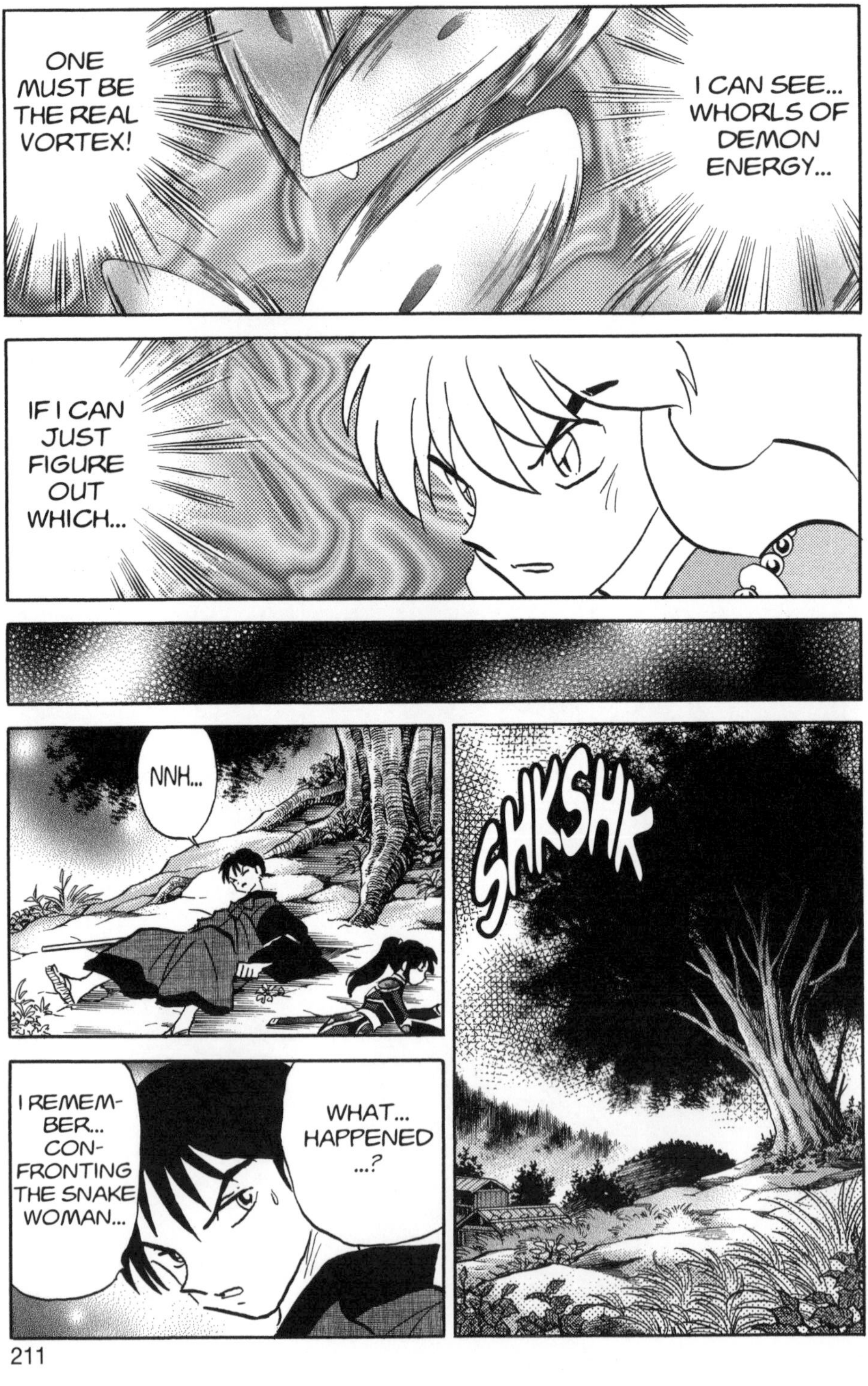
I CAN SEE... WHORLS OF DEMON ENERGY...
ONE MUST BE THE REAL VORTEX!
IF I CAN JUST FIGURE OUT WHICH...
SHKSHK
NNH...
WHAT... HAPPENED ...?
I REMEMBER... CONFRONTING THE SNAKE WOMAN...

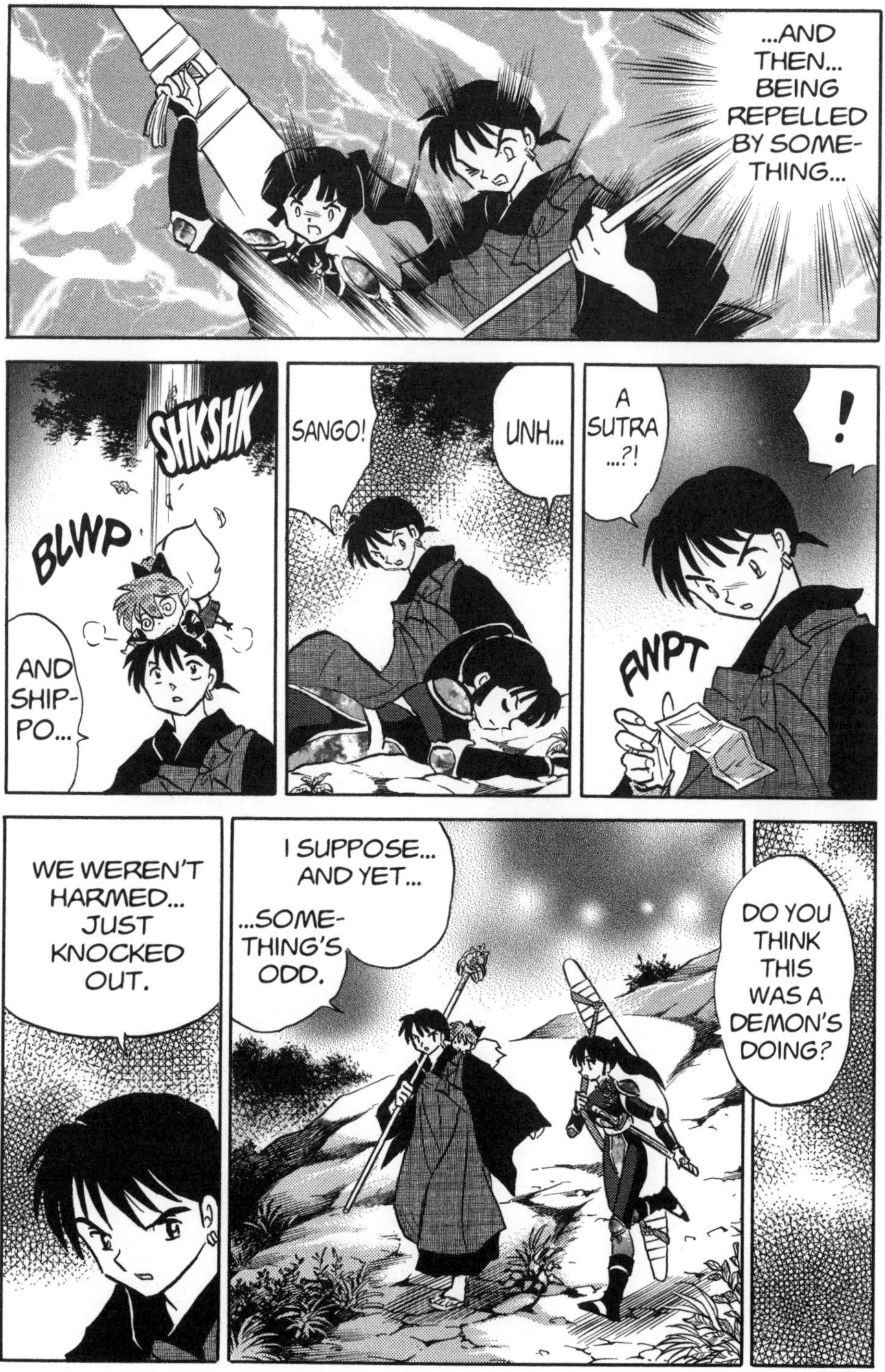
...AND THEN... BEING REPELLED BY SOME-THING...
!
A SUTRA ...?!
FWPT
UNH...
SANGO!
SHKSHK
BLWP
AND SHIP-PO...
DO YOU THINK THIS WAS A DEMON'S DOING?
I SUPPOSE... AND YET...
...SOME-THING'S ODD.
WE WEREN'T HARMED... JUST KNOCKED OUT.

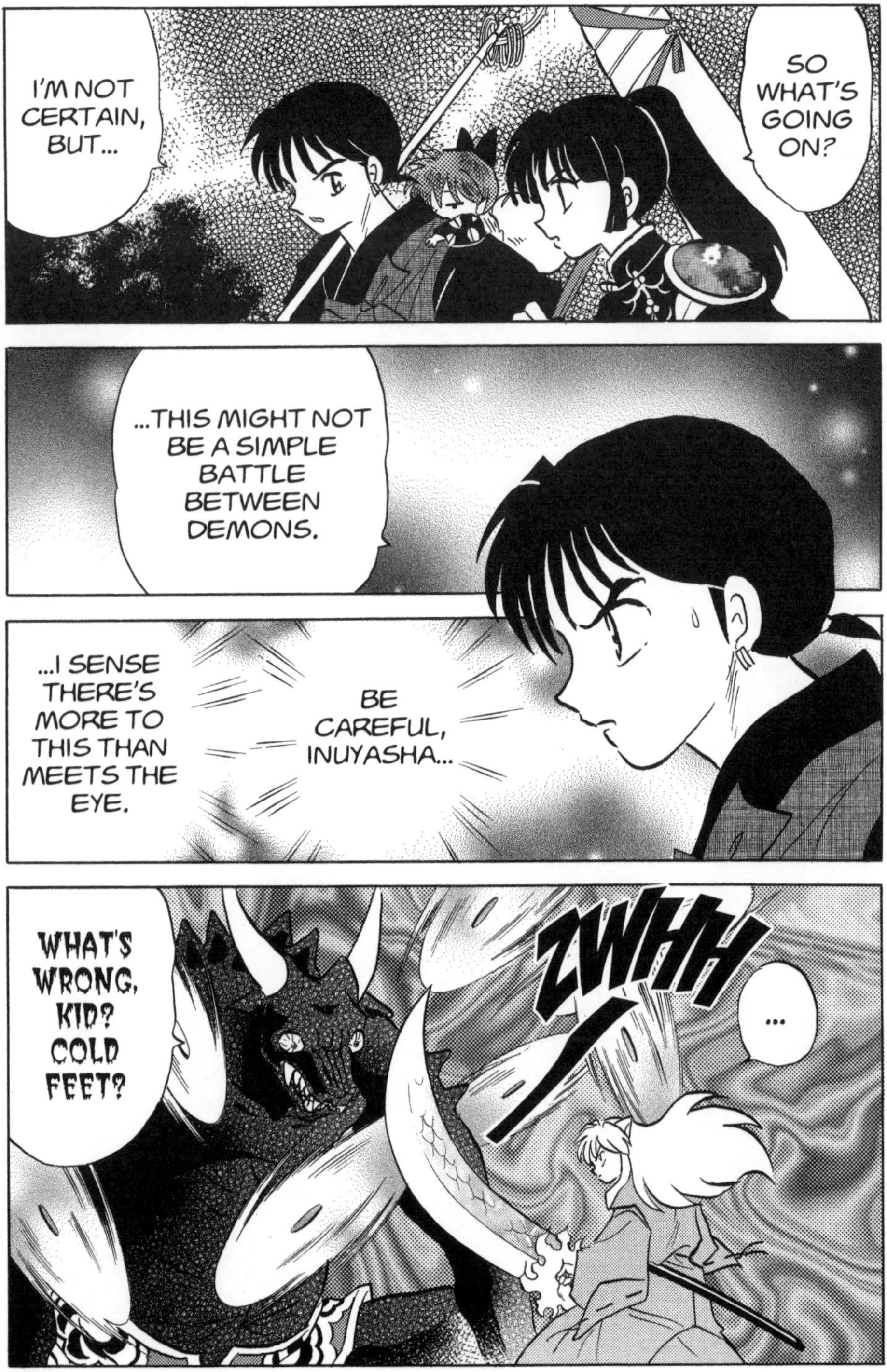
SO WHAT'S GOING ON?
I'M NOT CERTAIN, BUT...
...THIS MIGHT NOT BE A SIMPLE BATTLE BETWEEN DEMONS.
BE CAREFUL, INUYASHA...
...I SENSE THERE'S MORE TO THIS THAN MEETS THE EYE.
ZWHH
...
WHAT'S WRONG, KID? COLD FEET?

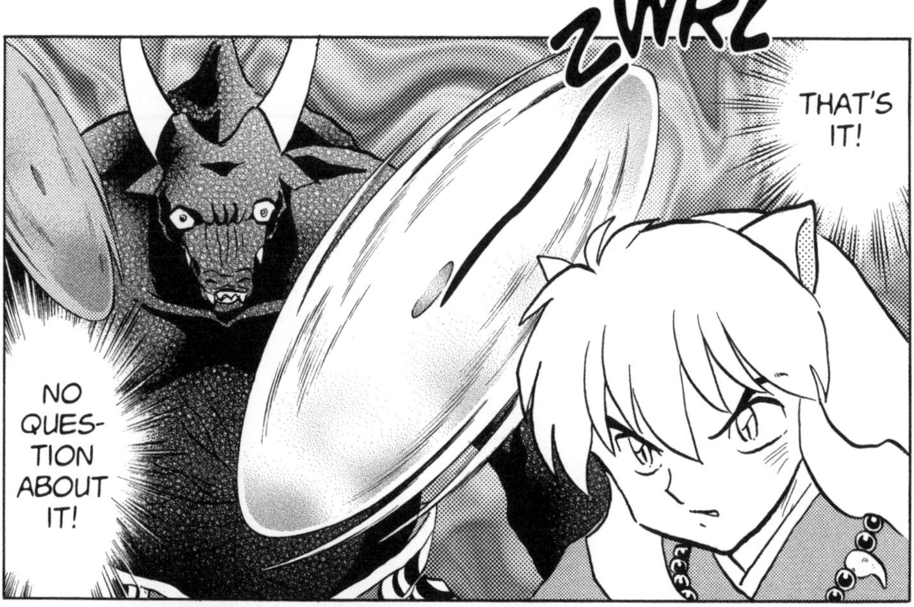
ZWRL
THAT'S IT!
NO QUES-TION ABOUT IT!

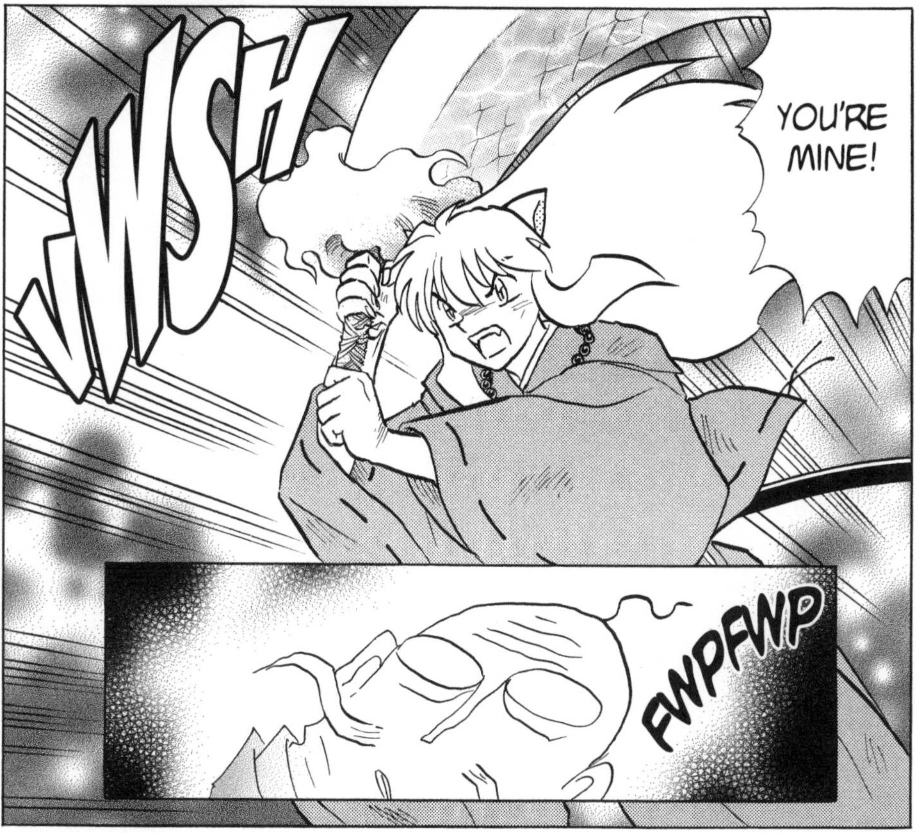
YOU'RE MINE!
VWSH
FWPFWP

SCROLL TWO
SCENT OF THE DEMON VORTEX

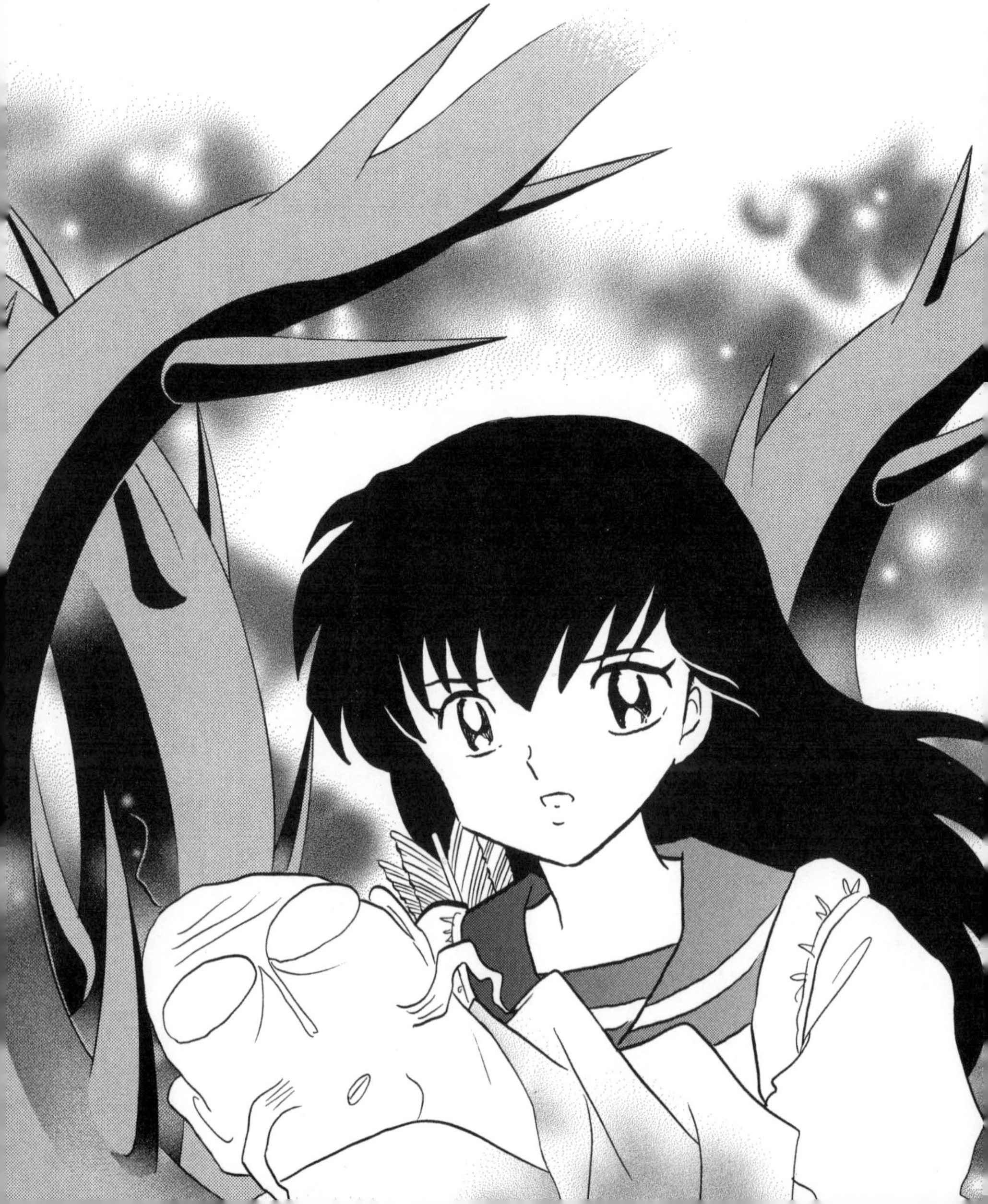

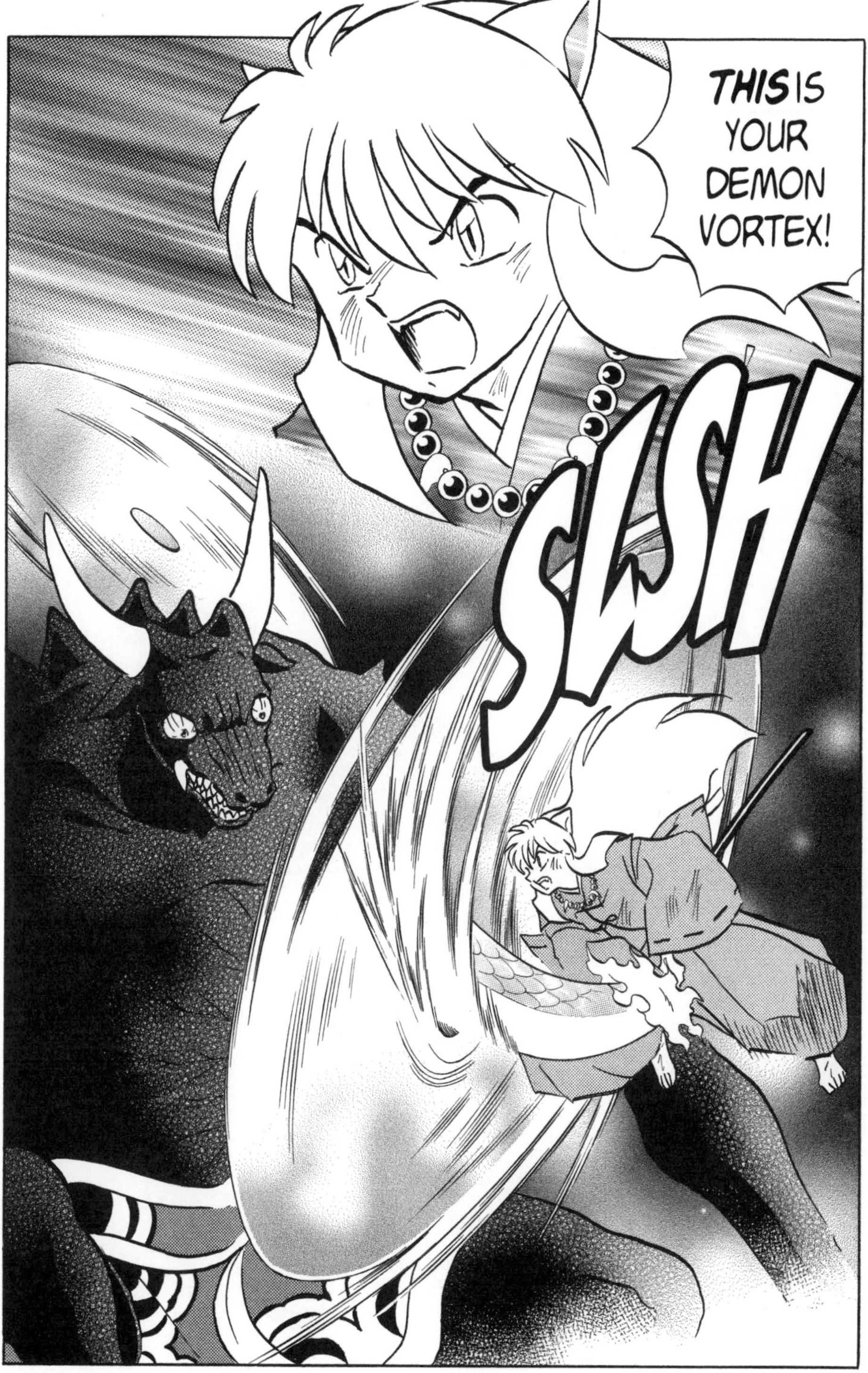
THIS IS YOUR DEMON VORTEX!
SLSH

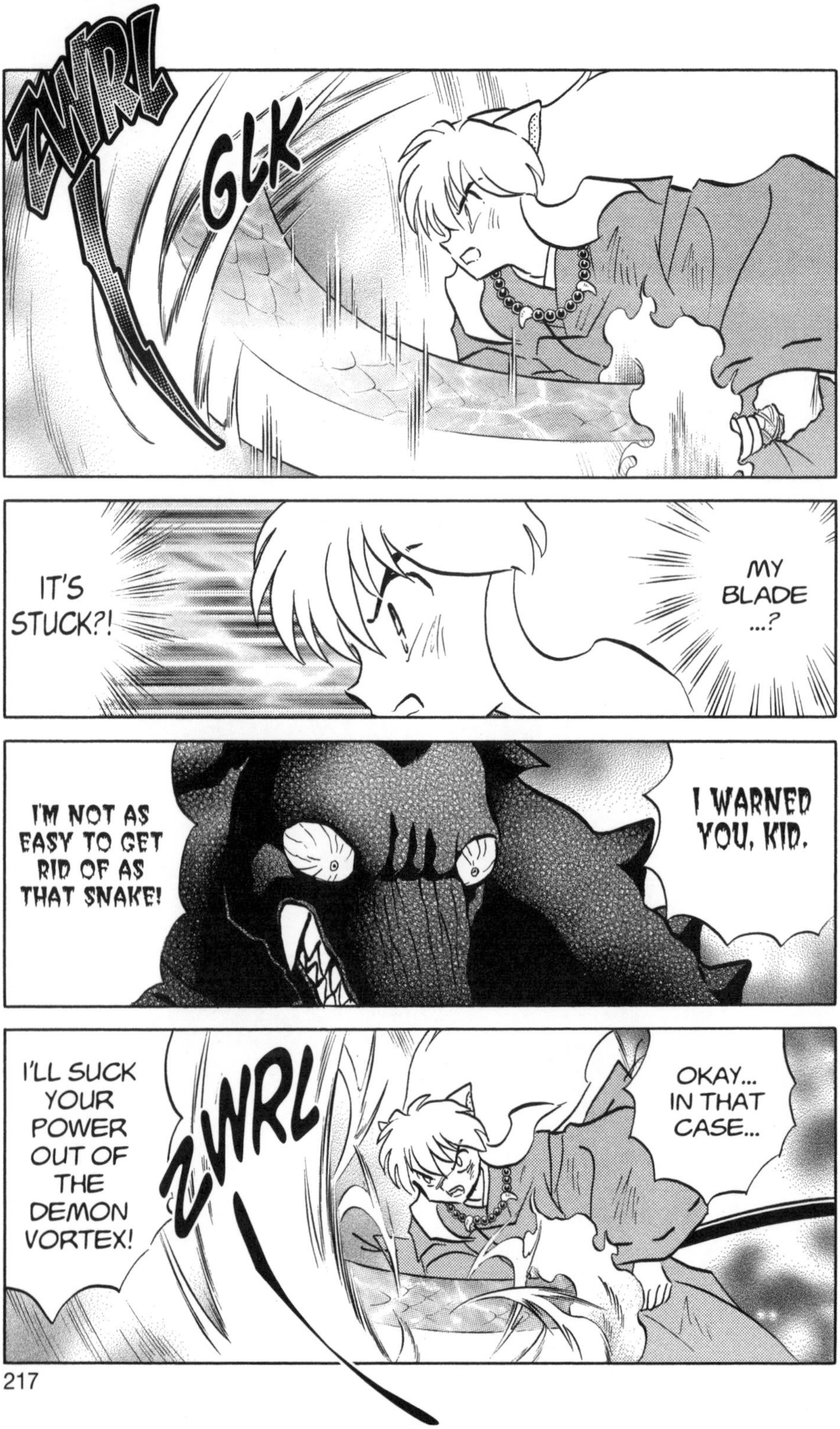
GLK
ZWRL
MY BLADE ...?
IT'S STUCK?!
I WARNED YOU, KID.
I'M NOT AS EASY TO GET RID OF AS THAT SNAKE!
OKAY... IN THAT CASE...
ZWRL
I'LL SUCK YOUR POWER OUT OF THE DEMON VORTEX!

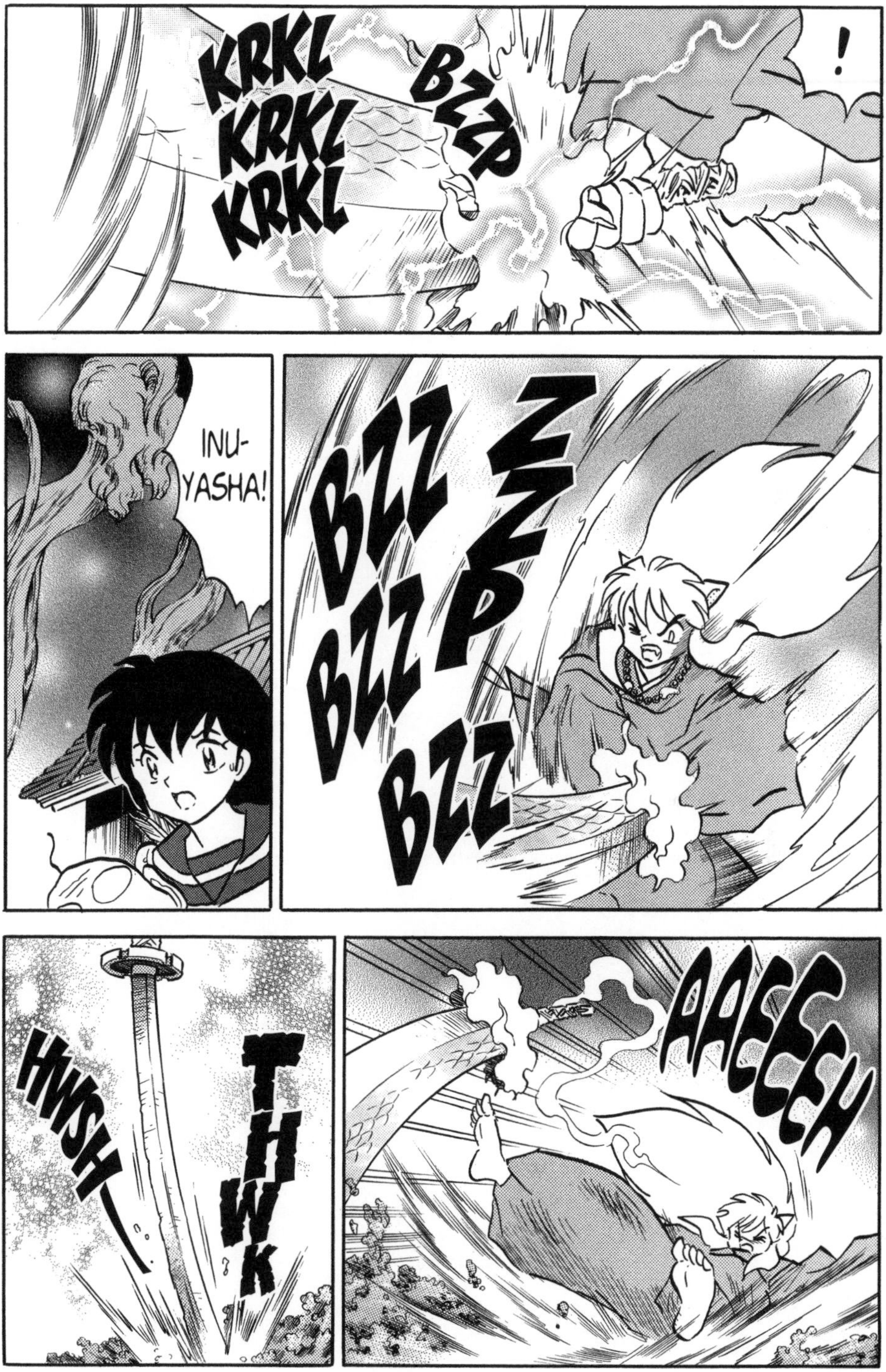
!
BZZP
KRKL
KRKL
KRKL
ZZ
BZZ
BZZP
BZZ
INU-YASHA!
AAEEEH
THWK
HWSH

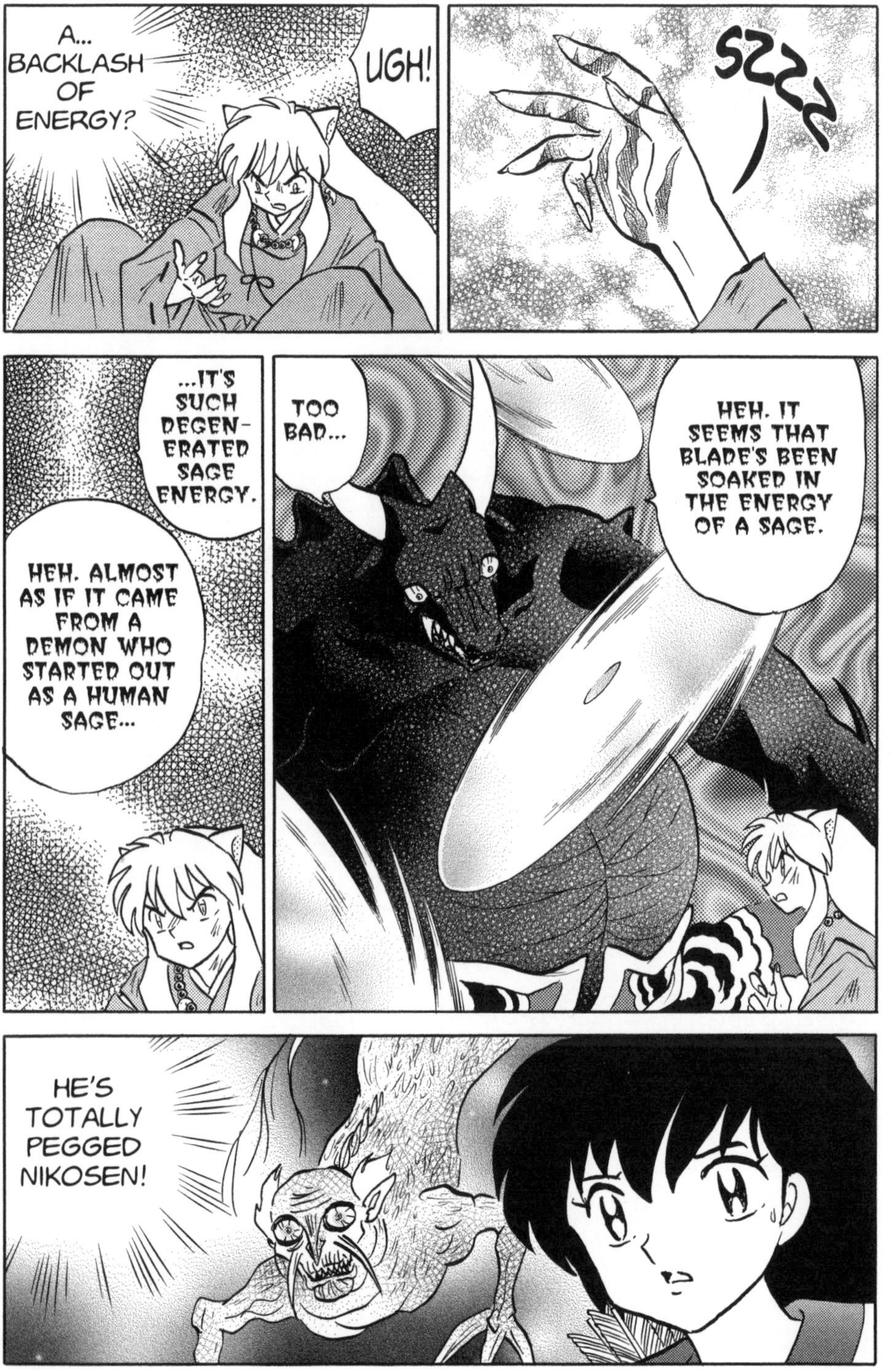
SZZZ
UGH!
A... BACKLASH OF ENERGY?
HEH. IT SEEMS THAT BLADE'S BEEN SOAKED IN THE ENERGY OF A SAGE.
TOO BAD...
...IT'S SUCH DEGEN-ERATED SAGE ENERGY.
HEH. ALMOST AS IF IT CAME FROM A DEMON WHO STARTED OUT AS A HUMAN SAGE...
HE'S TOTALLY PEGGED NIKOSEN!

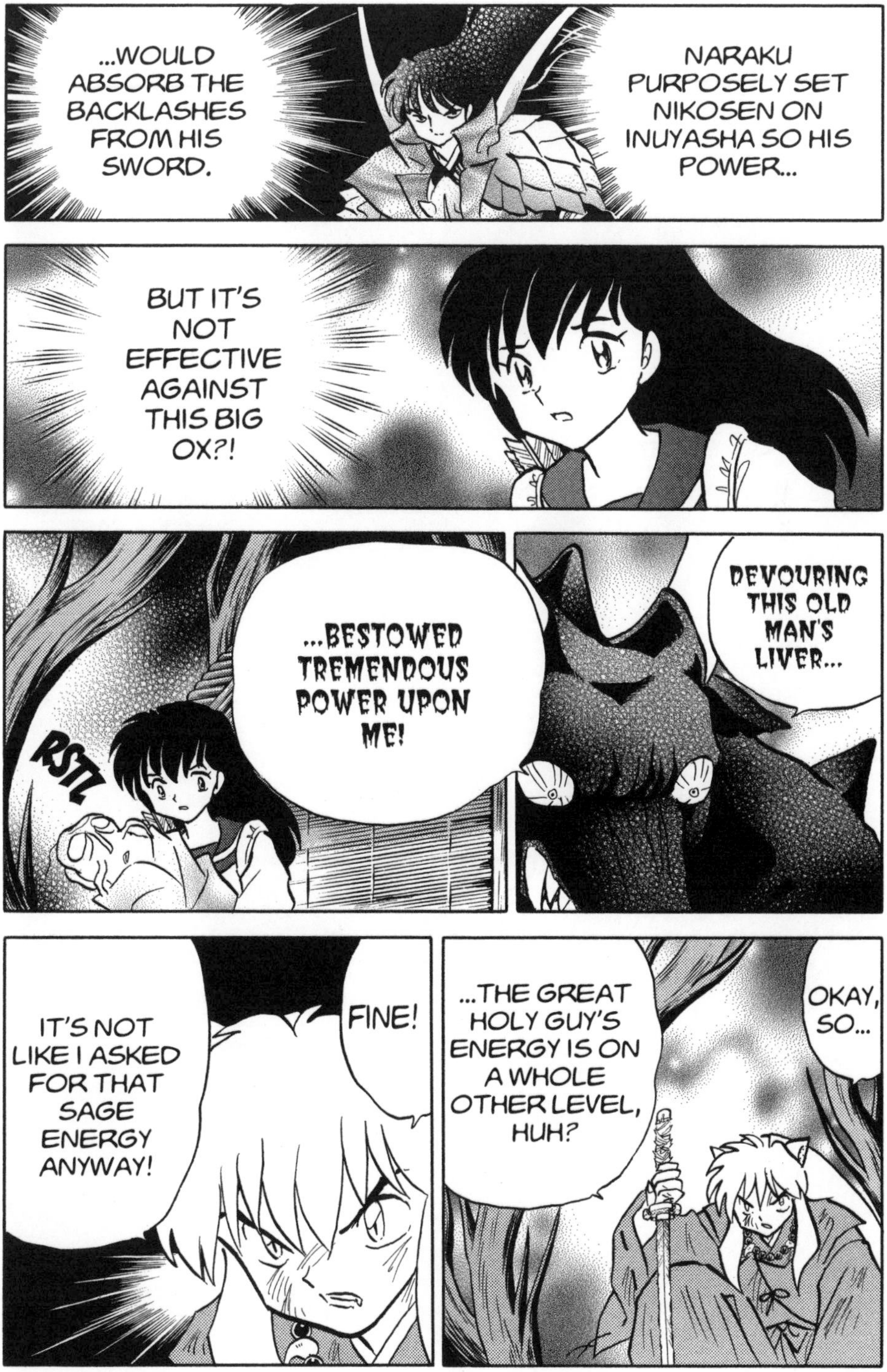
NARAKU PURPOSELY SET NIKOSEN ON INUYASHA SO HIS POWER...
...WOULD ABSORB THE BACKLASHES FROM HIS SWORD.
BUT IT'S NOT EFFECTIVE AGAINST THIS BIG OX?!
DEVOURING THIS OLD MAN'S LIVER...
...BESTOWED TREMENDOUS POWER UPON ME!
RSTL
OKAY, SO...
...THE GREAT HOLY GUY'S ENERGY IS ON A WHOLE OTHER LEVEL, HUH?
FINE!
IT'S NOT LIKE I ASKED FOR THAT SAGE ENERGY ANYWAY!

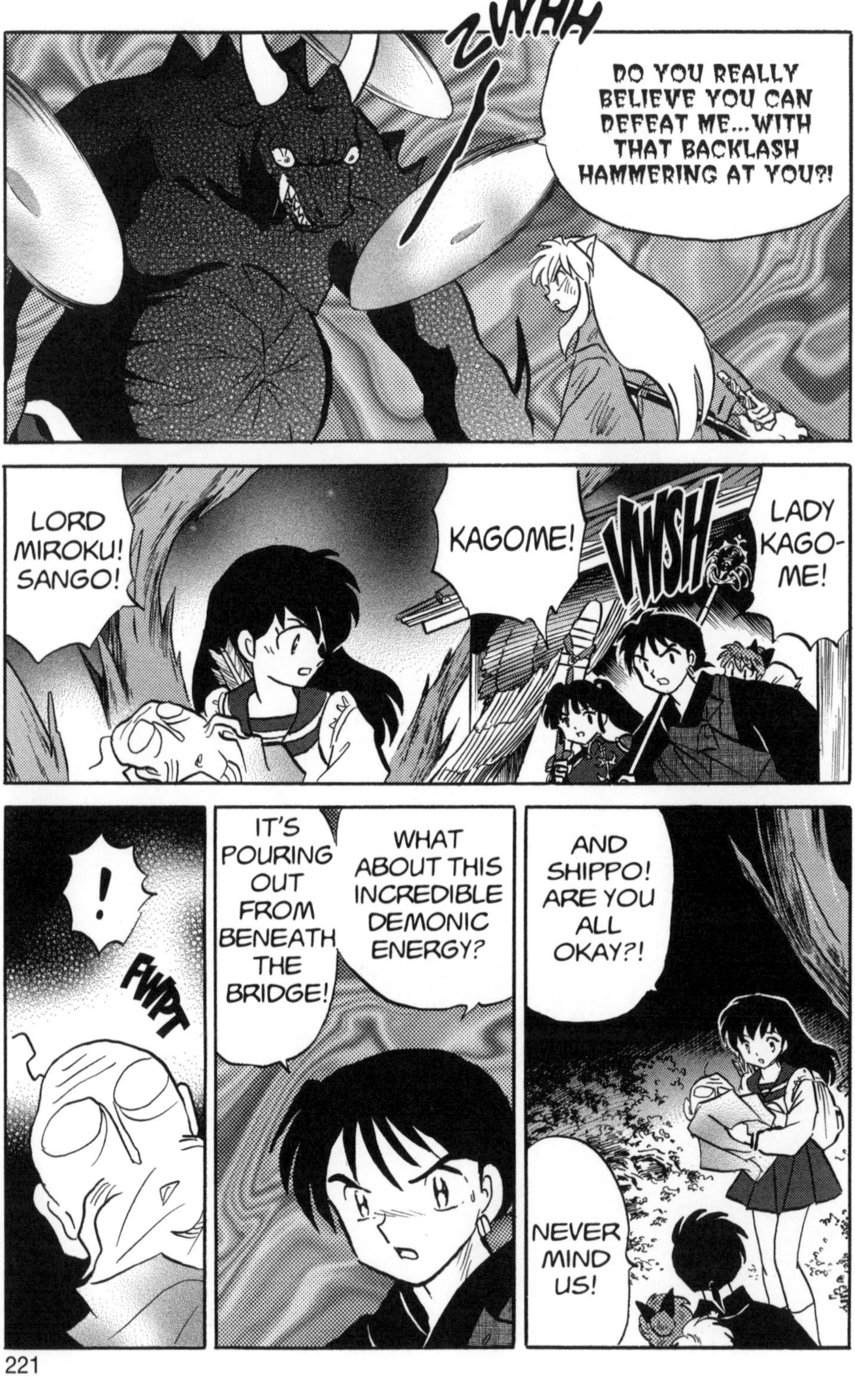
ZWHH
DO YOU REALLY BELIEVE YOU CAN DEFEAT ME...WITH THAT BACKLASH HAMMERING AT YOU?!
LADY KAGO-ME!
VWISH
KAGOME!
LORD MIROKU! SANGO!
AND SHIPPO! ARE YOU ALL OKAY?!
NEVER MIND US!
WHAT ABOUT THIS INCREDIBLE DEMONIC ENERGY?
IT'S POURING OUT FROM BENEATH THE BRIDGE!
!
FWPT

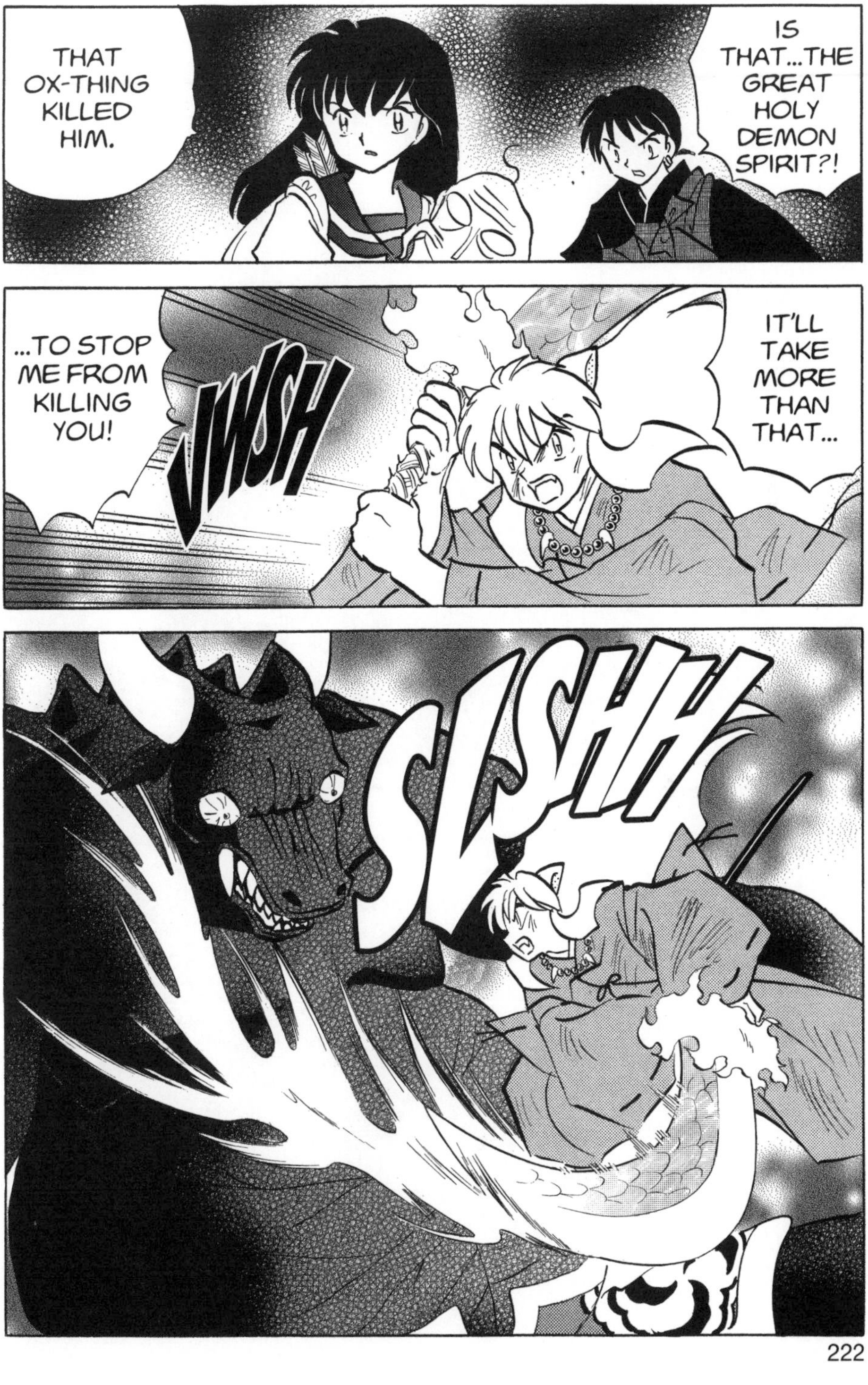
IS THAT...THE GREAT HOLY DEMON SPIRIT?!
THAT OX-THING KILLED HIM.
IT'LL TAKE MORE THAN THAT...
...TO STOP ME FROM KILLING YOU!
JWSH
SLSHH

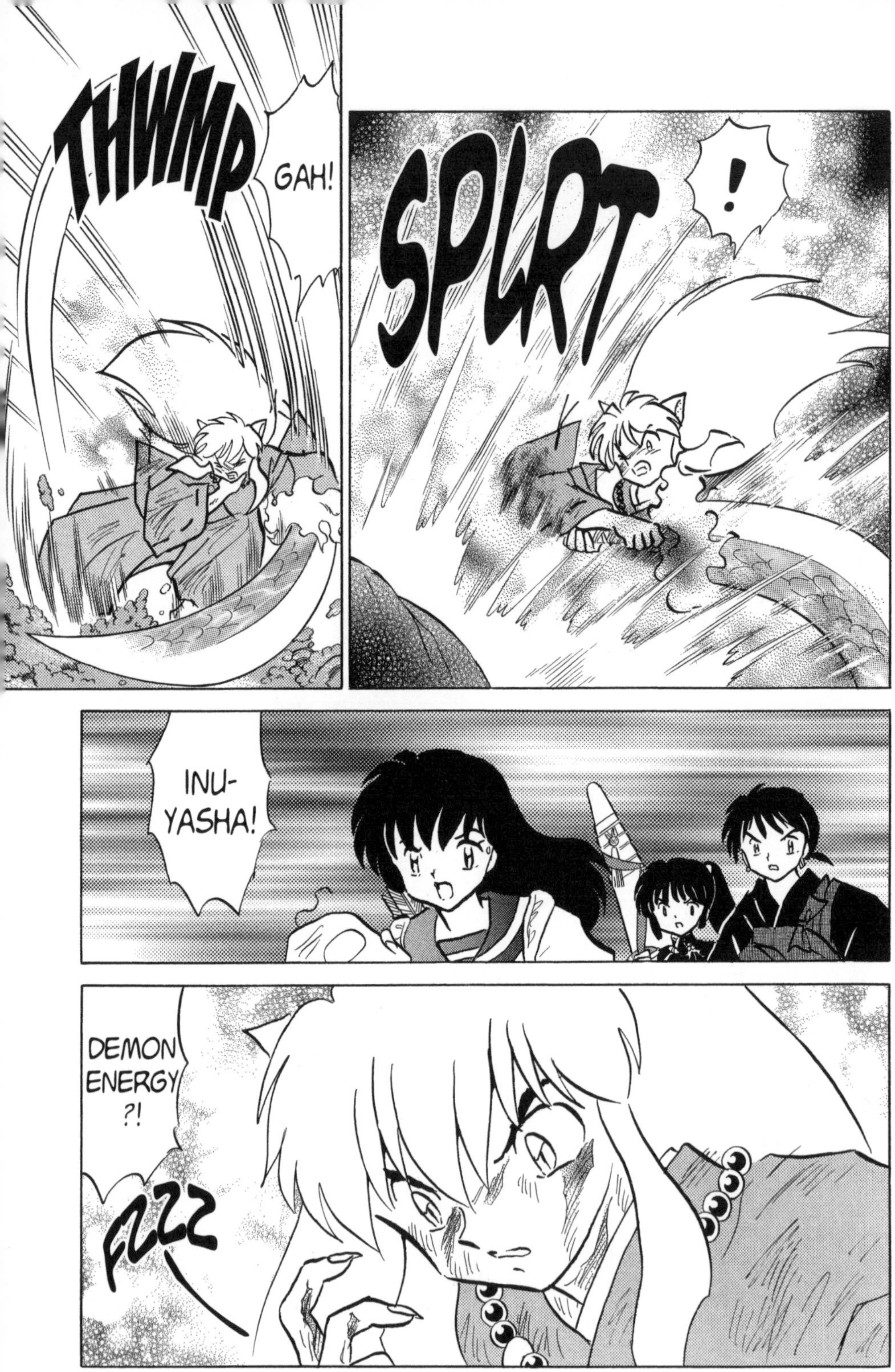
SPLRT
!
THWMP
GAH!
INU-YASHA!
DEMON ENERGY ?!
FZZZ

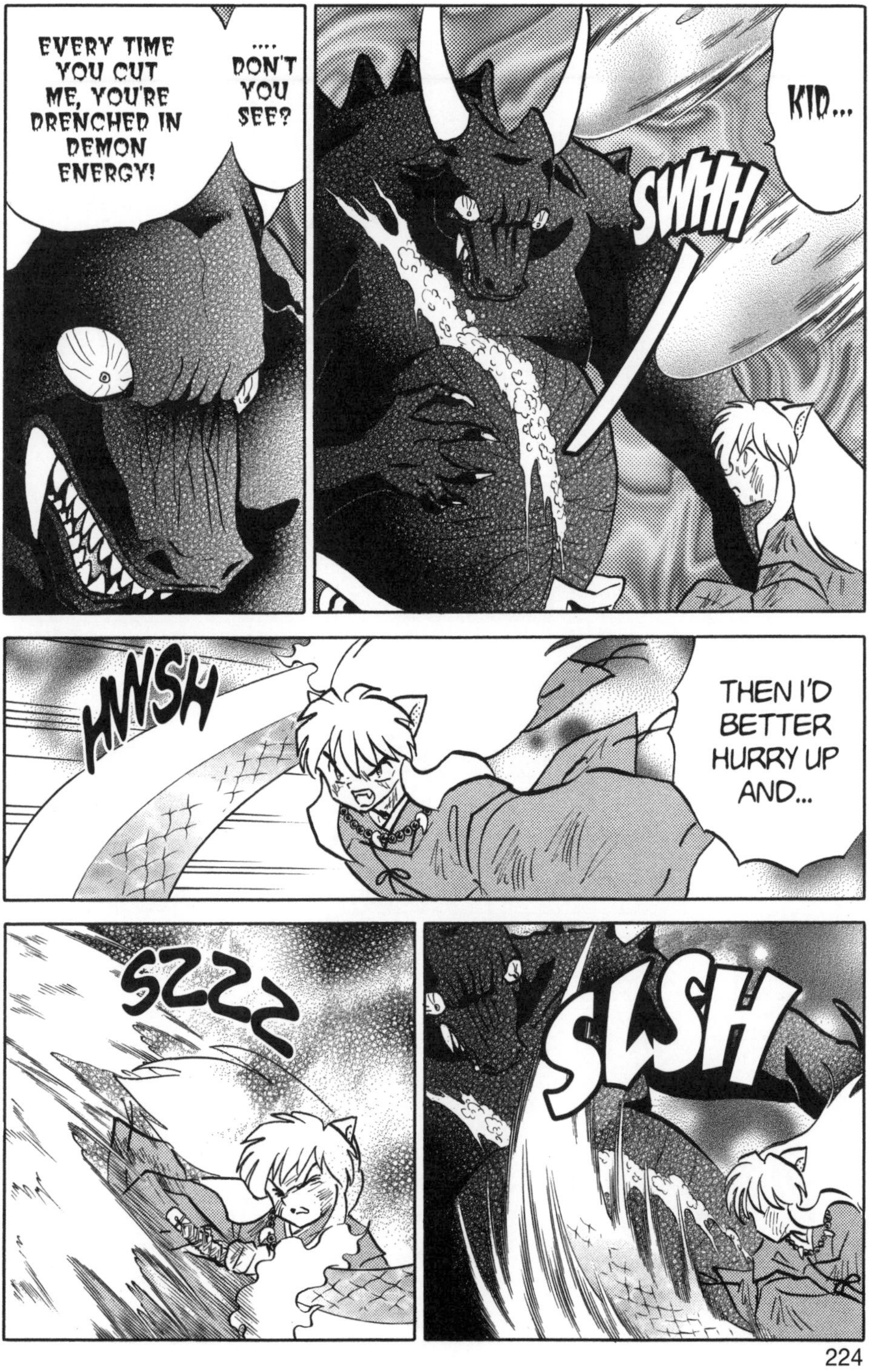
KID...
SWHH
.... DON'T YOU SEE?
EVERY TIME YOU CUT ME, YOU'RE DRENCHED IN DEMON ENERGY!
THEN I'D BETTER HURRY UP AND...
HWSH
SLSH
SZZZ

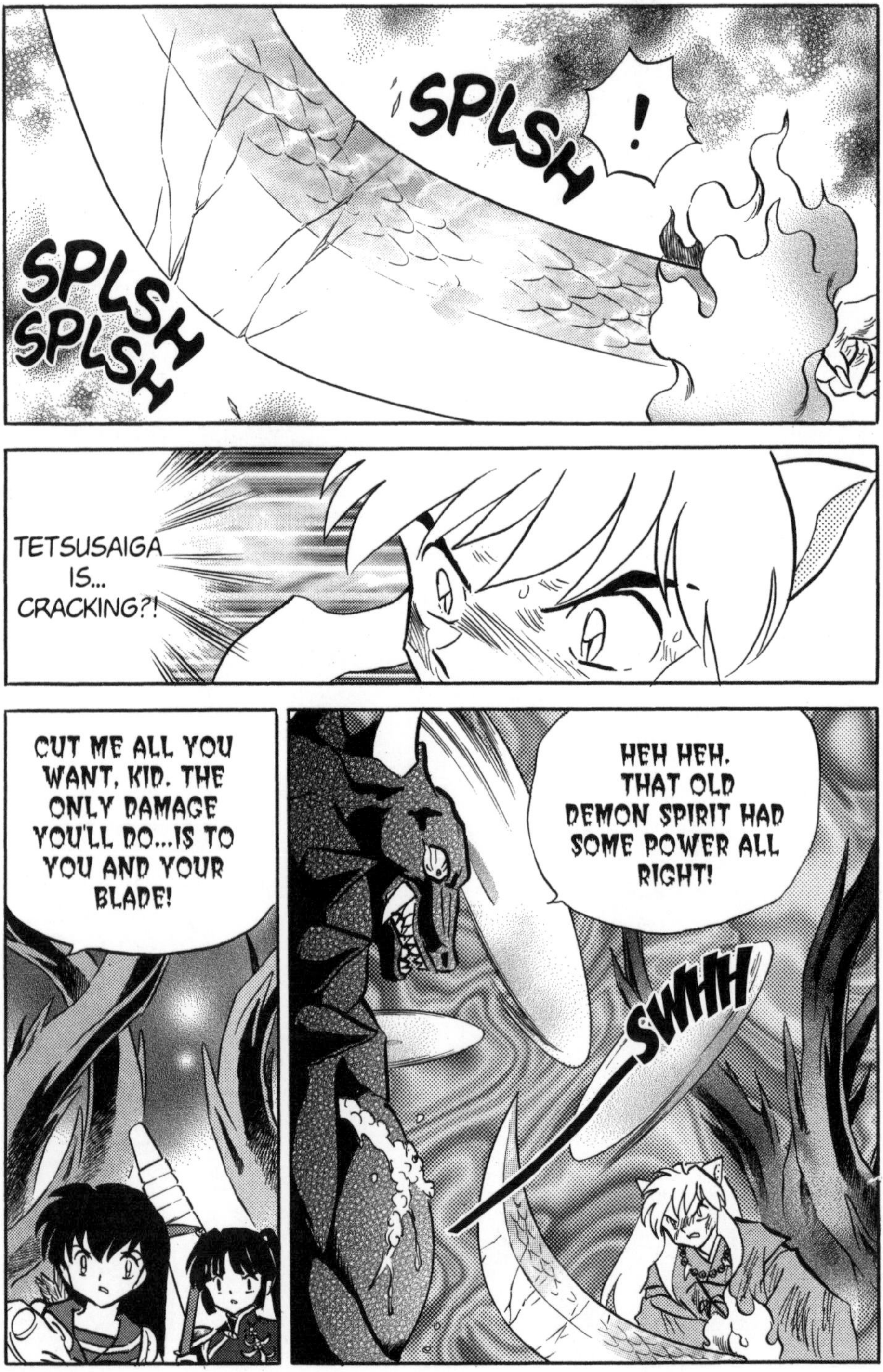
!
SPLSH
SPLSH
SPLSH
TETSUSAIGA IS... CRACKING?!
HEH HEH. THAT OLD DEMON SPIRIT HAD SOME POWER ALL RIGHT!
SWHH
CUT ME ALL YOU WANT, KID. THE ONLY DAMAGE YOU'LL DO...IS TO YOU AND YOUR BLADE!

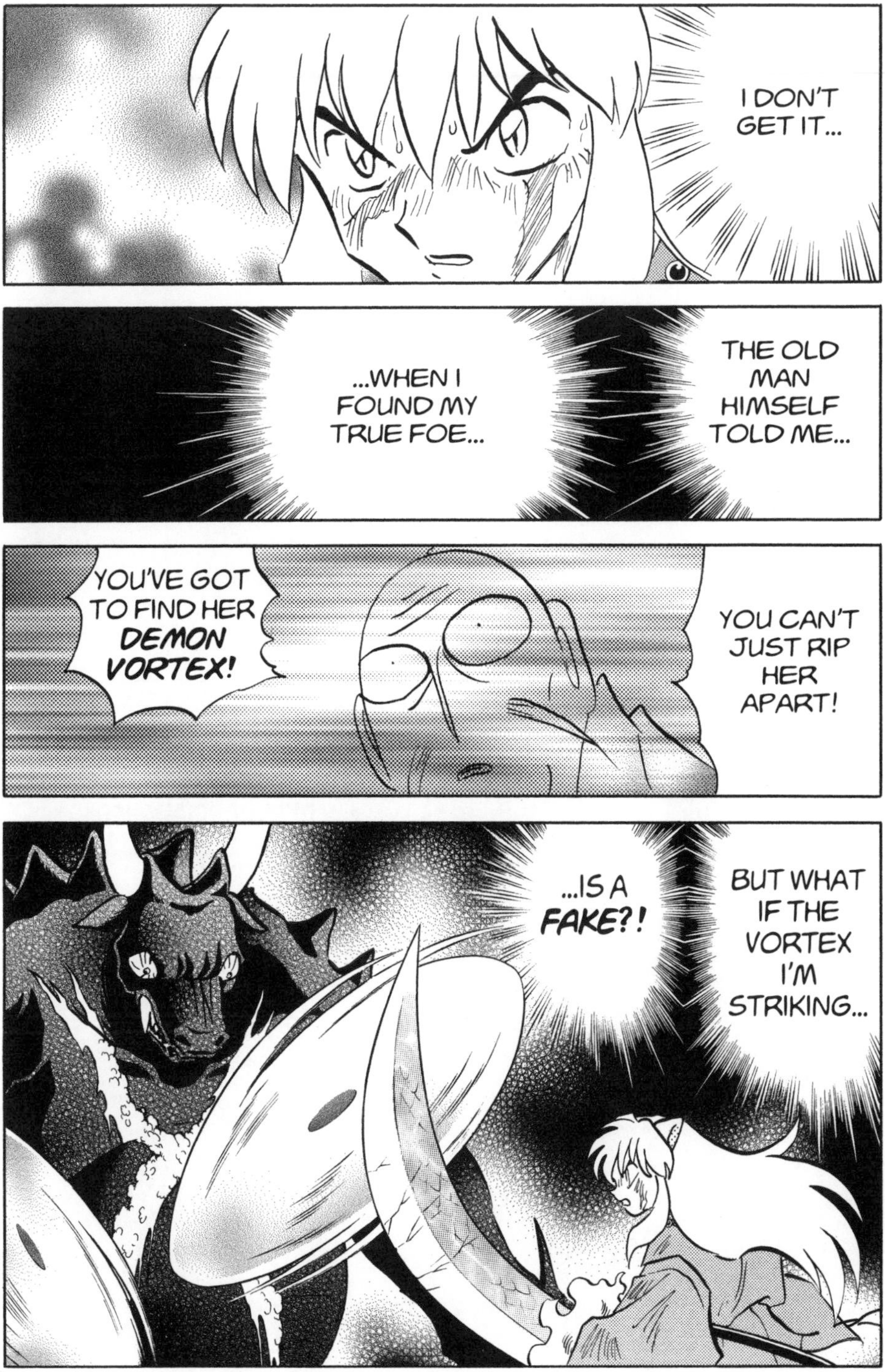
I DON'T GET IT...
THE OLD MAN HIMSELF TOLD ME...
...WHEN I FOUND MY TRUE FOE...
YOU CAN'T JUST RIP HER APART!
YOU'VE GOT TO FIND HER DEMON VORTEX!
BUT WHAT IF THE VORTEX I'M STRIKING...
...IS A FAKE?!

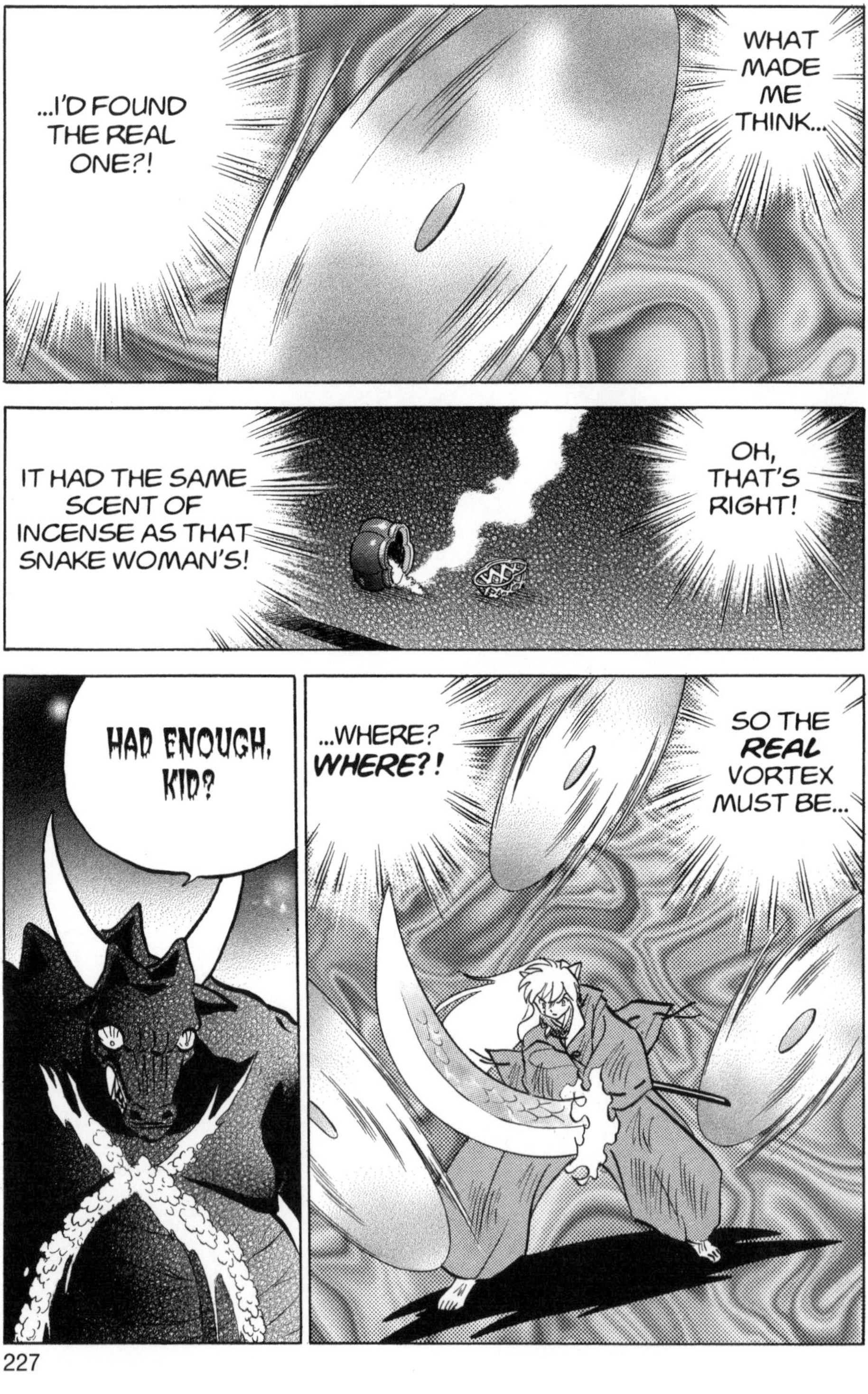
WHAT MADE ME THINK...
...I'D FOUND THE REAL ONE?!
OH, THAT'S RIGHT!
IT HAD THE SAME SCENT OF INCENSE AS THAT SNAKE WOMAN'S!
SO THE REAL VORTEX MUST BE...
...WHERE? WHERE?!
HAD ENOUGH, KID?

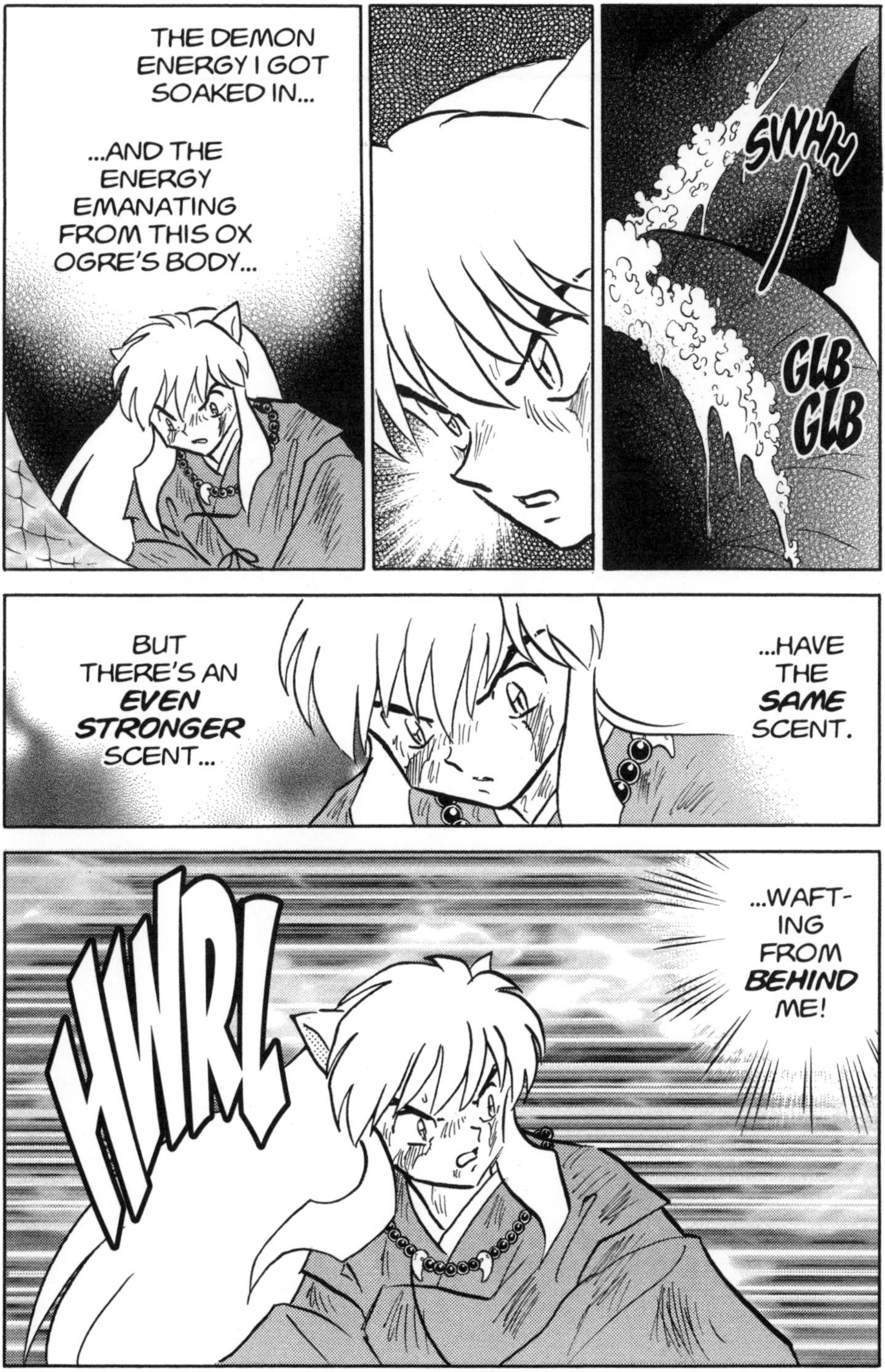
SWHH
GLB GLB
THE DEMON ENERGY I GOT SOAKED IN...
...AND THE ENERGY EMANATING FROM THIS OX OGRE'S BODY...
...HAVE THE **SAME** SCENT.
BUT THERE'S AN ***EVEN STRONGER*** SCENT...
...WAFT-ING FROM ***BEHIND*** ME!
HWRL

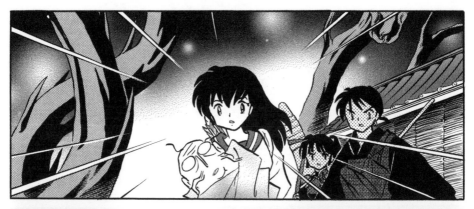

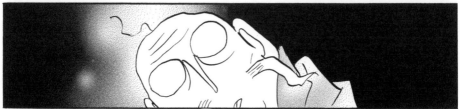

KAGOME!

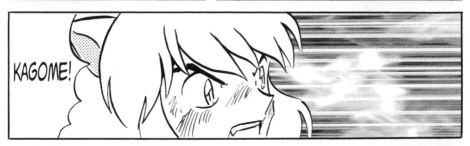

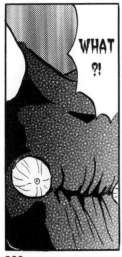

WHAT ?!

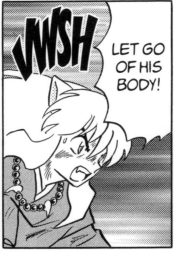

VWSH

LET GO OF HIS BODY!

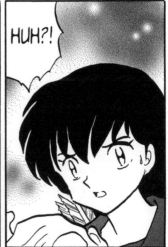

HUH?!

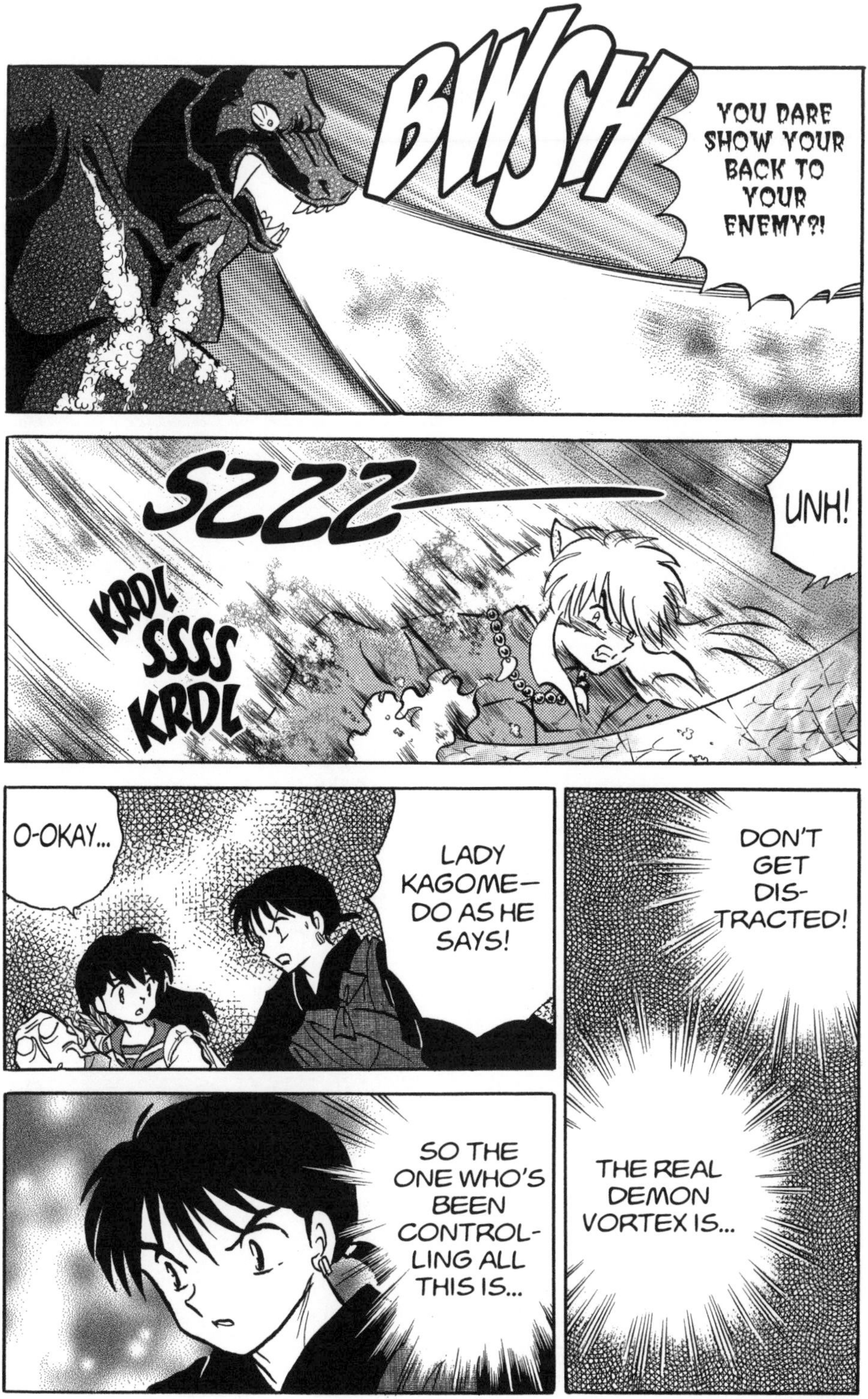
BWSH
YOU DARE SHOW YOUR BACK TO YOUR ENEMY?!
UNH!
SZZZ
KRDL SSSS KRDL
DON'T GET DIS-TRACTED!
THE REAL DEMON VORTEX IS...
LADY KAGOME— DO AS HE SAYS!
O-OKAY...
SO THE ONE WHO'S BEEN CONTROL-LING ALL THIS IS...

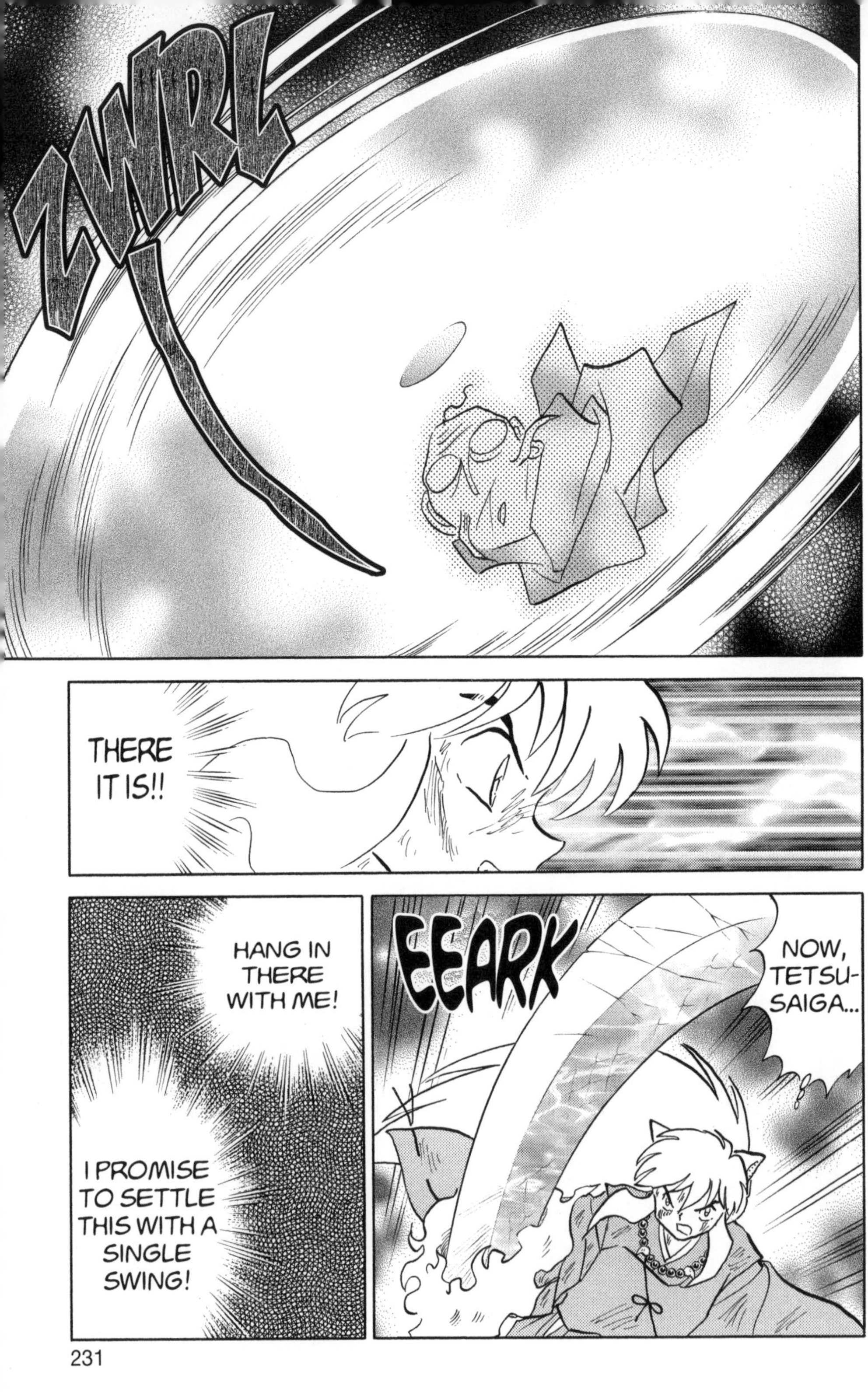

ZWIRL
THERE IT IS!!
NOW, TETSU-SAIGA...
EEARK
HANG IN THERE WITH ME!
I PROMISE TO SETTLE THIS WITH A SINGLE SWING!

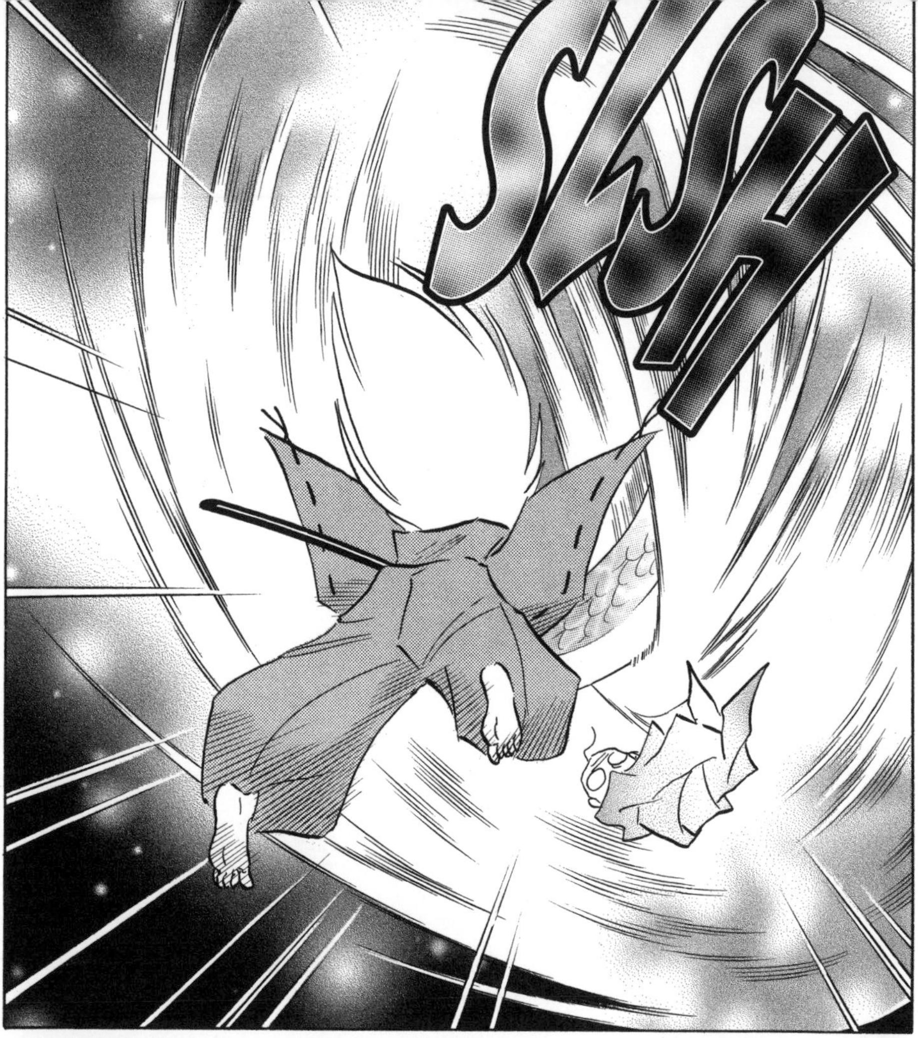
SWSH
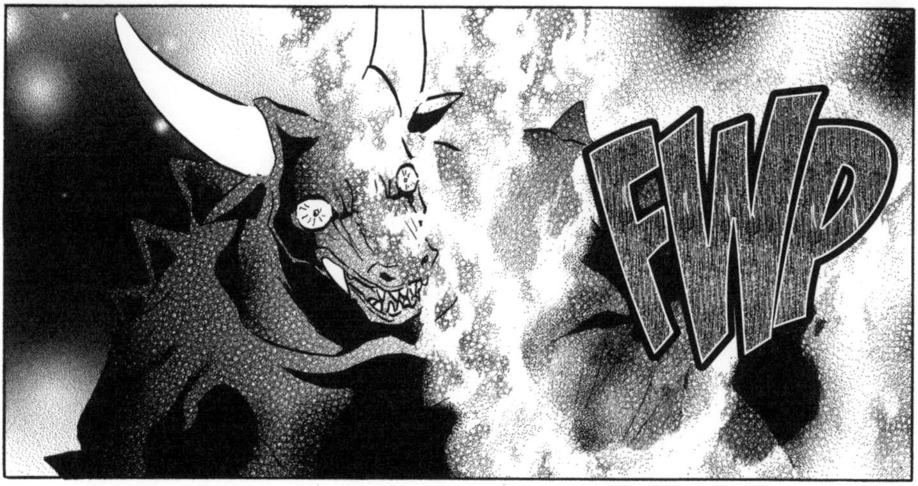
FWP

SCROLL THREE
TRAINING

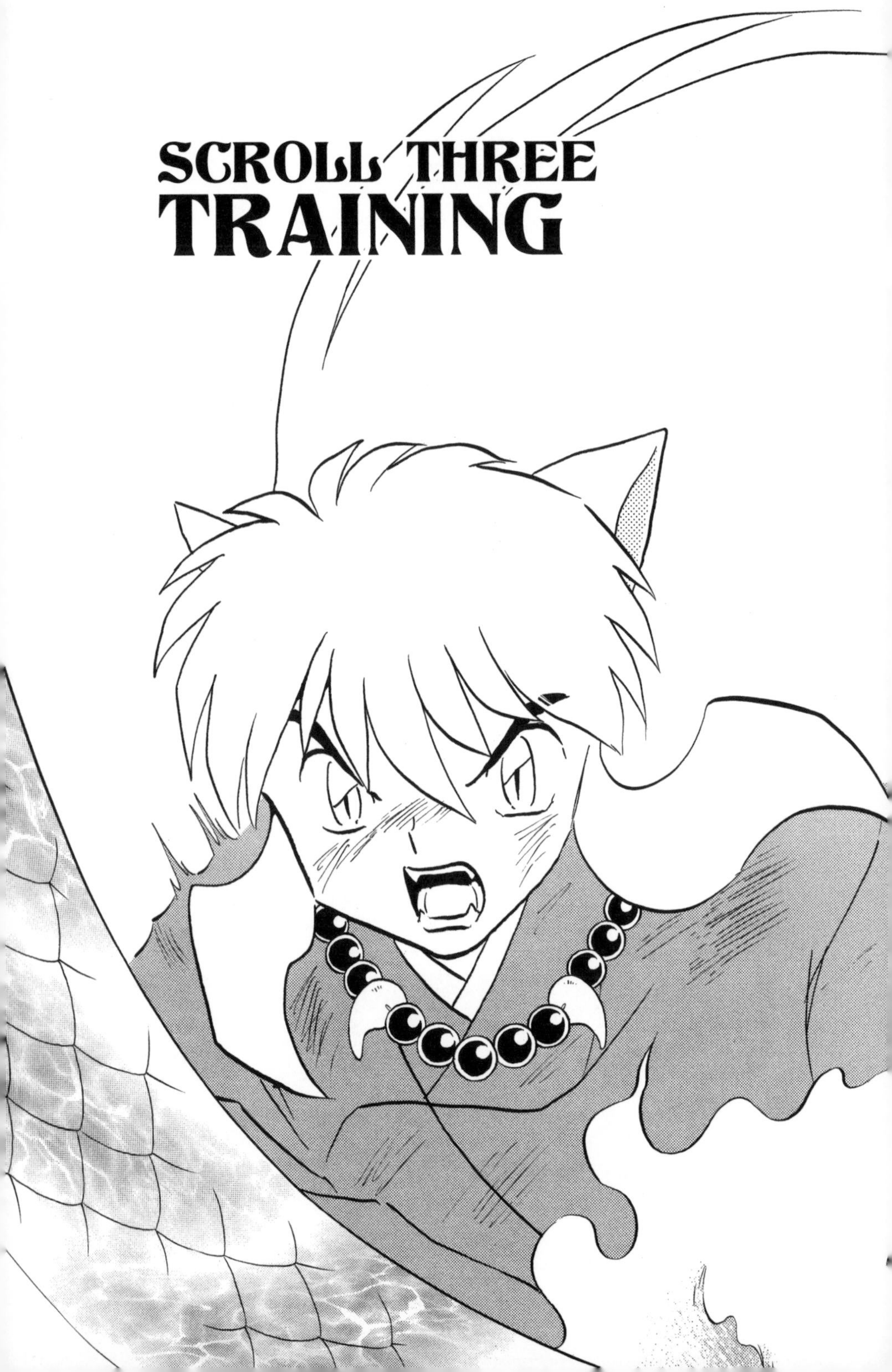

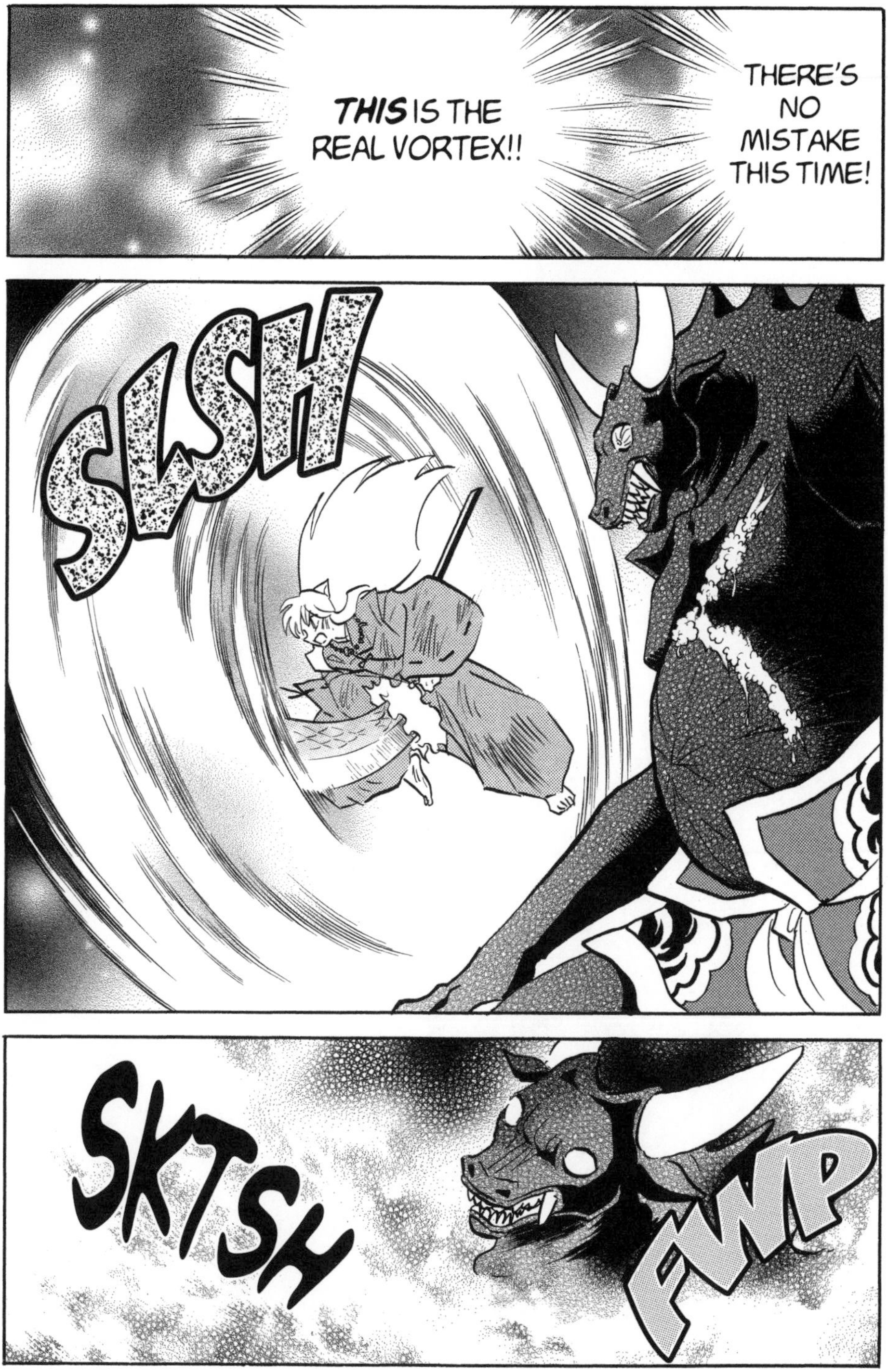
THERE'S NO MISTAKE THIS TIME!
THIS IS THE REAL VORTEX!!
SLSH
FWP
SKTSH

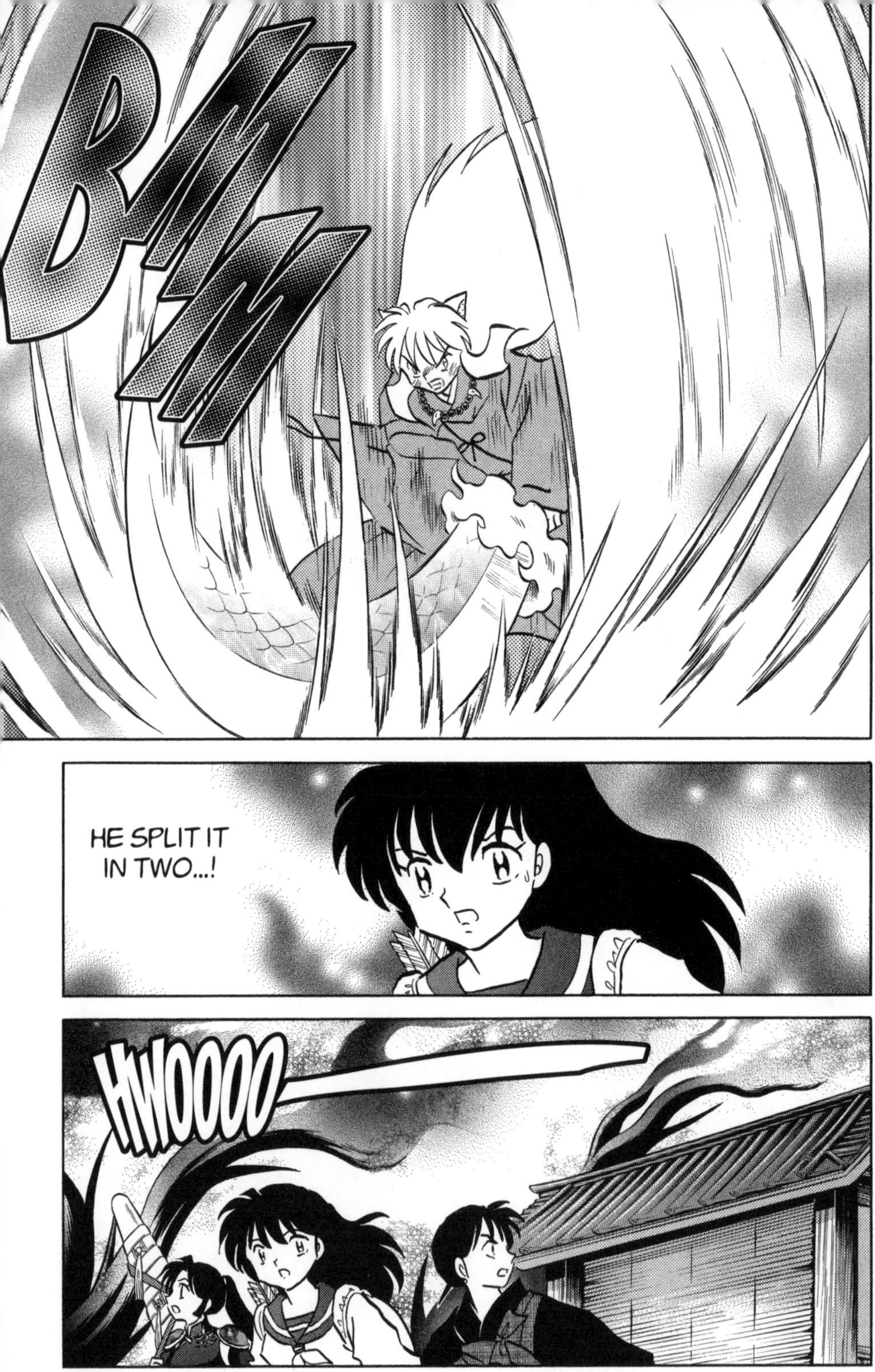

BAMM
HE SPLIT IT IN TWO...!
HWOOOO

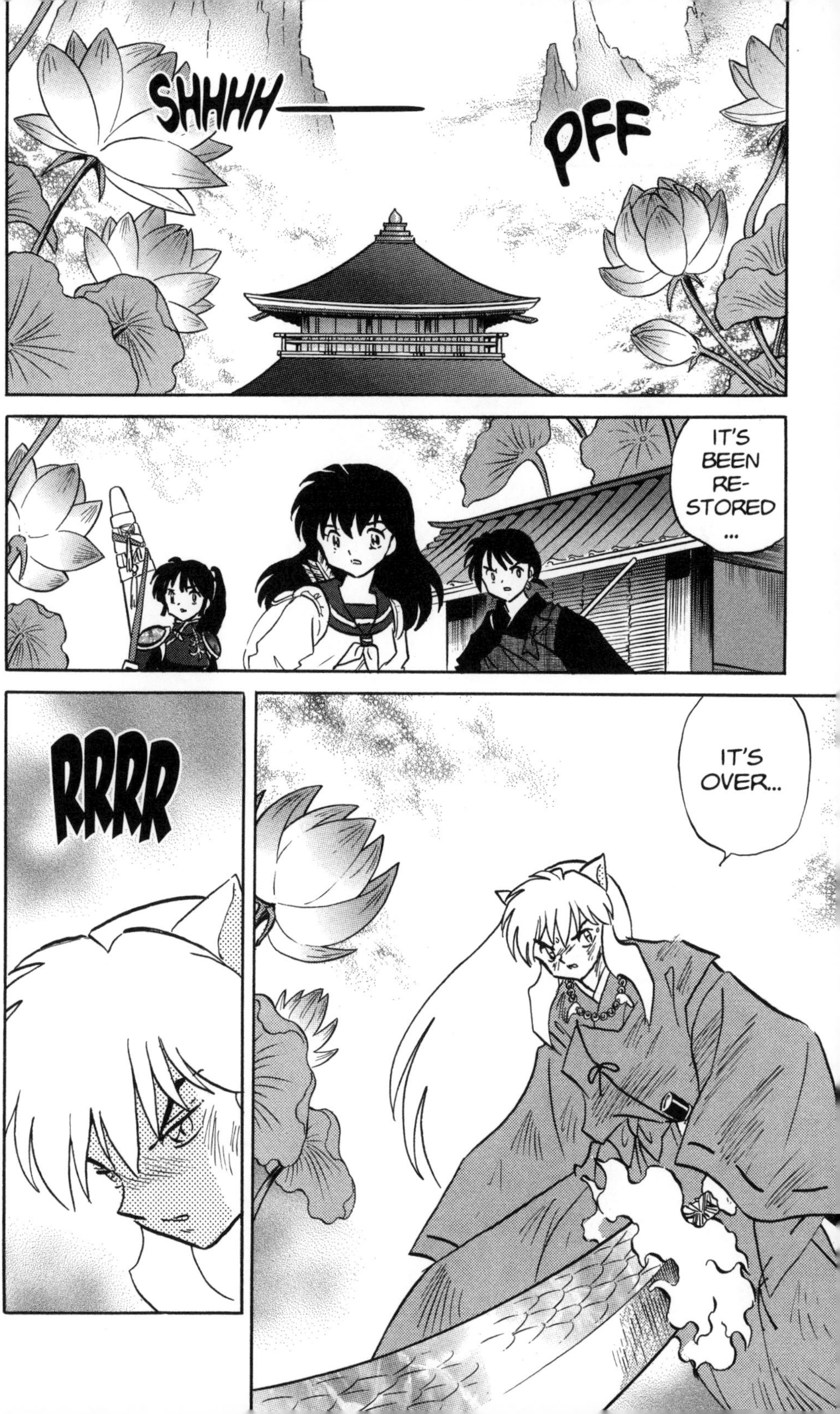
PFF
SHHHH—
IT'S BEEN RE-STORED...
IT'S OVER...
RRRR

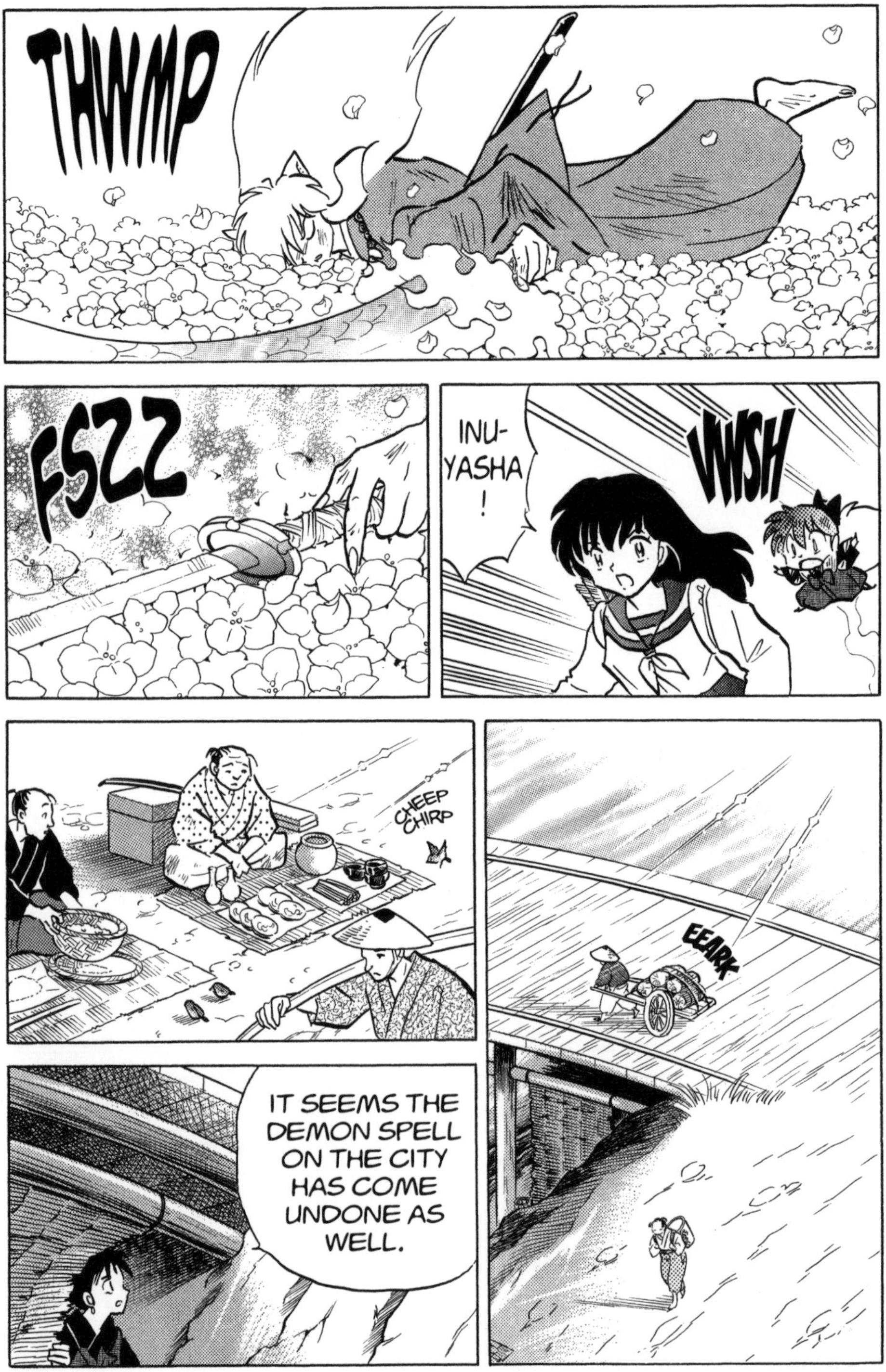
THWMP
INU-YASHA!
VWSH
FSZZ
EEARK
CHEEP CHIRP
IT SEEMS THE DEMON SPELL ON THE CITY HAS COME UNDONE AS WELL.

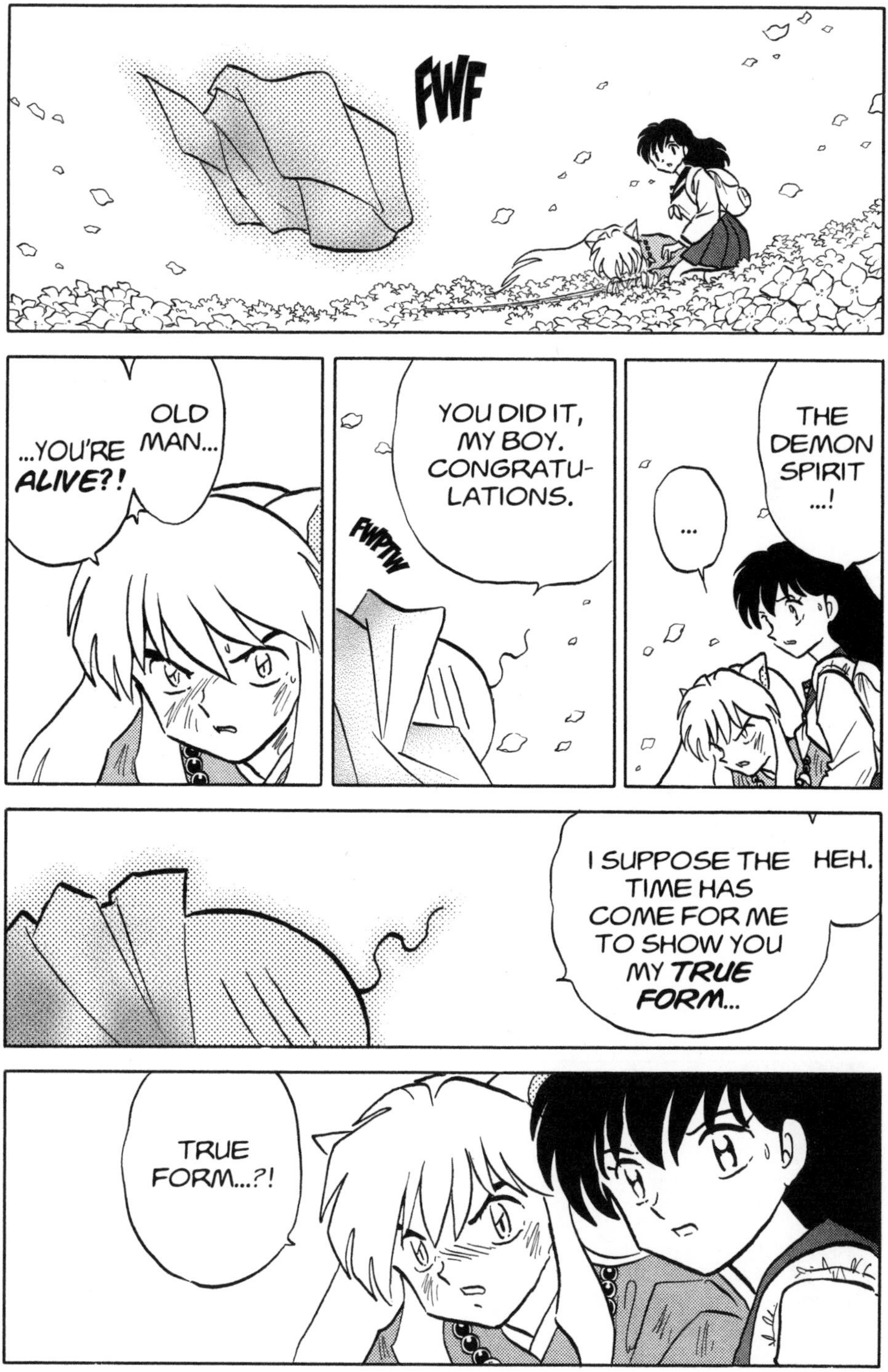
FWF
THE DEMON SPIRIT ...!
...
YOU DID IT, MY BOY. CONGRATU-LATIONS.
FWPTW
OLD MAN...
...YOU'RE **ALIVE?!**
HEH.
I SUPPOSE THE TIME HAS COME FOR ME TO SHOW YOU MY **TRUE FORM**...
TRUE FORM...?!

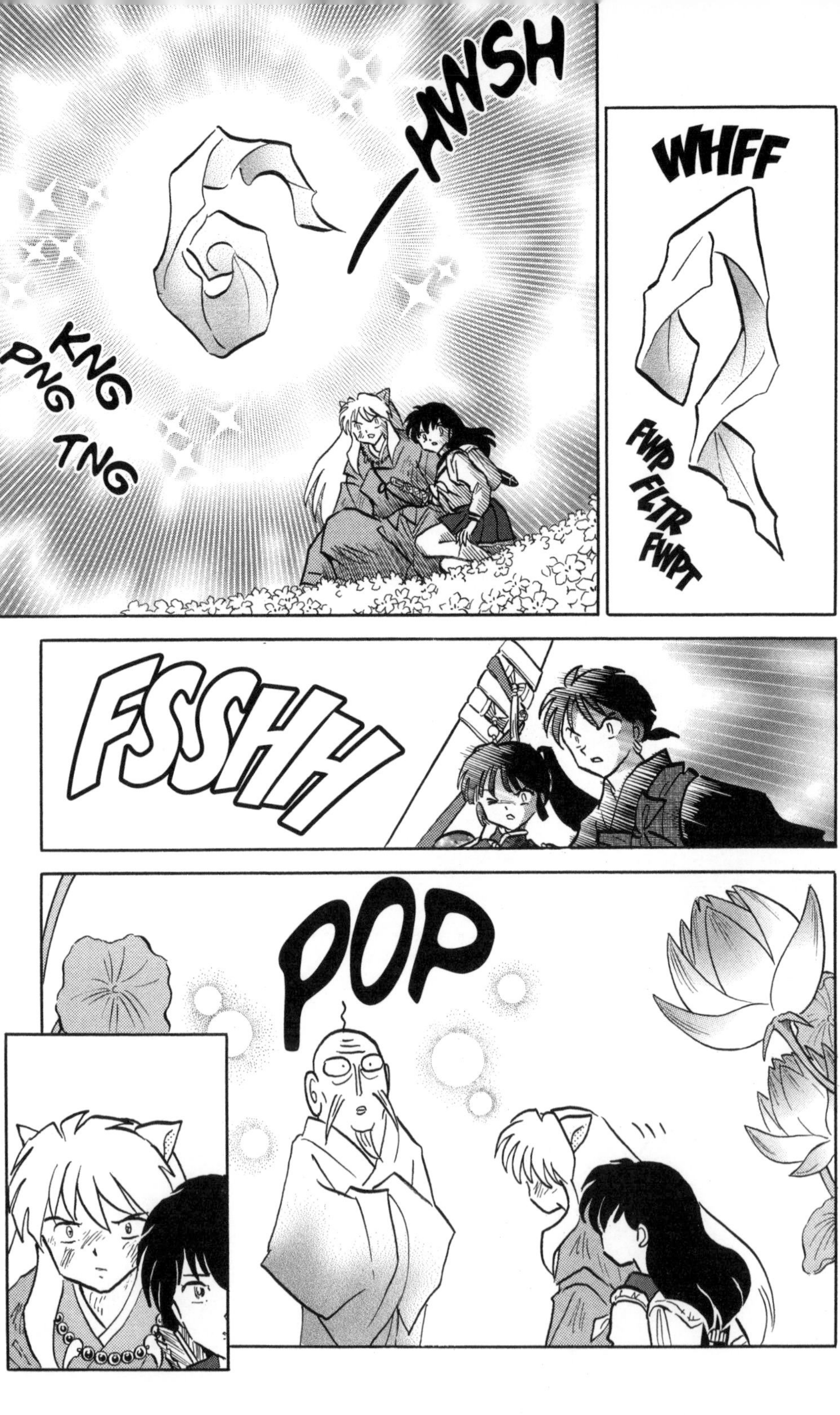
WHFF
FWP FLTR FWPT
HWSH
KNG PNG TNG
FSSHH
POP

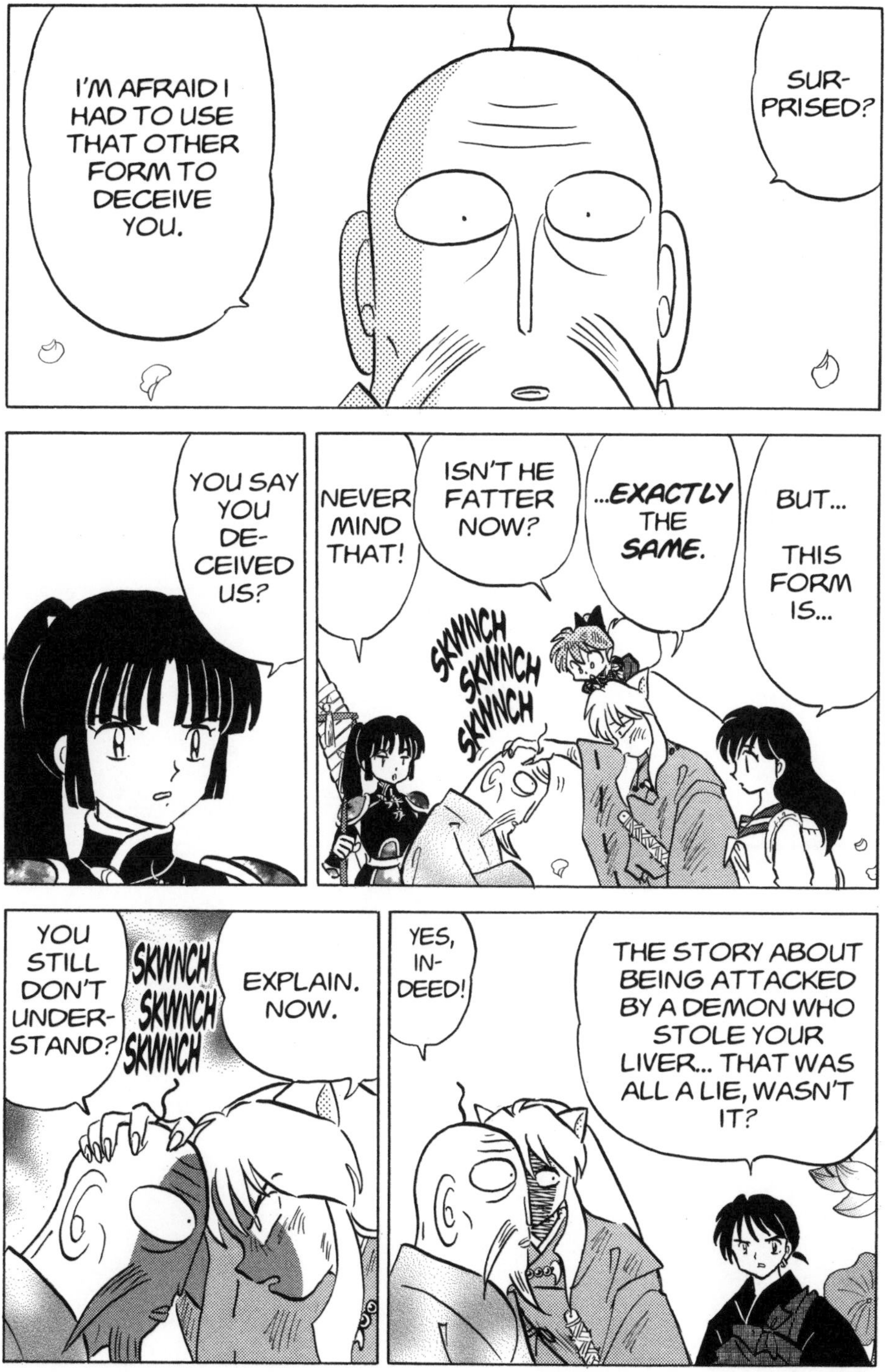
SUR-PRISED?
I'M AFRAID I HAD TO USE THAT OTHER FORM TO DECEIVE YOU.
BUT... THIS FORM IS...
...*EXACTLY* THE *SAME.*
ISN'T HE FATTER NOW?
NEVER MIND THAT!
SKWNCH SKWNCH SKWNCH
YOU SAY YOU DE-CEIVED US?
THE STORY ABOUT BEING ATTACKED BY A DEMON WHO STOLE YOUR LIVER... THAT WAS ALL A LIE, WASN'T IT?
YES, IN-DEED!
EXPLAIN. NOW.
SKWNCH SKWNCH SKWNCH
YOU STILL DON'T UNDER-STAND?

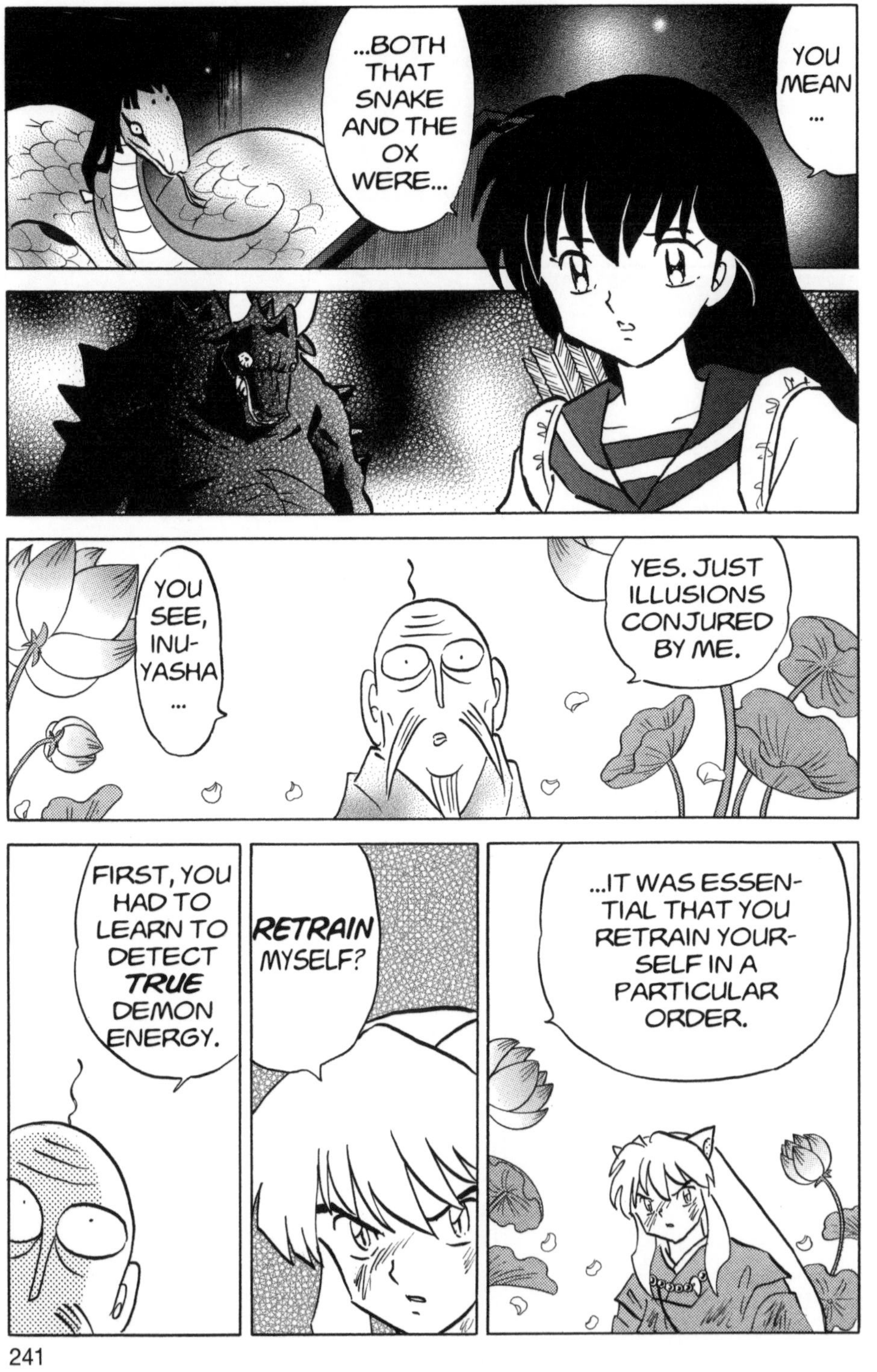
YOU MEAN...
...BOTH THAT SNAKE AND THE OX WERE...
YES. JUST ILLUSIONS CONJURED BY ME.
YOU SEE, INU-YASHA...
...IT WAS ESSEN-TIAL THAT YOU RETRAIN YOUR-SELF IN A PARTICULAR ORDER.
RETRAIN MYSELF?
FIRST, YOU HAD TO LEARN TO DETECT TRUE DEMON ENERGY.

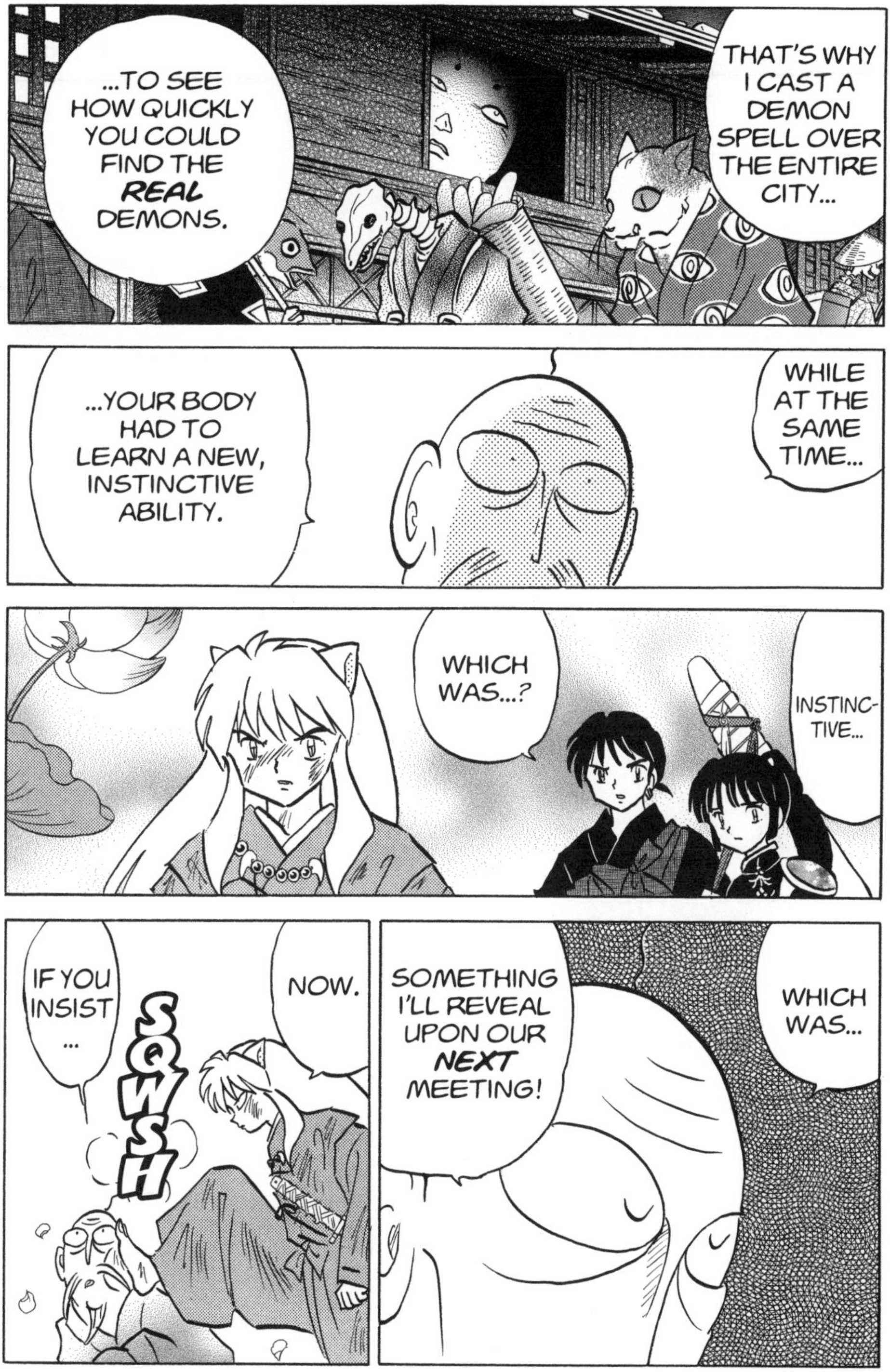
THAT'S WHY I CAST A DEMON SPELL OVER THE ENTIRE CITY...
...TO SEE HOW QUICKLY YOU COULD FIND THE *REAL* DEMONS.
WHILE AT THE SAME TIME...
...YOUR BODY HAD TO LEARN A NEW, INSTINCTIVE ABILITY.
INSTINC-TIVE...
WHICH WAS...?
WHICH WAS...
SOMETHING I'LL REVEAL UPON OUR *NEXT* MEETING!
NOW.
IF YOU INSIST...
SQWSH

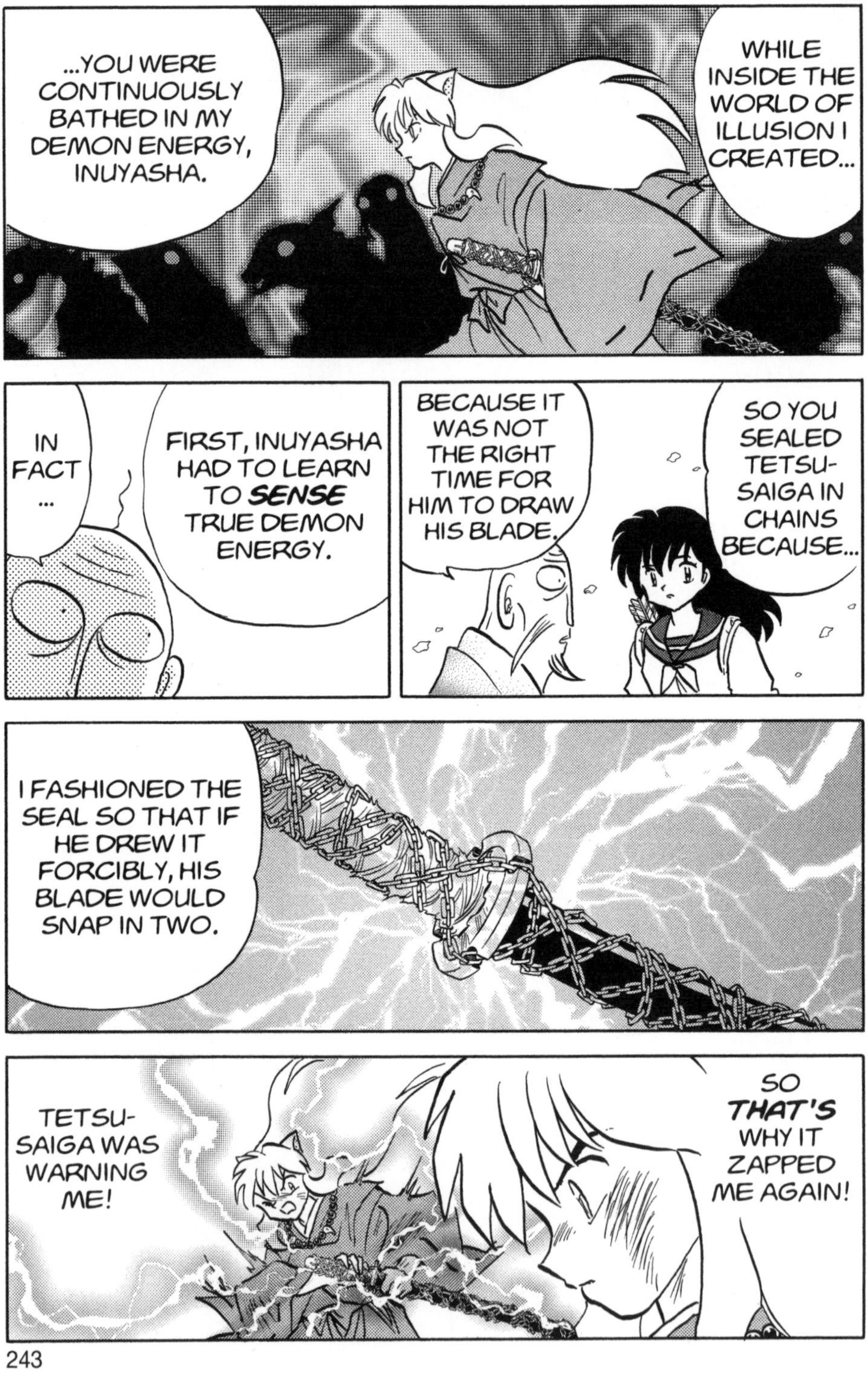
WHILE INSIDE THE WORLD OF ILLUSION I CREATED...
...YOU WERE CONTINUOUSLY BATHED IN MY DEMON ENERGY, INUYASHA.
SO YOU SEALED TETSU-SAIGA IN CHAINS BECAUSE...
BECAUSE IT WAS NOT THE RIGHT TIME FOR HIM TO DRAW HIS BLADE.
FIRST, INUYASHA HAD TO LEARN TO ***SENSE*** TRUE DEMON ENERGY.
IN FACT ...
I FASHIONED THE SEAL SO THAT IF HE DREW IT FORCIBLY, HIS BLADE WOULD SNAP IN TWO.
SO ***THAT'S*** WHY IT ZAPPED ME AGAIN!
TETSU-SAIGA WAS WARNING ME!

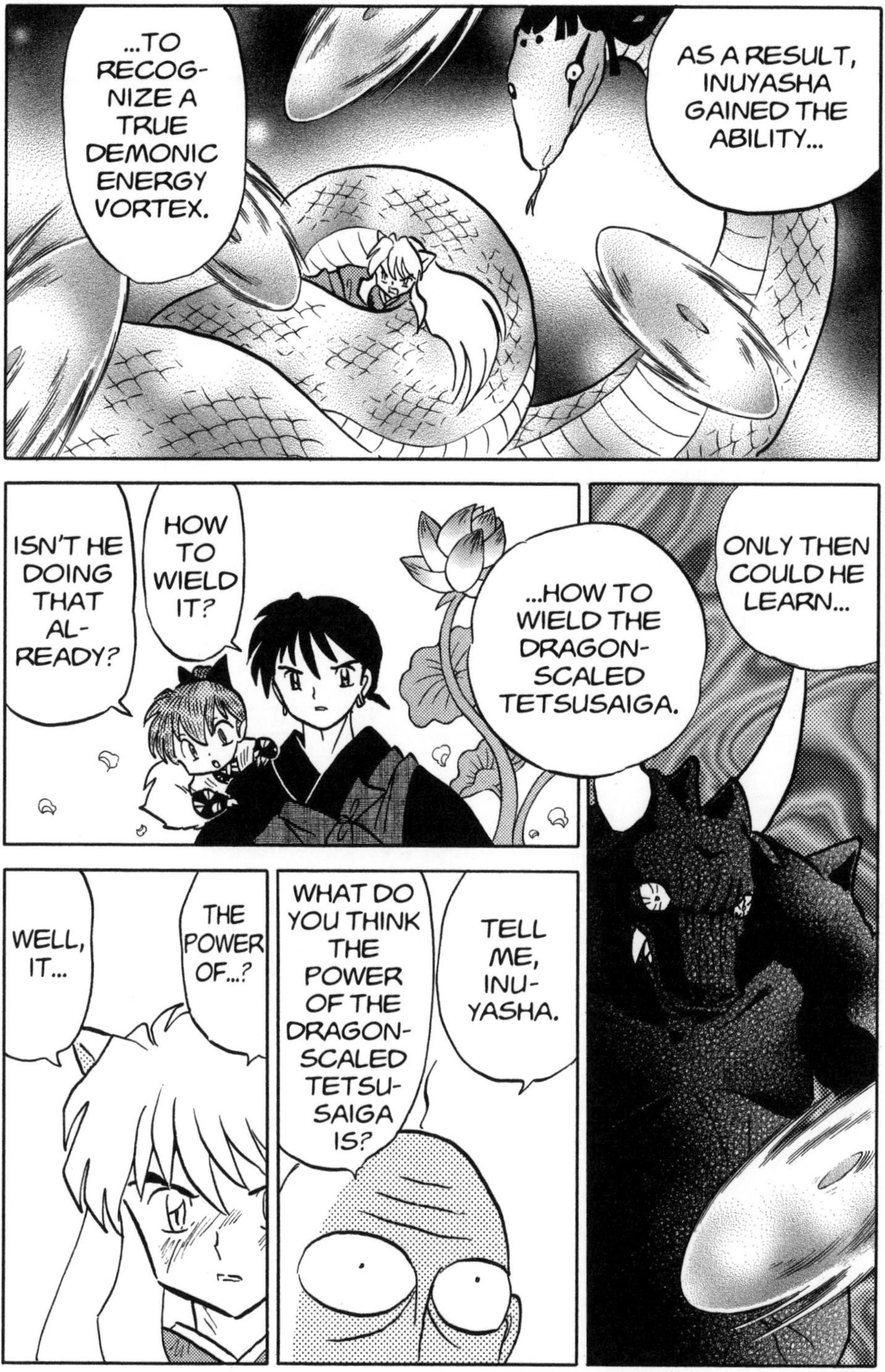
AS A RESULT, INUYASHA GAINED THE ABILITY...
...TO RECOGNIZE A TRUE DEMONIC ENERGY VORTEX.
ONLY THEN COULD HE LEARN...
...HOW TO WIELD THE DRAGON-SCALED TETSUSAIGA.
HOW TO WIELD IT?
ISN'T HE DOING THAT AL-READY?
TELL ME, INU-YASHA.
WHAT DO YOU THINK THE POWER OF THE DRAGON-SCALED TETSU-SAIGA IS?
THE POWER OF...?
WELL, IT...

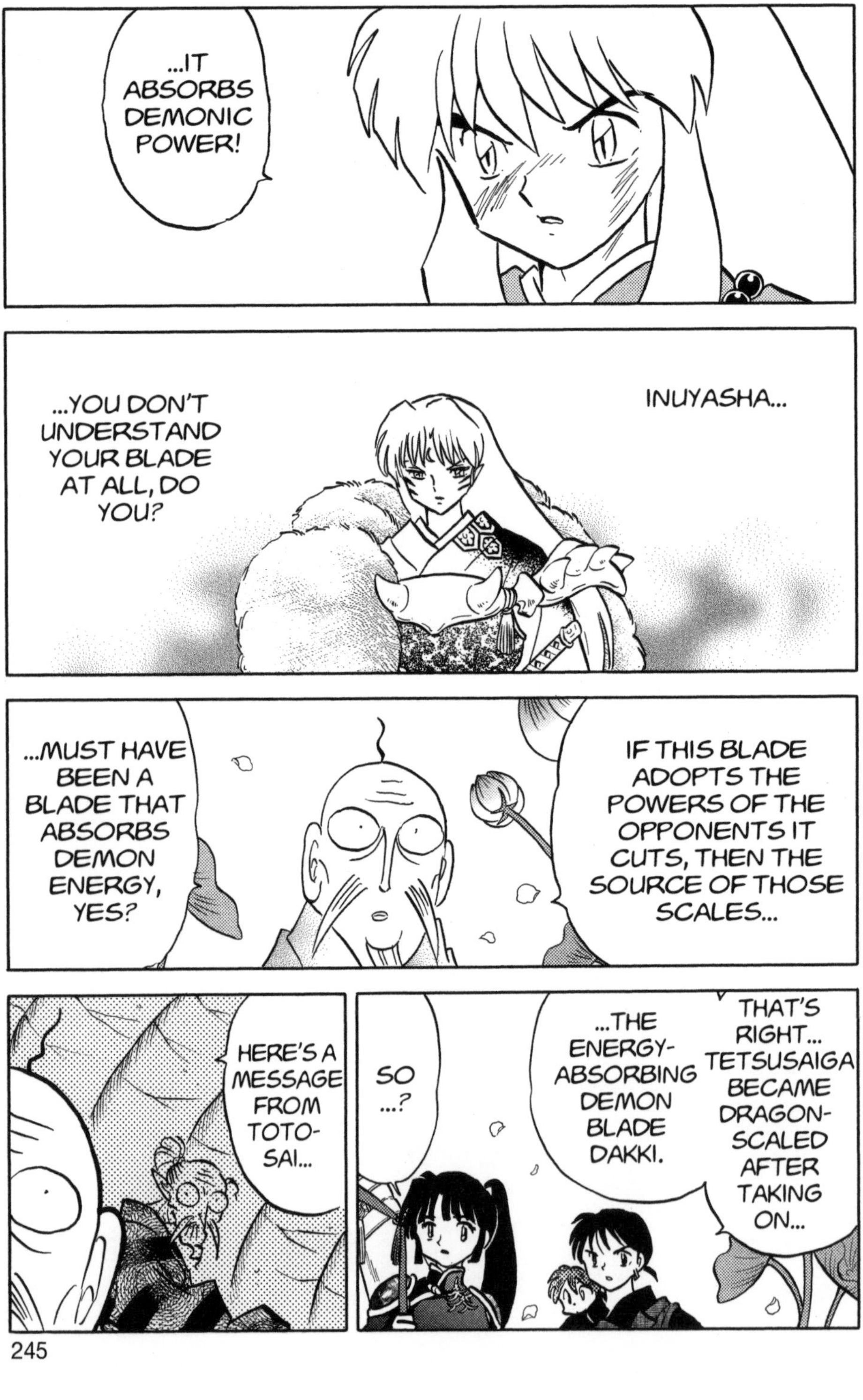
...IT ABSORBS DEMONIC POWER!
INUYASHA...
...YOU DON'T UNDERSTAND YOUR BLADE AT ALL, DO YOU?
IF THIS BLADE ADOPTS THE POWERS OF THE OPPONENTS IT CUTS, THEN THE SOURCE OF THOSE SCALES...
...MUST HAVE BEEN A BLADE THAT ABSORBS DEMON ENERGY, YES?
THAT'S RIGHT... TETSUSAIGA BECAME DRAGON-SCALED AFTER TAKING ON...
...THE ENERGY-ABSORBING DEMON BLADE DAKKI.
SO ...?
HERE'S A MESSAGE FROM TOTO-SAI...

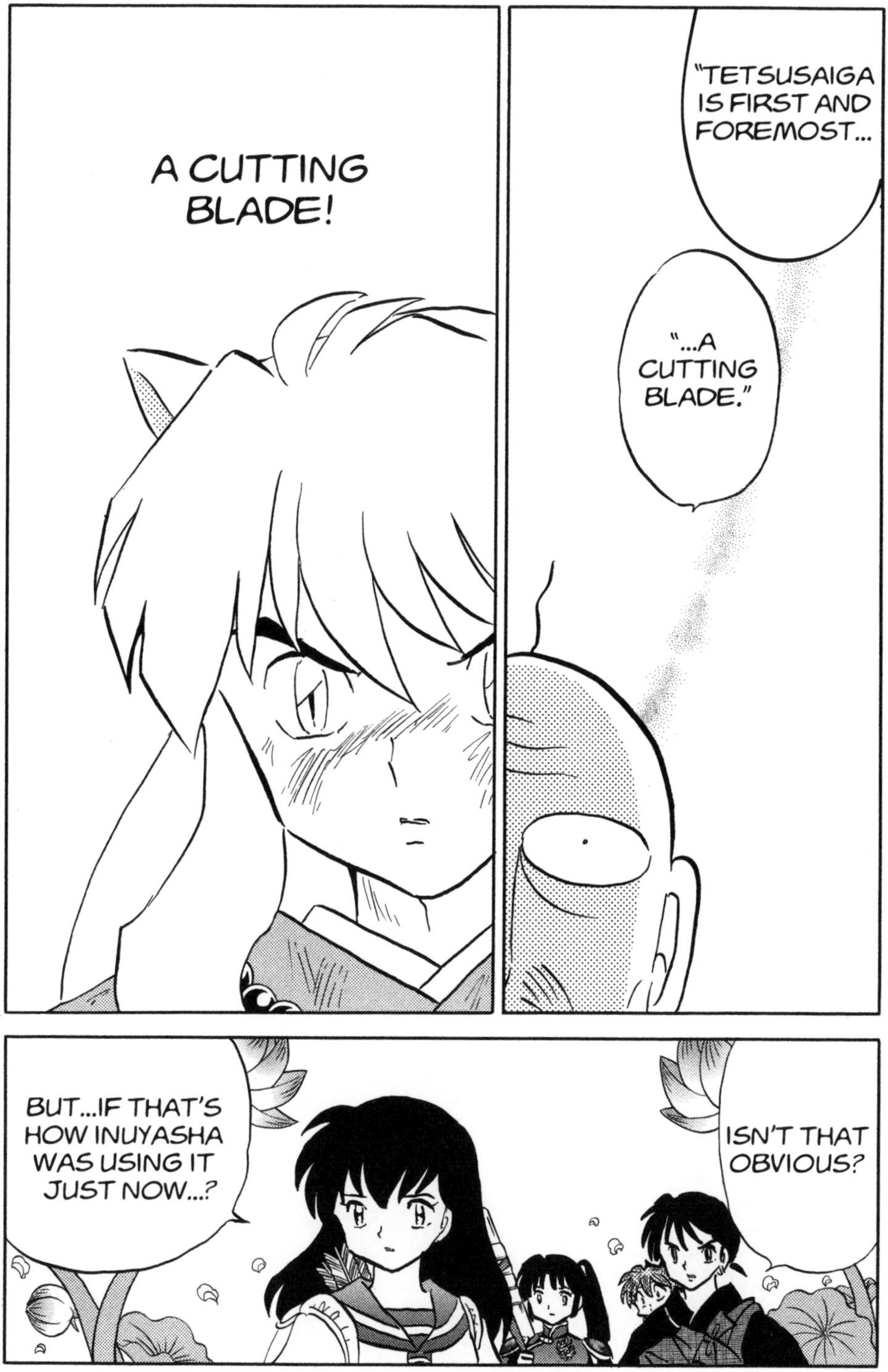
"TETSUSAIGA IS FIRST AND FOREMOST...
"...A CUTTING BLADE."
A CUTTING BLADE!
ISN'T THAT OBVIOUS?
BUT...IF THAT'S HOW INUYASHA WAS USING IT JUST NOW...?

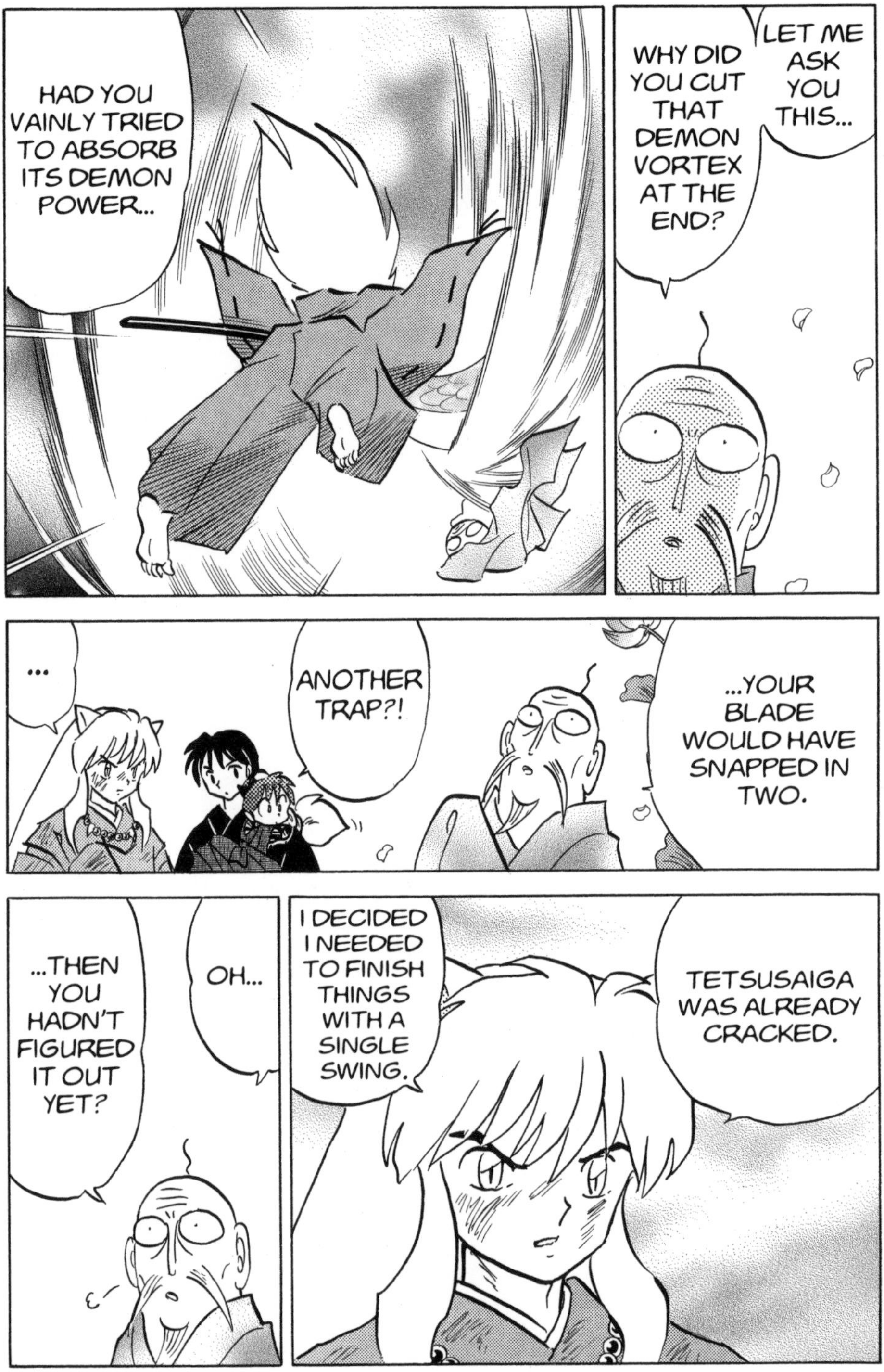
LET ME ASK YOU THIS...
WHY DID YOU CUT THAT DEMON VORTEX AT THE END?
HAD YOU VAINLY TRIED TO ABSORB ITS DEMON POWER...
...YOUR BLADE WOULD HAVE SNAPPED IN TWO.
ANOTHER TRAP?!
...
TETSUSAIGA WAS ALREADY CRACKED.
I DECIDED I NEEDED TO FINISH THINGS WITH A SINGLE SWING.
OH...
...THEN YOU HADN'T FIGURED IT OUT YET?

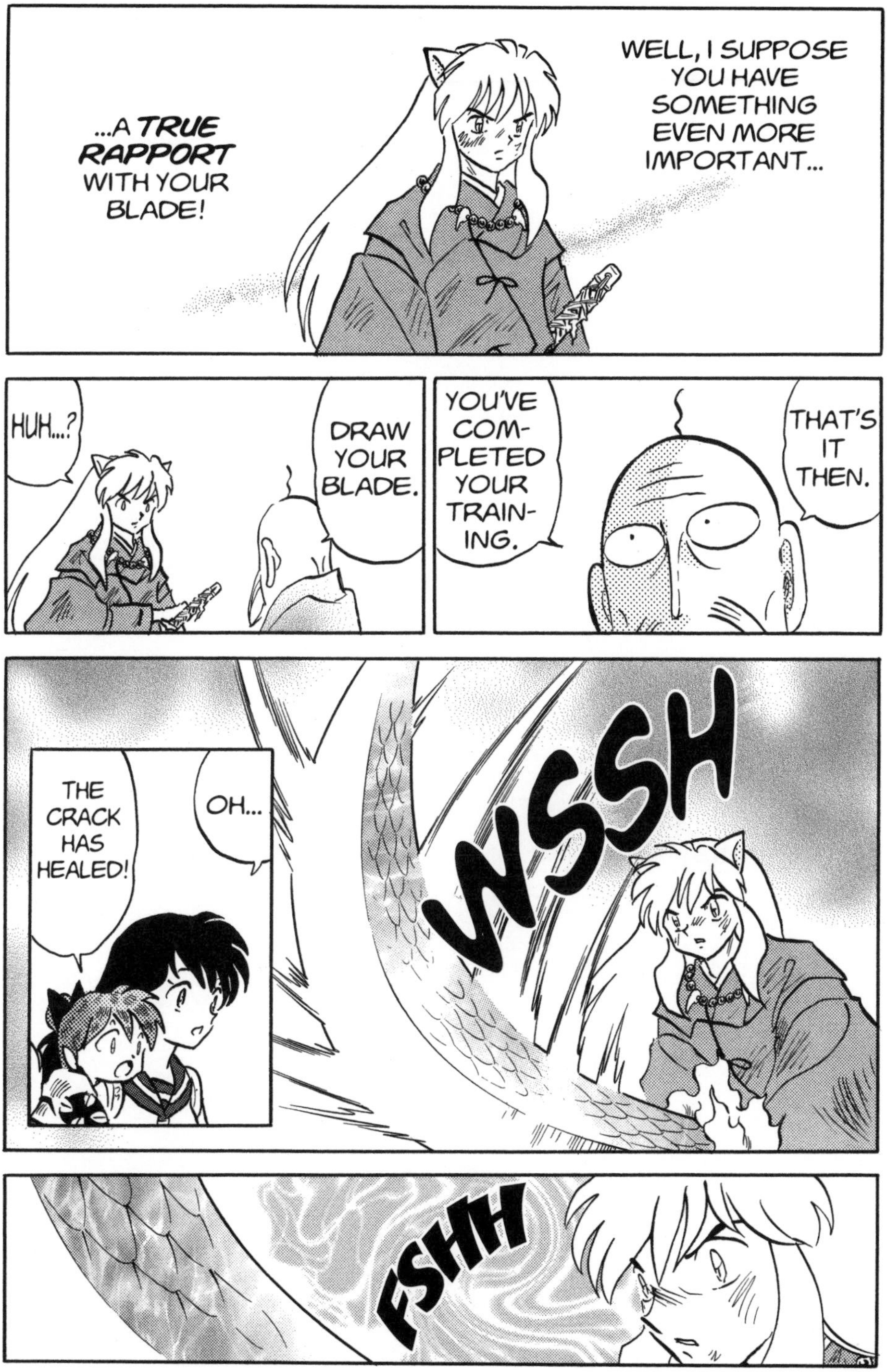
WELL, I SUPPOSE YOU HAVE SOMETHING EVEN MORE IMPORTANT...
...A **TRUE RAPPORT** WITH YOUR BLADE!
THAT'S IT THEN.
YOU'VE COMPLETED YOUR TRAINING.
DRAW YOUR BLADE.
HUH...?
WSSH
OH...
THE CRACK HAS HEALED!
FSHH

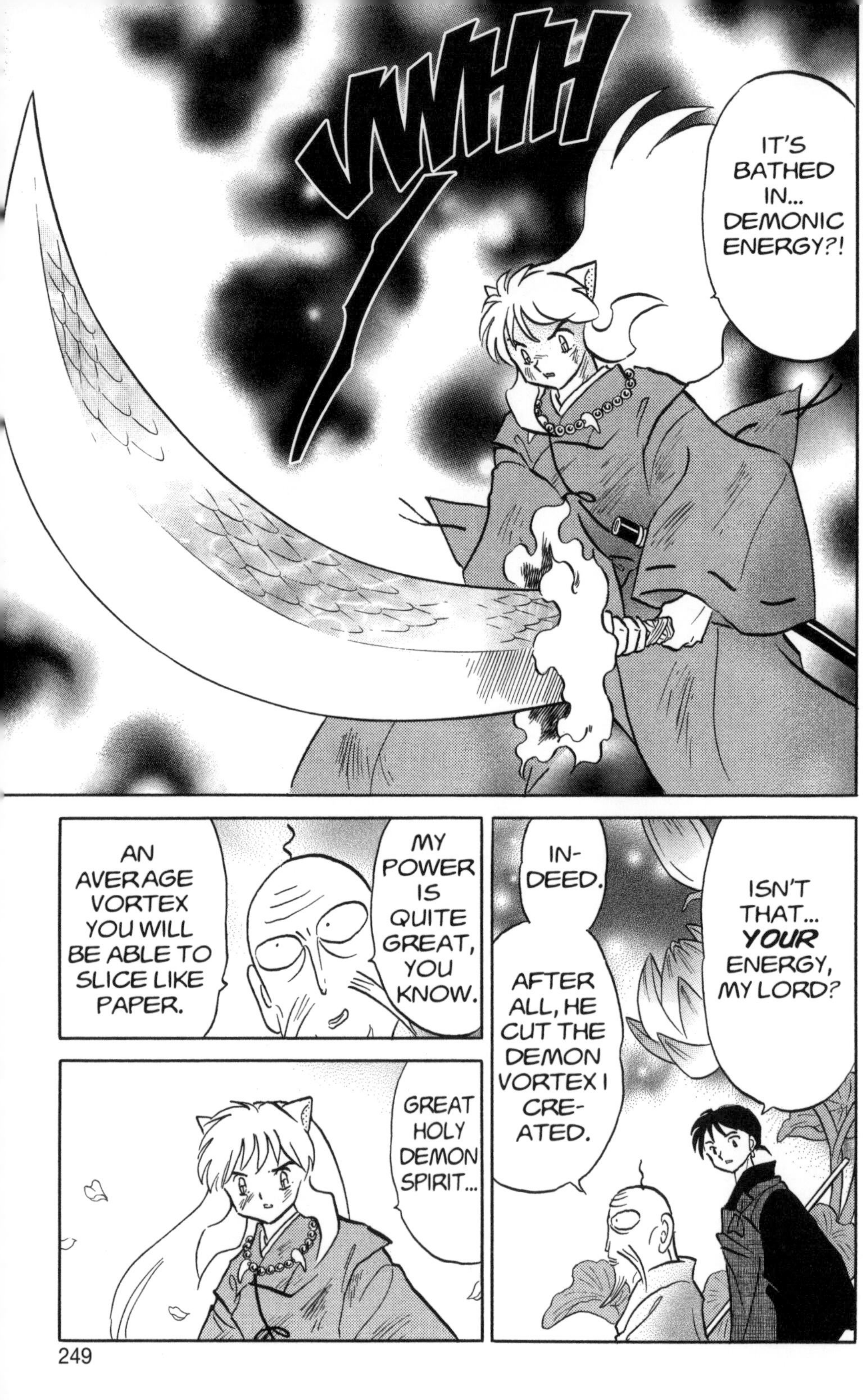
VWHHH
IT'S BATHED IN... DEMONIC ENERGY?!
ISN'T THAT... ***YOUR*** ENERGY, MY LORD?
IN-DEED.
AFTER ALL, HE CUT THE DEMON VORTEX I CRE-ATED.
MY POWER IS QUITE GREAT, YOU KNOW.
AN AVERAGE VORTEX YOU WILL BE ABLE TO SLICE LIKE PAPER.
GREAT HOLY DEMON SPIRIT...

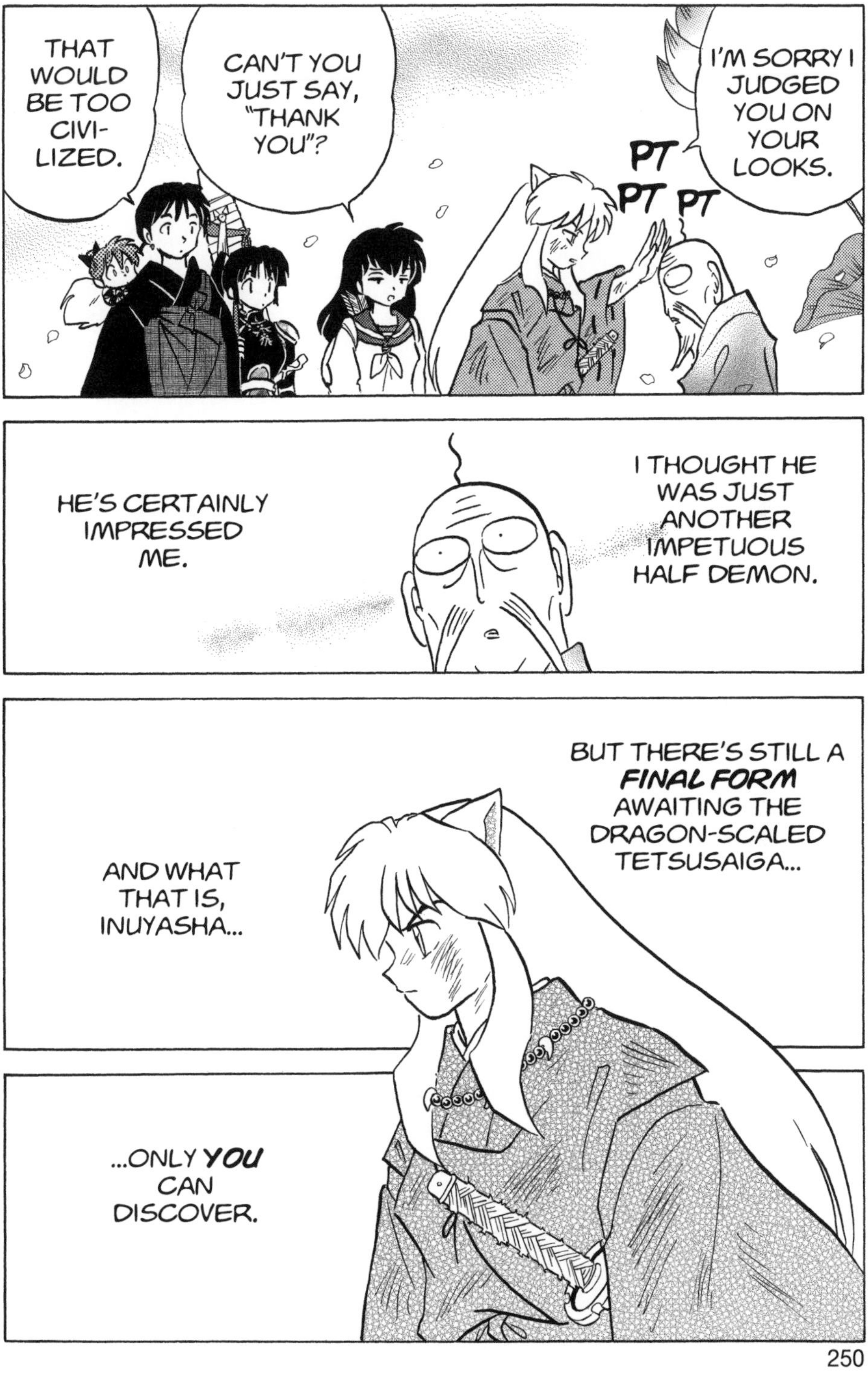
I'M SORRY I JUDGED YOU ON YOUR LOOKS.
PT PT PT
CAN'T YOU JUST SAY, "THANK YOU"?
THAT WOULD BE TOO CIVILIZED.
I THOUGHT HE WAS JUST ANOTHER IMPETUOUS HALF DEMON.
HE'S CERTAINLY IMPRESSED ME.
BUT THERE'S STILL A FINAL FORM AWAITING THE DRAGON-SCALED TETSUSAIGA...
AND WHAT THAT IS, INUYASHA...
...ONLY YOU CAN DISCOVER.

SCROLL FOUR
KAI

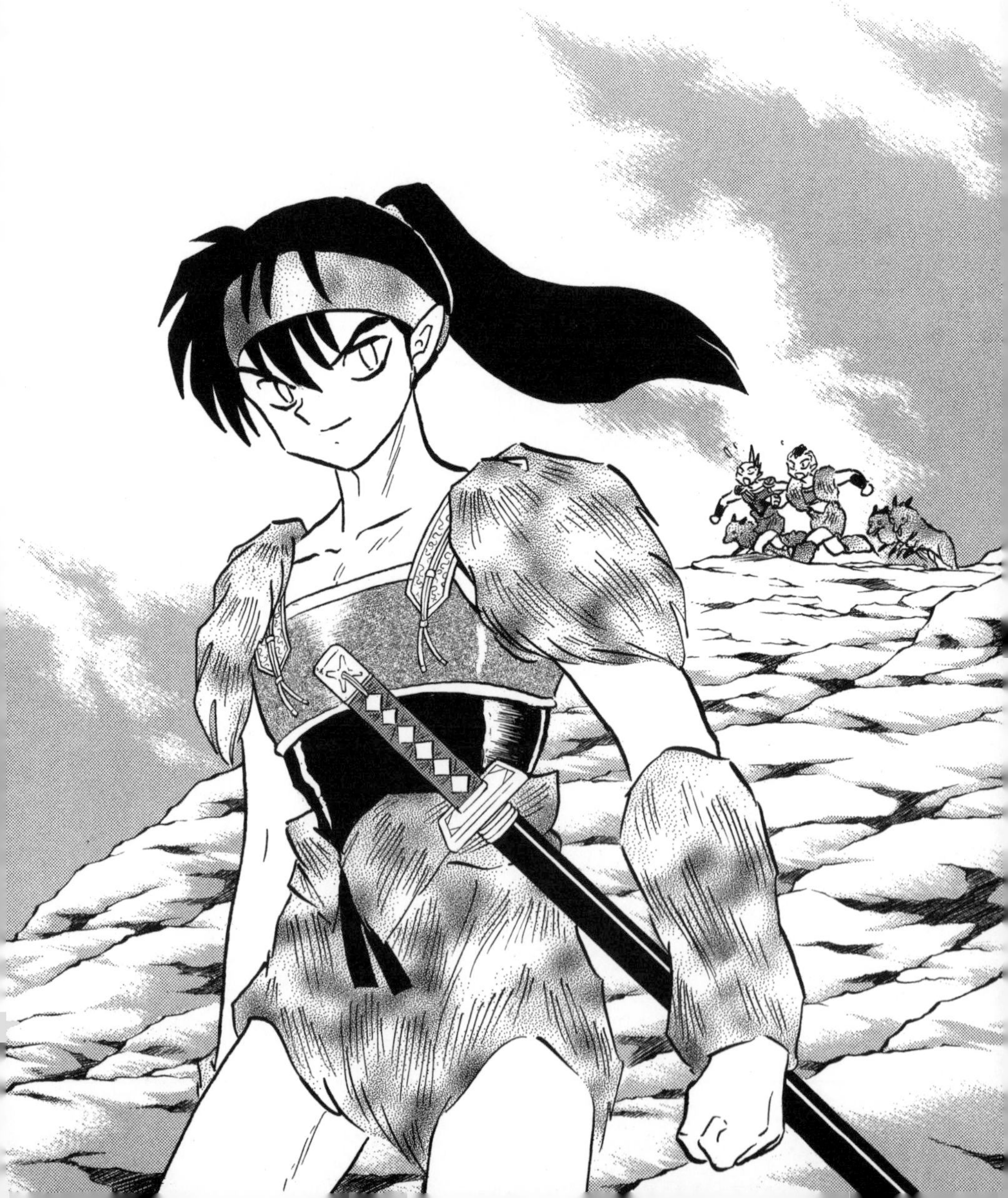

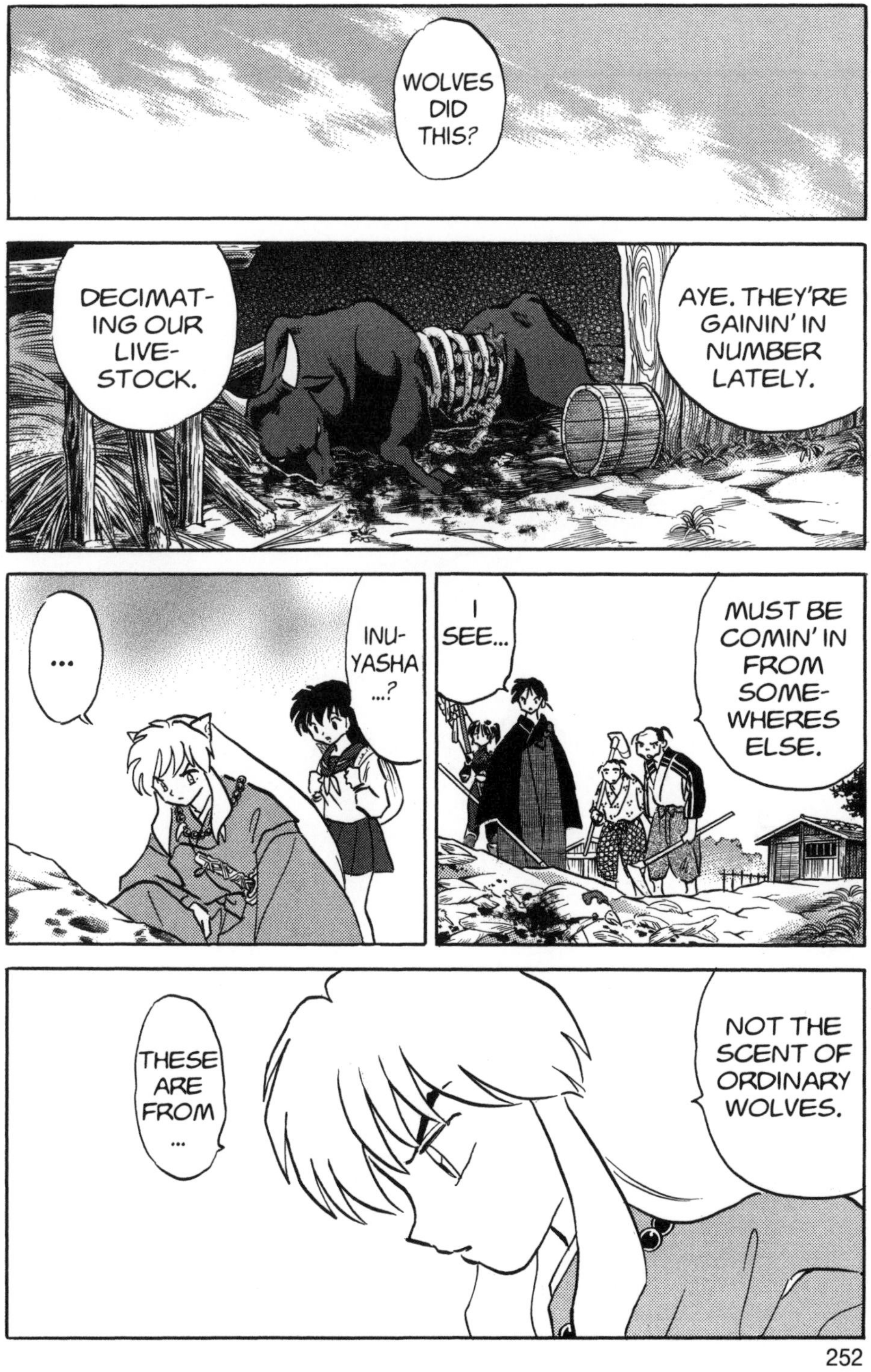
WOLVES DID THIS?
AYE. THEY'RE GAININ' IN NUMBER LATELY.
DECIMATING OUR LIVESTOCK.
MUST BE COMIN' IN FROM SOMEWHERES ELSE.
I SEE...
INU-YASHA...?
...
NOT THE SCENT OF ORDINARY WOLVES.
THESE ARE FROM...

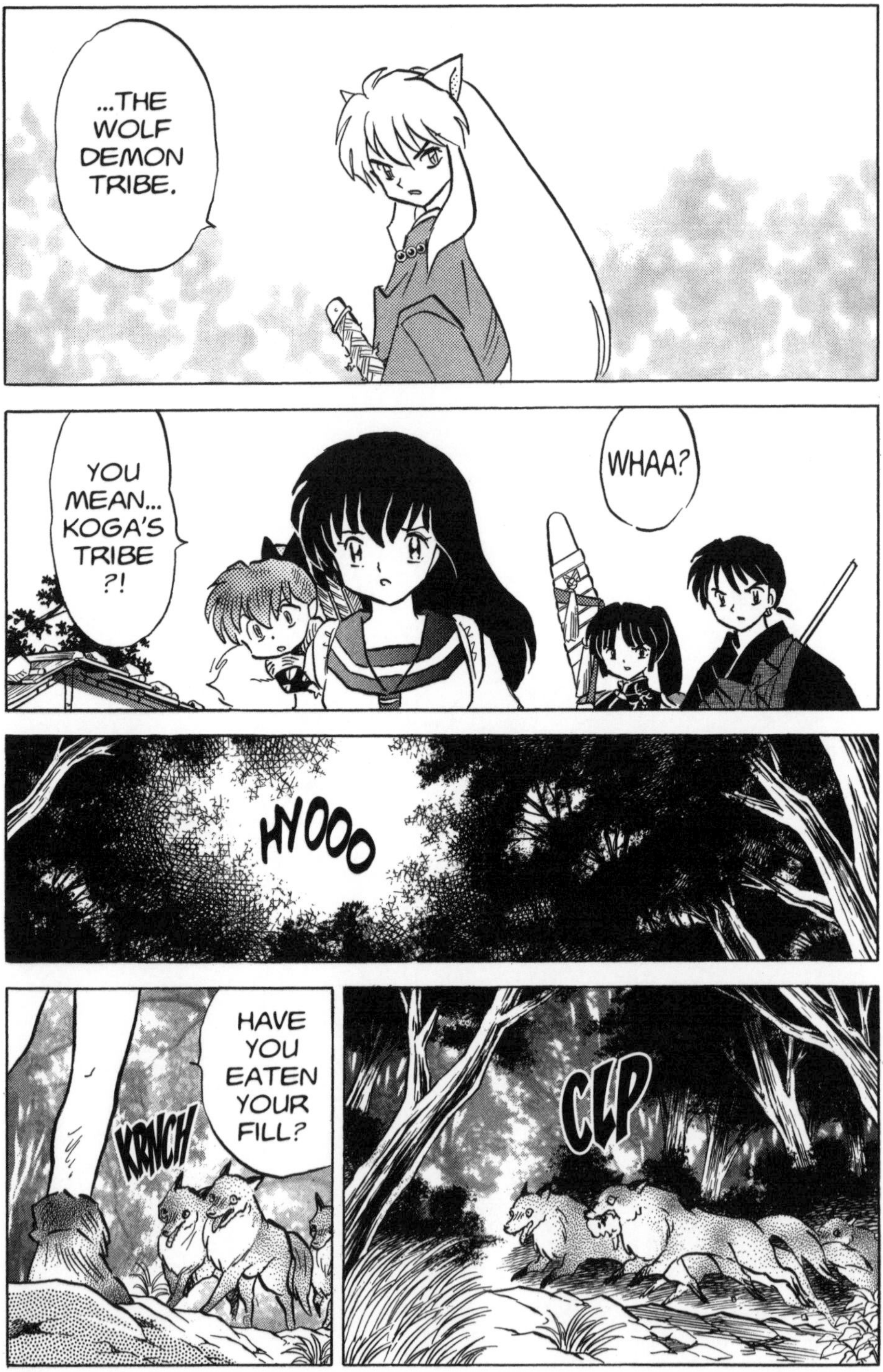
...THE WOLF DEMON TRIBE.
WHAA?
YOU MEAN... KOGA'S TRIBE ?!
HYOOO
CLP
HAVE YOU EATEN YOUR FILL?
KRNCH

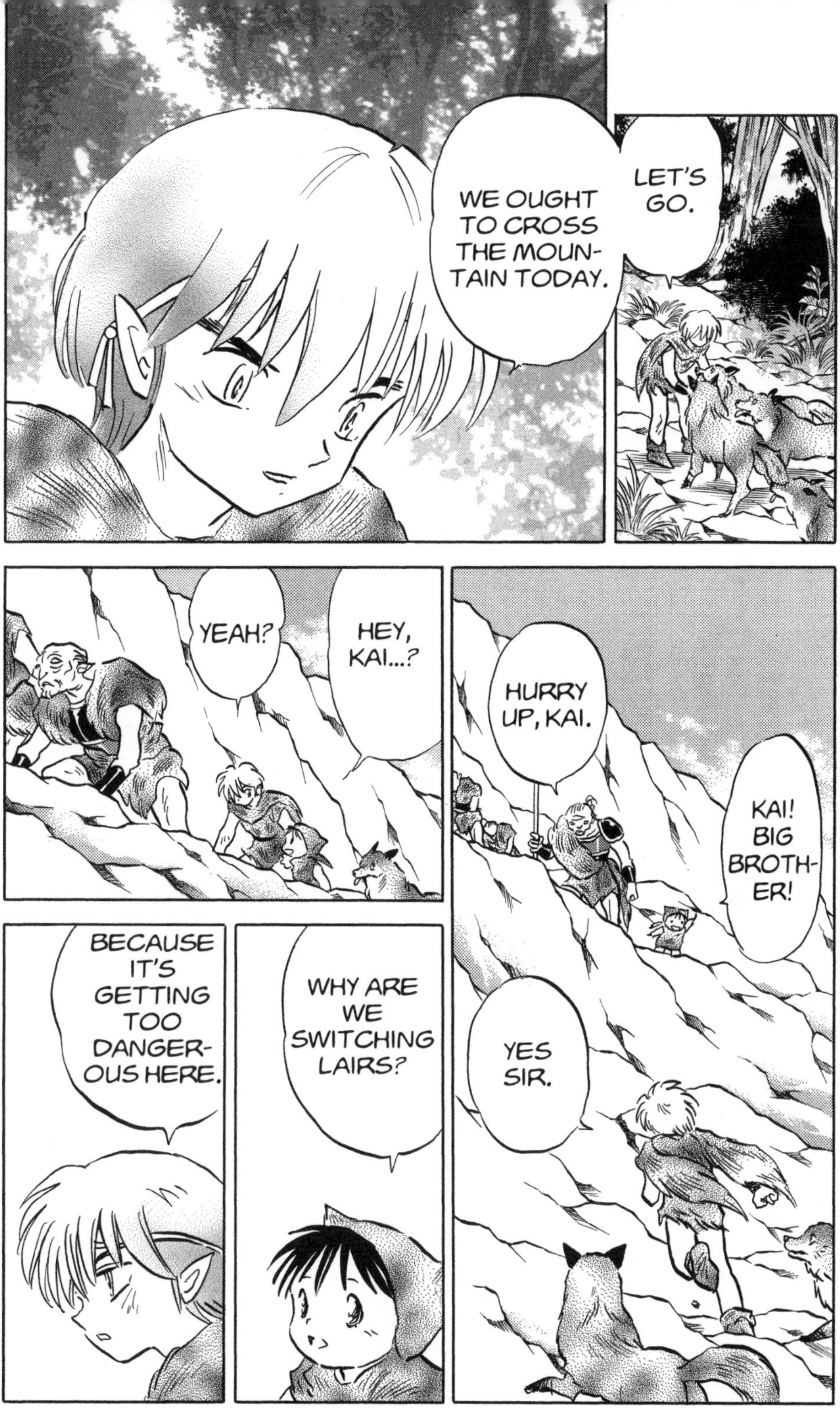
LET'S GO.
WE OUGHT TO CROSS THE MOUN- TAIN TODAY.
HURRY UP, KAI.
KAI! BIG BROTH- ER!
YES SIR.
HEY, KAI...?
YEAH?
WHY ARE WE SWITCHING LAIRS?
BECAUSE IT'S GETTING TOO DANGER- OUS HERE.

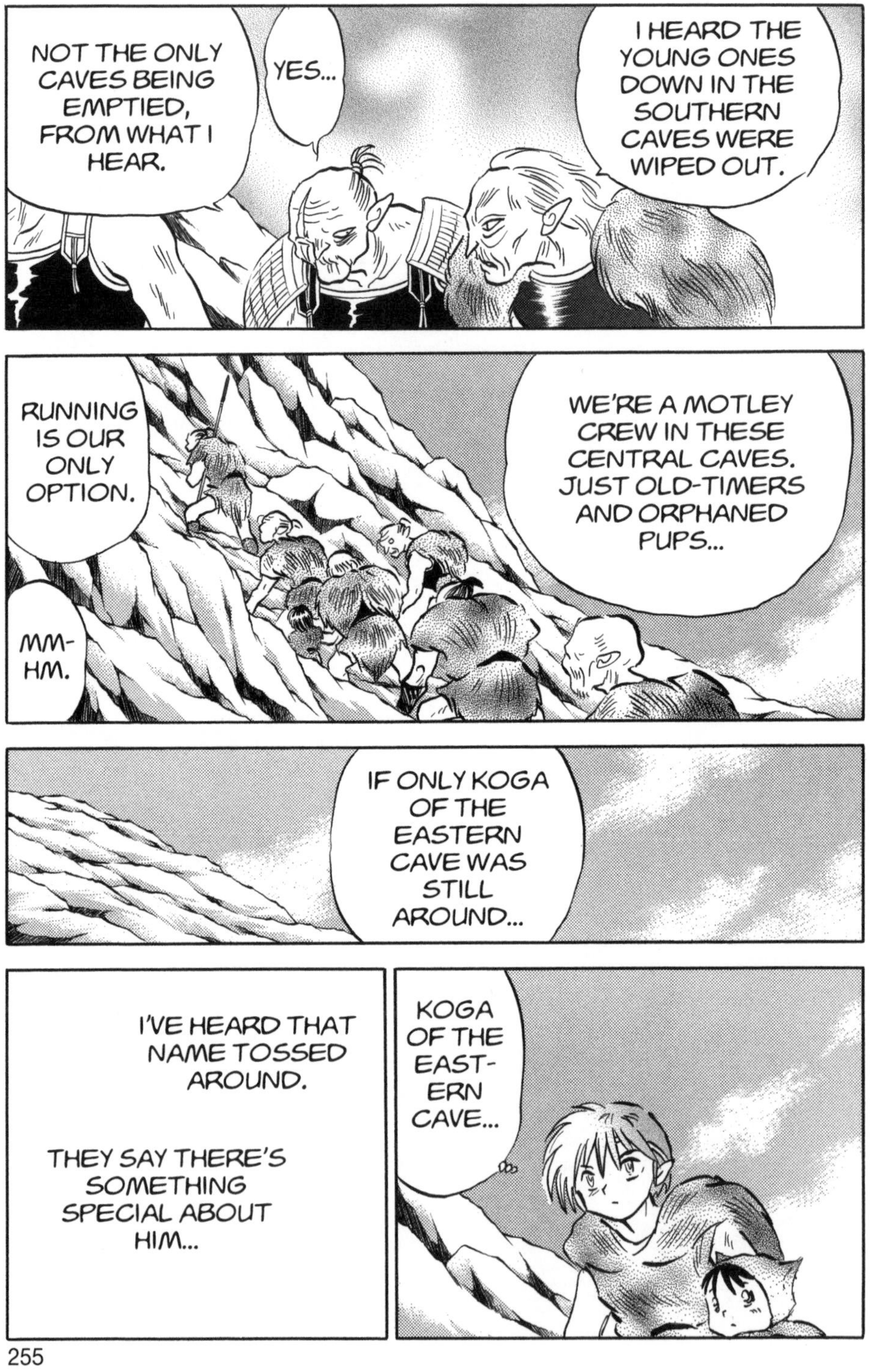
I HEARD THE YOUNG ONES DOWN IN THE SOUTHERN CAVES WERE WIPED OUT.
YES...
NOT THE ONLY CAVES BEING EMPTIED, FROM WHAT I HEAR.
WE'RE A MOTLEY CREW IN THESE CENTRAL CAVES. JUST OLD-TIMERS AND ORPHANED PUPS...
RUNNING IS OUR ONLY OPTION.
MM-HM.
IF ONLY KOGA OF THE EASTERN CAVE WAS STILL AROUND...
KOGA OF THE EAST-ERN CAVE...
I'VE HEARD THAT NAME TOSSED AROUND.
THEY SAY THERE'S SOMETHING SPECIAL ABOUT HIM...

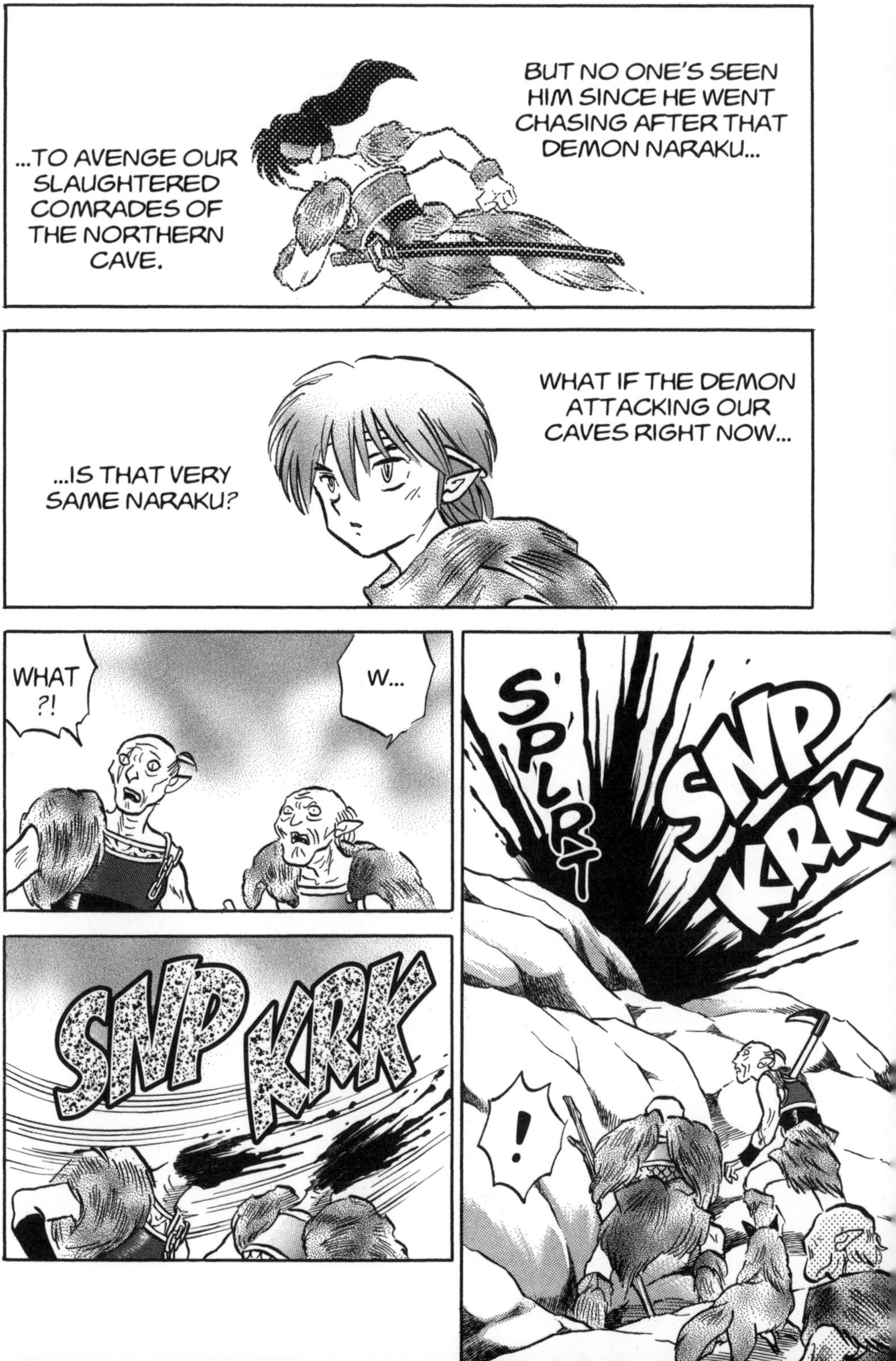
BUT NO ONE'S SEEN HIM SINCE HE WENT CHASING AFTER THAT DEMON NARAKU...
...TO AVENGE OUR SLAUGHTERED COMRADES OF THE NORTHERN CAVE.
WHAT IF THE DEMON ATTACKING OUR CAVES RIGHT NOW...
...IS THAT VERY SAME NARAKU?
SNP KRK
SPLRT
!
W...
WHAT ?!
SNP KRK

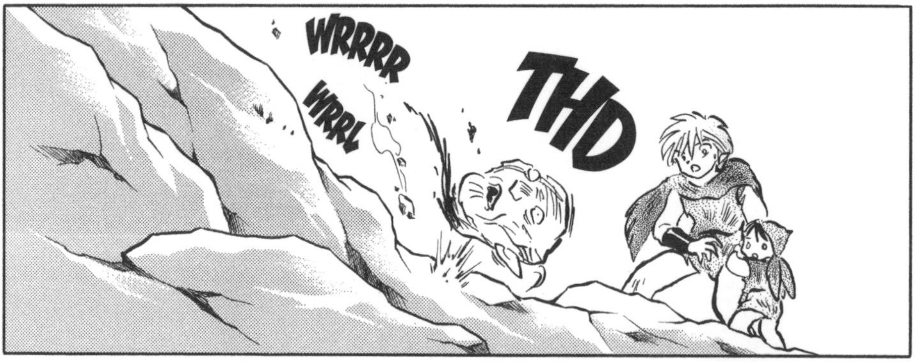
WRRRRR WRRL
THD

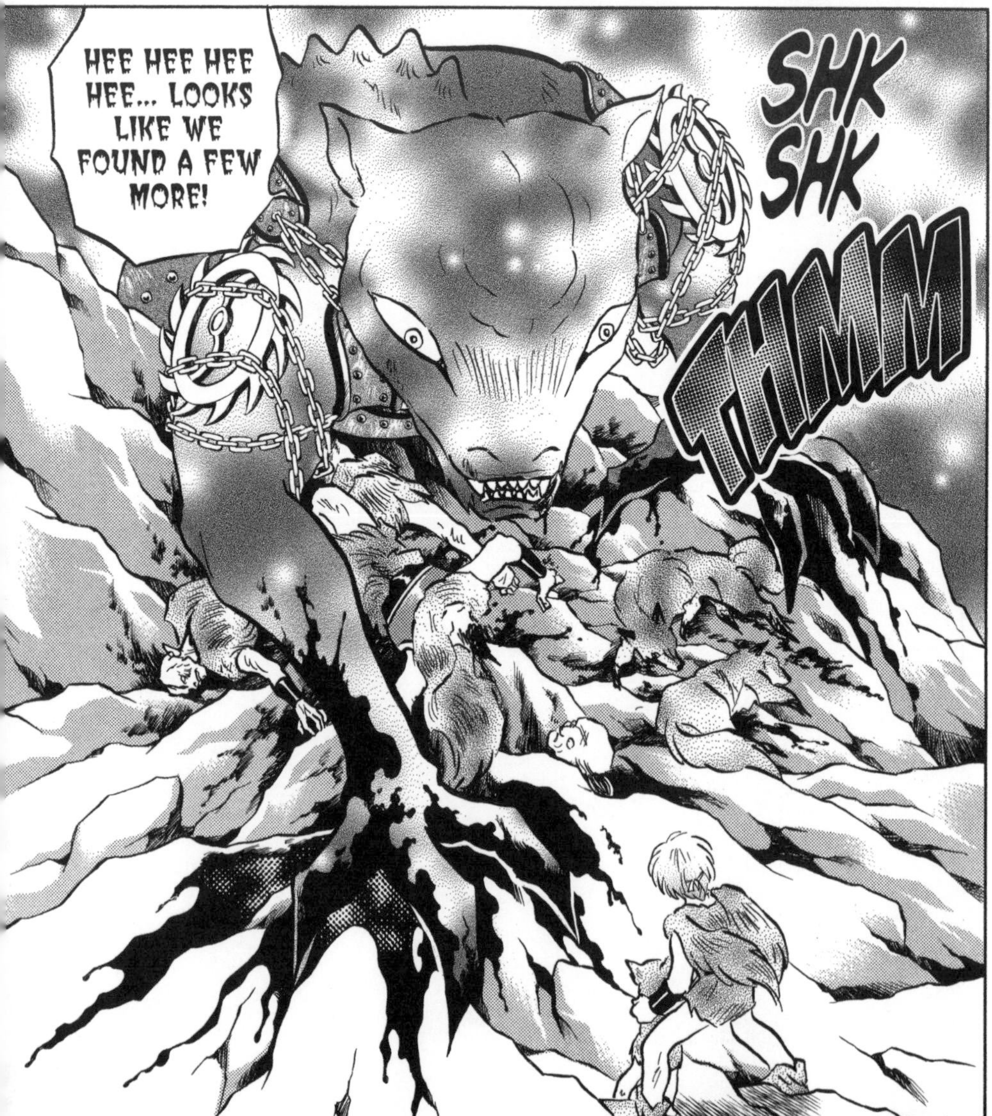
SHK SHK
THMMM
HEE HEE HEE HEE... LOOKS LIKE WE FOUND A FEW MORE!

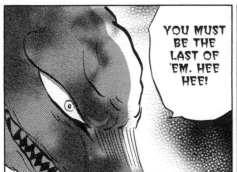

YOU MUST BE THE LAST OF 'EM. HEE HEE!

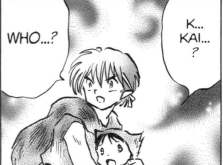

WHO...?

K... KAI...?

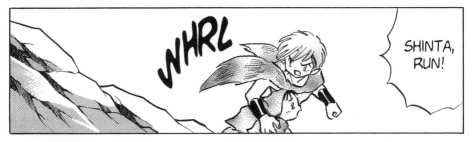

WHRL

SHINTA, RUN!

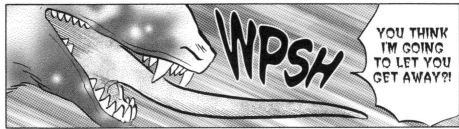

WPSH

YOU THINK I'M GOING TO LET YOU GET AWAY?!

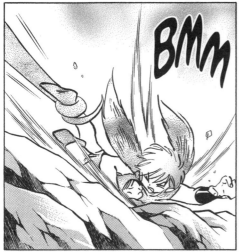

BMM

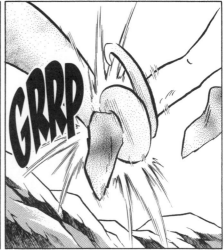

GRRP

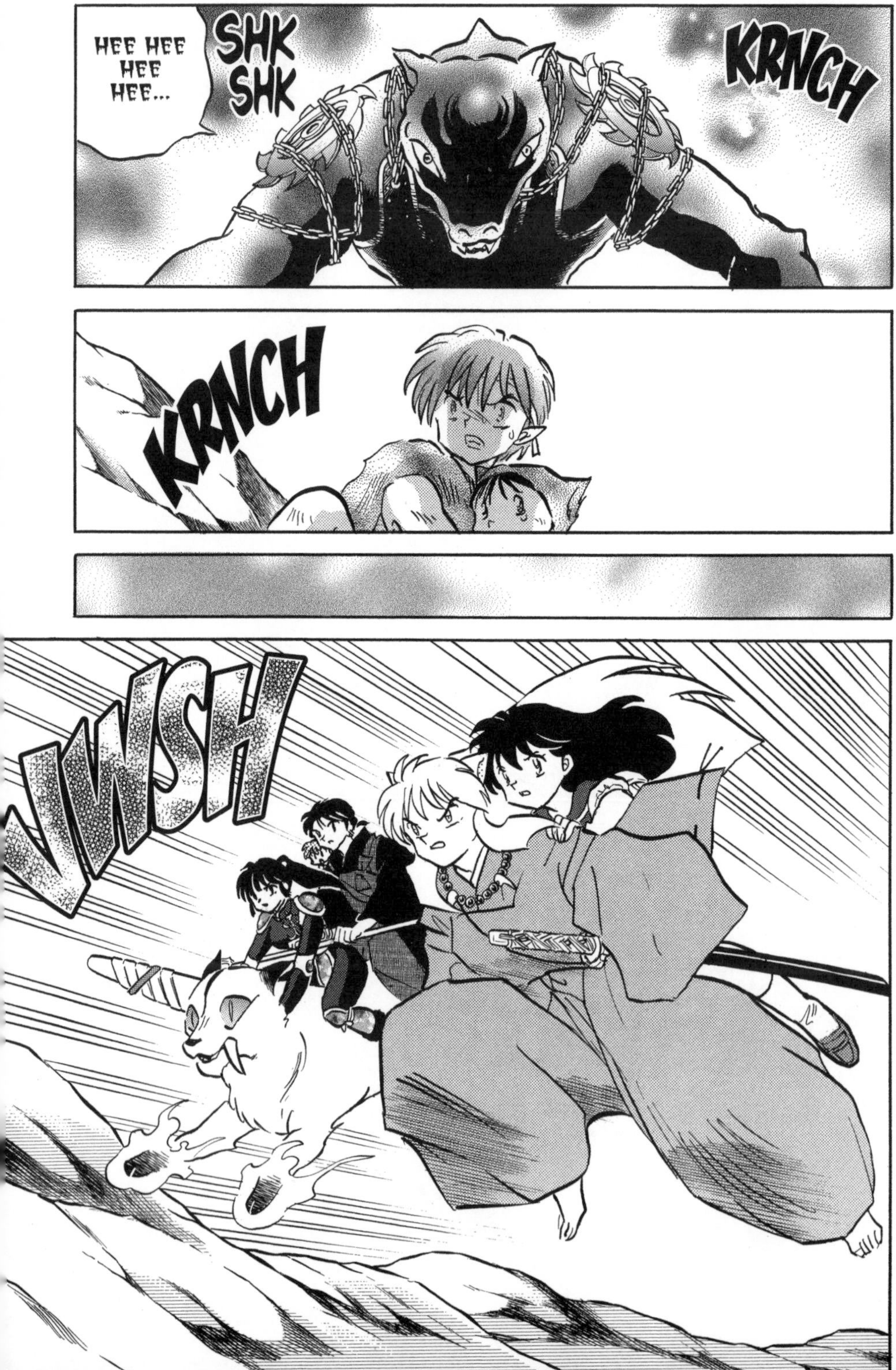
KRNCH
SHK SHK
HEE HEE HEE HEE...
KRNCH
VWSH

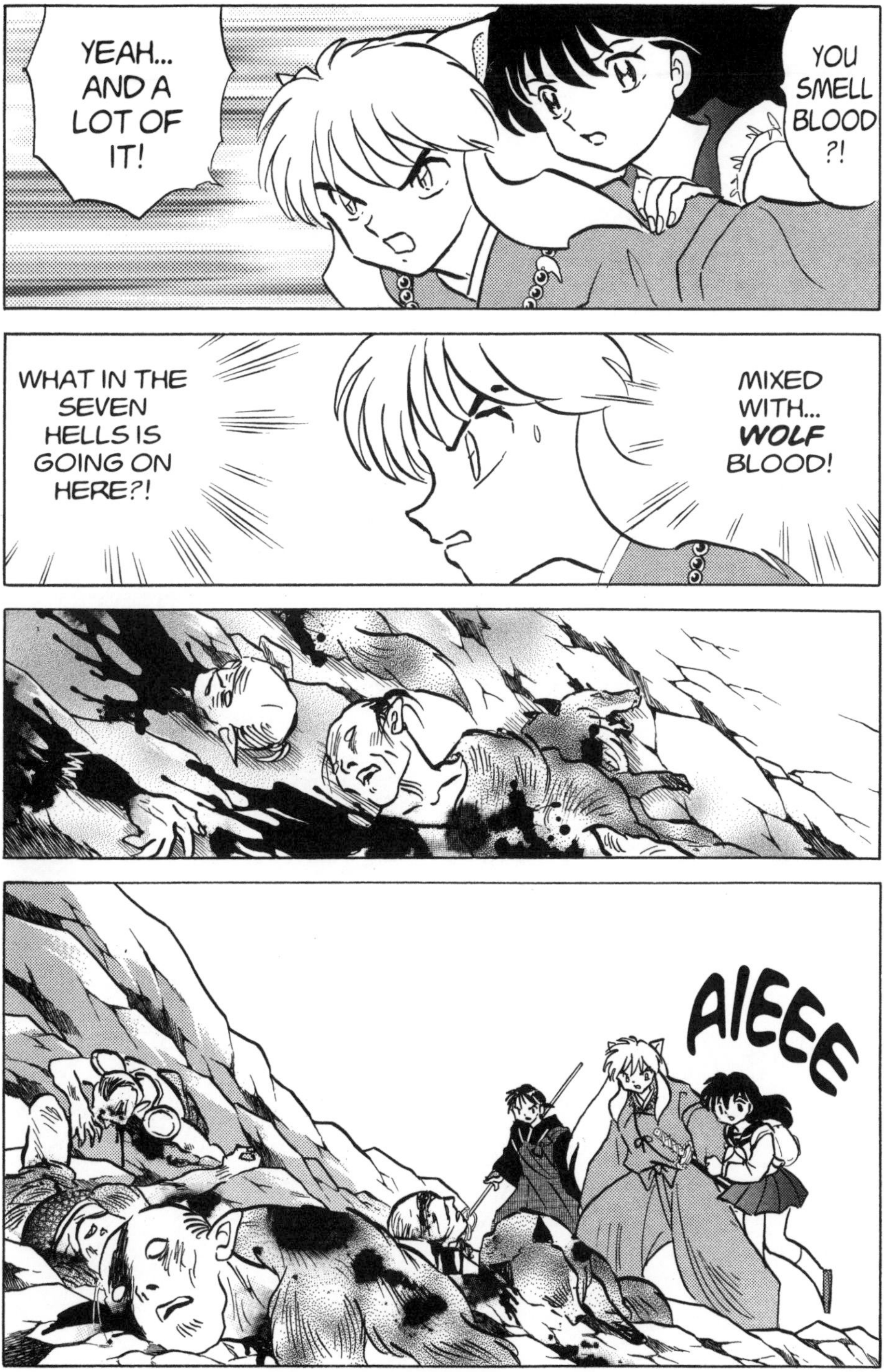
YOU SMELL BLOOD?!
YEAH... AND A LOT OF IT!
MIXED WITH... **WOLF** BLOOD!
WHAT IN THE SEVEN HELLS IS GOING ON HERE?!
AIEEE

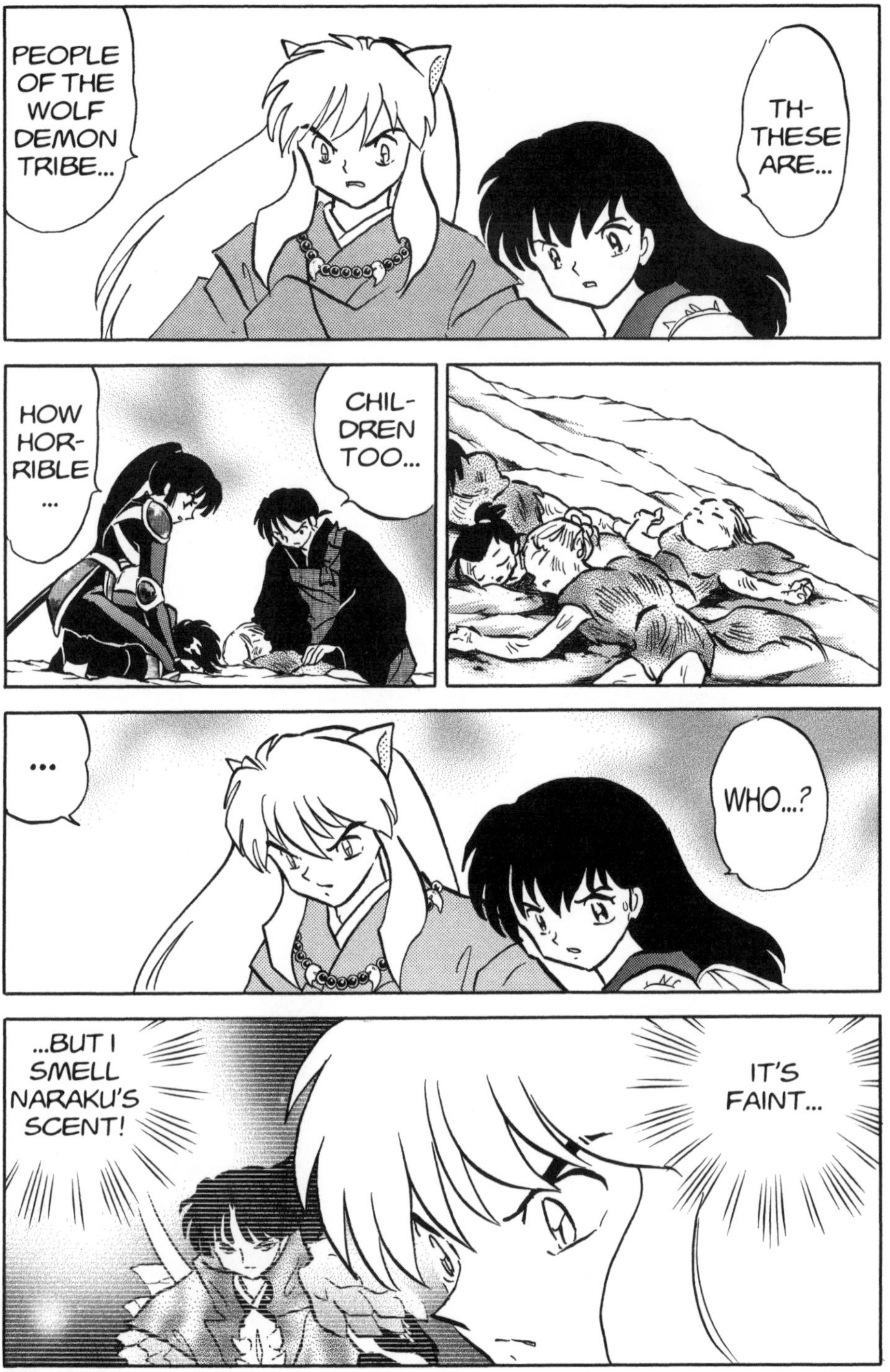
TH- THESE ARE...
PEOPLE OF THE WOLF DEMON TRIBE...
CHIL- DREN TOO...
HOW HOR- RIBLE ...
WHO...?
...
IT'S FAINT...
...BUT I SMELL NARAKU'S SCENT!

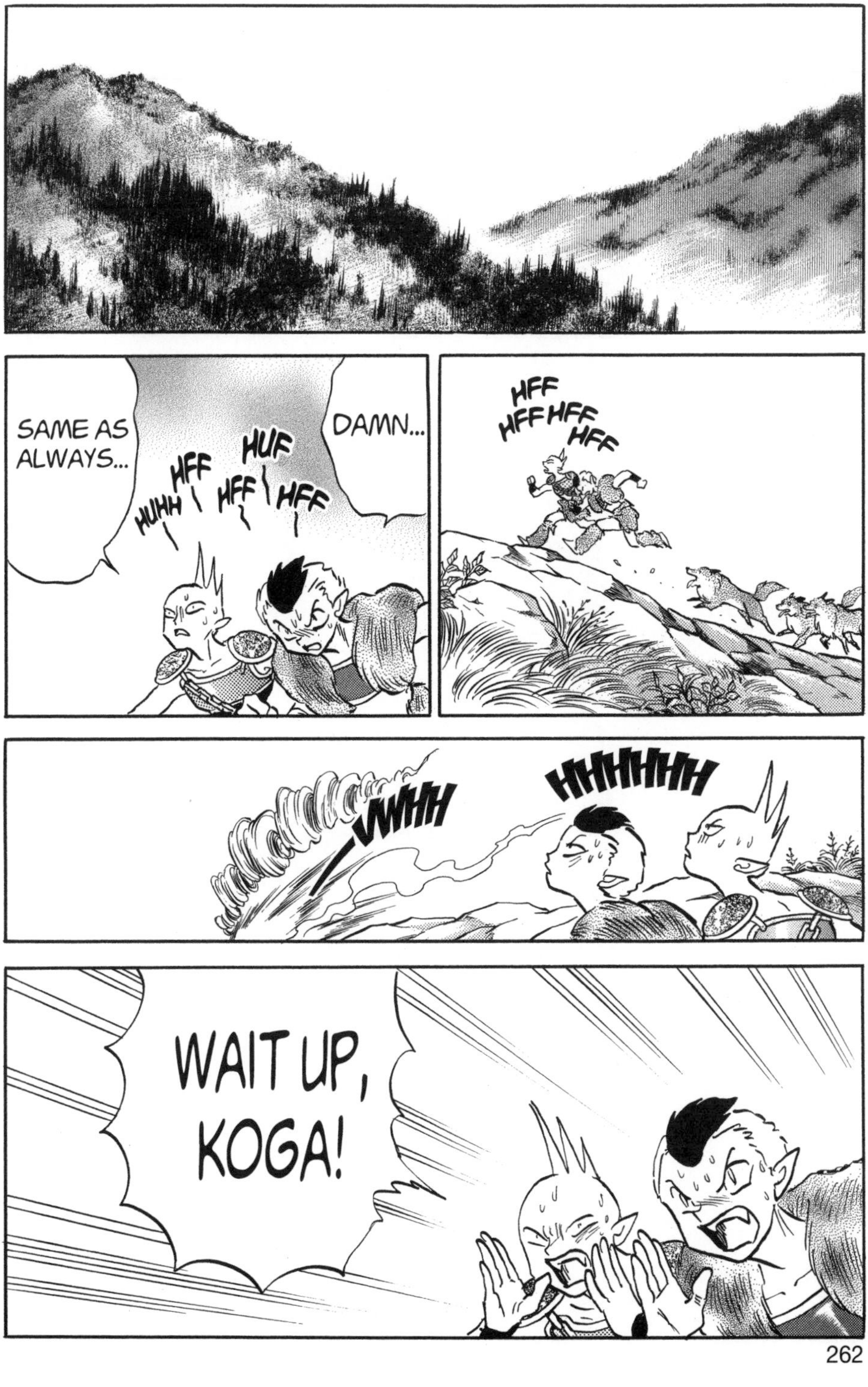
HFF
HFF HFF
HFF
DAMN...
HUF
HFF
HFF
HFF
HUHH
SAME AS ALWAYS...
HHHHHHHH
VWHH
WAIT UP, KOGA!

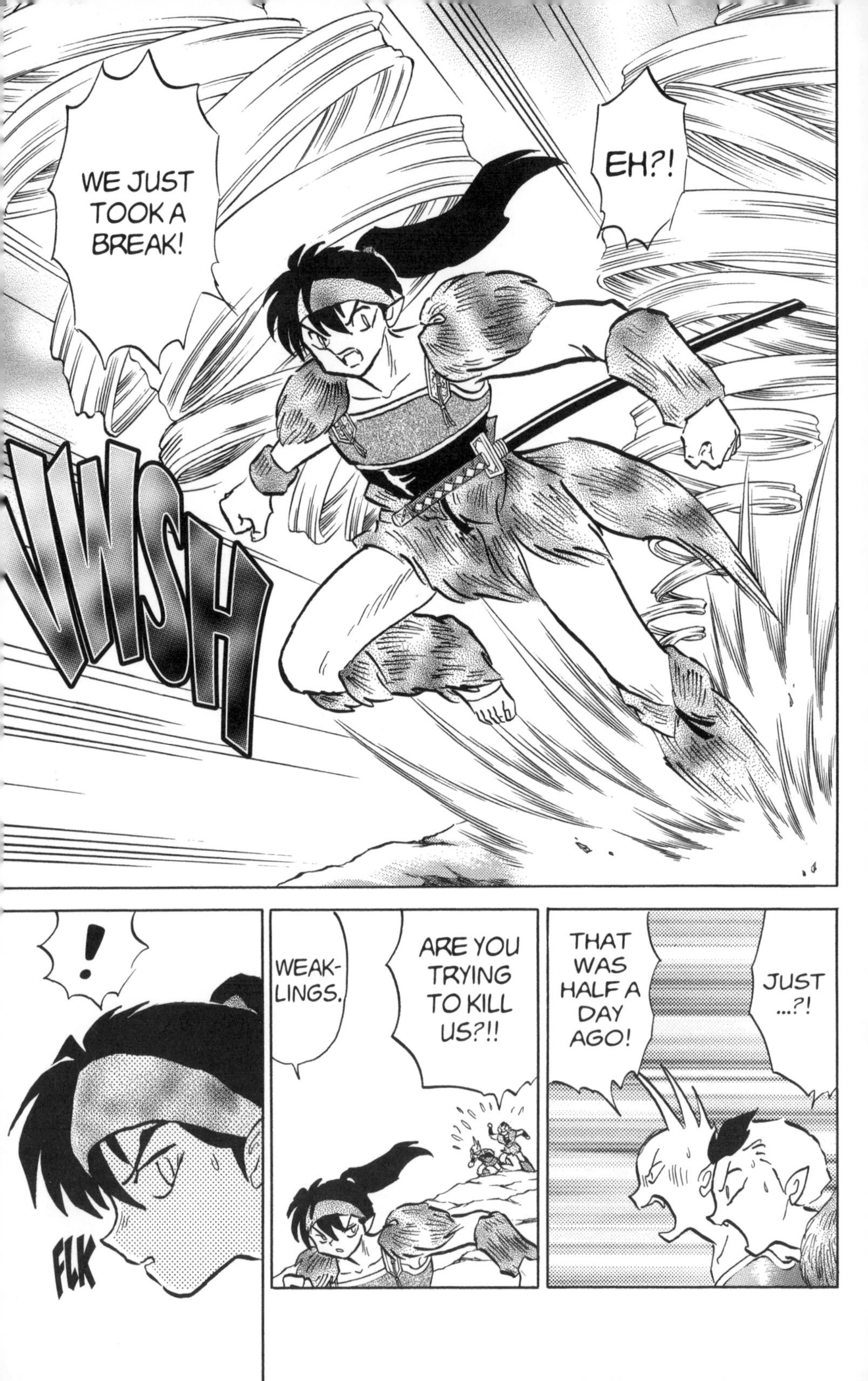
EH?!
WE JUST TOOK A BREAK!
VWISH
JUST ...?!
THAT WAS HALF A DAY AGO!
ARE YOU TRYING TO KILL US?!!
WEAK-LINGS.
!
FLK

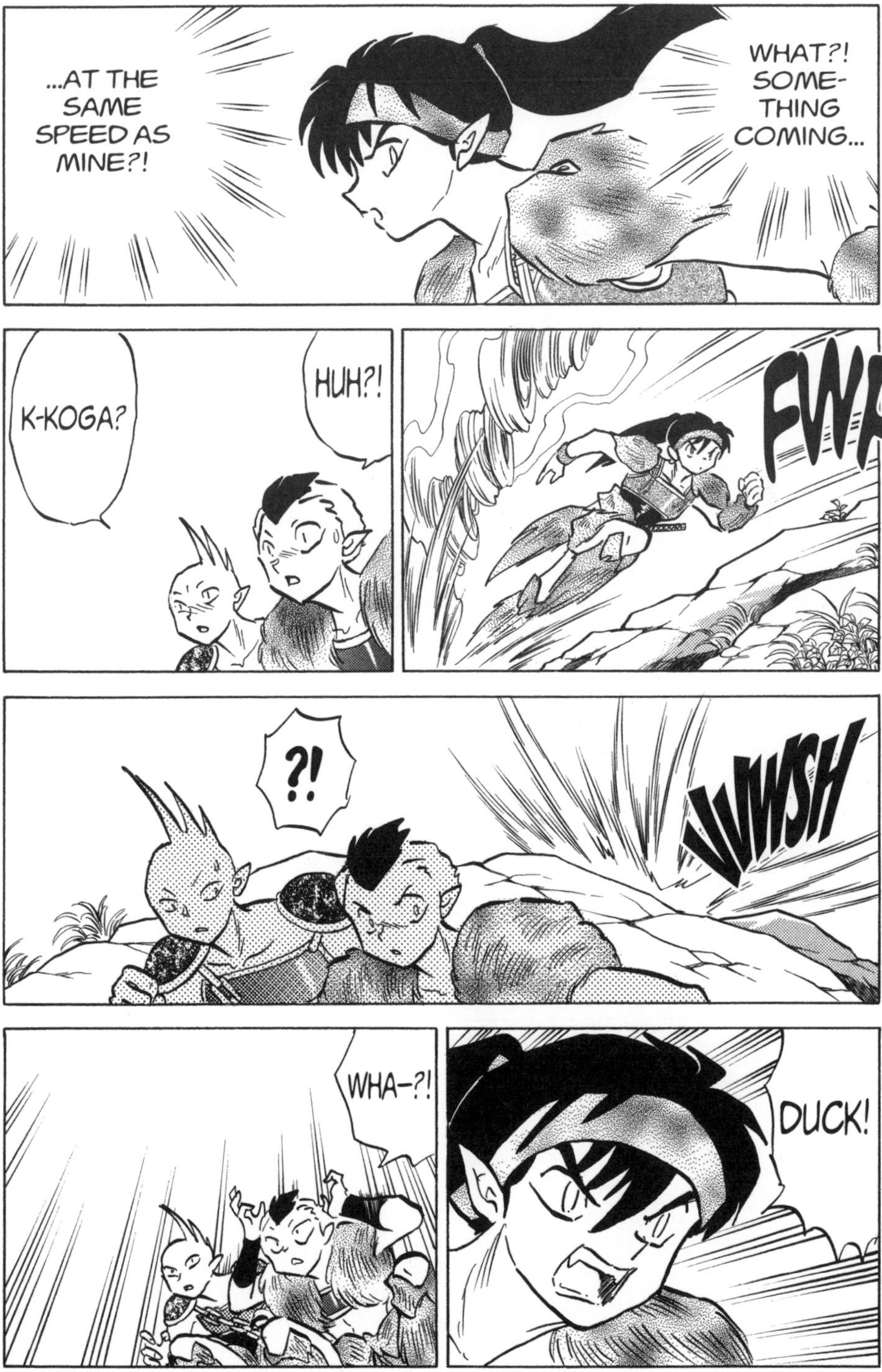
WHAT?! SOME-THING COMING...
...AT THE SAME SPEED AS MINE?!
FWP
HUH?!
K-KOGA?
VVWSH
?!
DUCK!
WHA-?!

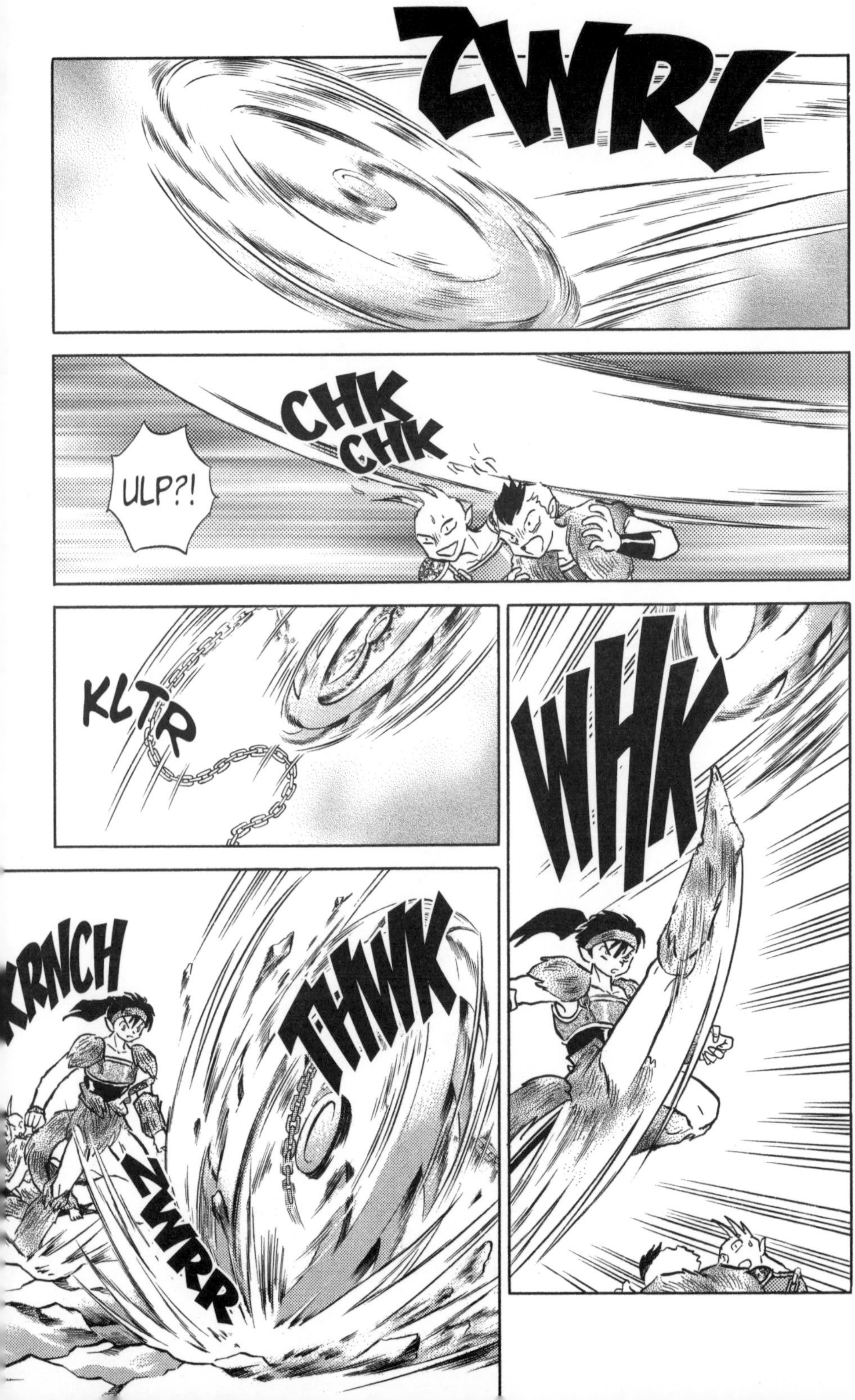
ZWRL
CHK CHK
ULP?!
WHK
KLTR
THWK
KRNCH
ZWRR

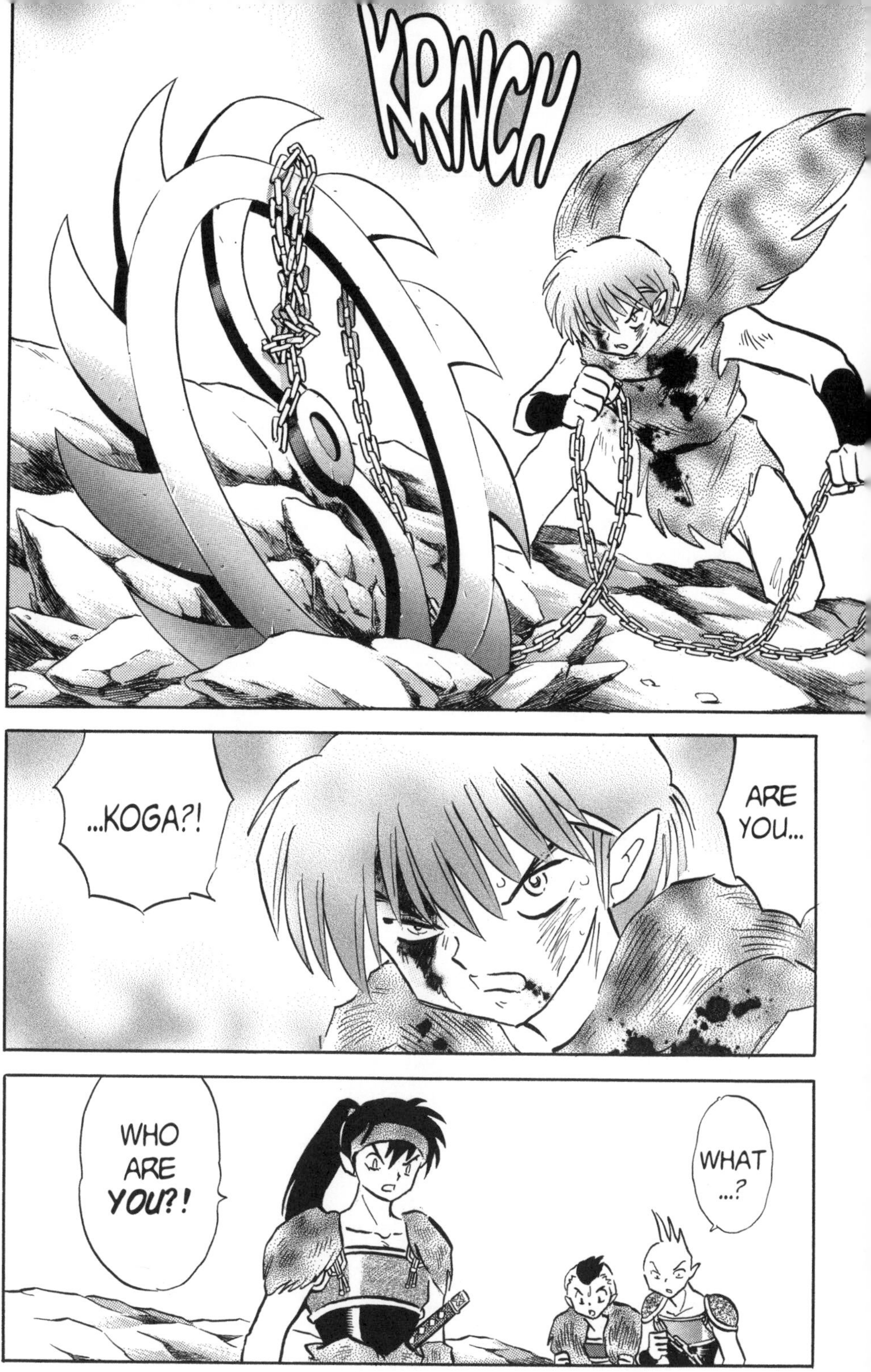
KRNCH
ARE YOU...
...KOGA?!
WHAT ...?
WHO ARE YOU?!

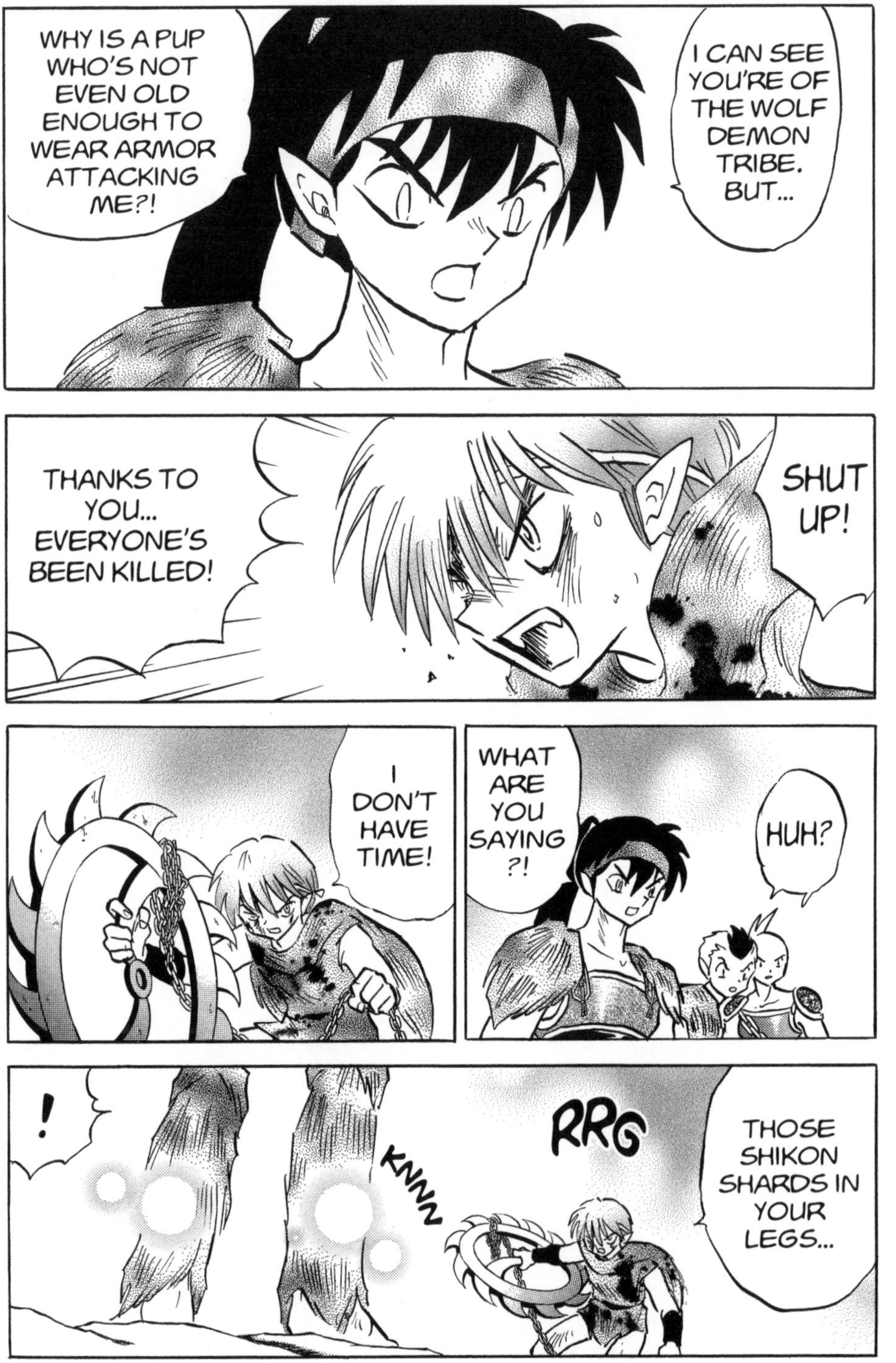
I CAN SEE YOU'RE OF THE WOLF DEMON TRIBE. BUT...
WHY IS A PUP WHO'S NOT EVEN OLD ENOUGH TO WEAR ARMOR ATTACKING ME?!
SHUT UP!
THANKS TO YOU... EVERYONE'S BEEN KILLED!
HUH?
WHAT ARE YOU SAYING?!
I DON'T HAVE TIME!
THOSE SHIKON SHARDS IN YOUR LEGS...
RRG
KNNN
!

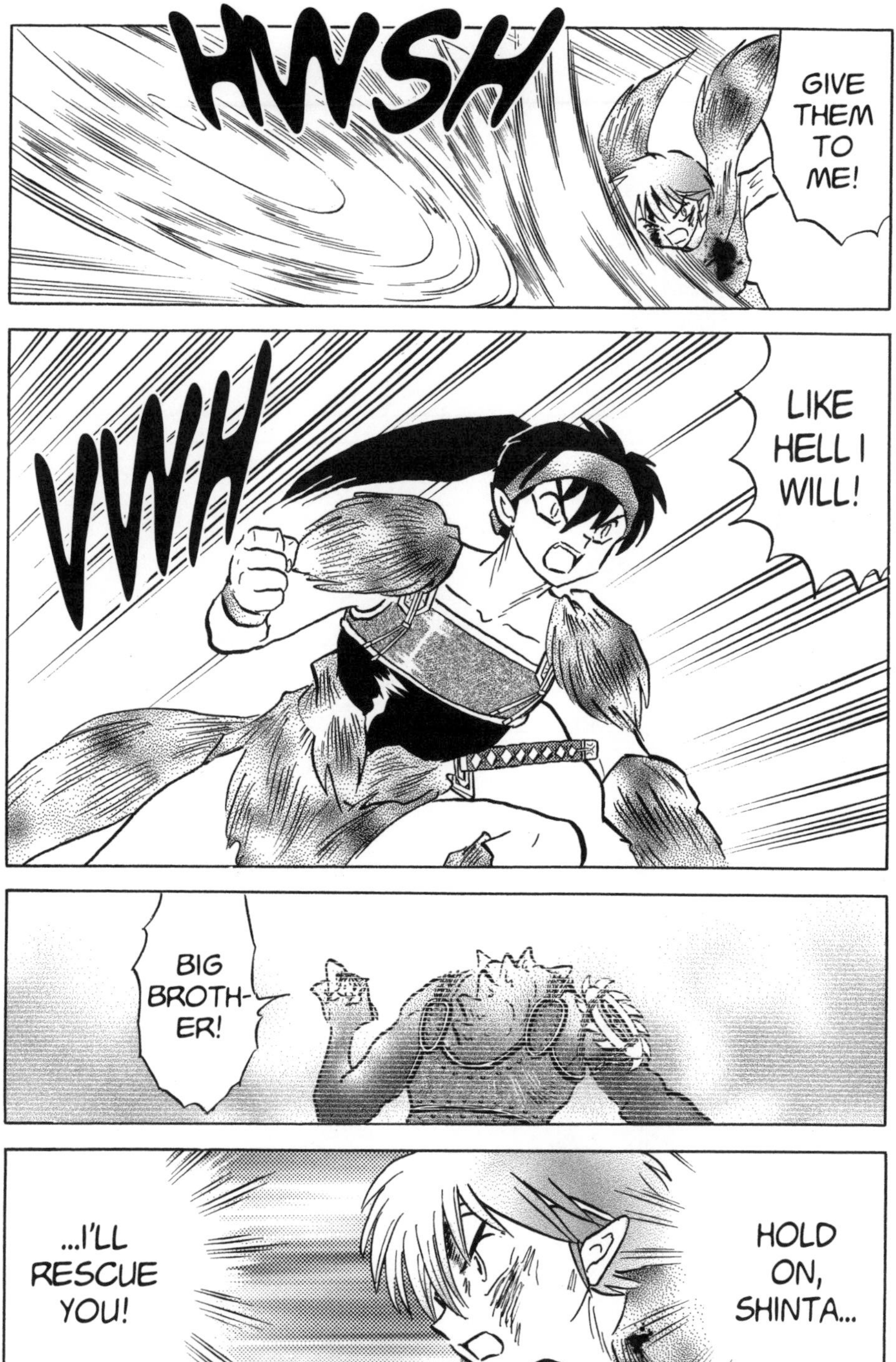
GIVE THEM TO ME!
HWSH
LIKE HELL I WILL!
VWH
BIG BROTH-ER!
HOLD ON, SHINTA...
...I'LL RESCUE YOU!

SCROLL FIVE
SUNDOWN

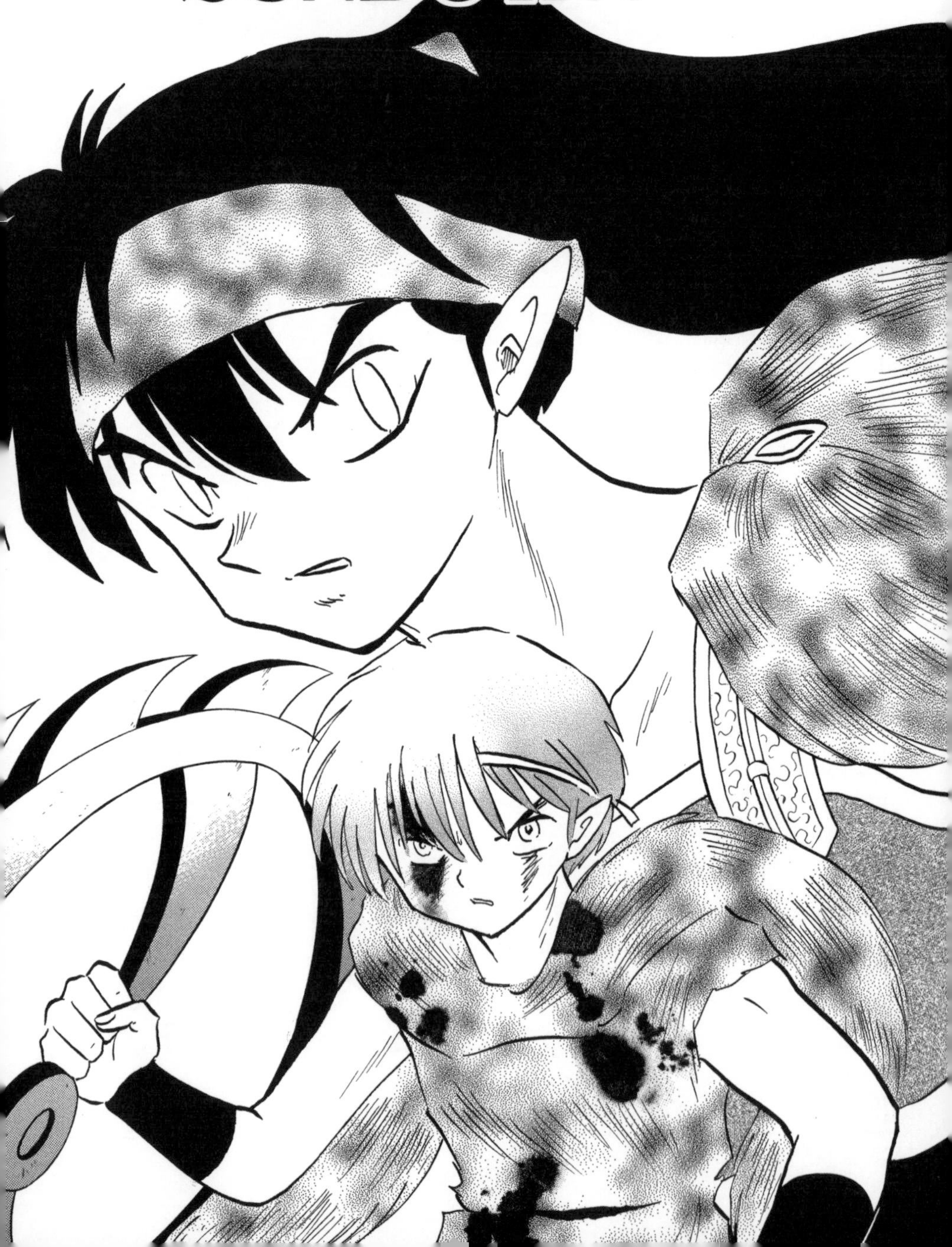

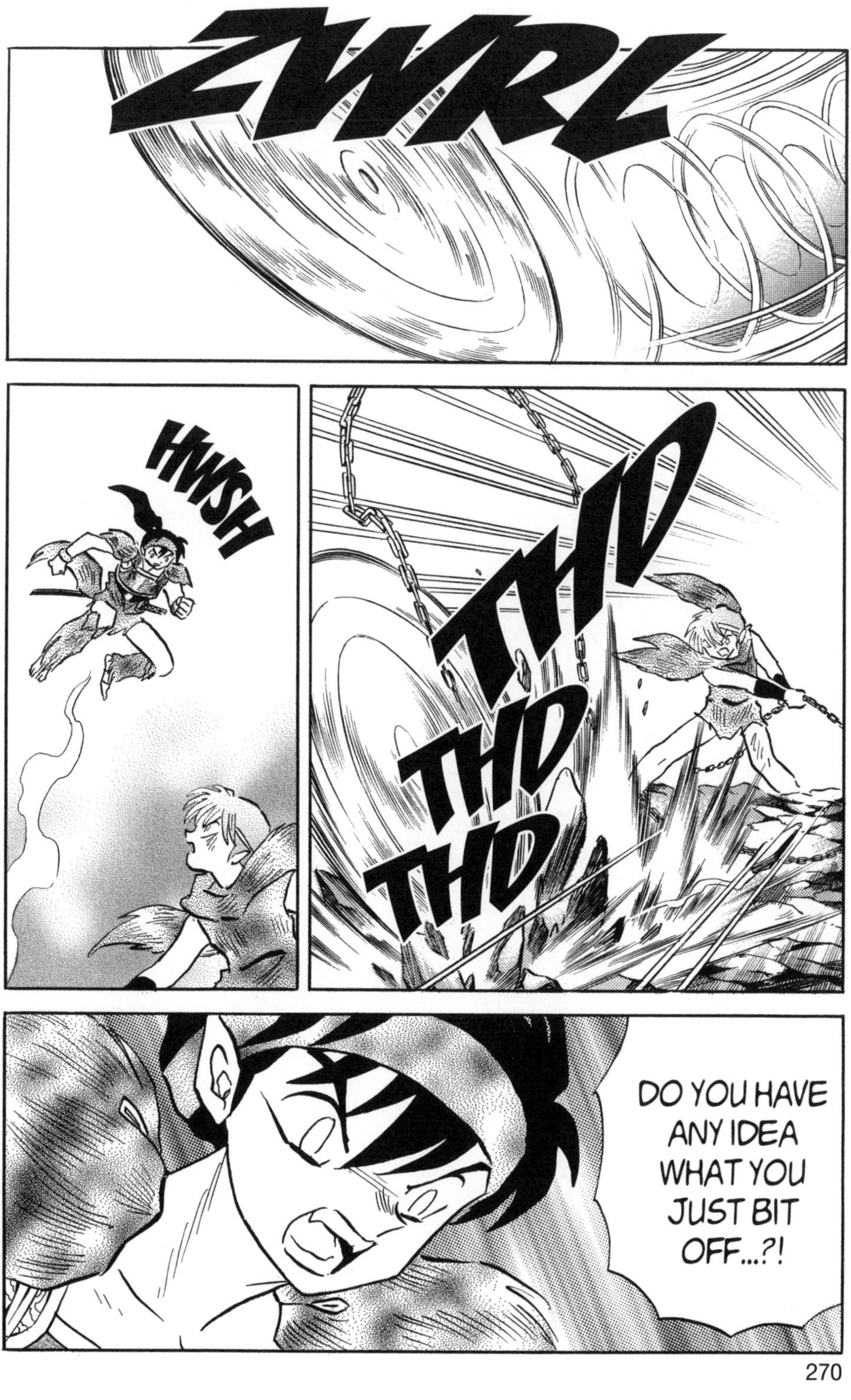
ZWRL
THD THD THD
HWSH!
DO YOU HAVE ANY IDEA WHAT YOU JUST BIT OFF...?!

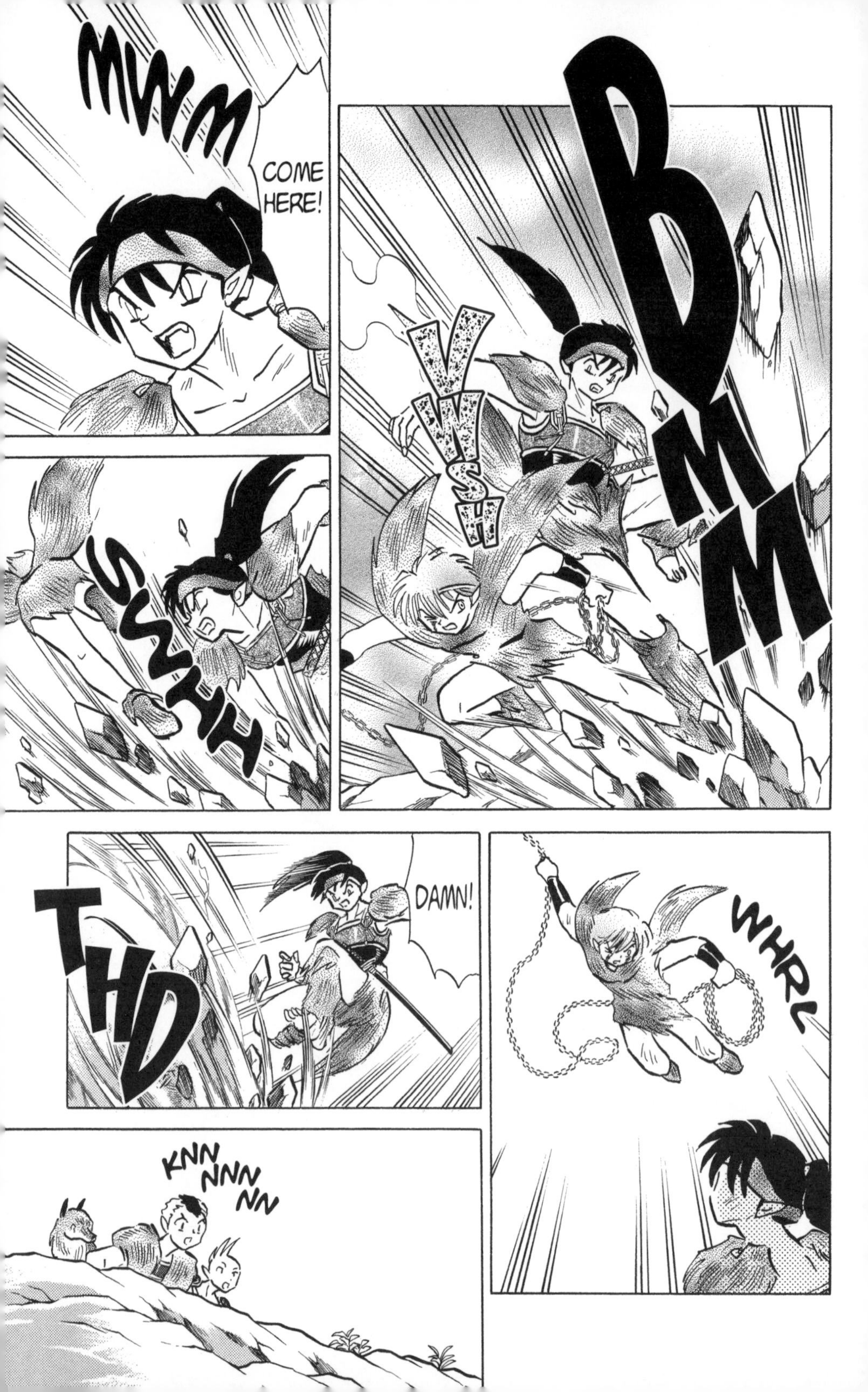
BMM
VWSH
MWM
COME HERE!
SWHH
WHRL
DAMN!
THD
KNN NNN NN

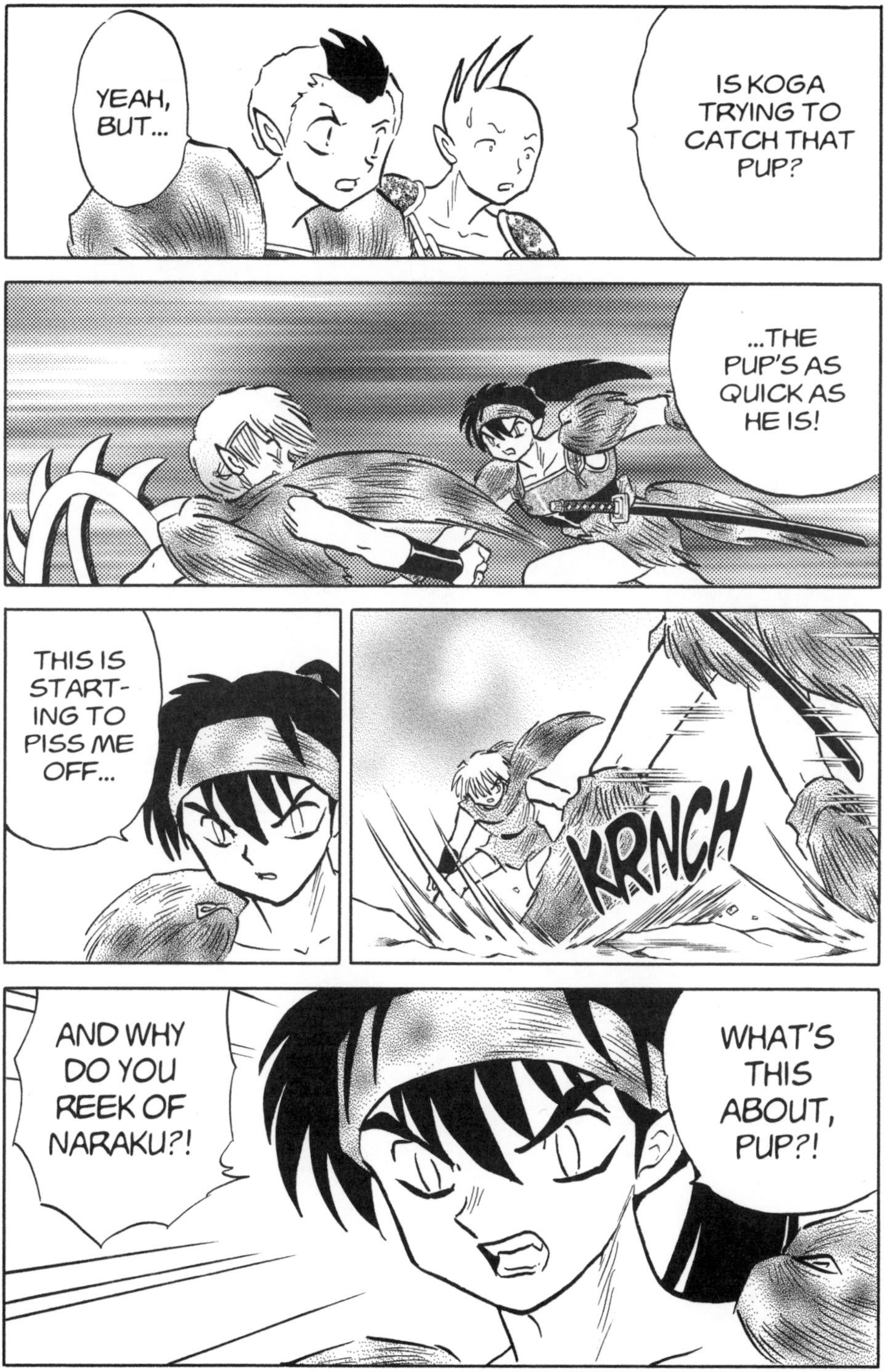
IS KOGA TRYING TO CATCH THAT PUP?
YEAH, BUT...
...THE PUP'S AS QUICK AS HE IS!
KRNCH
THIS IS START-ING TO PISS ME OFF...
WHAT'S THIS ABOUT, PUP?!
AND WHY DO YOU REEK OF NARAKU?!

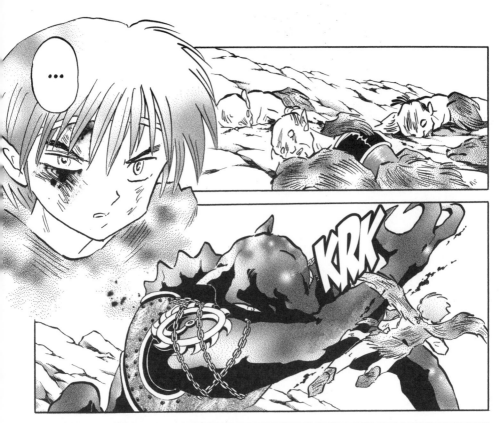

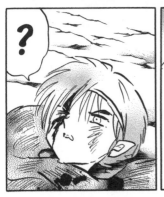

THAT'S ENOUGH.

IT'S POINT- LESS TO KILL **ALL** OF THEM.

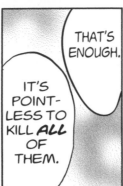

BIG BROTH- ER!

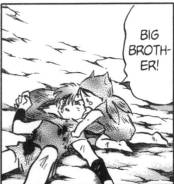

OH MY... POOR THING.

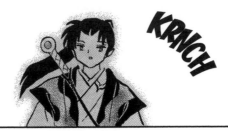

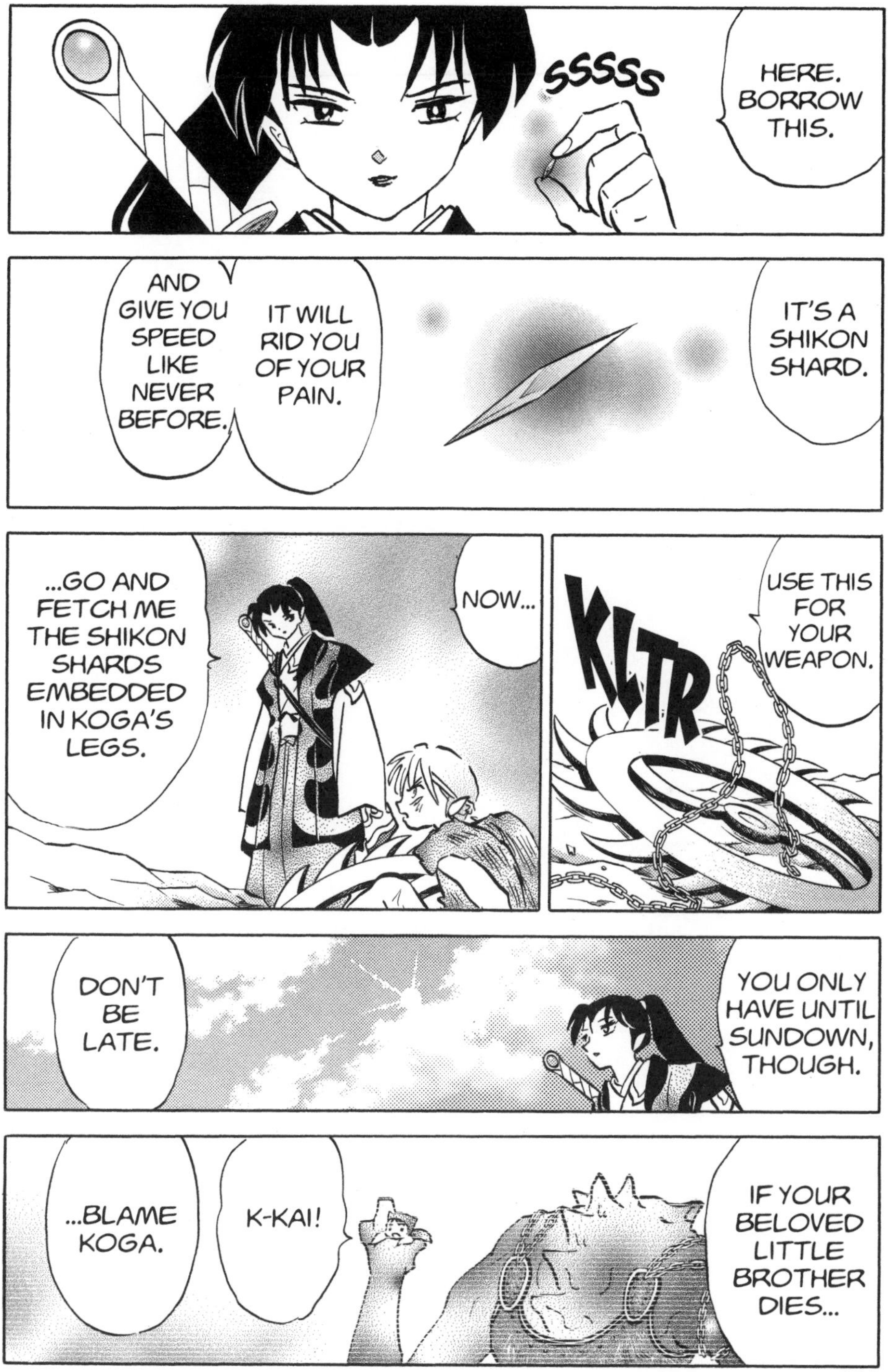
HERE. BORROW THIS.
SSSSS
IT'S A SHIKON SHARD.
IT WILL RID YOU OF YOUR PAIN.
AND GIVE YOU SPEED LIKE NEVER BEFORE.
USE THIS FOR YOUR WEAPON.
KLTR
NOW...
...GO AND FETCH ME THE SHIKON SHARDS EMBEDDED IN KOGA'S LEGS.
YOU ONLY HAVE UNTIL SUNDOWN, THOUGH.
DON'T BE LATE.
IF YOUR BELOVED LITTLE BROTHER DIES...
K-KAI!
...BLAME KOGA.

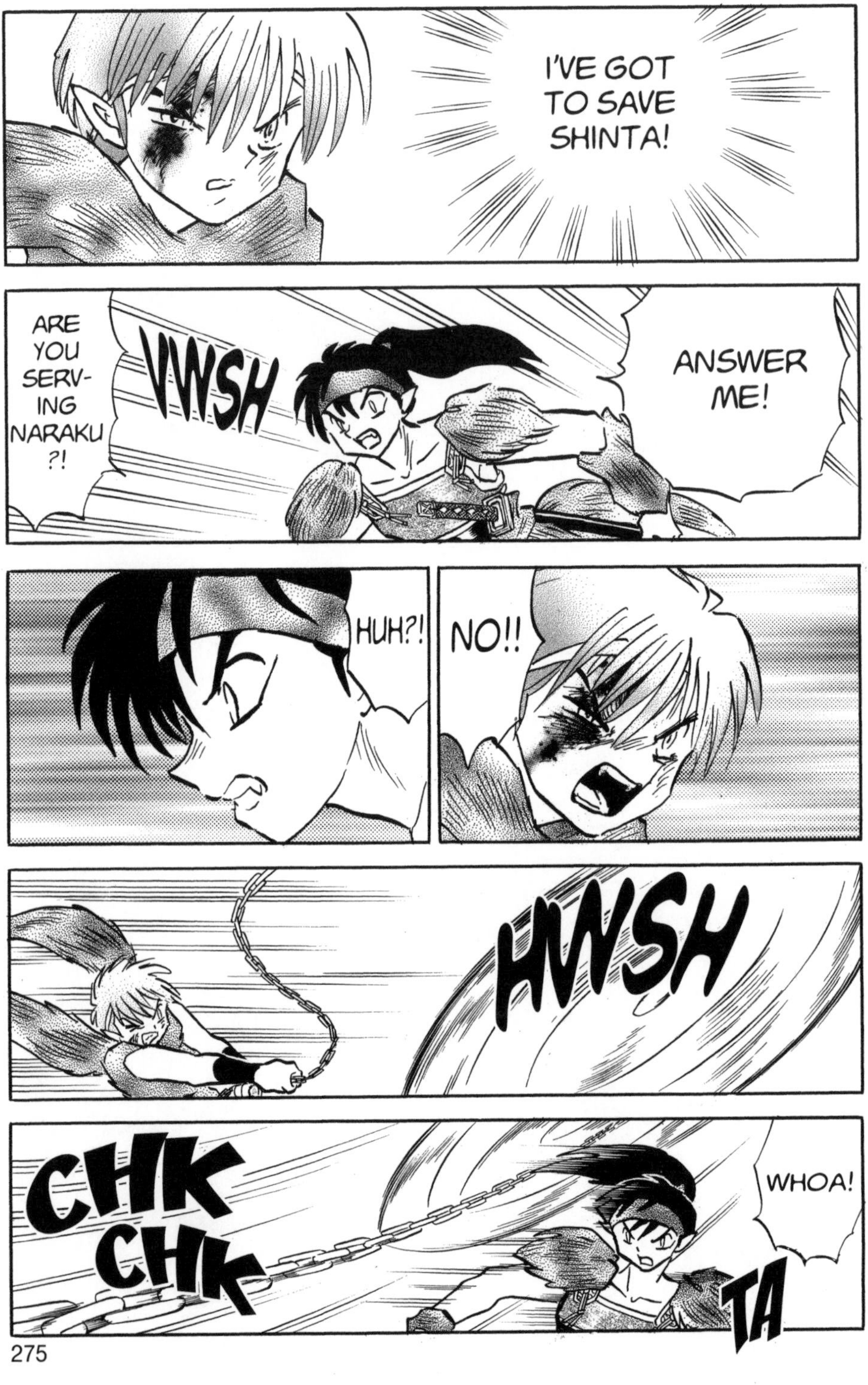
I'VE GOT TO SAVE SHINTA!
ANSWER ME!
VWSH
ARE YOU SERV-ING NARAKU?!
NO!!
HUH?!
HWSH
WHOA!
TA
CHK CHK

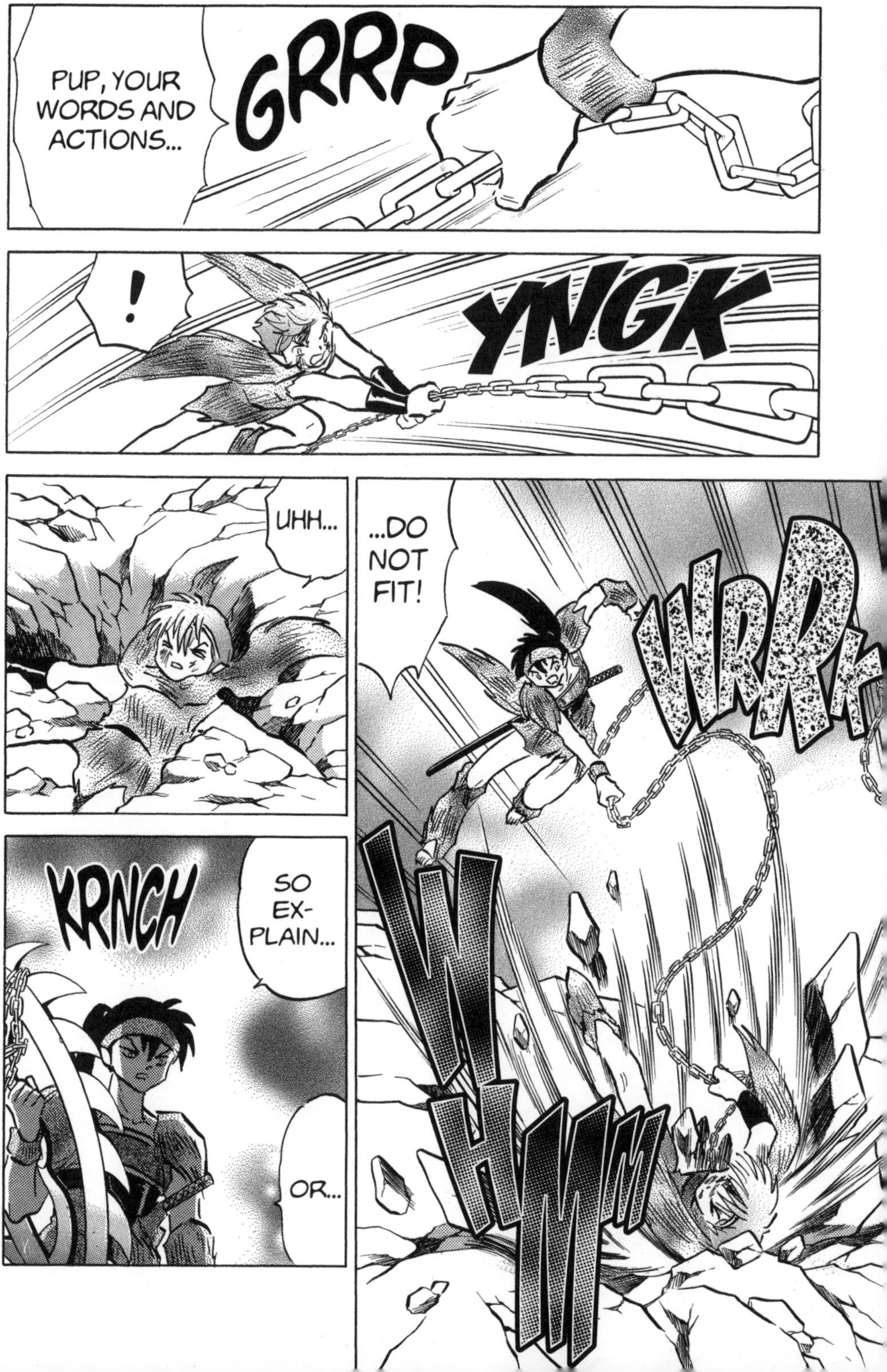
GRRP
PUP, YOUR WORDS AND ACTIONS...
YNGK
!
...DO NOT FIT!
WRRR
WHMMM
UHH...
KRNCH
SO EX-PLAIN...
OR...

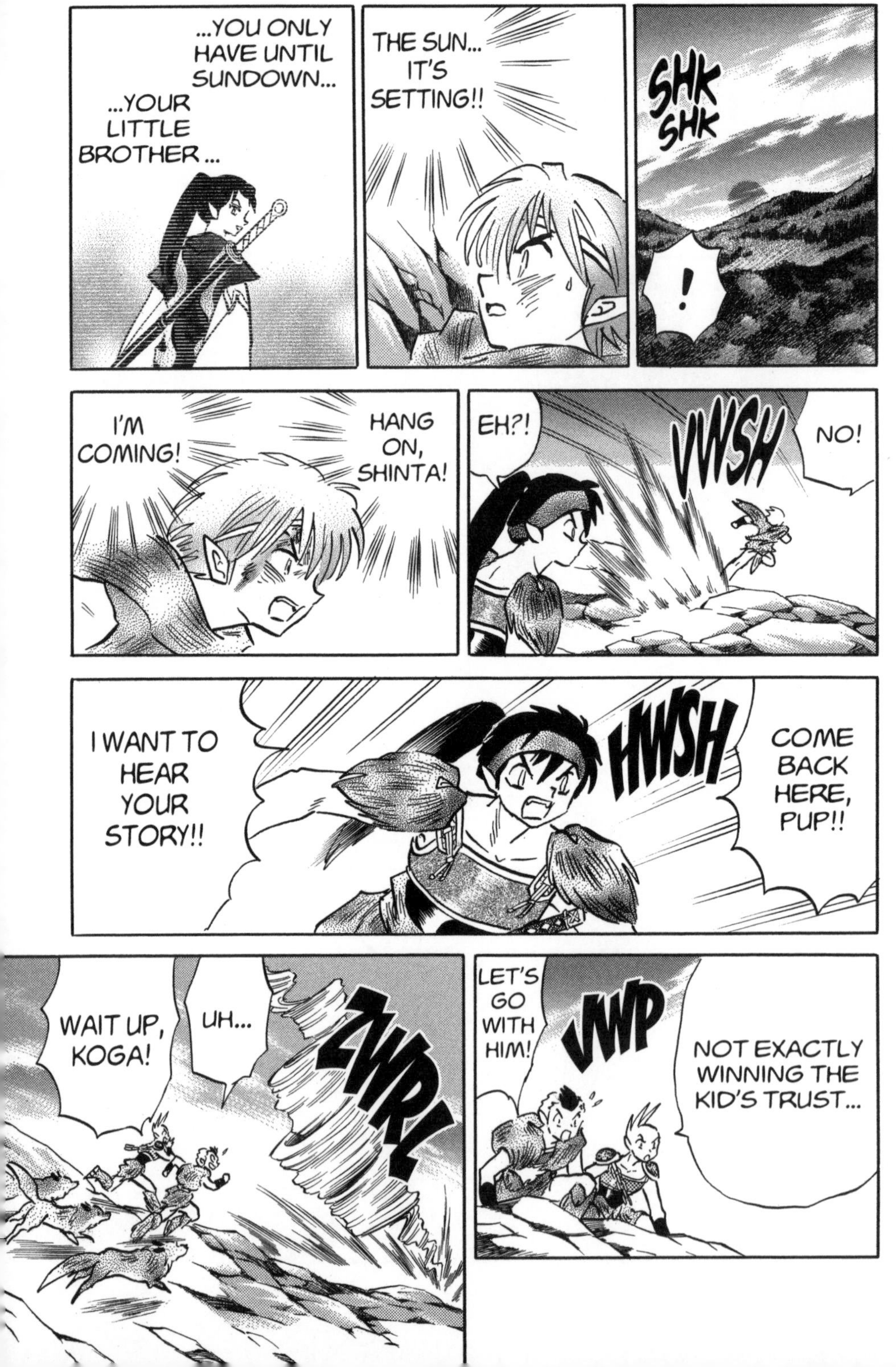
SHK SHK
!
THE SUN... IT'S SETTING!!
...YOU ONLY HAVE UNTIL SUNDOWN...
...YOUR LITTLE BROTHER ...
NO!
VWSH
EH?!
HANG ON, SHINTA!
I'M COMING!
COME BACK HERE, PUP!!
HWSH
I WANT TO HEAR YOUR STORY!!
NOT EXACTLY WINNING THE KID'S TRUST...
VWP
LET'S GO WITH HIM!
ZWRL
UH...
WAIT UP, KOGA!

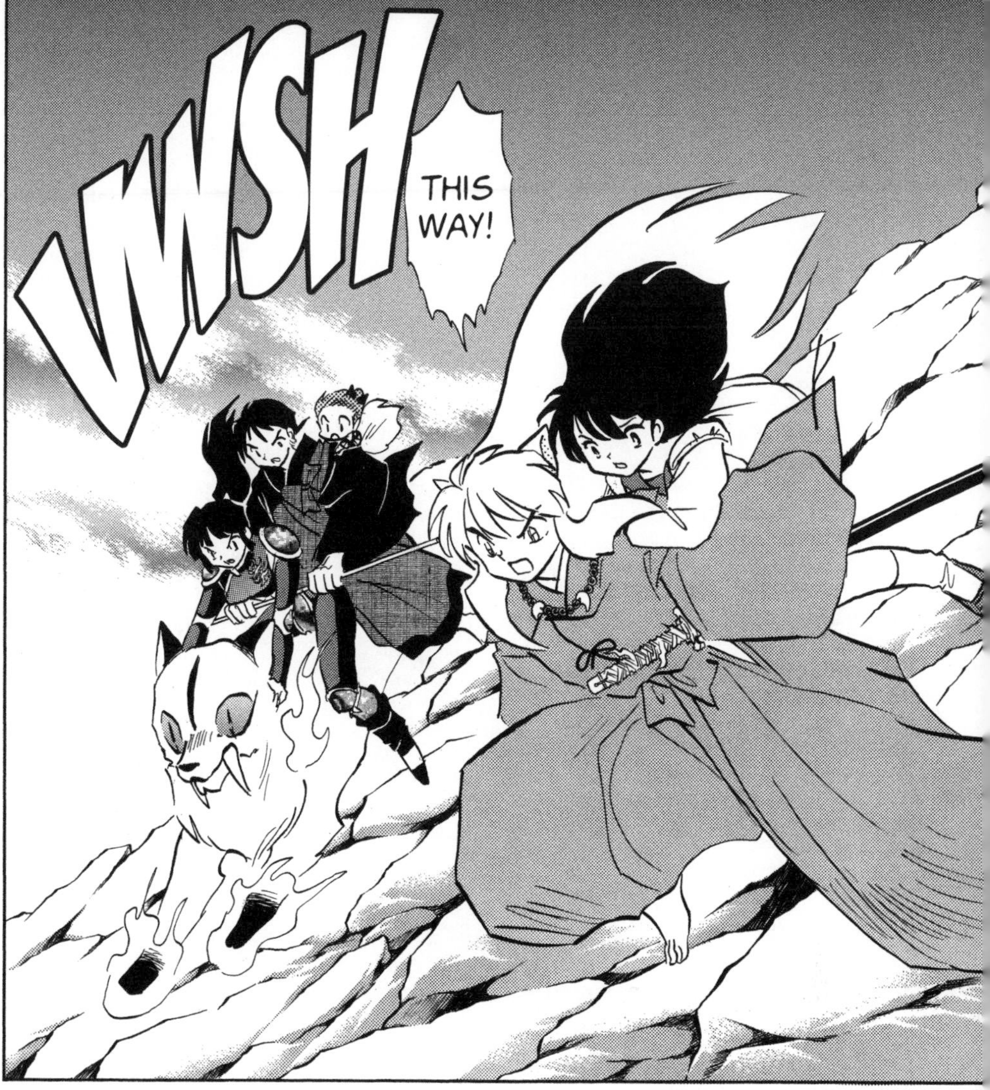
THIS WAY!
VWSH
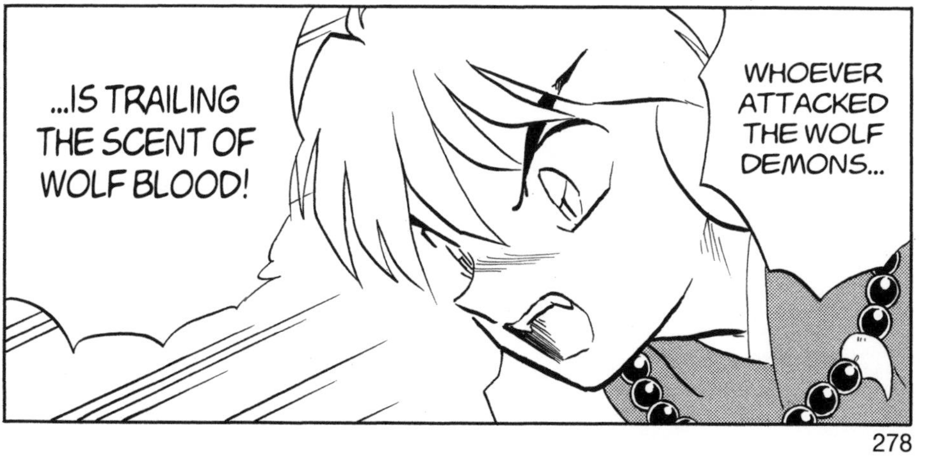
WHOEVER ATTACKED THE WOLF DEMONS...
...IS TRAILING THE SCENT OF WOLF BLOOD!

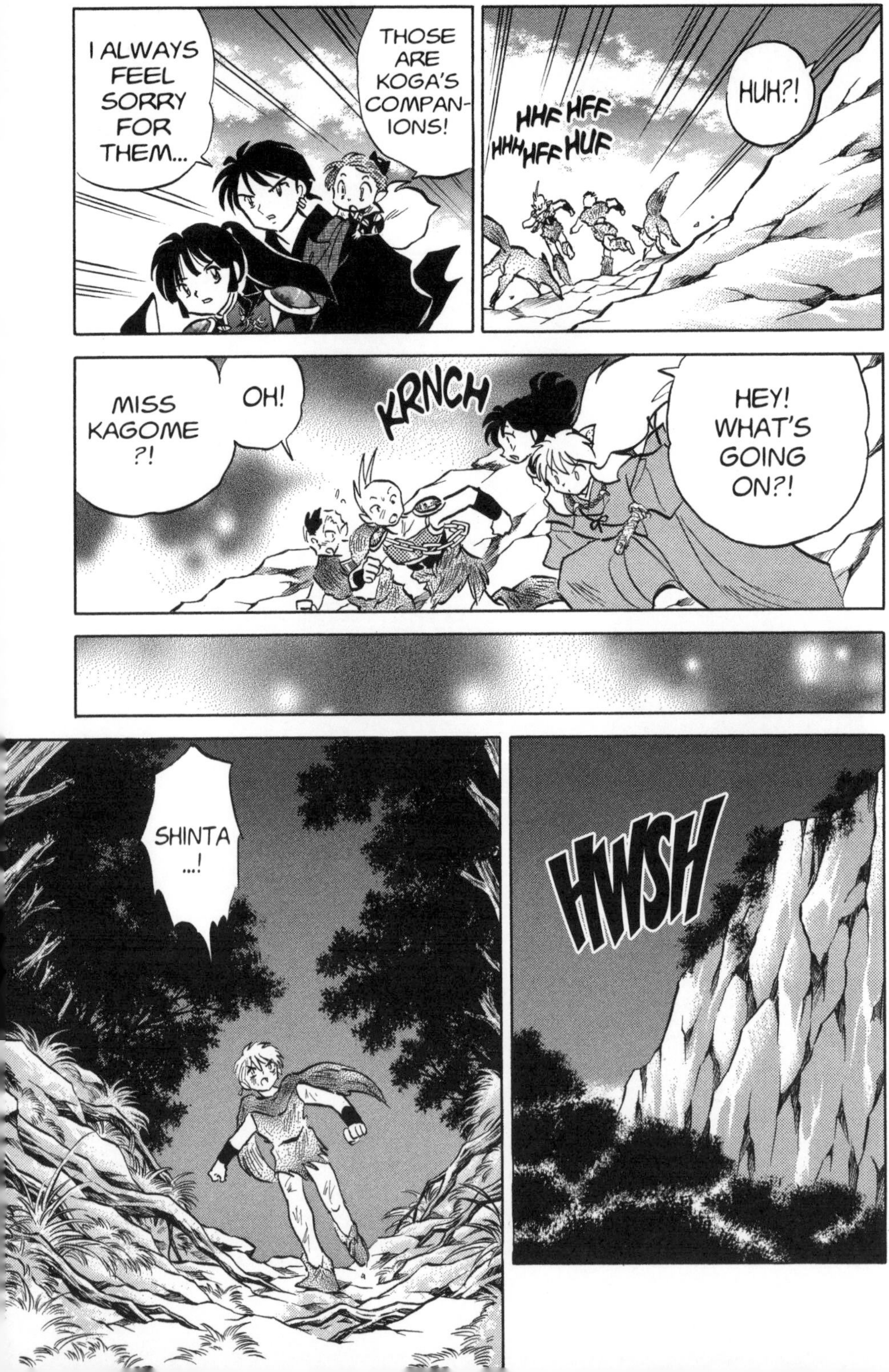
HUH?!
HHF HFF HHH HFF HUF
THOSE ARE KOGA'S COMPAN-IONS!
I ALWAYS FEEL SORRY FOR THEM...
HEY! WHAT'S GOING ON?!
KRNCH
OH!
MISS KAGOME?!
HWSH
SHINTA...!

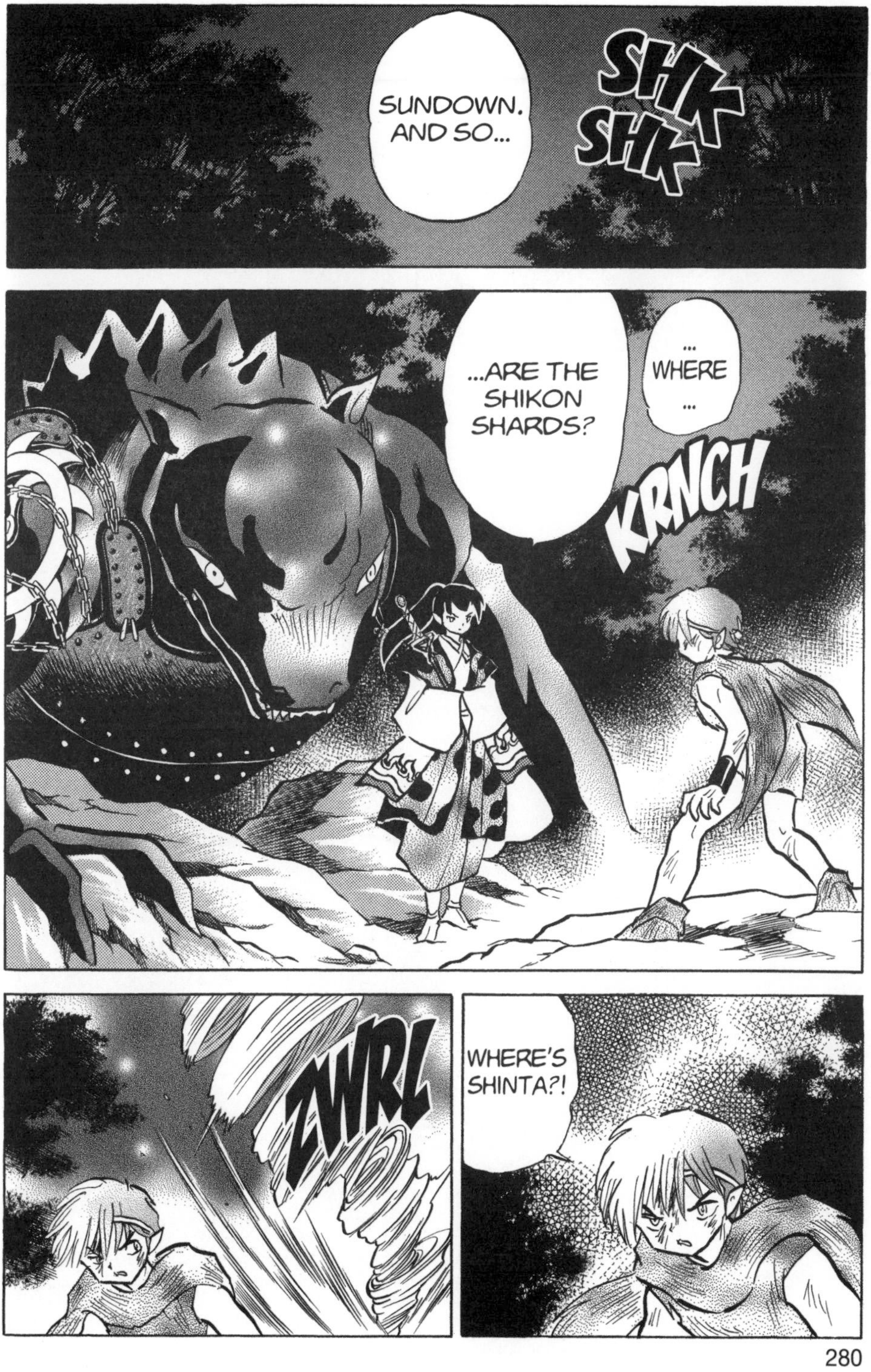
SHK
SHK
SUNDOWN. AND SO...
... WHERE ...
...ARE THE SHIKON SHARDS?
KRNCH
WHERE'S SHINTA?!
ZWRL

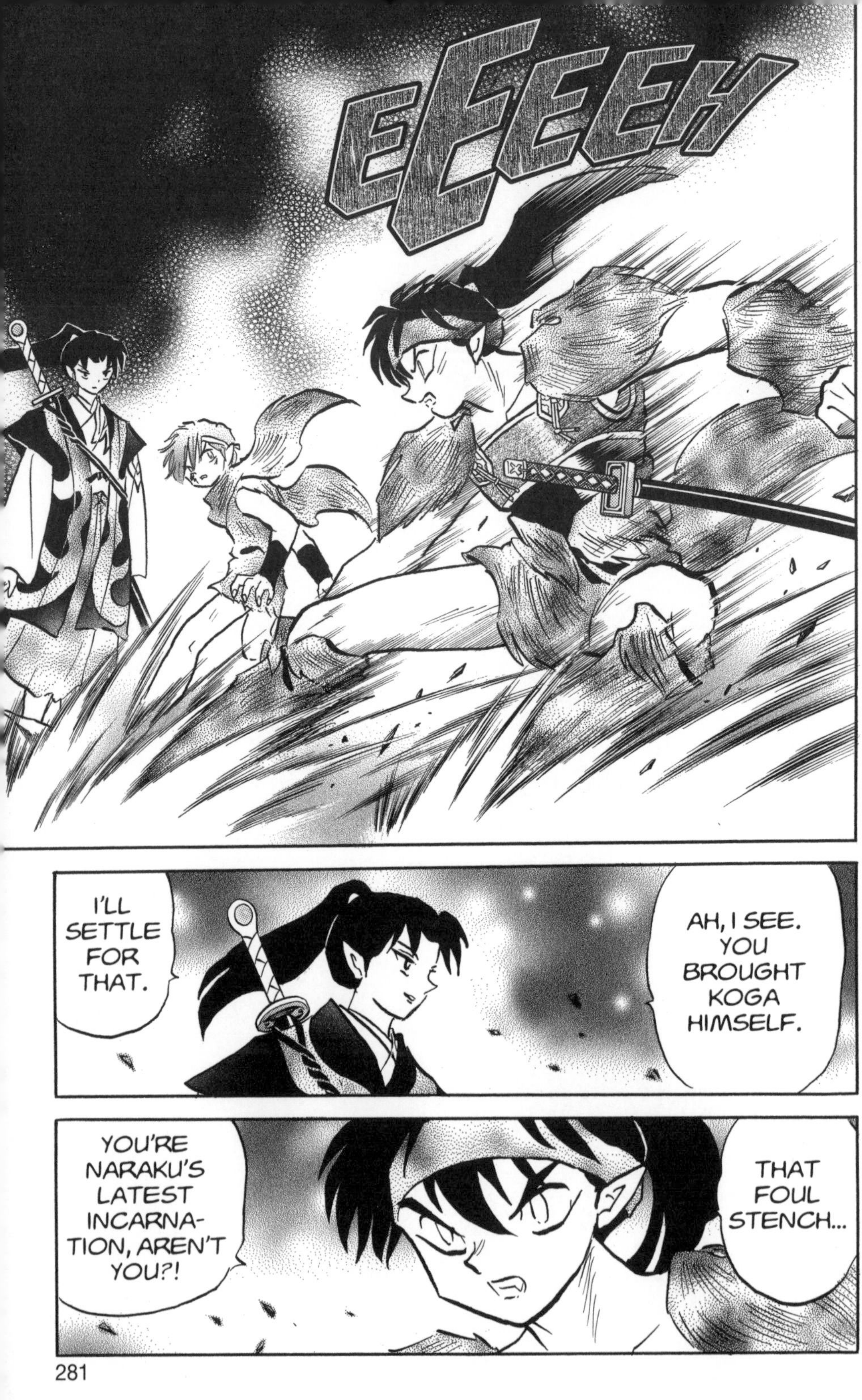
EEEEH
AH, I SEE. YOU BROUGHT KOGA HIMSELF.
I'LL SETTLE FOR THAT.
THAT FOUL STENCH...
YOU'RE NARAKU'S LATEST INCARNATION, AREN'T YOU?!

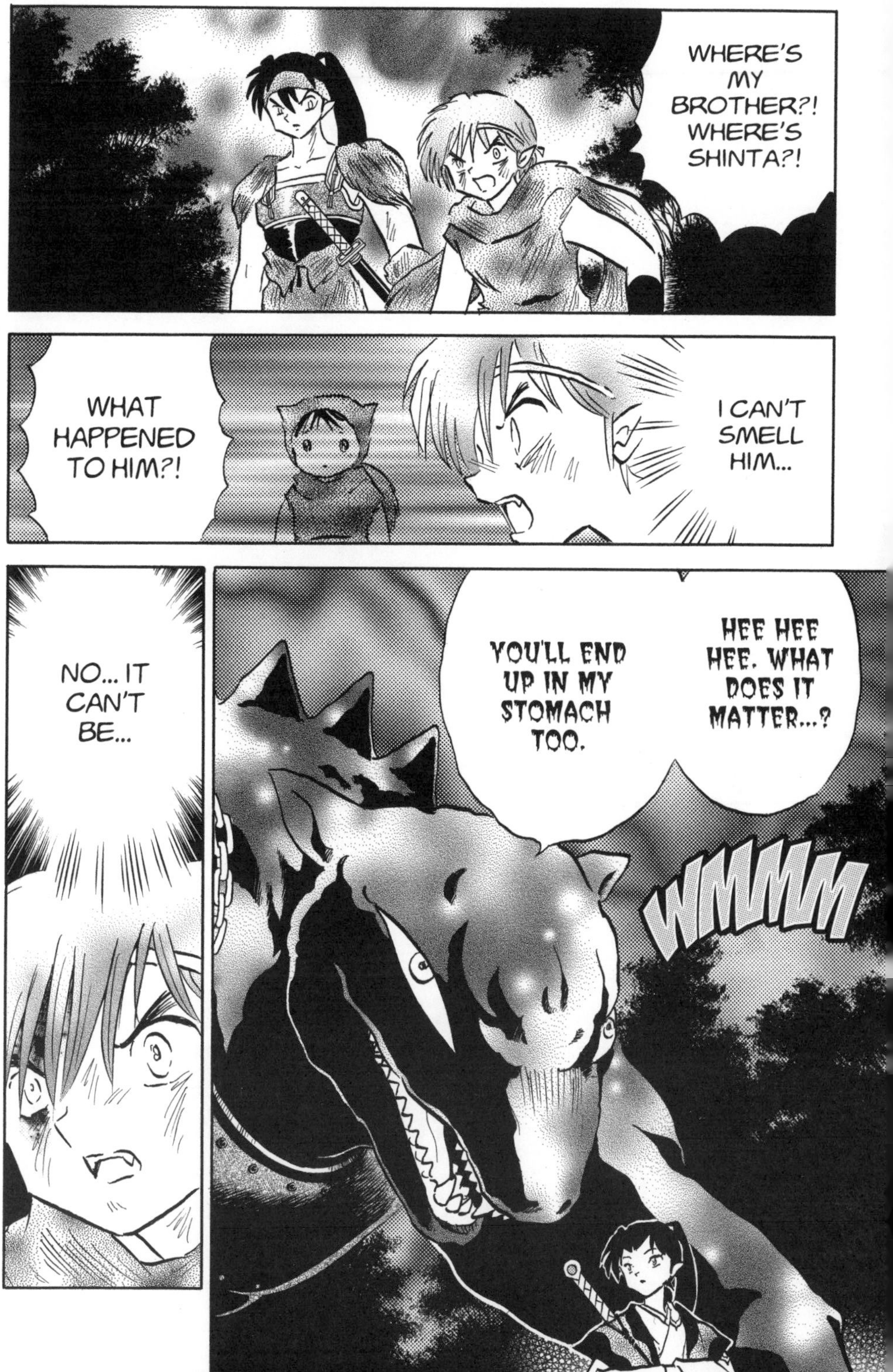
WHERE'S MY BROTHER?! WHERE'S SHINTA?!
I CAN'T SMELL HIM...
WHAT HAPPENED TO HIM?!
HEE HEE HEE. WHAT DOES IT MATTER...?
YOU'LL END UP IN MY STOMACH TOO.
WMMMM
NO... IT CAN'T BE...

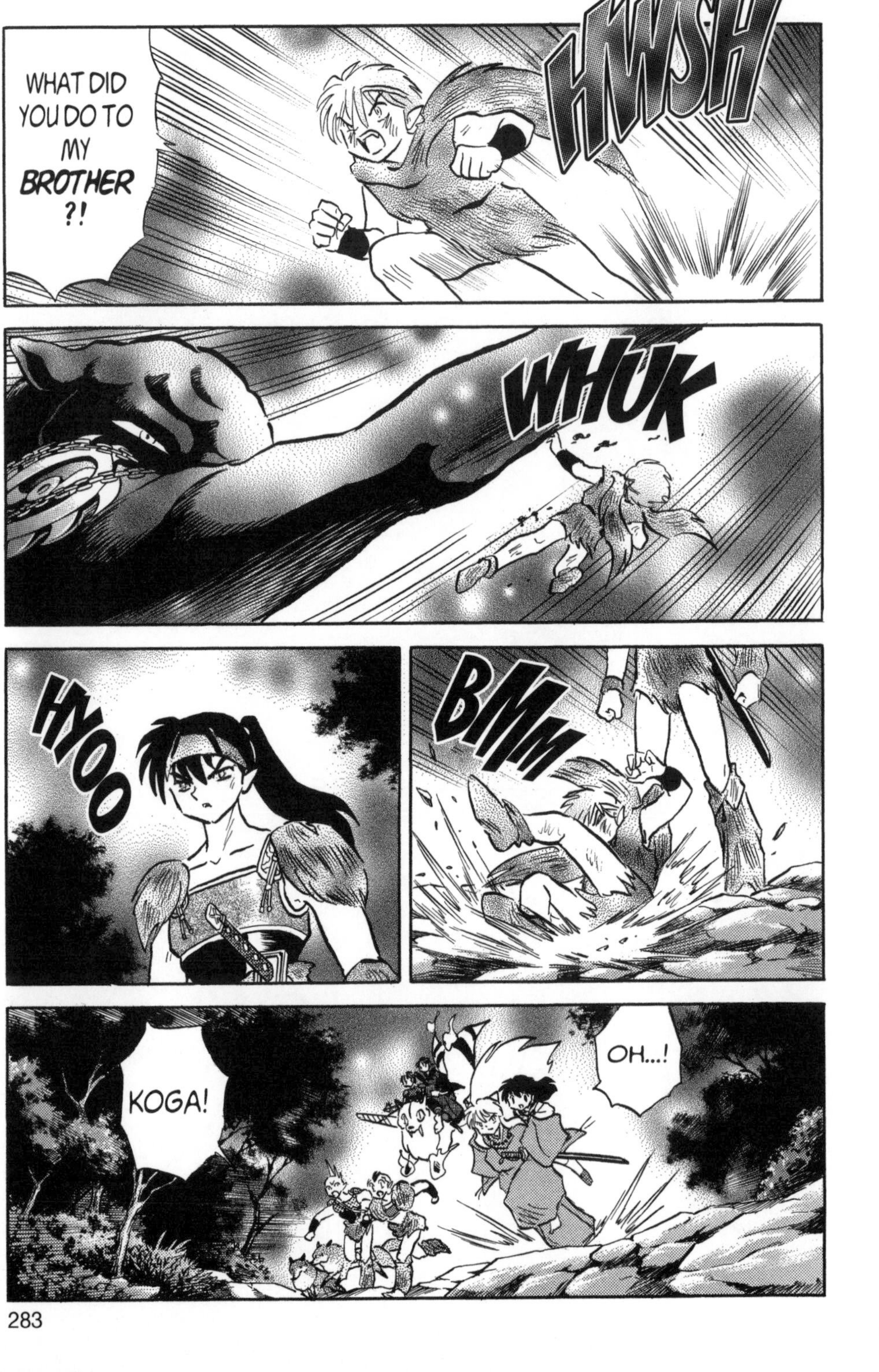
HWSH
WHAT DID YOU DO TO MY BROTHER?!
WHUK
BMM
HYOO
OH...!
KOGA!

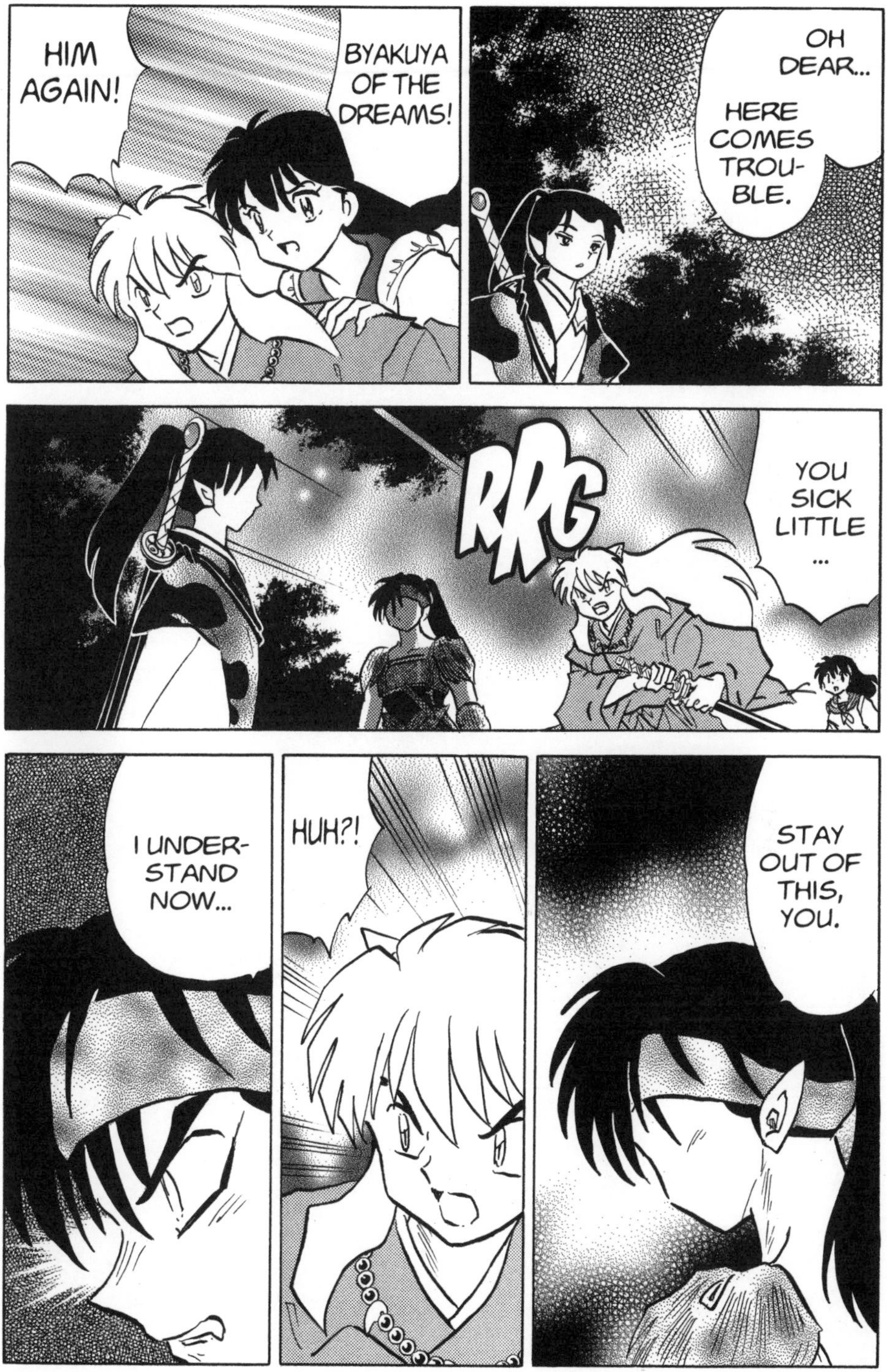
OH DEAR...
HERE COMES TROU-BLE.
BYAKUYA OF THE DREAMS!
HIM AGAIN!
YOU SICK LITTLE ...
RRG
STAY OUT OF THIS, YOU.
HUH?!
I UNDER-STAND NOW...

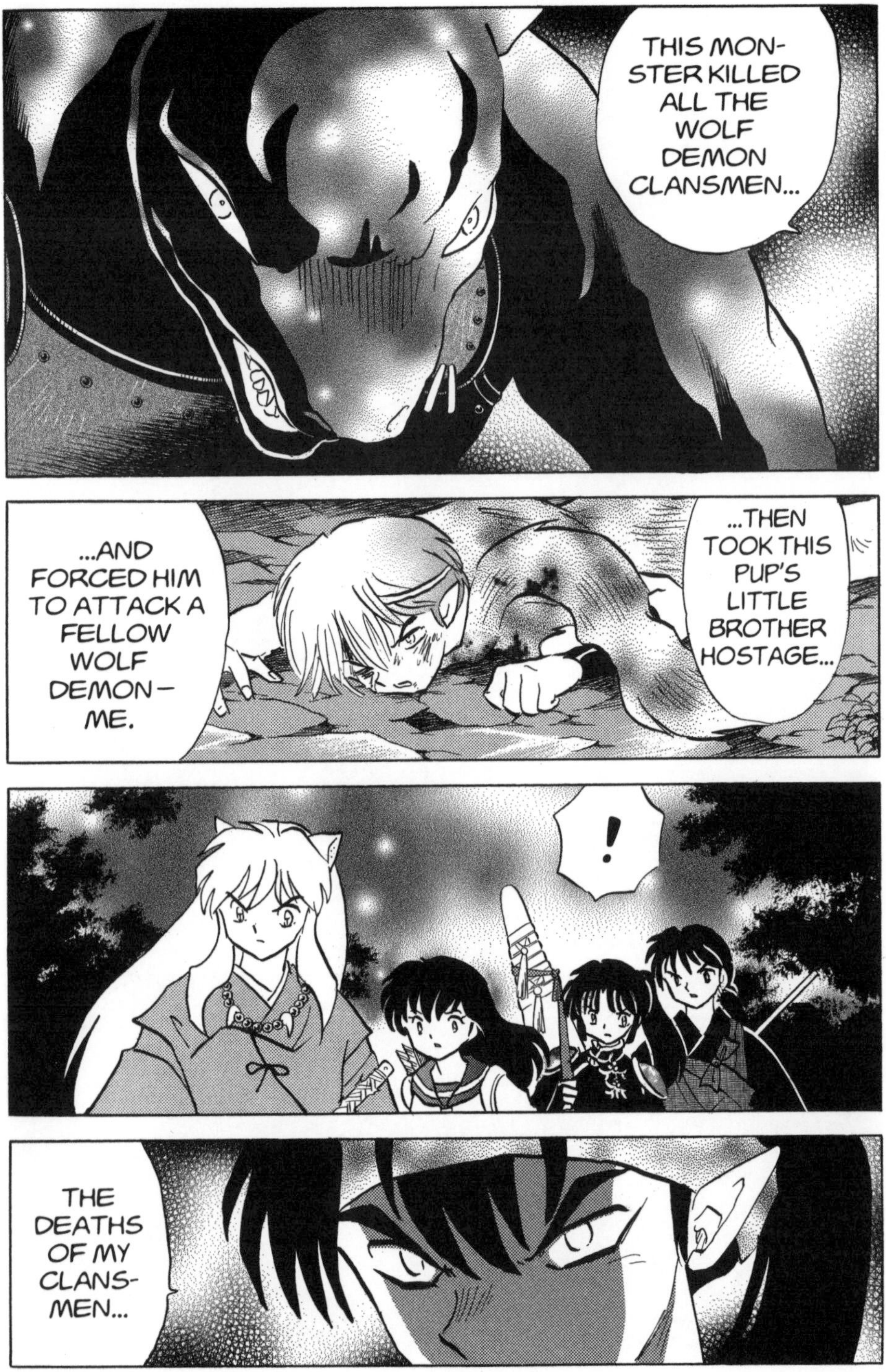
THIS MONSTER KILLED ALL THE WOLF DEMON CLANSMEN...
...THEN TOOK THIS PUP'S LITTLE BROTHER HOSTAGE...
...AND FORCED HIM TO ATTACK A FELLOW WOLF DEMON—ME.
!
THE DEATHS OF MY CLANSMEN...

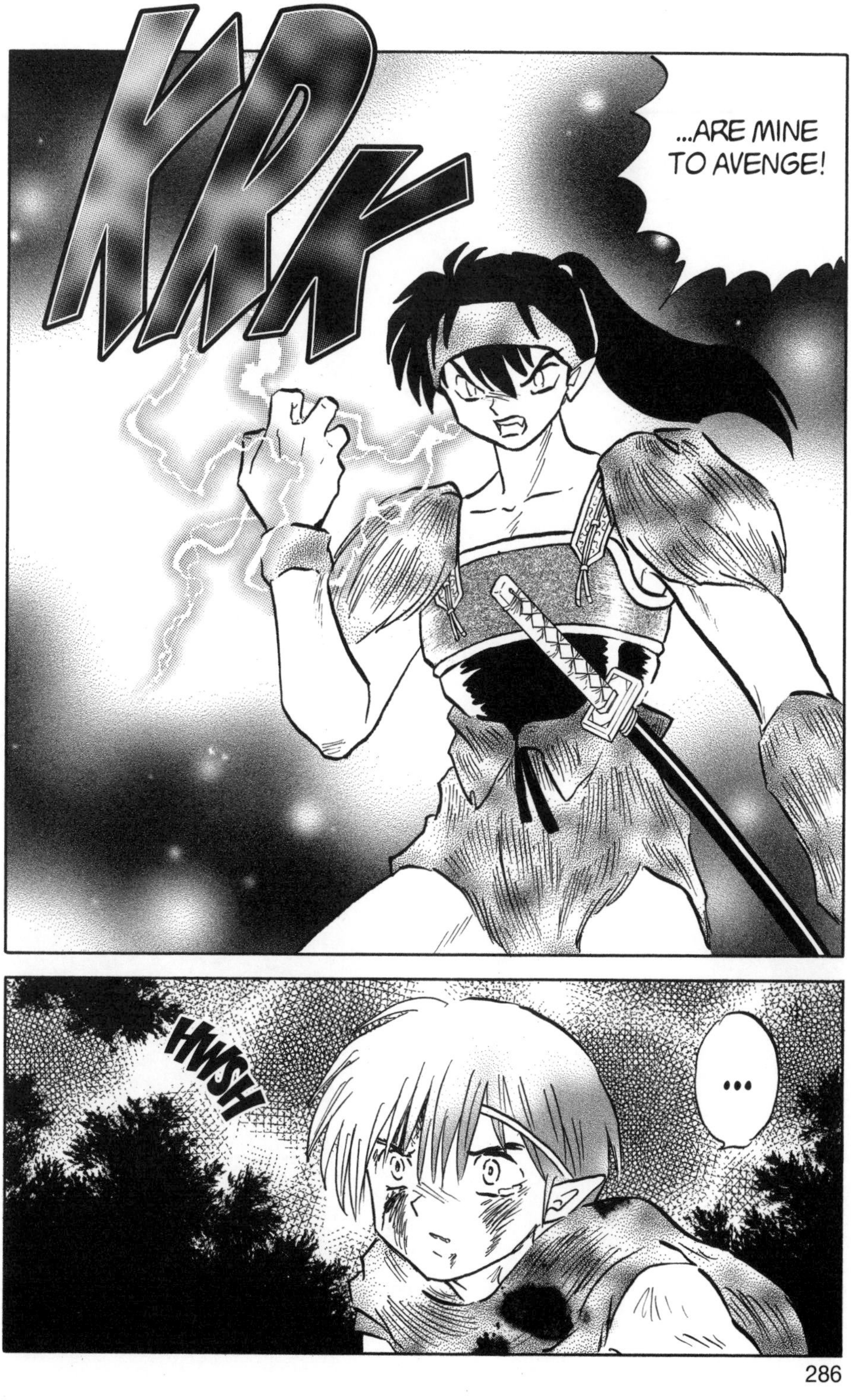
KRAK
...ARE MINE TO AVENGE!
...
HWSH

SCROLL SIX
THE GORAISHI'S MIGHT

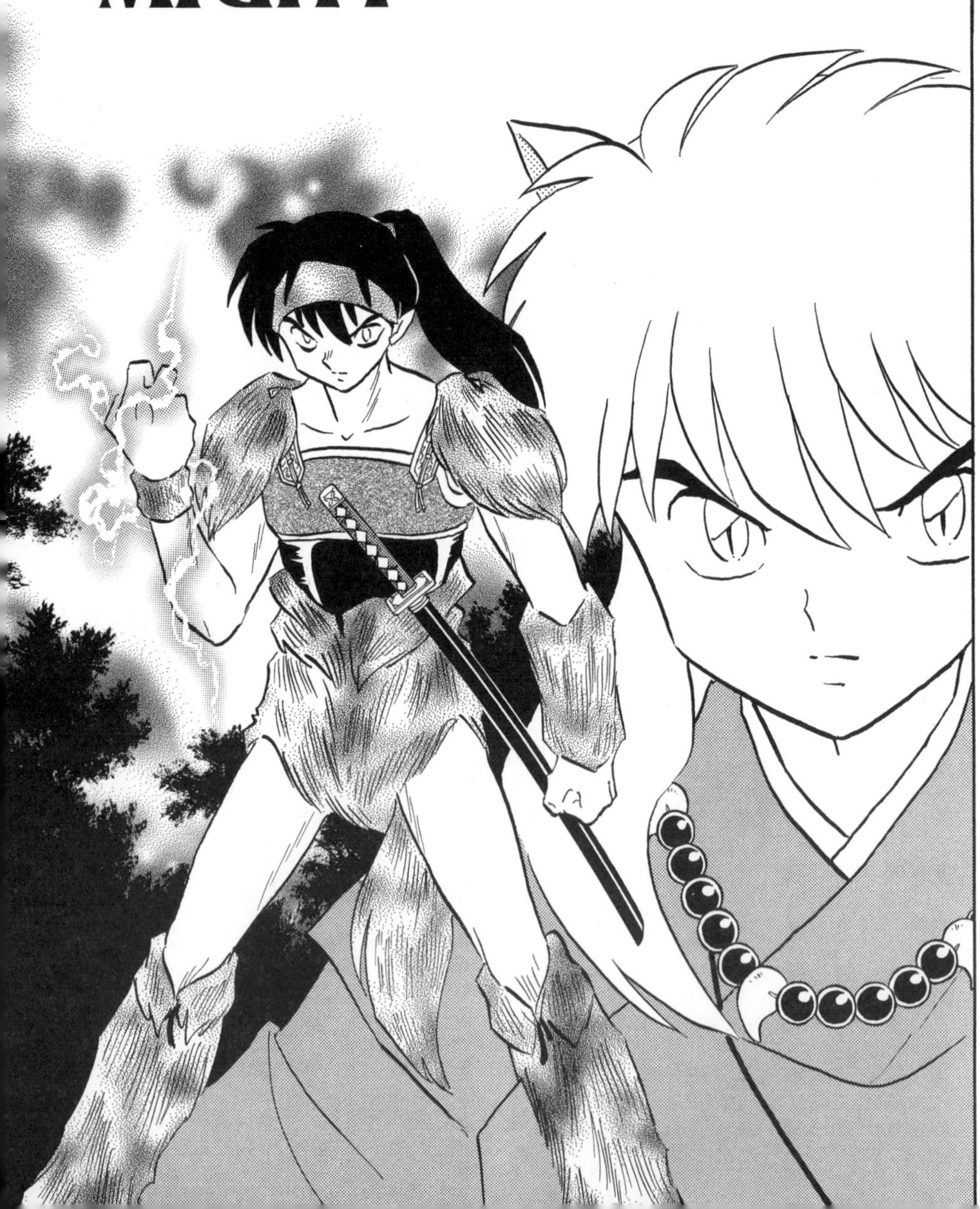

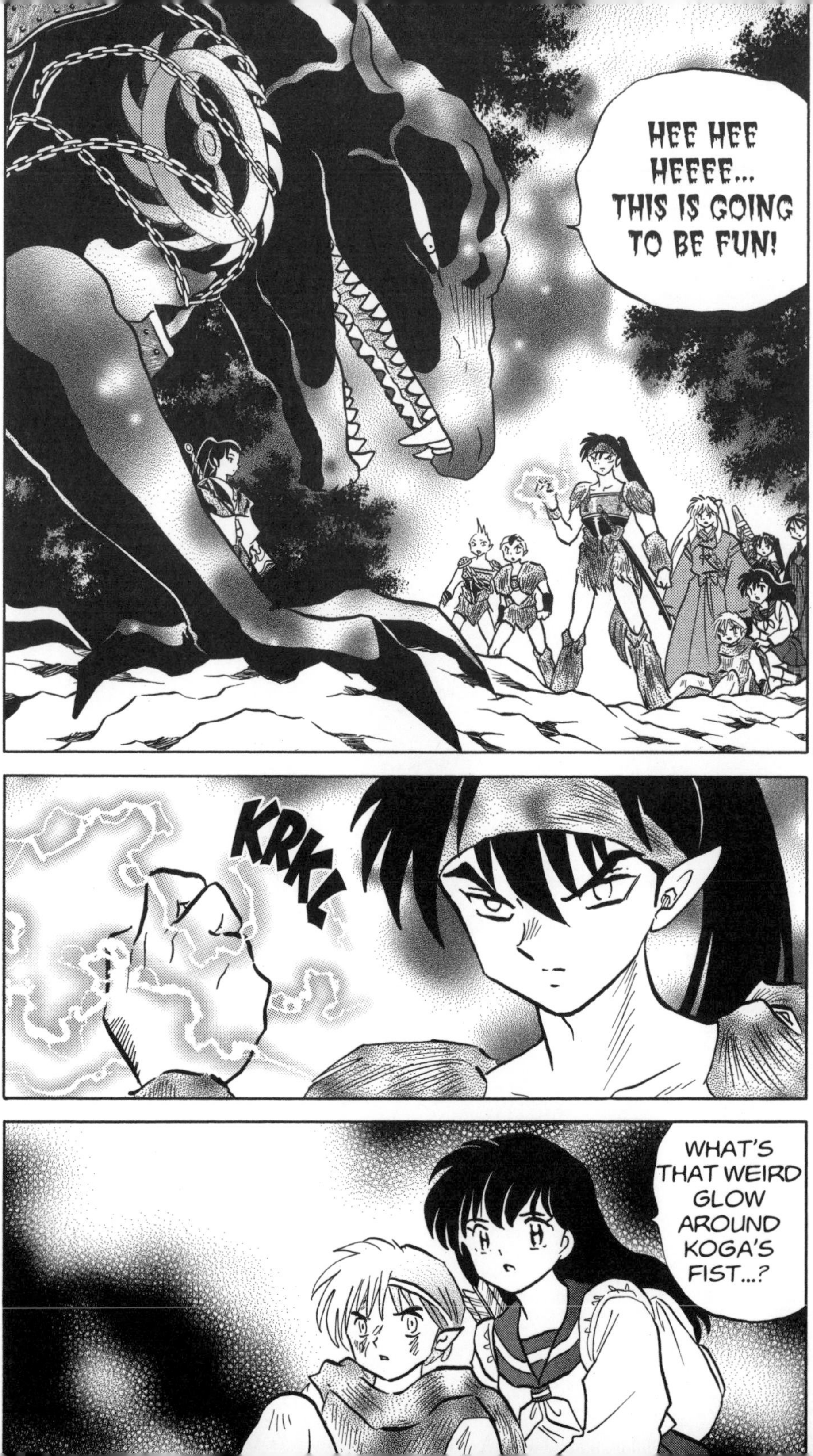
HEE HEE HEEEE... THIS IS GOING TO BE FUN!
KRKL
WHAT'S THAT WEIRD GLOW AROUND KOGA'S FIST...?

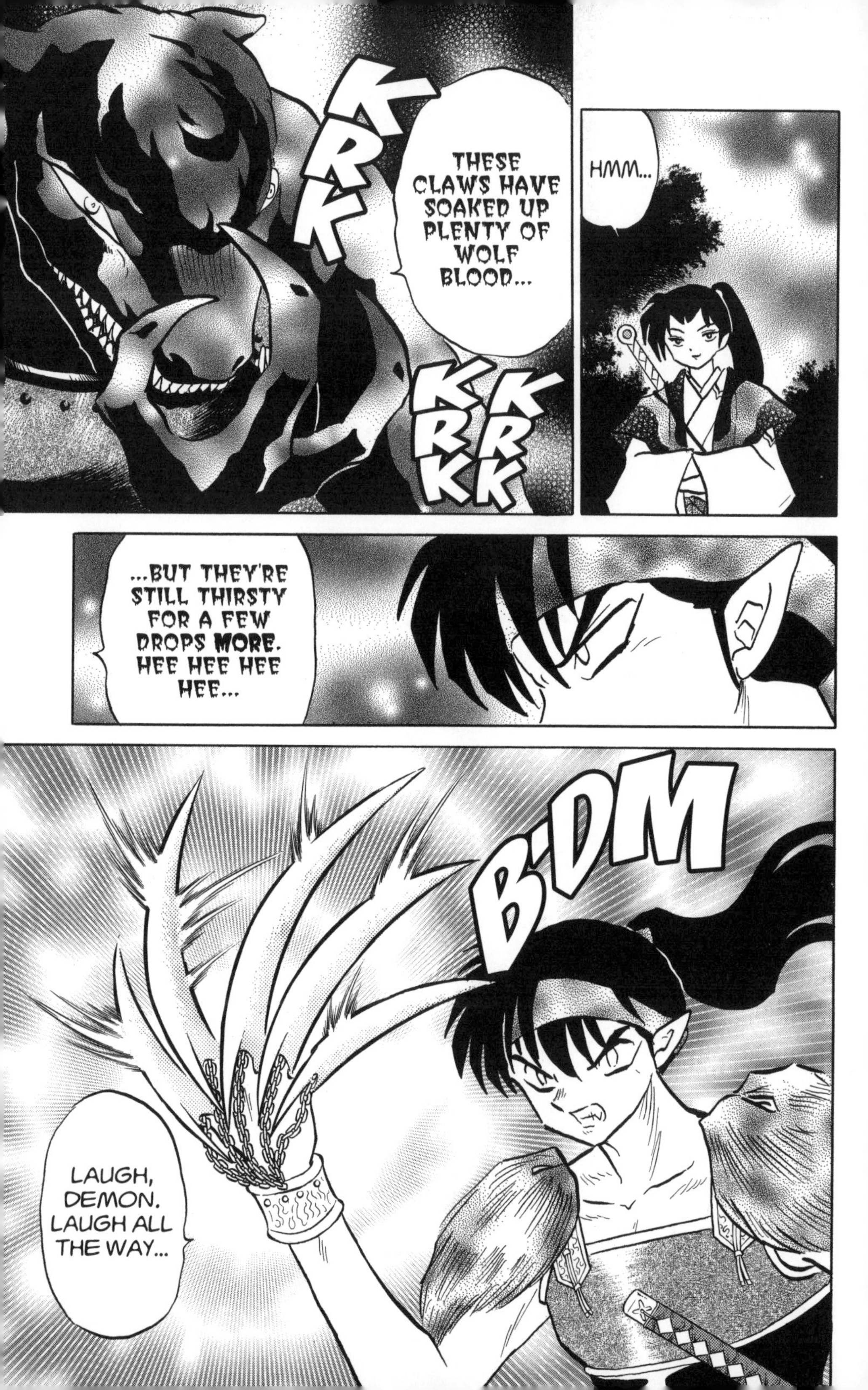
HMM...
KRK
THESE CLAWS HAVE SOAKED UP PLENTY OF WOLF BLOOD...
KRK KRK
...BUT THEY'RE STILL THIRSTY FOR A FEW DROPS MORE. HEE HEE HEE HEE...
B-DM
LAUGH, DEMON. LAUGH ALL THE WAY...

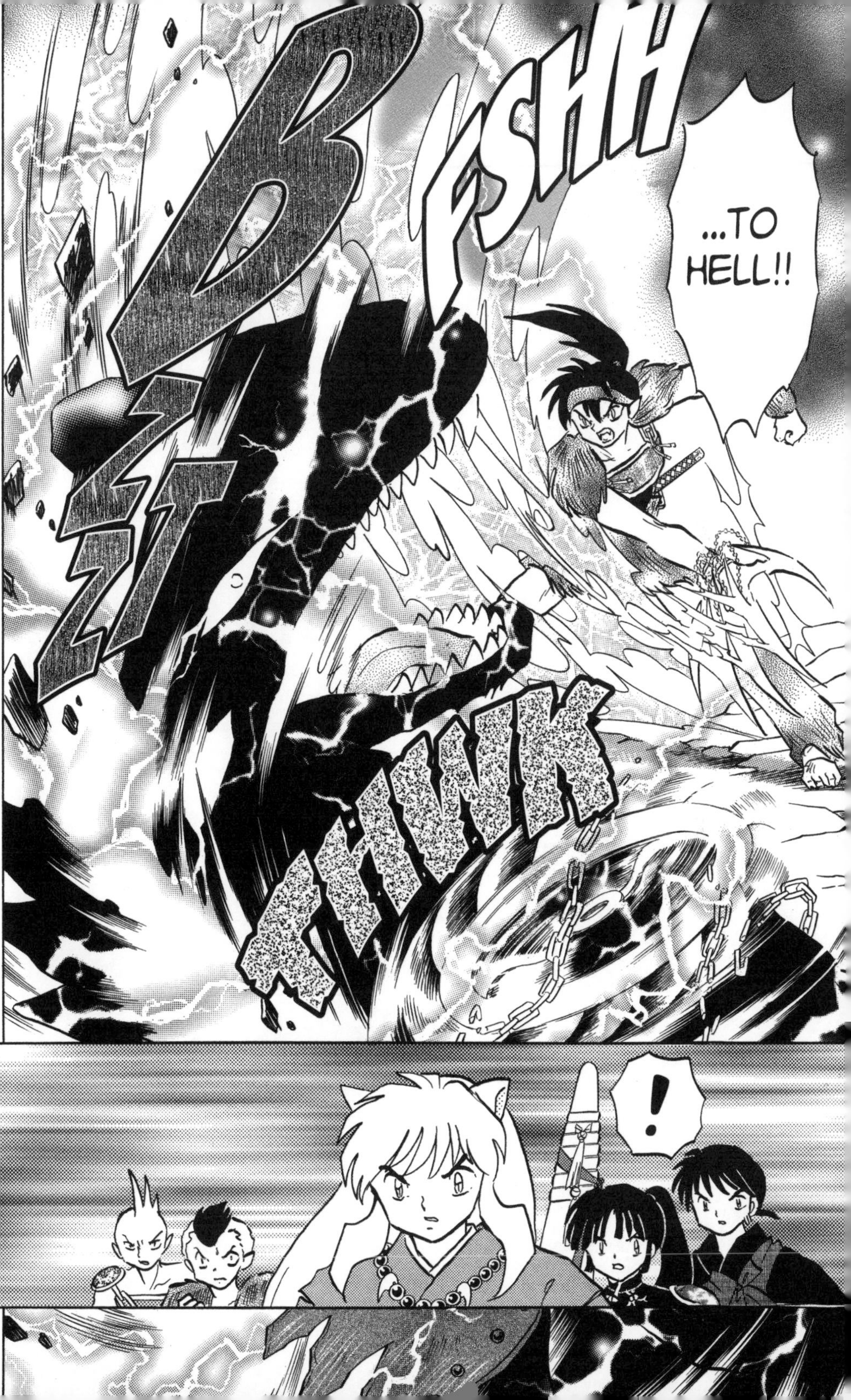...TO HELL!!
BFSHH
ZZT
KHUNK
!

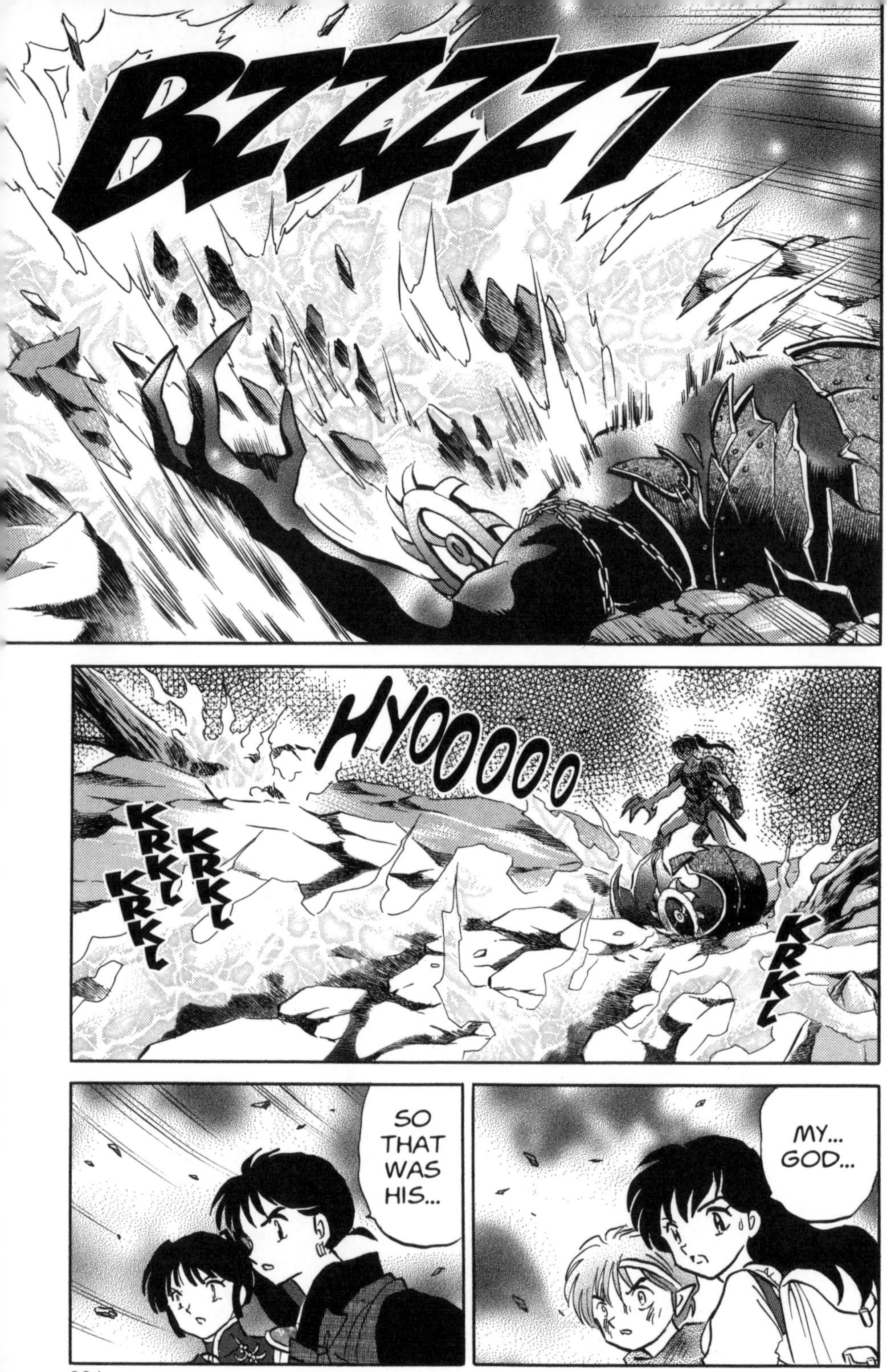
BZZZT
HYOOOOO
KRKL
KRKL
KRKL
KRKL
MY... GOD...
SO THAT WAS HIS...

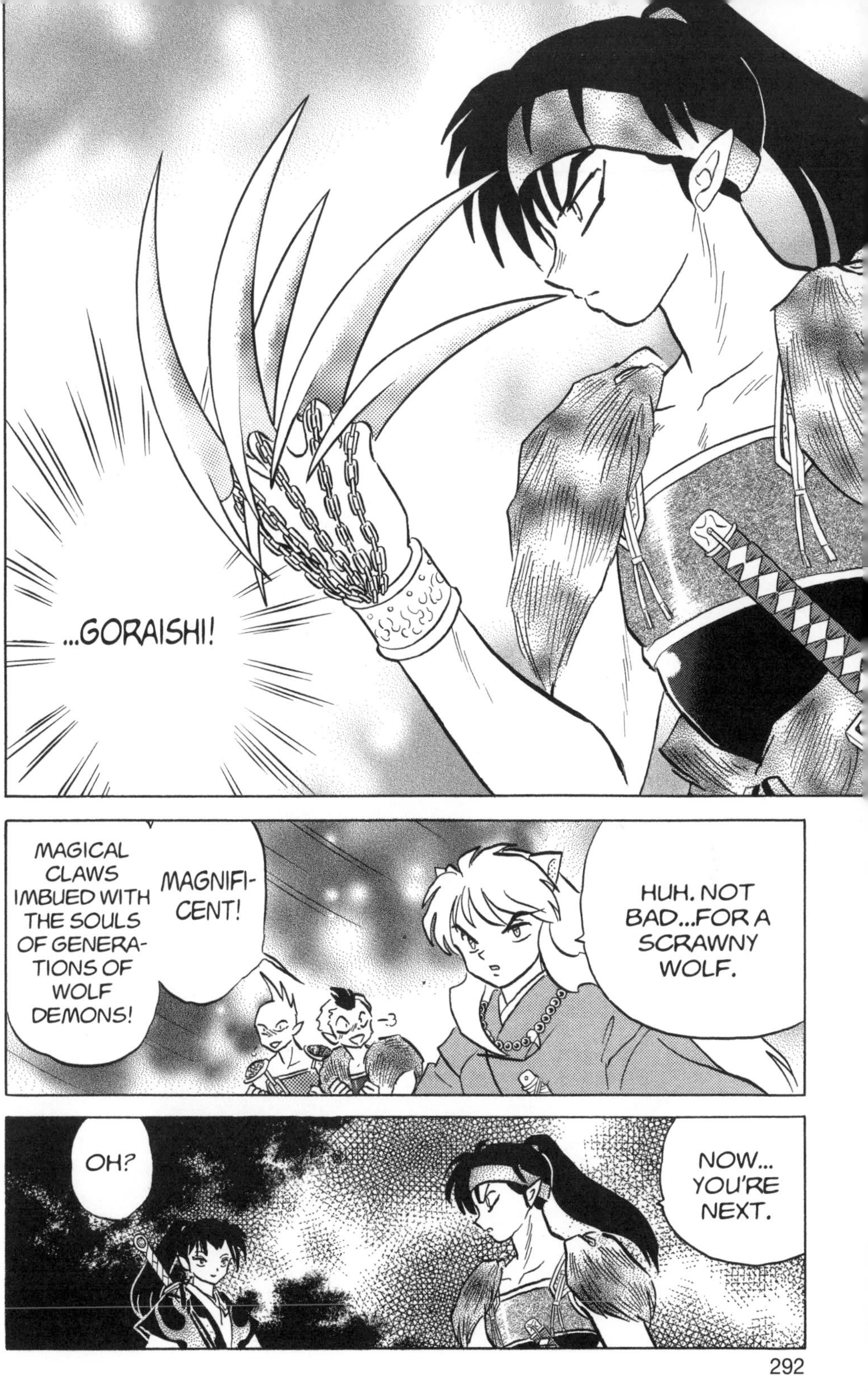
...GORAISHI!
HUH. NOT BAD...FOR A SCRAWNY WOLF.
MAGNIFI-CENT!
MAGICAL CLAWS IMBUED WITH THE SOULS OF GENERA-TIONS OF WOLF DEMONS!
NOW... YOU'RE NEXT.
OH?

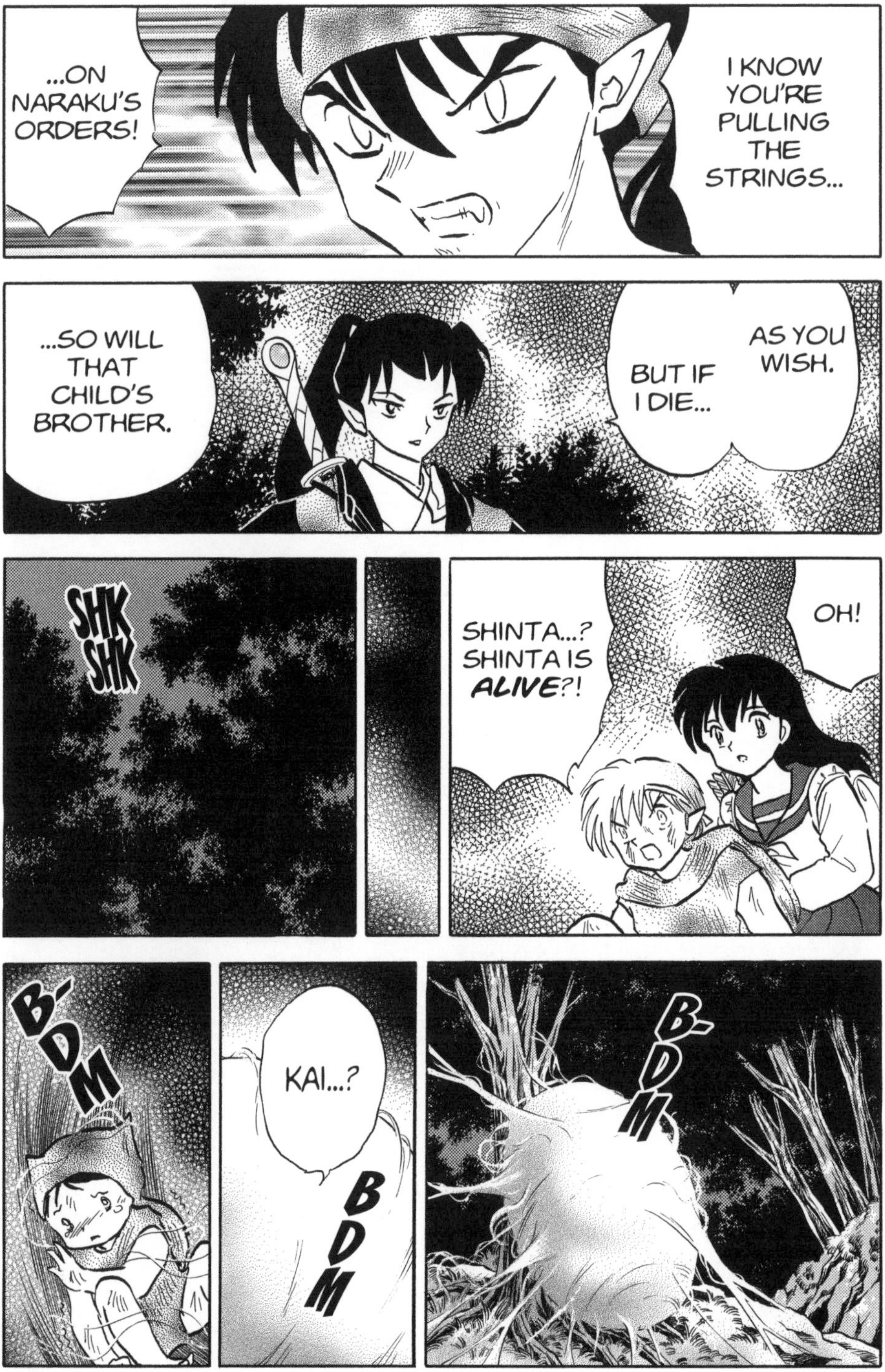
I KNOW YOU'RE PULLING THE STRINGS...
...ON NARAKU'S ORDERS!
AS YOU WISH.
BUT IF I DIE...
...SO WILL THAT CHILD'S BROTHER.
OH!
SHINTA...? SHINTA IS ***ALIVE***?!
SHK SHK
B-BDM
KAI...?
BDM
B-BDM

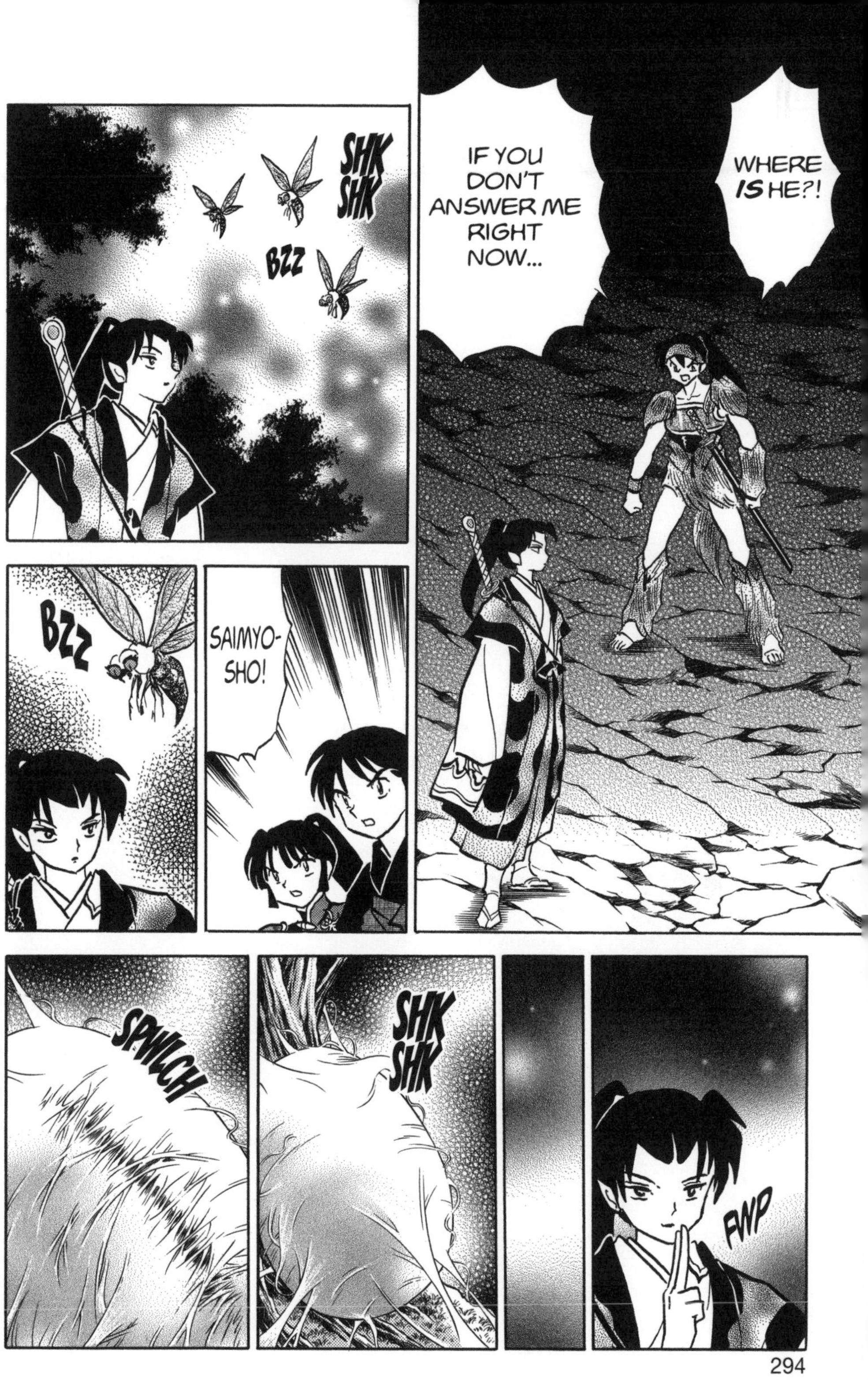
WHERE *IS* HE?!
IF YOU DON'T ANSWER ME RIGHT NOW...
SHK SHK
BZZ
SAIMYO-SHO!
BZZ
FWP
SHK SHK
SPWLCH

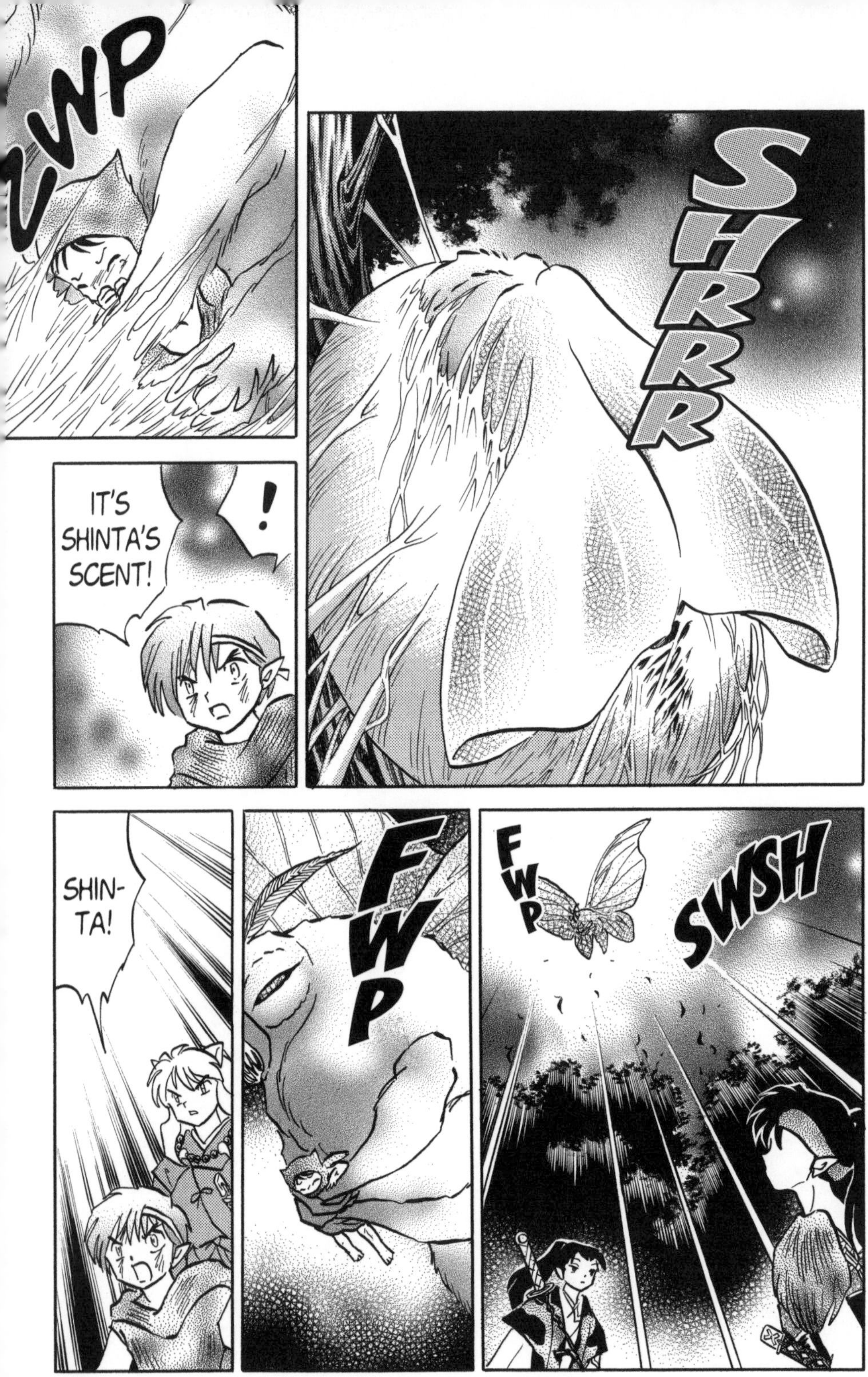
SHRRR
ZWP
!
IT'S SHINTA'S SCENT!
SWSH
FWP
FWP
SHIN-TA!

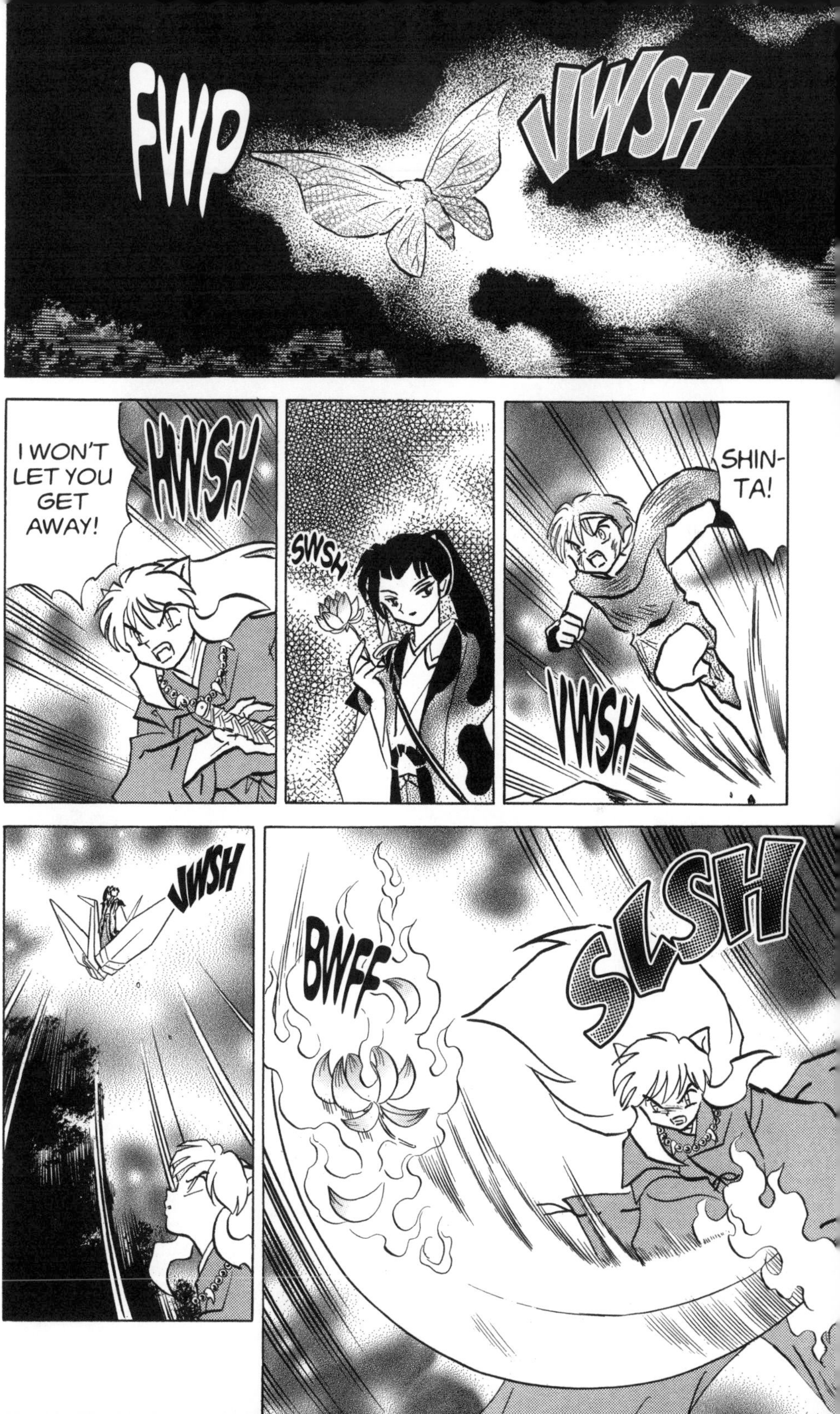
JWSH
FWP
SHIN-TA!
VWSH
SWSH
HWSH
I WON'T LET YOU GET AWAY!
SLSH
BWFF
JWSH

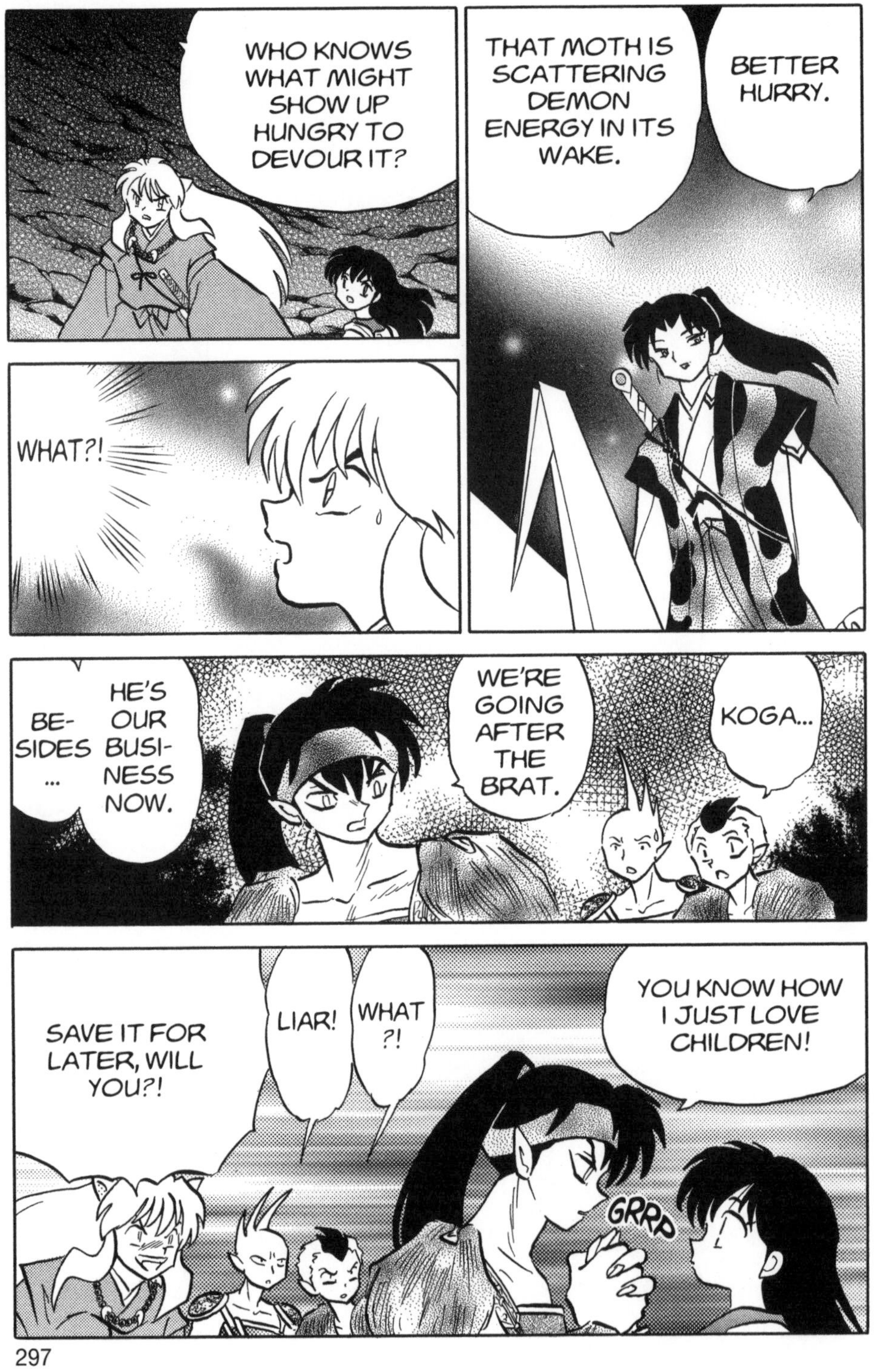
BETTER HURRY.
THAT MOTH IS SCATTERING DEMON ENERGY IN ITS WAKE.
WHO KNOWS WHAT MIGHT SHOW UP HUNGRY TO DEVOUR IT?
WHAT?!
KOGA...
WE'RE GOING AFTER THE BRAT.
HE'S OUR BUSINESS NOW.
BESIDES...
YOU KNOW HOW I JUST LOVE CHILDREN!
GRRP
WHAT?!
LIAR!
SAVE IT FOR LATER, WILL YOU?!

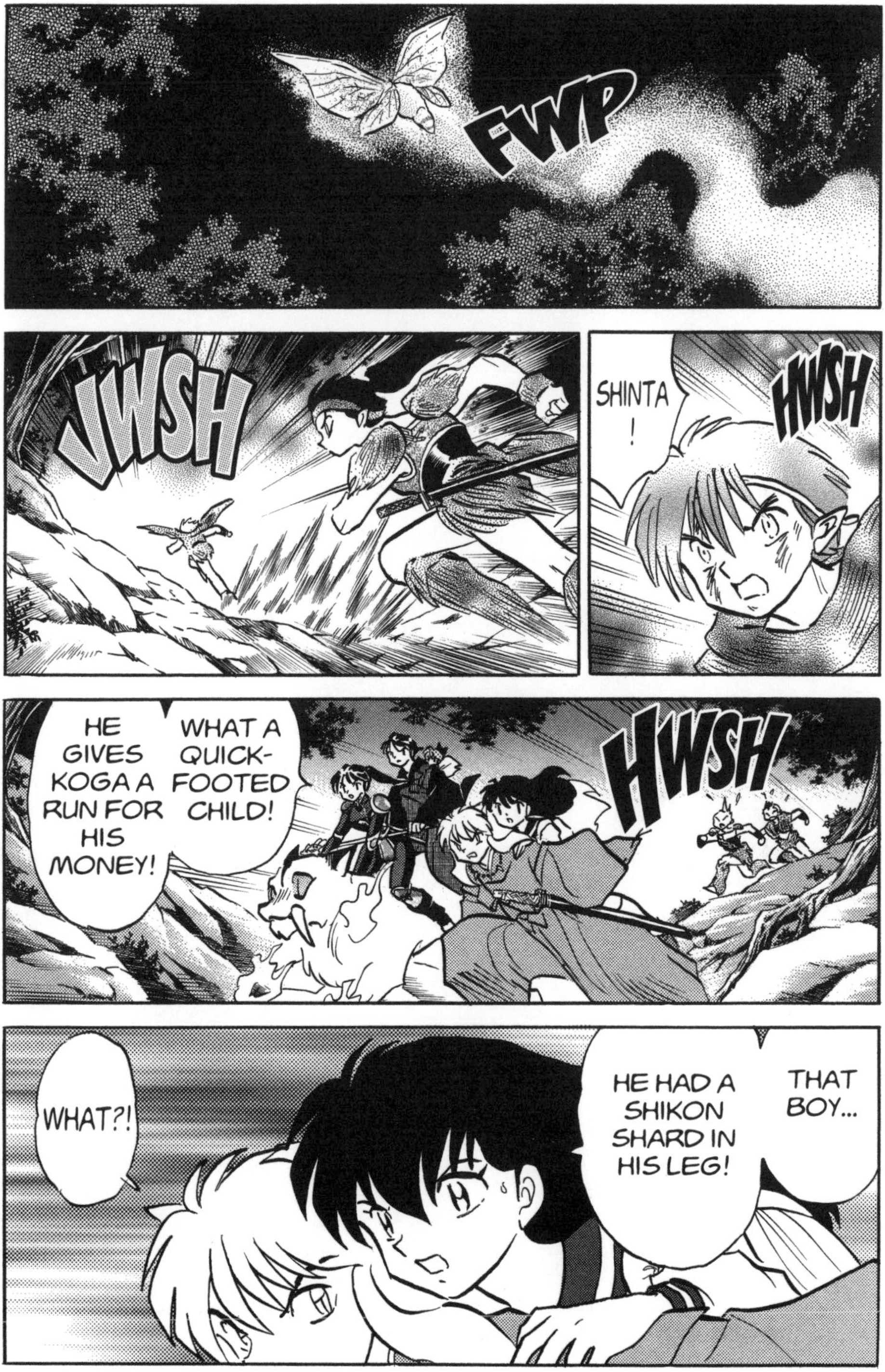
FWP
SHINTA!
HWSH
JWSH
HWSH
WHAT A QUICK-FOOTED CHILD!
HE GIVES KOGA A RUN FOR HIS MONEY!
THAT BOY...
HE HAD A SHIKON SHARD IN HIS LEG!
WHAT?!

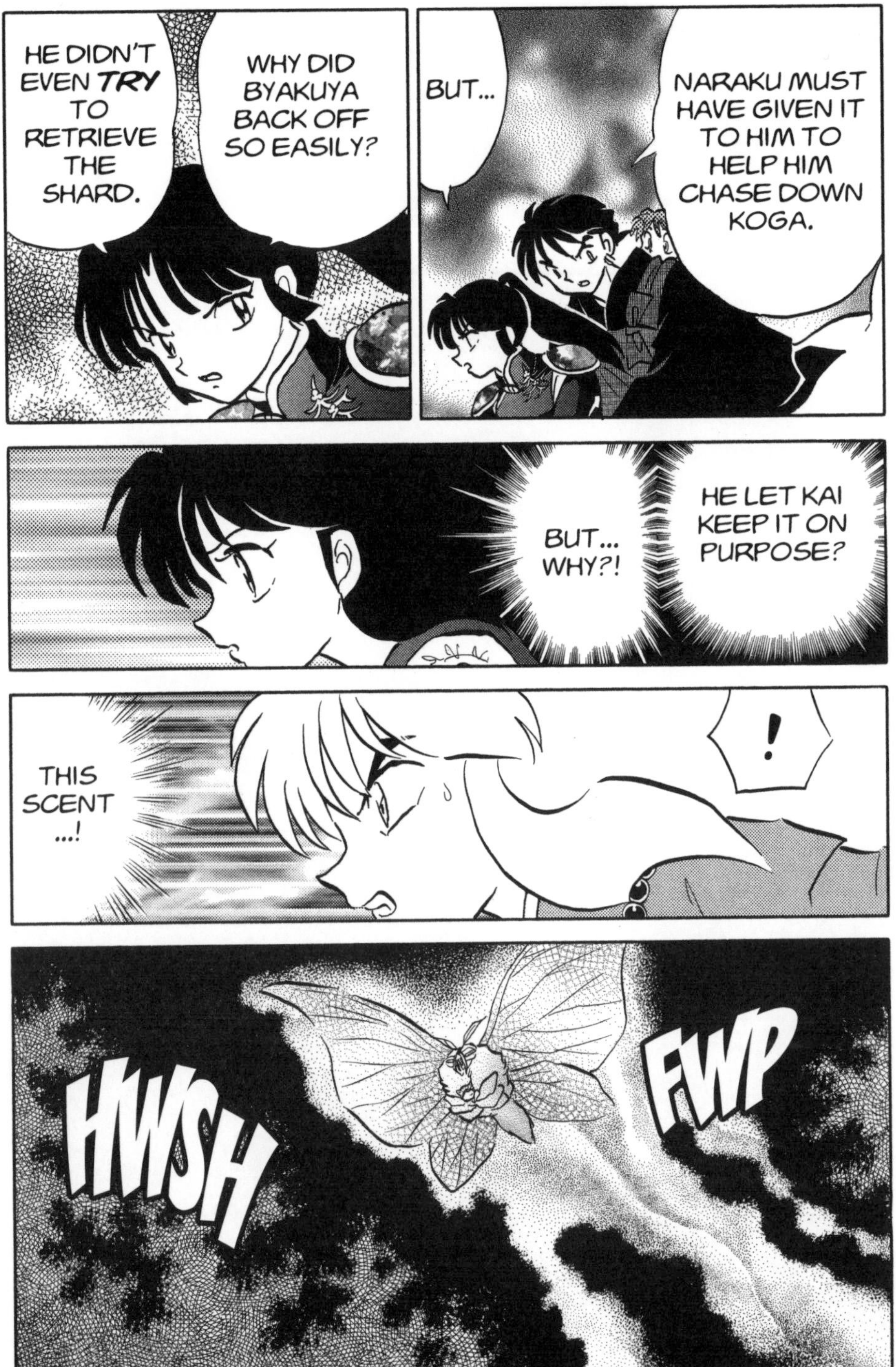
NARAKU MUST HAVE GIVEN IT TO HIM TO HELP HIM CHASE DOWN KOGA.
BUT...
WHY DID BYAKUYA BACK OFF SO EASILY?
HE DIDN'T EVEN TRY TO RETRIEVE THE SHARD.
HE LET KAI KEEP IT ON PURPOSE?
BUT... WHY?!
!
THIS SCENT ...!
FWP
HWSH

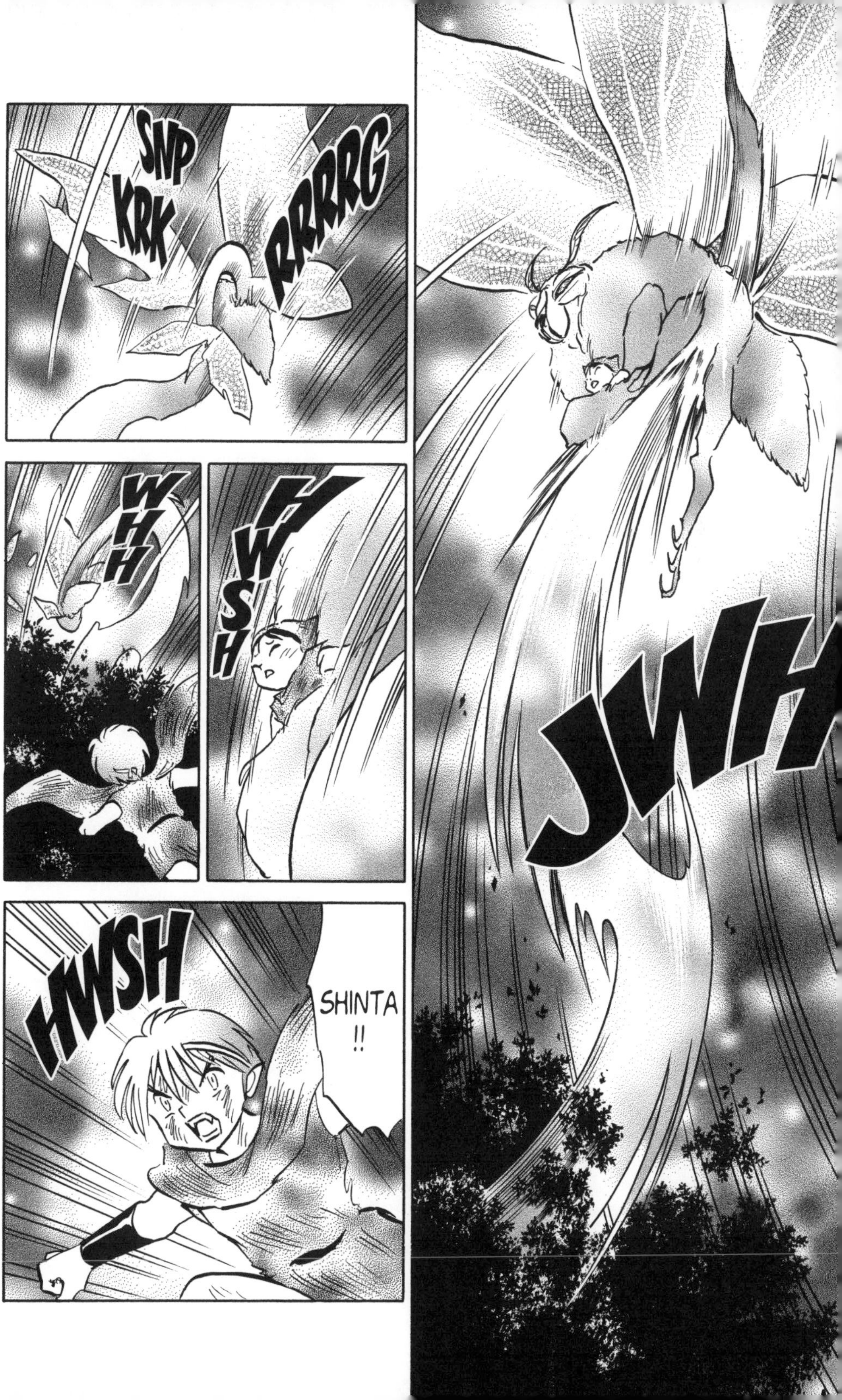
JWH
SNP
KRK
RRRRG
HWSH
WHH
HWSH
SHINTA !!

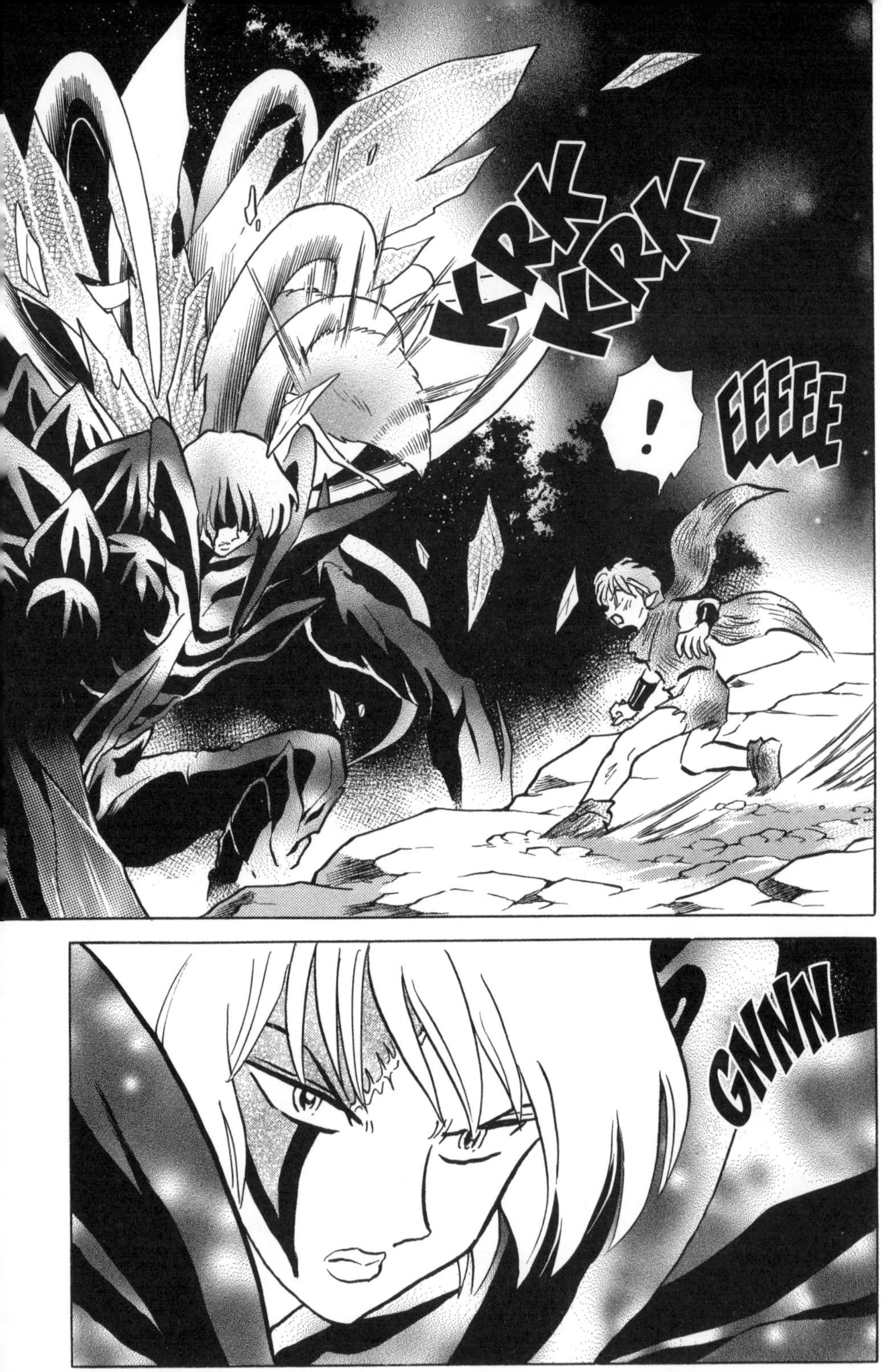
KRK KRK
EEEEE
!
GNNN

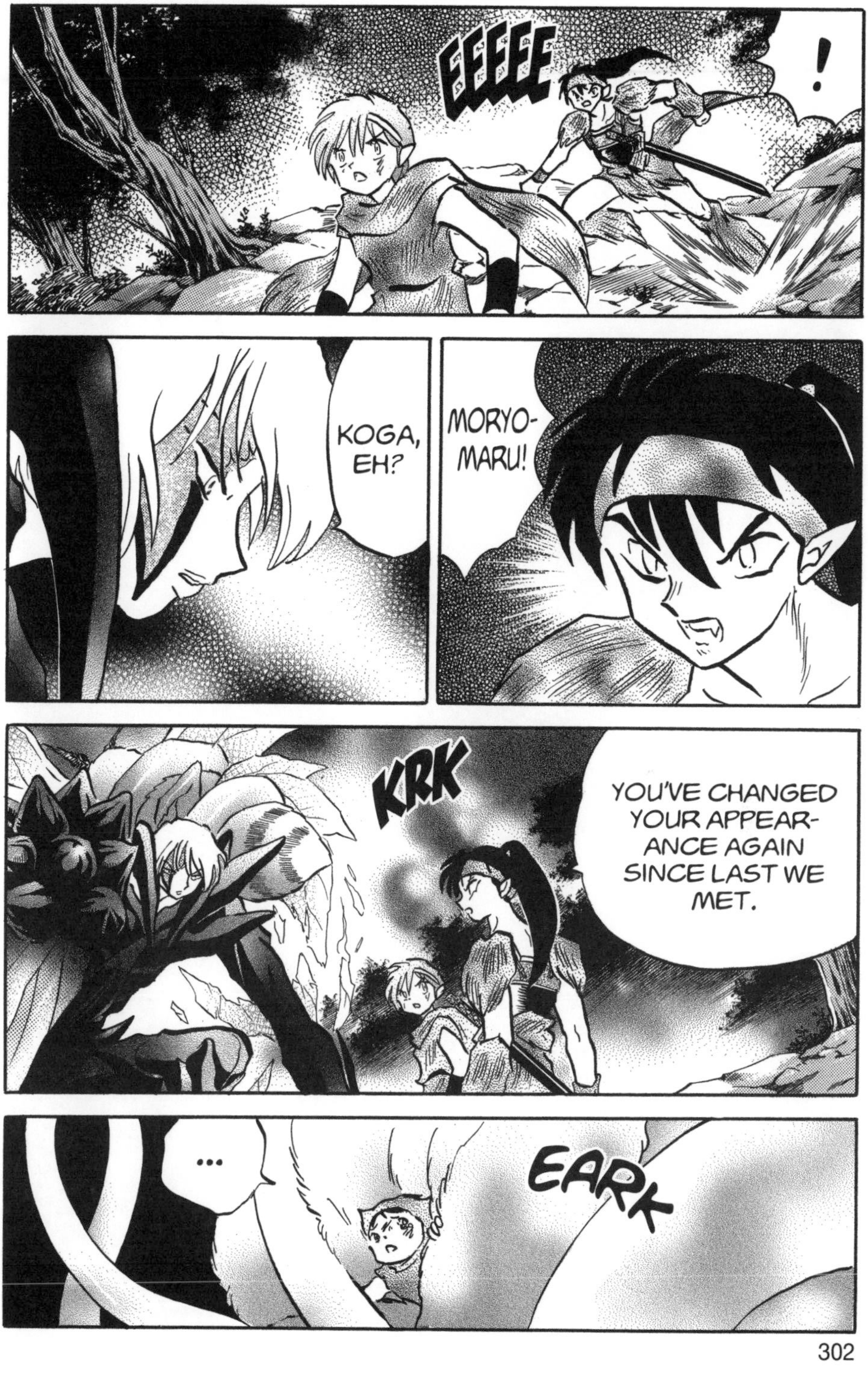
!
EEEEE
MORYO-MARU!
KOGA, EH?
YOU'VE CHANGED YOUR APPEAR-ANCE AGAIN SINCE LAST WE MET.
KRK
EARK
...

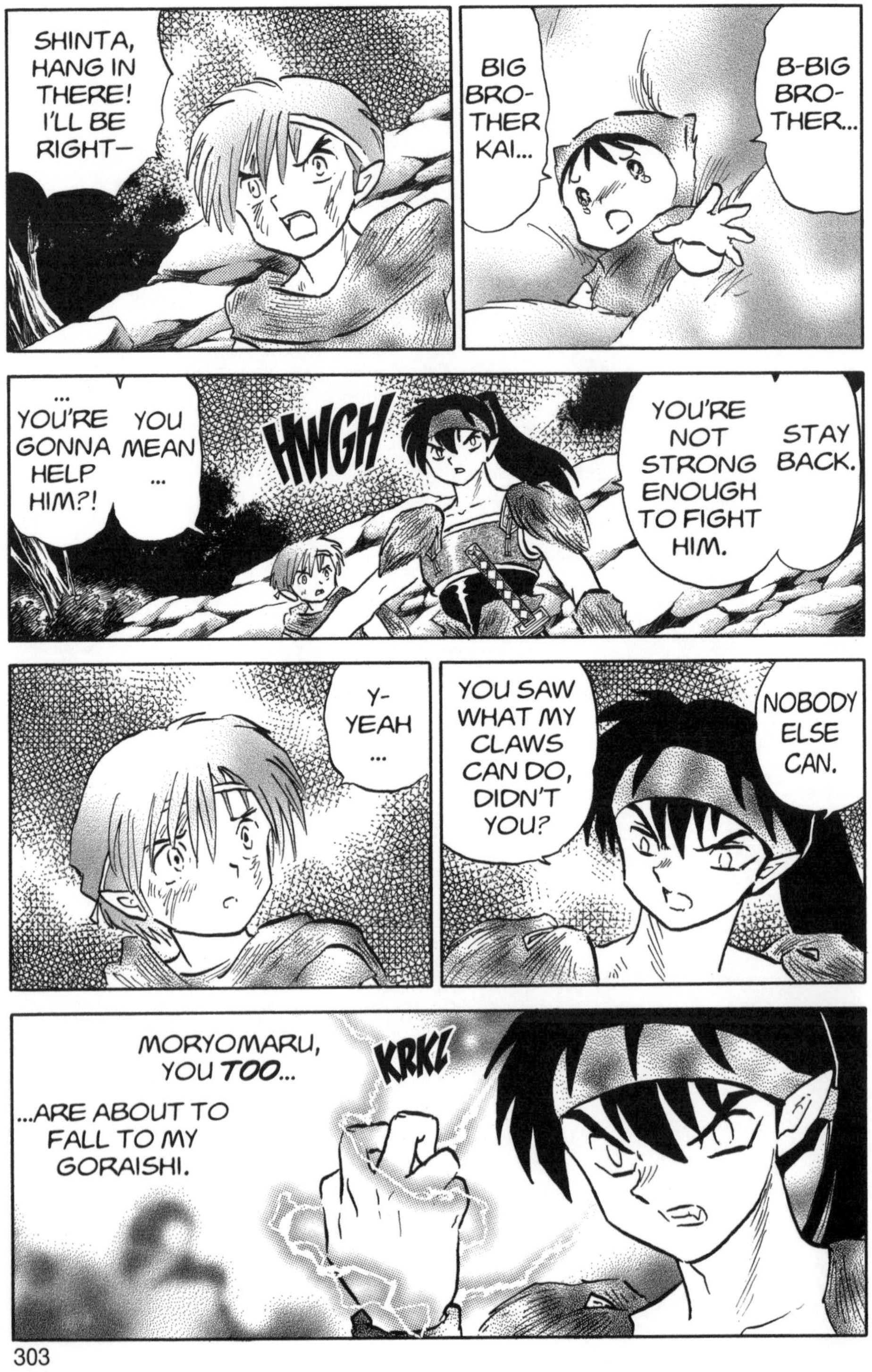

B-BIG BROTHER...
BIG BROTHER KAI...
SHINTA, HANG IN THERE! I'LL BE RIGHT—
STAY BACK.
YOU'RE NOT STRONG ENOUGH TO FIGHT HIM.
HWGH
YOU MEAN ...
... YOU'RE GONNA HELP HIM?!
NOBODY ELSE CAN.
YOU SAW WHAT MY CLAWS CAN DO, DIDN'T YOU?
Y-YEAH ...
KRKL
MORYOMARU, YOU **TOO**...
...ARE ABOUT TO FALL TO MY GORAISHI.

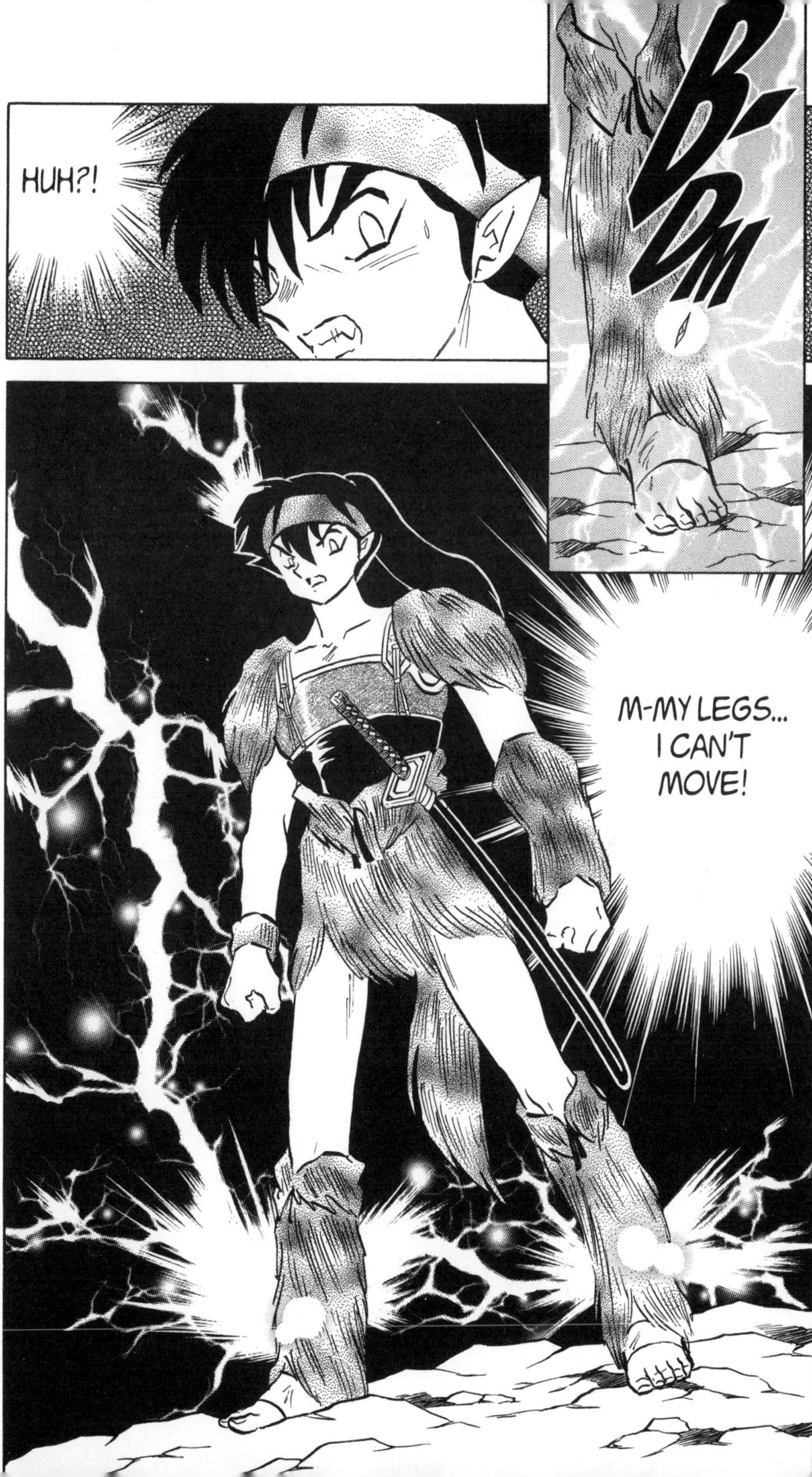
BADUM
HUH?!
M-MY LEGS... I CAN'T MOVE!

SCROLL SEVEN
MIDORIKO'S WILL

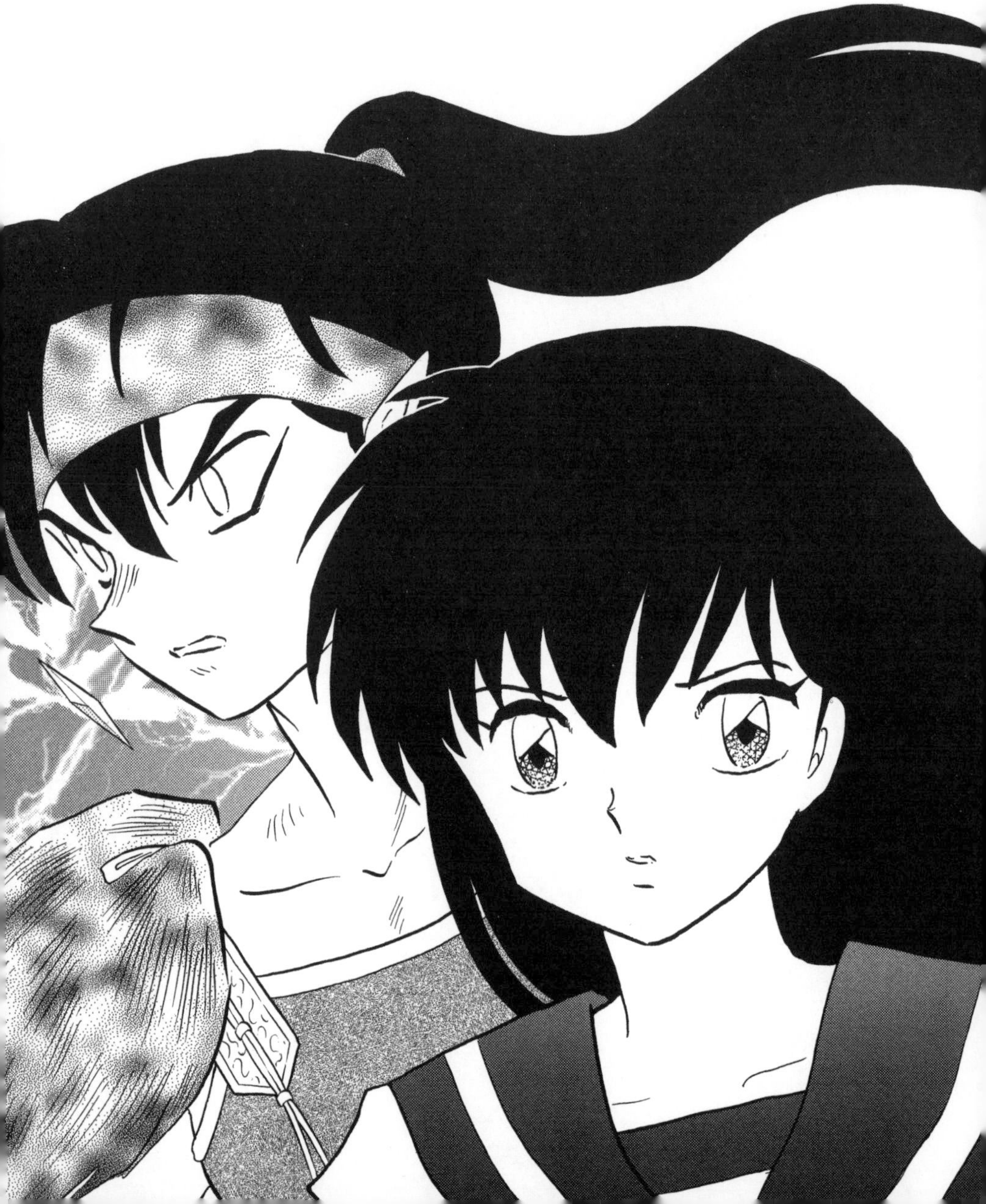

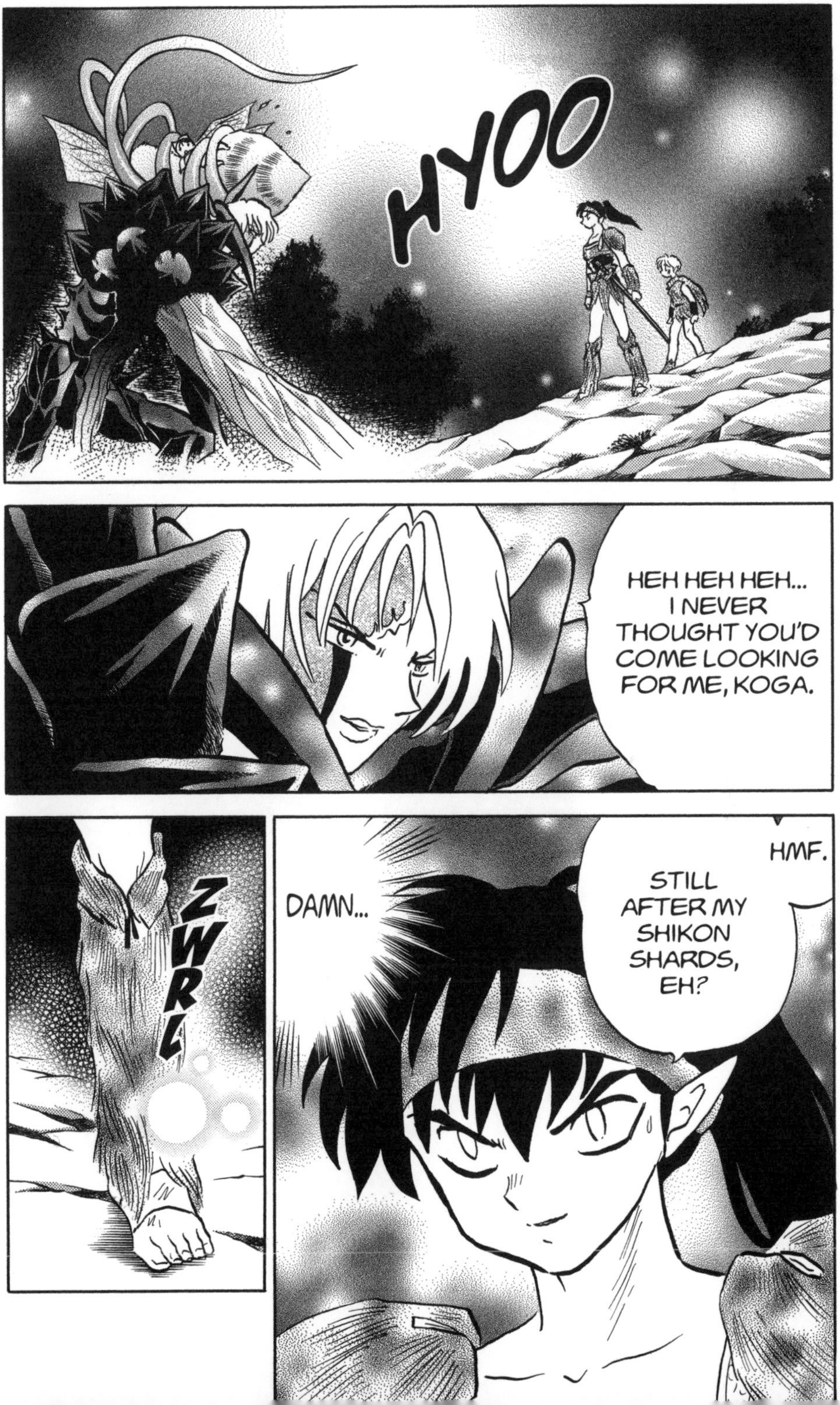
HYOO
HEH HEH HEH... I NEVER THOUGHT YOU'D COME LOOKING FOR ME, KOGA.
HMF.
STILL AFTER MY SHIKON SHARDS, EH?
DAMN...
ZWRL

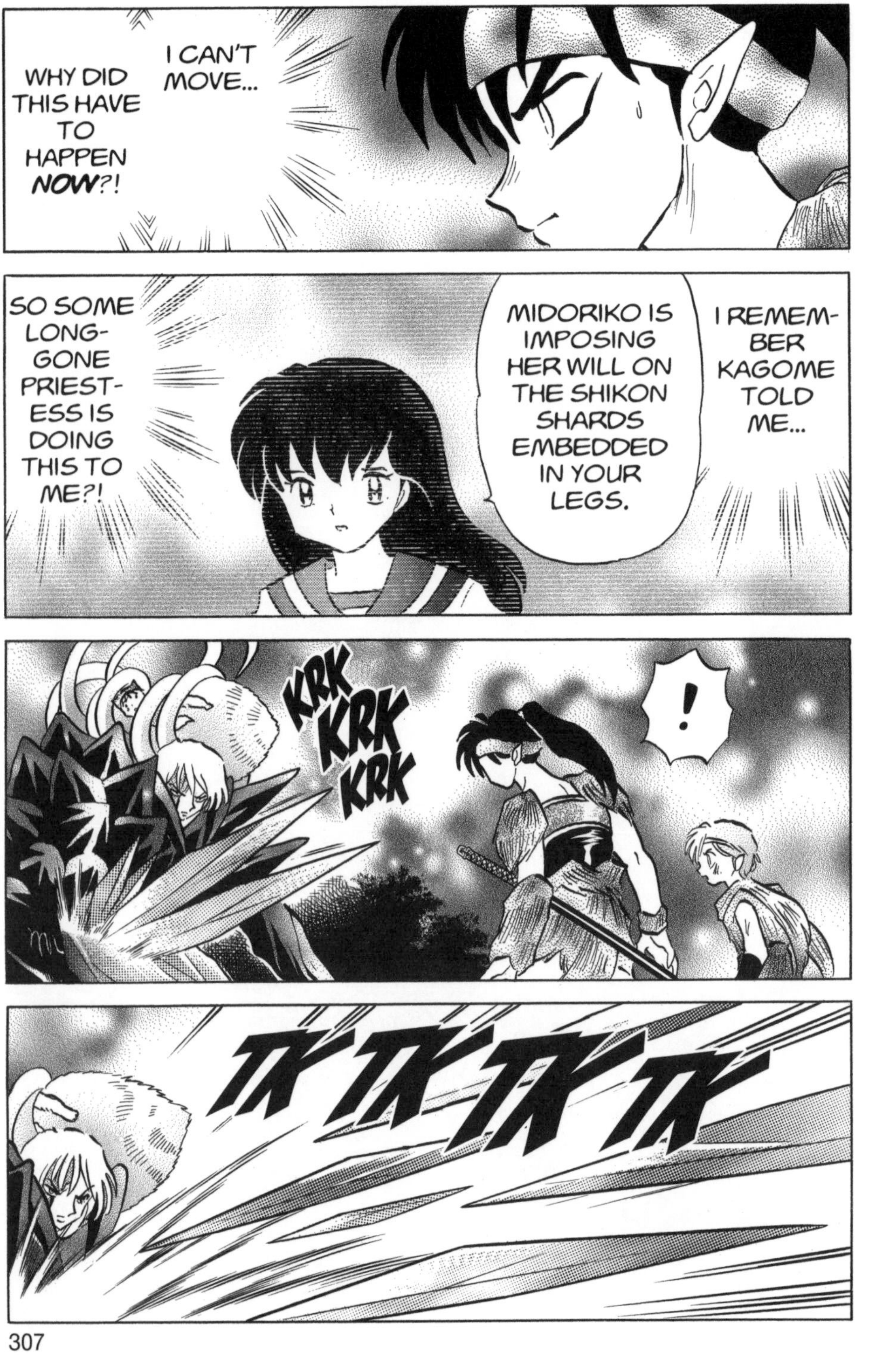
I CAN'T MOVE...
WHY DID THIS HAVE TO HAPPEN NOW?!
I REMEMBER KAGOME TOLD ME...
MIDORIKO IS IMPOSING HER WILL ON THE SHIKON SHARDS EMBEDDED IN YOUR LEGS.
SO SOME LONG-GONE PRIESTESS IS DOING THIS TO ME?!
!
KRK KRK KRK

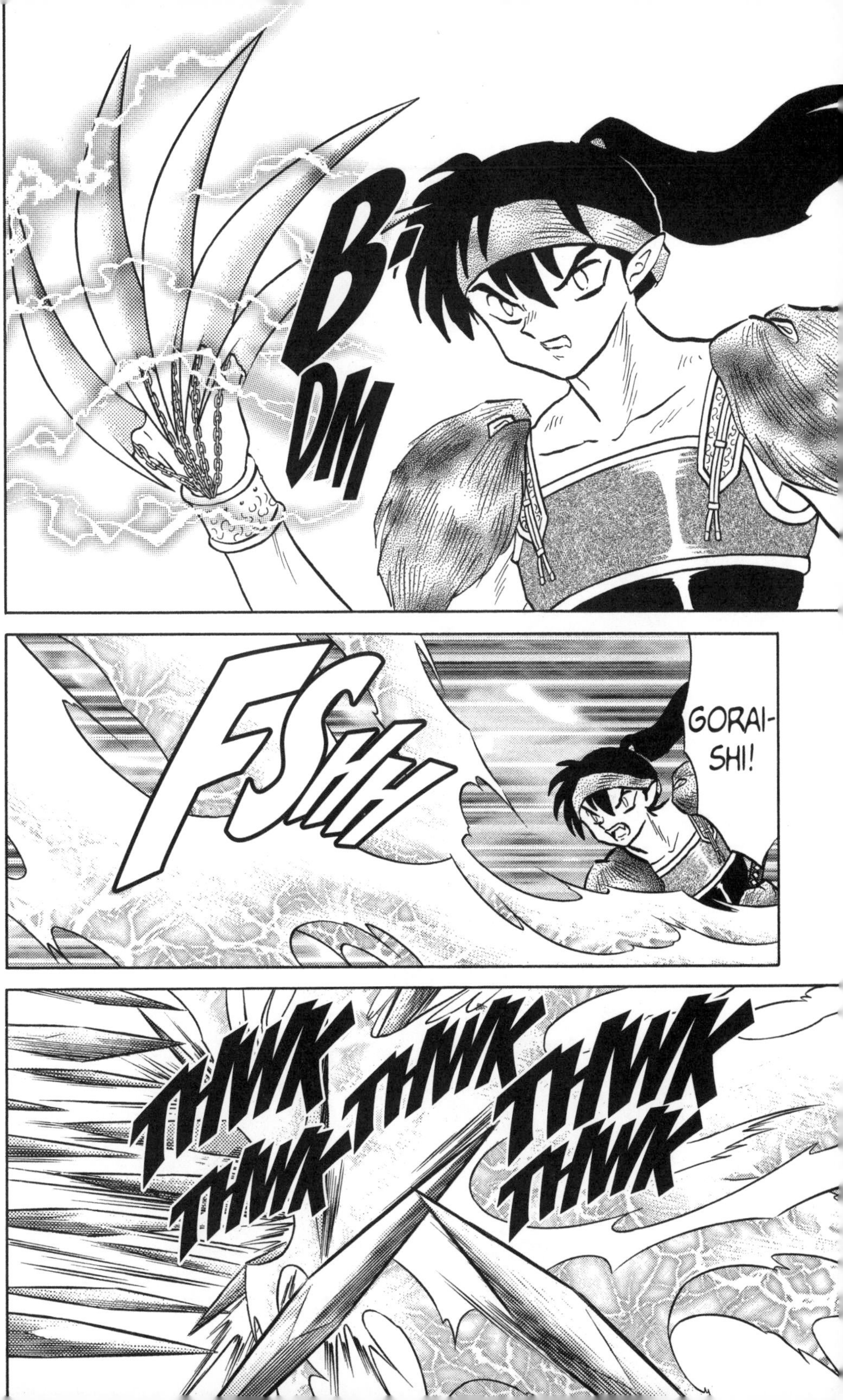
B-DM
GORAI-SHI!
FSHH
THNK THNK THNK THNK THNK THNK

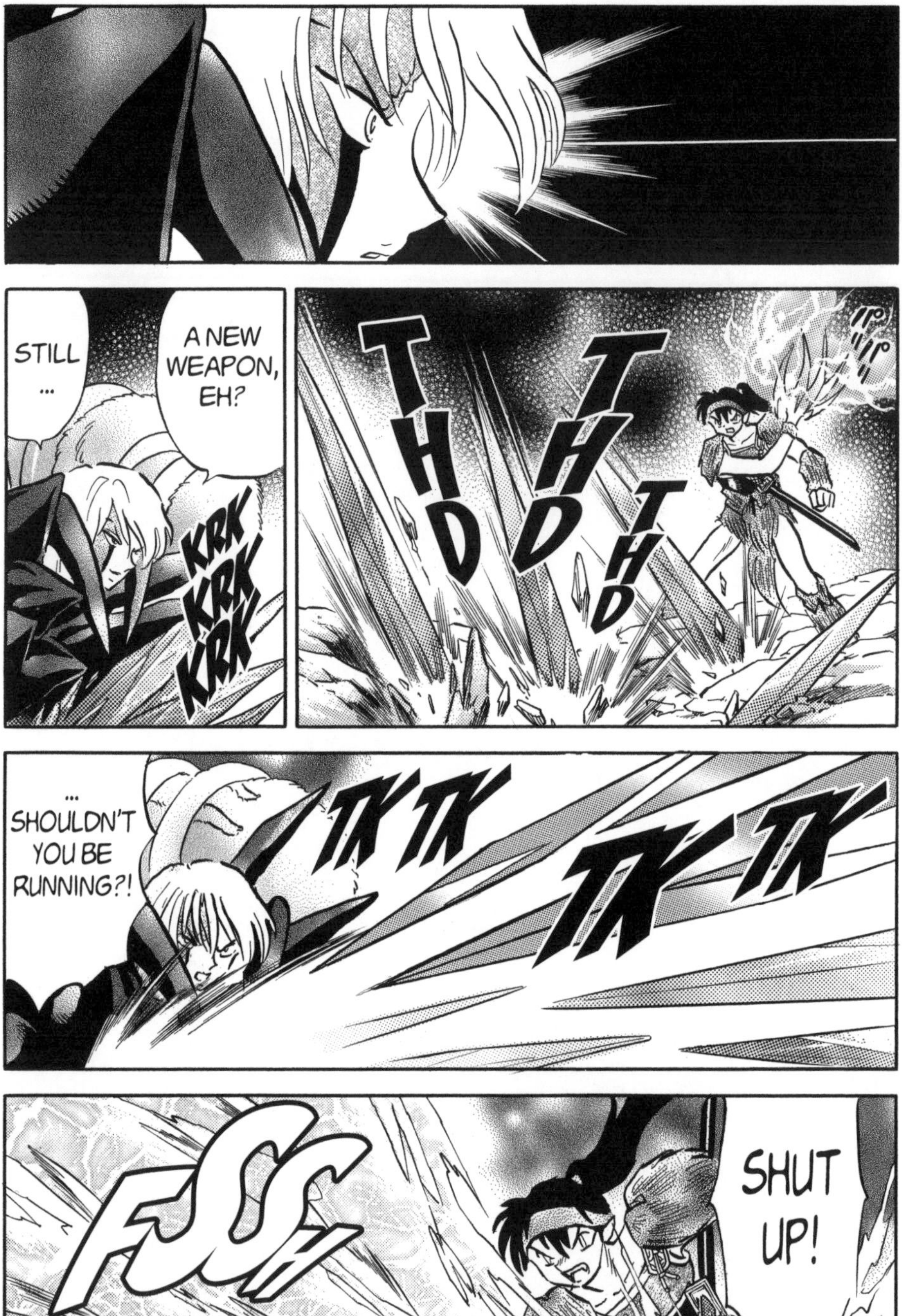
THD
THD
THD
A NEW WEAPON, EH?
STILL ...
KRK KRK KRK
... SHOULDN'T YOU BE RUNNING?!
SHUT UP!
FSSH

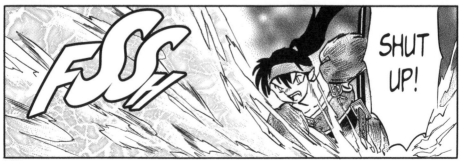

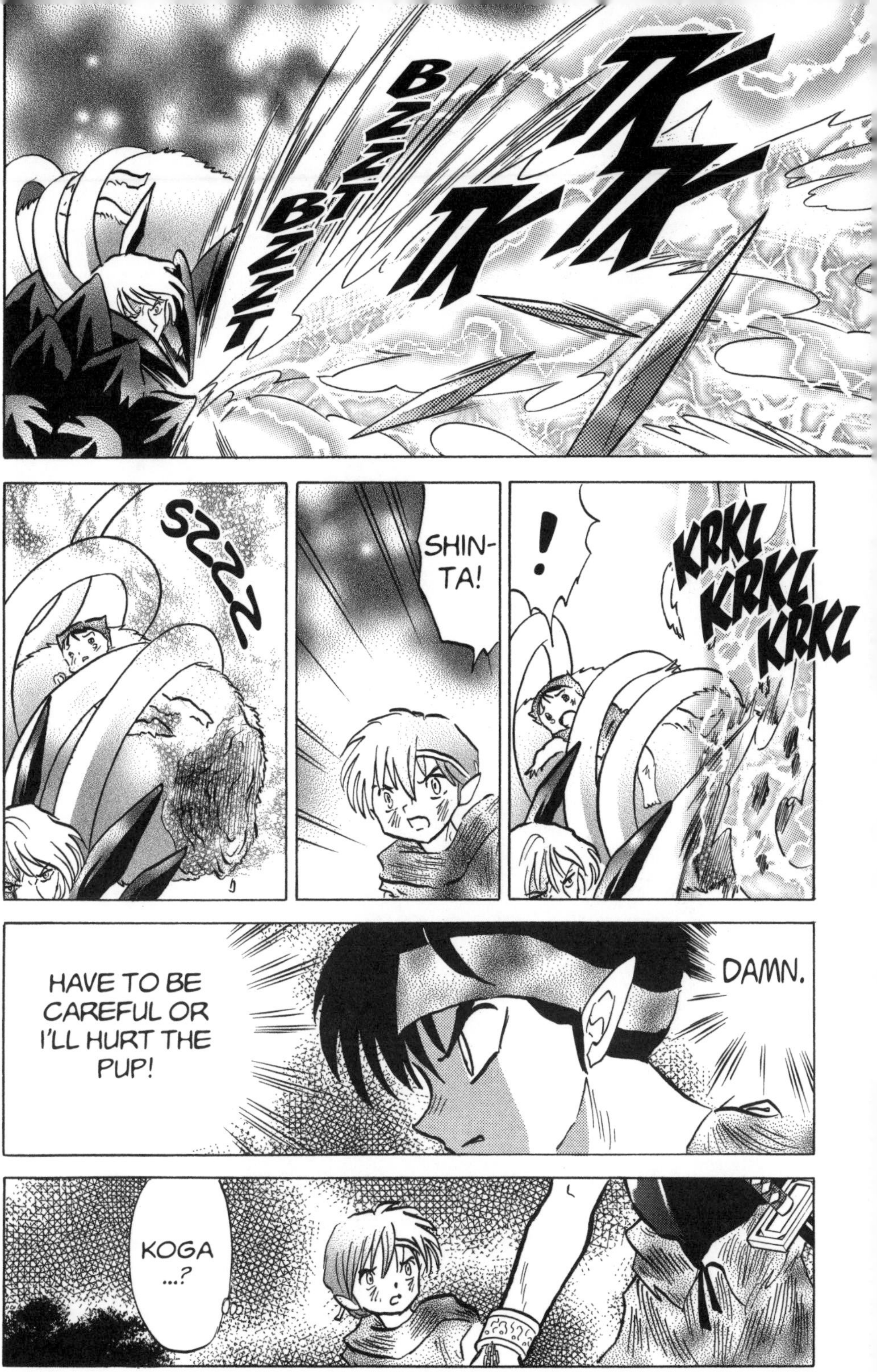
BZZZT
BT
BZZZT
!
KRKL KRKL KRKL
SHIN-TA!
SZZZ
DAMN.
HAVE TO BE CAREFUL OR I'LL HURT THE PUP!
KOGA ...?

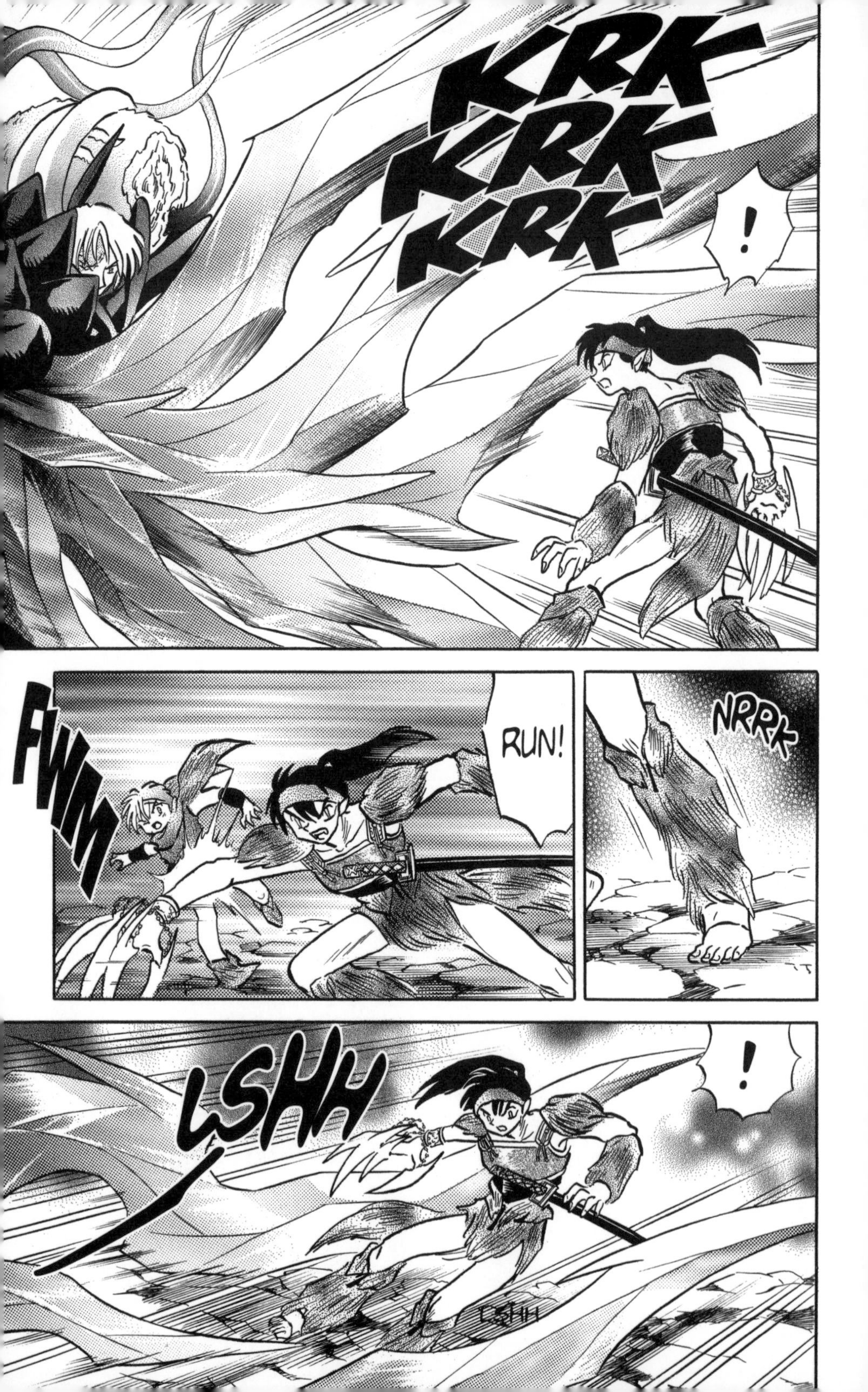
KRK
KRK
KRK
!
NRRK
RUN!
FWM
!
LSHH
LSHH

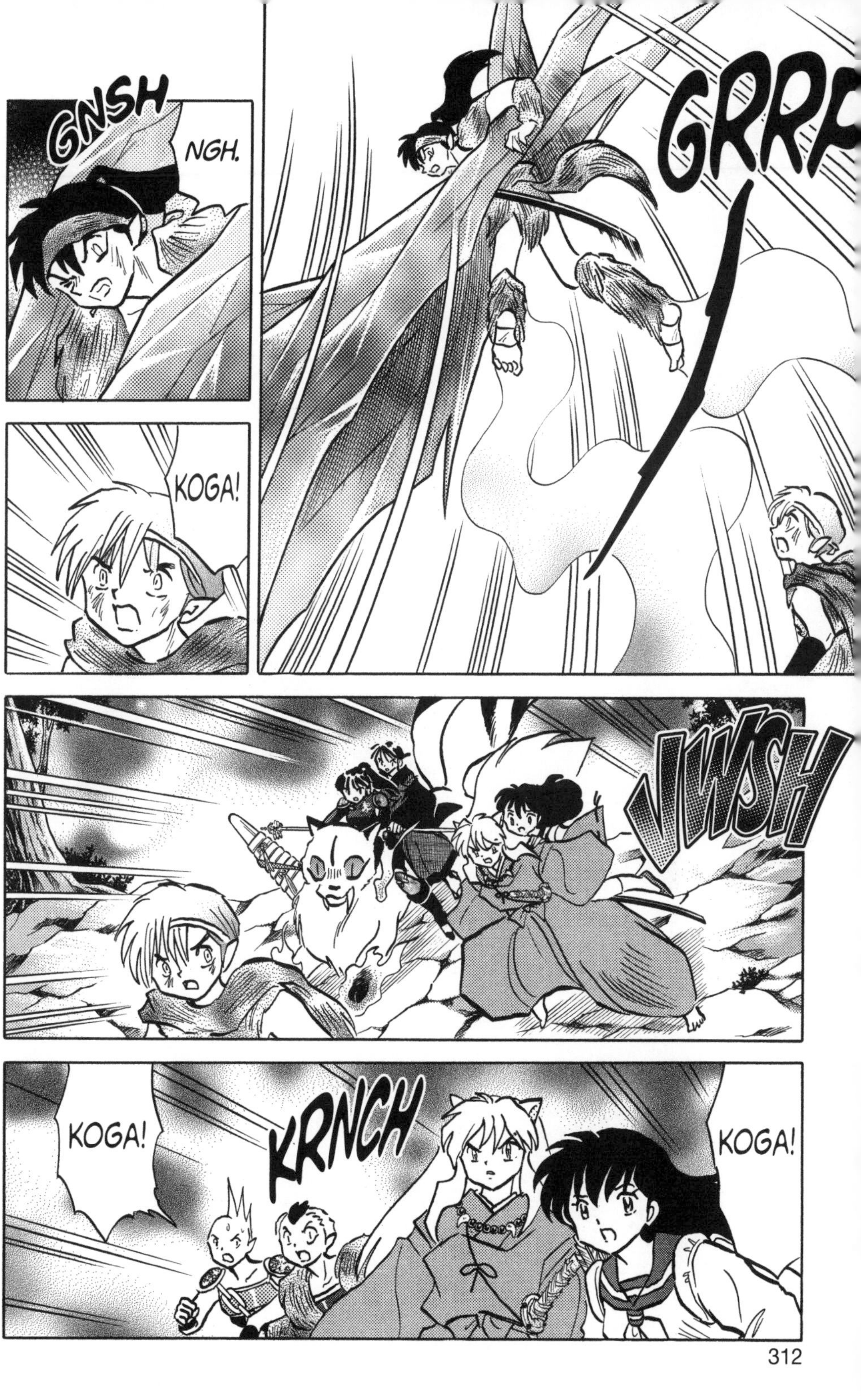
GRRF
GNSH
NGH.
KOGA!
JWSH
KOGA!
KRNCH
KOGA!

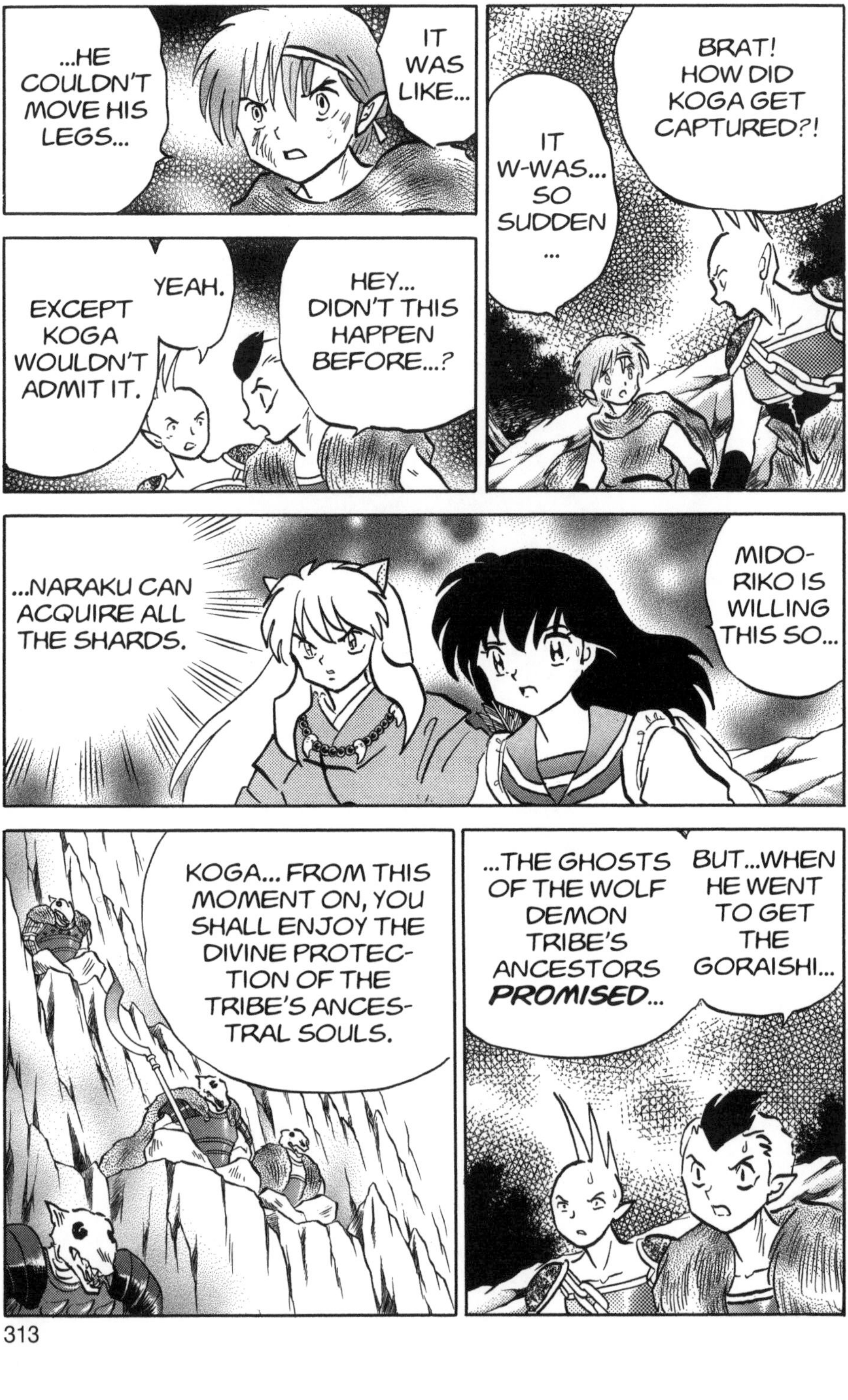
BRAT! HOW DID KOGA GET CAPTURED?!
IT W-WAS... SO SUDDEN ...
IT WAS LIKE...
...HE COULDN'T MOVE HIS LEGS...
HEY... DIDN'T THIS HAPPEN BEFORE...?
YEAH.
EXCEPT KOGA WOULDN'T ADMIT IT.
MIDO-RIKO IS WILLING THIS SO...
...NARAKU CAN ACQUIRE ALL THE SHARDS.
BUT...WHEN HE WENT TO GET THE GORAISHI...
...THE GHOSTS OF THE WOLF DEMON TRIBE'S ANCESTORS ***PROMISED***...
KOGA... FROM THIS MOMENT ON, YOU SHALL ENJOY THE DIVINE PROTEC-TION OF THE TRIBE'S ANCES-TRAL SOULS.

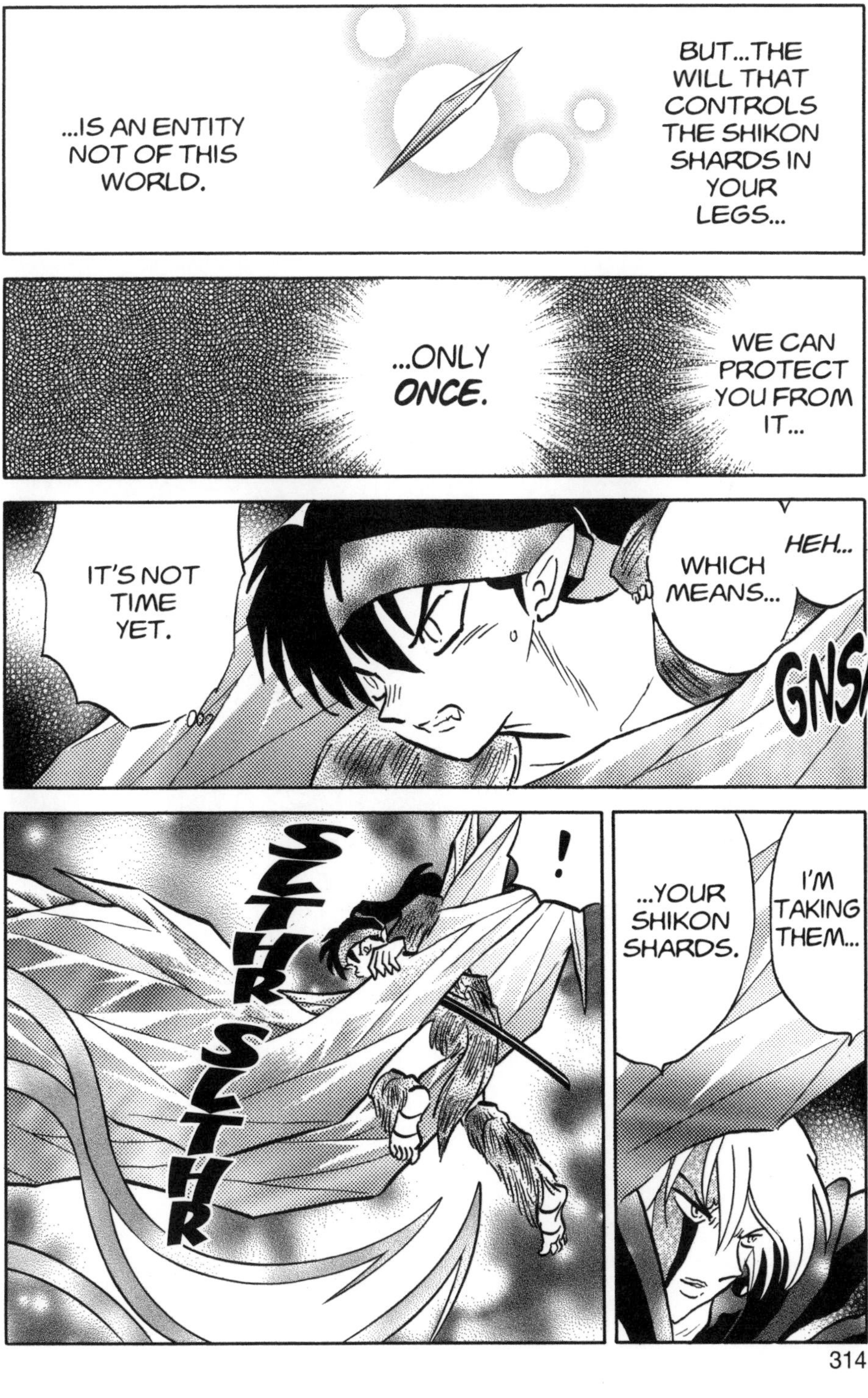
BUT...THE WILL THAT CONTROLS THE SHIKON SHARDS IN YOUR LEGS...
...IS AN ENTITY NOT OF THIS WORLD.
WE CAN PROTECT YOU FROM IT...
...ONLY ONCE.
HEH... WHICH MEANS...
GNSH
IT'S NOT TIME YET.
I'M TAKING THEM...
...YOUR SHIKON SHARDS.
!
SLTHR SLTHR

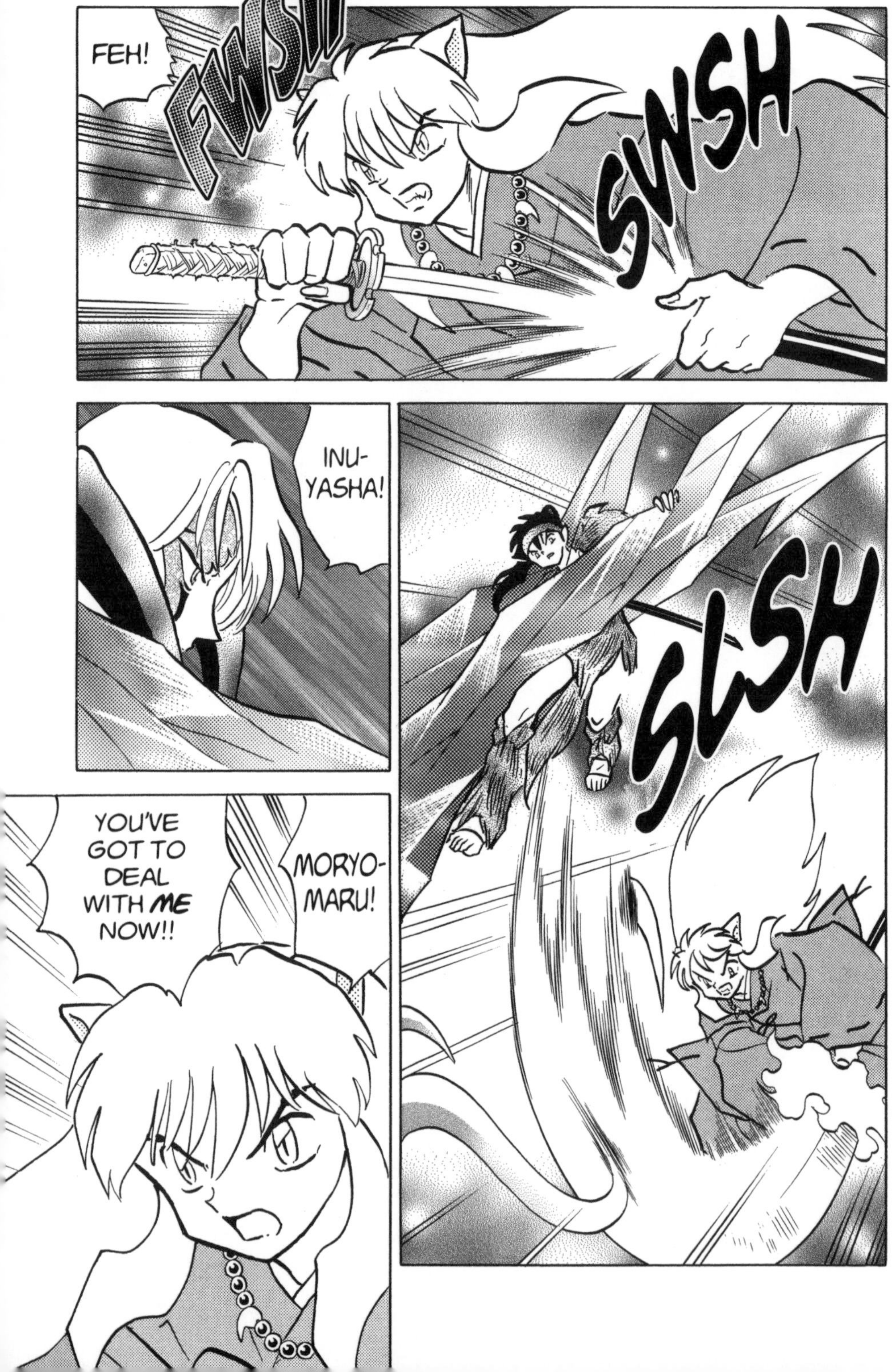
SWSH
FWSH
FEH!
SLSH
INU-YASHA!
MORYO-MARU!
YOU'VE GOT TO DEAL WITH *ME* NOW!!

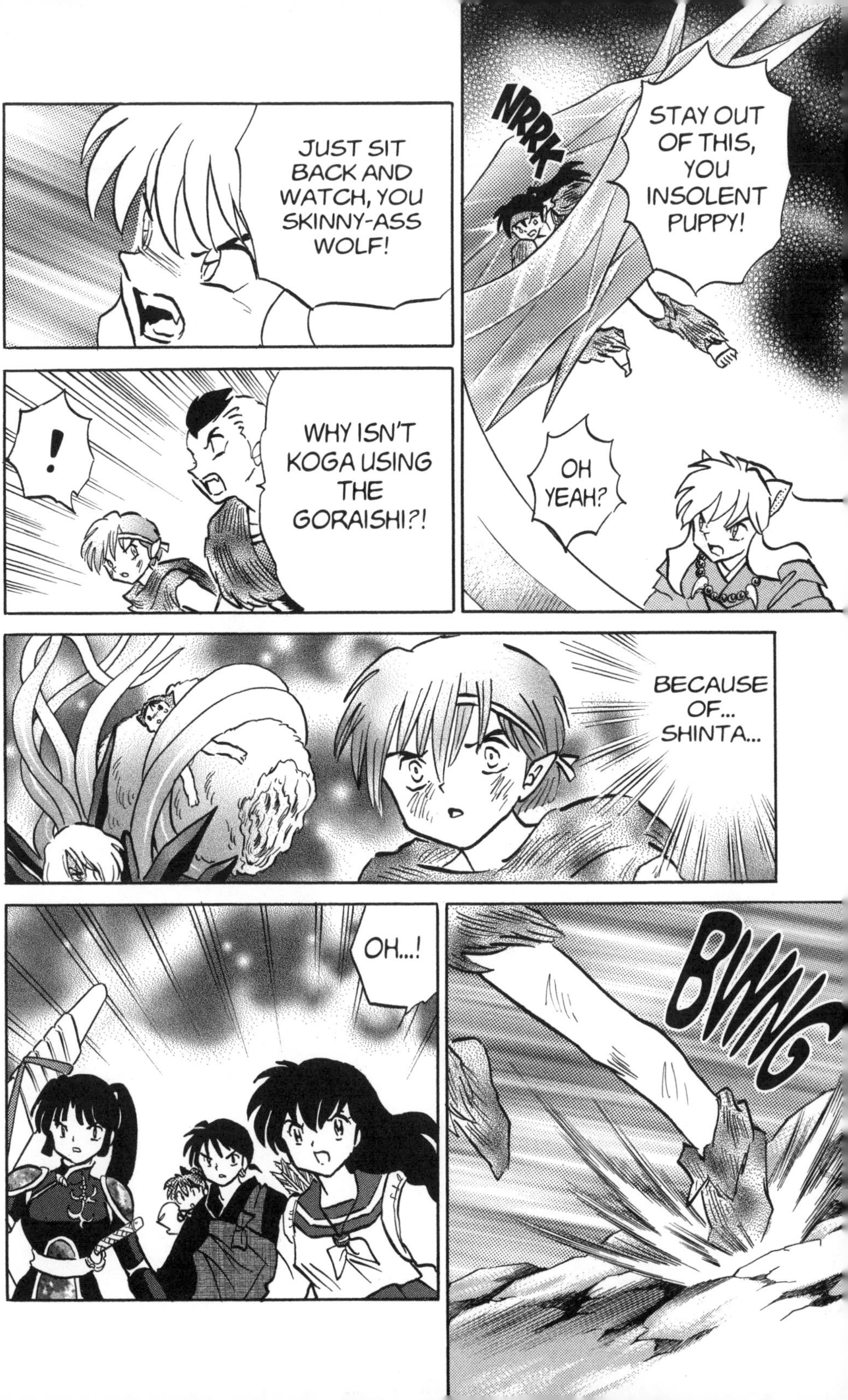
NRRK
STAY OUT OF THIS, YOU INSOLENT PUPPY!
OH YEAH?
JUST SIT BACK AND WATCH, YOU SKINNY-ASS WOLF!
WHY ISN'T KOGA USING THE GORAISHI?!
!
BECAUSE OF... SHINTA...
BWNG
OH...!

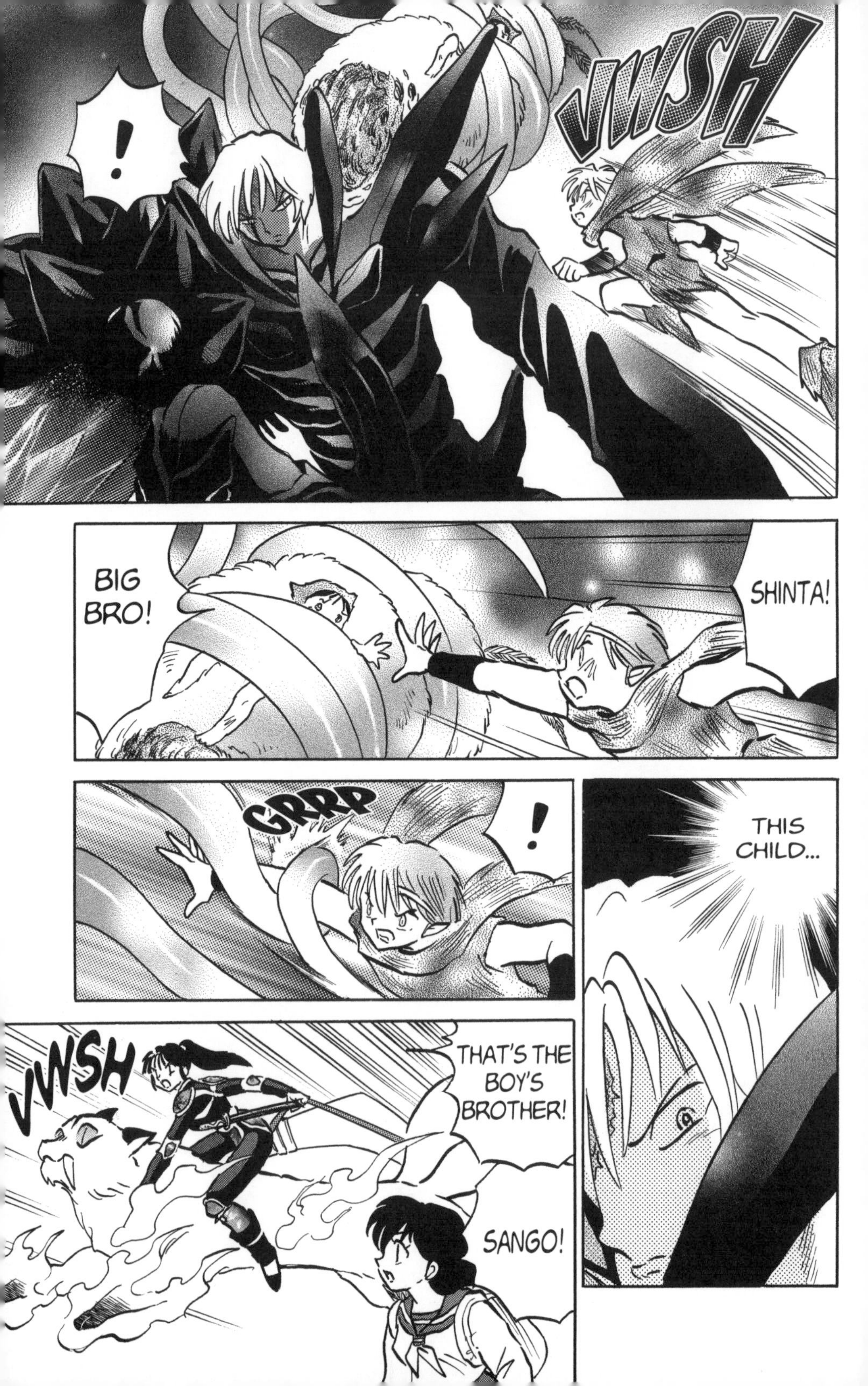
VWSH
!
SHINTA!
BIG BRO!
THIS CHILD...
!
GRRP
THAT'S THE BOY'S BROTHER!
SANGO!
VWSH

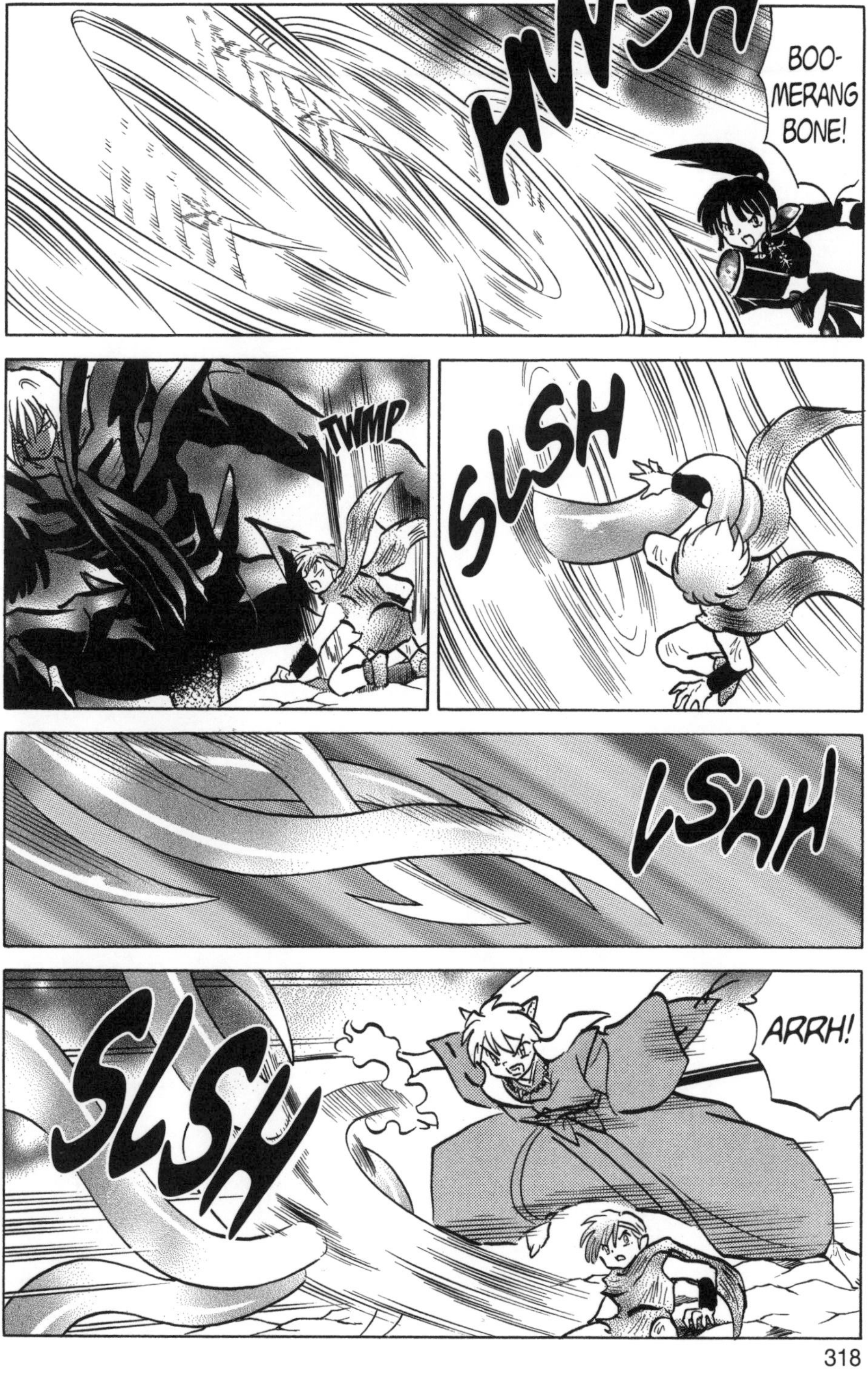
WNSH
BOO-MERANG BONE!
SLSH
TWMP
WSHH
ARRH!
SLSH

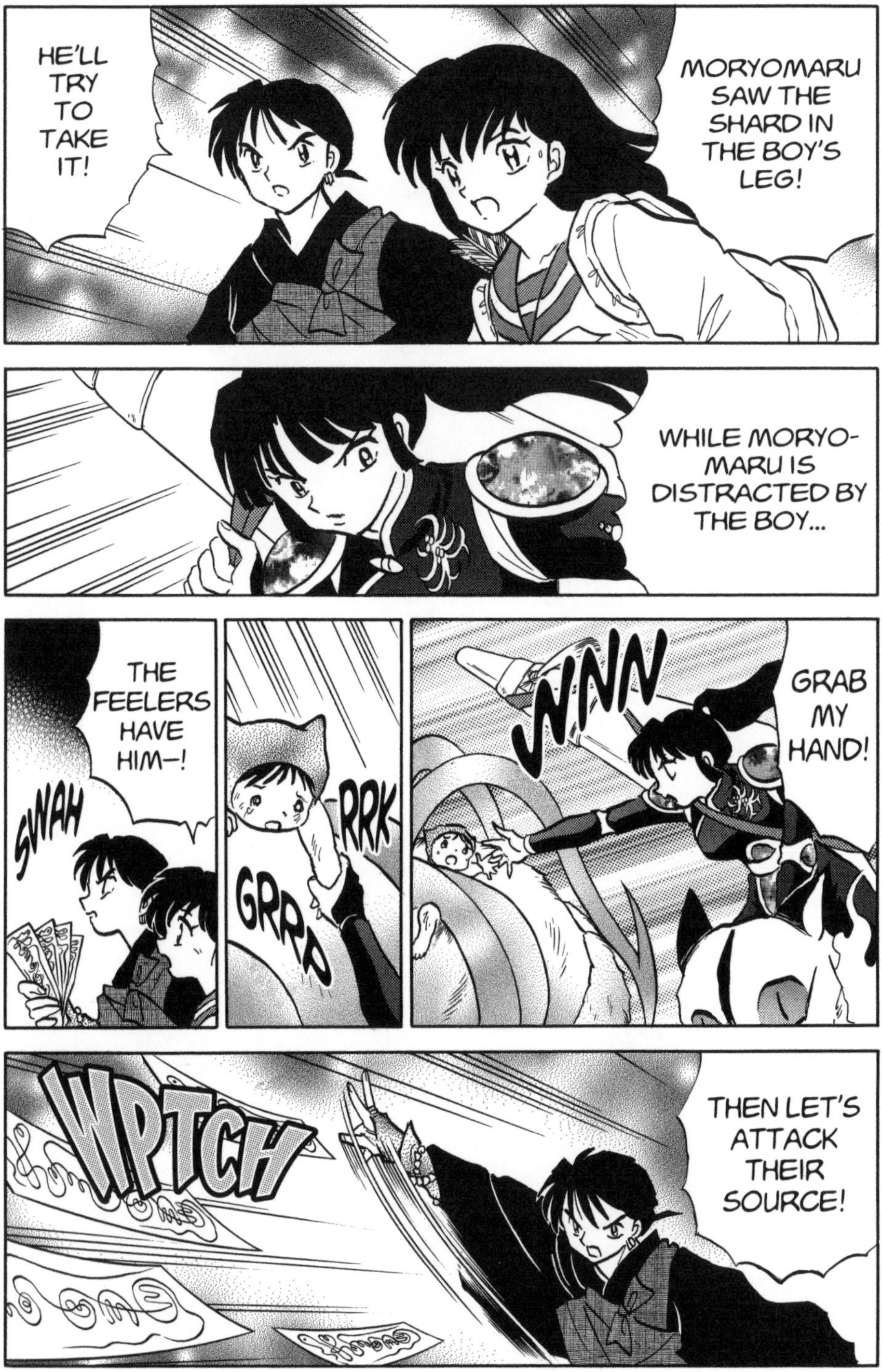
MORYOMARU SAW THE SHARD IN THE BOY'S LEG!
HE'LL TRY TO TAKE IT!
WHILE MORYO-MARU IS DISTRACTED BY THE BOY...
GRAB MY HAND!
WNN
RRK
GRRP
THE FEELERS HAVE HIM—!
SWAH
THEN LET'S ATTACK THEIR SOURCE!
WPTCH

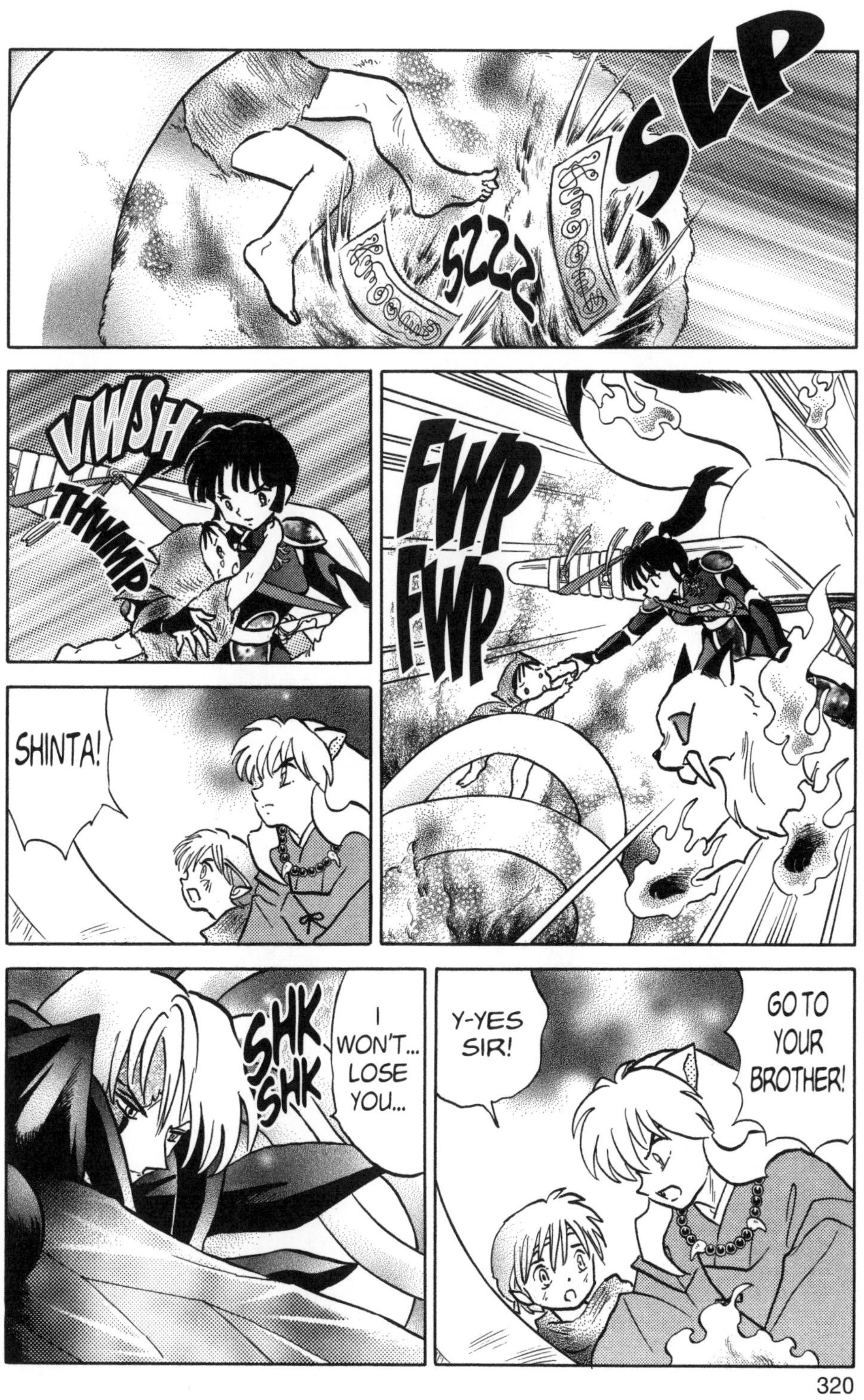
SLP
SZZZ
FWP
FWP
VWSH
THWMP
SHINTA!
GO TO YOUR BROTHER!
Y-YES SIR!
I WON'T... LOSE YOU...
SHK
SHK

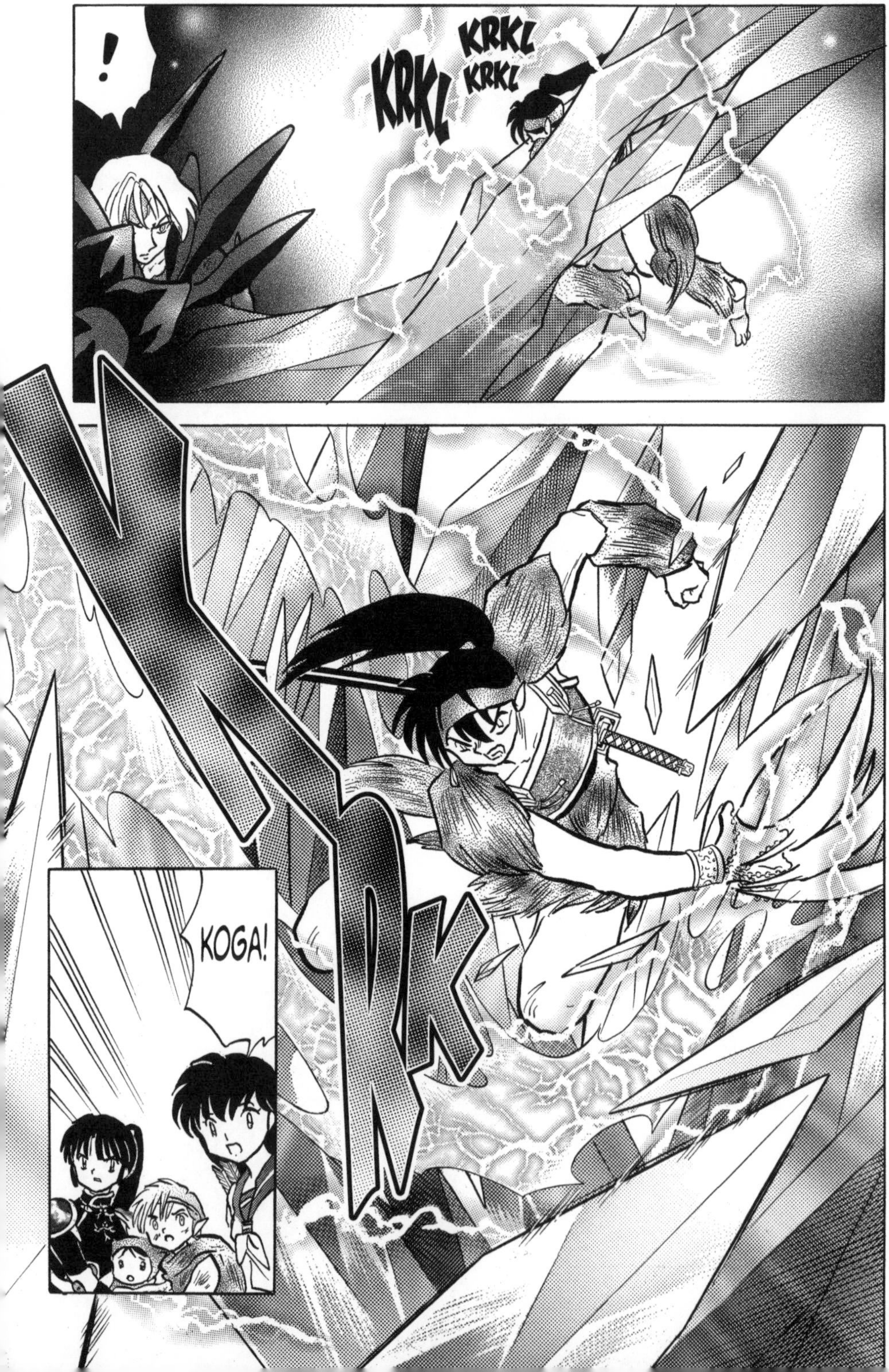
!
KRKL
KRKL
KRKL
VRK
KOGA!

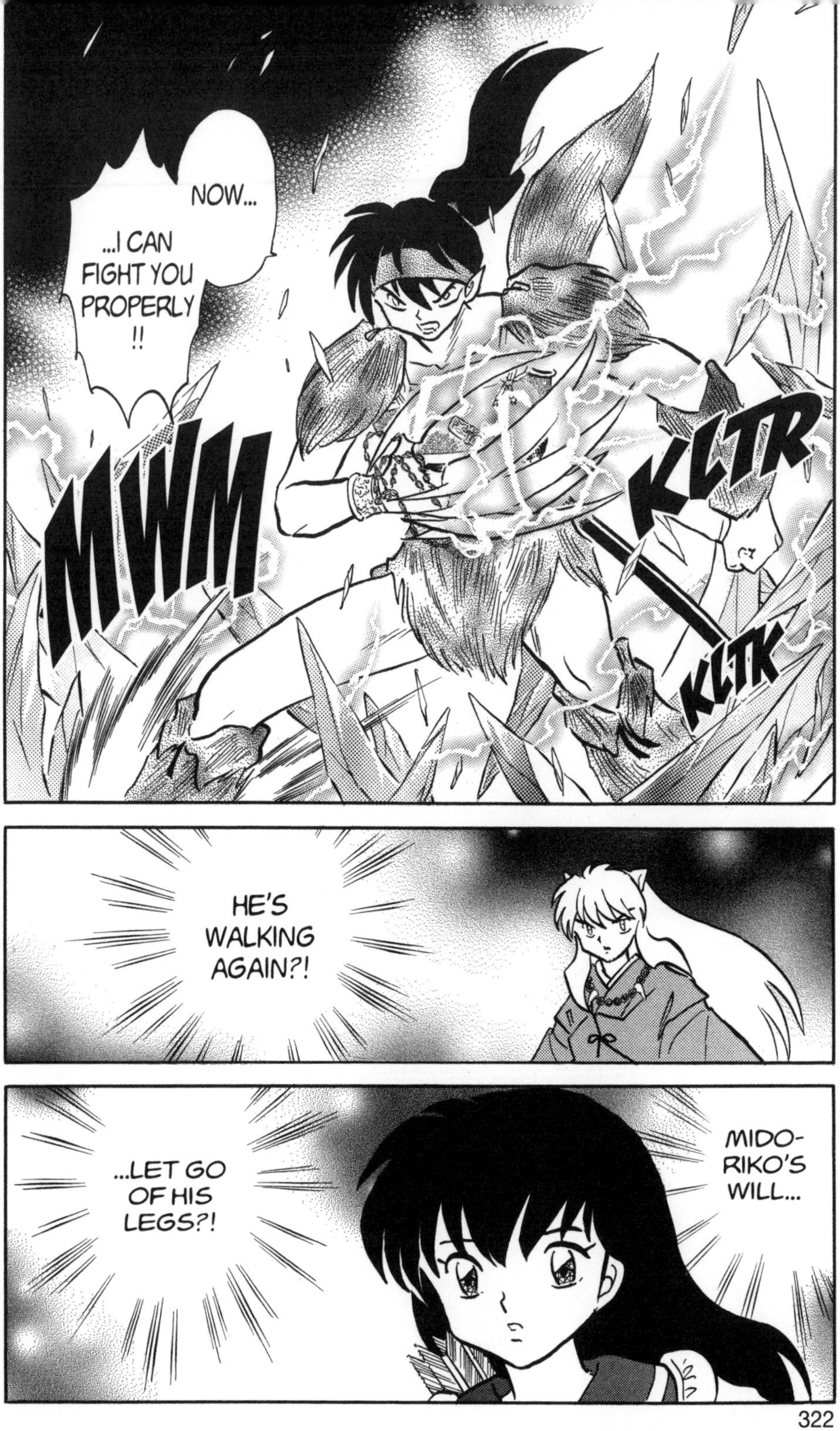
NOW...
...I CAN FIGHT YOU PROPERLY !!
KLTR
KLTK
MWM
HE'S WALKING AGAIN?!
MIDO-RIKO'S WILL...
...LET GO OF HIS LEGS?!

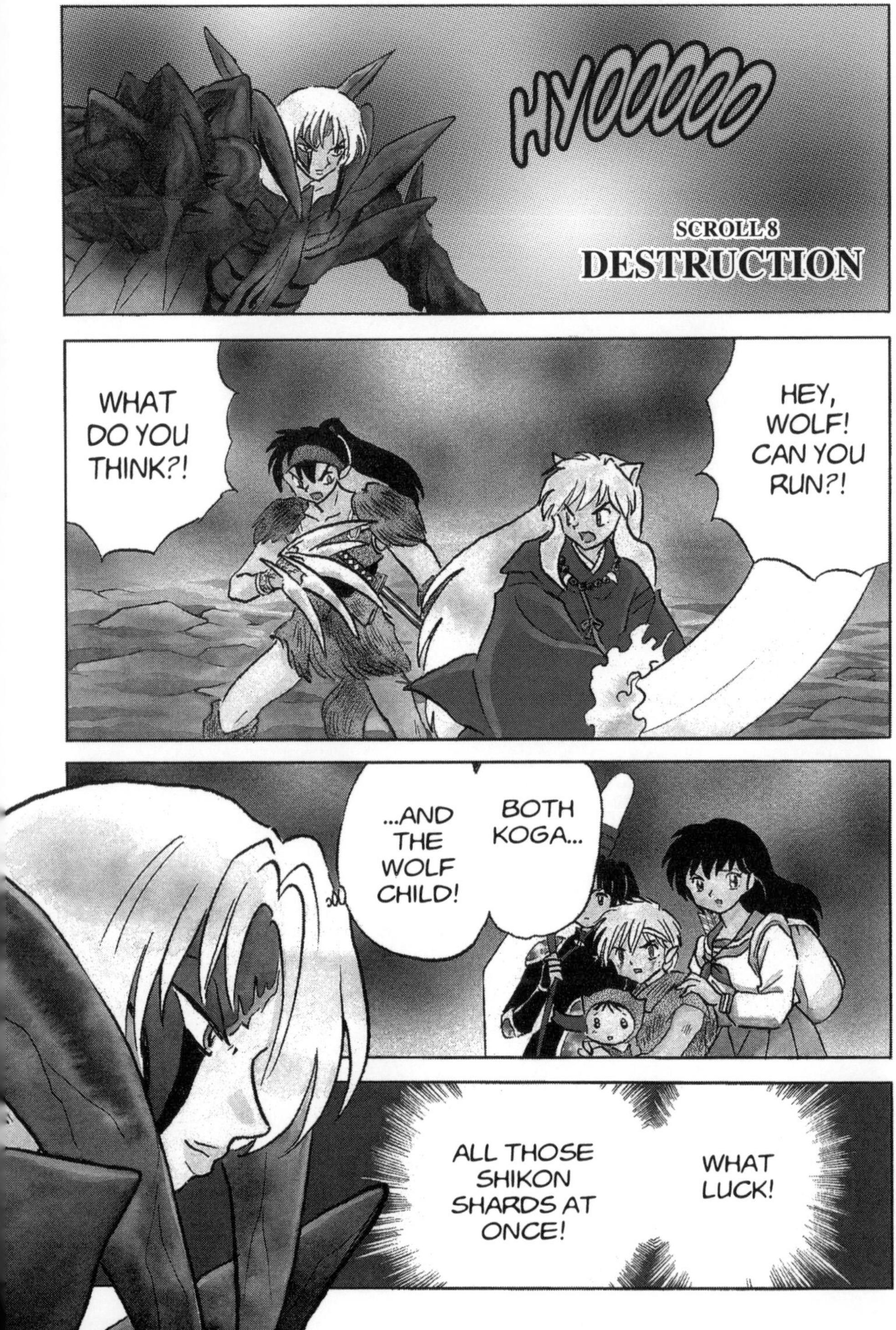
HYOOOOO
SCROLL 8
DESTRUCTION
HEY, WOLF! CAN YOU RUN?!
WHAT DO YOU THINK?!
BOTH KOGA...
...AND THE WOLF CHILD!
WHAT LUCK!
ALL THOSE SHIKON SHARDS AT ONCE!

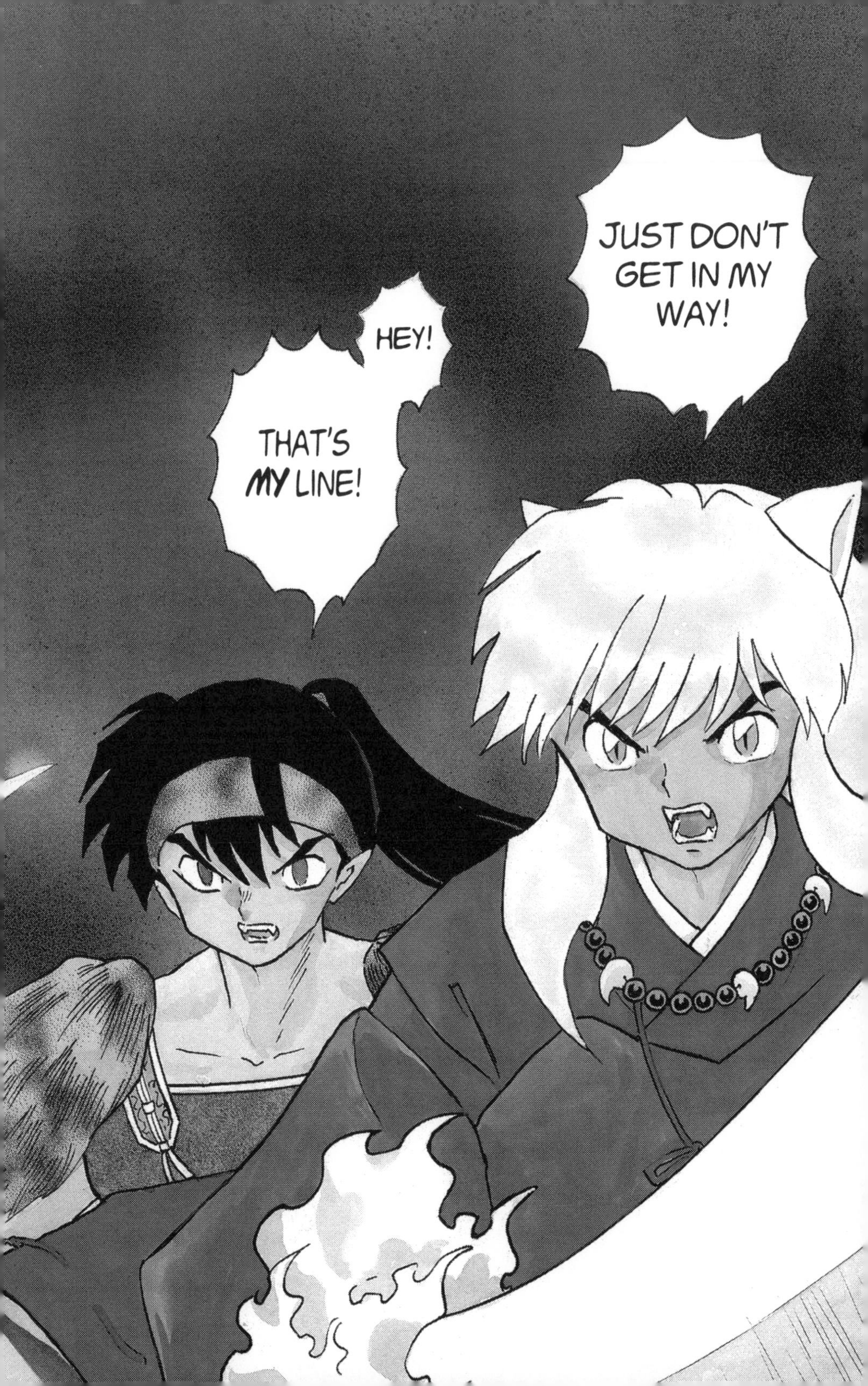
JUST DON'T GET IN MY WAY!
HEY!
THAT'S **MY** LINE!

SCROLL EIGHT
DESTRUCTION

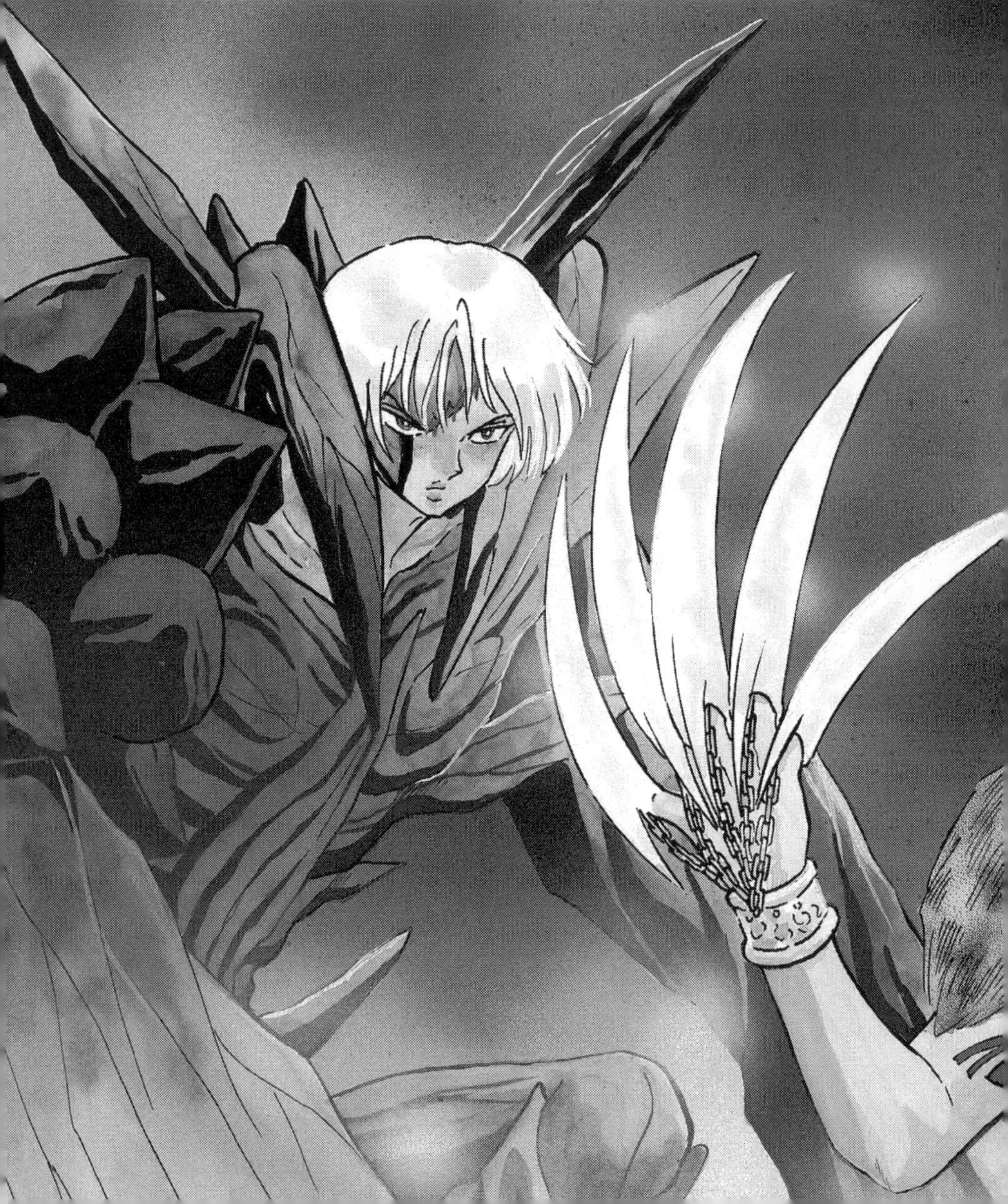

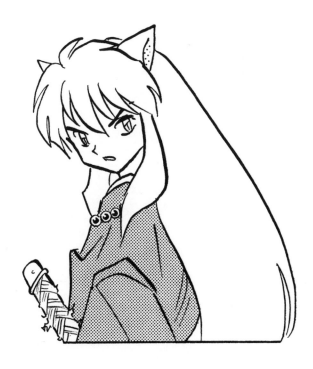

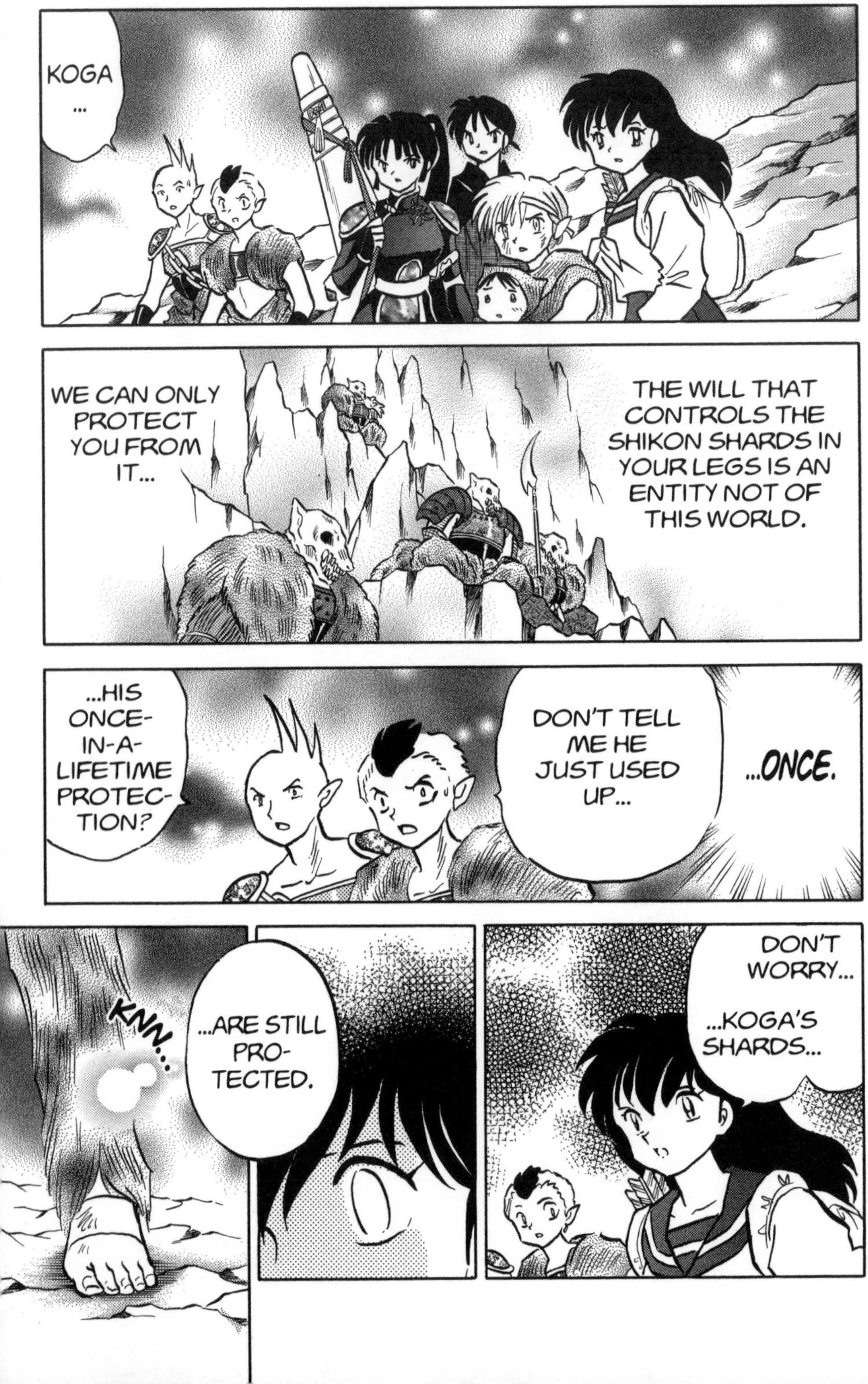
KOGA ...
THE WILL THAT CONTROLS THE SHIKON SHARDS IN YOUR LEGS IS AN ENTITY NOT OF THIS WORLD.
WE CAN ONLY PROTECT YOU FROM IT...
...ONCE.
DON'T TELL ME HE JUST USED UP...
...HIS ONCE-IN-A-LIFETIME PROTEC-TION?
DON'T WORRY...
...KOGA'S SHARDS...
...ARE STILL PRO-TECTED.
KNN...

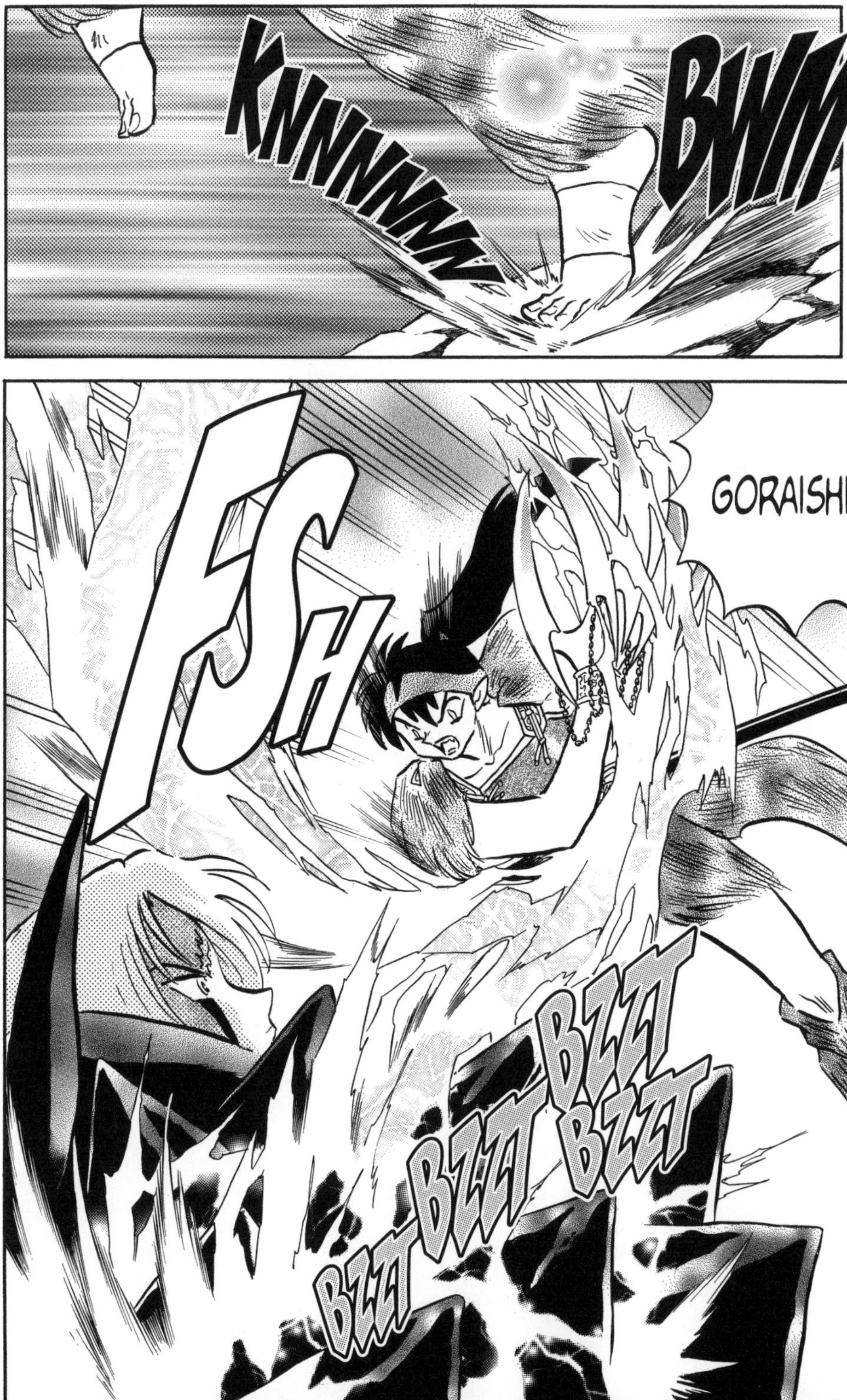
BWM
KNNNNNN
GORAISHI!!
FSH
BZZT BZZT BZZT BZZT

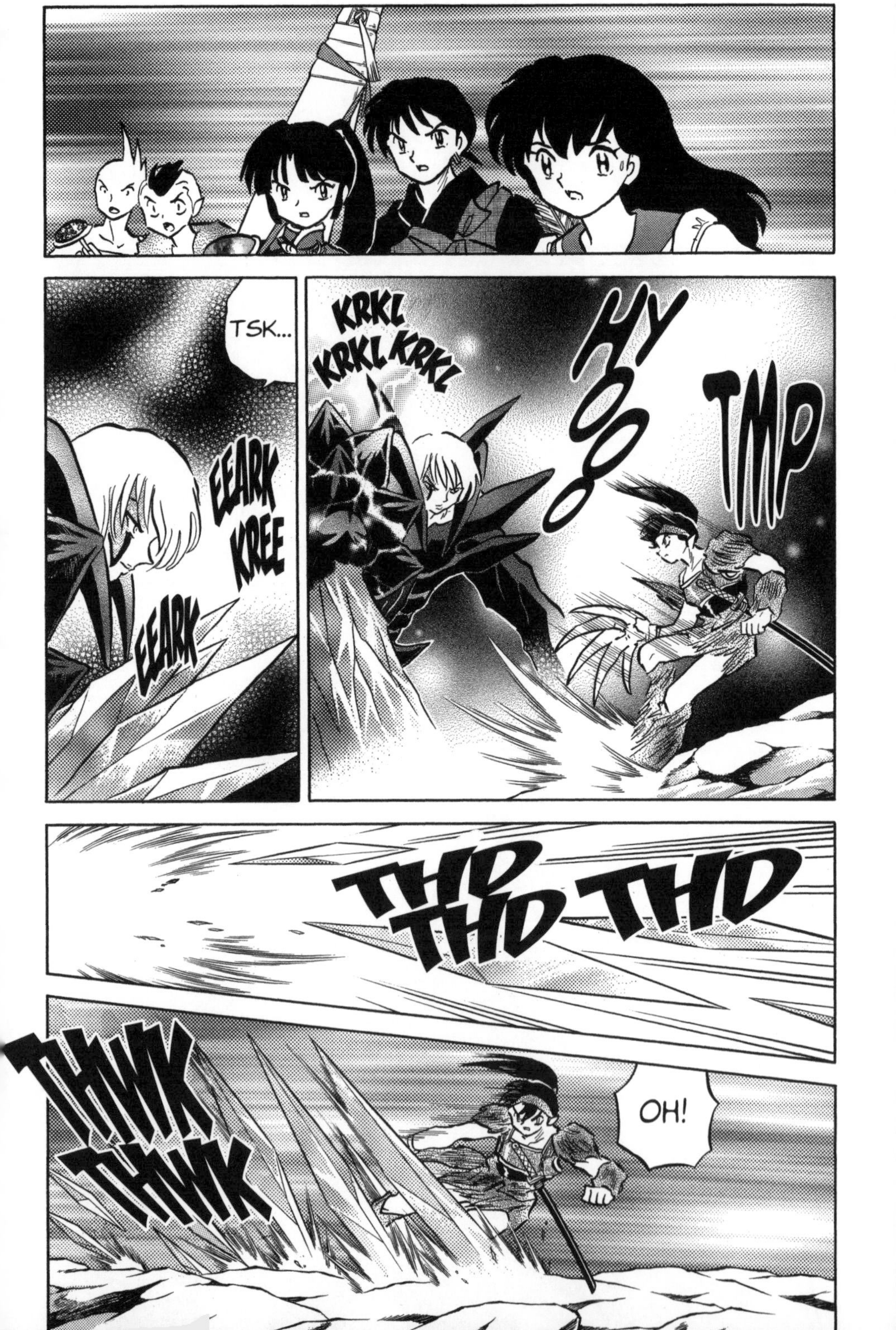
HYOOO
KRKL
KRKL KRKL
TMP
TSK...
EEARK KREE
EEARK
THD THD THD
OH!
THWK
THWK

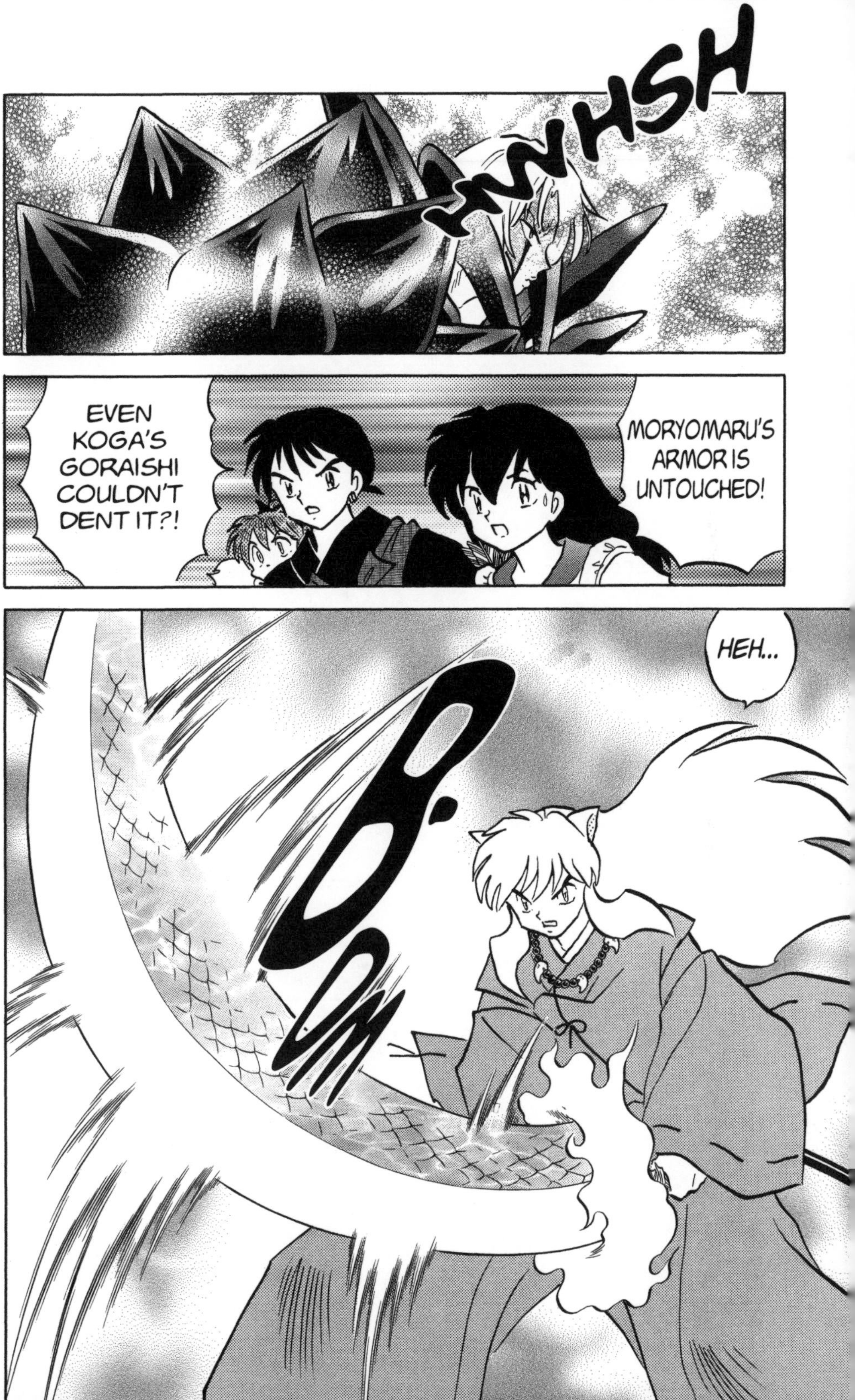
WHSH
MORYOMARU'S ARMOR IS UNTOUCHED!
EVEN KOGA'S GORAISHI COULDN'T DENT IT?!
HEH...
BOOM

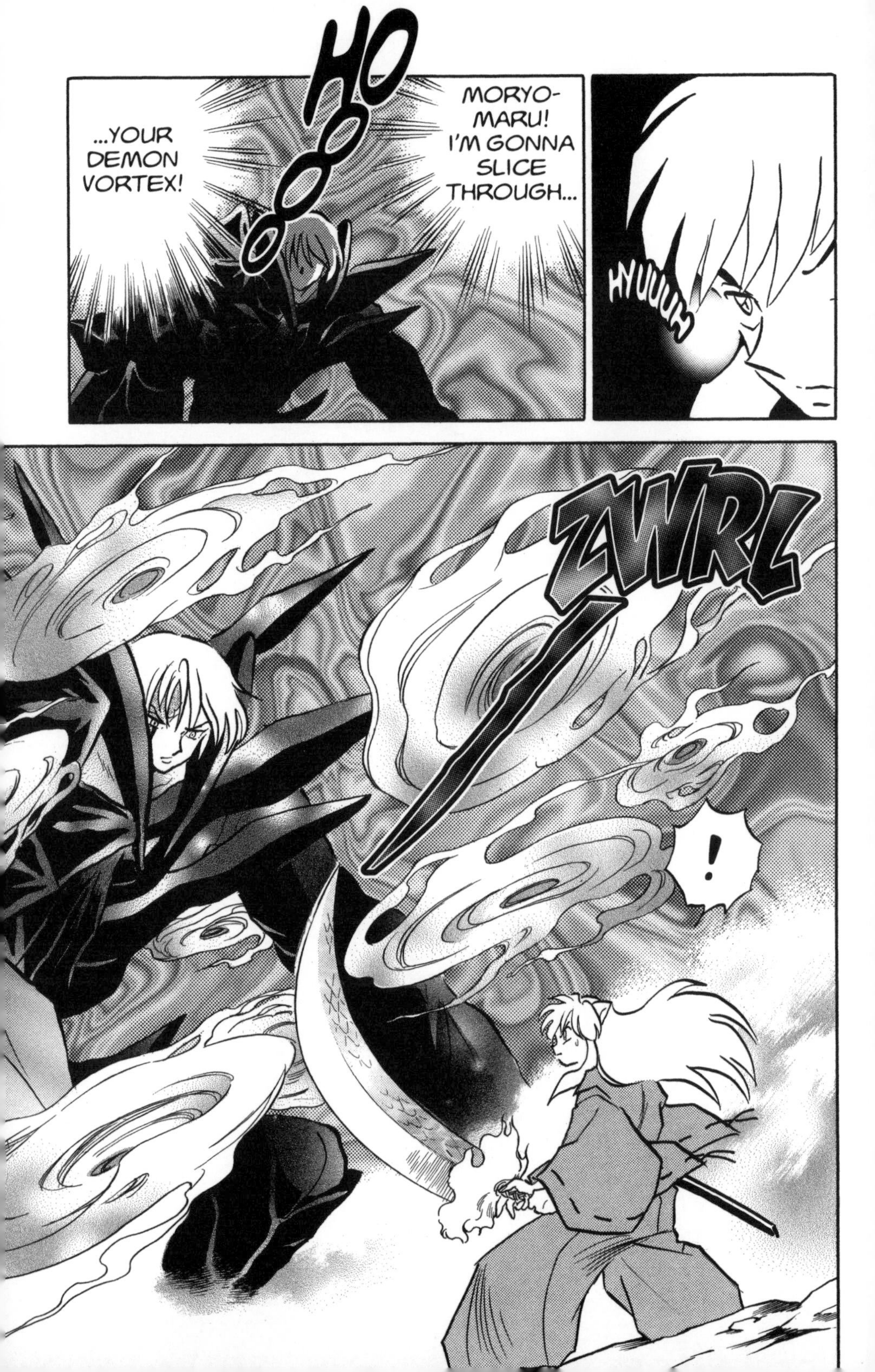
HYUUUH
MORYO-MARU! I'M GONNA SLICE THROUGH...
HOOOOO
...YOUR DEMON VORTEX!
ZWRL
!

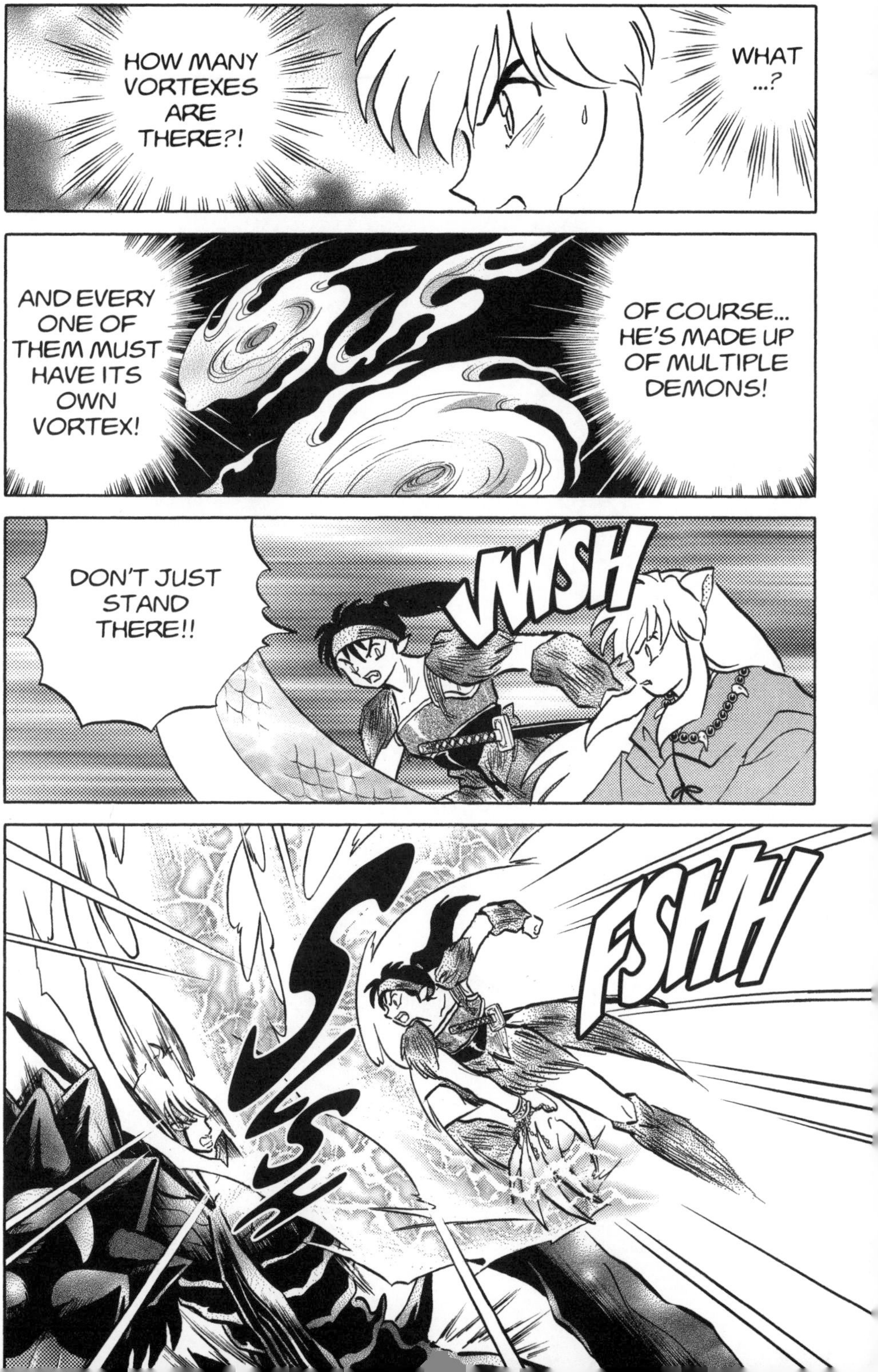
WHAT ...?
HOW MANY VORTEXES ARE THERE?!
OF COURSE... HE'S MADE UP OF MULTIPLE DEMONS!
AND EVERY ONE OF THEM MUST HAVE ITS OWN VORTEX!
VWSH
DON'T JUST STAND THERE!!
FSHH
SWSH

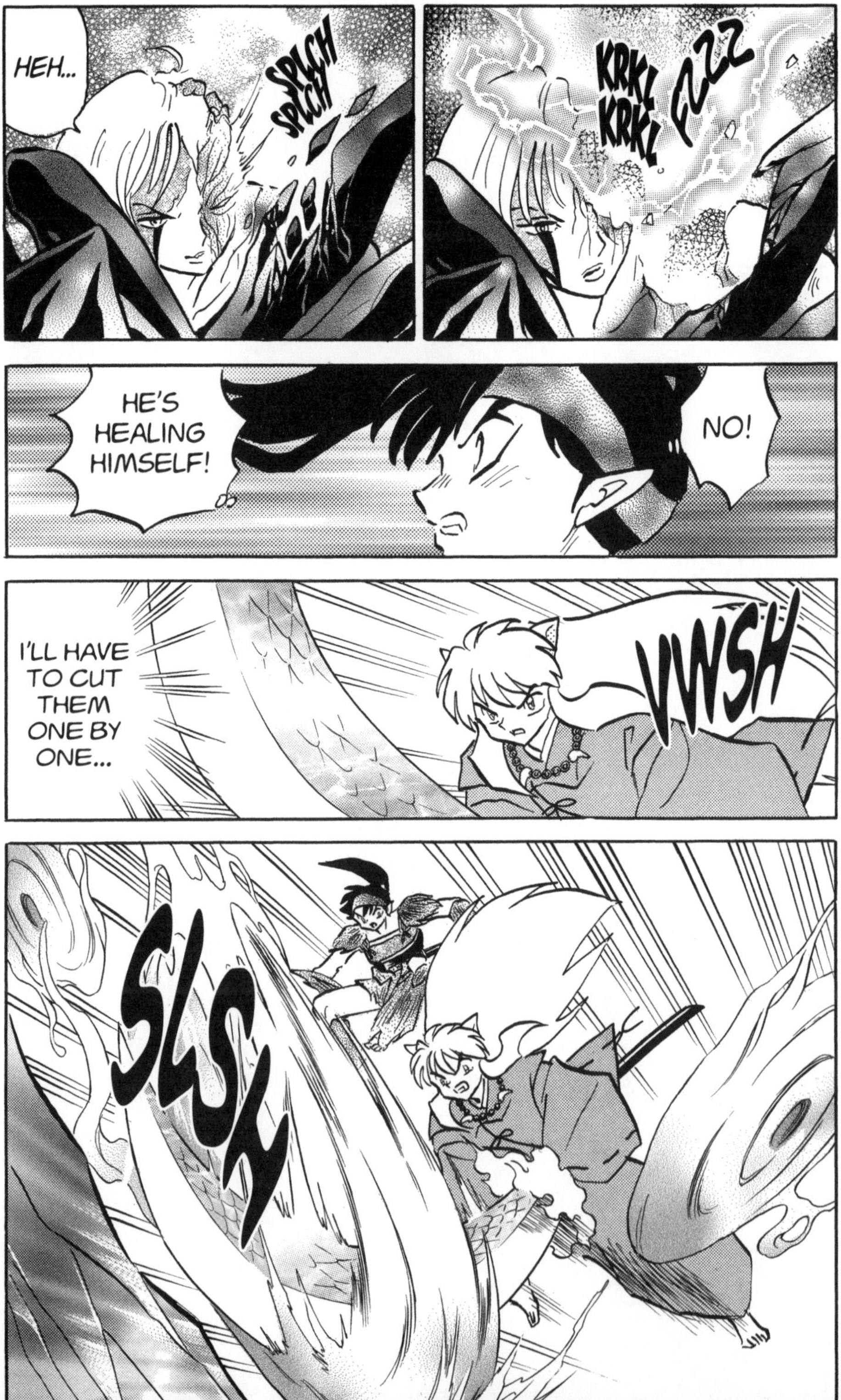
KRKL
KRKL
FZZZ
HEH...
SPLCH
SPLCH
NO!
HE'S HEALING HIMSELF!
VWSH
I'LL HAVE TO CUT THEM ONE BY ONE...
SLSH

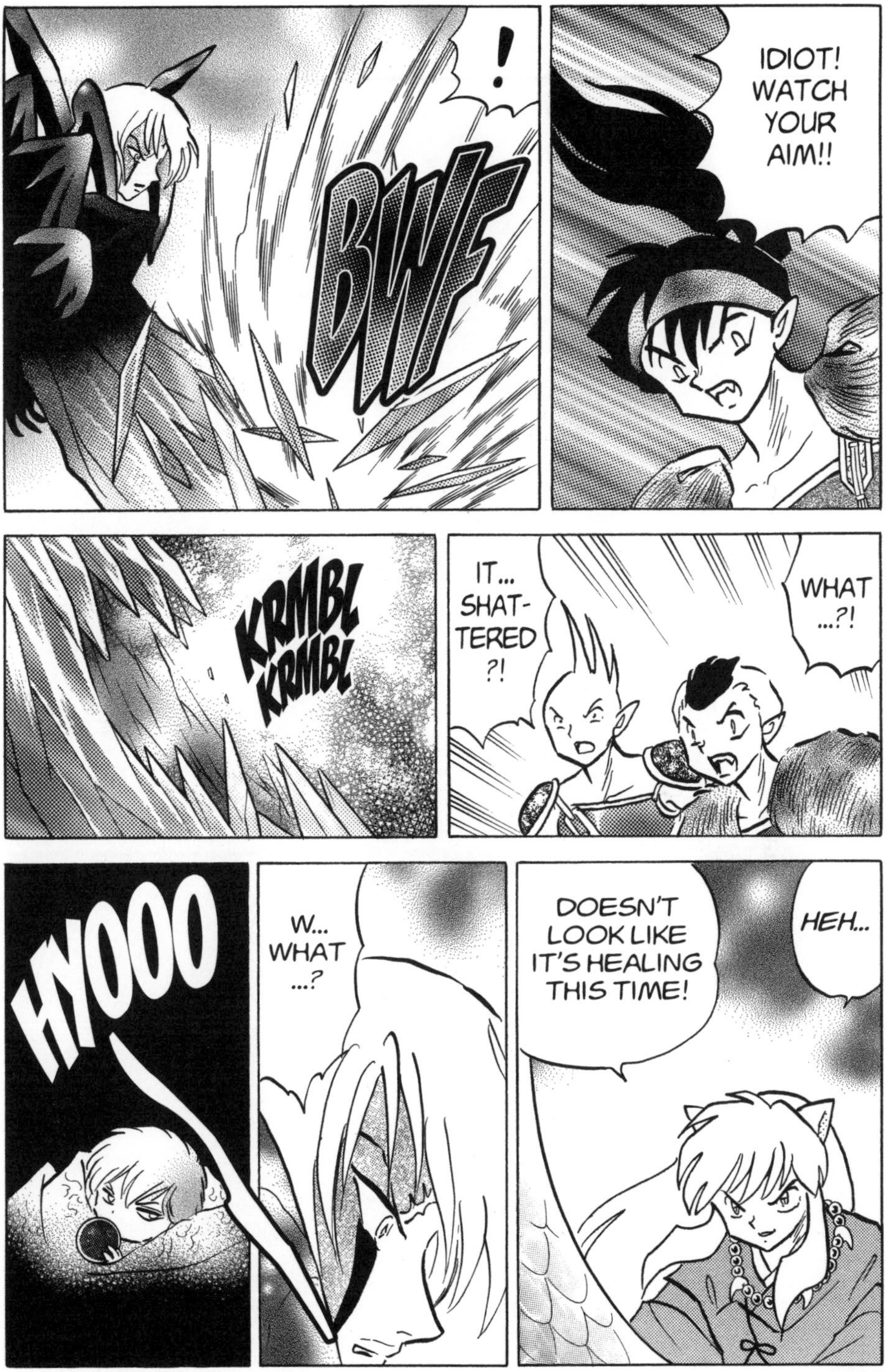
IDIOT! WATCH YOUR AIM!!
!
BWF
WHAT ...?!
IT... SHAT-TERED ?!
KRMBL KRMBL
HEH...
DOESN'T LOOK LIKE IT'S HEALING THIS TIME!
W... WHAT ...?
HYOOO

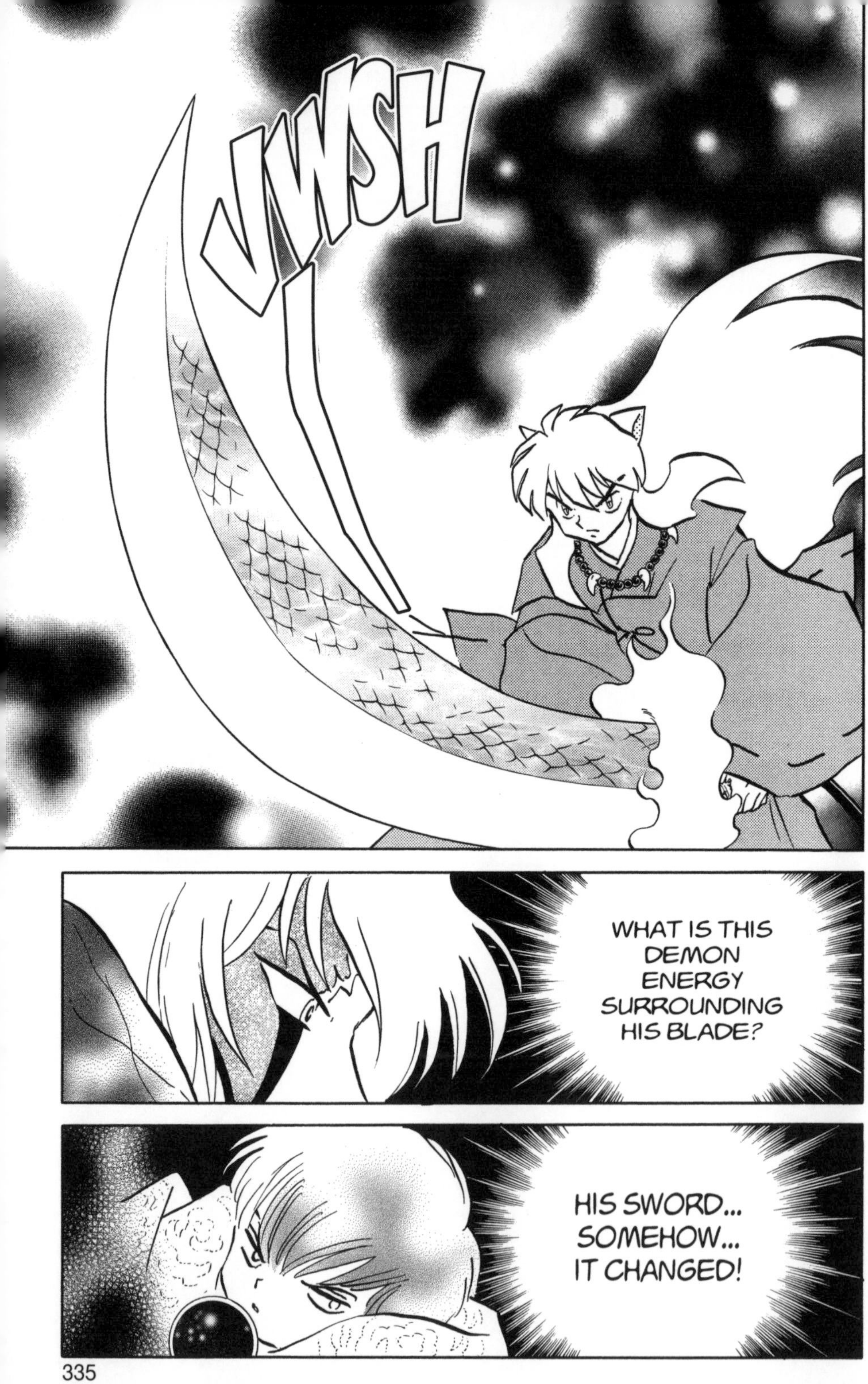
VWSH
WHAT IS THIS DEMON ENERGY SURROUNDING HIS BLADE?
HIS SWORD... SOMEHOW... IT CHANGED!

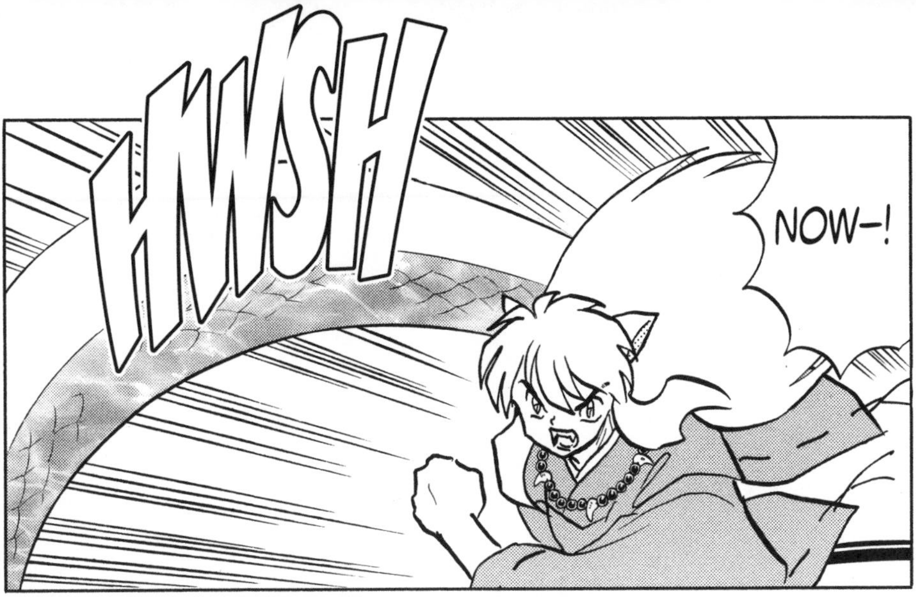
HWSH
NOW-!

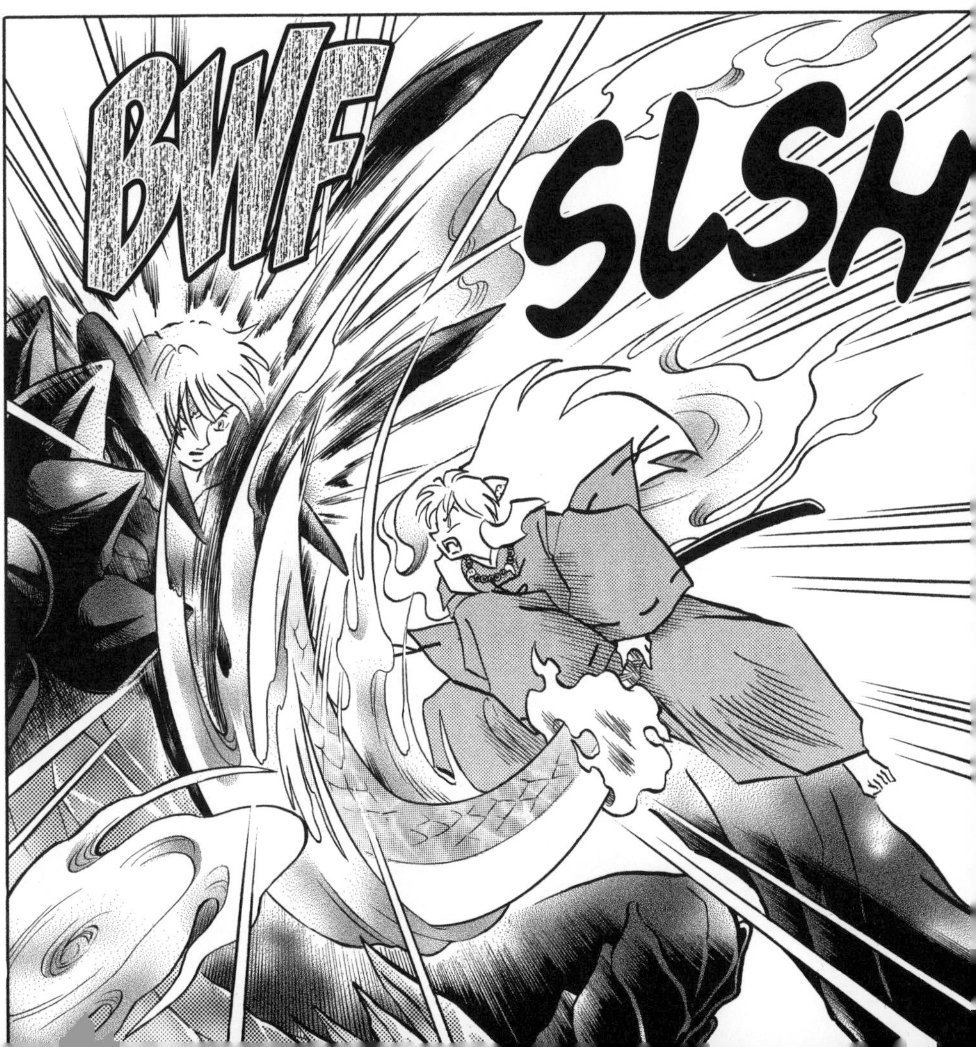
SLSH
BWF

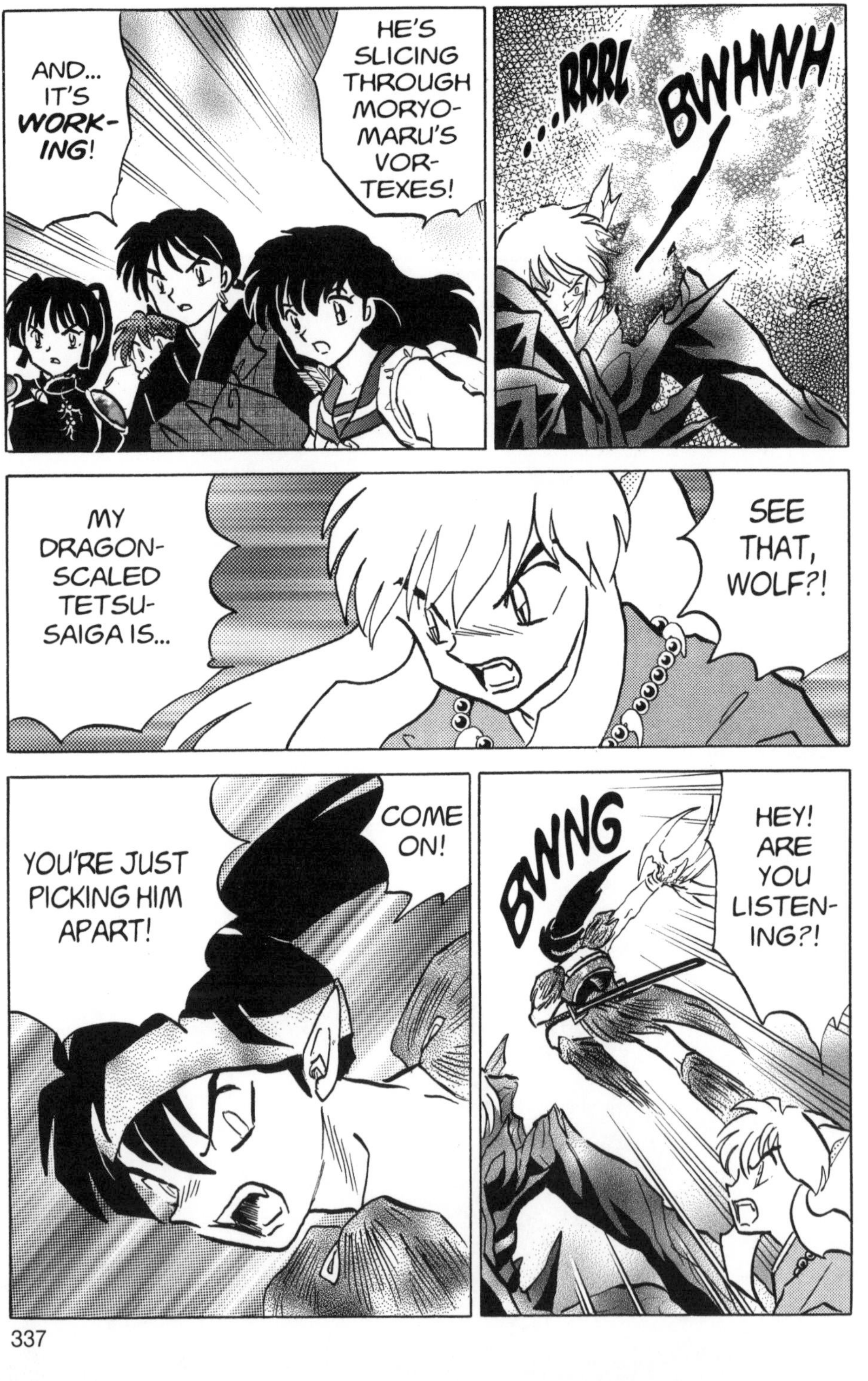
...RRRL
BWHNH
HE'S SLICING THROUGH MORYO-MARU'S VOR-TEXES!
AND... IT'S WORK-ING!
SEE THAT, WOLF?!
MY DRAGON-SCALED TETSU-SAIGA IS...
HEY! ARE YOU LISTEN-ING?!
BWNG
COME ON!
YOU'RE JUST PICKING HIM APART!

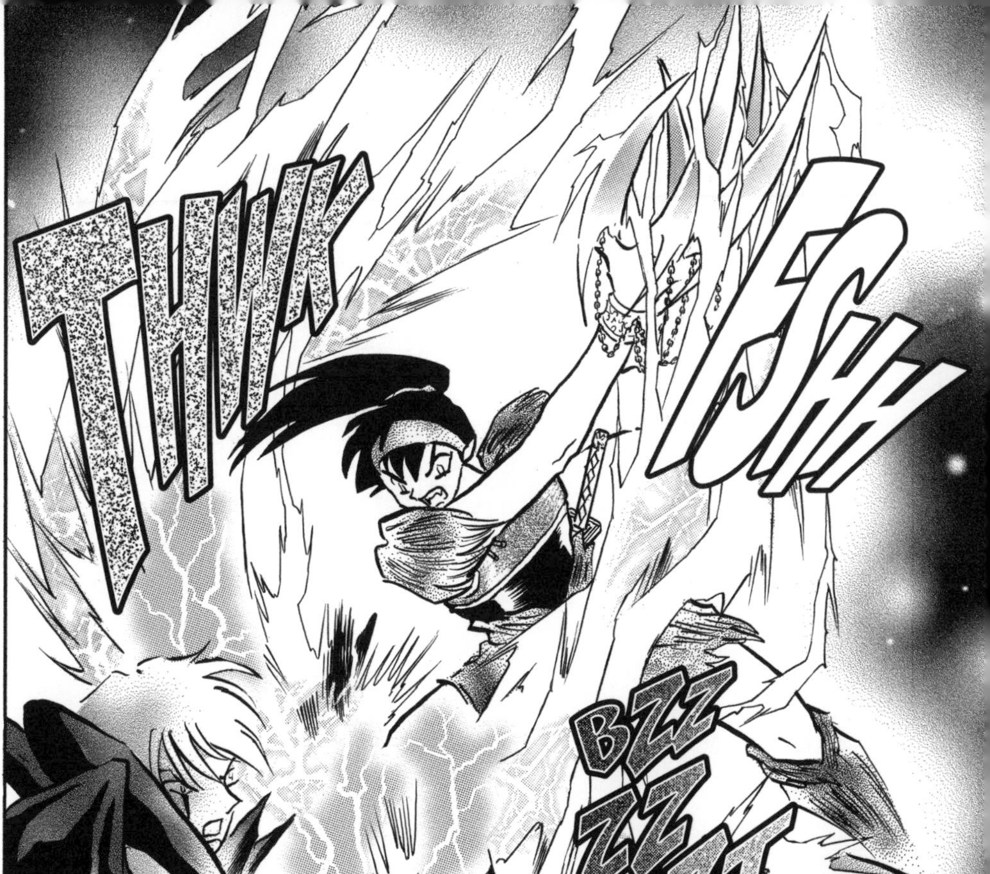
FSHH
THWK
BZZZZZZT
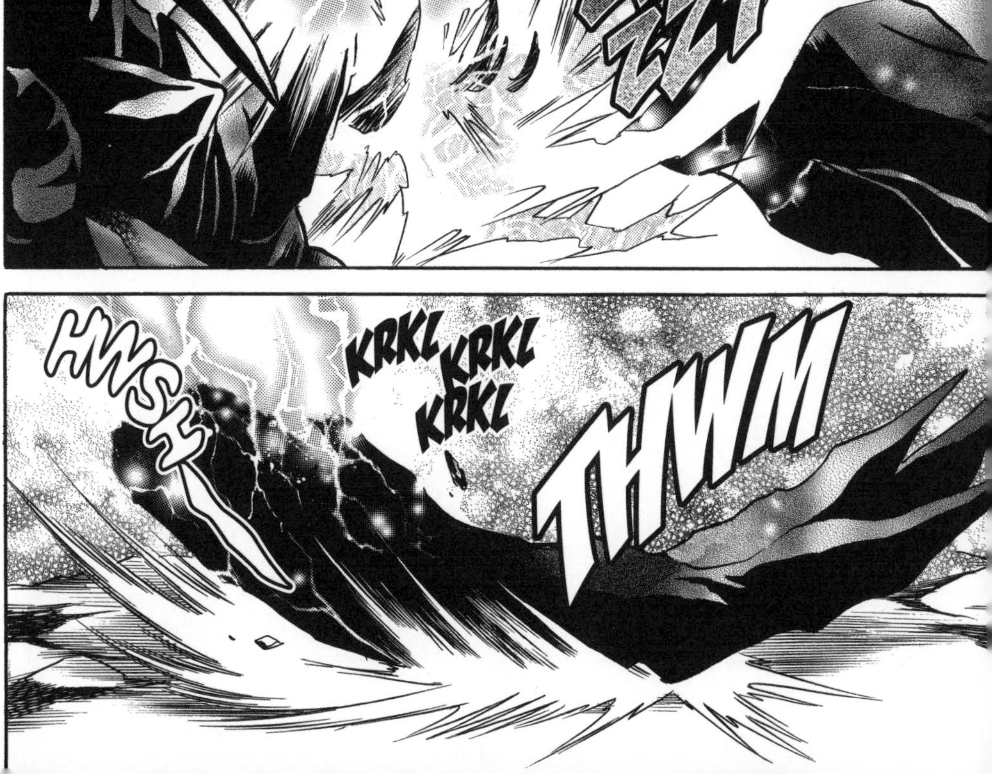
THWM
KRKL KRKL KRKL
HWSH

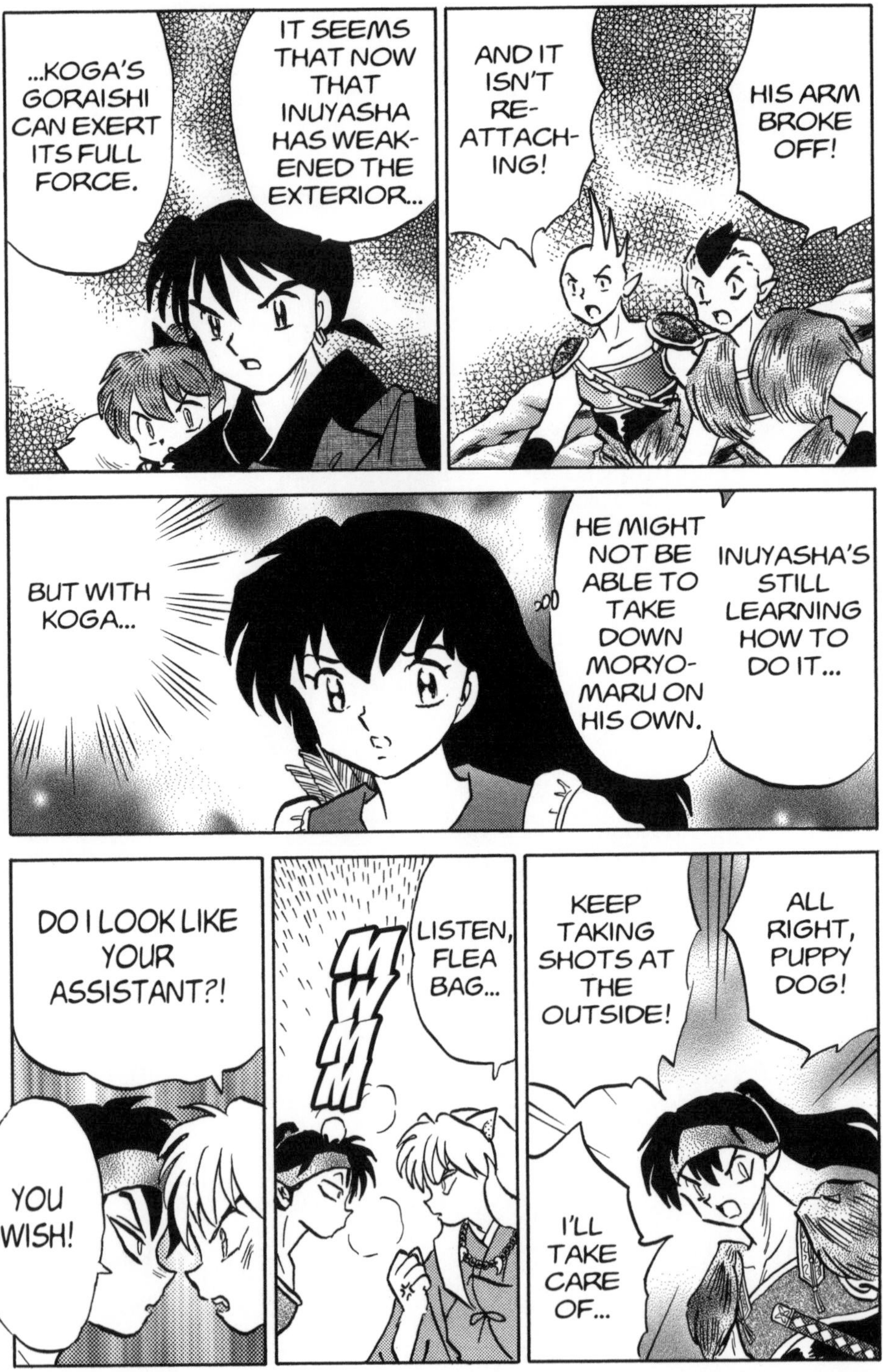
HIS ARM BROKE OFF!
AND IT ISN'T RE-ATTACHING!
IT SEEMS THAT NOW THAT INUYASHA HAS WEAKENED THE EXTERIOR...
...KOGA'S GORAISHI CAN EXERT ITS FULL FORCE.
INUYASHA'S STILL LEARNING HOW TO DO IT...
HE MIGHT NOT BE ABLE TO TAKE DOWN MORYOMARU ON HIS OWN.
BUT WITH KOGA...
ALL RIGHT, PUPPY DOG!
KEEP TAKING SHOTS AT THE OUTSIDE!
I'LL TAKE CARE OF...
LISTEN, FLEA BAG...
DO I LOOK LIKE YOUR ASSISTANT?!
YOU WISH!

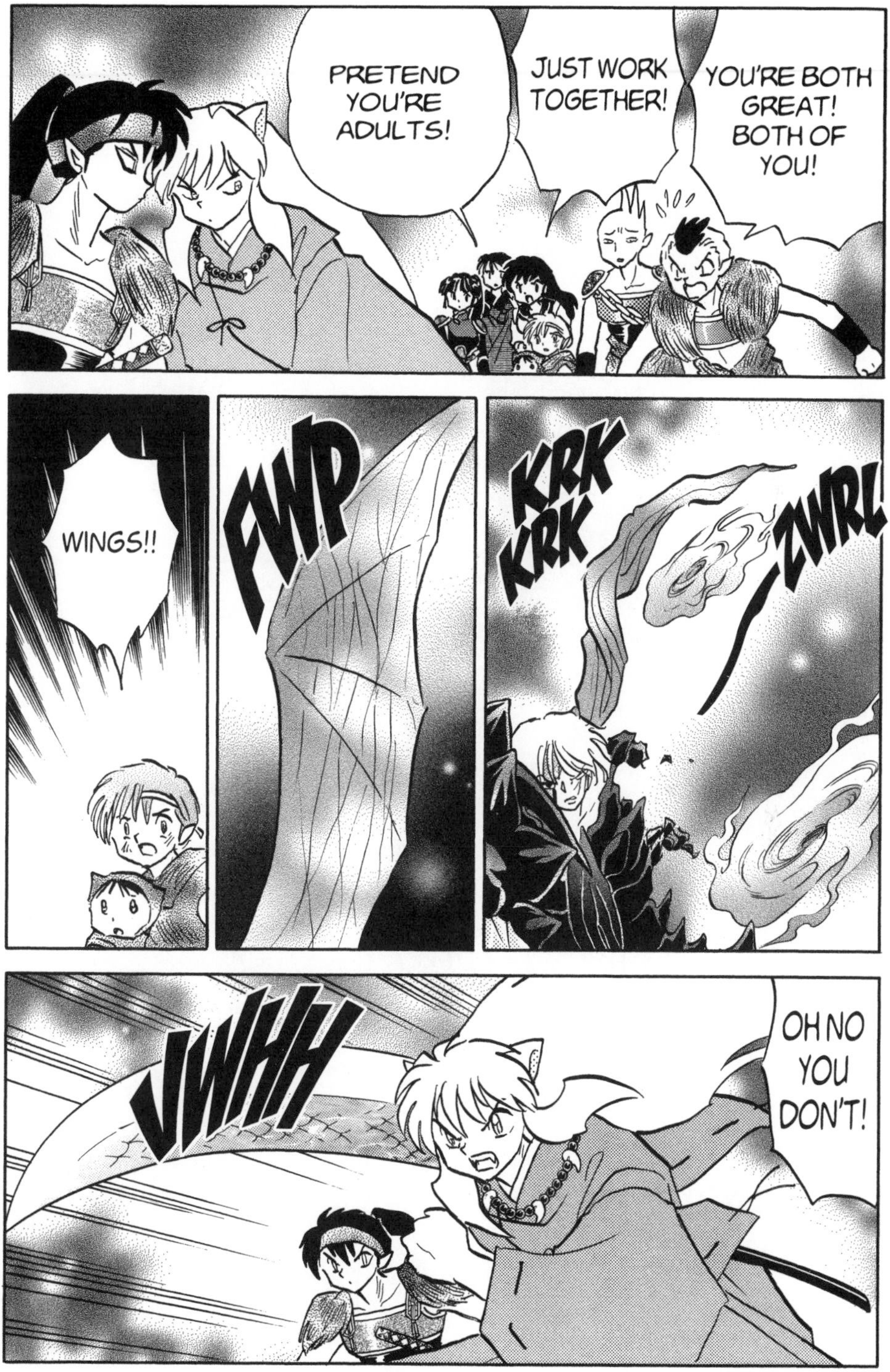
YOU'RE BOTH GREAT! BOTH OF YOU!
JUST WORK TOGETHER!
PRETEND YOU'RE ADULTS!
KRK KRK
ZWRL
FWP
WINGS!!
OH NO YOU DON'T!
JWHH

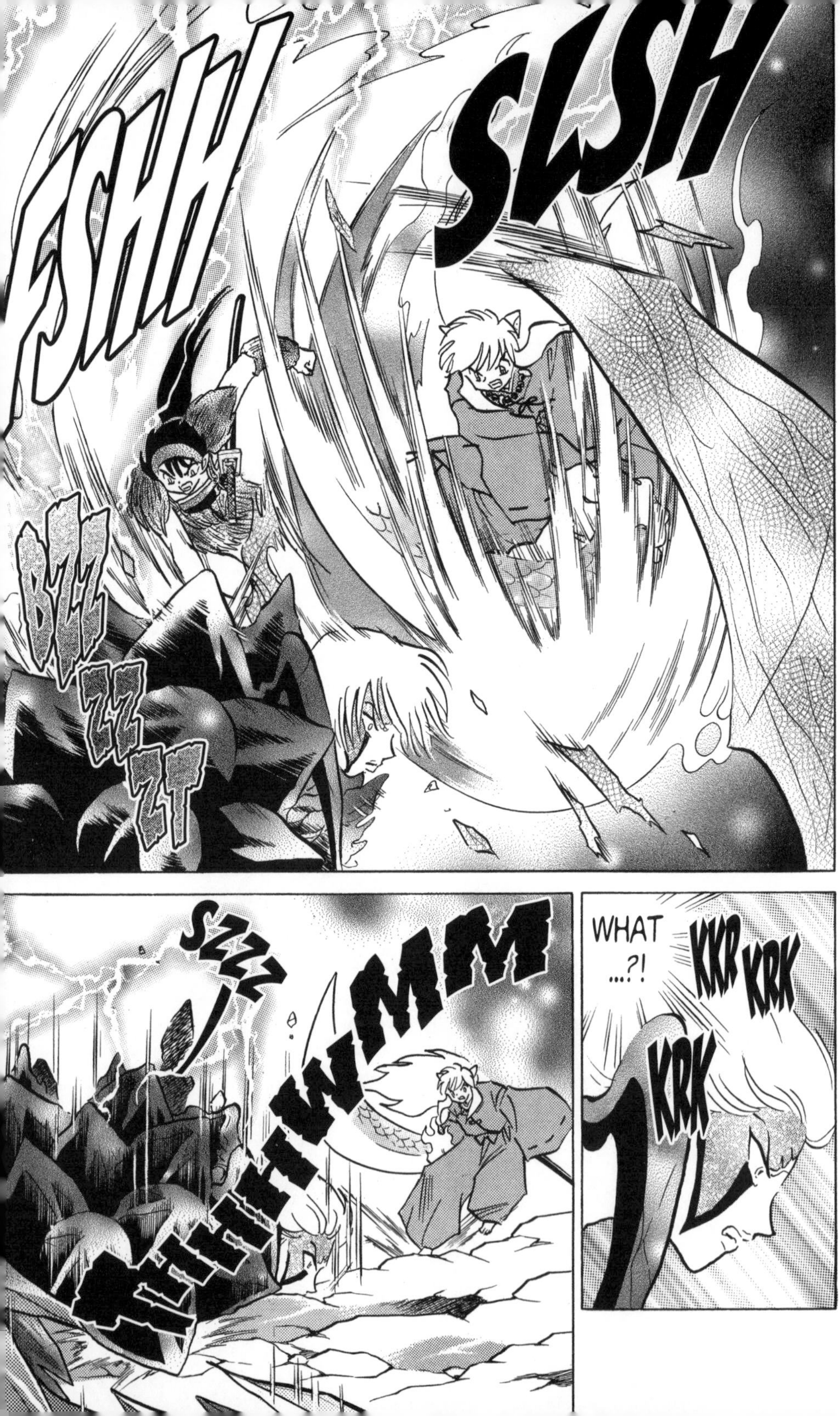
SLSH
FSHH
BZZZZZT
WHAT ...?!
KKR KRK
KRK
SZZZ

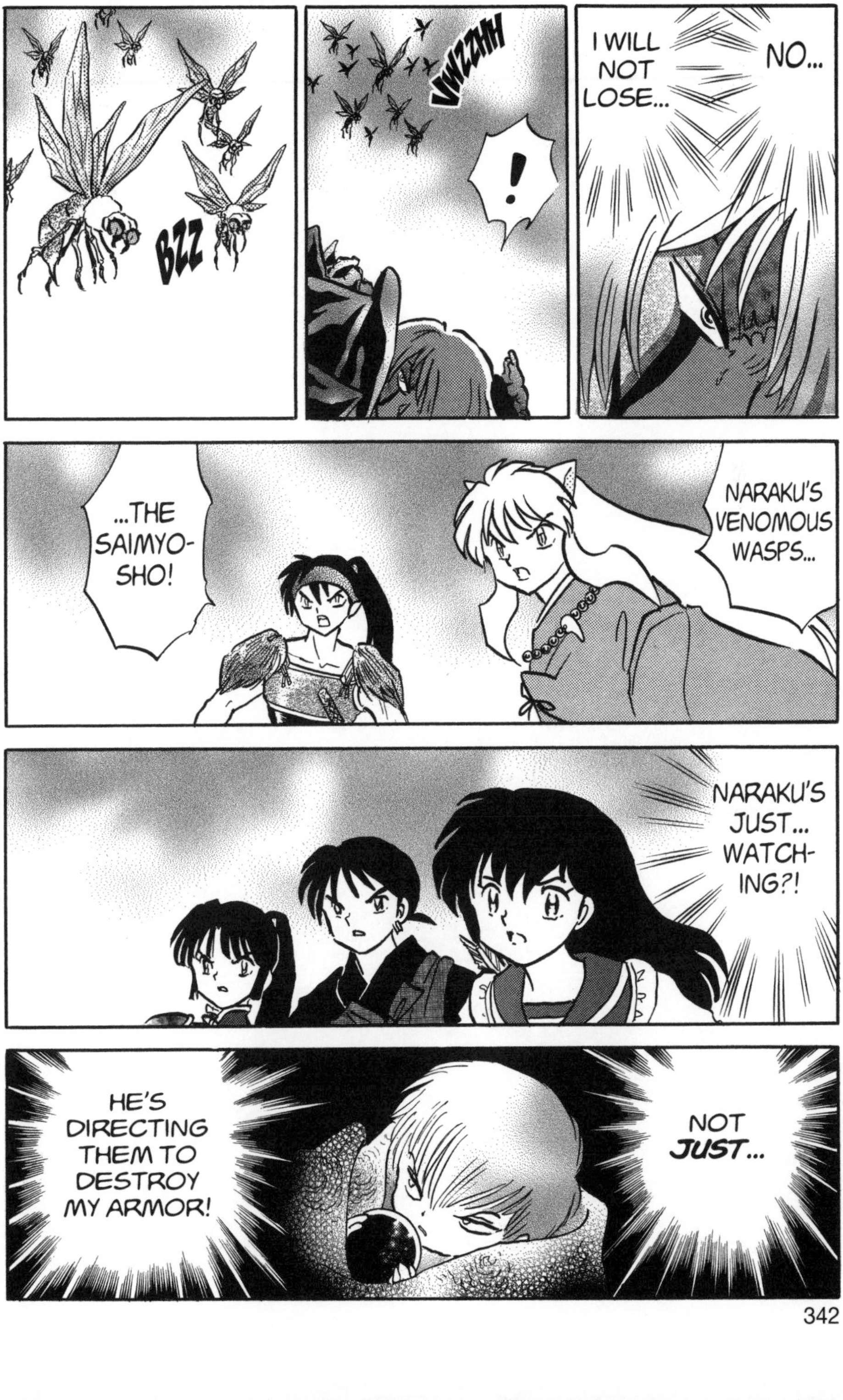
NO...
I WILL NOT LOSE...
VWZZHH
!
BZZ
NARAKU'S VENOMOUS WASPS...
...THE SAIMYO-SHO!
NARAKU'S JUST... WATCHING?!
NOT JUST...
HE'S DIRECTING THEM TO DESTROY MY ARMOR!

SCROLL NINE
THE INVISIBLE VORTEX

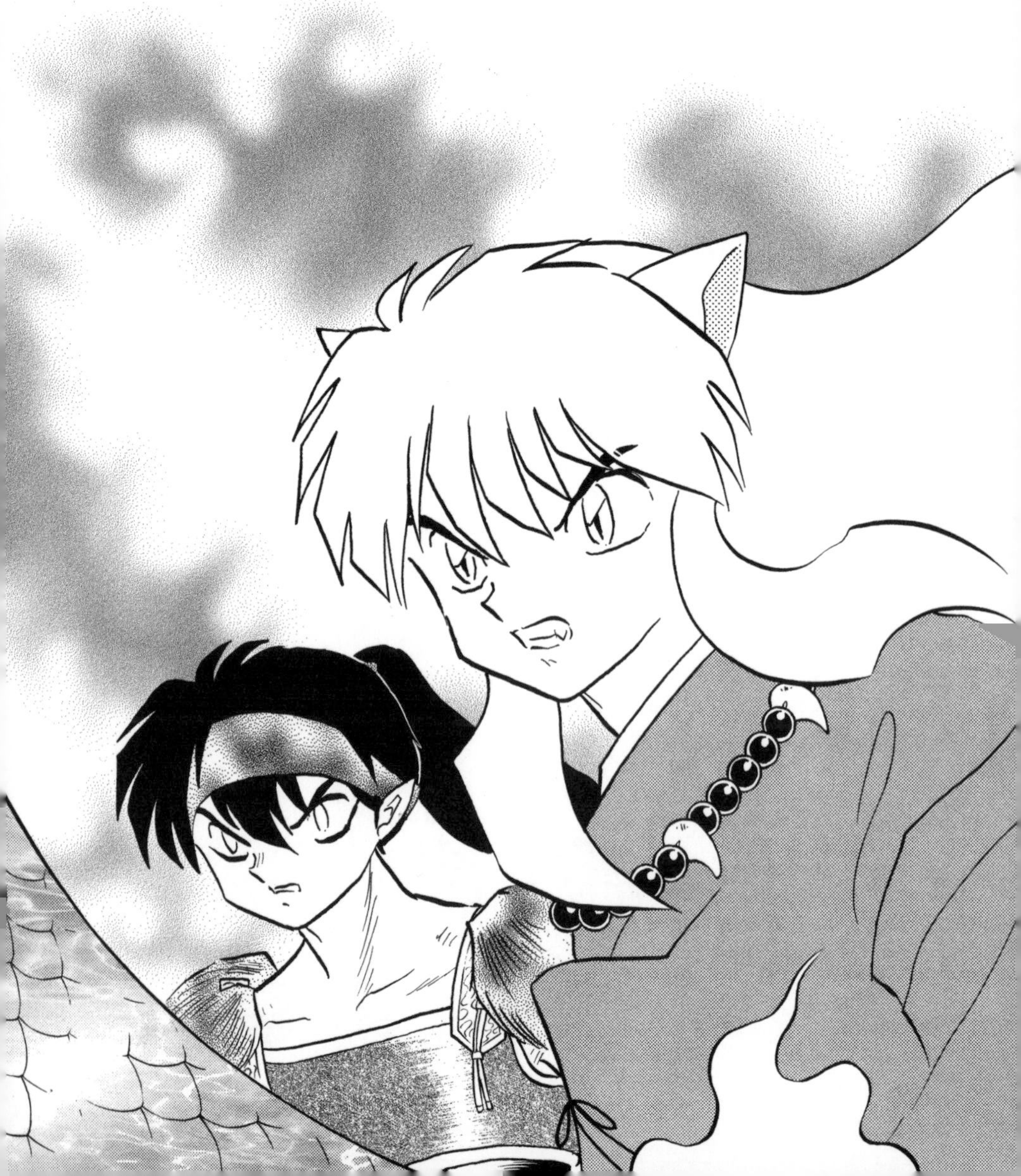

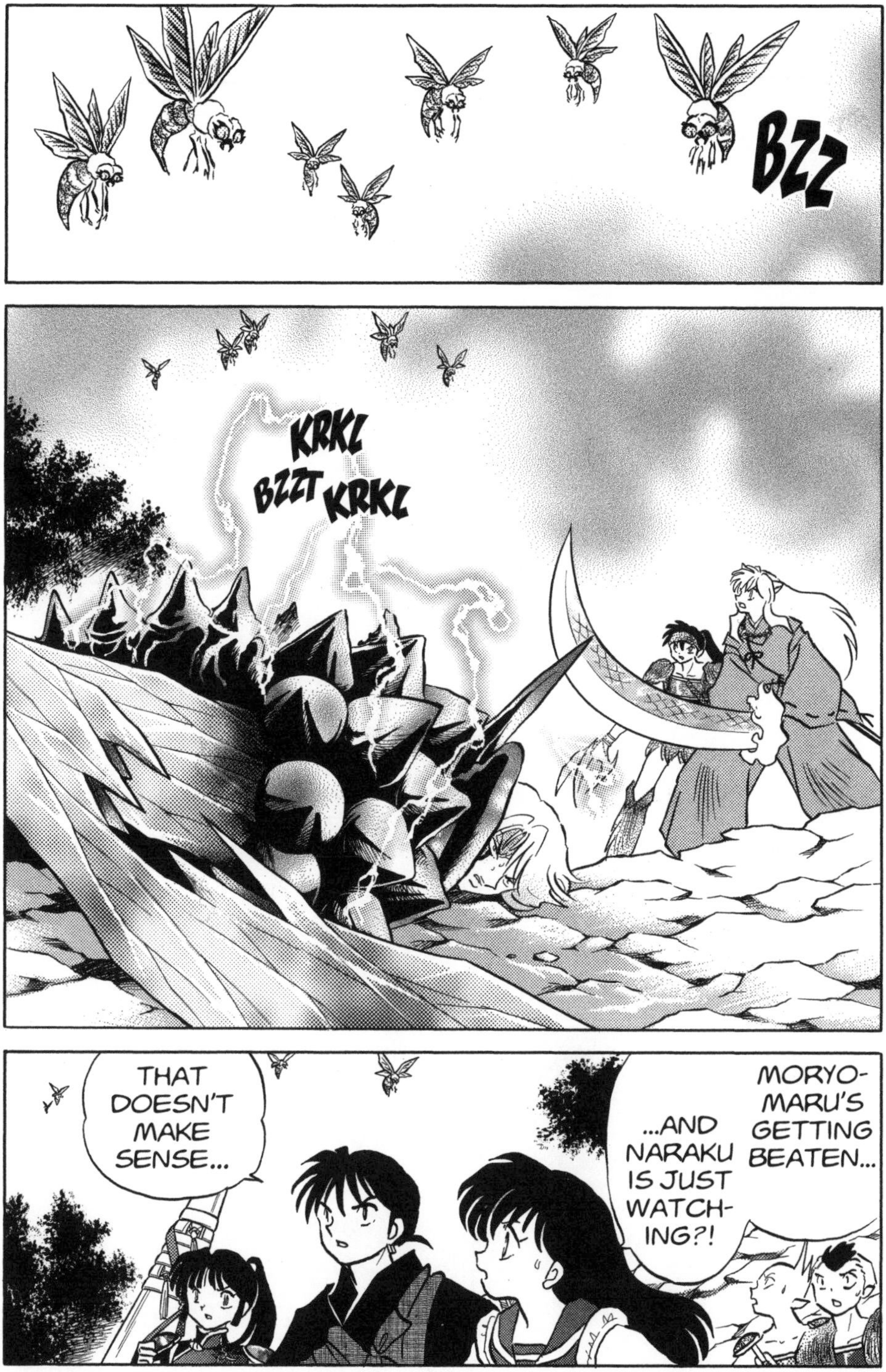
BZZ
KRKL
BZZT
KRKL
MORYO-MARU'S GETTING BEATEN...
...AND NARAKU IS JUST WATCH-ING?!
THAT DOESN'T MAKE SENSE...

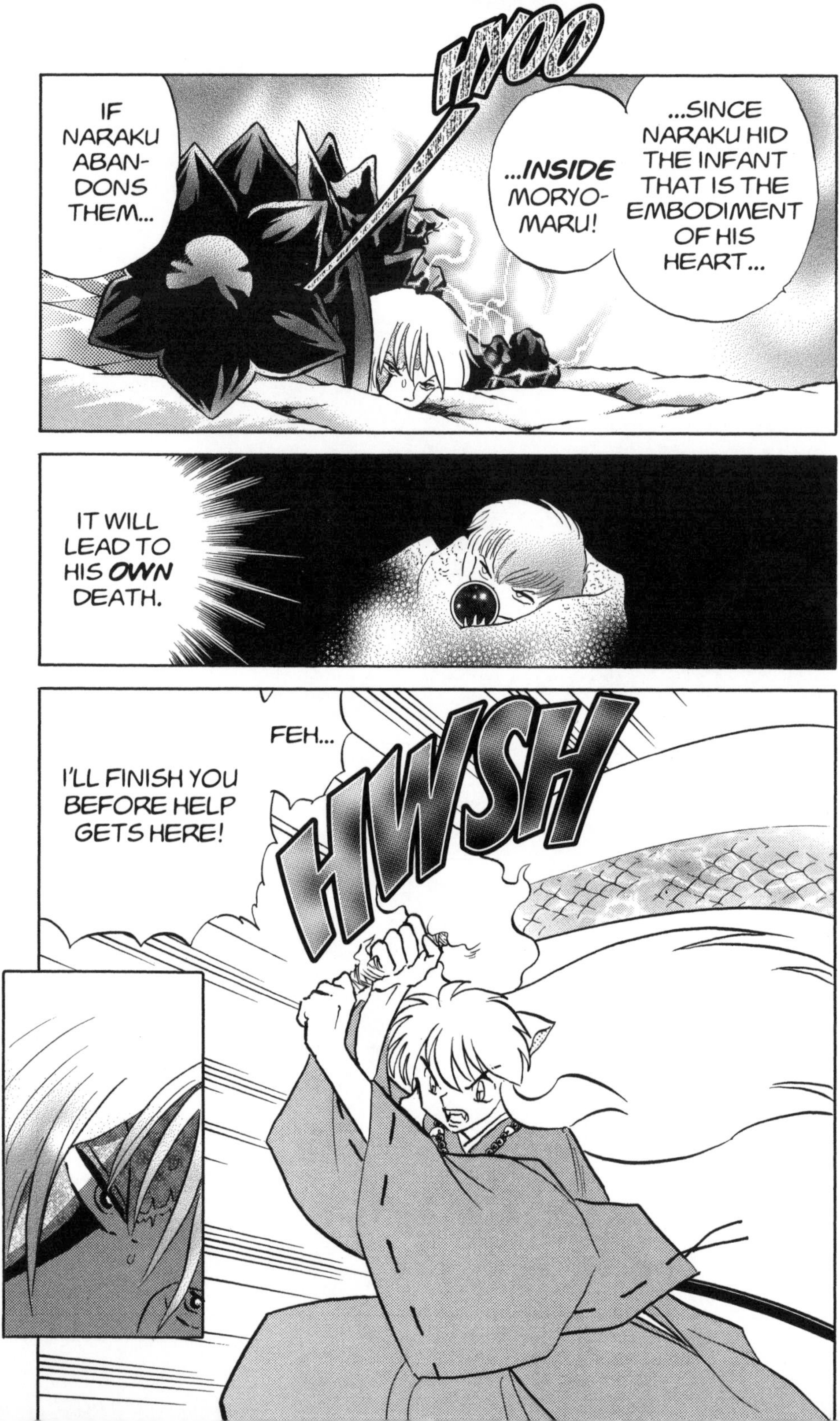
HYOO
...SINCE NARAKU HID THE INFANT THAT IS THE EMBODIMENT OF HIS HEART...
...INSIDE MORYO-MARU!
IF NARAKU ABAN-DONS THEM...
IT WILL LEAD TO HIS OWN DEATH.
HWSH
FEH...
I'LL FINISH YOU BEFORE HELP GETS HERE!

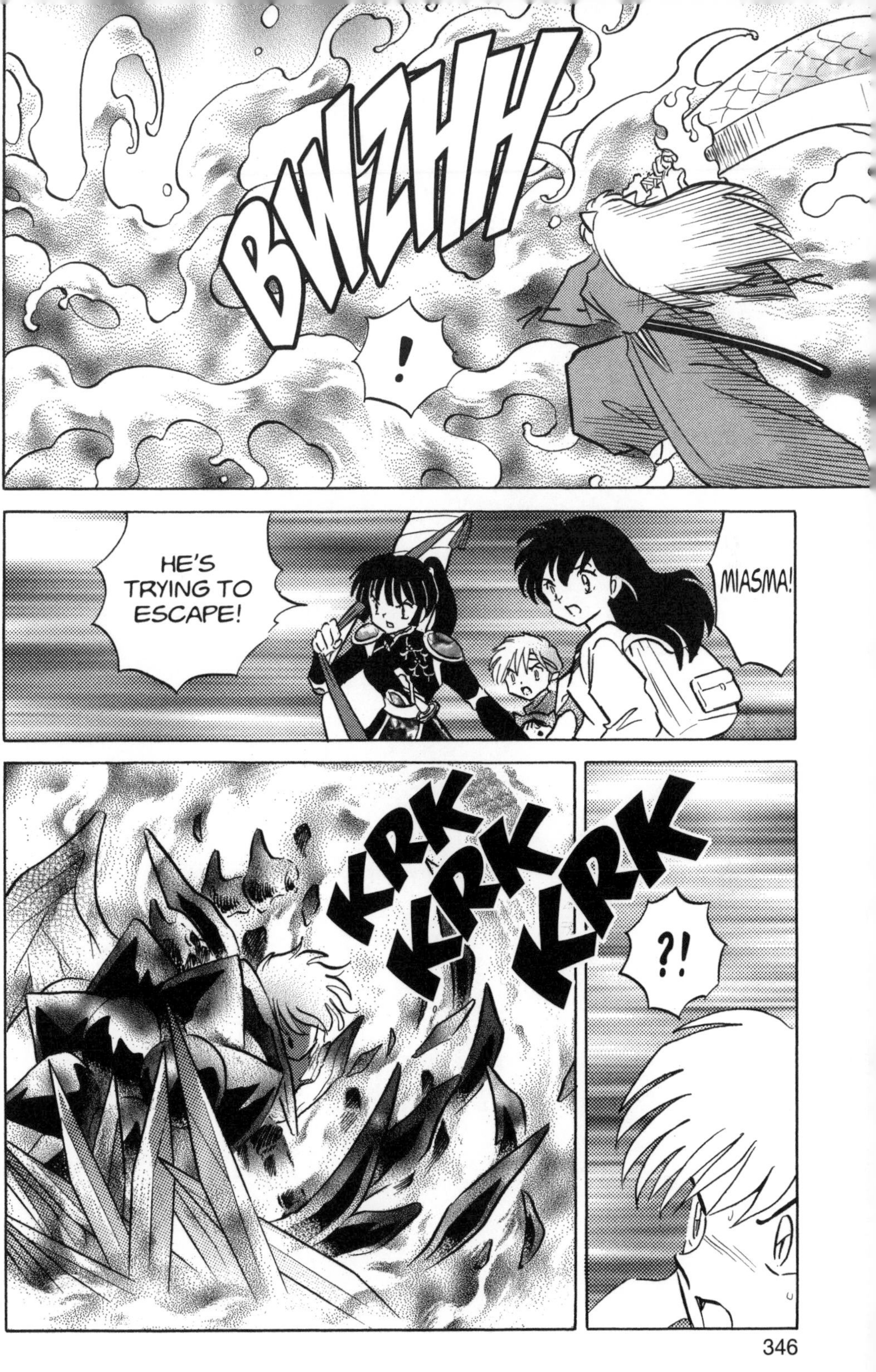
BWZHH
!
MIASMA!
HE'S TRYING TO ESCAPE!
?!
KRK KRK KRK

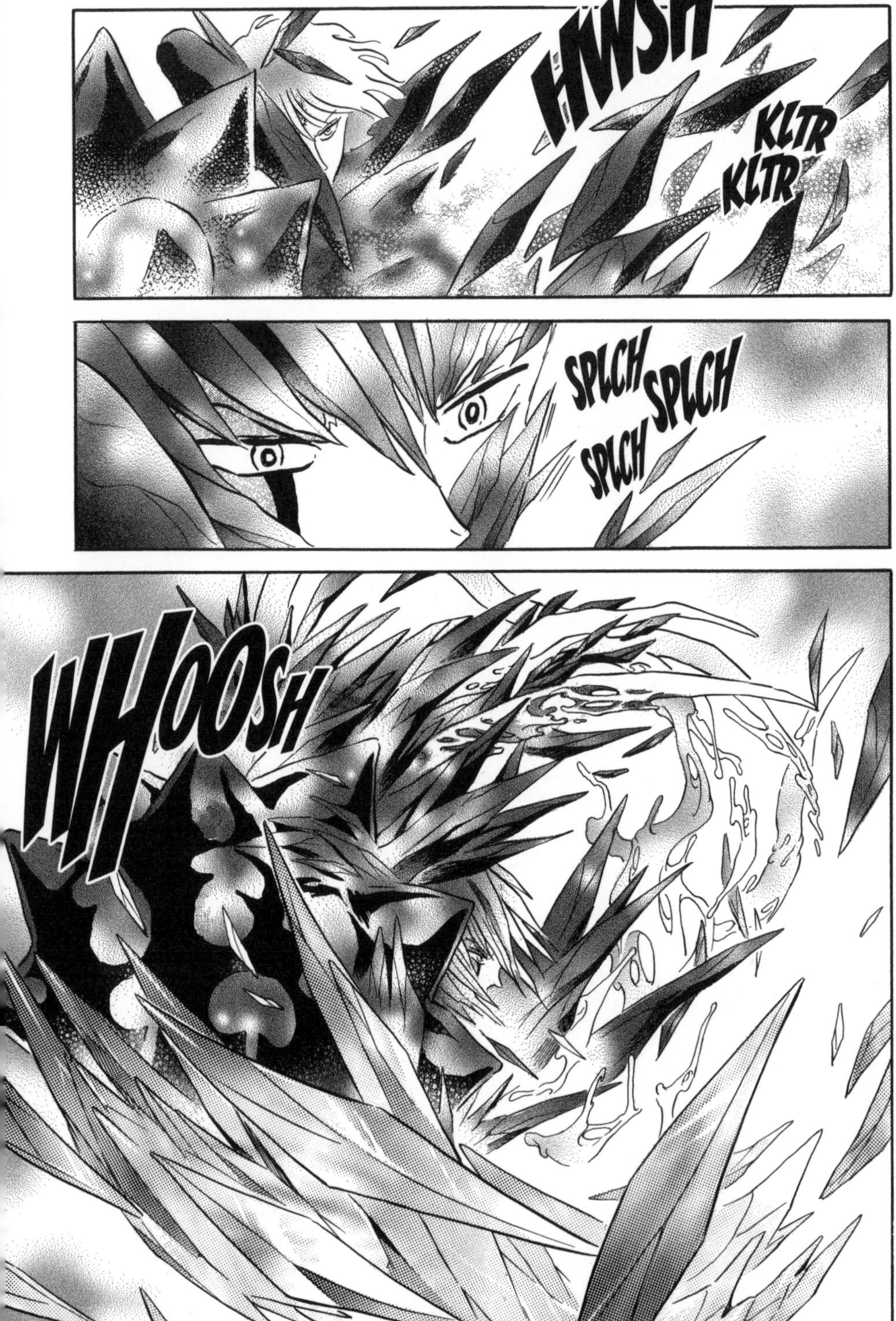
HWSH
KLTR
KLTR
SPLCH
SPLCH
SPLCH
WHOOSH

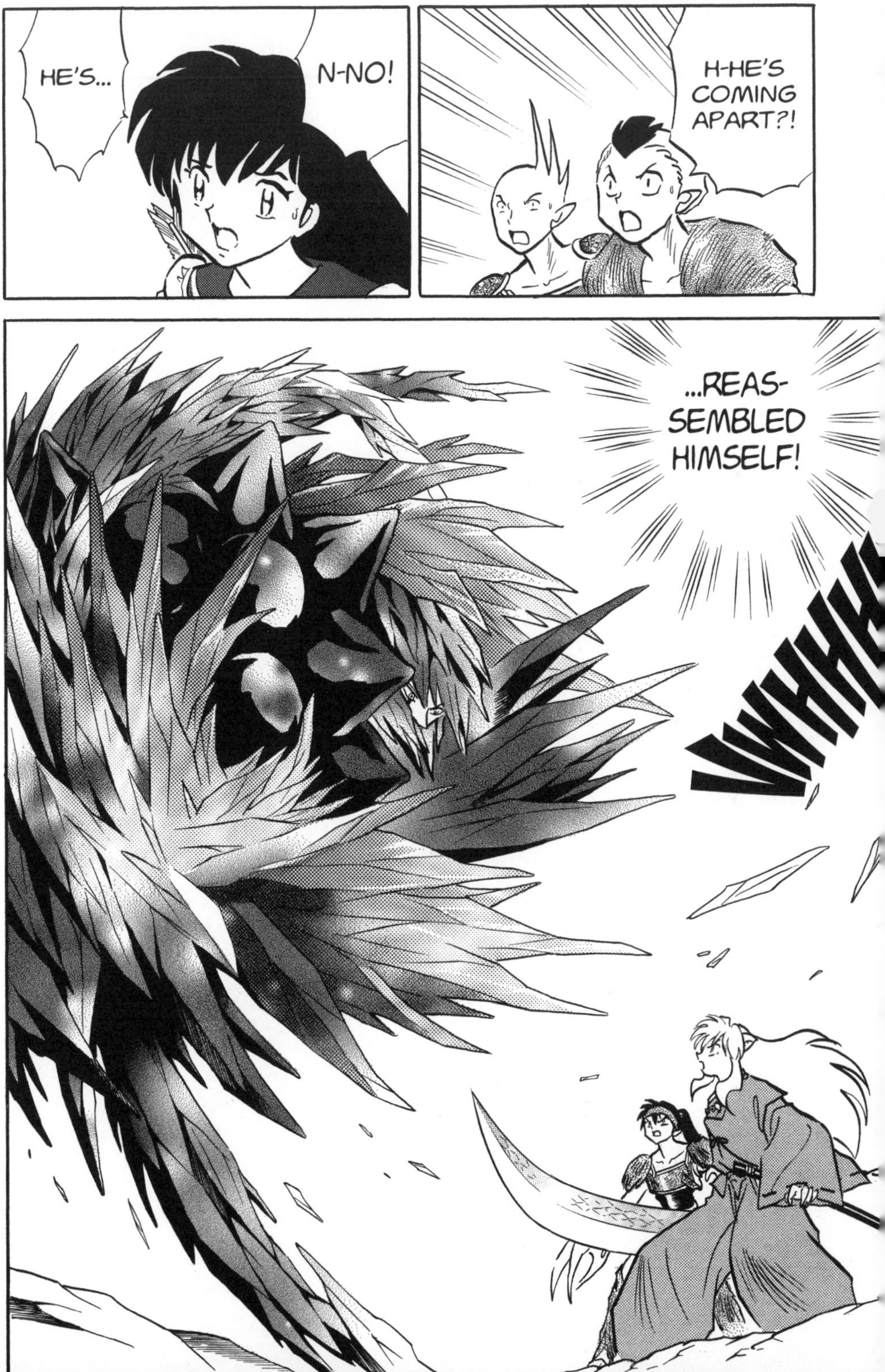
H-HE'S COMING APART?!
N-NO!
HE'S...
...REAS-SEMBLED HIMSELF!
VWHHH

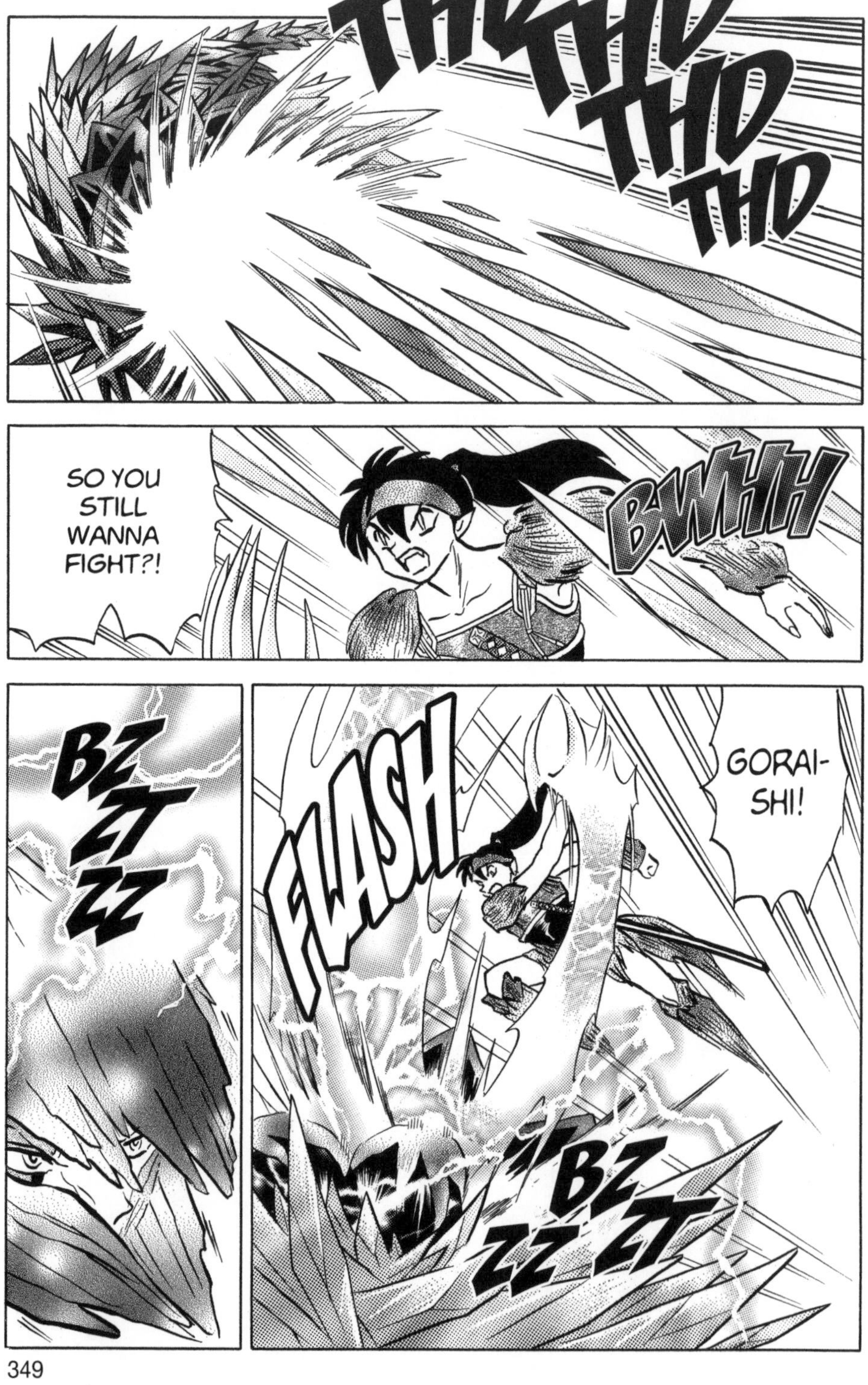
THD THD THD THD THD
BWHH
SO YOU STILL WANNA FIGHT?!
GORAI-SHI!
FLASH
BZZZZT
BZZZZ

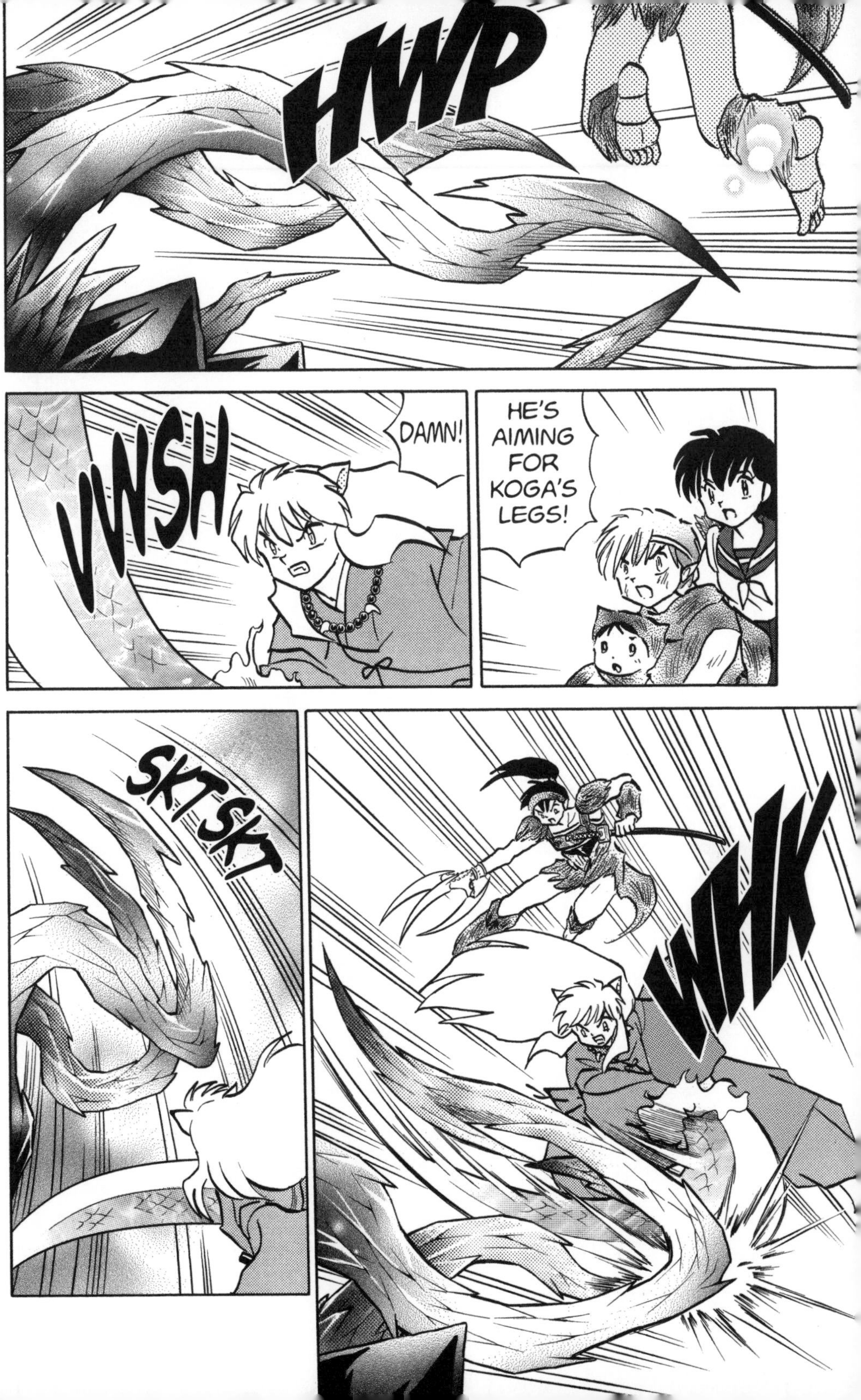
HWP
HE'S AIMING FOR KOGA'S LEGS!
DAMN!
VWSH
WHK
SKT SKT

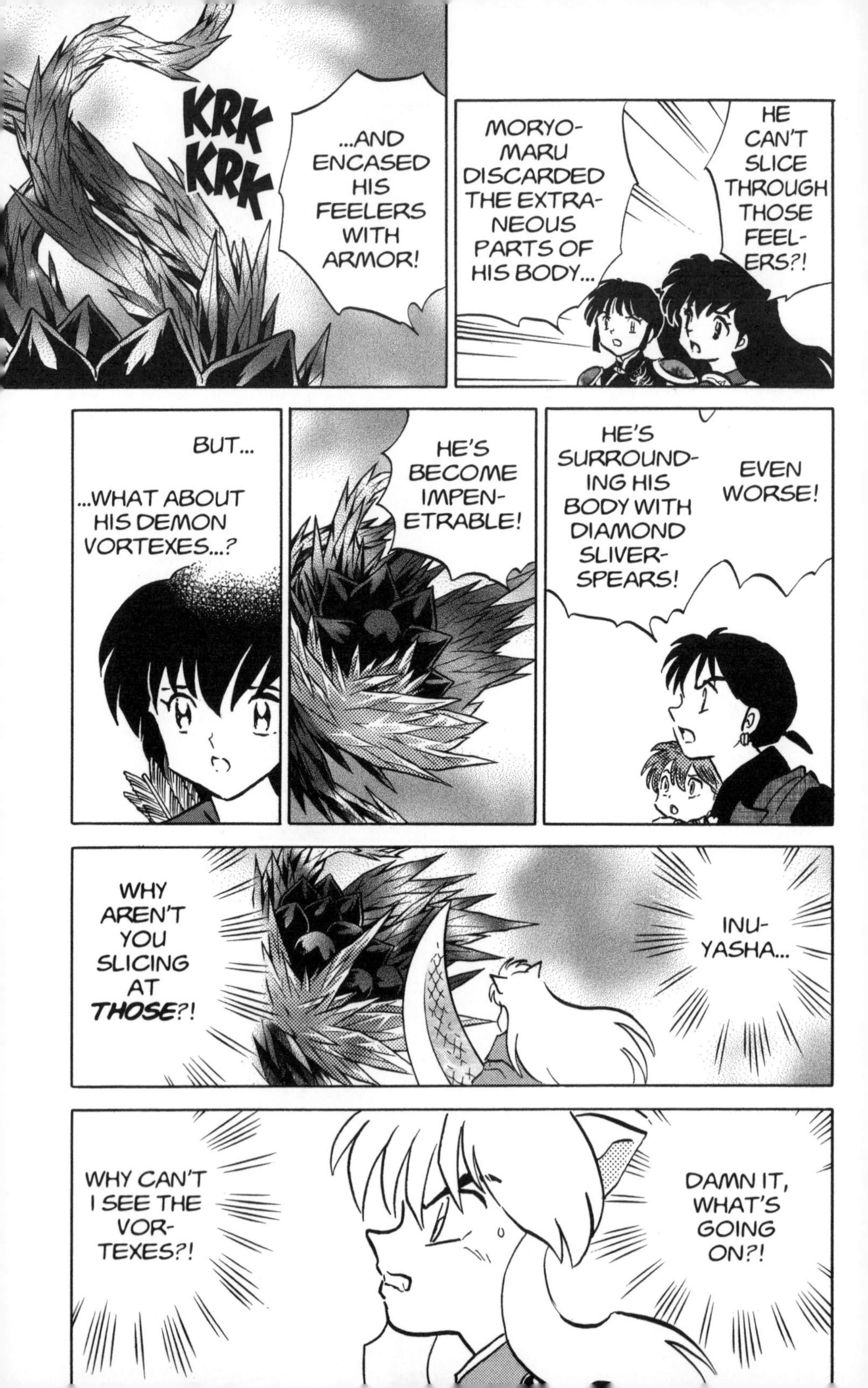
HE CAN'T SLICE THROUGH THOSE FEEL-ERS?!
MORYO-MARU DISCARDED THE EXTRA-NEOUS PARTS OF HIS BODY...
...AND ENCASED HIS FEELERS WITH ARMOR!
KRK KRK
EVEN WORSE!
HE'S SURROUND-ING HIS BODY WITH DIAMOND SLIVER-SPEARS!
HE'S BECOME IMPEN-ETRABLE!
BUT...
...WHAT ABOUT HIS DEMON VORTEXES...?
INU-YASHA...
WHY AREN'T YOU SLICING AT *THOSE*?!
DAMN IT, WHAT'S GOING ON?!
WHY CAN'T I SEE THE VOR-TEXES?!

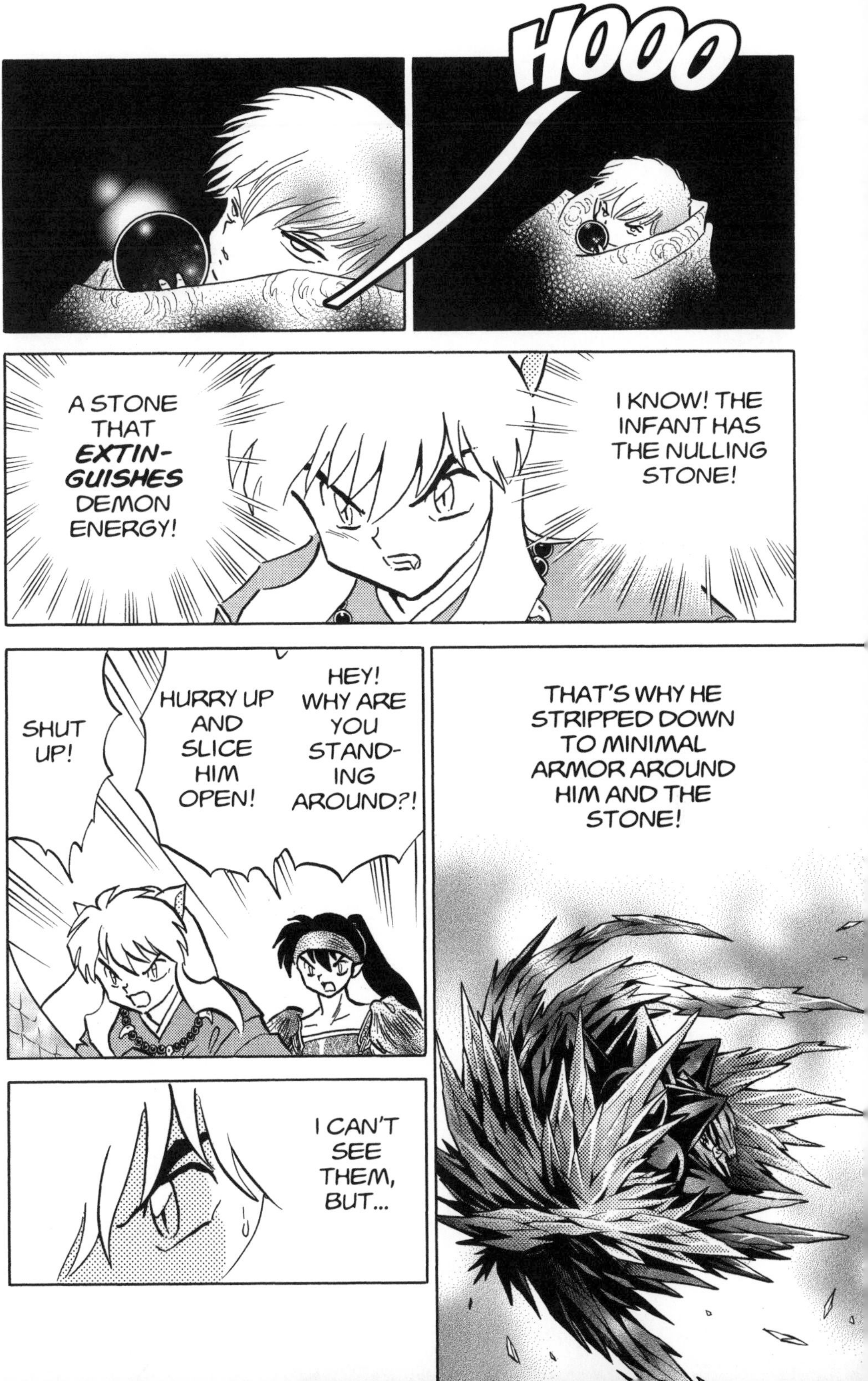
HOOO
I KNOW! THE INFANT HAS THE NULLING STONE!
A STONE THAT EXTIN-GUISHES DEMON ENERGY!
THAT'S WHY HE STRIPPED DOWN TO MINIMAL ARMOR AROUND HIM AND THE STONE!
HEY! WHY ARE YOU STAND-ING AROUND?!
HURRY UP AND SLICE HIM OPEN!
SHUT UP!
I CAN'T SEE THEM, BUT...

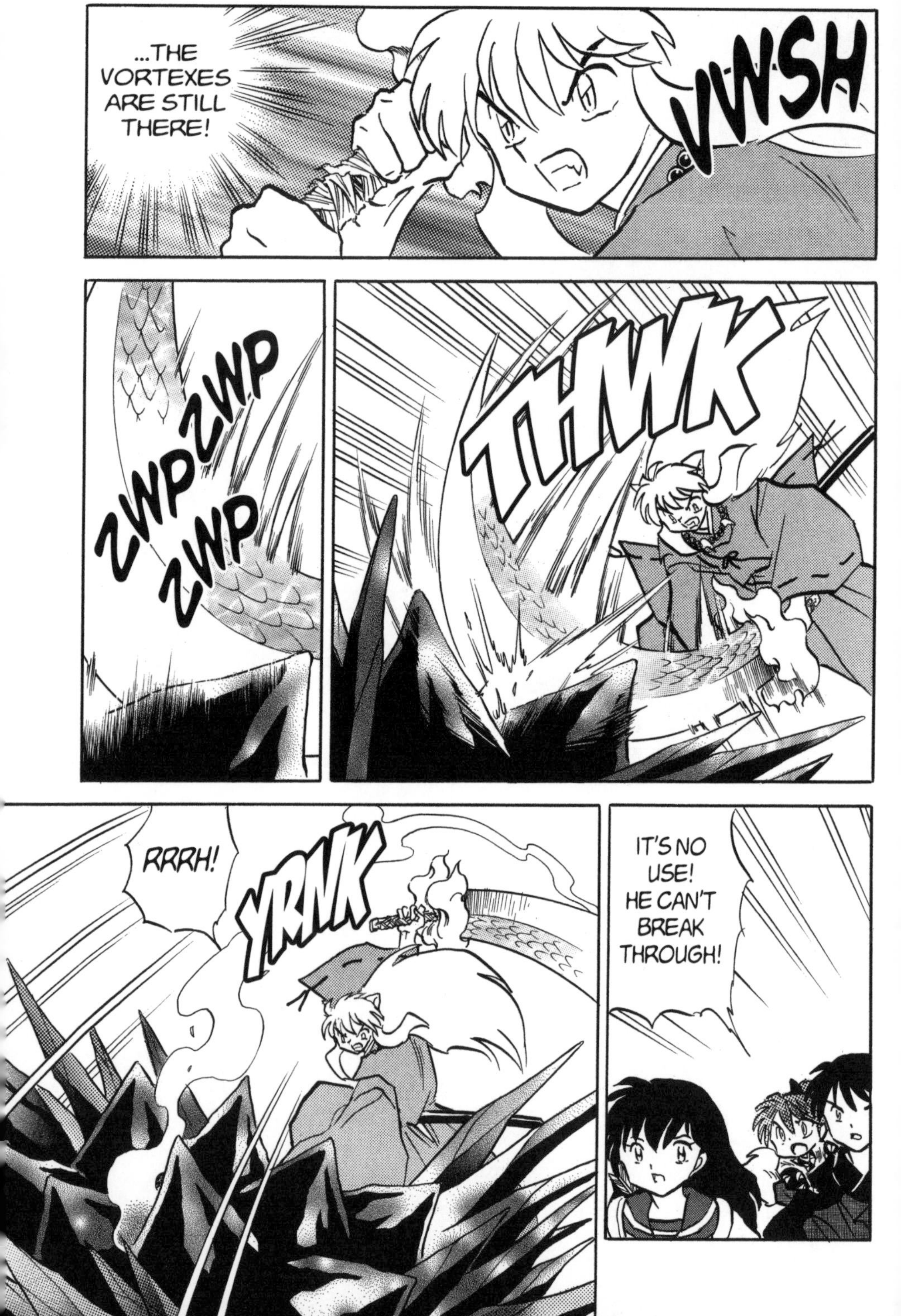
VVNSH
...THE VORTEXES ARE STILL THERE!
THWK
ZWP ZWP ZWP ZWP
IT'S NO USE! HE CAN'T BREAK THROUGH!
YRNK
RRRH!

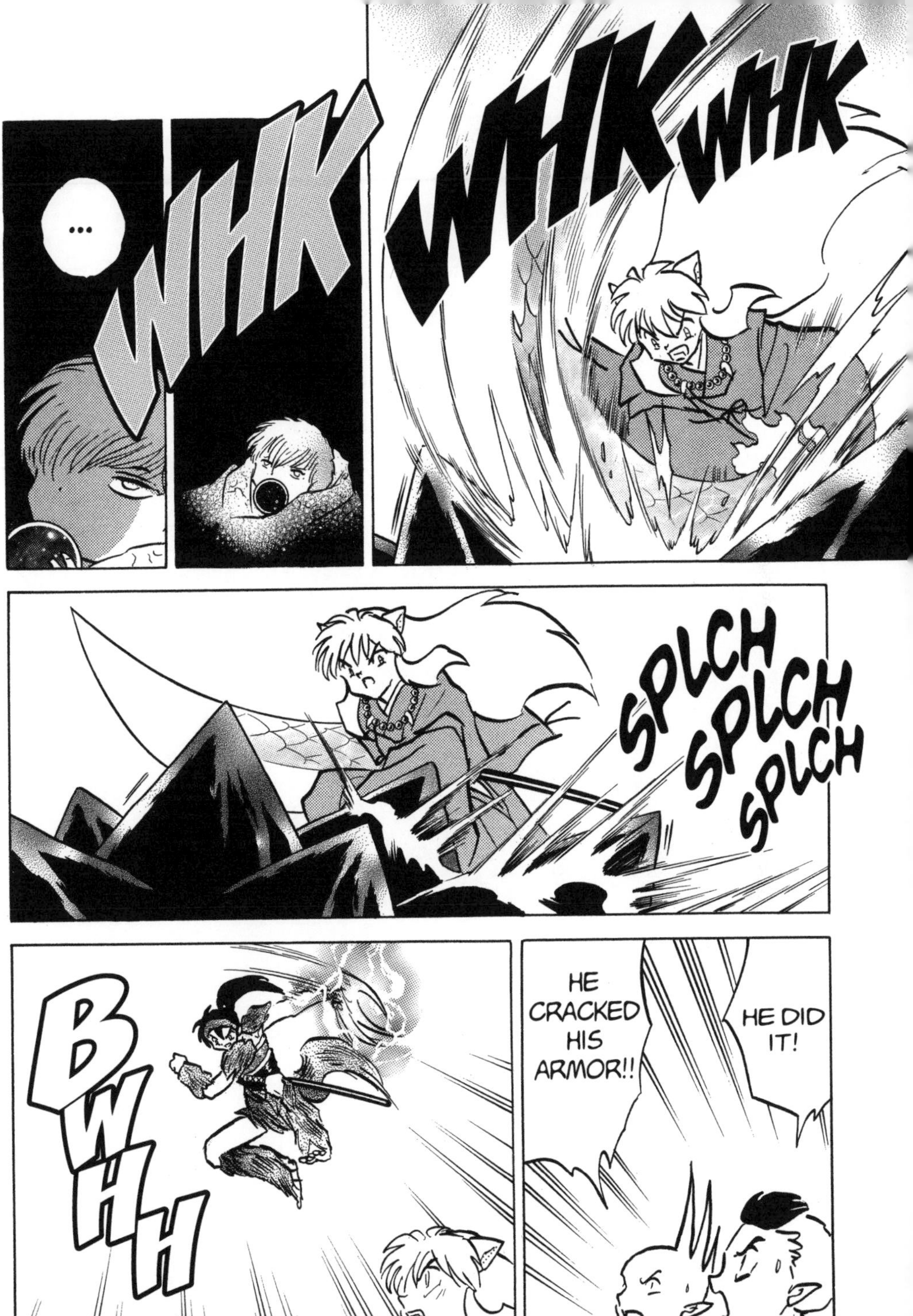
WHK
WHK
WHK
...
SPLCH
SPLCH
SPLCH
HE DID IT!
HE CRACKED HIS ARMOR!!
BWHH

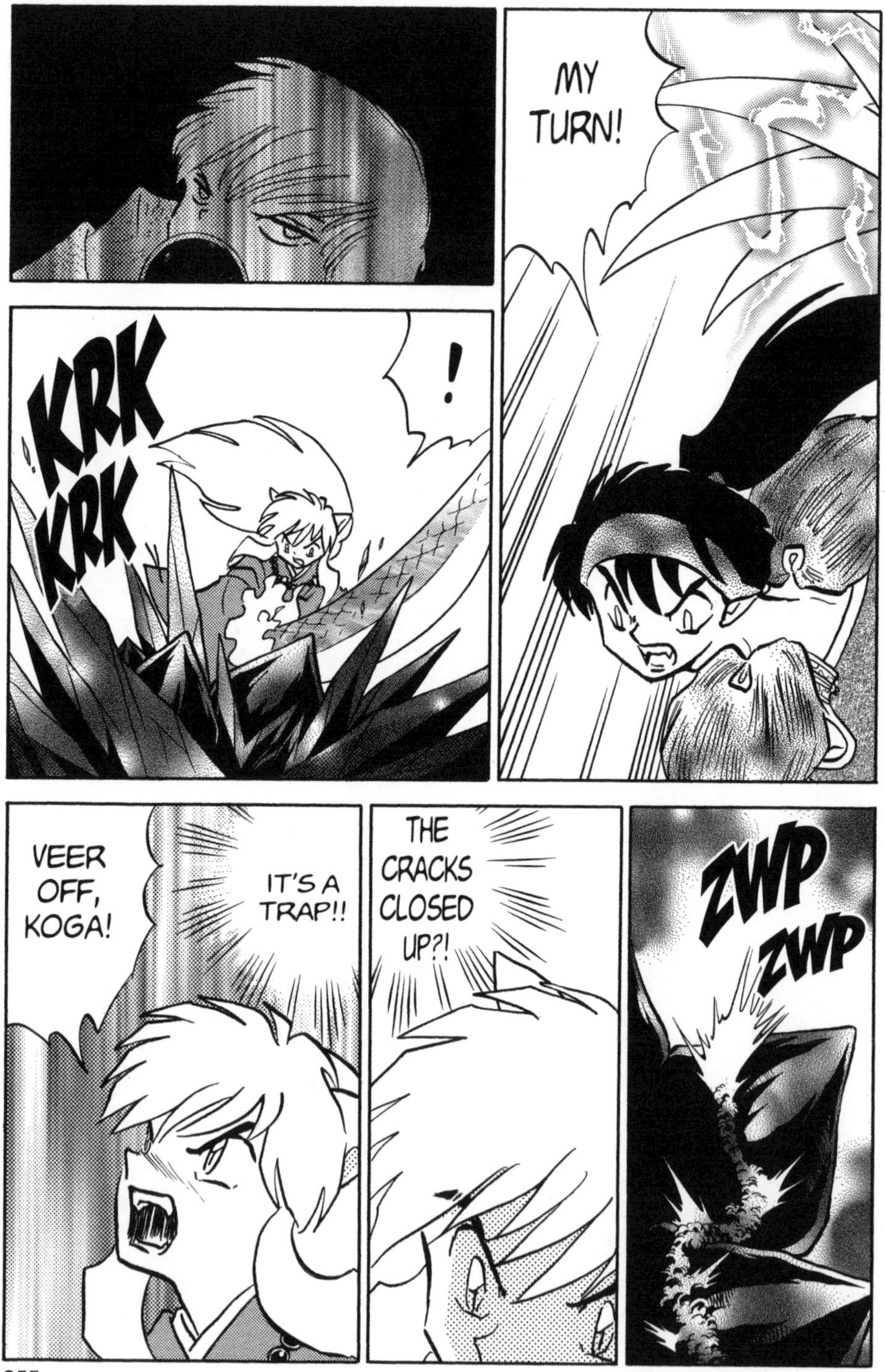
MY TURN!
KRK KRK
!
ZWP ZWP
THE CRACKS CLOSED UP?!
IT'S A TRAP!!
VEER OFF, KOGA!

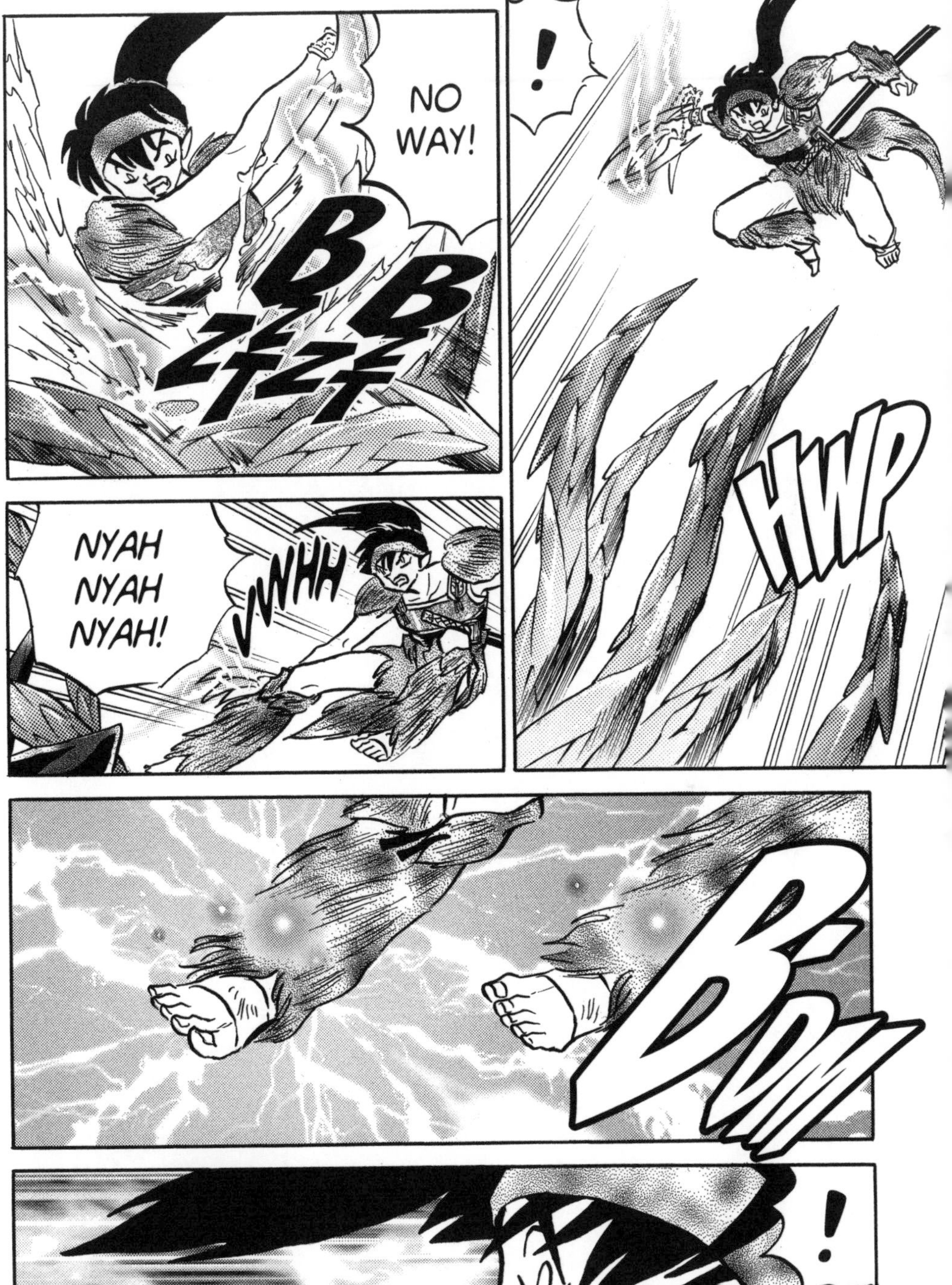
!
HWP
NO WAY!
BBZZZT
NYAH NYAH NYAH!
VWHH
BOOM
!

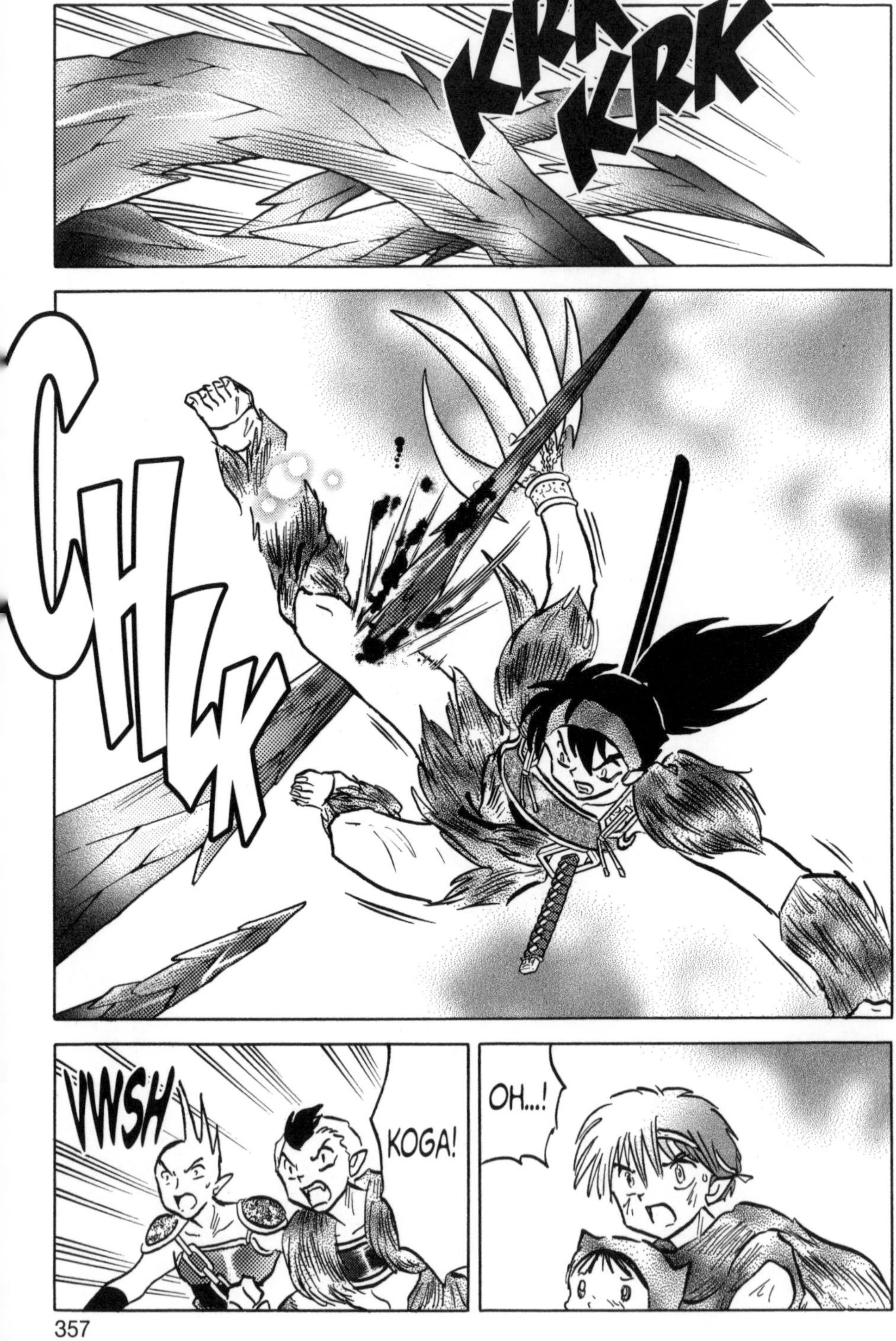
KRK KRK
CHUK
OH...!
VWSH
KOGA!

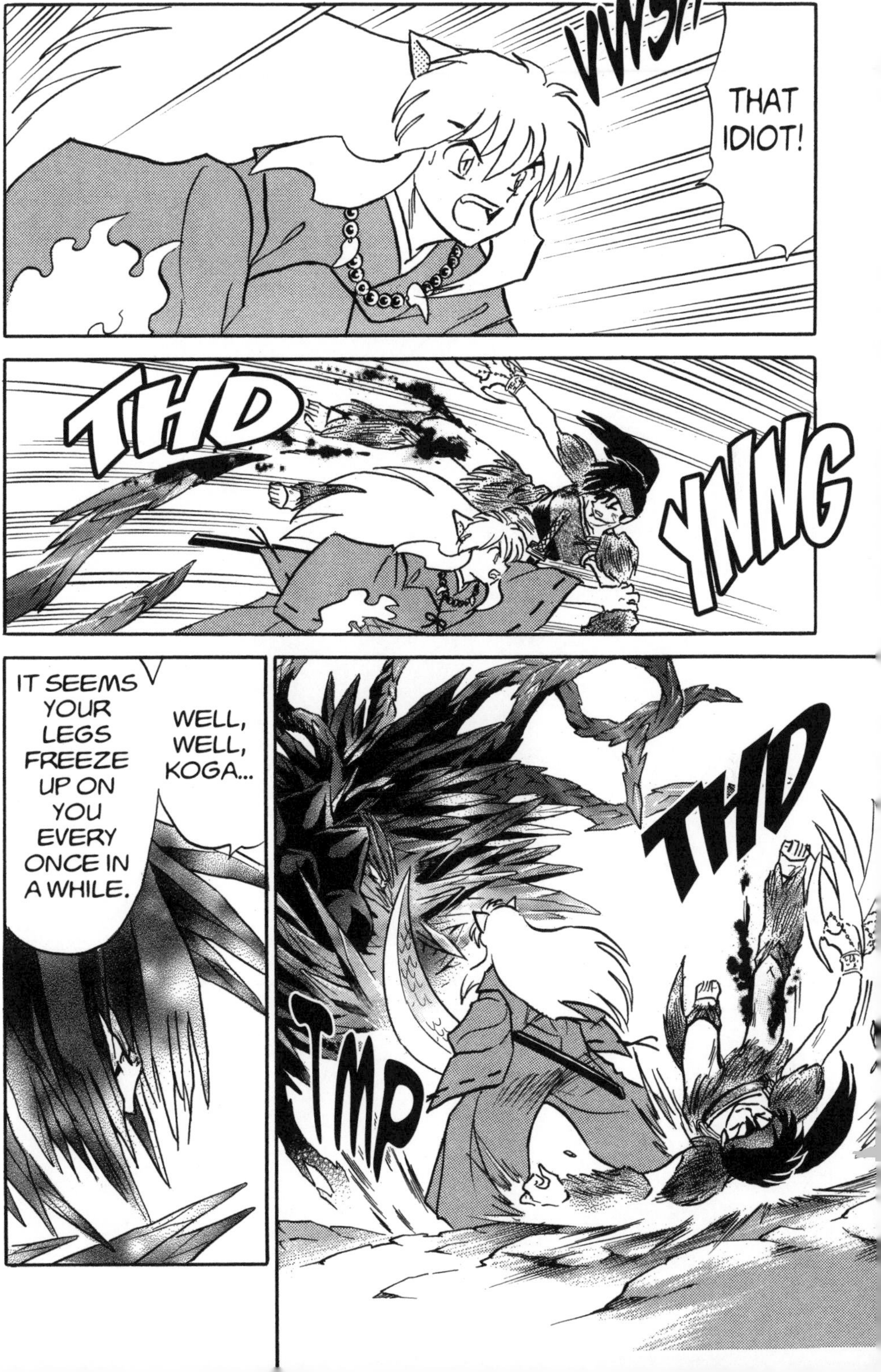
VWSH
THAT IDIOT!
YNNG
THD
THD
TMP
WELL, WELL, KOGA...
IT SEEMS YOUR LEGS FREEZE UP ON YOU EVERY ONCE IN A WHILE.

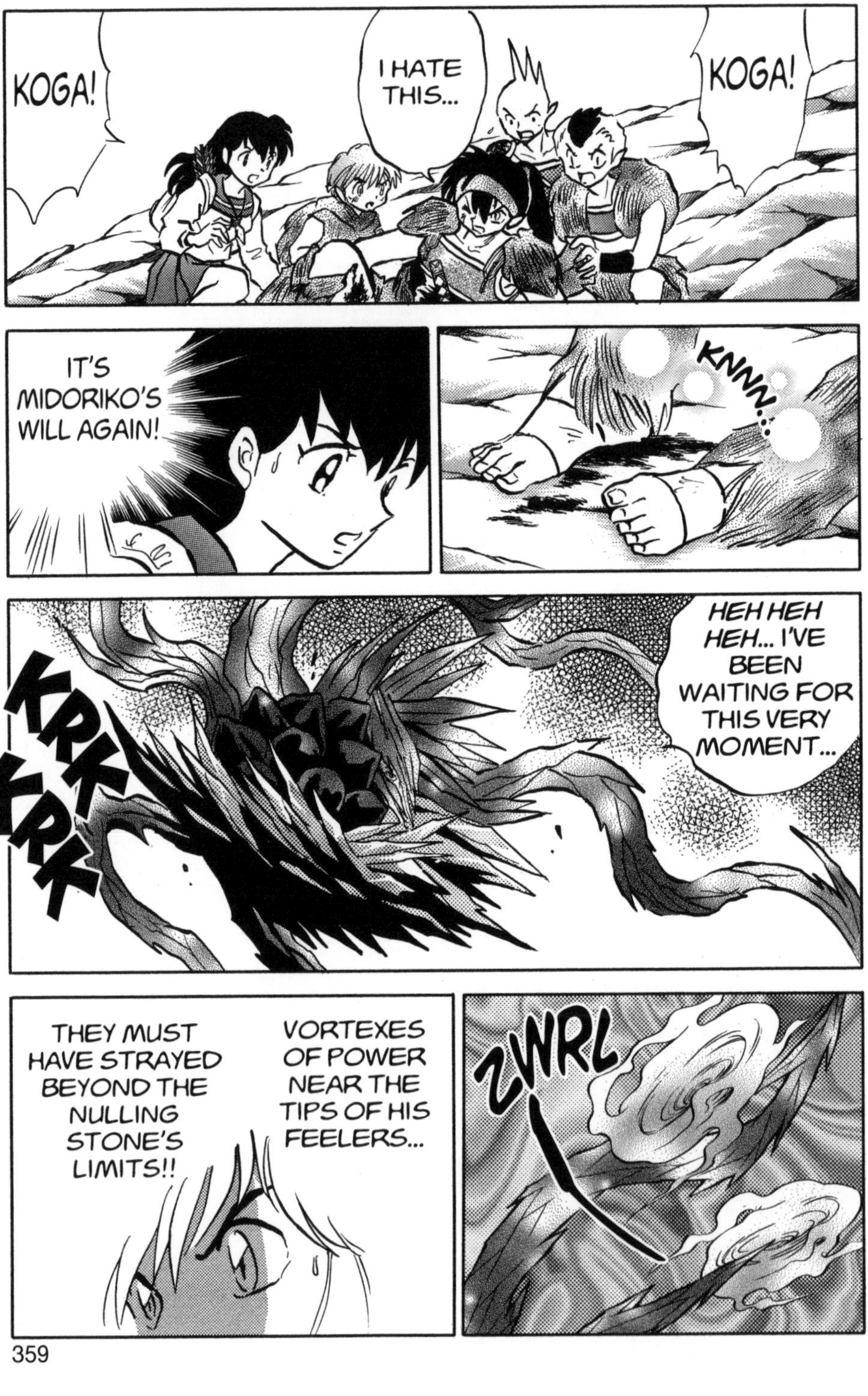
KOGA!
I HATE THIS...
KOGA!
KNNN...
IT'S MIDORIKO'S WILL AGAIN!
HEH HEH HEH... I'VE BEEN WAITING FOR THIS VERY MOMENT...
KRK KRK
ZWRL
VORTEXES OF POWER NEAR THE TIPS OF HIS FEELERS...
THEY MUST HAVE STRAYED BEYOND THE NULLING STONE'S LIMITS!!

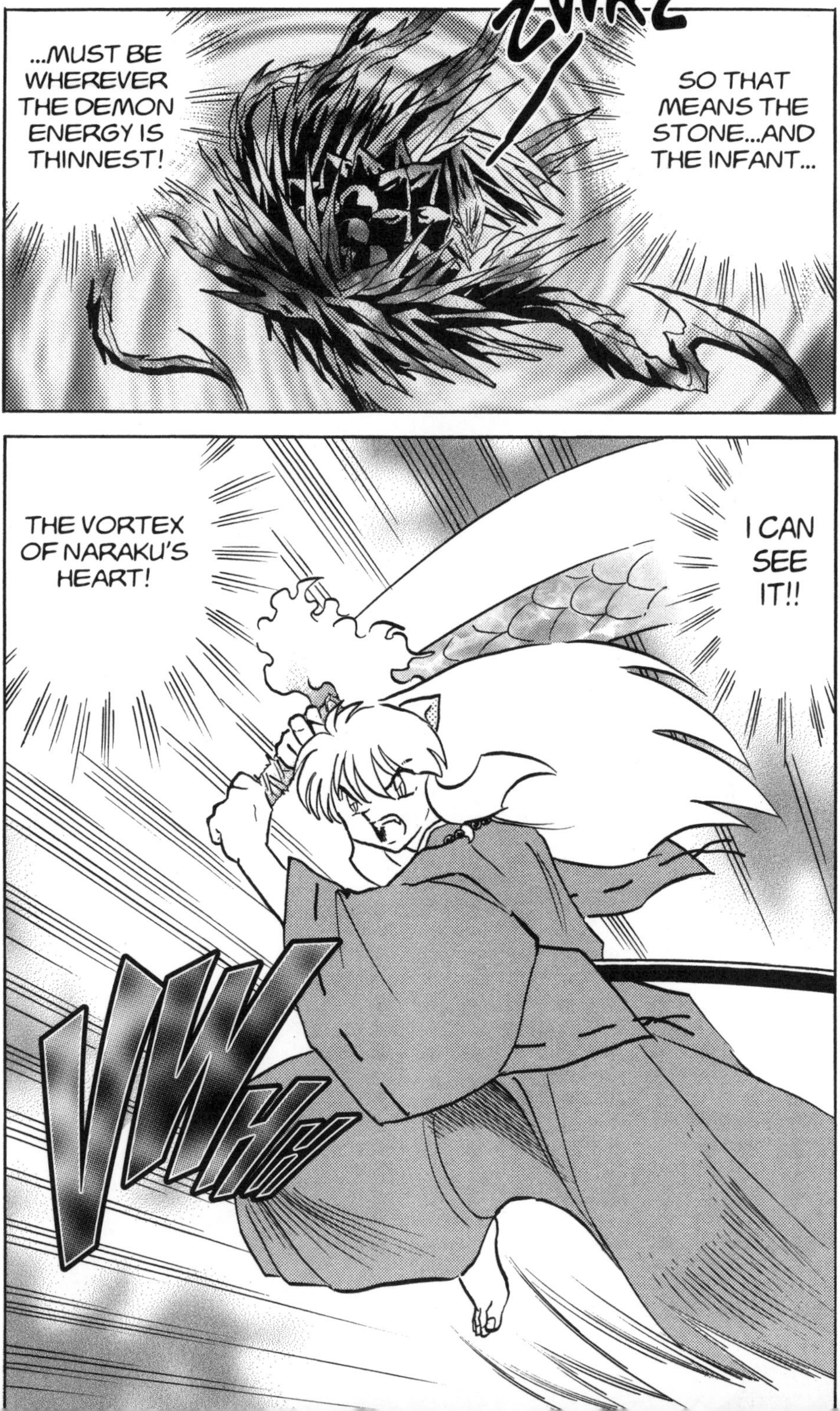
ZWRL
SO THAT MEANS THE STONE...AND THE INFANT...
...MUST BE WHEREVER THE DEMON ENERGY IS THINNEST!
I CAN SEE IT!!
THE VORTEX OF NARAKU'S HEART!
VWH

SCROLL TEN
KOGA'S DECISION

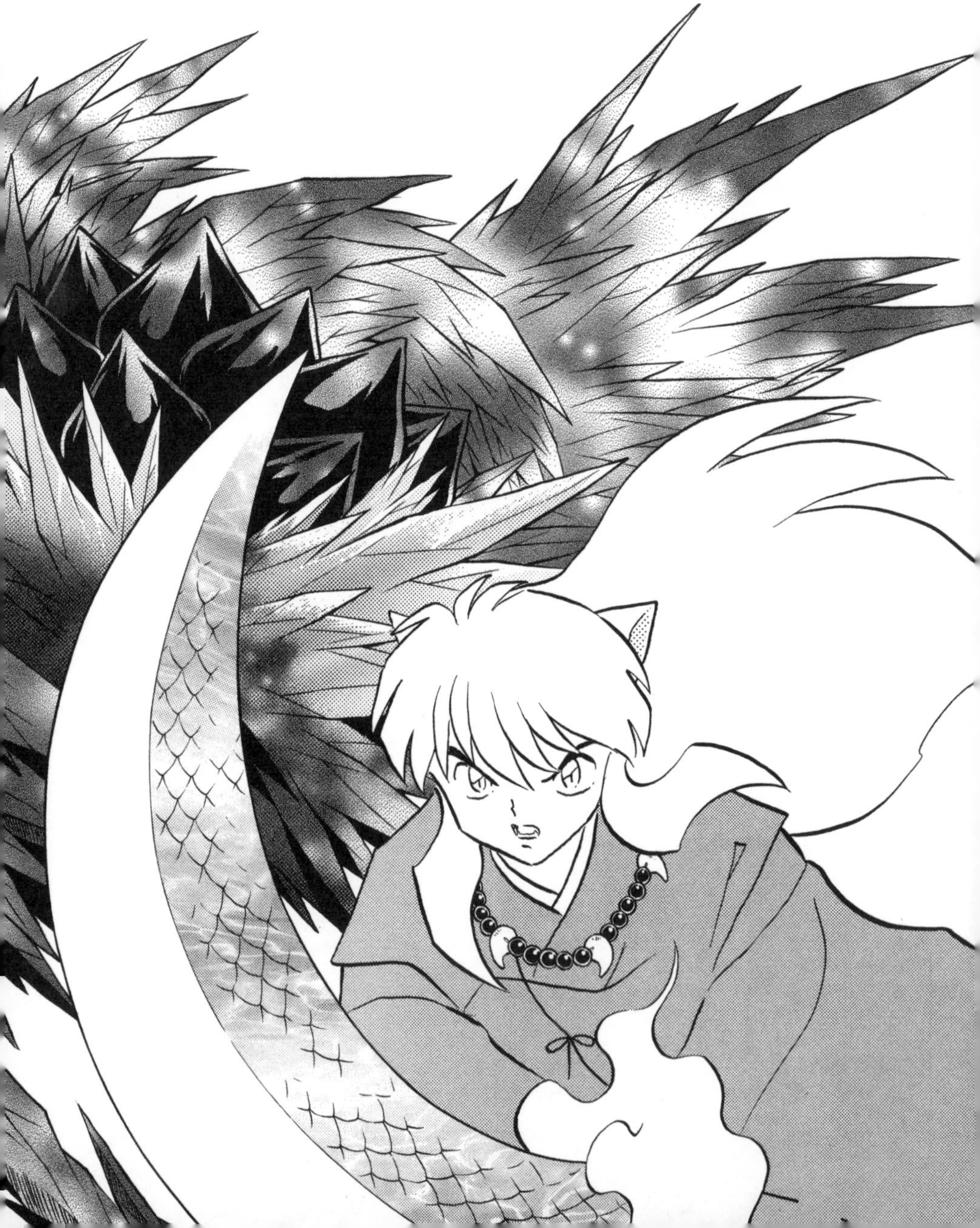

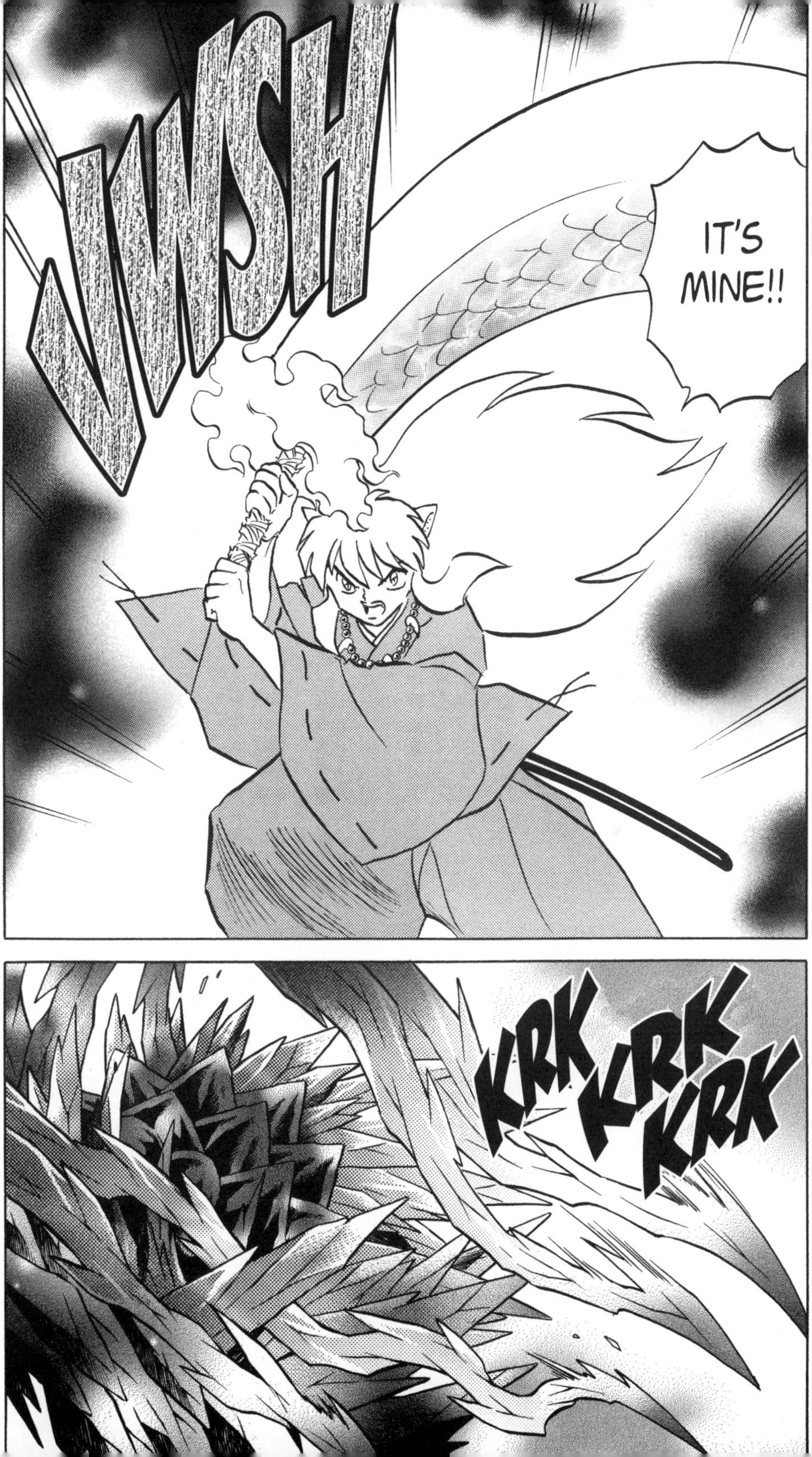
IT'S MINE!!
JWSH
KRK KRK KRK

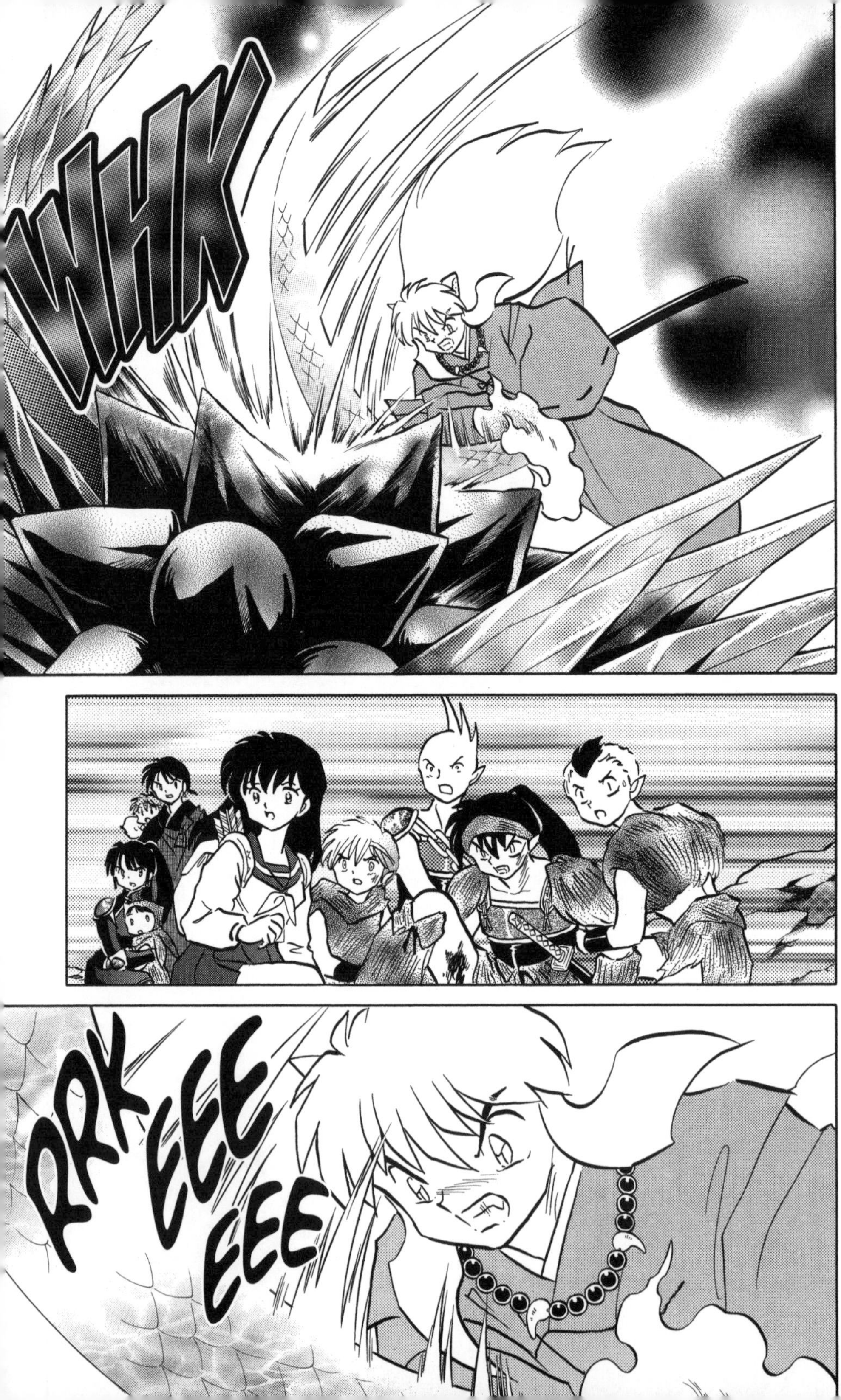
WHK
RRK EEE EEE

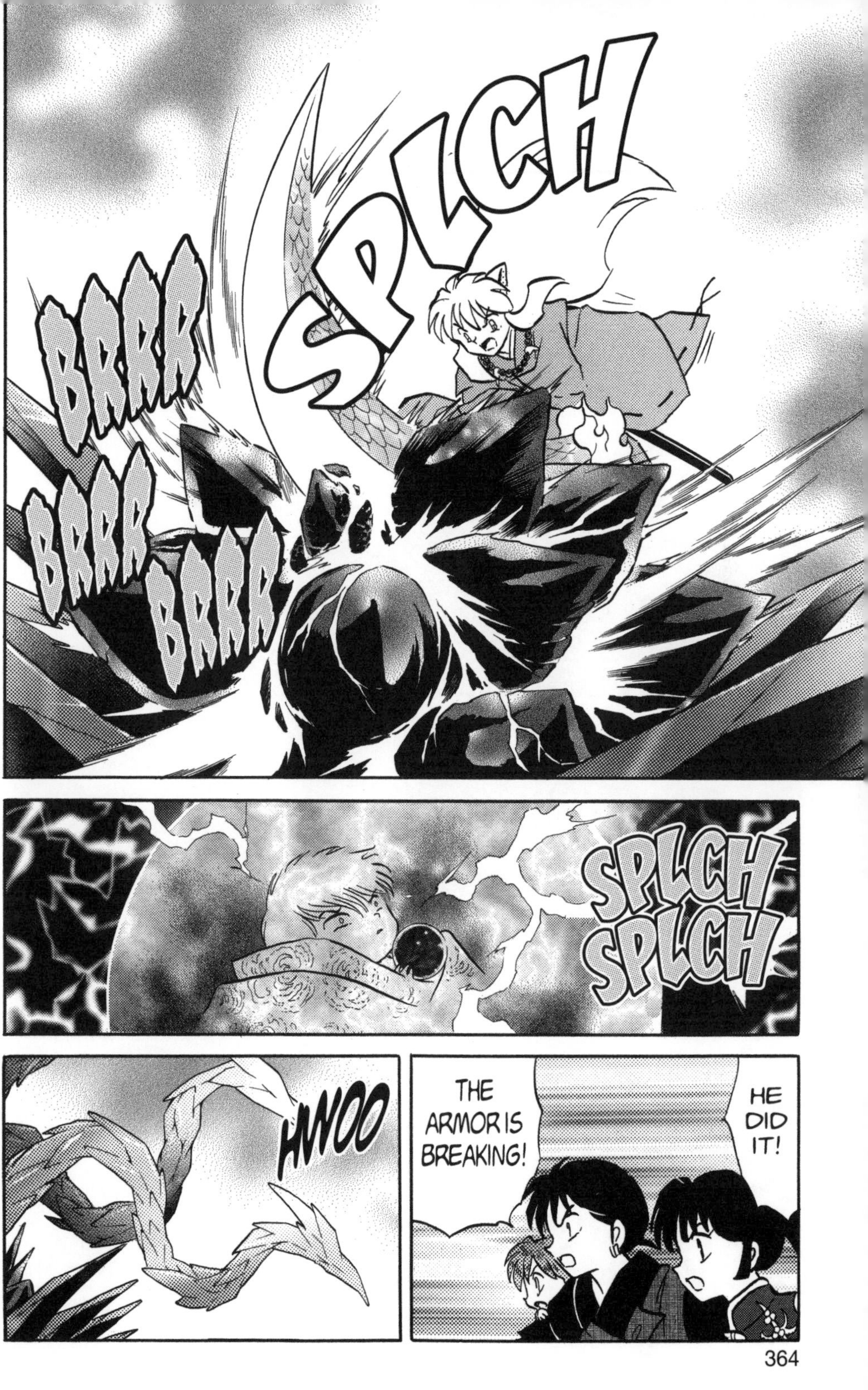
SPLCH
BRRR
BRRR
BRRR
SPLCH
SPLCH
HE DID IT!
THE ARMOR IS BREAKING!
HWOO

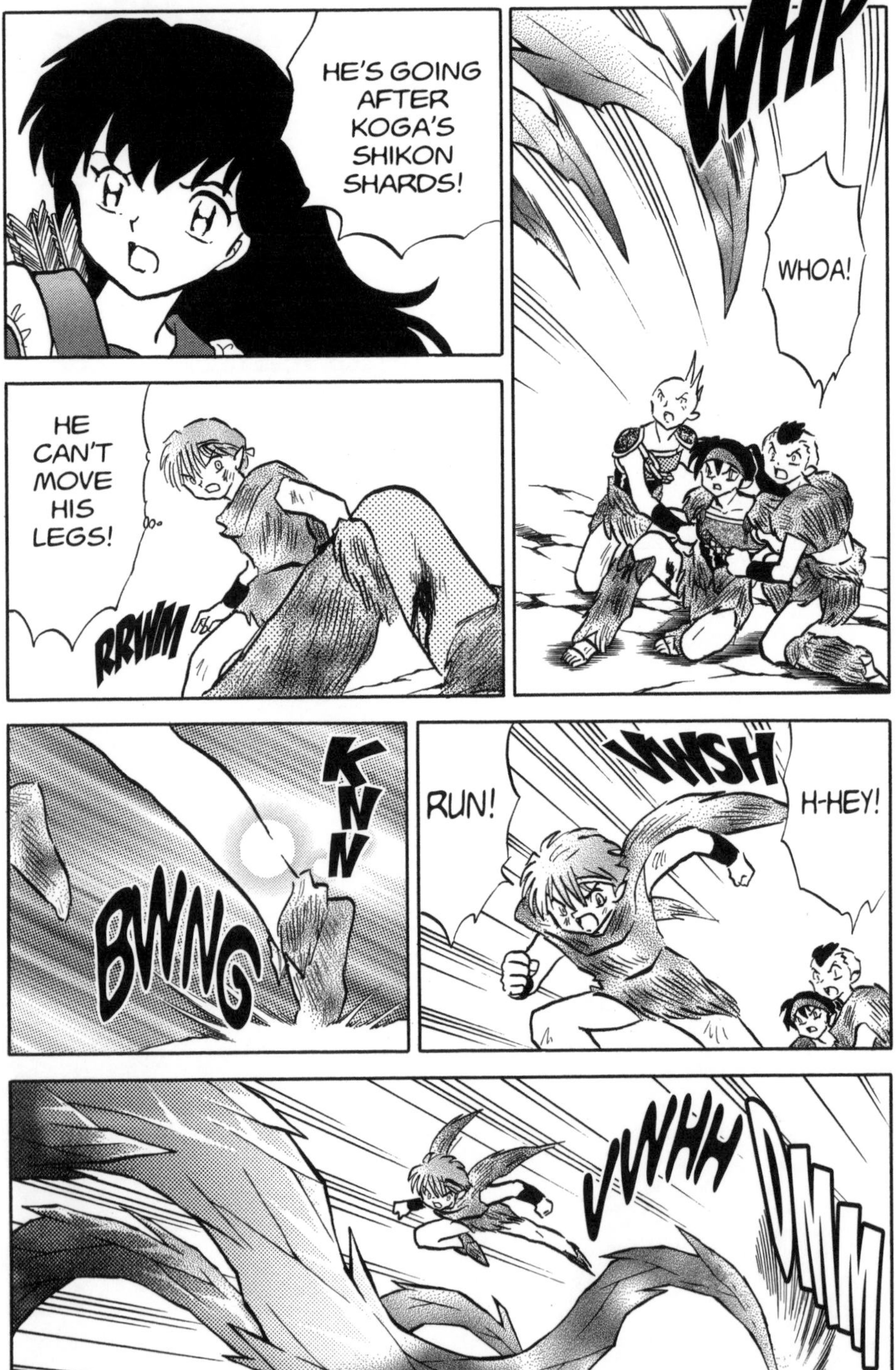
WHIP
WHOA!
HE'S GOING AFTER KOGA'S SHIKON SHARDS!
HE CAN'T MOVE HIS LEGS!
RRWM
VWSH
H-HEY!
RUN!
KNN
BWNG
VVHH

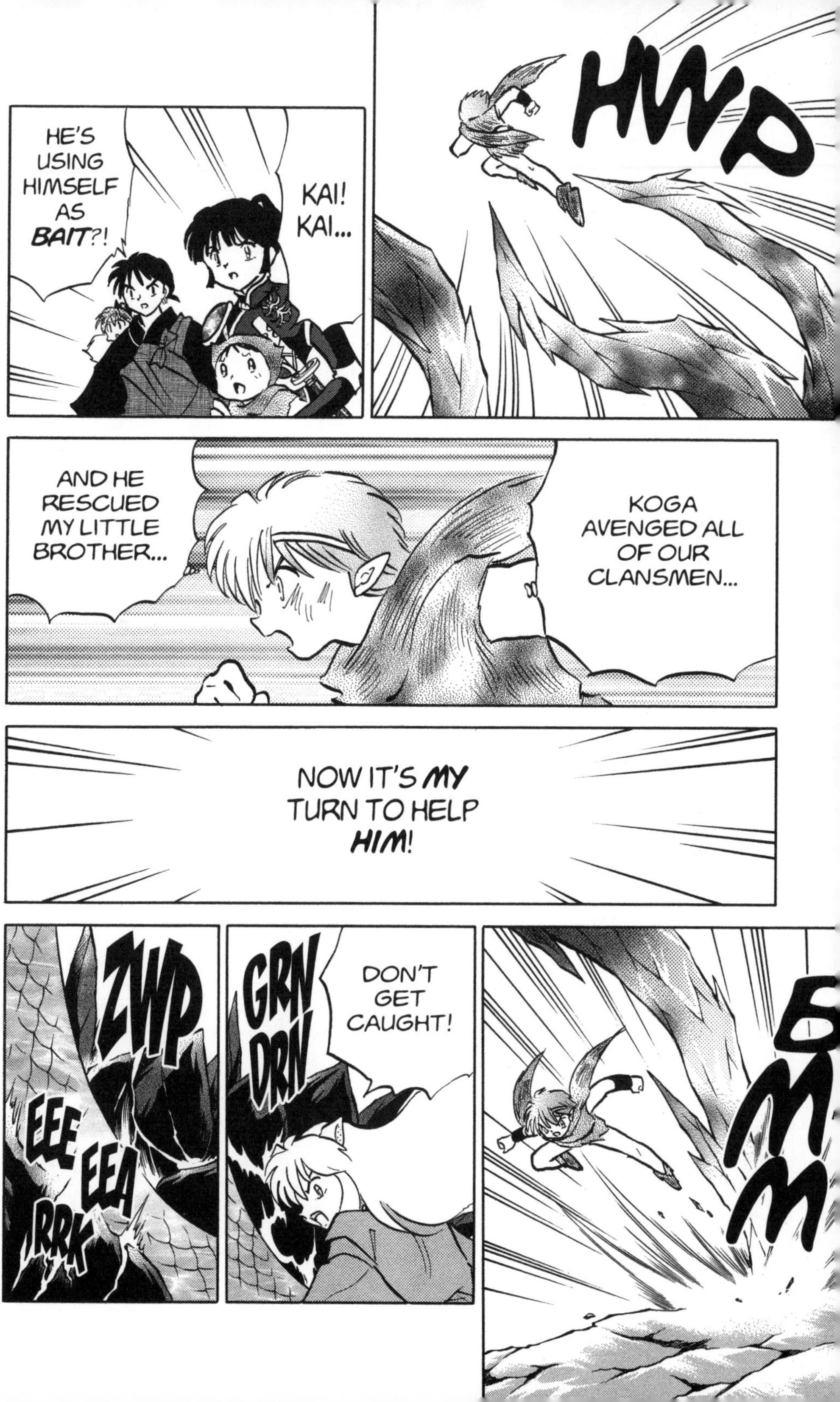
HWP
KAI! KAI...
HE'S USING HIMSELF AS BAIT?!
KOGA AVENGED ALL OF OUR CLANSMEN...
AND HE RESCUED MY LITTLE BROTHER...
NOW IT'S MY TURN TO HELP HIM!
DON'T GET CAUGHT!
GRN DRN
ZWP
EEE EEA RRK

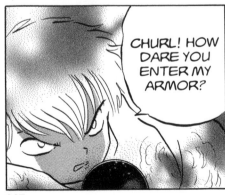

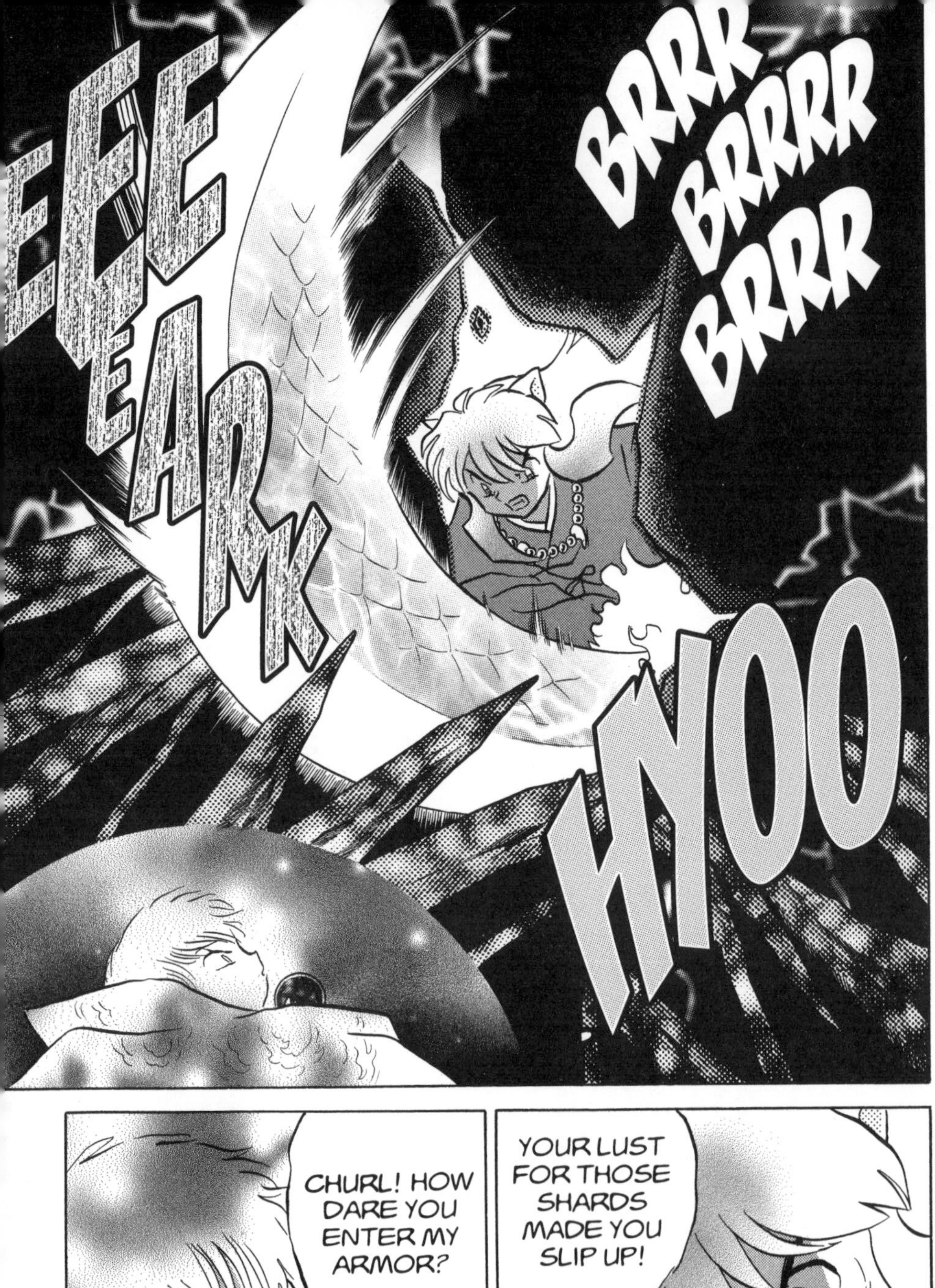
BRRR BRRRR BRRR
EEEEARK
HYOO
YOUR LUST FOR THOSE SHARDS MADE YOU SLIP UP!
CHURL! HOW DARE YOU ENTER MY ARMOR?

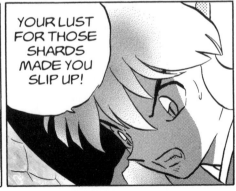

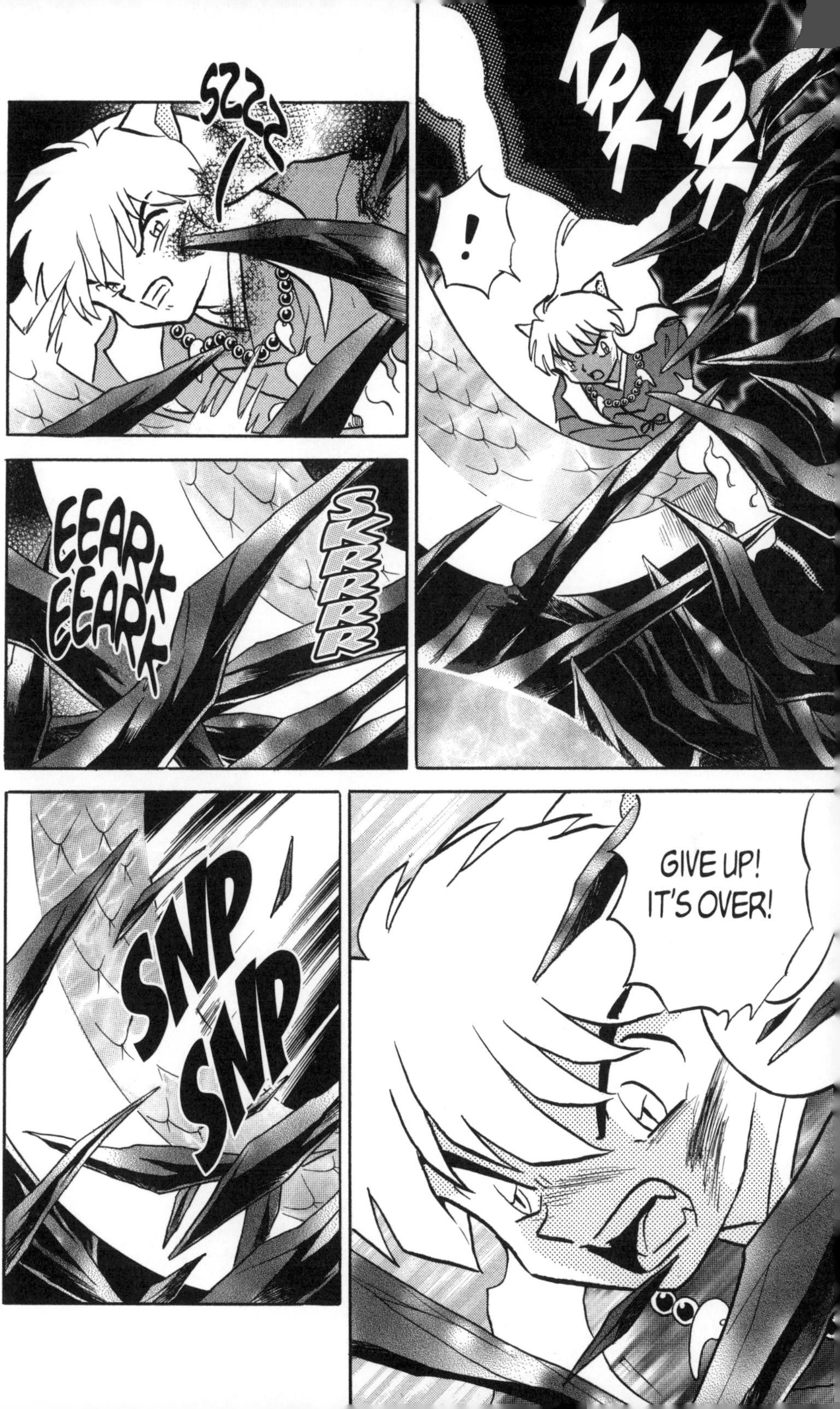
KRK KRK
!
SZZZ
EEARK EEARK
SKRRRR
GIVE UP! IT'S OVER!
SNP SNP

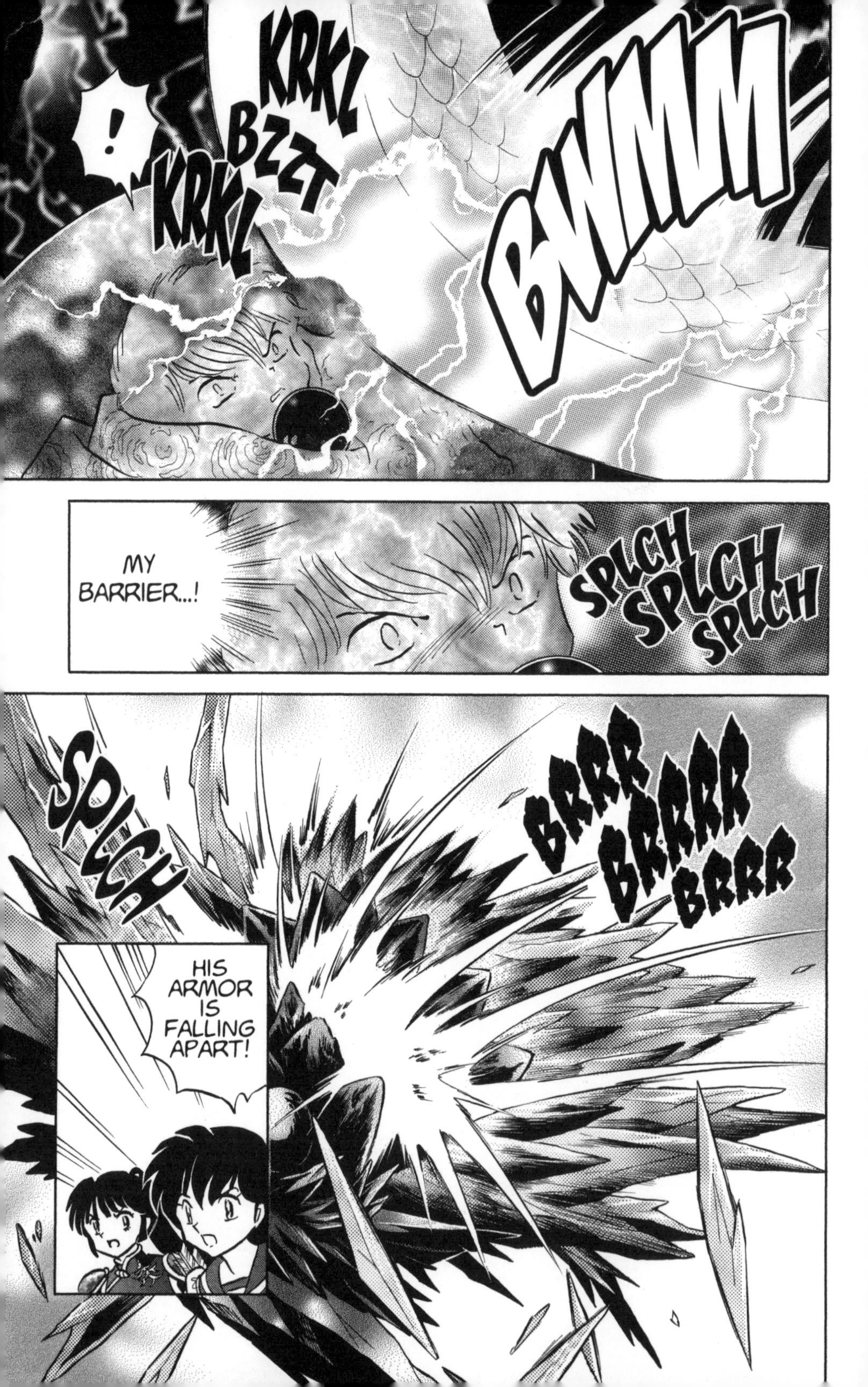

BVMMM
KRKL
BZZT
KRKL
!
SPLCH
SPLCH
SPLCH
MY BARRIER...!
BRRR
BRRRR
BRRR
SPLCH
HIS ARMOR IS FALLING APART!

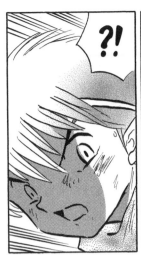

?!

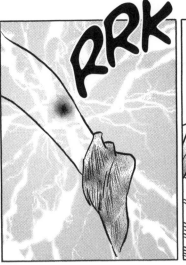

RRK

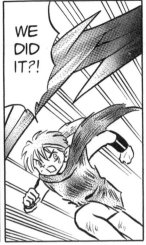

WE DID IT?!

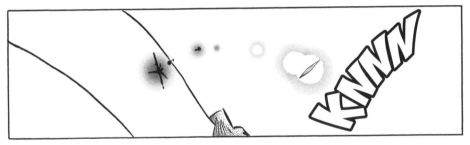

KNNN

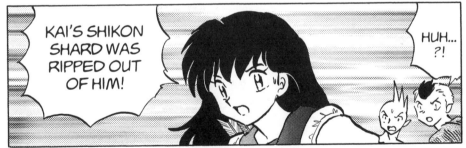

KAI'S SHIKON SHARD WAS RIPPED OUT OF HIM!

HUH... ?!

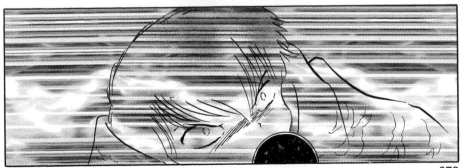

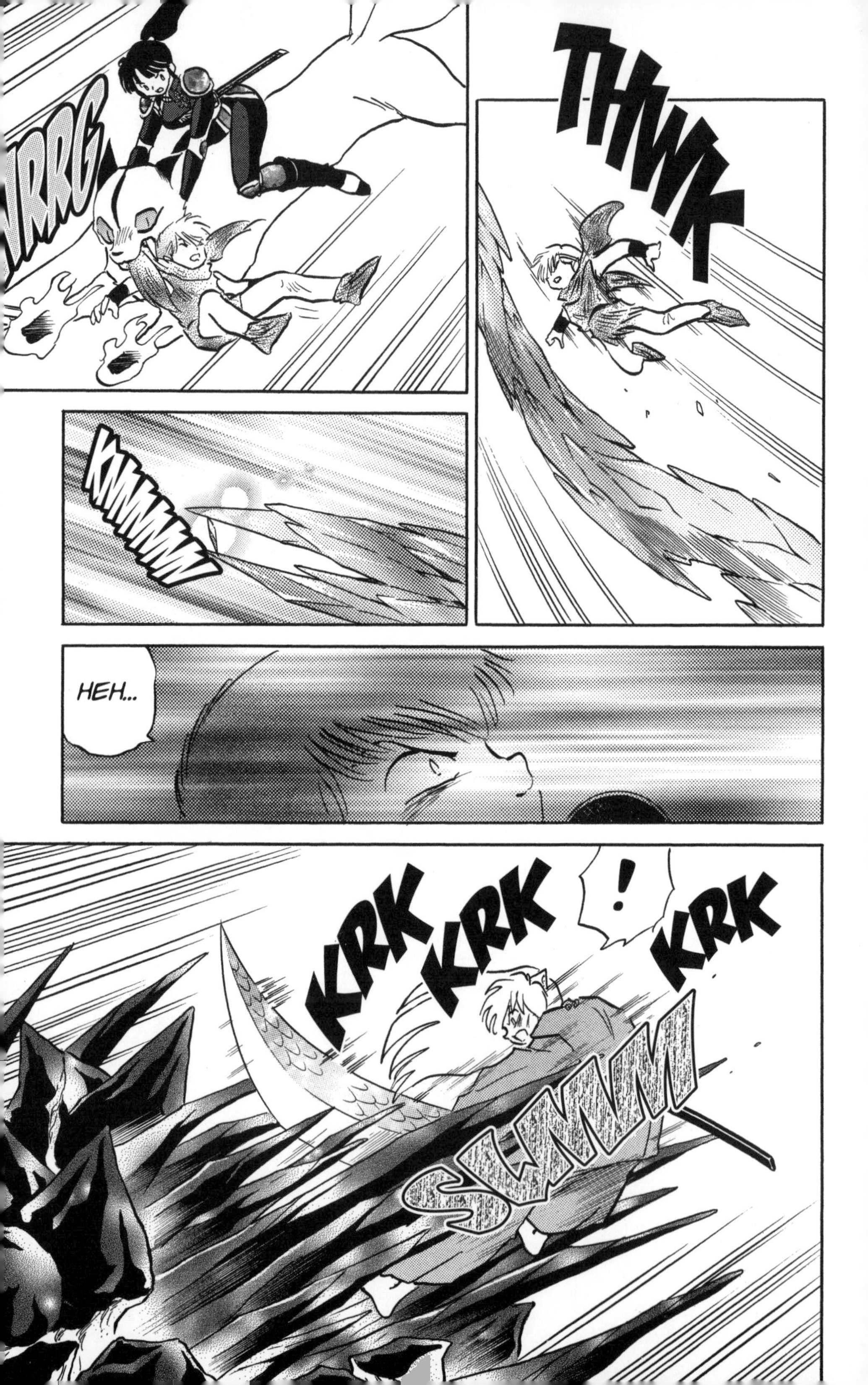
THWAK
RRG
KNNNNNNN
HEH...
!
KRK
KRK
KRK
SWMM

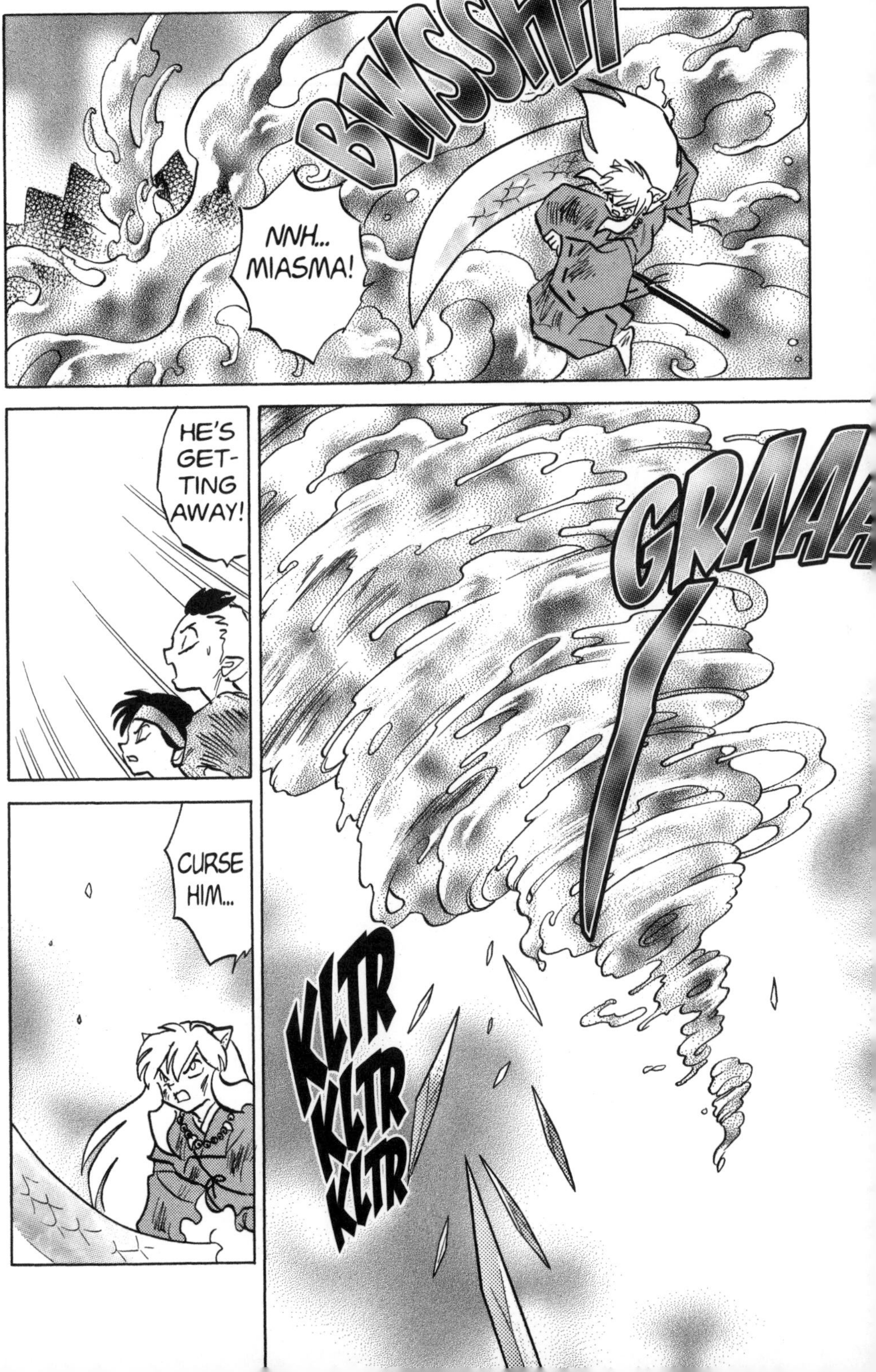
BWSSHH
NNH... MIASMA!
GRAAA
KLTR KLTR KLTR
HE'S GET- TING AWAY!
CURSE HIM...

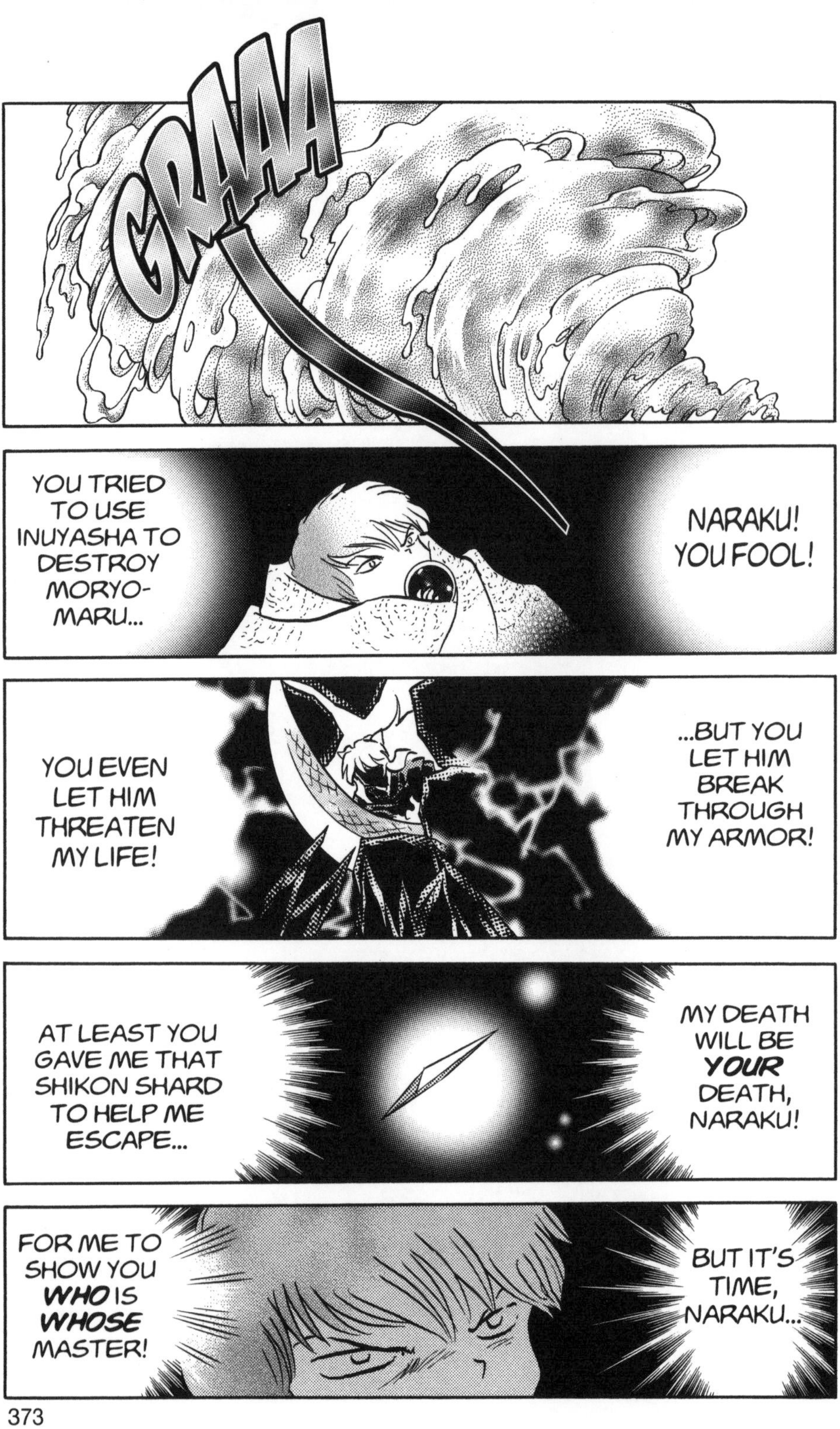
GRAAA
NARAKU! YOU FOOL!
YOU TRIED TO USE INUYASHA TO DESTROY MORYO-MARU...
...BUT YOU LET HIM BREAK THROUGH MY ARMOR!
YOU EVEN LET HIM THREATEN MY LIFE!
MY DEATH WILL BE ***YOUR*** DEATH, NARAKU!
AT LEAST YOU GAVE ME THAT SHIKON SHARD TO HELP ME ESCAPE...
BUT IT'S TIME, NARAKU...
FOR ME TO SHOW YOU ***WHO*** IS ***WHOSE*** MASTER!

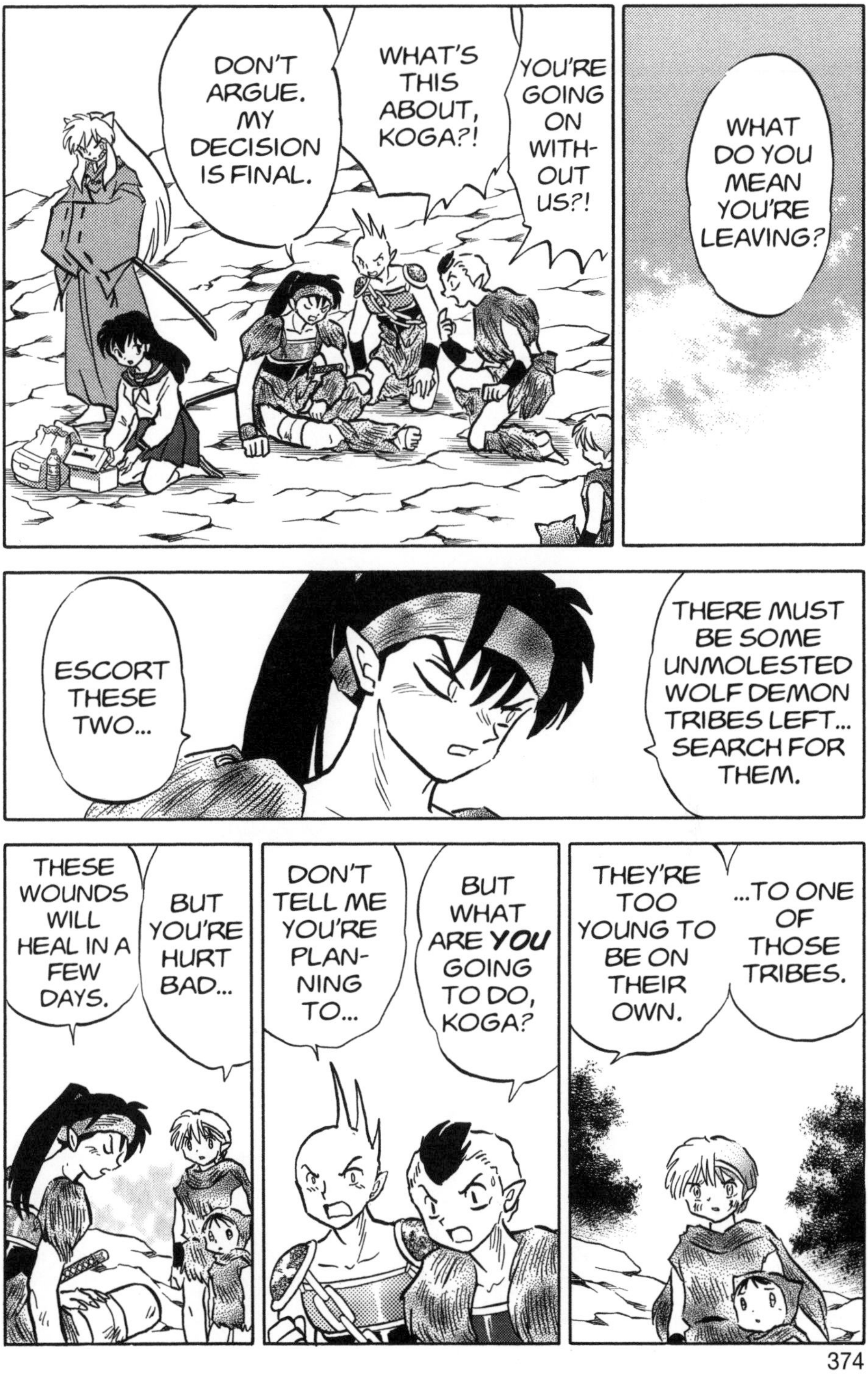
WHAT DO YOU MEAN YOU'RE LEAVING?
YOU'RE GOING ON WITH-OUT US?!
WHAT'S THIS ABOUT, KOGA?!
DON'T ARGUE. MY DECISION IS FINAL.
THERE MUST BE SOME UNMOLESTED WOLF DEMON TRIBES LEFT... SEARCH FOR THEM.
ESCORT THESE TWO...
...TO ONE OF THOSE TRIBES.
THEY'RE TOO YOUNG TO BE ON THEIR OWN.
BUT WHAT ARE *YOU* GOING TO DO, KOGA?
DON'T TELL ME YOU'RE PLAN-NING TO...
BUT YOU'RE HURT BAD...
THESE WOUNDS WILL HEAL IN A FEW DAYS.

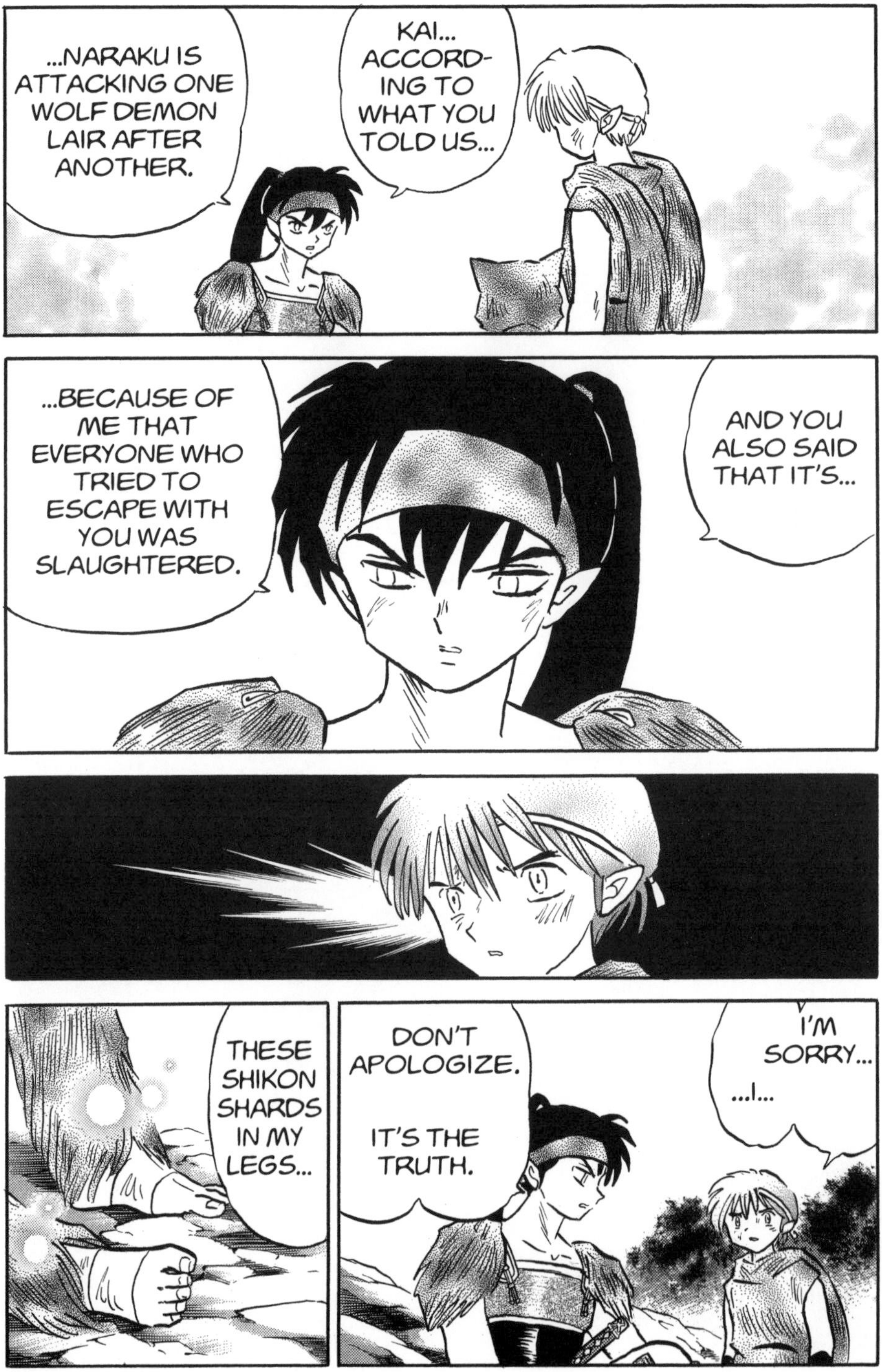
KAI... ACCORD-ING TO WHAT YOU TOLD US...
...NARAKU IS ATTACKING ONE WOLF DEMON LAIR AFTER ANOTHER.
AND YOU ALSO SAID THAT IT'S...
...BECAUSE OF ME THAT EVERYONE WHO TRIED TO ESCAPE WITH YOU WAS SLAUGHTERED.
I'M SORRY...
...I...
DON'T APOLOGIZE.
IT'S THE TRUTH.
THESE SHIKON SHARDS IN MY LEGS...

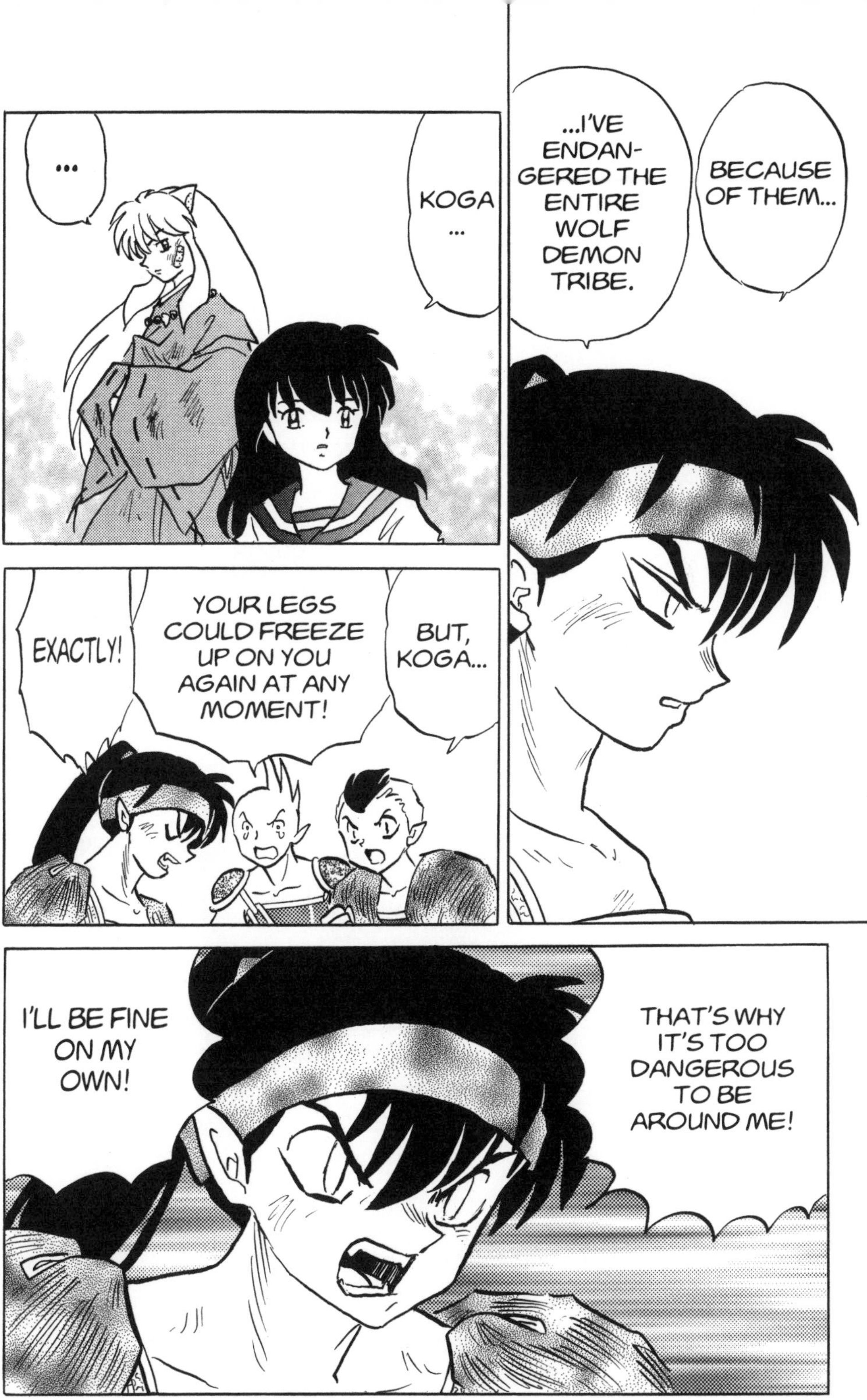
BECAUSE OF THEM...
...I'VE ENDANGERED THE ENTIRE WOLF DEMON TRIBE.
KOGA ...
...
BUT, KOGA...
YOUR LEGS COULD FREEZE UP ON YOU AGAIN AT ANY MOMENT!
EXACTLY!
THAT'S WHY IT'S TOO DANGEROUS TO BE AROUND ME!
I'LL BE FINE ON MY OWN!

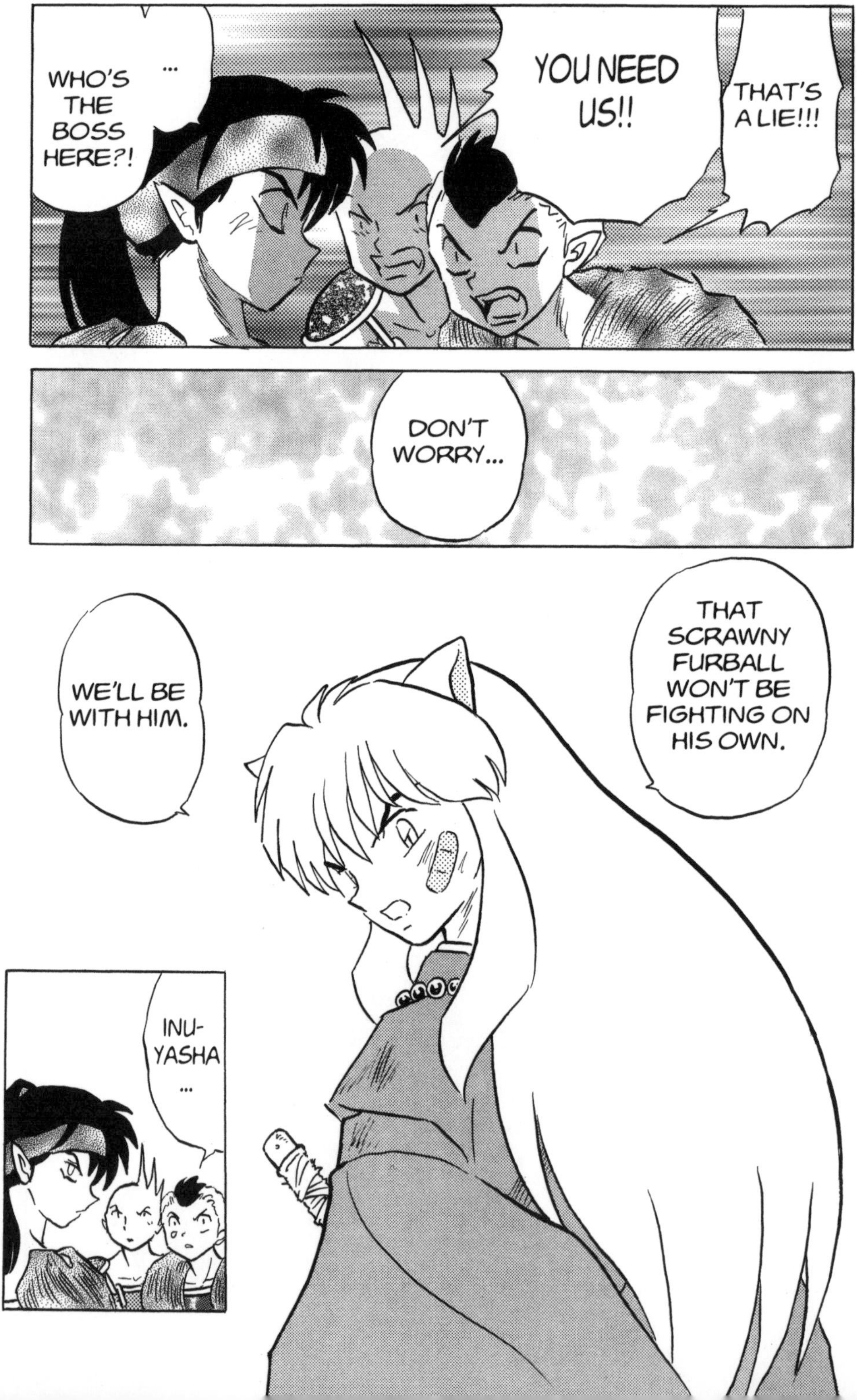
THAT'S A LIE!!!
YOU NEED US!!
...
WHO'S THE BOSS HERE?!
DON'T WORRY...
THAT SCRAWNY FURBALL WON'T BE FIGHTING ON HIS OWN.
WE'LL BE WITH HIM.
INU-YASHA ...

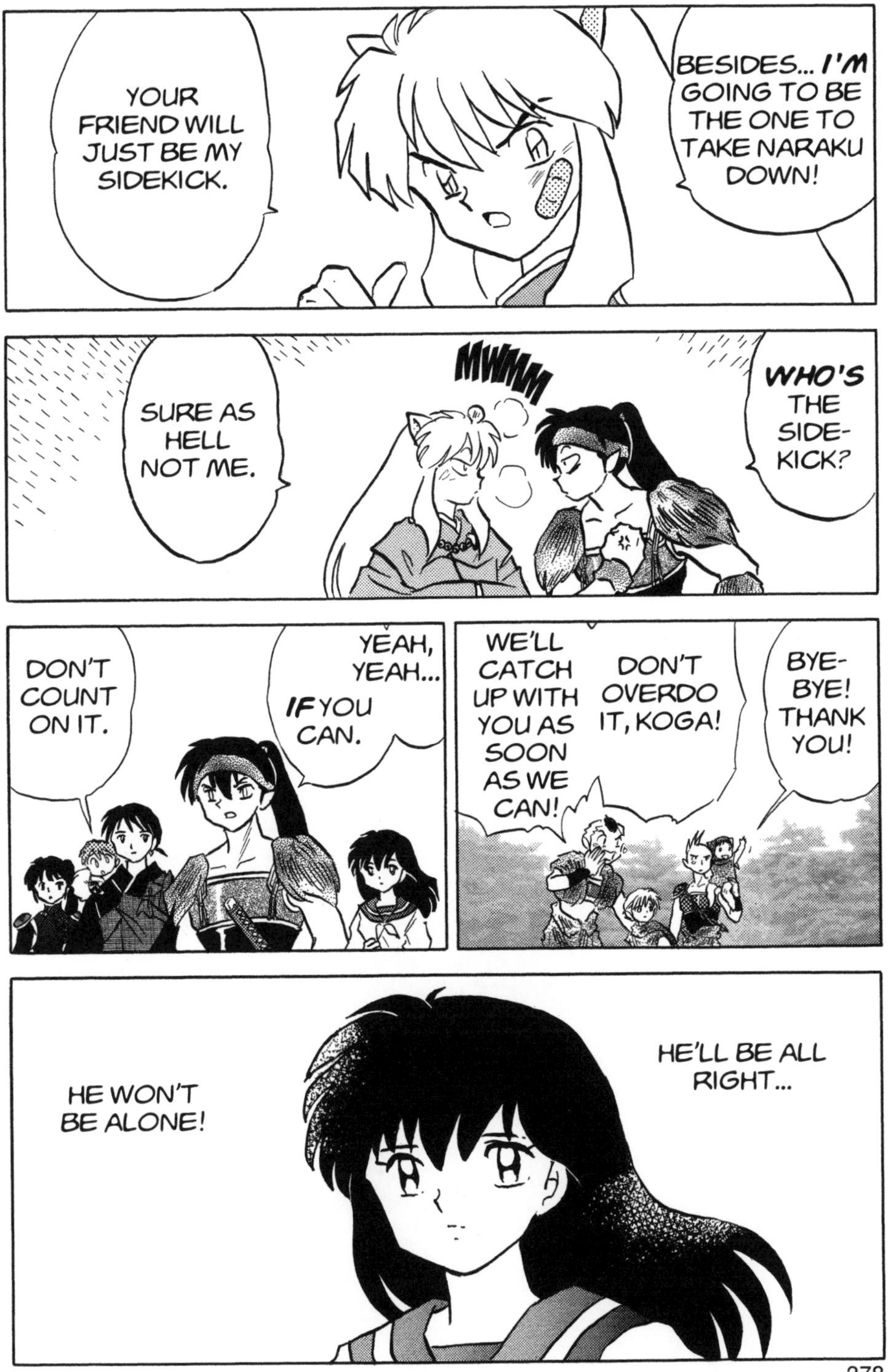
BESIDES... I'M GOING TO BE THE ONE TO TAKE NARAKU DOWN!
YOUR FRIEND WILL JUST BE MY SIDEKICK.
WHO'S THE SIDE-KICK?
MWMM
SURE AS HELL NOT ME.
BYE-BYE! THANK YOU!
DON'T OVERDO IT, KOGA!
WE'LL CATCH UP WITH YOU AS SOON AS WE CAN!
YEAH, YEAH... IF YOU CAN.
DON'T COUNT ON IT.
HE'LL BE ALL RIGHT...
HE WON'T BE ALONE!

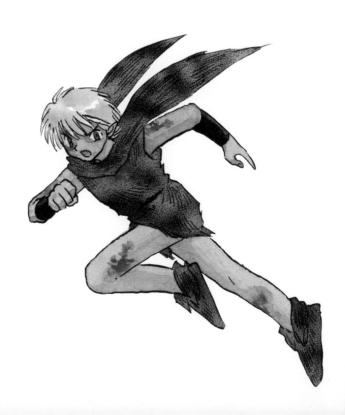

InuYasha

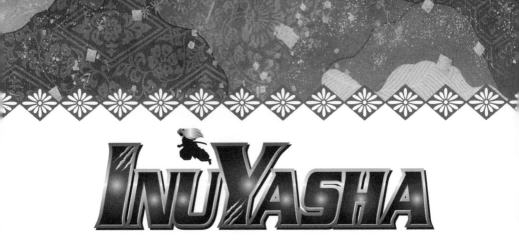

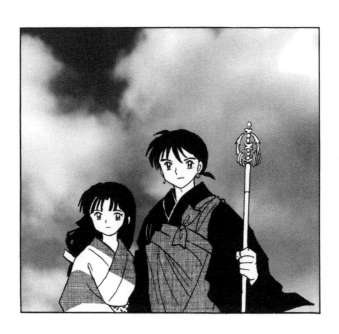

Volume 45

Absorption

SCROLL ONE
YOMEIJU

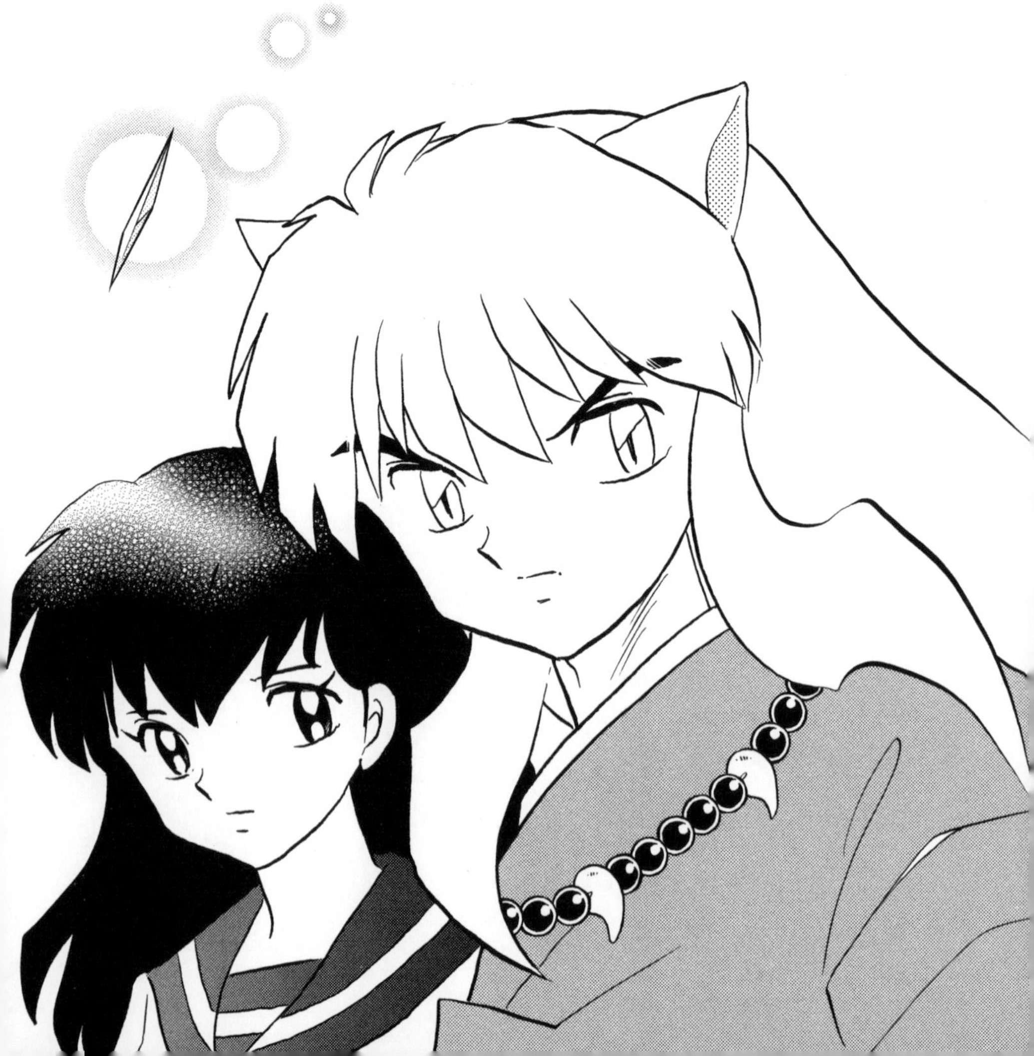

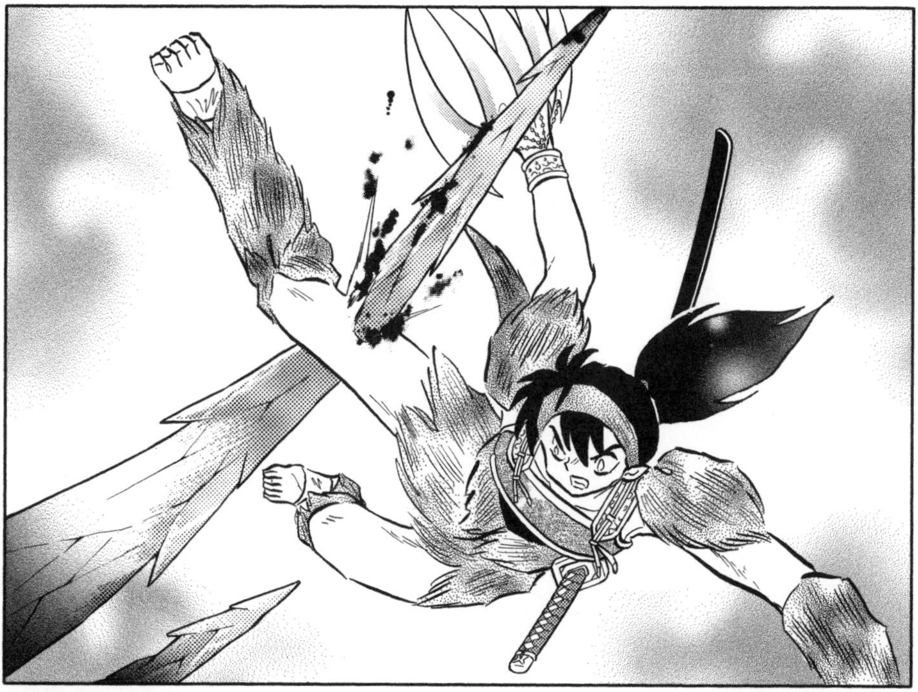

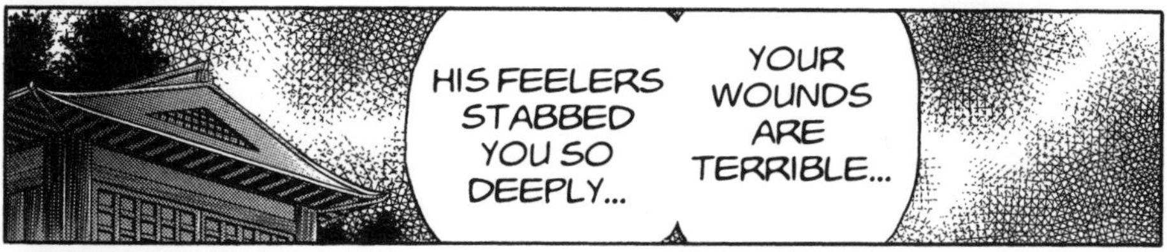
YOUR WOUNDS ARE TERRIBLE...
HIS FEELERS STABBED YOU SO DEEPLY...

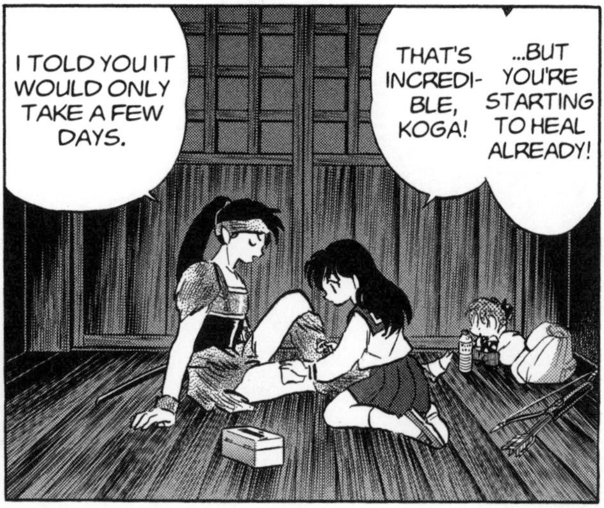
...BUT YOU'RE STARTING TO HEAL ALREADY!
THAT'S INCREDIBLE, KOGA!
I TOLD YOU IT WOULD ONLY TAKE A FEW DAYS.

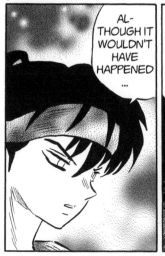

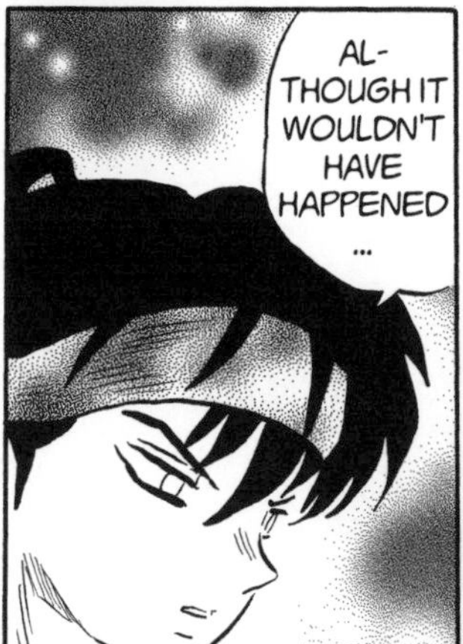
ALTHOUGH IT WOULDN'T HAVE HAPPENED ...

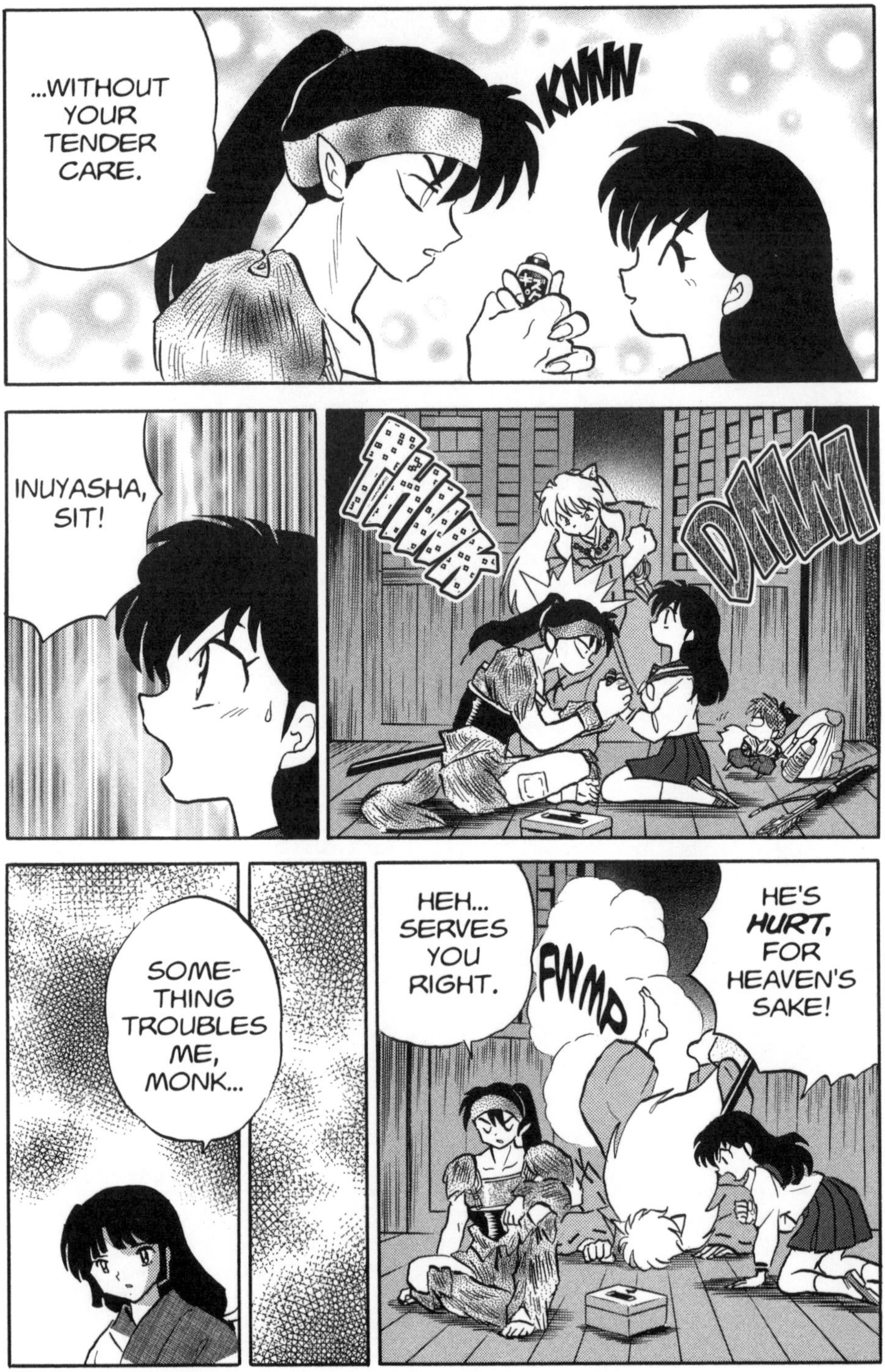
...WITHOUT YOUR TENDER CARE.
KNNN
DMMM
THWK
INUYASHA, SIT!
HE'S ***HURT,*** FOR HEAVEN'S SAKE!
FWMP
HEH... SERVES YOU RIGHT.
SOME-THING TROUBLES ME, MONK...

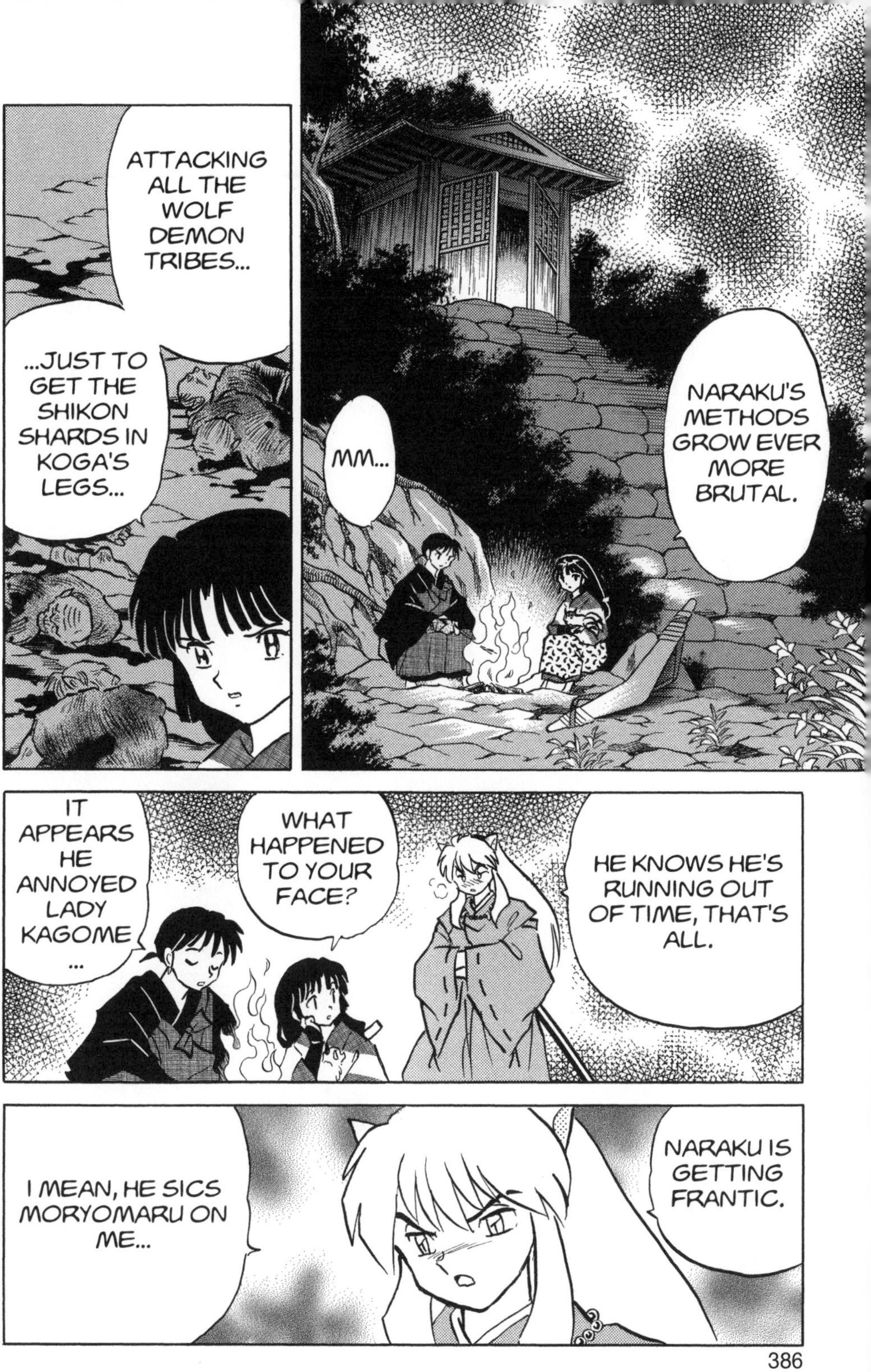
NARAKU'S METHODS GROW EVER MORE BRUTAL.
MM...
ATTACKING ALL THE WOLF DEMON TRIBES...
...JUST TO GET THE SHIKON SHARDS IN KOGA'S LEGS...
HE KNOWS HE'S RUNNING OUT OF TIME, THAT'S ALL.
WHAT HAPPENED TO YOUR FACE?
IT APPEARS HE ANNOYED LADY KAGOME...
NARAKU IS GETTING FRANTIC.
I MEAN, HE SICS MORYOMARU ON ME...

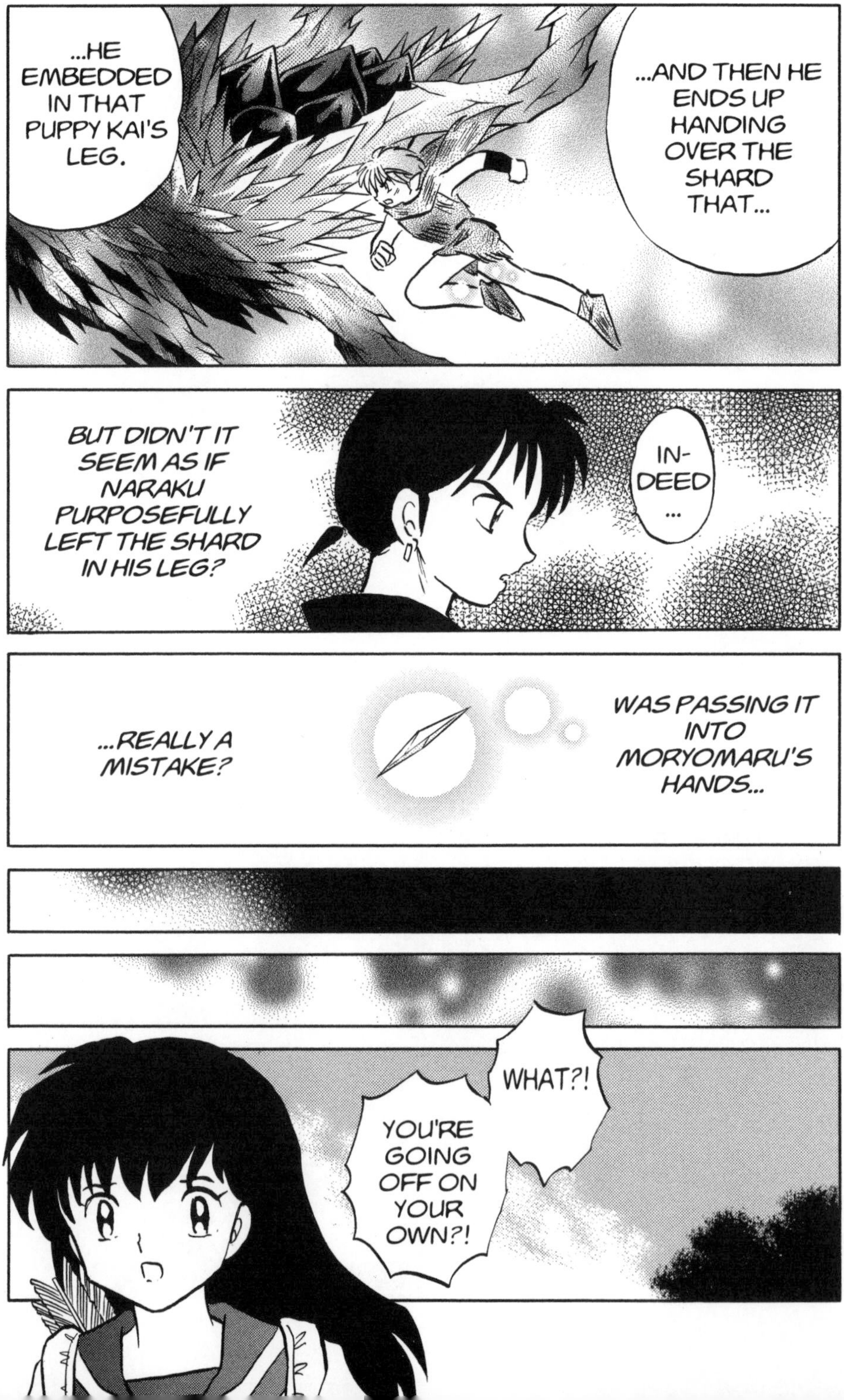
...AND THEN HE ENDS UP HANDING OVER THE SHARD THAT...
...HE EMBEDDED IN THAT PUPPY KAI'S LEG.
IN-DEED...
BUT DIDN'T IT SEEM AS IF NARAKU PURPOSEFULLY LEFT THE SHARD IN HIS LEG?
WAS PASSING IT INTO MORYOMARU'S HANDS...
...REALLY A MISTAKE?
WHAT?!
YOU'RE GOING OFF ON YOUR OWN?!

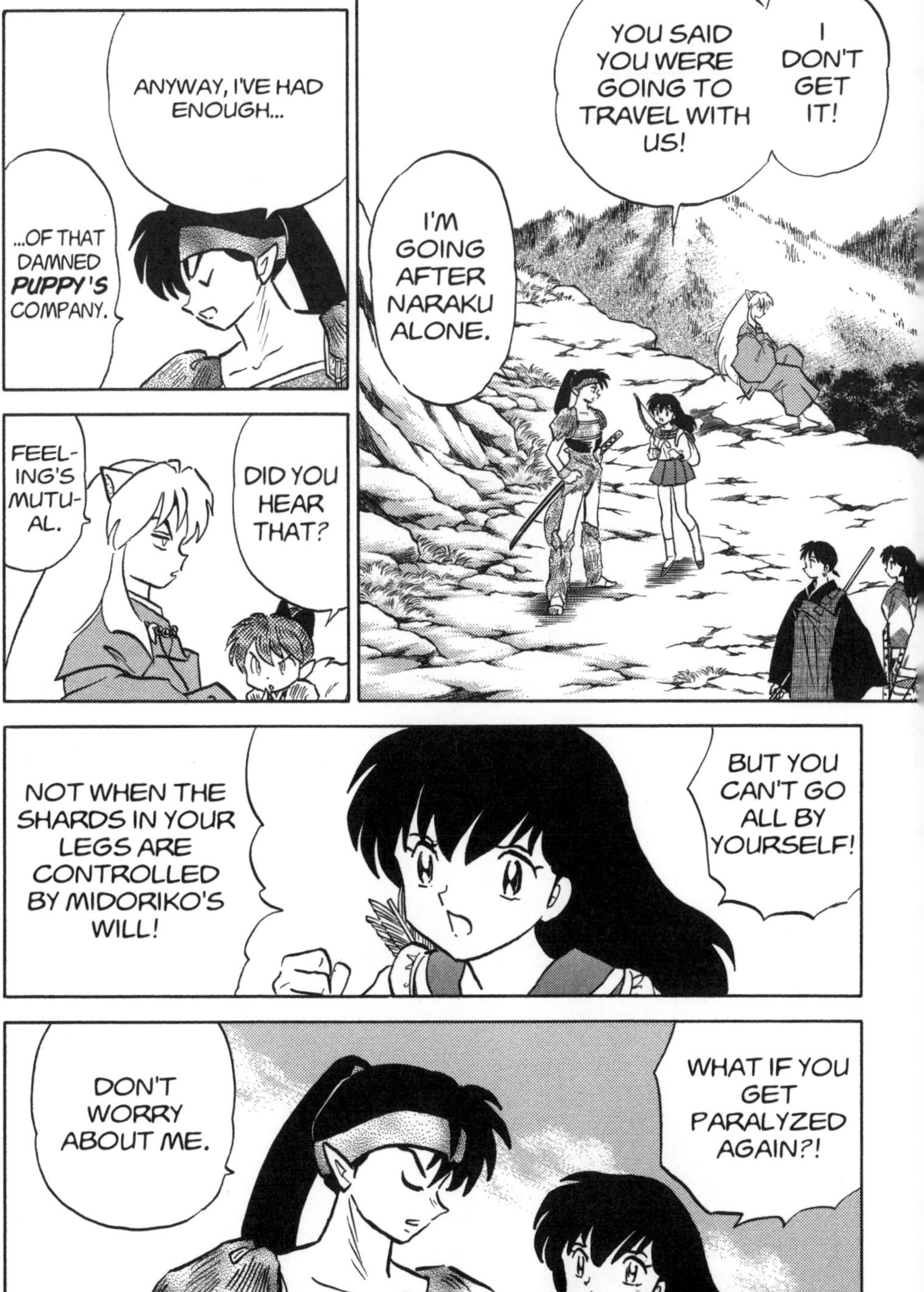
I DON'T GET IT!
YOU SAID YOU WERE GOING TO TRAVEL WITH US!
I'M GOING AFTER NARAKU ALONE.
ANYWAY, I'VE HAD ENOUGH...
...OF THAT DAMNED **PUPPY'S** COMPANY.
DID YOU HEAR THAT?
FEEL-ING'S MUTU-AL.
BUT YOU CAN'T GO ALL BY YOURSELF!
NOT WHEN THE SHARDS IN YOUR LEGS ARE CONTROLLED BY MIDORIKO'S WILL!
WHAT IF YOU GET PARALYZED AGAIN?!
DON'T WORRY ABOUT ME.

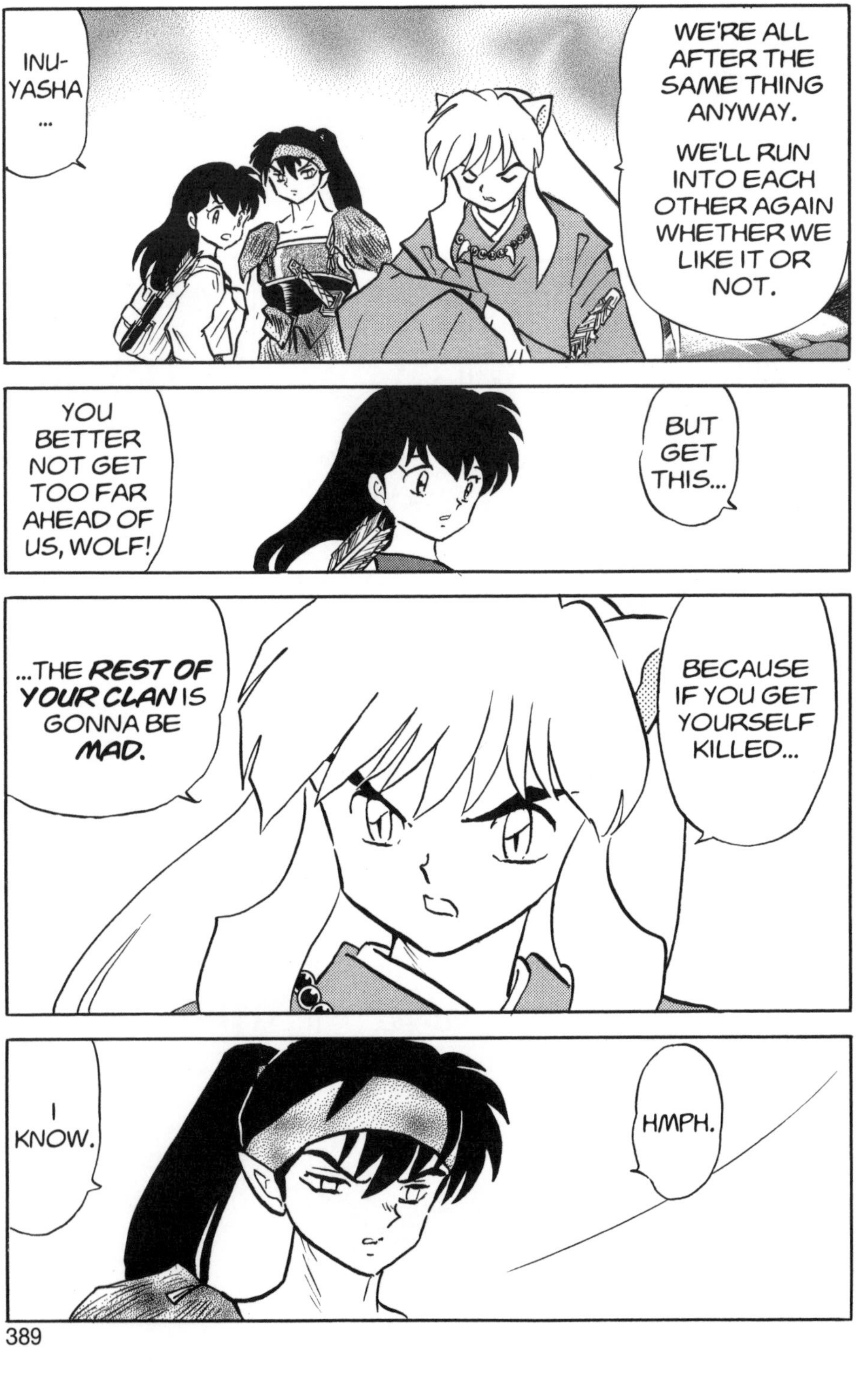
WE'RE ALL AFTER THE SAME THING ANYWAY.
WE'LL RUN INTO EACH OTHER AGAIN WHETHER WE LIKE IT OR NOT.
INU-YASHA ...
BUT GET THIS...
YOU BETTER NOT GET TOO FAR AHEAD OF US, WOLF!
BECAUSE IF YOU GET YOURSELF KILLED...
...THE **REST OF YOUR CLAN** IS GONNA BE **MAD.**
HMPH.
I KNOW.

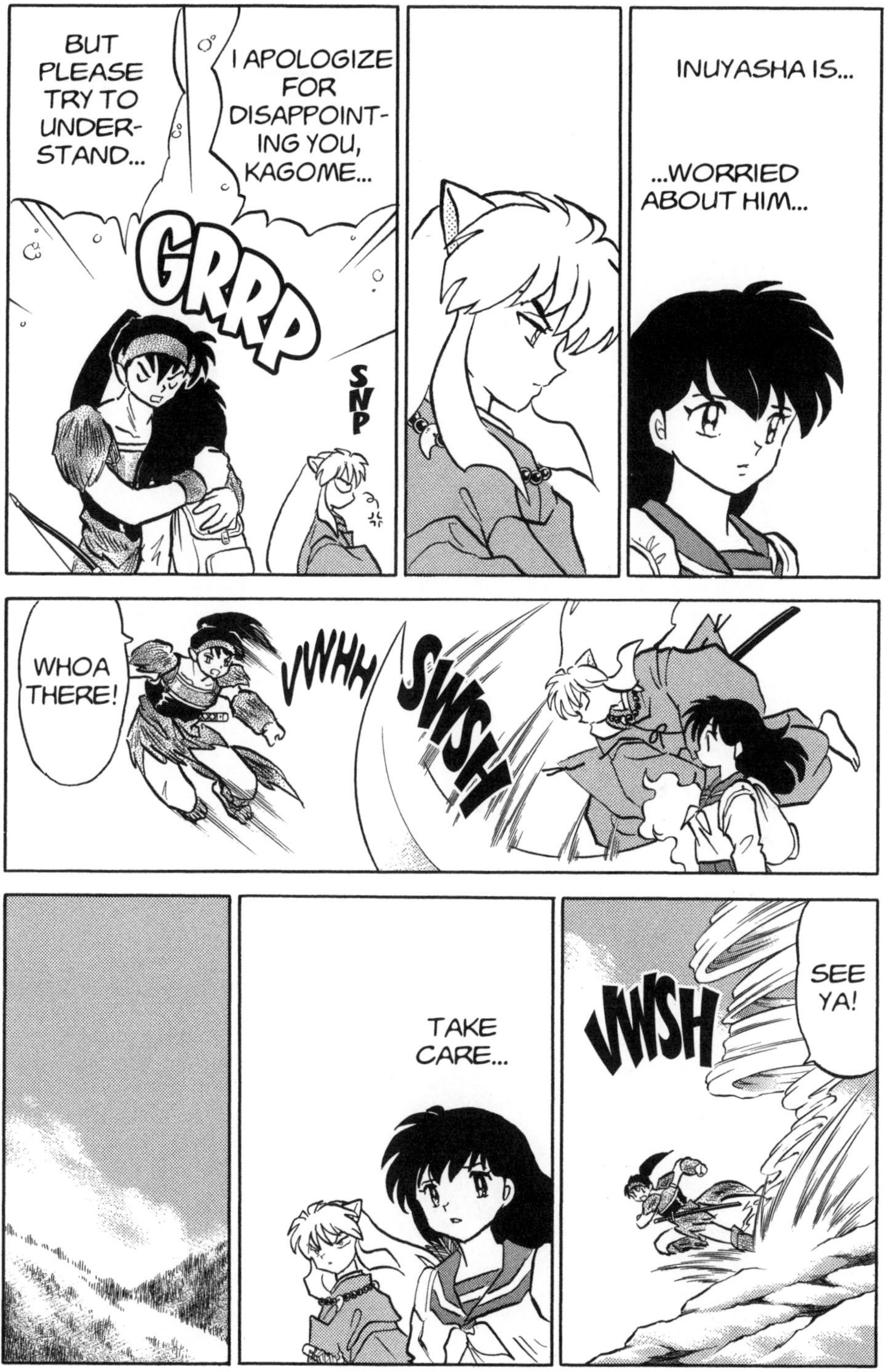
INUYASHA IS...
...WORRIED ABOUT HIM...
I APOLOGIZE FOR DISAPPOINT-ING YOU, KAGOME...
BUT PLEASE TRY TO UNDER-STAND...
GRRP
SNP
SWSH
VWHH
WHOA THERE!
SEE YA!
VWISH
TAKE CARE...

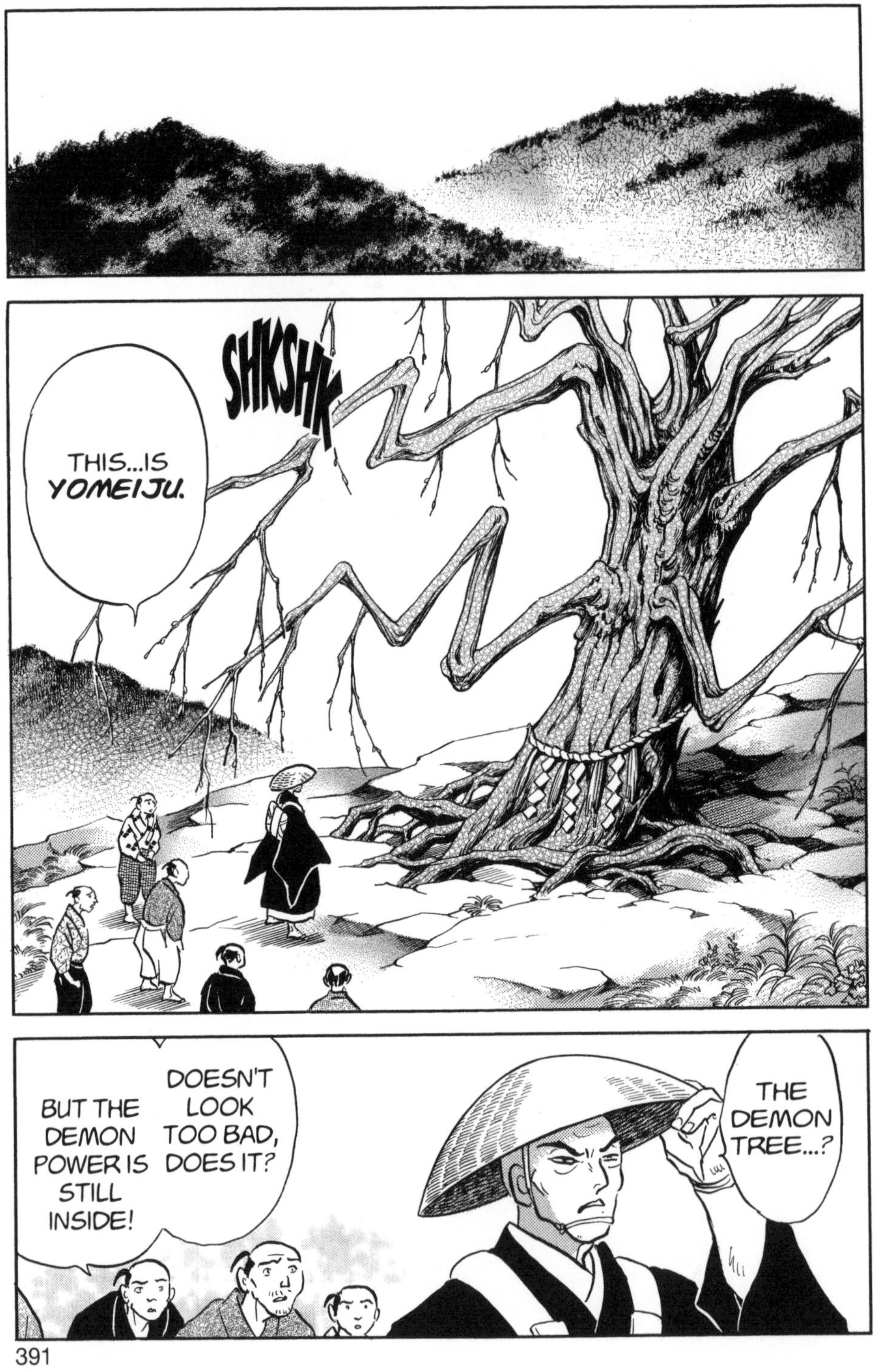
SHKSHK
THIS...IS YOMEIJU.
THE DEMON TREE...?
DOESN'T LOOK TOO BAD, DOES IT?
BUT THE DEMON POWER IS STILL INSIDE!

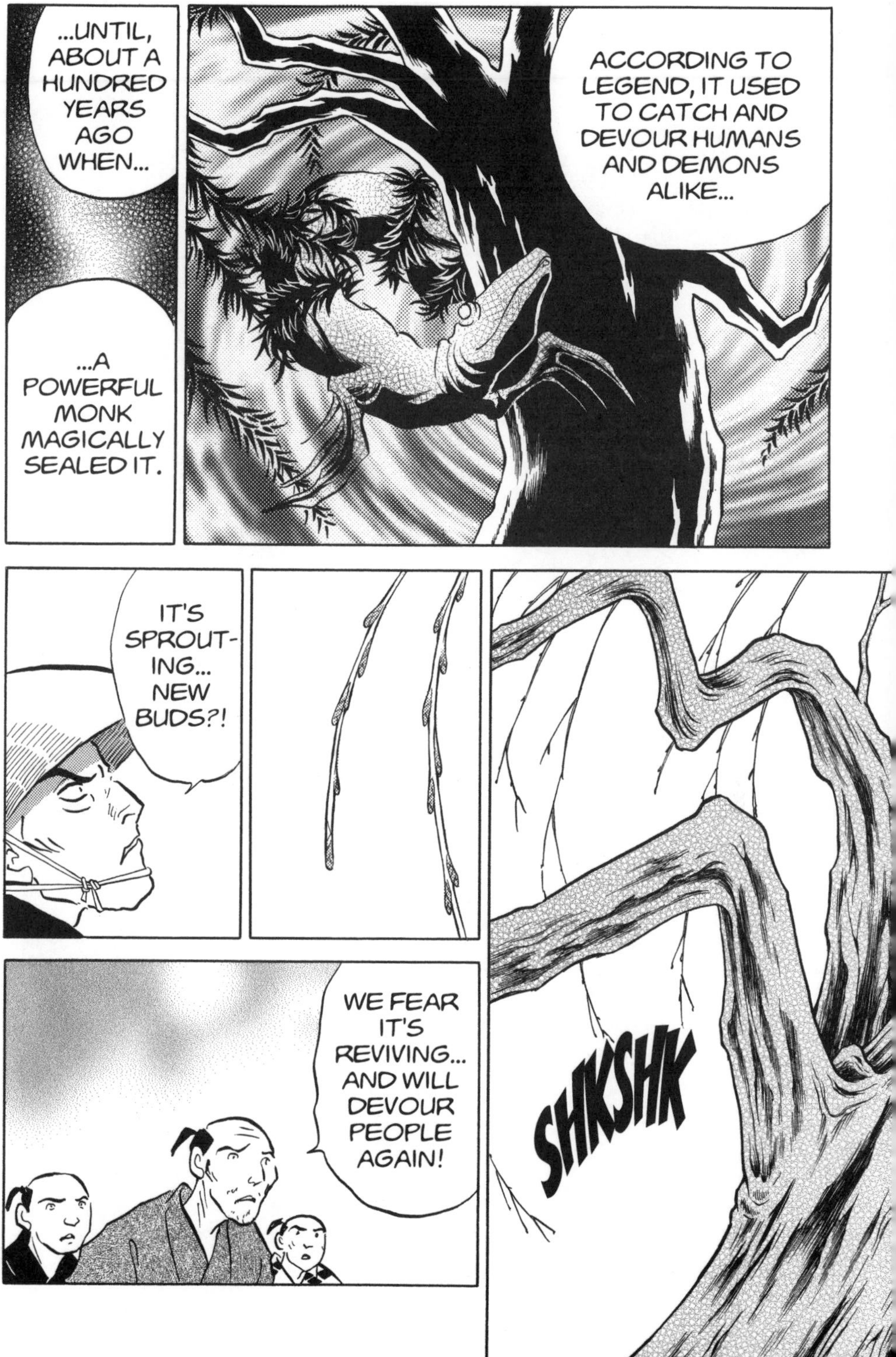
ACCORDING TO LEGEND, IT USED TO CATCH AND DEVOUR HUMANS AND DEMONS ALIKE...
...UNTIL, ABOUT A HUNDRED YEARS AGO WHEN...
...A POWERFUL MONK MAGICALLY SEALED IT.
SHKSHK
IT'S SPROUT-ING... NEW BUDS?!
WE FEAR IT'S REVIVING... AND WILL DEVOUR PEOPLE AGAIN!

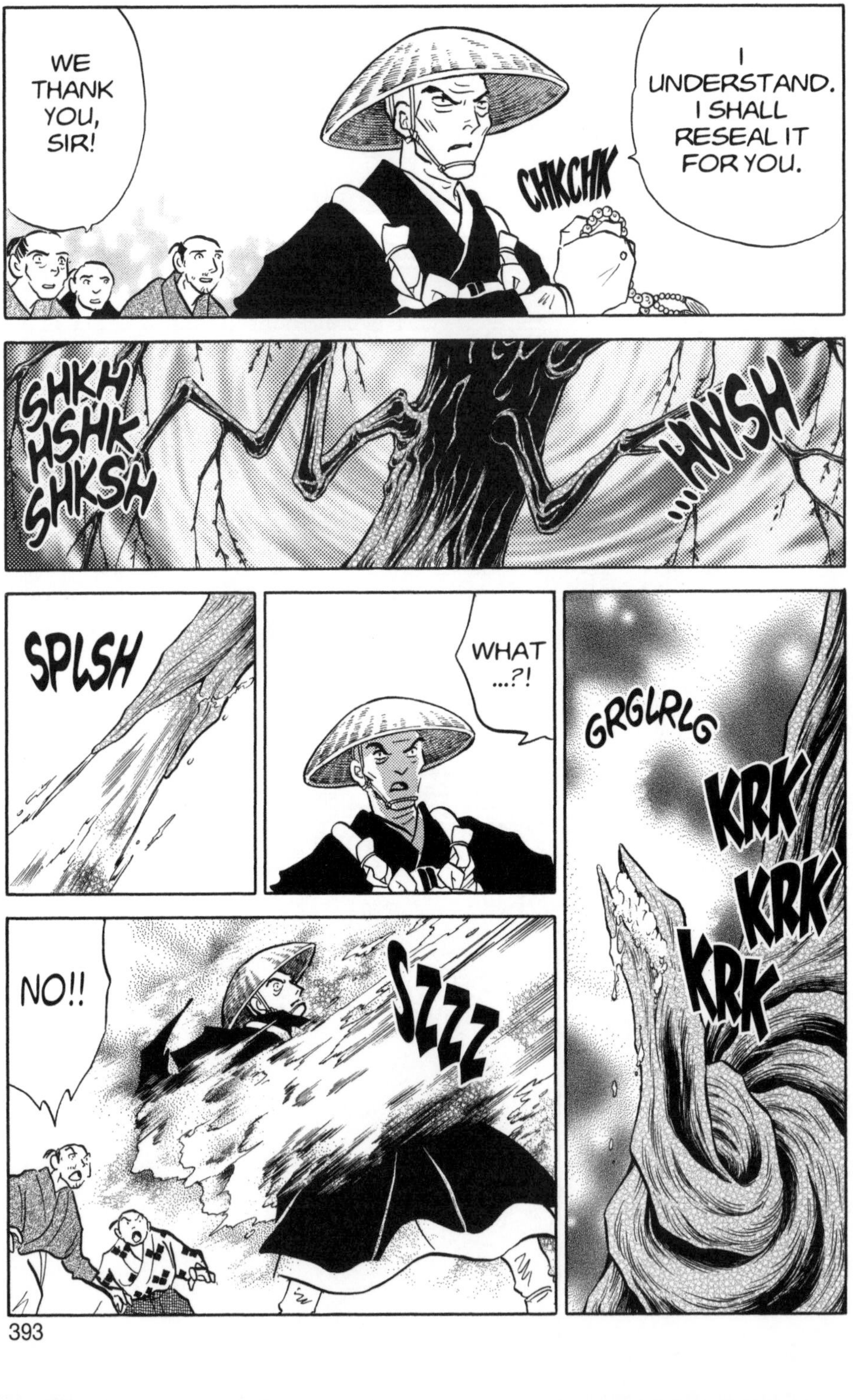
I UNDERSTAND. I SHALL RESEAL IT FOR YOU.
CHKCHK
WE THANK YOU, SIR!
SHKH HSHK SHKSH
...HWSH
GRGLRLG
KRK KRK KRK
WHAT ...?!
SPLSH
SZZZZ
NO!!

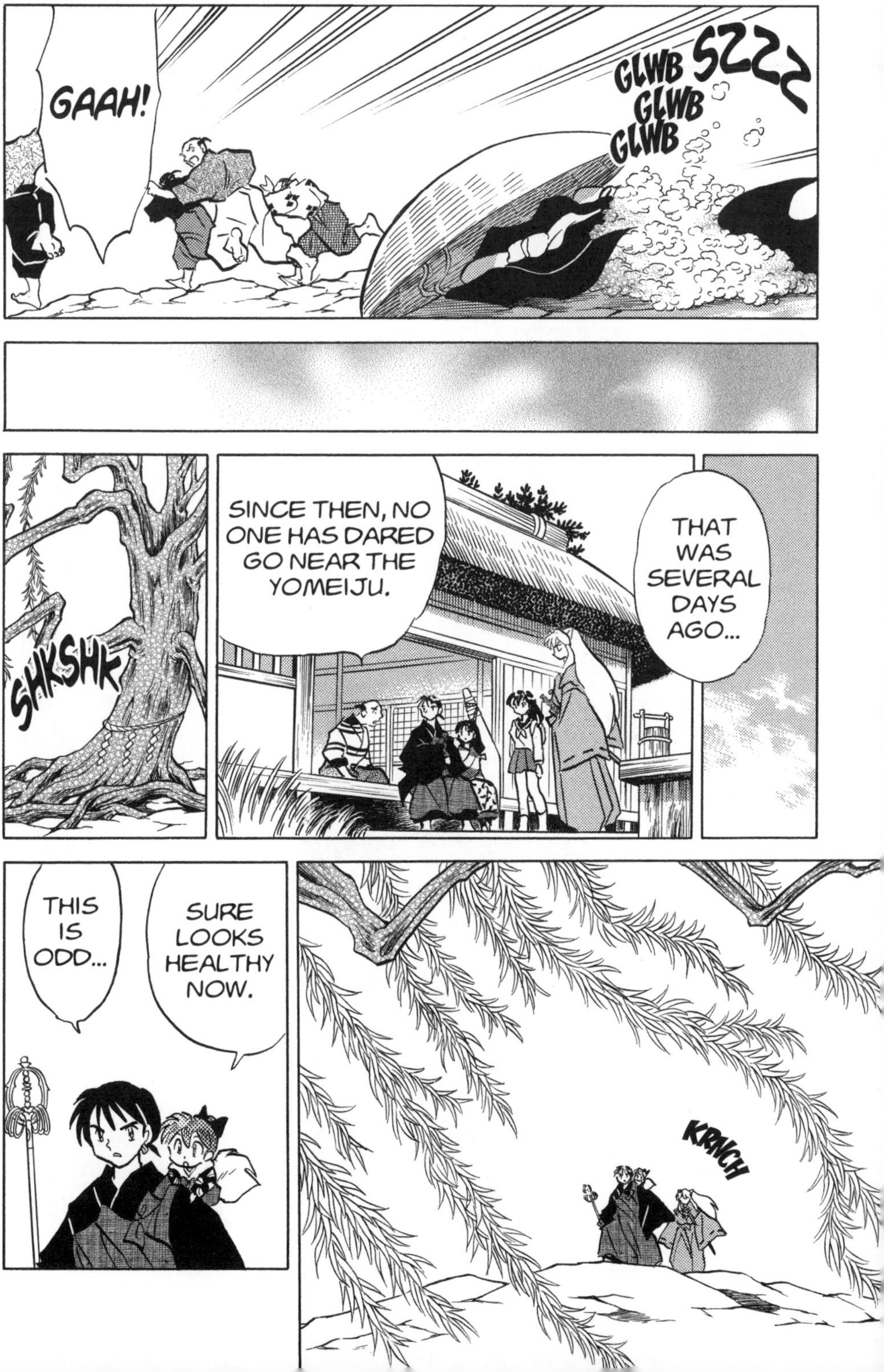
SZZZ
GLWB GLWB GLWB
GAAH!
THAT WAS SEVERAL DAYS AGO...
SINCE THEN, NO ONE HAS DARED GO NEAR THE YOMEIJU.
SHKSHK
KRNCH
SURE LOOKS HEALTHY NOW.
THIS IS ODD...

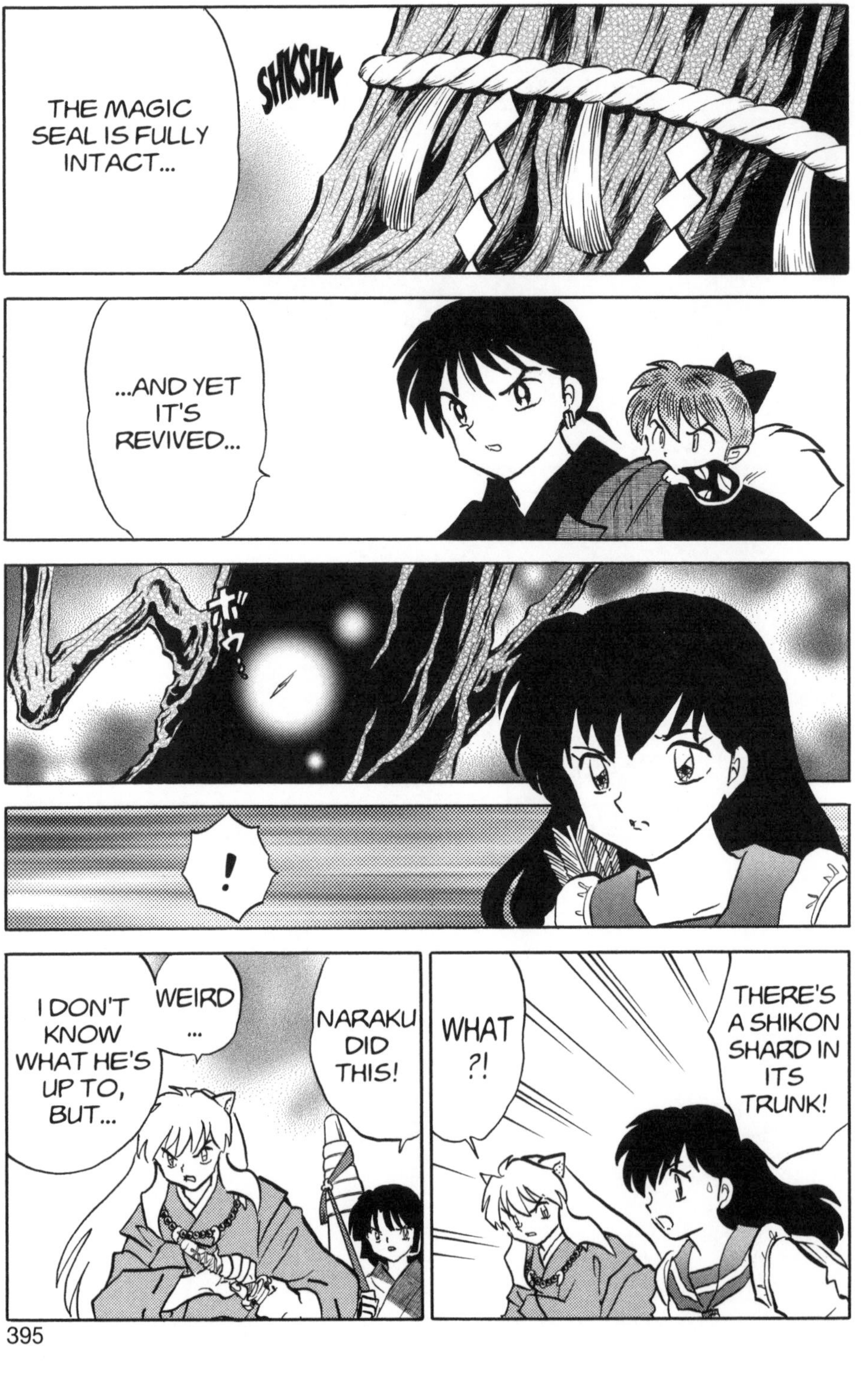
SHKSHK
THE MAGIC SEAL IS FULLY INTACT...
...AND YET IT'S REVIVED...
ボゥ
!
THERE'S A SHIKON SHARD IN ITS TRUNK!
WHAT?!
NARAKU DID THIS!
WEIRD...
I DON'T KNOW WHAT HE'S UP TO, BUT...

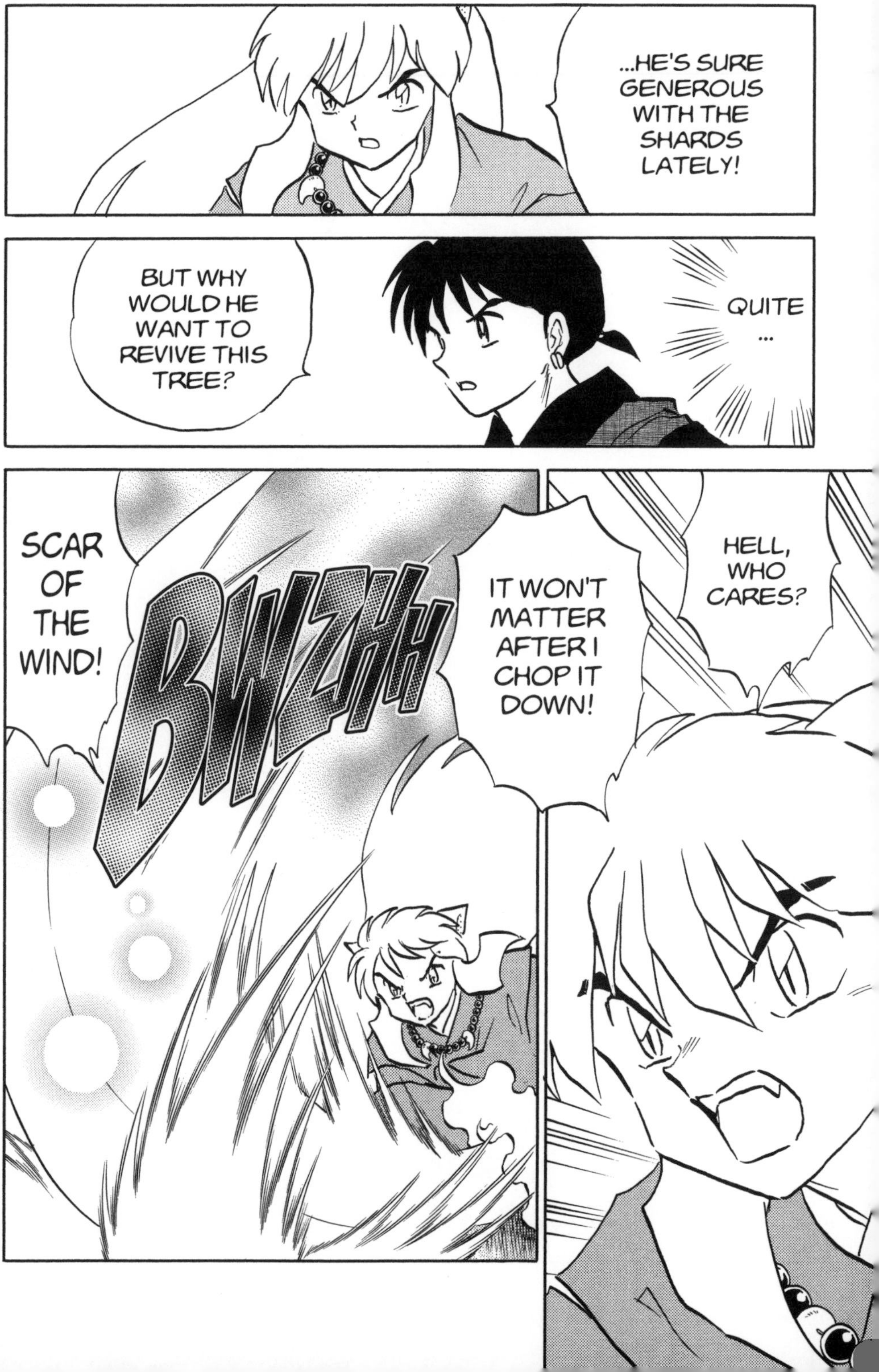
...HE'S SURE GENEROUS WITH THE SHARDS LATELY!
QUITE ...
BUT WHY WOULD HE WANT TO REVIVE THIS TREE?
HELL, WHO CARES?
IT WON'T MATTER AFTER I CHOP IT DOWN!
SCAR OF THE WIND!
BWZHHH

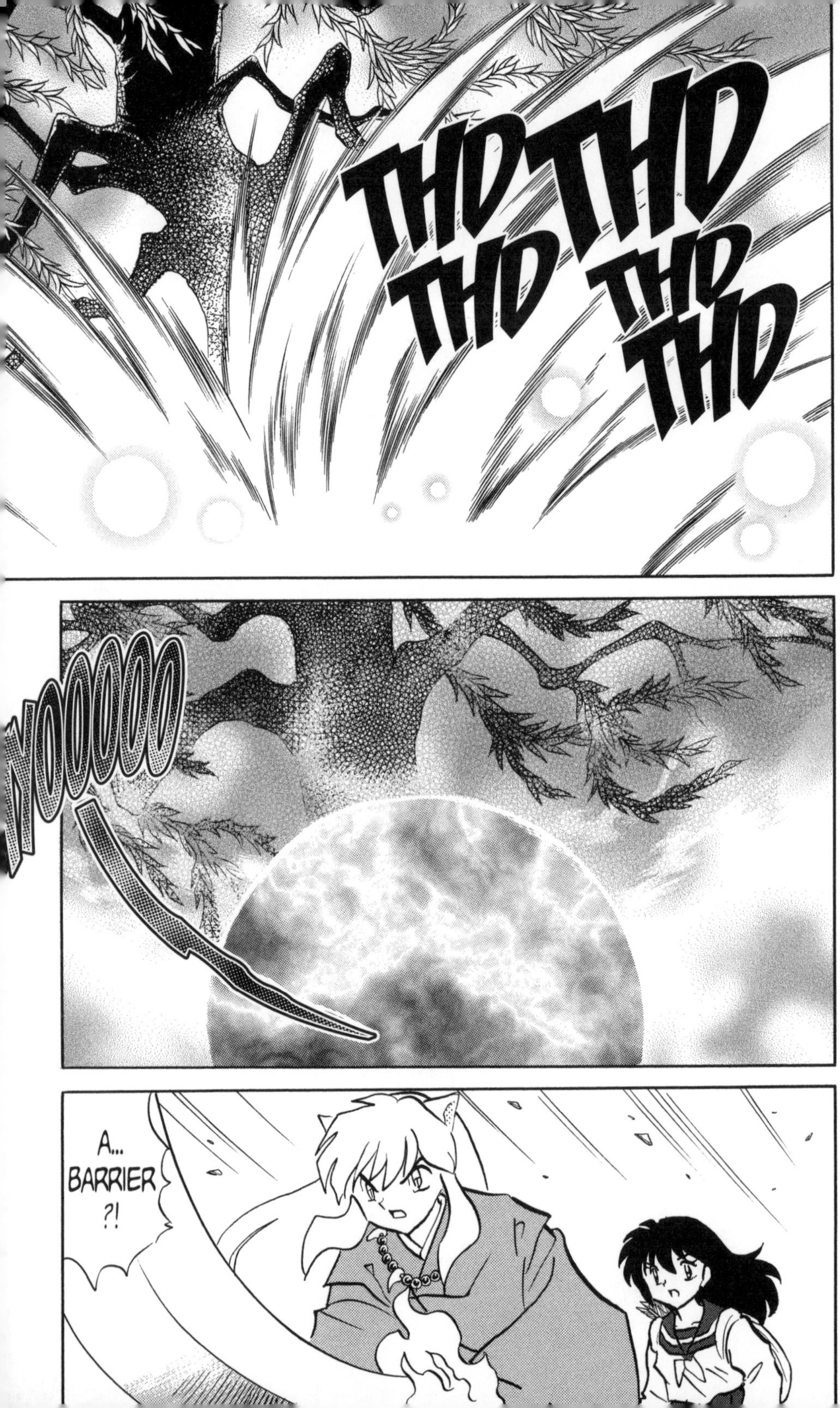
THD THD THD THD THD
WOOOOO
A... BARRIER ?!

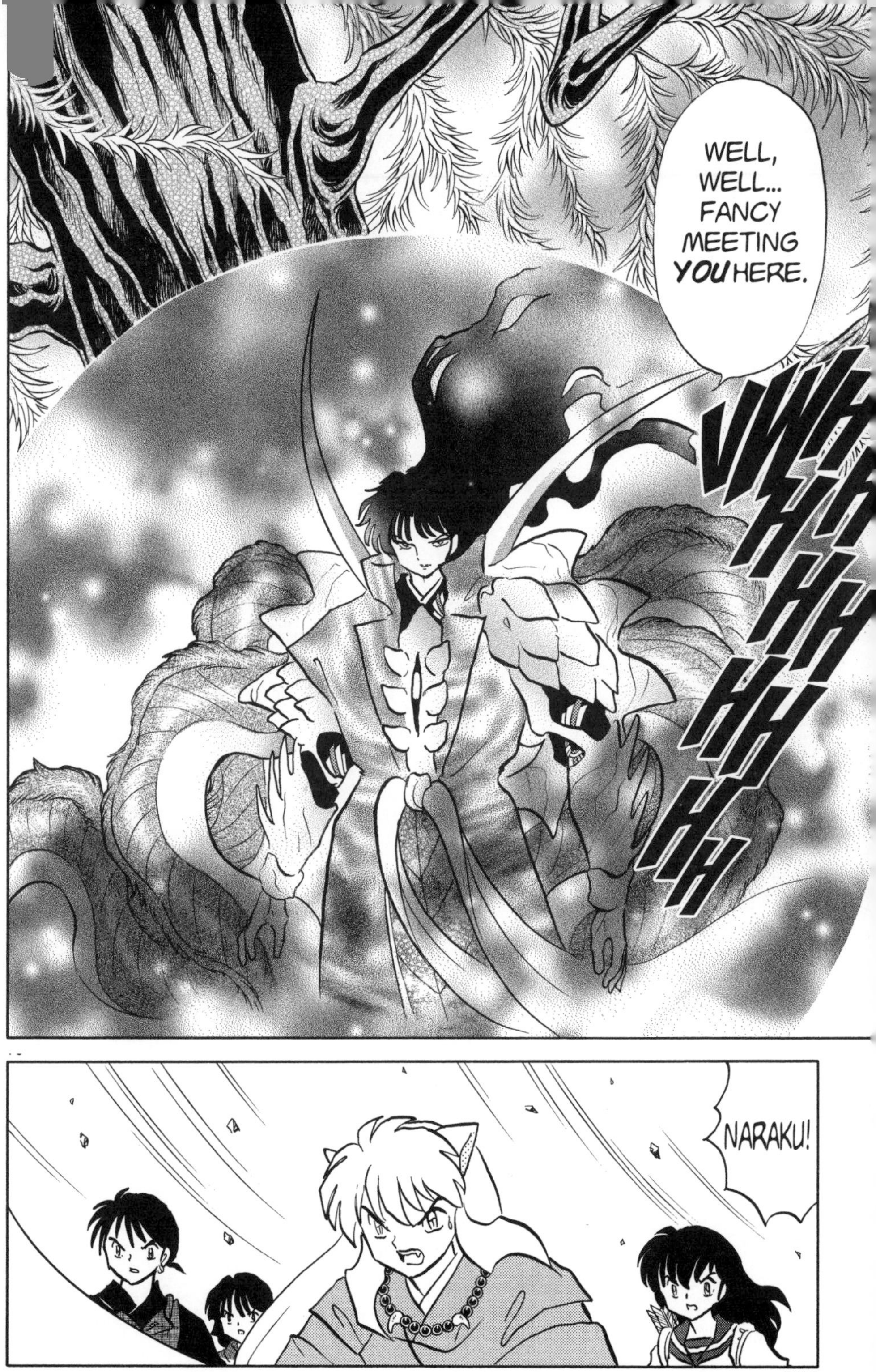
WELL, WELL... FANCY MEETING YOU HERE.
VWSHHHHHH
NARAKU!

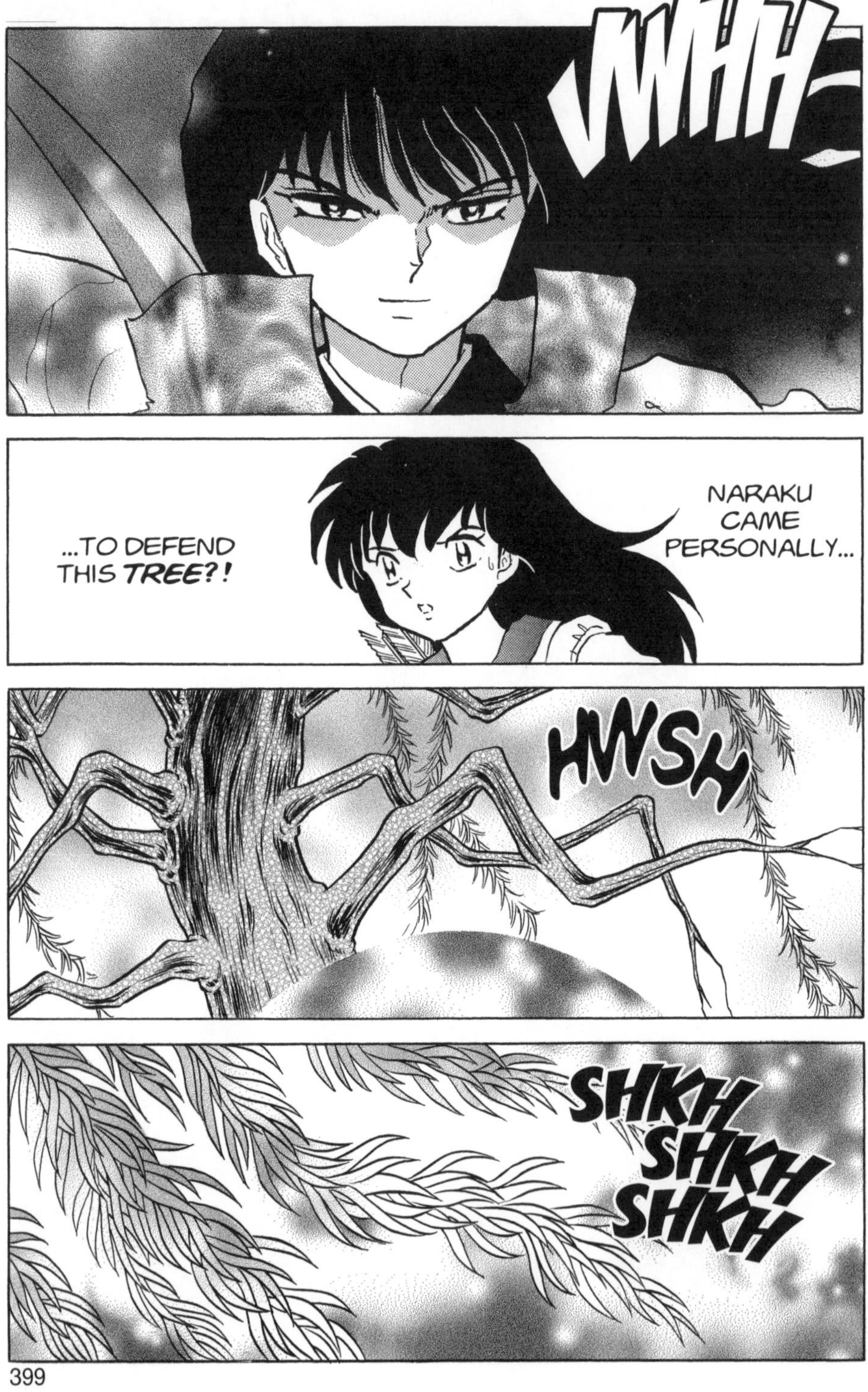
VWHH
NARAKU CAME PERSONALLY...
...TO DEFEND THIS TREE?!
HWSH
SHKH SHKH SHKH

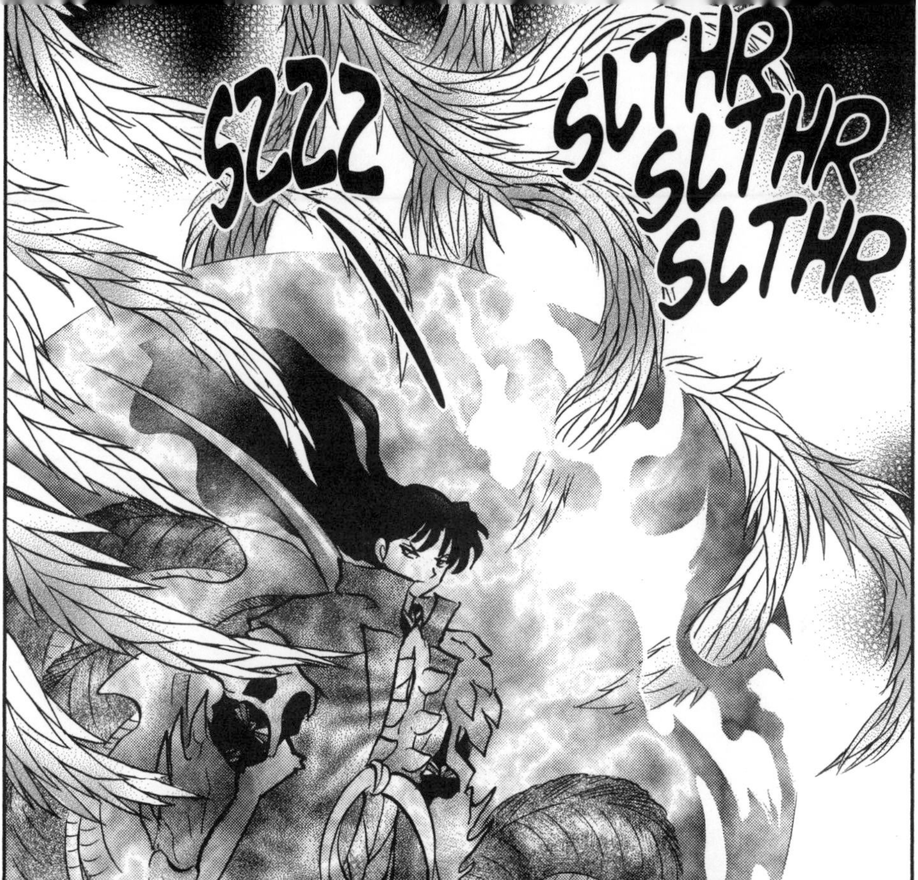
SLTHR SLTHR SLTHR SLTHR
SZZZ

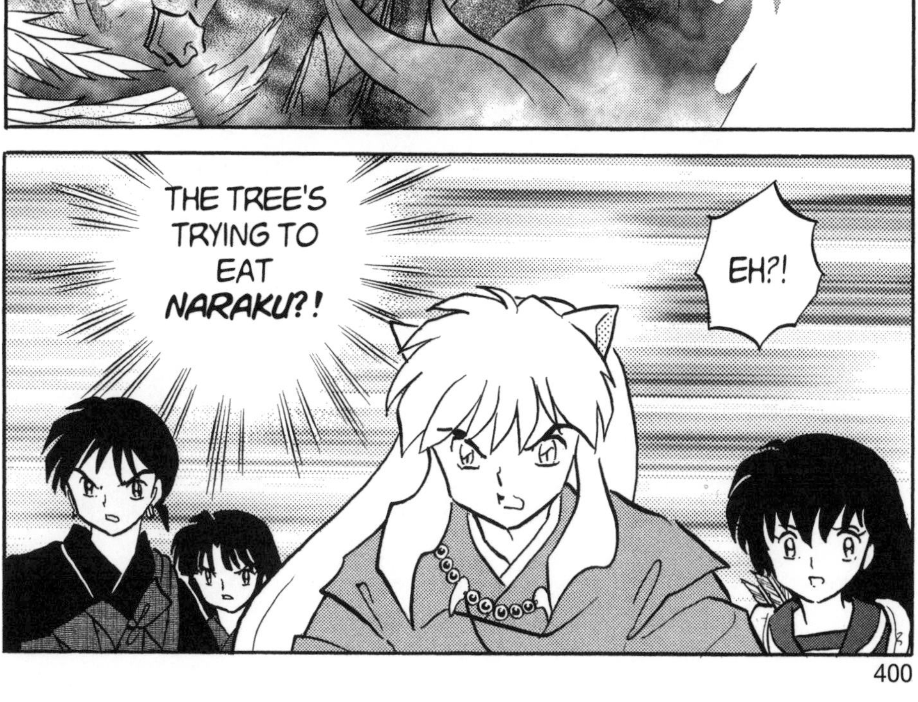
EH?!
THE TREE'S TRYING TO EAT **NARAKU?!**

SCROLL TWO
YOMEIJU'S POWER

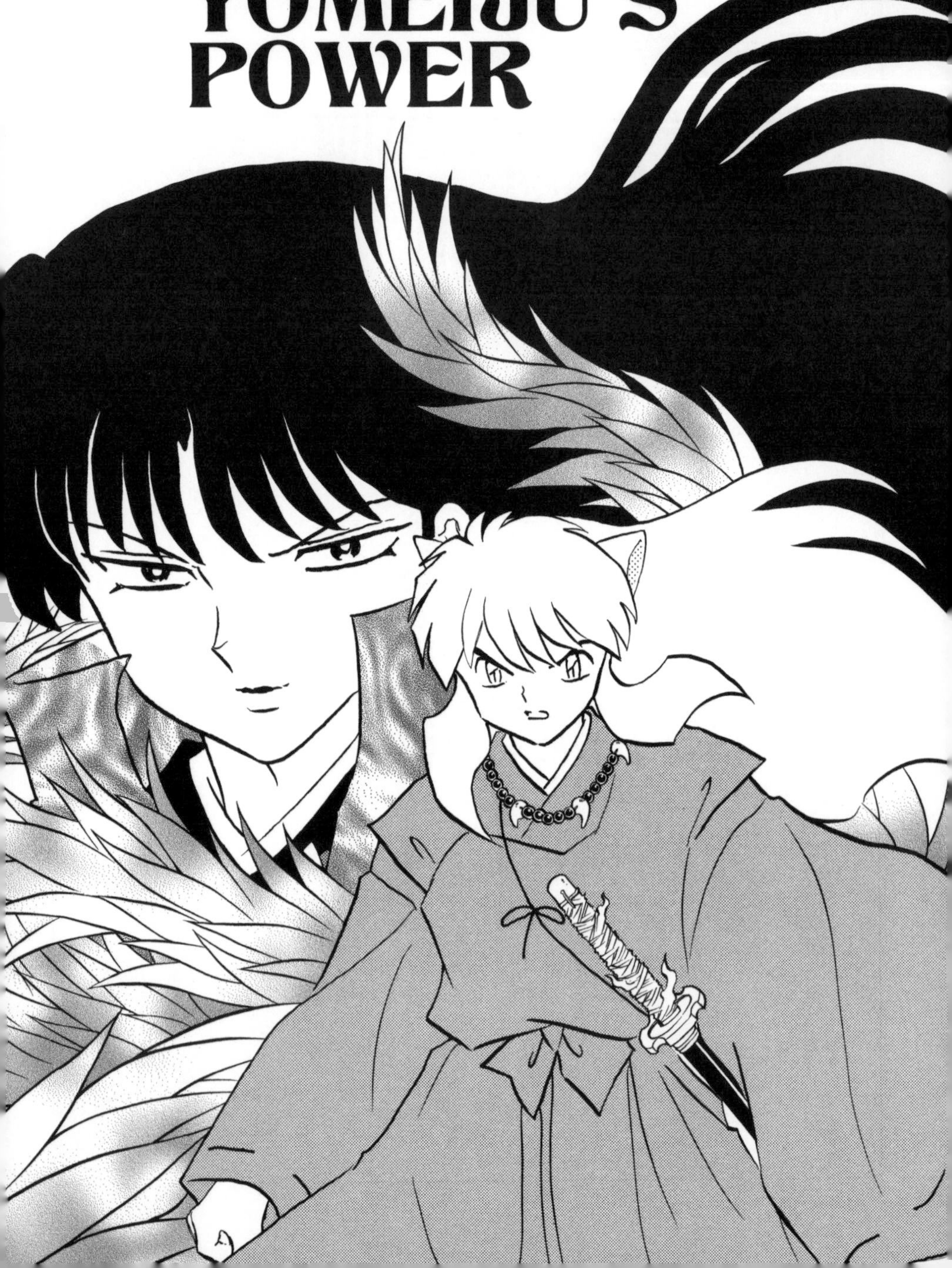

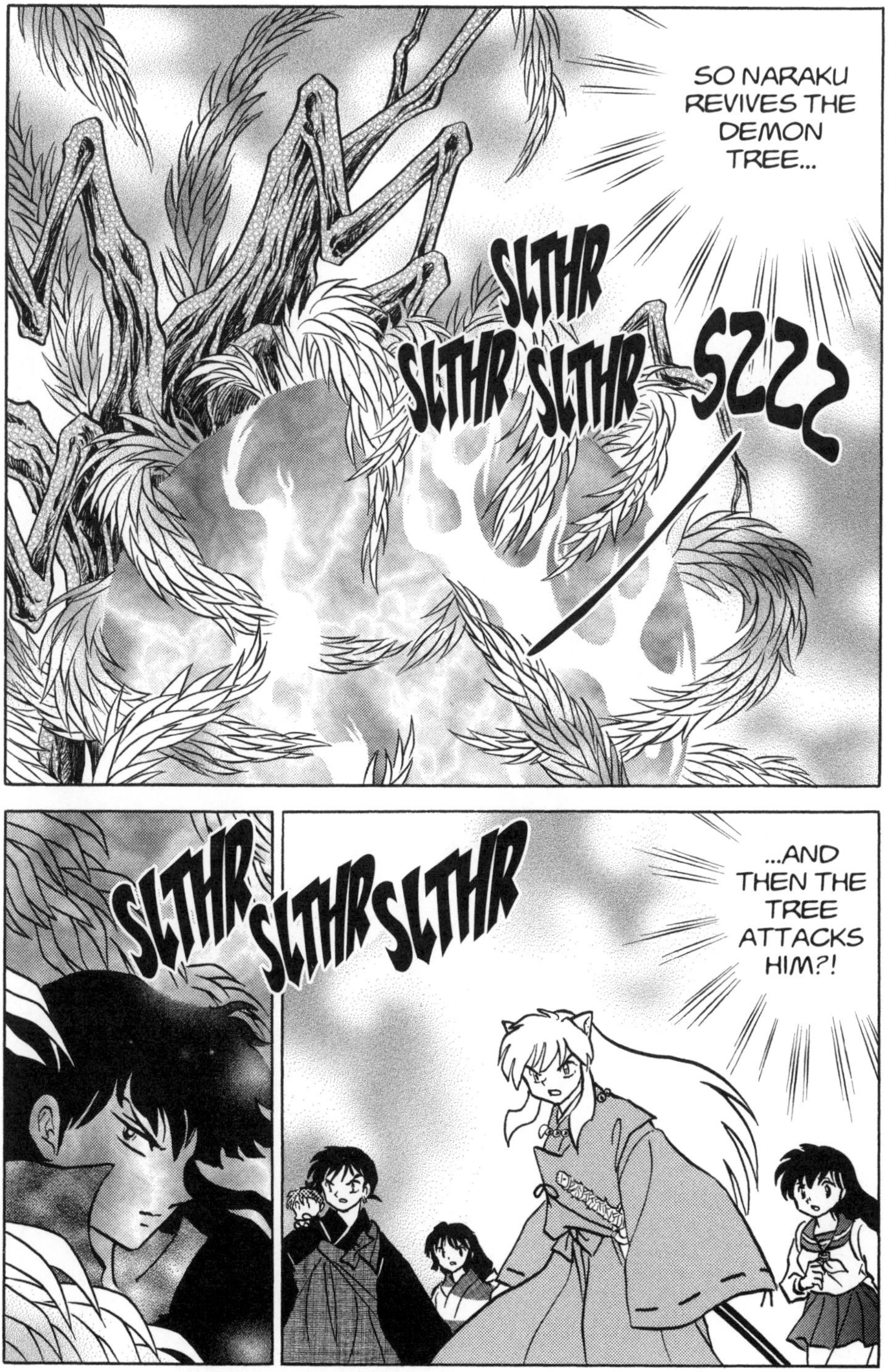
SO NARAKU REVIVES THE DEMON TREE...
SLTHR
SLTHR SLTHR
SZZZ
...AND THEN THE TREE ATTACKS HIM?!
SLTHR SLTHR SLTHR

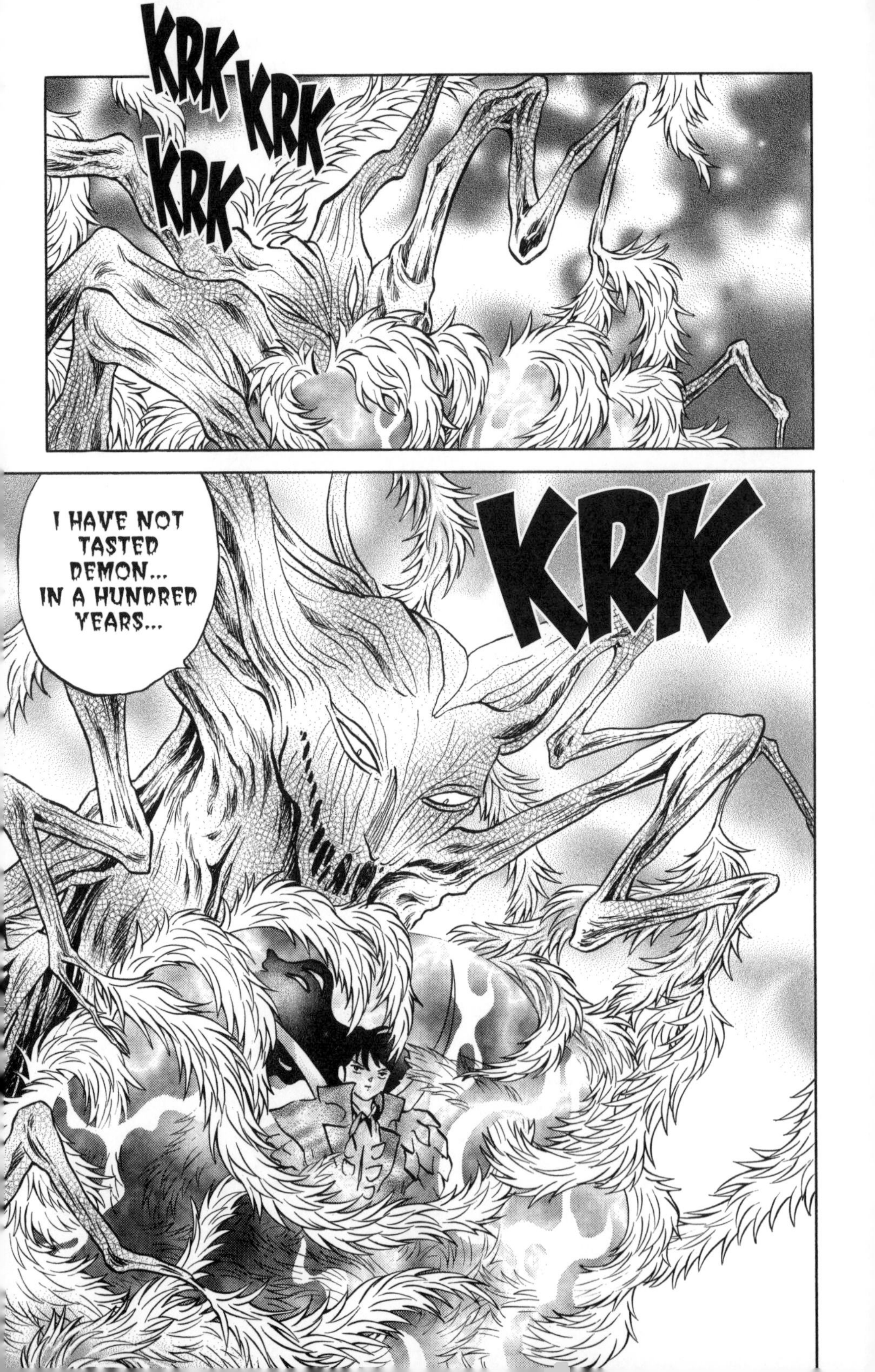
KRK KRK
KRK
KRK
I HAVE NOT TASTED DEMON... IN A HUNDRED YEARS...

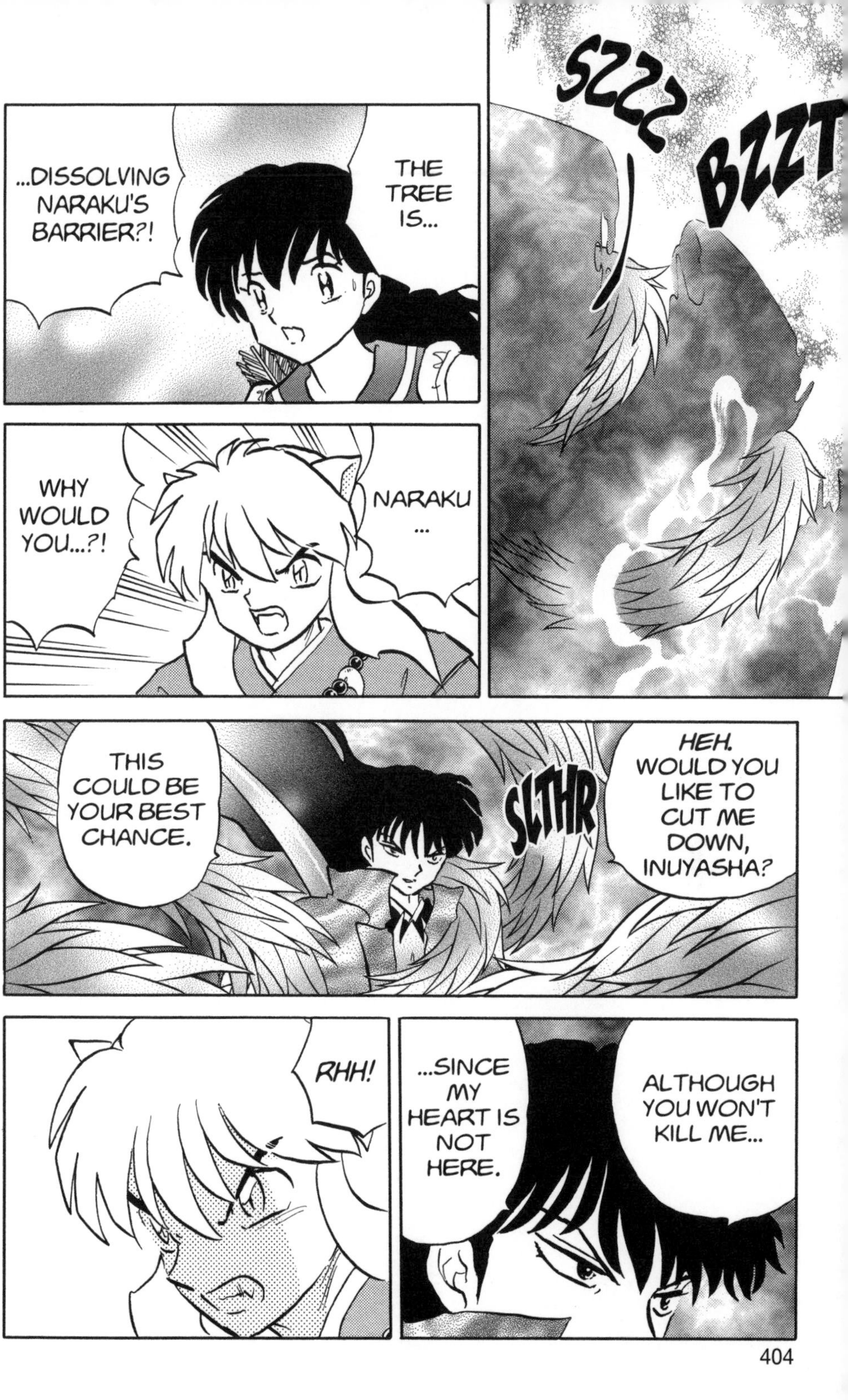
SZZZ
BZZT
THE TREE IS...
...DISSOLVING NARAKU'S BARRIER?!
NARAKU...
WHY WOULD YOU...?!
HEH. WOULD YOU LIKE TO CUT ME DOWN, INUYASHA?
SLTHR
THIS COULD BE YOUR BEST CHANCE.
ALTHOUGH YOU WON'T KILL ME...
...SINCE MY HEART IS NOT HERE.
RHH!

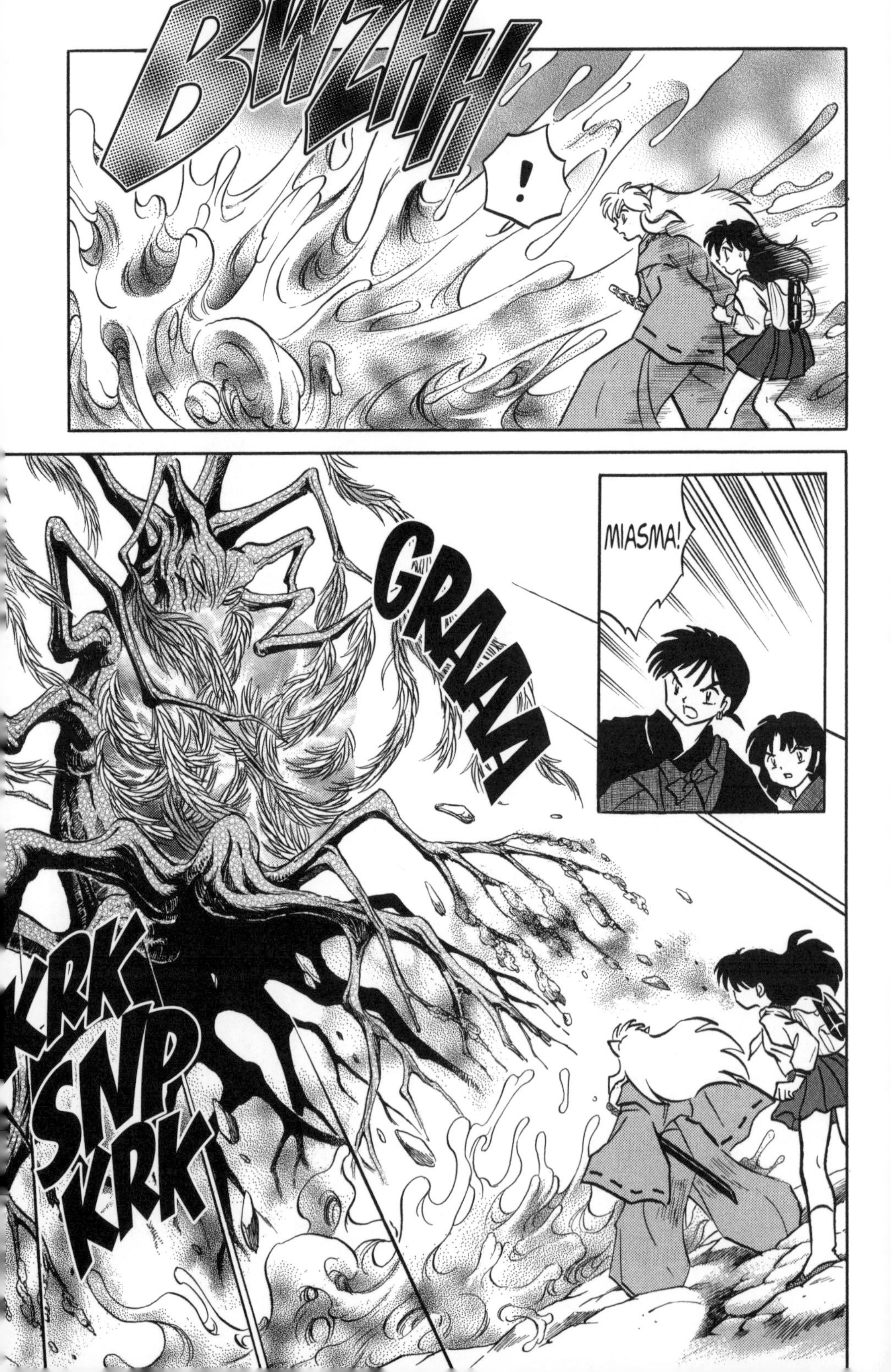
BWZHH
!
MIASMA!
GRAAAA
KRK
SNP
KRK

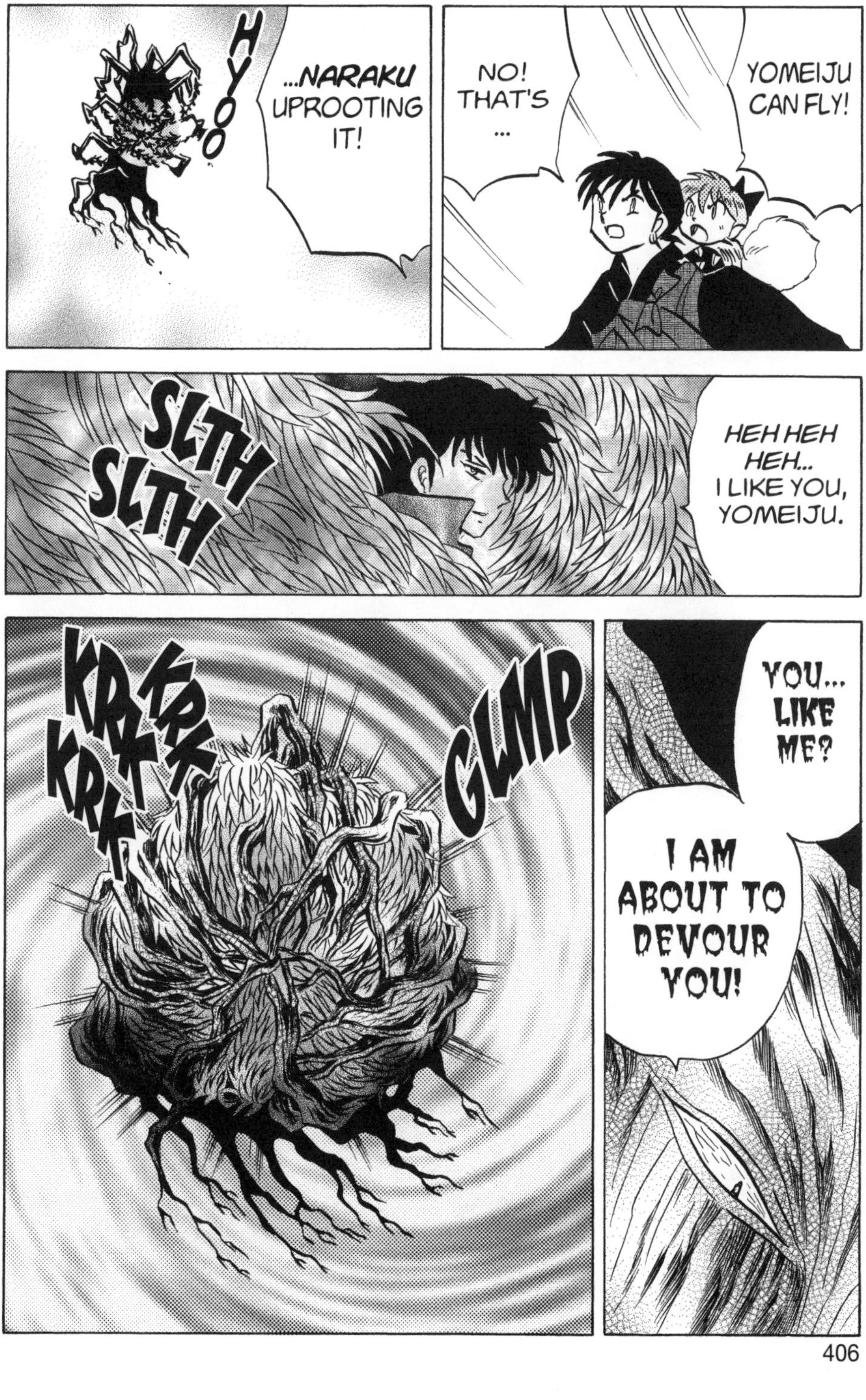
YOMEIJU CAN FLY!
NO! THAT'S ...
...NARAKU UPROOTING IT!
HYOOO
HEH HEH HEH... I LIKE YOU, YOMEIJU.
SLTH SLTH
YOU... LIKE ME?
I AM ABOUT TO DEVOUR YOU!
GLUMP
KRK KRK KRK KRK

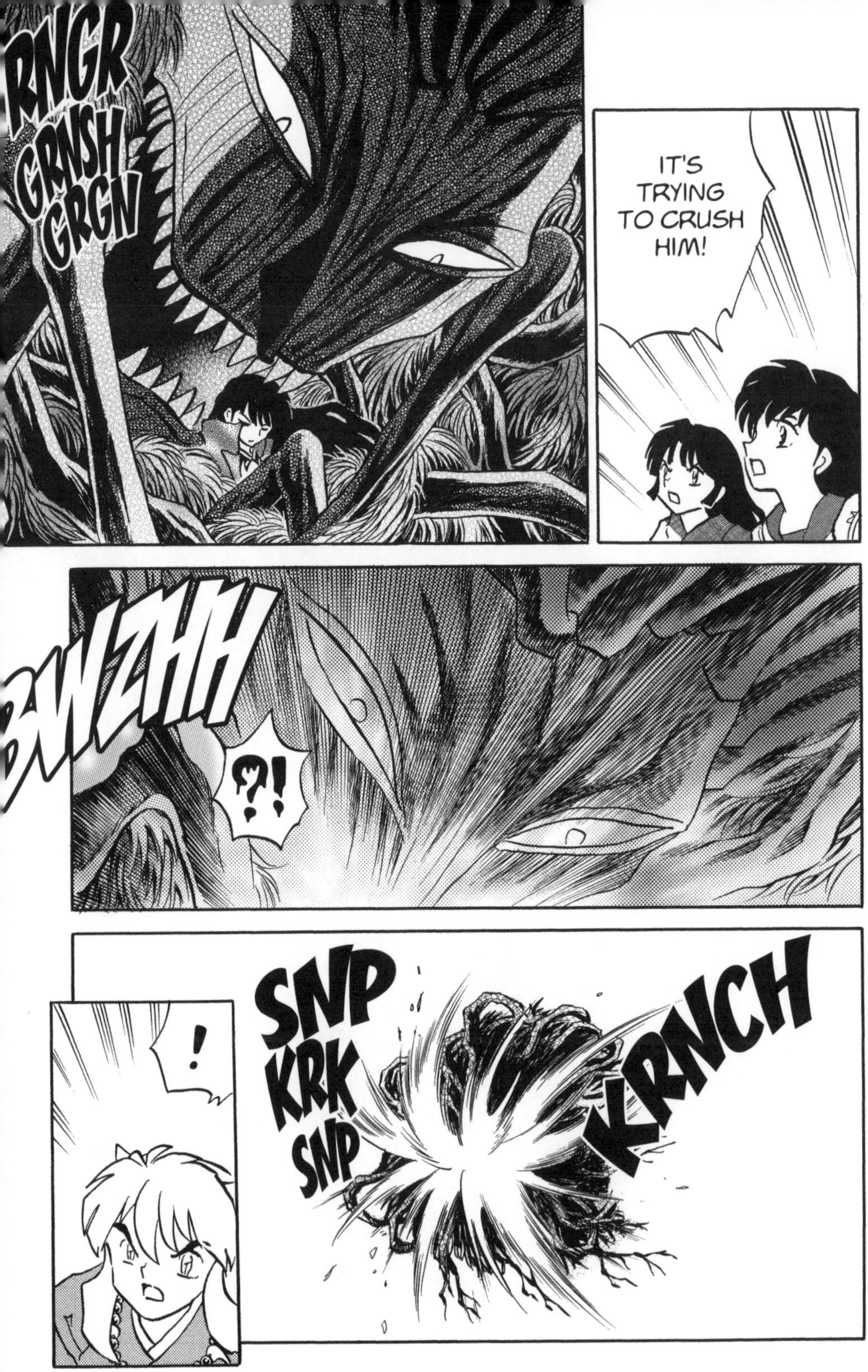
IT'S TRYING TO CRUSH HIM!
RNGR GRNSH GRGN
BWZHH
?!
KRNCH
SNP KRK SNP
!

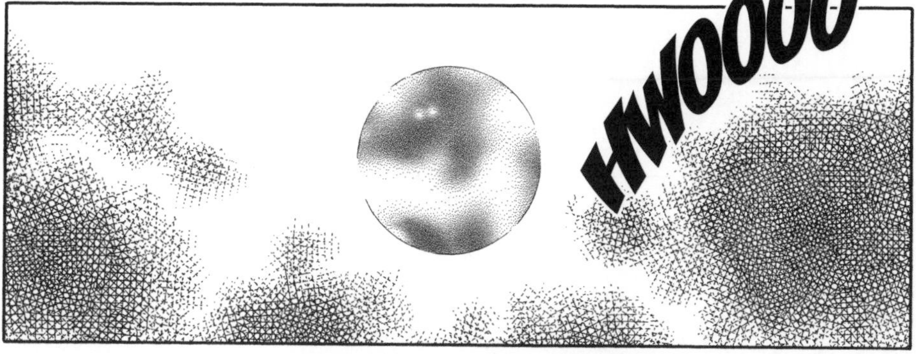
HWOOOO
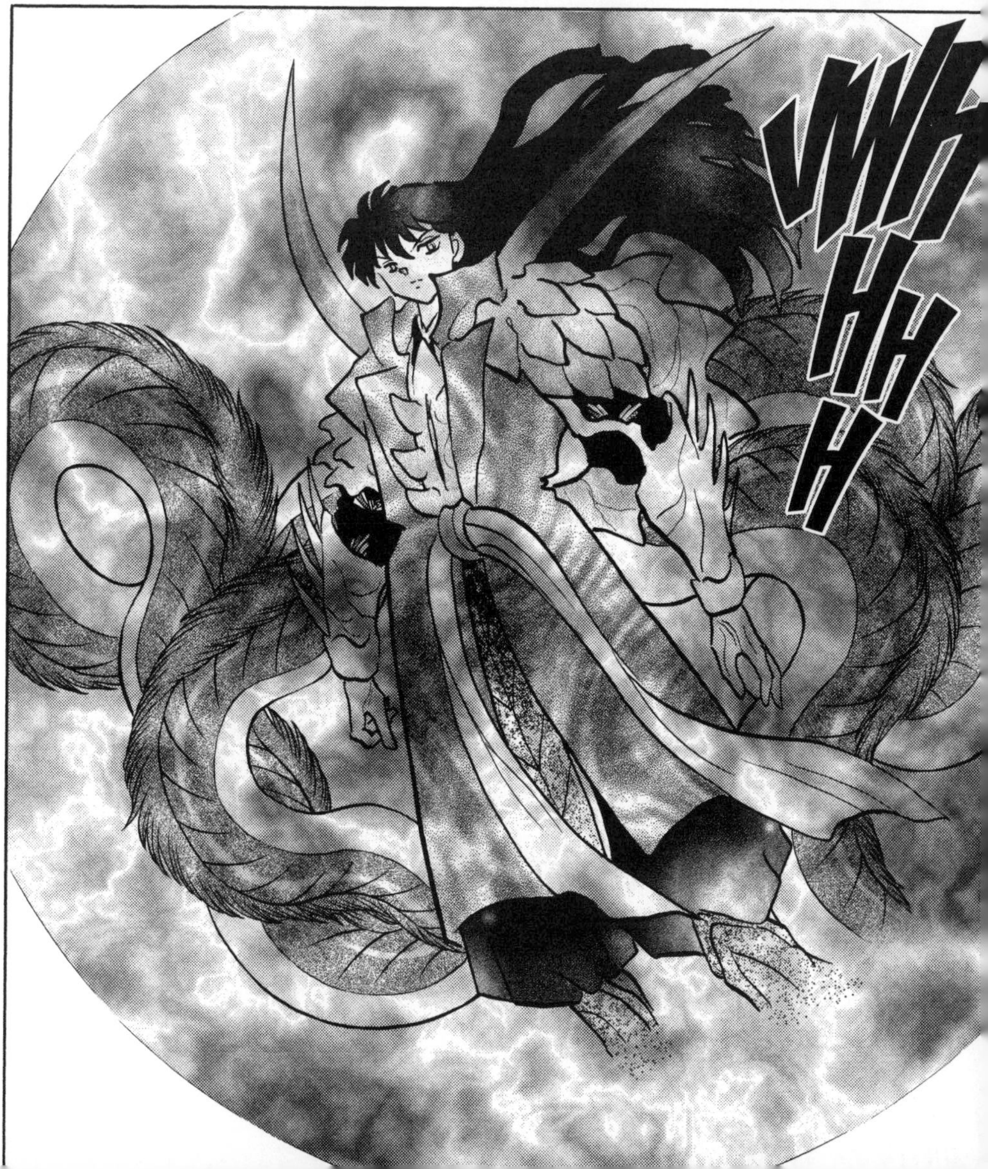
VWHHHH

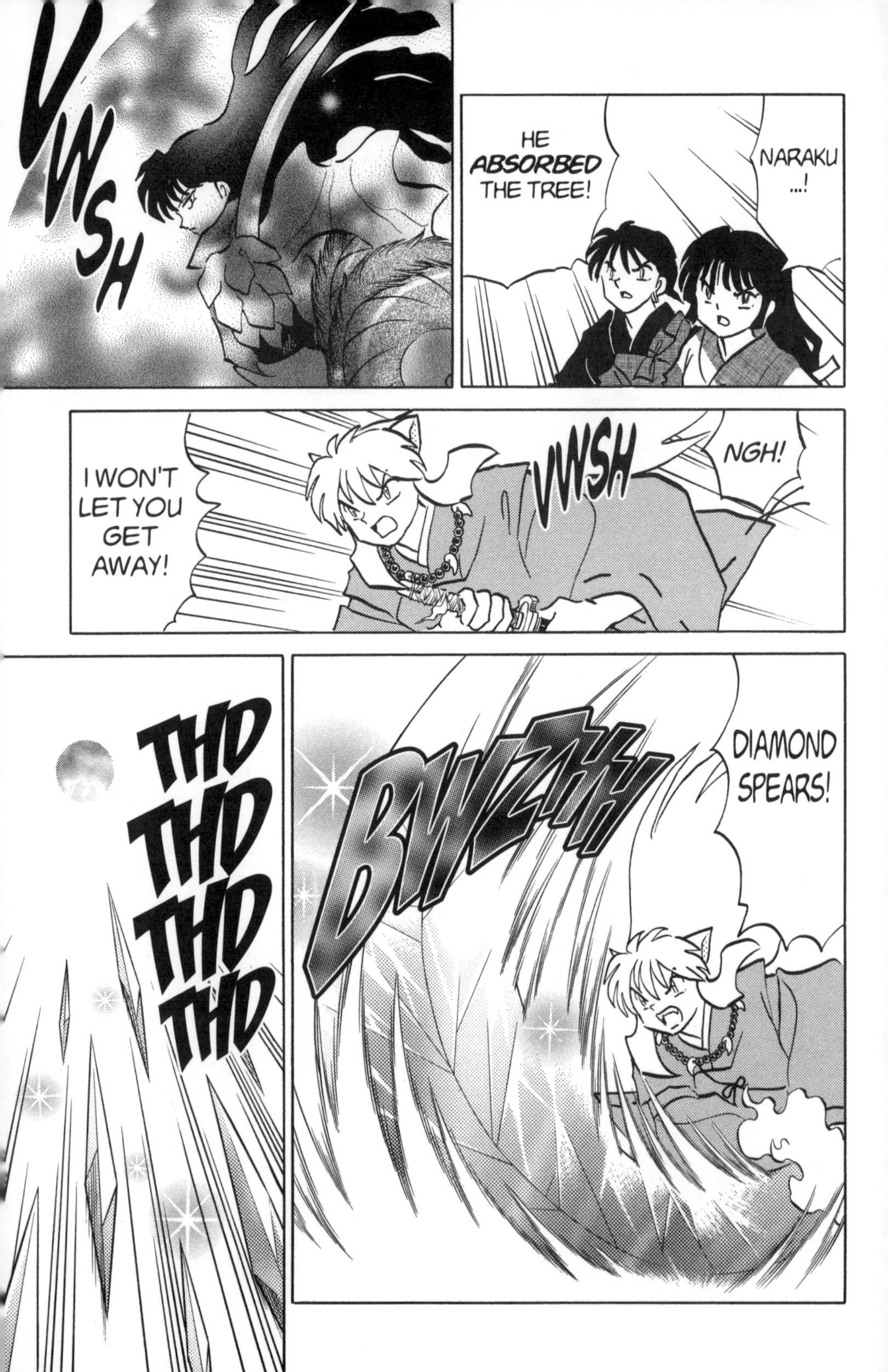
NARAKU ...!
HE ABSORBED THE TREE!
VWSH
NGH!
VWSH
I WON'T LET YOU GET AWAY!
DIAMOND SPEARS!
BWZHH
THD THD THD THD

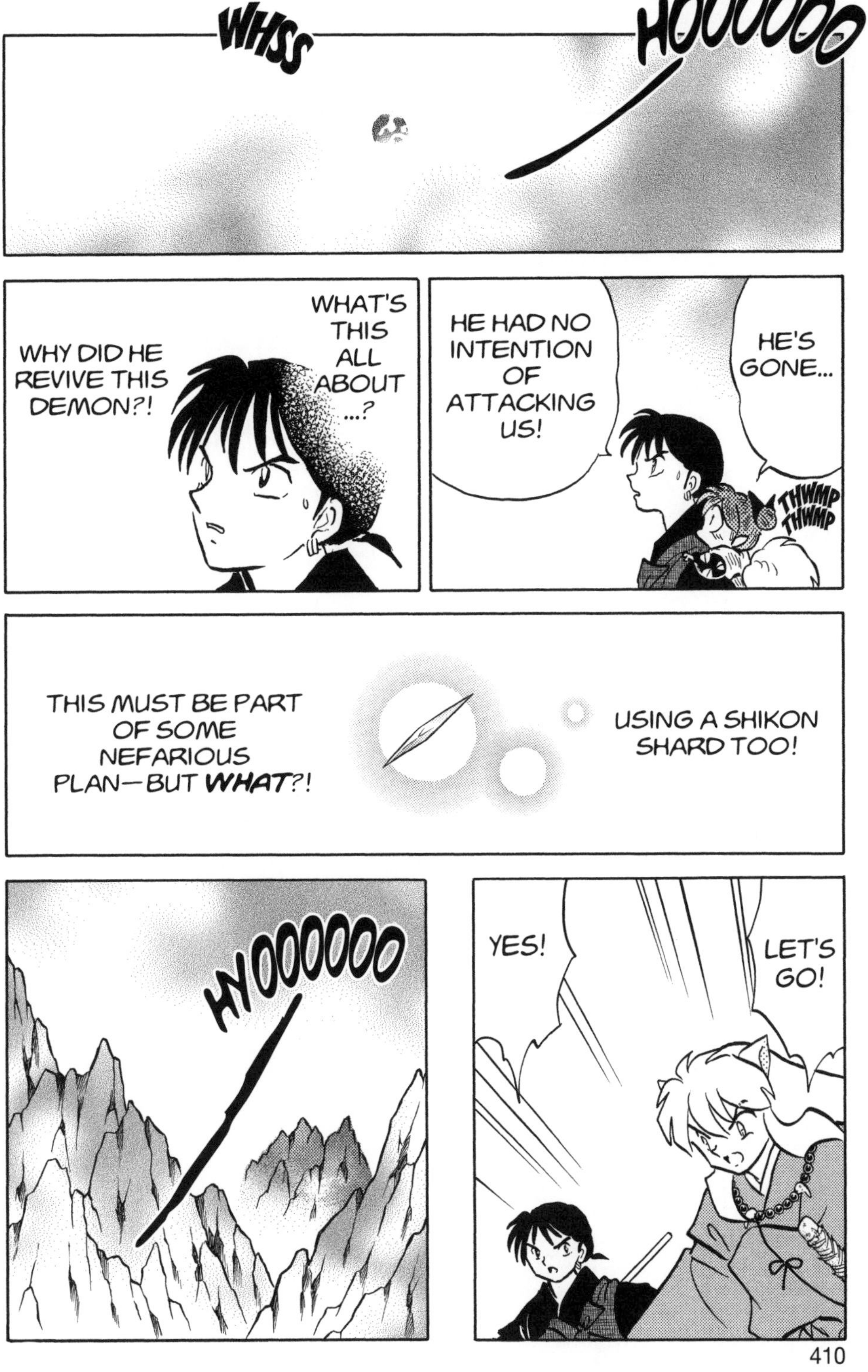
HOOOOOO
WHSS
HE'S GONE...
HE HAD NO INTENTION OF ATTACKING US!
THWMP THWMP
WHAT'S THIS ALL ABOUT ...?
WHY DID HE REVIVE THIS DEMON?!
USING A SHIKON SHARD TOO!
THIS MUST BE PART OF SOME NEFARIOUS PLAN—BUT **WHAT**?!
LET'S GO!
YES!
HYOOOOOO

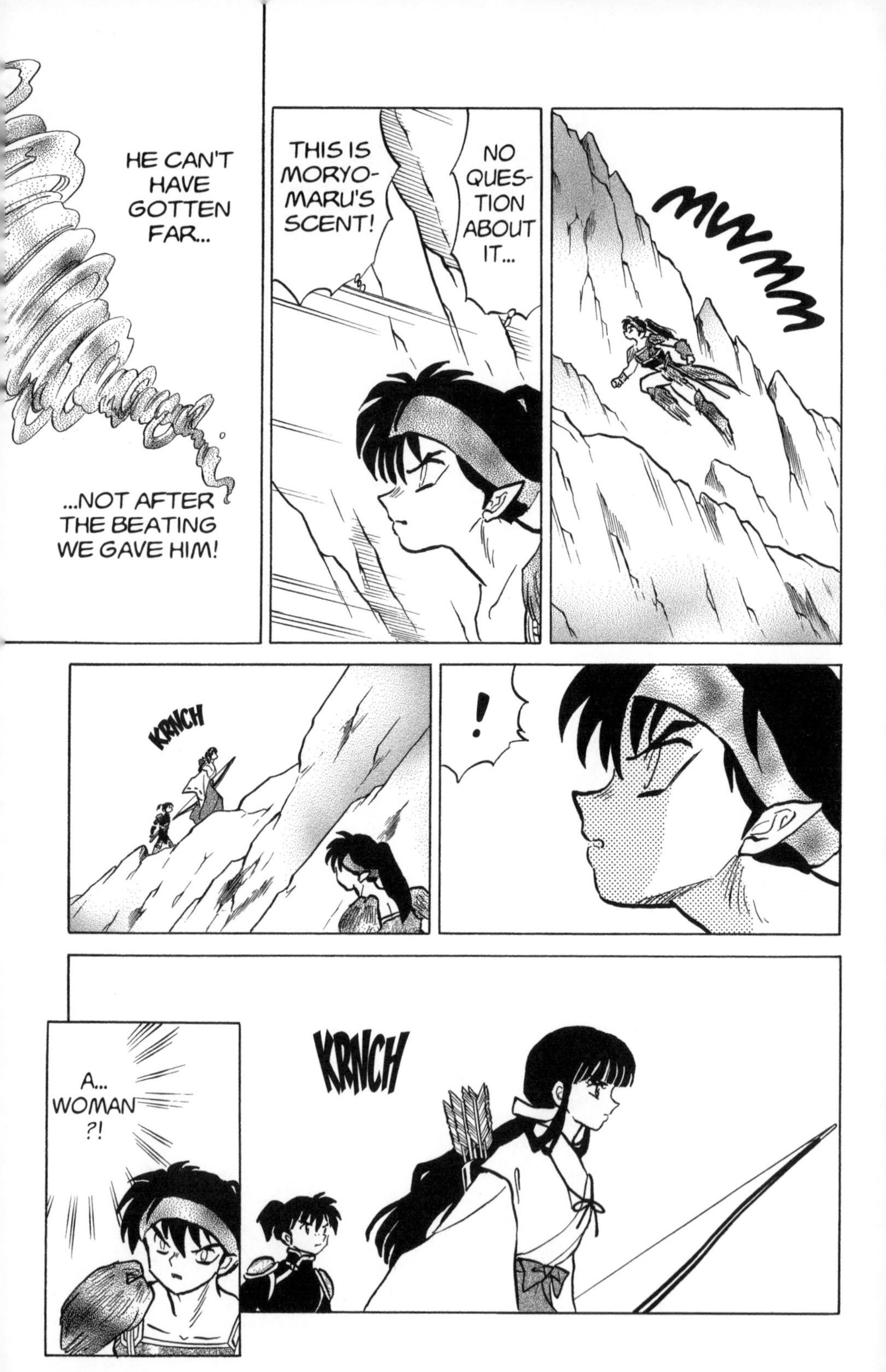
MWMM
NO QUESTION ABOUT IT...
THIS IS MORYOMARU'S SCENT!
HE CAN'T HAVE GOTTEN FAR...
...NOT AFTER THE BEATING WE GAVE HIM!
!
KRNCH
KRNCH
A... WOMAN ?!

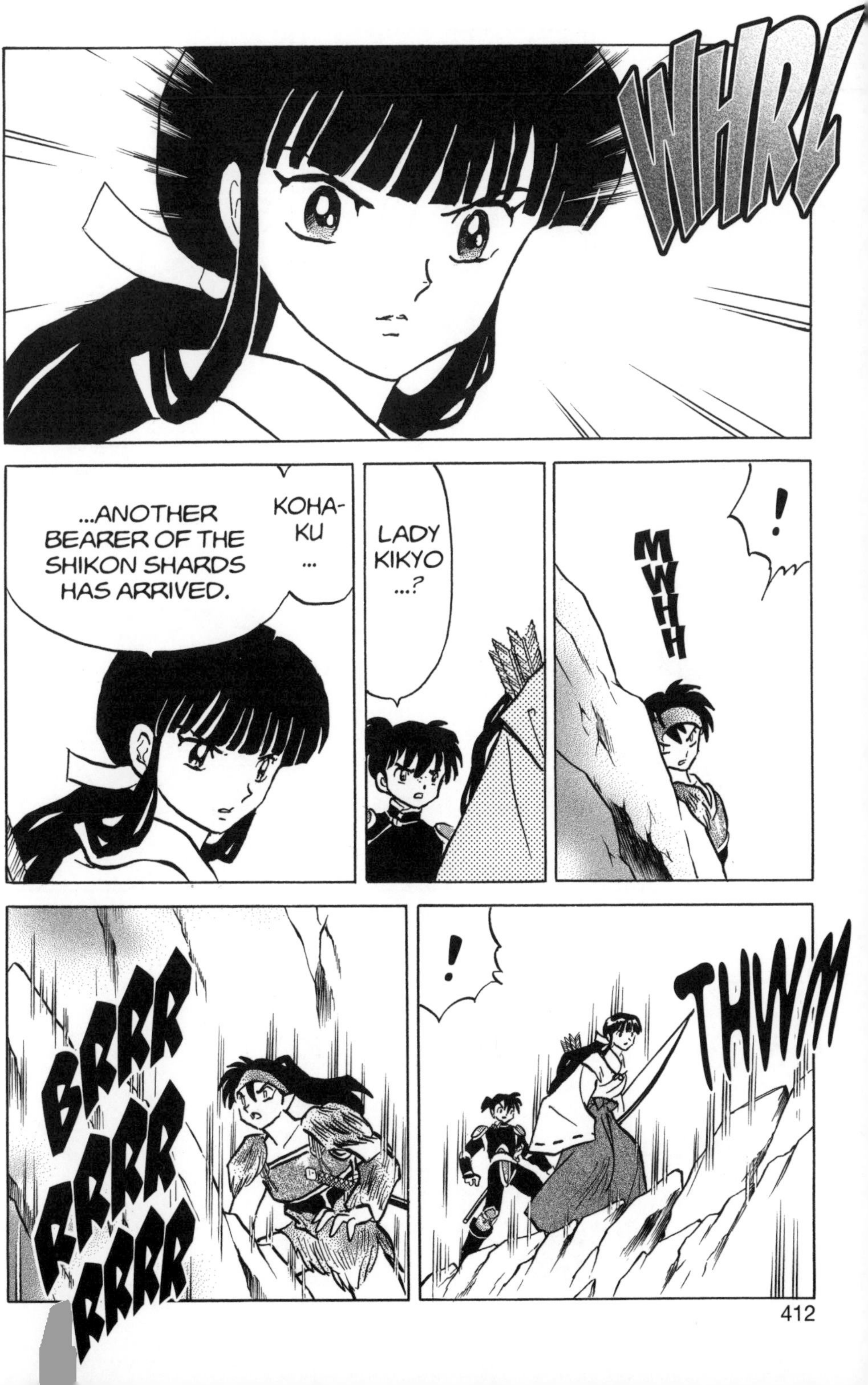
WHRL
!
MWHH
LADY KIKYO ...?
KOHAKU ...
...ANOTHER BEARER OF THE SHIKON SHARDS HAS ARRIVED.
!
THWM
BRRR RRRR RRRR RRRR

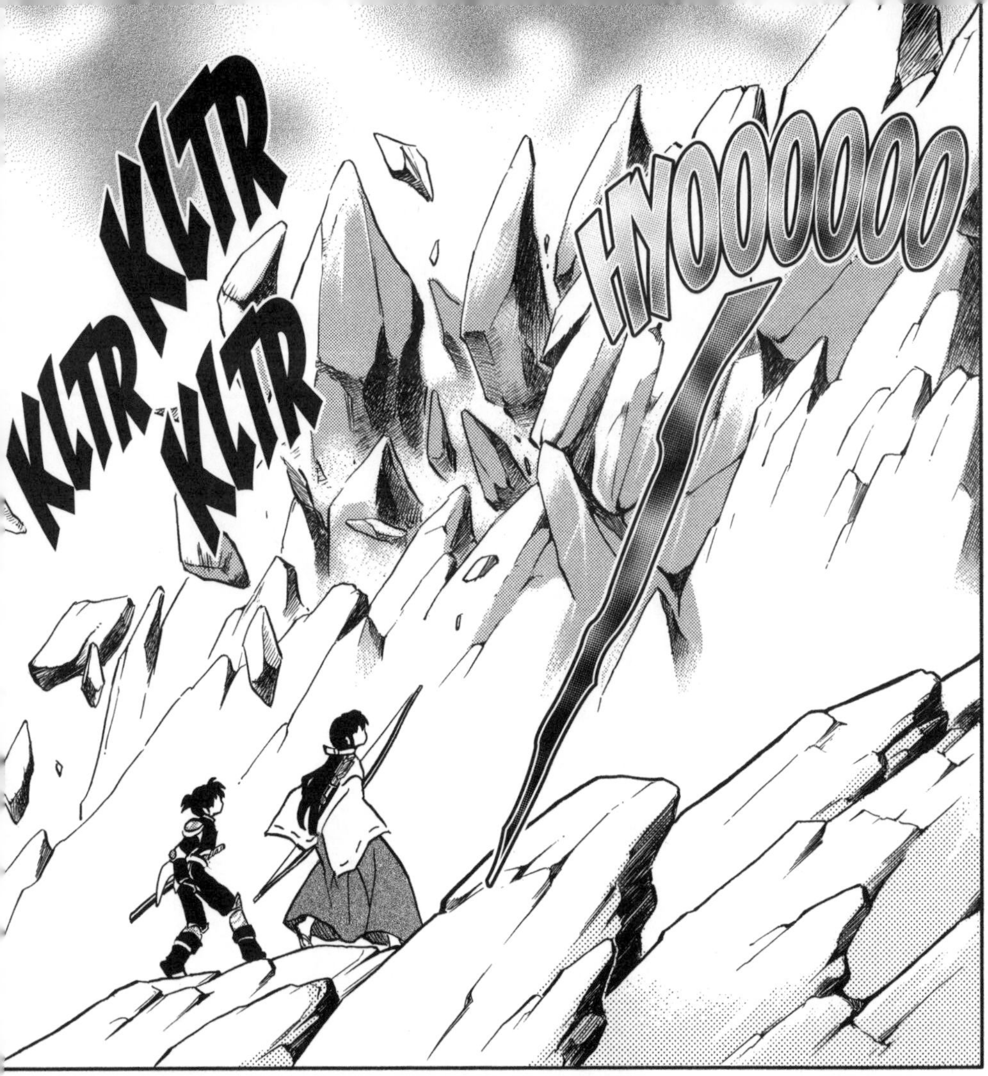
HYOOOOOO
KLTR KLTR
KLTR KLTR
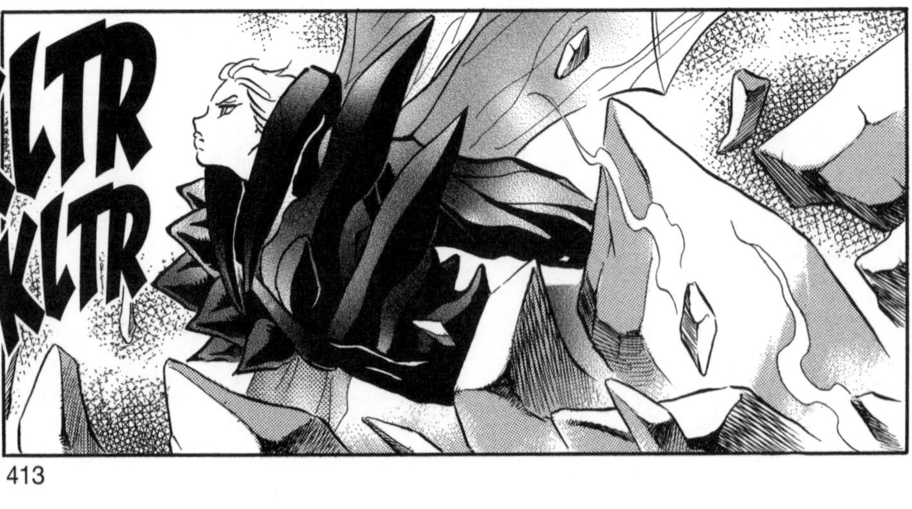
KLTR
KLTR

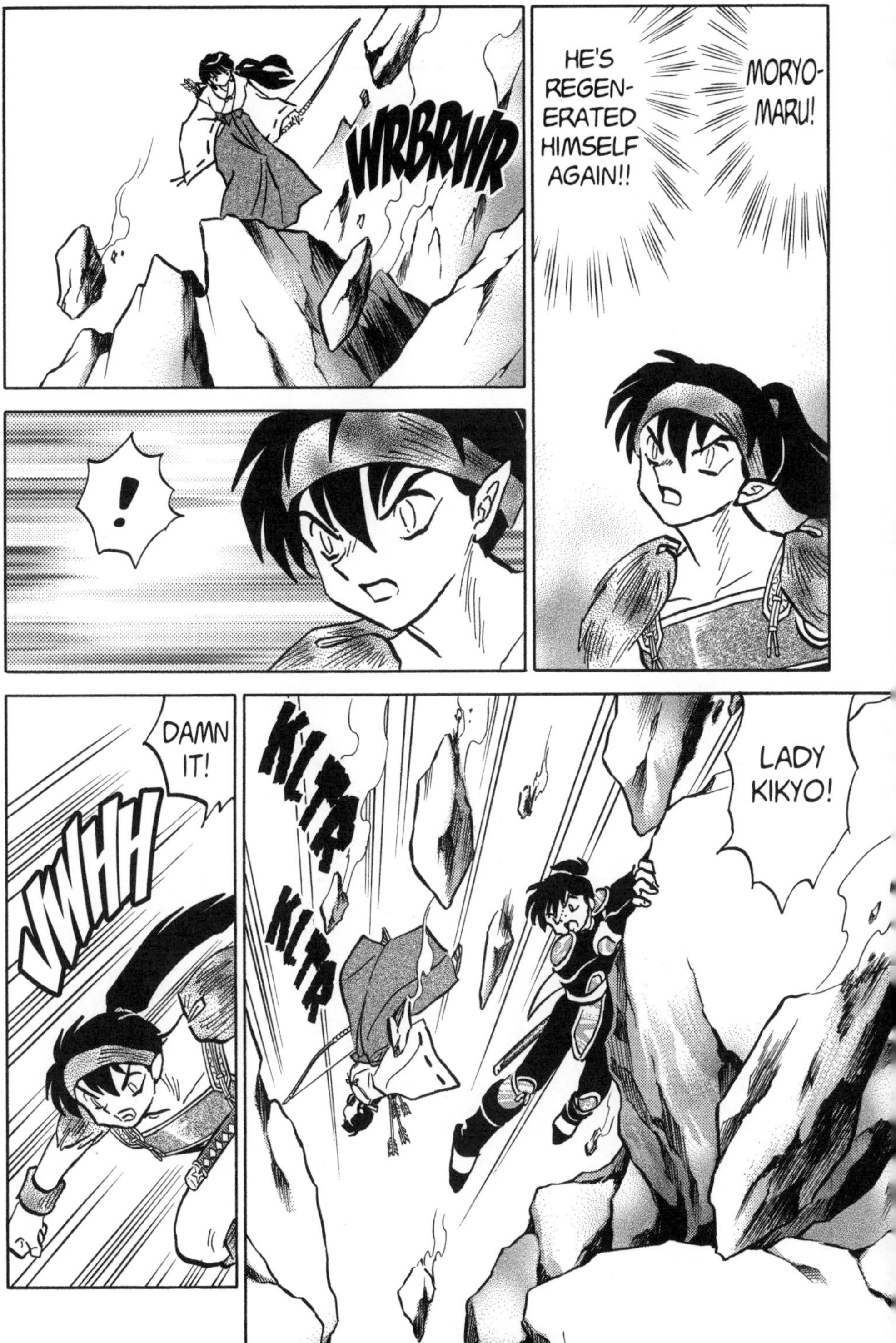
MORYO-MARU!
HE'S REGENERATED HIMSELF AGAIN!!
WRBRWR
!
LADY KIKYO!
KLTR KLTR
DAMN IT!
JWHH

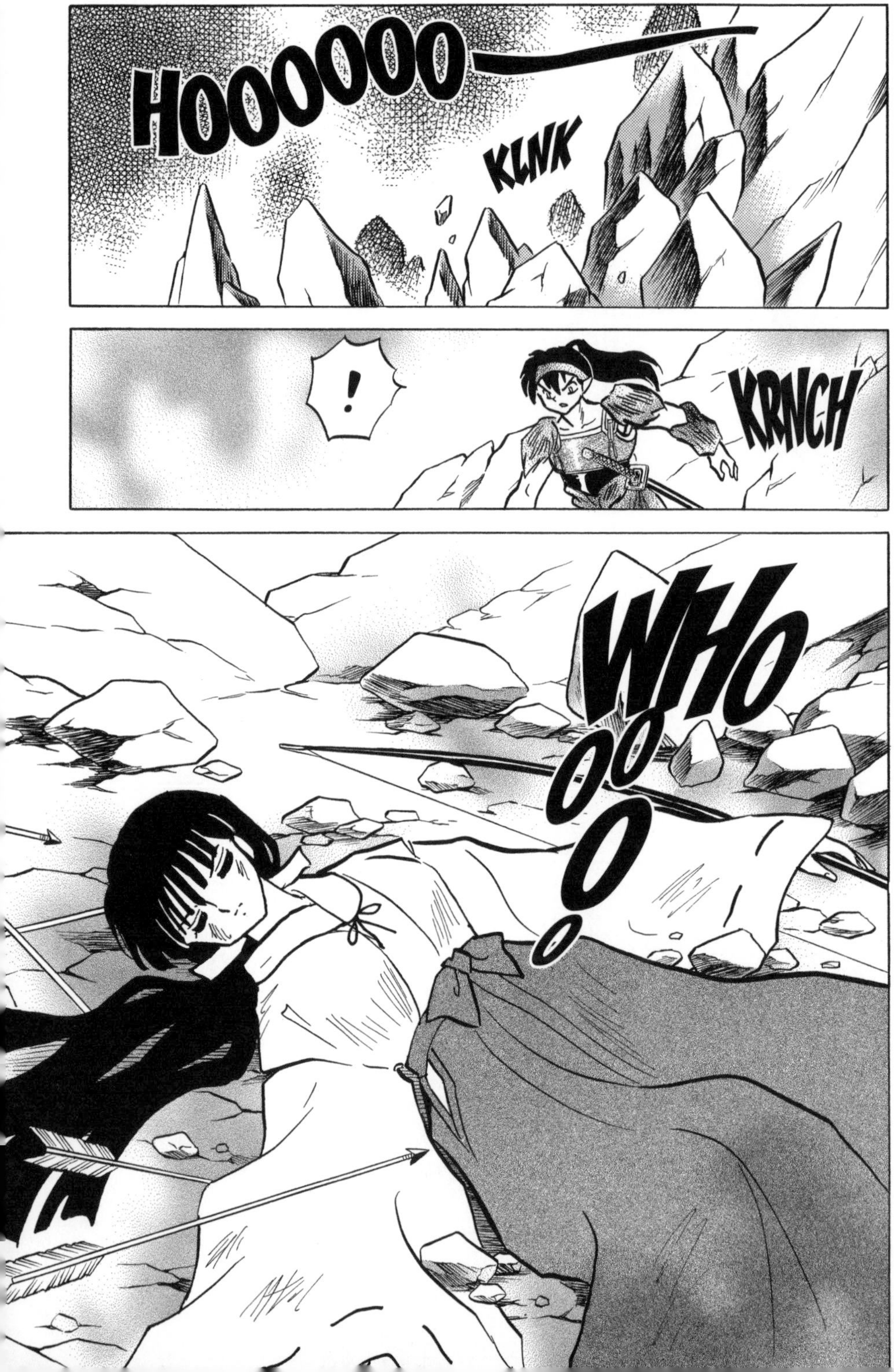
HOOOOOO
KLNK
KRNCH
!
WHOOOOO

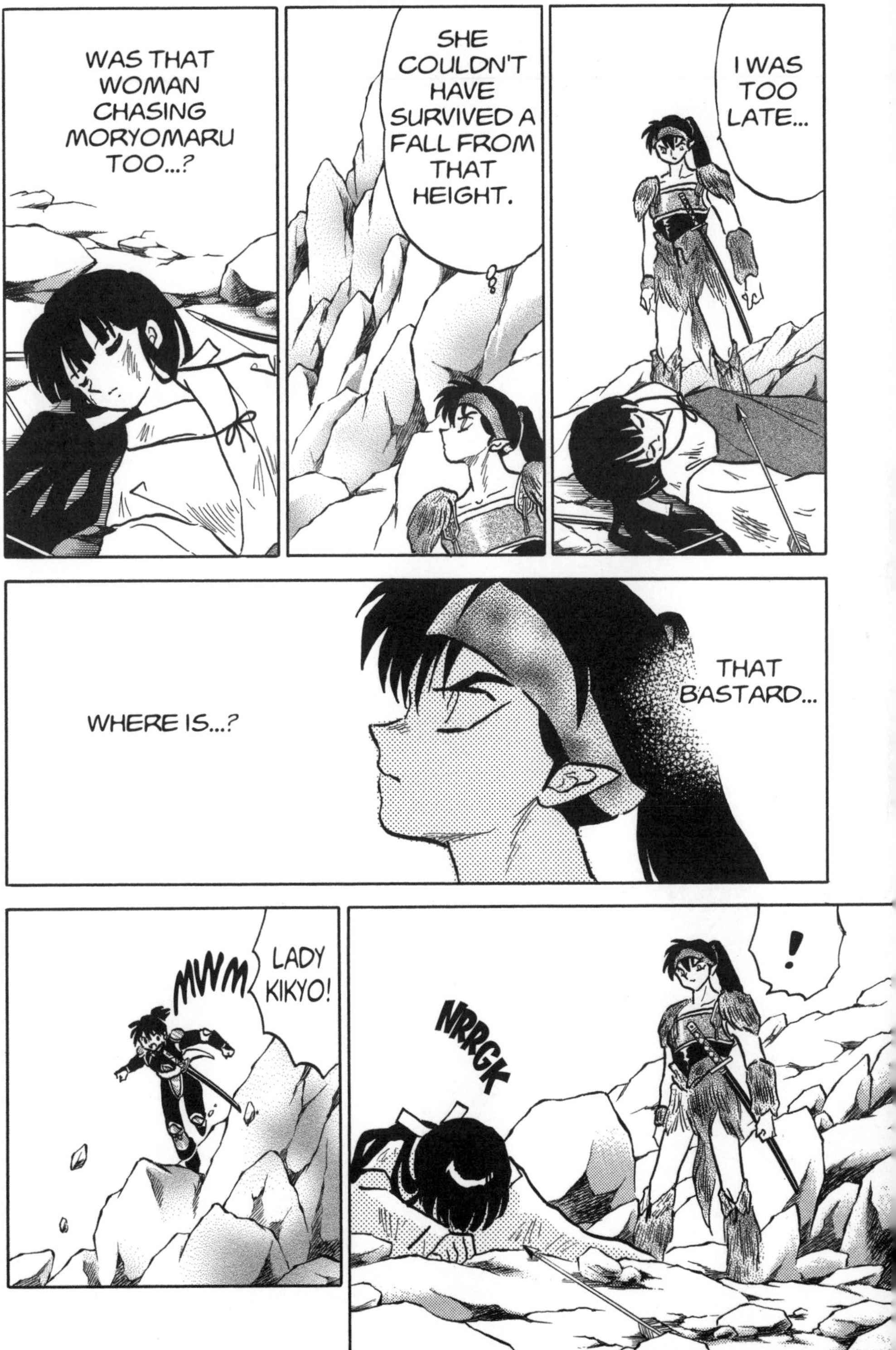
I WAS TOO LATE...
SHE COULDN'T HAVE SURVIVED A FALL FROM THAT HEIGHT.
WAS THAT WOMAN CHASING MORYOMARU TOO...?
THAT BASTARD...
WHERE IS...?
!
NRRGK
LADY KIKYO!
MWM

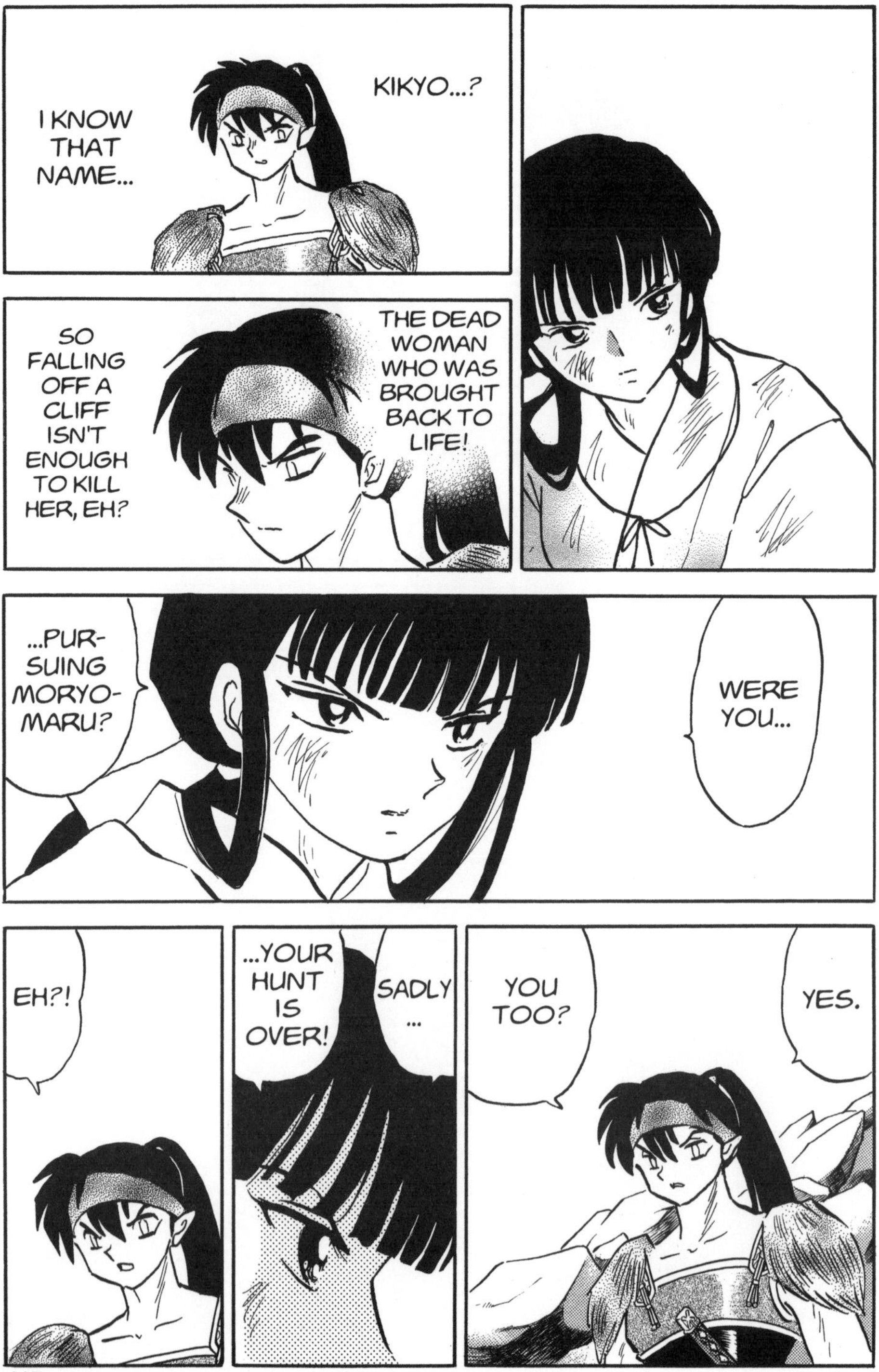
KIKYO...?
I KNOW THAT NAME...
THE DEAD WOMAN WHO WAS BROUGHT BACK TO LIFE!
SO FALLING OFF A CLIFF ISN'T ENOUGH TO KILL HER, EH?
WERE YOU...
...PUR-SUING MORYO-MARU?
YES.
YOU TOO?
SADLY...
...YOUR HUNT IS OVER!
EH?!

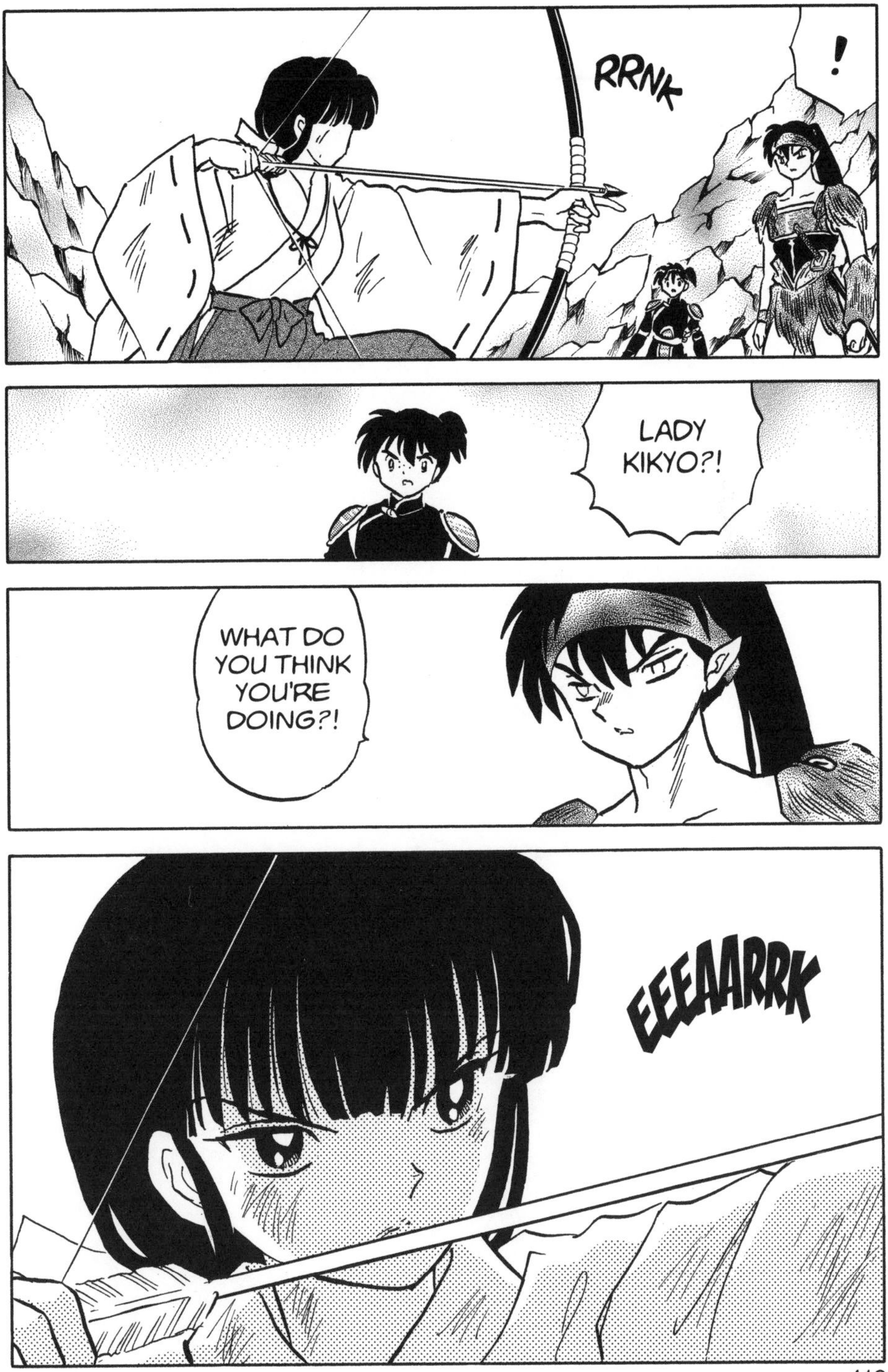
!
RRNK
LADY KIKYO?!
WHAT DO YOU THINK YOU'RE DOING?!
EEEAARRK

SCROLL THREE
CONFRONTATION

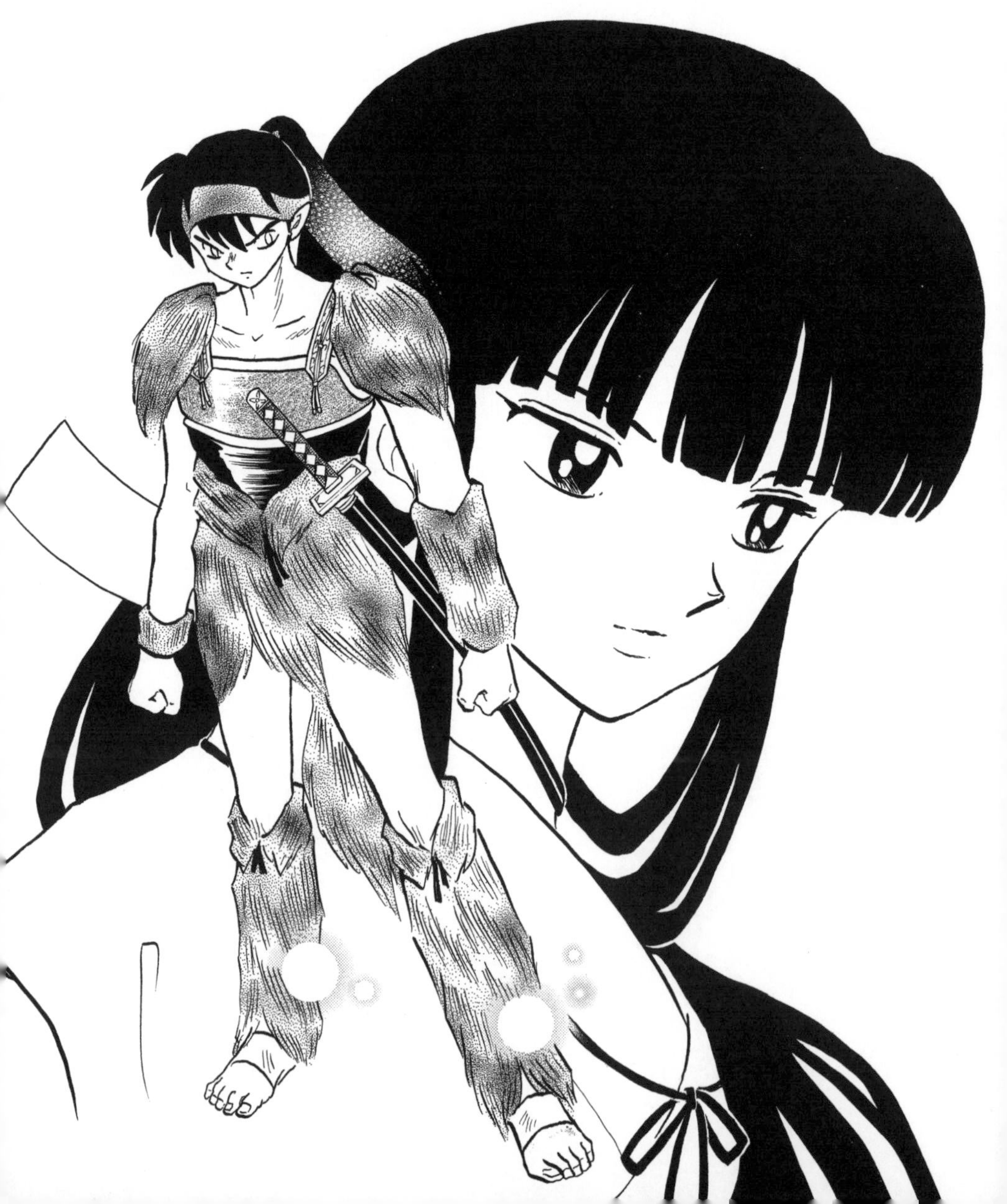

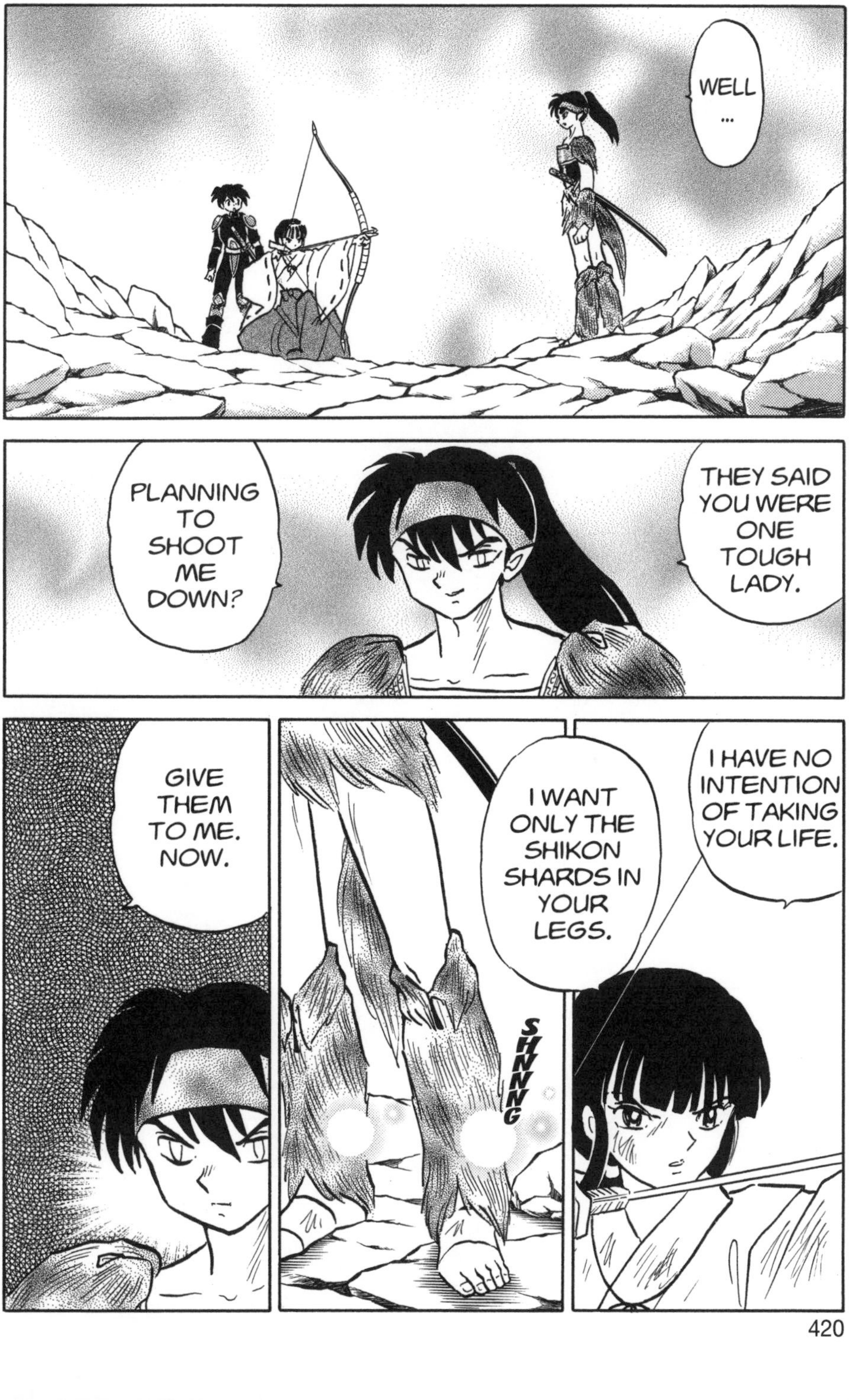
WELL ...
THEY SAID YOU WERE ONE TOUGH LADY.
PLANNING TO SHOOT ME DOWN?
I HAVE NO INTENTION OF TAKING YOUR LIFE.
I WANT ONLY THE SHIKON SHARDS IN YOUR LEGS.
SHNNNG
GIVE THEM TO ME. NOW.

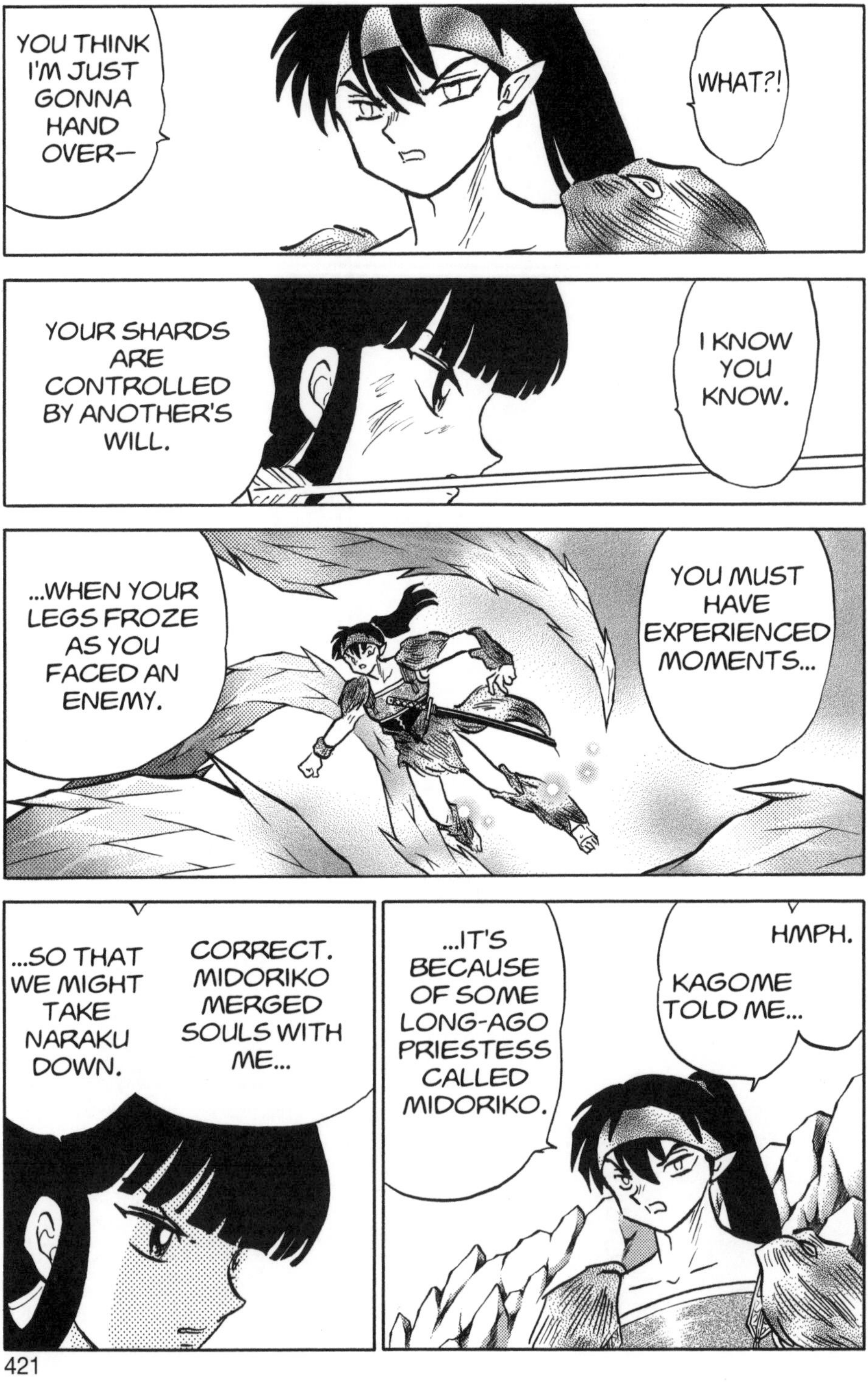
WHAT?!
YOU THINK I'M JUST GONNA HAND OVER—
I KNOW YOU KNOW.
YOUR SHARDS ARE CONTROLLED BY ANOTHER'S WILL.
YOU MUST HAVE EXPERIENCED MOMENTS...
...WHEN YOUR LEGS FROZE AS YOU FACED AN ENEMY.
HMPH.
KAGOME TOLD ME...
...IT'S BECAUSE OF SOME LONG-AGO PRIESTESS CALLED MIDORIKO.
CORRECT. MIDORIKO MERGED SOULS WITH ME...
...SO THAT WE MIGHT TAKE NARAKU DOWN.

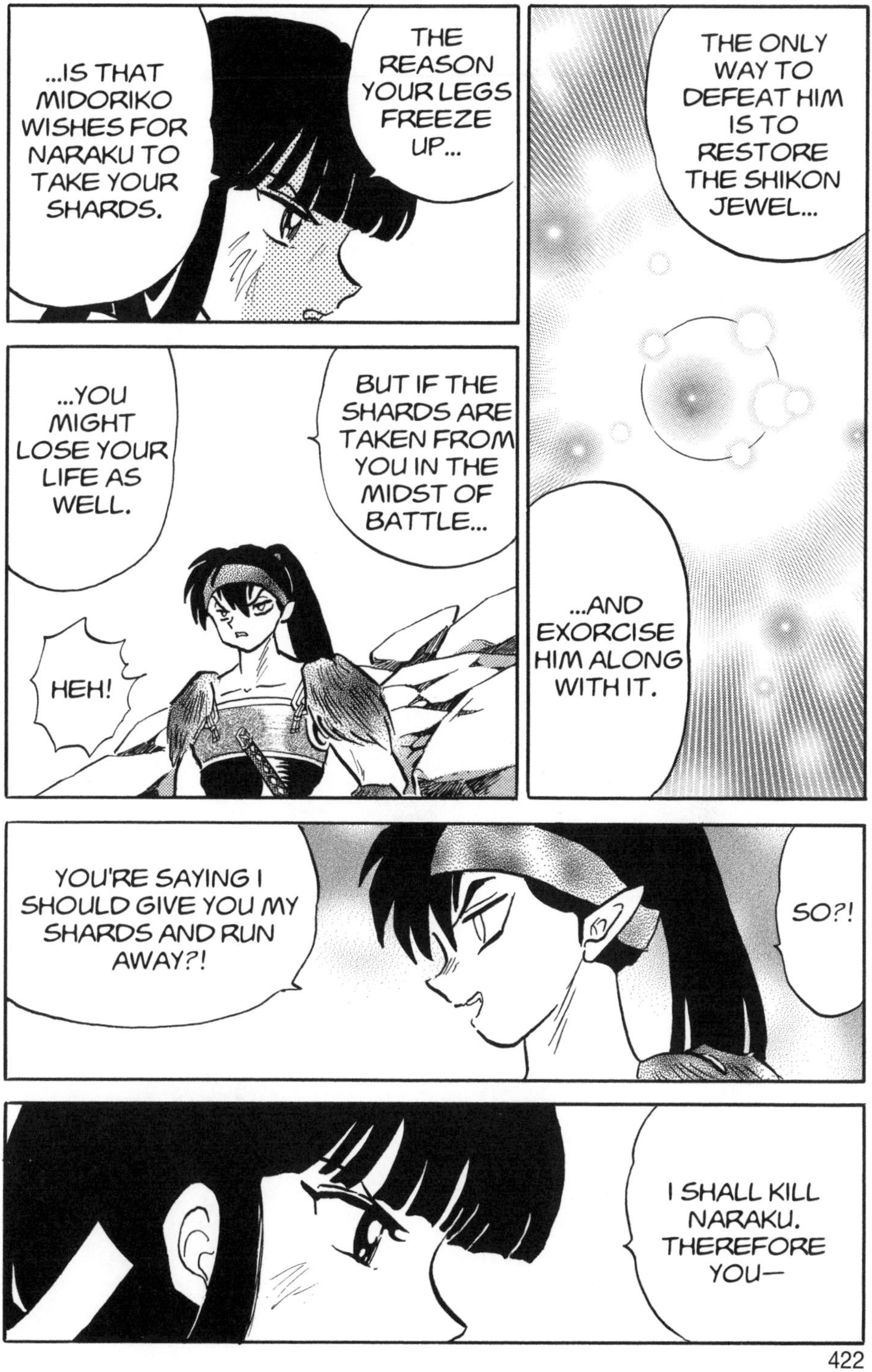
THE ONLY WAY TO DEFEAT HIM IS TO RESTORE THE SHIKON JEWEL...
...AND EXORCISE HIM ALONG WITH IT.
THE REASON YOUR LEGS FREEZE UP...
...IS THAT MIDORIKO WISHES FOR NARAKU TO TAKE YOUR SHARDS.
BUT IF THE SHARDS ARE TAKEN FROM YOU IN THE MIDST OF BATTLE...
...YOU MIGHT LOSE YOUR LIFE AS WELL.
HEH!
SO?!
YOU'RE SAYING I SHOULD GIVE YOU MY SHARDS AND RUN AWAY?!
I SHALL KILL NARAKU. THEREFORE YOU—

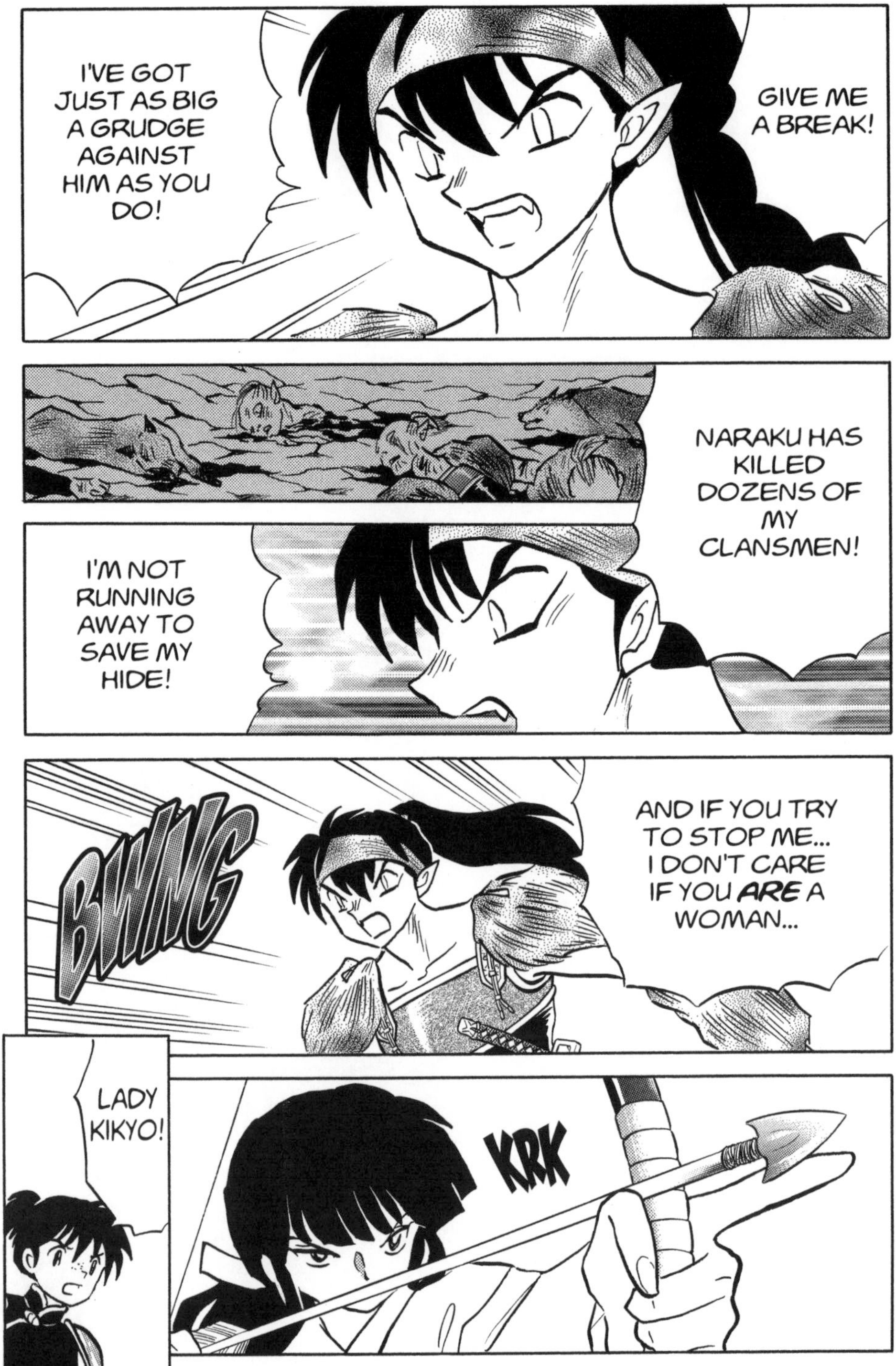
GIVE ME A BREAK!
I'VE GOT JUST AS BIG A GRUDGE AGAINST HIM AS YOU DO!
NARAKU HAS KILLED DOZENS OF MY CLANSMEN!
I'M NOT RUNNING AWAY TO SAVE MY HIDE!
AND IF YOU TRY TO STOP ME... I DON'T CARE IF YOU *ARE* A WOMAN...
BWING
KRK
LADY KIKYO!

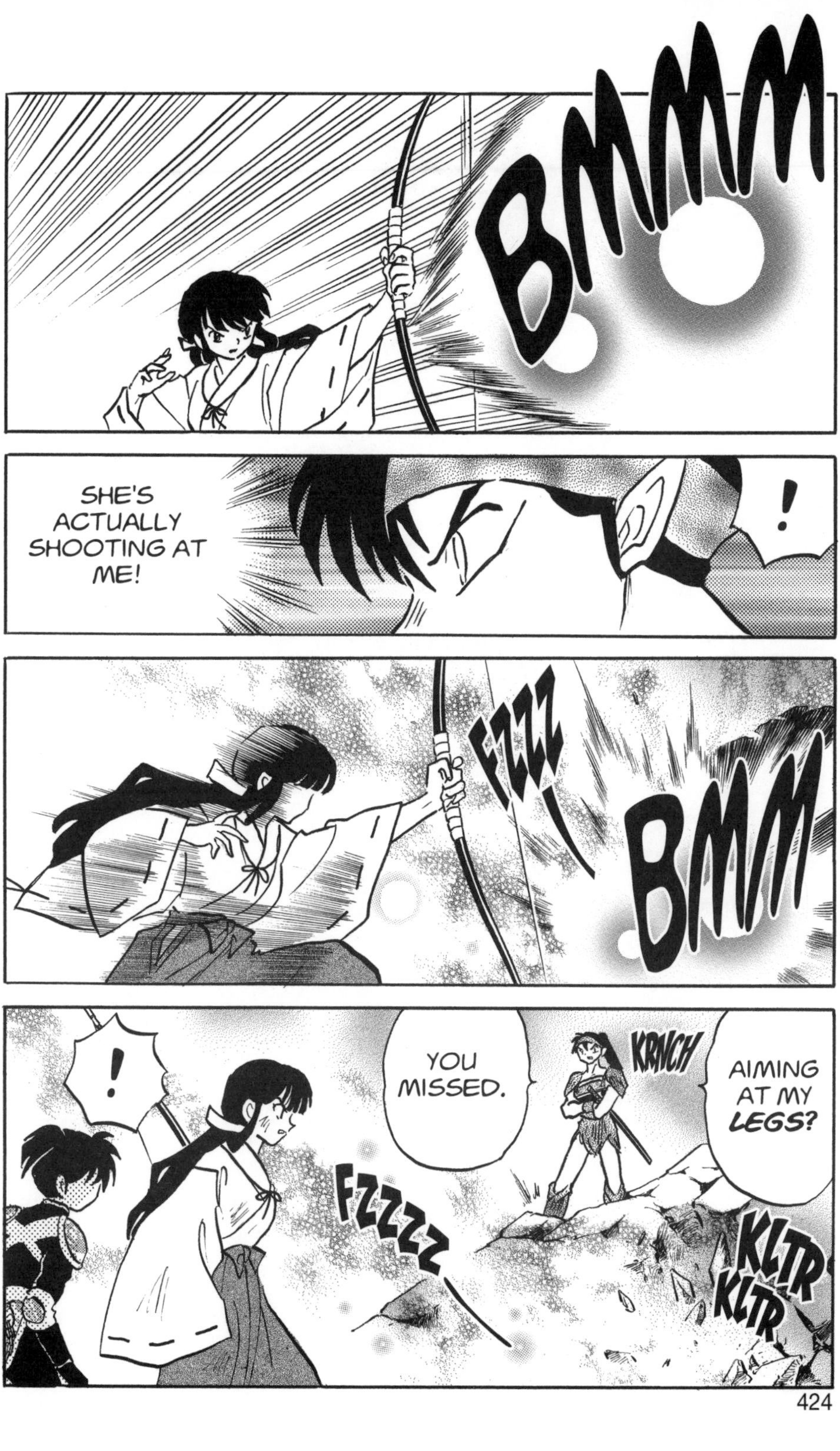
BMMM
!
SHE'S ACTUALLY SHOOTING AT ME!
BMM
FZZZ
KRNCH
AIMING AT MY ***LEGS?***
KLTR KLTR
YOU MISSED.
FZZZZ
!

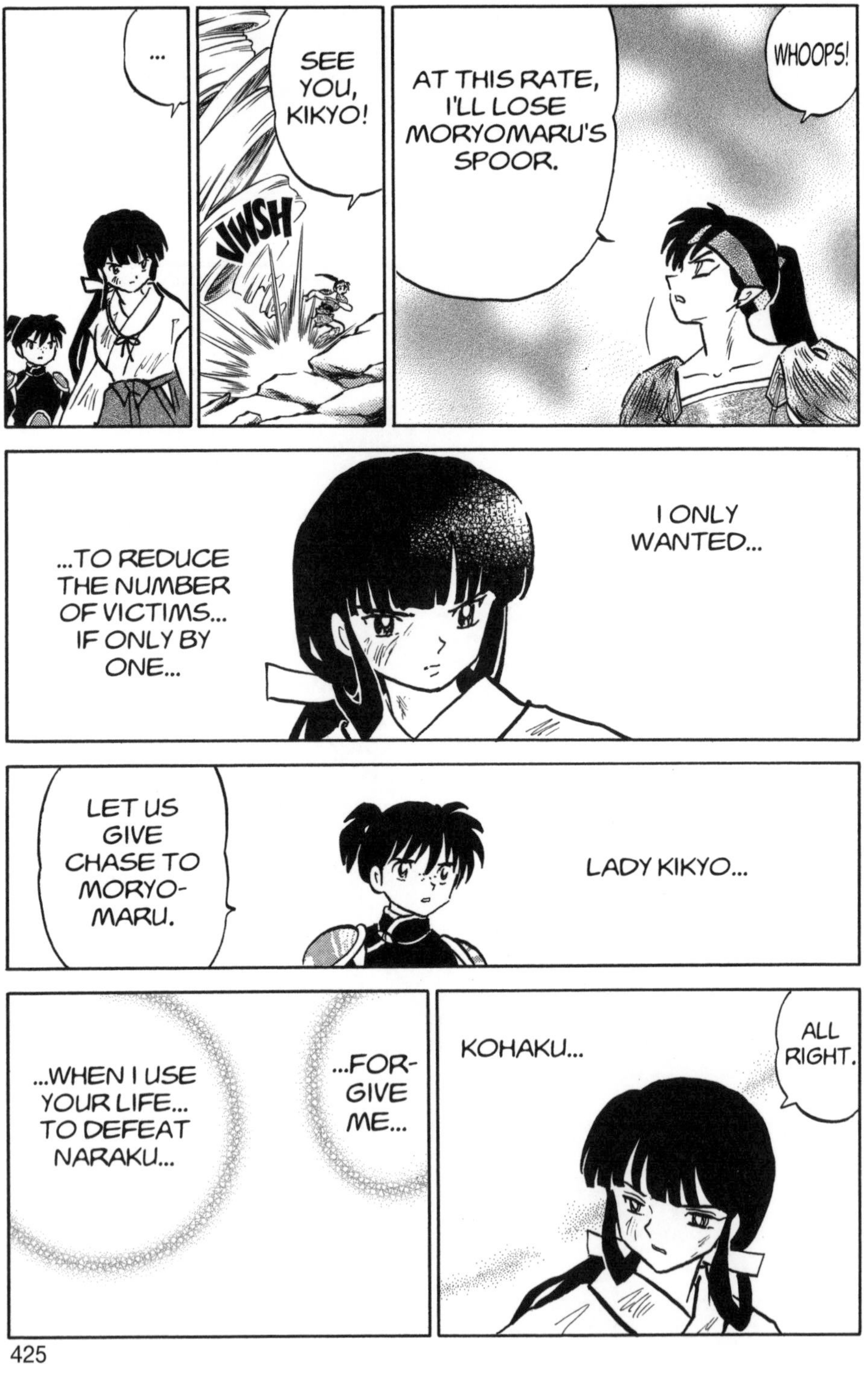
WHOOPS!
AT THIS RATE, I'LL LOSE MORYOMARU'S SPOOR.
SEE YOU, KIKYO!
JWSH
...
I ONLY WANTED...
...TO REDUCE THE NUMBER OF VICTIMS... IF ONLY BY ONE...
LADY KIKYO...
LET US GIVE CHASE TO MORYO-MARU.
ALL RIGHT.
KOHAKU...
...FOR-GIVE ME...
...WHEN I USE YOUR LIFE... TO DEFEAT NARAKU...

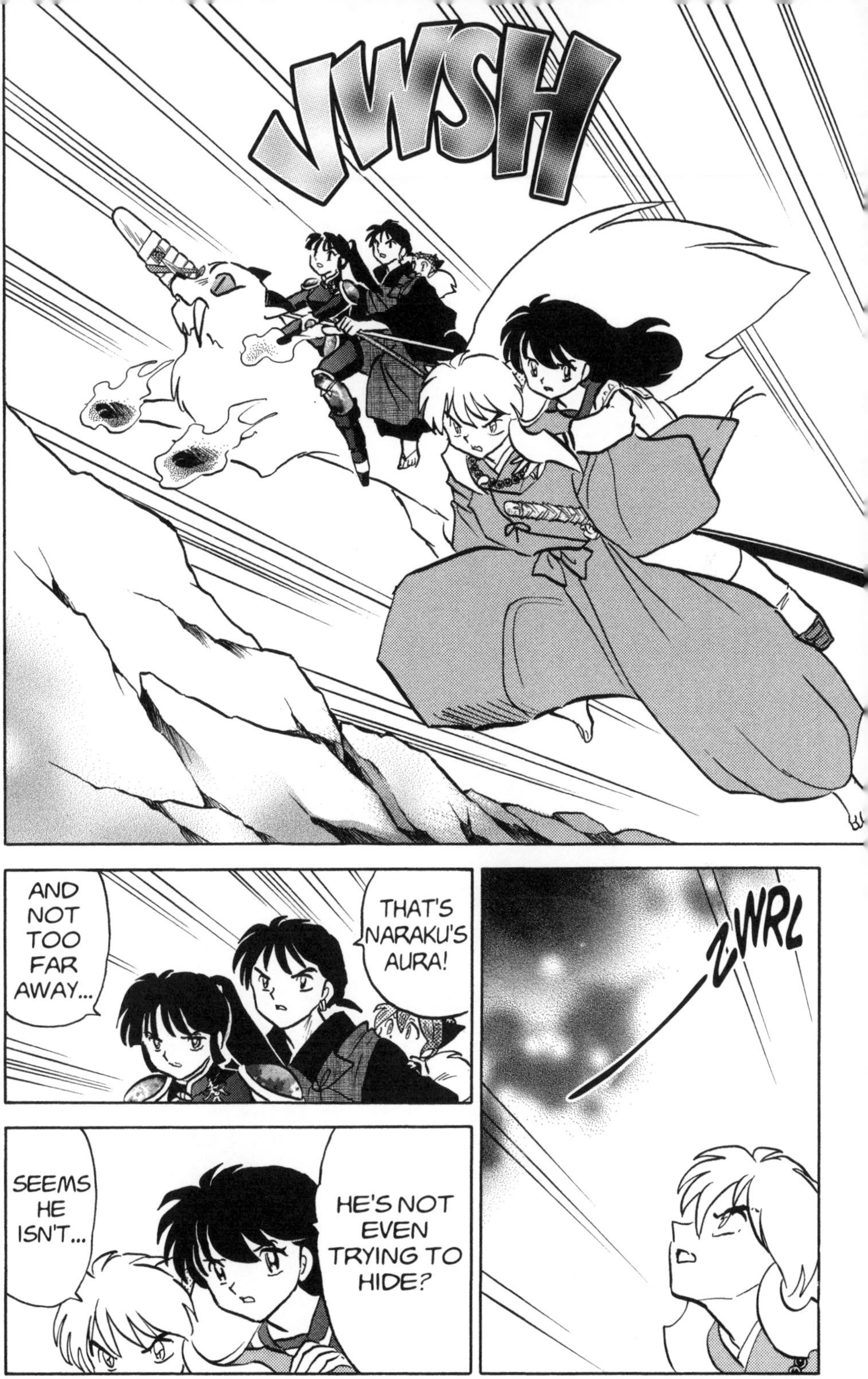
JWSH
ZWRL
THAT'S NARAKU'S AURA!
AND NOT TOO FAR AWAY...
HE'S NOT EVEN TRYING TO HIDE?
SEEMS HE ISN'T...

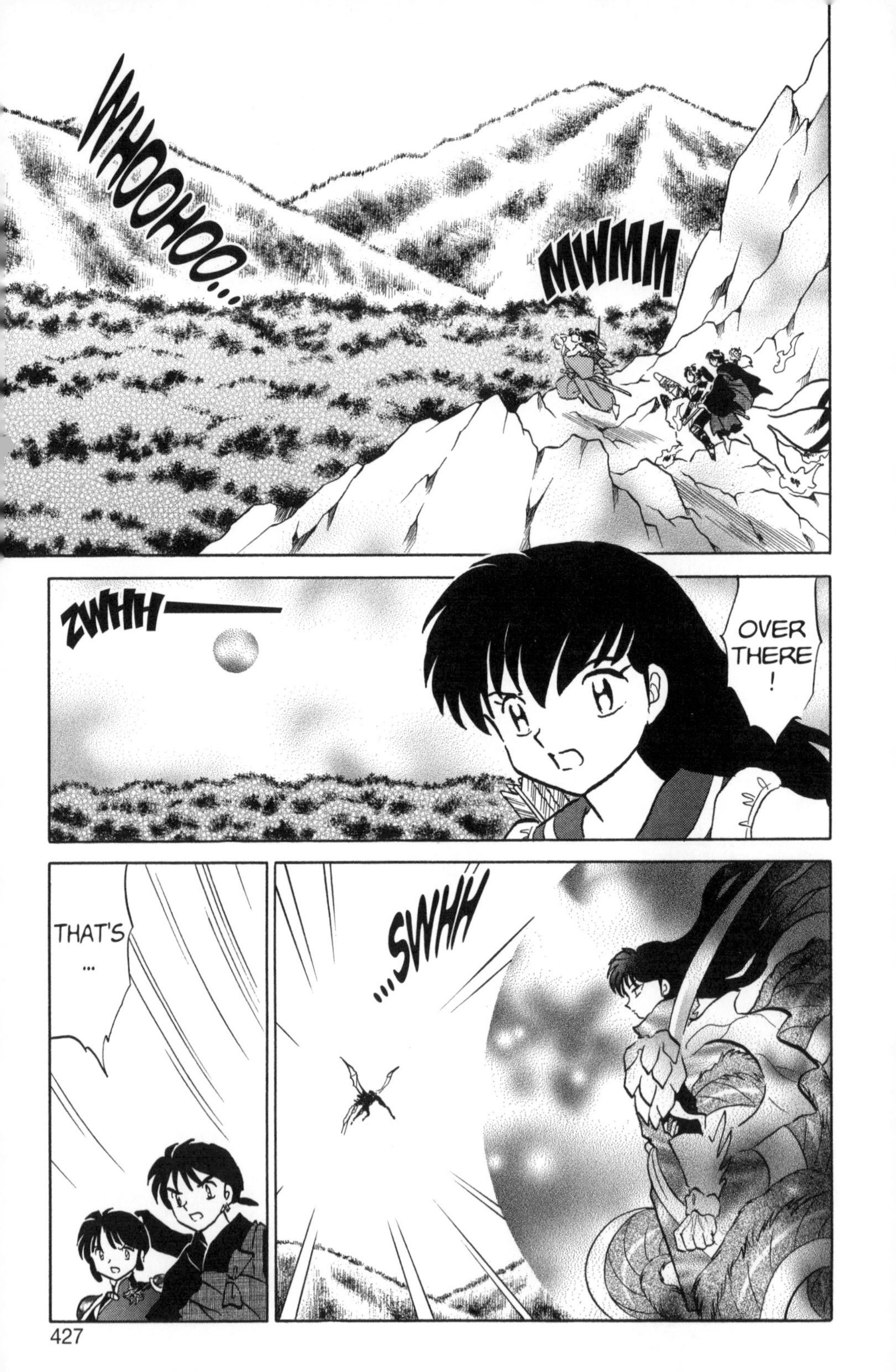
MWMM
WHOOHOO...
OVER THERE!
ZWHH
...SWHH
THAT'S ...

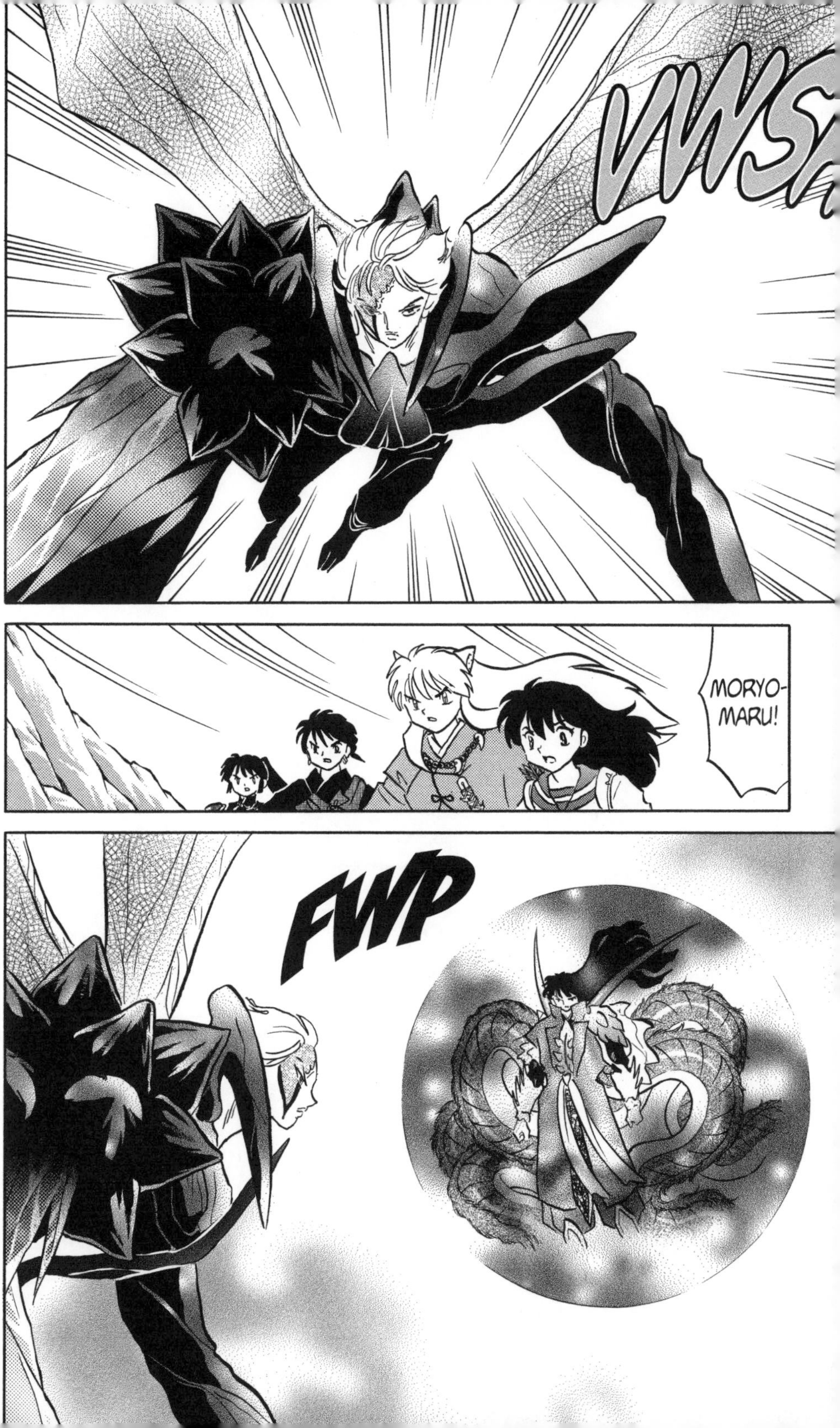
VWS
MORYO-MARU!
FWP

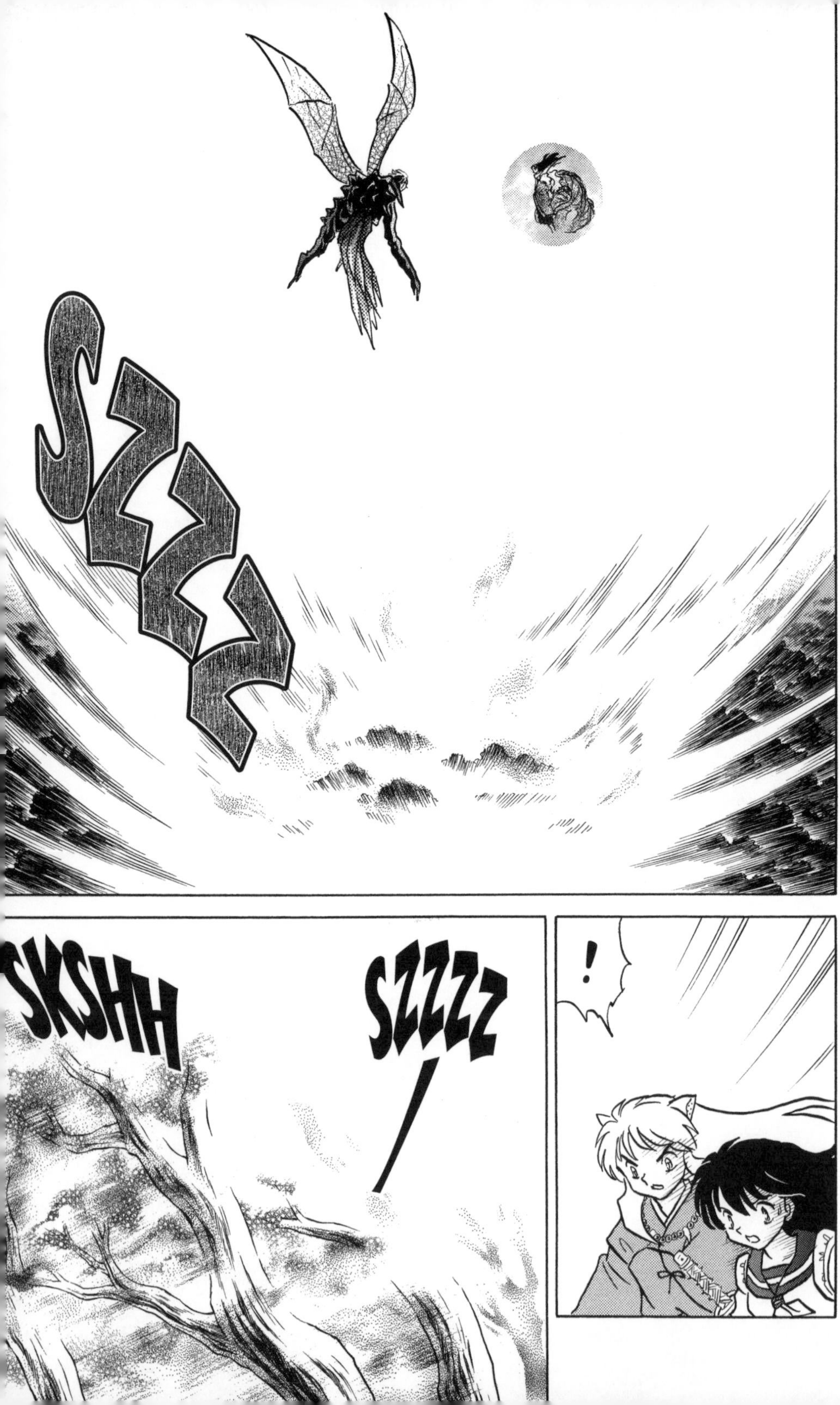
SZZZZ
!
SZZZZ
SKSHH

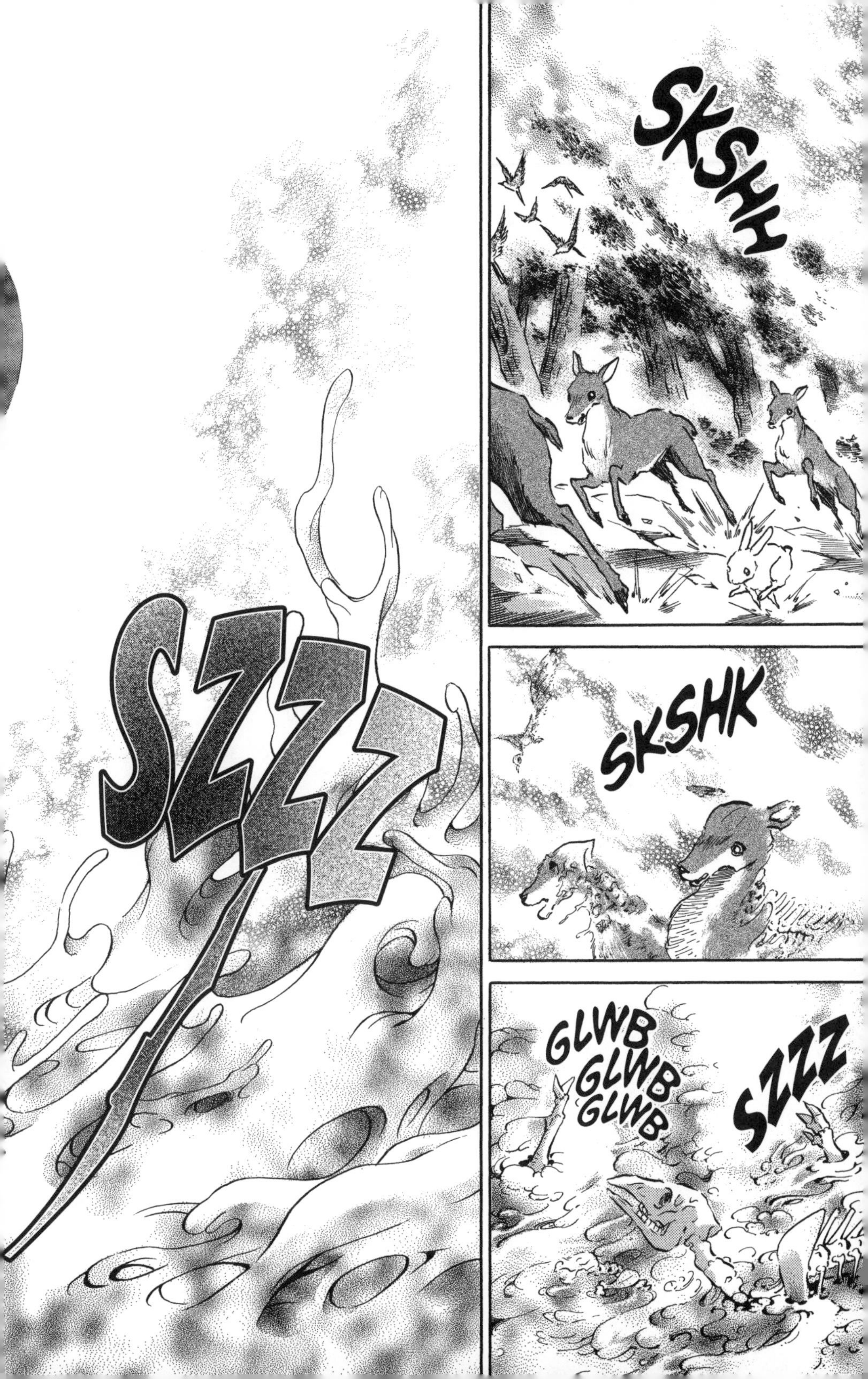
SKSHH
SKSHK
SZZZ
GLWB GLWB GLWB
SZZZ

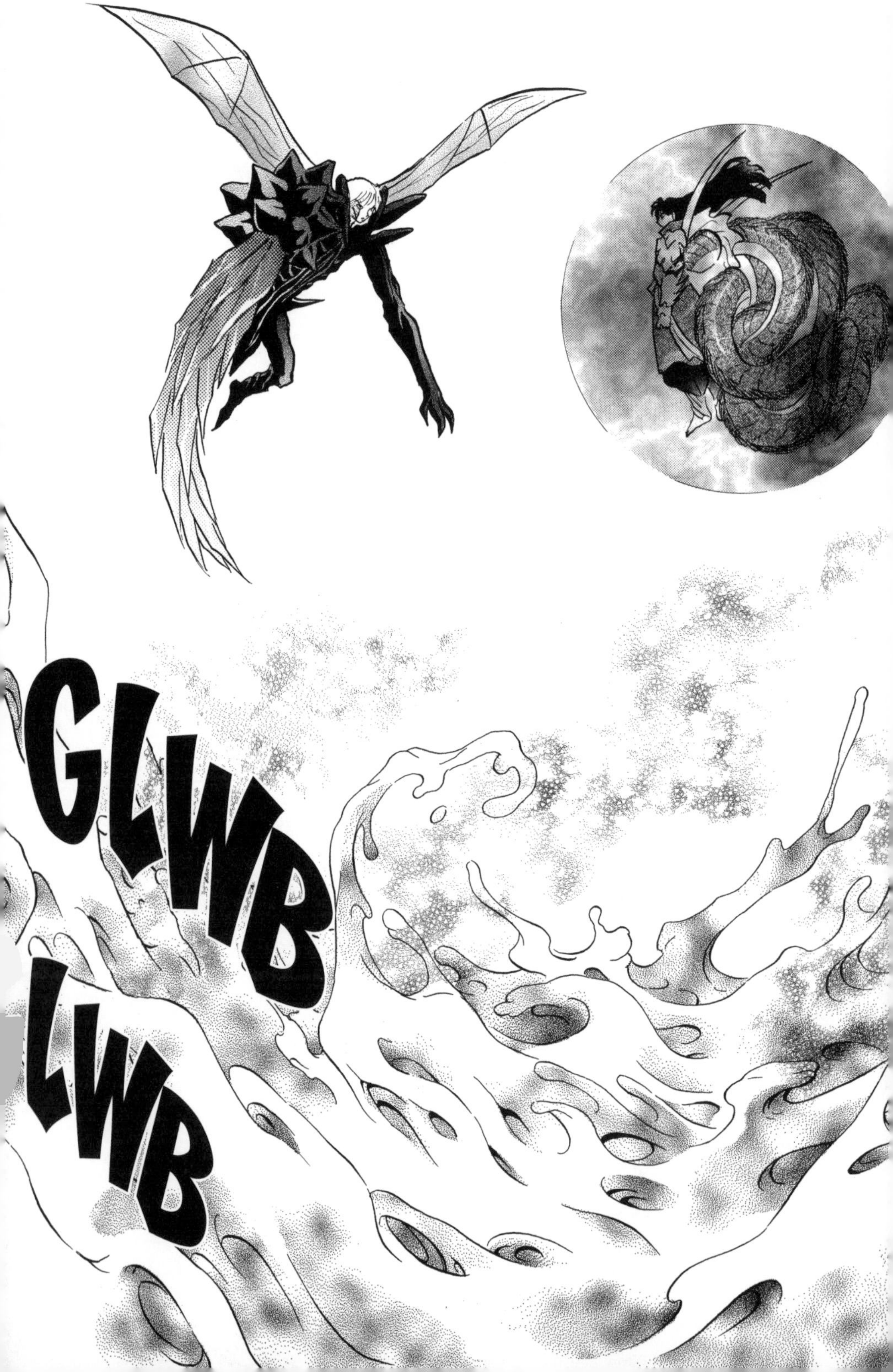
GLWB
LWB

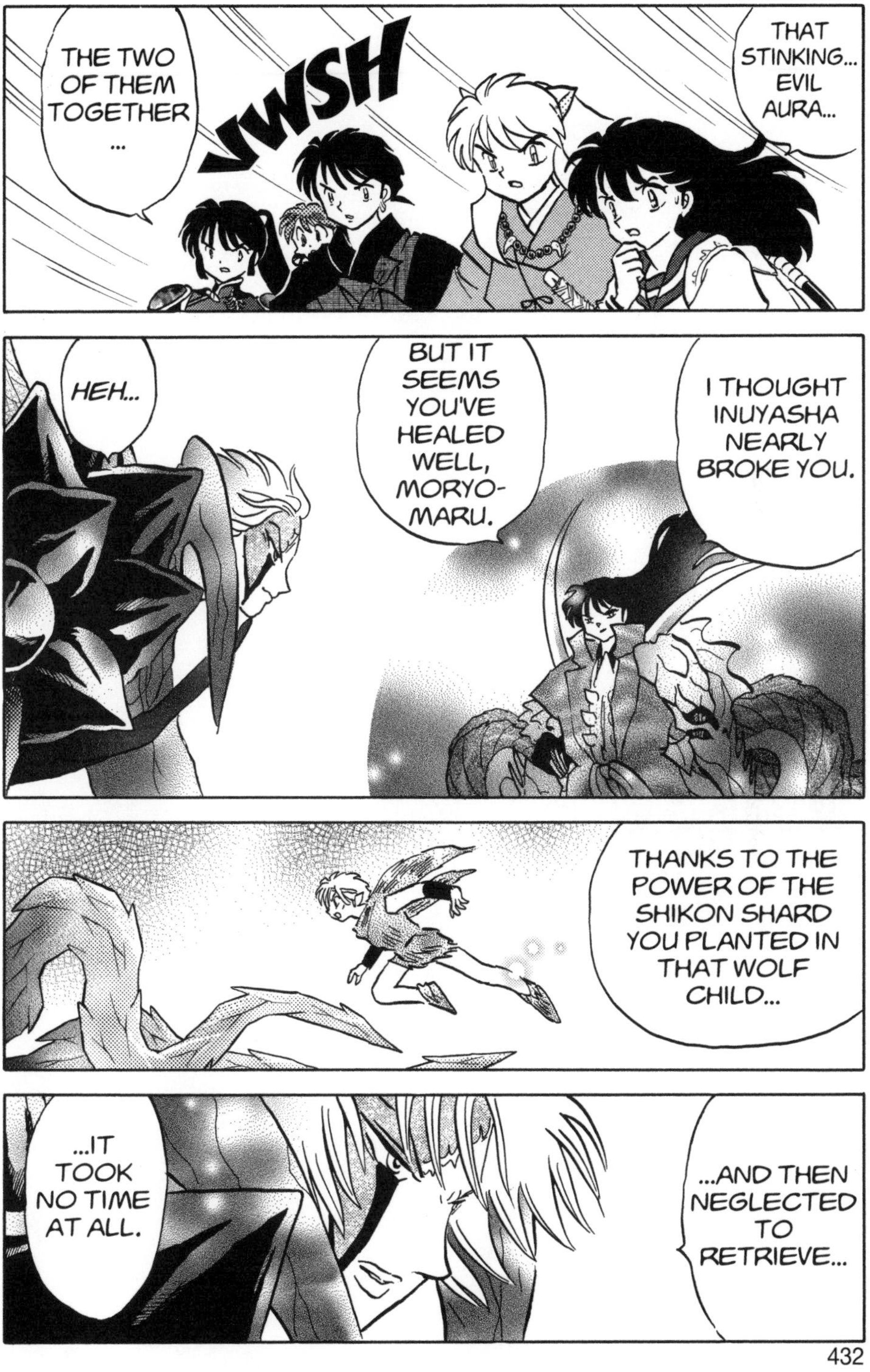
THAT STINKING... EVIL AURA...
VWSH
THE TWO OF THEM TOGETHER ...
I THOUGHT INUYASHA NEARLY BROKE YOU.
BUT IT SEEMS YOU'VE HEALED WELL, MORYO-MARU.
HEH...
THANKS TO THE POWER OF THE SHIKON SHARD YOU PLANTED IN THAT WOLF CHILD...
...AND THEN NEGLECTED TO RETRIEVE...
...IT TOOK NO TIME AT ALL.

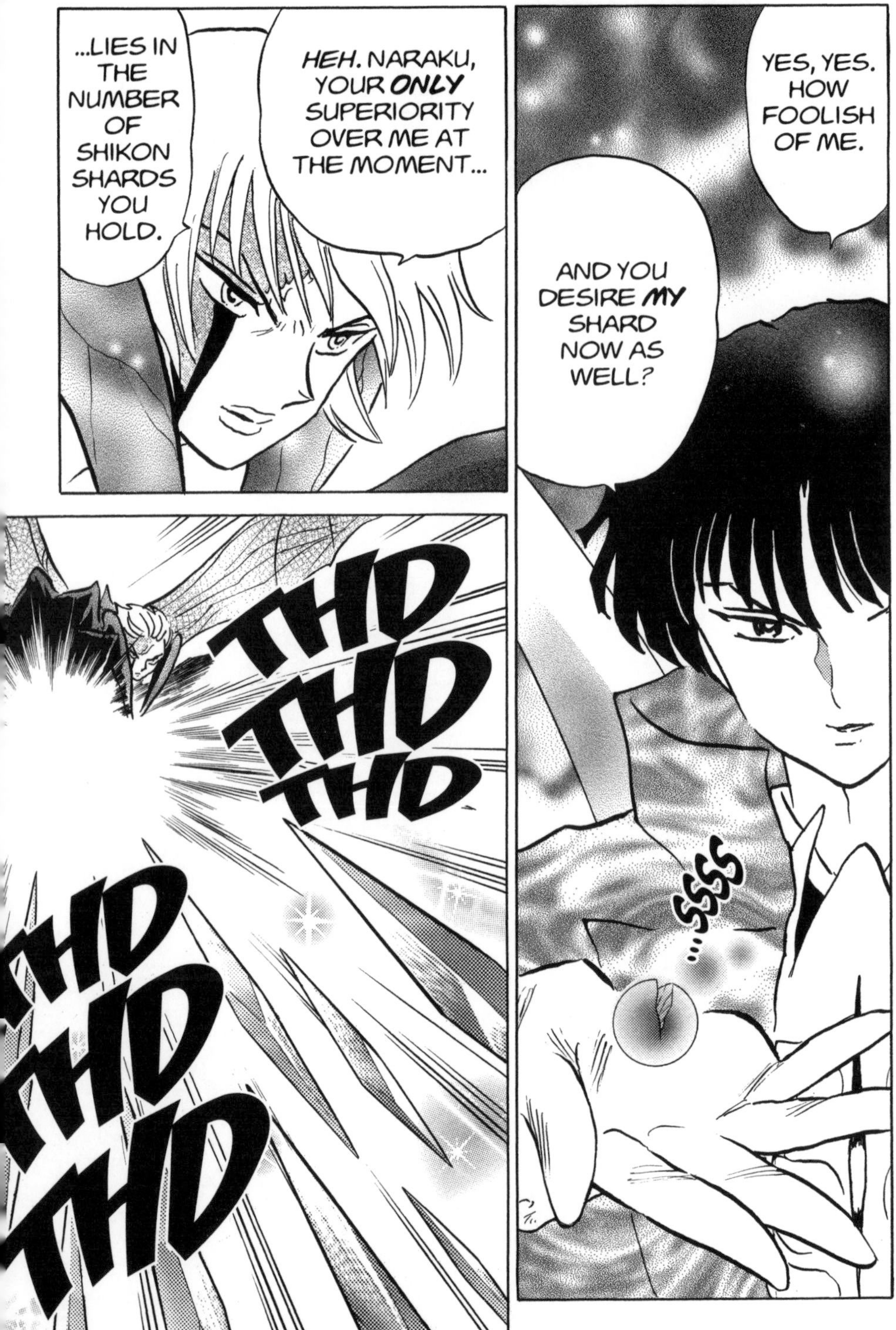
YES, YES. HOW FOOLISH OF ME.
AND YOU DESIRE *MY* SHARD NOW AS WELL?
...SSSS
HEH. NARAKU, YOUR ***ONLY*** SUPERIORITY OVER ME AT THE MOMENT...
...LIES IN THE NUMBER OF SHIKON SHARDS YOU HOLD.
THD THD THD
THD THD THD

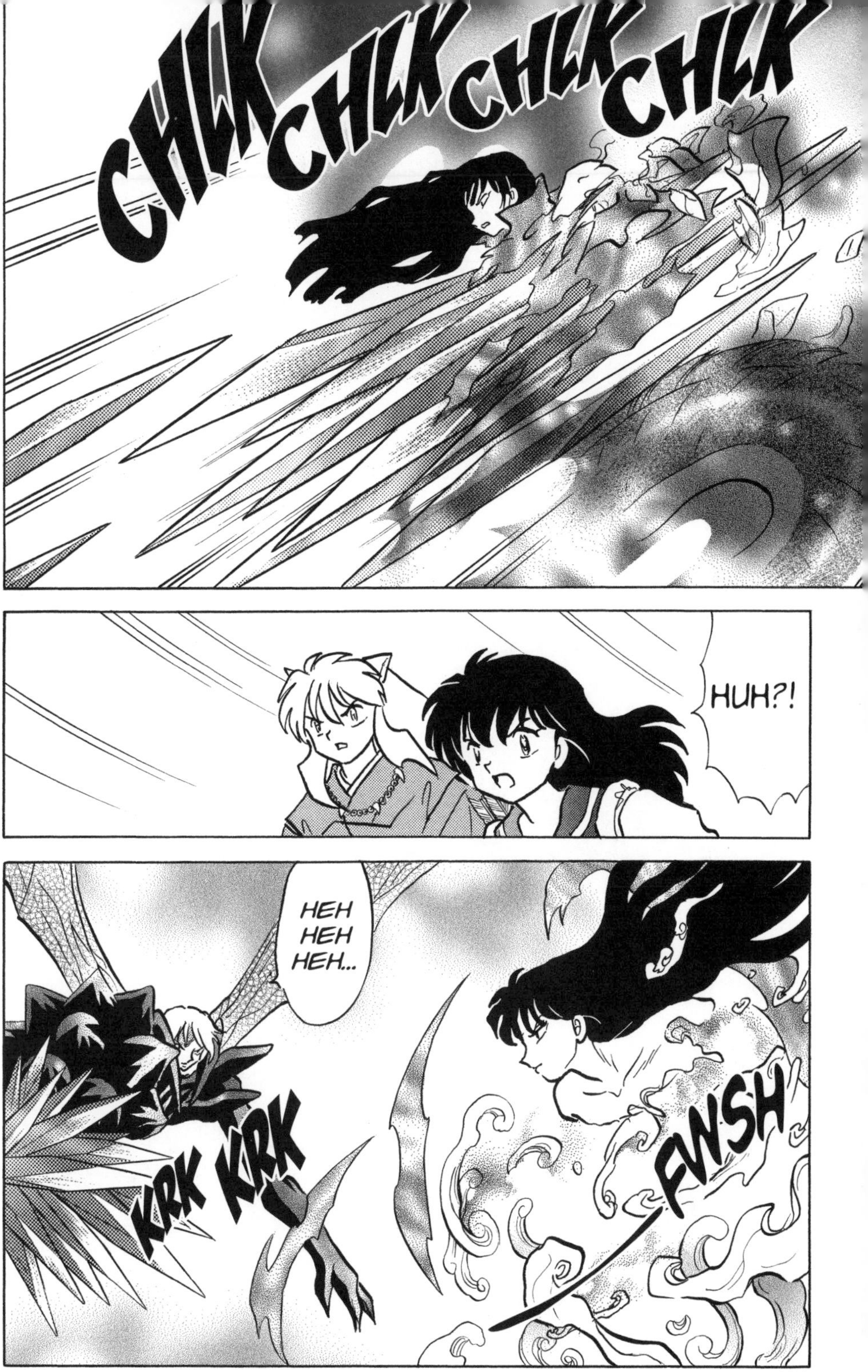
CHLK CHLK CHLK CHLK
HUH?!
HEH HEH HEH...
FWSH
KRK KRK

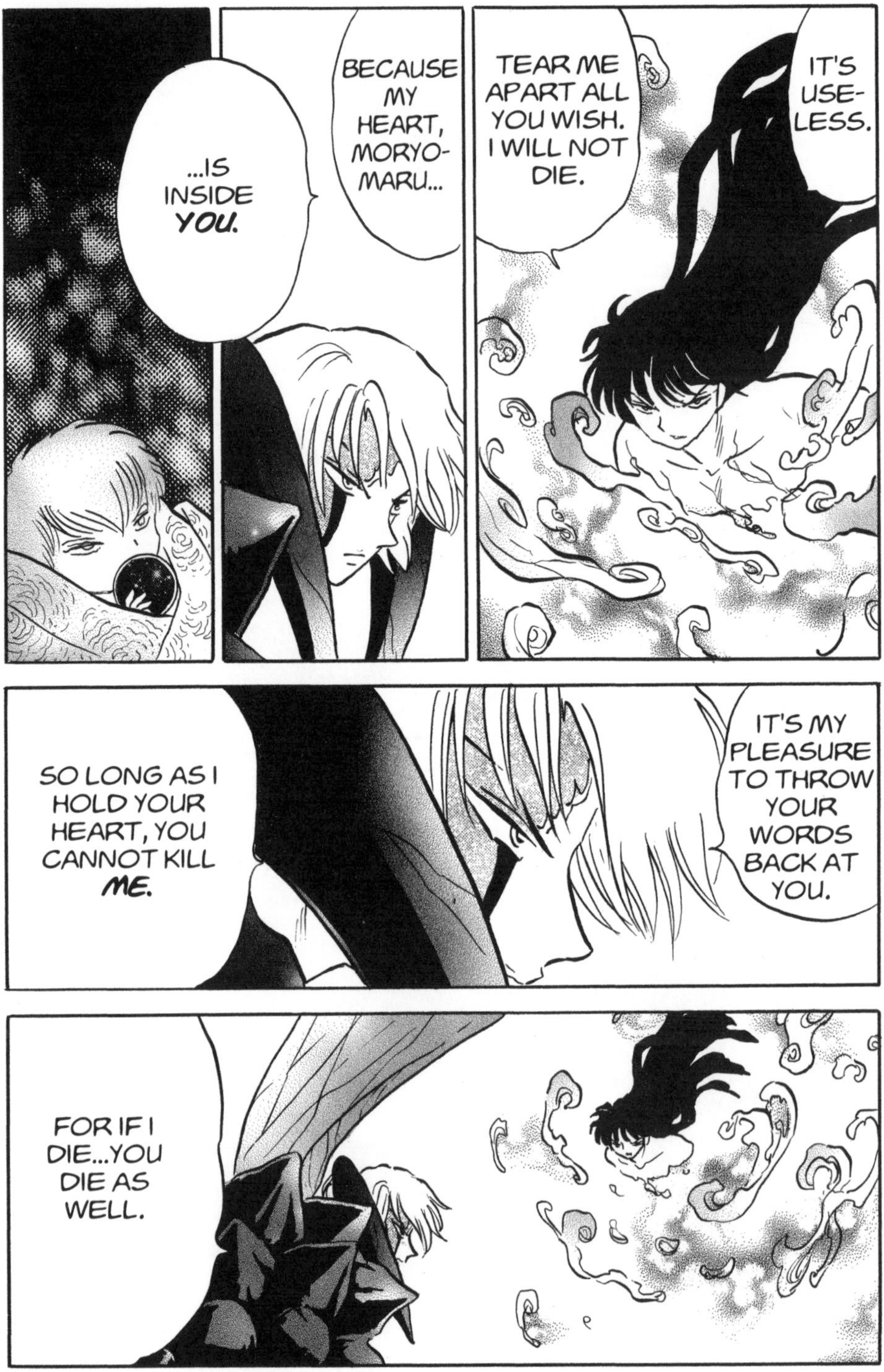
IT'S USELESS.
TEAR ME APART ALL YOU WISH. I WILL NOT DIE.
BECAUSE MY HEART, MORYOMARU...
...IS INSIDE *YOU.*
IT'S MY PLEASURE TO THROW YOUR WORDS BACK AT YOU.
SO LONG AS I HOLD YOUR HEART, YOU CANNOT KILL *ME.*
FOR IF I DIE...YOU DIE AS WELL.

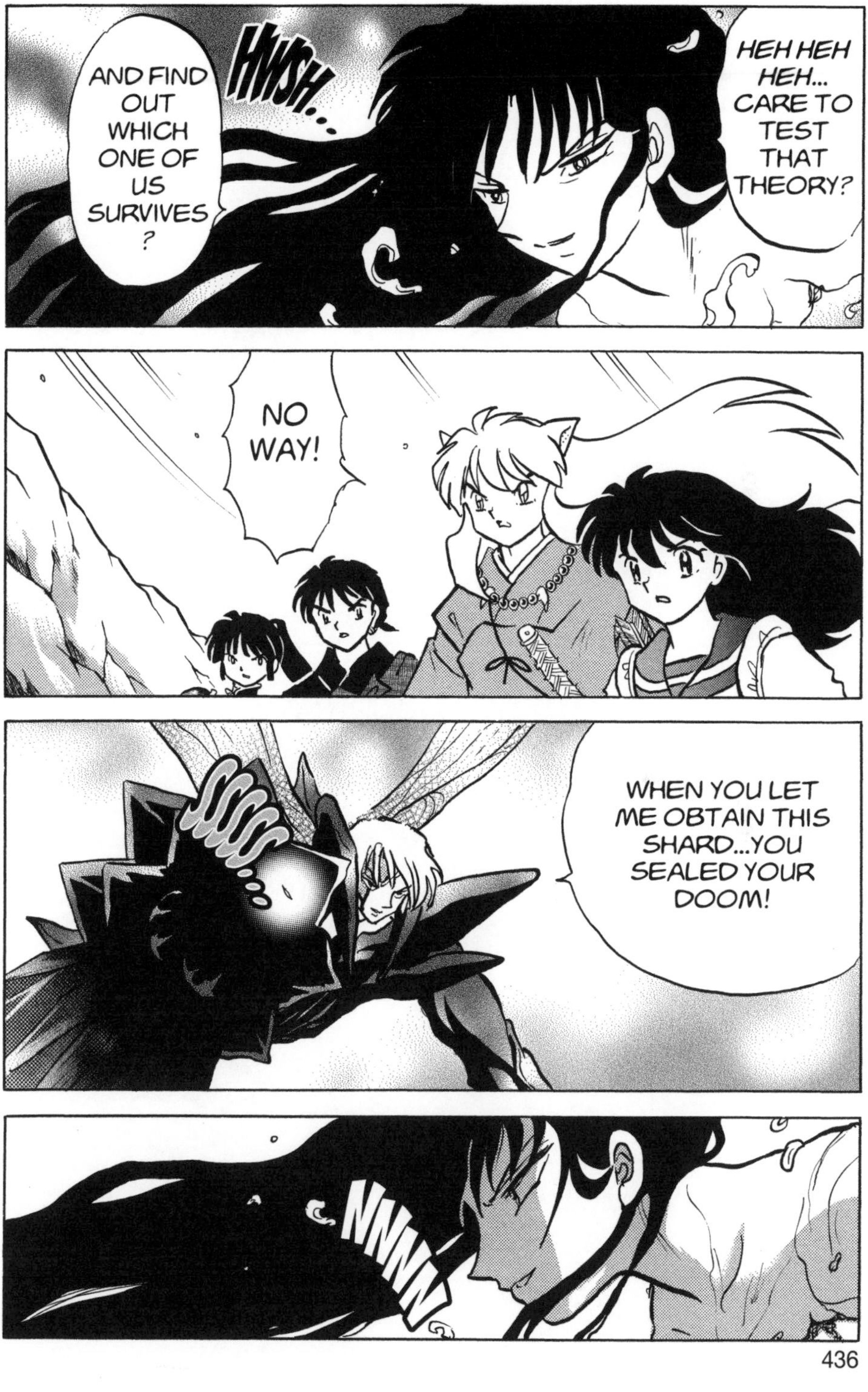
HEH HEH HEH... CARE TO TEST THAT THEORY?
HWSH...
AND FIND OUT WHICH ONE OF US SURVIVES?
NO WAY!
WHEN YOU LET ME OBTAIN THIS SHARD...YOU SEALED YOUR DOOM!
NNNN

SCROLL FOUR
ABSORPTION

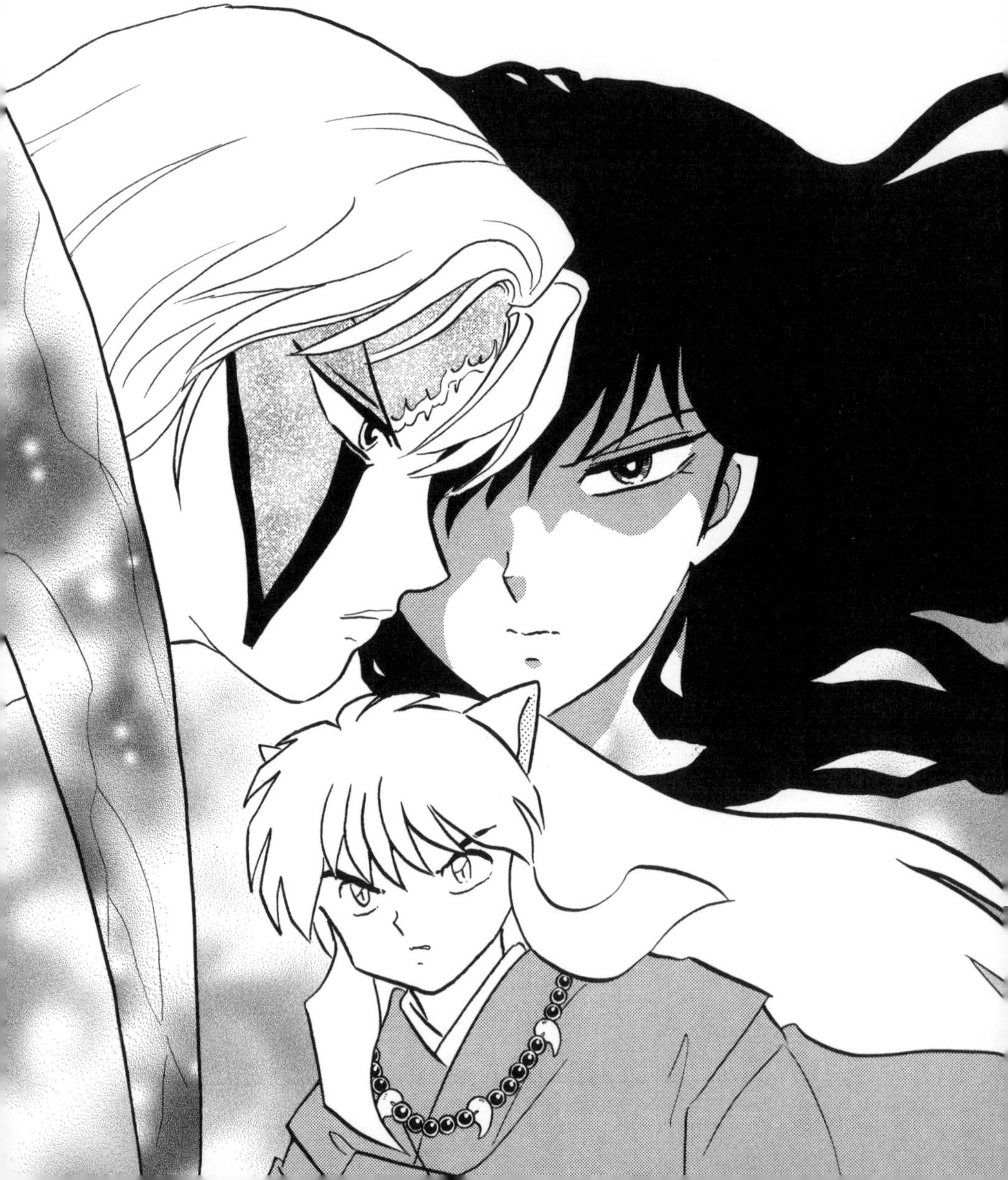

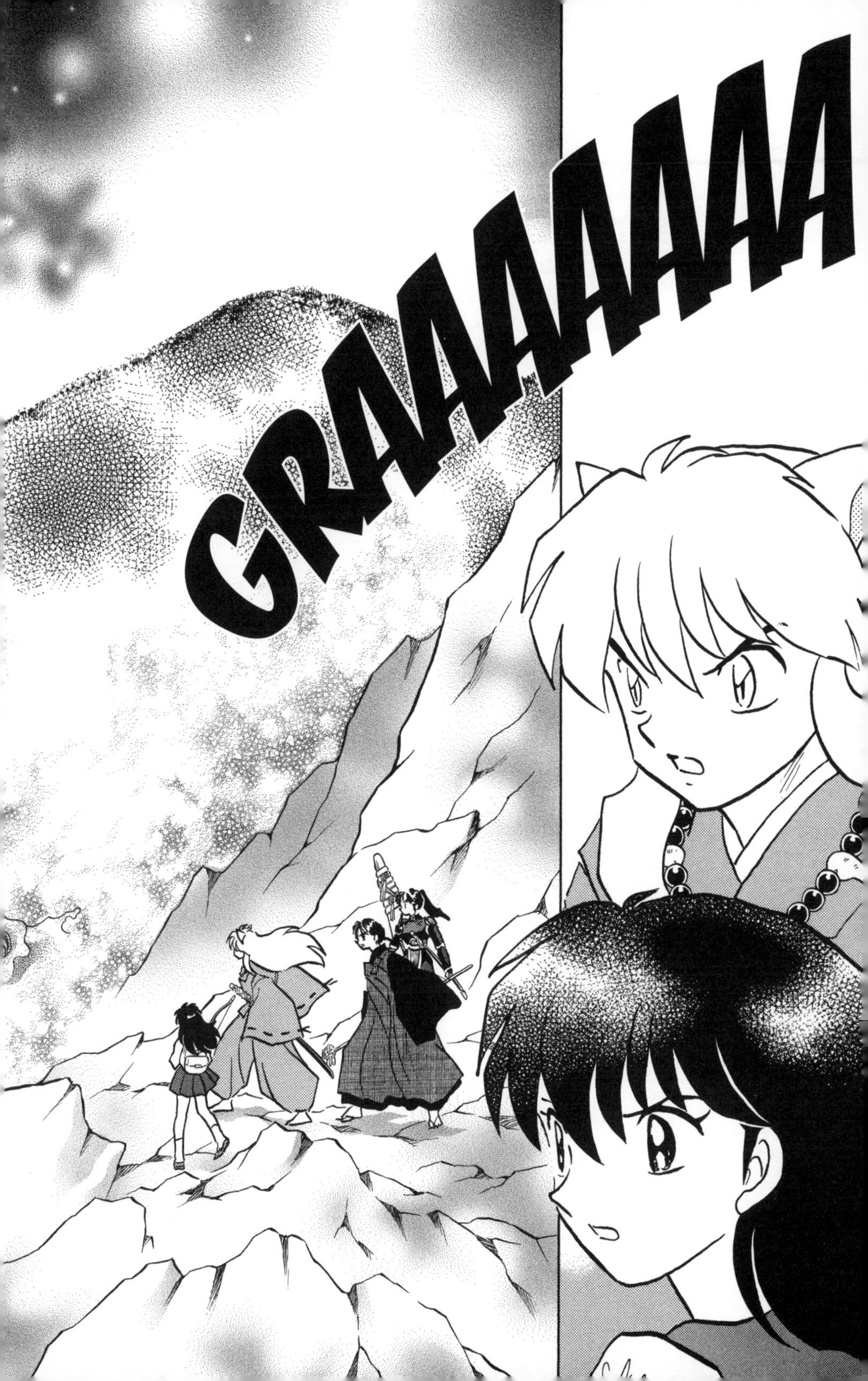
GRAAAAAAAA

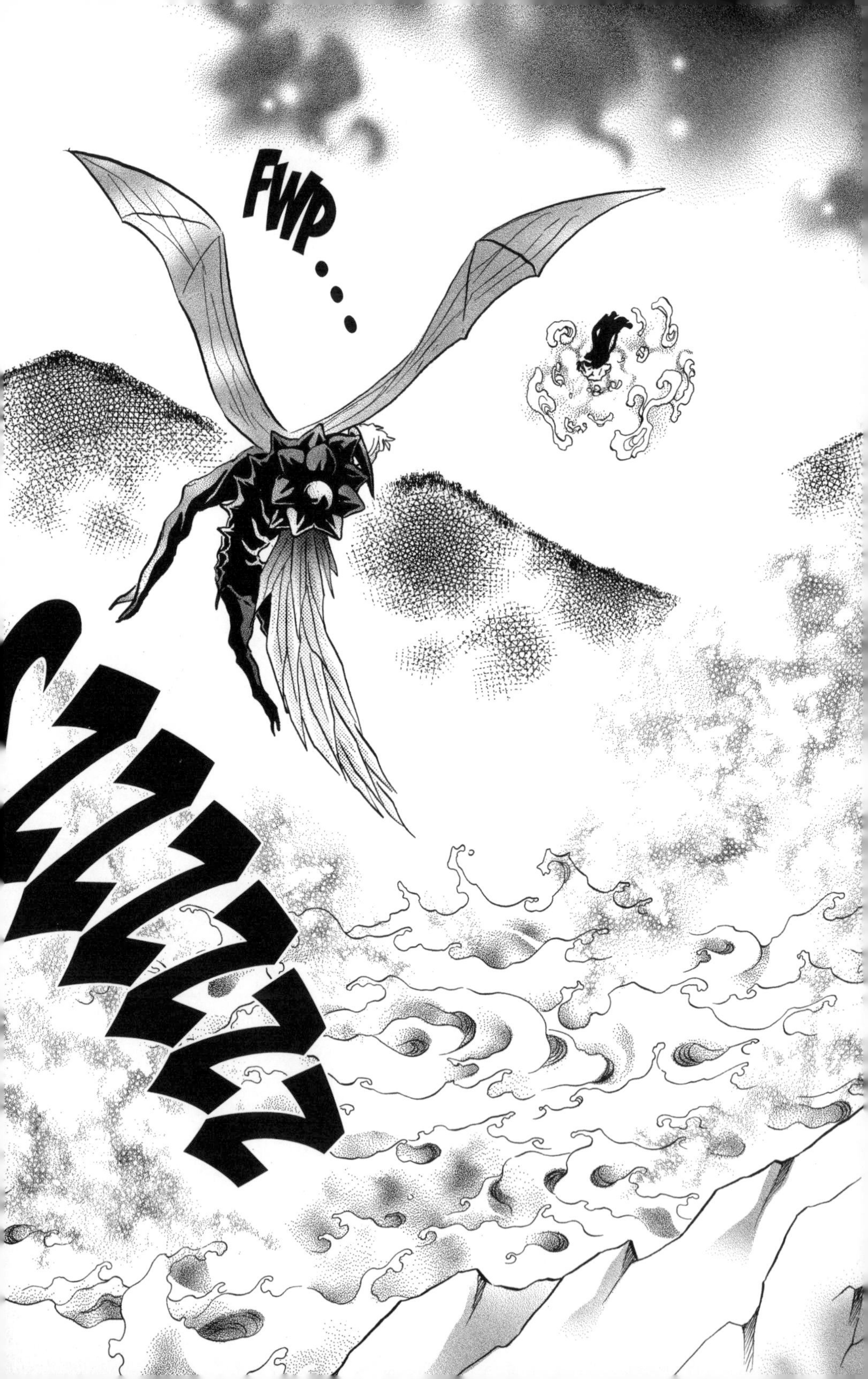
FWP...
SWZZZZ

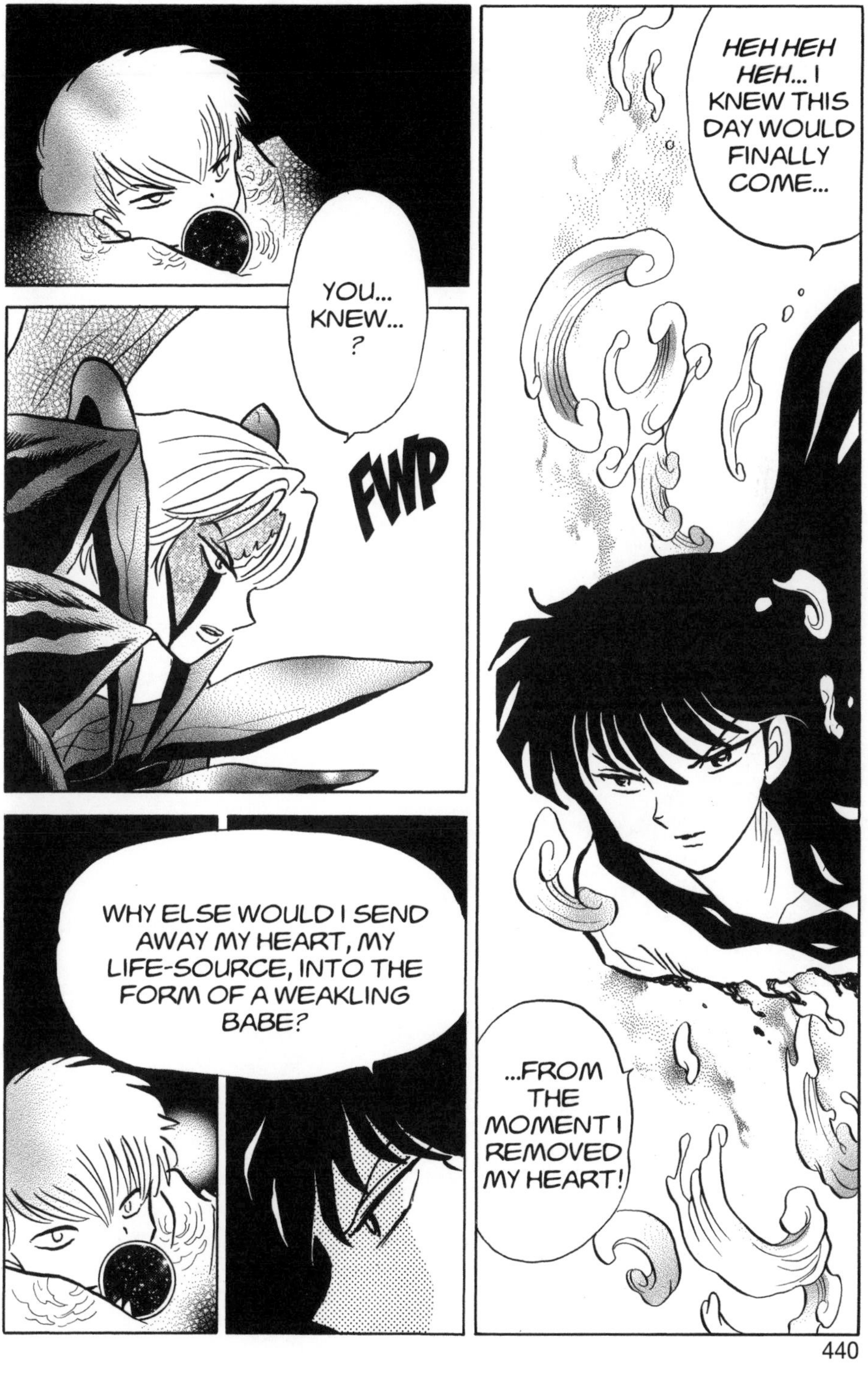
HEH HEH HEH... I KNEW THIS DAY WOULD FINALLY COME...
...FROM THE MOMENT I REMOVED MY HEART!
YOU... KNEW... ?
FWP
WHY ELSE WOULD I SEND AWAY MY HEART, MY LIFE-SOURCE, INTO THE FORM OF A WEAKLING BABE?

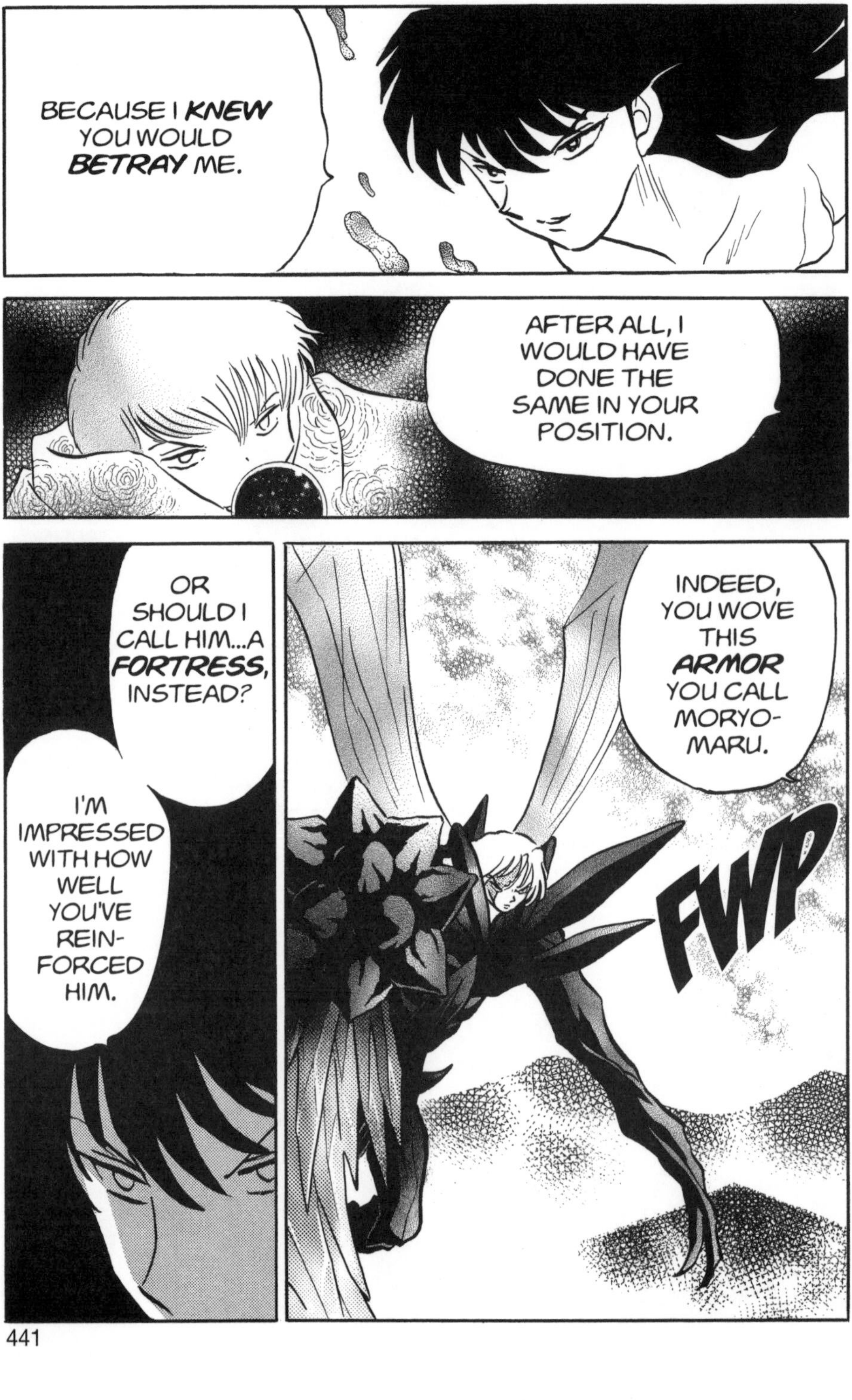
BECAUSE I **KNEW** YOU WOULD **BETRAY** ME.
AFTER ALL, I WOULD HAVE DONE THE SAME IN YOUR POSITION.
INDEED, YOU WOVE THIS **ARMOR** YOU CALL MORYO-MARU.
FWP
OR SHOULD I CALL HIM...A **FORTRESS**, INSTEAD?
I'M IMPRESSED WITH HOW WELL YOU'VE REIN-FORCED HIM.

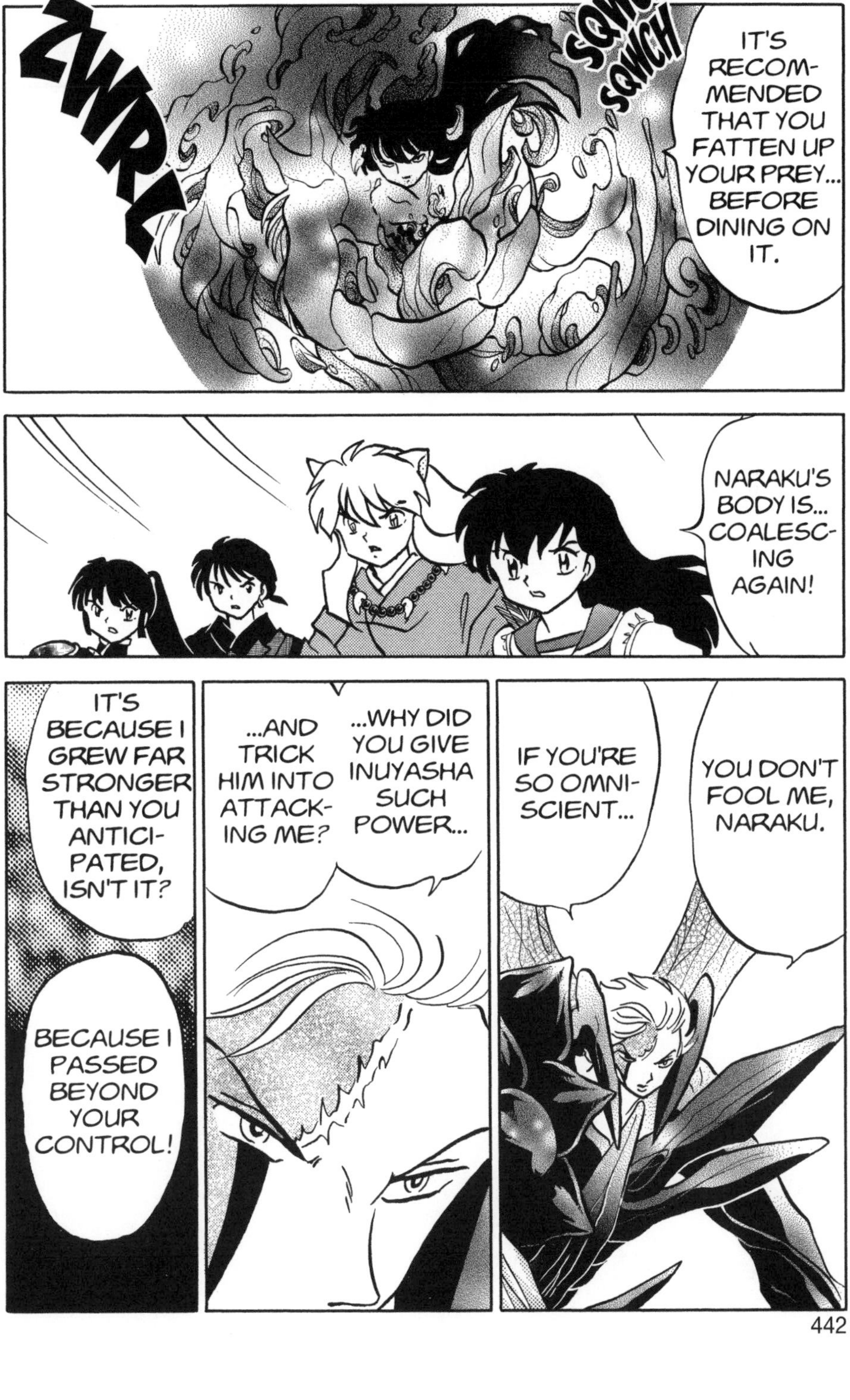
IT'S RECOMMENDED THAT YOU FATTEN UP YOUR PREY... BEFORE DINING ON IT.
SQWCH SQWCH
ZWRL
NARAKU'S BODY IS... COALESCING AGAIN!
YOU DON'T FOOL ME, NARAKU.
IF YOU'RE SO OMNISCIENT...
...WHY DID YOU GIVE INUYASHA SUCH POWER...
...AND TRICK HIM INTO ATTACKING ME?
IT'S BECAUSE I GREW FAR STRONGER THAN YOU ANTICIPATED, ISN'T IT?
BECAUSE I PASSED BEYOND YOUR CONTROL!

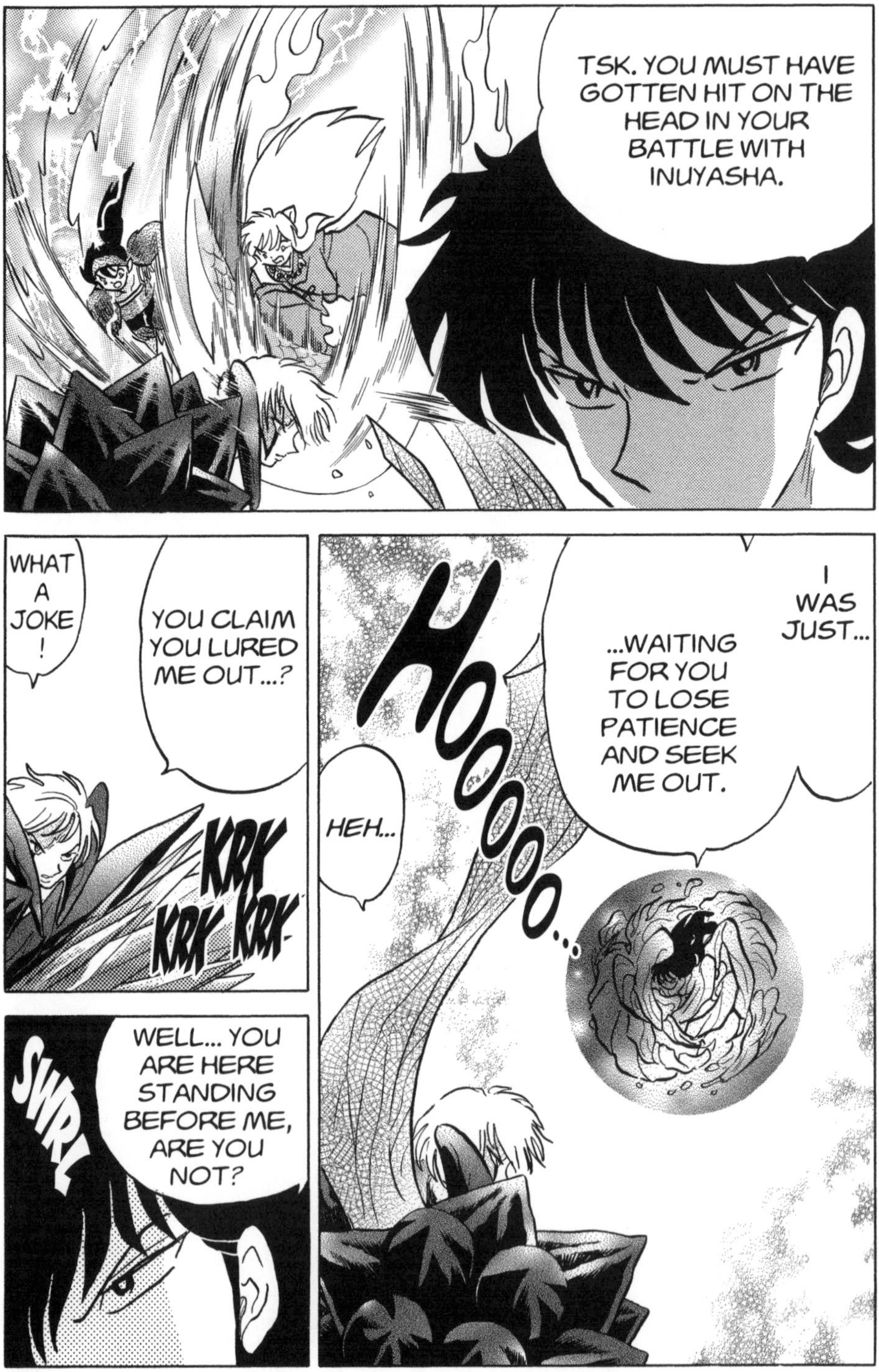
TSK. YOU MUST HAVE GOTTEN HIT ON THE HEAD IN YOUR BATTLE WITH INUYASHA.
I WAS JUST...
...WAITING FOR YOU TO LOSE PATIENCE AND SEEK ME OUT.
HOOOOOO...
HEH...
YOU CLAIM YOU LURED ME OUT...?
WHAT A JOKE!
KRK KRK KRK KRK
WELL... YOU ARE HERE STANDING BEFORE ME, ARE YOU NOT?
SWRL

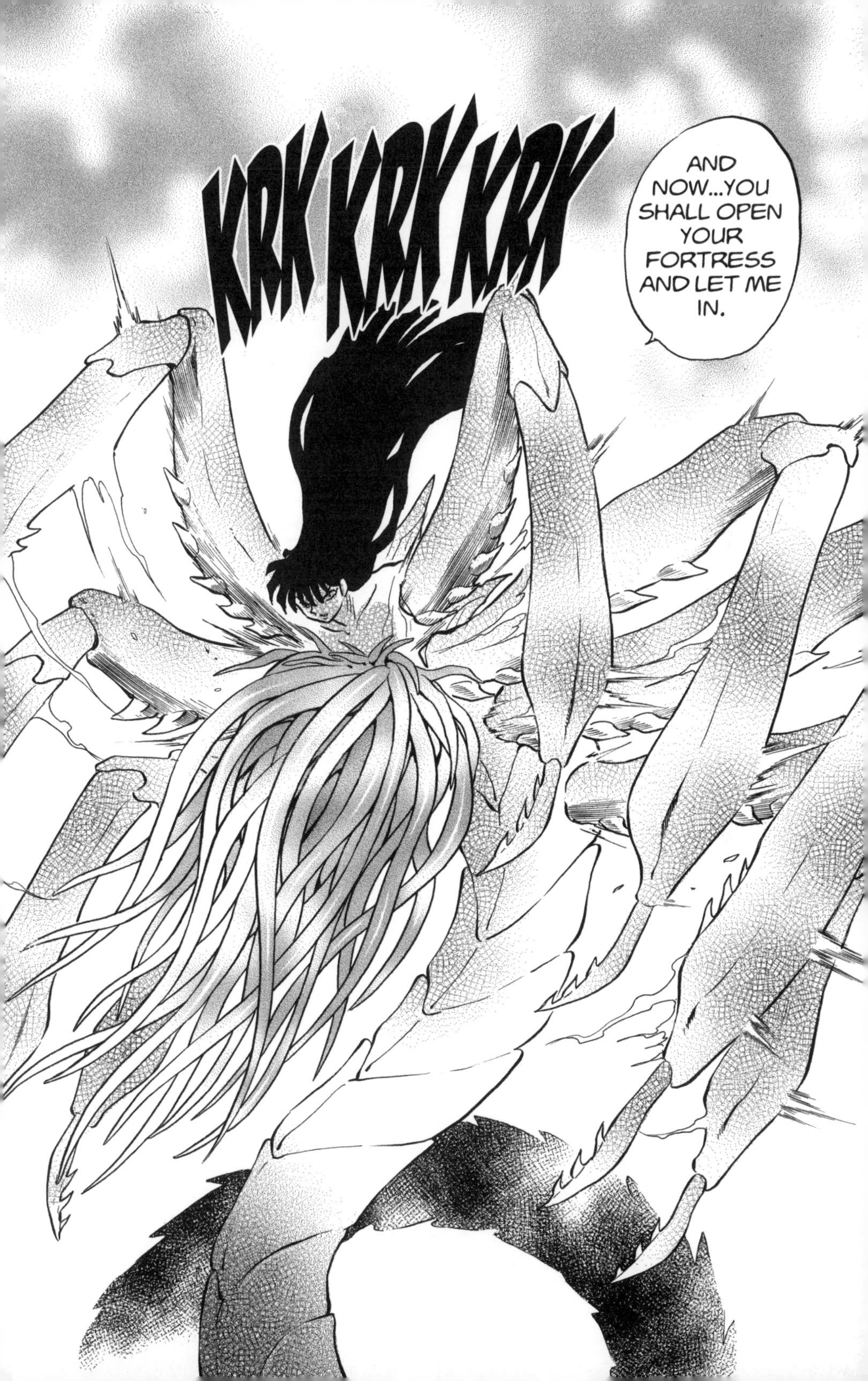
AND NOW...YOU SHALL OPEN YOUR FORTRESS AND LET ME IN.
KRK KRK KRK

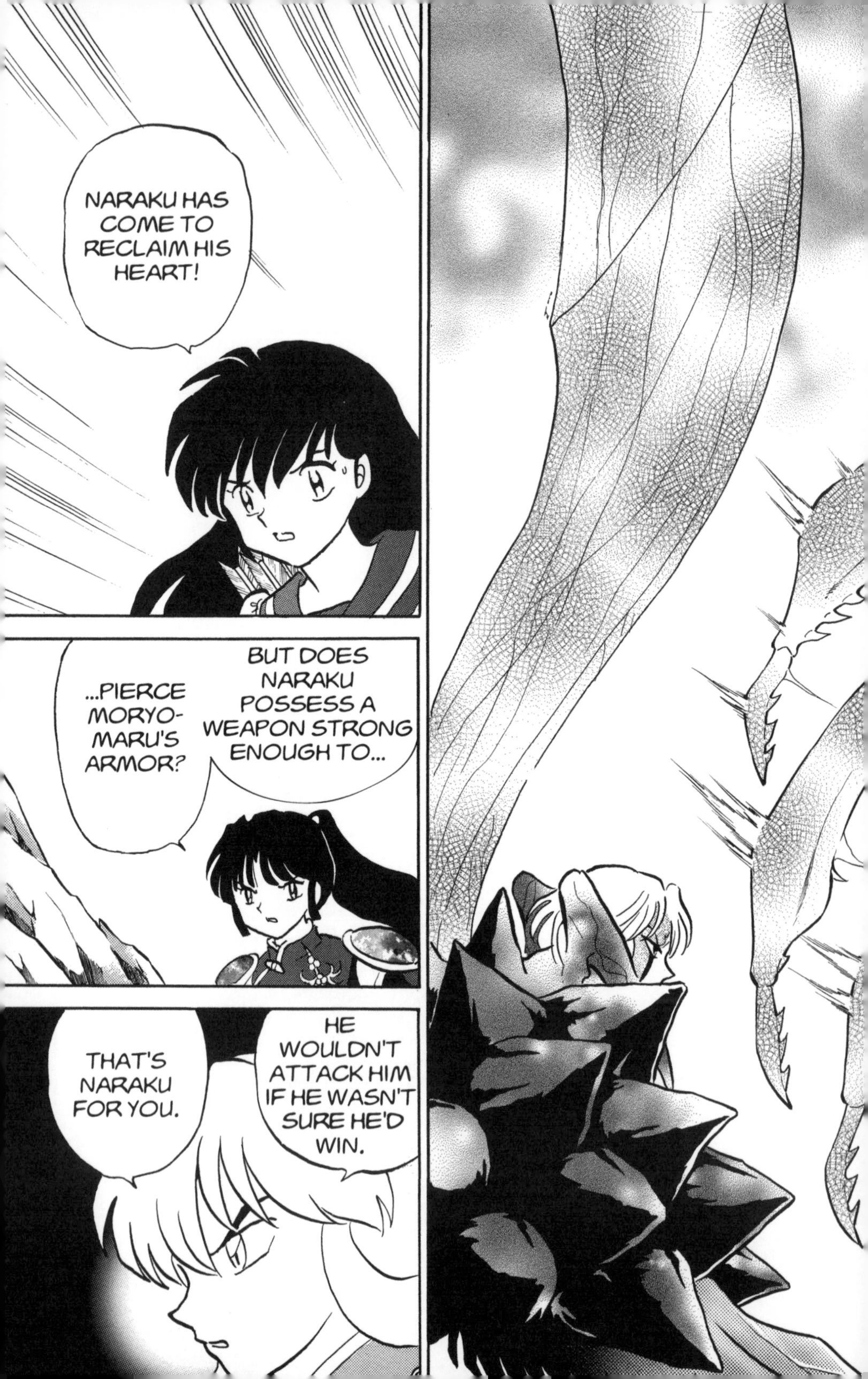
NARAKU HAS COME TO RECLAIM HIS HEART!
BUT DOES NARAKU POSSESS A WEAPON STRONG ENOUGH TO...
...PIERCE MORYO-MARU'S ARMOR?
HE WOULDN'T ATTACK HIM IF HE WASN'T SURE HE'D WIN.
THAT'S NARAKU FOR YOU.

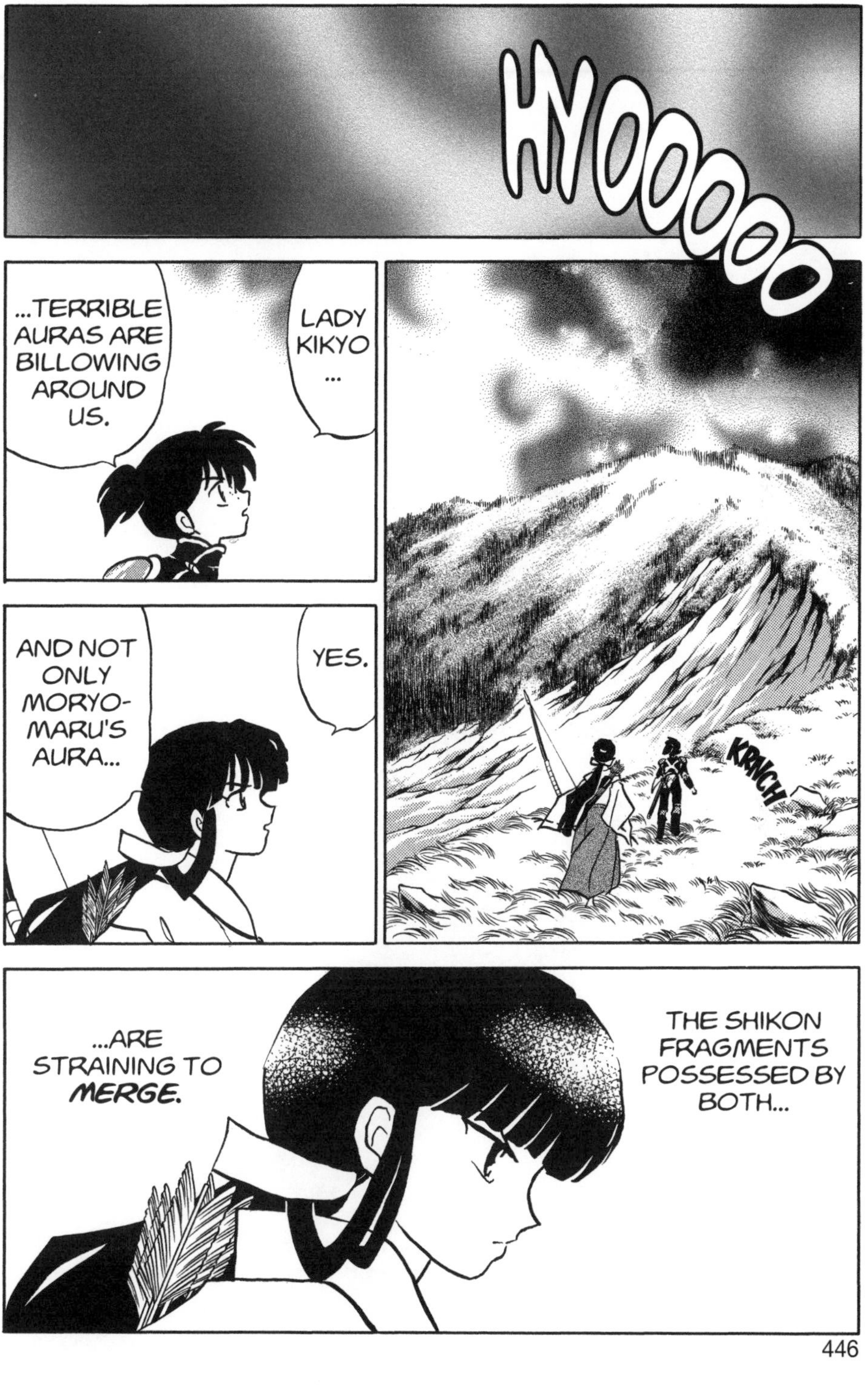
HYOOOOOO
KRNCH
LADY KIKYO...
...TERRIBLE AURAS ARE BILLOWING AROUND US.
YES.
AND NOT ONLY MORYO-MARU'S AURA...
THE SHIKON FRAGMENTS POSSESSED BY BOTH...
...ARE STRAINING TO *MERGE.*

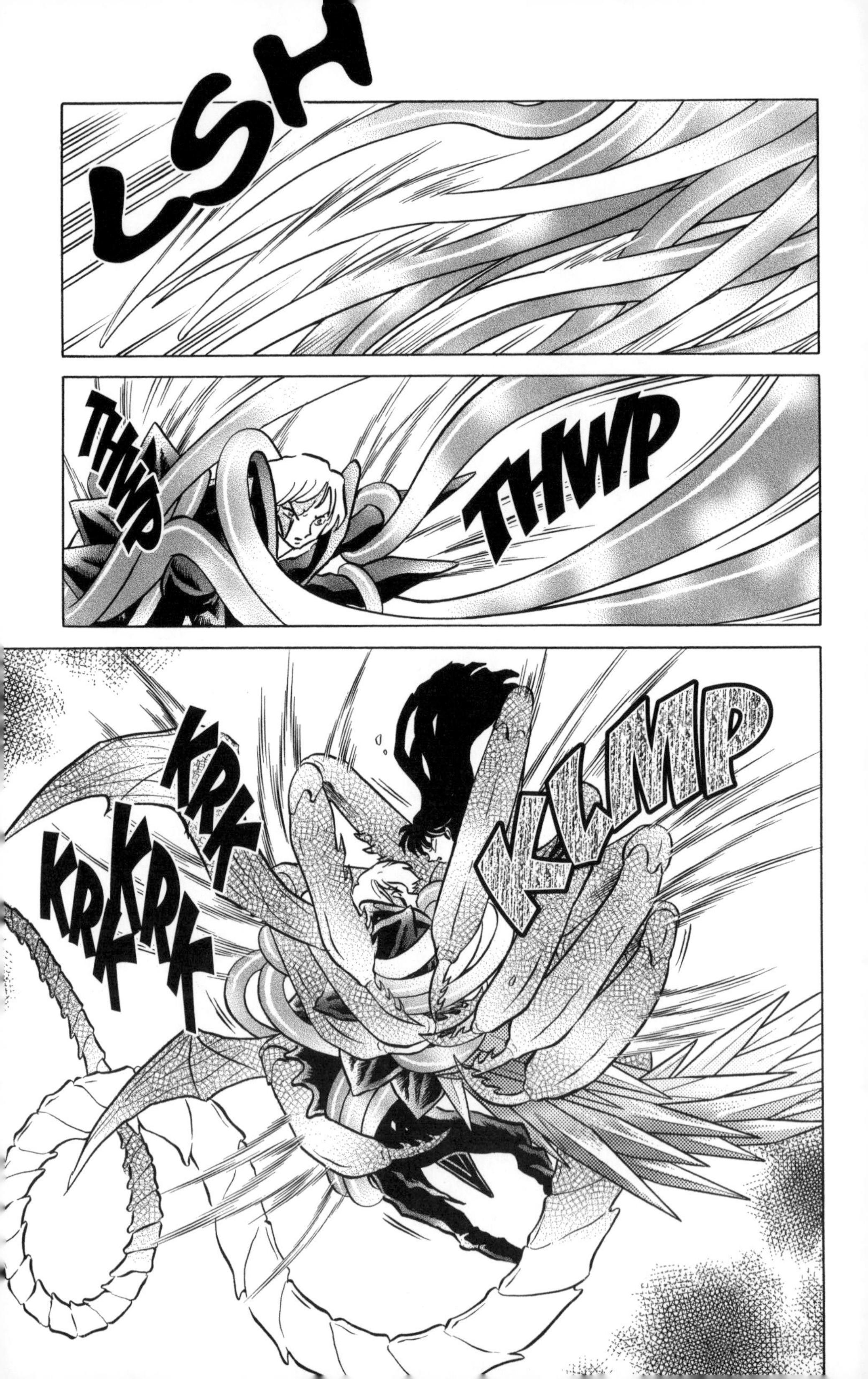
LSH
THWP
THWP
KLUMP
KRK
KRK
KRK

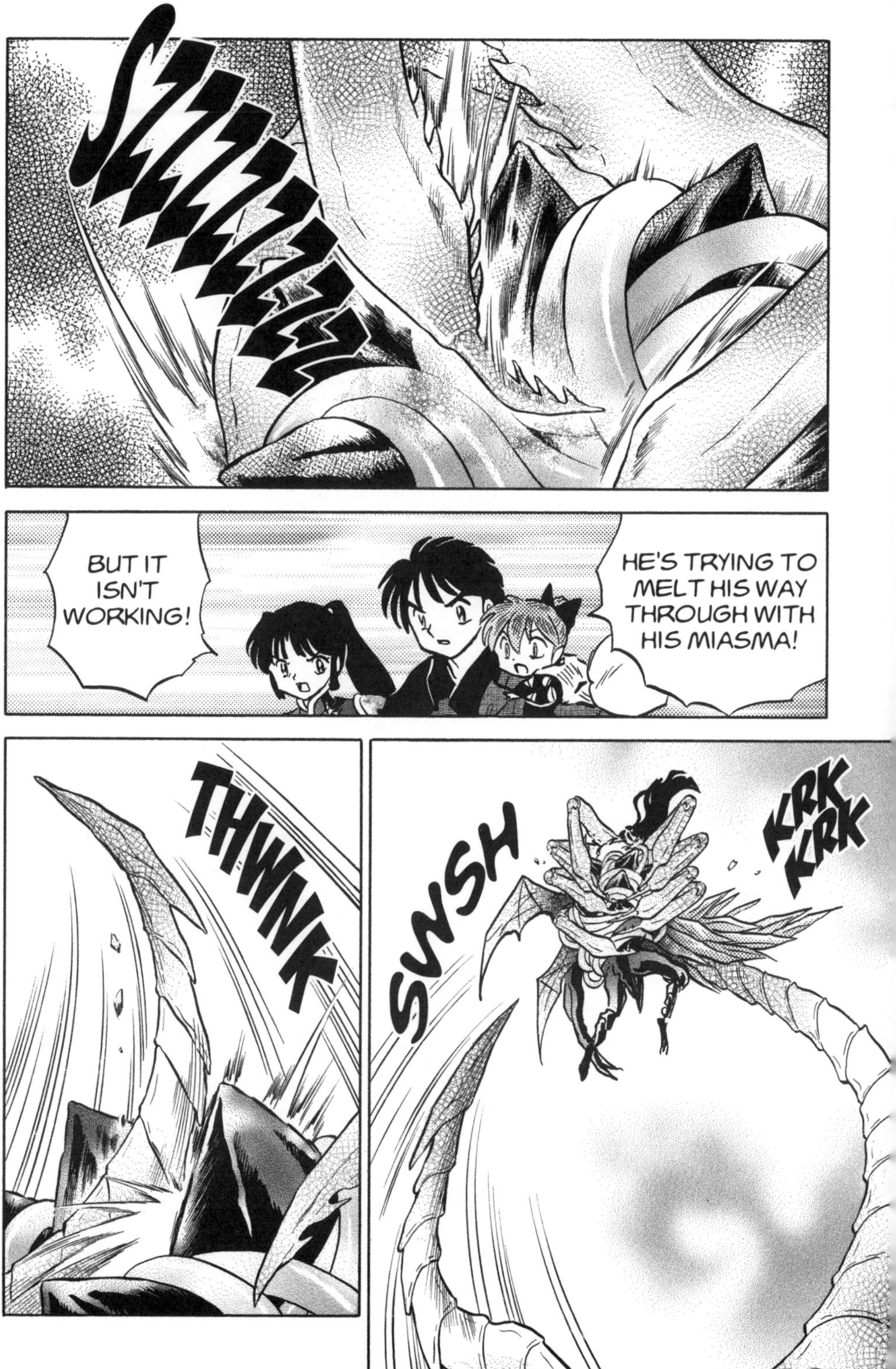
SZZZZZZZ
HE'S TRYING TO MELT HIS WAY THROUGH WITH HIS MIASMA!
BUT IT ISN'T WORKING!
KRK KRK
SWSH
THWNK

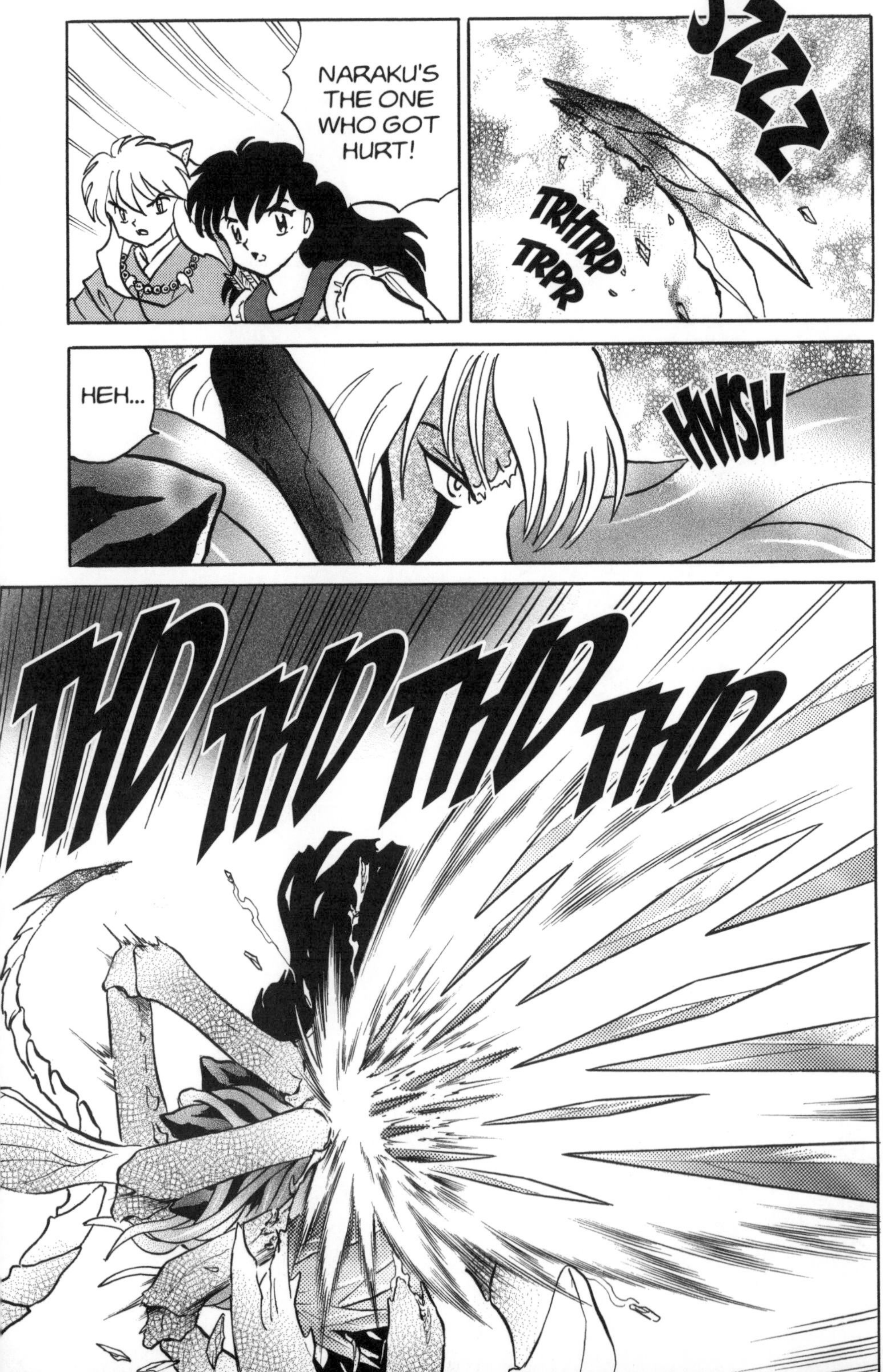
SZZZ
TRHTRP TRPR
NARAKU'S THE ONE WHO GOT HURT!
HWSH
HEH...
THD THD THD THD

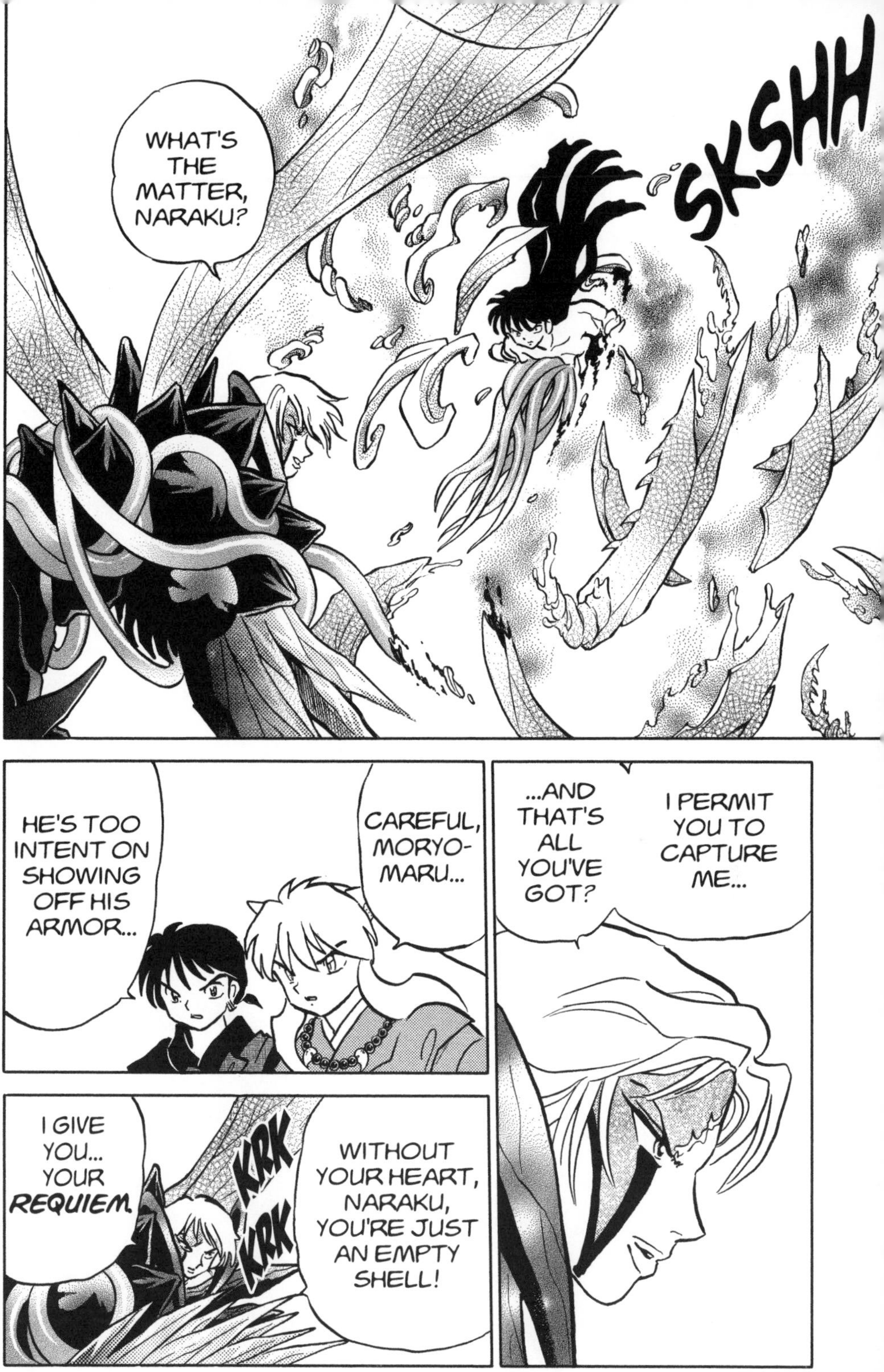
SKSHH
WHAT'S THE MATTER, NARAKU?
I PERMIT YOU TO CAPTURE ME...
...AND THAT'S ALL YOU'VE GOT?
CAREFUL, MORYO-MARU...
HE'S TOO INTENT ON SHOWING OFF HIS ARMOR...
WITHOUT YOUR HEART, NARAKU, YOU'RE JUST AN EMPTY SHELL!
KRK KRK
I GIVE YOU... YOUR ***REQUIEM.***

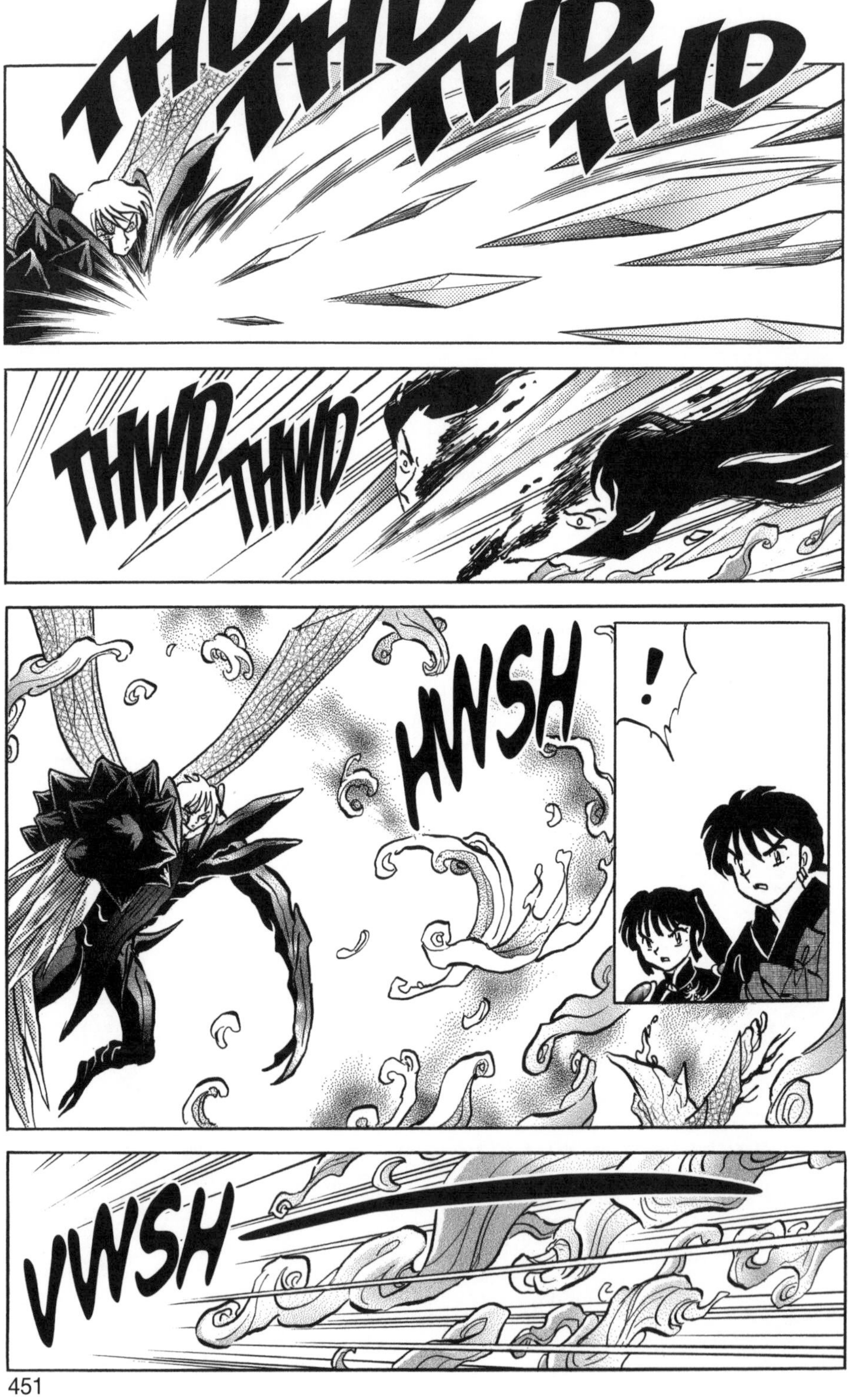
THD THD THD THD
THWD THWD
!
HWSH
VWSH

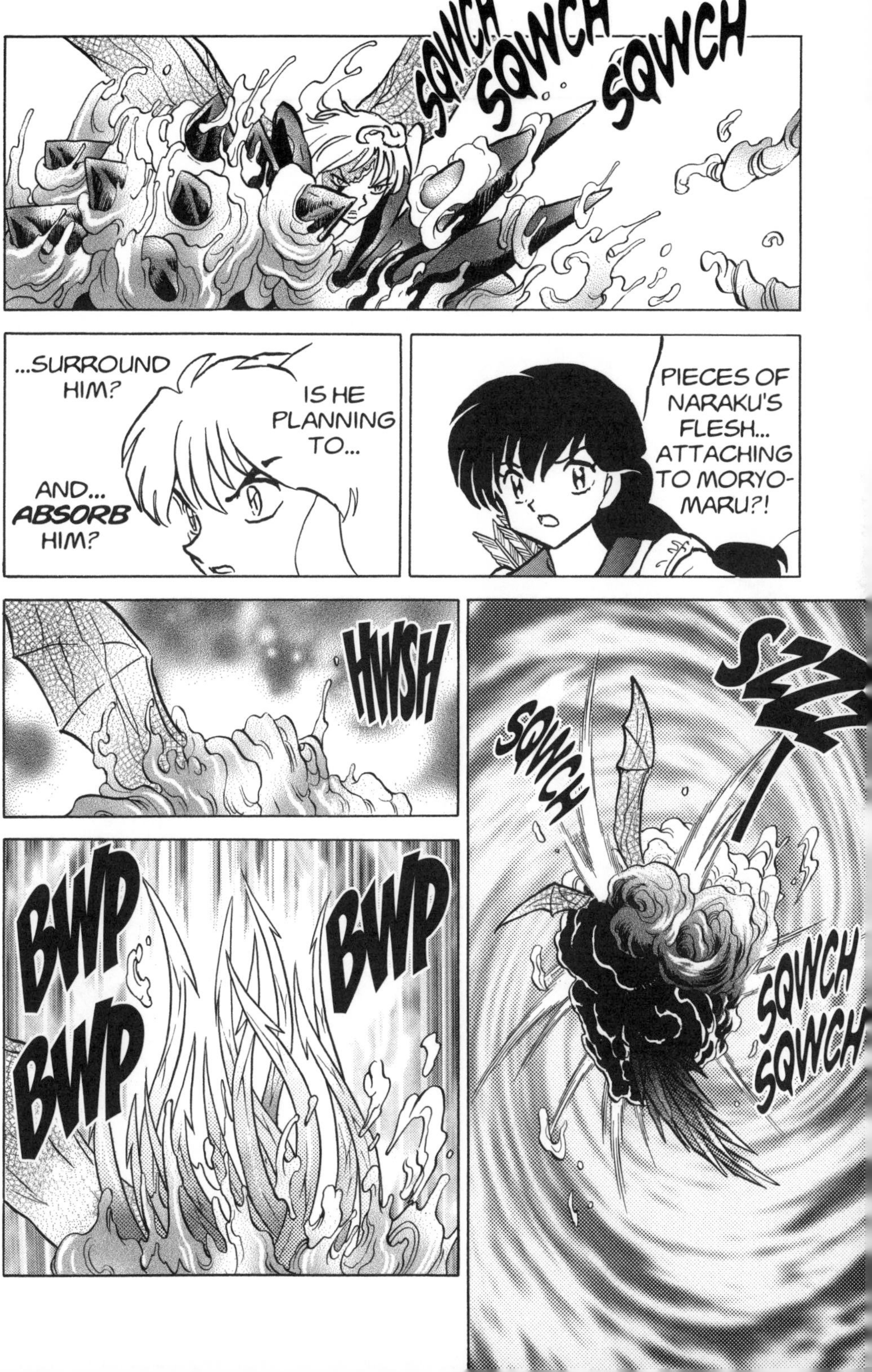
SQWCH
SQWCH
SQWCH
PIECES OF NARAKU'S FLESH... ATTACHING TO MORYO-MARU?!
IS HE PLANNING TO...
...SURROUND HIM?
AND... ABSORB HIM?
SZZZ
SQWCH
SQWCH SQWCH
HWSH
BWP
BWP
BWP

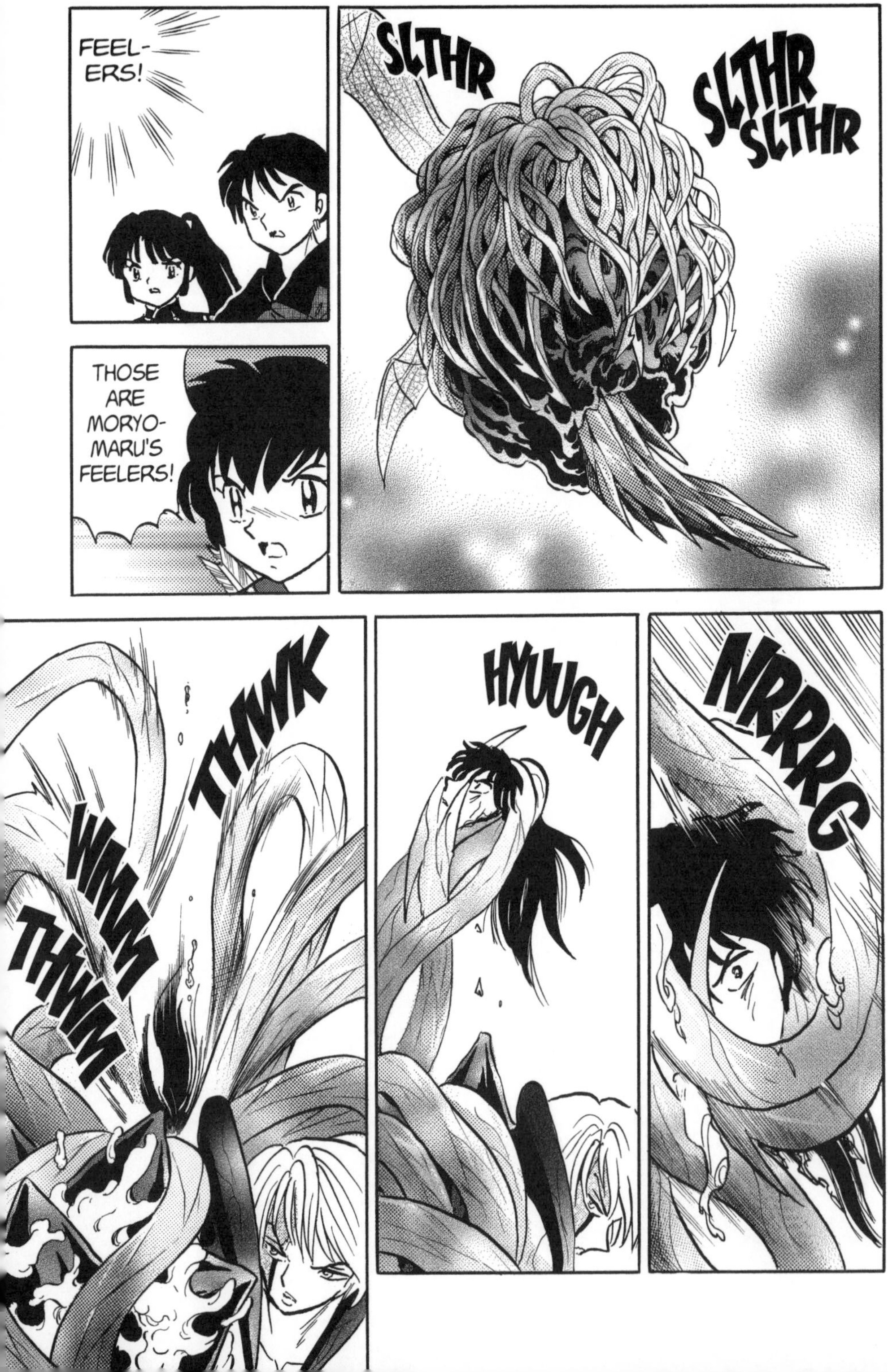
SLTHR
SLTHR SLTHR
FEEL-ERS!
THOSE ARE MORYO-MARU'S FEELERS!
NRRRG
HYUUGH
THWK
WMM THWM

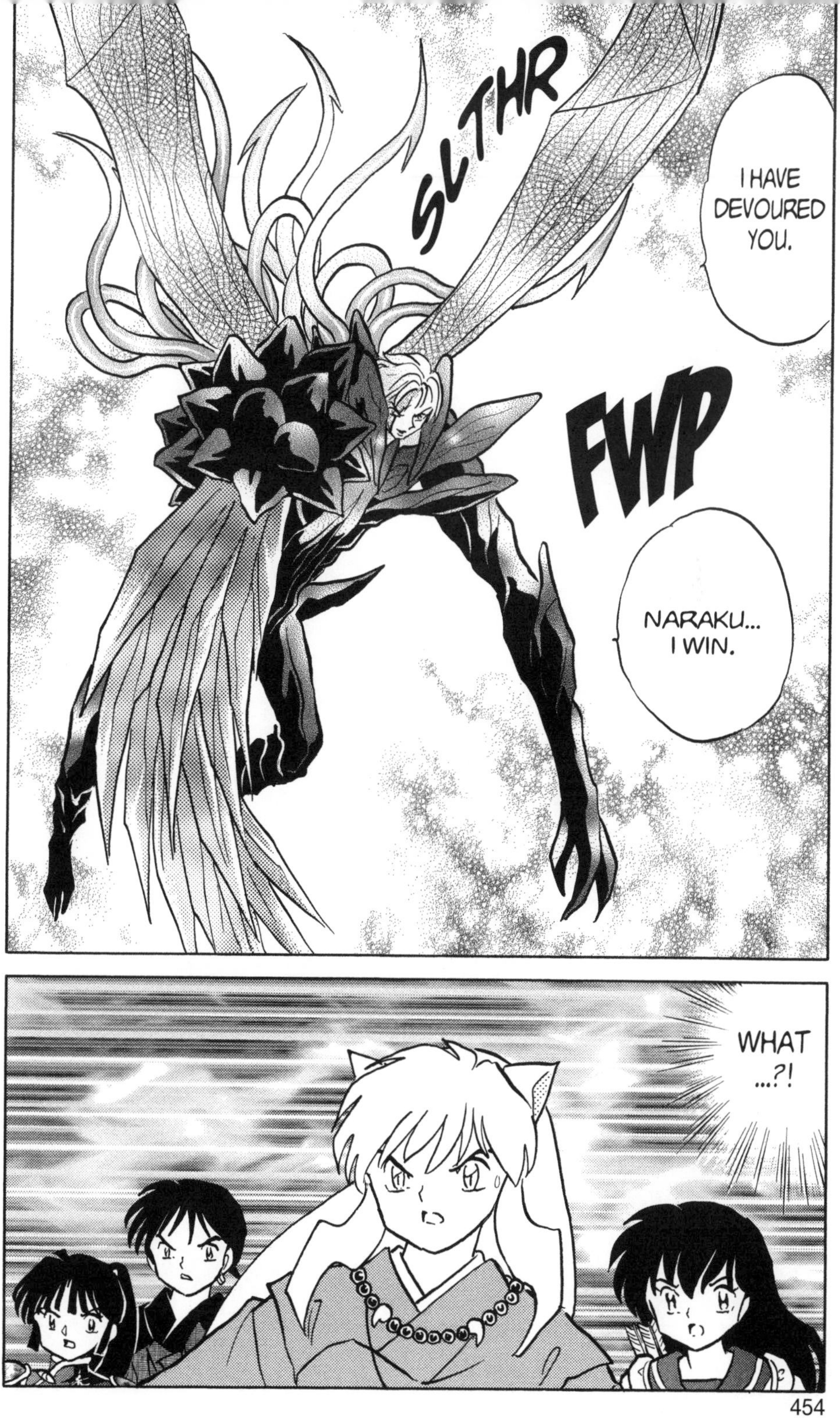
I HAVE DEVOURED YOU.
SLTHR
FWP
NARAKU... I WIN.
WHAT ...?!

SCROLL FIVE
NARAKU ERADICATED

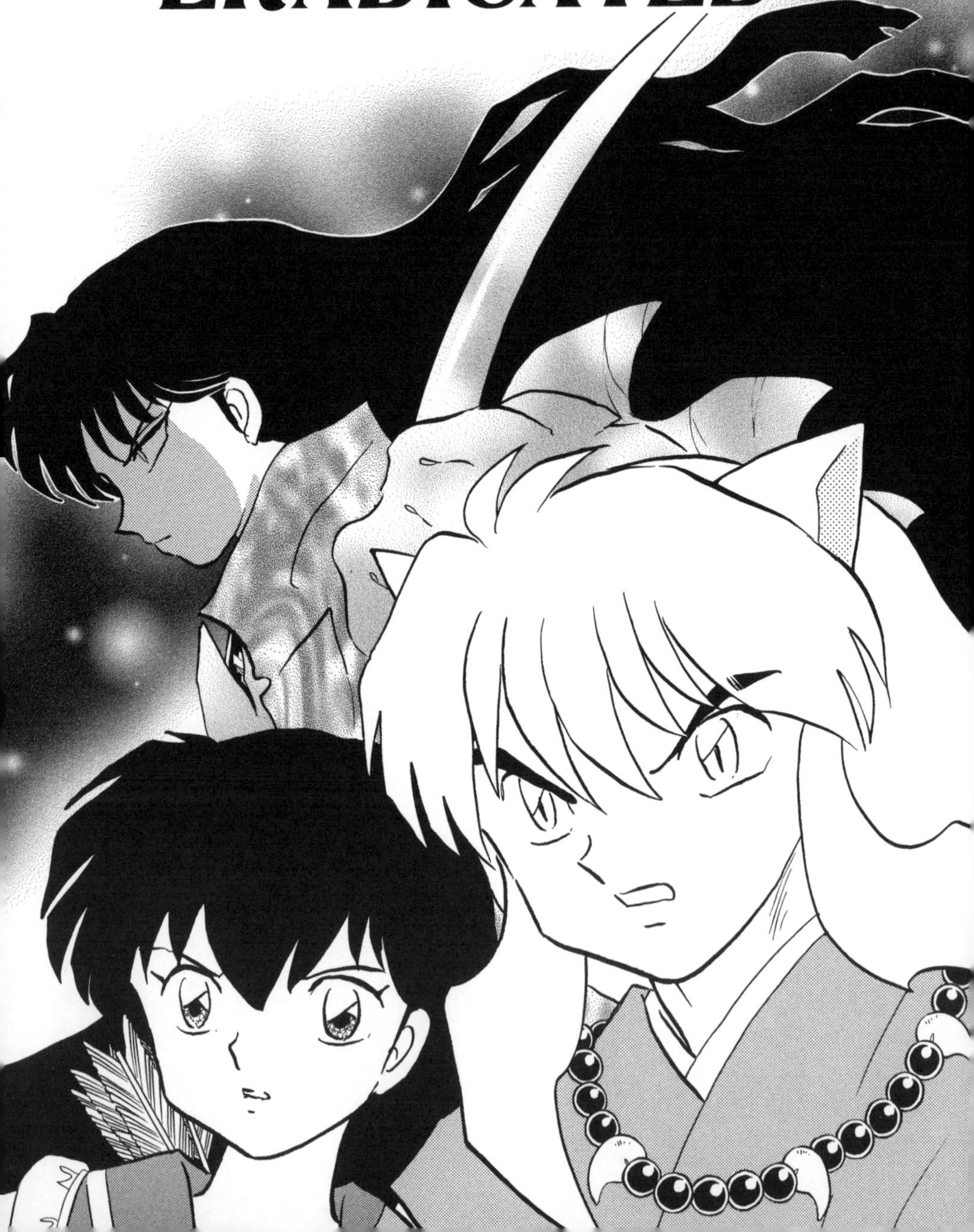

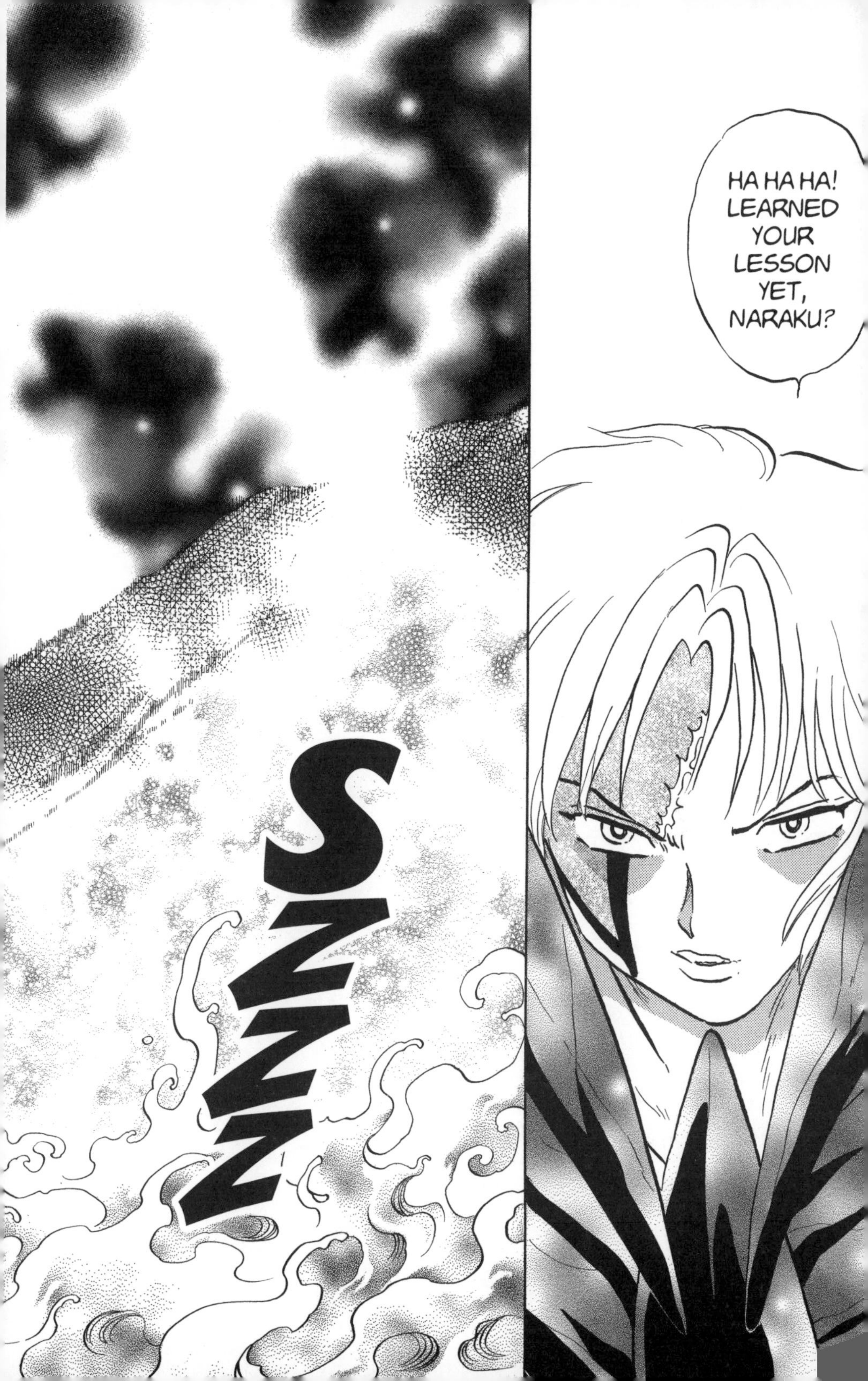
HA HA HA! LEARNED YOUR LESSON YET, NARAKU?
SNNNN

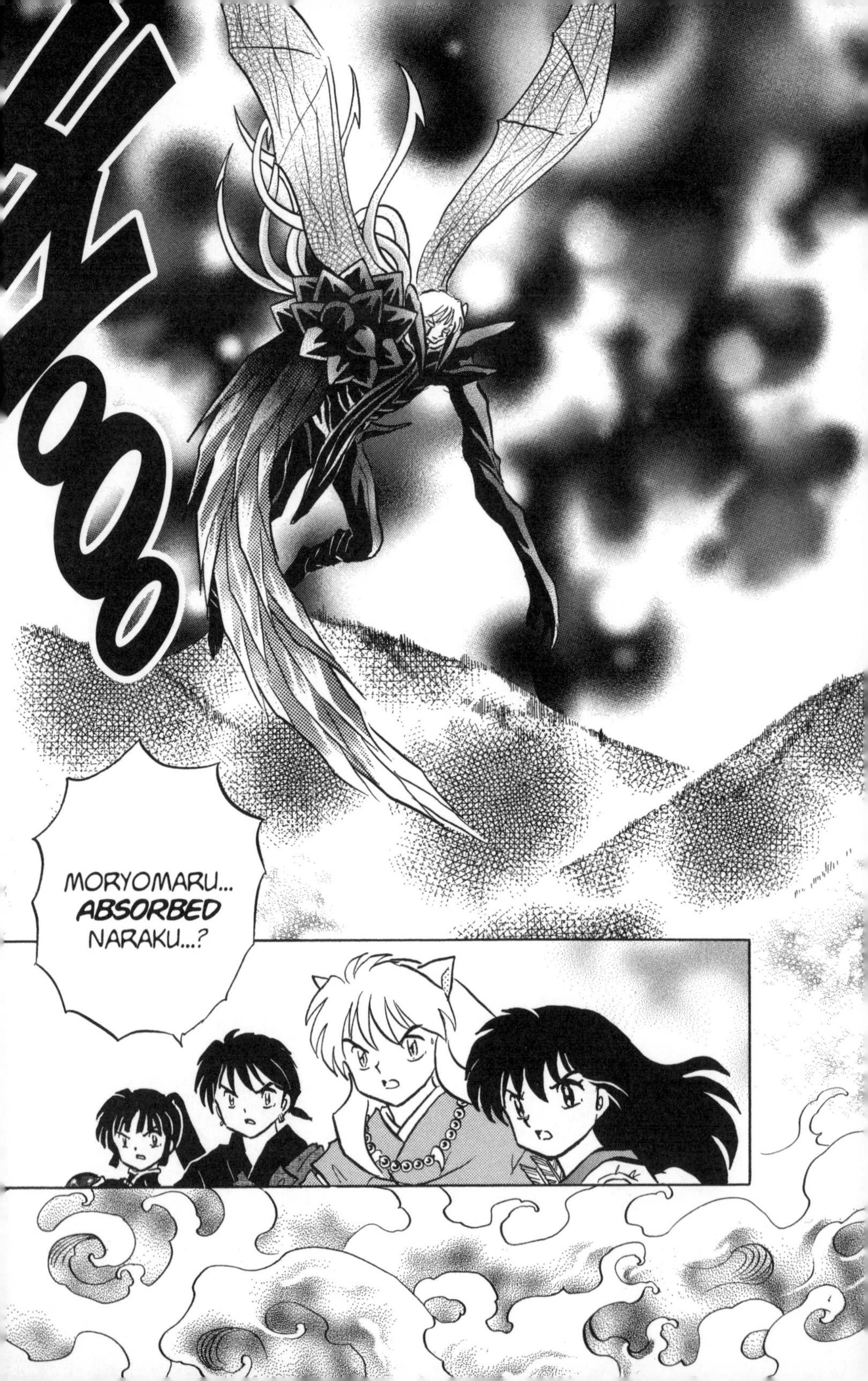
MORYOMARU... **ABSORBED** NARAKU...?

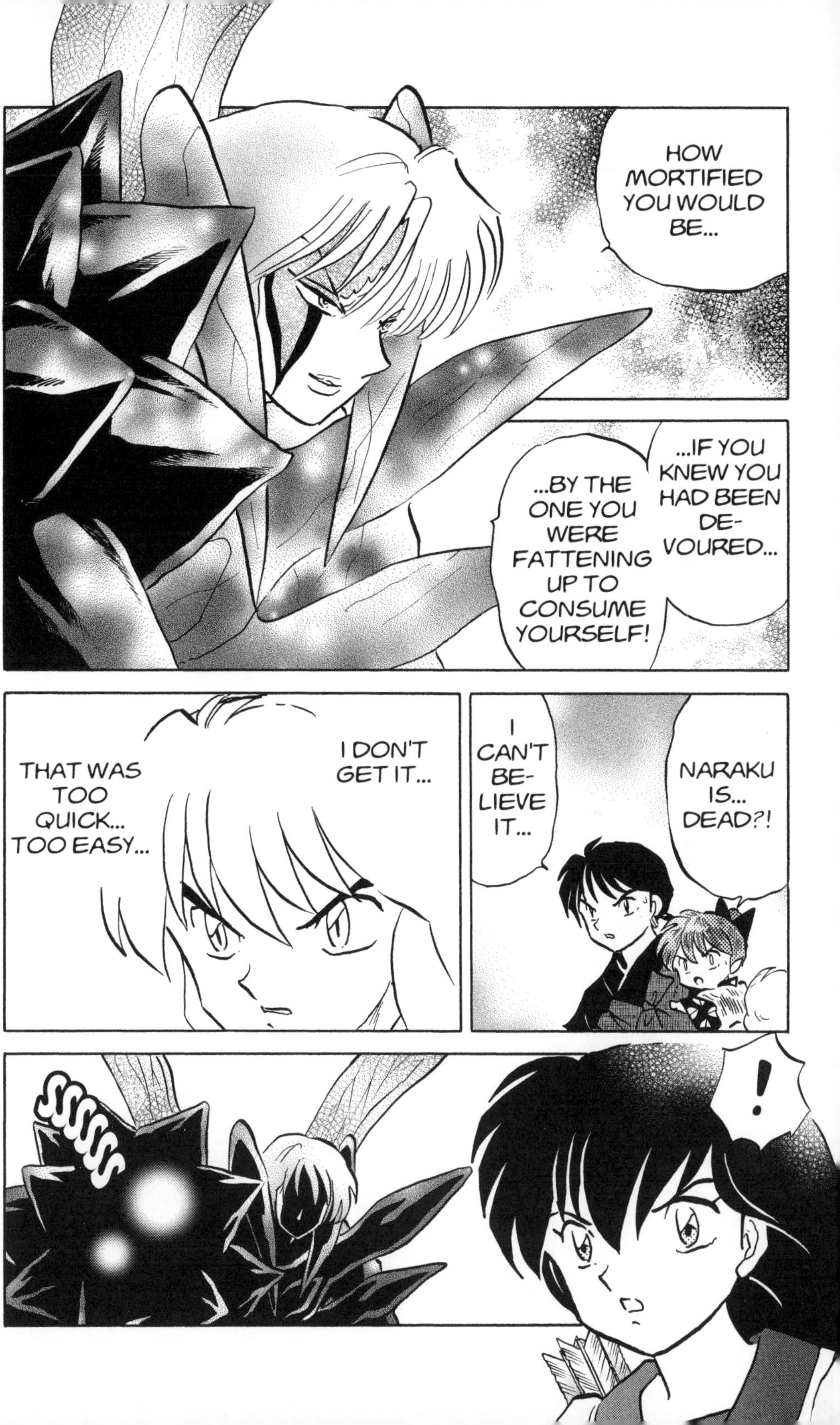
HOW MORTIFIED YOU WOULD BE...
...IF YOU KNEW YOU HAD BEEN DE-VOURED...
...BY THE ONE YOU WERE FATTENING UP TO CONSUME YOURSELF!
NARAKU IS... DEAD?!
I CAN'T BE-LIEVE IT...
I DON'T GET IT...
THAT WAS TOO QUICK... TOO EASY...
!
SSSSS

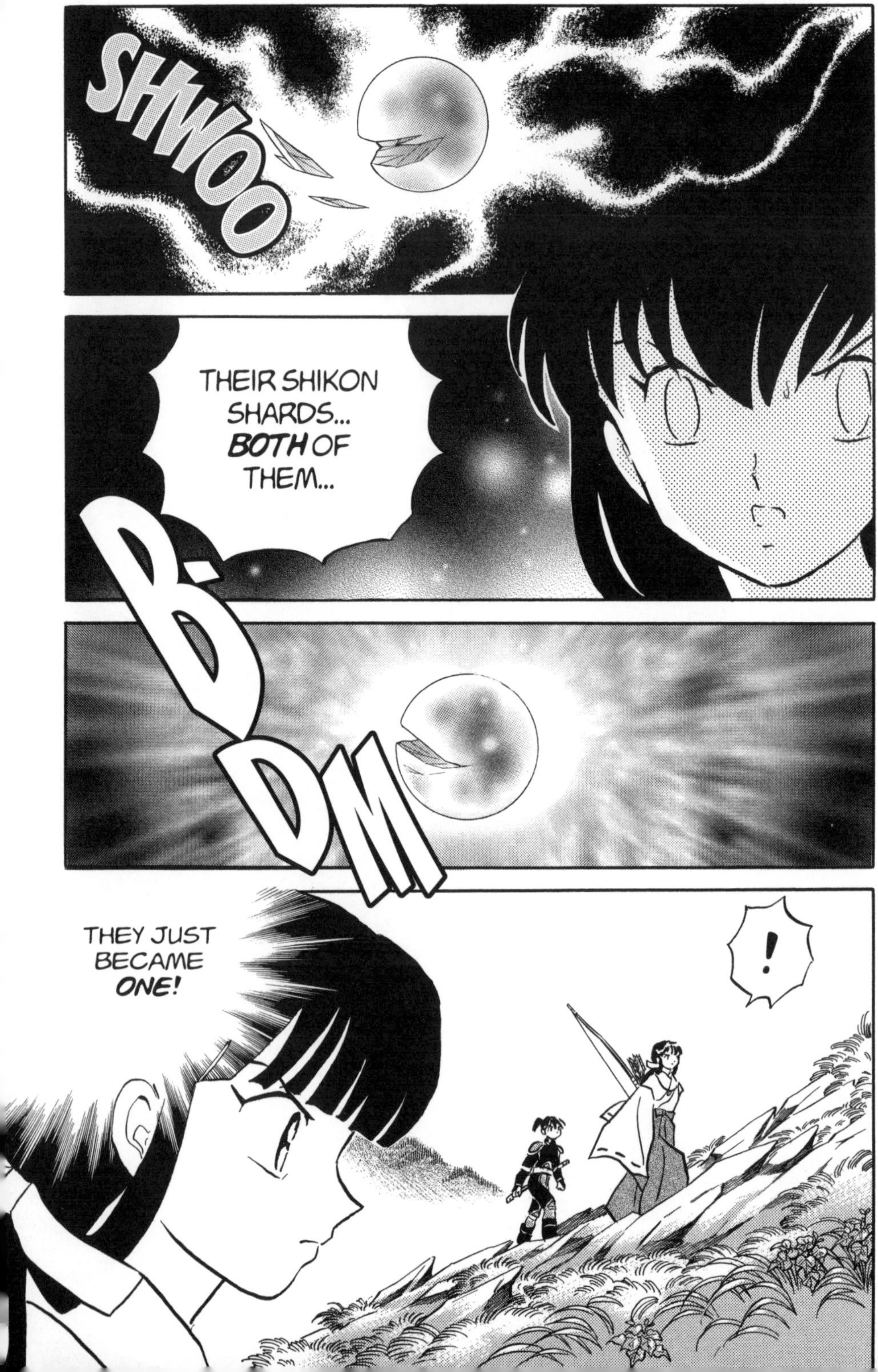
SHWOO
THEIR SHIKON SHARDS... BOTH OF THEM...
BADMM
!
THEY JUST BECAME ONE!

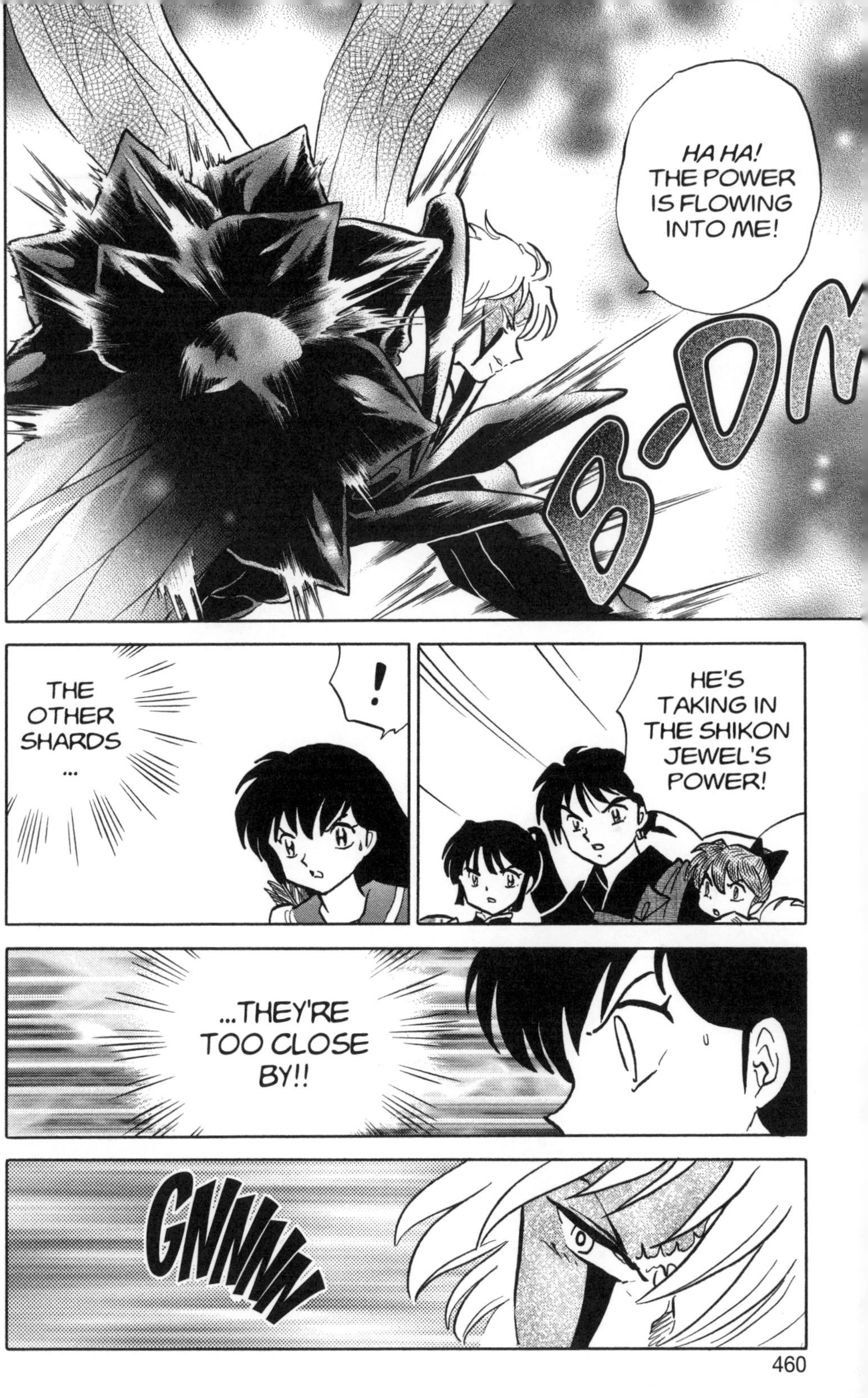
HA HA! THE POWER IS FLOWING INTO ME!
B-D
HE'S TAKING IN THE SHIKON JEWEL'S POWER!
!
THE OTHER SHARDS ...
...THEY'RE TOO CLOSE BY!!
GNNNN

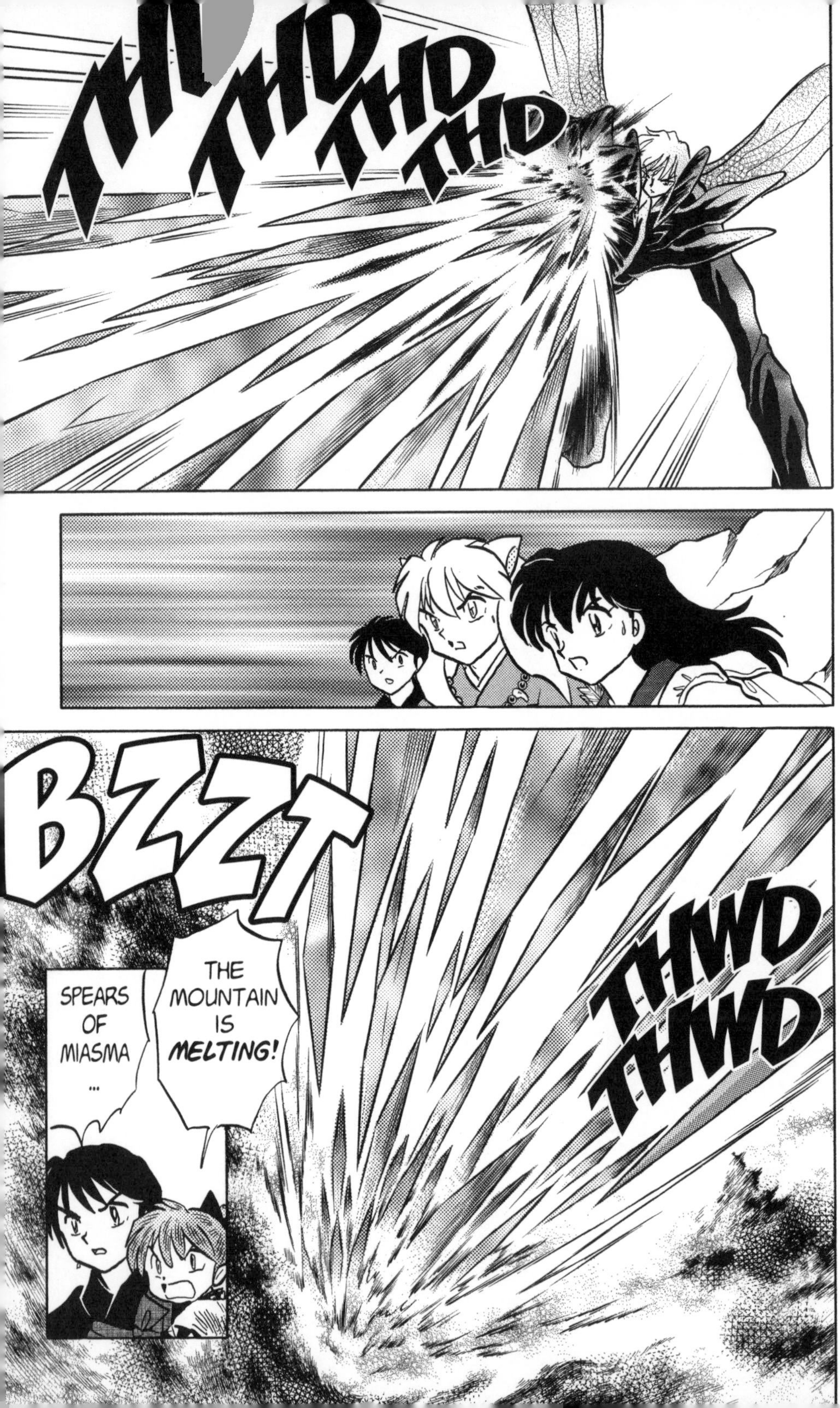
THD
THD
THD
THD
THWD
THWD
BZZT
THE MOUNTAIN IS *MELTING!*
SPEARS OF MIASMA ...

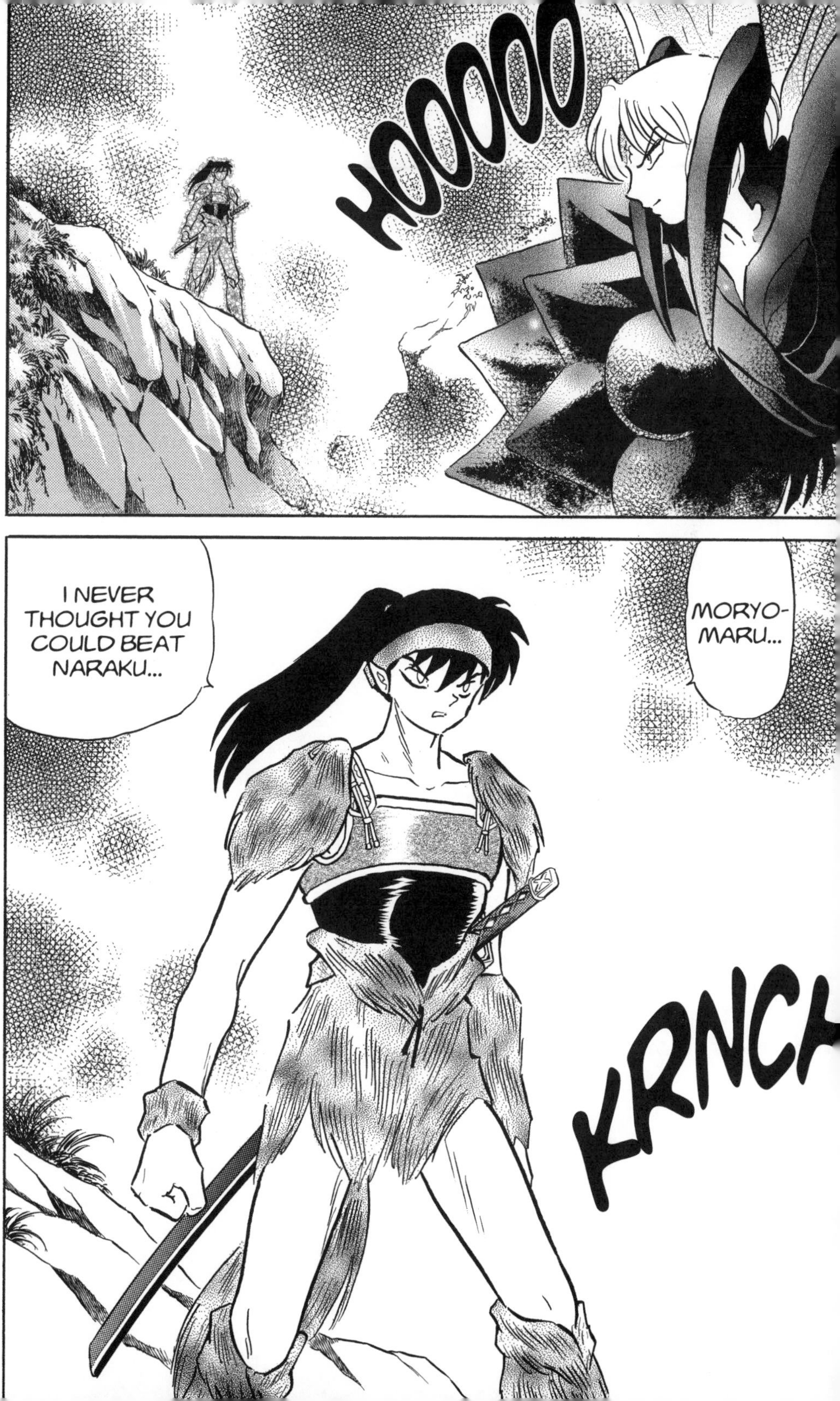
HOOOOO
MORYO-MARU...
I NEVER THOUGHT YOU COULD BEAT NARAKU...
KRNCH

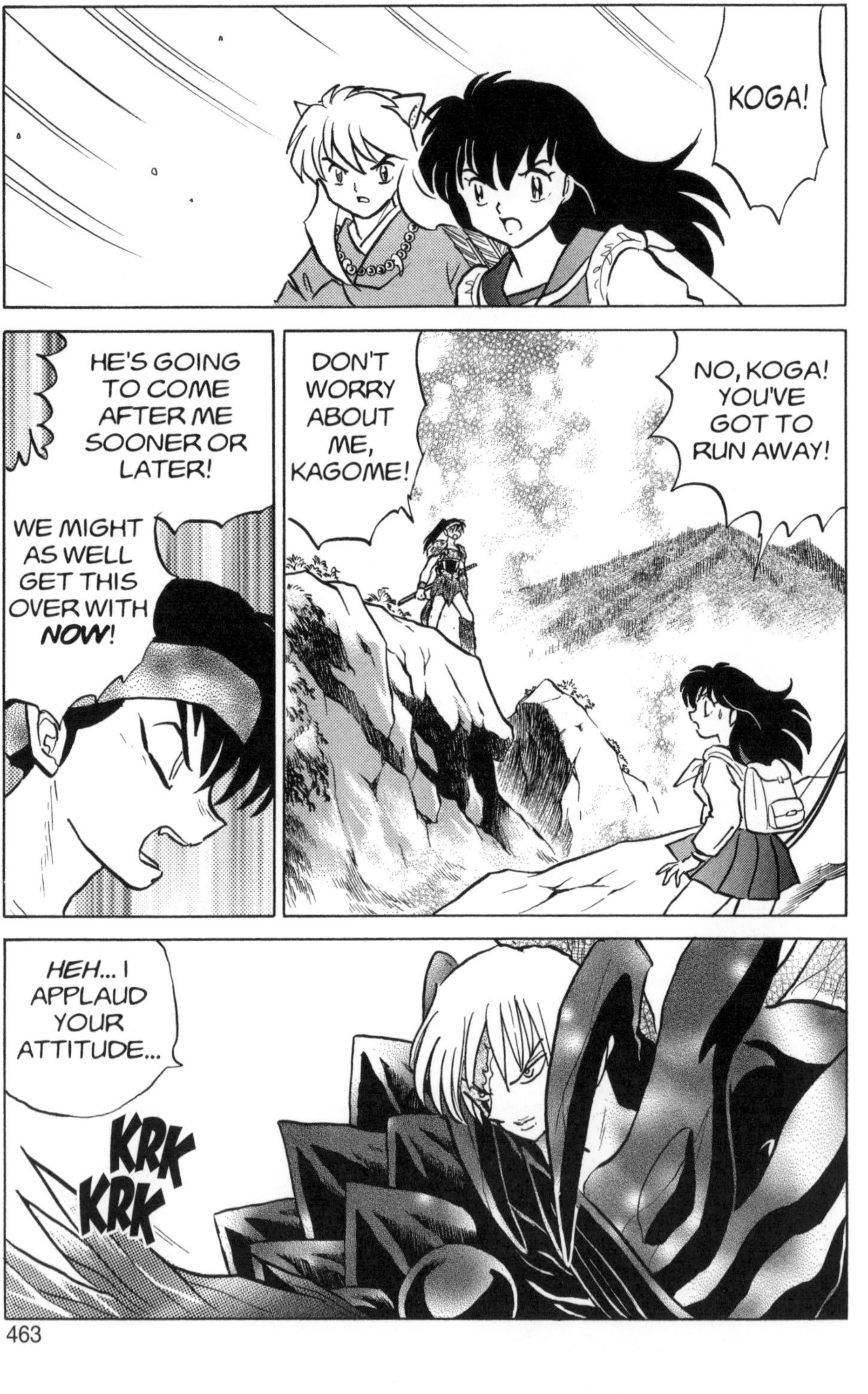
KOGA!
NO, KOGA! YOU'VE GOT TO RUN AWAY!
DON'T WORRY ABOUT ME, KAGOME!
HE'S GOING TO COME AFTER ME SOONER OR LATER!
WE MIGHT AS WELL GET THIS OVER WITH NOW!
HEH... I APPLAUD YOUR ATTITUDE...
KRK KRK

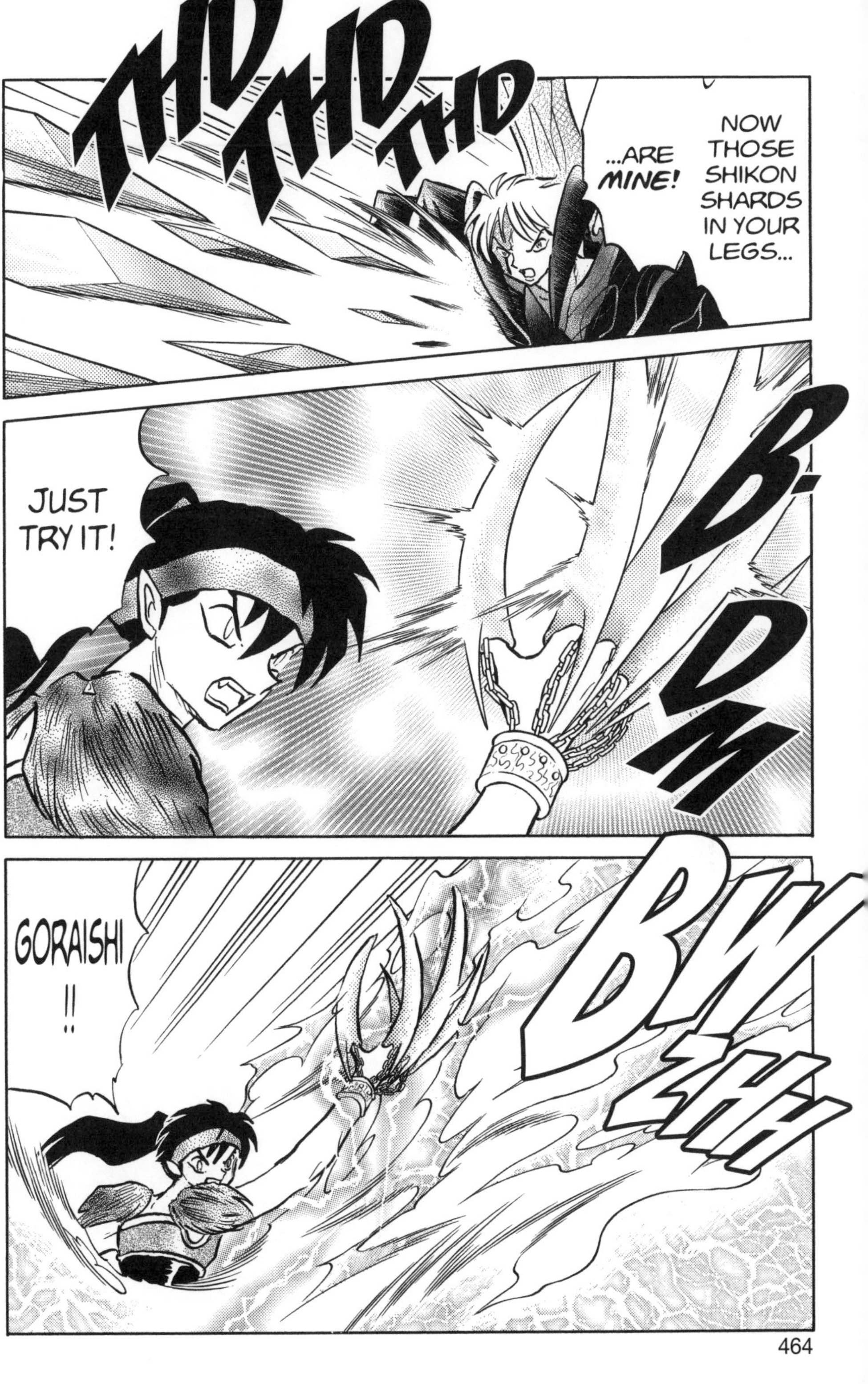
NOW THOSE SHIKON SHARDS IN YOUR LEGS...
...ARE MINE!
THD THD THD
B-DM
JUST TRY IT!
BW
ZHH
GORAISHI !!

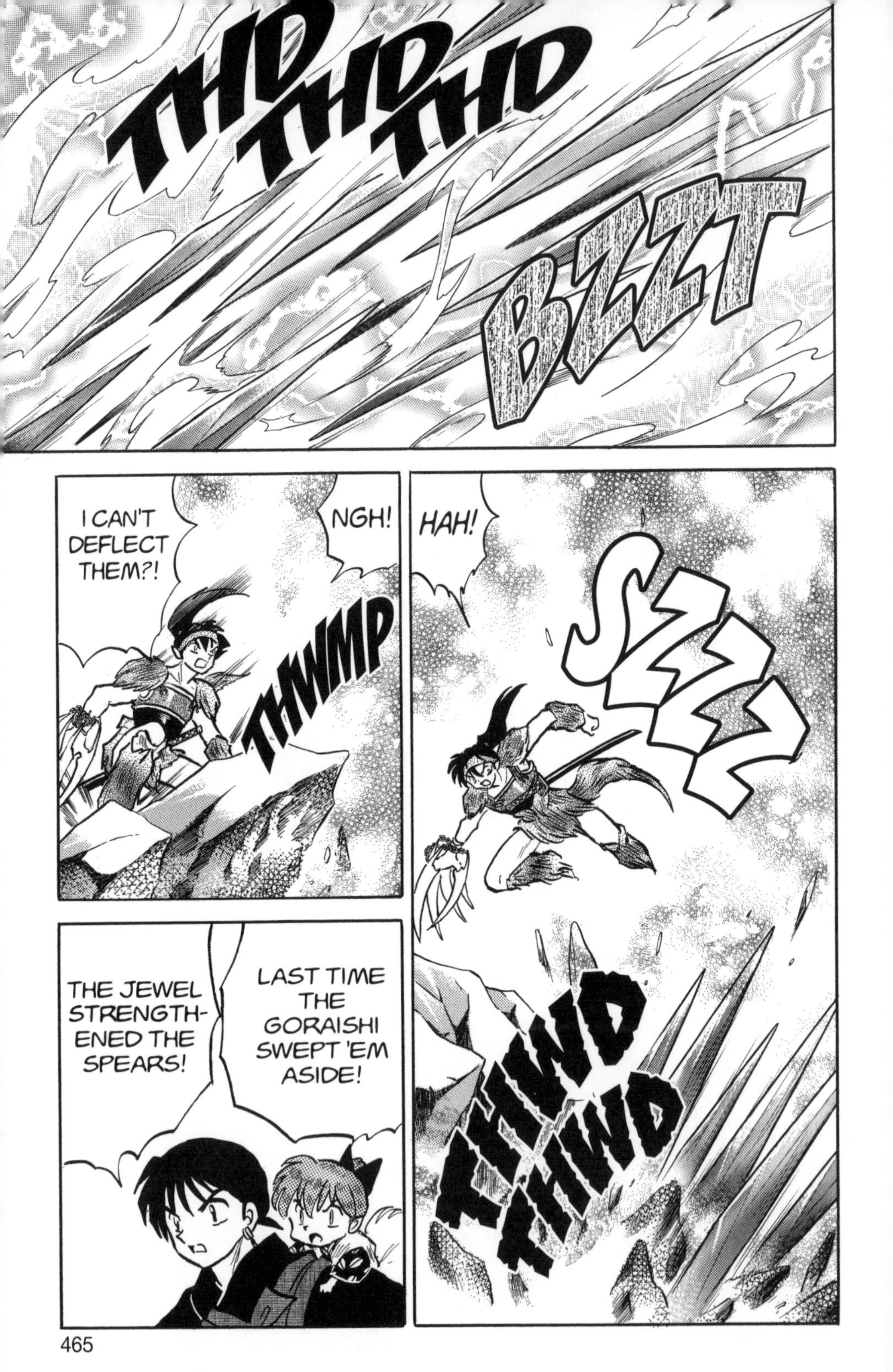
THD THD THD
BZZT
HAH!
SZZZ
THWD THWD
NGH!
I CAN'T DEFLECT THEM?!
THWMP
LAST TIME THE GORAISHI SWEPT 'EM ASIDE!
THE JEWEL STRENGTH-ENED THE SPEARS!

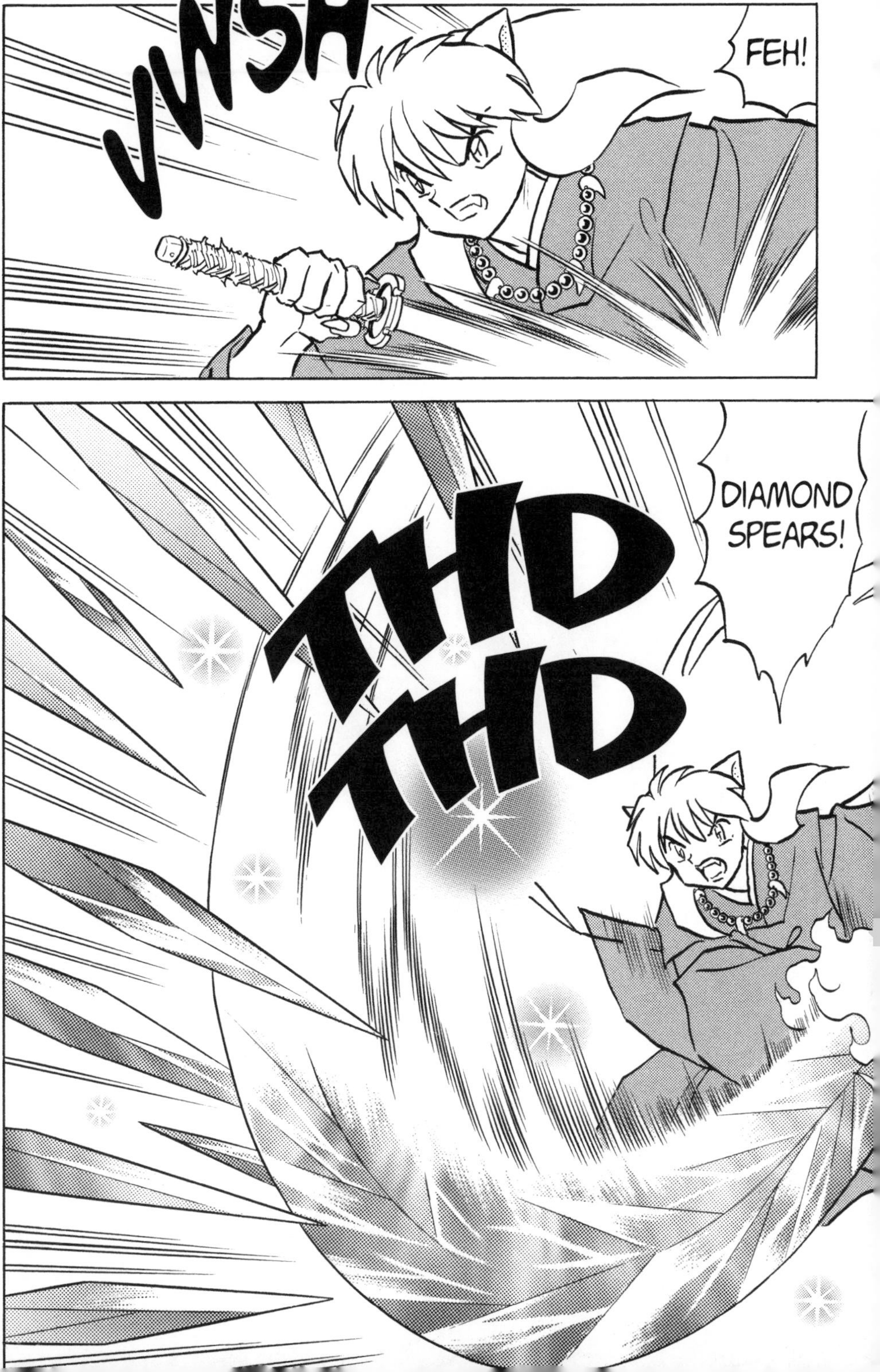
FEH!
VWSH
DIAMOND SPEARS!
THD THD

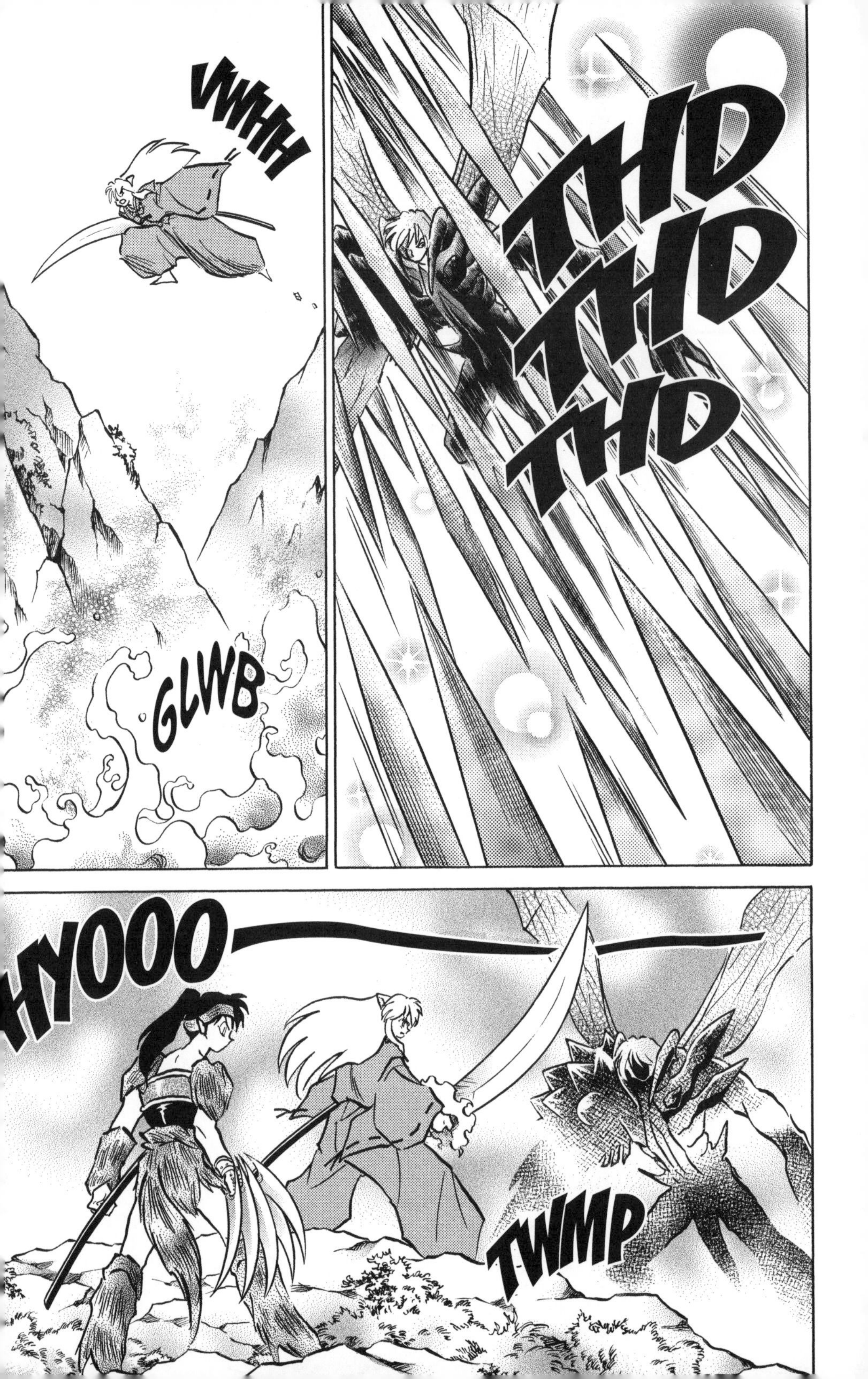
THD THD THD
VWHH
GLWB
HYOOO
TWMP

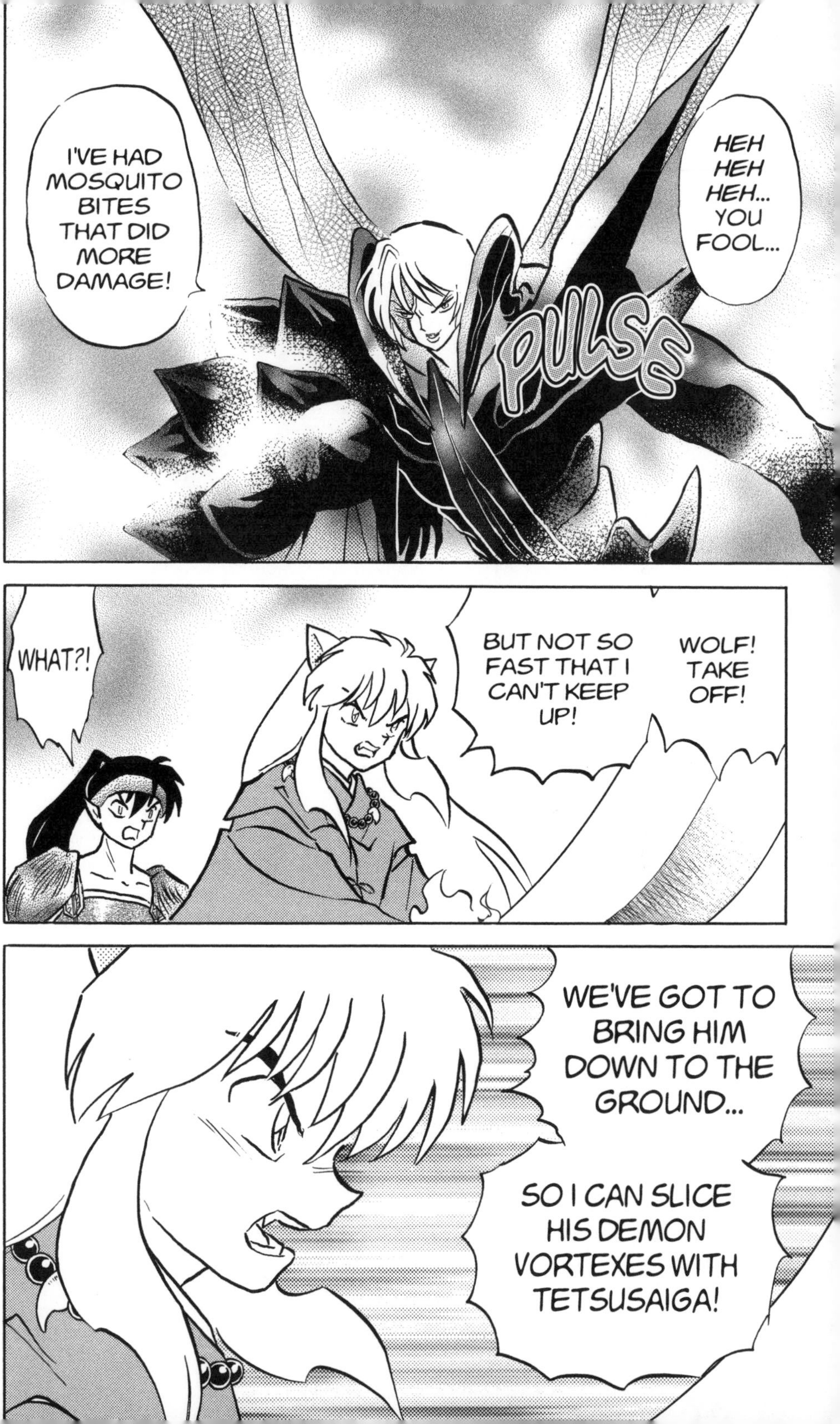
HEH HEH HEH... YOU FOOL...
PULSE
I'VE HAD MOSQUITO BITES THAT DID MORE DAMAGE!
WOLF! TAKE OFF!
BUT NOT SO FAST THAT I CAN'T KEEP UP!
WHAT?!
WE'VE GOT TO BRING HIM DOWN TO THE GROUND...
SO I CAN SLICE HIS DEMON VORTEXES WITH TETSUSAIGA!

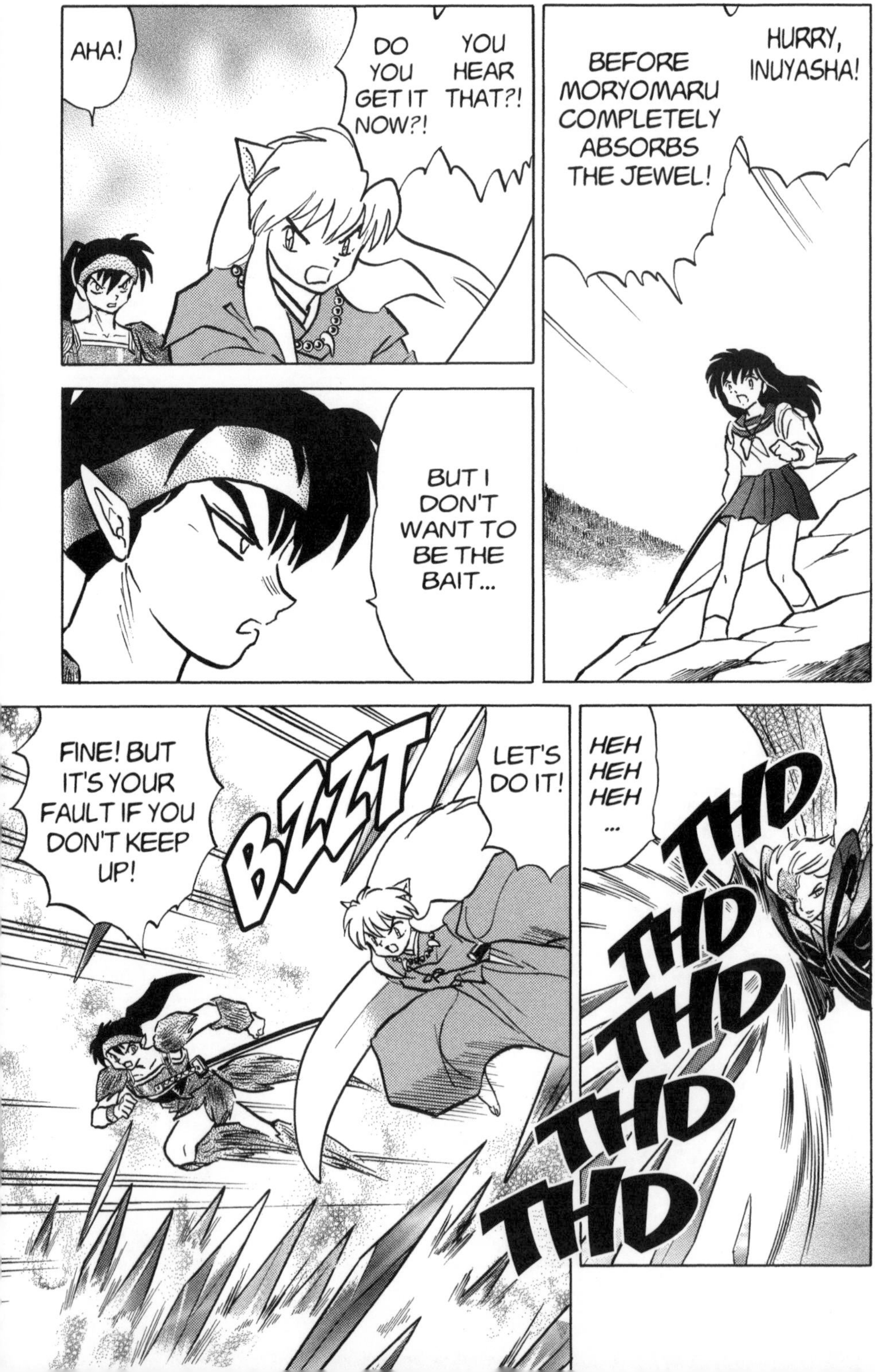
HURRY, INUYASHA!
BEFORE MORYOMARU COMPLETELY ABSORBS THE JEWEL!
YOU HEAR THAT?!
DO YOU GET IT NOW?!
AHA!
BUT I DON'T WANT TO BE THE BAIT...
HEH HEH HEH ...
THD THD THD THD THD
LET'S DO IT!
BZZZT
FINE! BUT IT'S YOUR FAULT IF YOU DON'T KEEP UP!

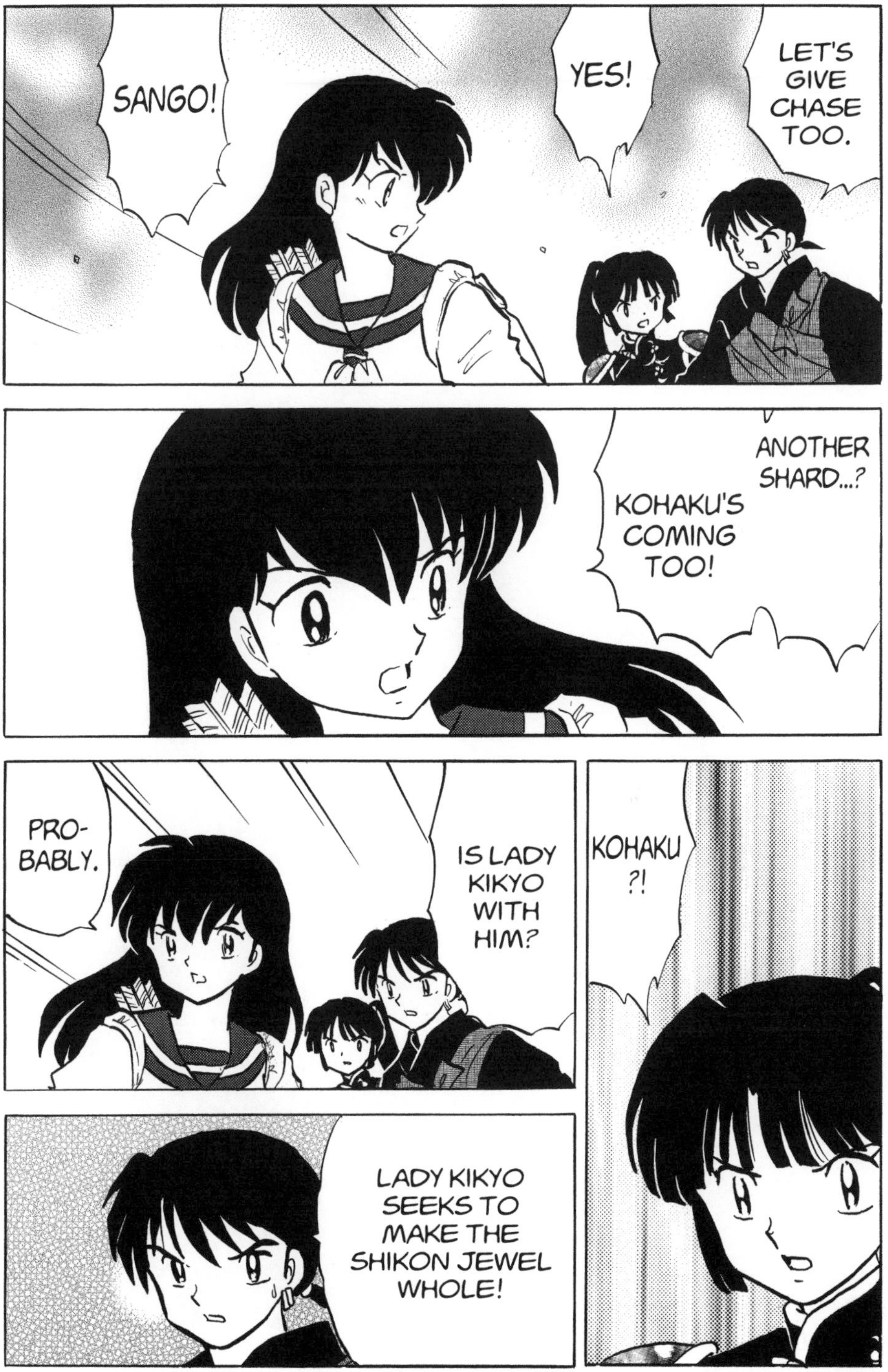
LET'S GIVE CHASE TOO.
YES!
SANGO!
ANOTHER SHARD...?
KOHAKU'S COMING TOO!
KOHAKU ?!
IS LADY KIKYO WITH HIM?
PRO-BABLY.
LADY KIKYO SEEKS TO MAKE THE SHIKON JEWEL WHOLE!

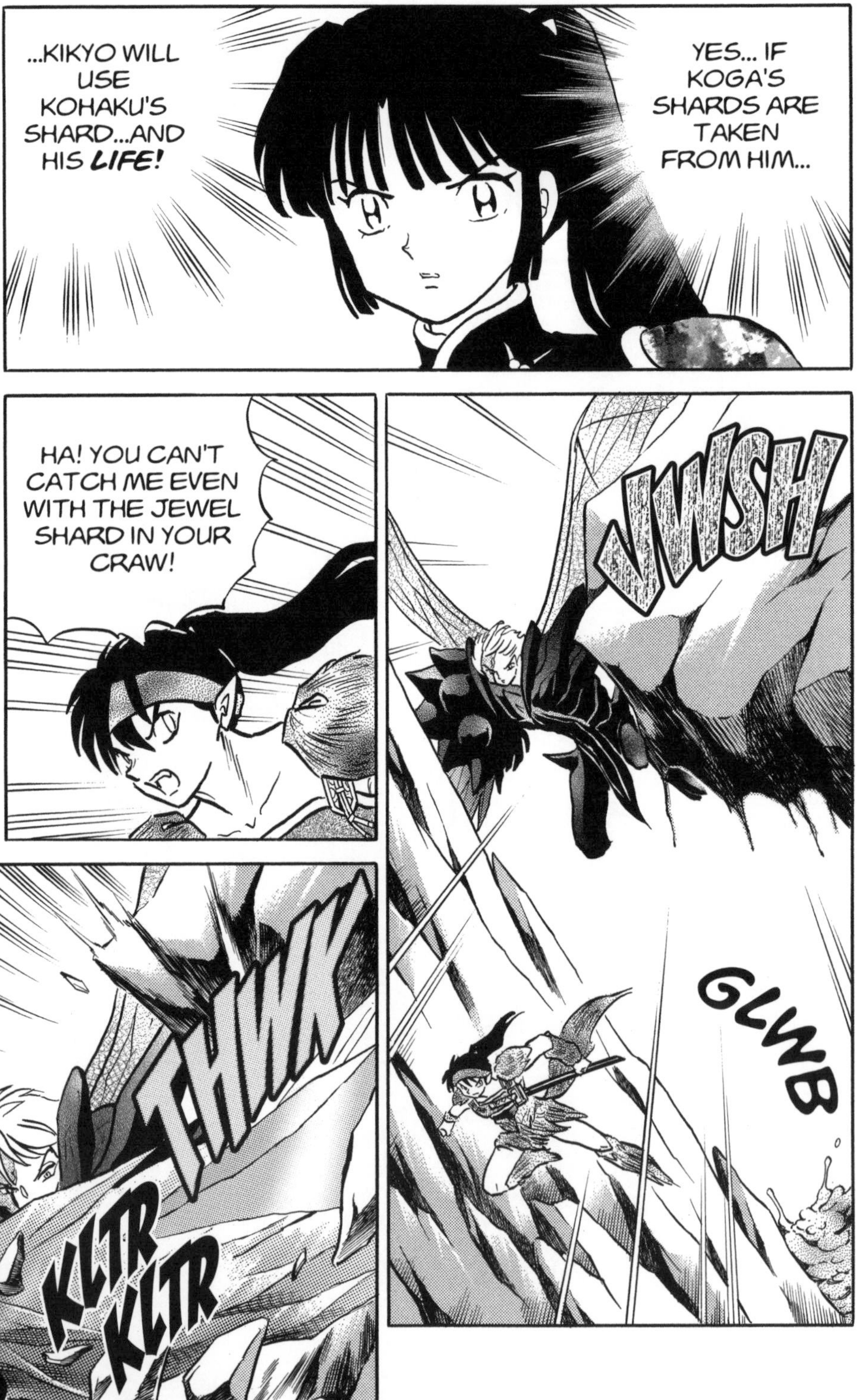
YES... IF KOGA'S SHARDS ARE TAKEN FROM HIM...
...KIKYO WILL USE KOHAKU'S SHARD...AND HIS *LIFE!*
JWSH
GLWB
HA! YOU CAN'T CATCH ME EVEN WITH THE JEWEL SHARD IN YOUR CRAW!
THWK
KLTR KLTR

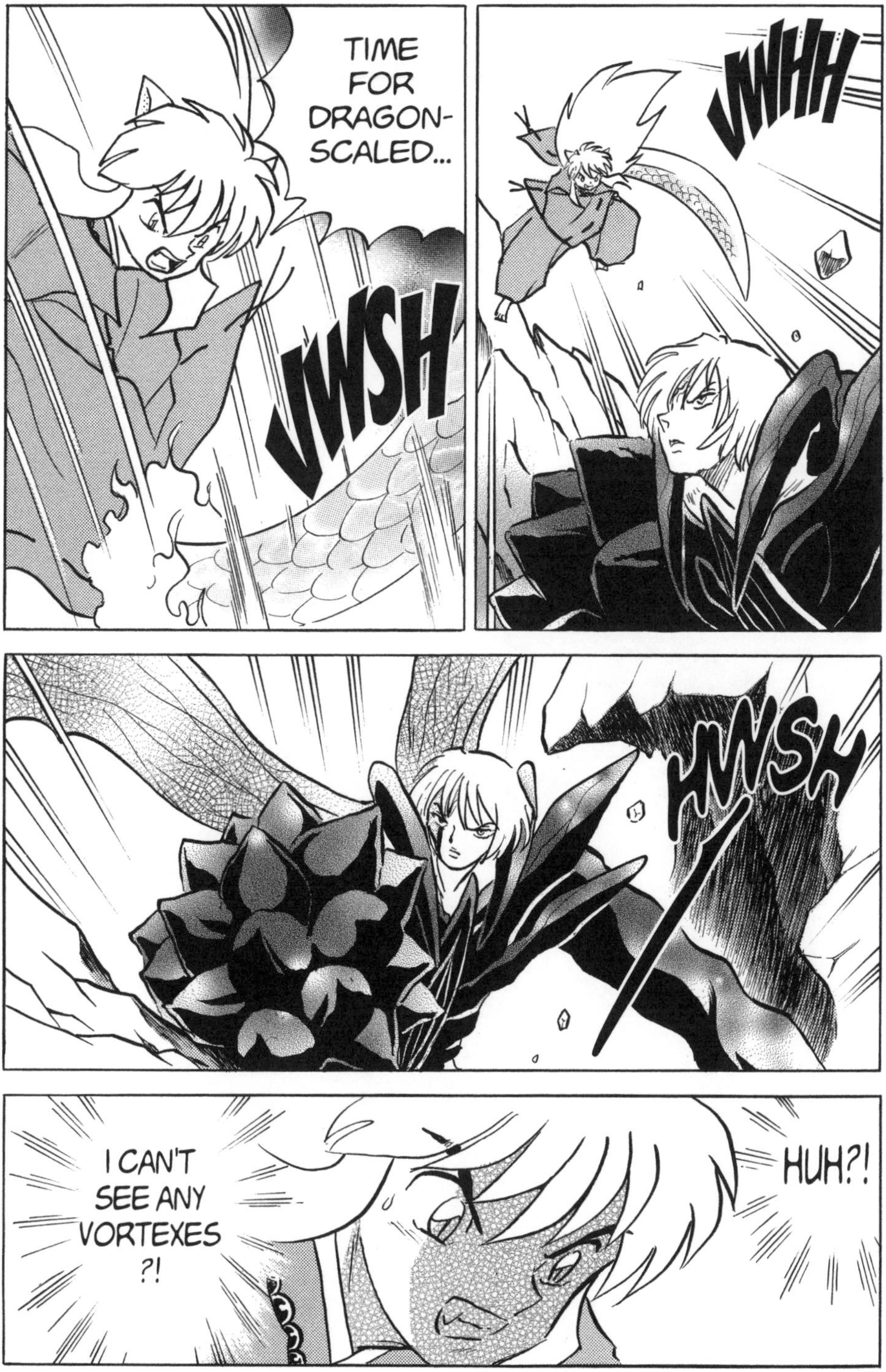
VWHH
TIME FOR DRAGON-SCALED...
VWSH
HWSH
HUH?!
I CAN'T SEE ANY VORTEXES ?!

SCROLL SIX
HEATED BATTLE

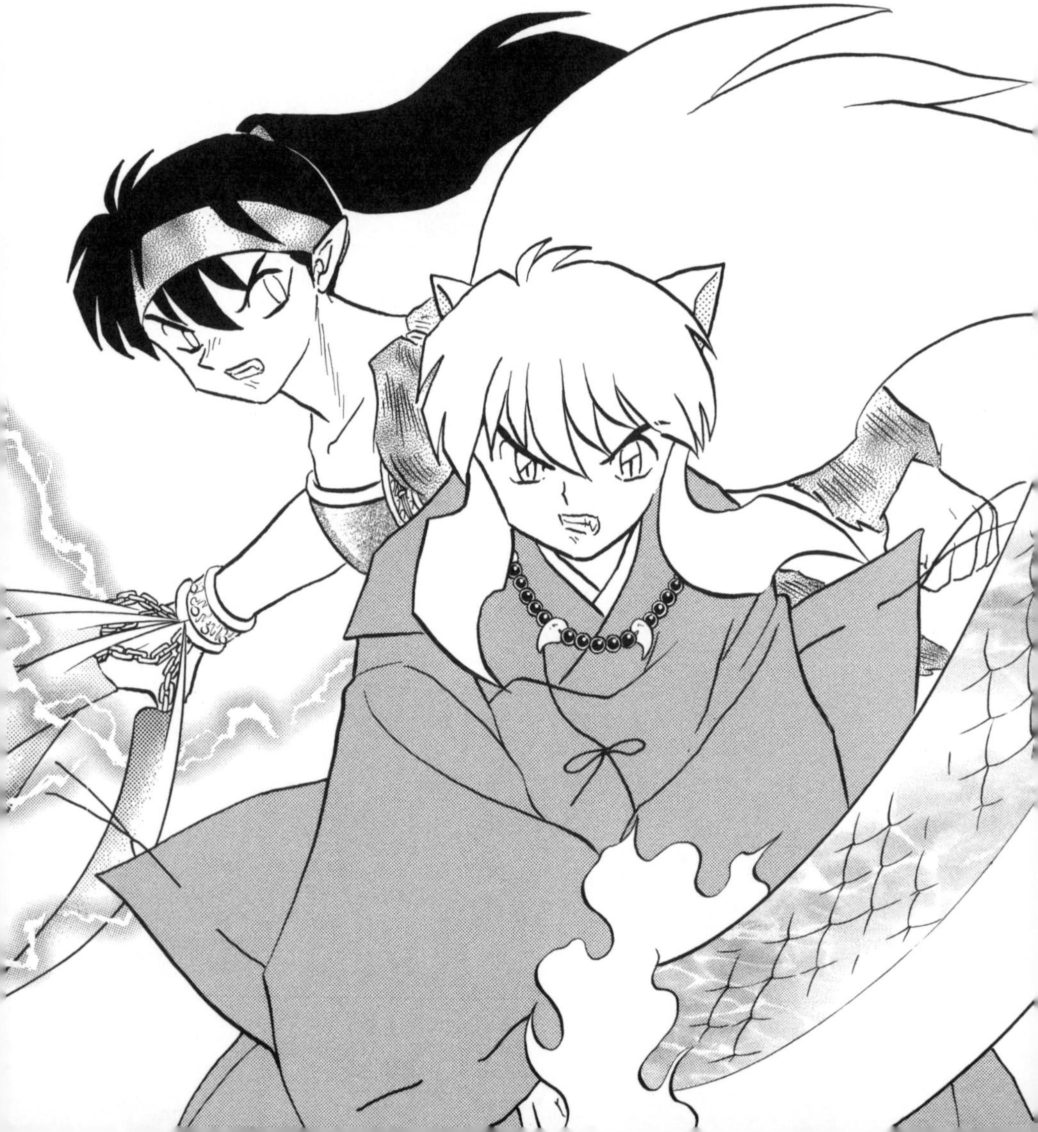

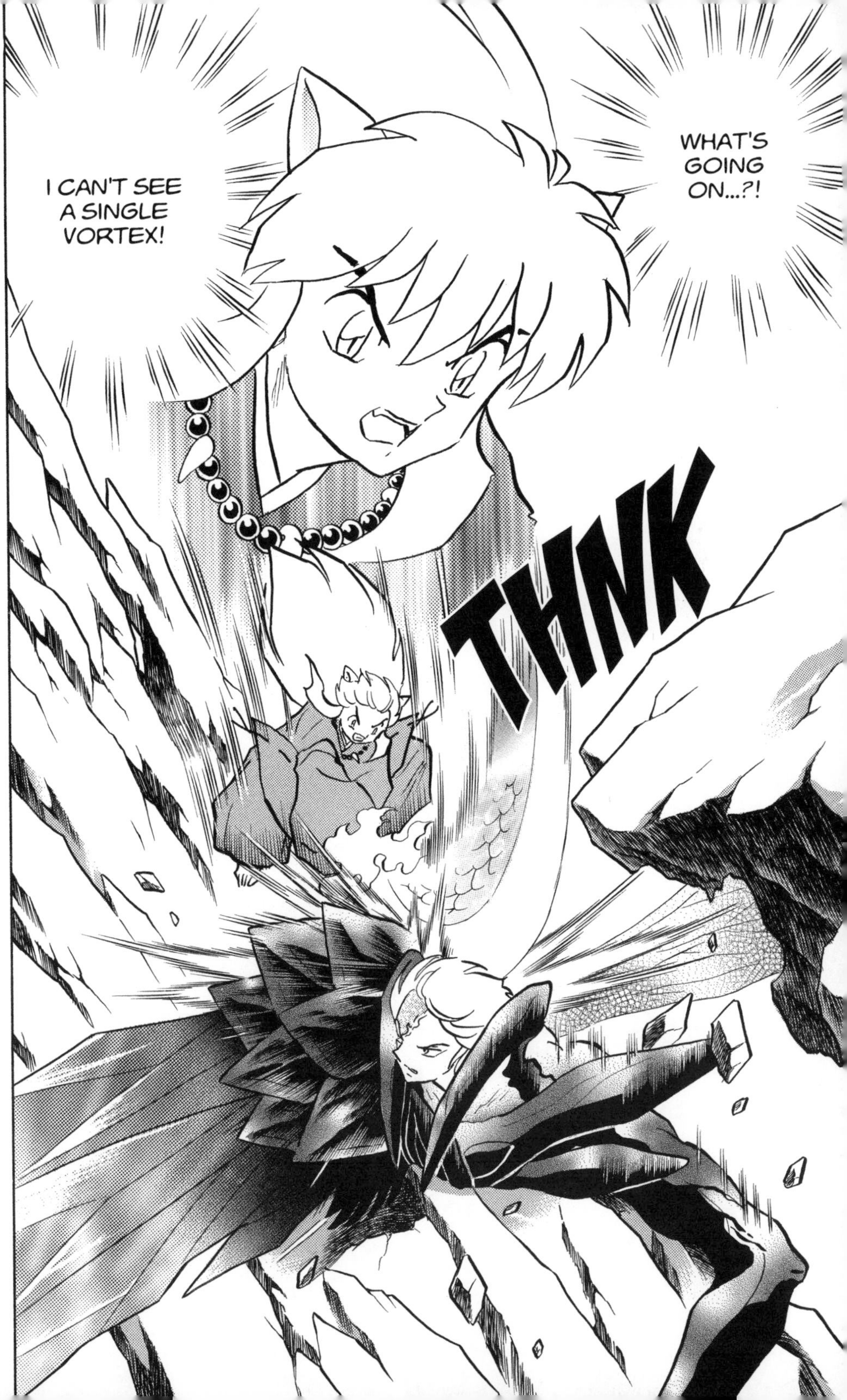
WHAT'S GOING ON...?!
I CAN'T SEE A SINGLE VORTEX!
THINK

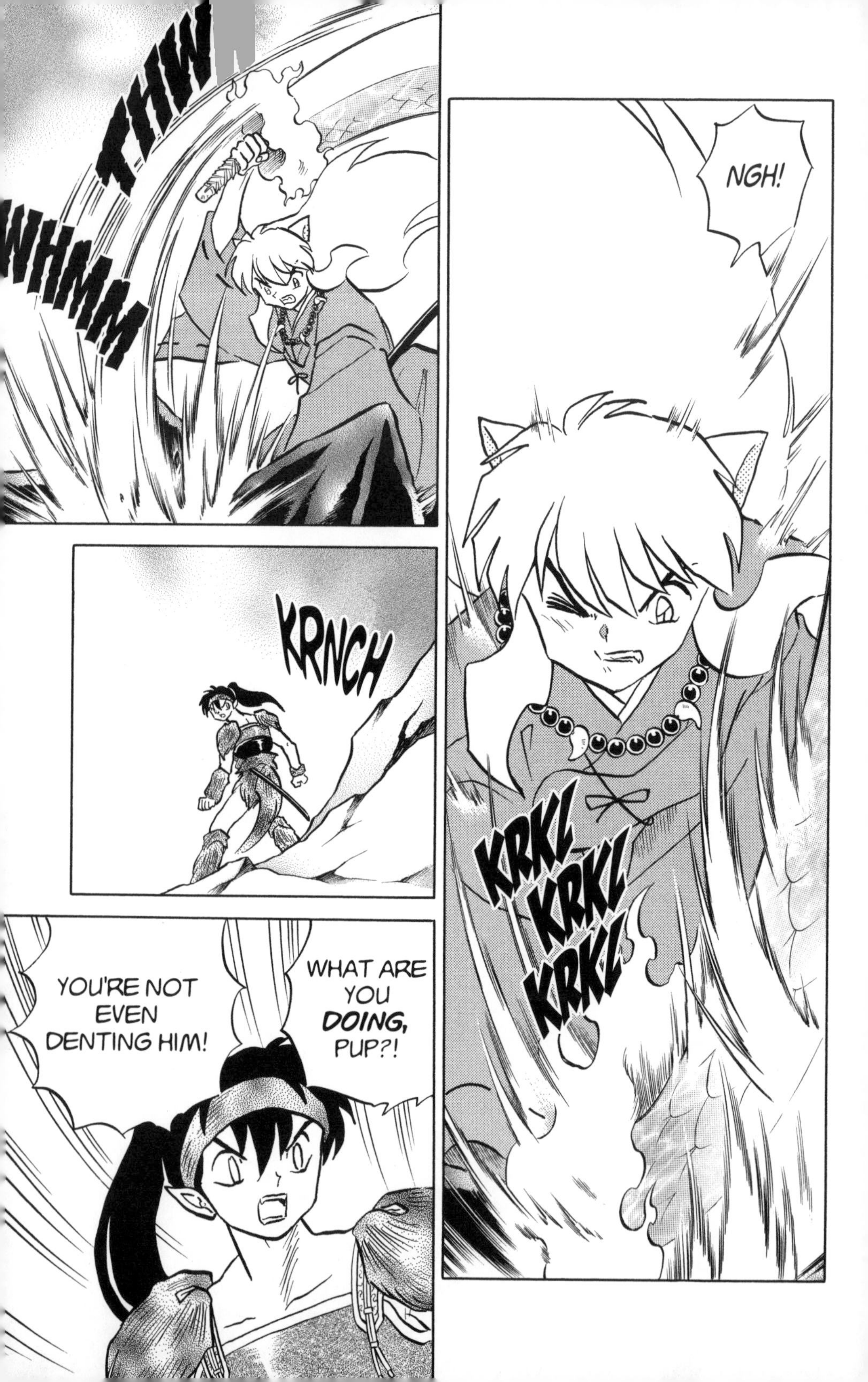
NGH!
KRKL KRKL KRKL
THWHMM
KRNCH
WHAT ARE YOU DOING, PUP?!
YOU'RE NOT EVEN DENTING HIM!

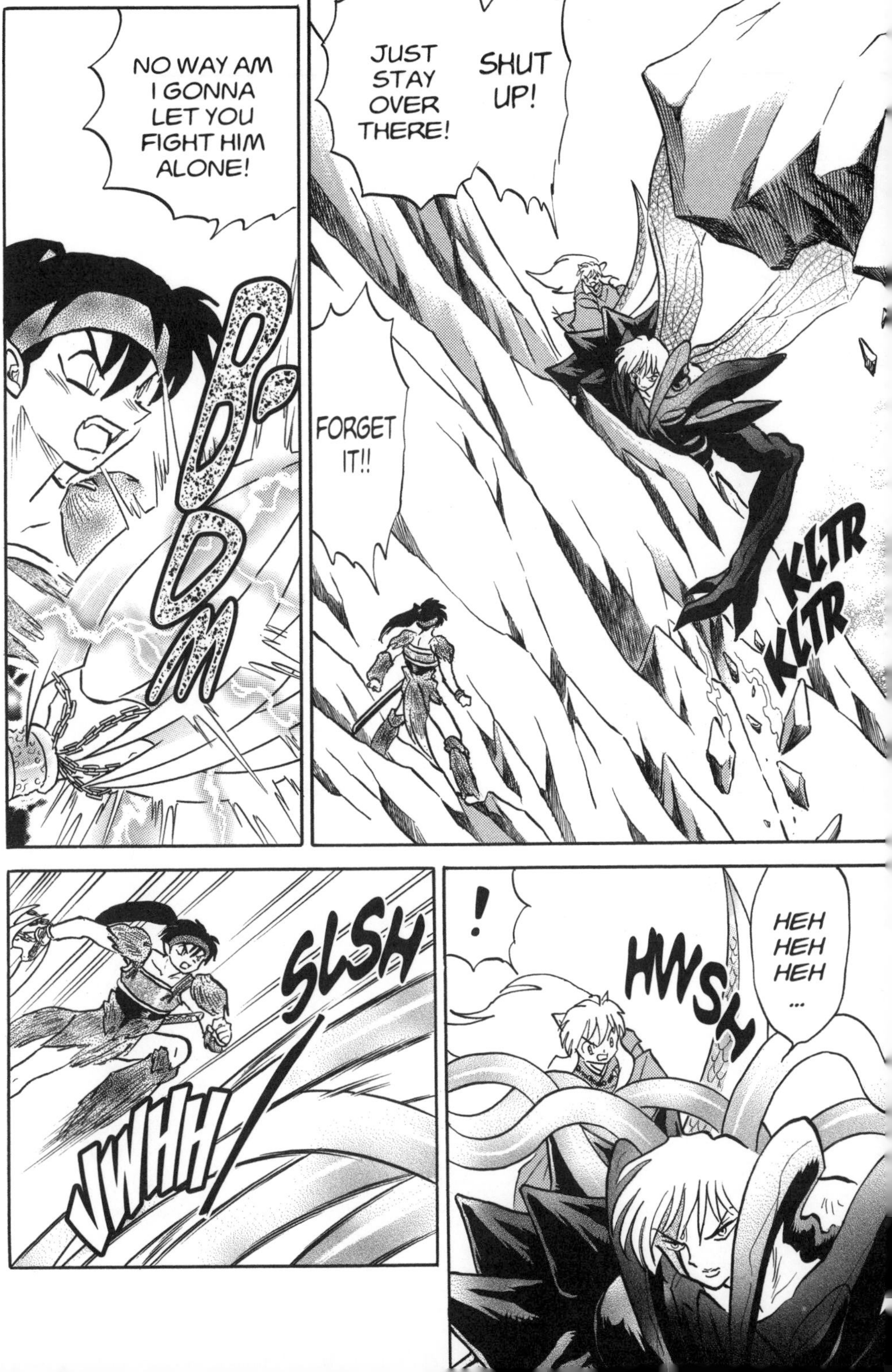

SHUT UP!
JUST STAY OVER THERE!
FORGET IT!!
KLTR KLTR
NO WAY AM I GONNA LET YOU FIGHT HIM ALONE!
BDDM
!
HWSH
HEH HEH HEH ...
SLSH
JWHH

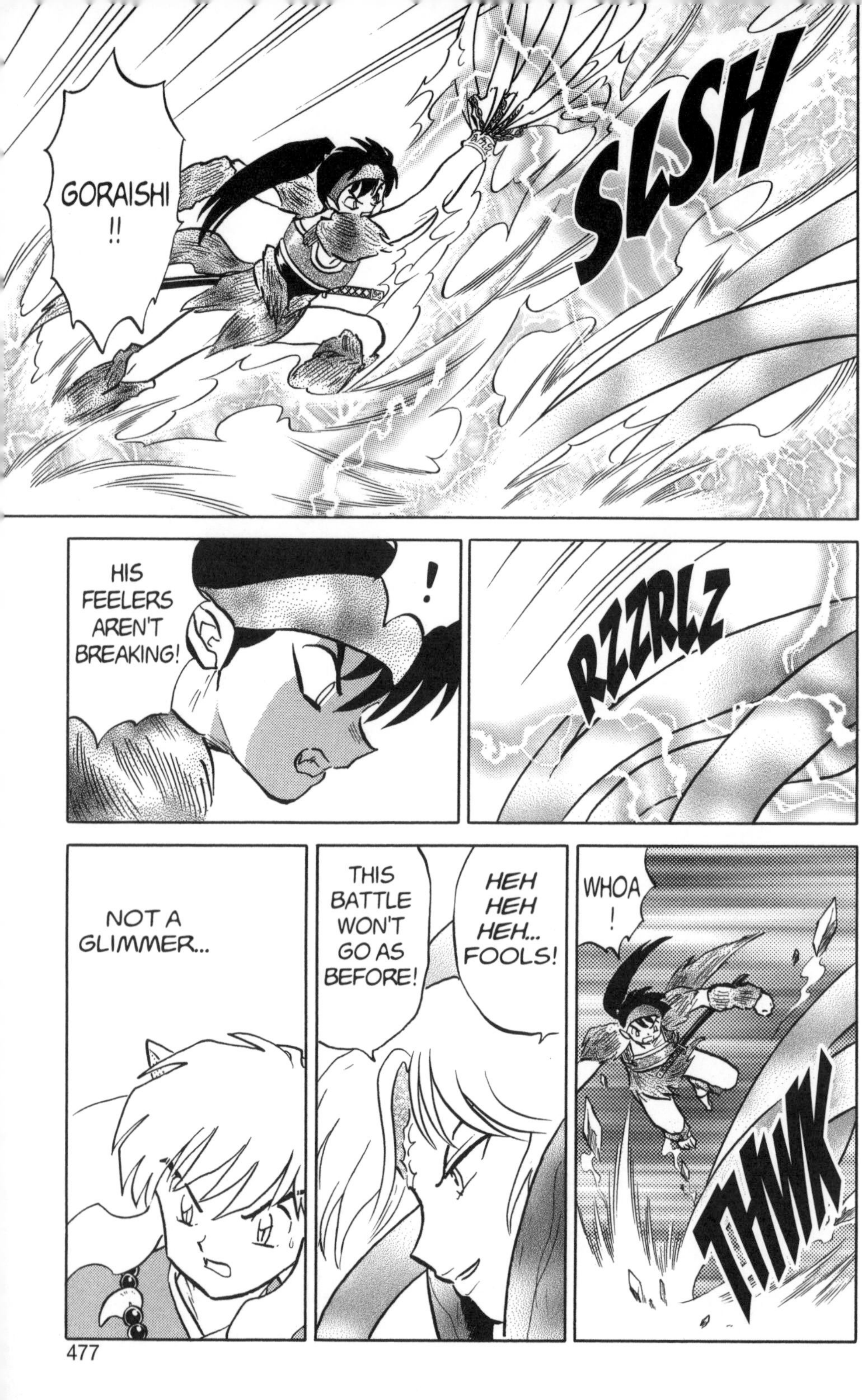
SLSH
GORAISHI !!
RZZRLZ
!
HIS FEELERS AREN'T BREAKING!
WHOA !
THWK
HEH HEH HEH... FOOLS!
THIS BATTLE WON'T GO AS BEFORE!
NOT A GLIMMER...

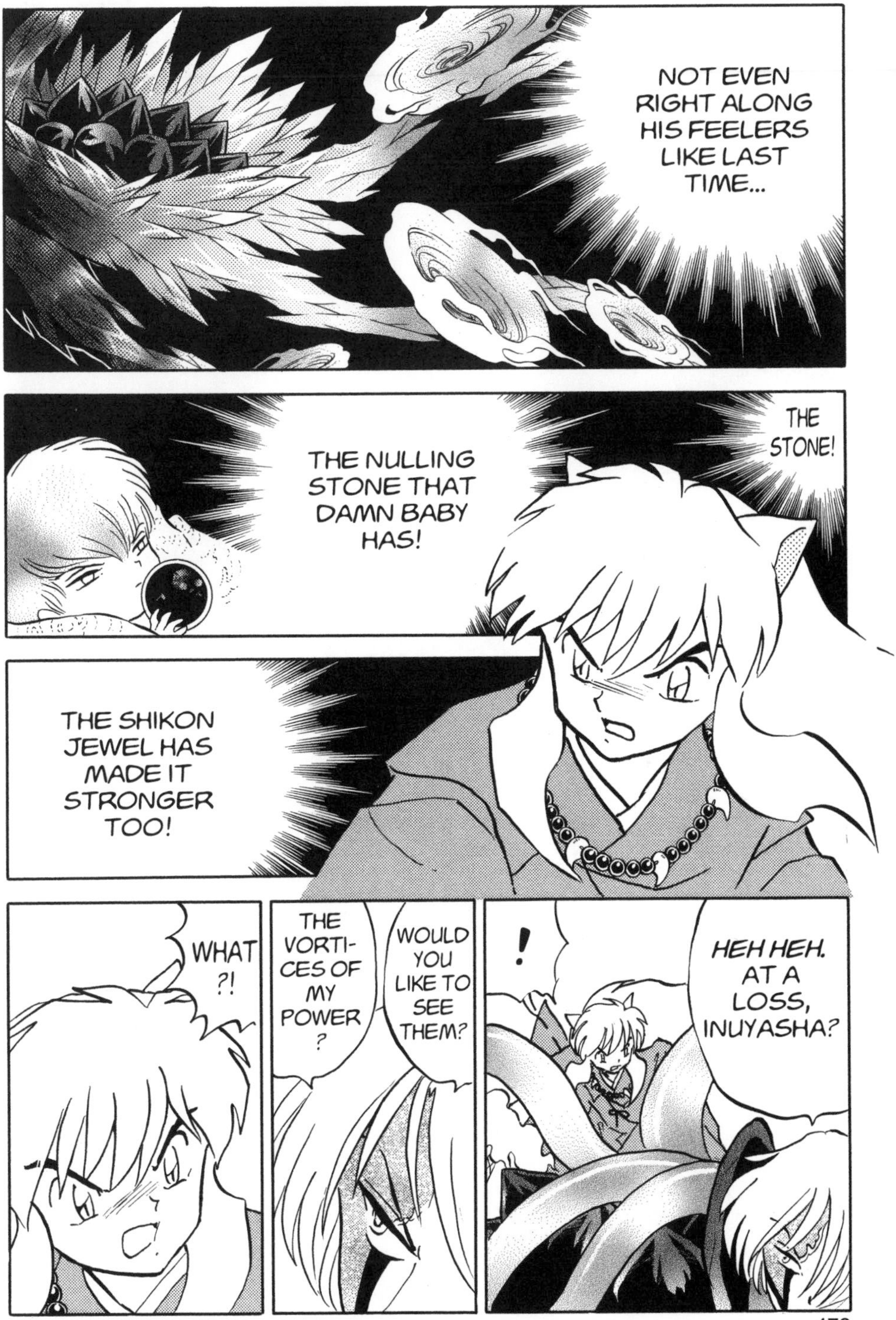

NOT EVEN RIGHT ALONG HIS FEELERS LIKE LAST TIME...
THE STONE!
THE NULLING STONE THAT DAMN BABY HAS!
THE SHIKON JEWEL HAS MADE IT STRONGER TOO!
!
HEH HEH. AT A LOSS, INUYASHA?
WOULD YOU LIKE TO SEE THEM?
THE VORTICES OF MY POWER?
WHAT?!

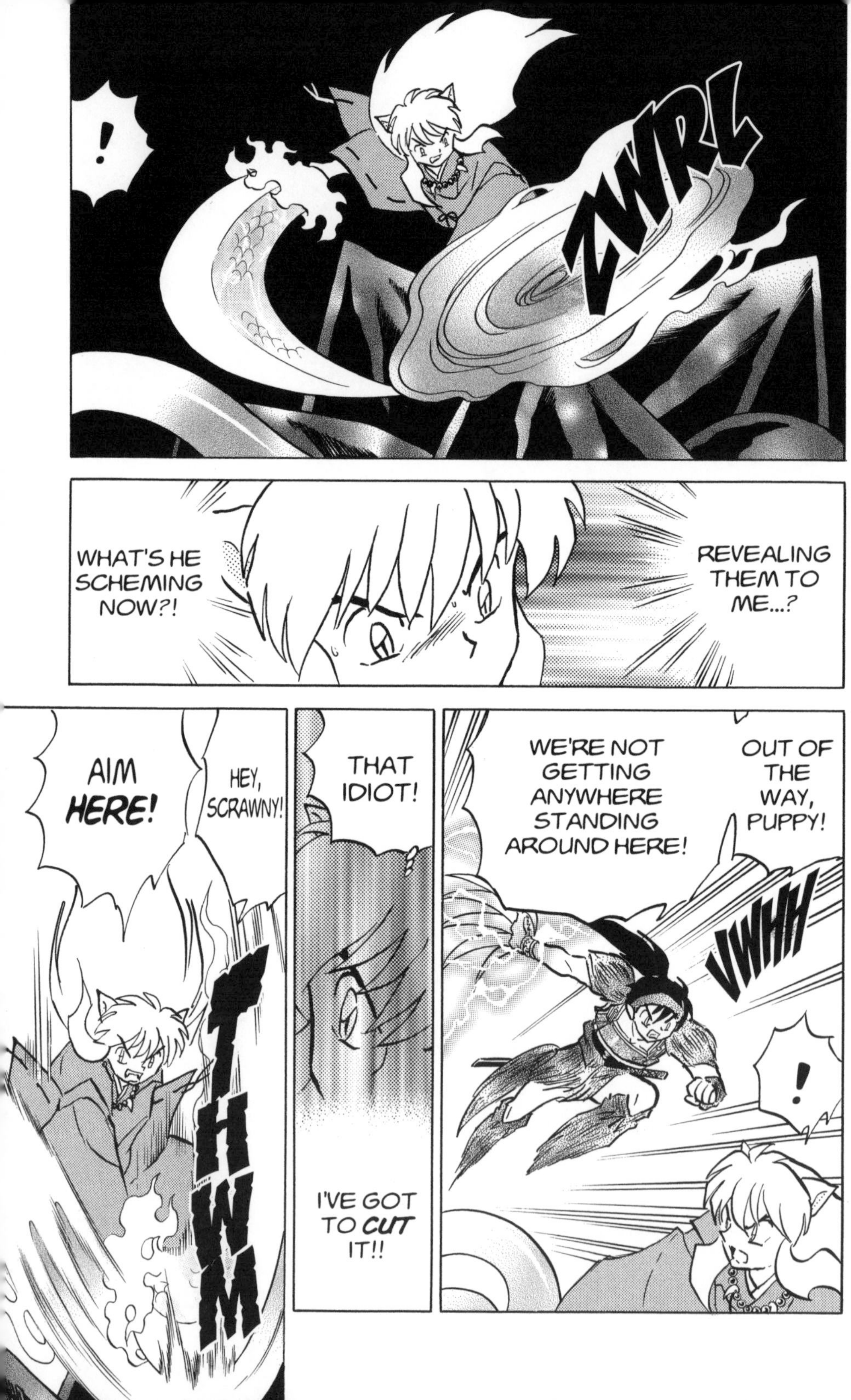
ZWRL
!
REVEALING THEM TO ME...?
WHAT'S HE SCHEMING NOW?!
OUT OF THE WAY, PUPPY!
WE'RE NOT GETTING ANYWHERE STANDING AROUND HERE!
VWHH
!
THAT IDIOT!
I'VE GOT TO CUT IT!!
HEY, SCRAWNY!
AIM HERE!
THWM

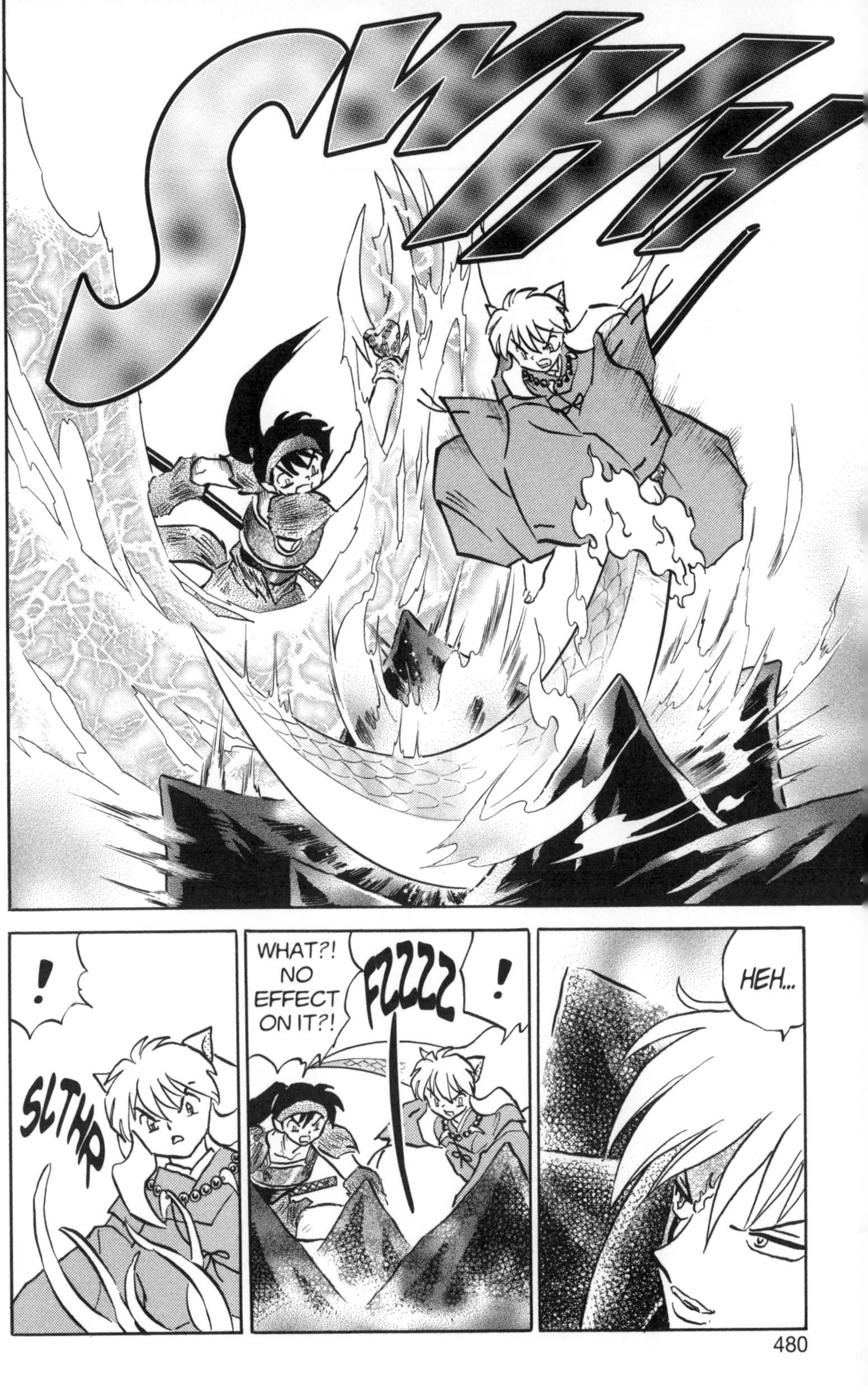

SWHH
HEH...
!
FZZZZ
WHAT?! NO EFFECT ON IT?!
!
SLTHR

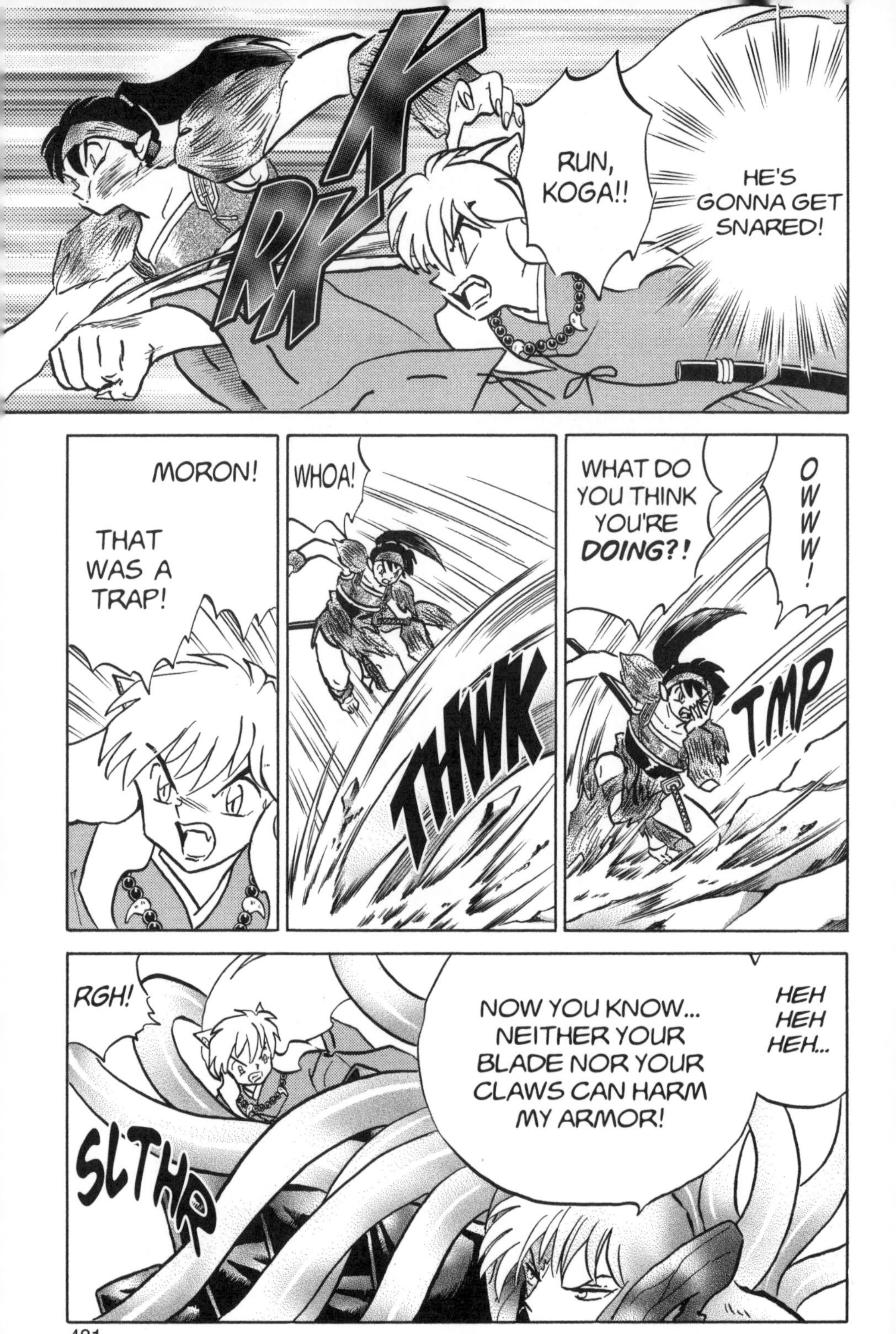
HE'S GONNA GET SNARED!
RUN, KOGA!!
WHAT DO YOU THINK YOU'RE **DOING?!**
OWWW!
TMP
WHOA!
THWK
MORON!
THAT WAS A TRAP!
HEH HEH HEH...
NOW YOU KNOW... NEITHER YOUR BLADE NOR YOUR CLAWS CAN HARM MY ARMOR!
RGH!
SLTHR

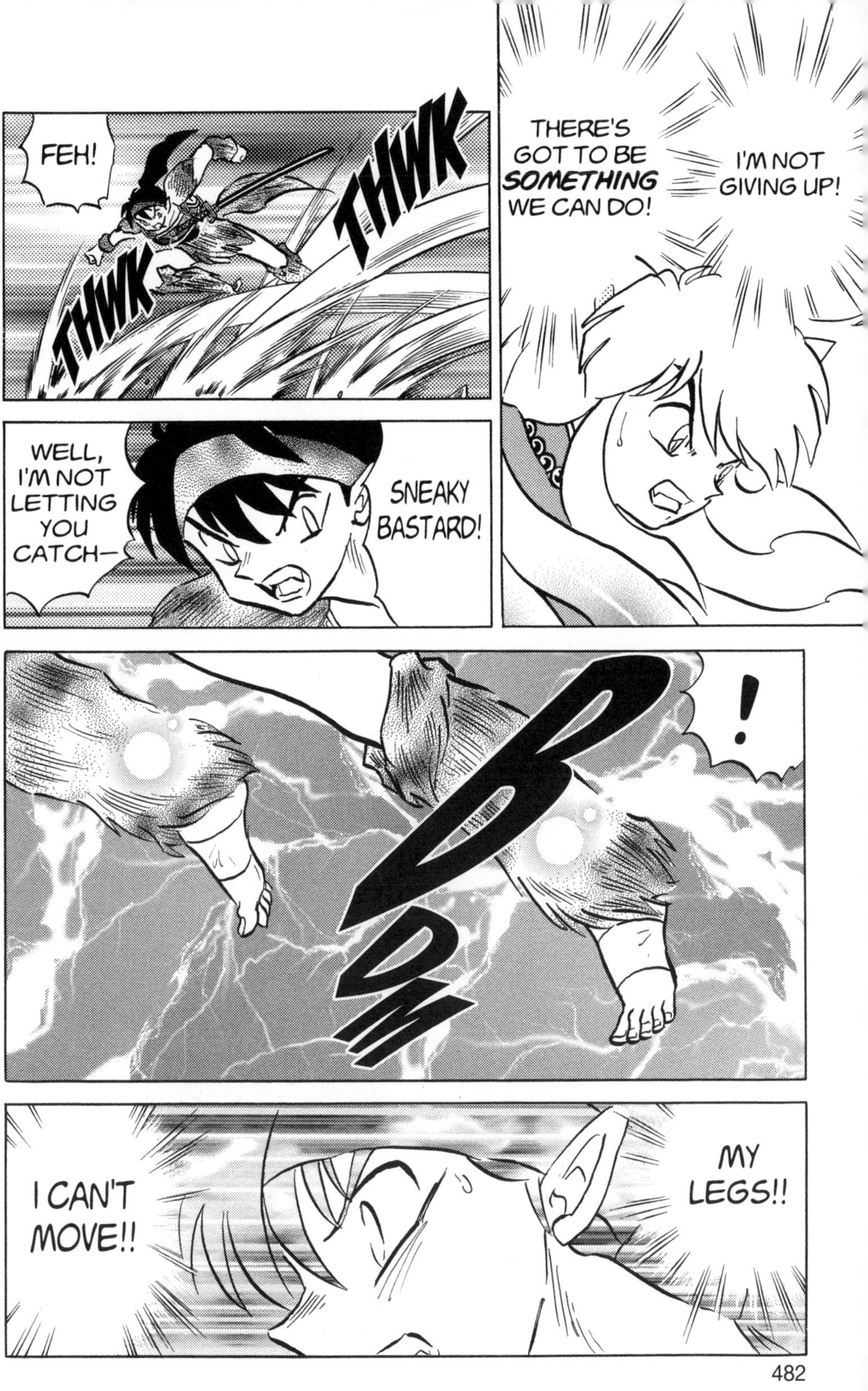
I'M NOT GIVING UP!
THERE'S GOT TO BE SOMETHING WE CAN DO!
THWK
THWK
FEH!
SNEAKY BASTARD!
WELL, I'M NOT LETTING YOU CATCH—
!
BDM
MY LEGS!!
I CAN'T MOVE!!

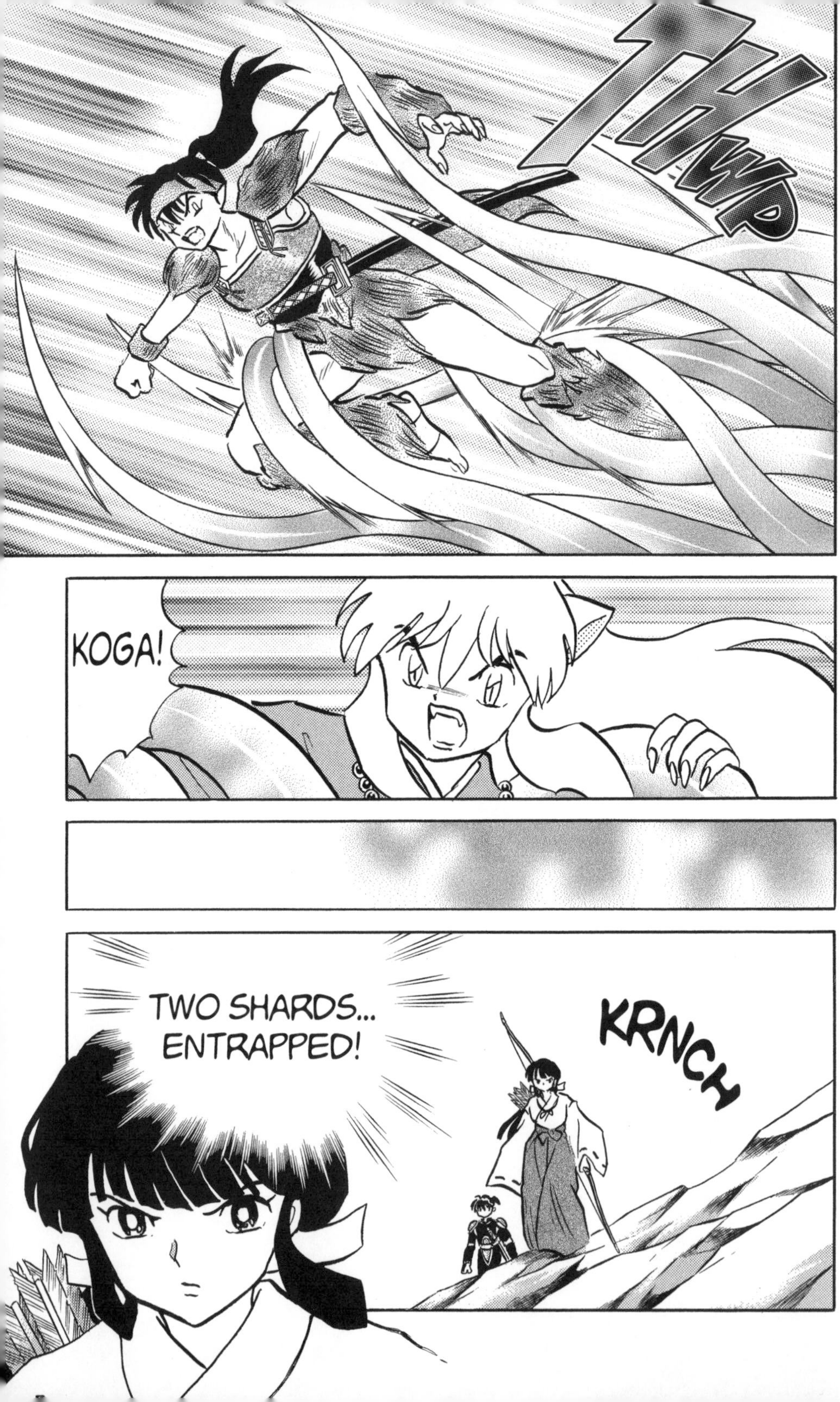
THWP
KOGA!
TWO SHARDS... ENTRAPPED!
KRNCH

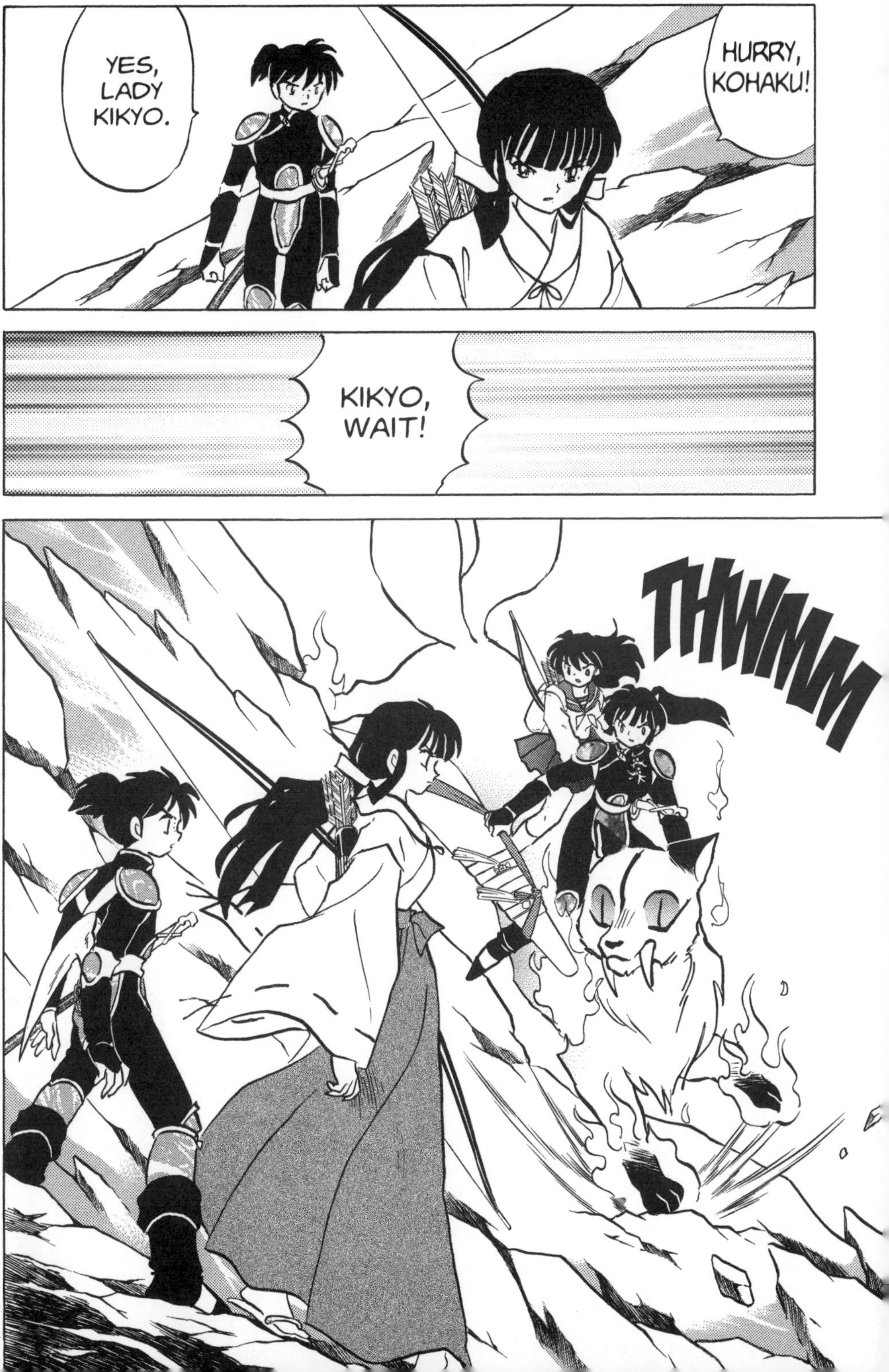
HURRY, KOHAKU!
YES, LADY KIKYO.
KIKYO, WAIT!
THWMMM

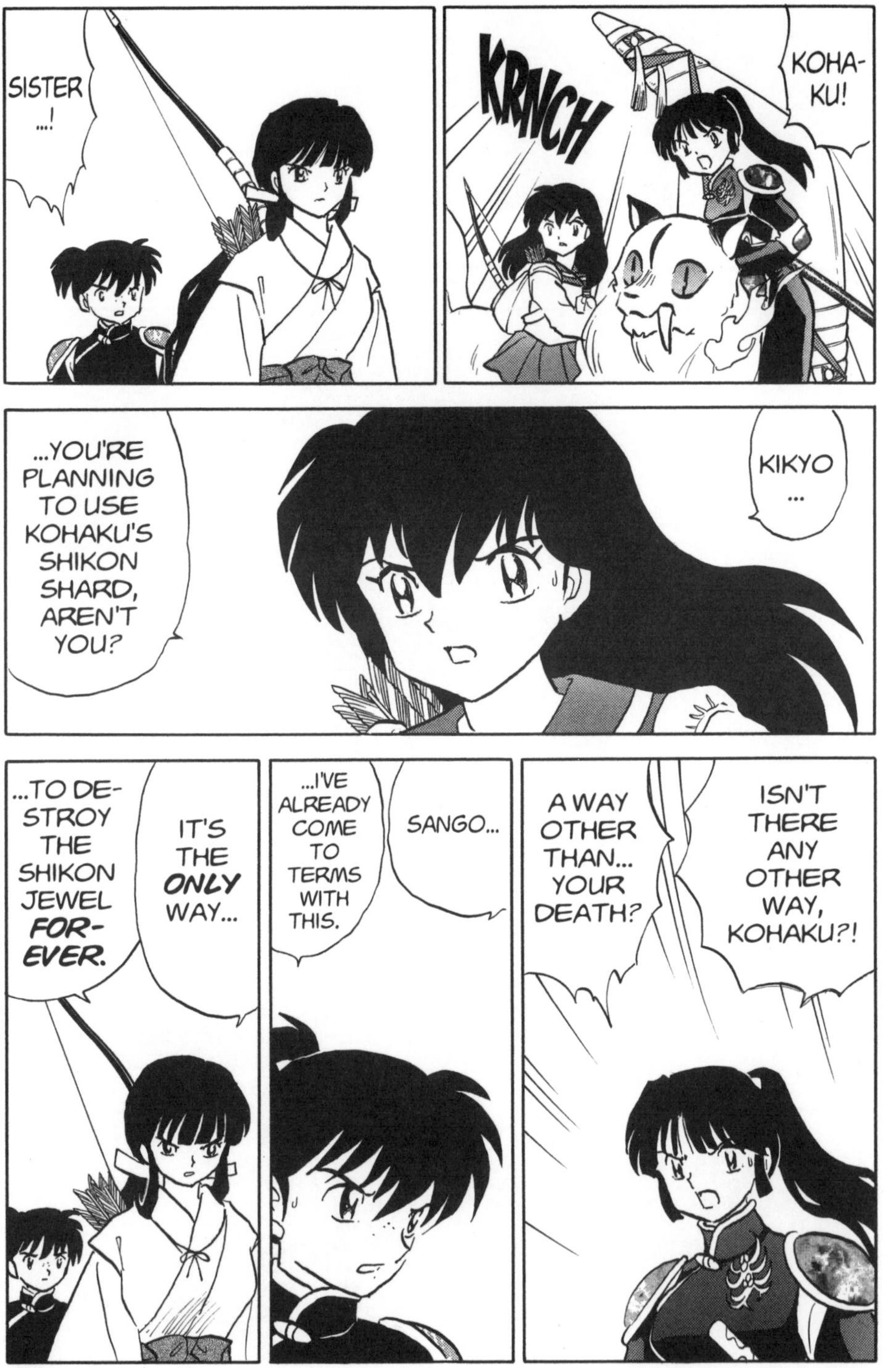
KOHA-KU!
KRNCH
SISTER ...!
KIKYO ...
...YOU'RE PLANNING TO USE KOHAKU'S SHIKON SHARD, AREN'T YOU?
ISN'T THERE ANY OTHER WAY, KOHAKU?!
A WAY OTHER THAN... YOUR DEATH?
SANGO...
...I'VE ALREADY COME TO TERMS WITH THIS.
IT'S THE ONLY WAY...
...TO DESTROY THE SHIKON JEWEL FOREVER.

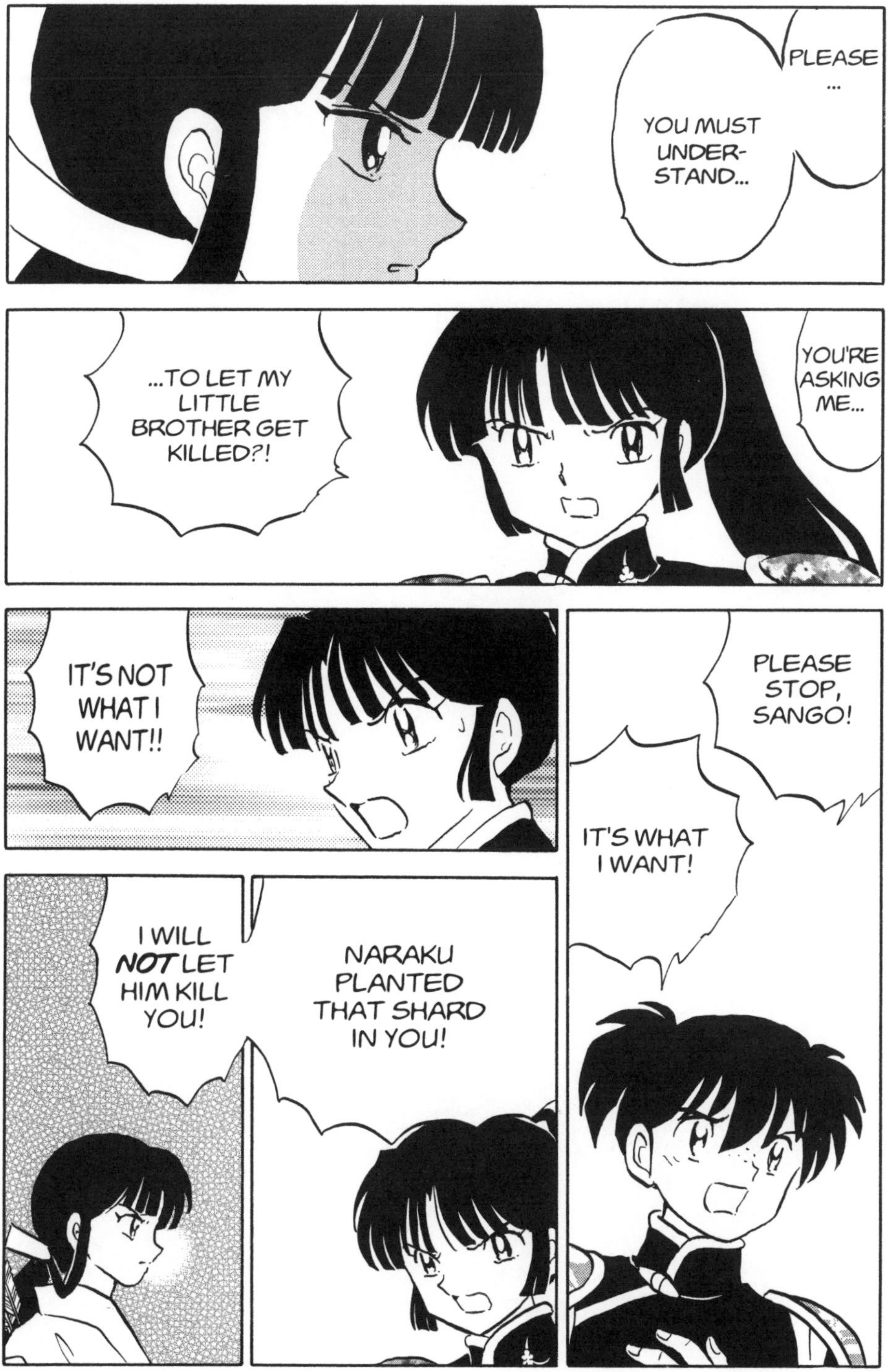
PLEASE ...
YOU MUST UNDER-STAND...
YOU'RE ASKING ME...
...TO LET MY LITTLE BROTHER GET KILLED?!
PLEASE STOP, SANGO!
IT'S WHAT I WANT!
IT'S NOT WHAT I WANT!!
NARAKU PLANTED THAT SHARD IN YOU!
I WILL **NOT** LET HIM KILL YOU!

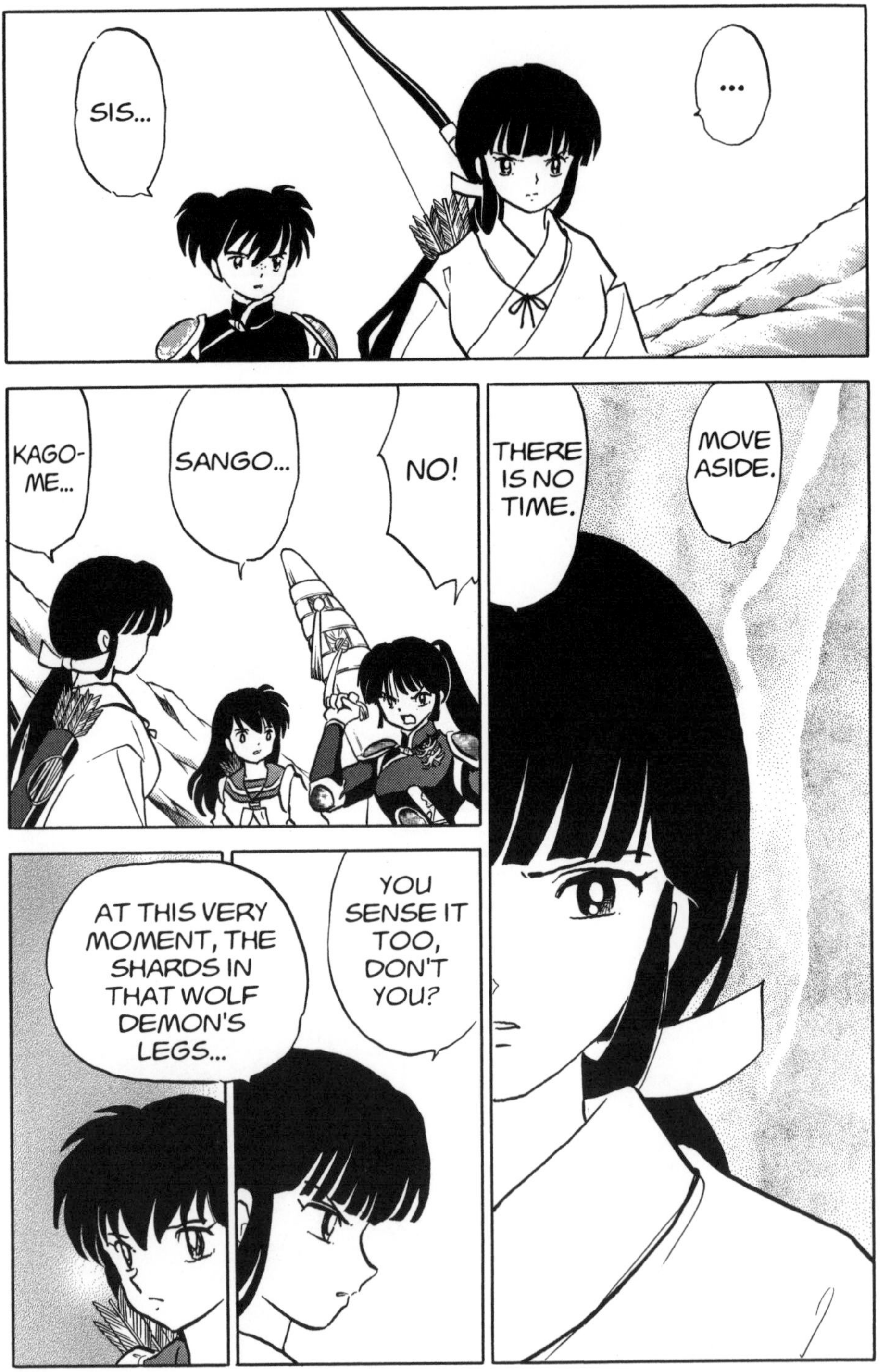
...
SIS...
MOVE ASIDE.
THERE IS NO TIME.
NO!
SANGO...
KAGOME...
YOU SENSE IT TOO, DON'T YOU?
AT THIS VERY MOMENT, THE SHARDS IN THAT WOLF DEMON'S LEGS...

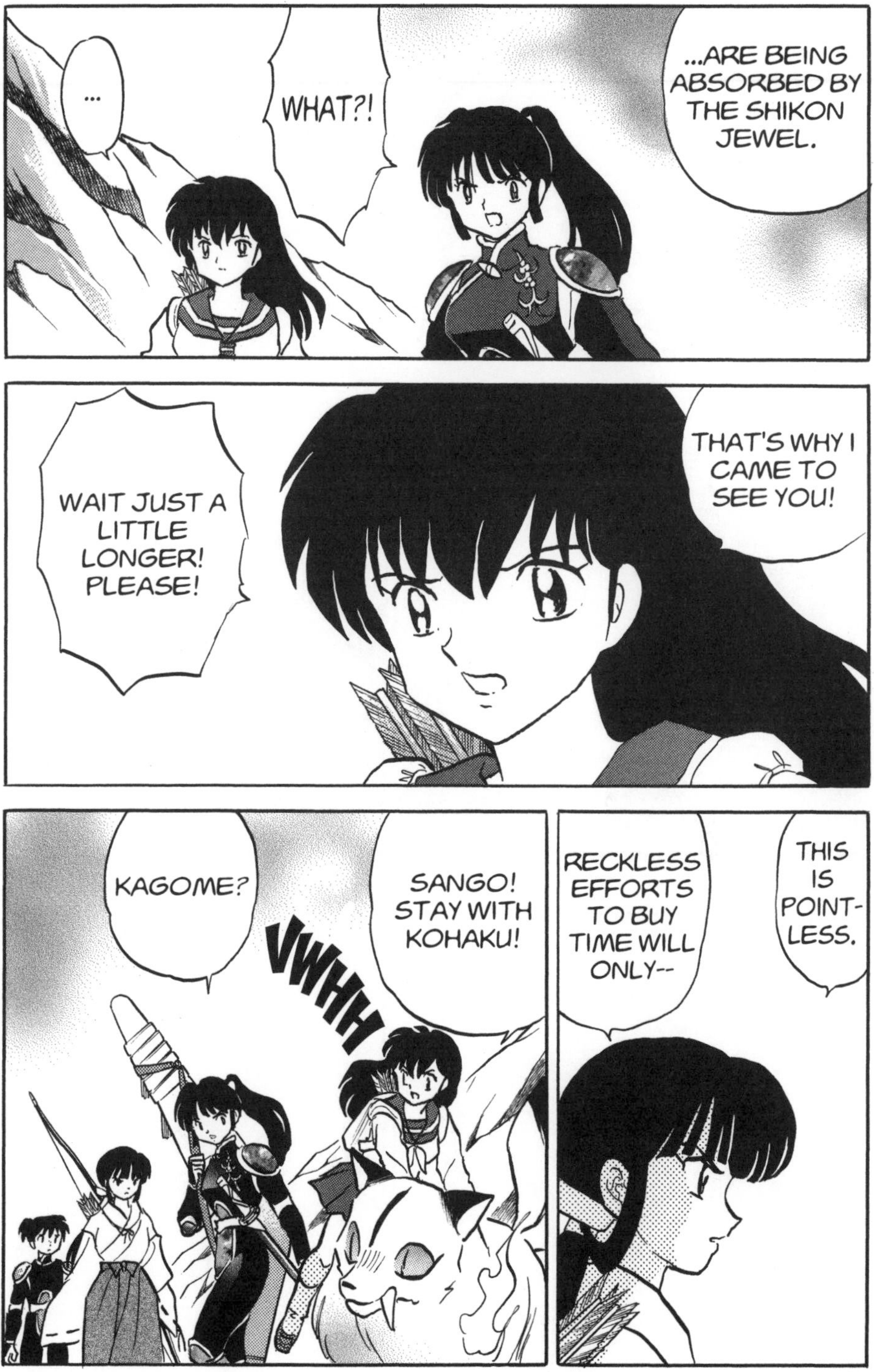
...ARE BEING ABSORBED BY THE SHIKON JEWEL.
WHAT?!
...
THAT'S WHY I CAME TO SEE YOU!
WAIT JUST A LITTLE LONGER! PLEASE!
THIS IS POINT-LESS.
RECKLESS EFFORTS TO BUY TIME WILL ONLY--
SANGO! STAY WITH KOHAKU!
VWHH
KAGOME?

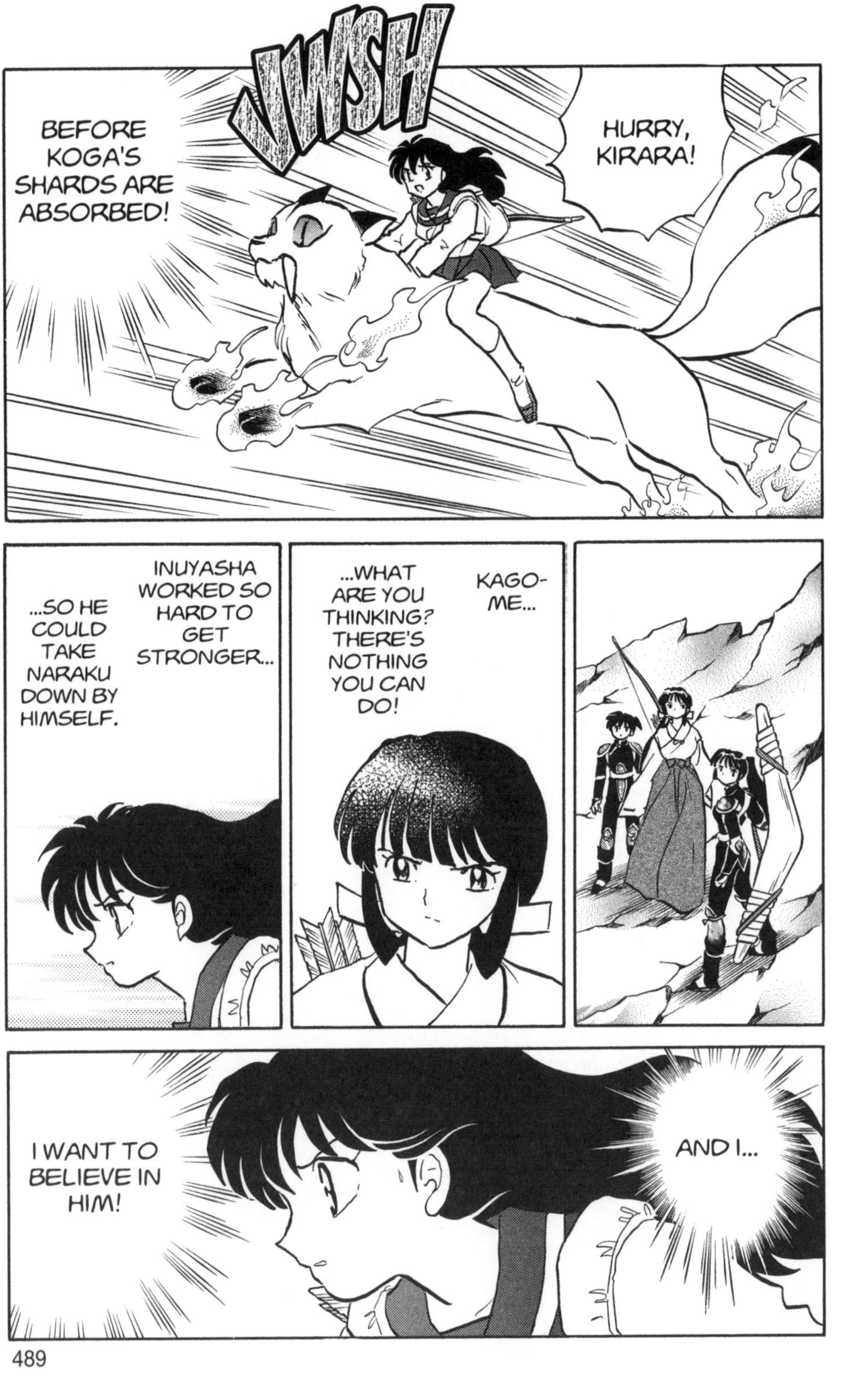
JWSH
HURRY, KIRARA!
BEFORE KOGA'S SHARDS ARE ABSORBED!
KAGO-ME...
...WHAT ARE YOU THINKING? THERE'S NOTHING YOU CAN DO!
INUYASHA WORKED SO HARD TO GET STRONGER...
...SO HE COULD TAKE NARAKU DOWN BY HIMSELF.
AND I...
I WANT TO BELIEVE IN HIM!

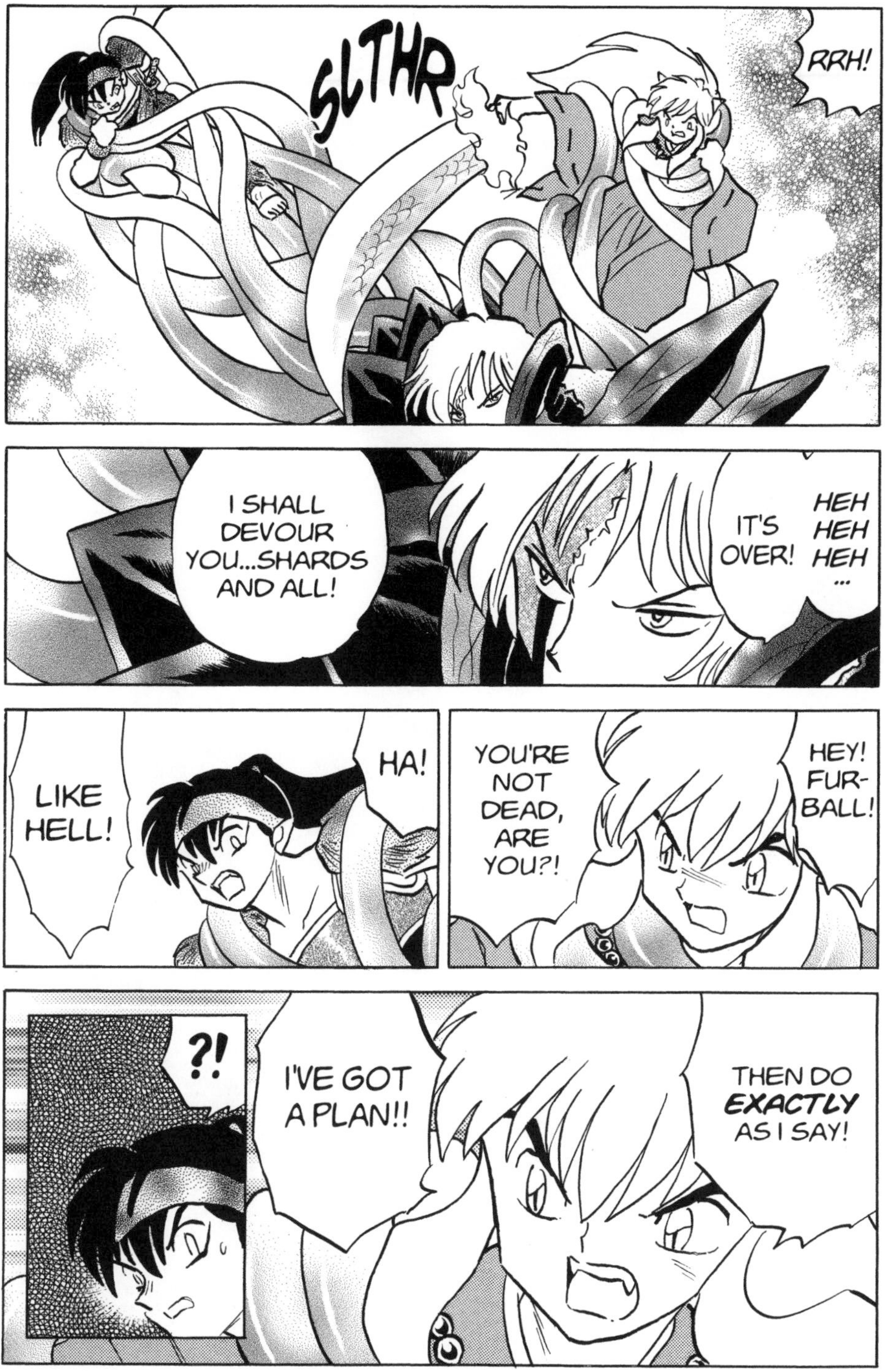
RRH!
SLTHR
HEH HEH HEH ...
IT'S OVER!
I SHALL DEVOUR YOU...SHARDS AND ALL!
HEY! FUR-BALL!
YOU'RE NOT DEAD, ARE YOU?!
HA!
LIKE HELL!
THEN DO **EXACTLY** AS I SAY!
I'VE GOT A PLAN!!
?!

SCROLL SEVEN
THE INFANT'S MISTAKE

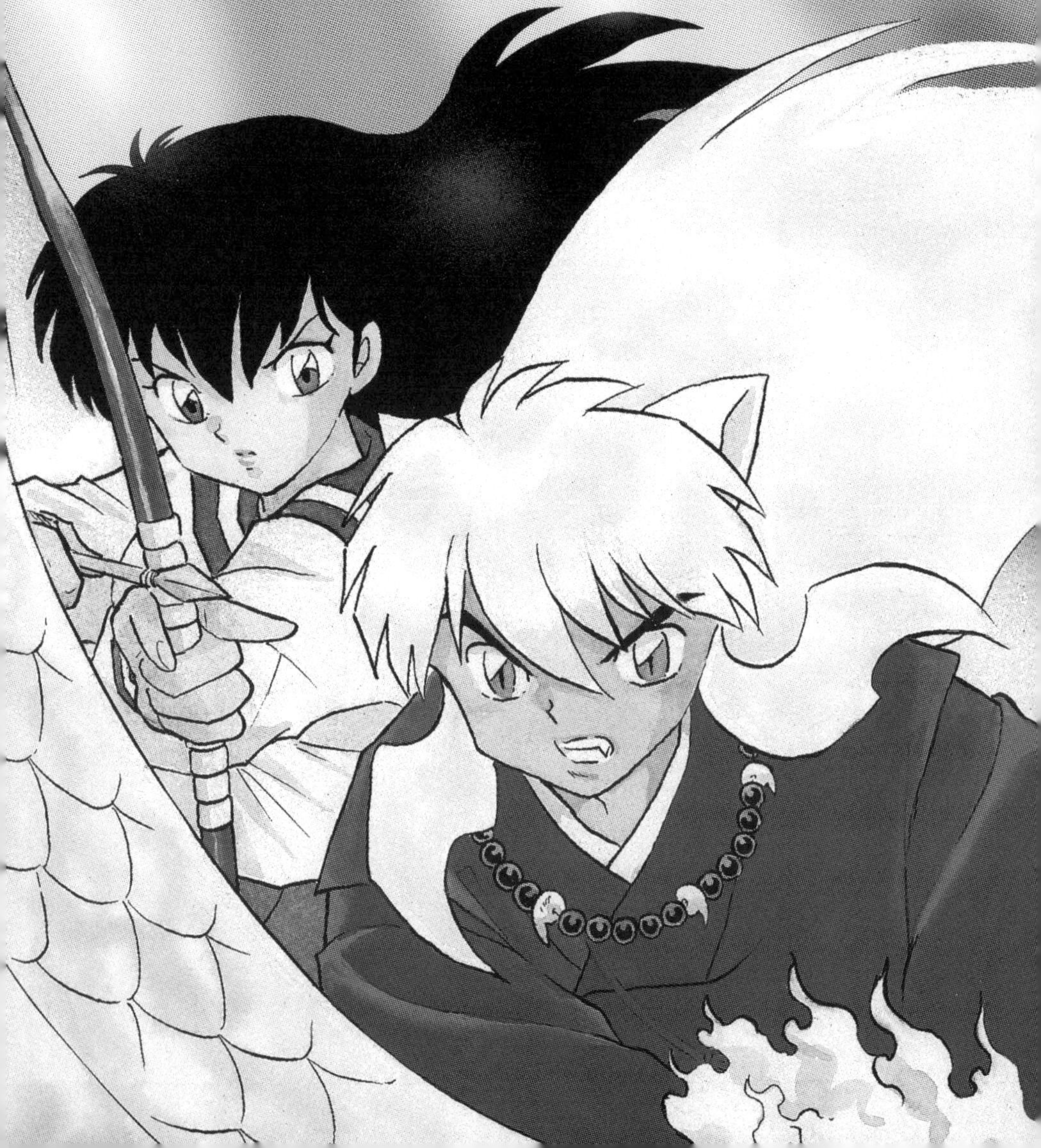

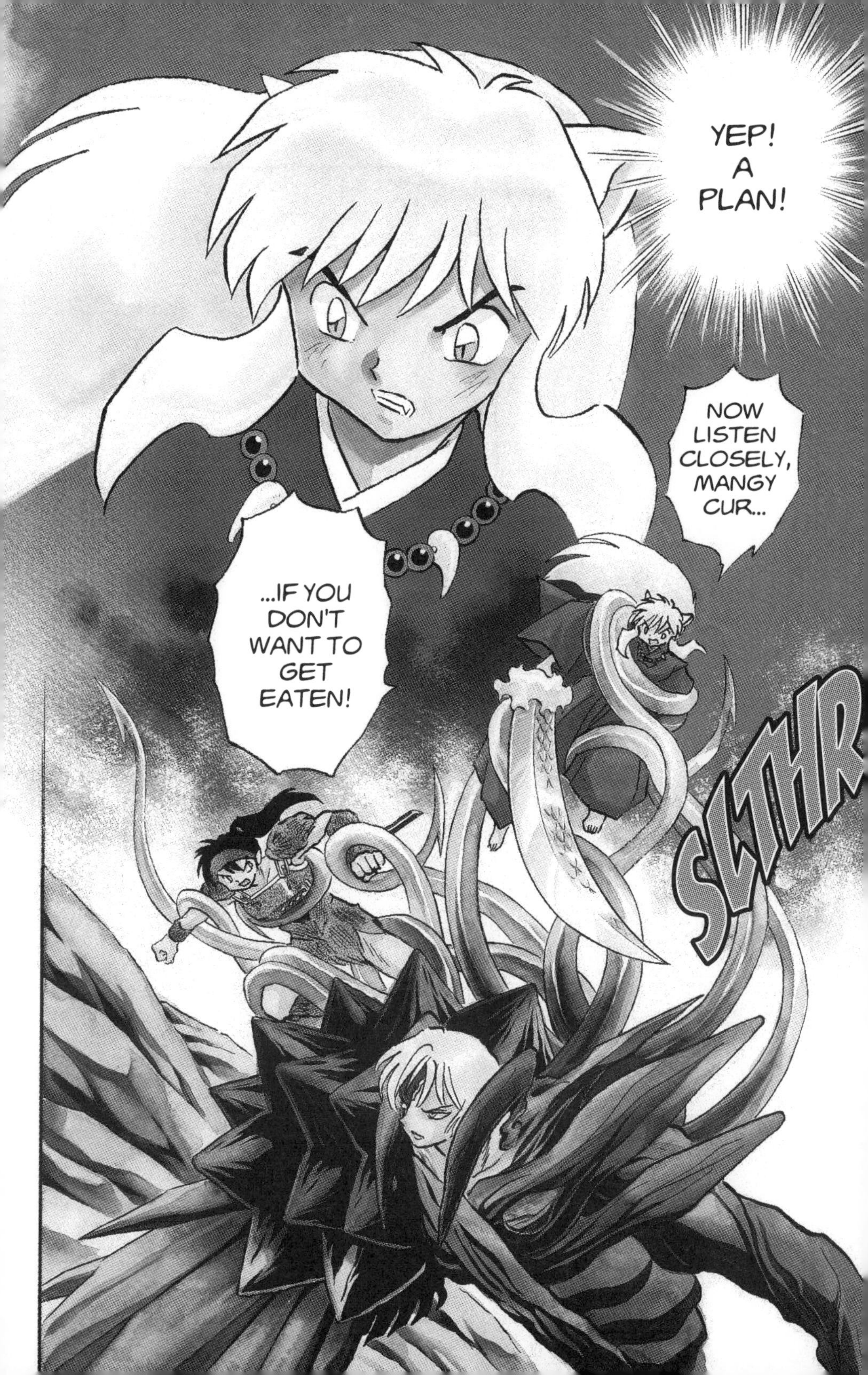
YEP! A PLAN!
NOW LISTEN CLOSELY, MANGY CUR...
...IF YOU DON'T WANT TO GET EATEN!
SLTHR

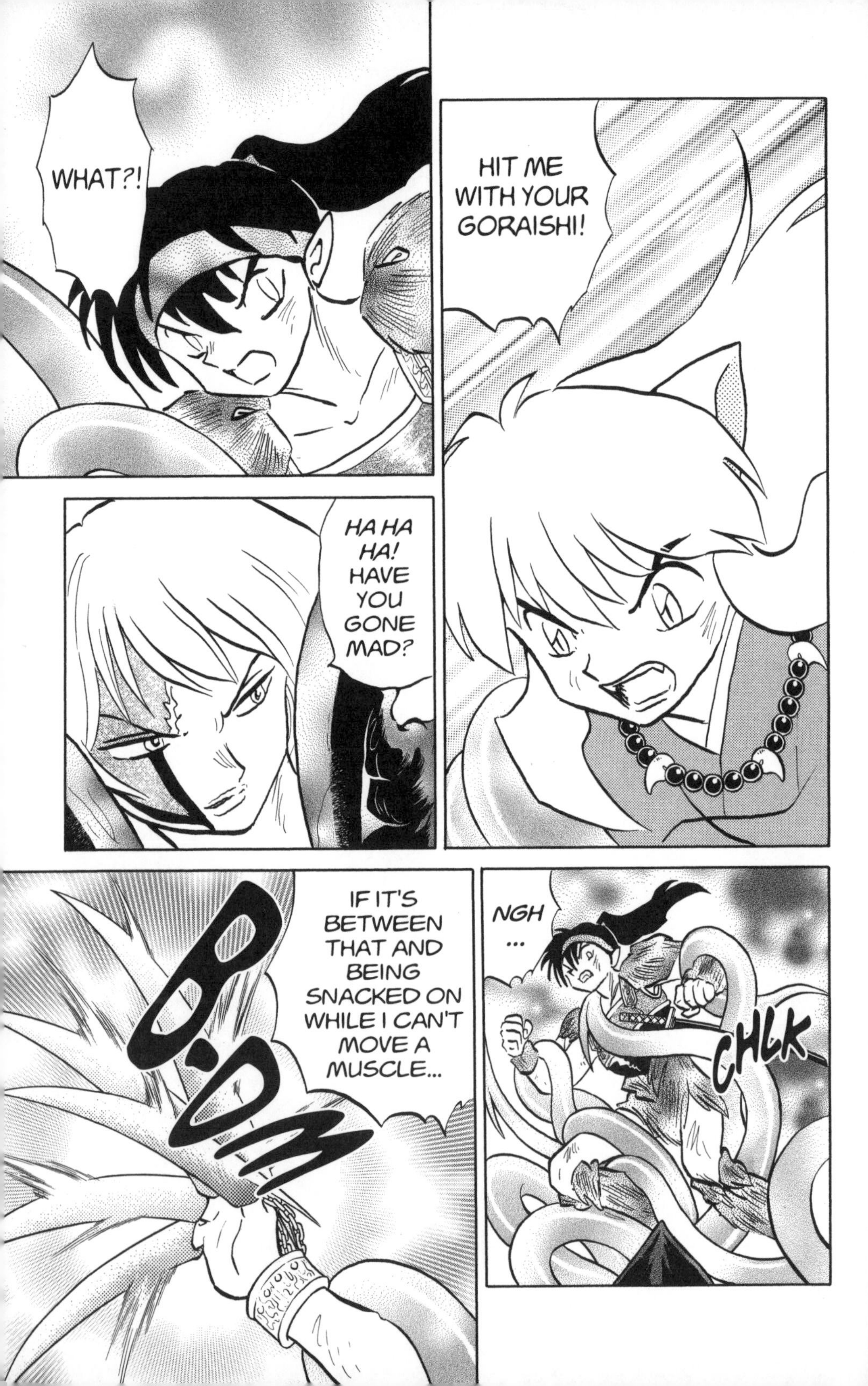
HIT ME WITH YOUR GORAISHI!
WHAT?!
HA HA HA! HAVE YOU GONE MAD?
NGH ...
CHLK
IF IT'S BETWEEN THAT AND BEING SNACKED ON WHILE I CAN'T MOVE A MUSCLE...
B-DM

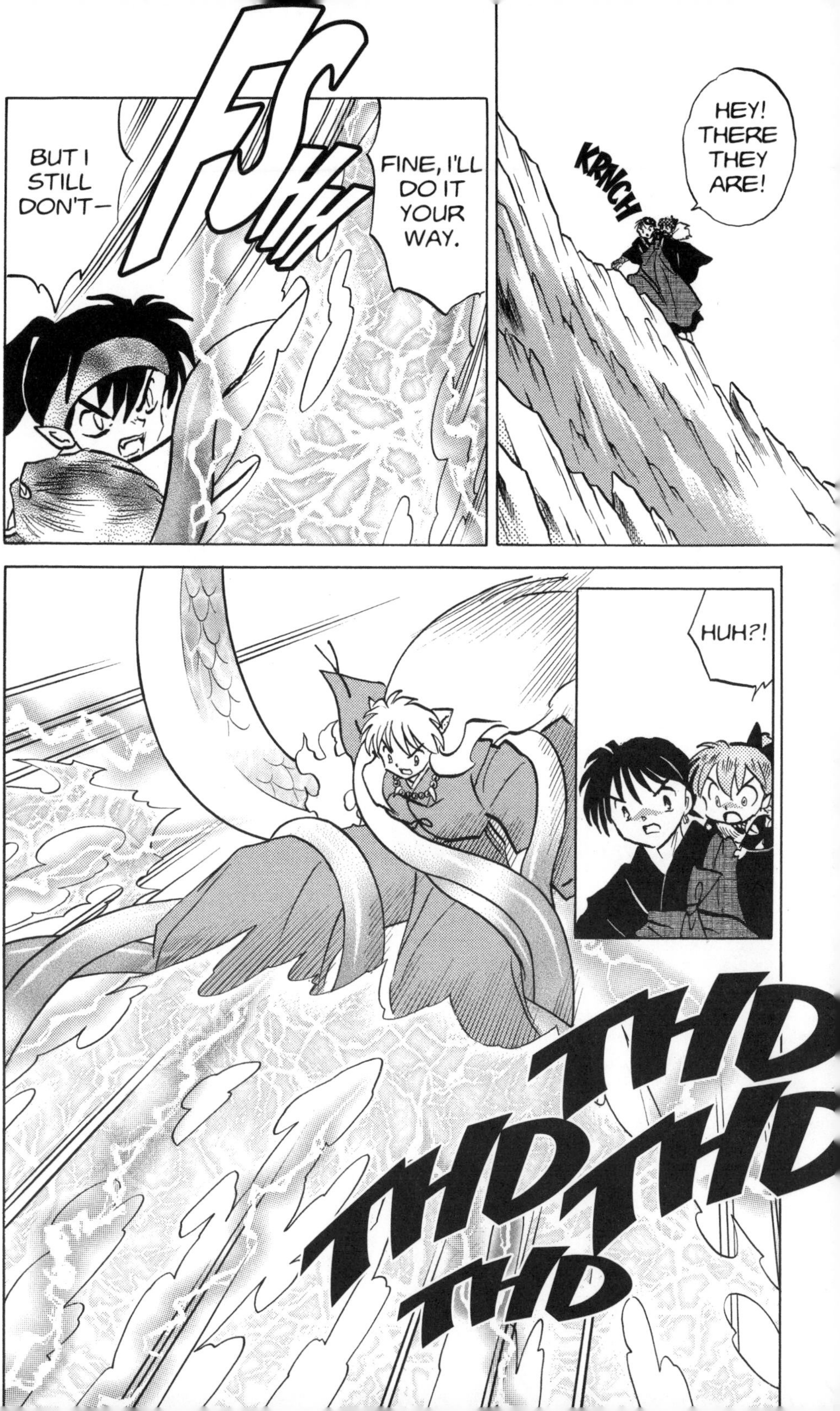
HEY! THERE THEY ARE!
KRNCH
FINE, I'LL DO IT YOUR WAY.
FSHH
BUT I STILL DON'T—
HUH?!
THD THD THD THD

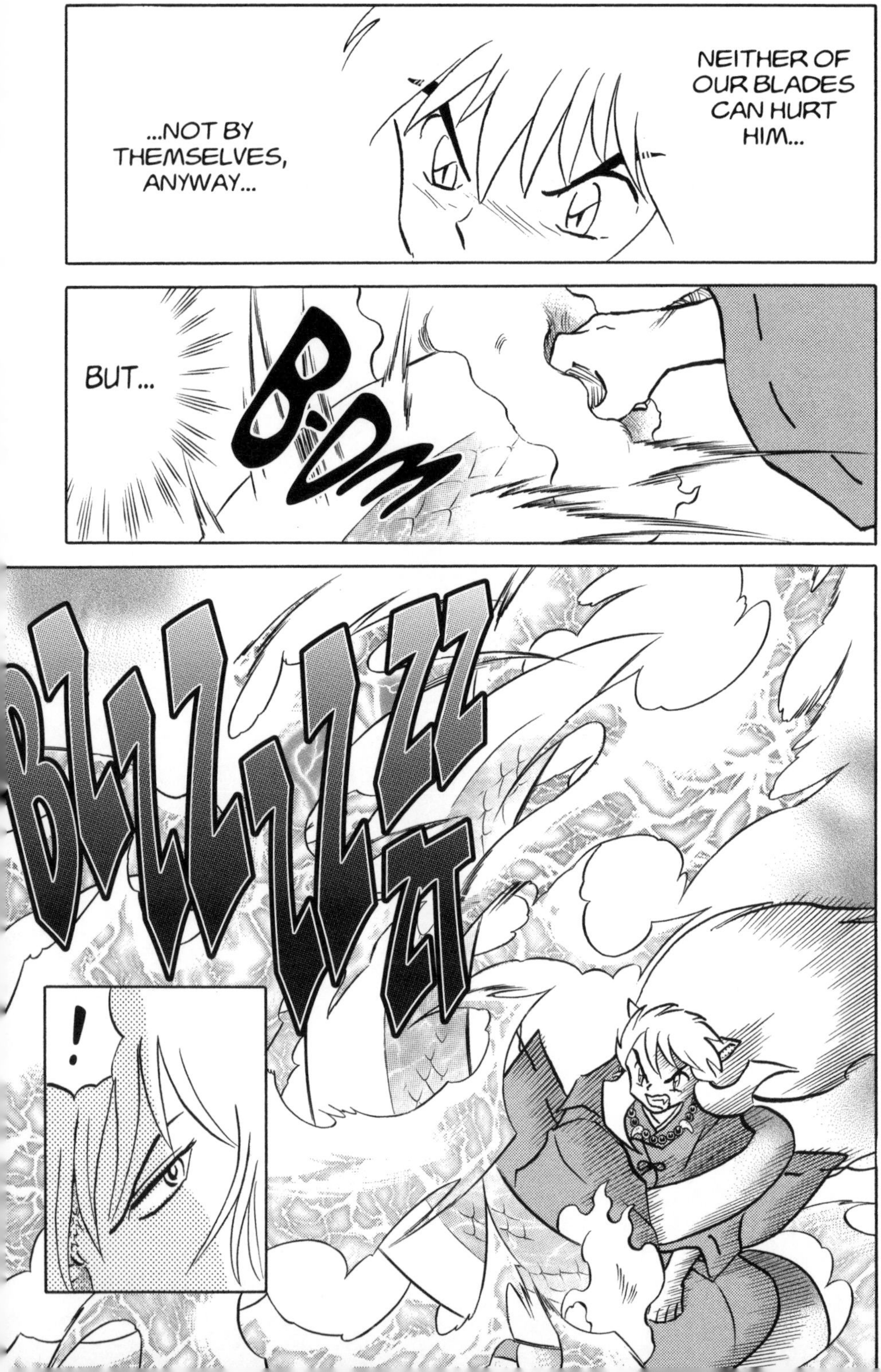
NEITHER OF OUR BLADES CAN HURT HIM...
...NOT BY THEMSELVES, ANYWAY...
BUT...
!

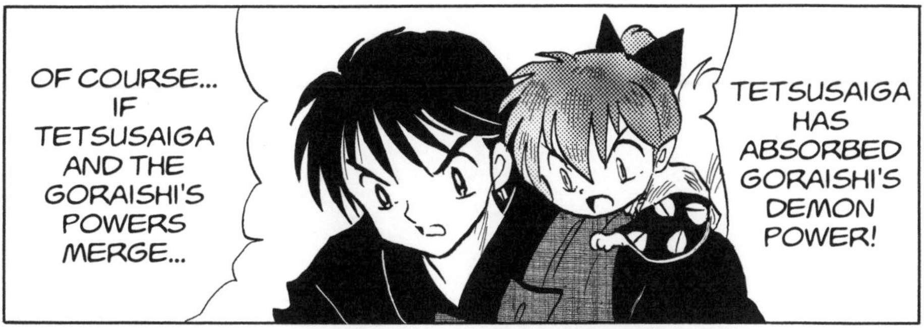
TETSUSAIGA HAS ABSORBED GORAISHI'S DEMON POWER!
OF COURSE... IF TETSUSAIGA AND THE GORAISHI'S POWERS MERGE...

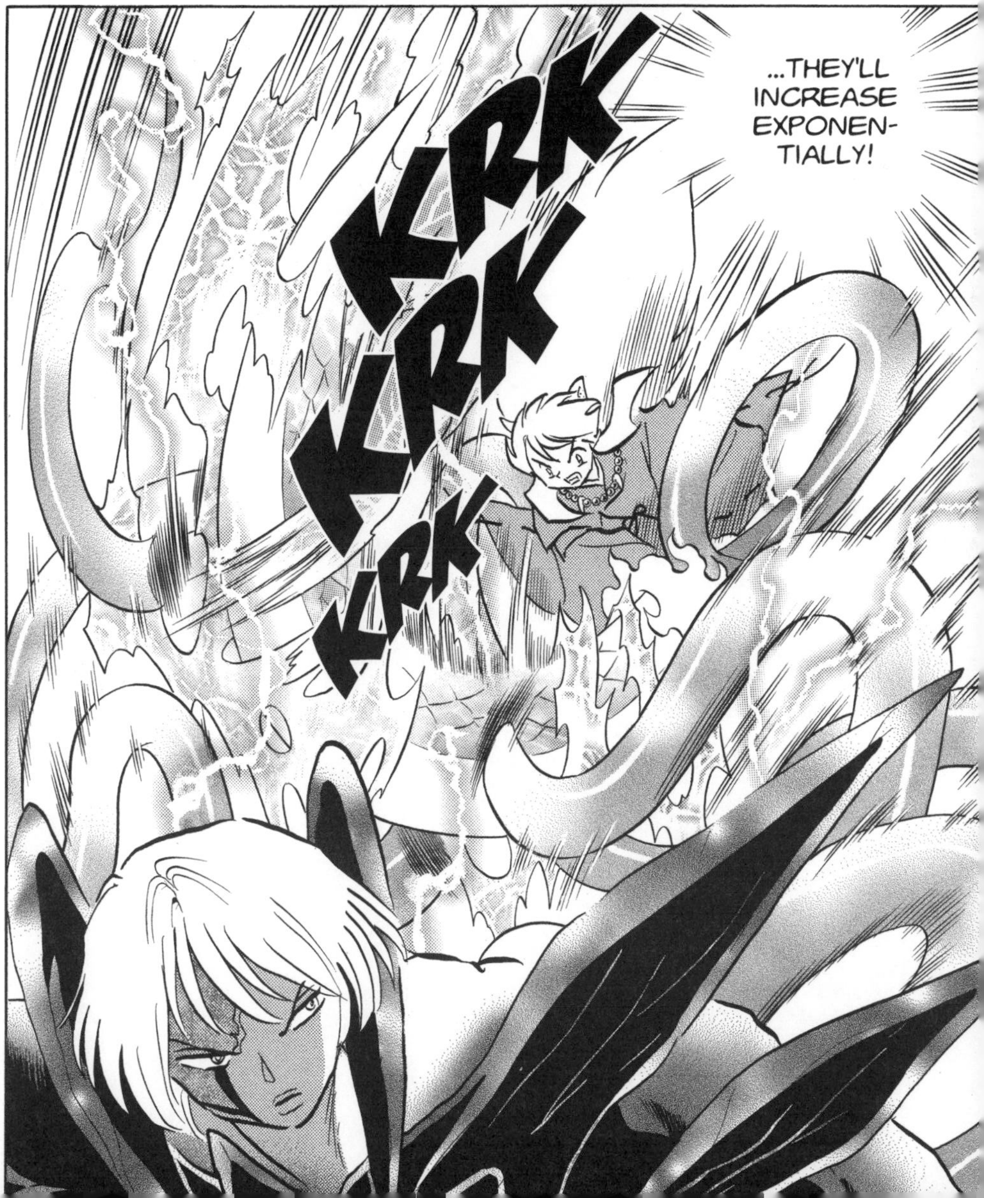
...THEY'LL INCREASE EXPONEN-TIALLY!
KRK KRK KRK KRK

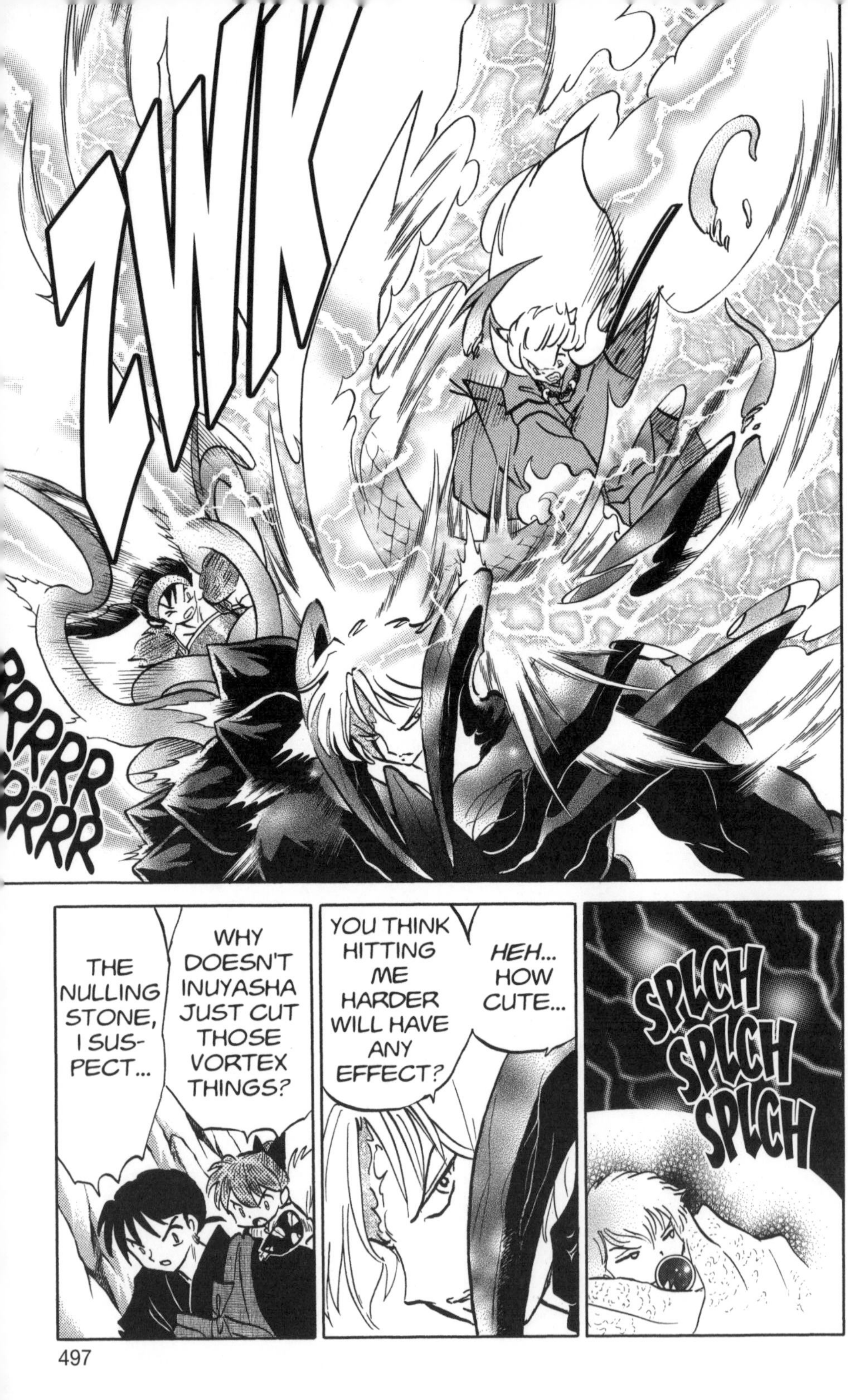
ZWIK
RRRRR RRRR
SPLCH SPLCH SPLCH
HEH... HOW CUTE...
YOU THINK HITTING ME HARDER WILL HAVE ANY EFFECT?
WHY DOESN'T INUYASHA JUST CUT THOSE VORTEX THINGS?
THE NULLING STONE, I SUS-PECT...

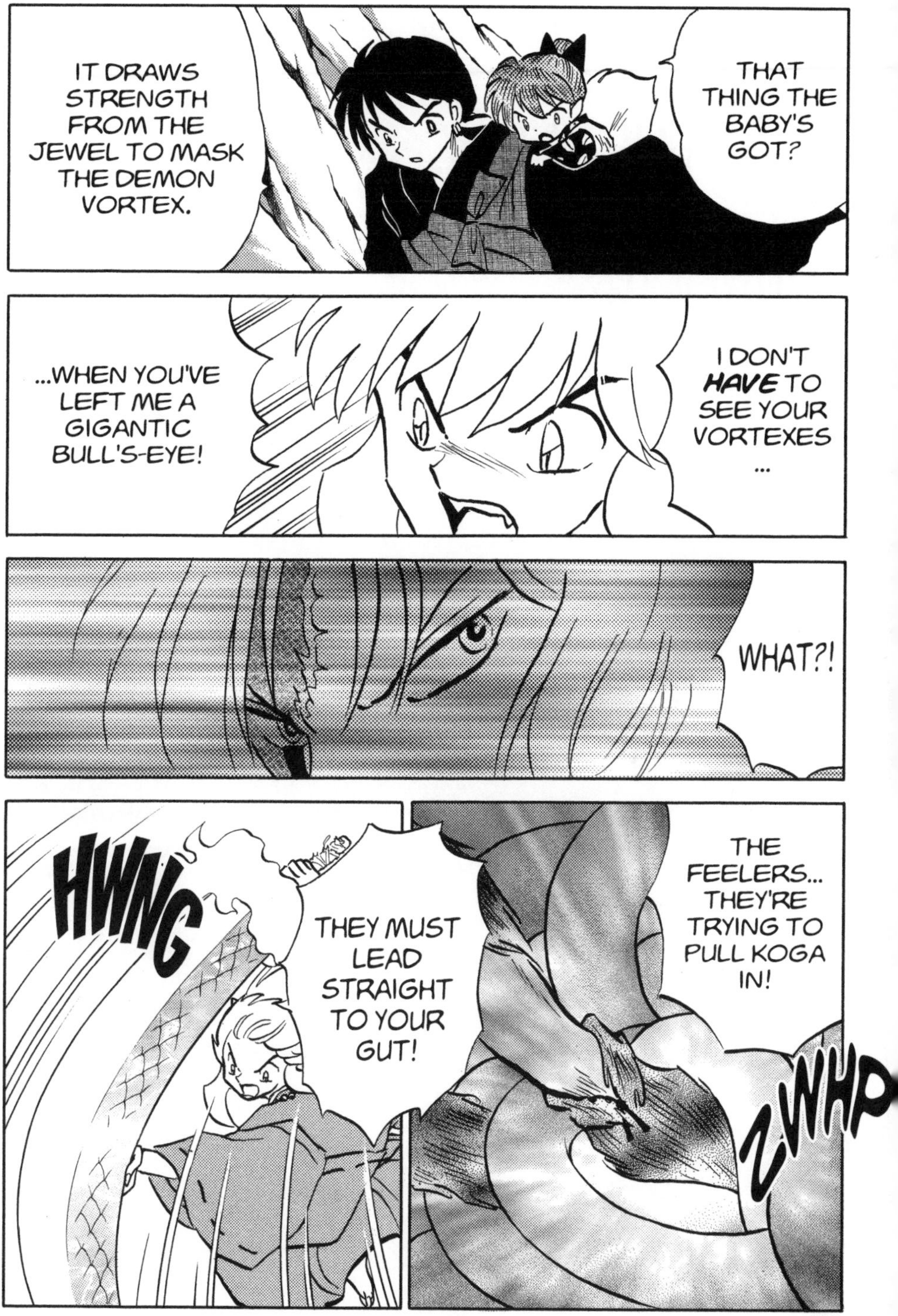
THAT THING THE BABY'S GOT?
IT DRAWS STRENGTH FROM THE JEWEL TO MASK THE DEMON VORTEX.
I DON'T *HAVE* TO SEE YOUR VORTEXES ...
...WHEN YOU'VE LEFT ME A GIGANTIC BULL'S-EYE!
WHAT?!
THE FEELERS... THEY'RE TRYING TO PULL KOGA IN!
ZWHP
THEY MUST LEAD STRAIGHT TO YOUR GUT!
HWNG

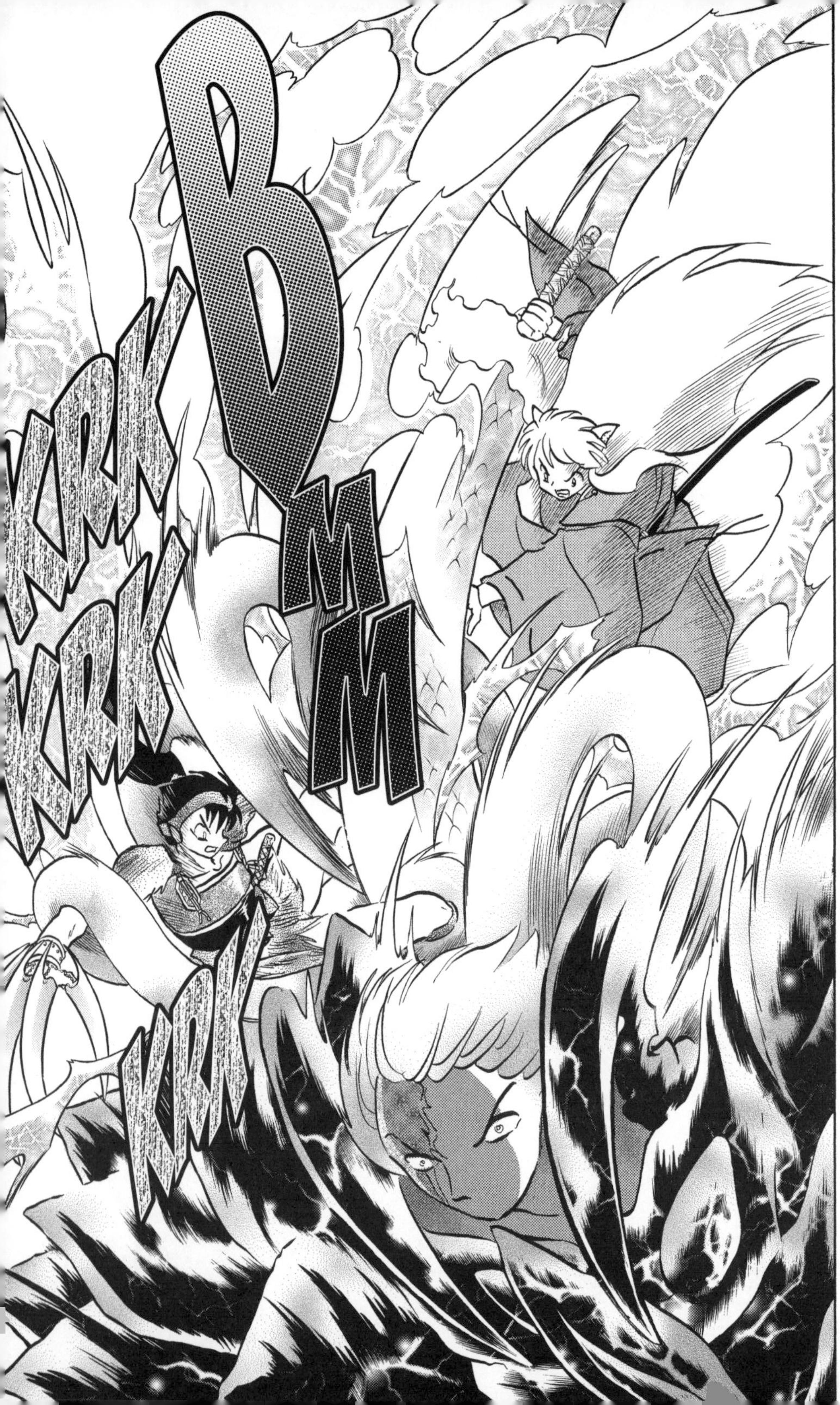
BMM
KRAK
KRAK
KRAK

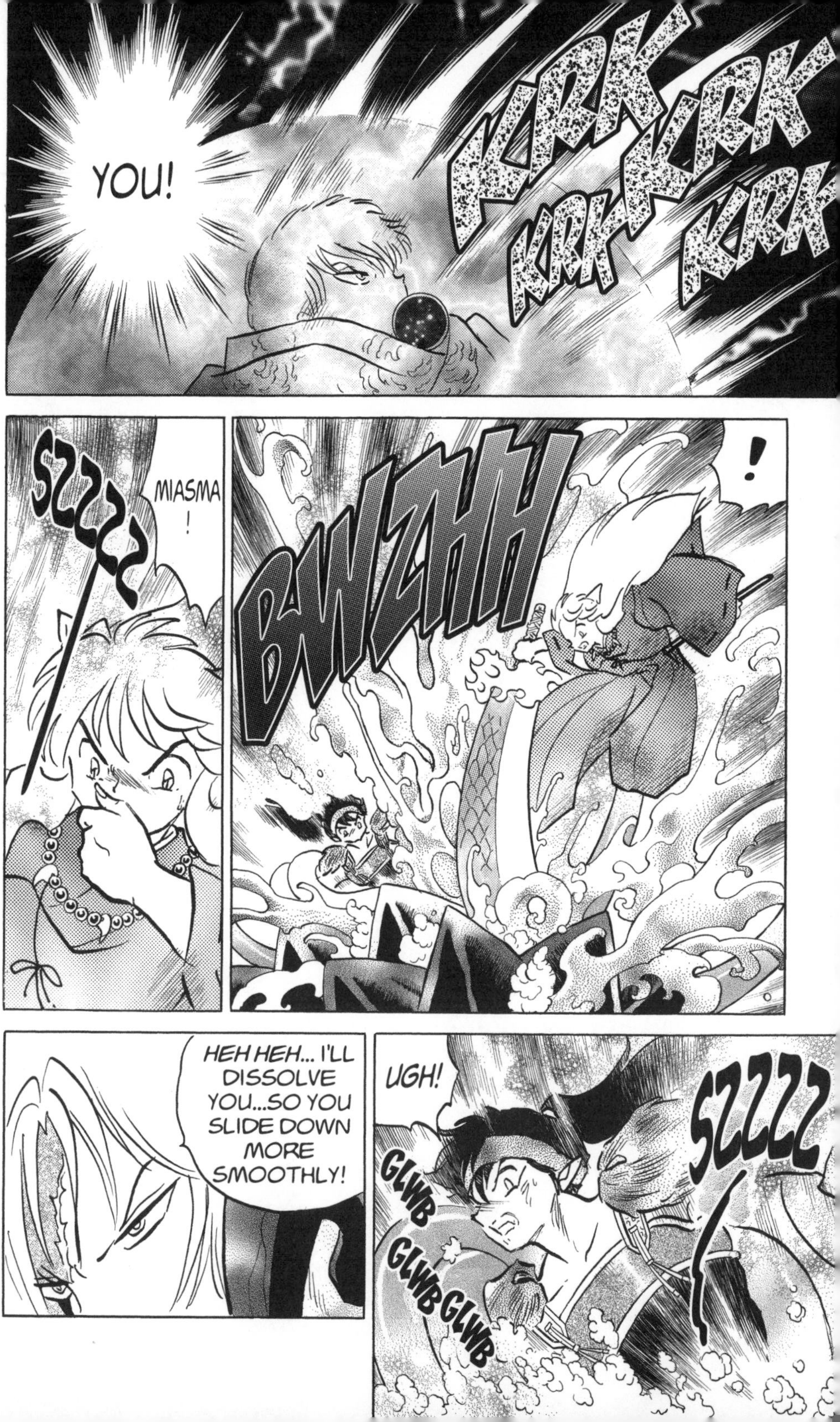
KRK KRK
KRK KRK
YOU!
!
BWZHH
SZZZZ
MIASMA
!
UGH!
SZZZZ
GLWB
GLWB
GLWB GLWB
HEH HEH... I'LL DISSOLVE YOU...SO YOU SLIDE DOWN MORE SMOOTHLY!

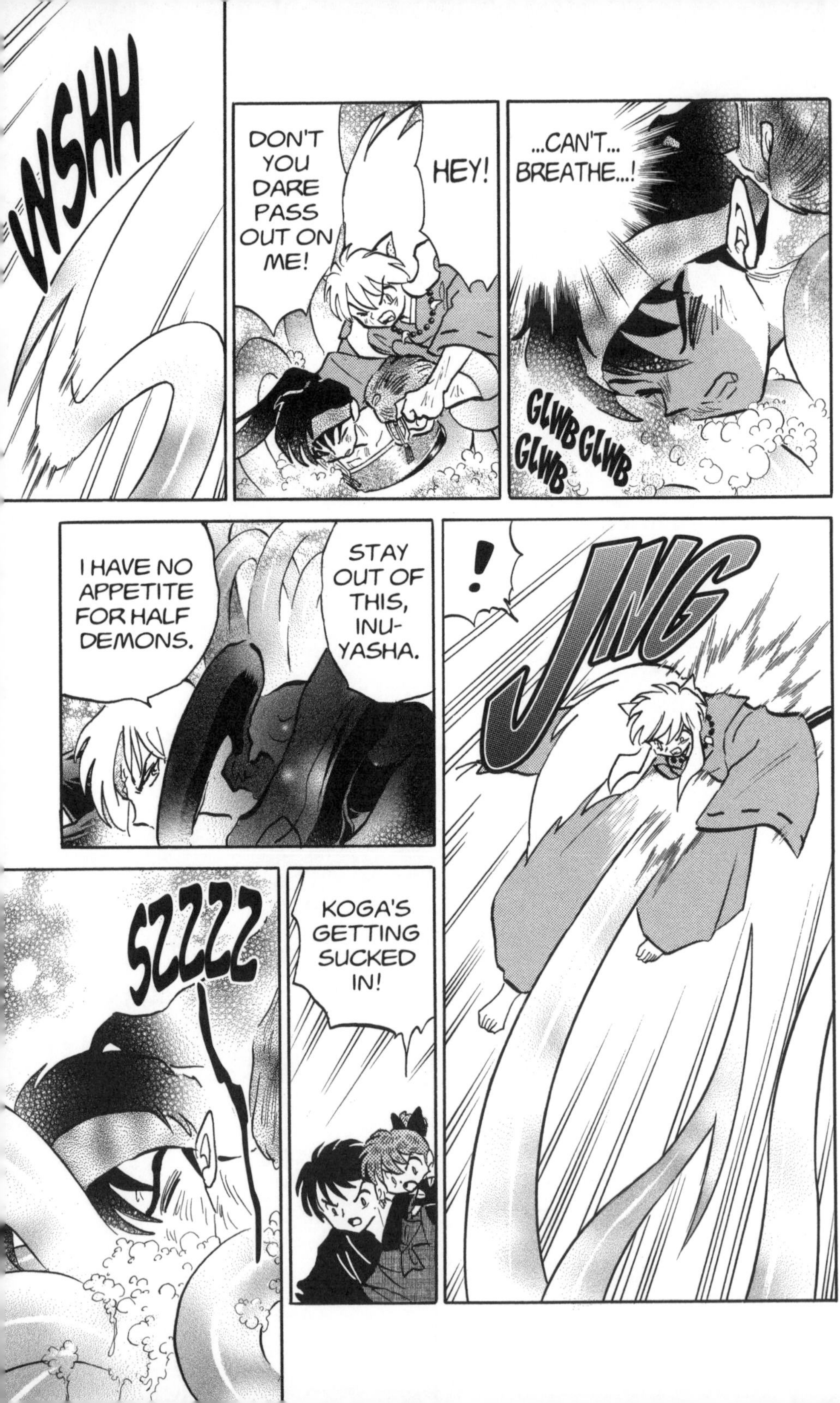
...CAN'T... BREATHE...!
GLWB GLWB GLWB
HEY!
DON'T YOU DARE PASS OUT ON ME!
WSHH
JING
!
STAY OUT OF THIS, INU-YASHA.
I HAVE NO APPETITE FOR HALF DEMONS.
KOGA'S GETTING SUCKED IN!
SZZZZ

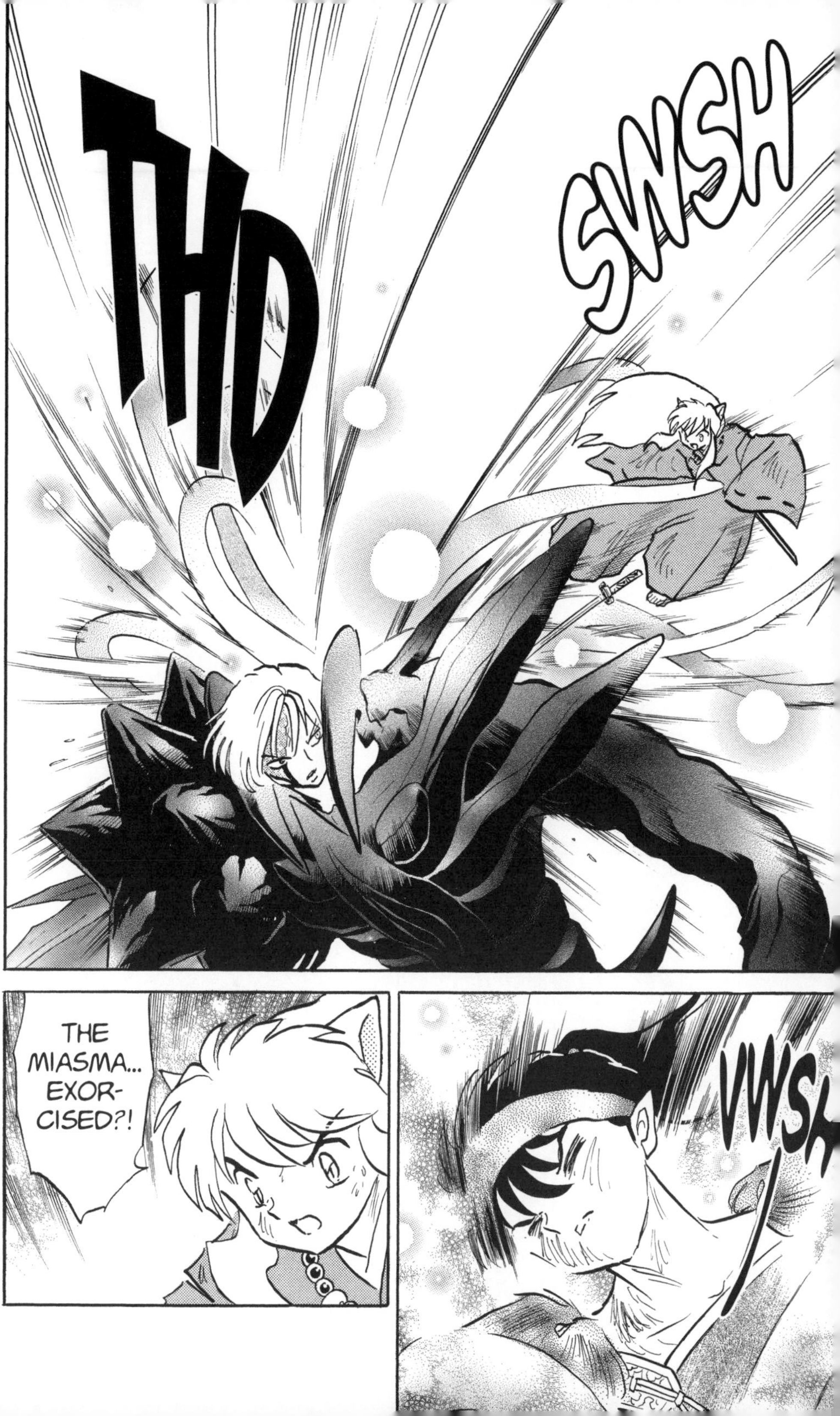
SWSH
THD
VWSH
THE MIASMA... EXOR-CISED?!

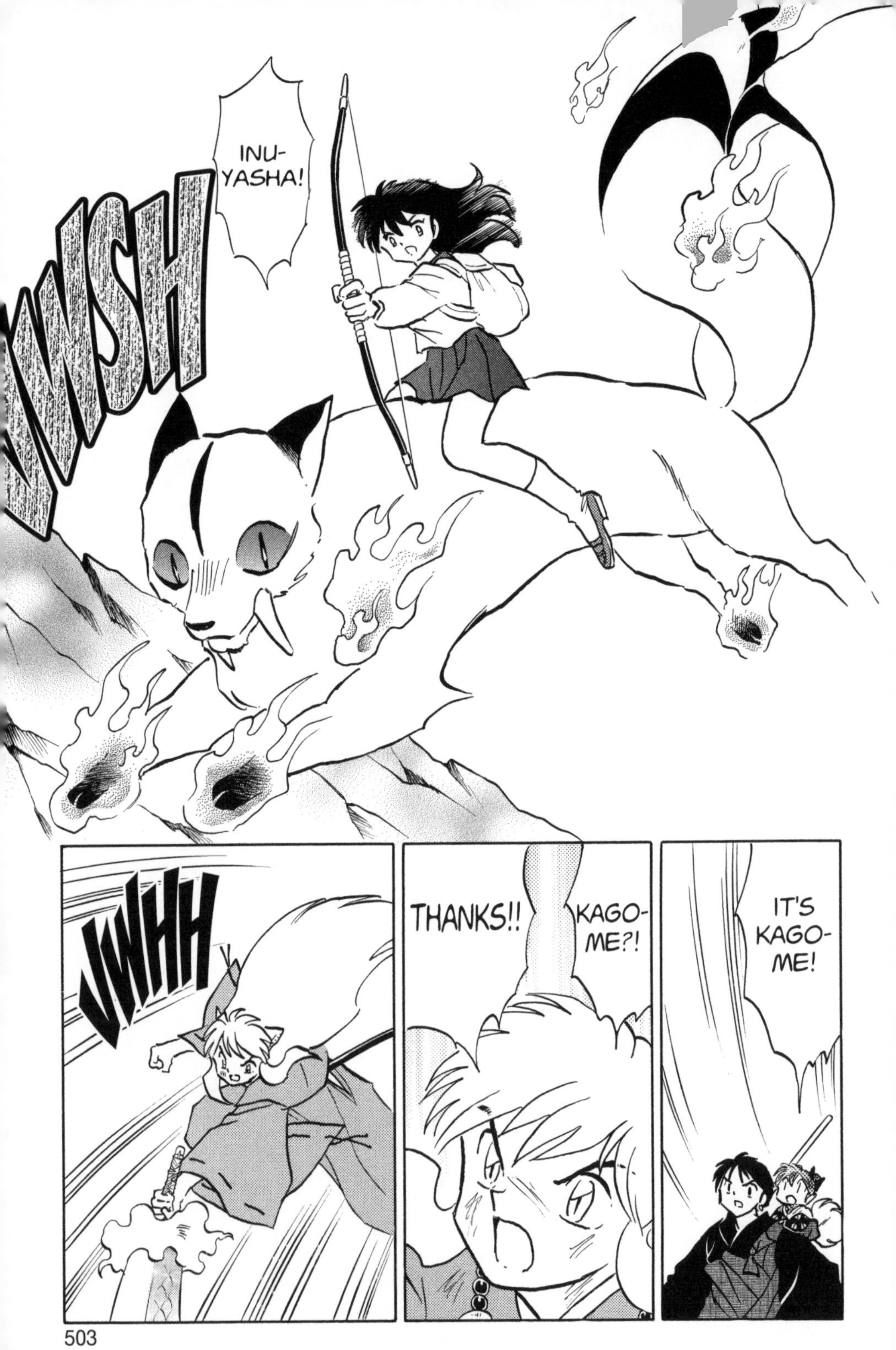
INU-
YASHA!
WWSH
IT'S
KAGO-
ME!
KAGO-
ME?!
THANKS!!
JWHH

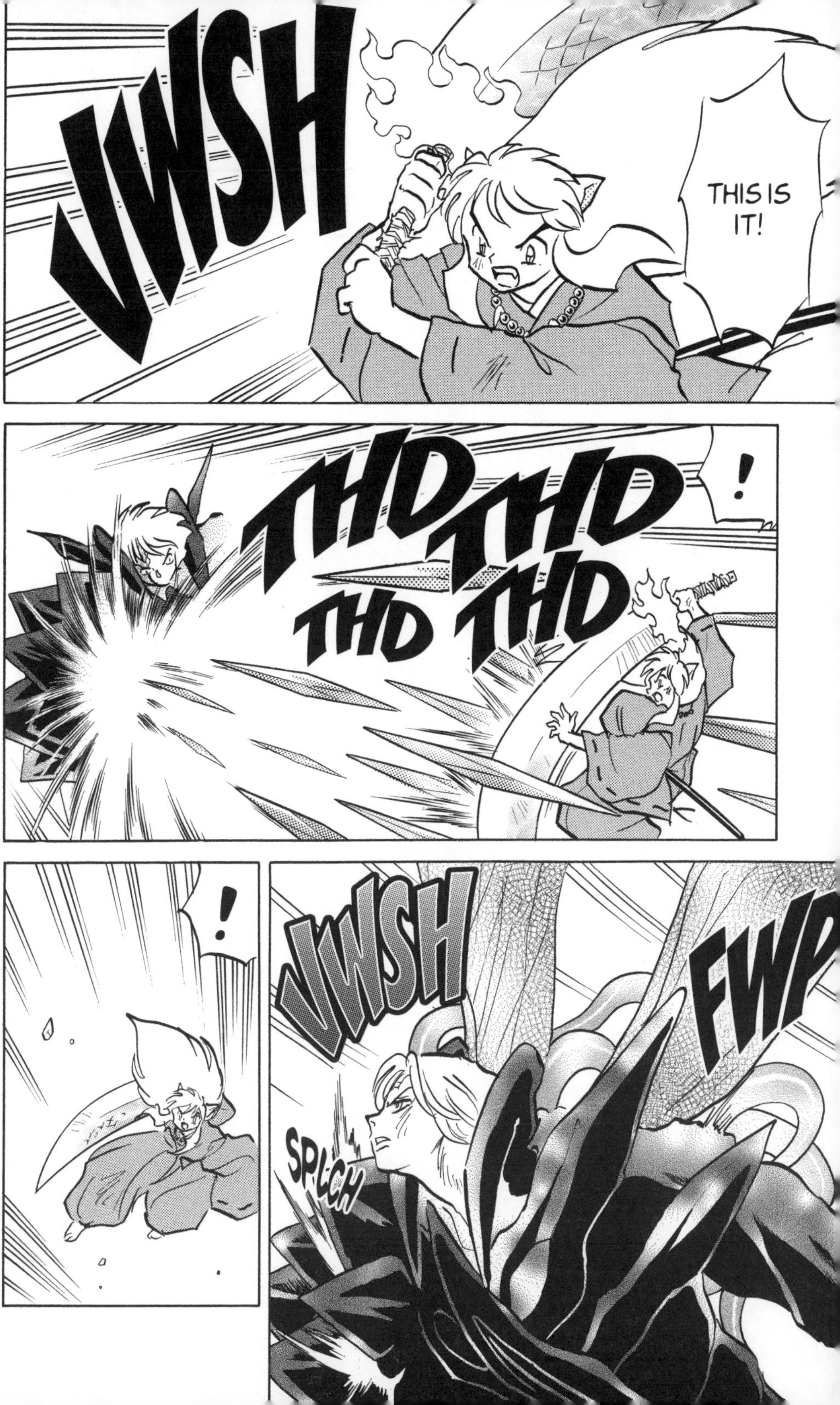
THIS IS IT!
JWSH
!
THD THD
THD THD
FWP
JWSH
SPLCH
!

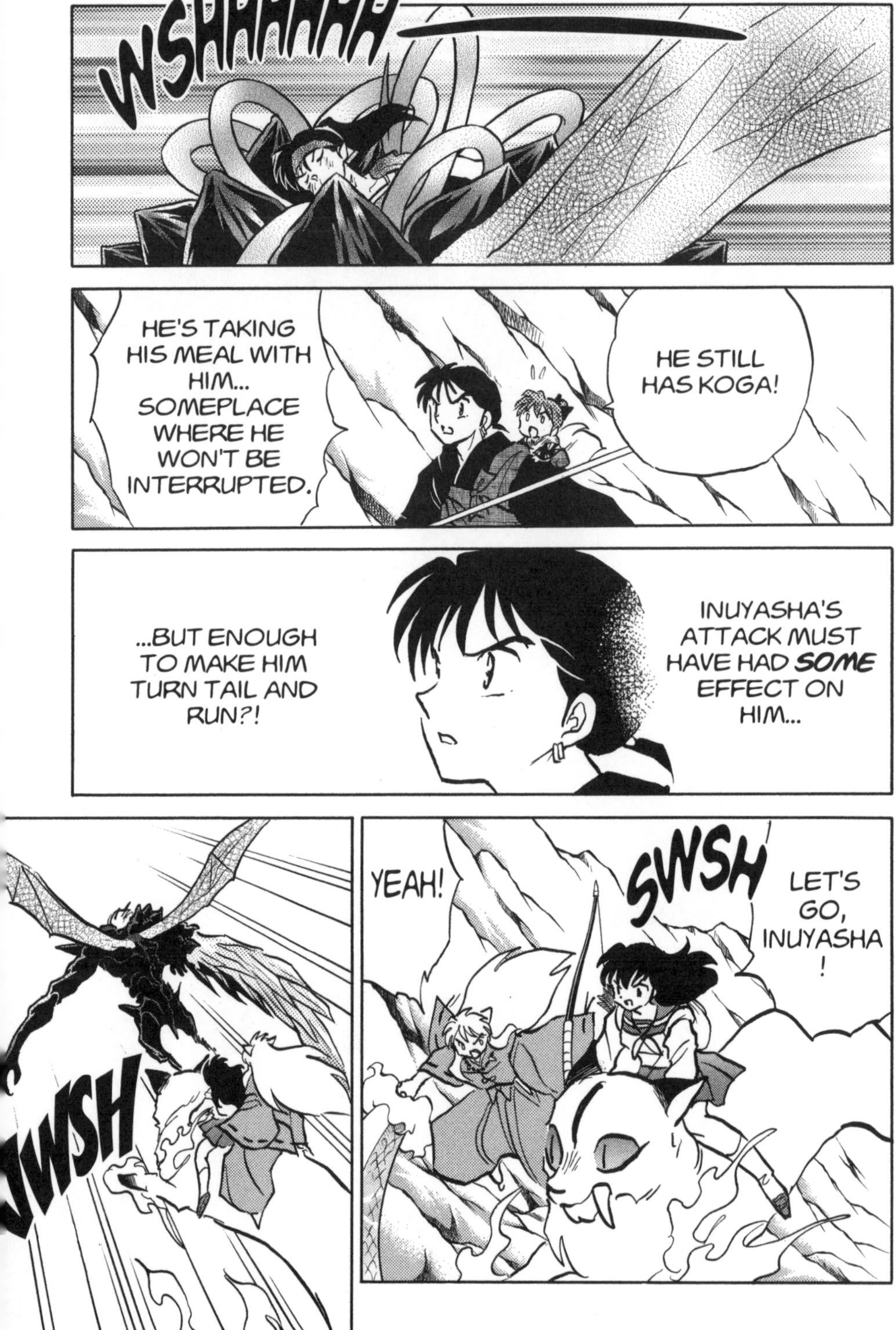
WSHHHHHH
HE STILL HAS KOGA!
HE'S TAKING HIS MEAL WITH HIM... SOMEPLACE WHERE HE WON'T BE INTERRUPTED.
INUYASHA'S ATTACK MUST HAVE HAD *SOME* EFFECT ON HIM...
...BUT ENOUGH TO MAKE HIM TURN TAIL AND RUN?!
LET'S GO, INUYASHA!
SWSH
YEAH!
WSH

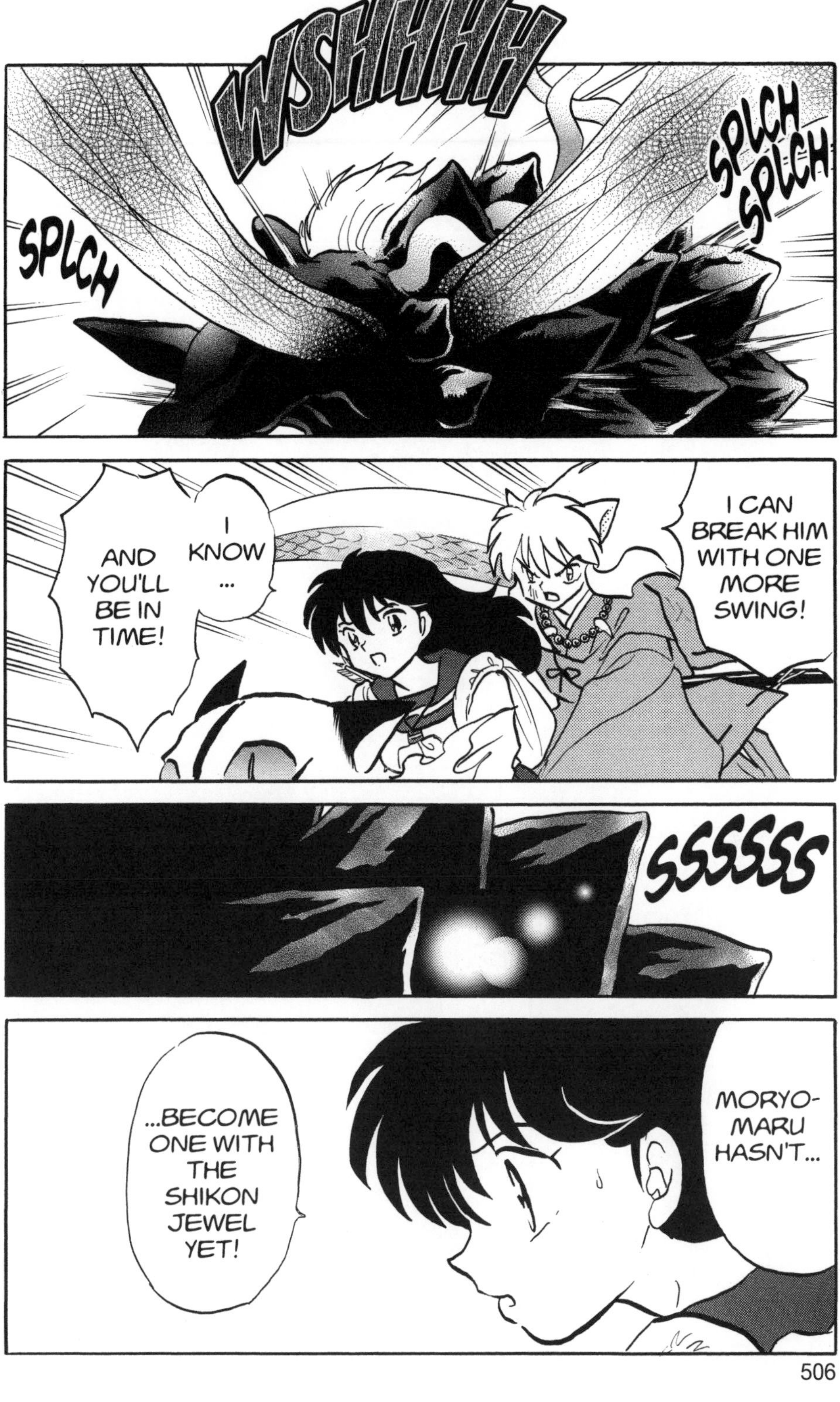
WSHHHH
SPLCH SPLCH
SPLCH
I CAN BREAK HIM WITH ONE MORE SWING!
I KNOW ...
AND YOU'LL BE IN TIME!
SSSSSS
MORYO-MARU HASN'T...
...BECOME ONE WITH THE SHIKON JEWEL YET!

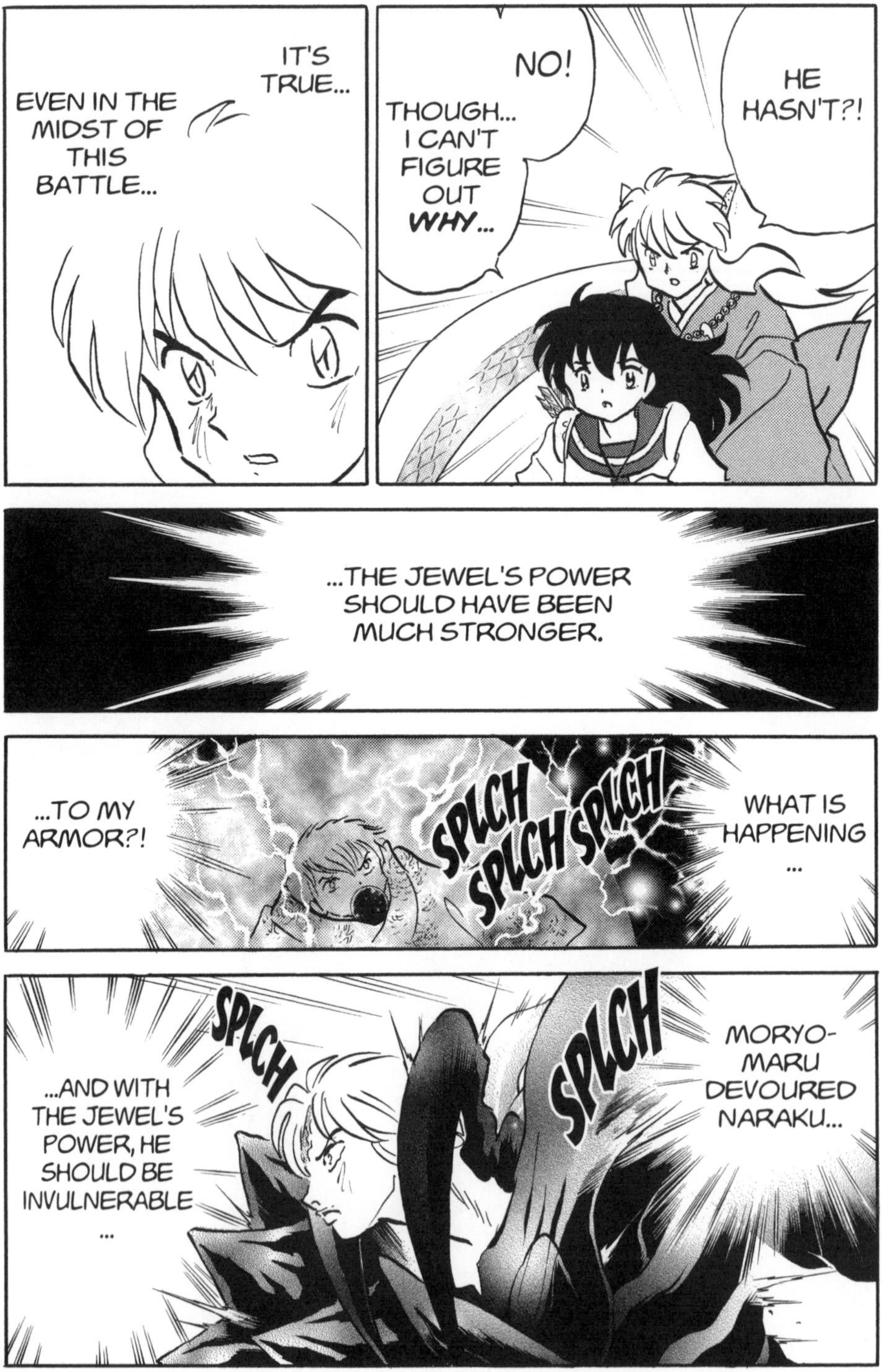
HE HASN'T?!
NO!
THOUGH... I CAN'T FIGURE OUT WHY...
IT'S TRUE...
EVEN IN THE MIDST OF THIS BATTLE...
...THE JEWEL'S POWER SHOULD HAVE BEEN MUCH STRONGER.
WHAT IS HAPPENING ...
SPLCH SPLCH SPLCH
...TO MY ARMOR?!
MORYO-MARU DEVOURED NARAKU...
SPLCH
SPLCH
...AND WITH THE JEWEL'S POWER, HE SHOULD BE INVULNERABLE ...

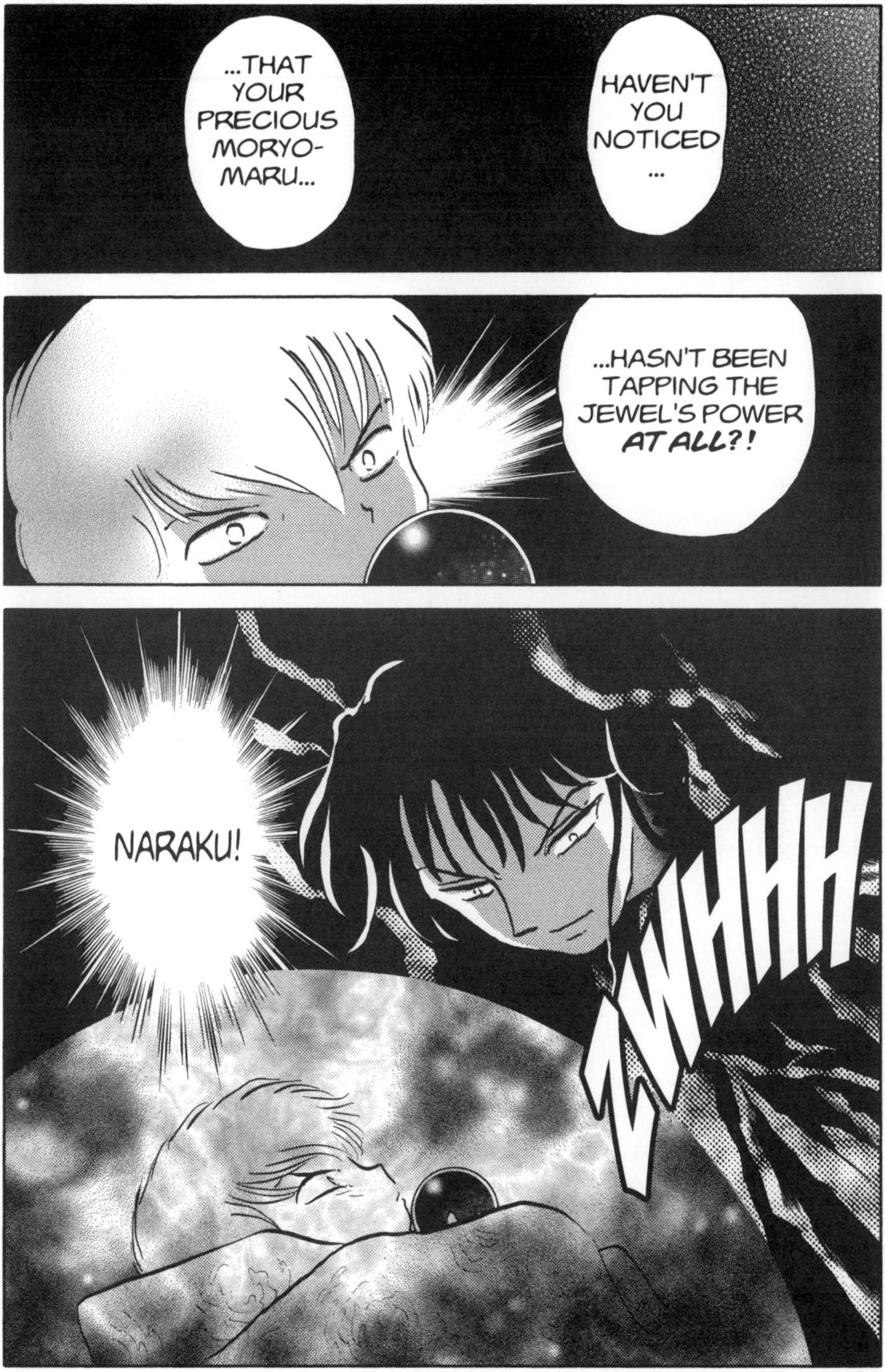
HAVEN'T YOU NOTICED ...
...THAT YOUR PRECIOUS MORYO-MARU...
...HASN'T BEEN TAPPING THE JEWEL'S POWER AT ALL?!
WHHHH
NARAKU!

SCROLL EIGHT
EROSION

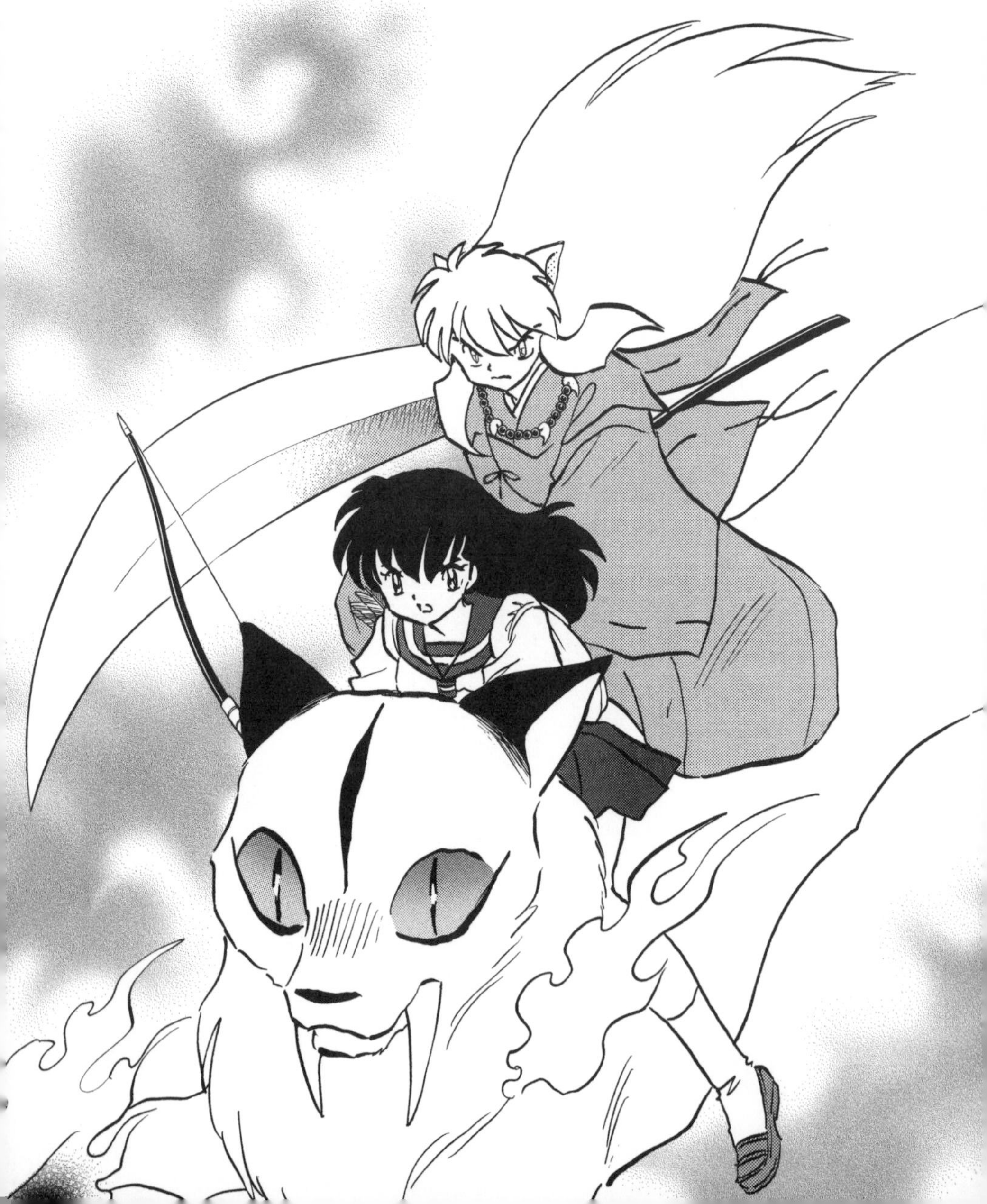

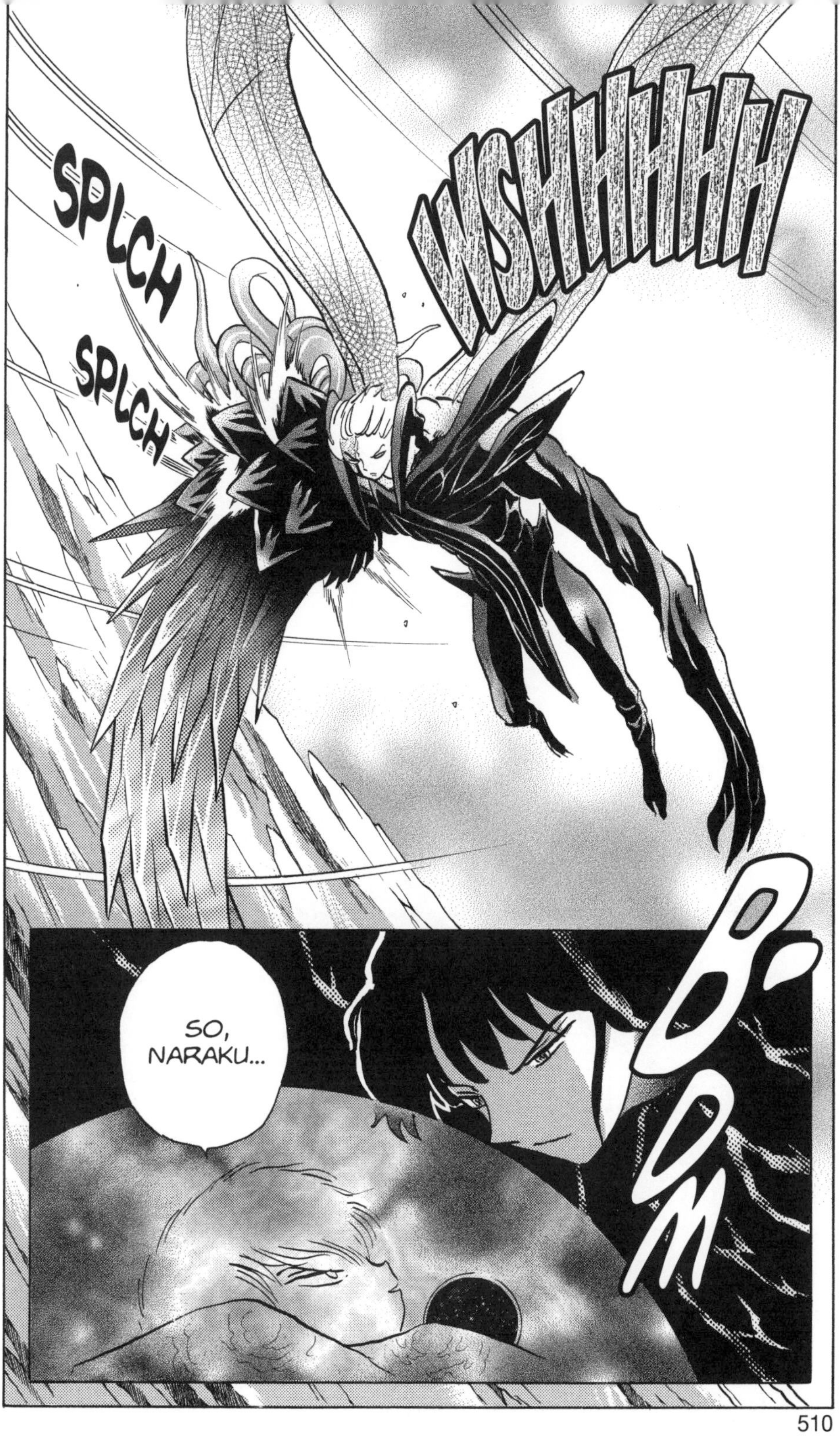
WSHHHHHH
SPLCH
SPLCH
BOOM
SO, NARAKU...

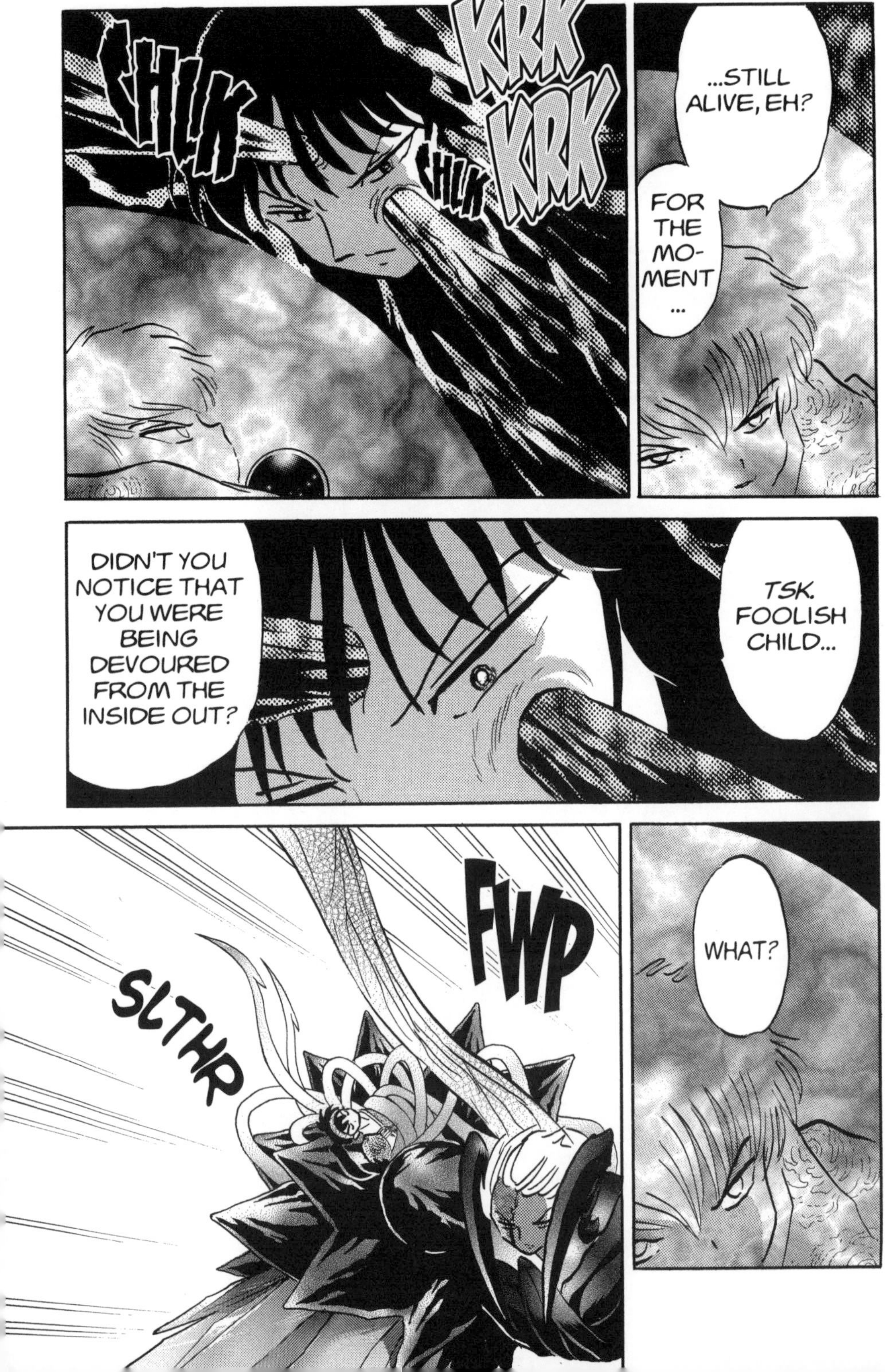
...STILL ALIVE, EH?
FOR THE MOMENT...
KRK KRK
CHLIK
CHLIK
TSK. FOOLISH CHILD...
DIDN'T YOU NOTICE THAT YOU WERE BEING DEVOURED FROM THE INSIDE OUT?
WHAT?
FWP
SLTHR

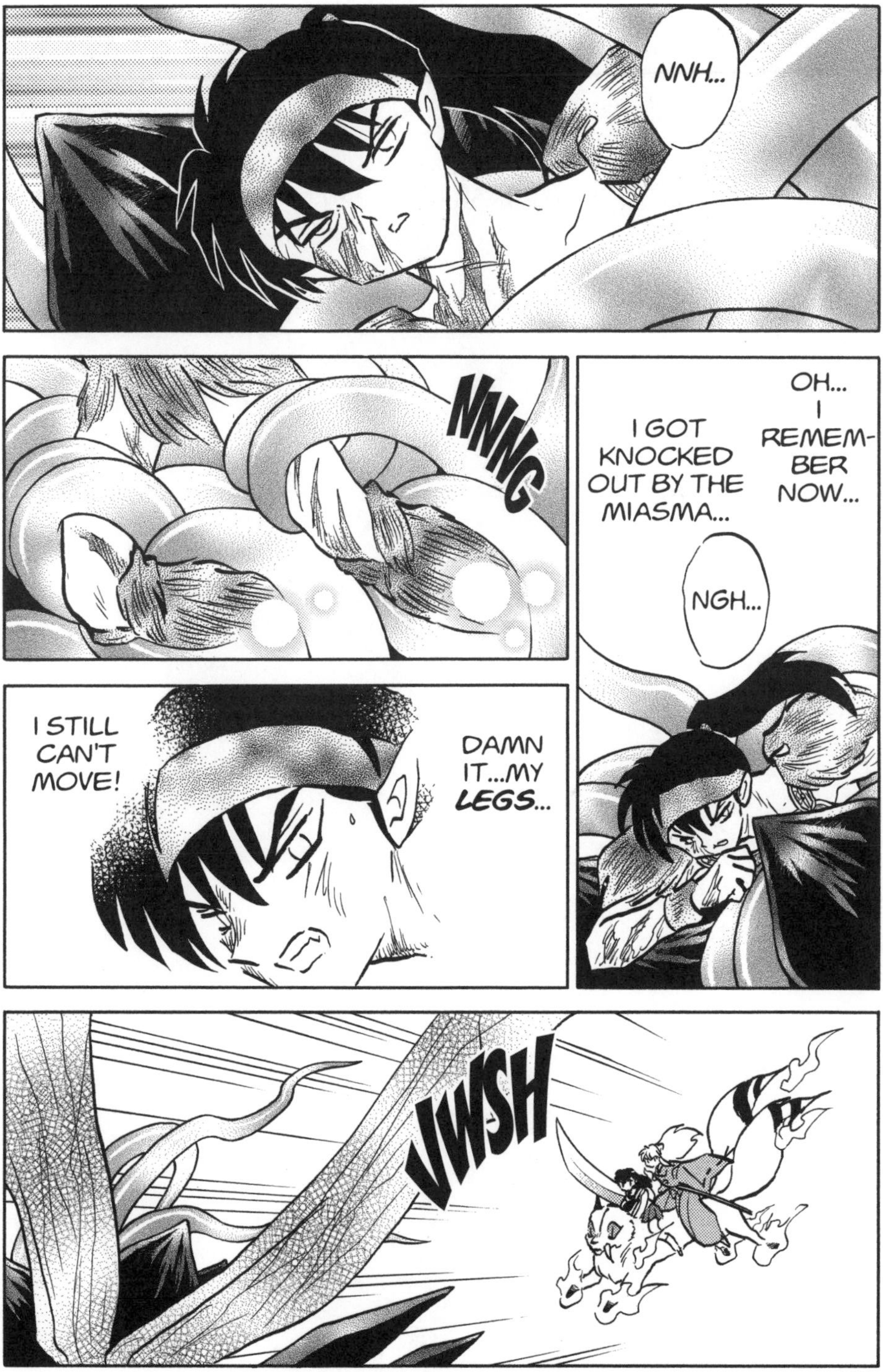
NNH...
OH... I REMEMBER NOW...
I GOT KNOCKED OUT BY THE MIASMA...
NGH...
NNNG
DAMN IT...MY *LEGS*...
I STILL CAN'T MOVE!
VWSH

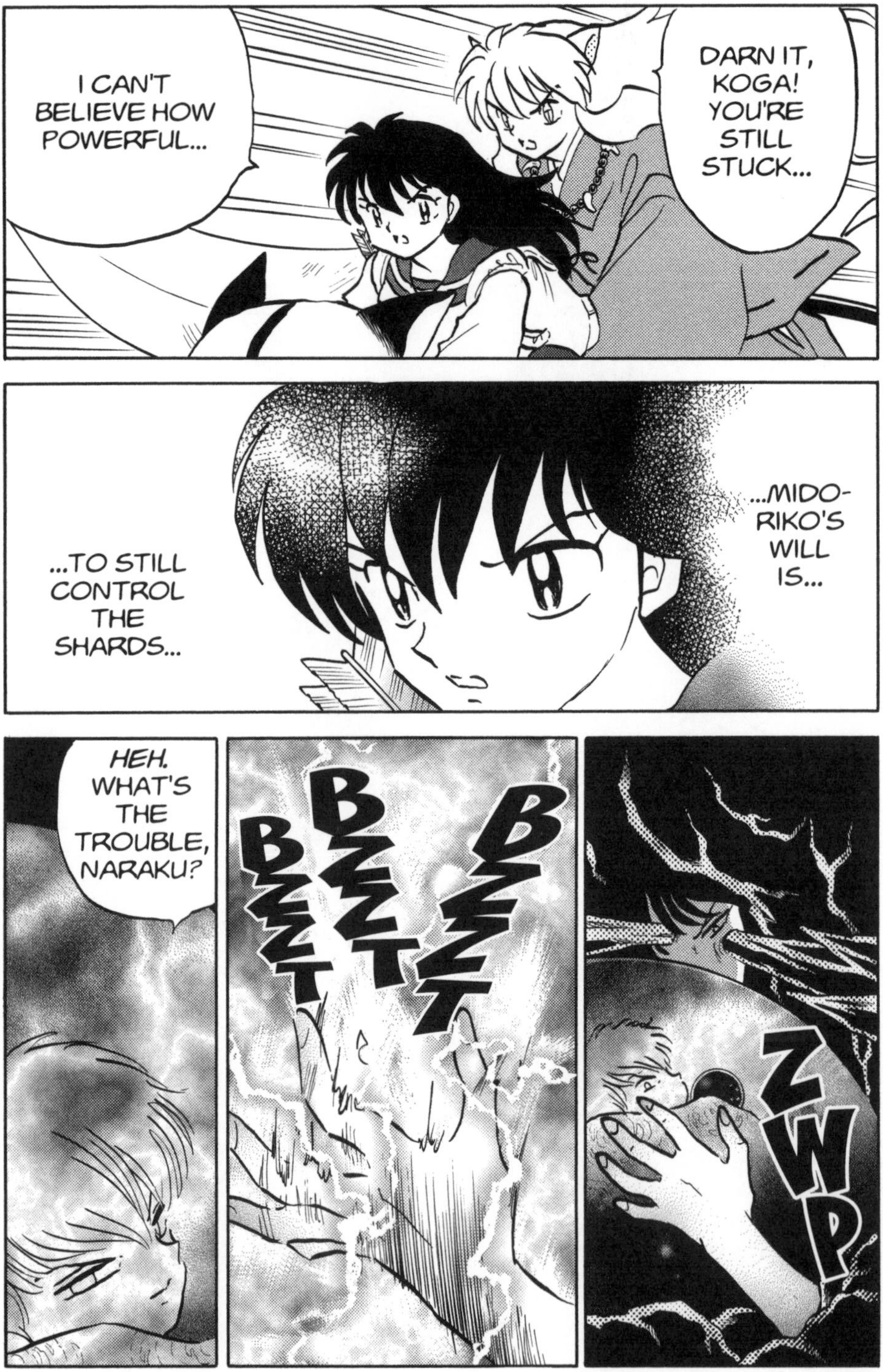
DARN IT, KOGA! YOU'RE STILL STUCK...
I CAN'T BELIEVE HOW POWERFUL...
...MIDO-RIKO'S WILL IS...
...TO STILL CONTROL THE SHARDS...
ZWP
BZZT BZZT BZZT
HEH. WHAT'S THE TROUBLE, NARAKU?

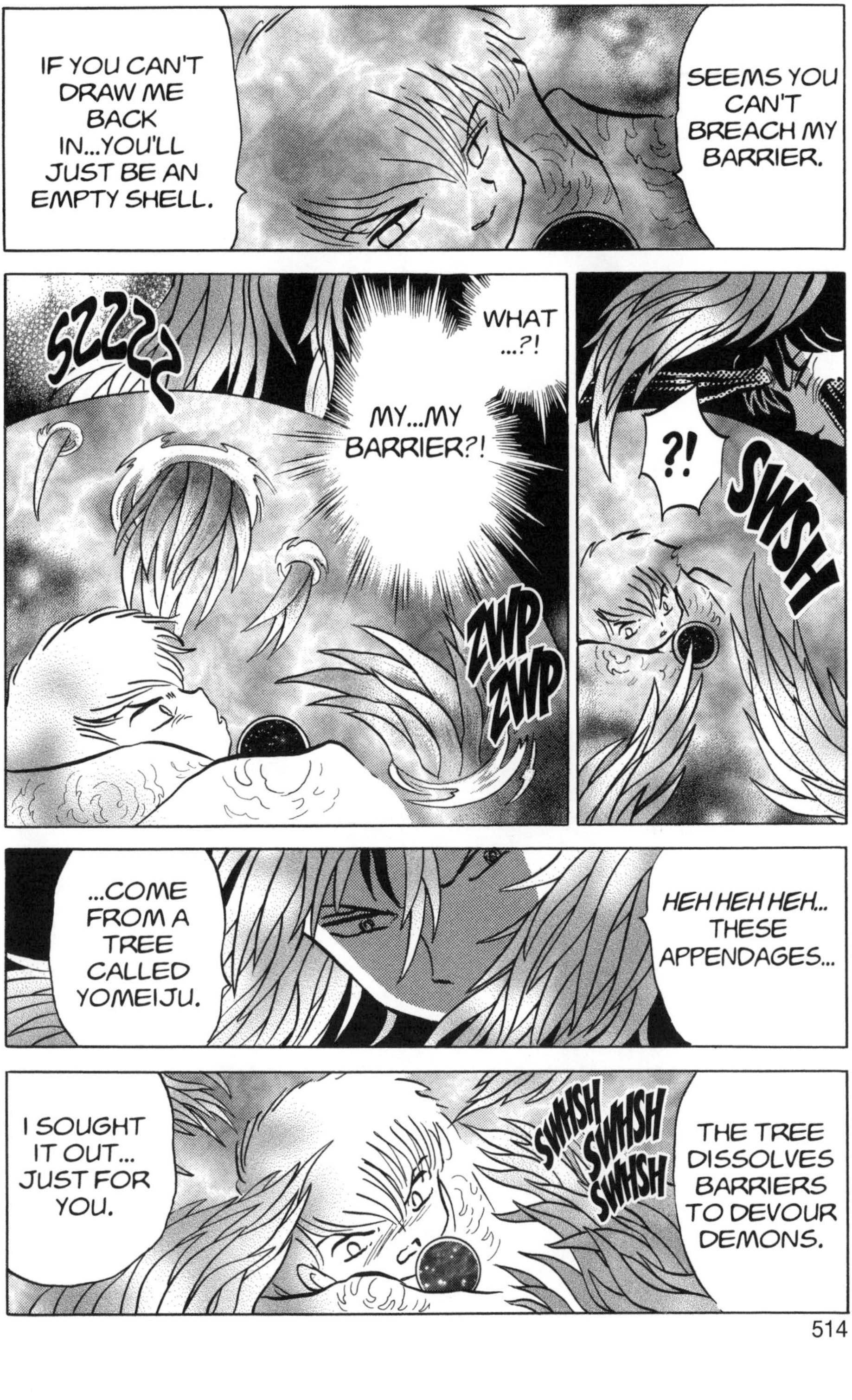
SEEMS YOU CAN'T BREACH MY BARRIER.
IF YOU CAN'T DRAW ME BACK IN...YOU'LL JUST BE AN EMPTY SHELL.
?!
SWSH
WHAT ...?!
SZZZZ
MY...MY BARRIER?!
ZWP ZWP
HEH HEH HEH... THESE APPENDAGES...
...COME FROM A TREE CALLED YOMEIJU.
THE TREE DISSOLVES BARRIERS TO DEVOUR DEMONS.
SWHSH SWHSH SWHSH
I SOUGHT IT OUT... JUST FOR YOU.

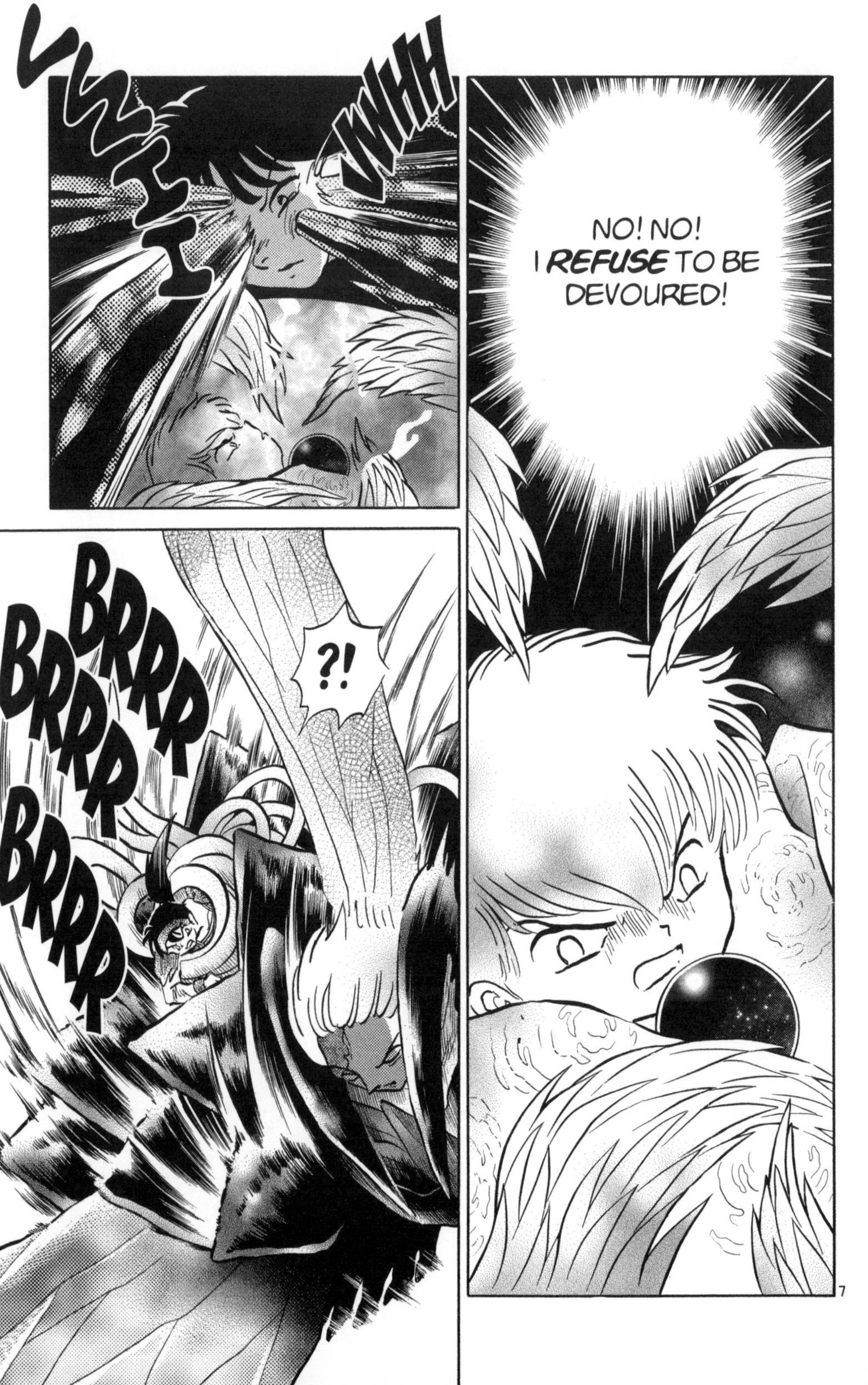
NO! NO!
I **REFUSE** TO BE
DEVOURED!
VWHH
BRRRR
BRRRR
BRRRR
?!

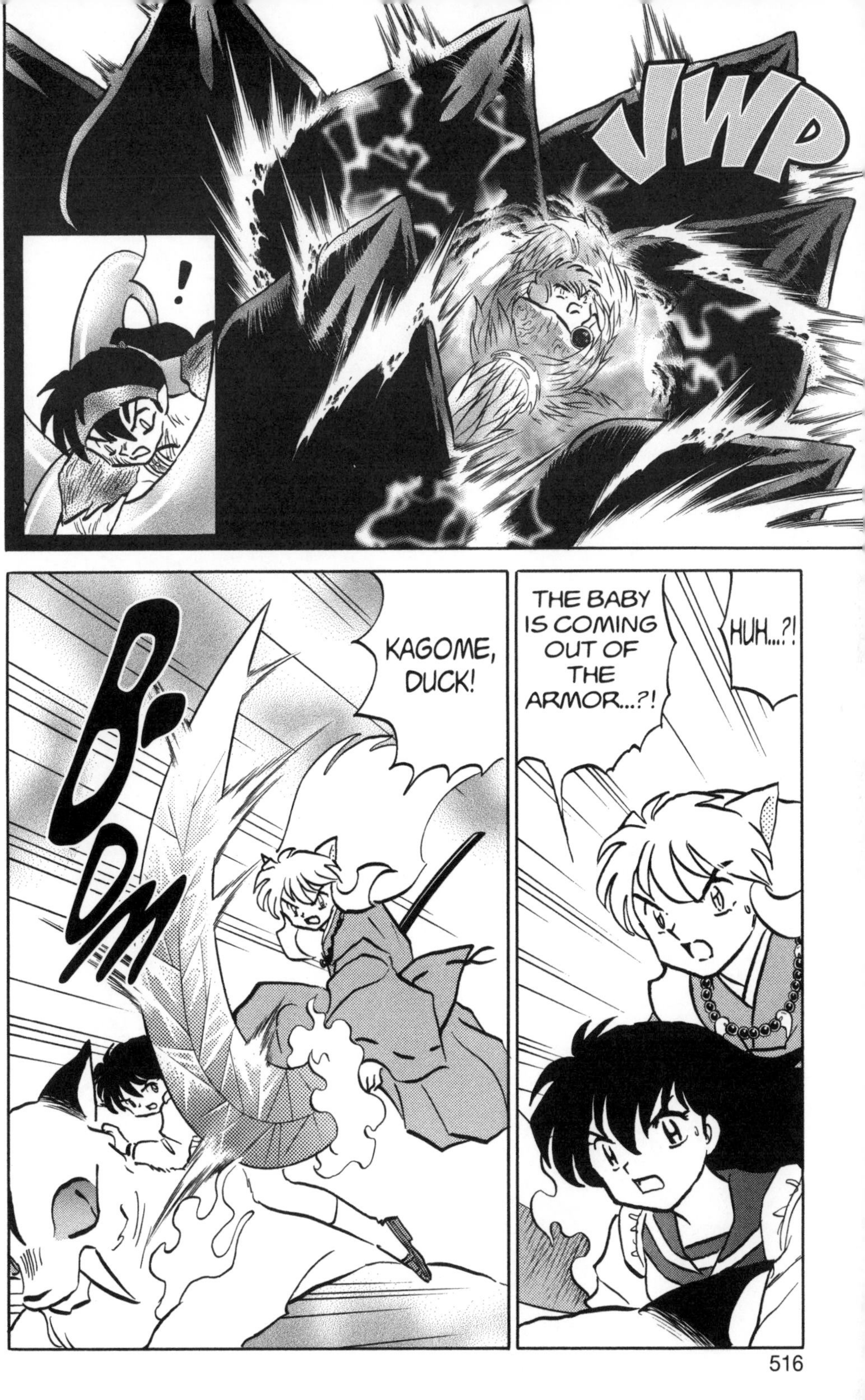
VWP
!
HUH...?!
THE BABY IS COMING OUT OF THE ARMOR...?!
KAGOME, DUCK!
BDOM

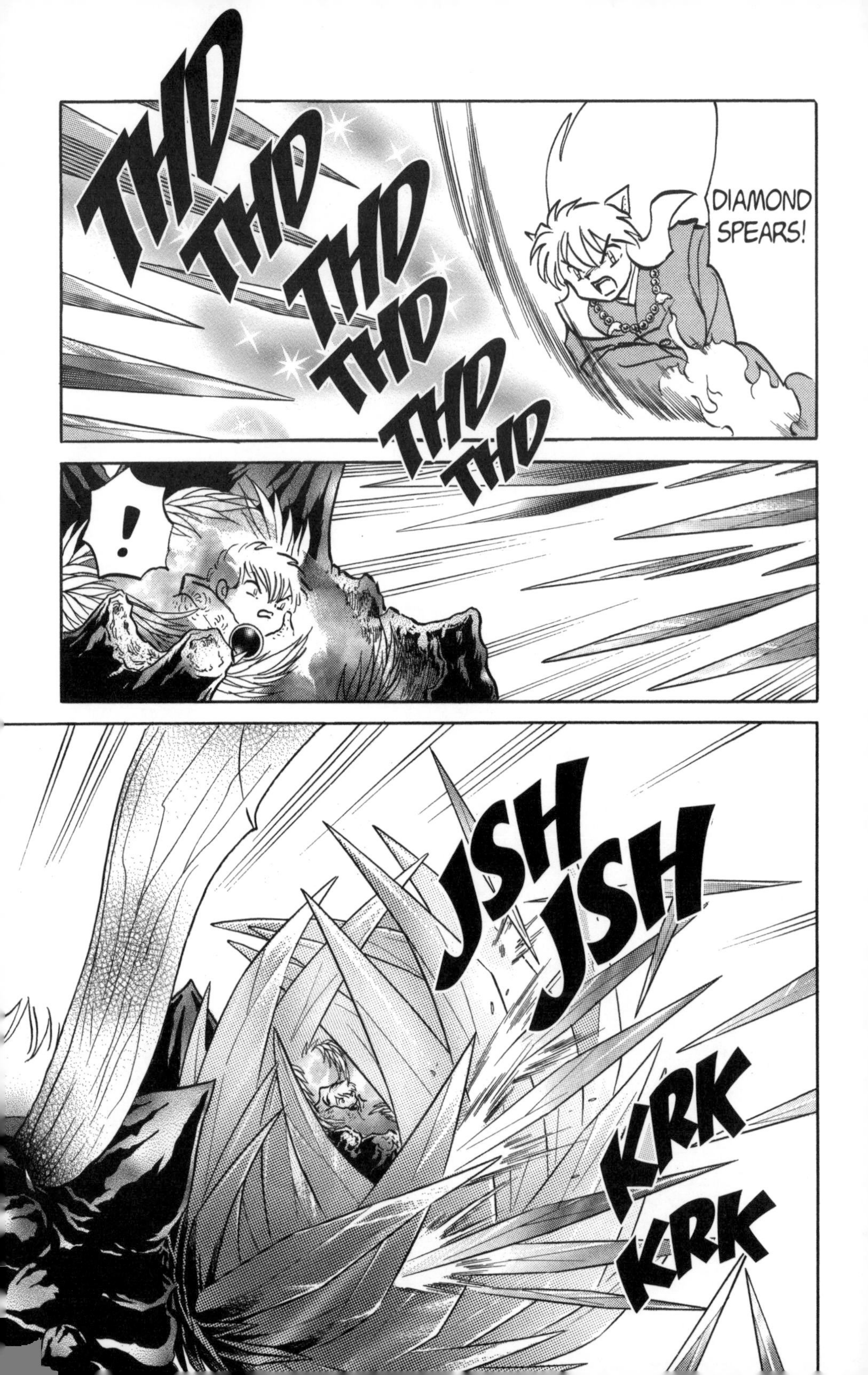
DIAMOND SPEARS!
THD THD THD THD THD THD
!
JSH JSH
KRK KRK

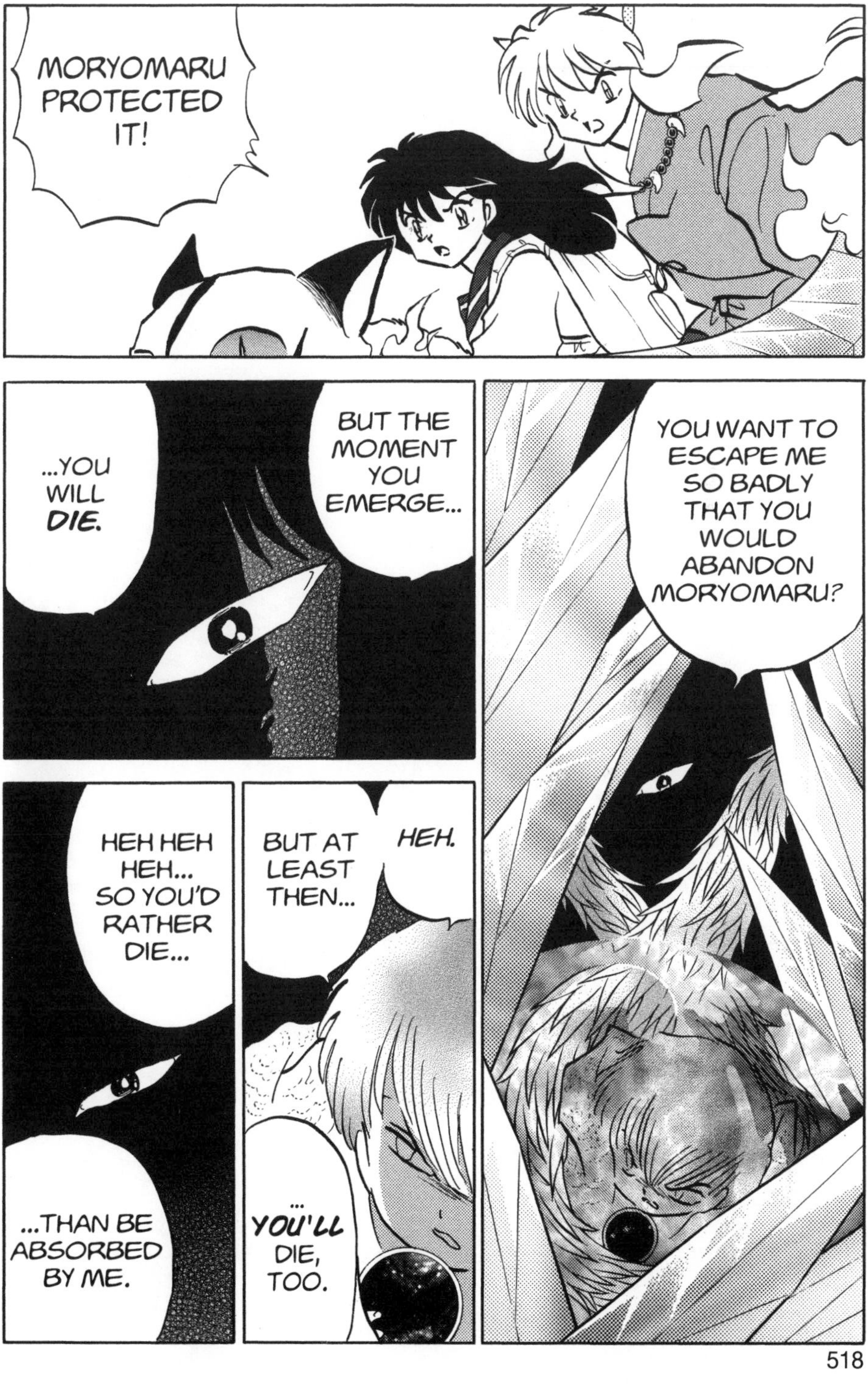
MORYOMARU PROTECTED IT!
YOU WANT TO ESCAPE ME SO BADLY THAT YOU WOULD ABANDON MORYOMARU?
BUT THE MOMENT YOU EMERGE...
...YOU WILL **DIE.**
HEH.
BUT AT LEAST THEN...
...**YOU'LL** DIE, TOO.
HEH HEH HEH... SO YOU'D RATHER DIE...
...THAN BE ABSORBED BY ME.

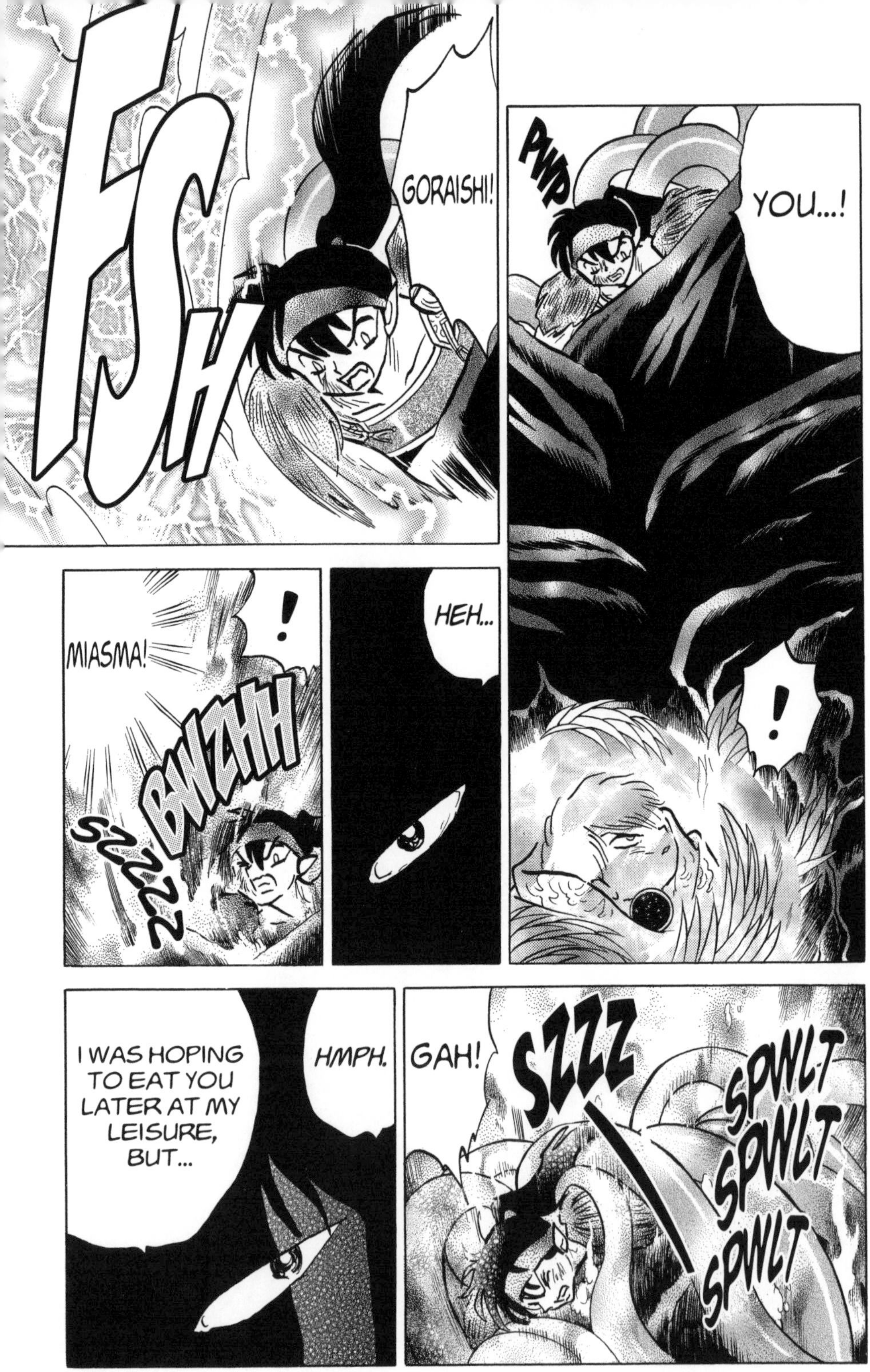
PWP
YOU...!
!
FSH
GORAISHI!
HEH...
!
MIASMA!
BWZHH
SZZZZ
GAH!
SZZZ
SPWLT
SPWLT
SPWLT
HMPH.
I WAS HOPING TO EAT YOU LATER AT MY LEISURE, BUT...

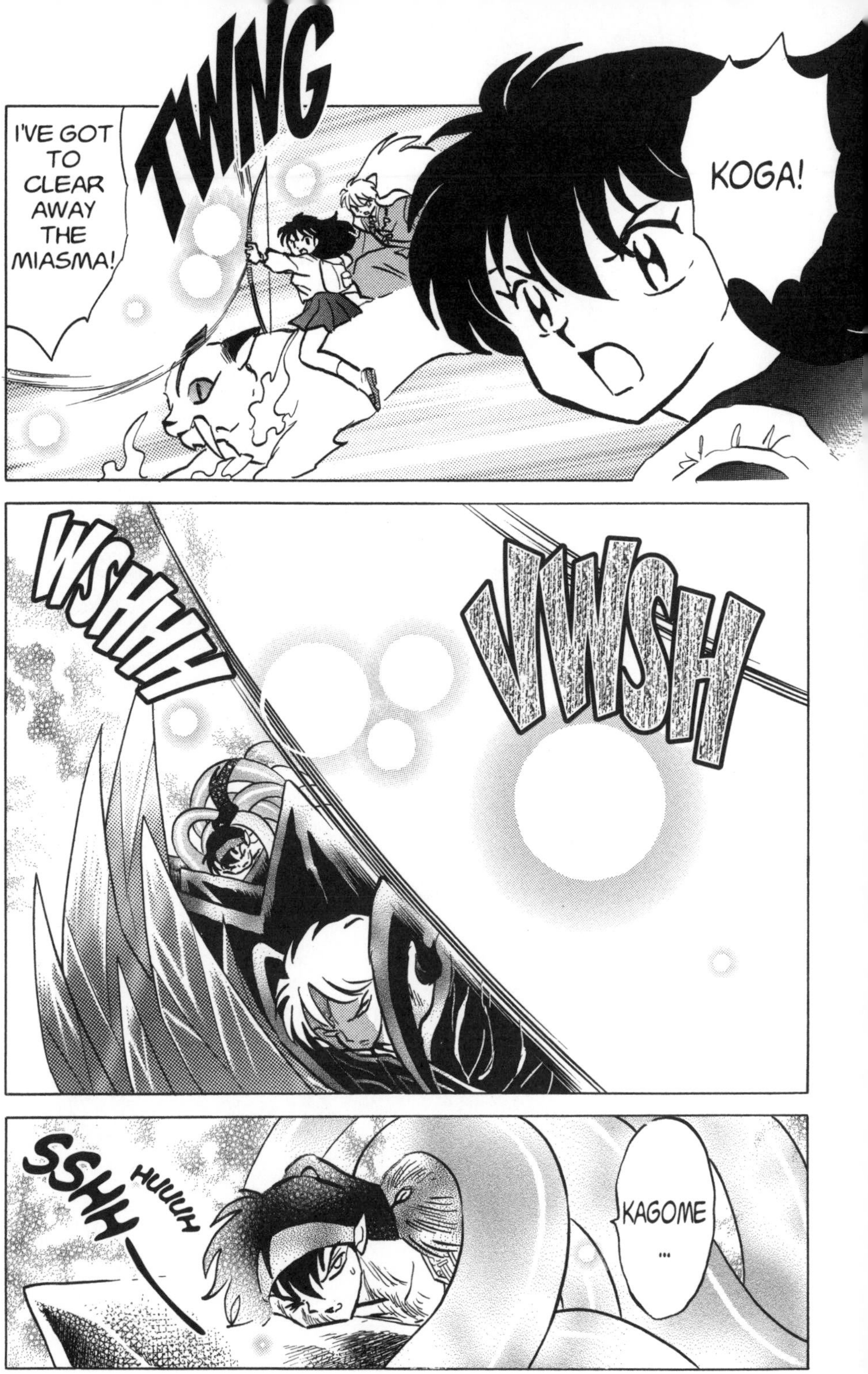
KOGA!
TWING
I'VE GOT TO CLEAR AWAY THE MIASMA!
VWSH
WSHHH
KAGOME ...
HUUUH
SSHH

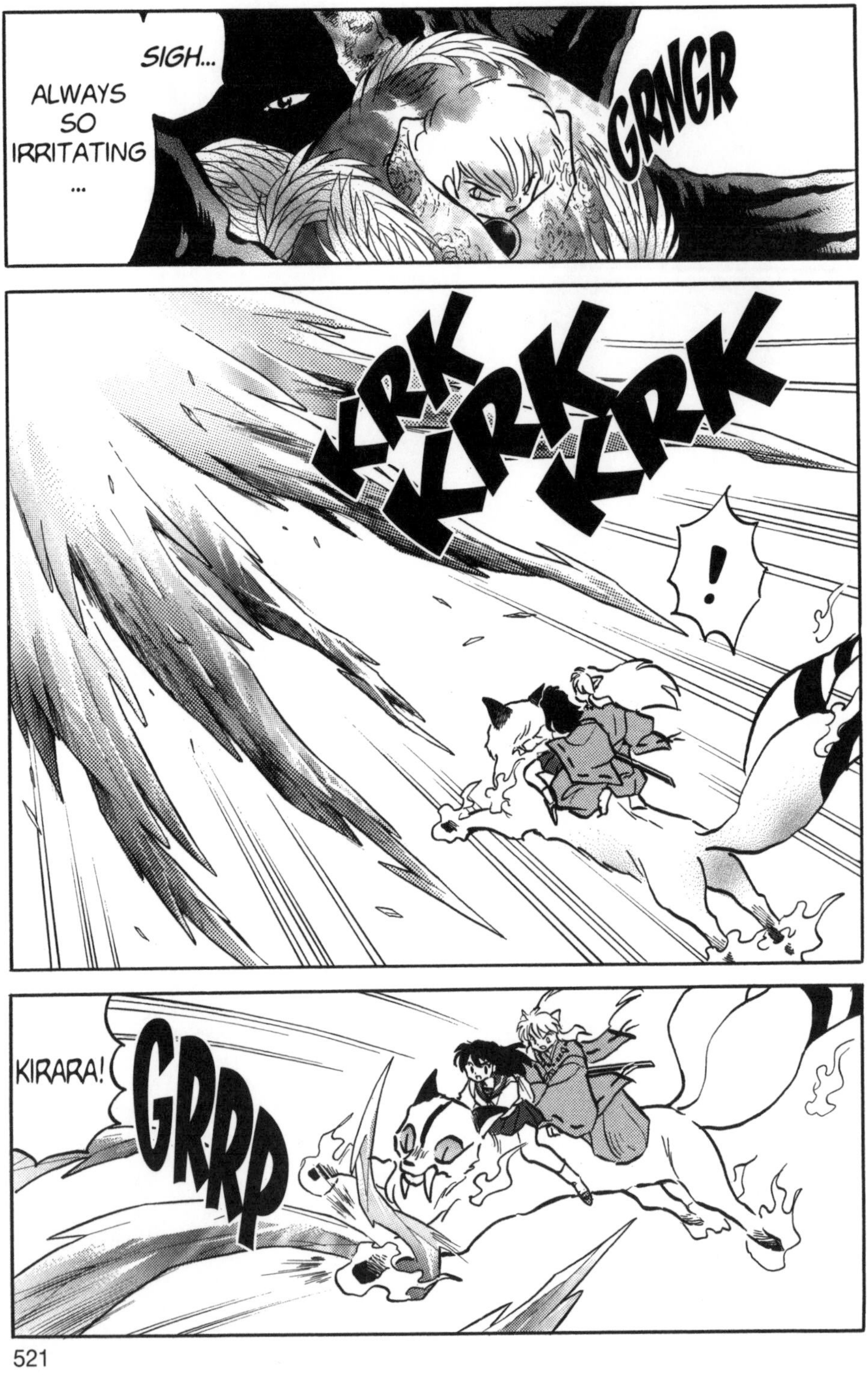
GRNGR
SIGH...
ALWAYS SO IRRITATING ...
KRK KRK KRK
!
GRRP
KIRARA!

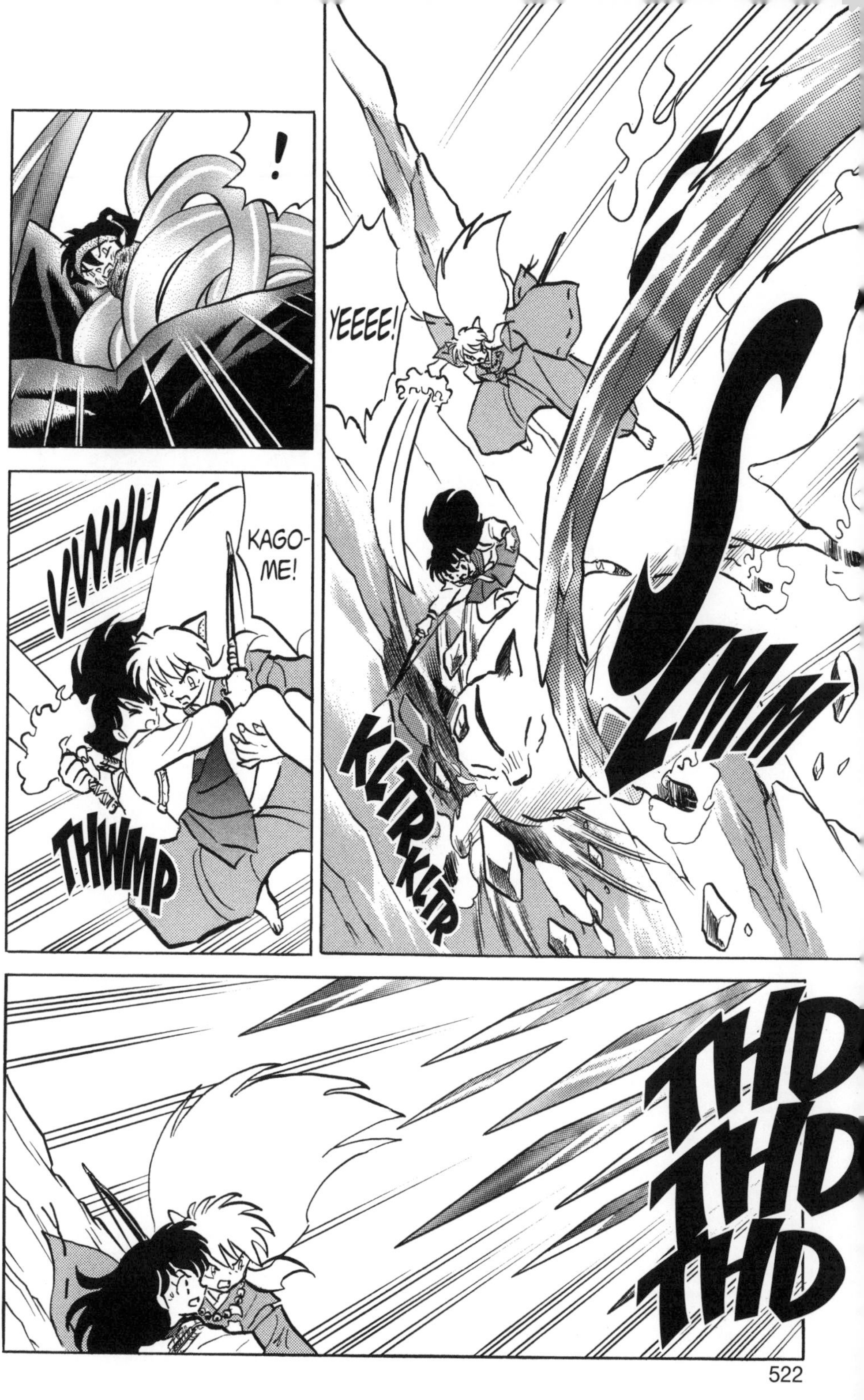
YEEEE!
KLTR KLTR
!
KAGO-
ME!
VWHH
THWMP
THD
THD
THD

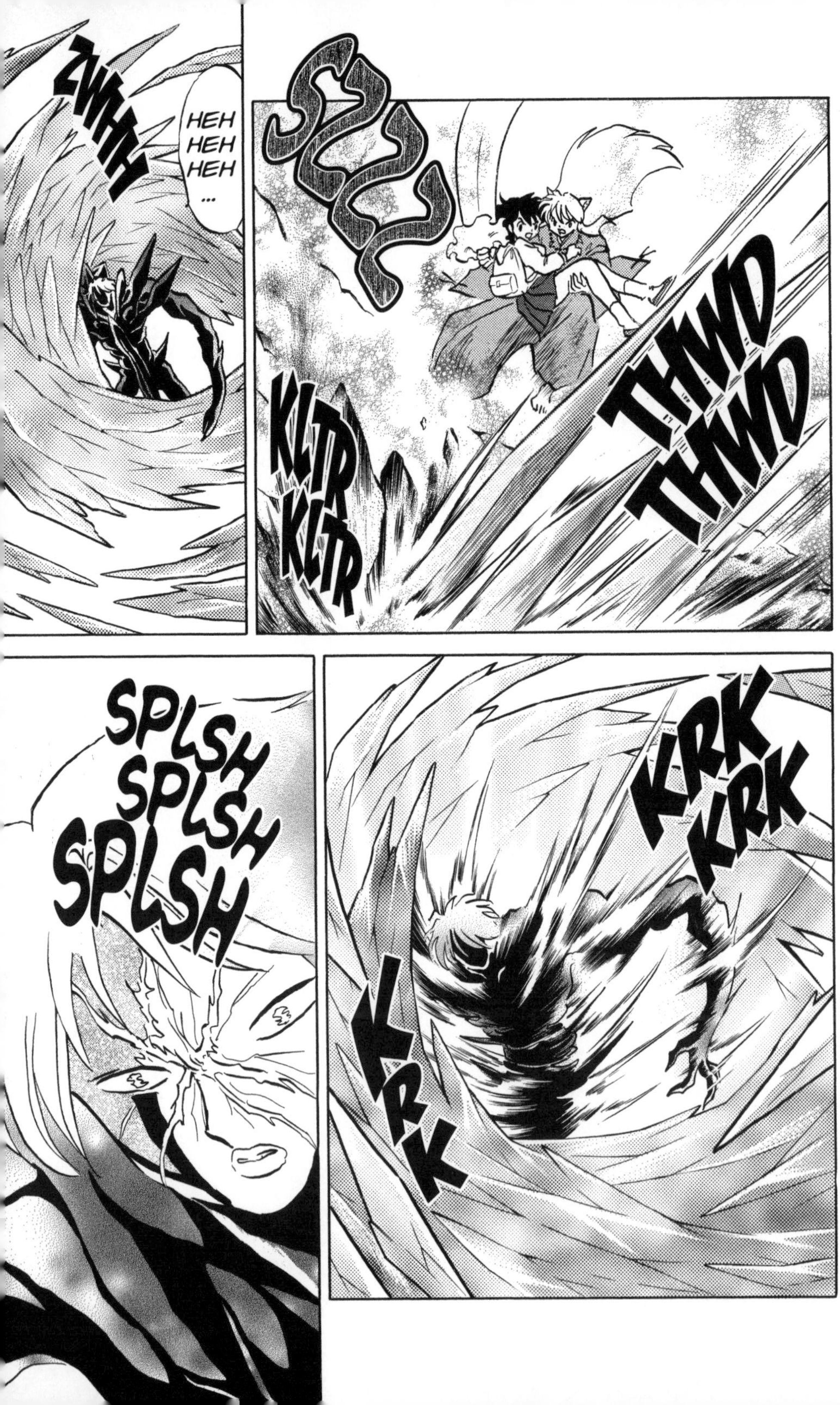
THWD THWD
KLTR KLTR
ZWHH
HEH HEH HEH ...
KRK KRK
KRK
SPLSH SPLSH SPLSH

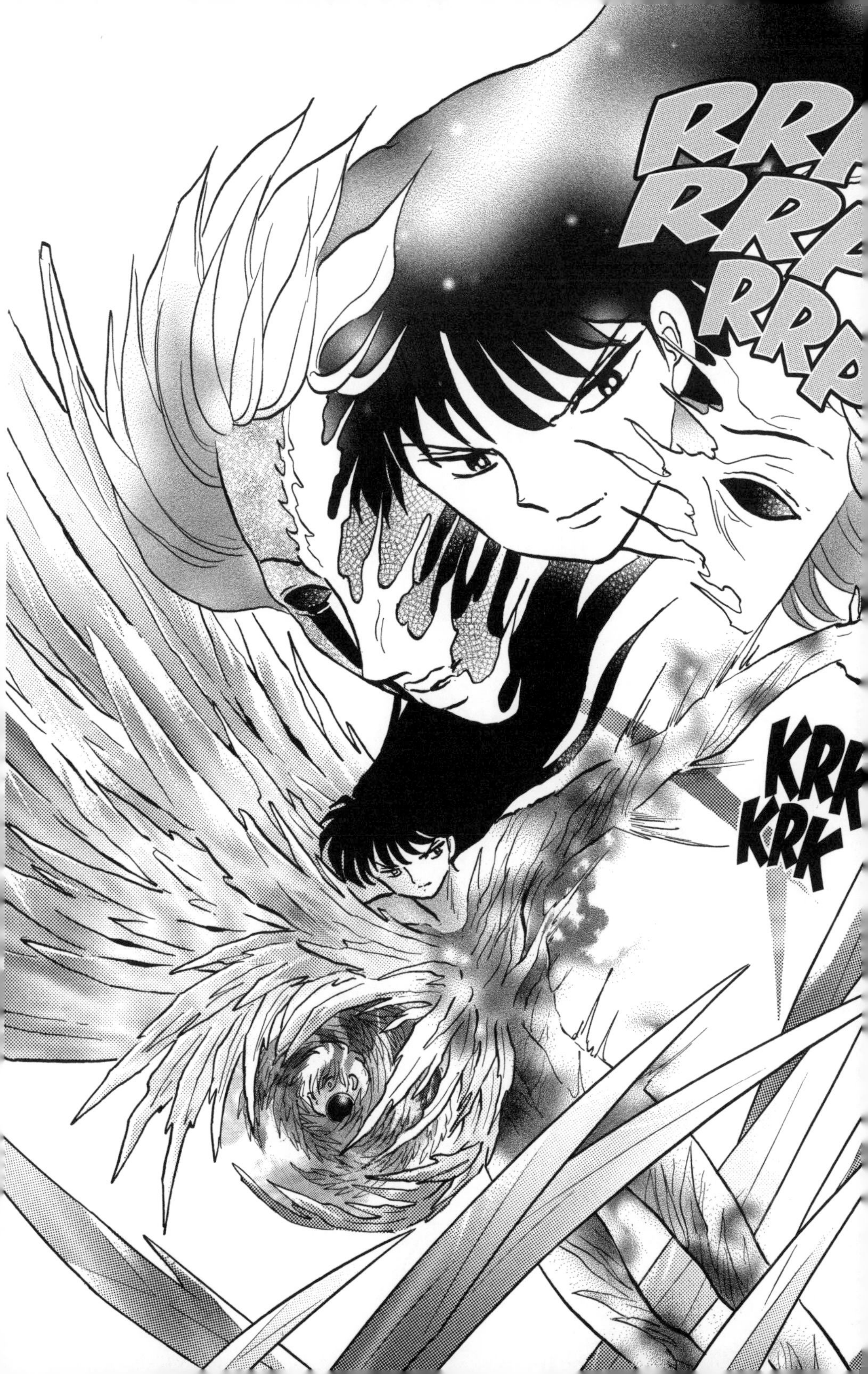
RRR RRR RRR
KRK KRK

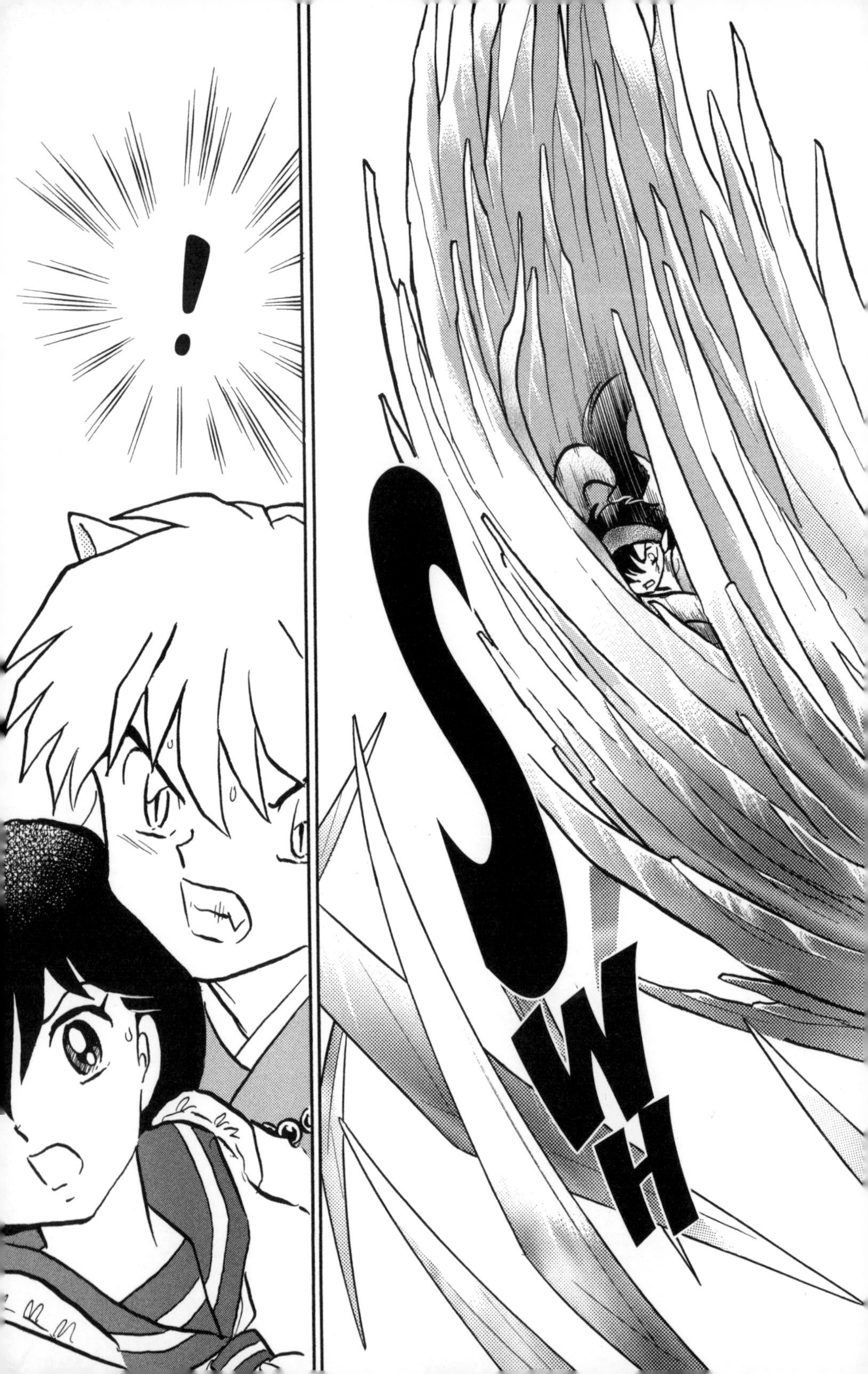
SWH
!

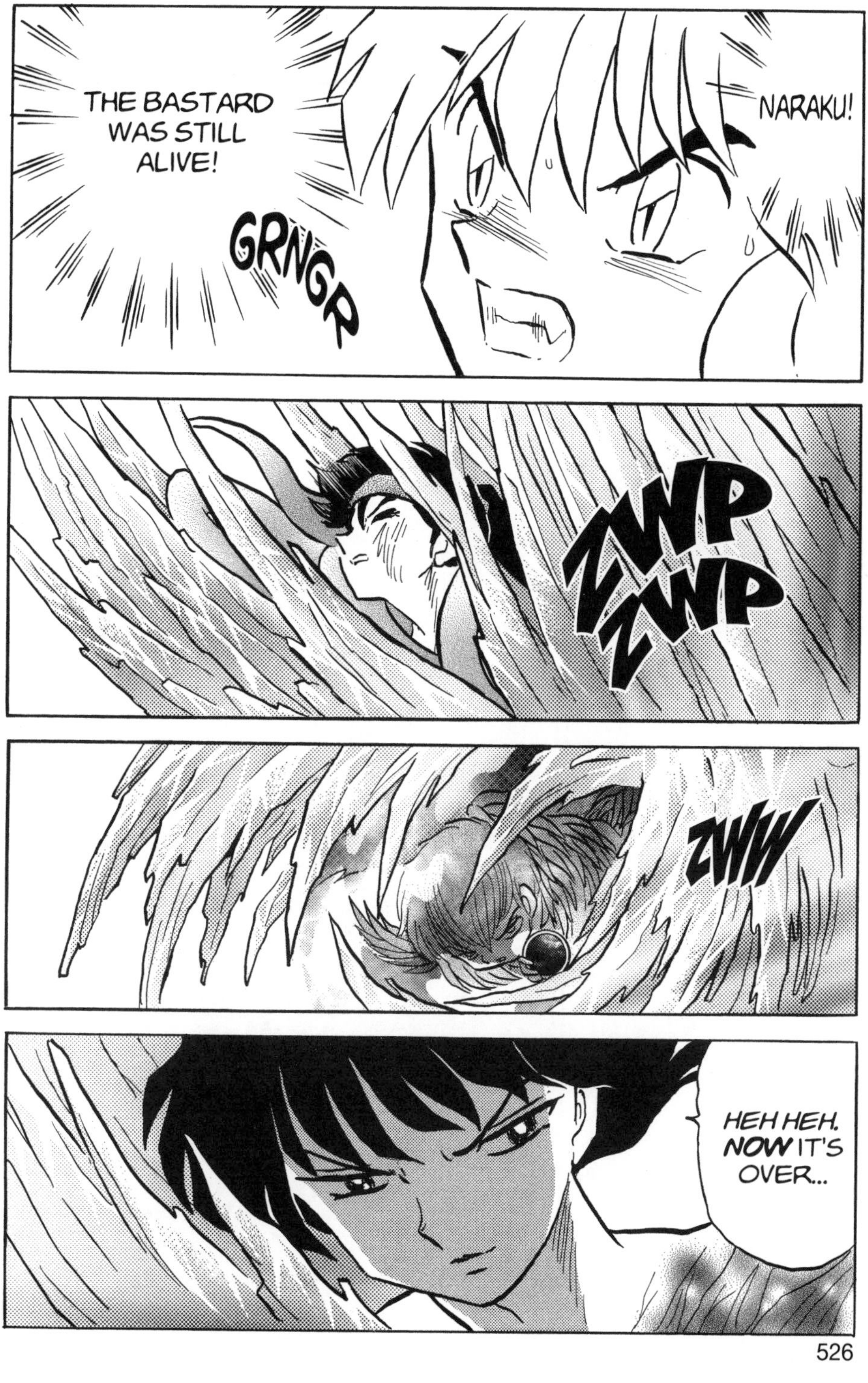
NARAKU!
THE BASTARD WAS STILL ALIVE!
GRNGR
ZWP ZWP
ZWW
HEH HEH. NOW IT'S OVER...

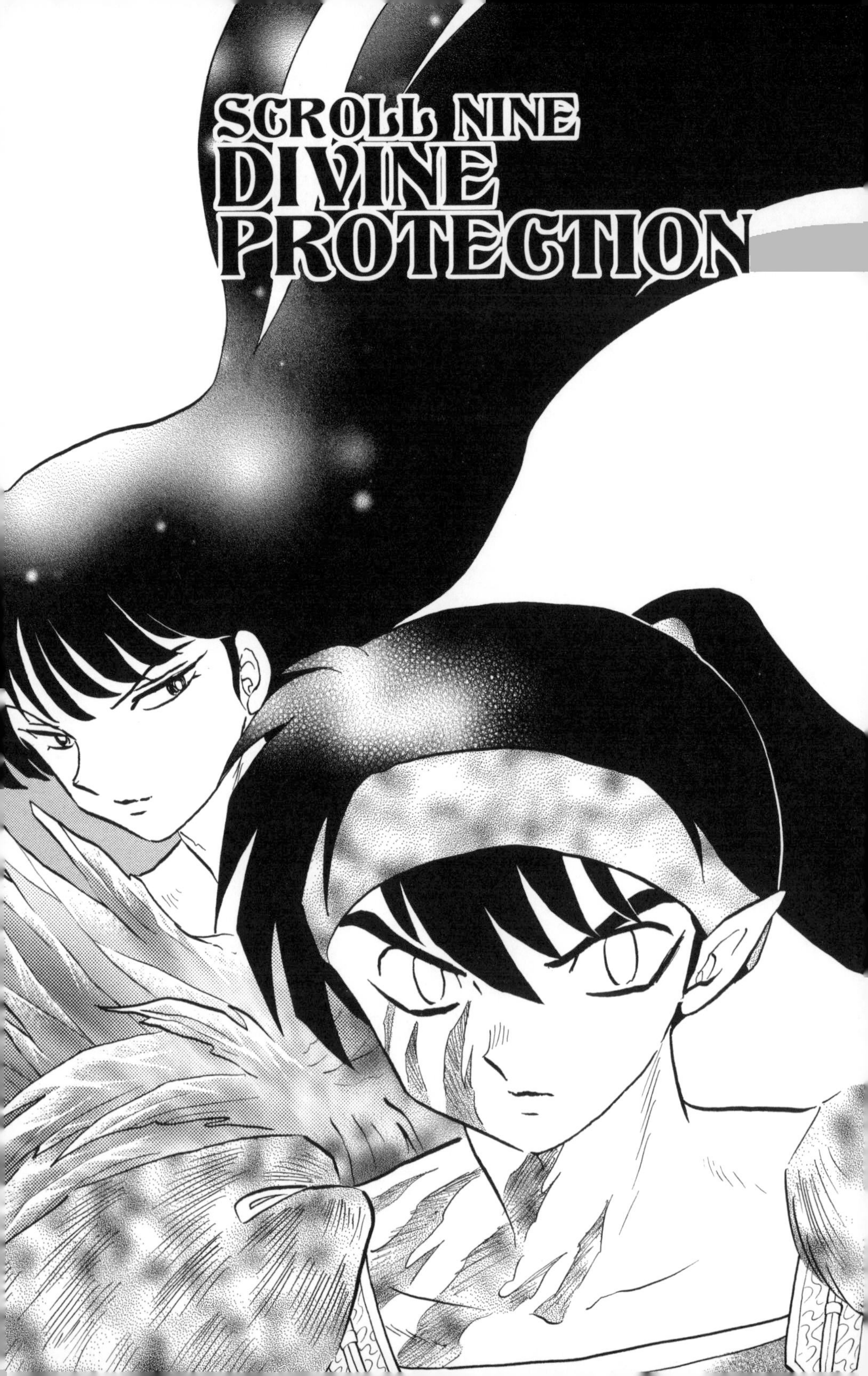
SCROLL NINE
DIVINE PROTECTION

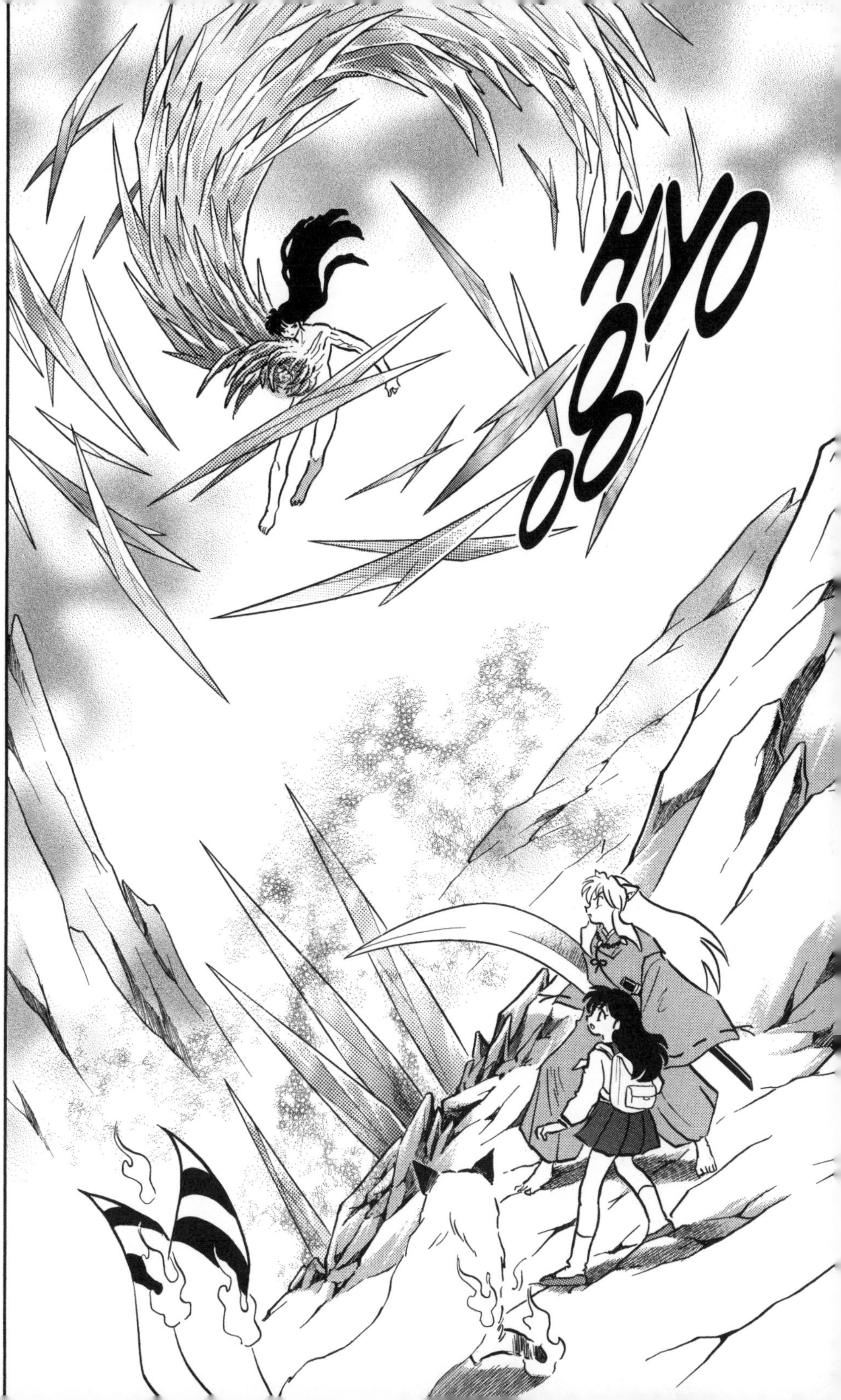
HYOOOOO

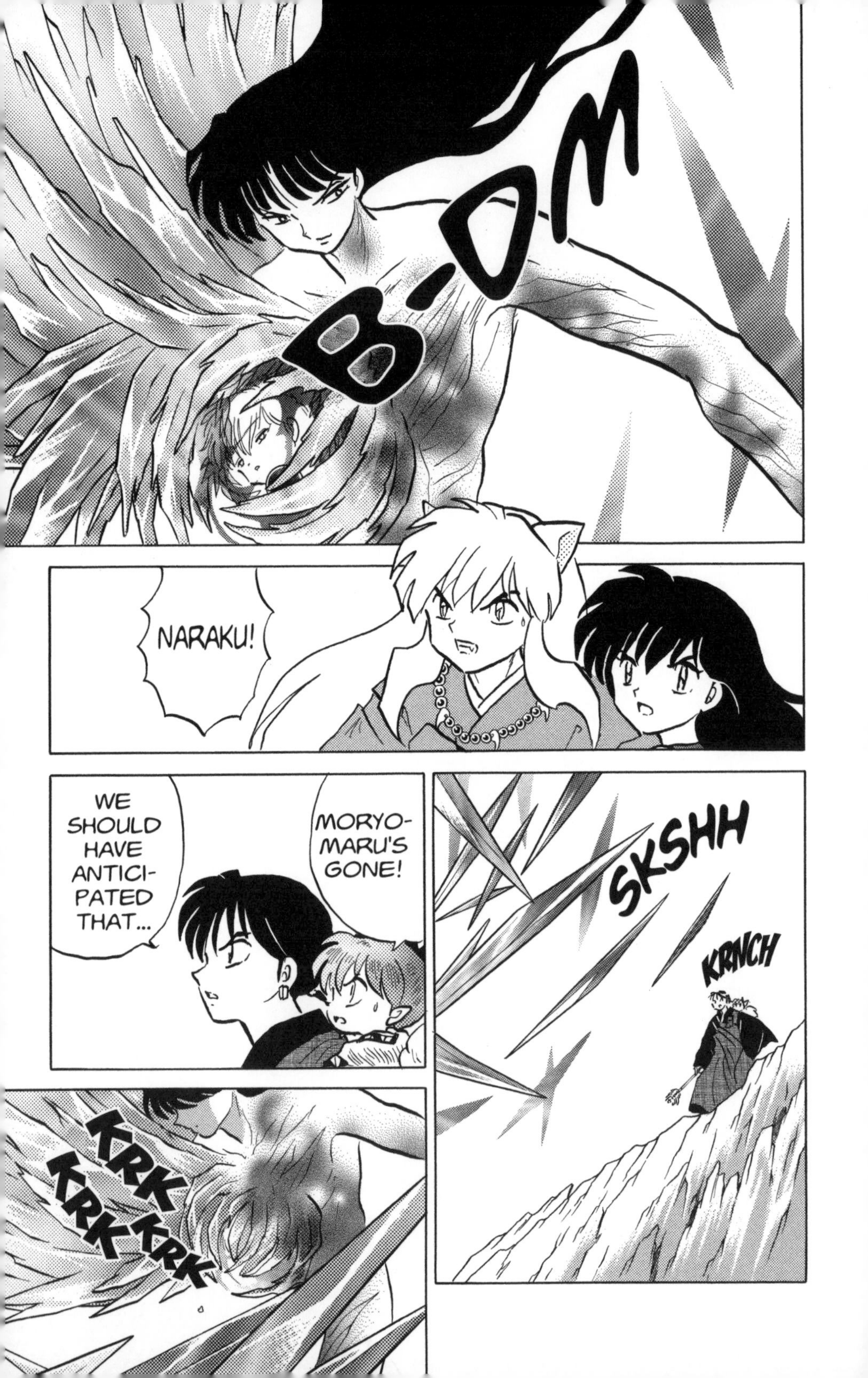
B-DOM
NARAKU!
SKSHH
KRNCH
MORYO-MARU'S GONE!
WE SHOULD HAVE ANTICI-PATED THAT...
KRK KRK KRK KRK

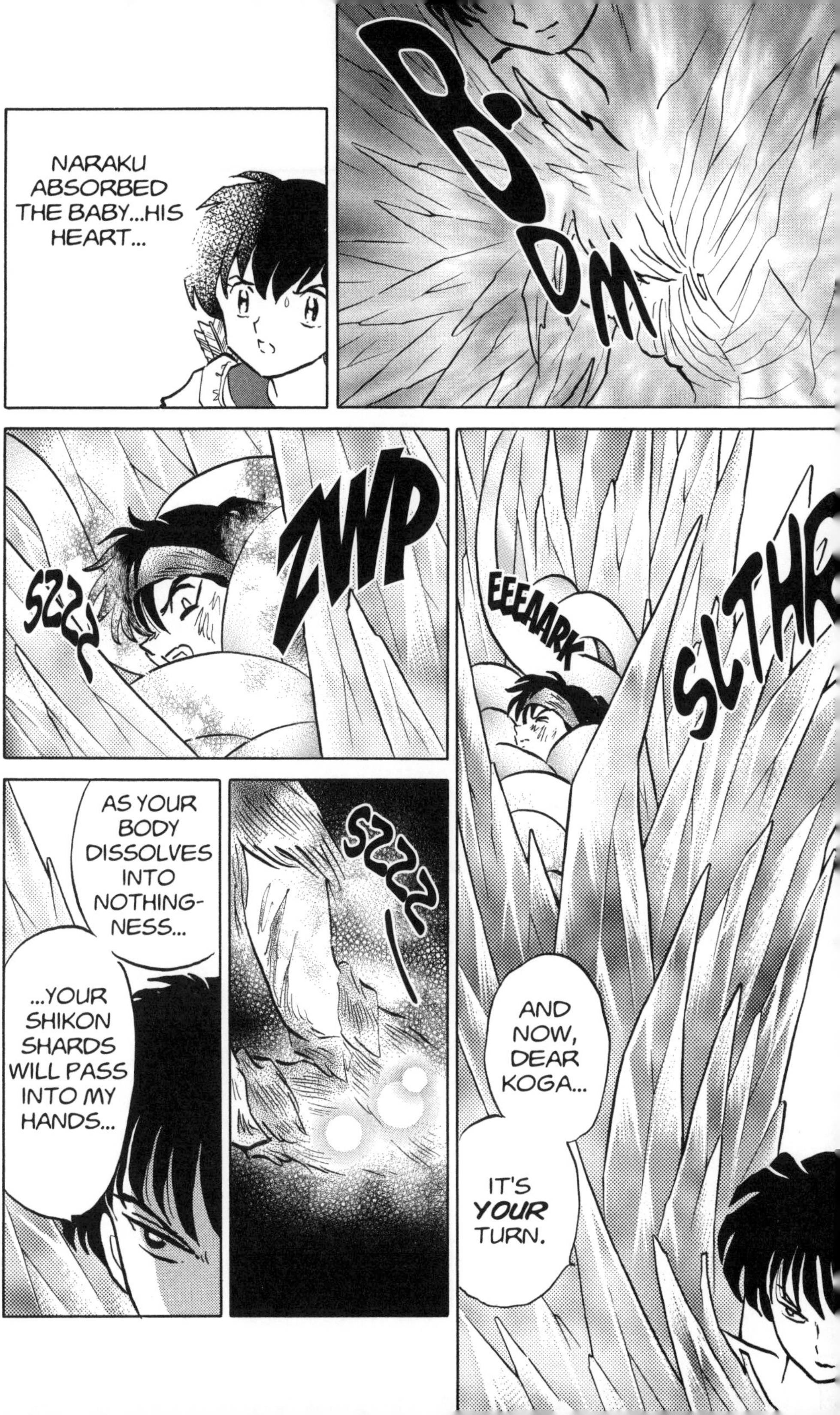
NARAKU ABSORBED THE BABY...HIS HEART...
EEEAARK
SLTHR
AND NOW, DEAR KOGA...
IT'S ***YOUR*** TURN.
ZWP
SZZZ
SZZZZ
AS YOUR BODY DISSOLVES INTO NOTHINGNESS...
...YOUR SHIKON SHARDS WILL PASS INTO MY HANDS...

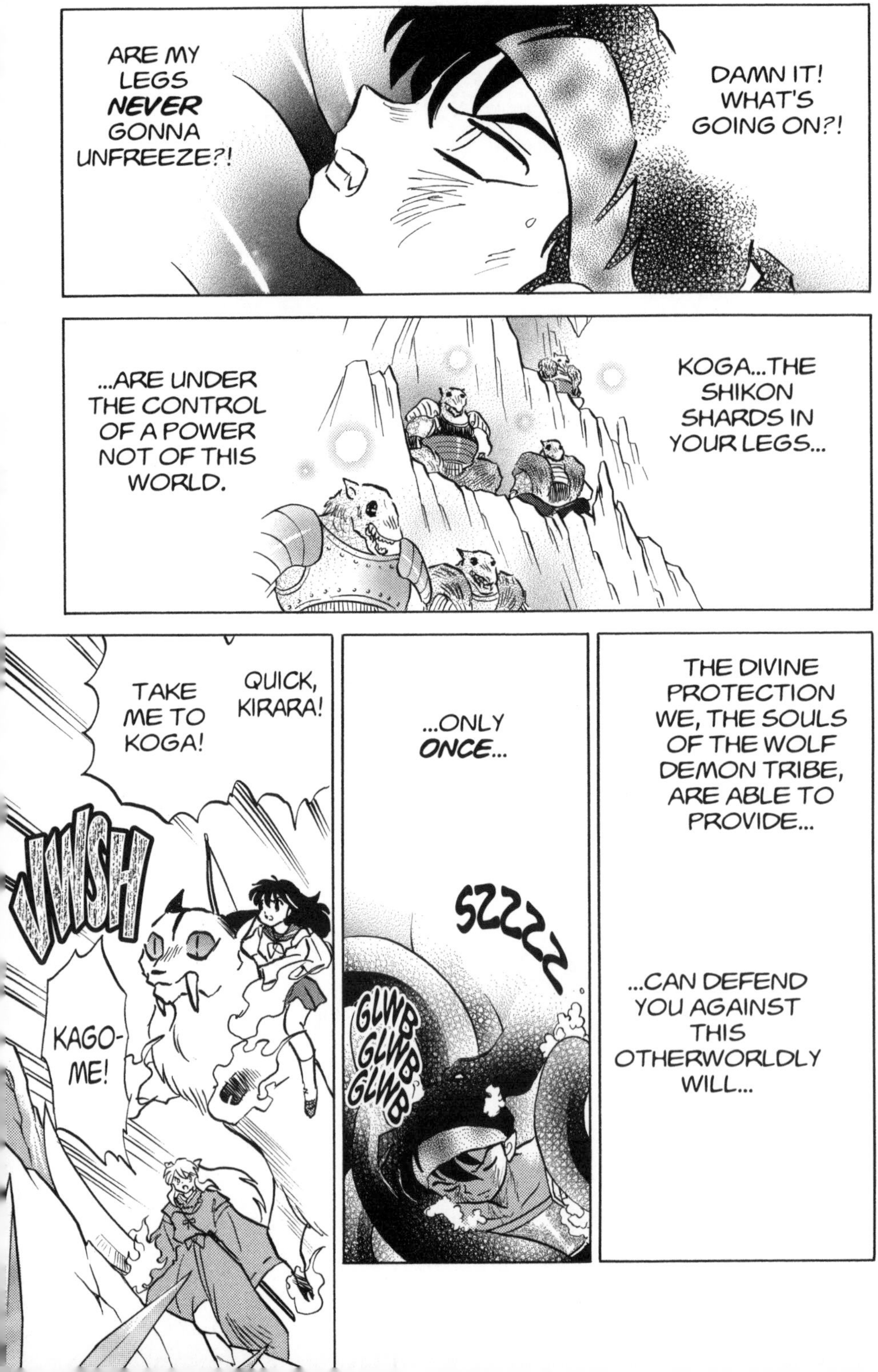

DAMN IT! WHAT'S GOING ON?!
ARE MY LEGS **NEVER** GONNA UNFREEZE?!
KOGA...THE SHIKON SHARDS IN YOUR LEGS...
...ARE UNDER THE CONTROL OF A POWER NOT OF THIS WORLD.
THE DIVINE PROTECTION WE, THE SOULS OF THE WOLF DEMON TRIBE, ARE ABLE TO PROVIDE...
...CAN DEFEND YOU AGAINST THIS OTHERWORLDLY WILL...
...ONLY **ONCE**...
SZZZZ
GLWB GLWB GLWB
QUICK, KIRARA!
TAKE ME TO KOGA!
JWSH
KAGO-ME!

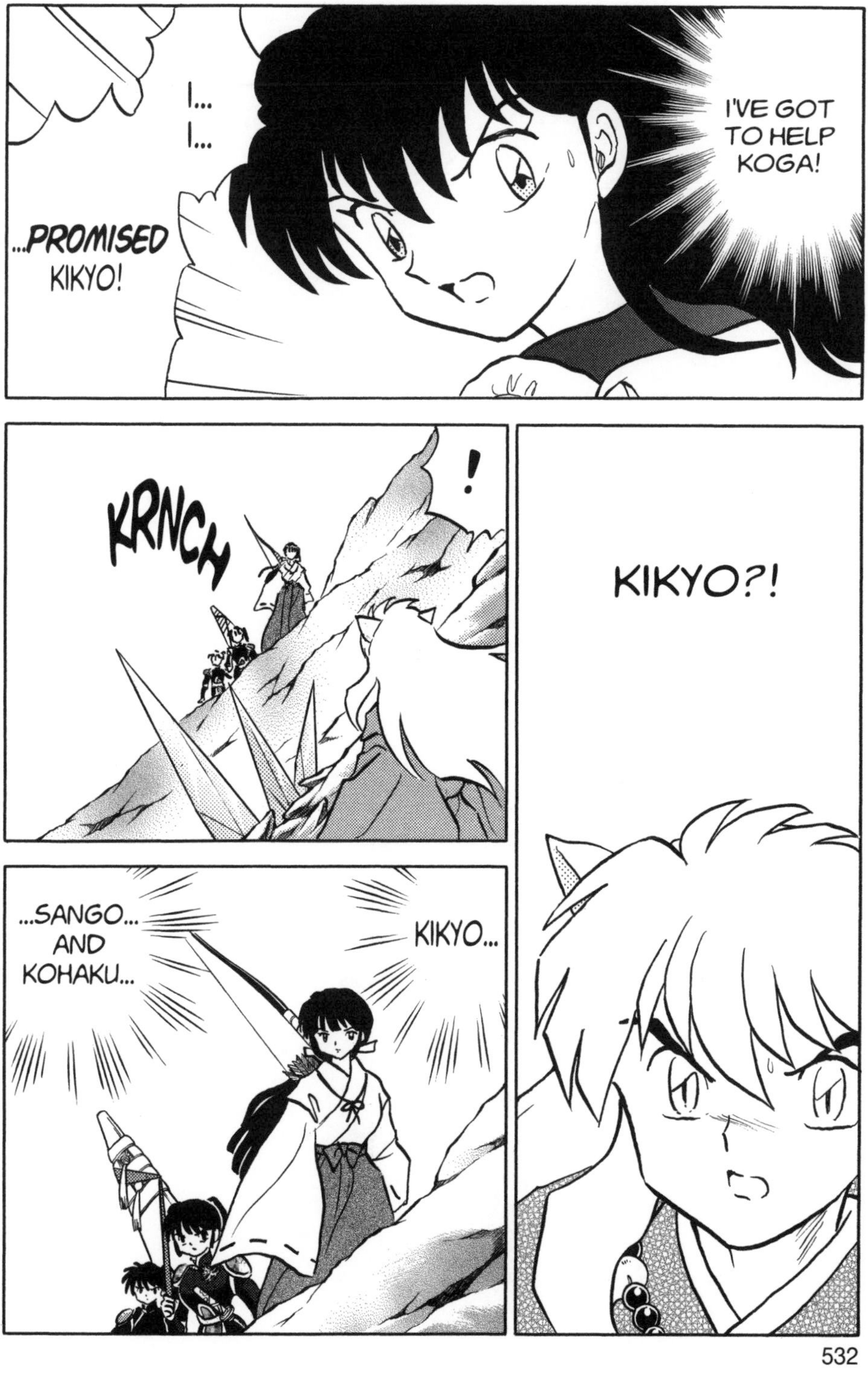
I'VE GOT TO HELP KOGA!
I... I...
...PROMISED KIKYO!
KIKYO?!
!
KRNCH
KIKYO...
...SANGO... AND KOHAKU...

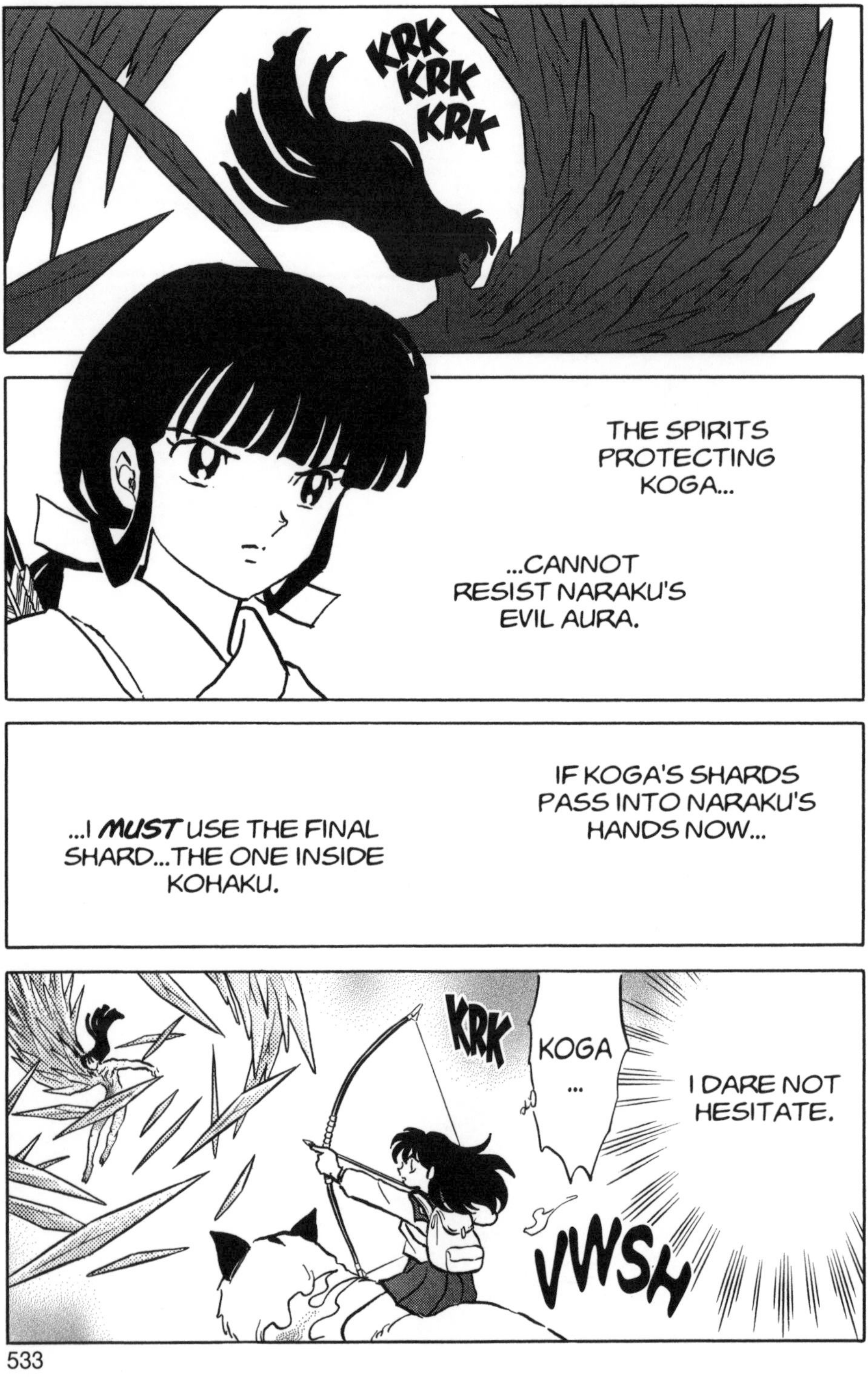
KRK KRK KRK
THE SPIRITS PROTECTING KOGA...
...CANNOT RESIST NARAKU'S EVIL AURA.
IF KOGA'S SHARDS PASS INTO NARAKU'S HANDS NOW...
...I *MUST* USE THE FINAL SHARD...THE ONE INSIDE KOHAKU.
I DARE NOT HESITATE.
KOGA ...
KRK
VWSH

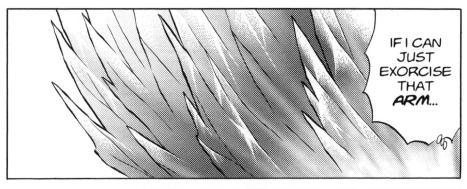

IF I CAN JUST EXORCISE THAT *ARM*...

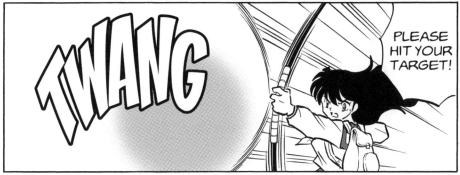

TWANG

PLEASE HIT YOUR TARGET!

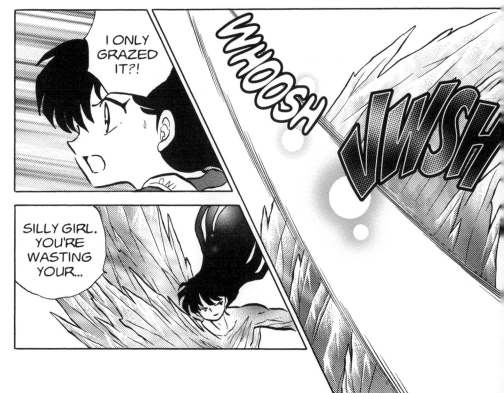

I ONLY GRAZED IT?!

WHOOSH

JWSH

SILLY GIRL. YOU'RE WASTING YOUR...

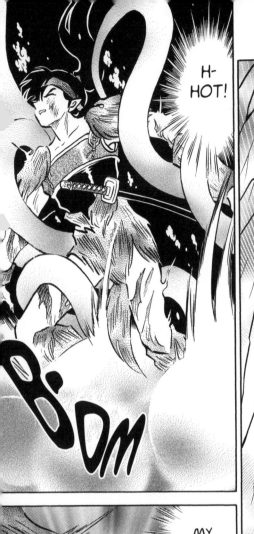

H-HOT!

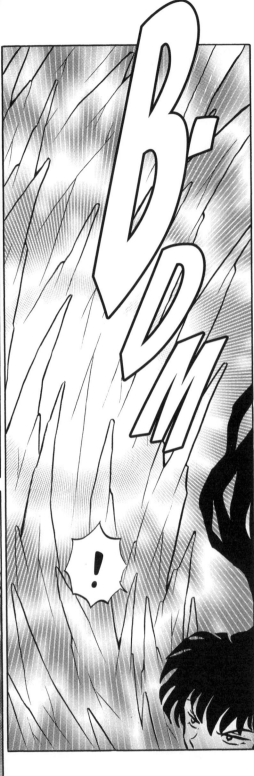

MY LEGS ...

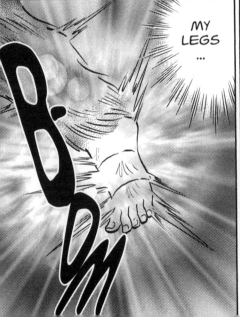

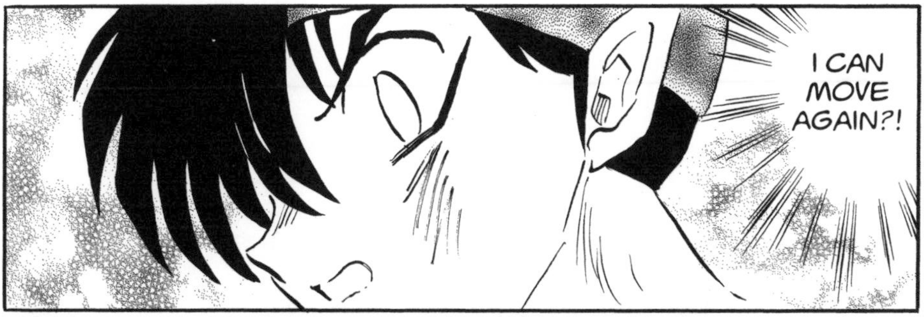
I CAN MOVE AGAIN?!

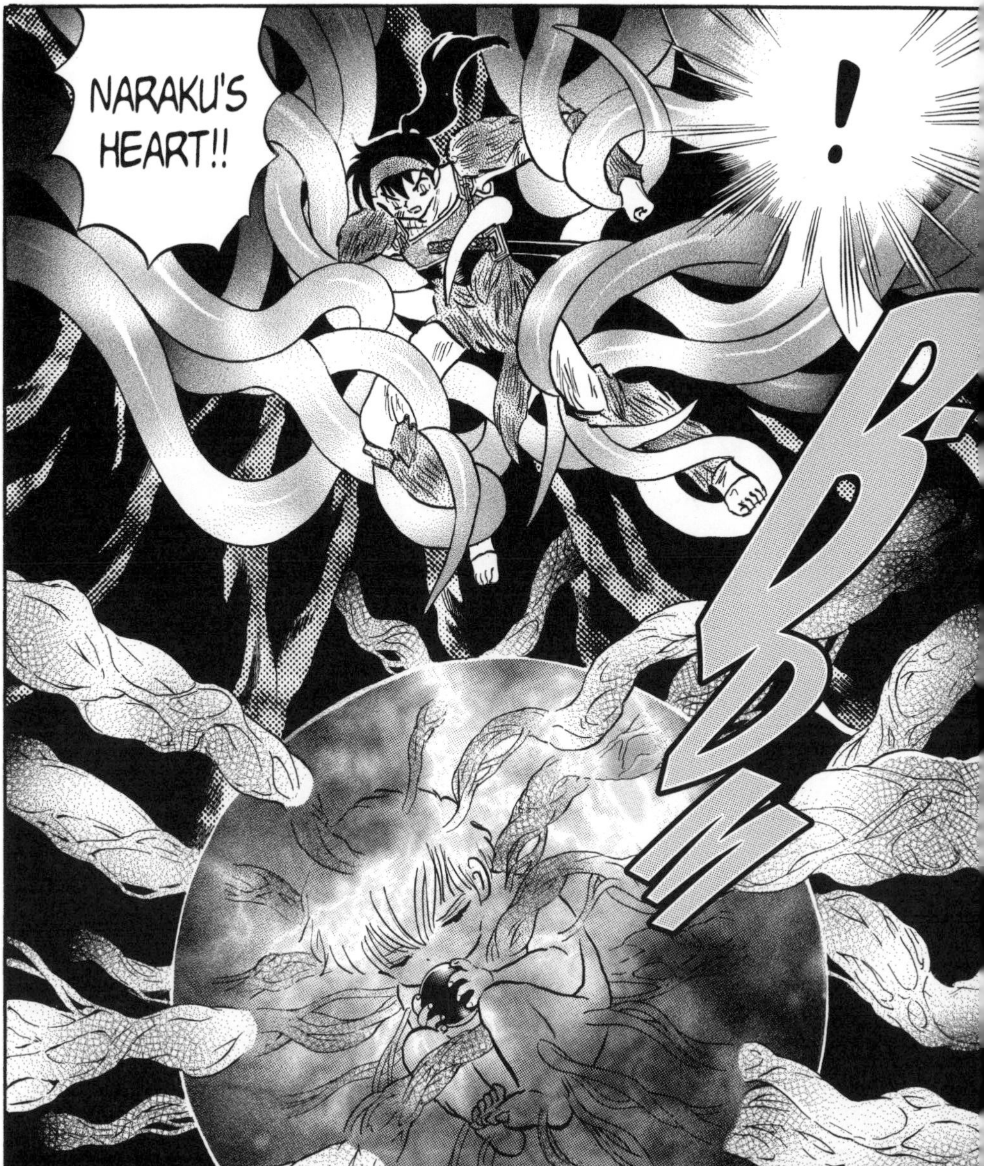
!
NARAKU'S HEART!!

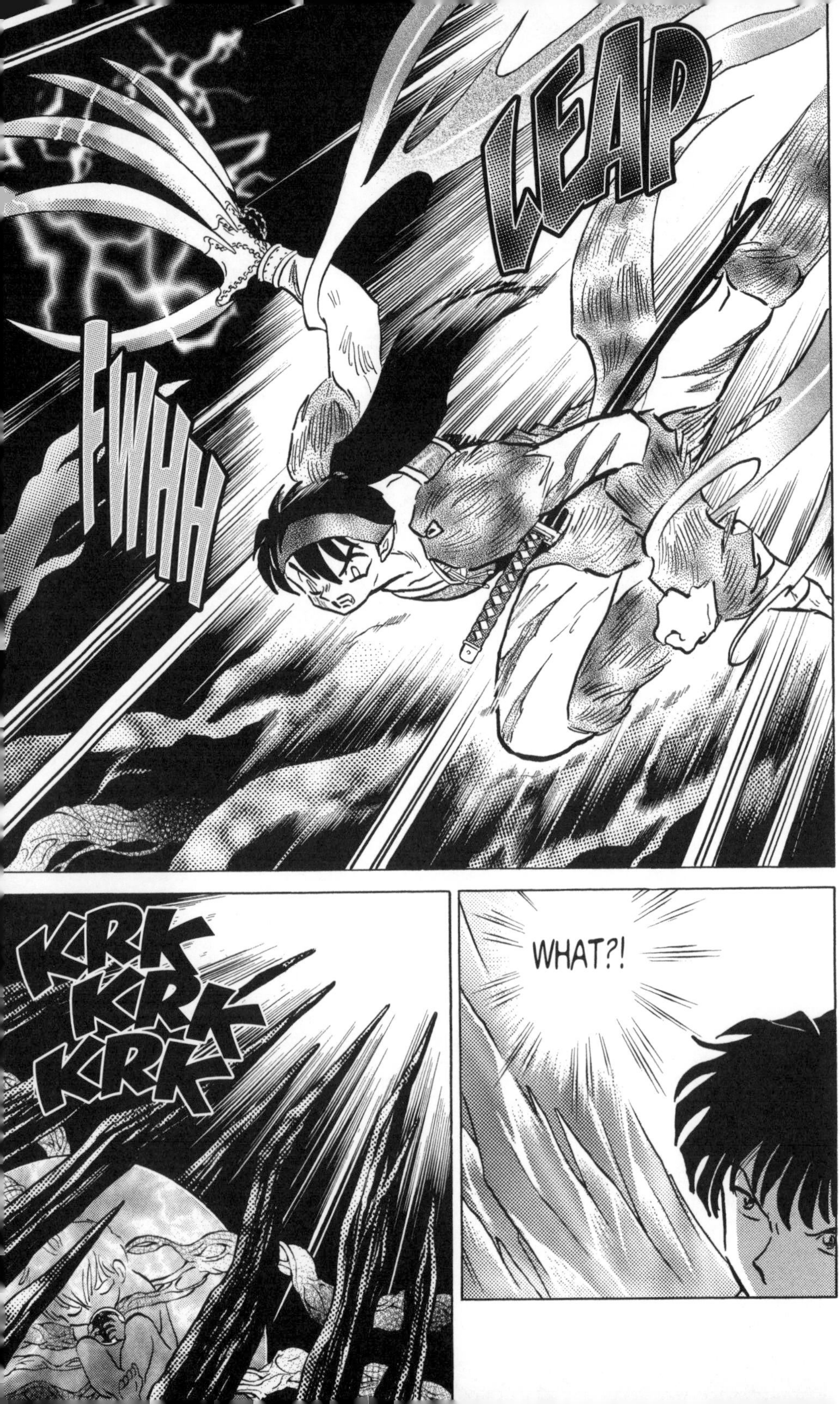
LEAP
FWHH
WHAT?!
KRK KRK KRK

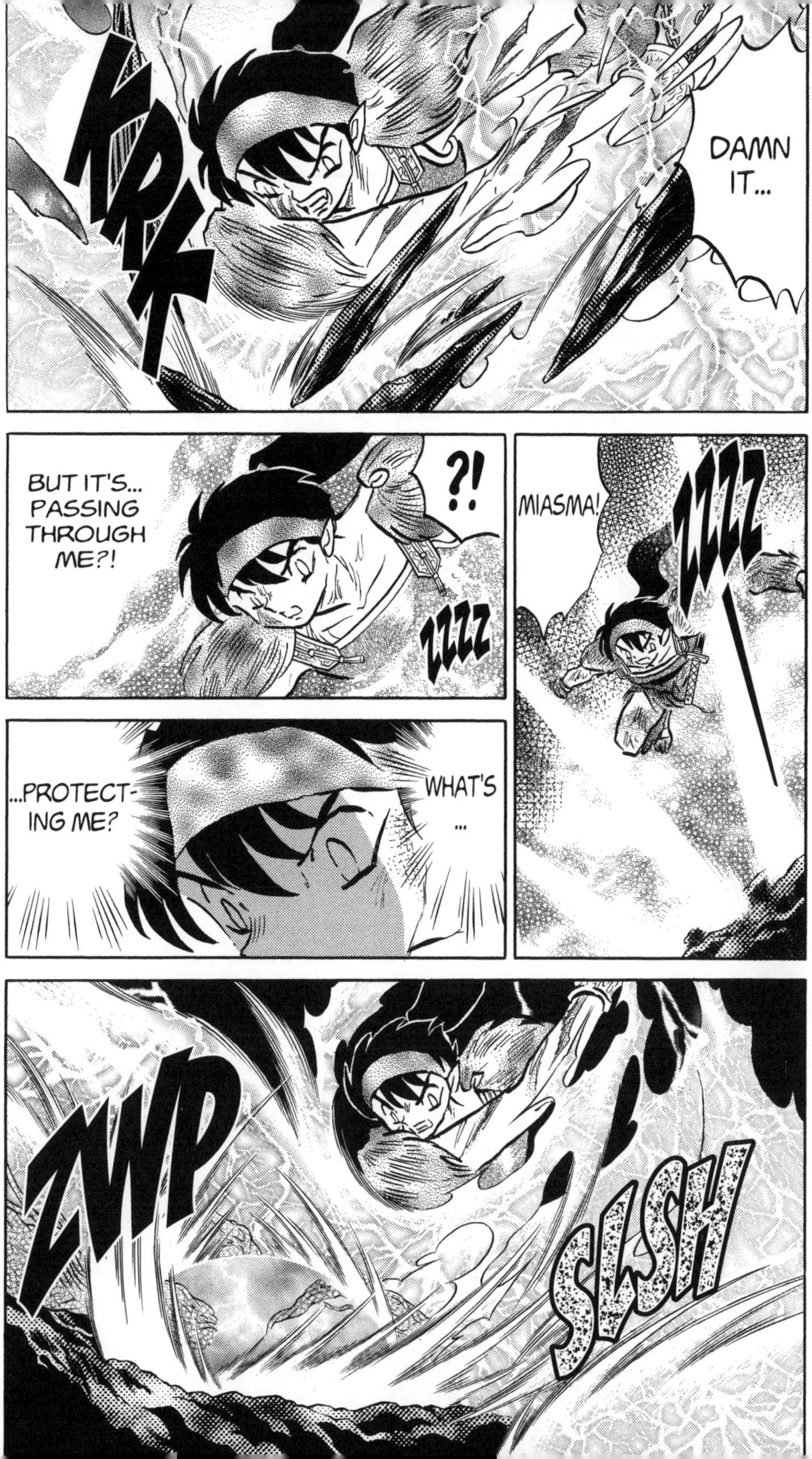
DAMN IT...
KRK
ZZZZ
MIASMA!
?!
BUT IT'S... PASSING THROUGH ME?!
ZZZZ
WHAT'S ...
...PROTECT-ING ME?
SLSH
ZWP

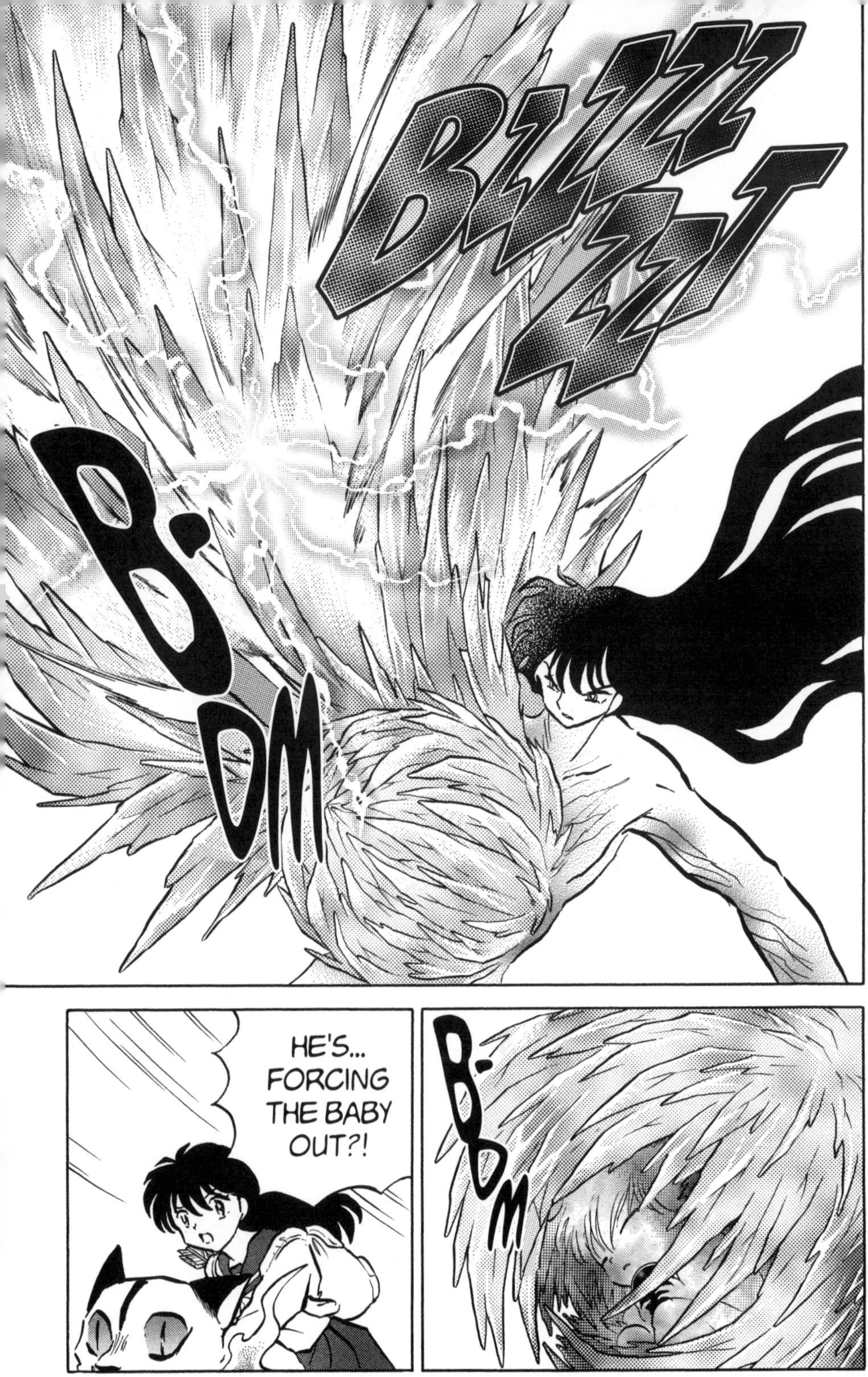
BZZZT
B-DOM
B-DOM
HE'S... FORCING THE BABY OUT?!

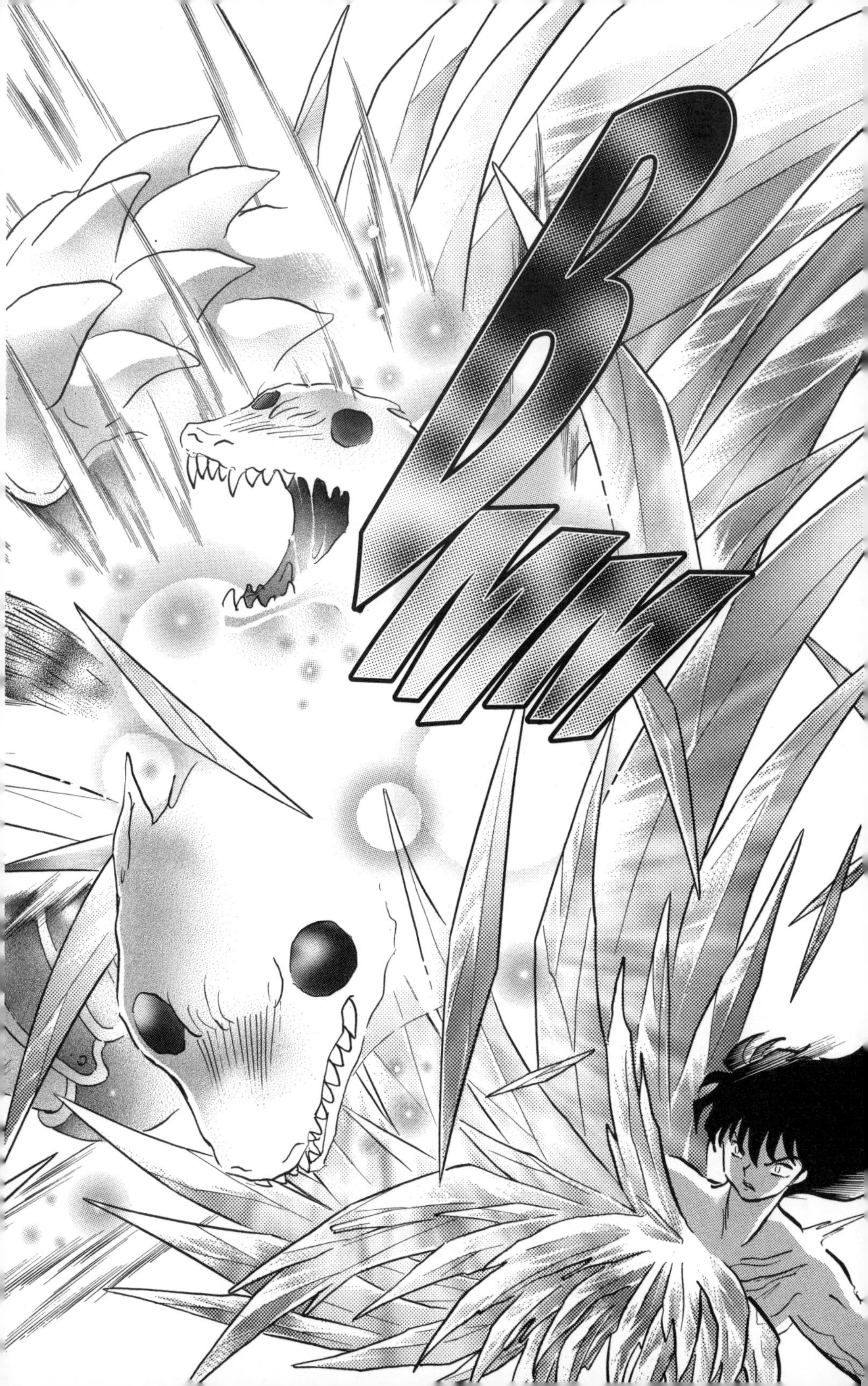
BMMM

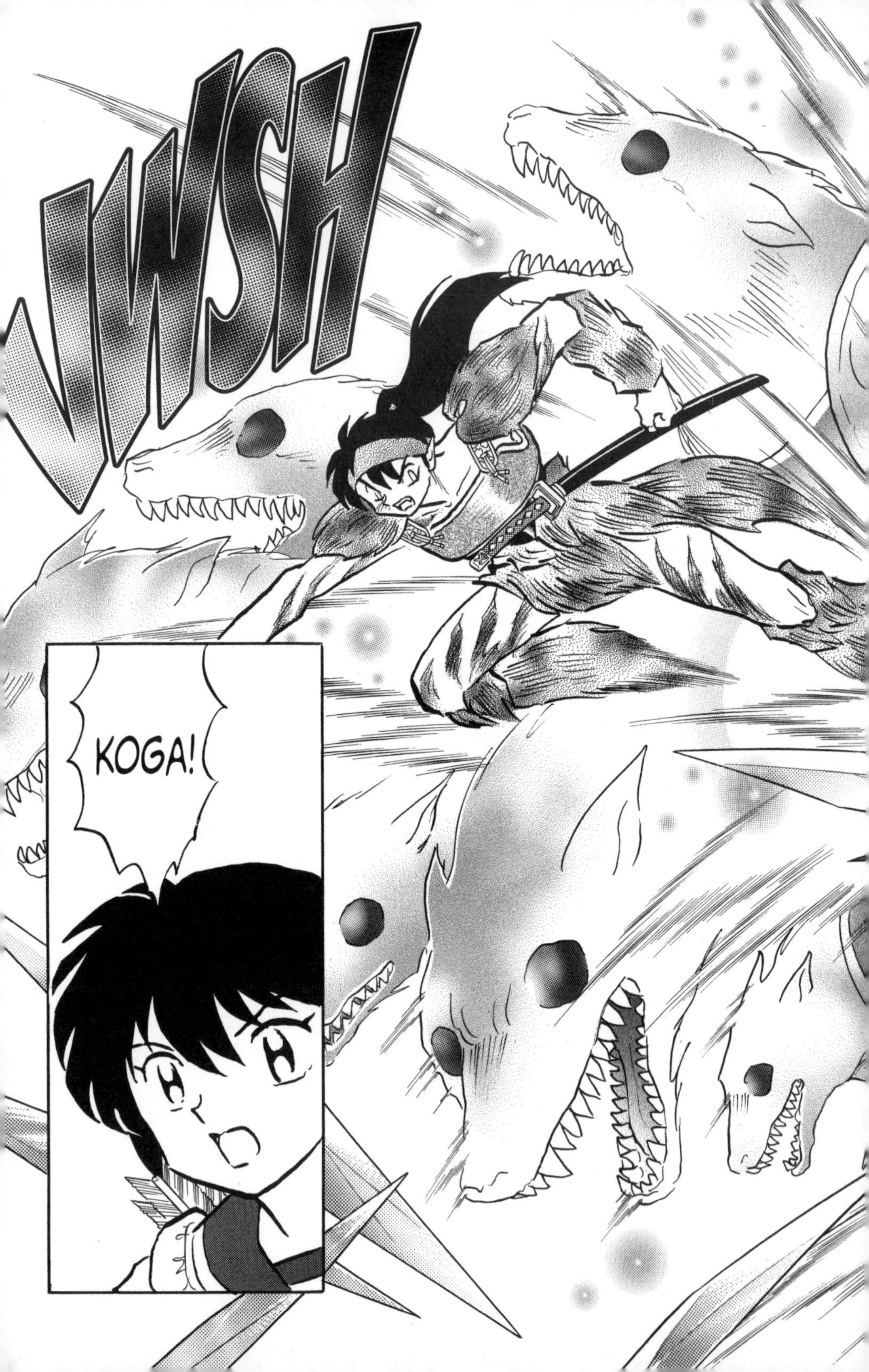
VWSH
KOGA!

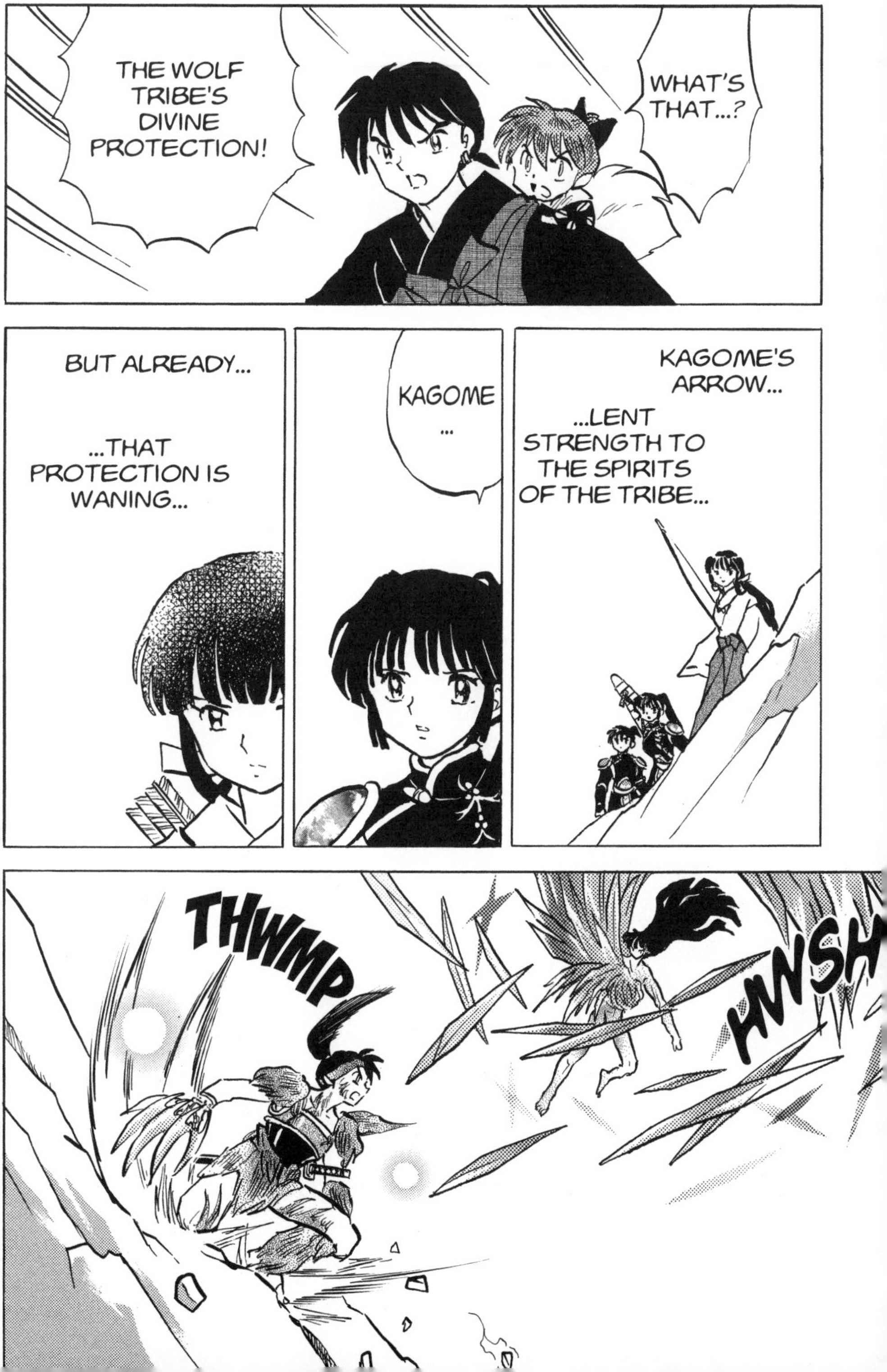
WHAT'S THAT...?
THE WOLF TRIBE'S DIVINE PROTECTION!
KAGOME'S ARROW...
...LENT STRENGTH TO THE SPIRITS OF THE TRIBE...
KAGOME...
BUT ALREADY...
...THAT PROTECTION IS WANING...
HWSH
THWMP

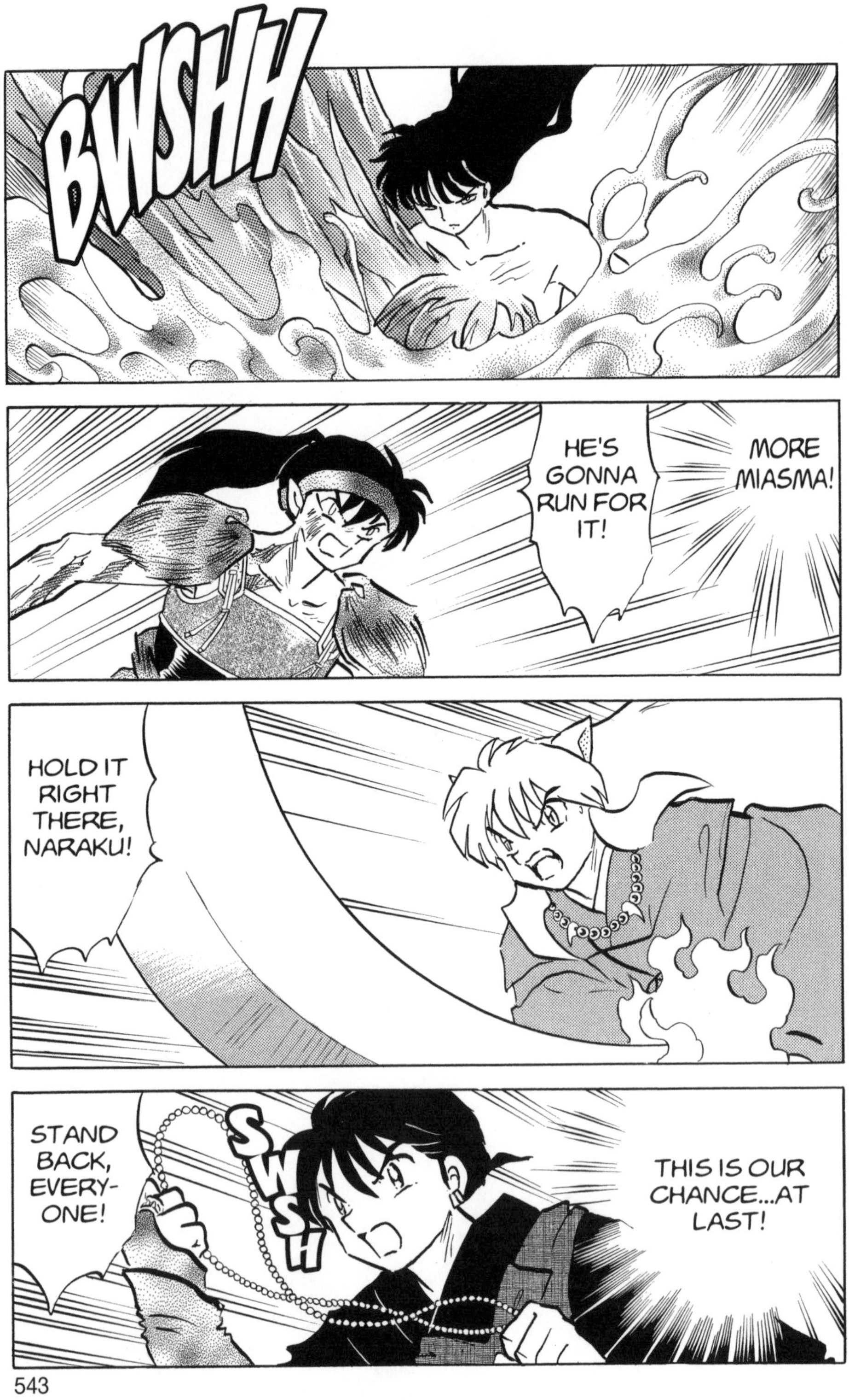
BWSHH
MORE MIASMA!
HE'S GONNA RUN FOR IT!
HOLD IT RIGHT THERE, NARAKU!
THIS IS OUR CHANCE...AT LAST!
SWSH
STAND BACK, EVERY-ONE!

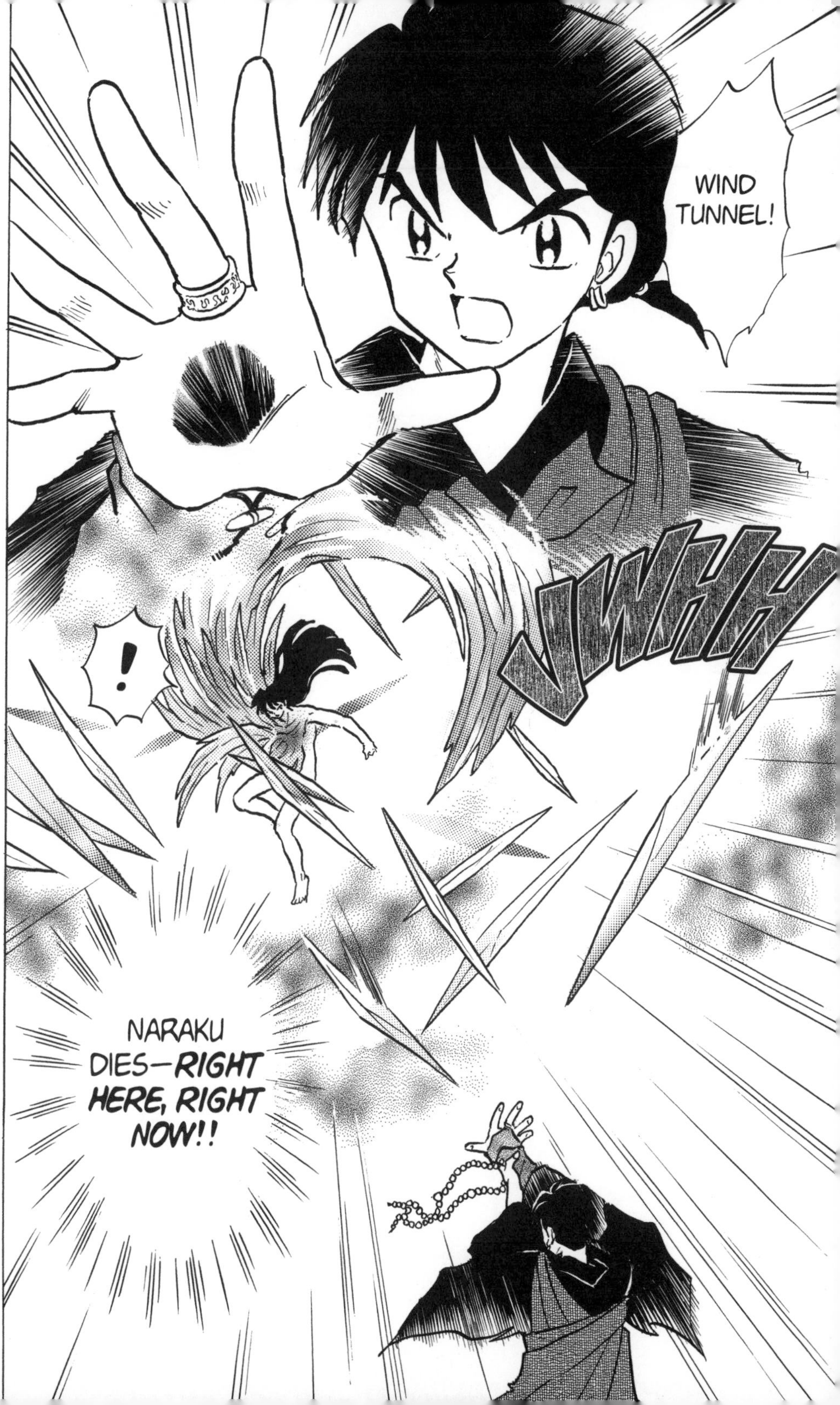
WIND TUNNEL!
JWHH
!
NARAKU DIES—*RIGHT HERE, RIGHT NOW!!*

SCROLL TEN
THE POISON OF THE MIASMA

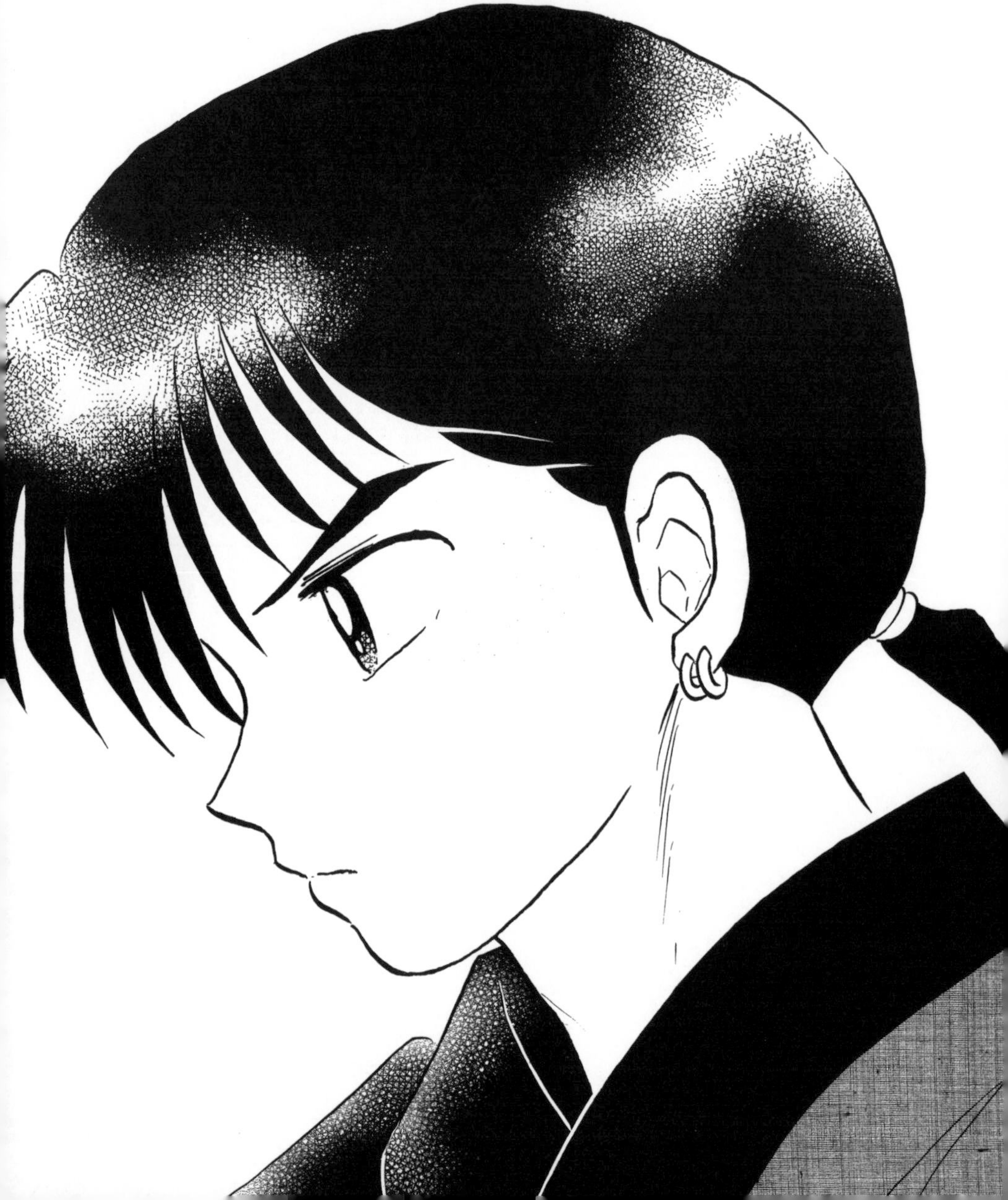

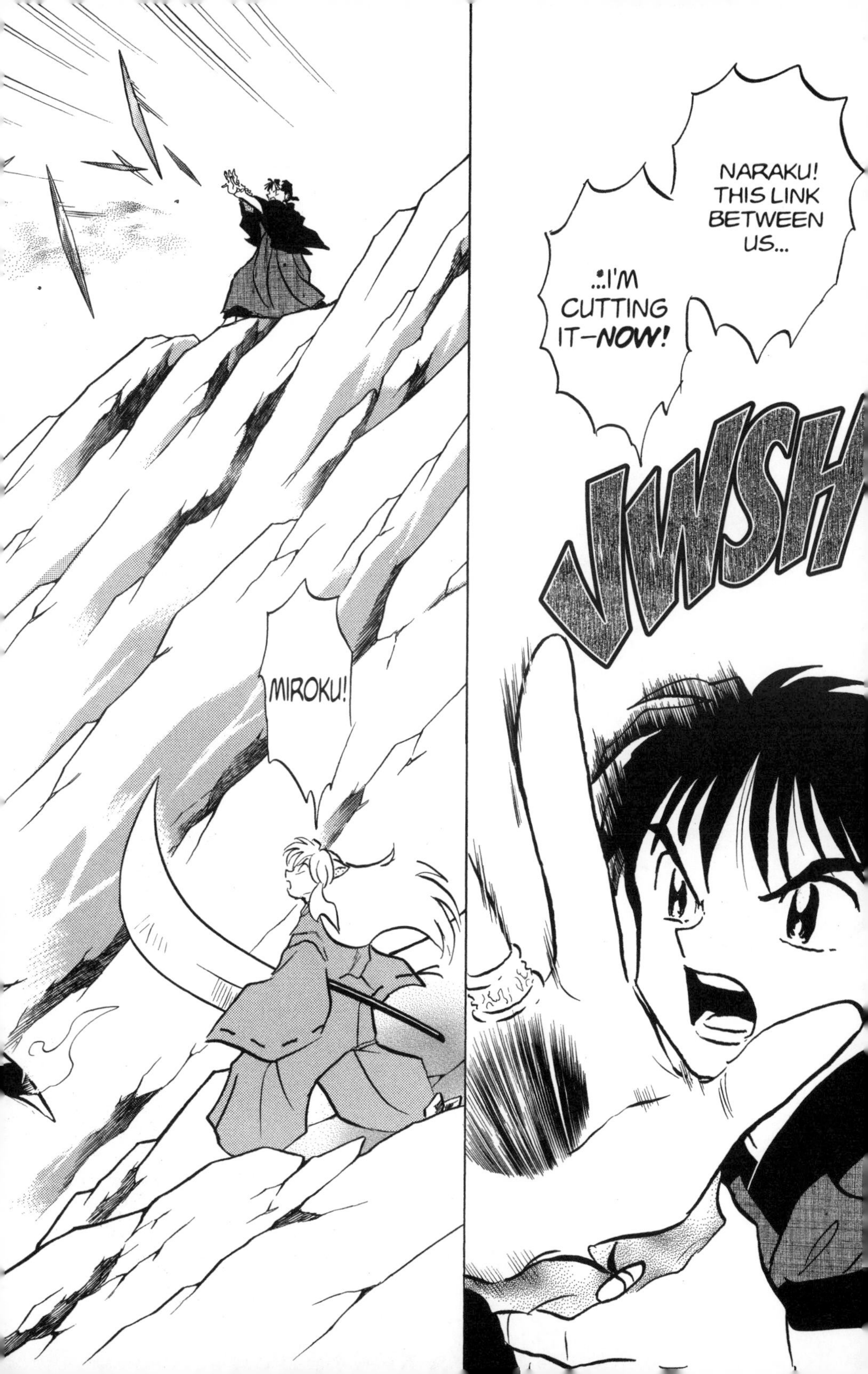
NARAKU! THIS LINK BETWEEN US...
...I'M CUTTING IT—*NOW!*
JWSH
MIROKU!

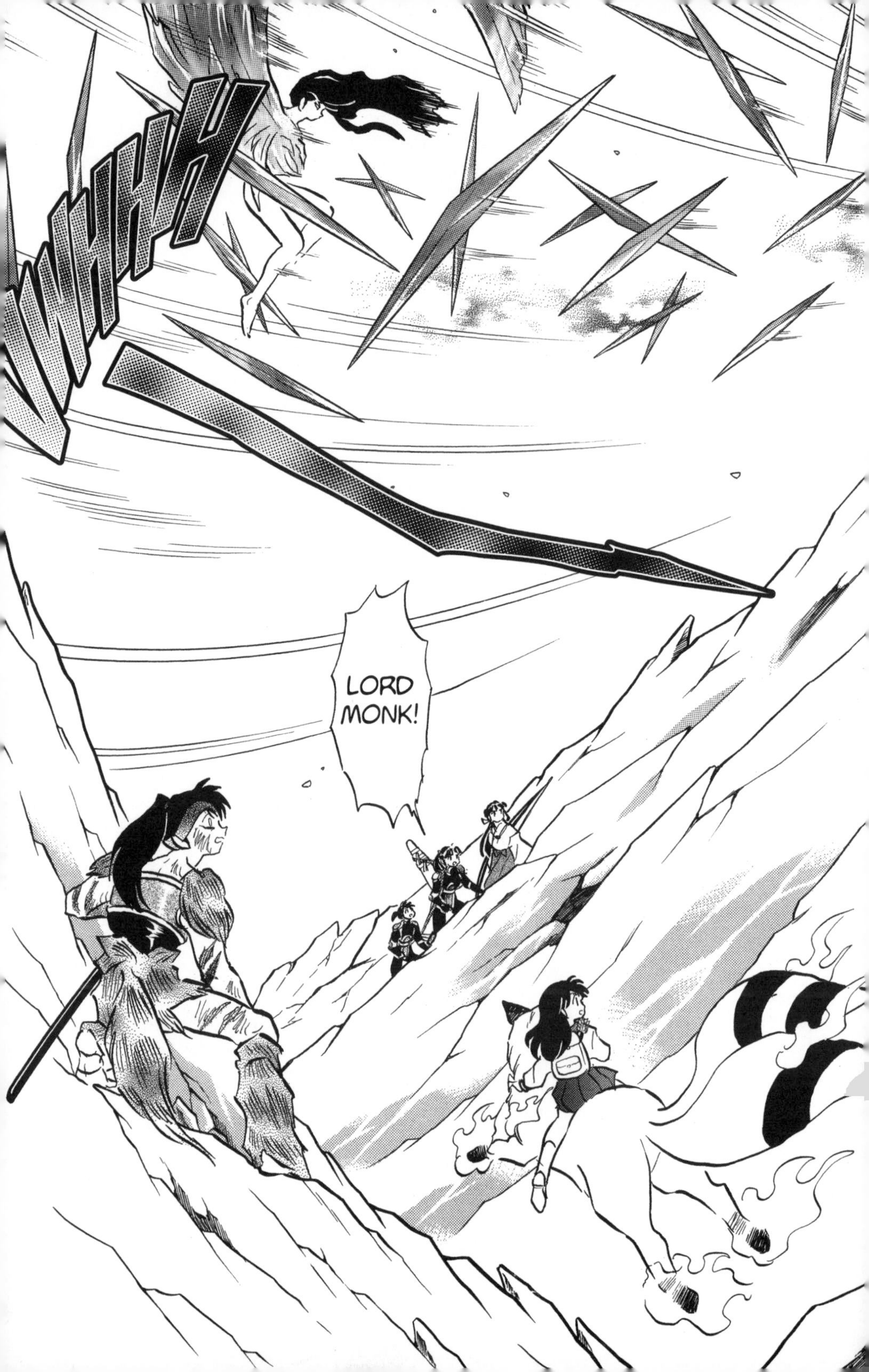
WHHHH
LORD MONK!

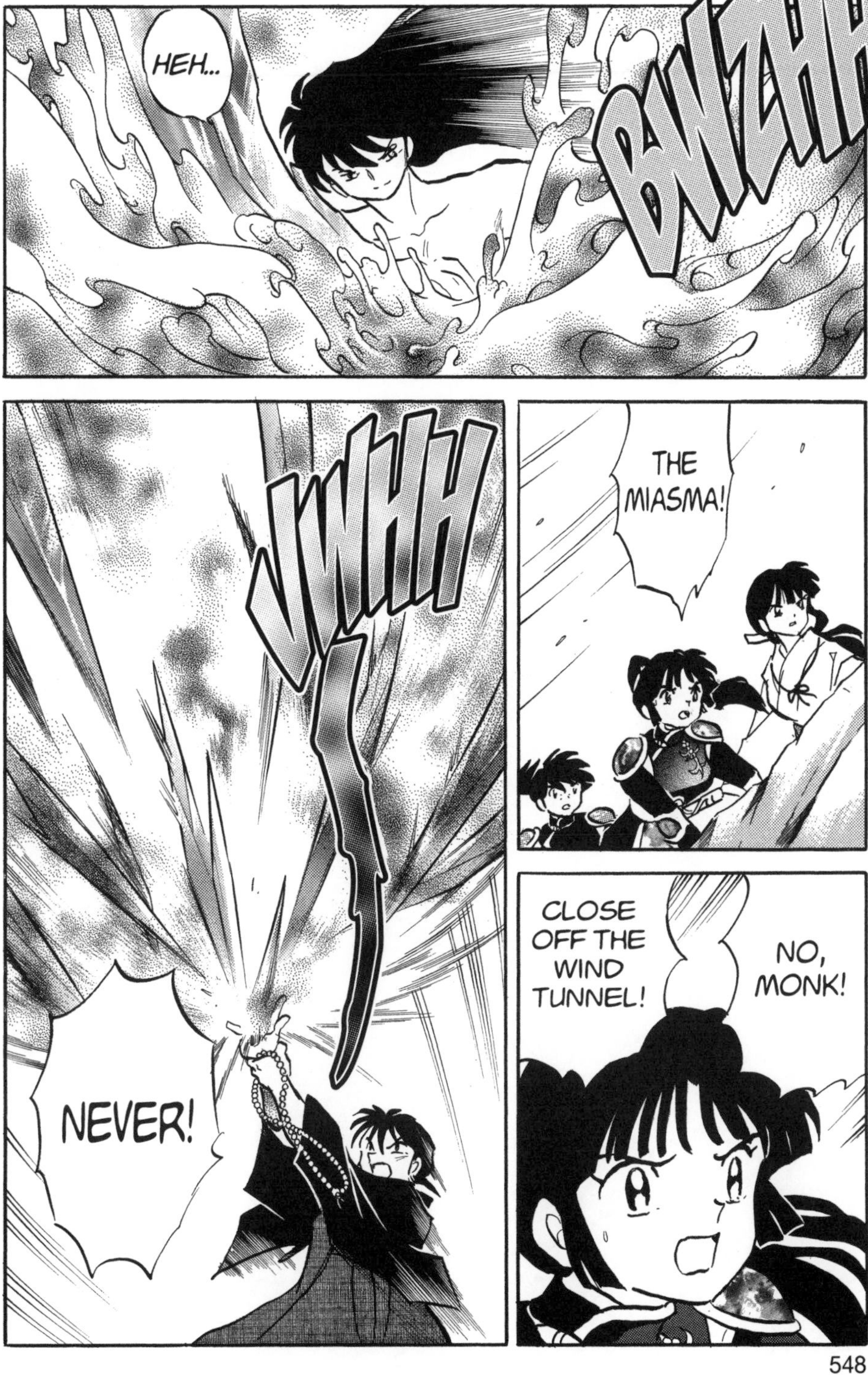
BWZHH
HEH...
THE MIASMA!
NO, MONK!
CLOSE OFF THE WIND TUNNEL!
JWHH
NEVER!

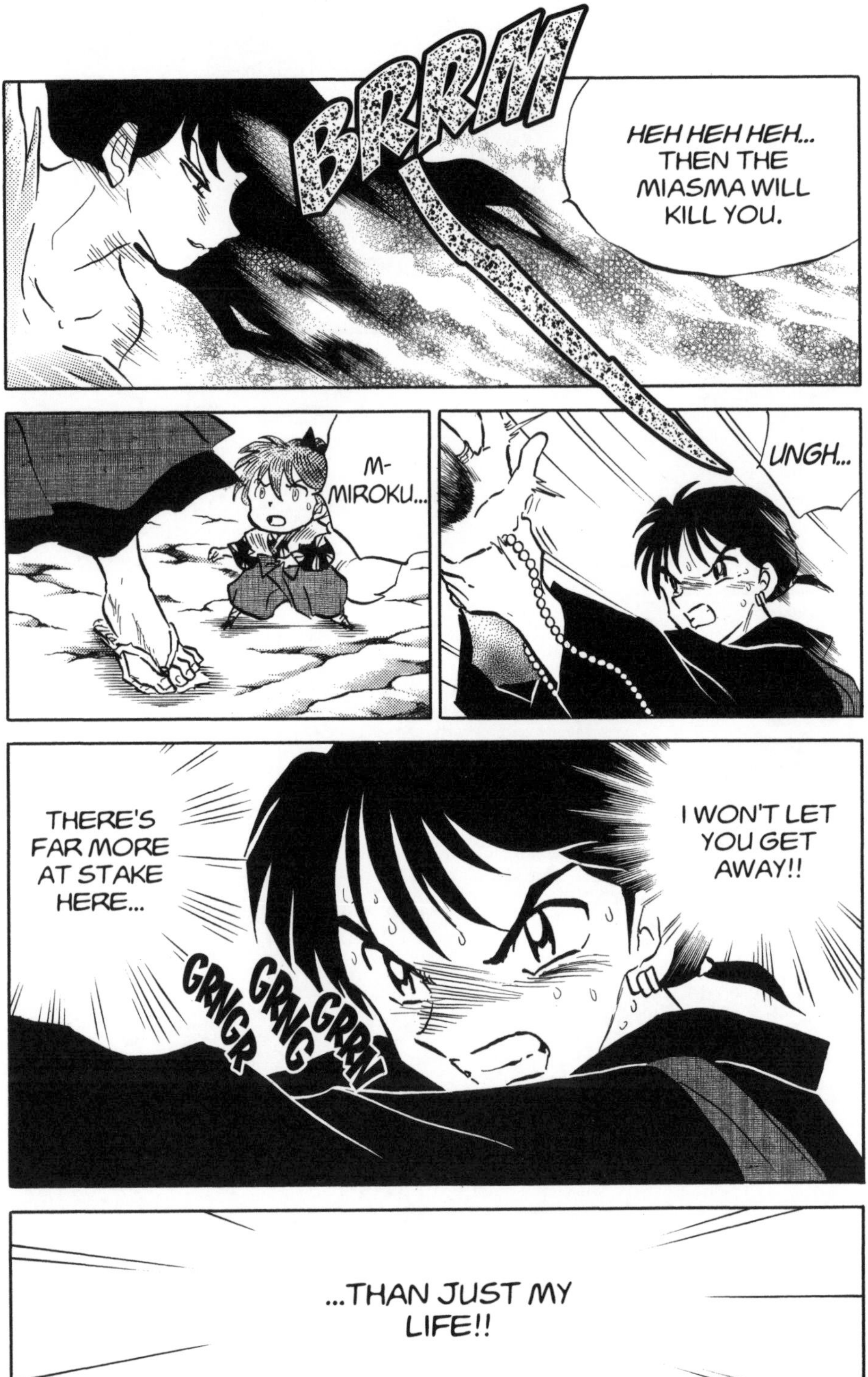
BRRM
HEH HEH HEH... THEN THE MIASMA WILL KILL YOU.
UNGH...
M-MIROKU...
I WON'T LET YOU GET AWAY!!
THERE'S FAR MORE AT STAKE HERE...
GRRRN
GRNG
GRNGR
...THAN JUST MY LIFE!!

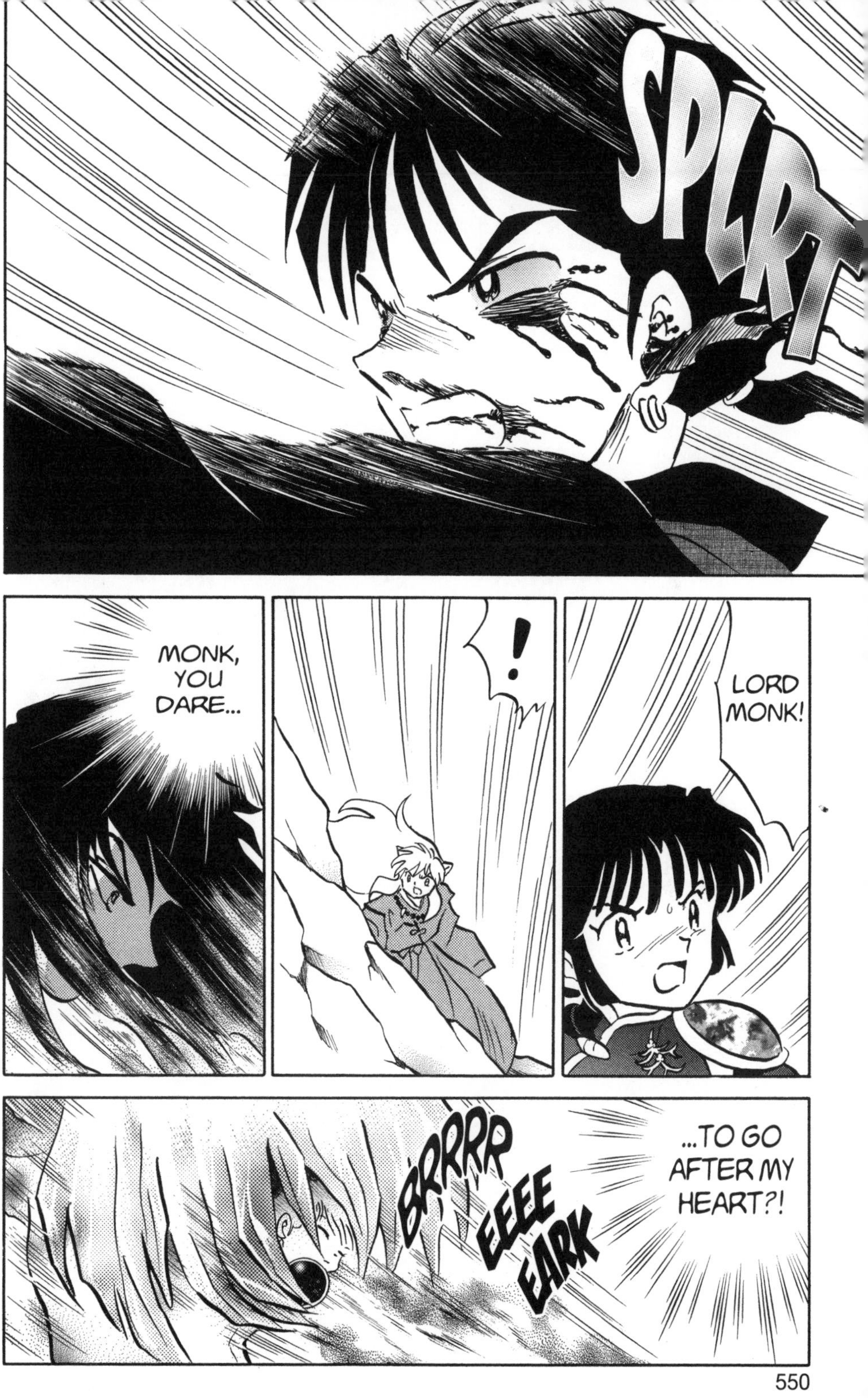
SPLRT
LORD MONK!
!
MONK, YOU DARE...
...TO GO AFTER MY HEART?!
BRRRR EEEE EARK

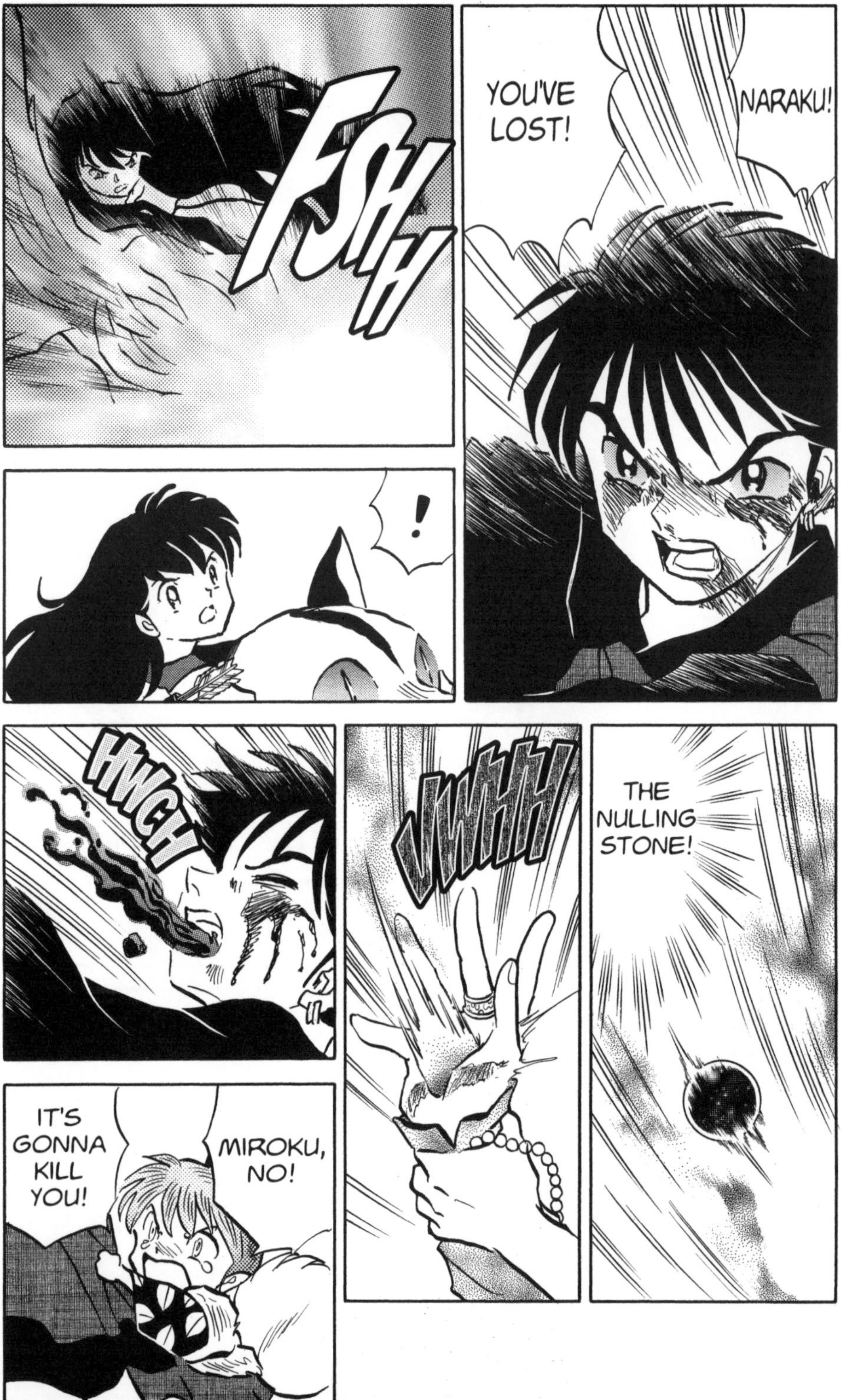
NARAKU!
YOU'VE LOST!
FSHH
!
THE NULLING STONE!
JWHH
HWCH
MIROKU, NO!
IT'S GONNA KILL YOU!

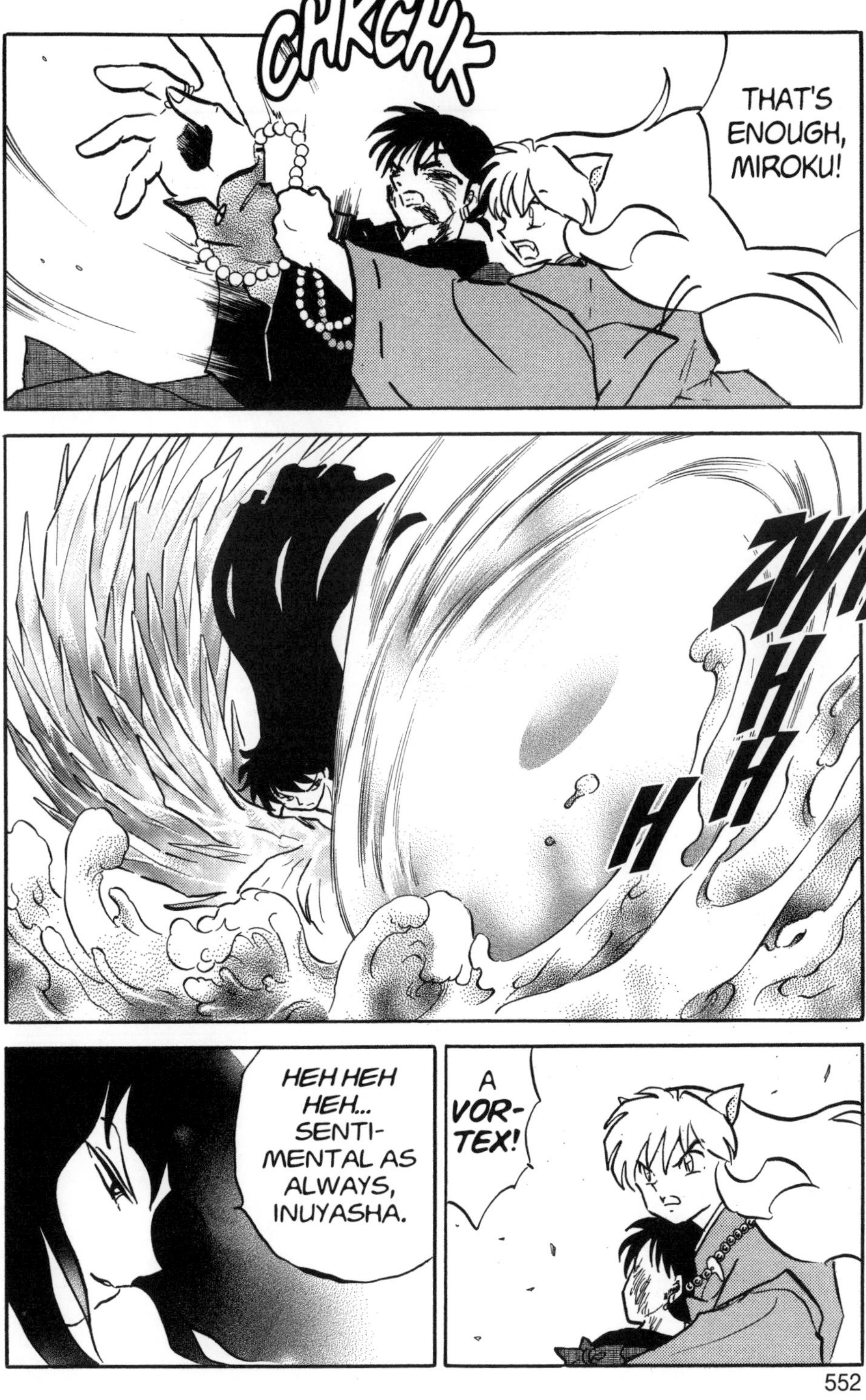
CHKCHK
THAT'S ENOUGH, MIROKU!
ZWHHHH
A VOR-TEX!
HEH HEH HEH... SENTI-MENTAL AS ALWAYS, INUYASHA.

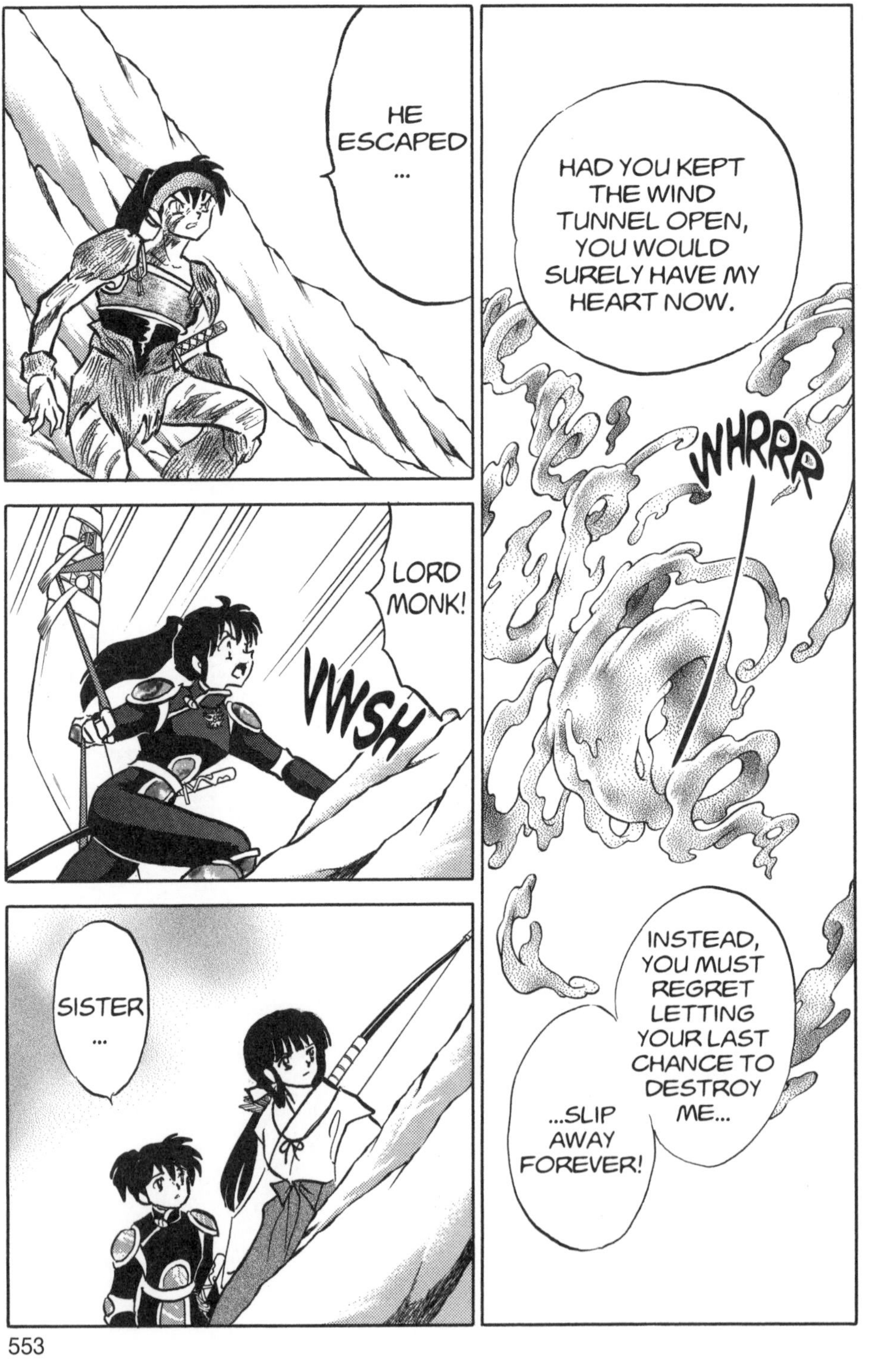
HAD YOU KEPT THE WIND TUNNEL OPEN, YOU WOULD SURELY HAVE MY HEART NOW.
WHRRR
INSTEAD, YOU MUST REGRET LETTING YOUR LAST CHANCE TO DESTROY ME...
...SLIP AWAY FOREVER!
HE ESCAPED ...
LORD MONK!
VWSH
SISTER ...

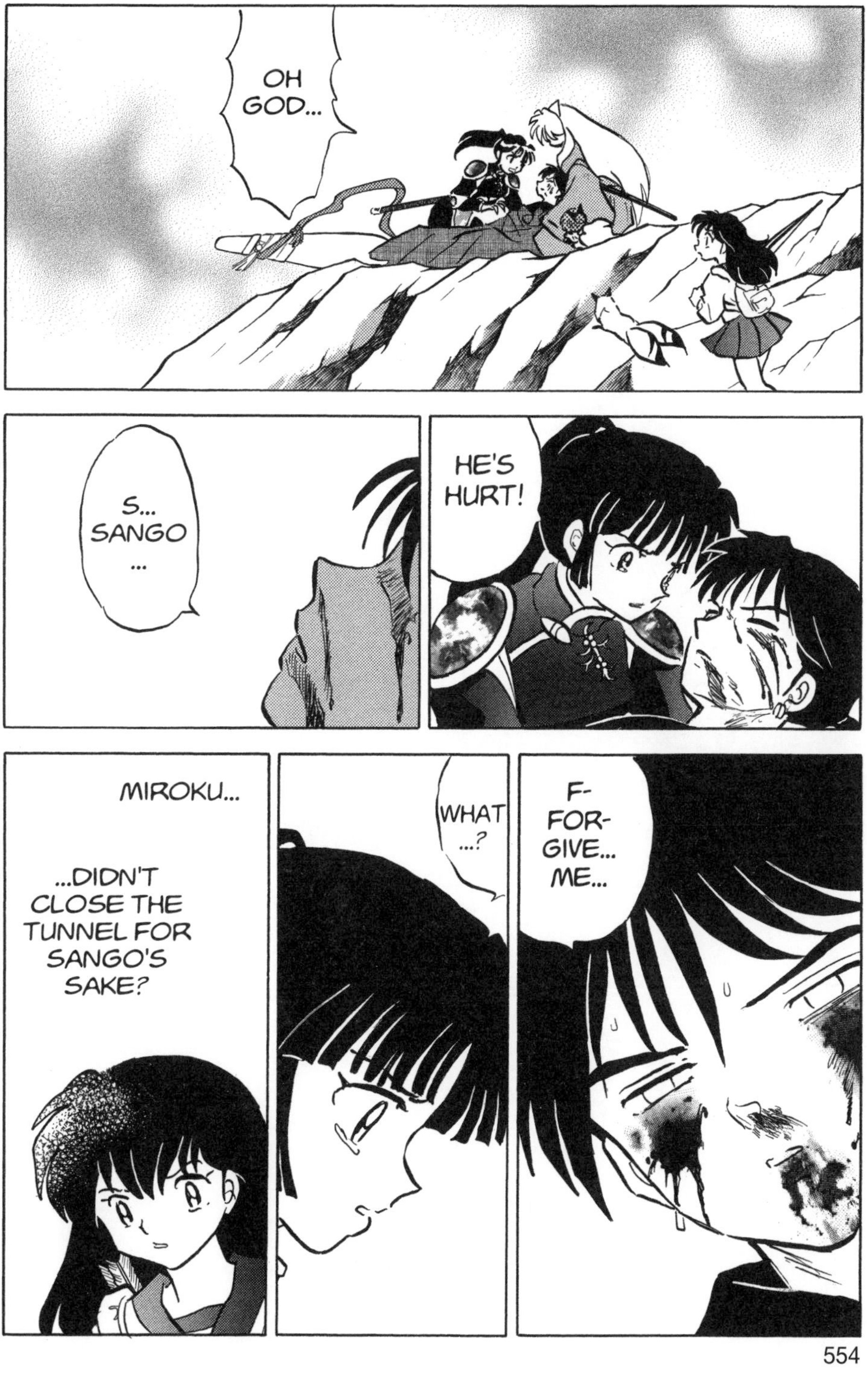
OH GOD...
HE'S HURT!
S... SANGO ...
F- FOR-GIVE... ME...
WHAT ...?
MIROKU...
...DIDN'T CLOSE THE TUNNEL FOR SANGO'S SAKE?

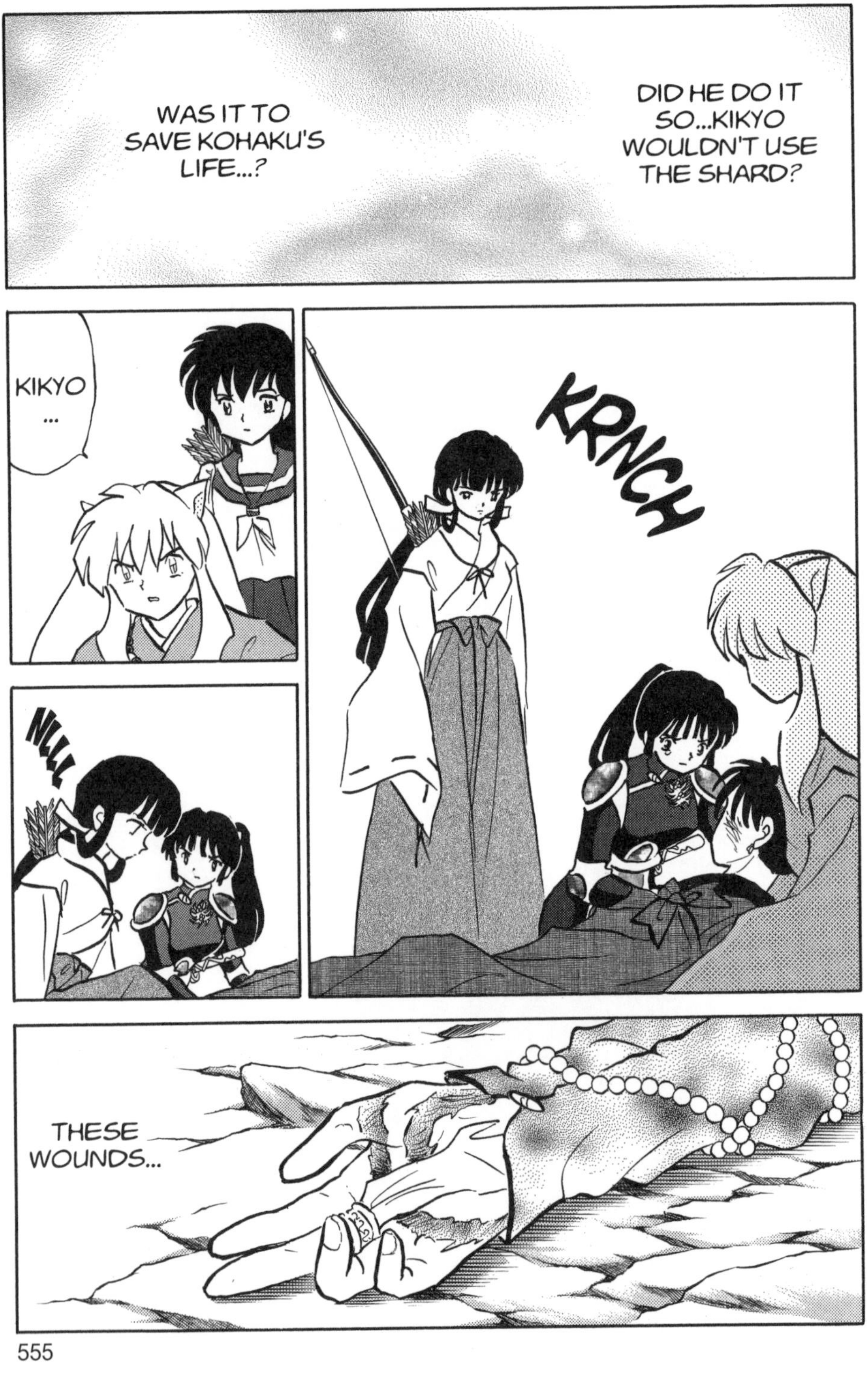
DID HE DO IT SO...KIKYO WOULDN'T USE THE SHARD?
WAS IT TO SAVE KOHAKU'S LIFE...?
KRNCH
KIKYO ...
NLLL
THESE WOUNDS...

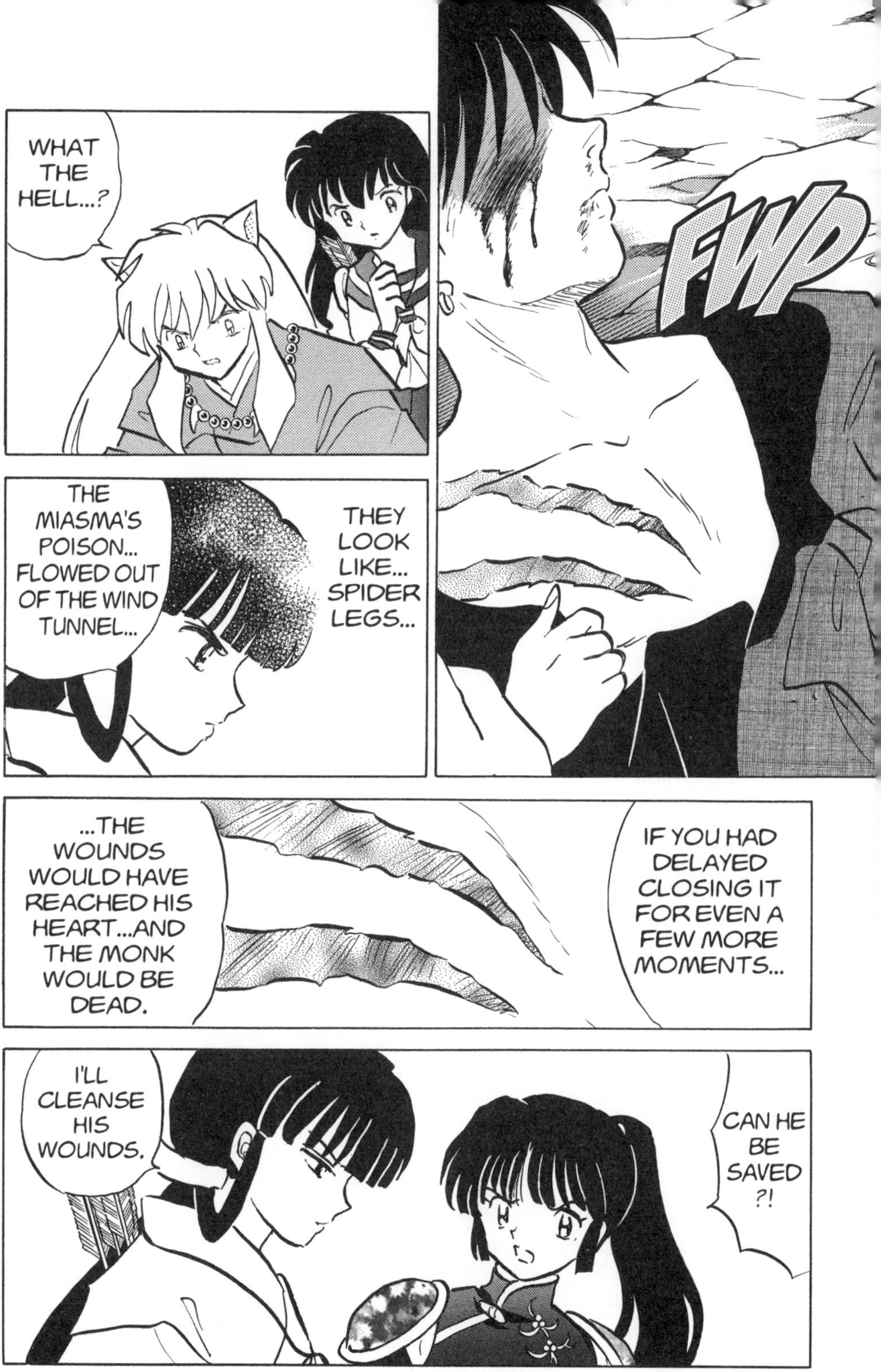
FWP
WHAT THE HELL...?
THEY LOOK LIKE... SPIDER LEGS...
THE MIASMA'S POISON... FLOWED OUT OF THE WIND TUNNEL...
IF YOU HAD DELAYED CLOSING IT FOR EVEN A FEW MORE MOMENTS...
...THE WOUNDS WOULD HAVE REACHED HIS HEART...AND THE MONK WOULD BE DEAD.
CAN HE BE SAVED?!
I'LL CLEANSE HIS WOUNDS.

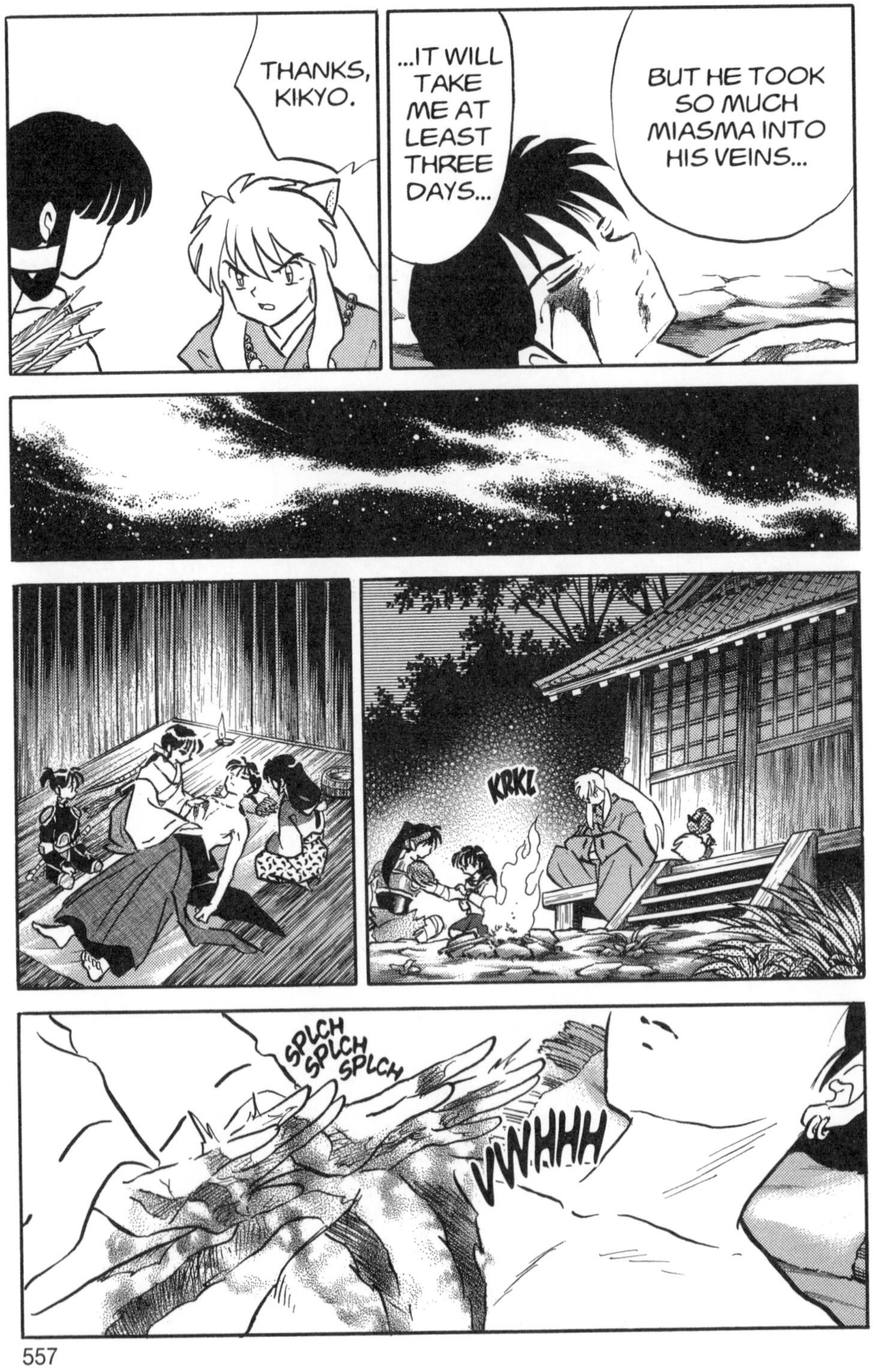
BUT HE TOOK SO MUCH MIASMA INTO HIS VEINS...
...IT WILL TAKE ME AT LEAST THREE DAYS...
THANKS, KIKYO.
KRKL
SPLCH SPLCH SPLCH
VWHHH

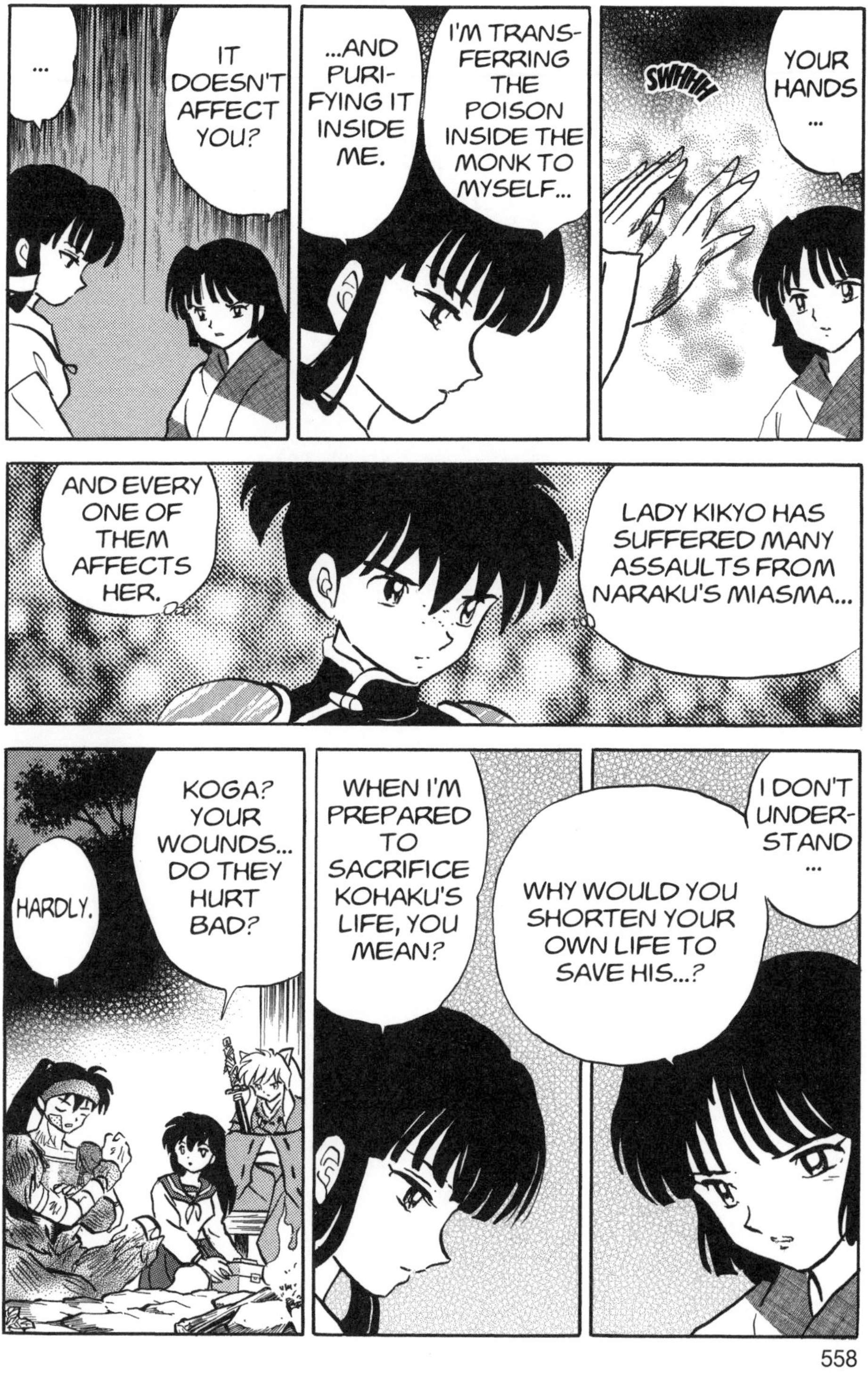
YOUR HANDS ...
SWHHH
I'M TRANS-FERRING THE POISON INSIDE THE MONK TO MYSELF...
...AND PURI-FYING IT INSIDE ME.
IT DOESN'T AFFECT YOU?
...
LADY KIKYO HAS SUFFERED MANY ASSAULTS FROM NARAKU'S MIASMA...
AND EVERY ONE OF THEM AFFECTS HER.
I DON'T UNDER-STAND ...
WHY WOULD YOU SHORTEN YOUR OWN LIFE TO SAVE HIS...?
WHEN I'M PREPARED TO SACRIFICE KOHAKU'S LIFE, YOU MEAN?
KOGA? YOUR WOUNDS... DO THEY HURT BAD?
HARDLY.

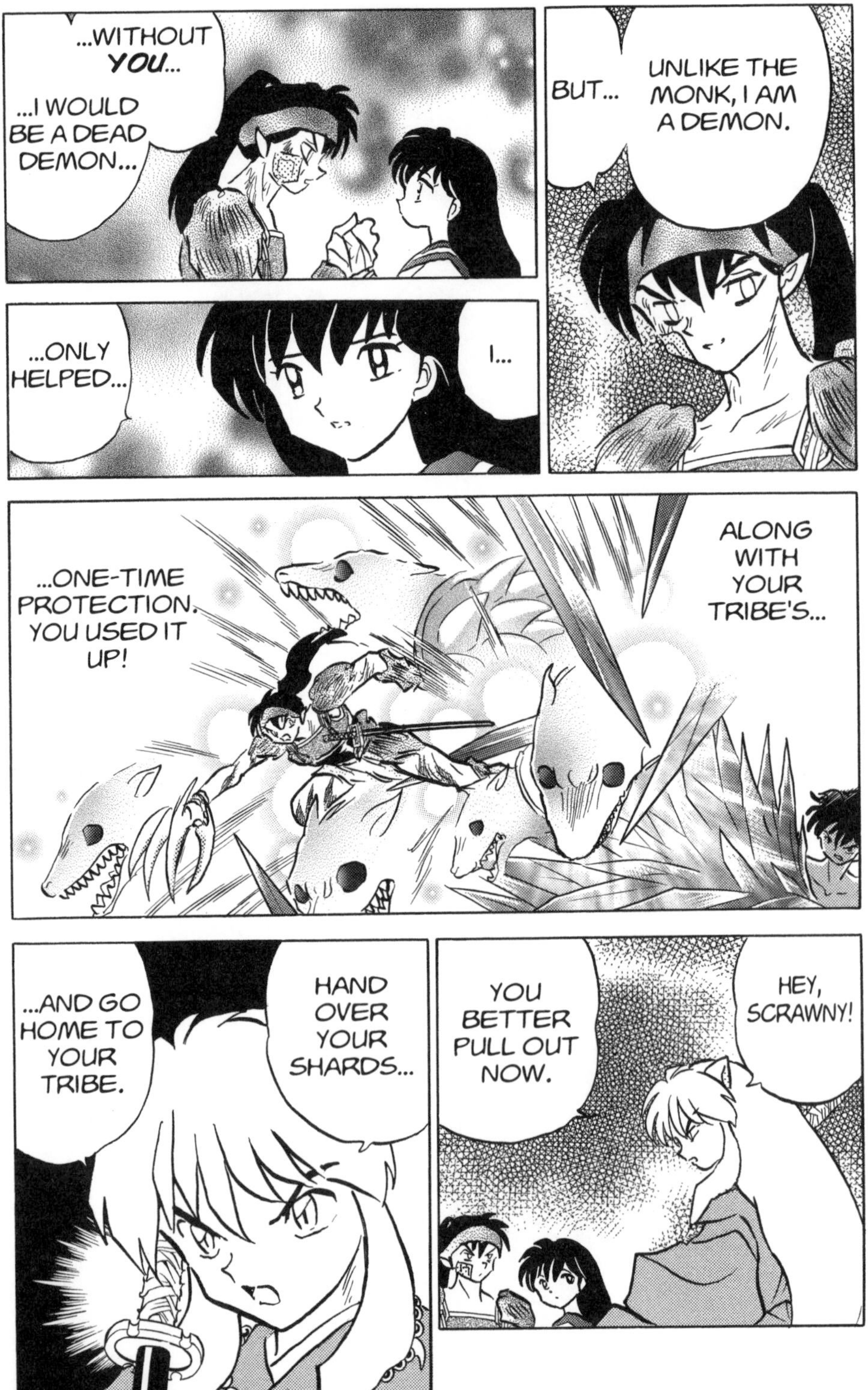
BUT...
UNLIKE THE MONK, I AM A DEMON.
...WITHOUT **YOU**...
...I WOULD BE A DEAD DEMON...
I...
...ONLY HELPED...
ALONG WITH YOUR TRIBE'S...
...ONE-TIME PROTECTION. YOU USED IT UP!
HEY, SCRAWNY!
YOU BETTER PULL OUT NOW.
HAND OVER YOUR SHARDS...
...AND GO HOME TO YOUR TRIBE.

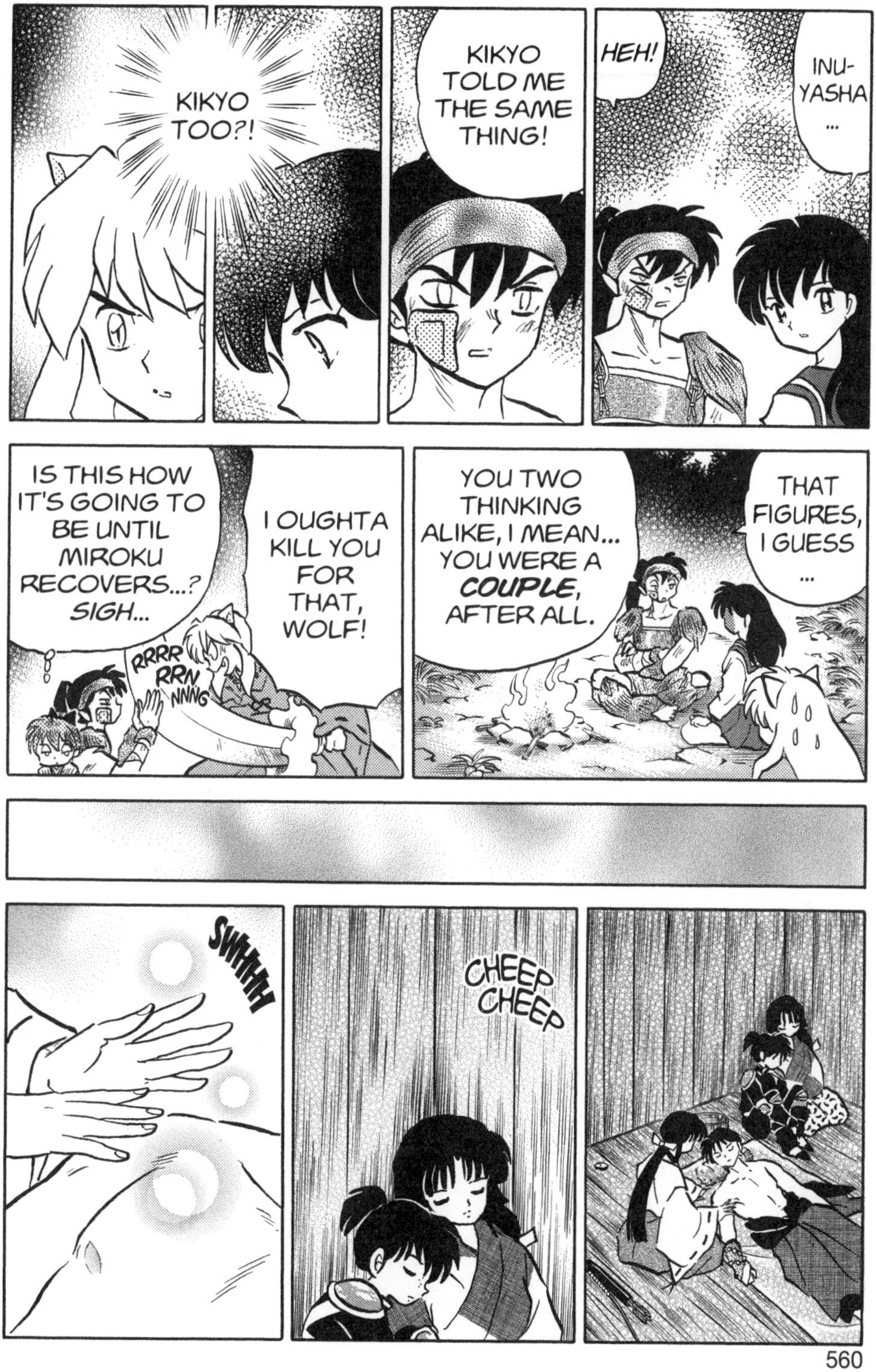
INU-YASHA ...
HEH!
KIKYO TOLD ME THE SAME THING!
KIKYO TOO?!
THAT FIGURES, I GUESS ...
YOU TWO THINKING ALIKE, I MEAN... YOU WERE A ***COUPLE***, AFTER ALL.
I OUGHTA KILL YOU FOR THAT, WOLF!
RRRR RRN NNNG
IS THIS HOW IT'S GOING TO BE UNTIL MIROKU RECOVERS...? *SIGH...*
CHEEP CHEEP
SWHHHH

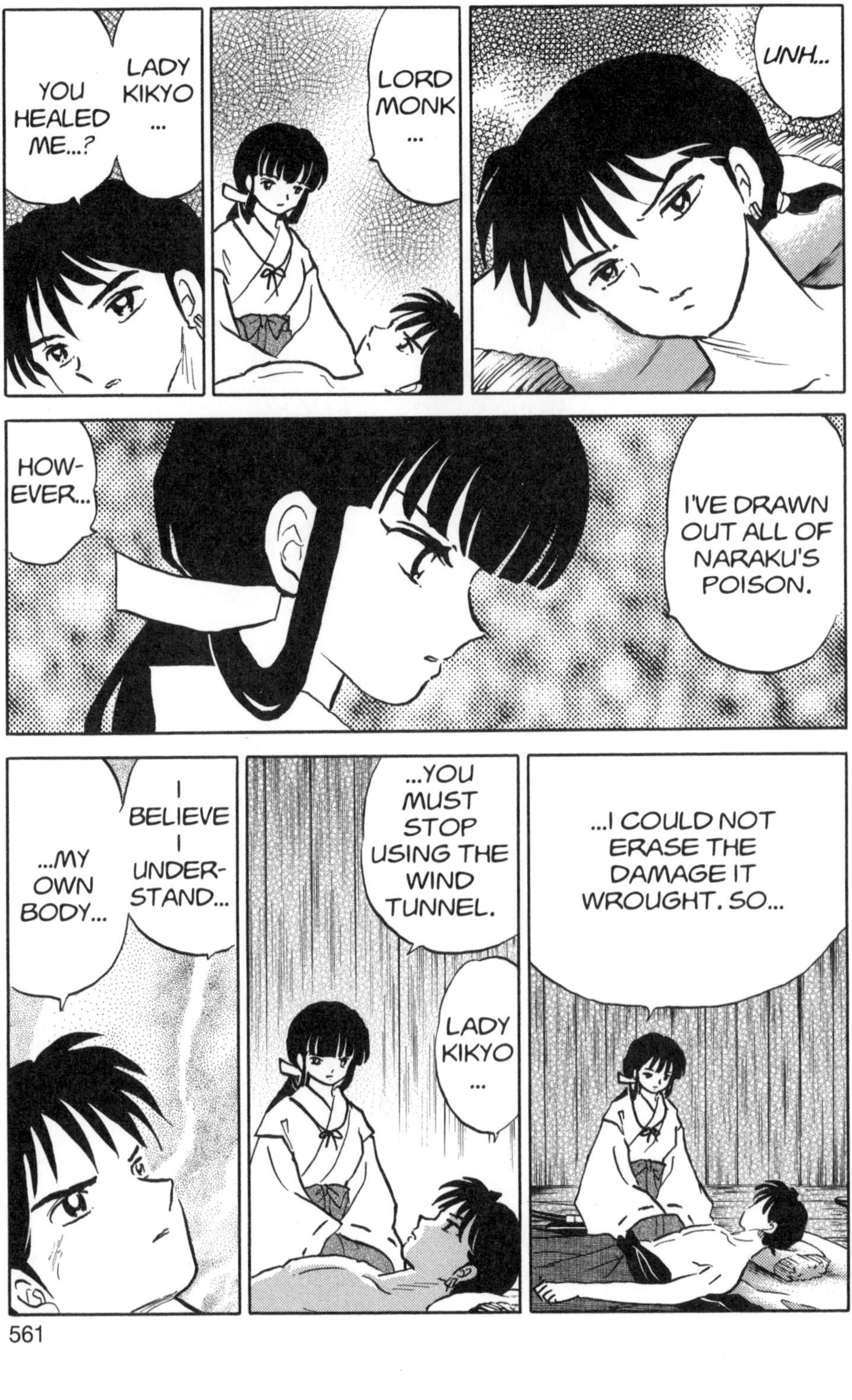
UNH...
LORD MONK ...
LADY KIKYO ...
YOU HEALED ME...?
I'VE DRAWN OUT ALL OF NARAKU'S POISON.
HOW-EVER...
...I COULD NOT ERASE THE DAMAGE IT WROUGHT. SO...
...YOU MUST STOP USING THE WIND TUNNEL.
LADY KIKYO ...
I BELIEVE I UNDER-STAND...
...MY OWN BODY...

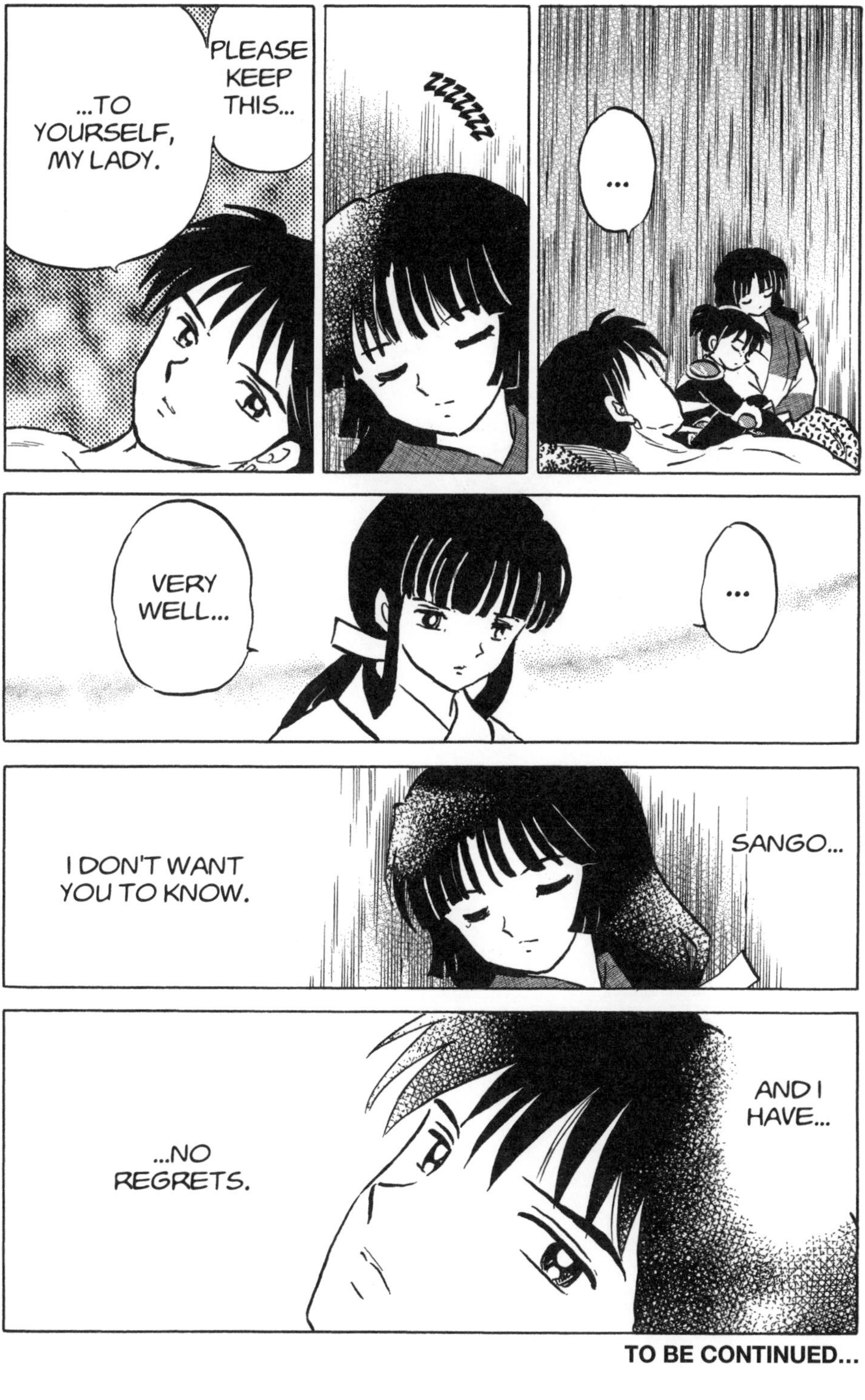
...
ZZZZZZZ
PLEASE KEEP THIS...
...TO YOURSELF, MY LADY.
...
VERY WELL...
SANGO...
I DON'T WANT YOU TO KNOW.
AND I HAVE...
...NO REGRETS.

TO BE CONTINUED...

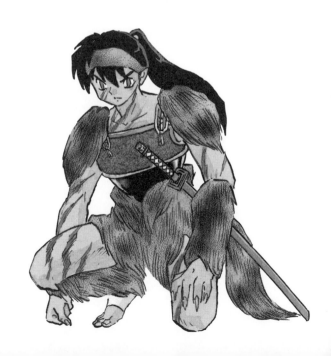

Original Cover Art Gallery

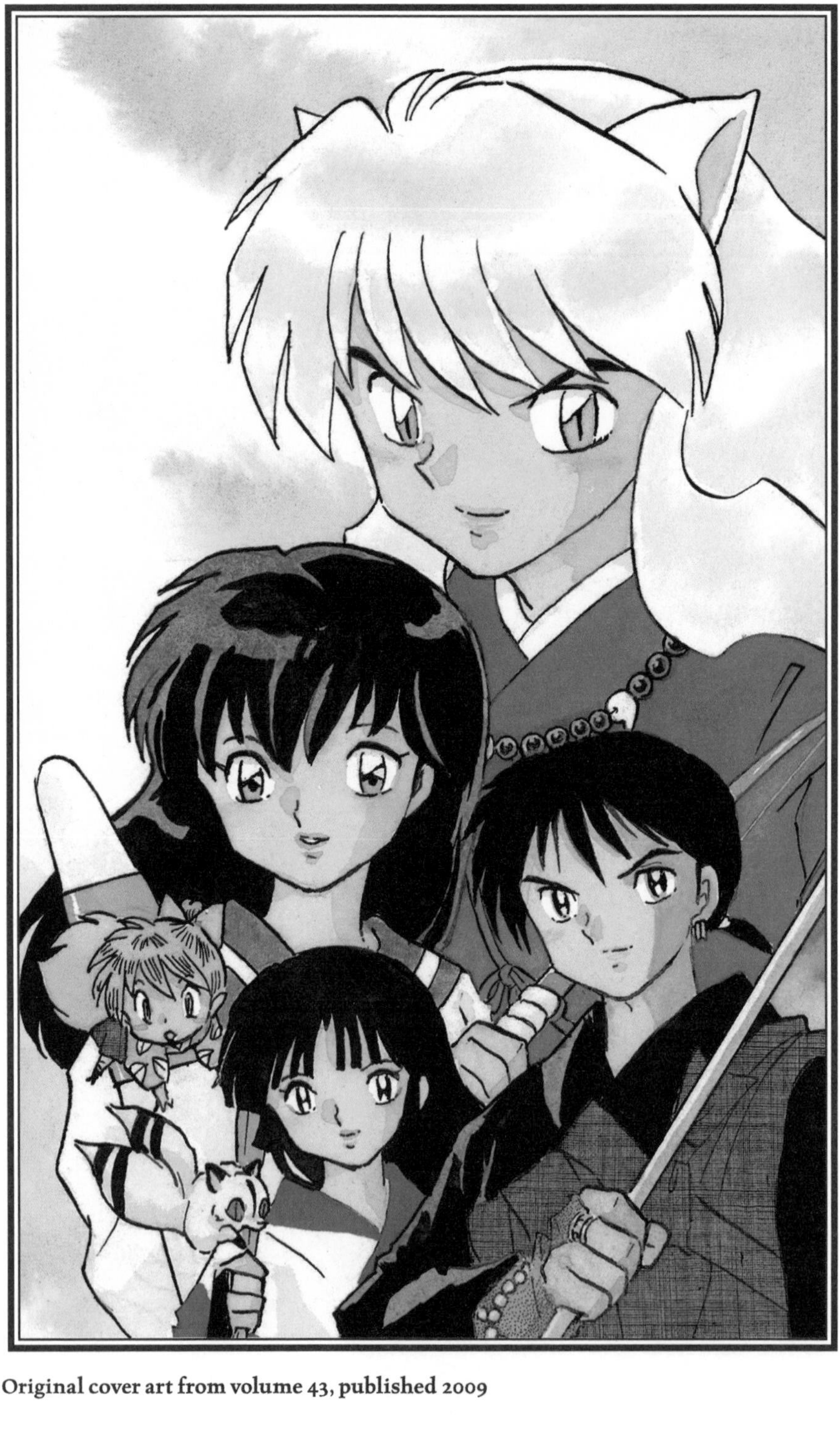

Original cover art from volume 43, published 2009

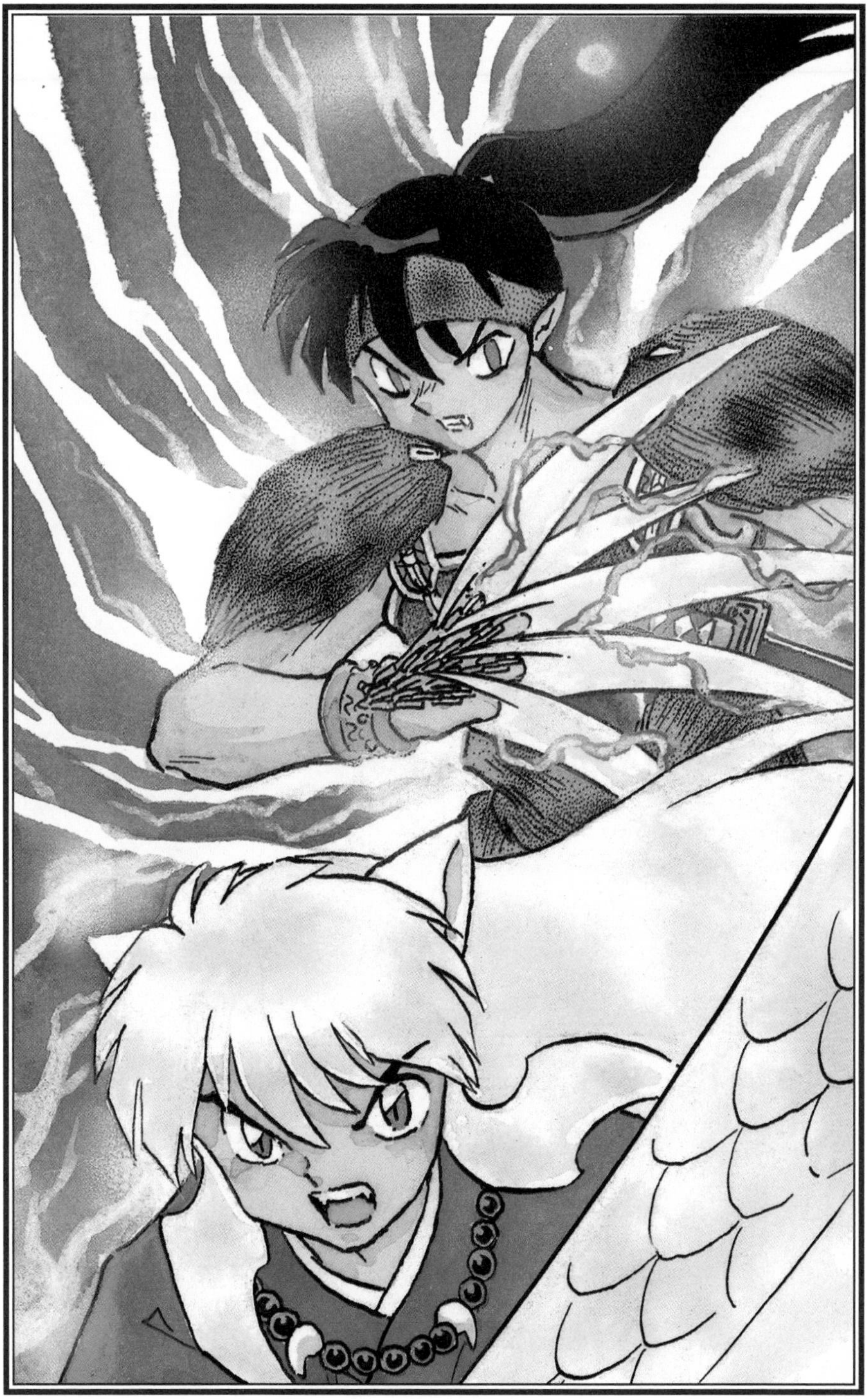

Original cover art from volume 44, published 2010

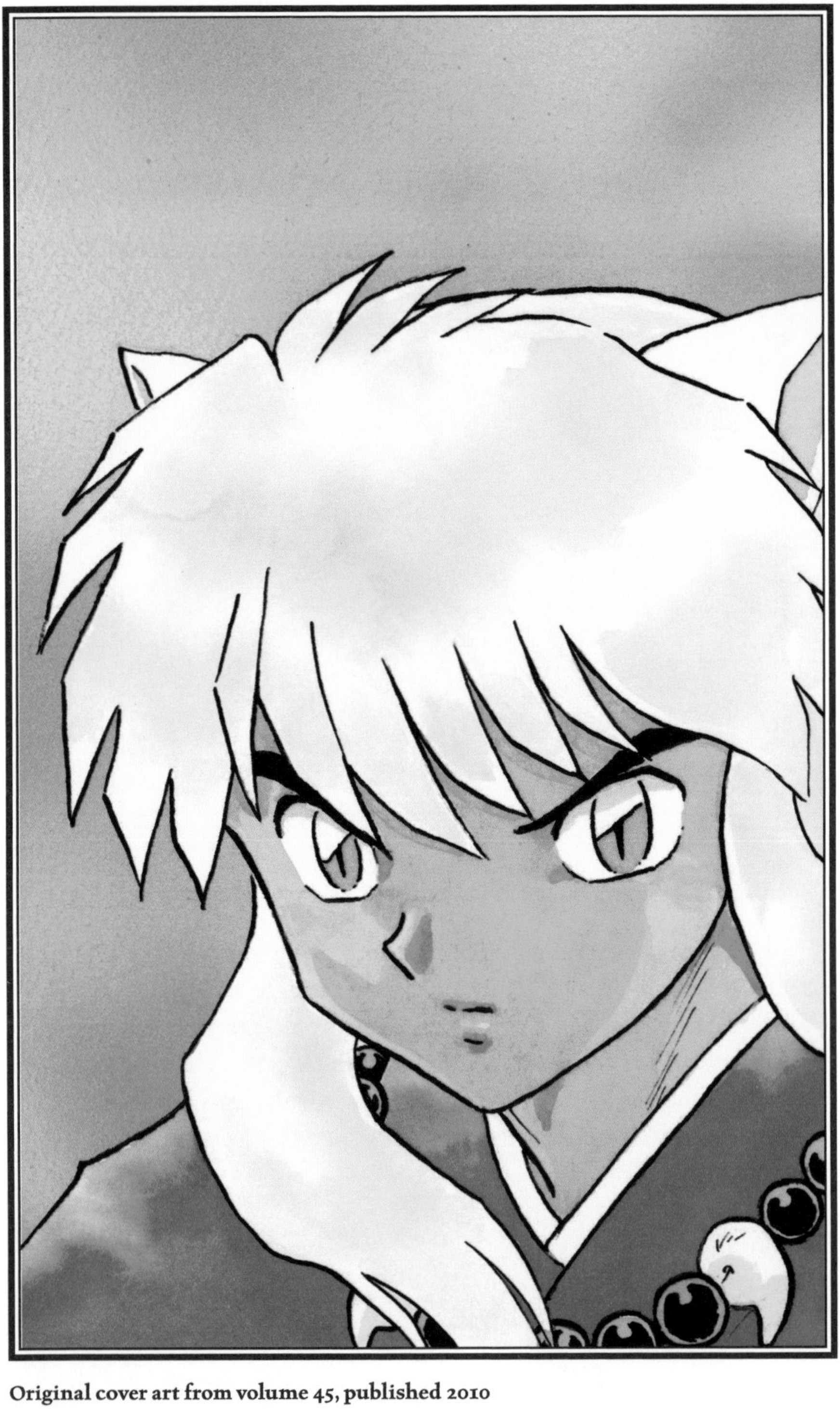

Original cover art from volume 45, published 2010

W9-CHV-626

Coming Next Volume

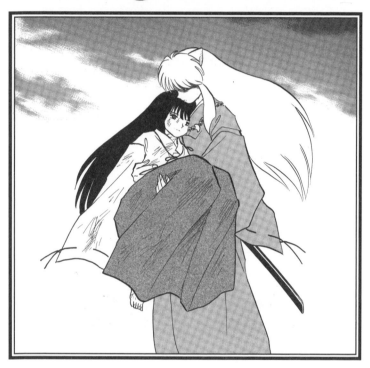

The forces of good and evil battle it out inside the very bodies of Kikyo and Naraku...and ultimately the Shikon Jewel itself. Then Inuyasha's half brother Sesshomaru is trapped in the world of the dead. Will he find the key that opens the door to the world of the living? Meanwhile, Inuyasha and the others stumble upon a strange village ruled by a demon with peculiar feeding habits...

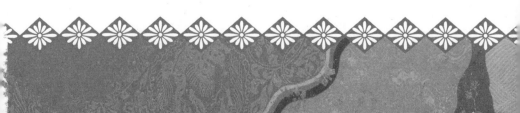